Lecture Notes in Computer Science 3399

Commenced Publication in 1973
Founding and Former Series Editors:
Gerhard Goos, Juris Hartmanis, and Jan van Leeuwen

Yanchun Zhang Katsumi Tanaka
Jeffrey Xu Yu Shan Wang Minglu Li (Eds.)

Web Technologies Research and Development – APWeb 2005

7th Asia-Pacific Web Conference
Shanghai, China, March 29 – April 1, 2005
Proceedings

Springer

Volume Editors

Yanchun Zhang
Victoria University of Technology, School of Computer Science and Mathematics
Ballarat Road, Footscray Park Campus, Melbourne, VIC 8001, Australia
E-mail: yzhang@csm.vu.edu.au

Katsumi Tanaka
Kyoto University, Department of Social Informatics
Yoshida Honmachi, Sakyo, Kyoto, 606-8501, Japan
E-mail: ktanaka@i.kyoto-u.ac.jp

Jeffrey Xu Yu
Chinese University of Hong Kong
Department of System Engineering and Engineering Management
Shatin, New Territories, Hong Kong
E-mail: yu@se.cuhk.edu.hk

Shan Wang
Renmin University of China, School of Information
Beijing 100872, P.R. China
E-mail: swang@ruc.edu.cn

Minglu Li
Shanghai Jiao Tong University, Department of Computer Science and Engineering
1954 Hua Shan Road, Shanghai 200030, P.R. China
E-mail: li-ml@cs.sjtu.edu.cn

Library of Congress Control Number: 2005922880

CR Subject Classification (1998): H.3, H.4, H.5, C.2, K.4

ISSN	0302-9743
ISBN-10	3-540-25207-X Springer Berlin Heidelberg New York
ISBN-13	978-3-540-25207-8 Springer Berlin Heidelberg New York

Springer is a part of Springer Science+Business Media

springeronline.com

Printed in Germany

Typesetting: Camera-ready by author, data conversion by Scientific Publishing Services, Chennai, India
Printed on acid-free paper SPIN: 11403531 06/3142 5 4 3 2 1 0

A Tribute to Prof. Yahiko Kambayashi (Feb 15, 1944–Feb 6, 2004)

We dedicate this book to our dear friend and colleague, APWeb 2005 Honorary General Chair, Prof. Yahiko Kambayashi, who passed away on February 6, 2004 after a short illness.

Prof. Kambayashi made many outstanding contributions to the database and Web information systems community. He was one of the pioneers and international leaders of research in database and information systems. He was a cofounder of the Web Information Systems Engineering (WISE) Society and the WISE conference series, and a cofounder and Co-editor-in-Chief of World Wide Web: Internet and Web Information Systems.

He was an IEEE Fellow, WISE Fellow, a winner of the 1995 ACM-SIGMOD Contribution award, a trustee of the VLDB Endowment, chairman of many major international conferences, and an editor of several international journals. Prof. Kambayashi received his Ph.D. from Kyoto University in 1970, and had been a full professor since 1984 at Kyushu University and Kyoto University. He published over 300 papers in major database and information systems journals and conferences such as Information Systems, SIGMOD, VLDB and ICDE. He was the author or editor of over 50 books and conference proceedings.

Prof. Kambayashi supervised over 40 Ph.D. students, many of whom are employed as faculty members at universities in Japan and worldwide. Many of us received support and guidance through his research collaborations and inspirations and his endless willingness to assist. We lost a pioneer, whose expertise, sage advice, and deep insights helped many of us. Those of us who knew him well lost a friend and will miss his generous hospitality and support.

He will be remembered as an outstanding researcher, leader, educator, mentor and friend. Prof. Kambayashi is survived by his wife and two sons. We are all saddened by his sudden departure and would like to express our heartfelt condolences and our deepest sympathy to his family through this book.

January 2005

Maria Orlowska
Mark Rusinkiewicz
John Mylopolous
Shan Wang
Katsumi Tanaka
Yanchun Zhang
Xiaofang Zhou
Qing Li

Preface

This volume contains papers selected for presentation at the 7th Asia Pacific Conference on Web Technology (APWeb 2005), which was held in Shanghai, China during March 29–April 1, 2005. APWeb is an international conference series on WWW technologies and is the primary forum for researchers and practitioners from both academia and industry to exchange knowledge on WWW-related technologies and new advanced applications.

APWeb 2005 received 420 submissions from 21 countries and regions worldwide, including China, Korea, Australia, Japan, Taiwan, France, UK, Canada, USA, India, Hong Kong, Brazil, Germany, Thailand, Singapore, Turkey, Spain, Greece, Belgium, New Zealand, and UAE. After a thorough review process for each submission by the Program Committee members and expert reviewers recommended by PC members, APWeb 2005 accepted 71 regular research papers (acceptance ratio 16.9%) and 22 short papers (acceptance ratio 5.2%). This volume also includes 6 keynote papers and 11 invited demo papers. The keynote lectures were given by six leading experts: Prof. Ah Chung Tsoi (Australia Research Council), Prof. Zhiyong Liu (National Nature Science Foundation of China), Prof. John Mylopoulos (University of Toronto), Prof. Ramamohanarao (Rao) Kotagiri (University of Melbourne), Prof. Calton Pu (Georgia Tech), and Prof. Zhiwei Xu (Chinese Academy of Sciences).

The conference was co-organized and supported by the National Institute of Information and Communications Technology (NICT), Japan, Shanghai Jiao Tong University, China, Victoria University, Australia, and it was also financially sponsored by National Natural Science Foundation of China, ARC Research Network on Enterprise Information Infrastructure (Australia), Microsoft Research Asia, the WISE Society, and the Database Society of China Computer Federation.

We wish to thank the APWeb conference Steering Committee, the APWeb 2005 Organizing Committee, and the Program Committee members and external reviewers for their dedication in promoting the conference and for their expertise in selecting papers. We wish also to thank the authors for submitting high-quality work to the conference.

With the large number of submissions, we received enormous help from many colleagues and volunteers. In particular, we thank Prof. Qing Li, Ms. Miranda Lee, Ms. Chengqin Ji and Ms. Zhihua Su for their support and help in registration, accommodation and local arrangements, and Dr. Hao Shi, Mr. Cameron Giles, Mr. Mike Ma and Mr. Guangdong Xu for their support in maintaining the paper review system.

Finally, we wish to pay our tribute to our Honorary General Chair, the late Prof. Yahiko Kambayashi, who was heavily involved in the early stage of planning of this conference. Prof. Kambayashi passed away on Feb. 6, 2004 after a short illness. Prof. Yahiko Kambayashi made many outstanding contributions to the Web information systems community. He was a cofounder of the Web Information Systems Engineering (WISE) Society and the WISE conference series, and a Co-editor-in-Chief of World Wide Web: Internet and Web Information Systems. We have lost a pioneer, whose expertise, sage advice, and deep insights helped many of us. Those of us who knew him well lost a friend and will miss his generous hospitality and support. Prof. Yahiko Kambayashi had been elected a WISE Fellow in early 2004 for his outstanding contribution to Web information systems research and his services to the WISE Society.

January 2005

Yanchun Zhang
Katsumi Tanaka
Jeffrey Xu Yu
Shan Wang
Minglu Li

Organization

Honorary General Chair

Yahiko Kambayashi†, Kyoto University, Japan

General Chair

Shan Wang, Renmin University of China, China

Program Committee Co-chairs

Yanchun Zhang, Victoria University, Australia
Katsumi Tanaka, Kyoto University, Japan

Publication Chair

Jeffrey Xu Yu, Chinese University of Hong Kong, China

Industrial Chair

Wei-Ying Ma, Microsoft Research Asia

Conference Organization Co-chairs

Minglu Li, Shanghai Jiaotong University, China
Aoying Zhou, Fudan University, China

Financial Chair

Qing Li, City University of Hong Kong, China

CCFDBS Liaison

Xiaofeng Meng, Database Society of China Computer Federation

Web Chair

Hao Shi, Victoria University, Australia

APWEB Steering Committee

Xiaofang Zhou (Chair), University of Queensland, Australia
Xuemin Lin, University of New South Wales, Australia
Hongjun Lu, Hong Kong University of Science and Technology, China
Jeffrey Xu Yu, Chinese University of Hong Kong, China
Yanchun Zhang, Victoria University, Australia

Program Committee

Jun Adachi, Japan
Toshiyuki Amagasa, Japan
Masatoshi Arikawa, Japan
James Bailey, Australia
Boualem Benatallah, Australia
Sourav S. Bhowmick, Singapore
Ulrik Brandes, Germany
Stephane Bressan, Singapore
Wentong Cai, Singapore
Jiannong Cao, Hong Kong, China
Jinli Cao, Australia
Sang K. Cha, Korea
Wojciech Cellary, Poland
Kuo-Ming Chao, UK
Somchai Chatvichienchai, Japan
Akmal Chaudhri, USA
Somchai Chatvichienchai, Japan
Jian Chen, China
Yi-Ping Phoebe Chen, Australia
Zheng Chen, China
Kai Cheng, Japan
David Cheung, Hong Kong, China
Kil-To Chong, Korea
Isabel Cruz, USA
Bin Cui, Singapore
Qianni Deng, China
Marie-Christine Fauvet, France
Ling Feng, Netherlands
Guangrong Gao, USA
Le Gruenwald, USA
Minyi Guo, Japan
Theo Haerder, Germany
Jun Han, Australia
Yoshinori Hara, Japan
Kenji Hatano, Japan
Xiangjian He, Australia
Jingyu Hou, Australia
Hui Hsiao, USA
Joshua Huang, Hong Kong, China
Maolin Huang, Australia
Patrick C.K. Hung, Canada
Weijia Jia, Hong Kong, China
Qingshan Jiang, China
Hai Jin, China
Kamal Karlapalem, India
Yutaka Kidawara, Japan
Markus Kirchberg, New Zealand
Hiroyuki Kitagawa, Japan
Yasushi Kiyoki, Japan
Huaizhong Kou, France
Shonali Krishnaswamy, Australia
Yong-Jin Kwon, Korea
Zoe Lacroix, USA
Alberto H.F. Laender, Brazil
Chiang Lee, Taiwan
Dik Lee, Hong Kong, China
Sanho Lee, Korea
Thomas Lee, USA
Chen Li, USA
Jianzhong Li, China
Jiuyong Li, Australia
Minglu Li, China
Qing Li, Hong Kong, China
Xue Li, Australia
Weifa Liang, Australia
Ee Peng Lim, Singapore
Chengfei Liu, Australia
Hong-Cheu Liu, Australia
Huan Liu, USA
Jianguo Lu, Canada

Jie Lu, Australia
Michael R. Lyu, Hong Kong, China
Wei-Ying Ma, China
Hong Mei, China
Weiyi Meng, USA
Xiaofeng Meng, China
Yuan Miao, Australia
Atsuyuki Morishima, Japan
Shinsuke Nakajima, Japan
Wee Keong Ng, Singapore
Anne Ngu, USA
Jun Ni, USA
Lionel M. Ni, Hong Kong, China
Jian Pei, USA
Gitesh Raikundalia, Australia
Keun Ho Ryu, Korea
Shazia Sadiq, Australia
Monica Scannapieco, Italy
Michel Schneider, France
Hao Shi, Australia
Timothy K. Shih, Taiwan
Keng Siau, USA
Dawei Song, Australia
William Song, UK
Jianwen Su, USA
Keishi Tajima, Japan
Kian Lee Tan, Singapore
Changjie Tang, China
Millist Vincent, Australia
Bing Wang, UK
Guoren Wang, China
Haixun Wang, USA
Hua Wang, Australia
Junhu Wang, Australia
Shengrui Wang, Canada
Wei Wang, USA
Wei Wang, Australia
Yan Wang, Australia
Gerald Weber, New Zealand
Ji-Rong Wen, China
Raymond Wong, Australia
Jie Wu, USA
Yi-Hung Wu, Taiwan
Vilas Wuwongse, Thailand
Jitian Xiao, Australia
Baowen Xu, China
Cheng-zhong Xu, USA
Kai Xu, Australia
Li Xu, USA
Jian Yang, Australia
Laurence T. Yang, Canada
Lianghuai Yang, China
Qiang Yang, Hong Kong, China
Yun Yang, Australia
Xun Yi, Australia
Hwan-Seung Yong, Korea
Masatoshi Yoshikawa, Japan
Arkady Zaslavsky, Australia
Karine Zeitouni, France
Koji Zettsu, Japan
Minjie Zhang, Australia
Shichao Zhang, Australia
Weining Zhang, USA
Xiaolong Zhang, China
Xiuzhen Zhang, Australia
Yongbing Zhang, Japan
Weimin Zheng, China
Shuigeng Zhou, China
Qiang Zhu, USA
Hai Zhuge, China

External Reviewers

Quan Bai
Hui Yang
Ruopeng Lu
Tony O'Hagan
Yoshinori Hijikata
Hiroko Kinutani
Yu Suzuki
Gi Whan Cho
Soon Chul Park
Yinsheng Li
Chen-Fang Tsai
Praveen Viswanath
J.-H. Chen
Hongkun Zhao
Jim Eales
Nalin Sharda
Don Watson
Ning-Han Liu
Chung-Wen Cho
Ding-Ying Chiu
Yao-Chung Fan

Jie Chen
Lifang Gu
Warren Jin
Peter Christen
Bin Wang
Chuan Yang
Xiangmin Zhou
Xinyu Chen
Edith Ngai
Xiaoqi Li
Pat Chan
Louis Lu
Yangfan Zhou
Chuhong Hoi
Kaizhu Huang
Haixuan Yang
Sim Kim Lau
Minsoo Lee
Hyokyung Bahn
Jung-Won Lee
Shermann S.M. Chan
Dickson K.W. Chiu
Chong-Wah Ngo
Zhe Shan
Jun Yang
Tianyi Zeng
Wei Jie
Quoc-Thuan Ho
Haifeng Shen
Xueyan Tang
Hee-Khiang Ng

Conference Co-organization

National Institute of Information and Communications Technology (NICT), Japan

Shanghai Jiao Tong University, China

Victoria University, Australia

Sponsors

National Institute of Information and Communications Technology (NICT), Japan

Shanghai Jiao Tong University, China

Victoria University, Australia

National Natural Science Foundation of China

ARC Research Network on Enterprise Information Infrastructure (Australia)

Microsoft Research Asia

WISE Society

Database Society of China Computer Federation

Table of Contents

Keynote Papers

Session 1: Classification and Clustering

Session 2: Topic and Concept Discovery

Session 3: Text Search and Document Generation

Session 4: Web Search

Session 5: Mobile and P2P

Session 6: XML (1)

Session 7: XML (2)

Session 8: Integration and Collaboration

Session 9: Data Mining and Analysis

Session 10: Web Browsing and Navigation

Session 11: Spatial Data

Session 12: Stream Data Processing

Session 13: Web Service

Session 14: Ontology

Session 15: Change Management

Session 16: Personalization

Session 20: Multimedia

Session 21: Object Recognition and Information Extraction

Session 22: Visualization and User Interfaces

Session 23: Delivery and Network

Session 24: Invited Demo Papers

---

*Notices: * denotes short paper.*

Databases and the Semantic Web: Data Semantics Revisited

Alexander Borgida[1] and John Mylopoulos[2]

[1] Dept. of Computer Science, Rutgers University, NJ, USA
borgida@cs.rutgers.edu
[2] Dept. of Computer Science, University of Toronto, Toronto, Canada
jm@cs.toronto.edu

Abstract. Two panels, held at SIGMOD'98 (Seattle, June 4) and CAiSE'98 (Pisa, June 11), discussed the topic of data semantics and its place in Databases research in the next millennium. The first, titled "Next Generation Database Systems Won't Work Without Semantics" included as panelists Philip Bernstein, Umesh Dayal, John Mylopoulos (chair), Sham Navathe and Marek Rusinkiewicz. The second one, titled "Data Semantics Can't Fail This Time!" included as panelists Michael Brodie, Stefano Ceri, John Mylopoulos (chair), and Arne Solvberg.

Atypically for panels, participants to both discussions generally agreed that data semantics will be the problem for Databases researchers to tackle in the near future. Stefano Ceri summed up well the sentiments of the discussions by declaring that

"... The three most important research problems in Databases used to be 'Performance', 'Performance', and 'Performance'; in years to come, the three most important and challenging problems will be 'Semantics', 'Semantics', and 'Semantics'..."

What is the data semantics problem? In what sense did it "fail" in the past? ...And why did the experts agree – unanimously – that the situation was about to change?

We review the data semantics problem and its long history in Databases research, noting the reasons why solutions of the past won't work in the future. We then review recent work on the Semantic Web and the directions it is taking. Finally, we sketch two new directions for research on data semantics.

This presentation is based on:

Borgida, A., Mylopoulos, J.: "Data Semantics Revisited". In: Proceedings VLDB Workshiop on *The Semantic Web and Databases* (SWDB'04), Toronto, August, (2004), Springer-Verlag LNCS, (to appear.)

Y. Zhang et al. (Eds.): APWeb 2005, LNCS 3399, p. 1, 2005.

DSL Weaving for Distributed Information Flow Systems

Calton Pu and Galen Swint

CERCS, College of Computing, Georgia Institute of Technology, 801 Atlantic Drive, Atlanta, Georgia, 30332-0280 USA
calton@cc.gatech.edu, swintgs@acm.org
http://www.cc.gatech.edu/projects/infosphere/

Abstract. Aspect-oriented programming (AOP) is a promising field for reducing application complexity. However, it has proven difficult to implement weavers for general purpose languages. Nevertheless, we felt some functionality for our information flow abstraction, Infopipes, might be best captures in aspects. In this paper, we describe a weaver built for domain specific languages (DSLs) related to Infopipes around an off-the-shelf XSLT processor. Aspects are written in XSLT, XML annotations are added to existing DSL generation templates, and XML directives are added to our Infopipes specification. Finally, we successfully demonstrate a generated+woven application that adds the quality of service (QoS) dimension CPU usage awareness to an image streaming application.

1 Introduction

Web services are gaining momentum in industry as a paradigm for building and deploying applications with a strong emphasis on interoperability between service providers. Inherent in this movement is the need to codify and monitor performance of applications or application components which are administered or purchased from another party. This has lead to the recognition and proposal of service level agreements (SLAs), which can capture expectations and roles in a declarative fashion [1,2]. One view of such agreements is that they constitute a domain specific language. As with any language, then, the question becomes how to map the "high" abstraction of the SLA language into a lower-level implementation. This amounts to run-time measurement, feedback, and adaptation interspersed into a web service-enable application.

In addition to viewing SLAs as a domain specific language, it is helpful to consider them as an aspect of a web-based application in the sense of Aspect Oriented Programming (AOP)[3]. This follows from noting that SLAs typically describe some application functionality that *crosscuts* application implementation which means that given a complete implementation of the application including service monitoring, then the SLA implementation code will be found in multiple components of the main application, and furthermore, the crosscutting code is heavily mixed, or *tangled*, in components where this crosscutting occurs.

AOP centers on the use of source code weavers to attack this problem crosscutting an tangling in an organized fashion. Currently, the most significant

Y. Zhang et al. (Eds.): APWeb 2005, LNCS 3399, pp. 2 – 14, 2005.

AOP tool has been the AspectJ weaver [4], developed after several years of effort, which supports the addition of aspect code to general Java applications. Applying the same techniques to C and C++ code, however, has been harder. The question arises, then, as to whether it is difficult to implement weavers for any language.

We built the AXpect weaver into the existing code generation framework, the Infopipe Stub Generator [5,6]. The ISG has three important parts: the intermediate representation, XIP; a repository of types and Infopipe descriptions; and a collection of templates written in XSLT.

This paper describes the architecture and implementation of the AXpect weaver in detail, as well as discusses a prototypical example application whereby a WSLA document is used to specify CPU usage policy between a server and client of a media stream. In section 2, we introduce the Infopipes abstraction for distributed applications. In section 3, we discuss the pre-existing code generator for our project, the ISG. In section 4, we present a close look at how we implement AOP in our system, and in section 5, we evaluate the weaver in the context of an example media application.

2 Infopipes

It has been long-recognized that RPC, while promising, has problems as a distributed programming paradigm. This mainly stems from the fact that a distributed application may have to deal with comparatively vast time scales, less security, and much greater divergence in resource availability than when operating on a single machine, even if it is a parallel machine. Consider that memory access and procedure call times may be measured in nano- or micro-seconds, but that web applications must address millisecond latencies – three to six orders of magnitude longer.

Infopipes are designed to take these differences into account, particularly for information flow applications. One reason for targeting information flow applications is that they are difficult to capture abstractly using RPC because their normal operation, sending a continuous stream of data, is innately mismatched to RPC's request/response scheme. Second, such applications often involve multiple processing steps, a concept that is again not addressed by RPC's encouragement of the client-server style. Finally, RPC completely obscures the communication taking place in the application, so that if latency, bandwidth, security, or some other property is needed then a developer must "uncover" the communication and insert new code to recover lost data about connection performance, and add any new functionality by hand which may be particularly difficult if some sort of end-to-end property is desired to be enforced. As we stated before, Infopipes expose the communication step, and make it much easier for a developer to capture connection information and implement properties around needed communication boundaries.

The Infopipes architecture is service-oriented – it encapsulates granules of distributed computation which are intended to be composited together [7] – just like those proposed for web service applications. While the ISG does not currently explicitly support XML as a wire format as is currently required to be Web Service compliant, it in no way excludes such a possibility, and even some previous unpublished Infopipe experiments have used XML as an *ad hoc* wire format. The ISG, in fact, already supports two completely different wire formats – PBIO, which is the wire format for ECho, and x86 byte-ordered data, as might come directly from a C program.

We have devised a prototype application to demonstrate Infopipes. The application is a video-streaming example in which the receiver of the video stream has Quality of Service requirements; it is constrained by its CPU resource and must provide feedback to the sender of the stream to control image arrival rate. Our code generator creates the communication setup, binding, and marshalling code and then automatically incorporates the QoS code which is parameterized in an external WSLA document. In the next section, we describe the implementation of our ISG to generate the base communication code. For this example, we will denote as our base application the sender and receiver's communication code with no QoS supporting code.

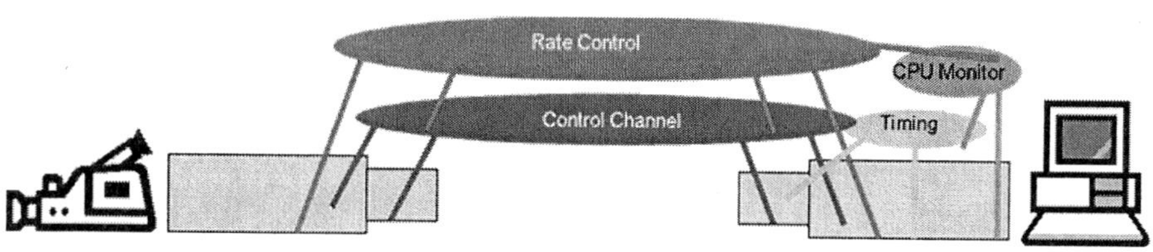

Fig. 1. The QoS-aware application

We can see that there the application requires several functions to be implemented to support its QoS needs: a control channel, for feedback information; timing tags and code to monitor the CPU usage from times gleaned; and a rate control channel which implements the actions to take based on observations from the CPU monitor.

3 The ISG

The ISG toolkit has been developed for the Infosphere project to automate the programming of Infopipes code for developers. It consists of a human-friendly descriptive language Spi (Specifying Infopipes), an intermediate descriptive language XIP (XML for Infopipes), a repository for persistence of defined Infopipes structures, and a hybrid C++/XSLT code generation engine.

For a developer, converting a Spi specification to compilable source code is a three-step process:

1. Create a Spi document to describe the information flow system.
2. Compile the Spi into XIP.
3. The XIP is then processed with the ISG.

The ISG can read the XIP, and as shown in Fig. 2 below (which also includes the AXpect weaver), it proceeds through multiple stages to generate the communication code for the application:

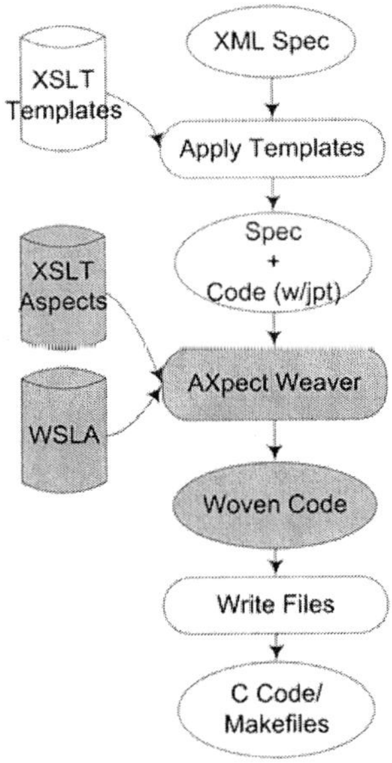

Fig. 2. ISG with support for AXpect weaving

```
<pipe class="ImagePipelinePlain">
   <subpipes>
     <subpipe name="imagesSource"
             class="SendingPipe"/>
     <subpipe name="imagesReceive"
             class="ReceivingPipe"/>
   </subpipes>
   <connections>
     <connection comm="tcp">
       <from pipe="imagesSource"
             port="out"/>
       <to pipe="imagesReceive"
           port="in"/>
     </connection>
    </connections>
</pipe>
```

Fig. 3. Example XIP Infopipe specification

1. The XIP is processed; new specifications go to the repository.
2. Previously defined specifications are retrieved and ISG constructs a full specification for a generated, termed a XIP+ document because it has a similar format, but is augmented with additional data.

3. Once the XIP+ document is completed, the XIP+ document is processed with our XSLT code generation templates. The result is another XIP+ document that also includes all the information from the source XIP+.
4. Code weaving can now be performed (see Section 4).
5. Code is written to directories and files ready for compilation.

The choice of XML for our intermediate format has proven to be beneficial even though XML's primary role is in the data connections between organizations. Instead of only inter-organizational data interchange, however, we use it for data interchange during the building of an application. This provides important advantages. First, it allows us to retain and add to semantic information that might otherwise be lost from stage-to-stage within the code generator. In particular, it allows us to capture domain information injected by virtue of operating in the Infopipes domain and with the Infopipes suite of domain languages. Such information is not readily preserved by general purpose programming languages. Second, it allows us to have one common wrapper format for multiple languages. Using XML, we can treat our code as data (which it is), and that fact allows us to modify the code after the generation phase. This technique is already widely used in programming languages, but is only recently catching on in code transformation. Examples in general purpose languages include LISP macros, C++ templates, and Java generics. Each of those, in some fashion, allows the programmer to create a type of data-code hybrid. Later, as needed, certain parameters can be changed and custom code can be created for an application.

4 Weaving

Weaving is a concept from AOP in which new pieces of code are executed in a controlled and automatic fashion near, around, or instead-of code in a core application. We devised a source-level weaver to insert new functionality on top of video application. The weaving integrates code to measure CPU statistics, provide feedback, and adapt to changing transmission environment. It has a goal of maintaining CPU usage receiver-side below a given level.

There are three key concepts that enable the weaver. First, we attach semantic tags to the source code that we generate. Second, we use XSLT describe the weaving process in the aspect, and third, we insert weaving directives into the Infopipes description file.

Any weaver must have some points in the target code that it can identify. These are the "joinpoints." In our case, we benefit from our domain specific arena. Because of this, we know that specific activities occur within each Infopipe with known ordering. For example, we know that each pipe has a start-up phase that includes starting up each inport and each outport, resolving bindings and names, and actually making connections. During these initializations, our pipe may initialize data structures for each inport or outport. In the code generation templates, there is template code for each of these "common tasks."

AOP has three types of advice: before, after, and around. A developer chooses a joinpoint using a pointcut, and then designates by keyword whether aspect code should execute before, after, or around (which subsumes instead-of) the selected joinpoint. One interesting subtlety is that in AXpect the explicit XML tags denote a semantic block of code, and not just a single point. This most closely relates to AspectJ "around" semantics. Still, we retain the before and after capability of the weaving, without loss of "power." One could also view it another way, in which the XML opening tag marks "before," the closing tag marks "after," and taken together the tags make up "around" semantics.

For a concrete example, consider a fragment of template for generating C code Infopipes. This template excerpt generates a startup function for the Infopipe. The startup function name is based on the name of the Infopipe. The XSL commands are XML tags which have the `xsl` namespace prefix (like the element `xsl:value-of` which retrieves the string representation of some XML element, attribute, or XSLT variable). The added joinpoint XML tag is bolded, and it denotes the beginning and ending of the code block that implements the startup functionality. We have reverse-printed the joinpoint XML for clarity, and printed the C code in bold to distinguish it from the XSLT.

```
// startup all our connections
int infopipe_<xsl:value-of select="$thisPipeName"/>_startup()
{
  // insert signal handler startup here
  <jpt:pipe point="startup">
  // start up outgoing ports <xsl:for-each select="./ports/outport">
  infopipe_<xsl:value-of select="@name"/>_startup(); </xsl:for-each>
. . .
  </jpt:pipe>
  return 0;
}
```

Sometimes a joinpoint does not denote code but language artifacts that are needed for code to be written correctly. In following example, we see that we can denote the header file for an inport. This allows the C developer of new aspect code to insert new function definitions at the appropriate scope.

```
#ifndef INFOPIPE<xsl:value-of select="$thisPortName"/>INCLUDED
#define INFOPIPE<xsl:value-of select="$thisPortName"/>INCLUDED

<jpt:header point="inport"  pipename="{$thisPipeName}" portname="{$thisPortName}">
int drive();
// init function
int infopipe_<xsl:value-of select="$thisPortName"/>_startup();
int infopipe_<xsl:value-of select="$thisPortName"/>_shutdown();
void infopipe_<xsl:value-of select="$thisPortName"/>_receiveloop();
// data comes in to this struct
extern <xsl:value-of select="$thisPortType"/>Struct
          <xsl:value-of select="$thisPortName"/>;
. . .
</jpt:header>
#endif // Infopipe<xsl:value-of select="$thisPortName"/>INCLUDED
```

Joinpoints remain with the code until the files are written to disk. After the generation phase, they serve as signposts to the weaver and aspects. If we consider our first example, then after generation for the pipe called "imageReceiver" there is this startup code:

```
// startup all our connections
int infopipe_imageReceiver_startup()
{
  <jpt:pipe point="startup">
  infopipe_inp_startup();
  infopipe_inp_receiveloop();
  </jpt:pipe>
  return 0;
}
```

At this point, obviously, the code looks very much like pure C ready for compilation, and most importantly, we and the AXpect weaver know *what* the code does in the context of the Infopipes domain. Interestingly, we find that so far only about 26 joinpoints are necessary for quite a bit of flexibility with respect to actions we can perform on the generated code. These joinpoints have evolved into some broad categories as evidenced in **Table 1**, below.

"Language Artifacts" help a developer structure his code properly. "Data" joinpoints relate to the structures that hold incoming/outgoing data. "Pipe" joinpoints define actions that occur during the overall running of the pipe. Communication layer joinpoints are needed because it is common for these packages to need to perform initialization, set-up, or tear down functionality only once per-application start, and some applications may need to build on this communication layer behavior or modify it. Last, we have joinpoints on the inports and outports themselves.

Table 1. Catalog of joinpoints in the C templates. These are expressed in a shorthand such that in the table below *type*:*point* equates to <jpt:*type* point="*point*"> in the XML/XSLT

Language Artifacts	Data	Pipe	Comm Layer	Inport	Outport
make:rule	data:define	pipe:userfunction	socket:socket	inport:startup	outport:marshall
header:pipe	data:initialize	pipe:startup	socket:bind	inport:read	outport:push
source:pipe		pipe:shutdown	comm-startup	inport:unmarshall	outport:startup
header:inport			comm-shutdown	inport:callmiddle	outport:shutdown
source:inport				inport:shutdown	
header:outport					
source:outport					
source:userdeclare					

The second ingredient of the AXpect weaver is an XSLT file that contains aspect code. Every AXpect file has two parts. First, the aspect has some pattern matching statement, written using XPath and utilizing the XSLT pattern matching engine, to find the proper joinpoint and the code to be inserted. This corresponds to the role of the pointcut in an AOP system like AspectJ. The pointcut in AXpect is an XPath predicate for an XSLT match statement in a fashion similar to this:

```
//filledTemplate[@name=$pipename][@inside=$inside]//jpt:pipe[@point='shutdown']
```

We can dissect the elements of the pointcut XPath statement:

`//filledTemplate[@name=$pipename][@inside=$inside]` –

structure-shy specification to find a filledElement template, which is a block of generated code and predicates to narrow filled templates returned to one for a particular pipe.

`//jpt:pipe[@point='shutdown']` – a specific joinpoint

Instead of keywords like AspectJ, the AXpect developer uses placement. The actual joinpoint and its contents are copied over by XSLT's `xsl:copy` instruction. A simple aspect for AXpect looks like this (the C code is bolded for distinction from the XSLT):

```
<xsl:template match="//filledTemplate[@name=$pipename]
          [@inside=$inside]//jpt:pipe[@point='shutdown']">
  fclose(afile);
  <xsl:copy>
    <xsl:apply-templates select="@*|node()"/>
  </xsl:copy>
</xsl:template>
```

It is now easy to see how aspect code, pointcuts and joinpoints, and advice mesh. The pointcut (in reverse print) we have already discussed, and it is contained in the match attribute to the xsl:template element. We can see the C code to close a file (fclose(afile)) is located before the xsl:copy command, which means that it will be executed before the rest of the shutdown code. The xsl:apply-templates is boilerplate XSLT that ensures the processor continues to pattern match to all elements and attributes of the generated document that lie inside the joinpoint element. (It is our plan, in fact, to eliminate having to write XSLT for aspects, and the accompanying boilerplate like the xsl:copy elements and to generate them from a higher level description.)

As a second example, we can examine a case where around is helpful:

```
<xsl:template match="//filledTemplate[@name=$pipename]
          [@inside=$inside]//jpt:source[@point='pipe']">
static  FILE *afile;
  <xsl:copy>
    <xsl:apply-templates select="@*|node()"/>
  </xsl:copy>
#include &lt;unistd.h&gt;
int main()
. . .
```

In this case we are structurally bound by the standards of C coding which advocate placing variable definitions at the top of a file and having functions declared at file scope. This means we weave on the joinpoint that defines the source file of the Infopipe. The declaration of the variable occurs before the main code of the Infopipe, and the definition and declaration of the main function occur after. Since `main()` is not generated by default we add it using an aspect and then call the Infopipe startup code which spawns a thread to handle service our incoming Infopipes connection.

One of the interesting results of using XSLT and XML for this system is that aspects can introduce new joinpoints in the form of new XML tags. This means that one aspect can build upon an aspect that was woven into the code earlier (order of aspect weaving will be discussed shortly). In our example scenario, we insert timing code to measure how long various pieces of Infopipe code take to run the user function which can be used later in calculating CPU usage.

```
<xsl:template match="//filledTemplate
                        [@name=$pipename][@inside=$inside]//jpt:inport">
  <jpt:time-probe point="begin">
  // take timing here
  gettimeofday(&amp;inport_<xsl:value-of select="@point"/>_begin,NULL);
  </jpt:time-probe>
  <xsl:copy>
    <xsl:apply-templates select="@*|node()"/>
  </xsl:copy>
  <jpt:time-probe point="end">
  gettimeofday(&amp;inport_<xsl:value-of select="@point"/>_end,NULL);
  </jpt:time-probe>
</xsl:template>
```

The timing code is bracketed with XML that declares it, and the CPU monitoring code can then select it with a pointcut just like any other joinpoint:

```
<xsl:template match="//filledTemplate[@name=$pipename][@inside=$inside]
                        //jpt:inport[@point='callmiddle']
                        //jpt:time-probe[@point='end' ">
```

This brings us to the third part of the AXpect weaver – specifying the aspects to apply in the XIP specification. This is a very simple process in which we add <apply-aspect> statements to the pipe descriptions:

```
<pipe class="vidSink" lang="C">
  <apply-aspect name="rate_controller.xsl" targetPct="20">
    <apply-aspect name="control_receiver.xsl" target="ppmIn"/>
    <apply-aspect name="cpumon.xsl" target="ppmIn">
      <apply-aspect name="timing.xsl"/>
      <apply-aspect name="sla_receiver.xsl" doc="uav.xml"/>
    </apply-aspect>
  </apply-aspect>
  <ports>
    <inport name="ppmIn" type="ppm"/>
  </ports>
</pipe>
```

Note that we can nest the apply-aspect elements to declare dependencies of one aspect upon another. Since we invoke the XSLT processor multiple times, and neither the XSLT standard nor Xalan-C supports self-invocation, the evaluation of these statements is handled in a C++ program using Xerces-C, which is the platform the ISG is built around. The weaver proceeds recursively through the following steps on each pipe:

1. Retrieves the first <apply-aspect> element from the pipe specification.
2. If the aspect contains more <apply-aspect> statements, then the AXpect applies those aspects first, and re-enters the process of weaving at this step.
3. The weaver retrieves the aspect code from disk (aspects are kept in a well-known directory).
4. Apply the aspect to the code by passing the aspect XSLT stylesheet, the generated code with joinpoints, and system XML specification to the Xalan-C XSLT processor. The result is a new XIP+ document that again

contains the specification, woven code, and joinpoints The weaving result serves as input for any aspects that follow the current aspect. This includes aspects which depend on the current aspect's functionality, or functionally independent aspects that are simply applied later.

5. Once all aspects are applied, the entire XML result document is passed to the last stage of the generator.

This algorithm implementation only required an additional 79 lines of C++ code be added to the generator application. The bulk of the weaver complexity is contained by the XSLT weaver.

5 Our Sample Application

We used the AXpect weaver and Infopipes to implement the sample application which we described earlier in the paper. We now discuss the implementation of aspects to fulfill the QoS requirements of the rate-adaptive image-streaming application.

The timing aspect hooks on to all join points that designate an executable block of code. This can be done in an efficient fashion by using the pattern matching to select entire sets of joinpoints around which to install timing code around. Complementing this is creating new variables to hold the timing measurements which we do by creating their names at aspect-weaving time.

On top of this we install the CPU monitoring code. This code installs around the join points for timing, specifically the timing points that designate the call to the middle-method code. Instead of using start-to-end elapsed time which would only provide a measure of how long it took to execute a joinpoint, we measure end-to-end so that we have a measure of the total time for the application to complete one "round-trip" back to that point. We can compare this to the system-reported CPU time to calculate the percentage of CPU used by this process.

The control channel sends data between the two ends of the Infopipe. We used a socket independent of the normal Infopipe data socket both to avoid the overhead of demultiplexing control information and application data and to piggyback this functionality on top of the OS demultiplexing which would be performed, anyway. Also, separating these two flows of information should improve the general robustness of the application as there is no possibility of errant application data being interpreted as control data or of misleading data being injected as control data somehow.

Finally, there is the SLA aspect. During weaving, it reads an external SLA document which specifies the metrics and tolerances of the values the SLA needs to observe and report. At run time, the SLA reads the CPU usage values and sends them through the control channel to the video; once received, the SLA acts based on the returned value. In our example, the SLA can set a variable to control if and for how long the sender enters `usleep()` to adjust its rate control.

We compiled the sample application and ran it with a "strong" sender, a dual 866MHz Pentium III machine and a "weak," resource-constrained receiver, a Pentium

II 400MHz. Running without any controls on resource usage, the video sender is able to capture roughly 36% of the receiver's CPU. Using the CPU control, we are able to bring the CPU usage back to a target 20±5% range.

We have observed so far that our aspect files are generally larger than they amount of code they actually generate. However, this tradeoff is appropriate considering the increase in locality of code and reusability (some of these aspects, such as timing and CPU monitoring, have been reused already in another demo). In fact, when we examine the files altered or created by the aspects in this application, we see that an aspect such as the sender-side SLA code can alter four of the generated files and then add two more files of its own. In all, the QoS-aware application is 434 lines longer than the base application that is not QoS aware. Without support from a weaver to help manage code, it would obviously be more difficult to keep track of these 434 lines if they are handwritten into the base set of 18 files versus the six AXpect files.

(See also http://www.cc.gatech.edu/projects/infosphere/online_demos/WeaveDemo)

6 Related Work

The AOP and code generation community is actively exploring the new possibilities in combining the two including SourceWeave.NET [8], Meta-AspectJ[9], two-level weaving [10], and Xaspects [11].

Before that, The AOP community has worked diligently on weavers for general purpose languages such as Java and C++. This has resulted in tools such as AspectJ, AspectWerkz, JBossAOP, and AspectC[4,13,14,15]. Generally, development of weavers for these platforms requires continual and concerted effort over a fairly long period of time. Other work has tackled separation of concerns for Java through language extensions, such as the explicit programming approach of ELIDE project [16].

DSLs have also often been implemented on top of weavers. Notable in this area is the QuO project, which uses a DSL then generates CORBA objects which are called from the execution path to run and be evaluated at the join point to implement quality of service. However, the QuO project does not weave source code. Instead, it alters the execution pathof the application therefore imposes invocation overhead [17]. Bossa uses AOP ideas to abstract scheduling points in OS kernels, but again does not do source weaving; each joinpoint triggers an event and advice registers at events in order to run [18]. Because of the use of aspects in conjunction with DSLs, the XAspects project is studying the use of aspects to implement families of DSLs. Still, this project uses AspectJ as the source weaver and therefore focuses only on Java as the target language [11]. The Meta-AspectJ package also targets enhancing the power of code generators and using code generation plus AOP to reduce complexities for implementing security and persistence [9]. Work has been done using XML in the AOP arena; however, this work has concentrated on using XML to denote the abstract syntax tree [18]; conversely, it has been used as the aspect language syntax as in SourceWeave.NET to weave aspect code in the bytecode of the .NET the Common Language Runtime (CLR) [8].

7 Conclusion and Ongoing Work

We have shown that even adding a relatively simple QoS requirement can entail widespread changes to an application and that those changes can be spread throughout the entire application. To address this, we described the AXpect weaver. The AXpect weaver can use information from a WSLA and integrate new code into source code generated from an Infopipes XML specification. Our target application used the weaver to add new functionality to a C program which realized an image-streaming with responsiveness to CPU usage constraints on the sender end of the image stream. For future work, we are continuing to explore the space of applications for weaving, and we have already demonstrated early application of the weaver to C++ programs with further plans for Java. Also, we are investigating Infopipes support for Web Service applications.

Acknowledgements

The authors are grateful for the input of Charles Consel (INRIA, University of Bordeaux, France); Ling Liu, Younggyun Koh, Wenchang Yan, and Sanjay Kumar (Georgia Institute of Technology, Atlanta, GA), and Koichi Moriyama (SONY Corp., Japan); Part of this work was done under DARPA funding.

References

1. M. Debusmann, and A. Keller, "SLA-driven Management of Distributed Systems using the Common Information Model," *IFIP/IEEE International Symposium on Integrated Management*. 2003.
2. Sahai, S. Graupner, V. Machiraju, and A. van Moorsel, "Specifying and Monitoring Guarantees in Commercial Grids through SLA," *Third International Symposium on Cluster Computing and the Grid*. 2003.
3. G. Kiczales, J. Lamping, A. Mendhekar, C. Maeda, C. V. Lopes, J.-M. Loingtier, J. Irwin. "Aspect-Oriented Programming." *Proceedings of the 15th European Conference of Object-Oriented Programming* (ECOOP 2001). June 2001.
4. G. Kiczales, E. Hilsdale, J. Hugunin, M. Kersten, J. Palm, W. G. Griswold. "An Overview of AspectJ." *Proceedings of the European Conference of Object-Oriented Programming* (ECOOP 1997). June 1997.
5. Pu, Galen Swint, C. Consel, Y. Koh, L. Liu, K. Moriyama, J. Walpole, W. Yan. Implementing Infopipes: The SIP/XIP Experiment, Technical Report GT-CC-02-31, College of Computing, Georgia Institute of Technology, May 2002.
6. G. Swint, C. Pu, and K. Moriyama, "Infopipes: Concepts and ISG Implementation," The 2nd IEEE Workshop on Software Technologies for Embedded and Ubiquitous Computing Systems, Vienna. 2004.
7. M. Papazoglou. "Service-Oriented Computing: Concepts, Characteristics, and Directions." Fourth International Conference on Web Information Systems Engineering (WISE'03). December 2003.
8. Jackson, S. Clarke. "SourceWeave.NET:Cross-Language Aspect-Oriented Programming." Proceedings of the Third International Conference on Generative Programming and Component Engineering (GPCE), Vancouver, Canada, October 24-28 2004.

9. Zook, S. S. Huan, Y. Smaragdakis. "Generating AspectJ Programs with Meta-AspectJ." Proceedings of the Third International Conference on Generative Programming and Component Engineering (GPCE), Vancouver, Canada, October 24-28 2004.
10. J. Gray, J. Sztipanovits, D. Schmidt, T. Bapty, S. Neema, and A. Gokhale, "Two-level Aspect Weaving to Support Evolution of Model-Driven Synthesis." *Aspect-Oriented Software Development.* Robert Filman, Tzilla Elrad, Mehmet Aksit, and Siobhan Clarke, eds. Addison-Wesley, 2004.
11. M. Shonle, K. Lieberherr, and A. Shah. Xaspect: An Extensible System for Domain Specific Aspect Languages. OOPSLA 2003. October 2003.
12. S. Sarkar, "Model Driven Programming Using XSLT: An Approach to Rapid Development of Domain-Specific Program Generators," www.XML-JOURNAL.com. August 2002.
13. J. Bonér, A. Vasseur. AspectWerkz. http://aspectwerkz.codehaus.org/.
14. JBoss. http://www.jboss.org/products/aop.
15. Y. Coady, G. Kiczales, M. Feeley, and G. Smolyn. "Using AspectC to Improve the Modularity of Path-Specific Customization in Operating System Code," in *Proceedings of the 8th European software engineering conference held jointly with 9th ACM SIGSOFT international symposium on Foundations of Software Engineering*, Vienna, Austria, 2001, pp. 88-98.
16. Bryant, A. Catton, K. de Volder, G. C. Murphy, "Explicit programming," *1st International Conference on Aspect-Oriented Software Development*, Enschede, The Netherlands, April 22-26, 2002.
17. J. P. Loyall, D.E. Bakken, R.E. Schantz, J.A. Zinky, D.A. Karr, R. Vanegas, and K.R. Anderson, "QoS Aspect Languages and Their Runtime Integration," *Proceedings of the 4th Workshop on Languages, Compilers, and Run-time Systems for Scalable Computers* (LCR98). Pittsburgh. May 28-30, 1998.
18. L.P. Barreto, R. Douence, G. Muller, and M. Südholt, "Programming OS Schedulers with Domain-Specific Languages and Aspects: New Approaches for OS Kernel Engineering," *International Workshop on Aspects, Components, and Patterns for Infrastructure Software* at AOSD, April 2002.
19. S. Schonger, E. Pulermüller, and S. Sarstedt, "Aspect-Oriented Programming and Component Weaving: Using XML Representations of Abstract Syntax Trees," *Proceedings of the 2nd German GI Workshop on Aspect-Oriented Software Development* (In: Technical Report No. IAI-TR-2002-1), University of Bonn, February 2002, pp. 59 – 64.

Broadening Vector Space Schemes for Improving the Quality of Information Retrieval

Kotagiri Ramamohanarao and Laurence A.F. Park

ARC Centre for Perceptive and Intelligent Machines in Complex Environments,
The Department of Computer Science and Software Engineering,
The University of Melbourne, Australia
{rao, lapark}@csse.unimelb.edu.au

Abstract. The vector space model (VSM) of information retrieval suffers in two areas, it does not utilise term positions and it treats every term as being independent. We examine two information retrieval methods based on the simple vector space model. The first uses the query term position flow within the documents to calculate the document score, the second includes related terms in the query by making use of term correlations. Both of these methods show significant improvements over the VSM precision while keeping the query time to speeds similar to those of the VSM.

1 Introduction

Information retrieval has been examined from many different angles. There have been many methods of retrieval designed to obtain precise results in a fast time from a simple key word based query. Of all of the methods, the most used during the last half century was the vector space method. It's simplicity provides it with great speed and little storage needed and its precision has been used as the baseline for many experiments. The vector space method of document retrieval suffers from two main problems: 1) Its disregard of term positions. 2) Its assumption of term independence. Term positions should be taken into account during the document scoring process. As a simple example, we will examine the documents:

> Document 1: "The smell of the bakery first appeared at five in the morning. The maroon delivery trucks passed through the town ten minutes later."
>
> Document 2: "The smell of diesel first appeared at five in the morning. The bakery delivery trucks passed through the town ten minutes later."

Given a query of "bakery trucks" each of these documents would be given the same score using the vector space method. The simplest method of distinguishing between the two is by observing the term positions. Only then can we see that document 2 is better suited to the query.

The former problem arrives from the document vector creation process. When documents are converted into vectors, we only examine the term occurrences

Y. Zhang et al. (Eds.): APWeb 2005, LNCS 3399, pp. 15–26, 2005.

though the document rather than the term positions. There have been many efforts to try to include term positions [4, 1, 5, 8]. These term proximity methods calculate the document scores based on the distances between the query terms within the document. These methods provide high precision results for specific cases, but have trouble trying to incorporate the term occurrence in the document scores and have also resulted in an increase in the query time and data storage.

In the former section of our paper, we present our new spectral based document retrieval system which is able to use term position information and present the results to the user in a time comparable to the vector space method.

The latter of the two problems is also found during the document vector creation. When creating our term space, we choose to assign the count of each unique term to a separate dimension, resulting in a vector space of M dimensions, where M is the number of unique terms in the document set. Our document score is based on the inner product of the query and document vectors, therefore all of the terms are treated as independent entities, which they are not. If our query is given as "red vehicles", neither of the previously examined documents would be retrieved, simply because they do not contain the query terms. If we were to somehow remove the term independence, we would want document 1 obtaining a higher score than document 2. Document 1 has terms related to both of the query terms ("maroon" and "truck"), while document 2 has terms related to only one of the query terms ("diesel" and "truck"). There have been many attempts to remove this term independence assumption. Manual and automatic thesauruses have been used [7], many versions of latent semantic analysis have been tried [2, 6], and more recently language models have been constructed [16, 3]. Each of these have their own method of removing the independence assumption but they all add to the query time and the document storage.

In the latter part of our paper, we present a novel method of breaking the term independence assumption which is a combination between the thesaurus method and the latent semantic analysis method and also allows us to retrieve documents in a time comparable to the vector space method.

The paper will proceed as follows: Section 2 will introduce our spectral based document retrieval method and discuss such aspects as term signal creation and use of phase in document scoring; Section 3 will follow by introducing our query mapping structure and how we can perform fast query term expansions using latent semantic analysis and speed ups used in the vector space method.

2 Spectral Based Retrieval

To make use of the positions of query terms in document, many have tried observing the features such as the query term proximities. If query terms occur frequently through the document, we must make many comparisons and take into account many positions in the document. Once we have made calculations based on the term proximity, we are left with the problem of how to incorporate the count of each term in the document. Relative to the vector space method, each of these calculations increases the query time and storage of the term positions increases the data storage.

Spectral based document retrieval [11, 15, 12, 14, 13] compares patterns of positions rather than individual positions. The patterns are set by our choice of spectral transformation. If we apply the spectral transformation to a document, we move from the term position domain to the term spectral domain. Each spectral component is independent of the others, therefore we only have to compare the one spectral component for each term in a document to obtain a score based on the query term positions. Therefore, by comparing query term spectra rather than query term positions we reduce the amount of comparison that need to be made.

In this section we will describe the spectral based retrieval process and each of its elements and provide experimental results showing the benefits over the vector space method.

2.1 Term Signals

The vector space method assigns a single number to each term-document element, the term occurrence in the document. This value contains no information about the position of the term in the document, only the amount of times it appears. Our spectral based retrieval method uses term signals in the place of the term occurrence value. A term signal is a sequence of numbers that represent the occurrence of the associated term in particular sections of the document. This is similar to providing the term count for each paragraph, but in our case we find the term count within a certain range of terms depending on the desired term signal length. If we choose to have term signals of length B (containing B elements) then the bth element of the term signal $\tilde{f}_{d,t}$ will be the count of term t in document d from words Nb/B to $N(b+1)/B-1$, where N is the document length in words. In other words, we split the document into B equal portions and term signal element b is the count of term t in document d's bth portion. The term signals are shown as:

$$\tilde{f}_{d,t} = [\ f_{d,t,0}\ f_{d,t,1}\ \cdots\ f_{d,t,B-1}\ ] \tag{1}$$

Once we have our term signals, we can see that they are a sequence of values that represent the approximate positions of each term in a document. The greater the value of B, the higher the accuracy of the term positions[1]. Since each term signal is a sequence, we are able to apply signal processing transformation to them to map them into a spectral domain. Transforms which we have investigated are the Fourier transform, the cosine transform, and the Wavelet transform using the Haar wavelet and Daubechies-4 wavelet.

2.2 The Spectral Domain

Once we have our set of term spectra for each document ($\tilde{\nu}_{d,t}$), we can now proceed with the query. When a query is given, the user generally wants the retrieval

[1] Note that if $B = 1$, the spectral method produces the same results as the vector space method.

system to return documents which have many occurrences of the query terms and the query terms should be within a small proximity within the document. Now that we have a set of term spectra, we cannot measure term proximity directly. We must take advantage of the complex nature of each spectrum. If we used the Fourier transform to obtain our term spectra, the resulting complex signal could be split into magnitude and phase signals. The magnitude of the term spectrum corresponds to the term count in the corresponding term signal. The phase of the term spectrum corresponds to the relative position of the term in the term signal.

Magnitude. The magnitude of the term spectrum $\tilde{f}_{d,t}$ is related to the occurrence of the tth term in the dth document, so it is important that we use this information in our document score calculations. The spectral transformation that we use is a linear transform, therefore each of the spectral component magnitudes is equally as important as the other. If a certain component magnitude is dominant in the spectrum, it implies that the term signal followed a certain pattern which is represented in the used transform. We take the magnitude of the term spectrum to be the sum of each of the spectral component magnitudes:

$$H_{d,b} = \sum_{t \in Q} H_{d,t,b} \tag{2}$$

Phase Precision. We have mentioned that we would like to give a high score to documents that have high magnitudes and similar phase for each spectral component of each query spectrum. If we have a set of query terms Q and each query term spectrum contains the elements:

$$\nu_{d,t,b} = H_{d,t,b} \exp\left(i\theta_{d,t,b}\right) \tag{3}$$

where $\nu_{d,t,b}$ is the bth spectral component of the term spectrum from term t in document d, $H_{d,t,b}$ is its magnitude, $\theta_{d,t,b}$ is its phase and $i = \sqrt{-1}$. Then, for any given magnitude, we would want the highest score to be attributed to the document that has the same phase in each spectral component for all of the query terms. So the highest score is given in the case:

$$\theta_{d,t_i,b} = \theta_{d,t_j,b} \qquad \forall i,j \in Q \tag{4}$$

As the phase of each component shifts, we want the score to reduce. Therefore if the spectral components are totally out of phase, we should assign a low score.

A good measure of similarity is variance, where low variance implies that each of the elements are similar. Unfortunately, we cannot use variance because phase is a radial value ($2\pi = 0$). Therefore we must look towards phase precision.

To find how similar vectors are, we an simply average them and observe the magnitude of the average vector. If the vectors are facing the same direction, the magnitude of the average will be large. If the vectors are facing in different directions, the averaging will cause the vectors to cancel each other, providing a small magnitude of the average. We can use this concept with our phases. If

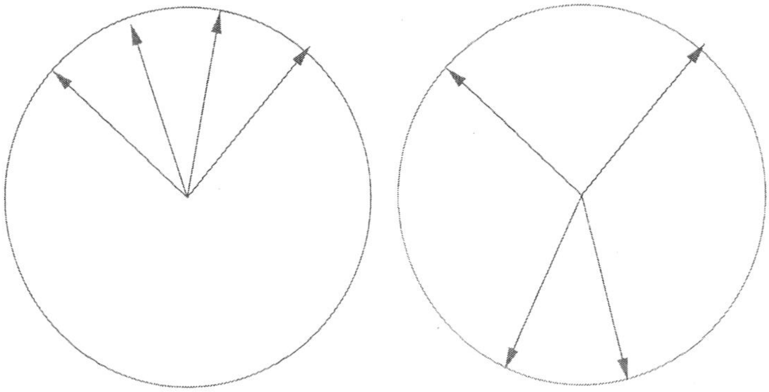

Fig. 1. A graphical example of phase precision. The left and right unit circles contain four unit vectors with assigned phases. The four vectors in the left unit circle face in a similar direction. Therefore the average magnitude of these will be close to 1. The four unit vectors in the right circle face in different directions. Therefore they will cancel each other when added and their average magnitude will be close to 0

we attach a unit magnitude to each of the phases, we can average them and take the magnitude of the average, called phase precision. If all of the phases are the same, the phase precision will be 1. If all of the phases are different, the phase precision will be close to zero (shown in figure 1). The phase precision equation is:

$$\Phi_{d,b} = \left| \frac{\sum_{t \in Q} \exp\left(i\theta_{d,t,b}\right)}{\#(Q)} \right| \tag{5}$$

where $\Phi_{d,b}$ is the phase precision of spectral component b in document d.

Combining Magnitude and Phase Precision. The magnitude and phase precision values are obtained for each spectral component, therefore we must combine them to obtain a single document score. The magnitude represents the occurrence of the query terms in the document and the phase precision is a measure of how similar query term positions are. We use the phase precision as a weighting factor to the magnitude calculation. This implies that is the query terms are in approximately the same positions, we will use the full magnitude values (since the phase precision weight will be 1) and as the query term position difference grows the phase precision weight will reduce and we will be using only a fraction of the magnitude values. We give the document score as:

$$s_d = \sum_{b=0}^{B-1} H_{d,b}\Phi_{d,b} \tag{6}$$

2.3 Experimental Results

Some experimental results are shown in table 1. The precision obtained after 5, 10, 15 and 20 documents is shown for the vector space model and our spectral

Table 1. Experiments using the AP2WSJ2 document set from TREC showing the precision at the top 5,10,15 and 20 documents. We can see that the spectral retrieval method obtains better precision than the Vector space methods for several different weighting schemes. This is due to the unique way in which the spectral document retrieval method uses term position information

Method	Weight	Precision 5	Precision 10	Precision 15	Precision 20
Spectral	Lnu.ltu	0.4960	0.4613	0.4391	0.4227
VSM	Lnu.ltu	0.4693	0.4493	0.4356	0.4180
Spectral	BD-ACI-BCA	0.4867	0.4647	0.4440	0.4193
VSM	BD-ACI-BCA	0.4440	0.4247	0.4142	0.3953
Spectral	AB-AFD-BAA	0.4947	0.4673	0.4493	0.4220
VSM	AB-AFD-BAA	0.4880	0.4493	0.4404	0.4217

based method for three high ranking weighting schemes [17]. The experiments were run on the AP2WSJ2 document set from TREC using the titles of queries 51 to 200. We can see that the spectral based method provides significantly better precision results for each weighting scheme.

3 Latent Semantic Query Mapping

To remove the assumption of term independence, methods such as thesauruses have been employed which expand the users query to include terms related to the original query terms. Other methods, such as latent semantic indexing, map the documents and query from the terms space into a reduced dimensional topic space. Documents and queries are compared as usual (using the inner product) in this topic space.

Our method [10] combines the two mentioned methods to produce a query expansion using latent semantic analysis. The query expansion data is placed in a mapping which occurs before the documents and query are compared. In this section we will describe the mapping creation process and display results of experiments of the vector space method with and without the query expansion.

3.1 Latent Semantic Analysis

If a word has latent semantics, it implies that there is a hidden meaning behind it. Latent semantic analysis (LSA) is the process which we follow in order to find the hidden meanings. LSA was first performed using singular value decomposition (SVD) [2] of the document-term index and later performed using maximum likelihood methods [6]. In each of the methods, we receive a mapping matrix which is able to map a vector from the term domain to the latent topic domain. If we focus on the SVD method, the decomposition gives us:

$$A = U\Sigma V' \tag{7}$$

where A is our document-term index, U is the set of orthonormal left singular vectors, Σ is the set of singular values, and V is the set of orthonormal right singular vectors. From this equation, we take our new set of document vectors to be $U\Sigma$ and our term to topic mapping as the matrix V. We can show that the mapping of the document-term index give us the set of mapped document vectors in the topic space:

$$\hat{A} = AV = U\Sigma \tag{8}$$

where $\hat{A}$ is the set of document vectors in the topic space. Queries are mapped into the topic space in the same way:

$$\hat{q} = qV \tag{9}$$

where $\hat{q}$ is the query in the topic space. Once all of our vectors are in the topic space, we compare them for similarity using the inner product:

$$s = \hat{A}\hat{q}' = AV(qV)' \tag{10}$$

$$= AVV'q' \tag{11}$$

where s is the set of document scores. We know that V is an orthonormal matrix, therefore $VV' = I$ (the identity matrix).

The SVD arranges the elements of the singular vectors in such a way that we can ignore the last few elements of each vector and still obtain similar results. If we take only the first n elements of the document and query vectors mapped into the topic space ($\hat{A}$ and $\hat{q}$) we are obtaining the best least squares estimate of the vectors in n dimensions. The magnitude of the singular values give us insight into the importance of the corresponding dimension of the singular vectors. If the singular value is zero, the corresponding dimension can be ignored with no change to A.

3.2 Latent Semantic Space

By reducing the dimensionality of the topic space, we are reducing the number of elements that we need to store and use in calculations. A typical reduction would take a document vector from its 100,000 dimension term space to a 100 dimensional topic space. But as the saying goes 'there is no free lunch'. The document vectors in the term space are very sparse, we can see that if there were only 100 unique terms in a document, 99.9% of the document vector elements would contain zeros and the majority of non-zero elements would contain the value of 1. This statistic leads to very high compression and also allows the system designer to implement fast scoring algorithms based on this knowledge. The query vector is also very sparse, usually containing only two or three non-zero elements. The document scores are based on the inner product of the document and query vector, therefore, the most number of multiplications required to obtain the score will be equal to the number of non-zero elements in the query vector. By mapping the document and query vectors to the latent topic space, we are mapping our sparse high dimensional vectors in to dense low dimensional vectors. By obtaining a dense query vector, we have to perform many more multiplications during the query process and hence, receive a longer query time. The

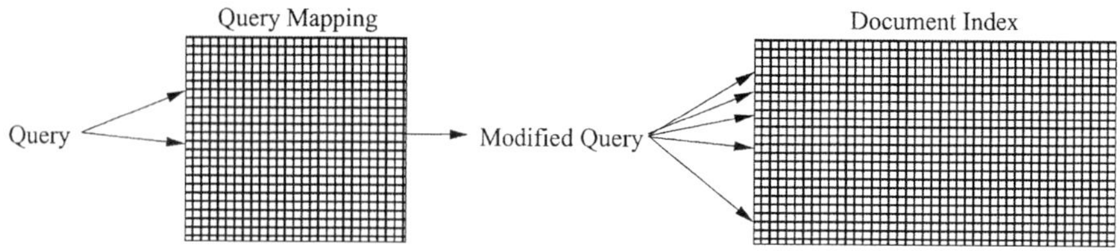

Fig. 2. To use the query map, the query selects the rows from the map corresponding to its query terms and combines these to obtain a modified query term set. This modified query is then applied to the document collection index in the usual fashion

compression of the stored document vectors in the reduced topic space would not be as compact as it was in the term space due to the unexpected data patterns.

Therefore an attempt to increase the precision by mapping into the topic space has caused an increase in query time and storage.

3.3 Latent Semantic Query Map

If we examine the equation where we have used the dimension reduced singular vectors to map our documents and query into the topic space (equation 10), we can see that it is possible to obtain the document scores by using the original sparse document vectors:

$$s = (AV)(V'q') = A(VV'q') = A(Mq') \tag{12}$$

where $M = VV'$. This equation shows that we are able to leave the document vectors in the term space and apply a simple mapping to the query to obtain the related query terms in the term space. By combining the term-topic mapping (V) with itself, we are creating a mapping which takes data from the term space to the topic space and then back to the term space. This will take the users query and map it to a set of weighted terms (shown in figure 2) where the weight reflects the query term's relevance to the query. This combined mapping benefits the retrieval process by: 1) leaving the documents in the sparse term space which allows us to use fast querying techniques. 2) providing us with an expanded query containing weighted terms, not unidentifiable topics. The second point is an important one, because it allows the user to review the expanded query and select terms which are appropriate for the query. The query can also be pruned automatically by setting a cutoff weight or choosing a set number of query terms. By reducing the number of query terms, we are also reducing the calculations required during the query process and the time required to complete the query.

We have reduced the query time and the storage required to store the document vectors, but we must also store the mapping.

3.4 Storing the Query Map

The query map (M) is a $m \times m$ matrix, where m is the number of unique query terms in the document set. It created by multiplying the term to topic mapping by the transpose of itself, therefore it is a dense square matrix, which is as compressible as $\hat{A}$.

To reduce the size of this matrix, we can examine the terms that occupy it. If we go back to the construction of the V matrix, we can recall that it is through the SVD of A. This leads to the following set of equations:

$$A = U\Sigma V' \quad (13)$$

$$A'A = (U\Sigma V')'(U\Sigma V') \quad (14)$$

$$= V\Sigma U'U\Sigma V' \quad (15)$$

$$= V\Sigma^2 V' \quad (16)$$

$$(A'A)V = V\Sigma^2 \quad (17)$$

The last line shows that V is the set of eigenvectors for the matrix $A'A$ which is the covariance matrix of A' or the covariance of the terms found in the document set. To establish a good estimate of the covariance of two variables, we need to take many samples. Therefore, if there are only a few occurrences of a term in the document set, its estimated covariance with other terms would not be accurate. This implies that we should remove the under sampled terms from the document term matrix before calculating the SVD.

Terms that appear in many documents provide us with little information as well. If they are included in the calculation of V, we will find that they would be about equally distributed amongst all topics and hence related to all terms. By including terms that appear in most documents into the query would not benefit the query since the term would simply add to the score of most documents (just as if we added a constant value to the document scores). Therefore we can reduce the query mapping size by excluding the terms that appear in many documents before the calculation of the SVD.

3.5 Fast Mapping

If we review the scoring process using the query mapping, we will observe that the mapping stage is exactly the same as the document score calculation stage. The two stages are: 1) Multiply the query vector with the mapping to receive the expanded query vector. 2) Multiply the expanded query vector with the document index to receive the document scores. This implies that all of the compression and fast querying techniques that are found while calculating the top document scores (such as quantisation and early termination [9]) can also be used to obtain the top weighted query terms related to the original query.

3.6 Experimental Results

We have provided a few experimental results showing the query mapping method and the Lnu.ltu vector space method using the titles of queries 51 to 200 from the TREC document set. Figure 3 shows results from three sets of experiments. The top four plots have precision on the y-axis and the number of documents a term must appear in to be included in the mapping (e.g. 200 implies that only

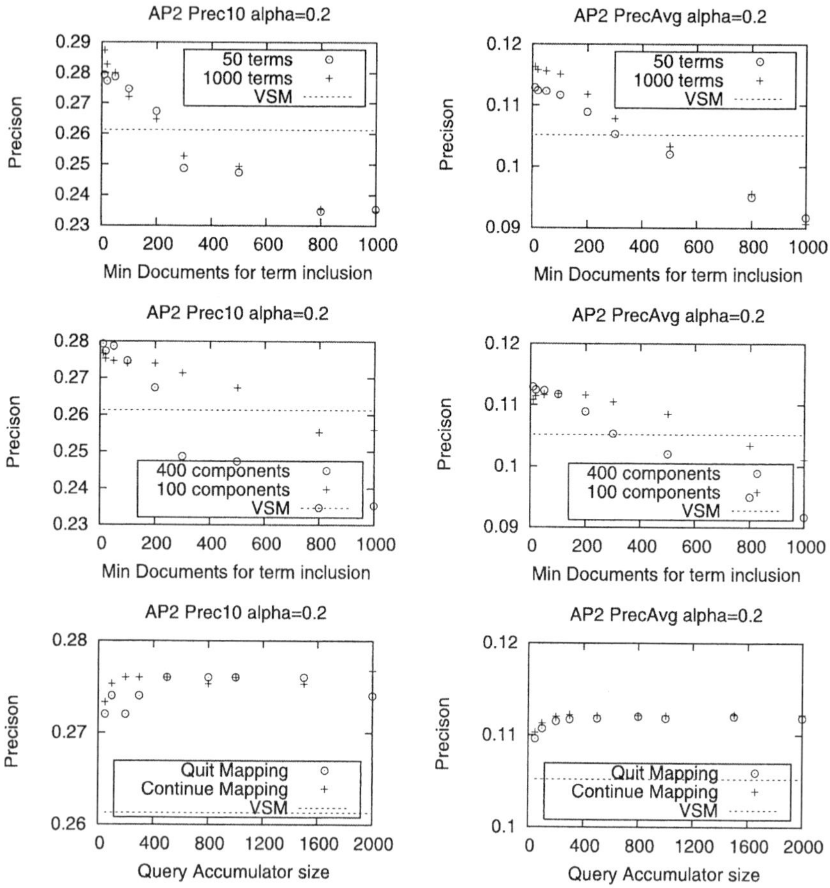

Fig. 3. Experimental results showing the precision of the vector space method using a query map

terms that appeared in more that 200 documents were included in the mapping) as the x-axis. The first two plots compare the precision at 10 documents and the average precision obtained by adjusting the number of expansion terms in the query. We can see that the 1000 term expansion provides only a slight improvement over the 50 term expansion. The second two plots provide the precision at 10 documents and the average precision obtained when changing the number of topic dimensions chosen. We can see that the 100 dimensional topic space provides a greater precision with a smaller mapping when compared to the 400 dimensional topic space.

The last two plots have precision on the y-axis and the number of query accumulators on the x-axis. They show the precision at 10 documents and the average precision obtained when the number of query term accumulators are varied. We can see that the Continue method provides higher precision, and if we choose 400 or more accumulators we achieve the best precision.

4 Conclusion

We have presented two separate methods of extending the vector space model in information retrieval and addressing the problems of including term position information and using term dependencies.

The first method labelled 'spectral based information retrieval' allows us to easily utilise the term positions by taking into account their term spectra. By combining query term spectra, we can produce greater document scores for those documents that have query terms within a smaller proximity when compared to those that span a larger proximity.

The second method entitled 'latent semantic query mapping' lets us perform query expansions on the users query based on the term relationships in the document set. The term relationships are found using singular value decomposition. This mapping can be stored in a fast retrieval index such as those found in the vector space model.

Each of these methods extends on the basic vector space model to obtain a generalised vector model of information retrieval. We have presented an extensive investigation of these methods in the papers [11, 15, 12, 14, 13, 10].

References

1. Charles L. A. Clarke and Gordon V. Cormack. Shortest-substring retrieval and ranking. *ACM Transactions on Information Systems*, 18(1):44–78, January 2000.
2. S. Deerwester, S. T. Dumais, G. W. Furnas, T. K. Landauer, and R. A. Harshman. Indexing by latent semantic analysis. *Journal of the the American Society for Information Science*, 41:391–407, 1990.
3. Jianfeng Gao, Jian-Yun Nie, Guangyuan Wu, and Guihong Cao. Dependence language model for information retrieval. In *Proceedings of the 27th annual international conference on Research and development in information retrieval*, pages 170 – 177, New York, NY, USA, 2004. ACM Press.
4. D. Hawking and P. Thistlewaite. Proximity operators - so near and yet so far. In Donna Harman, editor, *The Fourth Text REtrieval Conference (TREC-4)*, pages 131–144, Gaithersburg, Md. 20899, November 1995. National Institute of Standards and Technology Special Publication 500-236.
5. David Hawking and Paul Thistlewaite. Relevance weighting using distance between term occurrences. Technical Report TR-CS-96-08, The Australian National University, August 1996.
6. Thomas Hofmann. Probabilistic latent semantic indexing. In *Proceedings of the 22nd annual international ACM SIGIR conference on Research and development in information retrieval*, pages 50–57. ACM Press, 1999.
7. Y. Jing and W. B. Croft. An association thesaurus for information retrieval. In *RIAO 94 Conference Proceedings*, pages 146 – 160, New York, October 1994.
8. E. Michael Keen. Term position ranking: some new test results. In *Proceedings of the 15th annual international ACM SIGIR conference on Research and development in information retrieval*, pages 66–76. ACM Press, 1992.
9. Alistair Moffat and Justin Zobel. Self-indexing inverted files for fast text retrieval. *ACM Transactions on Information Systems (TOIS)*, 14(4):349–379, 1996.

10. Laurence Park and Kotagiri Ramamohanarao. Hybrid pre-query term expansion using latent semantic analysis. In *The Fourth IEEE International Conference on Data Mining*, November 2004.
11. Laurence A. F. Park, Marimuthu Palaniswami, and Ramamohanarao Kotagiri. Internet document filtering using fourier domain scoring. In Luc de Raedt and Arno Siebes, editors, *Principles of Data Mining and Knowledge Discovery*, number 2168 in Lecture Notes in Artificial Intelligence, pages 362–373. Springer-Verlag, September 2001.
12. Laurence A. F. Park, Marimuthu Palaniswami, and Kotagiri Ramamohanarao. A novel web text mining method using the discrete cosine transform. In T. Elomaa, H. Mannila, and H. Toivonen, editors, *6th European Conference on Principles of Data Mining and Knowledge Discovery*, number 2431 in Lecture Notes in Artificial Intelligence, pages 385–396, Berlin, August 2002. Springer-Verlag.
13. Laurence A. F. Park, Marimuthu Palaniswami, and Kotagiri Ramamohanarao. A novel document ranking method using the discrete cosine transform. *IEEE Transactions on Pattern Analysis and Machine Intelligence*, 27(1), January 2005.
14. Laurence A. F. Park, Kotagiri Ramamohanarao, and Marimuthu Palaniswami. A new implementation technique for fast spectral based document retrieval systems. In Vipin Kumar and Shusaku Tsumoto, editors, *2002 IEEE International Conference on Data Mining*, pages 346–353, Los Alamitos, California, USA, December 2002. IEEE Computer Society.
15. Laurence A. F. Park, Kotagiri Ramamohanarao, and Marimuthu Palaniswami. Fourier domain scoring : A novel document ranking method. *IEEE Transactions on Knowledge and Data Engineering*, 16(5):529–539, May 2004.
16. Munirathnam Srikanth and Rohini Srihari. Biterm language models for document retrieval. In *Proceedings of the 25th annual international ACM SIGIR conference on Research and development in information retrieval*, pages 425 – 426, New York, NY, USA, 2002. ACM Press.
17. Justin Zobel and Alistair Moffat. Exploring the similarity space. *ACM SIGIR Forum*, 32(1):18–34, Spring 1998.

A Neural Network Approach to Web Graph Processing

Ah Chung Tsoi[1], Franco Scarselli[2], Marco Gori[2], Markus Hagenbuchner[3], and Sweah Liang Yong[3]

[1] Australian Research Council, GPO Box 2702, Canberra, ACT 2601, Australia
[2] University of Siena, Siena, Italy
[3] Faculty of Informatics, University of Wollongong, Northfileds Ave., Wollongong, NSW 2522, Australia

Abstract. In this paper, we will provide an overview of some of the more recent developments in web graph processing using the classic Google page rank equation as popularized by Brins and Page [1], and its modifications, to handle page rank and personalized page rank determinations. It is shown that one may progressively modify the linear matrix stochastic equation underlying the Google page rank determinations [1] to one which may contain neural network formulations. Furthermore the capability of these modifications in determining personalized page ranks is demonstrated through a number of examples based on the web repository WT10G.

1 Introduction

The internet has grown to become ubiquitous in our daily lives. From a humble beginning in the early to mid 1990's, the internet has sustained a tremendous growth rate of approximately 1 million web page per day and it currently contains over 3 billion web pages.

From an information retrieval point of view, the internet presents an interesting case. It is one of the largest data repositories known to man, constantly growing and changing. Each web page may contain text, images, sound, video clips. Very few web pages contain intentionally coded metadata[1] which may facilitate their easy retrieval. Each web page is coded in a common format and language, known as the hypertext markup language (HTML). The specification of HTML is quite loose, and "forgiving". Thus, web pages containing some non-critical errors nevertheless still can be displayed when viewed by a user using a browser. Most web pages contain links to other web pages, which serve as "containers" of information. Such pointed web pages may contain the information itself, or they may in turn point to other web pages, which may serve as

[1] Each web page contains some metadata, e.g., anchor texts. However, such metadata are not designed specifically for information retrieval purposes.

Y. Zhang et al. (Eds.): APWeb 2005, LNCS 3399, pp. 27–38, 2005.

their "containers" of information. Thus, from a graph-theoretic point of view, each web page may be considered as a node, with incoming links from other nodes, and outgoing links pointing to other nodes. This is commonly known as web graphs.

There are two ways in which web pages may be retrieved from a user query: (a) matching the query to the content of web pages, and (b) through links. In approach (a), one simple way would be to match keywords from the user query with those occurring in the text in the web page; the one with the most matches will be ranked closest to the query. A common example is the Shared Point Portal© of Microsoft, in which sophisticated ways were used to weigh the words according to their occurrence in the total number of documents/web pages in the repository [2]; whether the word is a commonly occurred word, etc. In approach (b), an incoming link is considered as a "vote" of confidence from another web page. Thus, a web page with many incoming links, each of these links is coming from pages which themselves may have many incoming links would be considered as important as it is "most popular" from a "voting" point of view. One of the most celebrated formulations of the second approach is the work of Brins and Page [1] which is one of the mechanisms underlying the way in which the popular search engine: Google arranges query results and presents them to users. In this paper we will concentrate on approach (b) and we will not discuss approach (a) further.

The arrangement of this paper is as follows: in Section 2, we will provide a brief introduction to the page rank determination as given in [1]. In Section 3, we will show how Google's page rank equation can be modified to find personalized page ranks by the introduction of a forcing function term which can be considered as a basis expansion function, each basis being an identified topic which a person wishes to consider. In Section 4, we will show how the generalized linear matrix stochastic equation introduced in [1] discussed in Section 3 can be modified to become a multi-layered feedforward neural network. In Section 5 we will show a number of indicative experiments based on the web repository WT10G which demonstrate the potential of the proposed modifications to the Google page rank equation. Some conclusions are drawn in Section 6.

2 Page Rank Determination

The page rank, or page importance, as provided in [1], is independent of the content of the web pages, but solely dependent on the links among the web pages, and thus their topological structure. According to [1]:

$$x_i = d \sum_{j \in pa[i]} \frac{x_j}{h_j} + (1-d)e_i \ .$$

Here x_i is the page rank of the i-th web page, $i = 1, 2, \ldots, n$, the total number of web pages in the web repository is assumed to n. $pa[i]$ is the set of pages pointing to i, e_i is the default authority assigned to page i, h_j is the outdegree of j, and $d \in (0,1)$ is a dumping factor. When stacking all the x_i into an n-vector $\boldsymbol{X}$, we obtain

$$\boldsymbol{X} = d\boldsymbol{W}\boldsymbol{X} + (1-d)\boldsymbol{E}\ , \qquad (1)$$

where $W \in \mathcal{R}^{n \times n}$ is a matrix called transition matrix with elements $w_{i,j} = 1/h_j$ if there is a hyperlink from node j to node i, and h_j is the total number of outlinks of node j, and $w_{i,j} = 0$ otherwise. Thus, $\boldsymbol{W}$ is a non–null stochastic matrix, where each column either sums to 1 or to 0. In [1], the forcing factor $\boldsymbol{E} = [e_1, \ldots, e_n]'$ is a vector having all the elements equal to 1, i.e. $e_i = 1$ for each i, and $'$ denotes the transpose operator.

It may be shown that the solution to the page rank equation Eq(1) is unique and exists provided $\|d\boldsymbol{W}\|_1 < 1$ holds, where $\|\cdot\|_1$ denotes the norm 1 operator, i.e. $\|\boldsymbol{W}\|_1 = max_j(\sum_i |w_{i,j})|$. When the $\boldsymbol{W}$ satisfies the above hypothesis, the solution is given by $\boldsymbol{X} = (1-d)(\boldsymbol{I}_n - d\boldsymbol{W})^{-1}\boldsymbol{E}$, where $\boldsymbol{I}_n$ denotes the n–dimensional identity matrix.

3 Personalized Page Rank Determination

The page rank as determined by Eq(1) is valid for the entire web repository. Once the topology of the web repository is given, and d fixed, then the page ranks are fixed. There are circumstances where a user may wish to modify such page ranks. This is often referred to as personalized page ranks. The main idea underlying the approaches to personalized page ranks is that the concept of "page importance" is not absolute, but it depends on the particular needs of a user or a search engine. For example, the homepage of a large directory may be authoritative for a general purpose search engine, but not important for a portal specialized on the topic "Wine". Thus, the suggested solution consists of building different page ranks, each one specialized on a topic [3], a user [4] or a query [5].

One way in which the personalized page ranks can be constructed is to parameterize the page rank in Eq(1). We assume that a set of specialized page ranks $\boldsymbol{x}_1, \ldots, \boldsymbol{x}_m$ is available. These page ranks, which may be built using different kinds of features (e.g. the page content, the URL, etc.), should capture some of the page properties which are useful to estimate the authority of a document for a given user[2]. We will assume that a parameterization of the page rank can be obtained using a linear combination of these specialized page ranks. In other words, a parameterized page rank $\boldsymbol{x}(\boldsymbol{p})$ is constructed as follows:

$$\boldsymbol{x}(\boldsymbol{p}) = \sum_{h=1}^{m} \alpha_h \boldsymbol{x}_h \qquad (2)$$

where $\alpha_h \in \mathcal{R}$ are parameters which satisfy $\sum_{h=1}^{m} \alpha_h = 1$, and $\boldsymbol{p}' = [\alpha_1, \ldots, \alpha_m]'$. In fact, $\boldsymbol{x}(\boldsymbol{p})$, called adaptive page rank, can be personalized by varying the

[2] We will show how these specialized page ranks can be constructed in practice in Section 5.

parameter set $\boldsymbol{p}$. In the following, we will denote by $\boldsymbol{M} \in \mathcal{R}^{n \times m}$ the matrix $[\boldsymbol{x}_1, \ldots, \boldsymbol{x}_m]$ so that adaptive page rank is also defined by $\boldsymbol{x}(\boldsymbol{p}) = \boldsymbol{M}\boldsymbol{p}$.

Let us assume that there exist $\boldsymbol{e}_1, \ldots, \boldsymbol{e}_m$, such that, for each h, $\boldsymbol{x}_h$ is the solution of (1) when the forcing function is $\boldsymbol{e}_h$ and the transition matrix is the original $\boldsymbol{W}$ used in the page rank equation (1). Since $\boldsymbol{x}_h = (\boldsymbol{I}_n - d\boldsymbol{W})^{-1}\boldsymbol{e}_h$, $\boldsymbol{x}(p) = (\boldsymbol{I}_n - d\boldsymbol{W})^{-1} \left(\sum_{h=1}^{m} \alpha_h \boldsymbol{e}_h\right)$ holds. It follows that $\boldsymbol{x}(\boldsymbol{p})$ is the solution of

$$\boldsymbol{x}(\boldsymbol{p})_{t+1} = d\boldsymbol{W}\boldsymbol{x}(\boldsymbol{p})_t + \sum_{h=1}^{m} \alpha_h \boldsymbol{x}_h \,. \tag{3}$$

$$= d\boldsymbol{W}\boldsymbol{x}(\boldsymbol{p})_t + \boldsymbol{M}\boldsymbol{p} \tag{4}$$

Thus, $\boldsymbol{x}(\boldsymbol{p})$ is by itself a specialized rank whose default authorities are a linear combination of those used for computing $\boldsymbol{x}_1, \ldots, \boldsymbol{x}_m$.

The adaptive page ranks can be obtained by solving a quadratic programming problem [6], involving a quadratic cost function, e.g., expressing the square of difference of the distance between the page ranks as given by Eq(1), and those of Eq(4); a set of linear constraints which expresses user requirements, and the linear dynamical constraint Eq(4). Such solutions can be obtained quite quickly using common quadratic programming solution software [6].

4 Neural Network Formulations

It is interesting to ask the question: is it possible to replace the linear equation in Eq(1) by a nonlinear equation, e.g., a multi-layered feedforward neural network. The intuition is that a nonlinear forcing function may produce a better result than those provided by Eq(4), as there is no inherent reason why the underlying graph mapping function is linear. Indeed there are reasons to suspect that the underlying mapping function is nonlinear. It is noted that the page importance of each web page is a function of the page importance of those pages pointing to the page. The topology of the internet is such that there are relatively only a very small number of web pages pointing to a particular web page. In turn, these web pages are pointed to by a relatively small number of web pages, and so on. Hence, intuitively, it would be useful if we encode this limited neighborhood[3] dependency information in terms of a graph-dependent model. The page ranks as determined by Eq(1) on the other hand, does not have this graph-dependent notion. It assumes that potentially all web pages in the web graph can influence the page rank of an individual web page, or more generally one another. It depends on the topology of the web graph as encoded in the transition matrix to limit the influence of the other web pages which may not have any direct connections to the particular web page concerned or its parents, grand-parents, etc. Thus instead of relying on the transition matrix $\boldsymbol{W}$, in the graph-dependent

[3] Neighborhood here means the web pages pointing to a particular web page and their parents, and grand-parents, etc.

approach, it explicitly encodes the information in a graph-dependent fashion by only considering the parents, grand-parents, and generations before. In other words, the page importance is a function of where the web page is located in relation to its parents, grand-parents, etc. As we will implement the nonlinear dependency using a multi-layered feedforward neural network, we will call this a graph neural network.

To be more precise we will modify Eq(3) as follows:

$$\boldsymbol{x}(\boldsymbol{p})_{t+1} = \mathcal{N}(d\boldsymbol{W}\boldsymbol{x}(\boldsymbol{p})_t + \sum_{h=1}^{m} \alpha_h \boldsymbol{x}_h) \tag{5}$$

where $\mathcal{N}(\cdot)$ denotes a matrix nonlinear function. The implementation of this function can be realized using a multilayered feedforward neural network. In general, there is only one hidden layer, as it is known that such an architecture is a universal approximator to an arbitrary degree of accuracy provided that there is a sufficient number of hidden layer neurons [7].

The parameters of the multilayered feedforward neural network can be obtained by minimizing a quadratic cost function which, e.g., may express the square of the distance of the difference between the page ranks as determined by Eq(1) and those obtained by Eq(5), while satisfying the nonlinear equation Eq(5). The derivation is tedious though easy conceptually and hence omitted here.

5 Experimental Verifications

In this section, we will show a number of experiments using the web repository WT10G. The WT10G data set is provided by CSIRO, Australia and was prepared as a benchmark for the Text Retrieval Conference (TREC). The WT10G presents a snapshot of a portion of the World Wide Web. The collection paid special attention to the connectivity among the Web pages. Hence this set of Web collection is suitable for evaluations of search engine algorithms based on connectivity concepts. There are 1,692,096 documents from 11,680 servers contained in the dataset.

Nine topics have been considered: “Linux”, “Windows”, “Cooking”, “Wine”, “Sport”, “Tennis”, “Hockey”, “Surgery”, and “Cancer”. The association of pages to topics was carried out by a naive Bayesian classifier [8, 9]. Bayesian text classification consists of a learning and a production phase. During the learning phase some documents (about 20 in our experiments) which are known to address a topic are collected in order to produce a statistical analysis of the word occurrences. In the production phase, a classifier estimates, for each document in the dataset, the probability that it belongs to the topic by comparing the statistical data and the words of the document. The classifier assigns a document to a class when the probability is larger than a predefined threshold. In our case, the topic thresholds are defined by human inspection of the highest scored documents returned by the classifier. A more general approach was suggested in [10].

Since the presence of a huge number of different words affects the quality of the statistical analysis, both learning and production phases may include a feature extraction process which decreases the number of words considered for each document, selecting only the most useful ones [2]. In our case, feature extraction consists of three parts: (a) most common words (i.e. stop words) were removed; (b) a stemming procedure was applied[4]; and (c) during the production phase only the 20 most promising words were considered by selecting from the document those having the highest frequency in the training set[5].

Note that our feature extraction mechanism allows to recognize also the documents which discuss a number of topics at the same time, because the presence of many irrelevant words for the topic does not impair the extraction of the most relevant ones. Multi–topic documents are usually news wires, directories and other general content pages. Since, they play a different role with respect to documents dealing with a single topic, a special class "General" was built for them. We simply decided to include into topic "General" all the pages that were previously inserted in 3 or more topics. Finally, the topic "Other pages" was considered which includes all the documents not belonging to any classes indicated.

Table 1. The number of pages and the page rank (PR) average for each selected topic

	Windows	Linux	Cooking	Wine	Sport	Tennis	Hockey	Surgery	Cancer	General	Other
Pages	4,457	513	4,202	953	1,536	549	1,195	5,030	3,748	1,265	1,672,631
PR avg.	9.81	12.18	10.82	11.74	5.6	6.37	13.1	7.56	7.88	36.26	5.5

The first row of Table 1 shows the number of pages and the second row the mean of the page rank for each topics. Page rank is maximal on the class "General", where the average is much higher than those on other topics. This observation confirms the claim that the class of "general" pages plays a different role on the Web and contains directories and other well referenced documents.

Table 2 depicts the intersection of the topics. Element in row i and column j denotes the percentage of pages of topic i which have been classified also in topic j. Notice that some apparently unrelated topics have a non void intersection, e.g. Windows and Surgery. A manual inspection of the web pages concerned shows that the pages in these intersections are partially due to documents that actually discuss the two topics (e.g. pages about software for medical applications) and

[4] A stemmer produces word stems by removing the suffixes (e.g. in English "ing", "s", "es", "ed", and so on). The Porter stemmer [11] was used in our experiments.

[5] With respect to other feature extraction approaches, the selection of the most frequent words with respect to the training set produces a higher level of recall, i.e. $\frac{N_c}{N}$, where N_c is the number of documents found by the classifier and N the total number of documents on the topic. In fact, to find the few documents that discuss a specific topic in a very large dataset is a challenging problem.

Table 2. The distribution of the topics on the dataset. Cell in position i, j displays the percentage of the pages of topic i belonging also to topic j. By definition, classes "General" and "Other" (not displayed) do not intersect other classes

	Windows	Linux	Cooking	Wine	Sport	Tennis	Hockey	Surgery	Cancer
Windows	100	8	2	0	1	0	0	0	1
Linux	71	100	0	0	0	0	0	0	0
Cooking	2	0	100	15	2	0	0	2	2
Wine	1	0	66	100	1	0	0	0	0
Sport	4	0	5	0	100	2	11	3	2
Tennis	2	0	3	0	50	100	3	0	1
Hockey	1	0	3	0	15	2	100	0	0
Surgery	1	0	2	0	1	0	2	100	35
Cancer	1	0	3	0	1	0	0	47	100

partially due to general documents which our method was not able to move to the class "General"[6].

On the basis of these topics, eleven specialized page ranks $\boldsymbol{x}_1, \ldots, \boldsymbol{x}_{11}$ were computed, one for each topic. For each specialized rank, we used the same transition matrix $\boldsymbol{W}$ as Google's page rank and a forcing function $\boldsymbol{E}_i' = [e_{i,1}, \ldots, e_{i,n}]'$, where

$$e_{i,h} = \begin{cases} \frac{1}{Q} & \text{if } h \text{ belongs to topic } i \\ 0 & \text{otherwise} \end{cases}$$

and Q is a normalizing factor such that $\|\boldsymbol{E}_i\|_1 = N$ and N is the number of pages in the topic dataset. The normalization of the $\boldsymbol{e}_i$ allows to derive ranks with comparable values and simplifies the optimization process.

Table 3 shows the results of a statistical analysis carried out on specialized page ranks. Each row of the table compares a specialized page rank to the page rank as obtained in Eq(1), while the columns specify the set of pages where the comparison was carried out. For example, the cell of row "Wine" and column "Windows" displays the ratio of the average of the specialized page rank "Windows" on the pages of class "Wine" by the mean of page rank. Formally, cell in row i and column j is $\frac{r_{i,j}}{pr_j}$, where $r_{i,j}$ is the mean of the i–th specialized page rank on the pages of j-topic and pr_j is the mean of page rank on the pages of j-topic. Thus, the cells displaying values larger than one define the classes where the specialized ranks are larger than page rank.

The statistical analysis shows that specialized page ranks largely improve the scores of the pages about the corresponding topic and about related topics (see, for example, wine and cooking). The data also confirms that the improvement is large for smaller topics, where the rank is concentrated in a few pages. In

6 A further analysis has shown that the number of those spurious intersections decreases when class "General" is allowed to include more documents. For example, this can be achieved by using smaller topic thresholds, i.e. when counting the number of topics a document belonging to a topic, we consider also those topics for which the probability returned by the classifier is smaller but close to the topic threshold. However, since the classification accuracy is not important for the purposes of this paper, we skip over these refinements.

Table 3. The mean of specialized page ranks on the topics. Specialized page ranks are displayed in rows, the topics in columns. Cell in row i and column j is $\frac{r_{i,j}}{pr_j}$, where $r_{i,j}$ is the mean of the i–th specialized rank on the pages of j-topic and pr_j is the mean of Google's page rank on the pages of j-topic

	Windows	Linux	Cooking	Wine	Sport	Tennis	Hockey	Surgery	Cancer	General	Other
Windows	57.16	35.22	2.58	1.15	4.01	3.03	1.02	1.55	1.51	1.77	0.75
Linux	42.47	355.22	1.14	0.64	0.3	0.02	0.24	2.25	2.48	2.03	0.7
Cooking	2.35	0.71	53.73	44.85	7.56	3.81	2.2	2.45	3.07	1.91	0.71
Wine	1.4	0.55	44.01	214.68	3.57	2.96	1.48	1.79	1.63	2.55	0.7
Sport	2.63	0.33	4.08	1.56	243.24	109.85	20.45	2.21	2.26	2.04	0.67
Tennis	2.14	0.32	2.54	1.8	124.77	542.94	7.65	1.34	1.75	2.92	0.66
Hockey	1.96	0.39	2.85	0.99	54.92	14.76	163.19	1.12	0.76	2.73	0.68
Surgery	0.93	0.29	1.86	1.3	2.96	1.32	0.66	60.16	30.6	1.45	0.79
Cancer	0.86	0.31	2.31	1.22	2.75	1.78	0.39	30.82	74.48	1.35	0.79
General	2.2	1.92	2.89	2.23	9.76	6.13	3.28	3.91	4.85	49.25	0.74
Other	0.85	0.88	0.86	0.85	0.76	0.81	0.88	0.81	0.82	0.96	1.003

the limiting case of the class "Other", which contains most of the pages of the dataset, the improvement is very close to 1. Note also the scores of documents in apparently unrelated topics may be affected: the magnitude of the change, which is however much smaller than the modification which affects the related topics, is probably due to the web connectivity and the "closeness" of the topics on the web graph. For example, the rank of pages on "Linux" was improved because the rank on pages of "Windows" was improved.

In order to have more details on the distribution of each specialized page rank, the pages were sorted from the most important to the least important. Figure 1

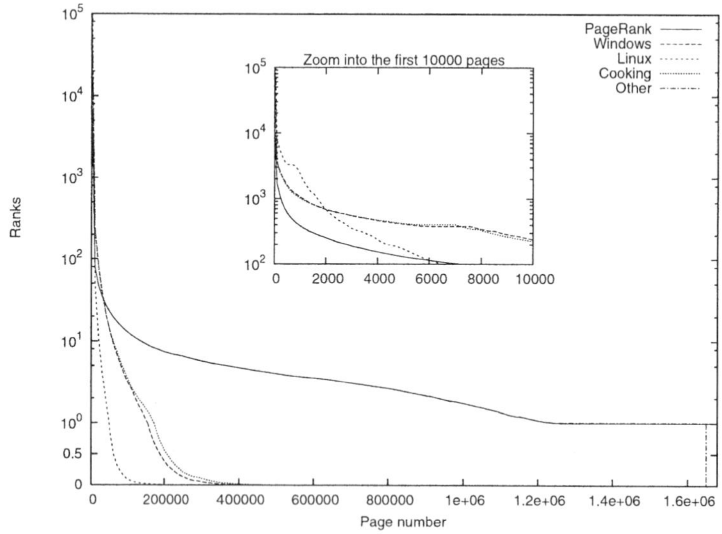

Fig. 1. The distribution of the page rank and the specialized page ranks on "Windows", "Linux", "Cooking" and "Other". The pages are represented on horizontal axis and the rank values on vertical axis

shows the distribution of the values of the page rank and the specialized page ranks on "Windows", "Linux", "Cooking" and "Other" pages[7].

The distribution displayed by the plots in Figure 1 is consistent with the intuitive idea underlining the concept of specialized page rank: it depends on the number of the pages of the topic. In fact, "Linux" is the topic with the smallest number of pages (see Table 1), "Cooking" and "Windows" are topics with moderate number of pages. On the other hand, Google's page rank can be seen as the specialized page rank of the topic which includes all the pages ($e' = [1, \ldots, 1]'$), and, "Other", which contains most of the pages, has similar magnitude as page rank. In topics with a small number of pages, the rank is concentrated in few pages, while in topics with larger number of pages, it is more widespread. The rank of the most important pages of topics with small number of pages may be up to 10 times larger than the corresponding ones of topics with large number of pages (see Figure 1).

However, the rank decreases faster for topics with small number of pages and becomes soon close to 0. In fact, specialized page ranks may be 0, since the pages not belonging to the topics have been assigned a zero default rank, i.e. $e_h = 0$. On the other hand, Google' page rank is never very close to zero, because $e_h = 1$ for each h, and the behavior of specialize page rank in the category of "Other" pages is similar to that of Google's page rank (the two plots overlap almost everywhere).

The goal of the next experiment is to study the basic properties of the proposed method of obtaining personalized page ranks. Acting as a user, interested in wine, we selected four pages on wine and designed three constraints to increase their scores. The constraints consisted of inequalities which require the adaptive page rank to be at least a 50% larger than their respective Google's page rank[8]. Moreover, in order to keep the scores of the documents that are not about wine as close as possible to their Google's page ranks, the optimization problem contained also the linear function and the constraints.

Table 4 shows the results achieved by the proposed algorithm. The table confirms that the scores of the three pages were actually augmented by 50%. Moreover, for each page, the absolute position in the ordering established by the adaptive page rank versus the position determined by Google's page rank is shown in Figure 2. Each point in the graph represents a page. The diagonal dashed line corresponds to the line $y = x$, and the points above such a line represent pages whose adaptive page rank is greater than the corresponding Google's page rank, whereas points under it represent pages whose adaptive page rank has decreased.

The top left hand graph in Figure 2 plots all the pages, the other graphs plot the pages which belong to the individual topics of interest. The "Wine" plot

[7] Other topics have been omitted to avoid cluttering of the graph, since their plots are similar.

[8] Note that it may be possible that the constraints may contain non self-consistent constraints. This can be resolved by using a modification of the theory considered in Section 3.

Table 4. The ranks, before and after optimization, of the constrained pages. Axis labels denotes the position of pages

	page 1	*page* 2	*page* 3	*page* 4
pagerank(*score*)	14.33	17.02	9.55	7.96
Adaptive(*score*)	26.01	25.54	16.19	14.58
pagerank(*absoluteposition*)	86,751	70,295	142,839	182,227
Adaptive(*absoluteposition*)	42,281	43,268	74,855	85,085

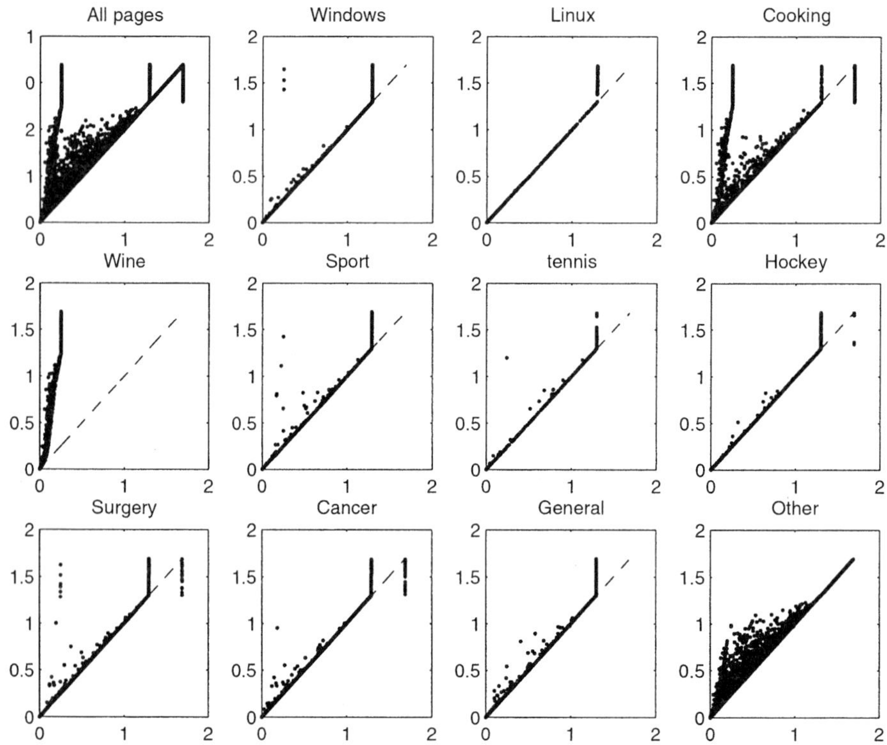

Fig. 2. Absolute position of pages before versus absolute position after optimization

shows that most of the pages on this topic gained a higher rank. On the other hand, for "Cooking", which is a related topic, there are different kinds of behaviors. There is a set of pages whose distribution closely resemble those observed on "Wine". In fact, some pages on "Cooking" belong also to the class "Wine" and received the same scores. Moreover, there are pages displayed above the line $y = x$ which are not related to the "Wine" pages. Finally, some documents are not about "Wine", but they are pointed to by pages on "Tennis". In fact, they have an intermediate behavior and lay just between the diagonal dashed line and the pages similar to "Cooking".

6 Conclusion

Grid is dynamic, open society of heterogeneous users and resources. We cannot predetermine user requirements and resource space. User requirements are always changing. Users and resources can join or leave grid at any time. Users in grid need both a flexible resource sharing mechanism and an effective knowledge sharing infrastructure. In grid environment, human-computer relationship is not limited to man-computer interaction any more, but also includes man-man collaboration.

GSML is collaboration oriented markup language. It can change the application logic on user's demand. GSML defines pipe as a standard-based function unit to operate versatile resources. There are two types of pipe: local and remote. Socket-based asynchronous events are used to be the medium of data and instruction. Events are organized into event-set to implement event barrier and pipes synchronization. GSML has similar characteristics with message passing programming languages in distributed systems.

In order to obtain collaboration, GSML applications are defined recursively so that different applications can import others as their own remote pipes. Events then can be sent to the remote applications. GSML provides a general-purposed collaboration infrastructure. We also develop a GSML tool suite to help users run GSML applications and edit GSML documents. GSML tools suite includes a composer and a browser. The composer gives users an easy way to organize the event flow visually. The browser includes a peer-server for local pipes, an event bus for pipes connection and a display container.

GSML is an important part of VEGA project. VEGA [12] stands: versatile resources, enabling intelligence, global uniformity and autonomous control. GSML focus on V and E problems. It uses pipes to represent and operate all kinds of resources and GSML-based collaboration to help users promoting their work efficiency. Together with VEGA GOS which aims to deal with G and A problems, GSML has made some significant progress.

Acknowledgements

We are pleased to acknowledge contributions by Lijuan Xiao, Xingwu Liu, Ge He, Chengchu Shu and Wei Li. This work is supported in part by the National Natural Science Foundation of China (Grant No. 69925205), the China Ministry of Science and Technology 863 Program (Grant No. 2002AA104310), and the Chinese Academy of Sciences Oversea Distinguished Scholars Fund (Grant No. 20014010).

References

1. Al Sairafi, S., Emmanouil, F. S.,Ghanem, M., Giannadakis, N., Guo, Y., Kalaitzopolous, D., Osmond, M., Rowe, A., Syed, J., Wendel, P.: The Design of Discovery Net: Towards Open Grid Services for Knowledge Discovery. International Journal of High Performance Computing Applications, Vol 17, Issue 3 (2003).
2. Berners-Lee, T., Hendler, J., Lassila, O.: The Semantic Web. Scientific American (May 2001), 35-43.

3. Boyd, L. L.: Architecture Patterns for Business Systems. The 4th Pattern Languages of Programming Conference Washington University Technical Report 97-34 (September 1997).
4. Esposito, D.: A First Look at Writing and Deploying Apps in the Next Generation of Windows. Microsoft MSDN Magazine, Vol. 19, No.1 (January 2004).
5. Foster, I., Kesselman, C. (eds.): The Grid 2: Blueprint for a New Computing Infrastructure. Morgan Kaufmann Publishers (2004).
6. Hyatt, D. (ed.): XML User Interface Language 1.0. http://www.mozilla.org/projects/xul/ (2001).
7. Jacob, R. J. K., Deligiannidis, L., Morrison, S.: A Software Model and Specification Language for Non-WIMP User Interfaces. ACM Transactions on Computer-Human Interaction, Vol. 6, No. 1 (March 1999), 1-46.
8. Leymann, F.: Web Services Flow Language 1.0. IBM Software Group, http://www-3.ibm.com/software/solutions/webservices/pdf/WSFL.pdf, (May 2001).
9. Thatte S. (ed.): Specification: Business Process Execution Language for Web Services Version 1.1. http://www-128.ibm.com/developerworks/library/ws-bpel/ (May 2003).
10. Thatte S.: XLANG Web Services for Business Process Design. http://www.gotdotnet.com /team/xml_wsspecs/xlang-c/ (2001).
11. Xu, Z., Li, W., Liu, D., Yu, H., Li, B.: The GSML Tool Suite: A Supporting Environment for User-level Programming in Grids. The Fourth International Conference on Parallel and Distributed Computing, Applications and Technologies (August 2003), 629-633.
12. Xu, Z., Li, W., Zha, Li., Yu, H., Liu, D.: Vega Grid: A Computer Systems Approach to Grid Research, Keynote speech paper at the Second International Workshop on Grid and Cooperative Computing, Shanghai, China (December 2003), 480-486.
13. Xu, Z., Liao, H., Li, B., Li, W.: Vega Grid and CSCW: Two Approaches to Collaborative Computing. The 8th International Conference on Computer Supported Cooperative Work in Design (May 2004), 10–17.

Some Issues for Fundamental Research on Information Sciences in China

Zhiyong Liu

National Natural Science Foundation of China, Beijing, China
zliu@nsfc.gov.cn

Abstract. Some background information for fundamental research in information sciences conducted in China will be introduced. Basic information of the topics and considerations for fundamental research supported by the National Natural Science Foundation of China (NSFC) will be emphasized in this talk. First, the state of the research and development of information technology will be introduced and analyzed with a comparison between China and some other countries. The comparison is in three aspects, including extent of the use of modern information facilities, development of computing technologies, and the state of development of IT devices in China. Secondly, hot topics of fundamental research on information sciences will be introduced, and some research areas supported by NSFC with priority with be described briefly. Thirdly, some research activities and achievements will be talked about, especially, research activities and achievements on some technologies and applications of the Internet and the Web will be described. In this talk, considerations and policies, including the policies for encouraging international coordination, of the NSFC will also be explained. The information of the prioritized areas of fundamental research will cover the next generation communication systems, networked computing, security, high performance computing, advanced information processing, micro- and nano- technologies, and technologies for opto- and opto-electronic devices.

Y. Zhang et al. (Eds.): APWeb 2005, LNCS 3399, p. 51, 2005.

An Incremental Subspace Learning Algorithm to Categorize Large Scale Text Data

Jun Yan[1], Qiansheng Cheng[1], Qiang Yang[2], and Benyu Zhang[3]

[1] LMAM, Department of Information Science, School of Mathematical Sciences, Peking University, Beijing, P.R. China 100871
yanjun@math.pku.edu.cn, qcheng@pku.edu.cn
[2] Department of Computer Science, Hong Kong University of Science and Technology, Hong Kong
qyang@cs.ust.hk
[3] Microsoft Research Asia, 49 Zhichun Road, Beijing, P.R. China 100080
byzhang@microsoft.com

Abstract. The dramatic growth in the number and size of on-line information sources has fueled increasing research interest in the incremental subspace learning problem. In this paper, we propose an incremental supervised subspace learning algorithm, called Incremental Inter-class Scatter (IIS) algorithm. Unlike traditional batch learners, IIS learns from a stream of training data, not a set. IIS overcomes the inherent problem of some other incremental operations such as Incremental Principal Component Analysis (PCA) and Incremental Linear Discriminant Analysis (LDA). The experimental results on the synthetic datasets show that IIS performs as well as LDA and is more robust against noise. In addition, the experiments on the Reuters Corpus Volume 1 (RCV1) dataset show that IIS outperforms state-of-the-art Incremental Principal Component Analysis (IPCA) algorithm, a related algorithm, and Information Gain in efficiency and effectiveness respectively.

1 Introduction

In the last decades, the emergence of the daily growth of databases on the Web classification or the face recognition has revived the old problem of incremental and on-line algorithm of subspace learning [5, 14]. Principal Component Analysis (PCA) and Linear Discriminant Analysis (LDA) are two most popular linear subspace learning algorithms [2, 6, 10-12, 18].

PCA is an unsupervised subspace learning algorithm. It aims at finding out the geometrical structure of data set and projecting the data along the directions with maximal variances. However, it discards the class information which is significant for classification tasks. Through Singular Value Decomposition (SVD)[9], PCA can find an optimal subspace in the sense of least square reconstruction error. Its computational complexity is $O(m^3)$, where m is the minor value between the sample number and the data dimension. LDA is a supervised subspace learning algorithm. It searches for the projection axes on which the data points of different classes are far from each

Y. Zhang et al. (Eds.): APWeb 2005, LNCS 3399, pp. 52–63, 2005.

other and at the same time where the data points of the same class are close to each other. Unlike PCA which encodes information in an orthogonal linear space, LDA encodes discriminating information in a linear separable space whose bases are not necessarily orthogonal.

The original PCA is a batch algorithm, which means that the data must be given once altogether. However, this type of batch algorithms no longer satisfies the applications that the data are incrementally received from various data sources, such as online sensors [13]. Thus, an incremental method is highly desired to compute adaptive subspace for the data arriving sequentially. Incremental Principal Component Analysis (IPCA) [1, 16] are designed for such a purpose and have been studied for a long time. However, IPCA ignores the valuable class label information of the training data and the most representative features derived from IPCA may not be the most discriminant ones. The Incremental Support Vector Machine (ISVM) techniques have been developed fleetly. But most of them are approximate and require several passed through the data to reach convergence. Researchers [3, 4] have proposed incremental supervised learning based on neural network [4], but the algorithm convergence and stability still remain questionable.

In this paper, we propose an incremental supervised subspace learning algorithm based on statistical efficiency by *incrementally* optimizing the *Inter-class Scatter* criterion, so-call *IIS*. It derives the online adaptive supervised subspace using data samples received sequentially and incrementally updates the eigenvectors of the inter-class scatter matrix. IIS does not need to reconstruct the inter-class scatter matrix whenever it receives new sample data, thus it is very fast computationally. We also proved the convergence of the algorithm in this paper. The experimental results on the synthetic datasets show that IIS can learn a subspace similar to but more robust than LDA; and the experimental results on a real text dataset, Reuters Corpus Volume 1 (RCV1) [8], compared with IPCA and Information Gain (IG) demonstrate that IIS yields significantly better micro F1 and macro F1 than two baseline algorithms – IPCA and Information Gain (IG).

The rest of the paper is organized as follows. We present the incremental subspace learning algorithm IIS and the proof of convergence in section 2. Then, we demonstrate the experimental results on the synthetic datasets and the real word data, the Reuter Corpus Volume 1 in Section 3. We conclude our work in Section 4.

2 Incremental Supervised Subspace Learning

As Introduced above, IPCA ignores the class label information and the most representative features found by IPCA are not always the most discriminating features. This motivates us to design a supervised subspace learning algorithm that efficiently utilizes the label information. In this work, we consider the scenario to maximize the Inter-class scatter criterion that aims to make the class centers as far as possible.

Denote the projection matrix from original space to the low dimensional space as $W \in R^{d \times p}$. In this work, we propose to incrementally maximize the Inter-class scatter (IIS) criterion $J_s = W^T S_b W$, where $S_b = \sum_{i=1}^{c} p_i (m_i - m)(m_i - m)^T$ is the inter-class scatter matrix the same as in LDA. It is obvious that W is the first k leading eigenvectors of the matrix S_b and the column vectors of W are orthogonal to each other.

In the following subsections, we will present the details on how to incrementally derive the leading eigenvectors of S_b; then the convergence proof and algorithm summary are also presented.

2.1 The First Eigenvector

Lemma-1: if $\lim_{n\to\infty} a_n = a$ then $\lim_{n\to\infty} \frac{1}{n}\sum_{i=1}^{n} a_i = a$.

Assume that a sample sequence is presented as $\{x_{l_n}(n)\}$, where $n=1, 2\ldots$. The purpose of IIS is to maximize the Inter-class scatter criterion $J_s(W) = W^T S_b W$. Here k is the dimension of transformed data, i.e. the final subspace dimension.

The Inter-class scatter matrix of step n after learning from the first n samples can be written as below,

$$S_b(n) = \sum_{j=1}^{c} \frac{N_j(n)}{n} (m_j(n) - m(n))(m_j(n) - m(n))^T$$

From the fact that $\lim_{n\to\infty} S_b(n) = S_b$ and the lemma-1, we obtain

$$S_b = \lim_{n\to\infty} \frac{1}{n} \sum_{i=1}^{n} S_b(i) \tag{1}$$

The general eigenvector form is $Au = \lambda u$, where u is eigenvector corresponding to the eigenvalue λ. By replacing the matrix A with the Inter-class scatter matrix at step we can obtain an approximate iterative eigenvector computation formulation with $v = \lambda u$:

$$\begin{aligned} v(n) &= \frac{1}{n}\sum_{i=1}^{n} S_b(i) u(i) \\ &= \frac{1}{n}\sum_{i=1}^{n}\sum_{j=1}^{c} \frac{N_j(i)}{i} (m_j(i) - m(i))(m_j(i) - m(i))^T u(i) \\ &= \frac{1}{n}\sum_{i=1}^{n}\Big(\sum_{j=1}^{c} p_j(n) \Phi_j(i) \Phi_j(i)^T\Big) u(i) \end{aligned}$$

where $\Phi_j(i) = m_j(i) - m(i)$, $v(n)$ is the nth step estimation of v and $u(n)$ is the nth step estimation of u. Once we obtain the estimate of v, eigenvector u can be directly computed as $u = v / \|v\|$. Let $u(i) = v(i-1)/\|v(i-1)\|$, we have the following incremental formulation:

$$v(n) = \frac{1}{n}\sum_{i=1}^{n}\Big(\sum_{j=1}^{c} p_j(n) \Phi_j(i) \Phi_j(i)^T\Big) v(i-1) \Big/ \|v(i-1)\|$$

$$i.e. \qquad v(n)=\frac{n-1}{n}v(n-1)+\frac{1}{n}(\sum_{j=1}^{c}p_j(n)\Phi_j(n)\Phi_j(n)^T)v(n-1)/\|v(n-1)\|$$

the formula can be rewritten as:

$$\begin{aligned} v(n) &= \frac{n-1}{n}v(n-1)+\frac{1}{n}(\sum_{j=1}^{c}\Phi_j(n)\Phi_j(n)^T)v(i-1)/\|v(i-1)\| \\ &= \frac{n-1}{n}v(n-1)+\frac{1}{n}\sum_{j=1}^{c}p_j(n)\alpha_j(n)\Phi_j(n) \end{aligned}$$

where $\alpha_j(n)=\Phi_j(n)^T v(i-1)/\|v(i-1)\|$, $j=1,2,...,c$.

For initialization, we set $v(0)$ as the first sample. Through this way, the subspace directions, i.e. the eigenvectors to be solved at time step n could be computed by the eigenvectors at time step n-1 and the new arrived data at time step n.

2.2 Higher-Order Eigenvectors

Notice that eigenvectors are orthogonal to each other. So, it helps to generate "observations" only in a complementary space for computation of the higher order eigenvectors. To compute the $(j+1)^{th}$ eigenvector, we first subtract its projection on the estimated j^{th} eigenvector from the data,

$$x_{l_n}^{j+1}(n)=x_{l_n}^{j}(n)-(x_{l_n}^{j}(n)^T v^j(n))v^j(n)/\left\|v^j(n)\right\|^2$$

where $x_{l_n}^1(n)=x_{l_n}(n)$. The same method is used to update $m_i^j(n)$ and $m^j(n)$ $i=1,2,...,c$ .Since $m_i^j(n)$ and $m^j(n)$ are linear combination of $x_{l_i}^j(i)$, where $i=1,2,...,n$, $j=1,2,...,k$, and $l_i\in\{1,2,...,C\}$, Φ_i are linear combination of m_i and m , for convenience, we can only update Φ at each iteration step by

$$\Phi_{l_n}^{j+1}(n)=\Phi_{l_n}^{j}(n)-(\Phi_{l_n}^{j}(n)^T v^j(n))v^j(n)/\left\|v^j(n)\right\|^2$$

In this way, the time-consuming orthonormalization is avoided and the orthogonality is always enforced when the convergence is reached, although not exactly so at early stages.

Through the projection procedure at each step, we can get the eigenvectors of S_b one by one. It is much more efficient compared with the time-consuming orthonor malization process.

2.3 Convergence Proof

Lemma-2: Let $A(n)=S_b(n)$, $A=S_b$, then for any large enough N

$$\lim_{n\to\infty} p\{\sup\left\|\frac{A(n)-A}{\|v(n-1)\|}v(n-1)\right\|\geq\varepsilon\}=0$$

Lemma-3: $v(n)$ is bounded with probability 1.

Theorem: Let v^* be a locally asymptotically stable (in the sense of Liapunov) solution to the Ordinary Differential Equation bellow:

$$\dot{v} = (\frac{A}{\|v\|} - I)v$$

with domain of attraction $D(v^*)$. If there is a compact set $\varphi \in D(v^*)$ such that the solution of the equation (**) below satisfies $P\{v(n) \in \varphi\} = 1$, then $v(n)$ converges to v^* almost surely. **Note**:

$$\begin{aligned} v(n) &= v(n-1) + \frac{1}{n}(A - I)v(n-1) + \frac{1}{n}(A(n) - A)v(n-1) \qquad ** \\ &= \frac{n-1}{n}v(n-1) + \frac{1}{n}u(n)u^T(n)v(n-1) \quad \text{if} \quad \|v(n-1)\| = 1 \end{aligned}$$

The convergence is a classical result from the theorems of stochastic approximation [7]. From the lemmas and theorem we can draw the conclusion of convergence [20].

Table 1. Algorithm Summary

for $n = 1,2,\ldots$, do the following steps,

Update $N_i(n), m_i(n), \Phi_i(n), m(n)$ following the aforementioned steps;

$$\Phi_i^1(n) = \Phi_i(n) \qquad i = 1,2,\ldots,c$$

for $j = 1,2,\ldots,\min\{K,n\}$

if $j = n$ then

$$v_j(n) = u_i^j(n),$$

else

$$\alpha_i^j(n) = \Phi_i^j(n)^T v^j(n-1) / \left\|v^j(n-1)\right\|^2$$

$$v^j(n) = \frac{n-1}{n}v^j(n-1) + \frac{1}{n}\sum_{i=1}^{c} p_i^j(n)\alpha_i^j(n)\Phi_i^j(n)$$

$$\Phi_i^{j+1}(n) = \Phi_i^j(n) - \Phi_i^j(n)^T v^j(n) v^j(n) / \left\|v^j(n)\right\|^2$$

$$u_i^{j+1}(n) = u_i^j(n) - u_i^j(n)^T v^j(n) v^j(n) / \left\|v^j(n)\right\|^2$$

End

2.4 Algorithm Summary

Suppose that at *Step* n, $x_{l_n}(n)$ is the input sample, which belongs to class l_n, $l_n \in \{1,2,\ldots,c\}$,. $N_i(n)$ is the total sample number of class i. $m_i(n)$ is the mean of class i. $m(n)$ is the mean of all samples. K is the dimension of subspace to be found by our algorithm. Set $\Phi_j(i) = m_j(i) - m(i)$. The full algorithm is as table 1. The solution of step n is $v_j(n)$, $j = 1,2,\ldots,K$.

2.5 Algorithm Property Analysis

The time complexity of IIS to train N input samples is $O(Ncdp)$, where c is the number of classes, d is the dimension of the original data space, and p is the target dimension, which is linear with each factor. Furthermore, when handling each input sample, IIS only need to keep the learned eigen-space and several first-order statistics of the past samples, such as the mean and the counts. Hence, IIS is able to handle large scale and continuous data.

IIS is also robust since IIS focuses on the mean of each class and all samples. That means that a little amount of mislabeled data could not affect the final solution. In fact, the robustness is determined by the criterion itself.

3 Experimental Results

We performed two sets of experiments. For intuition, in the first set of experiments, we used synthetic data that follow the normal distribution to illustrate the subspaces learned by IIS, LDA, and PCA, along with performance in a noise data. Since the web documents are large scale text data, thus to demonstrate the performance of our proposed algorithm on large scale text data, in the second set of experiments, we applied several dimension reduction methods on the Reuters Corpus Volume 1 (RCV1) dataset, and then compare the classification performance and the time cost. Reuters Corpus Volume 1 data set [8] contains over 800,000 documents. Moreover, each document is represented by a vector with the dimension about 300,000.

3.1 Synthetic Data

We generated a 2-dimension data set of 2 classes. Each class consists of 50 samples by following normal distribution with means (0, 1) and (0,-2), respectively; and the covariance matrix of them are *diag*(1, 25) and *diag*(2, 25). Figure 1 shows a scatter plot of the data set, along with the 1-d subspace learned by IIS, LDA, and PCA,

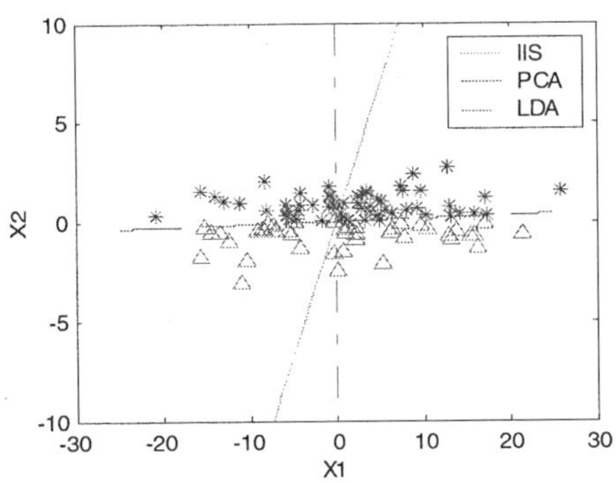

Fig. 1. Subspaces learned by IIS, LDA, and PCA

represented by the straight line, the dash dotted line, and the broken line, respectively. We can see that IIS can outperform PCA and yield comparable performance to LDA for classification.

To demonstrate the robustness of IIS against noise, we generated a 3-d data set of 3 classes each of which consists of 200 samples that follows the normal distribution with means (0, 5, 5), (0, 5, 10), and (5, 5, 10) and the same covariance matrixes Diag(5, 5, 5), where we performed IIS and LDA to learn the 2-d eigenspaces. We randomly provided several abnormal samples, and then compared the correlation between the "noise" eigenvectors and the "original" eigenvectors of each algorithm. Since $\|v - v'\| = 2(1 - v \cdot v')$, and $v = v'$ iff $v \cdot v' = 1$, the correlation between two unit eigenvectors is represented by their inner product, and the larger the inner product is, the more robustness against noise. The results are shown in Table 2.

Table 2. Correlation between the "noise" eigenvectors and the "original" eigenvector learned by IIS and LDA

Mislabeled Data Per Class	5	10	15	20
1ST Eigenvector of IIS	1	0.9999	0.9970	0.9963
2RD Eigenvector of IIS	1	0.9999	0.9990	0.9960
1ST Eigenvector of LDA	0.9577	0.8043	0.7073	0.6296
2RD Eigenvector of LDA	1	0.9992	0.9968	0.9958

We can see from table 1 that IIS is more robust against noises than LDA. With 20 mislabeled data (=10%) for each class, IIS can keep the inner product bigger than 99.6%. The intuitive reason for LDA being sensitive to noise comes from that LDA processes the matrix $S_w^{-1}S_b$. A small amount of mislabeled data can make S_w change, and even very little change of S_w makes S_w^{-1} change a lot. In other words, $S_w^{-1}S_b$ is very sensitive to the change of samples' label, and therefore the eigenvectors of $S_w^{-1}S_b$ are very sensitive to abnormal data.

Though the IIS has good performance on the synthetic data, our motivation to design it is to reduce the dimension of very large scale web documents or other large scale data sets, we conduct it on the widely used large scale text data RCV1 to introduce IIS.

3.2 Real World Data

To compare the effectiveness and efficiency of IIS to that of other subspace learning algorithms, we constructed classification experiments on the Reuters Corpus Volume 1 (RCV1) data set [8] which contains over 800,000 documents. We choose the data samples with the highest four topic codes (CCAT, ECAT, GCAT, and MCAT) in the "Topic Codes" hierarchy, which contains 789,670 documents. Then we split them into 5 equal-sized subsets, and each time 4 of them are used as the training set and the remaining ones are left as the test set. The experimental results reported in this paper are the average of the five runs. In these experiments, we use a single computer with Pentium(R) 4 CPU 2.80GHz, 1GB of RAM, Microsoft Windows XP Professional Version, to conduct the experiments. The coding language used by us is C++ 7.0. The most widely used performance measurement for text categorization problems are Precision, Recall and F1. Precision is a proportion which could be computed by the number of right categorized data over the number of all testing data. Recall is a proportion which could be computed by the number of right categorized data over the number of all the assigned data. F1 is a common measure in text categorization that combines recall and precision. We use two different *F1* measurements, i.e. micro *F1* and macro *F1* in our paper.

3.2.1 Experiment Setup

The dimensionality reduction algorithms are applies in the following manner:

- Apply the dimensionality reduction algorithm on a specific size of the training data to learn a subspace;
- Transform all the training data to the subspace;
- Train SVM by SMO [15];
- Transforming all the test data to the subspace;
- Evaluate the classification performance, using F1 value, on the transformed test data.

The dimension reduction algorithms applied are:

- The proposed IIS generating a 3-d subspace. We applied IIS on the first 10, 100, 1,000, 10,000, and 100,000 training data to study the convergence speed.
- Information Gain (IG). This is a state-of-the-art text classification method [17]. In this paper, we applied IG on all training data to generate 3-d and 500-d subspaces, denoted by IG3 and IG500, respectively. With the same dimension, IG3 performs as effective as ISBC; while IG500 will yields almost best classification performance, since SVM is insensitive to the number of feature [19].
- IPCA following the CCIPCA algorithm [16]. We also used IPCA to generate both 3-d and 500-d subspaces.

3.2.2 Effectiveness of IIS

The classification performances are summarized in Figure *2* and Figure *3*. From these figures, we can infer that the eigenspace learned by IIS on 100 input samples is significantly better than the ones learned by IPCA and IG3; and after learning 100,000 input samples (<20%), IIS can generate a comparable eigenspace to the one generated by IG500 in terms of classification performance. Hence, IIS is an effective subspace learning algorithm for classification tasks. On the other hand, we can see that IIS generated a near optimal eigenspace after just learning 10,000 samples. This indicates that in practice, the convergence speed of IIS is very fast.

The F1 value of each class is shown in Table 3. The inferior classification performance of ECAT is probably due to the uneven class distribution, as shown in Table 3.

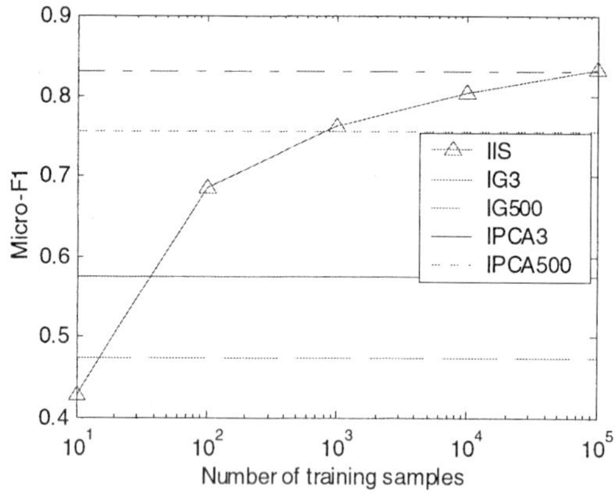

Fig. 2. Micro-F1 after reducing dimension by several subspace learning algorithms

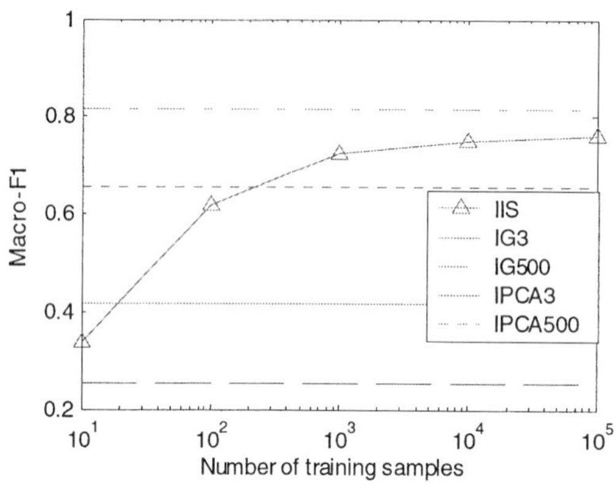

Fig. 3. Macro-F1 after reducing dimension by several subspace learning algorithms

3.2.3 Efficiency of IIS

The time spent of each algorithm in dimension reduction and classification training is reported in Table 4. We can see that the dimension reduction time of IIS is almost linear related to the number of input samples. Although the IG is faster than IIS, Its classification training time is much longer than that of IIS. The reason for IG500 being near square time complexity of SVM; while the possible reason for IG3 is that the optimization process of SVM is very slow if the margin between different classes is small which is unfortunately the case in the eigen-space of IG3.

Table 3. F1 values of each class using different dimension reduction algorithms

	CCAT	ECAT	GCAT	MCAT
IIS 3@10	0.596	0.117	0.443	0.192
IIS 3@100	0.711	0.213	0.762	0.793
IIS 3@1000	0.744	0.430	0.877	0.759
IIS 3@10000	0.873	0.443	0.875	0.850
IIS 3@100000	0.846	0.491	0.881	0.882
IG 3@ALL	0.696	0	0.524	0.451
IG 500@ALL	0.835	0.716	0.843	0.869
IPCA 3@ALL	0.632	0	0.376	0
IPCA 500@ALL	0.782	0.180	0.858	0.802
# SAMPLES (*10^5)	3.74	1.18	2.35	2.00

Table 4. Time costs (in seconds) of each dimension reduction algorithms

	DIMENSION REDUCTION TIME	CLASSIFICATION TRAINING TIME
IIS 3@10	1.85	1,298
IIS 3@100	17.1	11,061
IIS 3@1000	177	6,474
IIS 3@10000	2,288	7,560
IIS 3@100000	26,884	3,343
IG 3@ALL	136	52,605
IG 500@ALL	137	312,887
IPCA 3@ALL	28,960	25,374
IPCA 500@ALL	3,763,296	9,327

4 Conclusion and Future Works

In this paper, we proposed an incremental supervised subspace learning algorithm, IIS, which is a challenging issue of computing dominating eigenvectors and eigenvalues from incrementally arriving sample stream without storing the knowing data in advance. This proposed IIS algorithm is fast in convergence rate, low in the computational complexity, efficient, effective and robust. Experimental results on synthetic dataset and real text dataset demonstrate that it outperforms IPCA on classification tasks. It can be theoretically proved that IIS can find out the same subspace as LDA does if every class is uniformly distributed in all directions. In real word applications, this assumption can not always be satisfied; therefore intra-class scatter matrix in LDA is also very important for classification tasks. In the future work, we plan to extend the incremental supervised learning to consider both the inter-class and intra-class scatter matrices and we are currently exploring these extensions in theory and practice.

Acknowledgement

The authors would like to thank Ning Liu for the improvement of this paper.

References

[1] Artae, M., Jogan, M. and Leonardis, A., Incremental PCA for On-line Visual Learning and Recognition. In *Proceedings of the 16th International Conference on Pattern Recognition*, (Quebec City, QC, Canada, 2002), 781-784.

[2] Balakrishnama, S. and Ganapathiraju, A. Linear Discriminant Analysis - A brief Tutorial, Institute for Signal and Information Processing, MS, 1998.

[3] Chatterjee, C. and Roychowdhury, V.P. On self-organizing algorithms and networks for class-separability features. *IEEE Trans. on Neural Networks, 8* (3). 663 - 678.

[4] Hiraoka, K., Hidai, K., Hamahira, M., Mizoguchi, H., Mishima, T. and Yoshizawa, S., Successive Learning of Linear Discriminant Analysis: Sanger-Type Algorithm. In *Proceedings of the 14 th International Conference on Pattern Recognition*, (Barcelona, Spain, 2000), 2664-2667.

[5] Hoch, R., Using IR techniques for text classification in document analysis. In *Proceedings of the Proceedings of the 17th annual international ACM SIGIR conference on Research and development in information retrieval*, (Dublin, Ireland, 1994), Springer-Verlag New York, Inc., 31 - 40.

[6] Jolliffe, I.T. *Principal Component Analysis*. Springer-Verlag, 1986.

[7] Kushner, H.J. and Clark, D.S. *Stochastic Approximation Methods for Constrained and Unconstrained Systems*. Springer-Verlag, New York, 1978.

[8] Lewis, D., Yang, Y., Rose, T. and Li, F. RCV1: A new benchmark collection for text categorization research. *Journal of Machine Learning Research*.

[9] M.W., B. Large-scale sparse singular value computations. *International Journal of Supercomputer Applications, 6*. 13-49.

[10] Martinez, A.M. and Kak, A.C. PCA versus LDA. *IEEE Transactions on Pattern Analysis and Machine Intelligence, 23* (2). 228-233.

[11] Moghaddam, B. and Pentland, A. Probabilistic Visual Learning for Object Representation. *IEEE Trans. Pattern Analysis and Machine Intelligence, 19* (7). 696-710.

[12] Murase, H. and Nayar, S.K. Visual Learning and Recognition of 3D objects from Appearance. *International Journal of Computer Vision, 14* (1). 5-24.

[13] Muthukrishnan, S. Data stream algorithms and applications. *Rutgers/AT&T Shannon Labs*.

[14] Oja., E. Subspace methods of pattern recognition. *Pattern recognition and image processing series., 6* (John Wiley & Sons).

[15] Platt, J. Fast training of support vector machines using sequential minimal optimization. In *Advances in Kernel Methods: support vector learning*, MIT Press, Cambridge, MA, 1999, 185-208.

[16] Weng, J., Zhang, Y. and Hwang, W.-S. Candid Covariance-free Incremental Principal Component Analysis. *IEEE Trans. Pattern Analysis and Machine Intelligence, 25* (8). 1034-1040.

[17] Yang, Y. and Pedersen, J.O., A Comparative Study on Feature Selection in Text Categorization. In *Proceedings of the 14 th International Conference on Machine Learning*, (Nashville, Tennessee, 1997), 412-420.

[18] Yu, H. and Yang, J. A direct LDA algorithm for high-dimensional data with application to face recognition. *Pattern Recognition*, *34*. 2067-2070.

[19] Zhang, J., Jin, R., Yang, Y. and Hauptmann, A.G., Modified Logistic Regression: An Approximation to SVM and Its Applications in Large-Scale Text Categorization. In *Proceedings of the 20 th International Conference on Machine Learning*, (Washington, DC, 2003), 888-895.

[20] Zhang, Y. and Weng, J. Convergence analysis of complementary candid incremental principal component Analysis, Michigan State University, 2001.

Classifying Criminal Charges in Chinese for Web-Based Legal Services

Chao-Lin Liu and Ting-Ming Liao

Department of Computer Science, National Chengchi University, Taipei 11605, Taiwan
chaolin@nccu.edu.tw

Abstract. Along with the increasing accessibility of the Web, services available on the Web have expanded into several aspects of our lives. As a relatively new comer, Web-based legal services have become another front in the arena. For instance, through such services, people obtain rough pictures of the lawsuits of interest before they decide whether and how to approach their counselors. As a step toward offering online legal services, we propose algorithms for classifying criminal charges in Chinese based on the alleged criminal violations that the district attorney used to prosecute the defendants. The classification is not trivial because some prosecutions involve violations of multiple articles in the criminal law, and we wish to classify lawsuits as precisely as possible. We employ techniques of instance-based classification and introspective learning for the classification task, and achieve satisfactory initial results for classifying charges of larceny and gambling.

1 Introduction

Along with the quick expansion of the Web in the past decade, governments around the world have begun to offer services via the Web. Projects of e-governments in both developed and developing countries have proliferated in recent years [1]. In addition to accessing documents published by the governments, people are able to file relatively simple procedural applications on the Internet, and government agencies may reply and even return official documents in electronic formats, thereby saving time and costs of the whole society.

Providing legal information is a new comer among these Web services. This delayed offer is partially because the release of legal information may involve privacy problems. Nevertheless, modern techniques are available for releasing legal information without compromising privacy of individuals, and legal information services are available in the Chinese community already [2]. People in Taiwan may search for judicial documents of the past lawsuits via the Web using an interface similar to that of Google but more tailored for the needs of searching for judicial documents.

Despite this recent progress, there is still room for improving the current services. Purely offering judicial documents in their original forms does not help ordinary people very much, because understanding the contents of the judicial documents may not be a simple task for everyone. Providing a precise set of keywords to the search engines may

Y. Zhang et al. (Eds.): APWeb 2005, LNCS 3399, pp. 64 – 75, 2005.

require professional training in law in the first place. Hence, we believe that a user-friendly interface for ordinary people should allow users to simply provide a judicial document and ask for supports of users' interest. More specifically, we study methods that would analyze contents of prosecution documents and infer the infringed legal articles implied by the alleged actions in the contents. By doing so we allow users of our system to place queries with prosecution documents directly, avoiding the needs to first figuring out a set of keywords for querying our system.

Computer supports for legal applications are not new to the research community. In the past two decades, researchers have applied artificial intelligence techniques to a variety of applications in the legal domain, including computer-assisted sentencing; drafting, abstraction, and classification of legal documents; and education of legal practitioners [3]. However, we were not able to find many published results for processing legal documents that are written in Chinese. Lai and Huang use a small Chinese legal corpus in demonstrating the applicability of the Dependency Grammar for annotating Chinese documents [4]. Brown builds the CHINATAX system for inference problems that are related to the Commercial law of China [5]. In the past few years, we have been working on classification of judicial documents in Chinese for supporting legal consultation [6, 7, 8], and this paper reports some strengthening methods for our previous approaches.

In previous work, we apply techniques of *k*-nearest-neighbor (*k*NN) [9] for classifying lawsuits of criminal summary judgments. We train and refine our classifiers with real-world judicial documents to obtain a database of instances [8], and apply *k*NN methods for classifying query documents.[†] Under the constraint that each query document belongs to only one prosecution category, our system correctly classifies more than 85% of the query documents into one of the 13 prosecution categories. Although the past achievements look satisfactory, there are needs to improve the previous systems. Criminal summary judgments involve relatively simple lawsuits, and we can expand the applicability of our system into lawsuits involving general criminal law. In addition, classifying lawsuits based on the violated law articles will be more helpful than classifying lawsuits only based on the prosecution categories. Lawsuits belonging to a prosecution category may involve violation of multiple law articles, and we can classify these lawsuits into finer grains based on the violated articles.

In this paper, we deal with query documents that involve general criminal laws, and classify query documents based on the involved law articles. The classification task is distinctly more difficult than the previous one. Documents of lawsuits that belong to the same prosecution category contain similar descriptions of the criminal actions, and classify them into different combinations of violated law articles require professional training even for human experts. Consequently, the previous system did not perform well in such tasks. To confront this barrier, we employ concepts of introspective learning [10] for fine-tuning the influences of the leaned instances on the classification of the query documents. We run tests over query documents that involve larceny and gambling. When measured by the F measure, that will be explained in Section 4,

---

[†] We use **query documents** to refer to the documents that someone asks our system to classify.

experimental results indicate that the new system achieves 80% in the averaged F measures, outperforming its predecessor by about 10%.

We provide more background information about this research in Section 2, elaborate on the methods that we propose for enhancing the previous system in Section 3, report results of experimental comparison and evaluation of the previous and the current classifiers in Section 4, and wrap up this paper with discussions in Section 5.

2 Background

We provide more background information for this research, including the law articles that are of concerned in this paper and how we process judicial documents in Chinese. Since the current system aims at improving a previous system, we look into some details about the predecessor system for motivating the current research.

2.1 Laws Governing Larceny and Gambling in Chinese

Once judges determine the prosecution categories of the defendant, they have to decide what articles are applicable to the defendants. Not all prosecution categories require detailed articles that subcategorize cases belonging to the prosecution category, but some prosecution categories require more detailed specifications of the prosecutable behaviors than others. We concern ourselves with three articles for gambling and three articles for larceny in the criminal law in Taiwan [2].

Articles 266, 267, and 268 are for cases of gambling. Article 266 describes ordinary gambling cases, article 267 describes cases that involve people who make a living by gambling, and article 268 describes cases that involve people who provide locations or gather gamblers for making profits. Articles 320, 321, and 322 are for cases of larceny. Article 320 describes ordinary larceny cases, article 321 describes more serious larceny cases, and article 322 describes cases that involve people who make a living by stealing. A larceny case is considered as serious cases when the cases involve breaking in houses or relying on the use of weapons.

Applicability of these articles to a particular case depends on details of the facts cited in the prosecution documents. Very simple cases violate only one of these articles, while more complex ones call for the application of more articles. In addition, some combined applications of these articles are more normal than others in practice. Let A, B, C, D, E, and F denote types of cases that articles 266, 267, 268, 320, 321, and 322 are applied, respectively, and concatenated letters denote types of cases that articles denoted by each letter are applied. Based on our gathering of the published judicial documents, we observe some common types: A, C, AB, AC, D, DE, and DF. The cases of other combinations are so rare that we cannot reasonably apply and test our learning methods. Hence we will ignore those rare combinations in this paper.

2.2 Preprocessing Judicial Documents in Chinese

Unlike most western languages such as English, words in Chinese are not separated by spaces. This special feature requires computer software that does Chinese information processing to segment Chinese strings into words. A machine readable dictionary such as HowNet [11] is necessary and helpful, but does not solve all the problems. When there are multiple ways to segment a string, it is the de facto practice to segment a string into fewer numbers of words, all else being equal. Nevertheless, even with this so-called "preferring longer words" heuristic, it is not guaranteed that one can segment Chinese text correctly without the help of syntactic and even semantic level information. In some special cases, different segmentation of the same text string converts the original string to different meanings. The string "*Kai Fa Zhong Guo Jia*" is one of such peculiar examples.[‡] We can treat "*Kai Fa Zhong Guo Jia*" as either the combination of "*Kai Fa Zhong Guo*" (develop China) and "*Jia*" (expert) or the combination of "*Kai Fa Zhong*" (developing) and "*Guo Jia*" (country). The first segmentation interprets "*Kai Fa Zhong Guo Jia*" as "an expert for developing China" while the second "a developing country."

We adopt the wisdom collected from the research work in Chinese information processing for processing the judicial documents in Chinese. Since HowNet is not designed particularly for applications in the legal domain, some common legal terms are not available in HowNet. Hence we have to customize HowNet by augmenting it with some legal terms. We rely on the customized HowNet for segmenting Chinese strings, and employ the "preferring longer words" heuristic when necessary. If there are still ambiguities, we will choose one of the alternatives arbitrarily.

2.3 An Instance-Based Approach to Case Classifications

Instance-based learning [9] is a technique that relies on past recorded experience to classify future problem instances. *K*NN methods are very common among different incarnations of the concept of instance-based learning. By defining a distance measure between the past experience and the future problem instance, a system selects k past experiences that are most similar to the future problem instance, and classifies the future instance based on the classes of the selected k past experiences.

The quality of the distance measure is crucial to the success of a *k*NN-based system. Given a segmented Chinese text as we explained in Section 2.2, we can treat each past experience as a vector of Chinese words. The distance measure can be defined in ways similar to the vector models used in typical approaches to information retrieval [12], but we take a different approach particularly for legal reasoning.

Figure 1 provides a flowchart of our previous work. Major contributions of the previous work include an algorithmic way of generating instances for instance-based legal reasoning and a modification to the standard distance measures that are used in vector models for classifying judicial documents [8]. The first achievement allows us to relieve the concerns brought up by Brüninghaus and Ashley that relying on manually constructed cases instances constituted a major barrier for applying instance-base

‡ We romanize Chinese characters for LNCS publication requirements: Kai(開) Fa(發) Zhong(中) Guo(國) Jia(家).

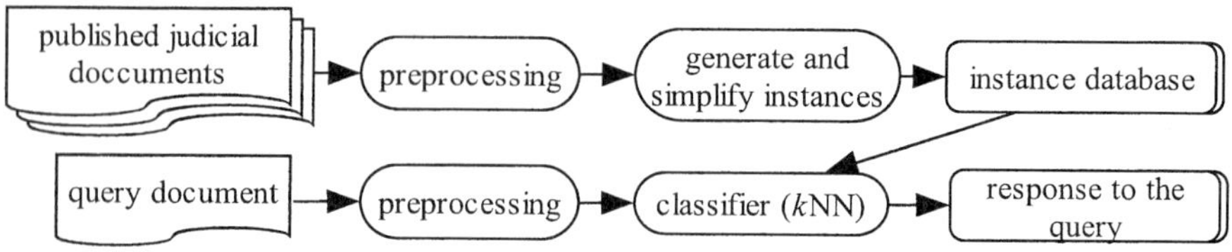

Fig. 1. A flowchart of our classifier

reasoning systems to real-world problems [13, 14]. We will not review details on how our algorithms simplify instances that are generated from judicial documents as it is not the main theme of this paper [8]. The simplification step removes relatively unimportant words from the learned instances for improving efficiency of the classifier. Since the published judicial documents include information about the finalized conviction, we can augment each instance with the finalized prosecution reason.

To classify a query document with an unknown prosecution reason, we preprocess the document with the segmentation methods we reported in Section 2.2, compare the similarity between the instances stored in the instance database and the query instance, and choose qualified instances from the instance database to vote on the prosecution reason of the query instance using a *k*NN method. The preprocessing step converts the query document to the same format of instances that are stored in the instance database, leaving the prosecution reason unspecified. For simple referrals, we call the instance that is converted from the query document as the **query instance** henceforth. In computing the distance between the query instance and the instances in the instance database, we consider not only the occurrences but also the orders of words. The orders of matched words must also match for the matched words to be used in the calculation of the similarity between the instances in the instance database and the query instance. In the previous work, we call the matched words with the same order as **ordered common words** or **OCW**s in short. When there are multiple choices of the OCWs, we choose the longest OCW for computing similarity between instances. The degree of similarity between instances is defined as the averaged portions of the OCW in the instances being compared, while we compute *portion* based on numbers of words in the instances of interest.

Let $I_i=(\tau_i,\kappa_i)$ denote the i-th instance in the instance database, where τ_i is the prosecution reason of the instance and κ_i is the list of ordered keywords that were converted from the original judicial document. Let $Len(\kappa)$ be a function that returns the number of words in an ordered list of words κ, and $OCW(I_i, I_j)$ a function that returns the longest OCWs of κ_i and κ_j. The degree of similarity between instances I_i and I_j is defined as follows.

$$s(I_i,I_j)=\left(\frac{Len(OCW(I_i,I_j))}{Len(I_i)}+\frac{Len(OCW(I_i,I_j))}{Len(I_j)}\right)\Big/2 \quad (1)$$

Example 1. *Let X-Y-Z-W-R represent the ordered word list containing five words in an instance, and X-K-Z-W-R-Y-W the ordered word list containing seven words in another* *instance. There are different OCWs between these instances, e.g., X-Z-W-R, X-R, and X-Y-W. The longest OCW is X-Z-W-R, and the degree of similarity between the instances that include these word lists is (4/5+4/7)/2.*

3 Introspective Learning

The design sketched in Section 2.3 provides pretty good performance for differentiating query documents under different prosecution reasons, such as gambling and larceny-related cases. When we attempted to apply the same methods to further classify gambling cases based on the violated articles as those explained in Section 2.1, the performance became less satisfactory. The main reason is mostly because lawsuits that belong to the same prosecution reason often share a significant number of words, so the differences between such cases are more subtle than the differences between cases of different prosecution reasons. As mentioned in Section 2.3, a key feature in our previous work is the algorithmic generation of instances that would then be used in a *k*NN-based classification. The downside of the past approach is that words in the segmented text have equal influence on the computation of similarity in (1). Some words should in fact be minimally relevant to the final judgments, some have weak influences, and some should have strong influences. It is clear that appropriate assignments of weights to keywords in κin the instances will help to identify the subtle differences, and we resort to the concept of introspective learning [9, 10] for strengthening our classifier.

3.1 Learning Weights of Keywords

We expand the representation for an instance by adding two elements related to the correctness of an instance when it votes. Each instance comprises of four parts, I_i=(τ_i,κ_i, υ_i, ω_i), where υ_i records the percentages of correct votes in different rounds of the training process and ω_i the vector of weights for each keyword in κ_i. Notice that the field τ_i contains the **cited articles** for the instances. For jumpstarting the training process, the very first value inυ_i is set to zero, and results of any additional training steps will be added to υ_i. Since weights of keywords reflect their relative importance in computing similarity between instances, we confine weights of all keywords to the range of [0, 1]. The initial weights for all keywords in every instance are set to 0.5. Figures 2 and 3 show the procedures for training the instances.

Figure 2 shows the main procedure. We split the acquired judicial documents into three sets. We use the first set to generate the original instances, the second set to evaluate the results of tuning weights of the instances, and the third set for final evaluation of our approach. We create the original instances with the procedures described in Section 2, and initialize values of υ_i and ω_i of each instance, except that instances are tagged with the violated articles not the prosecution reasons that are recorded in the training documents. The procedure *introlearn* takes the original set of instances and the second set of judicial documents as input. The second step in *introlearn* adjusts the weights in the original instances, and we explain the details of the procedure *adjust* shortly. The third step evaluates the adjusted instances by adopting the updated instances to classify documents of the second set. The classification will consider the weights of the keywords, and the new formula for computing similarity is provided in Section 3.2. If the overall quality of the classification in step 3 improves over the previous round of update, the training will continue; otherwise the training will terminate. We will provide the exact definition of "quality of classification" in Section 4.1.

> *Input*: an instance database $\mathcal{I}$, a set of judicial documents $\mathcal{D}$
> *Output*: an instance database with adjusted weights $\mathcal{I}'$
> *Local variables*: $\ell\mathcal{I}1$, $\ell\mathcal{I}2$
> *Steps*:
> 1. $\ell\mathcal{I}1 = \mathcal{I}$; classify documents in D with instances in $\ell\mathcal{I}1$
> 2. $\ell\mathcal{I}2 = adjust(\ell\mathcal{I}1)$
> 3. Classify documents in $\mathcal{D}$ with qualified instances in $\ell\mathcal{I}2$
> 4. If the overall performance improves, $\ell\mathcal{I}1 = \ell\mathcal{I}2$ and return to step 2; otherwise, return the contents of the current $\ell\mathcal{I}1$

Fig. 2. Procedure for weight assignments: *introlearn*

Figure 3 shows how we adjust the weights of the instances. The first step embraces the leave-one-out principle [9] to probe the effectiveness of the instances in $\mathcal{I}$. We use one of the instances in $\mathcal{I}$ as the query instance, classify this instance with other instances in $\mathcal{I}$, and record both correctness of the voting instances and the OCWs that qualify these instances for voting. Again, the classification will consider the weights of the keywords using the formula provided in Section 3.2. After using each instance in $\mathcal{I}$ as the query instance exactly once in step 1, we can compute the percentage of correct votes for each instance in $\mathcal{I}$, and record this statistic in υ_i. An instance with degrading performance between rounds of calling *adjust* or an instance that votes correctly less than 50% of the time in the most recent execution of *adjust* will not be allowed to vote at step 3 in *introlearn*.

> *Input*: an instance database $\mathcal{I}$
> *Output*: an instance database with adjusted weights $\mathcal{I}'$
> *Steps*:
> 1. Use the leave-one-out principle to classify each instance, and record the correctness and the longest OCWs of the voting instances
> 2. Update the percentage of correct voting υ_i of each instance in $\mathcal{I}$
> 3. Modify the weights of each term in the OCW of each instance in each voting action
> 4. Return the modified database $\mathcal{I}$

Fig. 3. Procedure for adjusting weights: *adjust*

The third step in *adjust* modifies the weights for each keyword in the instances, based on the data recorded at the first step. We modify the weights of keywords of an instance, if the keywords belong to the OCWs that qualify the instance for casting a vote on a query instance. If the cited articles of the instance are the same as those of the instance that is temporarily used as a query instance at step 1, we increase weights of all words in the OCWs; other wise we decrease their weights. We hope to improve the performance of the classifier by increasing/decreasing the weights of the keywords that participate in correct/incorrect voting of the instances.

The magnitudes of adjustment differ among keywords, and is defined as $\delta(\kappa)=\eta/\phi(\kappa)$, where $\phi(\kappa)$ depends on the distributions of the occurrences of a keyword κ in the training documents with different cited articles, and η is the learning rate similar to that used in learning weights of artificial neural networks [9]. We borrow the concept of inverse document frequency that is commonly employed in information retrieval systems—A term that appears in many different topics of documents is less useful for classifying documents. Let $\Pr(\alpha_i|\kappa)$ be the percentage of occurrences of κ in instances that are tagged with article α_i, where α_i is a combination of cited articles for a particular prosecution reason as explained in Section 2.1. Let A be the set of all such α_i under consideration. We set $P_{max}(\kappa)$ to the largest $\Pr(\alpha_i|\kappa)$ for all α_i in A, and $\phi(\kappa)$ to the number of α_i in A such that $\Pr(\alpha_i|\kappa)/P_{max}(\kappa)\geq 0.1$. We consider the occurrence of κ as ignorable when the relative frequency $\Pr(\alpha_i|\kappa)/P_{max}(\kappa)$ is small.

As we adjust the weights at step 3 in *adjust*, the weights might leave the range of [0, 1]. We will normalize the weights in the instance when this situation occurs. Let ω_{max} and ω_{min} be the maximum and minimum weights of the instance before normalization. We readjust each weight ω of the instance to $(\omega-\omega_{min})/(\omega_{max}-\omega_{min})$.

3.2 *k*NN Classification

Once we have finished training of the weights of the instance, we may classify query documents with a *k*NN method. The determination of similarity between instances takes the weights of keywords into consideration as shown below. The new score function is actually a generalization of the old formula given in (1), where we give equal weights to all words.

$$s_{new}(I_i,I_j)=\left(\frac{\text{total weights of } OCW(I_i,I_j)}{\text{total weights of keywords in } I_i}+\frac{\text{total weights of } OCW(I_i,I_j)}{\text{total weights of keywords in } I_j}\right)\Big/2 \quad (2)$$

In the experiments, we choose 10 instances that are most similar to the instance of the query document, compute the total scores in terms of similarity between the voting instances and the query instance, and set the cited articles that receive the highest total score. Take the classification of cases for gambling for instances. There are four types of cited articles: A, C, AB, and AC, as we explain in Section 2.1. Let V_A, V_C, V_{AB}, V_{AC} denote the set of voting instances of type A, C, AB, and AC, respectively, and q the query instance. The score of type A is defined in (3), and scores of type C, AB, and AC are defined analogously. We take the square of the similarity between the instances in the summation so that more similar instances have larger influences on the results of voting.

$$s_A=\sum_{i\in V_A} s_{new}^2(i,q) \quad (3)$$

3.3 Selecting System Parameters

We decided to take 10 votes in the classification in a less scientific way. We ran a small scale experiment, and found that using about 10 most similar instances led to the best final results. Hence we continued to select 10 most similar instances in main experiments. Analogously, we set the learning rate η mentioned in Section 3.1 to 0.02 based upon results of small-scale experiments.

4 Experimental Evaluations

4.1 Data Sources and Measures for Classification Quality

We evaluated the resulting classifier with judicial documents for gambling and larceny cases. Table 1 shows the quantities of the documents that we used to train and test the performance of our system. We acquired the documents from both the web site of the Judicial Yuan and the Pan-Chiao District Court, Taipei, Taiwan. The leftmost column shows types of documents using the codes that we explained in Section 2.1. As we mentioned in Section 3.1, we split our data into three sets: Tr_1 was used as $\mathcal{J}$ in *adjust* and *introlearn*, Tr_2 was used as $\mathfrak{D}$ the procedure *introlearn*, and the last set Eval was used in the final evaluation.

Table 1. Quantities of data

	Tr_1	Tr_2	Eval
A	500	100	807
C	435	100	244
AB	565	100	1787
AC	500	100	1004
D	200	100	100
DE	200	100	100
DF	200	100	100

Since our work is not different from traditional research in text classification, we continue to use standard measures for quality. Namely, we used Precision, Recall, and the F measure for system evaluation [12]. More specifically, let p_i and r_i be the Precision and Recall of an experiment, we computed the F measure as $(2\ p_i\ r_i)\ /(\ p_i + r_i)$. When we needed to summarize the classification quality for multiple types of cited articles, as we did in the procedure *adjust*, we took the arithmetic average of the F measures of all experiments under consideration.

4.2 Results and Analyses

Table 2 shows the performance of the resulting classifier. The leftmost column indicates the measures used to evaluate the classifier. The top rows indicate types of judicial documents and types of cited articles. Numbers in the cells show the performance of the classifiers without and with the augmented keyword weights. The numbers on the left hand sides of the arrows are performance of the classifier that does not employ keyword weights in computing the similarity between instances.

Weighting the keywords indeed improved the classification quality of our classifier. The averages of Precision, Recall, and the F measures increased for cases of both gambling and larceny. The improvement on the classification of cases of larceny was much more salient than the improvement on the classification of cases of gambling. One of the reasons for this divergence in improvements is that the previous classifier has achieved relatively good performance in classifying cases of gambling. The previous classifier got 0.80 and 0.60 when we took the averages of the F measures for cases of gambling and larceny, respectively. (The average of 0.77, 0.70, 0.90, and 0.80 is about 0.80.) In contrast, the new classifier got 0.83 and 0.76.

Table 2. Experimental results in terms of precision, recall, and F measures

	Types of cases of gambling			
	A	C	AB	AC
p_i	0.74→0.89	0.56→0.57	0.93→0.94	0.90→0.89
r_i	0.80→0.79	0.92→0.84	0.88→0.96	0.78→0.83
Fi	0.77→0.84	0.70→0.68	0.90→0.95	0.84→0.86

	Types of cases of larceny		
	D	DE	DF
p_i	0.50→0.70	0.79→0.86	0.87→0.78
r_i	0.97→0.93	0.30→0.61	0.59→0.76
Fi	0.66→0.80	0.43→0.71	0.70→0.77

Table 3 provides the confusion matrix [12] that shows how the cases of gambling were classified. The leftmost column shows types of the test documents, and the top row shows types that our classifier assigned to the documents. Numbers on the left hand sides of the arrows are results that came from the previous classifier, and numbers on the right hand sides are results for the new classifier. For instance, out of the 807 cases of type A, 645, 11, 108, and 43 cases were classified as type A, C, AB, and AC by the previous classifier.

Table 3. Experimental results for cases of gambling, in number of cases

	A	C	AB	AC
A	645 → 639	11 → 13	108 → 96	43 → 59
C	2 → 2	224 → 206	0 → 0	18 → 36
AB	**185 → 55**	2 → 1	**1574 → 1721**	26 → 10
AC	44 → 22	**166 → 140**	6 → 6	**788 → 836**

Statistics in the last two rows in Table 3 indicate that weighting keywords did help us to avoid classifying compositive cases, e.g., AB and AC, into simple cases, e.g., A and C. However, statistics in the second and third row indicate that some more simple cases were misclassified, thereby offsetting the overall improvement.

5 Discussions

We report an experience of developing a sample-based query mechanism for providing online legal services. We allow users to place queries with prosecution documents, relieving users the needs to figure out appropriate legal keywords. The current experiments examine whether our system can correctly analyze the contents of the query documents, and classify the query documents based on the involved law articles. The reported work build on and improve our previous system that relies only matching ordered keywords for case classification.

Legal case classification is a central issue in computer applications to the legal domain. For instance, Pannu attemps to find “important” features for classifying legal documents with genetic algorithms [15], and Thompson compares different approaches for case classification [16]. The approach we employed is special in that we consider the order of words in the instances. By doing so, we provide a chance for the algorithmically generated instances to catch the context of the legal case, and it is known that contextual information is important in making legal reasoning [17]. We further augment the case instances with weights of keywords so that we can classify the cases at the level of cited articles, which is clearly more difficult than classifying cases based just on prosecution reasons. A case of larceny can be subcategorized into different categories based on how the criminals committed the crime. Experiments indicate that our current approaches provide pretty good classification results. Although not perfect yet, the results shown in Table 2 are better than the classification quality reported in [16] while we confront a more difficut classification task.

Despite the encouraging outcomes, we plan to introduce more techniques for enhancing the classifier. It is clearly a weak spot in our current approaches that we have not considered to analyze the judicial documents from a semantic viewpoint. We can also try to employ other language-modeling techniques that are available in the natural language processing research community.

Acknowledgements

This paper is a partial translation of the Master’s thesis of the second author who worked under the supervision of the first author. We thank Dr. Jim-How Ho, who serves as a Judge at the Pan-Chiao District Court, Taipei, Taiwan, for his providing consultation in legal knowledge. This research was funded in part by Grants NSC-92-2213-E-004-004 and NSC-93-2213-E-004-004 from National Science Council of Taiwan.

References

1. Some web sites for e-governments in developed and developing countries: <www.bsi.de/fachthem/egov/>; <www.e-government.govt.nz/>; <www.e-gov.go.jp/>; <www.whitehouse.gov/omb/egov/>; <www1.worldbank.org/publicsector/egov/>; <e-government.cabinetoffice.gov.uk/Home/Homepage/fs/en>

2. Some web sites for legal information in Chinese: <www.sinolaw.net.cn/alyl.asp>; <www.judicial.gov.tw/>; <www.lawbank.com.tw>; <www.root.com.tw>
3. Information about the International Conferences on Artificial Intelligence and Law between 1987 and 2003: <www.sigmod.org/sigmod/dblp/db/conf/icail/>
4. T. B. Y. Lai and C. Huang, Dependency-based syntactic analysis of Chinese and annotation of parsed corpus, *Proc. of the 38th Annual Meeting of the Association for Computational Linguistics*, 255 262, 2000.
5. G. Brown, CHINATAX: Exploring isomorphism with Chinese law, *Proc. of the 4th Int. Conf. on Artificial Intelligence and Law*, 175-179, 1993.
6. C.-L. Liu, C.-T. Chang, and J.-H. Ho, Classification and clustering for case-based criminal summary judgments, *Proc. of the 9th Int. Conf. on Artificial Intelligence and Law*, 252-261, 2003.
7. C.-L. Liu and C.-T. Chang, Some case-refinement strategies for case-based criminal summary judgments, *Lecture Notes in Artificial Intelligence* 2871, 285-291, 2003.
8. C.-L. Liu, C.-T. Chang, and J.-H. Ho, Case instance generation and refinement for case-based criminal summary judgments in Chinese. *J. of Information Science and Engineering* **20**(4), 783-800, 2004.
9. T. Mitchell, Machine *Learning*, McGraw-Hill, 1997.
10. Z. Zhang and Q. Yang, Feature weight maintenance in case bases using introspective learning, *J. of Intelligent Information Systems* **16**(2), 95-116, 2001.
11. HowNet. http://www.keenage.com
12. C. D. Manning and H. Schütze, *Foundations of Statistical Natural Language Processing*, MIT Press, 1999.
13. S. Brüninghaus and K. D. Ashley, Toward adding knowledge to learning algorithms for indexing legal cases, *Proc. of the 7th Int. Conf. on Artificial Intelligence and Law*, 9-17, 1999.
14. S. Brüninghaus and K. D. Ashley, Improving the representation of legal case texts with information extraction methods, *Proc. of the 8th Int. Conf. on Artificial Intelligence and Law*, 42-51, 2001.
15. A. S. Pannu, Using genetic algorithms to inductively reason with cases in the legal domain, *Proc. of the* 5th *Int. Conf. on Artificial Intelligence and Law*, 175-184, 1995.
16. P. Thompson, Automatic categorization of case law, *Proc. of the* 8th *Int. Conf. on Artificial Intelligence and Law*, 70-77, 2001.
17. C. Hafner and D. Berman, The Role of Context in Case-based Legal Reasoning: teleological, temporal and procedural. *Artificial Intelligence and Law* **10**, 19-64, 2002.

A Unified Probabilistic Framework for Clustering Correlated Heterogeneous Web Objects

Guowei Liu, Weibin Zhu, and Yong Yu

Computer Science & Engineering Department,
Shanghai Jiaotong University, Shanghai, China
{gwliu, wbzhu, yyu}@sjtu.edu.cn

Abstract. Most existing algorithms cluster highly correlated data objects (e.g. web pages and web queries) separately. Some other algorithms, however, do take into account the relationship between data objects, but they either integrate content and link features into a unified feature space or apply a hard clustering algorithm, making it difficult to fully utilize the correlated information over the heterogeneous Web objects. In this paper, we propose a novel unified probabilistic framework for iteratively clustering correlated heterogeneous data objects until it converges. Our approach introduces two latent clustering layers, which serve as two mixture probabilistic models of the features. In each clustering iteration we use EM (Expectation-Maximization) algorithm to estimate the parameters of the mixture model in one latent layer and propagate them to the other one. The experimental results show that our approach effectively combines the content and link features and improves the performance of the clustering.

1 Introduction

Clustering techniques have been used to retrieve, filter and categorize documents available on the World Wide Web for their increasing size and dynamic content[2][22][18]. Document clusters can organize large bodies of text for efficient browsing and searching. Clustering techniques have also been used to cluster web users via web log mining [16][21]. Web pages in the discovered clusters that have not been explored by the user may serve as navigational hints for the user to follow. User queries have also seen a need to apply clustering techniques [20]. The discovered frequently asked questions and most popular topics on a search engine facilitate the query answering substantially.

Different types of objects are always highly correlated to each other. For example, users and web pages they visit, queries and the documents related to, etc. These kinds of relationships may serve as valuable information to be explored. Users of the same interest are likely to browse the pages on the same topic. Similar queries submitted may reveal the same information need of the users. Hence, the search engine may respond by feeding these users with the

Y. Zhang et al. (Eds.): APWeb 2005, LNCS 3399, pp. 76–87, 2005.

documents that highly overlap. A simple way to use these kinds of relationships is to view the links among them as additional features in clustering process. However, such a solution makes the dimensionality even higher without fully exploring the mutual reinforcement between the objects.

To make full use of the relationship to improve the clustering results, [23] proposes a unified framework for clustering heterogeneous data by using an iterative algorithm. This framework uses a two-layered graph with nodes in different layers representing different types of objects as a basis for clustering. However, this approach simply identifies the links by 0 or 1, which will lead to information loss during the process of link merging. Moreover, the link merging process will probably make the error clustering result in one layer be introduced to the other layer and degrade the clustering performance.

To solve the above problems, we propose a unified probabilistic framework for clustering correlated heterogeneous data objects, which differs from [23] by employing probabilistic model for clustering. We introduce two latent clustering layers, which serve as the mixture probabilistic models to generate the data objects. In each iteration we first use EM algorithm to estimate the parameters of the mixture model in a latent layer. The experimental results show that our algorithm converges after several iterations and the clustering performance is improved during the iterations. The comparative experiment presents that our approach outperforms this method proposed in [23].

The rest of the paper is organized as follows. In Section 2, we present the related work on current clustering algorithms. In Section 3, we describe how we estimate the mixture densities parameters via EM algorithm, which is the basis of our framework. In Section 4, a novel unified framework for clustering correlated heterogeneous objects is introduced. We show the experimental results of the proposed approach in Section 5. Finally, we conclude in Section 6.

2 Related Work

Data clustering is a well studied problem in machine learning [8]. For clustering the highly correlated objects, diverse approaches have been proposed. Some clustering methods cluster objects solely based on content features while other methods treat link information as additional features [14][6][17]. These algorithms incorporate the link information as a side-effect and have not fully explored the mutual reinforcement between the web data.

Aspect models are proposed to solve the problem of clustering correlated heterogeneous data. [13] introduces mixture models to cluster the co-occurrence data. [14] presents a systematic, domain-independent framework for unsupervised learning from dyadic data by statistical mixture models. Based on aspect models, probabilistic latent semantic analysis(PLSA) models are proposed [9][11], which provide a probabilistic approach for the discovery of latent variables. Due to its great flexibility, PLSA has been widely and successfully used in variety of application domain, including information retrieval [10], text learning [3][7], co-citation analysis [4] and Web usage mining [15].

Collaborative filtering is another important area where the correlated information is utilized. [19] [12] presents a formal statistical model of collaborative filtering, which characterizes the link information between the web objects in probabilistic manner. Variations of K-means clustering and Gibbs Sampling instead of EM algorithm are used to estimate the model parameters.

3 Mixture Densities Parameters Estimation via EM Algorithm

The mixture model framework defines a probabilistic generative model for the data. The model probability distribution, which is defined by a set of parameters Θ, consists of a mixture of components $c_s \in C = \{c_1, ..., c_{|C|}\}$. Each component is parameterized by a disjoint subset of Θ. A data x is created by first selecting a component according to the mixture cluster prior probabilities $p(c_s)$, then having this selected component generate a data according to its own parameters, with distribution $p(x|c_s)$. Thus, we can characterize the likelihood of data x with a sum of total probability over all mixture components:

$$P(x|\Theta) = \sum_{s=1}^{N_c} p(c_s) * p(x|c_s)$$

where the parameters are $\Theta = \{p(c_s), \theta_s; s = 1, ..., N_c\}$ such that $\sum_{s=1}^{N_c} p(c_s) = 1$ and each $p(x|c_s)$ is the density function of each component parameterized by θ_s.

EM (Expectation-Maximization) is a class of iterative algorithms for maximum likelihood estimation in problems with incomplete data [6]. The mixture-density model parameters estimation problem is probably one of the most widely used applications of the EM algorithm.

Given a set of data X, generated by the mixture model, if we consider X as incomplete and posit the existence of unobserved data items $Y = \{y_s\}_{s=1}^{N_c}$,whose values inform us which component density generated each data item. The incomplete-data log-likelihood expression for the data X is given by:

$$log(L(\Theta|X)) = log \prod_{i=1}^{N} p(x_i|\Theta) = \sum_{i=1}^{N} log(\sum_{s=1}^{N_c} p(c_s) * p(x_i|c_s))$$

Using EM algorithm we can get the expression for $p(c_s)$, and for some model, it is possible to get analytical expressions for θ_s. [1] introduces how to estimate the parameters of Gaussian Mixture Model using EM algorithm. Following the approach mentioned in [1], we can also estimate the parameters of other mixture models, such as Naïve Bayes Model and Multinomial Mixture Model.

4 A Unified Probabilistic Framework for Clustering Correlated Heterogeneous Objects

4.1 The Data Object Structure

We are given two different object layers P and U. Each data object has a content vector, which describes its content feature. Data objects from two different layers are related through weighted links, which can be described by a $N_p * N_u$ Matrix(N_p and N_u are the object numbers in layer P and U respectively). The weight of the links reveals the association extent between two layer objects. We normalize this matrix and name it as "object conjunction matrix" $\{p(p_i, u_j)\}(i = 1, ..., N_p; j = 1, ..., N_u)$. Figure 1 illustrates the data structure.

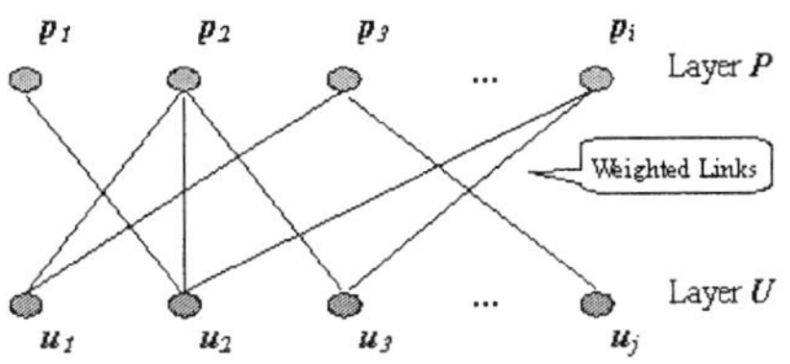

Fig. 1. Data Objects and Their Relationship

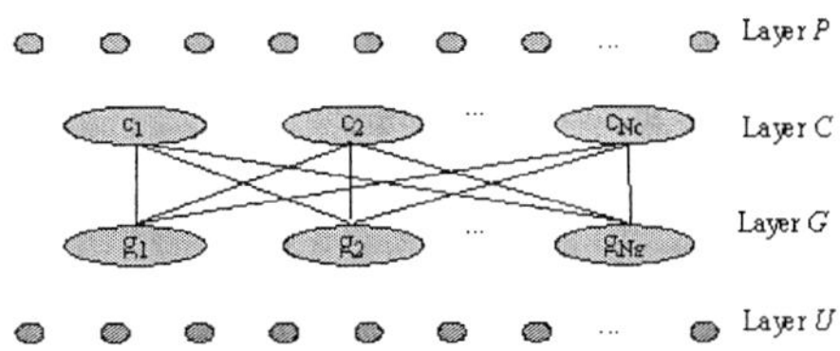

Fig. 2. Two Latent Layers of Mixture Model

4.2 Probabilistic Model with Two Latent Clustering Layers

In this subsection, a probabilistic model with two latent clustering layers is proposed. Firstly, two mixture models of the latent clustering layers are introduced. Then we introduce the model of the content feature and the link feature, and how the link vectors are calculated. Finally, we describe how the content and link features are combined by the probabilistic function in the mixture model. The calculated parameters of one layer mixture model will be propagated to the other layer by the "Component Conjunction Matrix".

Two Latent Clustering Layers. We propose a probabilistic model to generate the data objects in two layers. We assume the data objects in layer P(or U) can be clustered into N_c(or N_g) clusters and introduce two latent clustering layers C and G. Each latent clustering layer is a mixture model, which generates not only the content feature but also the link feature of its corresponding layer data objects. Latent clustering layer C(or G) consists of a mixture of N_c(or N_g) components. We make an assumption that one layer's data objects are independent of its opposite latent clustering layer. Figure 2 illustrates the framework, P and U are two **object layers**, C and G are two **latent clustering layers**. $c_s(s = 1, ..., N_c)$ are N_c components in the mixture model of layer C and $g_t(t = 1, ..., N_g)$ are N_g components in the mixture model of layer G.

Components from two different latent clustering layers are correlated through weighted links referred to as "component links", which can be viewed as the relationship between the components. We denote it by a $N_c * N_g$ normalized matrix, which is referred to as "Component Conjunction Matrix(CCM)" $\{p(c_s, g_t)\}$ $(s = 1, 2, ..., N_c; t = 1, 2, ..., N_g)$. CCM can be viewed as the prior associated probability of the component link (c_s, g_t). Thus the prior component probabilities $p(c_s)$ and $p(g_t)$ can be calculated:

$$p(c_s) = \sum_{t=1}^{N_g} p(c_s, g_t), \ (s = 1, ..., N_c) \tag{1}$$

$$p(g_t) = \sum_{s=1}^{N_c} p(c_s, g_t), \ (t = 1, ..., N_g) \tag{2}$$

If we can calculate CCM $\{p(c_s, g_t)\}$, parameters of distribution $p(p|c_s)$ and $p(u|g_t)$, according to Bayesian Theorem we can get the probability of p_i being generated by component c_s and the probability of u_j being generated by g_t:

$$p(c_s|p_i) = \frac{p(p_i|c_s) * p(c_s)}{\sum_{k=1}^{N_c} p(p_i|c_k) * p(c_k)} \tag{3}$$

$$p(g_t|u_j) = \frac{p(u_j|g_t) * p(g_t)}{\sum_{k=1}^{N_g} p(u_j|g_k) * p(g_k)} \tag{4}$$

Each component can be viewed as a virtual cluster, therefore the probability of p_i being generated by component c_s can be viewed as the probability of object p_i belonging to cluster c_s. Hence, the clustering of objects in layer P can be fulfilled, so can the clustering of objects in layer U.

Content and Link Features of Data Objects. We now describe how the data object of one layer is generated by its corresponding mixture model. Each data object has both content features and link features. Content features are the intensional attributes of each data object, denoted by a content vector. We can assume these content features of all data objects are generated by a content probabilistic model. For example, if the data objects in layer P are web pages, they can be represented by a keyword vector of term frequency, which can be assumed to be generated by Naïve Bayes generative model.

To handle the sparse data problem, links between the two object layers are mapped to those between the objects of one layer and the components of the opposite latent clustering layer. For a certain object p in layer P, its weighted links to all objects in layer U are mapped to the links to the components in latent layer G. We call these links the link feature of the data object and denote it by a link vector, which be calculated by the following expression:

$$\begin{aligned} p(g_t|p) &= \sum_{k=1}^{N_u} p(g_t, u_k|p) \\ &= \sum_{k=1}^{N_u} p(g_t|u_k, p) * p(u_k|p) \ (t = 1, ..., N_g) \\ &= \sum_{k=1}^{N_u} p(g_t|u_k) * p(u_k|p) \end{aligned} \tag{5}$$

Here $p(g_t|u_k)$ is the probability that u_k belongs to the component g_t, and can be calculated by equation 4. $p(u_k|p)$ can be calculated from "object conjunction matrix" $\{p(p_i, u_j)\}$ $(i = 1, ..., N_p; j = 1, ..., N_u)$. $p(g_t|p)$ $(t = 1, ..., N_g)$ is the weighted value of the link vector of p. Then we normalize this vector so as that the sum of each item equals to 1.

The link feature is useful for clustering the data objects. For example, in web page/user clustering, we want to cluster pages into page classes and cluster users into user groups. If two users are interested to a similar extent in the same classes of pages, these two users will have a high probability of belonging to the same user group; on the other hand, if two pages interest the same groups of users to a similar extent, these two pages will also have a high probability belonging to the same page class. So we can regard the link feature as a useful guide in object clustering.

The link vectors of all objects in object layer (without loss of generalization, here we denote by P) can be viewed as points in a space. Because of $\sum_{t=1}^{N_g} p(g_t|p) = 1$, the points are distributed on a hyperplane. If some points are assembled together on the hyperplane, they will have a high probability of being in the same cluster. The nearer the region is to the cluster center, the more dense the points are distributed. As mentioned above, the objects in layer P is generated by the mixture model of latent layer C, we assume the assembled points are generated by the component c_s. We need a suitable component model to generate them. Commonly, we will select the Gaussian Model. However, the points generated by a Gaussian model are not distributed on a hyperplane. In this paper, we take the Multinominal Model since the sample points generated by it are distributed on a hyperplane. However, each dimension value of the points generated by the Multinomial Model is discrete, so we make a modification by multiplying each dimension value of the link vectors $p(g_t|p)$ by a observation number N and rounding it to an integer. So $\sum_{t=1}^{N_g} N * p(g_t|p) = N$, the amplified link vectors of all objects in layer P are generated by a N_c-Multinomial Mixture Model. We think that our assumption on the distribution model is reasonable by taking into account all the properties of the points mentioned above.

Combination of Content and Link Features. The data object of one layer is generated by its corresponding mixture model. A data object p in object layer P is created by first selecting a mixture component according to the component prior probabilities, $p(c_s)$, then having this selected mixture component generate a data object according to its own parameters, with distribution $p(p|c_s)$. In this paper, we combine the content feature model and link feature model together by having $p(p|c_s)$ reflecting both content and link distribution $p_c(p|c_s)$ and $p_l(p|c_s)$. The probabilistic distribution for component c_s is defined as:

$$p(p|c_s) = (p_c(p|c_s))^{\alpha} * (p_l(p|c_s))^{1-\alpha} \tag{6}$$

where α is a predefined parameter. Thus, we can characterize the likelihood of data object p with a sum of total probability over all mixture components:

$$\begin{aligned} p(p|\Theta_c) &= \sum_{s=1}^{N_c} p(c_s) * p(p|c_s) \\ &= \sum_{s=1}^{N_c} p(c_s) * [(p_c(p|c_s))^{\alpha} * (p_l(p|c_s))^{1-\alpha}] \end{aligned} \tag{7}$$

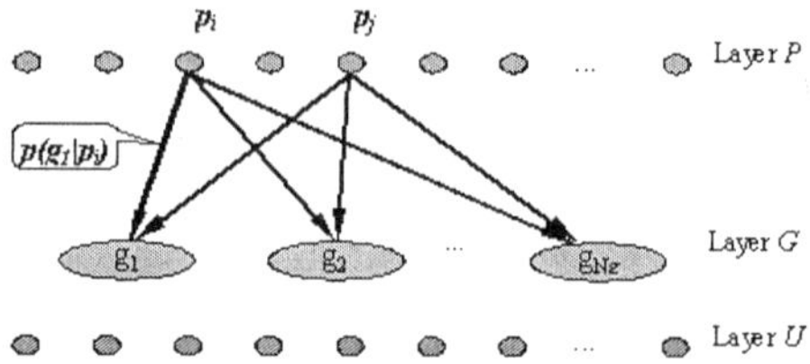

Fig. 3. Link Feature of Data Objects

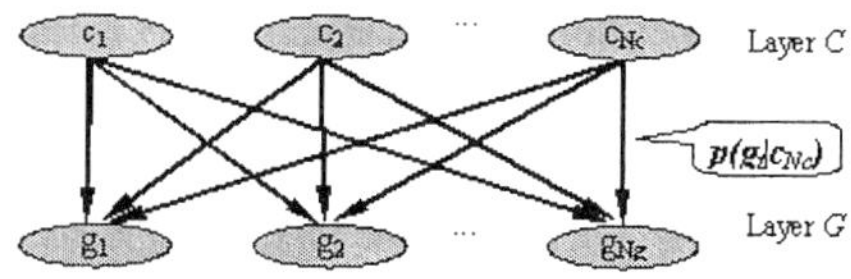

Fig. 4. Relationship from Components in One Layer to the Other Layer

where the parameters are $\Theta_c = \{p(c_s), \theta^c_{c_s}, \theta^l_{c_s}; s = 1, ..., N_c\}$ such that $\sum_i^{N_c} p(c_i) = 1$ and each $p_c(p|c_s)$ is the density function of each component of the content feature model parameterized by $\theta^c_{c_s}$ and each $p_l(p|c_s)$ is the density function of each component of the link feature model parameterized by $\theta^l_{c_s}$. As discussed in previous part, here we assume that $p_l(p|c_s)$ is a multinomial distribution.

Content feature density function is defined according to the model that the content feature obeys. For example, if objects in layer P are web pages, the content feature can be assumed to be generated by Naïve Bayes model. i.e. $\theta^c_{c_s} = \{p(w_r|c_s); (r = 1, ..., N_w)\}$

The CCM can be transformed to an equivalent form $\{p(c_s), p(g_t|c_s)\}$ $(s = 1, ..., N_c; t = 1, ..., N_g)$ by the following expressions:

$$\begin{aligned} p(c_s) &= \textstyle\sum_{t=1}^{N_g} p(c_s, g_t) \\ p(g_t|c_s) &= p(c_s, g_t)/p(c_s) \end{aligned} \tag{8}$$

As mentioned above, $p(c_s)$ is the prior probability of the component c_s. Because of $\sum_{t=1}^{N_g} p(g_t|c_s) = 1$, $p(g_t|c_s)$ can be viewed as the correlated extent for c_s to all components in the opposite latent layer (see Figure 4), and they also can be viewed as the means of multinomial distribution $p_l(p|c_s)$. i.e. $\theta^l_{c_s} = \{p(g_t|c_s), t = 1, ..., N_g\}$. Thus for a given object p with a link vector $N * p(g_t|p)$, the probability for it to be generated by a component c_s is:

$$p_l(p|c_s) = \frac{N!}{\prod_{k=1}^{N_g}(N * p(g_t|p))!} \prod_{k=1}^{N_g} p(g_t|c_s)^{N * p(g_t|p)} \tag{9}$$

where N is the observation number of the multinomial distribution, here we set it to be N_g. Thus we can use EM algorithm to estimate the parameters Θ_c of the mixture model.

On the other hand, a data object u in object layer U is also generated by a mixture model. We also combine the content feature model and link feature model together. The probabilistic distribution for component g_t is defined as:

$$p(u|g_t) = (p_c(u|g_t))^{\alpha} * (p_l(u|g_t))^{1-\alpha} \tag{10}$$

where α is the same predefined parameter as equation (5). The likelihood of data object u with a sum of total probability over all mixture components:

$$\begin{aligned} p(u|\Theta_g) &= \sum_{t=1}^{N_g} p(g_t) * p(u|g_t) \\ &= \sum_{t=1}^{N_g} p(g_t) * [(p_c(u|g_t))^{\alpha} * (p_l(u|g_t))^{1-\alpha}] \end{aligned} \tag{11}$$

Where the parameters are $\Theta_g = \{p(g_t), \theta^c_{g_t}, \theta^l_{g_t}; t = 1, ..., N_g\}$ such that $\sum_i^{N_g} p(g_i) = 1$ and each $p_c(u|g_t)$ is a density function of each component of the content feature model parameterized by $\theta^c_{g_t}$ and each $p_l(u|g_t)$ is density function of each component of the link feature model parameterized by $\theta^l_{g_t}$.

The CCM can also be transformed to an equivalent form $\{p(g_t), p(c_s|g_t)\}$ $(s = 1, 2, ..., N_c; t = 1, 2, ..., N_g)$ by the following expressions:

$$\begin{aligned} p(g_t) &= \sum_{s=1}^{N_c} p(c_s, g_t) \\ p(c_s|g_t) &= p(c_s, g_t)/p(g_t) \end{aligned} \tag{12}$$

They can be viewed as the parameters of the multinomial distribution which the link feature of u obeys. i.e. $\theta^l_{g_t} = \{p(c_s|g_t), s = 1, ..., N_c\}$ Thus we can use EM algorithm to estimate the parameters Θ_g of the mixture model.

The CCM can be transformed to two equivalent forms 8 and 12, which are a part of both the parameters Θ_c and Θ_g. Now we can see that this is an iterative process. We alternately estimate Θ_c and Θ_g using EM algorithm and update the CCM each time we get the estimation.

4.3 An Iterative Clustering Algorithm

Here we present the details of the iterative clustering algorithm. We can see how to use one equivalent form of CCM to update the other equivalent form, and actually update the CCM itself. Thus we iteratively update the CCM until it converges. The parameters of our algorithm are:

$$\Theta = \{p(c_s, g_t), \theta^c_{c_s}, \theta^l_{c_s}, \theta^c_{g_t}, \theta^l_{g_t}; (s = 1, ..., N_c; t = 1, ..., N_g)\},$$

where $\theta^l_{c_s} = \{p(c_s|g_t), s = 1, ..., N_c\}$ and $\theta^l_{g_t} = \{p(g_t|c_s), t = 1, ..., N_g\}$.

And we let:

$$\Theta_c = \{p(c_s), \theta^c_{c_s}, \theta^l_{c_s}; s = 1, ..., N_c\} \quad \text{and} \quad \Theta_g = \{p(g_t), \theta^c_{g_t}, \theta^l_{g_t}; t = 1, ..., N_g\},$$

so we can see $\Theta = \Theta_c \bigcup \Theta_g$.

The algorithm description:

1. Random the parameters Θ, including the parameters of probabilistic distribution $\{p(p|c_s)\}$, $\{p(u|g_t)\}$ and CCM $\{p(c_s, g_t)\}$.
2. Calculate $\{p(c_s)\}$ and $\{p(g_t|c_s)\}$ according to equation 8.
3. Let $\Theta^{'}_c = \{p(c_s), \theta^c_{c_s}; s = 1, ..., N_c\}$, use EM algorithm to estimate the parameters $\Theta^{'}_c$, which are the parameters of the content feature mixture model of layer C.

4. Update CCM according to the equation: $p(c_s, g_t) = p(g_t|c_s) * p(c_s)$.
5. Calculate the link vectors of data objects in layer U according to the equation: $p(c_s|u_j) = \sum_{k=1}^{N_p} p(c_s|p_k) * p(p_k|u_i), (j = 1, ..., N_u; s = 1, ..., N_c)$, where $p(c_s|p_k)$ is calculated according to equation 3 using Θ_c.
6. Calculate $\{p(g_t)\}$ and $\{p(c_s|g_t)\}$ according to equation 12.
7. Use EM algorithm to estimate the parameters Θ_g, which are the parameters of the mixture model of layer G.
8. Update CCM according to the equation: $p(c_s, g_t) = p(c_s|g_t) * p(g_t)$.
9. Calculate the link vector of the data objects in P layer according to the equation: $p(g_t|p_i) = \sum_{k=1}^{N_u} p(g_t|u_k) * p(u_k|p_i), (i = 1, ..., N_p; t = 1, ..., N_g)$, where $p(g_t|u_k)$ is calculated according to equation 4 using Θ_g.
10. Calculate $\{p(c_s)\}$ and $\{p(g_t|c_s)\}$ according to equation 8.
11. Use EM algorithm to estimate the parameters Θ_c, which are the parameters of the mixture model of layer C.
12. Update CCM according to the equation $p(c_s, g_t) = p(g_t|c_s) * p(c_s)$.
13. Go to step 5 until the parameters Θ converge.

Because at first the random CCM is not accurate, step 3 first clusters the data objects in layer P only according to their content features. Step 5 utilizes the parameters Θ_c to calculate the link vectors of objects in layer U. Then step 7 clusters the data objects in layer U according to both their content and link features by estimating the parameters Θ_g with initial values calculated at step 6. Similarly step 9 utilizes the parameters Θ_g to calculate the link vectors of objects in layer P. Then step 11 clusters the data objects in layer P according to both features by estimating the parameters Θ_c with initial values calculated at step 10. Θ_c is updated by Θ_g and vice versa until the process converges. CCM is viewed as the bridge between parameters Θ_c and Θ_g.

5 Experiments

Our first experiment is based on semi-synthetic data which simulates the documents having hyper-links pointing to other ones. The second experiment is based on real query log data, which shows that our algorithm also performs well in the real application.

5.1 Semi-synthetic Data

We conduct an experiment based on semi-synthetic data. First we select two groups of topics from Reuters Corpus Volume 1. The first group contains 12 topics and second one contains 8 topics. For each topic, we randomly select 100 to 300 documents to form a collection. The links between the documents of the two groups are randomly generated from a virtual probabilistic model. The similarity between the two collections is computed using the cosine function. The larger the similarity between the two collections is, the higher probability the two documents selected from these collections respectively will be considered as

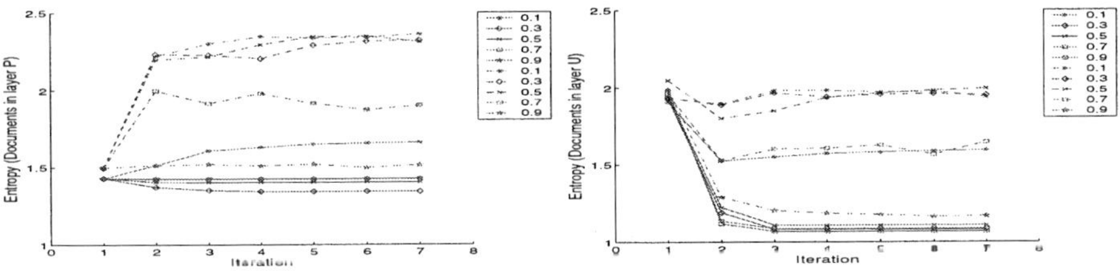

Fig. 5. Entropy. The numbers in the legend is the parameter α

related, that is, to have a link. The content feature of documents in both layers is assumed to be generated by the Naïve Bayes Model.

Because all the documents we use have class labels. We measure the clustering accuracy based on the entropy in information theory [5], which measures the uniformity or purity of a cluster. Assume n objects are clustered into N_c clusters, let S denotes the set of objects in a cluster, and the class label of each object $x_i \in S$ (where $i = 1, ..., |S|$) is denoted by $label(x_i)$, which takes values c_j(where $j = 1, ..., N_c$). The entropy of cluster S is defined by:

$$Entropy(S) = -\sum_{j=1}^{N_c} p_j * logp_j \quad \text{where} \quad p_j = \frac{|\{x_i | label(x_i) = c_j\}|}{|S|}$$

The weighted average entropy is defined by the weighted sum of cluster entropies, and it is the expected purity calculated on all clusters. The smaller the $Entropy_{avg}$ is, the more accurate the clustering result is.

$$Entropy_{avg} = \sum_{k=1}^{N_c} \frac{|S_k|}{n} Entropy(S_k)$$

Two experiments are conducted using the clustering algorithms of ours and the one proposed in [23], respectively. Figure 5 shows the variance of the $Entropy_{avg}$ in different iterations. The horizontal axis denotes the outer iteration times and the vertical axis denotes the $Entropy_{avg}$ of each iteration. The solid line and the dashed line denotes our approach and the approach in [23], respectively. As shown in the figure, the result entropy of our approach is lower than theirs and decreases during iterations, which indicates that the combination of the content and link feature by our approach does take effect in clustering the two layer objects. However, the fluctuation of the dashed line demonstrates that the result of the approach in [23] is not satisfactory. We can notice that the polyline depicted in our figure is different from that in [23]. We deduce that the reason is in [23] the inner iteration number of k-means is set to three and it is not guaranteed to converge. For comparability, we modify it by clustering the objects to convergence in each inner iteration. The results also show that our approach performs well when the parameter α ranges from 0.3 to 0.5.

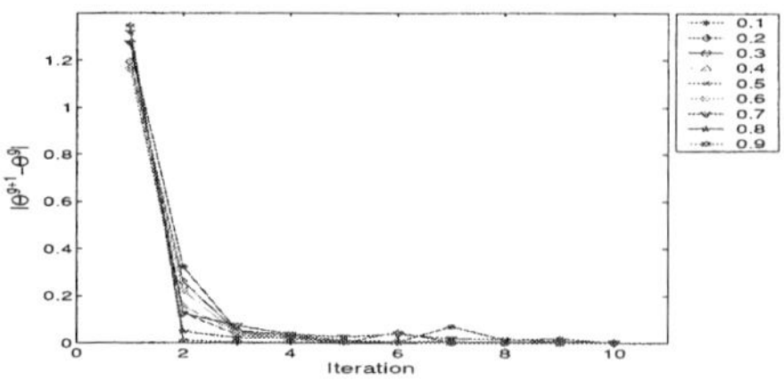

Fig. 6. Convergence. The numbers in the legend is the parameter α

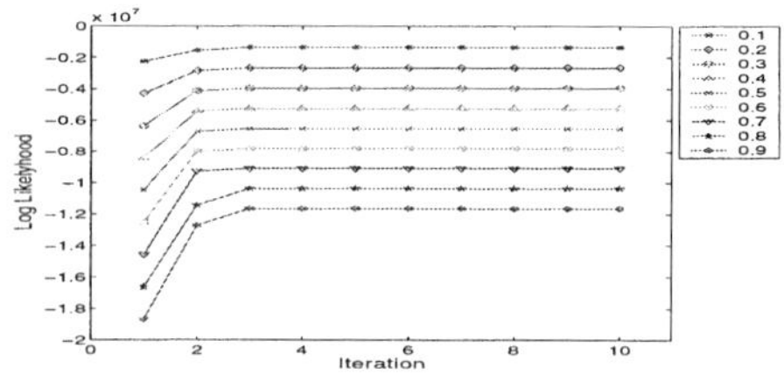

Fig. 7. Log Likelihood. The numbers in the legend is the parameter α

5.2 Real Data

We conducted experiments on a real data set, the MSN query log in Nov, 2003. After preprocessed, the MSN query log contains 5537 pages, 5163 queries and 16587 links between them. The cluster numbers of pages and queries are both set to 10. Figure 6 shows the convergence of the algorithm. The vertical axis denotes the value $|\Theta^{g+1} - \Theta^{g}|$, which is the closeness of the value Θ between the current and the previous iteration. We can notice it is converged to a low value after 4 to 6 iterations.

To evaluate our algorithm, we partitioned the preprocessed query logs into two parts, with 3/4 being the training data and 1/4 being the test data. Our clustering algorithm is run on the training data to train the model, and the log-likelihood of test data is calculated and depicted in Figure 7. The likelihood is the probability of all the test data being generated by the model trained based on the training data. The vertical axis denotes the log-likelihood of test data at each iteration with clustering from that without clustering. We can see that the log-likelihood is increased during each iteration, which indicates that the model trained based on the training data is becoming more and more accurate.

6 Conclusions

In this paper we propose a novel framework for clustering correlated objects. In the framework we combine the content and link feature of the data objects effectively. The iterative clustering algorithm uses one equivalent form of CCM to update the other equivalent form, and actually update the CCM itself. Finally we perform the experiments to demonstrate the effectiveness of our framework and the iterative clustering algorithm.

References

1. J. Bilmes. A gentle tutorial on the em algorithm and its application to parameter estimation for gaussian mixture and hidden markov models, 1997.
2. D. Boley, M. Gini, R. Gross, S. Han, K. Hastings, G. K. pis, V. Kumar, B. Mobasher, and J. Moore. Partitioning-based clustering for web document categorization. *Decision Support Systems*, 27(3), 1999.

3. T. Brants, F. Chen, and I. Tsochantaridis. Topic-based document segmentation with probabilistic latent semantic analysis. In *Proc. of the 11th international conference on Information and knowledge management*, 2002.
4. D. Cohn and T. Hofmann. The missing link - a probabilistic model of document content and hypertext connectivity. In *Neural Information Processing Systems*, 2001.
5. T. M. Cover and J. A. Thomas. Elements of information theory. 1991.
6. A. Dempster, N. Laird, and D. Rubin. Maximum-likelihood from incomplete data via the em algorithm. *Machine Learning*, 39, 1977.
7. E. Gaussier, C. Goutte, K. Popat, and F. Chen. A hierarchical model for clustering and categorising documents. In *Proc. of ECIR-02, 24th European Colloquium on Information Retrieval Research*, 2002.
8. J. Han and M. Kamer. *Data Mining: Concepts and Techniques.* Morgan Kaufmann, 2001.
9. T. Hofmann. Probabilistic latent semantic analysis. In *Proc. of Uncertainty in Artificial Intelligence, UAI'99*, Stockholm, 1999.
10. T. Hofmann. Probabilistic latent semantic indexing. In *Proc. of the 22nd Annual ACM Conference on Research and Development in Information Retrieval*, Berkeley, California, August 1999.
11. T. Hofmann. Unsupervised learning by probabilistic latent semantic analysis. *Mach. Learn.*, 42(1-2), 2001.
12. T. Hofmann. Latent semantic models for collaborative filtering. 2004.
13. T. Hofmann and J. Puzicha. Mixture models for co-occurrence and histogram data.
14. T. Hofmann and J. Puzicha. Unsupervised learning from dyadic data. Technical Report TR-98-042, Berkeley, CA, 1998.
15. X. Jin, Y. Zhou, and B. Mobasher. Web usage mining based on probabilistic latent semantic analysis. In *Proc. of the 2004 ACM SIGKDD international conference on Knowledge discovery and data mining*, 2004.
16. T. Morzy, M. Wojciechowski, and M. Zakrzewicz. Web users clustering. 2000.
17. J. Sinkkonen and S. Kaski. Clustering based on conditional distributions in an auxiliary space. *Neural Computation*, 14(1), 2002.
18. N. Slonim and N. Tishby. Document clustering using word clusters via the information bottleneck method. In *Proc. of the 23rd International ACM SIGIR Conference on Research and Development in Information Retrieval*, 2000.
19. L. Ungar and D. Foster. Clustering methods for collaborative filtering, 1998.
20. J. R. Wen, J. Y. Nie, and H. J. Zhang. Query clustering using user logs. 2002.
21. T. W. Yan, M. Jacobsen, H. Garcia-Molina, and U. Dayal. From user access patterns to dynamic hypertext linking. Technical Note CS-TN-97-42, Feb. 1997.
22. O. Zamir and O. Etzioni. Web document clustering: A feasibility demonstration. In *Proc. of the 21st Annual International ACM SIGIR Conference on Research and Development in Information Retrieval*, 1998.
23. H. J. Zeng, Z. Chen, and W. Y. Ma. A unified framework for clustering heterogeneous web object. In *Proc. of the 3rd WISE*, 2002.

CLINCH: Clustering Incomplete High-Dimensional Data for Data Mining Application*

Zunping Cheng[1], Ding Zhou[2], Chen Wang[1], Jiankui Guo[1], Wei Wang[1], Baokang Ding[1], and Baile Shi[1]

[1] Fudan University, China
{czp, chenwang, gjk, weiwang1, bkding, bshi}@fudan.edu.cn
[2] Pennsylvania State University, USA
dzhou@cse.psu.edu

Abstract. Clustering is a common technique in data mining to discover hidden patterns from massive datasets. With the development of privacy-maintaining data mining application, clustering incomplete high-dimensional data has becoming more and more useful. Motivated by these limits, we develop a novel algorithm **CLINCH**, which could produce fine clusters on incomplete high-dimensional data space. To handle missing attributes, CLINCH employs a prediction method that can be more precise than traditional techniques. On the other hand, we also introduce an efficient way in which dimensions are processed one by one to attack the "curse of dimensionality". Experiments show that our algorithm not only outperforms many existing high-dimensional clustering algorithms in scalability and efficiency, but also produces precise results.

Keywords: Clustering, Incomplete Data, High-Dimensional Data.

1 Introduction

The clustering is a primary technique in discovering hidden patterns from massive datasets. Common applications of cluster analysis involve scientific data exploration, information retrieval and text mining, spatial database applications, Web analysis, marketing, computation biology, and many others. [14]

Explosive progress in networking, storage, and processor technologies has led to deal with ultra large databases in data mining, which record tremendous, high-dimensional and transactional information. In tandem with this trend, concerns about informational privacy in data mining have emerged globally, for Data mining, with its promise to efficiently discover valuable, non-obvious information from large databases, is particularly vulnerable to misuse [5]. Specifically, a

* This paper was supported by the Key Program of National Natural Science Foundation of China (No. 69933010 and 60303008) and China National 863 High-Tech Projects (No. 2002AA4Z3430 and 2002AA231041).

Y. Zhang et al. (Eds.): APWeb 2005, LNCS 3399, pp. 88–99, 2005.

person: 1) may not divulge at all the values of certain fields; 2) may not mind giving true values of certain fields; 3) may be willing to give not true values but modified values of certain fields [5]. All these situations will lead to the creation of missing attributes, i.e. privacy concerns.

Available studies in this mostly focus on how to fill the missing attributes with appropriate values [3, 8, 16]. Given a point X_i with missing value in j^{th} dimension, a general approach is to find the K-Nearest Neighbors *(KNN)* of X_i and replace the missing attribute X_{ij} with the average of the jth values of its *KNN* [16]. However, when application is extended to deal with high-dimensional data, this method becomes unreliable in that high-dimensional data are sparse-prone, which makes the *KNN* search on it meaningless [14, 18].

Algorithms to deal with the incomplete high-dimensional data are relatively few. Moreover, these algorithms are mostly mathematic-prone. Viewing from the perspective of data mining application, little work has started. Mining on the incomplete data would be a more and more popular issue.

In this paper, we propose an efficient method to cluster on incomplete high-dimensional data. We employ the three-step framework, just the same as most grid-based algorithm [10, 1, 9, 7], in our clustering algorithm. The problem is mainly solved by identifying the dense units. Our approach identifies the units by processing dimension by dimension.

There are two contributions from this method: I) lots of points are pruned after several dimensions, therefore the total cost is cut down; II) we propose an innovative prediction mechanism to solve the problem of incomplete data. From experiments and complexity analysis, we can see that our approach outperforms many existing approaches while maintaining a reasonable precision.

The remainder of this paper is organized as follows. In Section 2, we state the clustering problem. In Section 3, Algorithm *CLIQUE* is introduced simply. Algorithm *CLINCH* is developed in Section 4. In Section 5, we evaluate the performance on synthetic and real datasets via comparing *CLINCH* with *CLIQUE* and *FilV-DBScan*. Related work is presented in Section 6. Section 7 concludes the paper.

2 Problem Statement

Definition 1 (DataSpace)
Given a set of K-dimensional data points $\{\overrightarrow{D_i}|i = 1, ..., n\}$, we have a K-by-n data matrix D: $D = \{\overrightarrow{D_1}, \overrightarrow{D_2}, ..., \overrightarrow{D_n}\}$, where $\overrightarrow{D_i} = \{d_{1i}, d_{2i}, ...d_{Ki}\}^T$. In a normalized incomplete data space D, d_{ij} could either be in $[0, 1]$ or "uncertain". *The* "uncertain" *indicates the missing of this attribute at this point.*

Definition 2 (Dimension)
Let a row of the data matrix D be $Dim_j = \{d_{j1}, d_{j2}, ..., d_{jn}\}$. We refer to Dim_j as the jth dimension of a data space. Apparently, a dimension is the set of jth attribute of all the points.

Definition 3 (Incompleteness)

Given a point $\overrightarrow{D_i}$, it has missing values if one or more of its attributes are uncertain. For example, $\overrightarrow{D_i}$ is a record in a 5-dimensional data space, $\overrightarrow{D_i} = \{0.25, uncertain, 0.15, uncertain, 0.20\}$, which means that record $\overrightarrow{D_i}$ has missing values in 2nd and 4th dimensions. Accordingly, the completeness ξ_j of jth the dimension follows:

$$\xi_j = \sum_{t=1}^{n} |\{d_{ji}|d_{ji} \neq uncertain, d_{ji} \in \overrightarrow{D_t}, i = 1, 2, ...n\}|.$$

Generally speaking, if $MAX(\xi_1, \xi_2, ..., \xi_m) \leq MININCOMPLETE$, the dataset is complete. Here, MININCOMPLETE is a threshold specified by users and can be used to obtain an algorithmic gain.

Definition 4 (Unit)

Given a data space D, each unit u is the intersection of one interval from each dimension. Formally, $u = \{[l_1, h_1), [l_2, h_2), ..., [l_k, h_k)\}$, where $[l_i, h_i)$ denotes the interval on the ith dimension. A unit is a dense unit if the points in this unit exceed a given support ϵ. Namely, we say a unit is dense under support of ϵ.

Definition 5 (Cluster)

Given a set of unit, a cluster is the maximal of connected dense units. Two points are in the same cluster if the units they belong to are connected or there exist a set of dense units that are each other connected.

Problem Statement: Given a set of data points D, desired number of intervals σ on each dimension and support ϵ, the problem is how to predict which units the points with missing value belong to and generate clusters.

3 Algorithm CLIQUE

In [1], *CLIQUE*, an automatic subspace clustering algorithm for high-dimensional data, was proposed. *CLIQUE* consists of mainly three steps: 1) searches for the dense units; 2) clusters are generated by grouping the connected dense units; 3) concise descriptions for each cluster are produced based on minimal cluster descriptions *MDL*.

Among these three phases, the only phase that accesses database is the dense unit generation. Accordingly, the step1 takes up most of the time spent in discovering clusters. Remember that in *CLIQUE*, k-dimensional dense unit candidates are generated by self-joining all the $k-1$-dimensional dense units. However, given any several dimensions of the whole high-dimensional dataspace, there would be over-numbered points in every unit. This produces too many dense units in the first several dimensions in *CLIQUE*. Although most of these units will be pruned as the dimension goes high, to self-join on these large amount of units in the first several dimensions, however, would square the overall runtime. This deteriorates *CLIQUE*'s performance on high-dimensional data.

To clarify, let's take a look at a simple example. Given a k-dimensional data space D, *CLIQUE* seeks the k-dimensional dense units level by level. Thus while generating all the 3-dimensional dense units, CILQUE self-joins the dense units in all 2-dimensional subspaces. Now let's estimate how large a number of dense units there will be if D is a high-dimensional database: in all, there are $C_k^2 = k \times (k-1)$ 2-dimensional subspaces. On every subspace, there will be $(I) \times (I)$ units, where (I) is the number of intervals on each dimension. Note when D are projected to any 2-dimensional subspaces, there will be over-numbered points in every units. This probably produces as many as $k \times (k-1) \times (I) \times (I)$ 2-dimensional dense units in all. Moreover, when such large number of units are self-joined, the cost time is squared.

4 Algorithm CLINCH

In this section, we introduce our approach *CLINCH* (i.e. **CL**ustering **IN**Complete **H**igh-dimensional data). We employ the framework like most grid-based clustering algorithms. Figure 1 illustrates the steps of algorithm *CLINCH*.

Input: Dataset D, support threshold $minsup$;
Output: A set of cluster's IDs;
Method: CLINCH(D, $minsup$)

```
1:  DenseUnitGen(D,minsup) //generate the dense units;
2:  Search for clusters with dense units set;
```

Fig. 1. Algorithm CLINCH

In the first step, we partition the space into several equi-sized units[1]. Then the units with points more than given support are marked as the dense units.

In the second step, the connected dense units are tagged the same ID as clusters. Two dense units are named to be "connected" if they share a common face [1]. Given a graph G, let every dense unit be a vertex in G. There is an edge between two dense units if and only if the two corresponding dense units are "connected". Then the problem of step 2 is equivalent to searching for the connected components in a graph. In implementation, we use depth-first search algorithm [2] in discovering these components. Since the problem is projected into the search of the graph, the clustering result will not be affected by the order of the records, ie. CLINCH is stable.

We propose to process the whole data space dimension by dimension. The phrase "dimension by dimension" means that 1) firstly dense units in *K-1-d* space are produced and then 2) dense units on *K-d* space are produced by combining

[1] In some paper, the interval assignments of partitioning of units are studied. Here we assume the space is partitioned evenly.

Input: Dataset D, support threshold $minsup$;
Output: A set of dense units;
Method: DenseUnitGen(D, $minsup$)

$DS \leftarrow$ determine and sort the order of $D's$ dimensions;
$UList \leftarrow$ FullDim(DS,$minsup$) //recognition on full dimensions;
IncompleteDim(DS,$minsup$,$UList$,$DimID$) //recognition on incomplete dimensions;

Fig. 2. Procedure DenseUnitGen

the mining results on *K-1-d* and dense intervals on the *Kth* dimension. At first, we sort all dimensions. Then we search for the dense units in the first several complete dimensions. Suppose there are β complete dimensions in all, we produce $\beta - dimensional$ dense units and pass them to the following step. Then the rest dimensions are processed with the received $\beta - dimensional$ dense units. At last a set of dense units will be generated in whole dimensions. Figure 2 shows the procedure for generating dense units.

4.1 Determine the Order of Dimension for Process

Intuitively, we firstly deal with the complete dimensions and then the incomplete ones. We handle the complete dimensions in the decreasing order of their entropies [7]. The entropy of a dimension is defined in [7, 10]. Since lager entropies mean more information, if we deal with dimensions with larger entropies, the prediction on the missing attributes will be more precise. After finishing all the complete dimensions, characteristics of clusters on this complete subspace are built through entropies, and will be employed for the prediction of missing attributes through the following incomplete dimensions. This process is similar to building a decision-tree for the first several dimensions, which would be used in later prediction [5]. Intuitively, we optimize the grouping of points for prediction if we follow the decreasing entropies. Similar idea has already been widely accepted in the study of classification algorithms [7].

On the other hand, we process the incomplete dimensions after all the complete ones are processed. For these incomplete dimensions, we handle them according to their completeness ξ_j. This is to guarantee that dimensions with more uncertain records are processed later, which maximizes the information used for prediction.

After the order of dimension is determined, we proceed to recognize the dense units.

4.2 Recognition on Full Dimensions

We benefit from the monotonicity introduced in [1]. If a unit is dense in its k-dimensional space, then it will be also dense in any of its $k-1$-dimensional space [1]. With this feature, we could prune many units in the first several

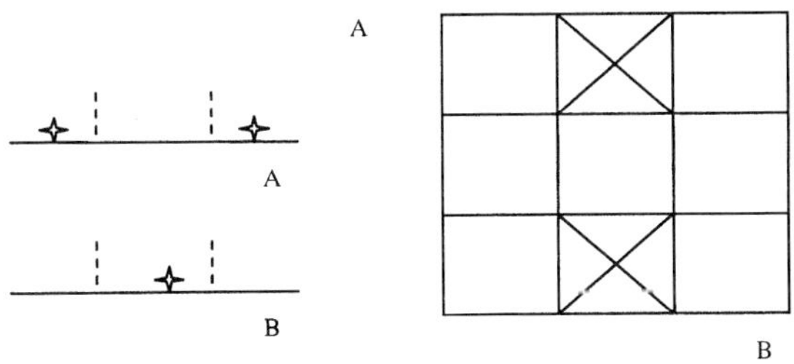

Fig. 3. Generation of 2-d candidates from 1-d dense units

Input: Dataset sorted by entropy of Dimension DS, support threshold $minsup$;
Output: a set of $\beta - dimensional$ units
Method: FullDim(DS, $minsup$)
1: $K \leftarrow$ number of complete dimensions;
2: $C_0 \leftarrow$ 1-dimensional dense units on DS_0;
3: $C[1, ...K-1] \leftarrow$ NULL;
4: for i from 1 to $K-1$
5: $U_i \leftarrow$ Generate the $1 - dimensional$ dense units on the dimension of $DS[i]$;
6: $C_i \leftarrow C_{i-1} \times U_i$; //generate the i-dim unit candidates from C_{i-1} and C_i;
7: scan subspace from DS_0 to DS_i and keep the dense units in C_i;

Fig. 4. Procedure FullDim

dimensions if we recognize the dense units dimension by dimension. Our process is illustrated in Figure 3: let A be the first dimension and B be the second. Figure 4 shows the pseudo-code of our approach.

In line 6 of Figure 4, i-dimensional unit candidates are generated from the $1-$ *dimensional* dense unit U_i and C_{i-1}. Thus the time cost of this step is bounded by the number of element in each dimension. Given every $k - dimensional$ dense unit is also dense in any of its $k-1$ subspace, our $k-1$ dense unit list C_{k-1} contains the dense units in $k - dimensional$. Then by also checking the ones on the ith dimension, we further limit the number of candidates for following prune. Line 7 then check on the subspace to maintain the truly dense one, whose implementation is straightforward.

Let's go back to the example in Section 2. Compared with the self-join of CLIQUE, the join of CLINCH only generate as many as $k \times (k-1) \times (I_{max}) \times (I_{max})$ dense units. Here, $I_{max} = MAX(\{I_i | i = 1, ..., k)\}$, I_i is the amount of dense unites of the ith dimension. Since $I_{max} \leq I$, it is clear that the join of CLINCH can get less cost than the self-join of CLIQUE. Furthermore, the employment of the dimension-by-dimension processing in the dense unit recognition not only ease the efficiency in the self-join step in *CLIQUE* but also provides the possibility to cluster incomplete data without filling the value beforehand.

4.3 Recognition on Incomplete Dimensions

After all the complete dimensions are processed, we pass the dense units to the step 3. Our idea is to employ the information from the processed several dimensions to predict those missing values. Based on the $dimension-by-dimension$ approach, we introduce a decision-tree like mechanism to enable predication for incomplete points. An example of such prediction is illustrated in Figure 5. Given four $3-dimensional$ points $A(0.4, 0.4, X)$, $B(0.5, 0.4, 0.8)$, $C(0.85, 0.45, 0.2)$ and $D(0.7, 0.5, 0.3)$, assume they are all complete in their first 2 dimension and their positions are illustrated as follow:

This algorithm is illustrated in Figure 6.

4.4 Time Complexity

The time complexity of Algorithm *CLINCH* mainly consists of three parts:

1. Sort the dimensions by their entropy.
2. Generate $1-dimensional$ dense unit.
3. Generate $k-dimensional$ units dimension by dimension.

Among these three steps, part 1 and 2 cost $O(k*n)$ and $O(n)$ respectively. On the other hand, the time complexity of part 3 is bounded by $O(\sum_{1}^{k-1} T_i)$, where T_i denotes the time in dealing with n points on i^{th} dimension. When it is complete in dimension i, time to handle n points is $O(n)$, otherwise the time depends on the completeness ξ_i. Formally,

$$T_i = \begin{cases} O(n) & \textit{The } i^{th} \textit{ dimension is complete} \\ O(n*(1-\xi_i) + \sum_{1}^{n*\xi_i} a_j) & \textit{Otherwise} \end{cases}$$

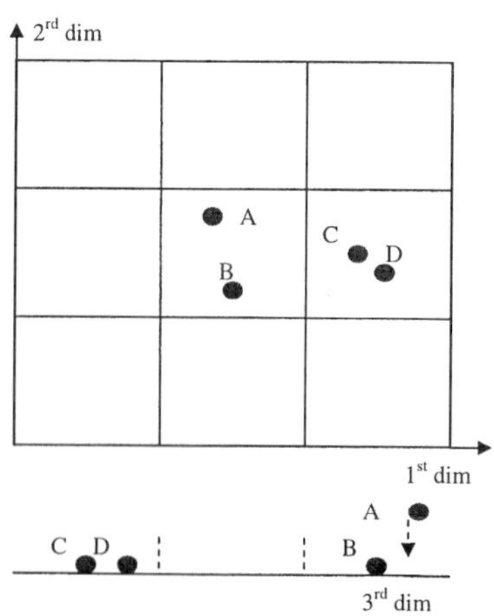

Fig. 5. Example for 3-dimensional units recognition

Input: Dataset sorted by entropy of Dimension DS, support threshold $minsup$, a set of $\beta - dimensional$ units $UList$, Dimension ID $DimID$;

Method: IncompleteDim(DS, $minsup$, $UList$, $DimID$)

```
C_(DimID-1) ← UList;
for i from DimID to DS.Dim − 1
    U_i ← Generate the 1 − dimensional dense Unit on the dimension of DS[i];
    C_i ← C_(i-1) ∪ U_i
    for every point P in the subspace form D[0...i]
        if P is complete in i^th dimension then
            determine which unit candidate P belongs to
        else
            find P's nearest complete neighbor Pnbr from S
            //S is the i − 1-dimensional unit that Pnbr belongs to
            record P and its Pnbr;
    include each incomplete point P to the i-dim unit Pnbr belongs to;
    remove the non-dense unit in C_i;
```

Fig. 6. Procedure IncompleteDim

Where a_j is the largest size of unit that an incomplete point needs to seek in for neighbor.

Overall, the time complexity is $O(k * n + \sum_{1}^{k-1} T_i + n)$, which is bounded by $O(k * n)$. This much outperforms the exponential time of CILQUE.

5 Experiments

In this section, we evaluate the performance of *CLINCH*. Criterion in estimating the performance of *CLINCH* includes its efficiency and quality of clustering results. In efficiency, we record the total CPU time for comparison with *CLIQUE* and the way introduced in [16] followed by *DBSCAN*. The efficiency was tested on both synthetic and real data. The synthetic data generator was introduced in [22]. The real dataset is from the completely specified database *MUSK2* from *UCI*[2] machine learning repository. We evaluate the precision in the way introduced in [21], which would be covered in details later. We implemented all the algorithms in C++. The experiments have been run on Pentium IV with 2.2 GHz containing 512MB DDR of main memory and Windows XP as operating system.

5.1 Efficiency

We use real data as well as synthetic data in the experiments. The synthetic data generator is introduced in [22]. We could set the number and size of clusters,

[2] http://www.cs.uci.edu/ mlearn

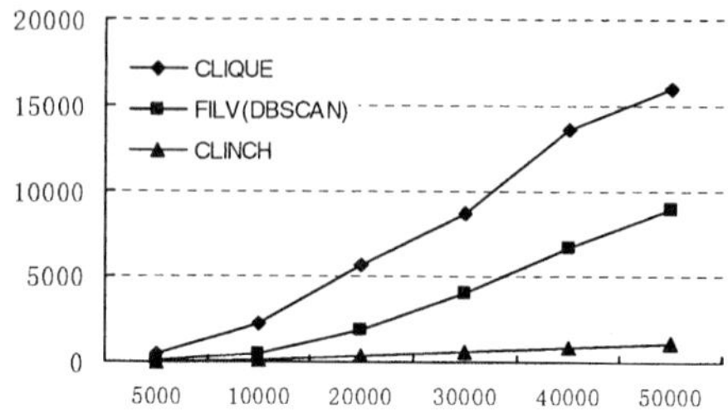

Fig. 7. Time vs. Dataset Size (50-d)

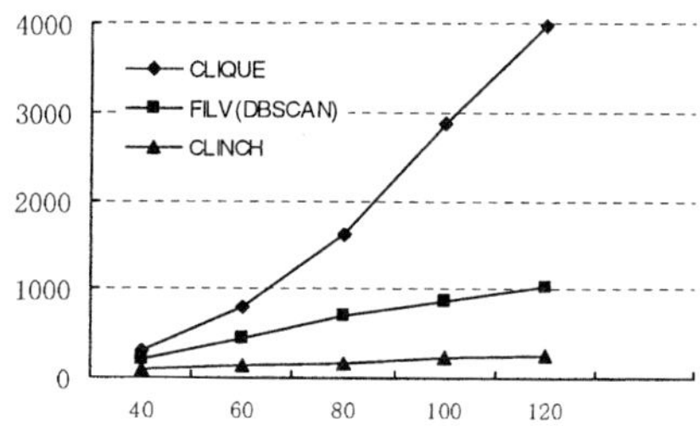

Fig. 8. Time vs. Dim (size of 10000)

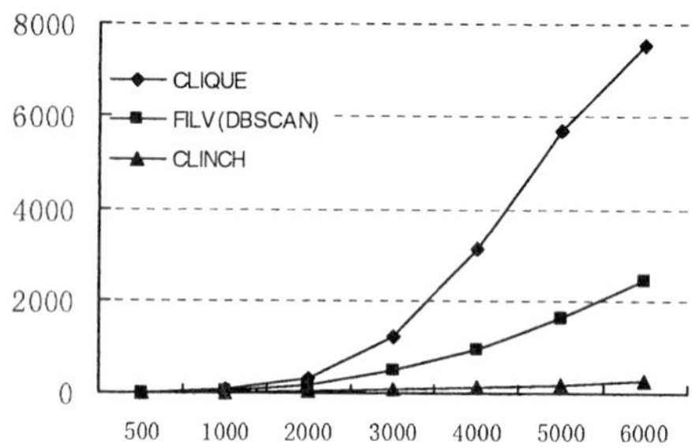

Fig. 9. Time vs. Dataset Size on MUSK2

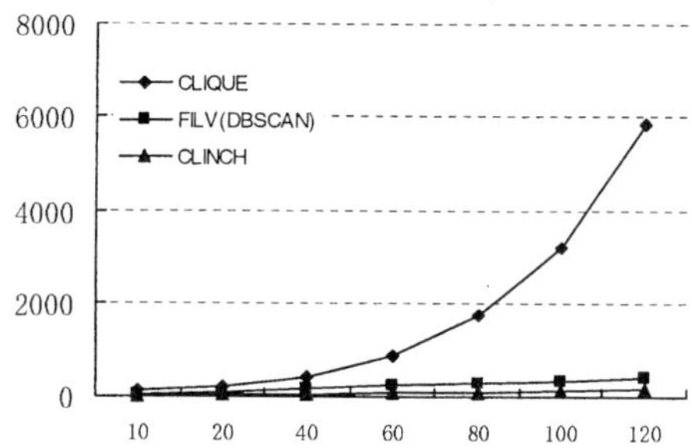

Fig. 10. Time vs. Dim on MUSK2

size and dimensionality of dataset etc. To test the performance of *CLINCH* on different size of real data, we extract a series of subsets of *MUSK2*. Experiments on the efficiency of *CLINCH* include its sensitivity to the dimensionality and size of dataset.

Using cluster generator, we set to generate 5 clusters of 50-dimensional database in different sizes. We could see from the figure 7 that *CLINCH* scales well with the increase of database size. Besides, *CLINCH*'s scalability with dimension was also investigated. We tested three algorithms on datasets with 10000 points. The effects of dimensions are shown in figure 8.

We also conducted the comparison on real dataset. The dataset is from the machine learning repository *MUSK2* from *UCI*. Scalability with dimension and database size is tested by retrieving either the subspaces of dimensions and subsets of data. Figure 9 and 10 show performances of *CLINCH* on different database sizes and dimensionality.

5.2 Precision

In this section we would study what precision the *CLINCH* maintains and could see that *CLINCH* produces the same clustering results if both performed on complete data.

We employ the dataset from completely specified *UCI* dataset *MUSK2* for experiments. We generate the incomplete data space by randomly removing some attributes of points.

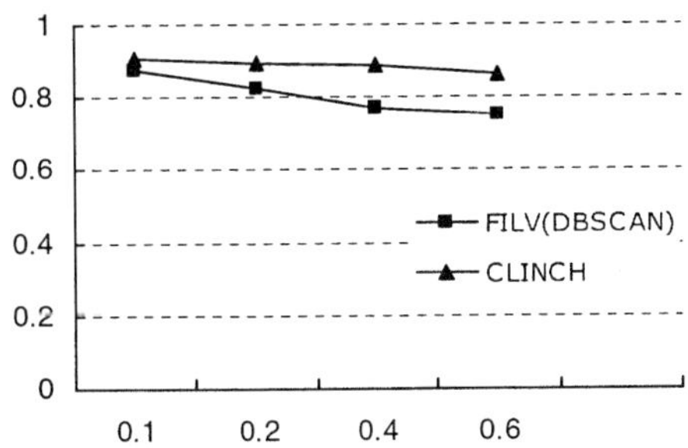

Fig. 11. Precision vs. Missing Dim

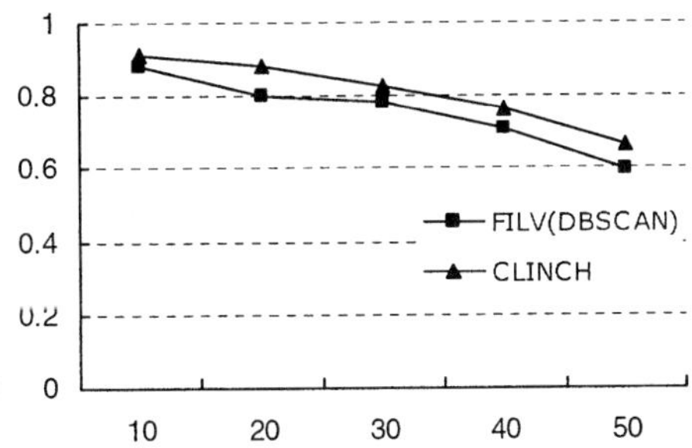

Fig. 12. Precision vs. Missing Percent

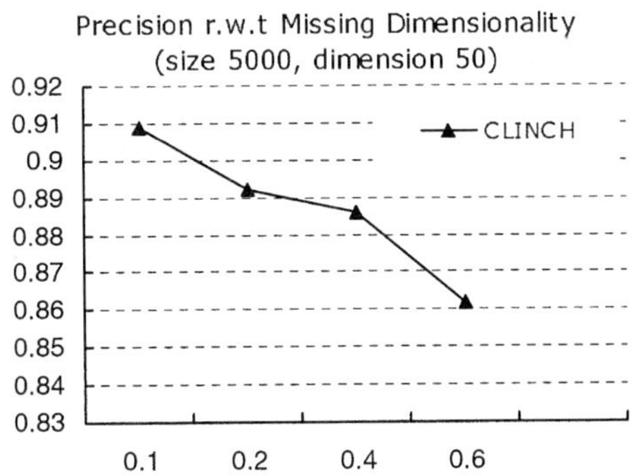

Fig. 13. Clinch Precision (compared with CLIQUE)

In the sea of filling-value algorithms for incomplete data, we choose the approach introduced in [16], which is simple and easy to implement. In assessing the quality of *CLINCH*, we benefit from the method introduced in [21]. Specifically, we measure the precision by solving the label-matching problem. We here compared our results with *CLIQUE*, which was taken as producing the acceptable grouping of points.

Figure 11 illustrates the precision with respect to the dimensionality that miss values.

Firstly, we could see from Figure 13 that the CLINCH produces very similar clustering results as CLIQUE. In figure 11, we set the missing percentage of every dimension to be a random value no larger than 0.5, we presume that dimension with a large missing percentage will be useless. Figure 12 show the effect of missing percentage. We randomly miss a certain percentage of the attributes in some dimensions, precision on which is illustrated above.

6 Related Work

Several approaches are proposed to fight the problem of clustering high-dimensional data. The first category is to perform dimensionality reduction before clustering: points are projected to lower dimensional space to ease the traditional on reduced data space [4, 6]; Another category in attacking the high-dimensional clustering is based on grid partitioning [1, 9, 7, 20]. Algorithms in this category first divide the space into rectangular units and keep the high-density ones. Then the high-density units are combined to their neighbors to form clusters and summaries.

Comparatively, in handling the points with missing attributes. Much work has been done on filling the missing attributes with appropriate values. Several simple, inexpensive and easy to implement techniques were introduced in [16]. Besides, imputation, statistical or regression procedures are widely used in estimating the missing values [13, 15]. Similar idea by reconstruction is also illustrated in [3]. However, these techniques are prone to estimation errors when the dimensionality increases. There are also some approaches that view this problem from a different angel: they extract principal components without elimination or imputation [11, 19]. Similar PCA-like methods for missing value estimation include [11, 17].

7 Conclusion

In this paper, we develop an effective and efficient method to clustering on incomplete high-dimensional data. Our two contributions include contributing a fast high-dimensional clustering technique as well as the proposal of an prediction technique based on it. Our experiments and theoretical proof show our algorithm CLINCH has a good performance both in efficiency and precision of clustering incomplete data. In the future, we would like to transplant the algorithm to other fields such as multimedia mining and pattern recognition. Meanwhile, to meet the need of documents classification, further study in super high-dimensional data is necessary.

References

1. R. Agrawal, J. Gehrke, D. Gunopulos,and P. Raghavan. Automatic subspace clustering of high-dimensonal data for data mining applications. In *proc of the ACM SIGMOD Conference*, 94-105, Seattle, WA, 1998.
2. A. Abo, J. Hopcroft and J. Ullman. The Design and Analysis of Computer Algorithms. Addison-Welsley, 1974..
3. C.C. Aggarwal and S. Parthasarathy. Mining Massively Incomplete Data Sets by Conceptual Reconstruction. In *proc of the Seventh ACM SIGKDD International Conference on Knowledge Discovery and Data Mining*, 2001.
4. C.C. Aggarwal, C. Procopius,J.L. Wolf, P.S. Yu and J.S. Park. Fast Algorithm for Projected Clustering. In *proc of the ACM SIGMOD Conference*, 61-72, Philadelphia, PA, 1999.
5. R. Agrawal and R. Srikant. Privacy Preserving Data Mining. In *ACM SIGMOD*, 2000.
6. C.C. Aggarwal and P.S. Yu. Finding generalized projected clusters in high dimensional spaces. Sigmod Record, 29,2,70-92, 2000.

7. C. Cheng, A. Fu and Y. Zhang. Entropy-based subspace clustering for mining numerical data. In *proc of the 5th ACM SIGKDD Conference.* 84-93, San Diego, CA, 1999.
8. Z. Ghahramani and M. I. Jordan. Learning from incomplete data. *Department of Brain and Cognitive Sciences, Paper No. 108*, MIT, 1994.
9. S. Goil,H. Nagesh and A. Choudhary. MAFIA: Efficient and scalable subspace clustering for very large data sets. Technicial Report CPDC TR 9906-010, Northwestern University, 1999.
10. J.W. Han. etc. Data Mining: Concepts and Techniques. Morgan Kaufmann Press, June, 2000.
11. K. Honda, A. Yamakawa, A. Kanda and H. Ichihashi. An application of fuzzy c-Means Clustering to PCA-Like method for missing value estimation. In *Proc. 16th Int. Conf. on Production Research*, Prague, Czech, July 2001.
12. I. Joliffe Principal Component Analysis. Springer-Verlag, New York, NY, 1986.
13. R. Little and D. Rubin. Statistical Analysis with Missing Data Values. Wiley Series in Prob. and Stat,1987.
14. P. Berkhin. Survey of Clustering Data Mining Techniques. In: *Accrue Sotware*, 2002.
15. J.R. Quinlan. Programs for Machine Learning. Morgan Kaufman, 1993.
16. J. Rodas and J. Gramajo. Classification and Clustering Study in Incomplete Data Domain. *Informatic Systems and Languages Department, Technical University of Catalonia.*, 2000.
17. T. Shibayama. A PCA-Like Method for Multivariate Data with Missing Values. Japanese Journal of Educational Psychology, Vol. 40, 257-265, 1992.
18. M. Steinbach, L.Ertöz and V. Kumnar. The Challenges of Clustering High Dimensional Data. In *Applications in Econophysics, Bioinformatics, and Pattern Recognition.*
19. H. Shum,K. Ikeuchi and R. Reddy. Principal Component Analysis with Missing Data and its Application to Polyhedral Object Modeling. IEEE Transaction on Pattern Analysis and Machine Intelligence, Vol 17, No. 9, 854-867, 1995.
20. D. Zhou, Z.P. Cheng,C. Wang,H.F. Zhou, W, Wang and B.L. Shi. SUDEPHIC: Self-tuning Density-based Partitioning and Hierarchical Clustering In *proc of the 9th International Conference on Database Systems for Advanced Applications*, Jeju Island, Korea, 2004.
21. H.Y. Zha,C. Ding, M. Gu, X.F. He and H. Simon. Spectral Relaxation for K-means Clustering. Neural Info. Processing Systems NIPS 2001.
22. M. Zait and H. Messatfa. A comparative study of clustering methods. Future Generation Computer Systems, 13(2-3): 149-159, November 1997.

Topic Discovery from Document Using Ant-Based Clustering Combination

Yan Yang[1], Mohamed Kamel[2], and Fan Jin[1]

[1] Yan Yang and Fan Jin, School of Computer and Communication Engineering, Southwest Jiaotong University, Chengdu, Sichuan, 610031, China
yangyan@nec.swjtu.edu.cn

[2] Mohamed Kamel, Pattern Analysis and Machine Intelligence Lab, Electrical and Computer Engineering, University of Waterloo, Waterloo, Ontario N2L 3G1, Canada
mkamel@uwaterloo.ca

Abstract. This paper presents a topic discovery approach based on multi-ant colonies clustering combination. The algorithm consists of three parts. First, each document is represented as a vector of features in a vector space model. Then a hypergraph model is used to combine the clusterings produced by three kinds of ant-based algorithms with different moving speed. Finally, the topic of each cluster is extracted by re-computing the term weights. Test results show that the number of topics can be adaptively determined and clustering combination can improve the system performance.

1 Introduction

With the explosive growth of the World Wide Web, it has become more and more difficult to discover information effectively and efficiently. There is a need for tools that can help analyze the contents of the information to discover and approximately describe the topics from document in order to meet users' information needs.

Clustering is an un-supervised learning technique used in the process of topic discovery from documents. It is a division of data into groups of similar objects. The classic clustering approaches include hierarchical algorithms, partitioning methods such as K-means, Fuzzy C-means, graph theoretic clustering, neural networks clustering, and statistical mechanics based techniques [1]. The ant-based clustering algorithm is inspired by the behavior of ant colonies in clustering their corpses and sorting their larvae. One of the first studies related to this domain is the work of Deneubourg et al. [2], who have proposed a basic model that allowed ants to randomly move, pick up and drop objects according to the number of similar surrounding objects so as to cluster them. Lumer and Faieta [3] have developed this model from Deneubourg et al.'s robotic implementation to exploratory data analysis (LF algorithm). The work of Ramos and Merelo [4] studied ant-clustering systems with different ant speeds for textual document clustering. Several combinations of the ant algorithm and K-means clustering algorithm, such as the AntClass algorithm by Monmarche [5], the CSIM by

Y. Zhang et al. (Eds.): APWeb 2005, LNCS 3399, pp. 100–108, 2005.

Wu et al. [6] and the ant–based clustering ensemble algorithm [7] have been proposed. Strehl and Ghosh studied three effective cluster ensemble techniques based on a hypergraph model [8].

After obtaining a clustering of a document collection, the topic of each cluster needs to be extracted. Ayad and Kamel investigated a novel topic discovery method based on aggregation of clustering generated by different clustering techniques [9]. K. J. Wu et al. studied another automatic topics discovery approach from hyperlinked documents, which combines a method of set construction, a clustering algorithm and an iterative principal eigenvector computation method [10].

Taking advantage of this existing work, we present in this paper a topic discovery approach based on multi-ant colonies clustering combination. The algorithm consists of three parts. First, each document is analyzed and represented as a vector of features in a vector space model. Then the hypergraph model is used to combine the clusterings produced by three kinds of ant-based algorithms with different moving speed such as constant, random, and randomly decreasing. Finally, the topic of each cluster is extracted by re-computing the term weights. Test evaluation shows that the number of topics can be adaptively determined and clustering combination can improve the system performance.

The remaining of this paper is organized as follows: Section 2 describes the system architecture and principles in each step. Section 3 reports the test results evaluating the performance of the proposed algorithm. Finally, Section 4 offers a summary of the paper.

2 Topic Discovery Based on Multi-ant Colonies Clustering Combination

2.1 Overview

Fig. 1 shows the system architecture for topic discovery from documents. The first step is the document indexing analysis that cleans and represents the textual content of the documents using the vector space model. The second step is called document clustering, which consists of three ant colonies with different moving speed followed by a clustering combination component. In the third step, the topic discovery finds an approximate description of the topic of each cluster using the highest weighted attributes.

2.2 Document Indexing Analysis

To discover the topics from textual contents of a document collection automatically, the document needs to be represented in a form suitable for the chosen clustering algorithm. The document indexing analysis usually is of the following step:

Cleaning. An important part of any text processing is the cleaning of a document. Cleaning a document is to get rid of unwanted elements of the document. The procedure for document cleaning in this algorithm includes removing tags, removal of stop-words, and stemming of words.

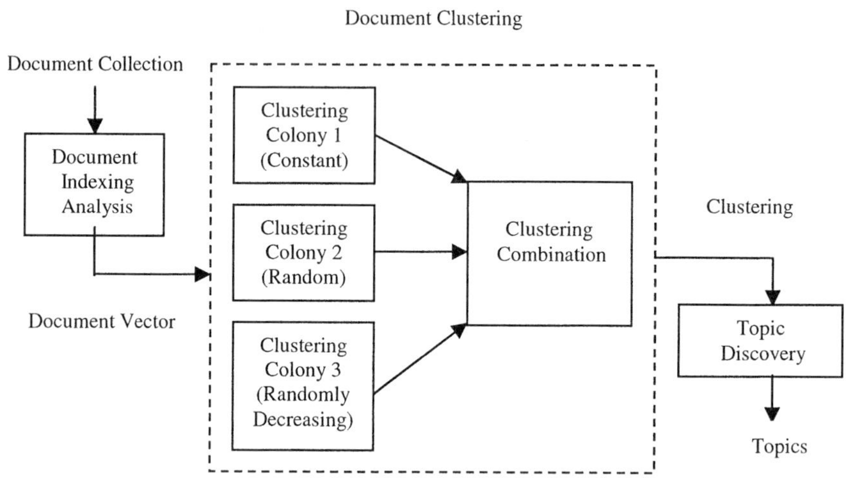

Fig. 1. System architecture for topic discovery from document

After removing tags, the textual contents are extracted ignoring the textual structure and organization. Stop-words are frequent words that carry no information such as "the", "and", "of", etc. It is often useful to eliminate these words. Finally, word stemming is the process of converting different forms of a word into one canonical form, called terms. Words like "walk", "walker", "walked", "walking" are all converted to a single word "walk". The Porter stemming [11] is a popular algorithm for this task.

Indexing. The most commonly used document representation is the so-called vector space model introduced by Salton in 1975 [12]. In the vector space model, each document is represented by a vector of words d. Each element of the vector reflects a particular word, or term, associated with the given document. In the term space, $d_i = \{w_{i1}, w_{i2}, ..., w_{in}\}$, where w_{ij}, $j = 1,...,n$ is the weight of term j in document i. The most common ways of determining the weight w_{ij} are based on the assumption that the best indexing terms are those that occur frequently in individual documents but rarely in the remainder of the collection. A well-known approach for computing term weights is the TF-IDF-weighting. The weight of a term j in a document i is given by:

$$w_{ij} = tf_{ij} \times \log(N / df_j) \tag{1}$$

where tf_{ij} is the term j frequency in the document i, or the number of occurrences of the term j in a document i. N is the total number of documents and df_j is the document frequency, that is the number of documents in which the term j occurs at least once. The inverse document frequency (*idf*) factor of this type is given by $\log(N / df_j)$.

The TF-IDF-weighting does not consider that documents may be of different lengths. For our algorithm, the TFC-weighting with length normalization is used as a term weighting equation for term j in a document i [13]:

$$w_{ij} = \frac{tf_{ij} \times \log(N / df_j)}{\sqrt{\sum_{k=1}^{n} [tf_{ik} \times \log(N / df_k)]^2}} \quad (2)$$

Reducing Dimensionality. When documents are represented as vectors, as described above, they belong to a very high-dimensional feature space because of one dimension for each unique term in the collection of documents. In order to reduce the dimension of the feature vector, the Document Frequency Thresholding is performed. Some terms whose document frequency are less than the predetermined threshold or appear in over 90% of the documents are removed. Further, only a small number of n terms with the highest weights in each document are chosen as indexing terms.

2.3 Document Clustering

In this module, there are two phases for clustering as shown in Fig. 1. The first phase consists of three clustering components using ant-based algorithm with different moving speed such as constant, random, and randomly decreasing, each of which generates a clustering. The second phase is the combination component that aggregates three clusterings produced from the previous phase and generates what is called a combined clustering using the hypergraph model.

Ant-Based Clustering Algorithm. The ant-based clustering algorithm is based on the basic model proposed by Deneubourg et al. [2] and some improvements [3][4][7]. First, the collection of document vectors is randomly projected onto a plane. Second, each ant chooses a document vector at random, and picks up or moves or drops down the vector according to picking-up or dropping probability with respect to the similarity of the current document vector within a local region. Finally, clusters are collected from the plane.

Let us assume that an ant is located at site r at time t, and finds a document vector $\mathbf{d}_i$ at that site. A measure of the average similarity of document vector $\mathbf{d}_i$ with the other vector $\mathbf{d}_j$ present in its neighborhood is given by:

$$f(d_i) = \max\left\{0, \frac{1}{s^2} \sum_{d_j \in Neigh_{s\times s}(r)} \left[1 - \frac{1 - Sim(d_i, d_j)}{\alpha(1 + (v-1)/v_{\max})}\right]\right\} \quad (3)$$

where $Neigh_{s\times s}(r)$ denotes a square of $s\times s$ sites surrounding site r. The parameter v denotes the speed of the ants, and $v_{\max}$ is the maximum speed. α defines a parameter to adjust the similarity between documents. $Sim(\mathbf{d}_i, \mathbf{d}_j)$ is the similarity between two document vectors $\mathbf{d}_i$ and $\mathbf{d}_j$ in the space of attributes. It is defined as the cosine of the angle between the vectors $\mathbf{d}_i$ and $\mathbf{d}_j$ (their dot product divided by their magnitudes):

$$Sim(d_i, d_j) = \frac{\sum_{k=1}^{n} (w_{ik} \cdot w_{jk})}{\sqrt{\sum_{k=1}^{n} (w_{ik})^2 \cdot \sum_{k=1}^{n} (w_{jk})^2}} . \quad (4)$$

As the two document vectors become more similar, $Sim(\mathbf{d}_i, \mathbf{d}_j)$ approaches 1, otherwise it approaches 0.

As shown in Equation (3), α defines a parameter to adjust the similarity between document vectors. Larger values of α will result in making the similarity between the vectors larger and forces vectors to lay the same clusters. When α is small, the similarity will decrease and may in the extreme result in too many separate clusters. The parameter α also determines the cluster number and the speed of convergence. The bigger α is, the smaller the cluster number, and the faster the algorithm converges.

Fast moving ants form clusters roughly on large scales, while slow ants group document vectors at smaller scales by placing vectors with more accuracy. So we develop three versions of clustering components (see Fig. 1) based on ants moving with different speed:

- *v is a constant*. All ants move with the same speed at any time;
- *v is random*. The speed of each ant is distributed randomly in $[1, v_{\max}]$, where $v_{\max}$ is the maximum speed;
- *v is randomly decreasing*. The speed term starts with large value (forming clusters), and then the value of the speed gradually decreases in a random manner (helping ants to cluster more accurately).

The picking-up and dropping probabilities both are a function of $f(\mathbf{d}_i)$ that converts the average similarity of a document vector into the probability of picking-up or dropping for an ant. The converted approaches are based on: the smaller the similarity of a document vector is (i.e. there aren't many documents that belong to the same cluster in its neighborhood), the higher the picking-up probability is and the lower the dropping probability is; on the other hand, the larger the similarity is, the lower the picking-up probability is (i.e. documents are unlikely to be removed from dense clusters) and the higher the dropping probability is. The sigmoid function is used as probability conversion function in our algorithm. Only one parameter needs to be adjusted in the calculation.

The picking-up probability P_p for a randomly moving ant that is currently not carrying a document vector to pick up a vector is given by:

$$P_p(d_i) = 1 - sigmoid(f(d_i)) \tag{5}$$

where

$$sigmoid(x) = \frac{1 - e^{-\rho x}}{1 + e^{-\rho x}} \tag{6}$$

has a natural exponential form. Parameter ρ is a slope constant and can speed up the algorithm convergence if it is increased.

The dropping probability P_d for a randomly moving loaded ant to deposit a document vector is given by:

$$P_d(d_i) = sigmoid(f(d_i))\,. \tag{7}$$

Clustering Combination. The idea of multi-ant colonies combination is inspired by the collaborative behavior of ant colonies. Combining clusterings starts by transforming the given clusterings into a suitable hypergraph representation as in [8]. Let d_i, $i = 1,2,...,N$ denote one document vector of a document collection, and a clustering of these N documents into k clusters can be represented as a label vector $\lambda \in I^N$. Given t groups clusterings with the q-th grouping $\lambda^{(q)}$ having $k^{(q)}$ clusters, the binary membership indicator matrix $H^{(q)} \in I^{N \times k^{(q)}}$ is constructed, in which each cluster is represented as a hyperedge (column). All entries of a row in the binary membership indicator matrix $H^{(q)}$ are 1, if the row corresponds to a document vector with known label. Rows for document vectors with unknown label are all zero. A concatenated block matrix

$$H = (H^{(1)} \ldots H^{(t)}) \tag{8}$$

defines the adjacency matrix of a hypergraph with N vertices and $\Sigma_{q=1}^{t} k^{(q)}$ hyper-edges. Each column vector $\mathbf{h}_a$ specifies a hyperedge h_a, where 1 indicates that the vertex corresponding to the row is part of that hyperedge and 0 indicates that it is not. Thus, we have mapped each cluster to a hyperedge and the set of clusterings to a hypergraph.

Usually, two objects are considered to be fully similar if they are in the same cluster, or they are fully dissimilar if they are not. So the similarity measure can be viewed as the fraction of clusterings in which two objects are in the same cluster. The next step of clustering combination is to compute the similarity matrix **Z** by:

$$\mathbf{Z} = \frac{1}{t} HH^T \tag{9}$$

where matrix H^T is the transposition of matrix **H**, **Z** is $N \times N$ sparse matrix.

In the final step, the ant-based clustering algorithm is used to re-cluster the documents again. The new similarity matrix **Z** is performed and the clustering that has the lowest outlier number, is used as an initial data set.

2.4 Topic Discovery

When clusterings are generated, the topic can be extracted by re-computing the terms weights of the revealed cluster structure as in [9]. It is assumed that the best terms are those that occur frequently inside the cluster but rarely in the other clusters. A TF-IDF-weighting approach is used to re-compute the terms weights as follows:

$$w_{ij} = tf_{ij} \times \log(C / cf_j) \tag{10}$$

where w_{ij} is the weight of term j in a cluster i. tf_{ij} is the term frequency in cluster i, that is, the number of occurrences of the term j in cluster i. The inverse cluster frequency $icf = \log(C / cf_j)$, where C is the total number of clusters and cf_j is the cluster frequency, or the number of clusters in which the term j occurs at least once.

For each cluster, the term weights obtained by Equation (10) give a way of finding approximate descriptions. The topic T_i is represented by a vector of l (*term*, *weight*) pairs with the highest weighted attributes as below:

$$T_i = [(term_{i1}, weight_{i1})(term_{i2}, weight_{i2})...(term_{il}, weight_{il})]. \tag{11}$$

3 Evaluation

The proposed algorithm was implemented in VC++6.0. Each document is represented as a vector of features in a vector space model using the TFC-weighting. The similarity between two documents is calculated using the cosine measure. Three different clusterings are generated using the ant-based clustering algorithm and combined. The topic of each cluster is represented using the highest weighted attributes. The goal of the test is to compare the quality of the results before and after the combination.

3.1 Test Data

Tests draw on data from the Reuters-21578 collection[1]. The documents in the Reuters-21578 collection were collected from the Reuters newswire in 1987. We sample only news documents that have TOPICS labels. The data set contains 10 different document collections each of size 300 documents that belong to a single-topic.

3.2 Performance Evaluation

The test is designed to compare the performance of topic extraction before and after the combination in terms of metrics: F-measure. The F-measure combines the ideas of precision and recall from the information retrieval literature [9]. For each manual topic T in the document collection, it is assumed that a cluster X^* corresponding to that topic is formed. In order to find X^*, the precision and recall of a topic T with respect to a cluster X are defined as:

$$precision(X,T) = n_{XT} / n_X \tag{12}$$

$$recall(X,T) = n_{XT} / n_T \tag{13}$$

where n_{XT} is the number of documents judged to be of topic T in cluster X, n_X is the number of documents in cluster X, and n_T is the number of documents judged to be of topic T in the whole collection.

The F-measure of a topic T is then given by

$$F(T) = \frac{2 \times precision(X,T) \times recall(X,T)}{precision(X,T) + recall(X,T)}. \tag{14}$$

With respect to topic T we consider the cluster with the highest F-measure to be X^*. That is F-measure becomes the score for topic T. The overall F-measure is computed by taking the weighted average of all values for the F-measure for each topic T as given by

$$F = \frac{\sum_{T \in M} \left(|T| \times F(T) \right)}{\sum_{T \in M} |T|} \tag{15}$$

where M is the set of manual topic, $|T|$ is the number of documents judged to be of topic T, and $F(T)$ is the F-measure for topic T.

3.3 Test Results

We tested 10 different documents each of size 300 documents using three kinds of ant-based clustering algorithms and their combination separately. Only 25 terms with the highest weights are chosen as indexing terms [14]. The average number of the space of attributes is 813. Table 1 gives the average value of the overall F-measure and the average number of clusters that was adaptively determined by the algorithm vs. the number of manual topics 12.8. We noted that the performance of the combination is better than the average performance of the single ant-based algorithm.

Table 1. Topic Extraction using Three Different Ant-based Clustering Algorithms and Combination

Algorithms	Average No. of Clusters	Average F-Measure
Ant colony 1	17.5	0.655
Ant colony 2	16.3	0.670
Ant colony 3	19.1	0.629
Average of three colonies algorithm	17.8	0.651
Combination	16.2	0.688

4 Summary

In this paper we introduced a method for topic discovery from document based on multi-ant colonies clustering combination. The topic of each cluster is extracted by re-computing the term weights. The overall F-measure was used for evaluating the performance of the proposed method. Test results show that the performance of the combination algorithm for topic extraction is better than the average performance of the single ant-based clustering algorithm.

Acknowledgements

This work was partially funded by the Key Basic Application Founding of Sichuan Province (04JY029-001-4) and the Science Development Founding of Southwest Jiaotong University (2004A15).

References

1. Berkhin, P.: Survey of Clustering Data Mining Techniques. Accrue Software Research Paper, 2002, [Online]. Available: http://www.accrue.com/products/researchpapers.htm
2. Deneubourg, J. L., Goss, S., Franks, N., Sendova-Franks, A., Detrain, C., Chretien, L.: The Dynamics of Collective Sorting: Robot-like Ant and Ant-like Robot. In Meyer, J. A., Wilson, S. W. (eds.): Proc. First Conference on Simulation of Adaptive Behavior: From Animals to Animats. Cambridge, MA: MIT Press (1991) 356-365
3. Lumer, E., Faieta, B.: Diversity and Adaptation in Populations of Clustering Ants. Proc. Third International Conference on Simulation of Adaptive Behavior: From Animals to Animats 3. Cambridge, MA: MIT Press (1994) 499-508
4. Ramos, V., Merelo, J. J.: Self-organized Stigmergic Document Maps: Environment as a Mechanism for Context Learning. In Alba, E., Herrera, F., Merelo, J.J. (eds.): AEB'2002 – 1st Spanish Conference on Evolutionary and Bio-Inspired Algorithms. Centro Univ. de Mérida, Mérida, Spain (2002) 284-293
5. Monmarché, N., Slimane, M., Venturini, G.: Antclass: Discovery of Clusters in Numeric Data by a Hybridization of an Ant Colony with the Kmeans Algorithm. Internal report No. 213, Laboratoire d'Informatique de l'Université de Tours, E3i Tours, [Online]. Available: http://www.antsearch.univ-tours.fr/publi/MonSliVen99b.pdf
6. Wu, B., Zheng, Y., Liu, S., Shi, Z.: CSIM: a Document Clustering Algorithm Based on Swarm Intelligence. IEEE World Congress on Computational Intelligence (2002) 477-482
7. Yang, Y., Kamel, M.: Clustering Ensemble Using Swarm Intelligence. IEEE Swarm Intelligence Symposium (2003) 65-71
8. Strehl, A., Ghosh, J.: Cluster Ensembles – a Knowledge Reuse Framework for Combining Partitionings. Proc. of AAAI, Edmonton, Canada. AAAI/MIT Press (2002) 93-98
9. Ayad, H., Kamel, M.: Topic Discovery from Text Using Aggregation of Different Clustering Methods. In Cohen, R., Spencer, B. (eds.): Advances in Artificial Intelligence, 15th Conference of the Canadian Society for Computational Studies of Intelligence, Calgary, Canada. (2002) 161-175
10. Wu, K. J., Chen, M. C., Sun, Y.: Automatic Topics Discovery from Hyperlinked Documents. Information Processing and Management, vol. 40. (2004) 239-255
11. Porter, M. F.: An Algorithm for Suffix Stripping. Program, vol. 14(3). (1980) 130-137
12. Salton, G., Wong, A., Yang, C.: A Vector Space Model for Automatic Indexing. Communications of the ACM, vol. 18(11). (1975) 613-620
13. Salton, G., Buckley, C.: Term Weighting Approaches in Automatic Text Retrieval. Information processing and Management, vol. 24(5). (1988) 513-523
14. Larsen, B., Aone, C.: Fast and Effective Text Mining Using Linear-time Document Clustering. In Chaudhuri, S., Madigan, D. (eds.): Proc. of fifth ACM SIGKDD Intl. Conf. on Knowledge Discovery and Data Mining. (1999) 16-22

A Pattern-Based Voting Approach for Concept Discovery on the Web

Jing Chen[1], Zhigang Zhang[2], Qing Li[1], and Xiaoming Li[2]

[1] Department of Computer Engineering and Information Technology,
City University of Hong Kong, 83 Tat Chee Avenue, Kowloon, Hong Kong
{jerryjin, itqli}@cityu.edu.hk
[2] Department of Computer Science and Technology,
School of Electronics Engineering and Computer Science,
Peking University, Beijing, China
zzg@net.cs.pku.edu.cn, lxm@pku.edu.cn

Abstract. Automatically discovering concepts is not only a fundamental task in knowledge capturing and ontology engineering processes, but also a key step of many applications in information retrieval. For such a task, pattern-based approaches and statistics-based approaches are widely used, between which the former ones eventually turned out to be more precise. However, the effective patterns in such approaches are usually defined manually. It involves much time and human labor, and considers only a limited set of effective patterns. In our research, we accomplish automatically obtaining patterns through frequent sequence mining. A voting approach is then presented that can determine whether a sentence contains a concept and accurately identify it. Our algorithm includes three steps: pattern mining, pattern refining and concept discovery. In our experimental study, we use several traditional measures, precision, recall and F1 value, to evaluate the performance of our approach. The experimental results not only verify the validity of the approach, but also illustrate the relationship between performance and the parameters of the algorithm.

1 Introduction

Domain-specific concepts are useful in a variety of traditional applications, including document summarizing, classification, clustering, indexing and query expansion [16, 17]. With the development of the Web, some new research areas and new applications are brought up, in which concept discovery also plays an important role. For example, in the Semantic Web area, concept discovery is a fundamental task of the knowledge capturing and ontology engineering processes. Although the potential benefit of concepts is large, the majority of current documents do not have an explicit declaration of the concepts presented. So automatically discovering concepts from text is necessary.

One way to extract concepts automatically from text is to use Natural Language Processing (NLP) to analyze syntax and semantics of the text [1]. Other

Y. Zhang et al. (Eds.): APWeb 2005, LNCS 3399, pp. 109–120, 2005.

applications try to avoid expensive NLP techniques and apply machine learning or statistical approaches to find rules or patterns to identify phrases as concepts [2]. Some emerging techniques also attempt to mine topic-specific concepts and definitions on the Web [3]. In [3], the authors first identify the sub-topics and salient concepts of a specified topic using some heuristics, and then find the informative pages containing definitions and descriptions for the users. In this paper, we apply a data mining approach, called frequent sequence mining, to automatically discover patterns from text. Our goal is to use these patterns to identify concepts from sentences.

A closely related work to ours is keyphrase extraction, for which there are two different ways. One is heuristics based, and the other is machine learning technique based. [6] and [7] present some heuristic methods for the extraction of medical terminologies and their definitions from online documents. [8] describes a system called GenEx for keyphrase extraction. GenEx has two components: the Extractor algorithm to process the input text and produce a set of keyphrases, and the Genitor genetic algorithm to tune the twelve parameters of Extractor to maximize its performance on training data. [9] presents an algorithm, Kea, to find important phrases from documents using a machine learning technique. In this study, two attributes are used to discriminate between keyphrases and non-keyphrases, namely, the TF*IDF score of a phrase and the distance into the document of a phrase's first appearance. Then, a Naive Bayes model is generated from a set of training documents where keyphrases are provided. In the concept extraction stage, Kea computes TF*IDF scores and distance values for all phrases in the new document, then the Naive Bayes model is applied to each phrase, computing the estimated probability of it being a keyphrase.

In this paper, we present a pattern based approach for concept discovery on the Web. The patterns used in our approach are automatically obtained through Web mining. Through the evaluation, we can see that using automatically mined patterns, the recall of concept discovery increases greatly without decrease in precision. Compared with heuristics based systems, our approach does not need the manual labor to describe predefined patterns; compared with the machine learning based methods, our algorithm is more flexible. Given a sentence, the algorithm proposed in this paper can determine whether this sentence contains a concept and if so, accurately identify it. In contrast, the machine learning based methods must use the whole Web page to determine the attributes of a candidate phrase, such as distance and TF*IDF value which rely on features of the whole page. Another advantage is that our concept discovery algorithm uses sentences as the input unit, while other machine learning based methods treat phrases as input unit, and they need to first generate a lot of candidate phrases by some mechanical heuristics. In order to evaluate the discovery ability of a pure pattern based approach, we do not use TF*IDF or distance to measure the importance of candidate phrases; moreover, we deliberately avoid any heuristic to select more important sentences from a Web page.

The remaining of the paper is organized as follows. In Section 2, we illustrate the process of pattern mining. Section 3 discusses the algorithm to refine patterns generated in the former step. The approach which automatically discovers concepts is given in Section 4. The evaluation results are presented in Section 5. In Section 6, we summarize our study and discuss some future work.

2 Pattern Mining

In the pattern mining stage, we aim to discover the frequent sequences that characterize the syntactic patterns of sentences containing concepts. This stage altogether includes two phases: corpora construction and frequent sequence mining. In the corpora construction phase, based on several manually constructed concept hierarchies, Web pages relevant to the concept hierarchies are retrieved through a search engine (Google). Web pages are segmented into sentences, and divided into two categories, the concept-relevant corpus and concept-irrelevant corpus. In the first corpus, each sentence contains at least one concept in the concept hierarchies; the second corpus includes the rest of the sentences. Then sentences in both corpora are preprocessed according to part-of-speech and the appearance of concepts. A frequent sequence mining approach is performed on the first corpus to discover frequent sequences that characterize the syntactic patterns of sentences containing one or more concepts. In the following, we will describe these processes in detail.

2.1 Corpora Construction

In many concept-based information retrieval models, a conceptual structure for mapping descriptions of information objects to concepts is widely used [10]. The authors of [10] divide such conceptual structures into 5 categories: conceptual taxonomy, formal or domain ontology, semantic linguistic network of concepts, thesaurus and predictive model. We make use of the first type, i.e. conceptual taxonomy, which is a hierarchical organization of concept descriptions. The main relationships among concepts in a conceptual taxonomy are aggregation (parent-child) and association (sibling). We will use 'concept hierarchy' to refer to conceptual taxonomy in the rest of this paper.

Initially, we collect several manually constructed concept hierarchies in different knowledge domains, including computer science, mathematics, chemistry, physics, botanical science, etc. However, it is not necessary for a hierarchy to be complete, as long as all aggregation and association relationships involved are accurate. Next, a query corresponding to each concept in a hierarchy is generated. We adopt a typical query expansion technique to produce the queries. Each concept which has a parent concept existing in the hierarchy will generate a query of the concept itself and its parent. The root concept of each hierarchy will generate a query of itself only. Then the queries are submitted to a search engine ([11]), and the top N retrieved documents are saved to our local disk. Duplicate pages are deleted from the dataset to avoid bias during the mining process.

For all pages retrieved, we segment each into sentences first, and then several operations are performed to the sentences in order to eliminate noisy words and concentrate on the more contributive ones. We define two types of uniform labels: concept related labels replace the appearance of concepts in a sentence, and part-of-speech labels are used to substitute articles and pronouns. The uniform labels still function as ordinary words, and the mining algorithm will ignore their difference from other words. If a sentence includes two or more appearances of concepts and two of them reflect an aggregation relationship in the concept hierarchy, then the parent concept is substituted by $\langle CD : ParentConcept\rangle$ and the child by $\langle CD : ChildConcept\rangle$, and all other concepts in this sentence is replaced by $\langle CD : OtherConcept\rangle$; if there is no aggregation relationship in the sentence, all concepts are replaced by label $\langle CD : Concept\rangle$. Articles and pronouns are substituted by $\langle CD : Article\rangle$ and $\langle CD : Pronoun\rangle$ respectively. Adjectives, adverbs, interjections, predeterminers are removed. The following is an example of the result of a processed sentence:

Original: An infinite series is a sum of infinitely many terms.
Result: $\langle CD : Article\rangle$ $\langle CD : Concept\rangle$ is $\langle CD : Article\rangle$ sum of terms.

Sentences with a concept related label are saved into the concept-relevant corpus, and the rest are saved into the concept-irrelevant one for further mining.

2.2 Frequent Sequence Mining

Sequential pattern mining is a data mining task that discovers frequent subsequences as patterns in a sequence database. The sequential pattern mining problem was first introduced in [12]: Given a set of sequences and a user-specified *min_support* threshold, the problem of sequential pattern mining is to find all the frequent subsequences, i.e., the subsequences whose occurrence frequency in the set of sequences is no less than *min_support*.

In our work, we simplify the sequential pattern mining problem as that every element in a sequence has only one item. The length of a sequence is then the number of elements in the sequence. We use the concept-relevant corpus as the input sequence set, regarding each sentence in the corpus as a sequence, and each word within as an element. So a sequence in our application is denoted as $\langle word_1 word_2 ... word_l\rangle$, and its length is the number of words in it. We use PrefixSpan [13] as our pattern mining algorithm.

In sequential pattern mining, *min_support* is an essential parameter, and *min_length* is widely used to constrain the minimum length of result sequences. In our work, we introduce a new parameter, *min_coverage*, to restrict the resulting patterns. *Min_coverage* is used to minimize the influence of a single knowledge domain (corresponding to a concept hierarchy) on the resulting patterns. Every knowledge domain has its own frequent vocabulary, hence tends to produce its own high frequency sequences. So we make sure that only the patterns that occur in no less than *min_coverage* domains can be recorded as resulting patterns. After the frequent pattern mining phase, the sequential patterns that are longer than *min_length* and occur no less than *min_support* times in at least *min_coverage* domains are recorded in the concept pattern set (CPS, or Concept Pattern Set). A detailed example is provided below.

Table 1. Example for Frequent Sequence Mining

seq_id	*domain_id*	*sequence*
1	1	$\langle abc \rangle$
2	1	$\langle ae \rangle$
3	2	$\langle bcde \rangle$
4	3	$\langle bce \rangle$

The sequence set is shown in Table 1. $Min\_support$ is set to 3, $min\_coverage$ 2, and min_length is 2.

Sub-sequence $\langle bc \rangle$ is a resulting sequence, its support is 3 since sequences 1, 3 and 4 all contain it, and its coverage is 3 since sequences 1, 3, and 4 belong to domains 1, 2, and 3 separately. Sub-sequence $\langle ce \rangle$ is not a resulting sequence since it fails to satisfy the constraint on support even though it satisfies the constraint on coverage.

3 Pattern Refining

We call a frequent sequence that characterizes the syntactic features of a sentence including concepts a concept representative pattern. Yet not all the patterns in CPS bear such a quality. Some of them are common syntactic patterns that may appear in any natural language sentence. For example, "this is for" and "$\langle CD : Pronoun \rangle$ should be" are both frequent sequences in natural language, but do not help much in finding concepts. So in the pattern refining phase, we first find out the frequent sequences in natural language.

3.1 Frequent Sequences in Natural Language

To distinguish concept representative patterns from common frequent patterns in natural language, we adopt the following method. As we have mentioned in Section 2.1, based on the same concept hierarchies, we have constructed another corpus that is composed of sentences not containing concepts, viz. the concept-irrelevant corpus. With the same mining algorithm, we use the concept-irrelevant corpus as input, and get another resulting pattern set (NPS, or Non-concept Pattern Set).

Obviously, the proportion of concept representative patterns in NPS is much fewer than that in CPS. And the common part of them is the patterns that are common in natural language, and should be filtered from CPS. The difference of CPS and NPS is called the final pattern set (FPS, or Final Pattern Set). Through experiment we find that the precision of the concept discovery system based on FPS is 11% higher than that based on CPS.

3.2 Pattern Credit Evaluation

Another obstacle to our goal is that even the most ideal pattern can sometimes find phrases that are not really concepts. A typical example would be the pattern "are examples of $\langle CD : ChildConcept\rangle$". It can find actual concepts like mathematical term "group" and "homology theory", but at the same time it distinguishes phrases like "this strategy" and "the more abstract statements" as well. We consider this as the drawback of pattern-based methods to identify concepts. To reduce the negative effects, we introduce a pattern evaluation technique to give credit to each pattern, and the credit will be used in the concept discovery process.

For each pattern in FPS, if all elements other than the concept related labels in the pattern can be found in a sentence and the order of the words in it are identical to that of the pattern, the pattern is called a 'matching' pattern of the sentence. The words in the sentence corresponding to the position of the concept related label are regarded as a concept. As we have discussed, almost all patterns make both right and wrong decisions. The proportion of times it makes a right decision to a wrong decision indicates the accuracy rate of the pattern.

A training set is needed to evaluate each pattern. In our context, the training set is a set of concepts and a set of sentences containing at least one of the concepts. Two extra concept hierarchies about algebraic structures and group theory are used to generate queries and gather Web pages containing the concepts. The training sentence set is comprised of sentences in the retrieved Web pages. For each concept hierarchy, a corresponding glossary is obtained from several online math dictionaries. Training sentences that do not contain any of the entries in the glossaries are deleted. Entries that do not appear in any sentence are removed. The current training set includes 48,053 sentences and 306 corresponding concepts.

We match each pattern in the FPS with all training sentences and make a decision for each - a positive decision by identifying a concept or a negative decision for regarding that the sentence contains no concept. For a positive decision, we compare the detected concept with the concept set. If it is found in the concept set, we consider it as a right decision, otherwise a wrong one. For negative decisions, we simply ignore them, because no single pattern can be versatile enough to discover any concept in any sentence. Thus we can get the accuracy rate of the pattern, which we define as the Credit of a pattern:

$$Credit = \frac{Right\_Decision\_Sum}{Right\_Decision\_Sum + Wrong\_Decision\_Sum} \quad (1)$$

For example, if the Credit of a pattern is 0.8, we get a conclusion that the pattern has made a positive decision that has an 80% probability to be right. In our context, this is equivalent to say a candidate concept is a real concept with an 80% probability. Also, if the Credit of a pattern is 0, we can conclude that the candidate concept discovered by the pattern is generally not a real concept. If the Credit is 0.5, it suggests that the pattern makes decisions quite randomly.

4 Concept Discovery Using Frequent Patterns

In the concept discovery phase, the following steps are performed to discover the concept:

Given a sentence, we try to match all patterns remaining in the FPS against it. The matched patterns will identify some phrases as candidate concepts. Then the probability for each phrase identified as a candidate concept is computed using the Credits obtained in the previous step. If the largest probability is larger than a threshold, the phrase with the largest probability is identified as a concept finally.

Generally speaking, given a sentence, there can be more than one 'matching' patterns for it. Some of them may identify the same phrase as a candidate concept; others may identify different words. To decide whether the 'matching' patterns have made a right decision and which phrase is the concept, a voting algorithm is designed as described in the following.

Upon completing the pattern credit evaluation phase, we get a Credit set $\{C_1, C_2, ..., C_i, ...\}$ corresponding to the final pattern set FPS= $\{p_1, p_2, ..., p_i, ...\}$. Consider a sentence S = $\{word_1, word_2, ..., word_j, ..., word_n\}$. Through matching each pattern with the sentence, some phrases are identified as candidate concepts. For each candidate concept, we can compute the probability that the candidate concept is really a concept according to the Credit of the patterns that identify the candidate concept. If a phrase, PH, is identified as a candidate concept by a set of patterns P' $\subseteq$ FPS, then the probability that PH is a real concept is:

$$Pr(PH|I(PH,P')) = \frac{Pr(PH, I(PH,P'))}{Pr(I(PH,P'))} = \frac{\prod\limits_{p_i \in P'} C_i}{\prod\limits_{p_i \in P'} C_i + \prod\limits_{p_i \in P'} (1 - C_i)} \qquad (2)$$

where I(PH,P') denotes that PH is identified as a concept by all patterns in P'. $Pr(PH|I(PH,P'))$ is the probability that PH is really a concept in condition that it is identified by all patterns in P'. $Pr(PH, I(PH,P'))$ is the probability that PH is really a concept and identified by P', which is to say that all patterns in P' made a right decision. Since all patterns make decisions independently, $Pr(PH, I(PH,P'))$ is equal with $\prod\limits_{p_i \in P'} C_i$. $Pr(I(PH,P'))$ is the probability that PH is identified by P', meaning either PH is really a concept and all patterns in P' made the right decision, or PH is not a real concept and all patterns in P' made a mistake. Thus, $Pr(I(PH,P'))$ equals to $\prod\limits_{p_i \in P'} C_i + \prod\limits_{p_i \in P'} (1 - C_i)$.

If $Pr(PH|I(PH,P'))$ is larger than 0.5, it means that the probability that PH is a concept is larger than the probability that it is not a concept. For example, assume our pattern set has three patterns, $\{p_a, p_b, p_c\}$, with the corresponding Credits $\{0.9, 0.3, 0.6\}$, and a sentence containing three words, $\{word_1 word_2 word_3\}$ is given. $Word_1$ is identified by p_a and p_b, and $word_2$ is identified by p_c, then $Pr(word_1|I(word_1, \{p_a, p_b\}))$ and $Pr(word_2|I(word_2, \{p_c\}))$ are computed as follows:

$Pr(word_1|I(word_1,\{p_a,p_b\})) = (0.9*0.3)/(0.9*0.3+(1-0.9)*(1-0.3)) = 0.27/(0.27+0.07) = 0.8$

$Pr(word_2|I(word_2,\{p_c\})) = 0.6/(0.6+(1-0.6)) = 0.6$

In this example, $Pr(word_1|I(word_1,\{p_a,p_b\}))$ and $Pr(word_2|I(word_2,\{p_c\}))$ are all larger than 0.5, so both of them can be regarded as concepts. But compared with $word_2$, $word_1$ has a larger possibility and is chosen as the final detected concept.

5 Preliminary Results

In this section, we first evaluate a previously proposed pattern-based concept discovery method ([3, 7, 14, 15]). Then we perform two experiments on our algorithm: the first experiment shows how the performance of the algorithm varies with the *min_coverage* parameter of the frequent sequence mining process, and compares the performance of our approach with the previous pattern-based method; the second shows how performance varies with the size of the training data. The test set is obtained in the same way as the training set and independent of the initial set for mining and the training set. It contains 133,980 sentences with 398 concepts corresponding to 2 concept hierarchies about atomic and molecular physics and computer architecture.

Precision, recall and F1 values are widely used to measure the effectiveness of information retrieval systems. Although recall is not a key issue in the Web context because of its richness in information, it is still an important factor in consideration for the efficiency of a system. In particular, the Web pages relevant to the user specified topic are retrieved by a search engine and collected by our system; then every Web page is parsed into a set of sentences. Finally, a set of automatically mined patterns are matched to each sentence to identify concepts within them. So if the patterns can achieve a higher recall, we can collect fewer Web pages with the highest relevance, and subsequently spend less time to parse the Web page set and get fewer sentences. This helps reduce the execution time significantly.

In most previous research on concept discovery, the following concept definition identification patterns are considered to be suitable for Web pages [3, 7, 14, 15]:

$\{is|are\}$ $[adverb]$ $\{called|known\ as|defined\ as\}$ $\{concept\}$
$\{concept\}$ $\{refer(s)\ to|satisfy(ies))\}$
$\{concept\}$ $\{is|are\}$ $[determiner]$
$\{concept\}$ $\{is|are\}$ $[adverb]$ $\{being\ used\ to|used\ to|referred\ to|$
$employed\ to|defined\ as|formalized\ as|described\ as|$
$concerned\ with|called\}$
$\{What\ is\}$ $[determiner]$ $\{concept\}$?
$\{concept\}$ $\{:|-\}$ $\{definition\}$
$\langle dt\rangle$ $\{concept\}$ $\langle dd\rangle$ $\{definition\}$
$Legend: \{\}$ $-$ $compulsory\ field$
$[]$ $-$ $optional field$
$adverb$ $-$ $e.g., usually, normally$
$definition$ $-$ $definition\ of\ a\ concept$

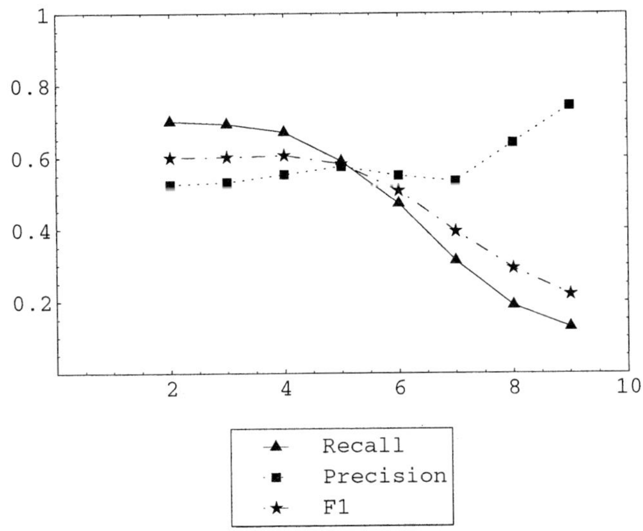

Fig. 1. Performance of using pattern sets with different domain coverage

Based on the patterns, the regular expression matching algorithm is applied to discover concepts from sentences. On our test set, the precision of the method is 48.5%, recall is 32.5% and F1 value is 0.389. We can see that the precision and recall are all low even though the patterns seem to be reasonable.

In our approach, there are two factors that can influence the performance: the pattern set used by the algorithm and the training set used to evaluate the patterns. And the former one depends on the parameters in the frequent sequence mining process, including *min_support*, *min_length* and *min_coverage*. From our experiment, we find that *min_support* and *min_length* do not have a fixed relationship with performance. So, in the following, we conduct the experiments that show how the performance of the algorithm varies with the *min_coverage* parameter as well as the size of the training data.

Table 2. *Min_coverage* and pattern sum of corresponding pattern set

min_coverage	*number of patterns*
2	112,000
3	68,948
4	19,068
5	4.350
6	1,068
7	210
8	41
9	5

Table 3. Performance comparison of the predefined pattern set and pattern sets with different domain coverage

Patternset	*Precision*	*Recall*	*F*1
Predefined pattern set	48.5%	32.5%	0.389
Pattern set with *min_coverage*=2	52.5%	70.0%	0.600
Pattern set with *min_coverage*=3	53.1%	69.3%	0.601
Pattern set with *min_coverage*=4	55.3%	67.0%	0.606
Pattern set with *min_coverage*=5	57.5%	58.9%	0.582
Pattern set with *min_coverage*=6	55.0%	47.1%	0.507
Pattern set with *min_coverage*=7	53.4%	31.2%	0.394
Pattern set with *min_coverage*=8	64.0%	18.9%	0.292
Pattern set with *min_coverage*=9	74.2%	12.8%	0.219

Table 2 shows the pattern sum of each pattern set with different *min_coverage*. Figure 1 shows how the performance of the algorithm varies with the coverage of the patterns. It can be seen from Table 2 that with the rising of *min_coverage*, from 2 to 9, the number of patterns dramatically decreases from 112,000 to 5 correspondingly. From Figure 1, we can see that recall also decreases sharply, from 0.7 to 0.13. Contrasting with the sharp decrease in the pattern sum and recall value, the precision varies very little when the coverage is less than 8, but it increases notably after the minimum coverage gets beyond 8. This means that the more domain areas a pattern is suitable for, the higher its precision is. From Table 3, we can see that the optimum performance of our system is achieved

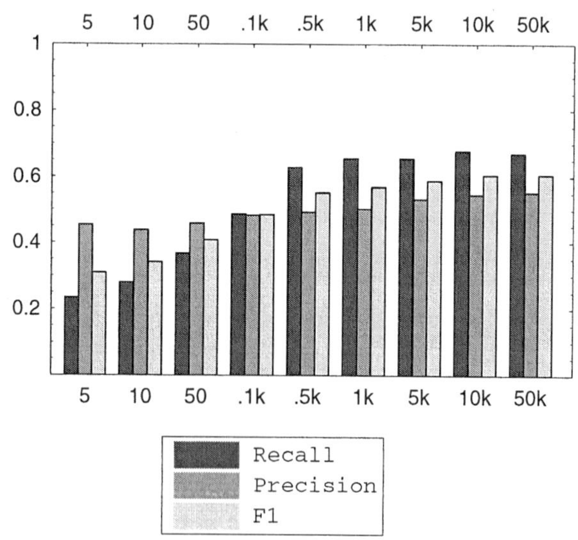

Fig. 2. Performance for different size of training set

when *min_coverage* is set to 4. Compared with the performance of previous pattern based methods, the recall and precision are both improved in our approach when the pattern sets with a *min_coverage* less than 8 are used. Precision is higher in all patterns sets, independent of the *min_coverage* parameter.

To illustrate how the performance varies with the amount of training data, we conduct the experiment on the same test set using the pattern set with *min_coverage* 4. Figure 2 plots the precision, recall and F1 values against the number of sentences for training, from 5 to 50,000. It can be seen that when the number of training sentences exceeds 50, the performance improves stably along with the increase in the training set size. If more than 5,000 sentences are used for training, however, little improvement in both recall and precision is gained by increasing the number of training samples further. The result shows that 5,000 sentences are sufficient to push the performance of our algorithm to its optimum.

The sentences collected in the test set come from Web pages. And Web pages are generally noisier and have fewer salient concepts than journal papers and technical reports from a digital library. Also, the concepts in Web pages are usually presented in special styles such as within the anchor text of a hyperlink instead of a full sentence in natural language. All these factors decrease the performance because our algorithm does not do any preprocessing on Web pages, nor does it deal with any of the peculiar properties of HTML.

In the future, more experiments will be conducted with several other training sets and test sets. Patterns will be evaluated with different training sets, and tested with different test sets, and the average performance will be obtained. Such an experiment can reduce the effect of the training and test set on the evaluation results, and then provide a more accurate evaluation.

6 Conclusions and Future Work

In this paper, we have presented a pattern based approach to concept discovery for any given sentence. In the approach, the patterns are automatically mined from the Web, and a voting algorithm is presented to identify concepts from sentences on the basis of all the patterns' decisions.

The result of our current system may sometimes contain none-exact concepts. For example, some other words such as adjective, adverb and a part of the sentence may appear in the result even though we have used a length parameter to constrain the length of the result. In our future work, we will conduct some refinement work on the result, aiming to identify the exact concept. And we will combine additional information such as TF*IDF and the importance of a sentence to improve the performance of the current approach. Another interesting work is that the pattern mining method can also be used to mine the sequences that characterize the syntactic patterns of sentences containing concept relationship descriptions. So the resulting patterns can be used to discover the relationship between concepts as well.

References

[1] LexiQuest Product White Paper, http://www.lexiquest.fr/products/LexiQuest Guide White Paper.pdf.

[2] Shigeaki Sakurai and Akihiro Suyama. Rule discovery from textual data based on key phrase patterns. Proceedings of the 2004 ACM symposium on Applied computing, 606-612, 2004.

[3] Liu, B., Chee W. Chin, Hwee T. Ng, Mining Topic-specific Concepts and Definitions on the Web, WWW 2003: 251-260, 2003.

[4] Woods, W. Conceptual indexing: A better way to organize knowledge. Technical Report, Sun Microsystems Laboratories, April 1997.

[5] Stanley Loh, Leandro Krug Wives, Jos Palazzo M. de Oliveira: Concept-Based Knowledge Discovery in Texts Extracted from the Web. SIGKDD Explorations 2(1): 29-39, 2000.

[6] Bennett, N.A., He, Q., Powell, K., Schatz, B.R. Extracting noun phrases for all of MEDLINE. In Proc. American Medical Informatics Assoc., 1999.

[7] J. Klavans and S. Muresan. "DEFINDER: Rule-based Methods for the Extraction of Medical Terminology and their Associated Definitions from On-line Text." Proc. AMIA, 201-202, CA, 2000.

[8] P. Turney. Learning to extract keyphrases from text. Technical Report, National Research Council, Institute for Information Technology, 1999.

[9] Eibe Frank and Gordon W. Paynter and Ian H. Witten and Carl Gutwin and Craig G. Nevill-Manning. Domain-Specific Keyphrase Extraction. IJCAI, 668-673, 1999.

[10] H-M. Haav, T.-L. Lubi, A Survey of Concept-based Information Retrieval Tools on the Web, A. Caplinkas and J. Eder (Eds), Advances in Databases and Information Systems, Proc. of 5th East-European Conference ADBIS*2001, Vol 2.: 29-41, 2001.

[11] Brin, S., Page, L.: The Anatomy of a Large-scale Hypertextual Web Search Engine, WWW7, 1998.

[12] Rakesh Agrawal and Ramakrishnan Srikant. Mining sequential patterns. Eleventh International Conference on Data Engineering, Taiwan, 3-14, 1995.

[13] J. Pei and J. Han and B. Mortazavi-Asl and H. Pinto and Q. Chen and U. Dayal and M.-C. Hsu,PrefixSpan: Mining Sequential Patterns Efficiently by Prefix Projected Pattern Growth, Proc. of the 17th Int. Conf. on Data Eng., 215-226, 2001.

[14] Cooper, R.J and Ruger, S.M. A simple question answering system. In Proceedings of TREC 9, 2000.

[15] Harabagiu, S., Moldovan, D., Pasca, M., Mihalcea, R., Surdeanu, M., Bunescu, R., Girju, R., Rus, V. and Morarescu, P. FALCON: Boosting knowledge for answer engines. In Proceedings of TREC 9, 2000.

[16] F. Lu, T. D. Johnsten, V. V. Raghavan, and D. Traylor. Enhancing internet search engines to achieve concept-based retrieval. In InForum'99, Oakridge, May 1999.

[17] Yonggang Qiu and Hans-Peter Frei. Concept-based query expansion. Proceedings of SIGIR-93, 16th ACM International Conference on Research and Development in Information Retrieval, 160-169, 1993.

A Similarity Reinforcement Algorithm for Heterogeneous Web Pages

Ning Liu[1], Jun Yan[2], Fengshan Bai[1], Benyu Zhang[3], Wensi Xi[4], Weiguo Fan[4], Zheng Chen[3], Lei Ji[3], Chenyong Hu[5], and Wei-Ying Ma[3]

[1] Department of Mathematical Science, Tsinghua University, Beijing, P.R. China
liun01@mails.tsinghua.edu.cn
fbai@math.tsinghua.edu.cn
[2] LMAM, Department of Information Science, School of Mathematical Science, Peking University, Beijing, P.R. China
yanjun@math.pku.edu.cn
[3] Microsoft Research Asia, 49 Zhichun Road, Beijing, P.R. China
[4] Computer Science, Virginia Polytechnic Institute and State University, U.S.A
[5] Lab for Internet Software Technologies, Institute of Software, CAS, Beijing, P.R. China

Abstract. Many machine learning and data mining algorithms crucially rely on the similarity metrics. However, most early research works such as Vector Space Model or Latent Semantic Index only used single relationship to measure the similarity of data objects. In this paper, we first use an Intra- and Inter- Type Relationship Matrix (IITRM) to represent a set of heterogeneous data objects and their inter-relationships. Then, we propose a novel similarity-calculating algorithm over the Inter- and Intra- Type Relationship Matrix. It tries to integrate information from heterogeneous sources to serve their purposes by iteratively computing. This algorithm can help detect latent relationships among heterogeneous data objects. Our new algorithm is based on the intuition that the intra-relationship should affect the inter-relationship, and vice versa. Experimental results on the MSN logs dataset show that our algorithm outperforms the traditional Cosine similarity.

1 Introduction

The performance of many data mining algorithms such as document clustering and text categorization critically depends on a good metric that reflects the relationship between the data objects in the input space [1] [30]. It is therefore important to calculate the similarity as effectively as possible [28].

Most early research works only used single relationship to measure the similarity of data objects. In the original vector space model (VSM) [23], "terms" (keywords or stems) were used to characterize queries and documents, creating a document-term relationship matrix where it is straightforward to compute the similarities between and among terms and documents by taking the inner product of the two corresponding row or column vectors. Dice, Jaccard and Cosine measurements[20] are a few classical methods that use the document-term relationship to measure the similarity of

Y. Zhang et al. (Eds.): APWeb 2005, LNCS 3399, pp. 121 – 132, 2005.

documents for retrieval and clustering purposes. Deerwester and Dumais [9, 10] thought that the concept in a document might not be well presented by keywords they contained. In their Latent Semantic Index (LSI) work, instead of directly using the document-term matrix to compute the similarity of text objects, they first use the Singular Vector Decomposition (SVD) method to map the document-term matrix into some lower dimension matrix where each dimension associates with a "hidden" concept, then the similarity of text objects (documents or queries) are measured by their relationships to these "concepts" rather than the key works they contained.

Other relationships such as reference relationships among scientific articles are also used to measure the similarity of data objects. Small [26] tried to measure the similarity of two journals by counting the number of journals they both cite, this method is also called co-citation. Kessler [14] measured the similarity of two journal papers by counting the number of journals that cite them both, this method is also called bibliographic coupling. Co-citation and bibliographic coupling had been successfully used to cluster scientific journals [18]. With the advent of World Wide Web, relationships within web objects such as the hyperlink relationship were also used to calculate the similarity of web objects. Dean [8] and Kleinberg [15] used hyper-links among a web pages community to discover similar web pages. Larson [16] and Pitkow [17] applied co-citation on the hyperlink structure of the web to measure the similarity of web pages. In the Collaborative Filtering [12] and Recommendedr Systems [21] field researchers tried to analyze the similarity of peoples by examining the people-document and people-artifacts relationship respectively.

The research works introduced above only used single type of relationship to measure the similarity of data objects. However, these approaches run into serious problems when various information applications require a more real and accurate similarity measuring method where multiple types of data objects and their relationship must be handled in an integrated manner. Thus in the extended VSM [11], feature vectors of data objects were lengthened by adding attributes from objects of other related spaces via inter-type relationships. By doing so, information from different sources are directly mapped into an enhanced Vector Space and similarity computation were obtained through the calculation on these enhanced feature vectors. The extended feature vector had been used for document search [25] or clustering purposes [6]. Following the same idea, Rocchio [22] and Ide [13] expand the query vector using the frequent terms appeared in the top documents retrieved by the query and improved the search effectiveness, the idea of using terms found in related documents to extend the query term vector is also referred to as "Query Expansion". Similarly, Brauen [4] modified document vector by adding or deleting the terms in the queries that relates to it. Changing document vectors by related query terms is also referred to as "Dynamic Document Space" method [24].

Recently, researchers have tried to calculate the similarity of two data objects by measuring the similarity of their related data objects. For example, Raghavan and Sever [18] tried to measure the similarity of two queries by calculating the similarity relationship of their corresponding search lists. Beeferman and Berger [3] clustered queries using the similarity of their clicked web pages and cluster web pages using the similarity of the queries that lead to the selection of the web pages. Wen [19] and Su

[27] calculated the query similarity based on both the query contents similarity and the similarity of the documents that retrieved by queries; they calculated the similarity of documents in a similar way. Although research works introduced above used inter-type relationships to help improve the similarity calculation of data objects, they did not consider the mutual reinforcement effect on similarities of the interrelated heterogeneous data objects. Most recently, Wang et, al [29] proposed an iteratively rein forcement clustering algorithm for multi-type data objects where the cluster results from one type of data objects is used to reinforce the clustering process of another data type. Their method was shown to be effective for clustering and is much related to the similarity reinforcement algorithm that we propose in this paper. Aiming at finding the best cluster for individual documents, Wang's algorithm may not be very precise when used to calculate the similarity of individual data objects.

Davidson [7] had proposed another much related idea. In his two page short paper, Davidson analyzed multiple term document relationships by expanding the traditional document-term matrix into a matrix with term-term, doc-doc, term-doc, and doc-term sub-matrices. He proposed that the links of the search objects (web-page or terms) in the expanded matrix could be emphasized. With enough emphasis, the principal eigenvector of the extended matrix will have the search object on top with the remaining objects ordered according to their relevance to the search object. Although his idea is sounding, he didn't point the reason that difference kind of relationship can be calculated in a unified manner in his paper. Then we propose a novel iterative similarity learning approach to measure the similarity among the objects combining inter-type relationship over the Intra- and Inter- Type Relationship Matrix (IITRM). Our proposed algorithm is based on an intuitive assumption that *the intra-relationship should affect the inter-relationship, and vice versa.* It can help detect latent relationships (such as latent term association discovered by LSI) among heterogeneous data objects, which can be used to improve the quality of various information applications that require the combination of information from different data sources. Experimental results the MSN logs dataset show that our algorithm outperforms the traditional Cosine similarity.

The rest of the paper is organized as follows: in Section 2, we will give the formal matrix to represent both intra- and inter- type relationships among data objects from heterogeneous data sources in a unified manner, which we call it as an Inter- and Intra-Type Relationship Matrix (IITRM) and the problem formulation of similarity measure. In Section 3, we will present an information-processing assumption that form the theoretical basis of our proposed study and the unified similarity calculating algorithm that we proposed. Some experimental results for this algorithm will also be reported in section 4. We conclude this paper and describe our future work in Section 5.

2 Intra- and Inter-type Relationship Matrix

In this section, we first will give the formal matrix that represents both intra- and inter- type relationships among data objects from two data sources in a unified manner, which we call it as the second-order Intra- and Inter- Type Relationship Matrix. Then we will present the Intra- and Inter- Type Relationship Matrix (IITRM) to represent a set of heterogeneous data objects and their inter-relationships.

2.1 Second-Order IITRM

Suppose we have *N* different data spaces S_1, S_2... S_N. Data objects within the same data space are connected via intra-type relationships $R_i \subseteq S_i \times S_i$. Data objects from two different data spaces are connected via inter-type relationships $R_{ij} \subseteq S_i \times S_j (I \neq j)$. The intra-type relationships R_i can be represented as an $m \times m$ adjacency matrix L_i (*m* is the total number of objects in data space S_i), where cell l_{xy} represents the inter-type relationship from the x_{th} object to the y_{th} object in the data space S_i. The inter-type relationship R_{ij} can also be represented as an $m \times n$ adjacency matrix L_{ij} (*m* is the total number of objects in S_i, and *n* is the total number of objects in S_j), where the value of cell l_{xy} represents the inter-type relationship from the x_{th} object in S_i to the j_{th} object in S_j.

Let's consider two data spaces $X = \{x_1, x_2, \cdots x_m\}$, and $Y = \{y_1, y_2, \cdots y_n\}$ and their relationships: R_x, R_y, R_{xy}, and R_{yx}. The adjacency matrices L_x and L_y stand for the intra-type relationship within the data spaces *X* and *Y*, respectively. L_{xy} and L_{yx} stand for the inter-type relationships from objects in *X* to objects in *Y* and inter-type relationships from objects in *Y* to objects in *X* respectively. If we merge data spaces *X* and *Y* into a unified data space *U*, then, previous inter- and intra- type relationships R_x, R_y, R_{xy}, and R_{yx} are now all part of intra-type relationships R_u in data space *U*. Suppose L_u is the adjacency matrix of R_u, then L_u is a $(m + n) \times (m + n)$ matrix, with cell l_{ij} representing the relationship from the *ith* object originally from *X*, (if $I \leq m$), or the *(i-m)th* object originally from *Y*,(if $i>m$), to the *jth* object originally from *X*, (if$i \leq m$), or the *(j-m)th* object originally from *Y*,(if $i>m$). It is not difficult to figure out that the matrix L_u is actually a matrix that combines L_x, L_y, L_{xy} and L_{yx} in such a way as shown in Eq. (1) below:

$$L_u = \begin{vmatrix} L_x & L_{xy} \\ L_{yx} & L_y \end{vmatrix} \tag{1}$$

In this paper, we call the matrix L_u as the Second-order Intra- and Inter- Type Relationship Matrix and denote as L_2^{IITRM}. The L_2^{IITRM} matrix can be used to explain a lot of real world information application scenarios. For example, if we only consider one data space: the web pages; and one type of intra-type relationship: the hyperlink relationship, the L_2^{IITRM} matrix is reduced to the link adjacency matrix of the web graph.

If we want to analyze how user-browsing behaviors can affect the "popularity" of a web page as defined in the PageRank algorithm [5], we would be actually analyzing two data spaces: *user*, *web page*, and one inter- (browsing), two intra- (hyperlink, user endorsement relationship) type similarities as shown in Figure1.

The figure can be represented as IITRM:

$$L_2^{IITRM} = \begin{vmatrix} L_{user} & L_{browse} \\ L^T_{browse} & L_{hyperlink} \end{vmatrix} \tag{2}$$

Where, L_{user} is the endorsement relationship matrix for user space, L_{bowse} is the browsing relationship matrix between user space and web page space; $L_{hyperlink}$ is the hyperlink adjacency matrix for web page space. Eq. (2) has provided a much generalized way of representing web objects and their relationships.

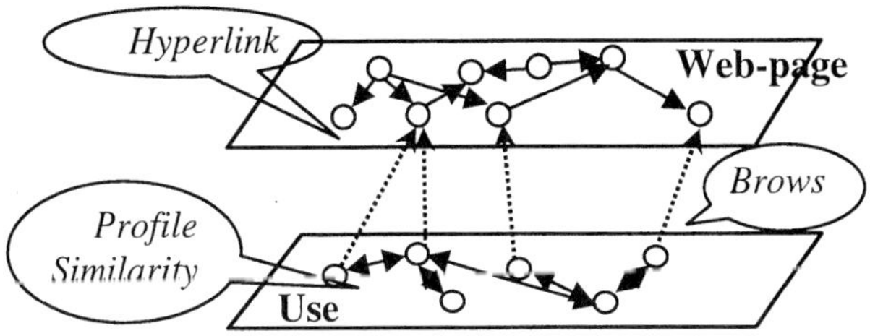

Fig. 1. A real world scenario for the Second-order IITRM

2.2 Intra- and Inter-type Relationship Matrix

As the second-order IITRM, we present the formal matrix that represents both intra- and inter- type relationships among data objects from heterogeneous data sources in a unified manner. Using the notations in the first paragraph of this section, Eq. (1) can easily lead to the definition of the intra- and inter- type Relationship Matrix L_N^{IITRM} for N interrelated data spaces, as shown in Eq. (3).

$$L_N^{IITRM} = \begin{vmatrix} L_1 & L_{12} & \cdots & L_{1N} \\ L_{21} & L_2 & \cdots & L_{2N} \\ \vdots & \vdots & \ddots & \vdots \\ L_{N1} & L_{N2} & \cdots & L_N \end{vmatrix} \tag{3}$$

As discussed above, our problem is reinforcing the similarity among the intra-type objects by combining the inter-type relationship. So we can divide N different data spaces $S_1, S_2 ... S_N$ into two data spaces S_x and $S_{\bar{x}}$, where $S_{\bar{x}}$ denotes all the data spaces except S_x. We can rewrite IITRM as below:

$$L_N^{IITRM} = \begin{vmatrix} L_x & L_{x\bar{x}} \\ L_{\bar{x}x} & L_{\bar{x}} \end{vmatrix} \tag{4}$$

3 Similarity Reinforcement Algorithm

In this section, we will further argue that the similarity relationships between data objects from heterogeneous data sources could also be iteratively reinforced by inter- and intra- type relationships among heterogeneous data spaces under a simple assumption. More specifically, this reinforcement process can also be modeled as an iterative calculation over IITRM. Following that is the convergence proof of this algorithm.

3.1 Similarity Reinforcement Algorithm

Firstly, let us interpret our basic assumption, "*the intra-relationship should affect the inter-relationship, and vice versa.*" We believe iteratively reinforcement the similarity of a set of heterogeneous data objects by their inter- and intra- type relationships can better predict the similarity of two data objects because the iterative similarity reinforcement calculation would discover some hidden similarities between data objects as illustrated in Figure 2.

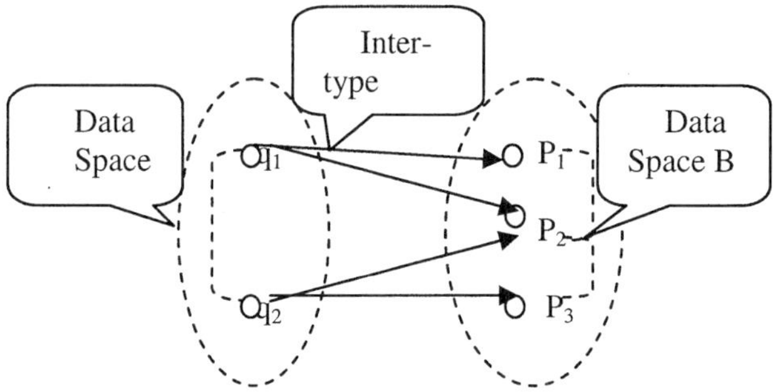

Fig. 2. An example of iterative similarity reinforcement calculation

In Figure 2, in the first step, data objects q_1 and q_2 in data space A are connected with objects p_1, p_2 and p_3 in data space via some inter-type relationship. The objects q_1 and q_2 in *A* are considered similar because they link to the same object p_2 in B. p_1 and p_2 are similar because they are linked by the same object q_1 in *A*, and p_2 and p_3 are similar for the same reason. In the second step, objects p_1 and p_3 in B also can be considered similar, because they are linked by similar objects q_1 and q_2 in *A*. The similarity measure procedure continues iteratively until the similarity values of the objects converge.

Therefore, under this assumption, we could model this iterative calculation as below equations over IITRM:

$$L_x^{k+1} = \lambda_1 L_{x\bar{x}} L_{\bar{x}}^k L_{\bar{x}x} \text{ and } L_{\bar{x}}^{k+1} = \lambda_2 L_{\bar{x}x} L_x^k L_{x\bar{x}} .$$

where λ_1 and λ_2 are the decay factors. We will prove that if $\lambda_1 < \|L_{\bar{x}x}\|_\infty^2$, $\lambda_2 < \|L_{x\bar{x}}\|_\infty^2$, the entries of similarity matrices will between zero and one in the proof of lemma 2 in the appendix. However, since the similarity of the same object should be one, we can assign the diagonal of the similarity matrix a score of 1. Then we rewrite the recursive equations as:

$$L_x^{k+1} = \lambda_1 L_{x\bar{x}} L_{\bar{x}}^k L_{\bar{x}x} + S_1^k \tag{5}$$

$$L_{\bar{x}}^{k+1} = \lambda_2 L_{\bar{x}x} L_x^k L_{x\bar{x}} + S_2^k \tag{6}$$

Where $S_1^k = I - diag(\lambda_1 L_{x\bar{x}} L_{\bar{x}}^k L_{\bar{x}x}), S_2^k = I - diag(\lambda_2 L_{\bar{x}x} L_x^k L_{x\bar{x}})$. In this paper, we call (5) and (6) the basic Similarity Equations of Similarity Reinforcement Algorithm (SRA). We choose initial value

$$L_{ij}^0 = \begin{cases} 1 & \text{if } i = j \\ 0 & \text{if } i \neq j \end{cases}$$

for the interactive iteration process. In other words, we take $L_x^0 = L_{\bar{x}}^0 = I$ to initialize this iteration algorithm. We experimented with various values for the parameters λ_1 and λ_2 in equation (5) and (6), and found little difference in the solution. In our experiments, we chose some small value ε so that if $\| L_i - L_{i-1} \| < \varepsilon$ the iterative process stops.

3.2 Convergence Proof

We give a proof summary of the existence and uniqueness for the basic Similarity Equations of our proposed Similarity Reinforcement Algorithm (SRA).

Definition 1. Suppose matrices $A \in R^{m\times n}$, $B \in R^{p\times q}$, then their *Kronecker Product* $A \otimes B$ is,

$$A \otimes B = \begin{pmatrix} a_{11}B & a_{12}B & \cdots & a_{1n}B \\ a_{21}B & a_{22}B & \cdots & a_{2n}B \\ \vdots & \vdots & & \vdots \\ a_{m1}B & a_{m2}B & \cdots & a_{mn}B \end{pmatrix}_{mp\times nq}$$

Definition 2. The *Row-First Vectorization* of a matrix $A \in R^{m\times n}$, denoted as $\vec{A}$, could be represented as $\vec{A} = (a_1, a_2, \cdots, a_m)^T$, where $a_i \in R^n$, $i = 1, 2, \cdots, m$ are row vectors of A.

Lemma 1. Supposes $A \in R^{m\times n}$ and $B \in R^{n\times n}$ are matrices, then $(\overrightarrow{ABA^T}) \in R^{m^2}$, moreover $(\overrightarrow{ABA^T}) = (A \otimes A)\vec{B}$.

Lemma 2. The matrices L_x and $L_{\bar{x}}$ defined in the basic SRA equations are bounded.

Lemma 3. The entries of matrices L_x and $L_{\bar{x}}$ defined in the basic SRA equations are non-decreasing.

Theorem 1. The interactive iteration basic SRA equations converge to a unique solution.

Proof: from lemma 2 and 3 we know that L_x and $L_{\bar{x}}$ are bounded and non-decreasing, so they converge to some solution. Let's prove the uniqueness of the solution.
Suppose $(L_x, L_{\bar{x}}), (L'_x, L'_{\bar{x}})$ are two different group of solutions of the basic SRA equations. Then,

$$\begin{cases} L_x^{k+1} = \lambda_1 L_{x\bar{x}} L_{\bar{x}}^k L_{\bar{x}x} + S_1^k \\ L_{\bar{x}}^{k+1} = \lambda_2 L_{\bar{x}x} L_x^k L_{x\bar{x}} + S_2^k \end{cases} \quad \text{and} \quad \begin{cases} L'^{k+1}_x = \lambda_1 L'_{x\bar{x}} L'^k_{\bar{x}} L'_{\bar{x}x} + S'^k_1 \\ L'^{k+1}_y = \lambda_2 L'_{\bar{x}x} L'^k_x L'_{x\bar{x}} + S'^k_2 \end{cases}.$$

For all the non-diagonal elements, change the representation by lemma 1. Entries of $\vec{L}_{\bar{x}}^k$ and $\vec{L}_x^{k+1}$ could be denoted as $l_{\bar{x}}^k(h)$, $l_x^{k+1}(g), h = 1, 2, \cdots, n^2, g = 1, 2, \cdots, m^2$. Suppose the element in L_x correspond to $l_x(g)$ is $l_x(i, j)$, we have

$$\begin{aligned} \left| L_x(g) - L'_x(g) \right| &= \left\| \lambda_1 ((L_{\bar{x}x})_i \otimes (L_{\bar{x}x})_j) \vec{L}_{\bar{x}} - \lambda_1 ((L_{\bar{x}x})_i \otimes (L_{\bar{x}x})_j) \vec{L}'_{\bar{x}} \right\| \\ &\le \left\| \lambda_1 ((L_{\bar{x}x})_i \otimes (L_{\bar{x}x})_j) \right\| \left\| (\vec{L}_{\bar{x}} - \vec{L}'_{\bar{x}}) \right\| \end{aligned}$$

For all the diagonal elements

$$|l_x(g)-l'_x(g)|=|1-1|=0\le\left\|\lambda_1((L_{\overline{x}x})_i\otimes(L_{\overline{x}x})_j)\right\|\left\|(\vec{L_{\overline{x}}}-\vec{L_{\overline{x}}}')\right\|.$$

Then $\left\|L_x-L_x'\right\|<\left\|\vec{L_{\overline{x}}}-\vec{L_{\overline{x}}}'\right\|$.

On the other hand $\left\|\vec{L_{\overline{x}}}-\vec{L_{\overline{x}}}'\right\|<\left\|L_x-L_x'\right\|$.

This leads to the conclusion that $\vec{L_x}=\vec{L_x}',\vec{L_{\overline{x}}}=\vec{L_{\overline{x}}}'$.

4 Experiments

In this section, we discuss the experimental data set, evaluation metric, and the experimental results based on cosine similarity and our proposed SRA. This experiment is performed on a real MSN click-through log data to find similar queries. Our proposed SRA achieves 80.6% improvement on the precision of similar queries.

4.1 Dataset

In order to study the effectiveness of SRA for measuring the similarity of web objects, experiments are conducted on a real user query click-through log collected by the MSN Web search engine in December, 2003. It contains about 4.2 million query requests recorded sampled from a period of six hours. The log we obtained has already been processed into a predefined format, i.e. each query request is associated with the URL of one clicked web page. A single query (or web page URL) can occur multiple times in the query click-through log.

Before running the experiments, some preprocessing steps are applied to the queries and web page URLs. All queries are converted to lower-cases, stemmed by the Porter algorithm. The stop-words in the queries are removed. After these steps, the average query length is about 2.7 words. All URLs are converted into canonical form by performing such tasks as replacing unsafe characters with their escape sequences and collapsing sequences like "..\..". Each URL is considered as a feature, while each query is treated as an object. (We can also treat URLs as objects, and treat queries as features). Our proposed algorithm can solve similarities between objects and between features at the same iteration.) The weight for a query on a URL is the frequency of the query leading to the URL.

4.2 Evaluation Metrics

Since our proposed algorithm aims to find better similarity between objects by combing the inter-type relationship, we developed an operational measure of precision to evaluate the performance. Given an object as input, we ask 10 volunteers to identify the correct similar objects from the top N returned results by each algorithm. The precision is defined as

$$Precision = \frac{|M|}{|N|} \tag{7}$$

where $|N|$ is the number of top N similar objects to be evaluated, and $|M|$ is the number of correct similar objects tagged by the volunteers. The final relevance judgment for each object is decided by majority vote. In our experiment, $|N|$ is set as 10.

4.3 Finding Similar Queries

In this experiment, the volunteers were asked to evaluate the precision of results for the selected 10 queries (which are air tickets, auto trader, bank of America, cannon cameras, Disney, mapquest, msn content, Presario 2100, united airlines, and weather report). Figure 3 shows the comparison of the SRA approach with cosine similarity. We found that SRA outperforms the cosine similarity in precision by 80.6%.

Through careful study of the query "*Presario 2100*" which was a popular laptop model, we found that our proposed algorithm not only can filter some un-related queries, but also can find some close-related laptop models. In Table 1 the tag "Y" represents that the query is similar to the given query "*Presario 2100*"; "N" indicates "not similar". Although the cosine similarity returns some similar queries (the 1st – 5th results), it suffers from the "topic drift" issue (the 6th – 10th results), e.g. "*Presario 2100*" and "*Linux Compaq 2100*" share some clicked web pages, however, those web pages discuss how to install Linux in Presario 2100, and therefore, those common clicked web pages is actually a kind of "noise feature" for "*Presario 2100*", which causes "*Linux Compaq 2100*" to be returned as a similar query by cosine similarity. On the other hand, SRA finds out similar models which are not revealed by the cosine similarity. Although different models have many different clicked web pages, those clicked web pages are computed as "similar" since they are queried by "similar" queries, such as "*Compaq Presario*", "*Compaq notebook*", "*Compaq laptop*", etc. Hence, different models have higher similarity based on SRA than based on cosine similarity.

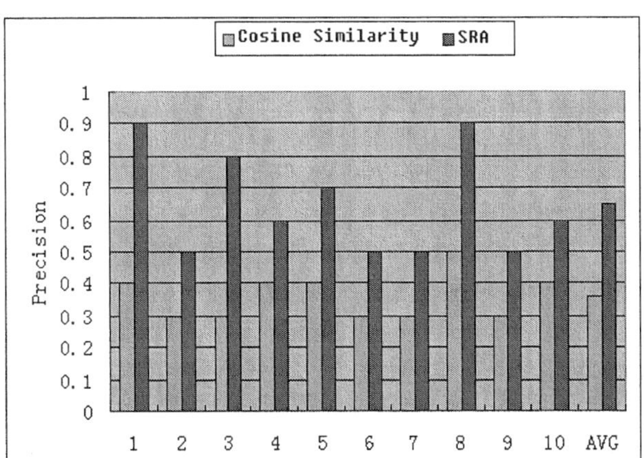

Fig. 3. Precision of similarity between queries

Table 1. Similar queries for "Presario 2100"

	Cosine Similarity		SRA	
1	Compaq Presario	Y	Compaq Presario	Y
2	Compaq notebook	Y	Compaq notebook	Y
3	Compaq laptop	Y	Compaq laptop	Y
4	online Compaq Presario	Y	online Compaq Presario	Y
5	Compaq Presario laptop	Y	Compaq Presario laptop	Y
6	compaque	N	Compaq Presario 9642	Y
7	Notebook price compare	N	Presario 2800 sale	Y
8	Compaq support	N	Compaq 2575us	Y
9	Linux Compaq 2100	N	Presario 9642	Y
10	Used Compaq reseller	N	Compaq batteries	N

5 Conclusion and Future Works

In this paper, we first use an Inter- and Intra- Type Relationship Matrix (IITRM) to represent a set of heterogeneous data objects and their inter-relationships. Then we propose a novel iterative similarity learning approach to measure the similarity among the objects combining inter-type relationship over the Intra- and Inter- Type Relationship Matrix (IITRM).

In our future work we will explore the efficiency, effectiveness, and generality of the SRA approach. We note that there is considerable room for improvement in the quality of clustering of both Web pages and queries. We believe that SRA could be successfully applied to improve the effectiveness of clustering. Finally, we plan to apply our approach to more complex settings, such as in digital libraries, where there are more types of objects, so as to demonstrate further the generality of SRA. Besides, we will give some variations of SRA in our future work.

Acknowledgement

Jun Yan thanks the support of Professor Qiansheng Cheng.

References

[1] Atnafu, S., Brunie, L. and Kosch, H., Similarity-Based Operators and Query Optimization for Multimedia Database Systems. In Proceedings of the International Database Engineering and Application Symposium, (Grenoble, France, 2001), 346-355.

[2] Baeza-Yates, R. and Ribeiro-Neto, B. Modern Information Retrieval. Addison Wesley Longman, 1999.

[3] Beefermand, D. and Berger, A., Agglomerative clustering of a search engine query log. In Proceedings of the the Sixth ACM SIGKDD International Conference on Knowledge Discovery and Data Mining, (Boston, MA, 2000), 407-415.

[4] Brauen, T.L. Document Vector Modification. Prentice-Hall, Inc., Englewood Cliffs, New Jersey, 1971.

[5] Brin, S. and Page, L. The Anatomy of a Large-Scale Hypertextual Web Search Engine. Computer Networks and ISDN Systems, 30. 107-117.

[6] Chakrabarti, S., Dom, B.E., Kumar, S.R., Raghavan, P., Rajagopalan, S., Tomkins, A., Gibson, D. and Kleinberg, J.M. Mining the Web's Link Structure. IEEE Computer, 32 (8). 60-67.

[7] Davison, B.D., Toward a unification of text and link analysis. In Proceedings of the 26th annual international ACM SIGIR conference on Research and development in information retrieval, (Toronto, Canada, 2003), 367-368.

[8] Dean, J. and Henzinger, M.R., Finding Related Pages in the World Wide Web. In Proceedings of the the 8th international conference on World Wide Web, (1999).

[9] Deerwester, S., Dumais, S.T., Landauer, T.K., Furnas, G.W. and Harshman, R.A. Indexing by latent semantic analysis. Journal of the Society for Information Science, 41(6). 391-407.

[10] Dumais, S.T., Furnas, G.W., Landauer, T.K. and Deerwester, S., Using latent semantic analysis to improve information retrieval. In Proceedings of the CHI'88: Conference on Human Factors in Computing, New York: ACM, 281-285.

[11] Fox, E. Extending the Boolean and Vector Space Models of Information Retrieval with P-Norm Queries and Multiple Concept Types. Cornell University Dissertation.

[12] Herlocker, J.L., Konstan, J.A., Borchers, A. and Riedl, J., An algorithmic framework for performing collaborative filtering. In Proceedings of the 22nd annual international ACM SIGIR conference on Research and development in information retrieval, (Berkeley, California, 1999), 230-237.

[13] Ide, E. New experiments in relevance feedback. Prentice Hall, 1971.

[14] Kessler, M.M. Bibliographic coupling between scientific papers. American Documentation, 14. 10-25.

[15] Kleinberg, J.M. Authoritative sources in a hyperlinked environment. Journal of the ACM (JACM), 46 (5). 604-632.

[16] Larson, R.R., Bibliometrics of the World-Wide Web: An exploratory analysis of the inte lectual structure of cyberspace. In Proceedings of the the Annual Meeting of the American Society for Information Science, (Baltimore, Maryland, 1996).

[17] Pitkow, J. and P.Pirolli, Life, death, and lawfulness on the electronic frontier. In Proceedings of the the Conference on Human Factors in Computing Systems, (Atlanta, Georgia, 1997).

[18] Popescul, A., Flake, G., Lawrence, S., Ungar, L.H. and Giles, C.L., Clustering and identifying temporal trends in document database. In Proceedings of the the IEEE advances in Digital Libraries, (Washington, D.C., 2000).

[19] J-R.Wen, J., Nie, J.-Y. and Zhang, H.-J. Query Clustering Using User Logs. ACM Transactions on Information Systems (TOIS), 20 (1). 59-81.
[20] Rasmussen, E. Clustering algorithm. Information Retrieval: Data Structure and Algorithms.
[21] Resnick, P. and Varian, H.R. Recommender Systems. Communications of the ACM, 40(3). 56-58.
[22] Rocchio, J.J. Relevance feedback in information retrieval. Prentice Hall Inc., Englewood Cliffs, NJ, 1971.
[23] Salton, G. Automatic Information Organization and Retrieval. McGraw-Hill, 1968.
[24] Salton, G. and McGill, M.J. Introduction to Modern Information Retrieval. McGraw-Hill Book Co., New York, 1983.
[25] Shaw, J.A. and Fox, E.A., Combination of multiple searches. In Proceedings of the the 3rd Text Retrieval Conference (TREC-3), (1995), 105.
[26] Small, H. A new measure of the relationship between two documents. Co-citation in the scientific literature, 24. 265-269.
[27] Su, Z., Yang, Q., Zhang, H.-J., Xu, X. and Hu, Y., Correlation-based Document Clustering using Web Logs. In Proceedings of the the 34th Hawaii International Conference On System Science, (Hawaii, U.S.A., 2001).
[28] Tosun, A.S. and Ferhatosmanoglu, H., Vulnerabilities in Similarity Search Based Systems. In Proceedings of the 11th International Conference on Information and Knowledge Management (CIKM), (McLean,VA, 2002).
[29] Wang, J.D., Zeng, H.J., Chen, Z., Lu, H.J., Tao, L. and Ma, W.-Y., ReCoM: reinforcement clustering of multi-type interrelated data objects. In Proceedings of the the ACM SIGIR Conference on Research and Development in Information Retrieval, (Toronto, Canada, 2003), 274-281.
[30] Zhai, C. and Lafferty, J., Model-based Feedback in the Language Modeling Approach to Information Retrieval. In Proceedings of the the 10th ACM International Conference on Information and Knowledge Management (CIKM), (Atlanta, US, 2001), 403-410.

Constraint-Based Graph Mining in Large Database*

Chen Wang, Yongtai Zhu, Tianyi Wu, Wei Wang, and Baile Shi

Fudan University, China
{chenwang, yt_zhu, tywu, weiwang1, bshi}@fudan.edu.cn

Abstract. Currently, constraints are increasingly considered as a kind of means of user- or expert-control for filtering those unsatisfied and redundant patterns rapidly during the web mining process. Recent work has highlighted the importance of constraint-based mining paradigm in the context of frequent itemsets, sequences, and many other interesting patterns in large database. However, it is still not clear how to push various constraints systematically into graph mining process. In this paper, we categorize various graph-based constraints into several major classes and develop a framework *CabGin* (i.e. Constraint-based Graph Mining) to push them into mining process by their categories. Non-monotonic aggregates like average also can be pushed into *CabGin* with minor revision. Experimental results show that *CabGin* can prunes a large search space effectively by pushing graph-based constraints into mining process.

1 Introduction

It has been well recognized that mining frequent patterns such as itemsets, sequences, trees and graphs plays an essential role in many important data mining tasks. There have been many studies on efficient and effective frequent graph mining. *AGM* [3], *FSG* [4], *gSpan* [11], *CloseGraph* [12], *FFSM* [2], and *AdiMine* [10] have been presented for improving scalability on mining subgraphs one after one. However, the extraction is not always tractable for the user-defined support thresholds, especially when the data is dense or highly correlated. Even if it is tractable, the size of the output can be huge. The lack of focus leads to many uninteresting subgraphs to be derived.

During the past five years, the user has been allowed to express his focus in constraint-based mining, by means of a class of constraints for representing application requirements. The cost for mining frequent patterns and the size of the output can be reduced effectively by pushing constraints deep into mining process. Many constraint-based algorithms for mining frequent patterns such as itemsets [5, 7] and sequences [1, 8] have been developed. However, there is little work on constraint-based graph mining.

---

* This research is supported in part by the Key Program of National Natural Science Foundation of China (No. 69933010 and 60303008), China National 863 High-Tech Projects (No. 2002AA4Z3430 and 2002AA231041).

Y. Zhang et al. (Eds.): APWeb 2005, LNCS 3399, pp. 133–144, 2005.

A lot of applications and data, e.g. chemical compounds and weblogs, are structure-critical. The user always expects to obtain focused frequent graphs containing certain subgraphs in these applications. For example, in structural analysis of chemical compounds, chemists wish to extract certain molecule structures which not only satisfies support threshold but also contains special substructures. Therefore, it is important to perform a systematic study on constraint-based graph mining. *"How can we characterize various kinds of constraints in graph mining? How can we push constraints deep into graph mining process for efficient extraction?"* These two problems motivate us to study more.

In this paper, we examine different classes of constraints based on semantics and then characterize them. The concepts of monotonic, anti-monotonic and succinct constraints are extended to context of graph mining. We also point out some non-monotonic constraints to be commonly appeared in graph mining. A framework, called *CabGin*, is built to push constraints deep into mining process based on *Adi-Mine* [10]. Moreover, some tough aggregate constraints such as average can also be pushed deep into mining process with minor revision. Our performance study shows that *CabGin* can prune a large search space effectively and reduce many unfocused, uninteresting frequent graphs.

The remainder of this paper is organized as follows. Section 2 characterizes various kinds of constraints in graph mining. In Section 3, we develop a framework *CabGin* to mine graphs with constraints. In Section 4, we evaluate the performance on synthetic datasets via comparing with *gSpan* and *Adi-Mine*. Related work is introduced in Section 5. We conclude the paper in section 6.

2 Constraints in Graph Mining

A *labeled graph* can be represented by a 4-tuple, $G = (V, E, L, l)$, where V is a set of vertices, $E \subseteq V \times V$ is a set of edges, L is a set of labels, $l : V \cup E \to L$ in which l is a function assigning labels to the vertices and edges. Given an undirected graph G, if a path exists between any two vertices, G is called a *connected graph*. In the case that G is a directed graph, the above definition applies to the undirected graph obtained by ignoring directions of edges in G. Graph $G = (V, E, L, l)$, *subgraph* $G_s = (V_s, E_s, L_s, l_s)$ of G fulfills the following condition: $V_s \subseteq V$, $E_s \subseteq E$. It is denoted as $G_s \subseteq G$.

Let constraint $\mathcal{C}$ for a graph pattern α be a boolean function $\mathcal{C}(\alpha)$. The problem of constraint-based graph mining is to find the complete set of graph patterns satisfying a given constraint $\mathcal{C}$. Given a constraint $\mathcal{C}$, the complete set of graph patterns satisfying $\mathcal{C}$ is denoted as $SAT(\mathcal{C})$.

From the application point of view, we present the following six categories of constraints based on the semantics. Although this is not complete, it covers most of useful constraints in applications.

Constraint 1 (Element Constraint). *An element constraint specifies what are the particular individual or groups of elements that should or should not be presented in the graphs. The elements consist of two parts: vertices and edges in* *graphs. It is the form of* $C_{vertex}(\alpha) \equiv (\varphi_i : 1 \leq i \leq SizeOfVertices(\alpha), \alpha[i]\theta V)$, *or* $C_{edge}(\alpha) \equiv (\varphi_i : 1 \leq i \leq SizeOfEdges(\alpha), \alpha[i]\theta V)$, *where* V *is a subset of elements,* $\varphi \in \{\forall, \exists\}$ *and* $\theta \in \{\in, \notin\}$.

Constraint 2 (Size Constraint). *A size constraint specifies the requirement on the size of graph patterns, where the size can be either the number of edges or the number of vertices.*

Constraint 3 (Super-Graph Constraint). *A super-graph constraint specifies what are the particular individual or groups of subgraphs that should or should not be appeared in the graphs. It is the form of* $C_{Graph}(\alpha) \equiv (\varphi p\theta\alpha, p \in P)$, *where* P *is a set of particular subgraphs,* $\varphi \in \{\forall, \exists\}$ *and* $\theta \in \{\in, \notin\}$.

Constraint 4 (Distance Constraint). *A distance constraint specifies the requirement on a set of distances, where the distance should be the number of edges from one particular vertex to the other.*

Constraint 5 (Aggregate Constraint). *An aggregate constraint is the constraint on an aggregate of vertices of edges in a graph, where the aggregate function can be* ***sum, avg, max, min****, etc.*

In the previous studies of constraint-based frequent patterns mining [5, 7], constraints can be categorized into several major classes such as monotonicity, anti-monotonicity and succinctness.

Table 1. Characterization of Commonly Used Constraints

Characterization	Constraints	Anti	Mono	Succ
Element	$C_{vertex}(\alpha) \equiv (\forall i : \alpha[i]\theta V, \theta \in \{\in, \notin\})$	Yes	No	Yes
	$C_{vertex}(\alpha) \equiv (\exists i : \alpha[i]\theta V, \theta \in \{\in, \notin\})$	No	Yes	Yes
	$C_{edge}(\alpha) \equiv (\forall i : \alpha[i]\theta V, \theta \in \{\in, \notin\})$	Yes	No	Yes
	$C_{edge}(\alpha) \equiv (\exists i : \alpha[i]\theta V, \theta \in \{\in, \notin\})$	No	Yes	Yes
Size	$C_{size}(\alpha) \equiv (SizeOfVertices(\alpha) \leq s)$	Yes	No	Yes
	$C_{size}(\alpha) \equiv (SizeOfVertices(\alpha) \geq s)$	No	Yes	Yes
	$C_{size}(\alpha) \equiv (SizeOfEdges(\alpha) leqs)$	Yes	No	Yes
	$C_{size}(\alpha) \equiv (SizeOfEdges(\alpha) geqs)$	No	Yes	Yes
Super-Graph	$C_{graph}(\alpha) \equiv (\exists p\theta\alpha, p \in P, \theta \in \{\in, \notin\})$	No	Yes	Yes
Distance	$C_{distance}(\alpha) \equiv (Distance(v_1, v_2) \leq d)$	Yes	No	No
	$C_{distance}(\alpha) \equiv (Distance(v_1, v_2) \geq d)$	No	Yes	No
Aggregate	$C_{max}(\alpha) \equiv (max(\alpha) \leq v)$	Yes	No	Yes
	$C_{max}(\alpha) \equiv (max(\alpha) \geq v)$	No	Yes	Yes
	$C_{min}(\alpha) \equiv (min(\alpha) \leq v)$	No	Yes	Yes
	$C_{min}(\alpha) \equiv (min(\alpha) \geq v)$	Yes	No	Yes
	$C_{sum}(\alpha) \equiv (sum(\alpha)\theta v, \theta \in \{\leq, \geq\})$	No	No	No
	$C_{avg}(\alpha) \equiv (avg(\alpha)\theta v, \theta \in \{\leq, \geq\})$	No	No	No

Definition 1 (Anti-monotonic Constraint). *An anti-monotonic constraint is a constraint C_a such that for all subgraphs s belonged in a graph S satisfy C_a if S satisfies it.*

Definition 2 (Monotonic Constraint). *A monotonic constraint is a constraint C_m such that for all super-graphs s derived from a graph S satisfy C_m if S satisfies it.*

Notice that a disjunction or a conjunction of anti-monotonic (monotonic) constraint is also an anti-monotonic (monotonic) constraint.

Definition 3 (Succinct Constraint)

1. *An edge $E_s \subseteq E$ is a succinct edge set if it can be expressed as $\sigma_p(E)$ for some selection predicate p, where σ is the selection operator.*
2. *$SP \subseteq 2^E$ is a succinct powerset if and only in there exist a fixed number of succinct edge $E_1, ..., E_m \subseteq I$, such that SP can be expressed in terms of the strict powersets of $E_1, ..., E_m$ using union.*
3. *Finally, a constraint C_s is succinct provided $SAT(C_s)$ can be expressed in terms of limited number of succinct graph sets using union and minus.*

Based on the above definition, the anti-monotonic, monotonic and succinct characteristics of some commonly used constraints for graph mining are shown in table 1. After characterized into several major classes, constraints will be easily pushed deep into *CabGin* introduced in next subsection.

3 Framework CabGin

3.1 Preliminary Knowledge on Graph Mining

In this paper, we focus on undirected labeled simple graph. We use 4-tuple, $G = (V, E, L, l)$, to represent a labeled graph. *Subgraph* $G_s = (V_s, E_s, L_s, l_s)$ of G fulfills the following condition: $V_s \subseteq V$, $E_s \subseteq E$. It is denoted as $G_s \subseteq G$. Given a set GS of graph structured data, the *support* $sup(G_s)$ of an subgraph G_s is defined as a ratio of number of graph data including G_s to the total number of graph data in the dataset GS.

Definition 4 (Isomorphism and Subgraph Isomorphism). *An isomorphism is a bijective function $f : V(G) \rightarrow V(G')$, such that (1) $\forall u \in V(G)$, $l_G(u) = l_{G'}(f(u))$, and (2) $\forall (u,v) \in E(G)$, $(f(u), f(v)) \in E(G')$ and $l_G(u,v) = l_{G'}(f(u), f(v))$. A subgraph isomorphism from G to G′ is an isomorphism from G to a subgraph of G′.*

Given a graph dataset, $GS = \{G_i \mid i = 0, ..., n\}$, and a minimum support, *minsup*, if g is isomorphic to a subgraph of G, then $\varsigma(g, G) = 1$, otherwise $\varsigma(g, G) = 0$. $\sigma(g, GS) = sum_{G_i \in GS}\varsigma(g, G)$, $\sigma(g, GS)$ denotes the occurrence frequency of g in GS, i.e. the support of g in GS. *Frequent Subgraph Mining* is to find each graph, g, such that $\sigma(g, GS)$ is greater than or equal to *minsup*.

Here, we import the knowledge of lexicographic ordering system introduced by X. Yan et al. [11], including its definition and property. The details on them refer to [11].

3.2 Mining Graph with Constraints

The high level structure of framework *CabGin* is shown in figure 1. While mining frequent subgrahps, *CabGin* grows the size of subgraphs by adding edges one by one. The framework mainly consists of two part: preprocessing graph set (Lines 1-5) and mining frequent subgraphs (Lines 6-15).

```
Input:    graph database GS, support threshold minsup and a set of constraints C;
Output:   all frequent subgraphs satisfied with minsup and C;
Method:   CabGin(GS, minsup, C)
 1:  if there are any succinct constraint in C
 2:      scan GS once, and filter graphs unsatisfied with succinct constraints;
 3:  scan GS once again, and find the frequent edges in GS;
 4:  initialize those edges ordered by constraints and support assembly in ADB;
 5:  S ← NULL; //initial the set of constraint-based frequent subgraphs with empty
 6:  for each edge e in ADB
 7:      checkup ← NULL; //initial the set of checking results over all constraints
 8:      Check-Constraints(e, C, checkup);
 9:      if checkup of any anti-monotonic constraints in C is false
10:          break;
11:      if checkup of all constraints in C are true
12:          S ← S ∪ {e};
13:      ApDB ← createPDB(e); //create a new adjacency-projected database;
14:      Subgraph-Mining(ADB, ApDB, minsup, C, checkup)
15:      remove e from ADB;
```

Fig. 1. Framework CabGin

The Part of Preprocessing Graph Set (Lines 1-5): The original dataset could be shrunk by cutting those graphs unsatisfied with a few succinct constraints, which would never be considered in the subsequent process. The operation (in line 1-2) could help to scan and process the graph set as small as possible in the whole mining process. As a result, check all succinct constraints in $\mathcal{C}$ firstly for decreasing the size of graph set GS. Then, scan the graph set once again and find all frequent edges by support threshold *minsup*. Next, construct adjacency database ADB for edges in graph set GS ordered by constraints and support. The data structure ADB is used to store the edge information and the detail about it will be described in the following section. Because a few constraints such as element constraint will affect the appearance of certain edges in frequent subgraphs, the edges must be processed as early as possible for cutting search space. Therefore, the edges correlated with constraints will be initialized into ADB and ordered by their support firstly. Afterward, initialize the rest of edges in GS and put them into ADB by their support. At last, initial the set of constraint-based frequent subgraphs with empty and get ready for next part.

The Part of Mining Frequent Subgraphs with Constraints (Lines 6-15): For each edge in adjacency database ADB, the following steps are taken one by one. In the circular steps, algorithm initials the checking results *checkup* for all constraints in $\mathcal{C}$ with empty at first. Then, call a procedure Check-Constraints (in line 8) to check whether the current pattern e satisfies all kinds of constraints in $\mathcal{C}$. According to the checking results, the procedure will revise the corresponding items in *checkup* and return it. After checking constraints, firstly pay attention to those anti-monotonic constraints in $\mathcal{C}$. If the pattern e unsatisfies any anti-monotonic constraint, the algorithm will break off and jump out from the current circulation. According to the property of anti-monotonic constraint, the algorithm could trim the search space in that any super patterns containing e would never satisfy the constraints. Afterwards, if the pattern e satisfies all constraints in $\mathcal{C}$, e would be added into the set S of frequent subgraphs. In order to mine all subgraphs containing the edge e, we need to create a new adjacency-projected database $ApDB$ like line 13. The $ApDB$ mainly consists of those edges which is adjacent to e in the GS. Procedure Subgraph-Mining grows all nodes in the DFS Code Tree [11], shown in figure 3, rooted at the edge e in the current round. The detailed process of Subgraph-Mining will also be introduced in the following section. At last, shrink the adjacency database ADB by removing the edge after all descendants of this 1-edge graph have been searched.

Adjacency Database for Edges. In order to mark an edge in a graph uniquely, we often represent it with a 5-tuple $(i, j, l_i, l_{(i,j)}, l_j)$ in which i and j are the identity of left and right vertex respectively, l_i, l_j, and $l_{(i,j)}$ represent the labels of the vertices and the edge between them. To further distinguish an edge from a graph set, another factor of identity of a graph must be considered. In the part of preprocessing graph set, the dominating problem is how to represent the original graph set with an efficient data structure. Therefore, we propose an idea of using adjacency database for edges in stead of original graph set as shown in figure 2. Recording edges information, each of which includes a 5-tuple and graph identity, and their adjacency information in each graph as a database, we can easily represent a graph set with it. The proof of this property is omitted in this section. Adjacency database in *CabGin* can be more convenient to mining constraint-based frequent subgraphs than sparse adjacency list presented in gSpan [11]. In figure 2, there are three essential objects: ***Edge***, ***InGraph***, and ***Identity***. Left vertex label, right vertex label, and edge label in ***Edge*** are equivalent to l_i, l_j, and $l_{(i,j)}$ in a 5-tuple respectively. Graph identity for each edge in a graph set is also registered in ***InGraph***. Left vertex ID and right vertex ID in ***Identity*** represent i and j in 5-tuple. Meanwhile, we link all adjacent edges in each graph by their ***Identity***.

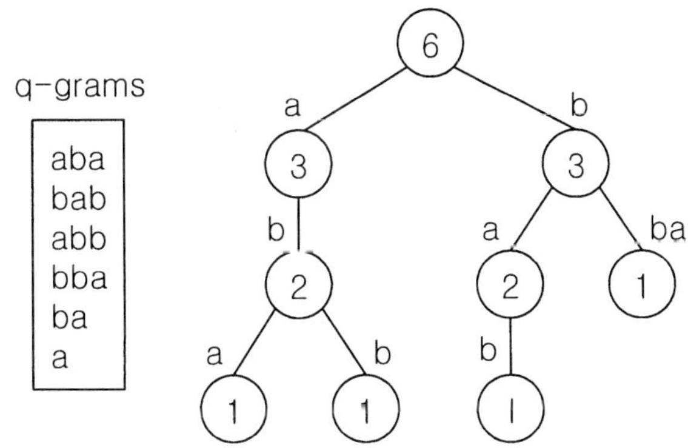

Fig. 3. Q-grams and CQ-tree for a string ababba

that are among all the pieces of length q (called q-grams*) and all suffixes of the last q-gram present in τ. In the tree, every edge has a label obtained from the common prefixes, and every node has a count value for keeping the number of occurrences of a string created by concatenating labels from the root to the node.*

For a string ababba, for example, Fig. 3 shows its q-grams and CQ-tree, where q is 3. The CQ-tree consists of q-grams aba, bab, abb, bba and suffixes ba, a of the last q-gram.

An insertion of a substring (a q-gram or a suffix of the last q-gram) to a CQ-tree implies that the counts of all prefixes of the substring increase by 1, which is extended to Theorem 1.

Theorem 1. *For a given string σ, the CQ-tree keeps the exact count values of all substrings whose lengths are equal to or less than q, and which exist in σ. This can be simply applied to more than one string.*

Proof. *When a q-gram $\sigma[i : i+q-1]$ is inserted into a CQ-tree, the count values of all prefixes $\sigma[i : i]$, $\sigma[i : i+1]$, $\ldots$, $\sigma[i : i+q-1]$ of the q-gram increase by 1. With inserting q-grams of string σ into the tree one by one, i varies from 1 to the length of σ, thus all substrings that are length q or below q are counted.* □

The basic ideas of a CQ-tree are *label-pruning* and *pre-pruning*, while a CS-tree follows *node-pruning* and *post-pruning*. In Fig. 1, a node having count 1 and label abba to be the tail of ababba would be pruned later due to its small count. In short, the *node* is pruned *later*. In contrast, the first q-gram aba can be thought of being created by cutting the tail of string ababba to length q string before inserted into the CQ-tree, as can be seen in Fig. 3. These ideas allow the CQ-tree to be quickly constructed.

The building time of a CQ-tree is in $O(q \cdot N)$ cpu time. Whenever a q-gram is extracted with scanning strings in a database character by character, the q-gram traverses the CQ-tree for comparing labels with itself at most q times. So, the tree can be built in one scan of the database and with the maximum number of comparisons $q \cdot N$.

The size of the CQ-tree becomes biggest when every node has all possible edges because the maximum height of the tree is q, and the maximum edges that a node can have is the alphabet size $|\Sigma|$. At the moment, the CQ-tree becomes a full n-ary tree (in here, $n = |\Sigma|$), and its size is $D \cdot (|\Sigma|^{q+1} - 1)/(|\Sigma| - 1)$, where D is the size of a node, and the rest is the number of nodes. Due to the limit of memory space, the size of the tree must be no more than the given memory space M as shown in (5).

$$D \cdot \frac{|\Sigma|^{q+1} - 1}{|\Sigma| - 1} \leq M \tag{5}$$

By rearranging (5) in terms of q,

$$q \leq log_{|\Sigma|} \frac{M}{D}(|\Sigma| - 1) \tag{6}$$

is obtained.

Note that the maximum size of the CQ-tree has nothing to do with the sizes and numbers of strings in a database. In other words, although strings in the database get more and longer, the maximum size of the tree does not change. Only q-gram length q and the alphabet size $|\Sigma|$ as characteristics of strings affect the maximum size of the tree. Also, it should be noted that an appropriate q can be decided by (6) before building the CQ-tree.

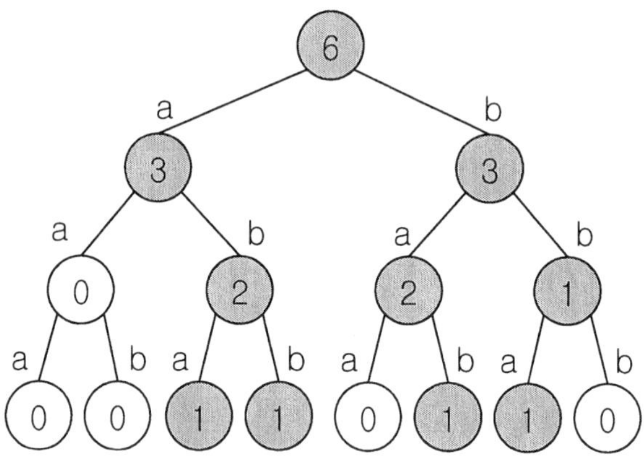

Fig. 4. A full binary tree mapped from a CQ-tree in Fig. 3

0	1	2	3	4	5	6	7	8	9	10	11	12	13	14
6	3	3	0	2	2	1	0	0	1	1	0	1	1	0

Fig. 5. An array for a full binary tree in Fig. 4

3.3 Mapping CQ-Tree to Full n-ary Tree

Even though a CQ-tree can be implemented in various ways [9, 10, 4, 2], there is a more compact data structure for the CQ-tree under a condition that the alphabet size of a database is small (*e.g.* DNA sequences): an array representing a full n-ary tree. That is, the CQ-tree is mapped to a full n-ary tree, and is stored in an array [5].

In Fig. 3, Fig. 4, and Fig. 5, a CQ-tree is changed to a full binary tree, and then stored in an array. During the change, 5 number of nodes having 0 count are newly created in the full binary tree, and a node is added by splitting two nodes on the path bba to three ones.

The major benefit given from the mapping to a full n-ary tree is that the full n-ary tree can be expressed in a one-dimensional array without wasting space because of any labels and pointers that link a parent node with child nodes.

4 Count Estimation with Lower and Upper Bounds

In this section, we present how to get the count estimation and the lower and upper bounds. Suppose that length-n pattern σ is given against a CQ-tree, which provides all the counts of length-q or below length-q substrings ($n > q$). The count is simply estimated by MO [7]. By adjusting Equation (4) to the CQ-tree, we can get

$$C_{\sigma[1:n]} \simeq \frac{\prod_{i=1}^{n-q+1} C_{\sigma[i:i+q-1]}}{\prod_{i=1}^{n-q} C_{\sigma[i+1:i+q-1]}}. \tag{7}$$

If the denominator of (7) is 0, $C_{\sigma[1:n]}$ must be 0, because the count of a string is 0 if its any substring has 0 as the count.

Now, we present the next lemma as a basis for the lower and upper bounds.

Lemma 1. *For two strings α and β, $\alpha\beta$ denotes the concatenation of α and β, and $\bar{\beta}$ denotes the set of all strings except for β. Then, the next formulae are satisfied.*

(a) $C_\alpha = C_{\alpha\beta} + C_{\alpha\bar{\beta}}$
(b) $C_\alpha \geq C_{\alpha\beta}$ and $C_\beta \geq C_{\alpha\beta}$

Lemma 1(a) implies that the string α has, as its following string, β or any other strings except for β. Lemma 1(b) is easily obtained from Lemma 1(a), because all the counts are positive or zero in Lemma 1(a).

First, we consider the upper bound of C_σ. The upper bound is obtained by extending Lemma 1(b). The count of pattern σ must be equal to or below the counts of all q-grams present in σ as follows:

$$(C_\sigma \leq C_{\sigma[1:q]}) \wedge (C_\sigma \leq C_{\sigma[2:q+1]}) \wedge \cdots \wedge (C_\sigma \leq C_{\sigma[n-q+1:n]}). \tag{8}$$

Thus the upper bound of C_σ is

$$\min_{i=1}^{n-q+1} (C_{\sigma[i:i+q-1]}). \tag{9}$$

Second, we consider the lower bound of C_σ.

Lemma 2. *For three strings α, β, and γ, $C_{\alpha\beta\gamma} \geq C_{\alpha\beta} + C_{\beta\gamma} - C_\beta$ is satisfied.*

Proof. From Lemma 1(a),

$$\text{(i) } C_{\beta\bar{\gamma}} = C_\beta - C_{\beta\gamma} \text{ and (ii) } C_{\alpha\beta\bar{\gamma}} = C_{\alpha\beta} - C_{\alpha\beta\gamma}$$

are obtained. From Lemma 1(b),

$$\text{(iii) } C_{\beta\bar{\gamma}} \geq C_{\alpha\beta\bar{\gamma}}$$

is also done. By substituting the left and right terms of (iii) with (i) and (ii), we can get

$$\text{(iv) } C_\beta - C_{\beta\gamma} \geq C_{\alpha\beta} - C_{\alpha\beta\gamma}.$$

Consequently, Lemma 2 is proved by rearranging (iv). □

Lemma 2 implies that the lower bound of $C_{\alpha\beta\gamma}$ is $C_{\alpha\beta} + C_{\beta\gamma} - C_\beta$.

Theorem 2. *For a string σ of length n, the count of σ can be bounded by all the counts of its q-grams and (q-1)-grams as follows:*

$$C_{\sigma[1:n]} \geq \sum_{i=1}^{n-q+1} C_{\sigma[i:i+q-1]} - \sum_{i=2}^{n-q+1} C_{\sigma[i:i+q-2]}. \tag{10}$$

Proof. We will prove Theorem 2 by the mathematical induction. When n is $q+1$ as the initial condition, the theorem is satisfied by replacing α, β, and γ of Lemma 2 with $\sigma_{[1:1]}$, $\sigma_{[2:q]}$, and $\sigma_{[q+1:q+1]}$, respectively. In other words,

$$\begin{aligned} C_{\sigma[1:q+1]} &\geq C_{\sigma[1:1]\sigma[2:q]} + C_{\sigma[2:q]\sigma[q+1:q+1]} - C_{\sigma[2:q]} \\ &= C_{\sigma[1:q]} + C_{\sigma[2:q+1]} - C_{\sigma[2:q]} \\ &= \sum_{i=1}^{2} C_{\sigma[i:i+q-1]} - \sum_{i=2}^{2} C_{\sigma[i:i+q-2]} \end{aligned} \tag{11}$$

Then, we assume that when n is k (in here, $k > q+1$), the theorem is true, that is,

$$C_{\sigma[1:k]} \geq \sum_{i=1}^{k-q+1} C_{\sigma[i:i+q-1]} - \sum_{i=2}^{k-q+1} C_{\sigma[i:i+q-2]}. \tag{12}$$

From now on, on the basis of the above assumption and Lemma 2, we will try to show that the theorem is satisfied, when n is $k+1$. First, when Lemma 2 has $\alpha = \sigma[1:k-q]$, $\beta = \sigma[k-q+1:k]$, and $\gamma = \sigma[k+1:k+1]$,

$$C_{\sigma[1:k+1]} \geq C_{\sigma[1:k]} + C_{\sigma[k-q+1:k+1]} - C_{\sigma[k-q+1:k]}. \tag{13}$$

Then, applying Formula (12) to Formula (13) yields

$$C_{\sigma[1:k+1]} \geq \left(\sum_{i=1}^{k-q+1} C_{\sigma[i:i+q-1]} - \sum_{i=2}^{k-q+1} C_{\sigma[i:i+q-2]} \right) + C_{\sigma[k-q+1:k+1]} - C_{\sigma[k-q+1:k]}. \tag{14}$$

Once again, by Lemma 2,

$$C_{\sigma[k-q+1:k+1]} \geq C_{\sigma[k-q+1:k]} + C_{\sigma[k-q+2:k+1]} - C_{\sigma[k-q+2:k]} \tag{15}$$

is obtained, hence Formula (14) is changed into

$$C_{\sigma[1:k+1]} \geq \sum_{i=1}^{k-q+1} C_{\sigma[i:i+q-1]} - \sum_{i=2}^{k-q+1} C_{\sigma[i:i+q-2]} + (C_{\sigma[k-q+1:k]} + C_{\sigma[k-q+2:k+1]} - C_{\sigma[k-q+2:k]}) - C_{\sigma[k-q+1:k]}. \tag{16}$$

Finally, by rearranging Formula (16), we can get

$$\begin{aligned} C_{\sigma[1:k+1]} &\geq \sum_{i=1}^{k-q+1} C_{\sigma[i:i+q-1]} + C_{\sigma[k-q+2:k+1]} - \sum_{i=2}^{k-q+1} C_{\sigma[i:i+q-2]} - C_{\sigma[k-q+2:k]} \\ &= \sum_{i=1}^{k-q+2} C_{\sigma[i:i+q-1]} - \sum_{i=2}^{k-q+2} C_{\sigma[i:i+q-2]}, \end{aligned} \tag{17}$$

which is the theorem on the time that n is $k+1$. In summary, we first showed that the theorem is true, when n is $q+1$. Then, it was also shown that if when n is k, the theorem is true, so is it when n is $k+1$. Consequently, Theorem 2 is proved. □

From Theorem 2, the lower bound of C_σ is

$$\max(0, \sum_{i=1}^{n-q+1} C_{\sigma[i:i+q-1]} - \sum_{i=2}^{n-q} C_{\sigma[i:i+q-2]}), \tag{18}$$

because the count cannot be negative. It should be noted that the CQ-tree has all the exact counts used in the lower and upper bounds. Namely, the CQ-tree supports both of the bounds well.

Example 1. Given $C_{\mathsf{bcd}} = 40$, $C_{\mathsf{abcd}} = 20$, and $C_{\mathsf{bcde}} = 30$, estimate C_{abcde} together with the lower and upper bounds.

Solution 1.

- $C_{\mathsf{abcde}} \simeq C_{\mathsf{abcd}} \times C_{\mathsf{bcde}} / C_{\mathsf{bcd}} = 15$
- $B_{upper} = \min(C_{\mathsf{abcd}}, C_{\mathsf{bcde}}) = 20$
- $B_{lower} = \max(0, C_{\mathsf{abcd}} + C_{\mathsf{bcde}} - C_{\mathsf{bcd}}) = 10$

5 Experiments

In this section, we experimentally show the building time and space of a CQ-tree, and examine if the CQ-tree supports MO estimation technique well. All the experiments were performed on a 1 GHz Pentium 3 processor with 768 MBytes of main memory and 40 GBytes hard disk. The operating system was Linux Release 7.1.

5.1 Data Sets

We conducted experiments with two data sets: Data set 1 (the first and second human chromosomes) that was provided by NCBI (National Center for Biotechnology Information) on the website [13], and Data set 2 that was created by changing Data set 1. The descriptions of the data sets are as follows.

Data set 1. The sizes of the first and second human chromosomes are about 228 MB and 223 MB, respectively. In the data set, there are 5 characters used: `A`, `C`, `G`, `T` and `N`, where `N` is used to represent an unidentified character. The number of occurrences of each character except `N` is about 100 millions, but `N` occurs about 1 million times. The exact numbers of these occurrences are shown in Table 1.

Data set 2. Data set 2 is created by removing `N` in Data set 1. So, the alphabet size of Data set 2 is 4, and the size of Data set 2 is a little smaller than the one of Data set 1.

5.2 Building CQ-Tree

We built 5 number of CQ-trees expressed in arrays with varying the q-gram length from 6 to 10. Table 2 shows the occupied spaces of the CQ-trees when the node size is 4 bytes. The building times of the CQ-trees that we generated are shown in Table 3. The building time of a CQ-tree is in $O(q \cdot N)$, where N is fixed in our experiments, hence the building times were roughly linear to q.

Table 1. Specifications of Data Sets

character	A	C	G	T	N
counts	136,512,829	94,518,252	94,464,939	136,210,212	1,400,357

Table 2. Space for CQ-tree (Mbytes)

The q-gram length	6	7	8	9	10
Data set 1	0.08	0.39	1.9	9	48
Data set 2	0.02	0.09	0.3	1.3	5

Table 3. Building time of CQ-tree (seconds)

The q-gram length	6	7	8	9	10
Data set 1	102	113	148	184	237
Data set 2	102	113	131	180	222

5.3 Count Estimation

For looking into the accuracy of a CQ-tree, we randomly generated 1000 number of length-11 queries, and then measured the error rate

$$error\ rate = \frac{|\text{ actual count} - \text{estimated count }|}{\text{actual count}}. \tag{19}$$

Table 4 shows the experimental results.

Table 4. Error rate of CQ-tree

The q-gram length	6	7	8	9	10
Data set 1	0.65	0.59	0.40	0.29	0.22
Data set 2	0.64	0.58	0.50	0.46	0.27

6 Conclusion

In the recent years, the problem of estimating substring selectivity has been focused on with the popularity of web, LDAP directories, XML, and so on. For the problem, a CS-tree has been usually used as the meta data that keeps statistical information. However, the CS-tree has two drawbacks: One is that some counts in the CS-tree may be incorrect, which results from occasional prunings. The other is that it is almost impossible to construct the CS-tree over long strings.

So, we proposed a CQ-tree that consists of q-grams obtained from strings in a database. The CQ-tree retains the exact counts of all substrings whose lengths are q or below q, and can be built in one scan of strings in the database. Moreover, in the case that the alphabet size is small like DNA sequences, the CQ-tree can be compactly expressed in an array without storing any labels or pointers by mapped into a full n-ary tree. As a result, more information can be maintained in the limited space.

On the basis of the CQ-tree, we return the lower and upper bounds that the number of occurrences of a query can reach to, together with the estimated count of the query pattern. The bounds are mathematically proved. We believe that the bounds presented are helpful to a user or a query optimizer.

References

1. Z. Chen, H. V. Jagadish, F. Korn, N. Koudas, S. Muthukrishnan, R. T. Ng, and D. Srivastava. Counting twig matches in a tree. In *ICDE*, pages 595–604, 2001.
2. M. Farach, P. Ferragina, and S. Muthukrishnan. Overcoming the memory bottlenect in suffix tree construction. In *39th Annual Symposium on Foundations of Computer Science*, pages 174–185, 1998.
3. E. R. Fiala and D. H. Greene. Data compression with finite windows. In *Comm. of the ACM*, volume 32, pages 490–505, 1989.
4. R. Grossi and J. S. Vitter. Compressed suffix arrays and suffix trees with applications to text indexing and string matching. In *ACM Symposium on Theory of Computing*, pages 397–456, 2000.
5. E. Horowitz, S. Sahni, and D. Mehta. *Fundamentals of data structures in C++*. W H Freeman & Co., 1995.
6. H. V. Jagadish, O. Kapitskaia, R. T. Ng, and D. Srivastava. Multi-dimensional substring selectivity estimation. In *VLDB*, pages 387–398, 1999.
7. H. V. Jagadish, R. T. Ng, and D. Srivastava. Substring selectivity estimation. In *PODS*, pages 249–260, 1999.
8. H. V. Jagadish, R. T. Ng, and D. Srivastava. On effective multi-dimensional indexing for strings. In *ACM SIGMOD*, pages 403–414, 2000.
9. P. Krishnan, J. S. Vitter, and B. Iyer. Estimating alphanumeric selectivity in the presence of wildcards. In *ACM SIGMOD*, pages 282–293, 1996.
10. E. M. McCreight. A space-economical suffix tree construction algorithm. In *Journal of the ACM*, volume 23, pages 262–272, 1976.
11. G. Navarro and R. Baeza-Yates. A practical q-gram index for text retrieval allowing errors. In *CLEI Electronic Journal*, volume 1, 1998.
12. G. Navarro, E. Sutinen, J. Tanninen, and J. Tarhio. Indexing text with approximate q-grams. In *Combinatorial Pattern Matching*, pages 350–363, 2000.
13. NCBI, 2001. http://ncbi.nlm.nih.gov.
14. P. Weiner. Linear pattern matching algorithms. In *IEEE 14th Annual Symp. on Switching and Automata Theory*, pages 1–11, 1990.

An Efficient Topic-Specific Web Text Filtering Framework

Qiang Li and Jianhua Li

Modern Communication Institute, Shanghai Jiaotong univ.,
Shanghai 200030, P. R. China
liqiang@sjtu.edu.cn

Abstract. In this paper, an efficient topic-specific Web text filtering framework is proposed. This framework focuses on blocking some topic-specific Web text content. In this framework, a hybrid feature selection method is proposed, and a high efficient filtering engine is designed. In training, we select features based on CHI statistic and rough set theory, then to construct filter with Vector Space Model. We train our frame with huge datasets, and the result suggests our framework is more effective for the topic-specific text filtering. This framework runs at server such as gateway, and it is more efficient than a client-based system.

1 Introduction

With the proliferation of harmful Internet content such as pornography, violence, hate messages and objectionable content, effective content-filtering systems are essential.

At present, there are four content-filtering approaches: Platform for Internet Content Selection (PICS), URL blocking, keyword filtering, and intelligent content analysis [1]. PICS is a voluntary self-labeling system. Each Web content publisher is totally responsible for rating the content, so that is very difficult for all Web content's publisher to filter Web pages according to the embedded PICS rating labels. URL blocking technique restricts or allows access by comparing the requested Web page's URL. This approach has advantages for its speed and efficiency. However, this approach requires implementing a URL list, and it can identify only the sites on the list. And keeping the list up-to-date is very difficult. That is, unless the list is updated constantly, the system's accuracy will decrease over time owing to the explosive growth of new Web sites. Keyword filtering compares offensive words and phrases on a retrieved Web page against those in a keyword dictionary of prohibited words and phrases. Blocking occurs when the number of matches reaches a predefined threshold. However, it is well known for overblocking. The high overblocking rate is often unacceptable and greatly jeopardizes the system's capability. So intelligent content analysis, which can automatically classify Web content, is needed. On the other hand, web-filtering systems are either client- or server-based [2]. A client-based system performs Web content filtering solely on the computer where it is installed, without consulting remote servers about the nature of the Web content that a user tries to access. A server-based system provides filtering to computers on the local area network where it is installed.

In this paper, an efficient topic-specific filtering framework for Web text based on intelligent content analysis is proposed. The paper is organized as follows: A hybrid feature selection method is briefly introduced in Section 2. Section 3 presents the

Y. Zhang et al. (Eds.): APWeb 2005, LNCS 3399, pp. 157 – 163, 2005.

efficient framework to filter the topic-specific text. The filter engine is introduced in Section 4. Section 5 describes experimental data set and presents the experimental result. Finally the conclusions are summarized in Section 6.

2 Feature Selection

Feature subset selection is very important when learning on text data [3]. Because a high number of features may slow down the process of text preprocessing, sometimes even hard to get result, and at the same time a good subset can even get better result than using full features. And to make our system fit for topic-specific text filtering in real-time such as embedding this model in firewall or gateway, we need to further select more accurate and few features. In [3], we know there are many feature selection methods such as DF, CHI statistic, information gain, mutual information, but the number of features selected by one of these methods is still high for good result. Fortunately, with Rough sets theory proposed by Pawlak in 1982 [4], it can also be used to select subset more accurately from thousands of features. But the existing attributes reduction methods based on rough set are not applicable for very large data set because of the high time and space complexity.

Rough Set Attribute Reduction removes redundant conditional attributes from nominal datasets, retaining the information content intact whilst reducing the mount of knowledge involved. In [5], a feature subset selection algorithm named QUICKREDUCT Algorithm is proposed base on the attribute dependency. The Algorithm only produce one possible minimum reduct, which is not enough to judge whether the new Web text is relevant to the topic or not. So we proposed a new algorithm which produce *m reducts*, the number *m* needed to be given by the designer. The special point is that between these reducts there are no common attributes, so these attributes have more powerfully capability to classify new objects. This Attributes Reduction algorithm is extended from the QUICKREDUCT Algorithm.

```
Input: C, the set of all feature attributes;
       D, the set of class attributes.
Output:  the unit of m reducts MR, MR ⊆ C
  MR=Φ
  for i=1 to m
      R:=Φ,
      do
            T:=R,
            for each x∈C-R
            if γ_{R∪{x}}(D) > γ_T(D)   T:=R∪{x},
            R:=T,
      until γ_R(D)=γ_C(D),
      C=C-R,
      MR=MR∪R,
  end for
  return MR
```

We proposed a hybrid feature selection method. We use CHI statistic methods to select features firstly (step one), and then we use the rough set theory to further reduce the number of the features (step two). Thus more accurate and few features are extracted. The feature selection architecture is shown in Fig 1.

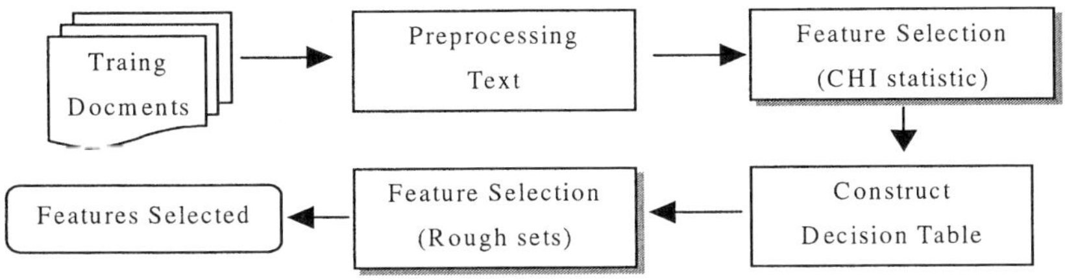

Fig. 1. Feature Selection Architecture

3 System Architecture

The topic-specific Web text filtering framework is composed of training offline phase and filtering online phase. The system architecture is shown in Fig 2.

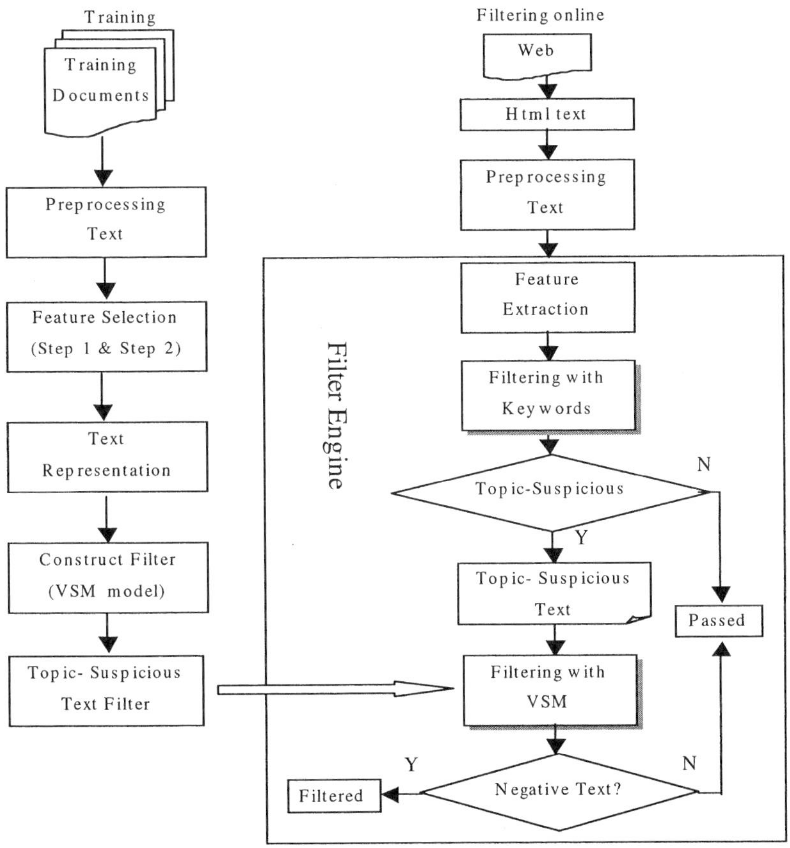

Fig. 2. System Architecture to Filter Topic-Specific Web Text

The main sub-modules are:

Feature selection. In this phase we use CHI statistic and rough set based attribute reduction to select features (see section 2).
Keywords filtering. Using keywords is to distinguish the suspicious text from normal text.
VSM classifier. In this phase we use vector space model (VSM) [6,7] to distinguish the negative text from suspicious text.
Filter engine. To improve the system speed, we employ the finite state automata theory to construct the filtering engine (see section 4).

4 Filtering Algorithms

In this section, after the feature selection (step 1& step 2), we can use the words to built class vectors respectively, which appeared in the selected features. The steps to construct the filter are as following:

Step 1. Computing the center vector for each class,
Step 2. Representing the incoming text into vector,
Step 3. Computing the similarity between incoming text vector and center vector of each class,
Step 4. Classifying the incoming text into the class with maximal similarity.

The similarity between incoming text vector and center vector of each class is computed by the cosine formula.

$$\mathrm{Sim}(d_i,d_j)=\frac{\sum_{k=1}^{m} W_{ik}\times W_{jk}}{\sqrt{(\sum_{k=1}^{m} W_{ik}^2)(\sum_{k=1}^{m} W_{jk}^2)}}$$

Where d_i denotes the incoming text vector, d_j denotes the center vector of each class, W_{ik} denotes the weight of term t_k in incoming text, W_{jk} denotes the weight of term t_k in center vector of jth class, m denotes the number of selected features.

5 Filtering Engine

In our system, the speed to extract features and judge whether the incoming Web text is relevant to the topic or not is very important, so we employ the finite-state automata theory to improve this need. Finite-state automata theory has been used in various language processing [8]. For the DFSA Method, three functions: *goto*, *failure*, and *output* are initially constructed from a given set of patterns. The pattern matching process now becomes the state transition process, which begins with the start state. The *goto function* continues mapping a state and an input character from the string into another state. If a final state is reached, the patterns specified by the *output function* are matched. During the state transition process, the *goto function* outputs the fail message, when an input character causes a mismatch. When it occurs, the *failure function* is used to choose a state, and the state transition restarts from that state.

In application, we first construct finite-state automata based on the selected features. Then the FSA is always running at server. Once incoming text stream is captured, we can use the *look up function* to get the words, which appeared in the selected features. On the other hand, these keywords stationed at the server can be replaced with other words only re-trained by large text corpora to fit the different needs for content filtering in the future.

6 Experiment and Result

We choose a Chinese dataset as our datasets, which is captured from Web. This dataset, which are relevant to some topic, includes two classes. One class is positive for the topic, which includes 949 documents; the other class is about objectionable content for the topic as negative, which includes 1464 documents. We firstly separate Chinese text into words, then prune infrequent words and high frequency words, and delete preposition, pronoun, auxiliary words, measure words, etc, and we only hold the noun, verb, adjective and some phrases. Thus we get a vocabulary of about 5139 words in this phase.

Next, we use CHI statistic to select features primarily, thus we get a vocabulary of 1384 words in this phase. To make our system fit for the application and to embed this model gateway for real-time text filtering, we need to further select more accurate features. So next we use rough set to further reduce those attributes, and rough set have this function in nature.

We primarily use the term frequency-inverse document frequency (TF-IDF) to establish the particular degree of important of term in a document. We denote $w = value$ (TF-IDF). Since rough set is suited to nominal datasets, we quantize the normalized space into 11 values calculated by floor ($10w$). Next we construct decision table for the 2413 documents based on these 1384 selected words. Then we use the rough set method we proposed to further reduce the number of the features. Then we use vector space model (VSM) to build the topic filter using the selected features based on the training data sets. And we get 343 negative documents for testing, which are got from other objectionable Web Sites. The result is shown in Table 1. We can see that when m is only 1 (that is only one reduct), the performance is better than unreduced training data set, but the performance is poor in testing data set (only 91.01%). When m is 3, the performance gives same accuracy almost as in unreduced training data set or testing data set. In this phase, 129 words are found, and we find these words are all more relevant to the positive and negative documents; moreover, underlying semantics between these words is preserved.

We run our system with the filter engine in our gateway for unseen web text by keywords firstly filtering suspicious text from normal text and further judging by VSM Classifier based on the selected keywords to distinguish the negative text from suspicious text when in need, we get good accuracy. See Table 2.

Table 1. The Result in Training Sets and Testing Sets

VSM Classifier	Original	Number of reducts		
		m=1	m=2	m=3
Numbers of attributes	1384	18	67	129
Precision of training set	95.69%	96.41%	96.31%	95.99%
Precision of testing set	99.42%	91.01%	97.68%	98.84%

Table 2. The Result in Gateway for Unseen Web Pages

Getting Web Pages	Classifier	Blocked Web Pages	Precision	Recall
4863	Keywords (step1)	550	88.69%	92.63%
	VSM (step2)	343	95.74%	95.74%

7 Conclusions

In this paper, an efficient topic-specific Web text filtering framework is proposed. This framework focuses on blocking some topic-specific Web text content. Especially, we proposed a hybrid feature selection method based rough set theory, and to improve the system speed, we employ the finite state automata theory in language processing to construct the filtering engine. The result suggests our framework is more effective for the topic. This system runs at server, it is more efficient than a client-based system. The future work is about two: one the one hand, we will combine URL blocking technique to improve system speed; on the other hand, we will consider relevant feedback technique to improve the capability to adapt to the rapid penetration of the Web.

Acknowledgements

This research is supported by the National Natural Science Foundation of China under NO.60402019, and the National 863 High-Tech Research Plan of China under NO.2003AA142160.

References

1. Pui Y.Lee, Siu C.Hui, Alvis Cheuk M.Fong: Neural Networks for Web Content Filtering. IEEE Intelligent Systems.Volume, 17 (2002) 48-57.
2. Chen Ding, Chi-Hung Chi, Jing Deng, Chun-Lei Dong: Centralized Content-Based Web Filtering and Blocking: How Far Can It Go. In Proceeding of IEEE International Conference on Systems, Man and Cybernetics, (1999) 115-119
3. Monica Rogati, Yiming Yang: High-performing feature selection for text classification. CIKM'02 Virginia, USA, November (2002) 659-661.

4. Z.Pawlak: Rough sets. International Journal of Information and computer Science. 11(5) (1982) 341-356.
5. Alexios Chouchoulas, Qiang Shen: Rough set-aided keyword reduction for text categorization. Applied Artificial Intelligence, 15(9) (2001) 843–873.
6. G.Salton, A.Wong, C.S.Yang: A vector space model for automatic indexing. Comm.ACM 18 (11) (1975) 613-620.
7. Jianfeng Pang, Dongbo Bu, Shuo Bai: Research and Implementation of Text Categorization System Based on VSM. Compute Application Research. (9) (2001) 23-26.
8. Jang-Jong Fan, Keh-Yih Su: An efficient algorithm for matching multiple patterns. IEEE Transactions on Knowledge and Data Engineering. 5(2) (1993) 339-351.

An Extension of UML Activity Diagram for Generation of XPDL Document

Hye-Min Noh, Bo Wang, Cheol-Jung Yoo, and Ok-Bae Chang

Department of Computer Science, Chonbuk National University,
664-14, 1ga, Duckjin-Dong, Duckjin-Gu, Jeonju, South Korea
{hmino, bowing, cjyoo, okjang}@chonbuk.ac.kr

Abstract. Currently there are a variety of different tools that may be used to analyze, model, describe and document a business process. However, it is difficult to exchange the information of a business process created in different tools because of the distinct information formats used in different tools. The XML Process Definition Language(XPDL) forms a common interchange standard. Generally a business process model can be represented by the UML activity diagram, but there is a difficult task to directly generate an XPDL document from a business process model represented by the standard activity diagram. In the paper we will propose an approach to generate an XPDL document from a business process model represented by the extended UML activity diagram and provide an implementation for the approach.

1 Introduction

The XPDL specification uses XML as the mechanism for process definition interchange. A Process Definition is defined as: The representation of a business process in a form that supports automated manipulation, such as modeling, or enactment by a workflow management system. The process definition consists of a network of activities and their relationships, criteria to indicate the start and termination of the process, and information about the individual activities, such as participants, associated IT applications and data, etc[1].

The UML activity diagram also can create business process model in forms of sets of activities and transitions between them[2, 3, 4]. However, it is difficult to directly map the business process model represented by the standard UML activity diagram to the process definition organized in XPDL because some elements in the standard UML activity diagram can not be directly associated to entities defined in the process definition. Hence the paper will propose a method of generating an XPDL document from a business process model represented by an extended activity diagram.

The paper consists of five sections. The following section discusses issues for relate works. The third section describes the XPDL document structure and entity definitions associated to modeling elements of UML activity diagram. The method of a mapping from the business process model represented by extended activity diagram to the XPDL document will be depicted in the fourth section. Section 5 presents our conclusion and future work. The references will be listed in the end.

Y. Zhang et al. (Eds.): APWeb 2005, LNCS 3399, pp. 164 – 169, 2005.

2 Issues for Related Works

Currently a tool for business process modeling has been implemented, which could create extended activity diagram for modeling business processes or workflows. In order to make the generated business process model available for other modeling tools or workflow systems, there must be a common interchange standard existing for information exchange among the diverse tools. Fortunately XPDL uses XML as the mechanism for process definition interchange. XPDL specification provides the workflow process definition interface that defines a common interchange format. The interface also defines a formal separation between the development and run time environments, enabling a process definition, generated by one modelling tool, to be used as input to a number of different workflow run-time products[5].

A business process model can be expressed conveniently by using the UML activity diagram[6]. Now the key problem is how to generate a XPDL document from a business process model represented by UML activity diagram. A solution will be proposed in the fourth section.

3 XPDL Document Structure and Associated Entities

The content of a XPDL document mainly describes Process Definition(s). The top-level entities are contained within a process definition[7].

The top-level entities are:

***Workflow Process Definition*:** The Process Definition entity provides contextual information that applies to other entities within the process.

***Workflow Process Activity*:** An activity represents work, which will be processed by a combination of resource specified by participant assignment and/or computer applications specified by application assignment.

***Transition Information*:** Activities are related to one another via flow control conditions. Each individual transition has three elementary properties, the from-activity, the to-activity and the condition under which the transition is made.

***Workflow Participant Declaration*:** This provides descriptions of resources that can act as the performer of the various activities in the process definition.

***Resource Repository*:** The resource repository for the fact that participants can be humans, programs, or machines.

***Workflow Application Declaration*:** This provides descriptions of the IT applications or interfaces which may be invoked by the workflow service to support, or wholly automate, the processing associated with each activity, and identified within the activity by an application assignment attribute(s).

***Workflow Relevant Data*:** This defines the data that is created and used within each process instance during process execution.

***System and Environment Data*:** This is data which is maintained by the workflow management system or the local system environment

***Data Types and Expressions*:** The meta-model (and associated XPDL) assumes a number of standard data types (string, reference, integer, float, date/time, etc.); such data types are relevant to workflow relevant data, system or environment data or participant data.

According to the descriptions of the top-level entities in process definition, a business process model represented by UML activity diagram can be mapped into the elements contained both in "workflow process activity" entity and in "transition information" entity.

4 Mapping from Business Process Model to XPDL Document

The task of the mapping from business process model represented by the UML activity diagram to the corresponding XPDL document actually is to generate the corresponding information in the format of XPDL from each element in source business process model and put the information into the appropriate positions in XPDL document structure. Considering that one "activity" element in UML activity diagram can not be definitely associated to one entity in XPDL, we just refine activity into three different types of activities which can be directly related to the 'regular' three different implementation types of activities respectively. Table 1 shows the associations between the elements of extended activity diagram and entities defined in XPDL.

Fig. 1 presents a process called 'EOrder' which is used to present an electrical order process.

Table 1. Associations between the Elements of Extended Activity Diagram and the Entities Defined in XPDL

Element notation	Description	Corresponding entity in XPDL
	A start state explicitly shows the beginning of a workflow.	Route activity.
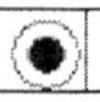	An end state explicitly shows the end of a workflow on an activity diagram.	Route activity.
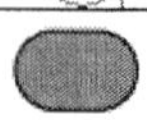	An activity with the type of "No Implementation" which is implemented by manual procedures.	A "regular" activity whose implementation type is "No Implementation".
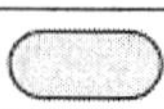	An activity with the type of "Tool" whose implementation is supported by (one or more) application(s).	A "regular" activity whose implementation type is "Tool".
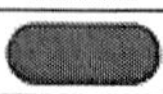	An activity with the type of "Subflow" which is Implemented by another process.	A "regular" activity whose implementation type is Subflow"
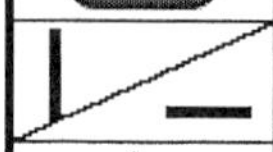	Vertical/Horizontal synchronization defines forks and joins representing parallel workflow.	Route activity with transition restriction with the attribute of join/split.
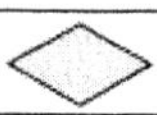	A decision represents a specific location on an activity diagram where the workflow may branch based upon guard conditions.	Route activity with transition restriction of split with XOR type.
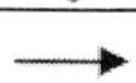	From one state to another state when certain conditions are satisfied	Transition

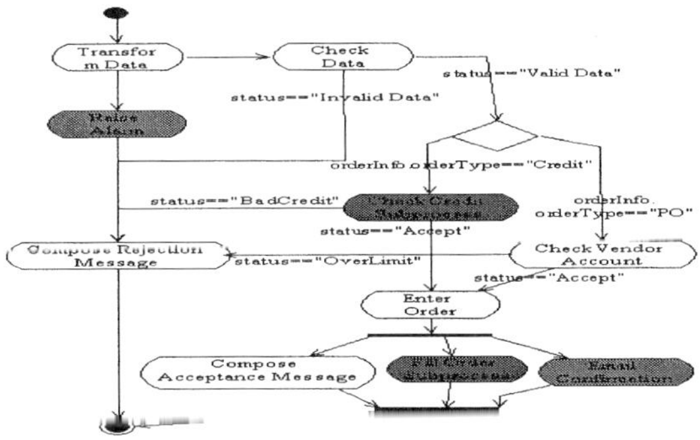

Fig. 1. EOrder Process

4.1 The Mapping of "Start State" Element and "End State" Element

The "start state" and "end state" element can be mapped to the "route activity" entity defined in XPDL. A route activity has neither a performer nor an application and its execution has no effect on workflow relevant data or application data. Fig. 2 shows the XPDL representations of "start state" element and "end state" element in the "EOrder" process model.

<Activity Id="5"> <Description>This is a start!</Description> <Route/> <ExtendedAttributes> .... </ExtendedAttributes>	</Activity> 6-1 The XPDL of The "Start state" Element <Activity Id="6"> .... </Activity> 6-22 The XPDL of The "End state" Element

Fig. 2. XPDL Representations of "Start State" and "End State" in the "EOrder" Process

4.2 The Mapping of Activity Element

Activity elements with three different colours of green, yellow and blue can be mapped to "regular" activity entities with three different implementation types which are defined in XPDL: "No Implementation", "Tool", and "Subflow" respectively. Fig. 3 shows XPDL representations of activities in the "EOrder" process.

<Activity Id="58" Name="Raise Alarm"> <Implementation> <No/></Implementation> <ExtendedAttributes>	.... </ExtendedAttributes> </Activity> 7-1 Activity"Raise Alarm" with "No Implementation" Type	<Activity Id="17" Name="Transform Data"> .... </Activity> ....

Fig. 3. XPDL representations of activities in the "EOrder" Process

"No Implementation" type means that the implementation of this activity is not supported by workflow using automatically invoked applications or procedures. "Tool" type means that the activity is implemented by (one or more) tools. A tool may be an application program. "Subflow" type means that the activity is refined as a subflow.

4.3 The Mapping of Synchronization Element

A synchronization element can be mapped to a route activity with "Transition Restriction" attribute with kind of "join" or "split", which is defined in XPDL Fig. 4 shows XPDL representations of a "fork" kind synchronization element and a "join" kind synchronization element in the "EOrder" process.

```
<Activity Id="9">
<Route/>
<TransitionRestrictions>
<TransitionRestriction>
<Split Type="AND">
........................
</Split>
.........................
</TransitionRestrictions>
<ExtendedAttributes>
.................................................
</Activity>
8-1 the "Fork" Kind Synchronization Element
<Activity Id="33">
<Route/>
<TransitionRestrictions>
<TransitionRestriction>
 <Join Type="AND"/>
</TransitionRestriction>
</TransitionRestrictions>
.............................
</Activity>
8-2 the "Join" Kind Synchronization Element
```

Fig. 4. XPDL Representations of Synchronization Elements in the "EOrder" Process

4.4 The Mapping of Decision Element

A decision element can be mapped to a route activity entity with transition restriction of split kind with XOR type, which is defined in XPDL. Fig. 5 shows the XPDL representation of "Check Order Type" decision element in the "EOrder" process.

```
<Activity Id="12" Name="Check Order Type">
<Route/>
<TransitionRestrictions>
<TransitionRestriction>
<Split Type="XOR">
<TransitionRefs>
..............................
</TransitionRefs>
</Split>
</TransitionRestriction>
</TransitionRestrictions>
<ExtendedAttributes>
...........................
</ExtendedAttributes>
</Activity>
```

Fig. 5. XPDL Representation of "Check Order Type" Decision Element in the "EOrder" Process

4.5 The Mapping of Transition Element

A transition element can be mapped to a transition entity defined in XPDL. The transition entities describe possible transitions between activities and the conditions that enable or disable them (the transitions) during workflow execution. Fig. 6 shows XPDL representations of all transition elements in the "EOrder" process.

```
<Transitions>
<Transition Id="1" From="9" To="8"/>
...............................................
<Condition Type="OTHERWISE"/>
</Transition>
<Transition Id="18" From="33" To="6"/>
..........................................................
<Condition>status == "Valid Data"</Condition>
</Transition>
.................................
```

Fig. 6. XPDL Representations of All Transition Elements in the "EOrder" Process

So far, we have proposed the method of the mapping from the business process model represented by extended activity diagram to XPDL document. The complete structure of XPDL document and the related detail information about associated XPDL entity definitions should be referred to in XPDL specification. Fig. 7 presents a demonstration of the implementation of automatic XPDL document generation corresponding to the method.

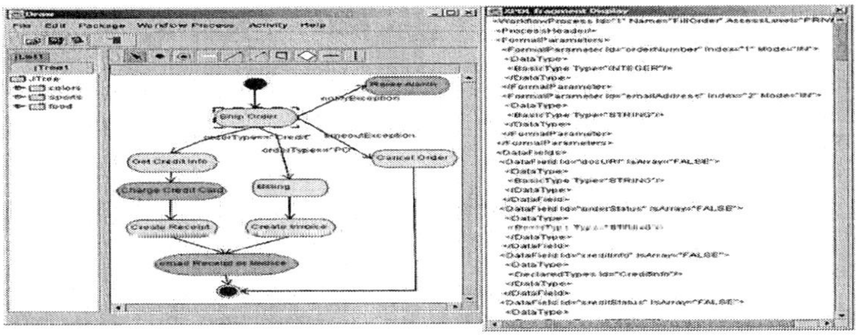

Fig. 7. The Demonstration of Implementation of Automatic XPDL Document Generation

5 Conclusions and Future Works

In the paper we proposed the approach of the mapping from the business process model represented by extended activity diagram to XPDL document and provide the implementation for that approach.

The approach proposed in this paper provides the important guidance for the mapping from other similar business process models, which are used in different software products, to XPDL document. The approach can successfully generate XPDL document from business process model presented by UML activity diagram. Now the implementation still can not generate the complete XPDL document from business process model presented by UML activity diagram because the XPDL document contains some data information that can not be obtained directly from the UML activity diagram. Therefore, In the future it is necessary to improve the implementation for the complete XPDL document generation.

References

1. Alexander, I. A.: A Co-Operative Task Modeling Approach to Business Process Understanding. Workshop on Object-Oriented Business Process Modeling, ECCOOP (1998)
2. Aissi, S., Malu, P., Srinivasan, K.: 2002. E-business Process Modeling: The Next Big Step. Computer, Vol. 35, Issue. 5, pp. 55-62, Geoffrey Sparks. An Introduction to UML: The Business Process Model. www.sparxsystems.com.au, Geoffrey Sparks (2002)
3. Hans-Erik Eriksson, Magnus Penker: Business Modeling with UML: Business Patterns and Business Objects. John Wiley & Sons Inc (2000)
4. Jim Heumann: Introduction to Business Modeling Using the Unified Modeling Language(UML). Rational Software (2001)
5. Object Management Group (OMG): OMG Unified Modeling Language Specification. http://www.rational.com (2002)
6. Oliver Wiegert: Business Process Modeling & Workflow Definition with UML. SAPAG (1998)
7. Workflow Management Coalition(WfMC): Workflow Process Definition Interface XML Process Definition Language(XPDL) Specification. http://www.wfmc.org. (2002)

Block-Based Language Modeling Approach Towards Web Search

Shengping Li, Shen Huang, Gui-Rong Xue, and Yong Yu

Department of Computer Science and Engineering,
Shanghai Jiao Tong University, Shanghai 200240, China
{lishengping, huangshen, grxue, yyu}@sjtu.edu.cn

Abstract. Using probabilistic Language Modeling approach in Information Retrieval, model for each document is estimated individually. However, with Web pages becoming more complex, each of them may contain some *blocks* discussing different topics. Consequently, the performance of statistic model for web document tends to be degraded by the mixture of topics. In this paper, we argue that segmenting Web page into several relatively independent blocks will assist the language modeling and a Block-based Language Modeling (BLM) approach is proposed. Different with normal method, BLM refines the modeling process into two parts: the probability of a query occurring in a block, and the probability of a block occurring in a Web page. Then given a query, those pages with more relevant blocks tend to be retrieved. Experimental results show that when unigram model is used, our approach outperforms original language modeling for web search in most cases.

1 Introduction

Today web search engine has become one of the most useful tools for web surfers, and many search models have been built up. In recent years, language modeling based information retrieval has been successfully applied to traditional document retrieval [1,14,15]. It's intuitive to borrow the idea of statistic language modeling for web search. However, numerous problems stem from the miscellaneous content of the Web page, i.e. a page may contain multiple blocks with different topics. First, if the query keywords occur in different blocks, the whole page is likely to be irrelevant. This can not be detected by current language modeling based retrieval which takes a whole document as a single model. Second, not all blocks focus on the same topic and noisy information like navigation bars, copyrights, contact information etc., is usually embedded in Web pages. The two problems both challenge the validity of the statistic language modeling and degrade the retrieval performance. In order to solve them, we should fully exploit the block information within a Web page.

To segment a Web page into regions or blocks effectively, some methods are proposed under different scenarios [2-8]. These approaches mostly use HTML tag and DOM tree analysis with some heuristic rules. Especially, VIPS [12] tried to learn the importance of blocks using both spatial and content features. Furthermore, based on

Y. Zhang et al. (Eds.): APWeb 2005, LNCS 3399, pp. 170 – 182, 2005.

previous work, some research efforts have shown that segmenting a Web page into several relatively independent blocks can enhance web search [10], web link analysis [13] and web data mining [11]. Similarly, we claim that block information will also benefit language modeling of web documents.

Language modeling approaches to information retrieval are attractive and promising because they connect the problem of retrieval with that of language model estimation, which have been studied extensively in other application areas such as speech recognition. The basic idea of these approaches is to estimate a language model for each document, and then rank documents by the likelihood of the query according to the estimated language model [1]. Zhai and Lafferty [14] studied the smoothing method for language modeling based information retrieval. Berger and Lafferty [15] proposed a more advanced model which characterized the retrieval process as a user translating a document into a query. However, all above approaches did not explore how the block information embedded in the web documents would affect the performance of language modeling-based information retrieval.

By these motivations, in this paper, we try to find a perfect marriage of language modeling and Web page segmentation, which can improve the search for the Web page that contains several topics or noisy information. We first devise a DOM tree-enabled *Structure indUction-based Page Segmentation (SUPS)* algorithm to partition the page, and then a *Block-based Language Modeling (BLM)* approach is proposed. BLM is constructed based on following three assumptions: first, a Web page can be segmented into independent parts of blocks and different blocks may represent different topics; second, query terms are regarded as more relevant to the Web page when they co-occur in the same block than when they are distributed over different blocks; third, the block which has more similar language model with the Web page is more relevant with the major idea of the whole page. And such blocks should contribute more for the relevance of the Web page to a query.

The major contributions of this paper are:

- A block based language modeling approach is proposed towards web search for the pages containing multi-blocks or multi-topics. BLM refines the modeling process into two parts: the probability of a query occurring in a block, and the probability of a block occurring in a Web page. By breaking a page into blocks containing independent topics, block-based language modeling for web search can obtain higher performance than its original one.
- A flexible segmentation algorithm, SUPS, is devised to automatically partition Web page. SUPS is based on DOM tree analysis and implements several common used methods of page segmentation.
- A user study is performed to evaluate the performance of the proposed approach, whose results show that using two evaluation metrics, BLM has about 8.34% and 16.28% improvements over the existing language modeling based method.

The remainder of the paper is organized as follows. In section 2, we review some related work. Section 3 briefly introduces SUPS page segmentation algorithm. Section 4 describes the details of our BLM approach. Experimental results and some discussion are provided in Section 5. Finally we make a conclusion and give the direction of future work in Section 6.

2 Related Work

Many research efforts [2- 4] divided the page based on the type of the tags including <P>, <TABLE>, <UL>, <H1>~<H6>, etc. In [5-7], some visual cues were used in DOM analysis. Chen [5] attempted to understand authors' intention by identifying Object function instead of semantic understanding. Yang [6] aimed to automatically analyze semantic structure of HTML pages based on detecting visual similarities of content objects on Web pages. Cai [7] proposed their VIPS approach to extract the content structure for a Web page by using page layout features. Besides, Embley [8] used some heuristic rules to discover record boundaries, which assist data extraction from the Web page. Our SUPS algorithm integrates DOM analysis, visual cues and heuristic rules together to identify obvious blocks. Song et al. [12] presented how to use the spatial and content features of each block to learn their importance. Different with it, our segmentation method does not try to measure the importance of block.

How to exploit segmentation information to help web mining and information retrieval tasks has been studied in recent years[9-11, 13]. Yi et al.[11] make use of the common presentation to map the styles of a page and its owner site. Noisy information in the page is cleaned for document classification and clustering. Cai et al.[13] showed that block information can improve link analysis like HITS[17] and PageRank[18]. By extracting the page-to-block, block-to-page relationships from link structure and page layout analysis, the authors constructed a semantic graph over the WWW so that each node exactly represents a single semantic topic.

As to web information retrieval, some researches are made on improving traditional approaches. Yu et al.[9] detected the semantic content structure in a Web page. The authors used the segmentation result to assist the selection of query expansion terms in pseudo-relevance feedback. Cai et al.[10] expanded the idea in [9] and conducted comparative experiments on block-level query expansion and retrieval using four segmentation approaches. To our best knowledge, most block-enhanced retrieval methods focus on using block information to perform query expansion, or using blocks-retrieval based ranking score to revise the original document-retrieval based score. BLM revises the model estimation and query generation of language modeling for information retrieval, while no retrieval model is modified in previous work.

Ponte and Croft [1] proposed a non-parametric language model which integrated document indexing and document retrieval. It inferred a language model for each document and estimated the probability of query generation in each model. Zhai and Lafferty [14] tried to solve a core problem in language modeling, *smoothing*, which adjusts the maximum likelihood estimator so as to correct the inaccuracy due to data sparseness. Berger and Lafferty [15] proposed a simple, well motivated model of the document-to-query translation process, and described an algorithm for learning the parameters of this model in an unsupervised manner from a collection of documents. According to the experimental reports in those papers, language model really outperformed other models on some data sets. However, all these approaches took the document as atomic unit for statistics and came up against the difficulties mentioned before. We claim that the blocks with single topic are more precise for model estimation. Thus in BLM, the model is estimated on a much smaller block granularity.

3 Structure Induction-Based Page Segmentation

Before explaining the idea of BLM, we briefly introduce our algorithm for page segmentation. Given that Document Object Model (DOM) provides each Web page a fine-grained structure and each subtree can represent a block, we first identified the block layout of Web page by constructing a DOM style HTML tag tree. Then we devise a heuristic rule based reasoning engine to induce the intention of the Web page designer. Two measurements, Degree of Isolation (DoI) and Degree of Coherence (DoC), are introduced for each node. DoI indicates the degree that a subtree can be differentiated from its siblings and DoC indicates the degree that a subtree can be viewed as an integral block. DoI is calculated by a top-town scan that begins with the root element, and is adjusted based on some visual cues such as tag, color, text and size etc. DoC is calculated by a bottom-up scan that begins with the leaf elements, and the coherence of parent node is adjusted based on the coherence of its children, which is also learned from visual cues. We call this method *Structure indUction-based Page Segmentation (SUPS).* Some details will be depicted in Section 5.1.

4 Block-Based Language Modeling

In this section, we first describe the basic idea of language modeling for information retrieval. Next, we explain how to improve such idea using block information.

4.1 Basic Language Modeling for Information Retrieval

To retrieval task, Language Modeling approach (LM) treats each document as a language model and the generation of queries as a random process. In [1], it is assumed that query terms occurred independently in a particular language model. If $\hat{p}(Q \mid M_d)$ is the probability of the query given the language model of document d and $\hat{p}(t \mid M_d)$ is the probability of each term t ($t \in Q$) under the term distribution for d, then $\hat{p}(Q \mid M_d)$ can be estimated by $\hat{p}(t \mid M_d)$ as following[1]:

$$\hat{p}(Q \mid M_d) = \prod_{t \in Q} \hat{p}(t \mid M_d) \times \prod_{t \notin Q} \left(1.0 - \hat{p}(t \mid M_d)\right) \tag{1}$$

In this formula, the first item is the probability of producing the terms in the query and the second item is the probability of not producing other terms. Maximum Likelihood Estimate (MLE) is used to estimate $\hat{p}(t \mid M_d)$ using the document collection:

$$\hat{p}_{ml}(t \mid M_d) = \frac{tf_{(t,d)}}{dl_d} \tag{2}$$

$tf_{(t,d)}$ is the raw frequency of term t in document d and dl_d is the total number of tokens in d. However, two practical problems exist: first, a probability of zero will be

[1] Actually, it is a kind of unigram language model. Although bigram and trigram models are not discussed in this paper, similar work can be done to enhance them by block information.

assigned to a document that is missing one or more of the query terms; second, only one document sample is used and the confidence for the maximum likelihood estimator is not high enough. For the first problem, a feasible way is to assign an average term probability in the whole collection to a document that is missing one or more of the query terms. I.e., $\frac{cf_t}{cs}$, where cf_t is the raw count of term t in the collection and cs is the total number of tokens in the collection. As to the second problem, LM introduces another estimator from a larger amount of data:

$$\hat{p}_{avg}(t) = \frac{\left(\sum_{d(t \in d)} p_{ml}(t \mid M_d)\right)}{df_t} \tag{3}$$

where df_t is the document frequency of t. This is a robust statistic in the sense that it is estimated from a lot of more data. However, we cannot assume that every document containing t is drawn from the same language model. So there is some risk in using the mean and it should be minimized. The risk $\hat{R}(t,d)$ for a term in a document can be modeled using the geometric distribution [16], then we can use this risk function as a mixing parameter in our calculation of $\hat{p}(t \mid M_d)$.

4.2 Language Modeling Improved by Block Information

In the language modeling mentioned above, it is assumed that a whole document talks about a unique topic and can be used to generate the query. However, with the Web page getting more and more miscellaneous, the performance of this statistical model tends to be degraded. We notice two common problems for the normal language modeling when it is applied to web documents containing multi-blocks.

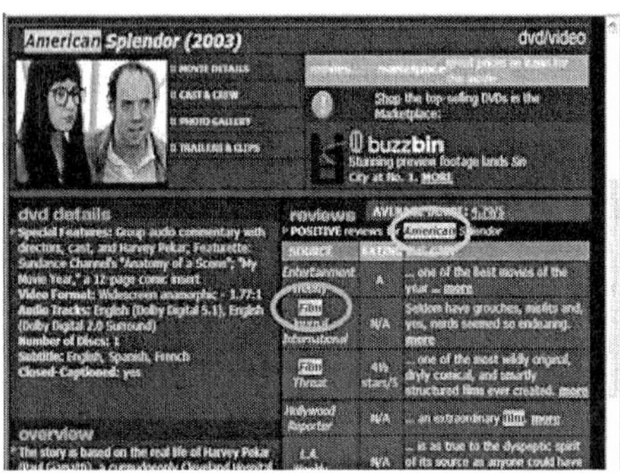

Fig. 1. A sample Web page in our test collection, with the query terms occurring in different blocks

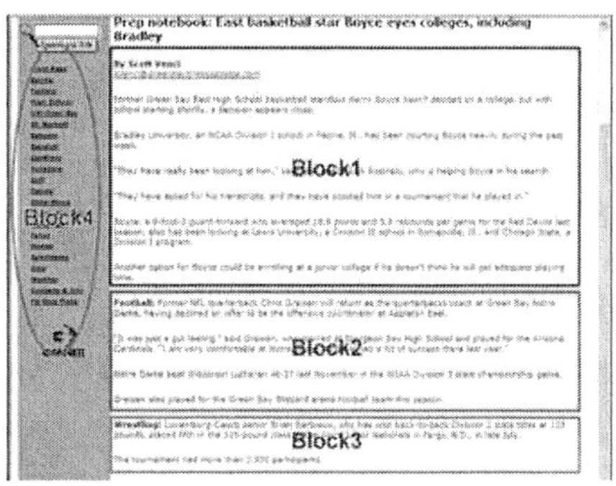

Fig. 2. A sample Web page in our test collection, which contain several blocks with different topics

First, let's suppose the query is "American film" and the Web pages discussing American film should be retrieved. For the sample in Figure 1, if we take the whole

Web page as a single model, it may easily generate the query "American film" and be judged as relevant. This is what we really don't expect because "American" here is a part of the movie title while "Film" is part of the reviewer name. The page does not mention anything about American film. If the representation clue that the two terms occurs in different blocks is used, this page will not be considered relevant any more. Actually, in such scenario, different models should be estimated for each block, instead of a single one for the whole document.

The second problem is about the multi-topics of one Web page. See the sample in Figure 2, several topics are discussed, including a basketball star (Block1), football (Block2), wresting (Block3) and a navigation bar (Block4). Such documents should be less relevant than those only talk about basketball star. In another word, we want to measure the "topic consistence" of the blocks in one page.

After these observations, we propose *Block-based Language Modeling (BLM)*. The assumptions behind such approach are:

- Web pages contain several blocks and they may discuss different topics.
- Query terms are regarded as more relevant to the Web page when they co-occur in the same block than when they are distributed over different blocks.
- The block which has more similar language model with the Web page is more relevant with the major idea of the whole page. And such blocks should contribute more for the relevance of the Web page to a query.

Then BLM refined the modeling into two major components:

- The probability of a query occurring in a block $\hat{p}(Q \mid M_B)$, where M_B means the estimated model for a block. I.e. language models are estimated not on the basis of whole Web page, but on the blocks within one page. In the case mentioned above, each $\hat{p}(Q \mid M_B)$ will be less than $\hat{p}(Q \mid M_d)$ because not all terms co-occurs in the same block.
- The probability of the block occurring in the Web page $\hat{p}(B \mid M_d)$, where B is a block. If a web focuses on one topic, the model of each block tends to be more compatible with that of whole page. In our BLM approach, we use the probability $\hat{p}(B \mid M_d)$ to represent the consistence between block and whole page.

Then the $\hat{p}(Q \mid M_d)$ can be revised as

$$\sum_{i=1}^{|B|} \hat{p}(Q \mid M_{Bi}) \cdot \hat{p}(B_i \mid M_d) \tag{4}$$

where $|B|$ is the number of all the blocks within a page, B_i is the *ith* block, and M_{Bi} is the model of B_i estimated using language model.
Actually, we find that the formula can also be derived with Bayesian rules:

$$\hat{p}(Q \mid M_d) = \sum_{i=0}^{|B|} \hat{p}(Q, B_i \mid M_d) = \sum_{i=0}^{|B|} \hat{p}(Q \mid B_i, M_d) \cdot \hat{p}(B_i \mid M_d) = \sum_{i=0}^{|B|} \hat{p}(Q \mid B_i) \cdot \hat{p}(B_i \mid M_d) \tag{5}$$

here $\hat{p}(Q \mid B_i, M_d) = \hat{p}(Q \mid B_i)$ because once a block is given, it only occurs in a unique document. Compared with the normal method, we use language modeling to estimate the model of each block. So $\hat{p}(Q|B_i)$ should be replace with $\hat{p}(Q|M_{Bi})$, finally we get formula (6), which is consistent with formula (4).

$$\hat{p}(Q|M_d) = \sum_{i=0}^{|B|} \hat{p}(Q|B_i) \cdot \hat{p}(B_i|M_d) \approx \sum_{i=0}^{|B|} \hat{p}(Q|M_{Bi}) \cdot \hat{p}(B_i|M_d) \tag{6}$$

One potential problem for this approach is that, blocks often have different length. For the longer block, the probability that all terms of it occur simultaneously will be very low, i.e. the estimated value of $\hat{p}(B|M_d)$ will be very low. For shorter block, the estimated value will be higher compared to longer one. This make the shorter block more "consistent" with the whole page, which contradicts with our intuition that longer block will dominate the content of a document. So we propose another version of BLM, in which $\hat{p}(B|M_d)$ is normalized using the length of block:

$$\hat{p}(Q|M_d) \approx \sum_{i=0}^{|B|} \hat{p}(Q|M_{Bi}) \cdot \sqrt[|Bi|]{\hat{p}(B_i|M_d)} \tag{7}$$

where $|B_i|$ is the number of term tokens in block B_i. We call this *block length normalization*.

5 Experiment

In this section, we first briefly introduce the segmentation algorithm SUPS. Then the data set, score method and evaluation metrics are presented. Finally, the performance of BLM is compared with that of the normal language modeling approach.

5.1 Page Segmentation

The designers of Web pages often use HTML tags such as <TD>, <HR>, <DIV>, <LI> etc. to organize content layout. For example, different topics are often put within different <TD> tags or separated by different <HR> tags. Our SUPS approach explores the web content structure and divides it into different topics. It is composed of following four steps:

1. Convert the HTML based Web page to XML based DOM tree. The major rules we apply for parse includes: (1) the non-presentation or non-decoration tags such as script, comment, process instrument, control, and identity declaration are dropped; (2) The end element tag for <BR>, <LI>, <DL> are appended if they are missing; (3) The <IMG> and <A> tags are omitted and only their text information is kept; (4) A virtual blank <Separator/> tag is devised to distinguish visual block boundaries. We will substitute a single <Separator/> for each <HR> tag, successive <BR> tags and blank layout tags whose "width" and "height" properties are not zero. Finally we can get a well-formed DOM tree rooted with <HTML> element.
2. Calculate Degree of Isolation (DoI). DoI is used to describe the difference between a block and its other siblings. First, DoI of node N is initialized with $1/c$ where c is the child nodes count of N's parent node. Then we traverse the

block. If <Separator/> node NS is found, we will uniformly assign its DoI to its left sibling nodes and right sibling nodes before removing NS. By a top-down iterative process, DoI of all nodes can be calculated.
3. Calculate Degree of Coherence (DoC). DoC is used to measure the confidence that a block can be regarded as an integral part. We define following heuristic rules: (1) If a node only contains text, its DoC is 1; (2) If a node has only one child node, it has the same DoC with the child node; (3) A node's DoC decreases in inverse ratio to its height in the tree. (4) The more structures a node's children share, e.g. tag name, background color, font type and font color, the more coherent the subtree is. Based on above rules, we can compute the DoC value for each node by a bottom-up iterative process.
4. Extract blocks from DOM tree. We define two set, Candidate Block Set S1 and Block Set S2. Two permitted threshold, PDoI and PDoc, are defined for DoI and DoC respectively. After that, the segmentation is performed in both top-down and bottom-up manners: (1) agglomeration process by DoI. DOM tree is traversed by breadth first policy and if the node DoI is greater than PDoI, put this block into S1; otherwise, merge it with neighbor block that has smaller DoI until the sum of DoI is greater than PDoI; (2) separation process by DoC: for each block in S1, if its DoC is greater than PDoC, put it into S2, otherwise, partition this block by repeating process (1); (3) When Set S1 is empty, stop our algorithm.

In short, SUPS combines top-town and bottom-up iterative calculation, and integrates heuristic rules and structure induction in a single model. Using this algorithm, Web page can be automatically partitioned into isolated blocks. The granularity of partition can be controlled by PDoI and PDoC.

5.2 Experiment Setup

We got the data set in following way: first 9 queries are excerpted from a query log[2]. Then for each one of them, we used Google web API [3] to randomly select 40 pages from top 120 results ranked by Google. The random selection ensures that some pages are relevant while some are less or not relevant. Then a web crawler tried to download these 360 pages. A embed DOM builder dynamically translated such HTML pages to well-formed DOM trees which were later parsed and partitioned into blocks by SUPS algorithm. Because some URLs were not available at download time and some not well-formed pages cannot be translated to DOM tree, we got only 296 pages and 1949 blocks finally. Table 1 shows more details.

We ask 7 volunteers to mark a score for each Web page in terms of its relevance to corresponding query. These volunteers are all graduate students engaging in information retrieval. The result will be affected by personal opinions. We hope following instructions can help volunteers provide objective evaluation as much as possible:

[2] A query log from MSN search engine: http://search.msn.com/
[3] Google Web API: http://www.google.com/apis/

- Rank 10: relevant, the page exactly matches the query.
- Rank 5-7: some relevant, the page refers to some aspects of the query.
- Rank 1-3: less relevant, only a tiny aspect of the query is mentioned.
- Rank 0: not relevant at all.

Table 1. The test data set and some statistics. "Page Num" means the number of the Web page about one topic, "Avg Page Length" means averge number of term tokens in each page, "Block Num" means the whole number of blocks about one topic, "Avg Block Num" means average number of blocks in each page and "Avg Block Length" means average number of term tokens in each block

Query	Page Num	Avg Page Length	Block Num	Avg Block Num	Avg Block Length
American film	39	317	292	7.5	42.4
basketball star	40	243.2	281	7	34.7
Apple corporation	33	246.1	202	6.1	40.3
Web service	39	227.1	247	6.3	36
Web service enhancement	31	223.8	194	6.3	35.5
IIS 5 isolation mode	22	271.6	141	6.4	42.4
Web mining	33	222.6	202	6.1	36.5
Harvard university	30	111.8	164	5.5	20.3
Car manufacturer	29	262.7	226	7.8	33.7

We use the average scores to rank the pages and call the final ranking "standard ranking", which will be used to evaluate both LM and BLM approaches.

5.3 Evaluation Metrics

We use two metrics, KDist and top n score, to evaluate the performance. First, to evaluate the quality of whole ranking, we measure the average "distance" between "standard ranking" and the ranking generated by different language modeling approaches. The KDist distance measure, based on Kendall's - τ rank correlation and used for comparing induced rank orders is defined as follows:

Consider two partially ordered lists of Web pages, τ_1 and τ_2 , each of length m. Let U be the union of the Web pages in τ_1 and τ_2 . If δ_1 is U - τ_1 , then let τ_1' be the extension of τ_1 , where τ_1' contains δ_1 appearing after all the Web pages in τ_1 .[4] We extend τ_2 analogously to yield τ_2' . KDist is then defined as:

$$\mathrm{KDist}(\tau_1, \tau_1) = \frac{|\{(\mu,\nu) : \tau_1', \tau_2' \text{ disagree on order of } (\mu,\nu), \mu \neq \nu\}|}{(|U|)(|U|-1)} \tag{8}$$

In other words, KDist(τ_1 , τ_2) is the probability that τ_1' and τ_2' disagree on the relative ordering of a randomly selected pair of distinct nodes $(\mu,\nu) \in U \times U$. In the current

[4] The Web pages in δ are placed with the same ordinal rank at the end of τ .

work, we only compare lists containing the same sets of Web pages, so that KDist is identical to Kendall's τ distance. Let "standard ranking" as τ_s, LM ranking vector as τ_{LM}, and BLM ranking vector as τ_{BLM}. In order to compare LM ranking and BLM ranking, we compute KDist(τ_s, τ_{LM}) and KDist(τ_s, τ_{BLM}). The lower the value is, the better the model performs.

The other metric we used is what we called *top n scores*. We think this metric is also very important because in most cases, web surfers only care about the top ranked pages. The scores of top n pages ranked by one model are summed up and the sum is compared with that of "standard ranking". The ratio η is given out as following:

$$\eta_m = \frac{sum \text{ scores of top n ranked pages returned by model m}}{sum \text{ scores of top n ranked pages in standard ranking pages}}. \tag{9}$$

5.4 Results and Analysis

The baseline, LM, is implemented using the unigram language model introduced in [1] because of its simplicity and effectiveness. Our BLM improves this model using block information and two versions are implemented: BLM with no normalization (BNN) and BLM with block length normalization (BBN). Figure 3 shows the KDist results and Figure 4 presents the improvements over baseline:

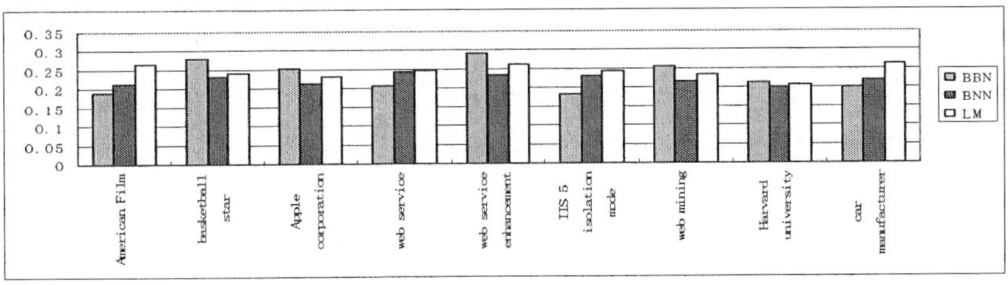

Fig. 3. KDist distances using different models. The lower the value, the better the ranking is compared with "standard ranking"

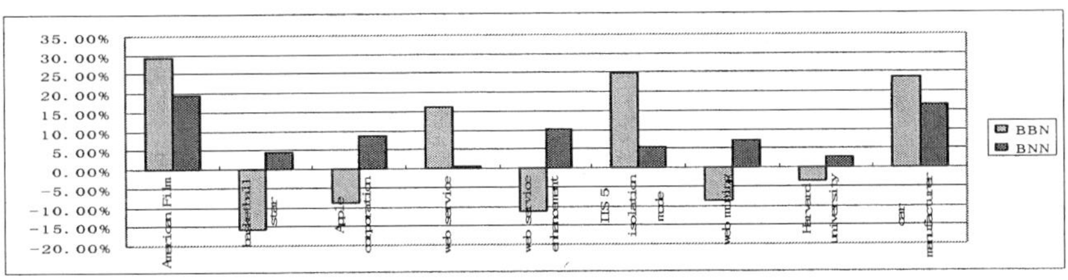

Fig. 4. Improvement of KDist distances using BBN and BNN models

As it can be seen from the figures, BLM with no normalization (BNN) can enhance the page ranking in all 9 queries. But when we normalize the block length

(BBN), the results are polarized, i.e. for some queries BBN obtains much greater improvement than BNN, while for others, BBN worsen the ranking result. We observed the result data and found two potential reasons for the polarization of BBN:

- For longer block, while $\hat{p}(B_i \mid M_d)$ tends to be tiny, $\hat{p}(Q \mid M_{Bi})$ is likely to be higher because longer block has higher probability to generate a query.
- Short block is more prone to be dominated by noisy terms. If block normalization is applied, in formula 7, the weight of noisy will be increased and the performance will be degraded.

In future, we will investigate whether block length is a key issue to concern. Nevertheless, we can see that in Figure 5, BBN can obtain about 5.06% while BNN achieve 8.34% improvement when the improvement averaged on the whole dataset.

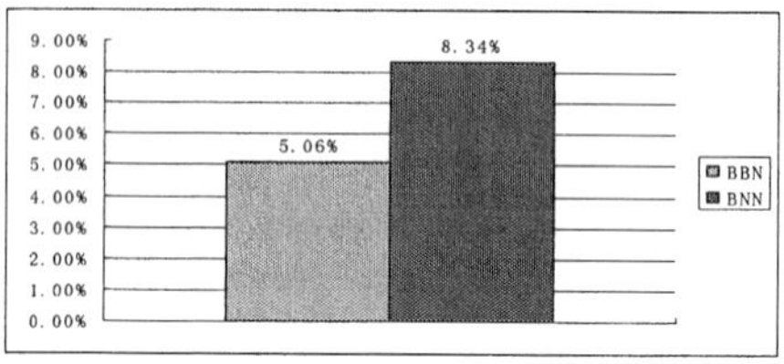

Fig. 5. Average KDist improvement using BBN and BNN models

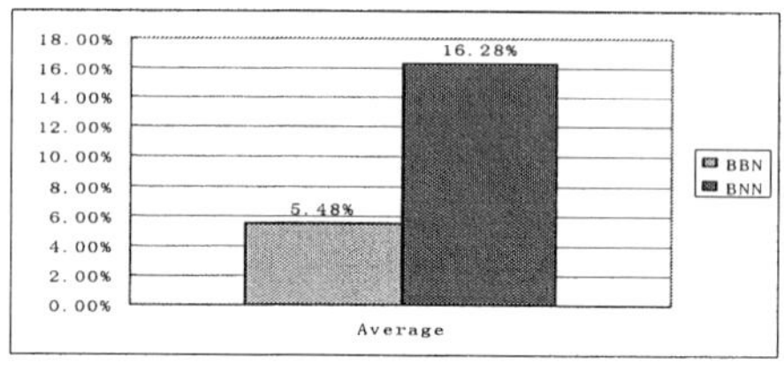

Fig. 6. Average improvement of top 10 ranked pages' scores using BBN and BNN models

As to the other metric, Figure 6 presents the average improvement on the whole dataset and Figure 7 shows the improvement of top 10 score for each topic. Compared with LM, BBN and BNN obtain 5.48% and 16.28% improvements respectively. Here the polarization problem also exists for BBN.

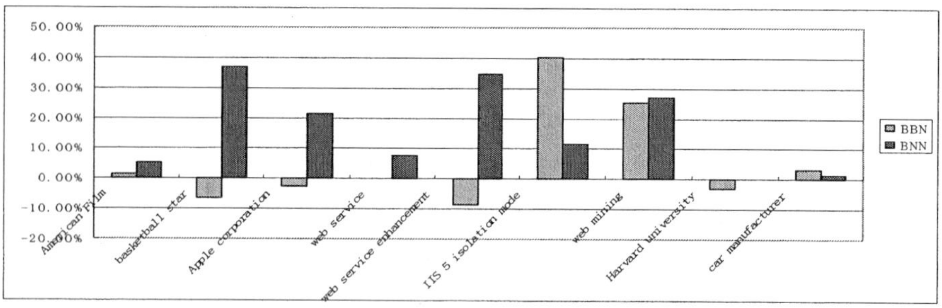

Fig. 7. Improvement of top 10 ranked pages' scores using BBN and BNN models

In summary, our experiment shows BLM approach outperforms the normal one in most cases. Especially, BNN improves 8.34% and 16.28% according to KDist and top 10 score respectively.

6 Conclusion and Future Work

In this paper, we proposed Block-based Language Modeling (BLM), a novel approach to integrate Web page segmentation and language modeling. It contains two major components: The probability of a query occurring in a block and the probability of the block occurring in the Web page. The first one means that we estimate the model not for page, but for blocks in page. The second used to measure the degree a page focuses on a single topic. Experimental results show this approach is promising and some interesting issues can be further investigated.

In future, we try to find more sophisticated block normalization method and the idea of BLM will be tested on larger collections like TREC 2001.

References

1. Ponte, J. and Croft, W., A Language Modeling Approach to Information Retrieval, in Proc. 21st annual international ACM SIGIR conference on Research and development in information retrieval, 1998 SIGIR.
2. Kaasinen, E., Aaltonen, M., Kolari, J., Melakoski, S., and Laakko, T., Two Approaches to Bringing Internet Services to WAP Devices, in Proc. 9th International World Wide Web Conference, 2000, pp. 231-246.
3. Lin, S. H. and Ho, J. M., Discovering Informative Content Blocks from Web Documents, in Proc. ACM SIGKDD'02, 2002.
4. Wong, W. and Fu, A. W., Finding Structure and Characteristics of Web Documents for Classification, In ACM SIGMOD Workshop on Research Issues in Data Mining and Knowledge Discovery(DMKD), Dallas, TX., USA, 2000.
5. Chen, J., Zhou, B., Shi, J., Zhang, H., and Wu, Q., Function Based Object Model towards Website Adaptation, in Proc. 10th International World Wide Web Conference, 2001.
6. Yang, Y. and Zhang, H., HTML Page Analysis Based on Visual Cues, in 6th International Conference on Document Analysis and Recognition, Seattle, USA, 2001.
7. Cai, D., Yu, S., Wen, J.R., and Ma, W.Y., Extracting Content Structure for Web Pages based on Visual Representation, In the 5th Asia Pacific Web Conference, 2003.
8. Embley, D. W., Jiang, Y., and Ng, Y.-K, Record-boundary discovery in Web documents, in Proc. 1999 ACM SIGMOD international conference on Management of data, Philadelphia PA, 1999, pp. 467-478.
9. Yu S., Cai D., Wen, J.R. and Ma, W.Y., Improving pseudo-relevance feedback in Web information retrieval using Web page segmentation, in Proc. 12th World Wide Web Conference, Budapest, Hungary, 2003.
10. Cai, D., Yu, S. , Wen, J.R., Ma, W.Y., Block-based Web Search, in Proc. 27th annual international ACM SIGIR conference on Research and development in information retrieval, 2004.
11. Yi, L., Liu, B. and Li, X. Eliminating Noisy Information in Web Pages for Data Mining, In Proc. ACM SIGKDD International Conference on Knowledge Discovery and Data Mining(KDD-2003), Washington, DC, USA, August, 2003.
12. Song, R., Liu, H., Wen, J.R., Learning Block Importance Models for Web Pages, In Proc. 13th World Wide conference (WWW2004), May 2004.

13. Cai, D., He, X., Wen, J.R. and Ma, W.Y., Block-level Link Analysis. In Proc. 27th annual international ACM SIGIR conference on Research and development in information retrieval, 2004.
14. Zhai, C., and Lafferty, J. A Study of Smoothing Methods for Language Models Applied to Ad Hoc Retrieval, In Proc. ACM SIGIR conference on Research and development in information retrieval, 2001.
15. Berger, A. and Lafferty, J. Information Retrieval as Statistical Translation. In Proc. ACM SIGIR conference on Research and development in information retrieval, 1999.
16. Zelen, M. and Severo, N. "Probability Functions" Handbook of Mathematical Functions. National Bureau of Standards Applied Mathematics Series No. 55, 1964.
17. Kleinber, J. Authoritative Sources in a Hyperlinked Environment, Journal of the ACM, Vol. 46, No. 5, pp. 604-622, 1999.
18. Page, L., Brin, S., Motwani, R. and Winograd, T. The PageRank Citation Ranking: Bringing Order to the Web, Technical Report, Stanford University, Stanford, CA, 1998.

Level-Based Link Analysis

Guang Feng[1,⋆], Tie-Yan Liu[2], Xu-Dong Zhang[1], Tao Qin[1], Bin Gao[3], and Wei-Ying Ma[2]

[1] MSPLAB, Department of Electronic Engineering, Tsinghua University, Beijing 100084, P. R. China
{fengg03, qinshitao99}@mails.tsinghua.edu.cn, zhangxd@tsinghua.edu.cn

[2] Microsoft Research Asia, No.49 Zhichun Road, Haidian District, Beijing 100080, P. R. China
{t-tyliu, wyma}@microsoft.com

[3] LMAM, School of Mathematical Sciences, Peking University, Beijing 100871, P. R. China
gaobin@math.pku.edu.cn

Abstract. In order to get high-quality web pages, search engines often resort retrieval pages by their ranks. The rank is a kind of measurement of importance of pages. Famous ranking algorithms, including PageRank and HITS, make use of hyperlinks to compute the importance. Those algorithms consider all hyperlinks identically in sense of recommendation. However, we find that the World Wide Web is actually organized with the natural multi-level structure. Benefiting from the level properties of pages, we can describe the recommendation of hyperlinks more reasonably and precisely. With this motivation, a new level-based link analysis algorithm is proposed in this paper. In the proposed algorithm, the recommendation weight of each hyperlink is computed with the level properties of its two endings. Experiments on the topic distillation task of TREC2003 web track show that our algorithm can evidently improve searching results as compared to previous link analysis methods.

1 Introduction

With the explosive growth of the Web, it becomes more and more difficult for surfers to find valuable pages in such huge repository. Consequently, search engines come forth to help them to retrieve appropriate and valuable web pages.

At the very beginning, almost all search engines worked in the same manner as conventional information retrieval systems where only relevance scores are utilized to sort pages for a certain query. Whereas, researchers found that this scheme merely led to a poor result in the web. The top-ranking pages were often not the most valuable ones and sometimes were even rubbish. In other words, high relevance score does not mean high quality.

⋆ This work was performed at Microsoft Research Asia.

Y. Zhang et al. (Eds.): APWeb 2005, LNCS 3399, pp. 183–194, 2005.

In order to get high-quality pages, search engines turned to resort retrieval pages by their importance. PageRank [2] and HITS [6] are two of the most popular algorithms, which utilize hyperlinks to compute the importance of each page. Taking relevance and rank into account, the quality of top-ranking retrieval pages can be improved by much.

More generally speaking, PageRank, HITS and other methods that use hyperlinks to measure the importance of pages are referred to as link analysis algorithms in the literature. The hyperlink between two web pages is treated as a kind of recommendation from source to destination. If there is a hyperlink from page A to page B, we believe A endorses B for its importance. Hence, the Web can be considered as a tremendous voting system. With the continuous iteration of voting, each page will get a stable measurement of its importance eventually.

Previous works [1][2][3][4][6][8] showed the effectiveness and efficiency of link analysis algorithms, which consider each hyperlink to be identical in sense of recommendation. However, we argue it is not the best way of utilizing hyperlinks although it has worked well. Optimally, different hyperlinks should have different weights in the voting process. For example, a hyperlink from the portal of a website to a common page should have stronger recommendation than a hyperlink from the common page to the portal. And we believe that the weight of a hyperlink should be decided by the level properties of its two ending pages.

With such a motivation, we introduce a new concept to link analysis algorithms, named *level-based link analysis*. Compared to previous algorithms, each hyperlink will be assigned a weight to express its strength of recommendation. By applying this concept, almost all previous link analysis algorithms can be refined with only a little modification to the adjacent matrix of web graph. In following sections, we will show how to combine traditional link analysis methods with this level-based concept in details.

The rest of this paper is organized as follows. In Section 2, we review some previous works to show the common process of link analysis. In Section 3, we describe the level-based link analysis in details. The experiments and corresponding results are shown in Section 4. Finally, we give the concluding remarks and future works in Section 5.

2 Related Works

We might feel that hyperlinks make up a great part of the Web from the saying "The Web is a hyperlinked environment" [6]. In the literature, link analysis algorithms have shown their success in measuring the importance of pages. Among them, PageRank and HITS are two of the widely-recognized representatives.

Before dropping in the detailed descriptions of them, we will give some basic definitions first. In many works, the Web were modelled as a directed graph

$$G = < V, E > ,$$

where $V = \{1, 2, \cdots, n\}$ is the collection of nodes, each of which represents a page; and $E = \{< i, j > | i, j \in V\}$ is the collection of edges, each of which represents a hyperlink. For example, $< i, j >$ means a hyperlink from page i to page j.

The adjacent matrix A of the web graph is defined as follows:

$$A_{ij} := \begin{cases} 1, & \text{if} < i, j > \in E \\ 0, & \text{otherwise} \end{cases} . \tag{1}$$

That is, if there is a hyperlink from page i to page j, $A_{ij} = 1$. Otherwise, $A_{ij} = 0$. This matrix is the core component of link analysis algorithms.

2.1 HITS

The HITS algorithm assigns two numeric properties to each page, called authority score and hub score. The higher authority score a page has, the more important it will be. If a page points to many pages with high authority score, it will obtain a high hub score. If a page is pointed by many pages with high hub score, it will obtain a high authority score symmetrically. Hub scores and authority scores exhibit a mutually reinforcing relationship. We can obtain the two scores of each page in an iterative manner.

Let $a = (a_1, a_2, \cdots, a_n)^T$ and $h = (h_1, h_2, \cdots, h_n)^T$ denote the authority and hub scores of the web graph respectively. Without regard to normalization, the iteration process can be formulated as follows [9]:

$$a_i^{(t+1)} = \sum_{j:<j,i>\in E} h_j^{(t)} , \tag{2}$$

$$h_i^{(t+1)} = \sum_{j:<i,j>\in E} a_j^{(t)} . \tag{3}$$

Representing them with matrix, the above equations will be

$$a^{(t+1)} = A^T h^{(t)} = \left(A^T A\right) a^{(t)} , \tag{4}$$

$$h^{(t+1)} = A a^{(t)} = \left(A A^T\right) h^{(t)} . \tag{5}$$

It can be proved that the stable values of a and h (denoted by a^* and h^*) will be the principal eigenvectors of $A^T A$ and AA^T respectively, when $A^T A$ as well as AA^T has unique principal eigenvector [5].

2.2 PageRank

The PageRank algorithm assigns one numeric property, called PageRank, to each page to represent its importance. This algorithm simulates a random walk process in the web graph. Suppose there is a surfer in an arbitrary page of the Web. At each step, he/she will transfer to one of the destination pages of the hyperlinks on the current page with probability ε, or to another page in the whole graph with probability $1 - \varepsilon$. This process can also be formulated in an iterative manner.

Firstly, normalize each row of the adjacent matrix A with its sum and get a probability matrix $\overline{A}$. Then the above random walk can be represented as

$$\overline{\overline{A}} = \varepsilon \overline{A} + (1 - \varepsilon) U \ , \tag{6}$$

where U is a uniform probability transition matrix, all elements of which equal to $1/n$ (n is the dimension of U). Denote $\pi = (\pi_1, \pi_2, \cdots, \pi_n)^T$ as the PageRank of the whole web graph. It can be computed through the below iterative process:

$$\pi^{(k+1)} = \overline{\overline{A}}^T \pi^{(k)} \ . \tag{7}$$

Again, the stable value of π corresponds to the principal eigenvector of $\overline{\overline{A}}^T$ when $\overline{\overline{A}}^T$ has unique principal eigenvector [5].

3 Level-Based Link Analysis

In this section, we illustrate the concept of level-based link analysis. First, we discuss how to compute the weight of each hyperlink so as to define the level-based adjacent matrix. Then we show how to add this concept to existing link analysis algorithms.

3.1 Weight of the Hyperlink

As aforementioned, the existing link analysis methods treat all hyperlinks identically in sense of recommendation. However, as we know, the Web is not organized with a flat structure but multi-level structure. Thus, hyperlinks should be treated non-identically. Then comes the problem of how to define the difference between two hyperlinks. To tackle it, we make use of the level properties of pages in the website. In particular, this can be illustrated by Fig.1, where a website is denoted by a tree; the circles denote pages; the solid lines denote hyperlinks while the dash lines denote the organization structure.

Suppose i_1, i_2 and j are three web pages. As we can see, there are two hyperlinks pointing to j from i_1 and i_2 respectively. Denote the level property of page i by l_i. If i is on the highest level, let $l_i = 1$. And l_i increases by one when i goes down to the next level of the tree. Here we use $w_{j|i}$ to represent the weight of the hyperlink from i to j and use $anc(i, j)$ to denote the ancestor of these two pages.

We show three cases of organization and hyperlinks in Fig. 1(a) to (c). The question is which hyperlink is stronger in sense of recommendation with respect to j, the one from i_1 or from i_2. To answer this question, we design two intuitive and reasonable rules as follows.

Rule 1. *In the case shown in* Fig.1(a), *where the joint-ancestor of* i_1 *and* j *is the same as the joint-ancestor of* i_2 *and* j, *we claim that* $< i_1, j >$ *has stronger recommendation than* $< i_2, j >$, *i.e.*

$$w_{j|i_1} > w_{j|i_2}$$
$$\text{when } l_{i_1} < l_{i_2} \text{ and } l_{anc(i_1,j)} = l_{anc(i_2,j)} \ .$$

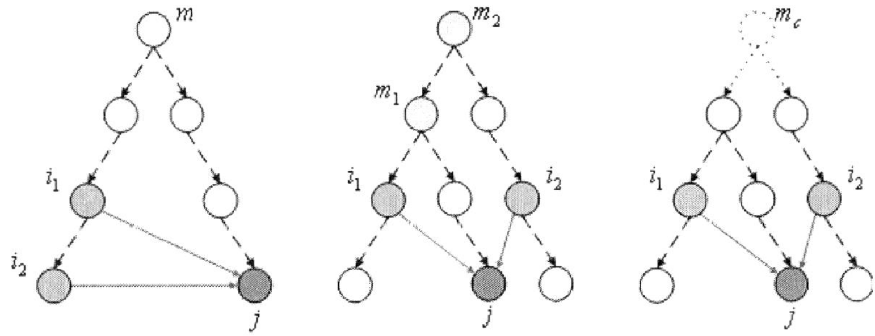

(a) (b) (c)

Fig. 1. Illustration for weight of the hyperlink

Generally speaking, a higher-level page will choose its hyperlinks more cautiously. Once a hyperlink appears in it, it means that the destination of the hyperlink is endorsed with much deliberation of the author. Thus, the hyperlink would probably have strong recommendation. So, we claim that the hyperlink from a higher-level page will have larger weight than the hyperlink from a lower one when other conditions are the same.

Rule 2. *In the case shown in* Fig.1(b), *where the joint-ancestor* m_1 *of* i_1 *and* j *is not the same as the joint-ancestor* m_2 *of* i_2 *and* j, *we claim that* $< i_2, j >$ *has stronger recommendation than* $< i_1, j >$, *i.e.*

$$w_{j|i_1} < w_{j|i_2}$$

$$\textit{when } l_{i_1} = l_{i_2} \textit{ and } l_{anc(i_1,j)} > l_{anc(i_2,j)} \ .$$

This claim is also fairly reasonable. Suppose the site with the portal m_2 focuses on the sports (its URL is http://www.***sports.com). And m_1 is the entry point of one sub-topic of that site. For example, the URL of m_2 is* http://www.***sports.com/football. As i_1 and j are in the same site and share the same topic, it is very common that there is a hyperlink between them. However, such a hyperlink may have more organizational sense than recommendation. Comparatively, the hyperlink between i_2 and j would represent more recommendation.

According to above discussion, we can define the *primary weight* of the hyperlink as follows:

$$\tilde{w}_{j|i} = \frac{1}{l_i \cdot l_{anc(i,j)}} \ . \tag{8}$$

In particular, if i and j have no ancestor, as shown in Fig.1(c), we can not come out a realization of (8). In this case, we construct a virtual page in the higher level than any existing pages, denoted by m_c (the dotted circle in Fig.1(c)). We consider this virtual page as the parent of the pages in the top level, or the root of all web sites. The level property of this virtual page is denoted by l_0. To guarantee the denominator in (8) is not zero, let $l_0 = 0.1$.

With the above discussions, we can define the *primary level-based adjacent matrix* $\tilde{L}$ as follows:

$$\tilde{L}_{ij} := \begin{cases} \tilde{w}_{j|i}, & \text{if} < i,j > \in E \\ 0, & \text{otherwise} \end{cases} . \tag{9}$$

The reason for which we emphasize "primary" here is that we will get the final-version of level-based adjacent matrix after taking more information into consideration as shown in the next sub section.

3.2 Level-Punishment

Intuitively, the higher level a page is on, the more important it is. Therefore, a page's importance should be punished by its level property l_i. Take HITS for example. After replacing A by $\tilde{L}$, (4) and (5) can be rewritten as follows:

$$a^{(t+1)} = \tilde{L}^T h^{(t)} = \left(\tilde{L}^T \tilde{L}\right) a^{(t)} , \tag{10}$$

$$h^{(t+1)} = \tilde{L} a^{(t)} = \left(\tilde{L} \tilde{L}^T\right) h^{(t)} . \tag{11}$$

We denote the level-punishment matrix by $P = diag(1/l_1, 1/l_2, \cdots, 1/l_n)$ and introduce it into the calculation of (10) and (11). Then we have

$$a^{(t+1)} = P \cdot \tilde{L}^T h^{(t)} = \left(P\tilde{L}^T P\tilde{L}\right) a^{(t)} , \tag{12}$$

$$h^{(t+1)} = P \cdot \tilde{L} a^{(t)} = \left(P\tilde{L} P\tilde{L}^T\right) h^{(t)} . \tag{13}$$

If define

$$L = P\tilde{L} , \tag{14}$$

we can obtain

$$a^{(t+1)} = L^T h^{(t)} = \left(L^T L\right) a^{(t)} , \tag{15}$$

$$h^{(t+1)} = L a^{(t)} = \left(L L^T\right) h^{(t)} . \tag{16}$$

Equation (15) and (16) is called level-based HITS (LBHITS) algorithm. Compared with (4) and (5), we only replaced A by L in LBHITS, where

$$L_{ij} = \frac{1}{l_i} \cdot \tilde{w}_{j|i} = \frac{1}{l_i \cdot l_j \cdot l_{anc(i,j)}} . \tag{17}$$

Up to now, we can reformulate the weight of the hyperlink as follows:

$$w_{j|i} = \frac{1}{l_i \cdot l_j \cdot l_{anc(i,j)}} . \tag{18}$$

Generally speaking, as long as replacing A by L in conventional link analysis algorithms, we can always obtain the level-based version of the original link analysis algorithms accordingly. We omit the corresponding deductions here for simplicity.

3.3 Convergence of Level-Based Link Analysis

In this subsection, we give the proofs of the convergence of LBHITS and level-based PageRank(LBPR). For other level-based link analysis algorithms, the proofs are similar.

Lemma 1. *If A is a symmetric matrix and x is a vector not orthogonal to the principal eigenvector of A, then*

$$\lim_{k \to \infty} A^k x = x^* \ ,$$

when the principal eigenvector of A is unique. And x^* equals to the unique principal eigenvector [5].

Theorem 1 (Convergence of LBHITS). *Replacing A by L in* (4) *and* (5)*, a and h will converge to a_L^* and h_L^* respectively.*

Proof. Let $h^{(0)}$ denote the arbitrary initial value of authority. Then after k steps of iteration, we can easily obtain

$$a^{(k)} = (L^T L)^{k-1} L^T h^{(0)} \ ,$$

$$h^{(k)} = (L L^T)^k h^{(0)} \ .$$

In terms of above lemma, because $h^{(0)}$ is an arbitrary value, we suppose it is not orthogonal to the principal eigenvector of LL^T. Hence, $h^{(k)}$ converges to a limit h_L^*. In the same way, $L^T h^{(0)}$ can be also considered to be not orthogonal to the principal eigenvector of $L^T L$ so that $a^{(k)}$ converges to a limit a_L^*. □

Theorem 2 (Convergence of LBPR). *Replacing A by L in computing LBPR, π will converge to π_L^*.*

Proof. After replacement, we can obtain

$$\overline{\overline{L}} = \varepsilon \overline{L} + (1 - \varepsilon) U \ .$$

Because L is finite and non-negative, $\overline{L}$ is finite and non-negative, too. Besides, U is a uniform probability transition matrix with any element positive so that $\overline{\overline{L}}$ must be finite and absolutely positive. Thereby $\overline{\overline{L}}$ is an irreducible probability transition matrix. It must have stationary distribution which can be computed as follows.

$$\overline{\overline{L}}^T \pi = \pi \ .$$

□

4 Experiments

In our experiments, the topic distillation task of TREC2003 web track was used to evaluate our algorithms. The data corpus in this task was crawled from .gov domain in 2002. It contains 1,247,753 documents, 1,053,111 of which are html files. We only used these html files in our experiments.

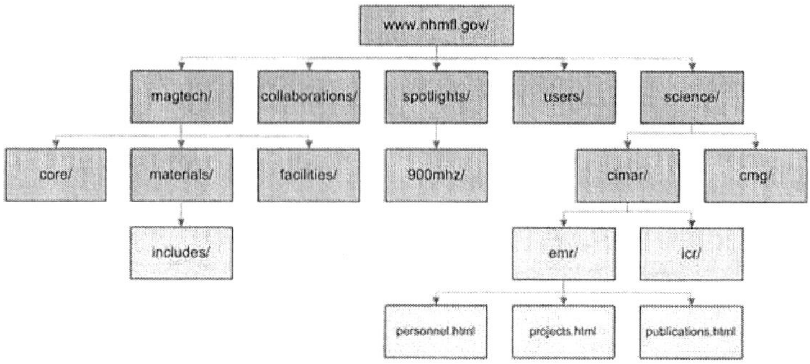

Fig. 2. A typical sitemap structure

There are totally 50 queries in this task. The number of positive answers (provided by the TREC committee) for each query ranged from 1 to 86 with an average of 10.32.

In order to realize the level-based link analysis, we will first show how to construct the sitemap. After that, we will describe the implementation of the baseline algorithms and then show the improved retrieval performance after introducing the link-based analysis to the retrieval framework.

4.1 Sitemap Construction

The sitemap is usually referred to as a regular service which is provided by many websites to represent their organizational structures. However, in our experiments, the sitemap is a data structure and contains more information than its original. The sitemap records the level properties of pages and the hierarchical structure of the website. In other words, it must record the parent-child relationship of pages. There is a constraint here that each page can have only one parent. In our current implementation, we define the sitemap strictly as a tree. A typical sitemap is showed in Fig. 2. Because the sitemap is implicit in many websites, we need an algorithm to construct it from the relationship among web pages automatically. For this purpose, we make use of the URLs of each page to construct sitemap according to the following rules.

1. For the URL whose format is like http://www.abc.gov/.../index.*, we regularize it to the same as http://www.abc.gov/.../. For the cases of default.*, home.* and homepage.*, we also regularize them in the same way.
2. For those pages with only one-level URL such as http://www.usgs.gov/ and http://www.bp.gov/, we treat them as the roots of new sitemaps.
3. For those pages with multi-level URL, we will find a parent for them. For example, the parent of http://www.aaa.gov/.../bb/ is http://www.aaa.gov/.../ while the parent of http://www.aaa.gov/.../bb/cc.* is* http://www.aaa.gov/.../bb/. If such parents happen to be not included in the data corpus (which means that these pages are missing in crawler process), we simply treat the original page as the root of a new sitemap.

In such a way, we construct a simple sitemap to display the structure of a website. We acknowledge the above process is not very accurate, but sitemap construction is not the focus of our paper although we can foresee that the better sitemap we have, the more effective our level-based link analysis will be.

4.2 Algorithm Confirmation

In web information retrieval system, when a query is submitted, we firstly compute the relevance score of each page with respect to the query and select top n relevant pages. Secondly, we integrate the relevance score and the rank score linearly into the final score that is used to resort the top n pages, formulating as follows:

$$Score = \alpha \cdot relevance + (1 - \alpha) \cdot rank \ . \tag{19}$$

In our experiment, we use BM2500 [10] as the relevance weighting function. The retrieval result without regard to rank scores is called baseline, where the mean average precision(MAP) is 0.1367 and the precision at ten(P@10) is 0.108. Compared with the best result of TREC2003 participants (with MAP of 0.1543 and P@10 of 0.1280), this baseline is reasonable.

Specifically, the rank in (19) used in both HITS and LBHITS are the authority values. To illustrate the advantage of our level-based link analysis algorithm, we choose HITS for comparison.

As we know, HITS is a query-dependent algorithm. In the original paper [6] of HITS, the size of the root set is 200 and the in-link parameter is 50. Besides, the intrinsic links are removed before computing authority and hub scores. We implement the HITS algorithm strictly according to the above descriptions.

In the implementation of our LBHITS algorithm, we use the same root set and in-link parameter as in the original HITS algorithm. However, we don't remove intrinsic links. The reason for removing intrinsic links is that "intrinsic links very often exist purely to allow for navigation of the infrastructure of a site" [6]. However, as we have punished the weight of these intrinsic links in our algorithm thus we don't need to remove them at all.

4.3 Experimental Result

In this subsection, we listed the retrieval performance of both HITS and LBHITS on the TREC 2003 topic distillation task.

We resort the relevance documents according to the composite score to select top-1000 pages for evaluation. Both MAP and P@10 are used to evaluate the performance of the algorithms.

In Fig.3 and Fig.4, we listed MAP and P@10 with respect to different α. The curves of both HITS+Relevance and LBHITS+Relevance converge to the baseline when $\alpha = 1$.

From the above figures, we can see when purely using the importance, LBHITS has already been better than HITS, although the corresponding performance is very low. After combining with relevance scores, both HITS+Relevance and LBHITS+Relevance get improvement over the baseline. For LBHITS+Relevance, the

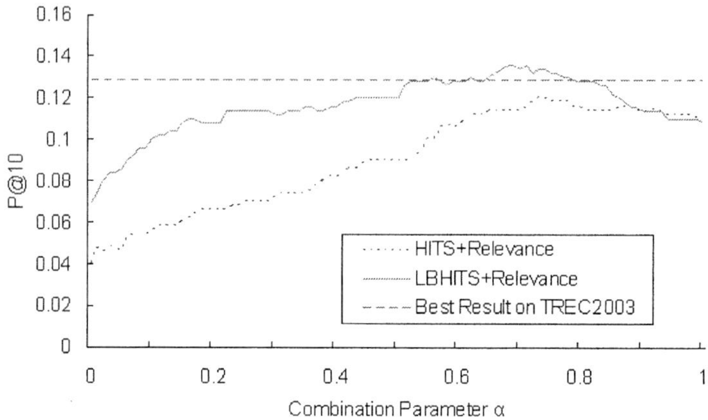

Fig. 3. Comparison of P@10 for Topic Distillation Task on TREC2003

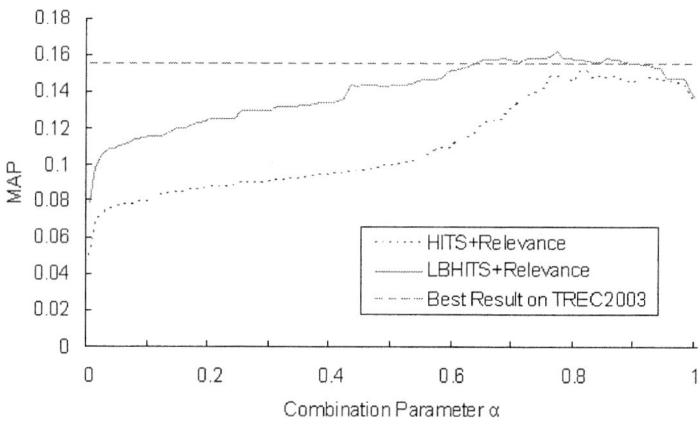

Fig. 4. Comparison of MAP for Topic Distillation Task on TREC2003

best P@10, 0.136, is achieved when $\alpha = 0.68$. This is better than HITS+Relevance and the baseline by 13.3% and 25.9% respectively. And the best MAP, 0.162, is achieved when $\alpha = 0.77$. This corresponds to 7% and 18.5% improvements over HITS+Relevance and the baseline.

Furthermore, HITS+Relevance performed worse than the best result of TREC 2003 while LBHITS+Relevance sometimes performs better than the best result. For the best case, LBHITS+Relevance achieves 6.3% and 5.0% improvements over the best result of TREC 2003 in sense of MAP and P@10 respectively.

Table 1. Retrieval Performance Comparison

Methods	P@10	MAP
Baseline	0.108	0.1367
HITS only	0.040	0.0502
LBHITS only	0.070	0.0789
HITS+Relevance	0.120	0.1514
LBHITS+Relevance	0.136	0.1620
Best Result on TREC2003	0.128	0.1543

As the experiments exhibit, level-based link analysis is effective and in accordance with our theoretical analysis in the previous sections. At the end of this section, we place the retrieval performance of all algorithms tested in our experiments in a table for a comprehensive comparison.

5 Conclusions

In this paper, we refine the previous link analysis algorithms by introducing the level properties of pages. We discuss the reasoning and propose how to define the weight of the hyperlink based on the level properties of its two endings. Through our experiments, we prove that the level-based link analysis can give rise to higher retrieval performance than the previous algorithms.

For the future works, there are still many issues that need to be explored. First, how to define the weight of the hyperlink to better represent the influence of the level property is still a challenge. In section 3, we just discover the trend of the weight with respect to the changing endings. However, it is just a naïve attempt. There must be some more precise and effective approaches to represent the strength of recommendation of the hyperlink. Second, as we have shown, the level property can improve the performance of rank. It is natural that we want to know whether it can improve the performance of relevance as well. Because the Web is naturally organized with multi-level structure, we believe that the level property should influence every aspect of researches on the Web, including the relevance and many other basic components.

References

1. Bharat, K. and Henzinger, M. R.: Improved algorithms for topic distillation in a hyperlinked environment. In Proc. 21st Annual Intl. ACM SIGIR Conference, pages 104-111. ACM, 1998
2. Brin, S. and Page, L.: The anatomy of a large-scale hypertextual Web search engine. In The Seventh International World Wide Web Conference, 1998.
3. Chakrabarti, S.: Integrating the Document Object Model with hyperlinks for enhanced topic distillation and information extraction. In the 10th International World Wide Web Conference, 2001.

4. Chakrabarti, S., Dom, B., Gibson, D., Kleinberg, J., Raghavan, P. and Rajagopalan, S.: Automatic resource list compilation by analyzing hyperlink structure and associated text. In Proc. of the 7th Int. World Wide Web Conference, May 1998.
5. Golub, G. H. and Van Loan, C. F.: Matrix Computations. Johns Hopkins Univ. Press, 1996.
6. Kleinberg, J.: Authoritative sources in a hyperlinked environment. Journal of the ACM, vol. 46, No. 5, pp. 604-622, 1999.
7. Langville, A. N. and Meyer, C. D.: Deeper Inside PageRank. Internet Mathematics, 2004.
8. Lempel, R. and Moran, S.: The stochastic approach for linkstructure analysis (SALSA) and the TKC effect. Proc. 9th International World Wide Web Conference, 2000.
9. Ng, A. Y., Zheng, A. X. and Jordan, M. I.: Link analysis, eigenvectors and stability. International Joint Conference on Artificial Intelligence (IJCAI-01), 2001.
10. Robertson, S. E.: Overview of the okapi projects. Journal of Documentation, Vol. 53, No. 1, 1997, pp. 3-7.

A Formal Approach to Evaluate and Compare Internet Search Engines: A Case Study on Searching the Chinese Web[†]

Kin F. Li[1], Yali Wang[1], Shojiro Nishio[2], and Wei Yu[1]

[1] Department of Electrical and Computer Engineering, University of Victoria
[2] Graduate School of Information Science and Technology, Osaka University

Abstract. The Internet has become an indispensable tool for finding information quickly using a search engine. The usefulness of the information retrieved, is open to questions. It depends on the keyword used, the search criteria, the judgement of the user, and also on the effectiveness of the search engine. There are some published works, mostly online, that evaluate Internet search engines. Most of them, however, are either informal, focused on a few aspects, subjectively qualitative, or ad-hoc without a rigorous approach. In this work, we propose a formal mathematical model to evaluate and compare search engines. As a case study, five popular Chinese search engines are examined.

1 Introduction

Pokorny provided an overview on existing web search engine architectures and concluded that current web search techniques are inefficient with respect to robustness, flexibility, and precision, and there is much room for improvements in new search techniques [15]. Each search engine has its own characteristics and effectiveness as different algorithms are used in the various stages of the web mining process. It is not an easy task to isolate and examine these algorithms' efficiency and effectiveness, not to mention that these trade secrets are often well guarded and difficult to obtain. Usually, one judges how good a search engine is by determining the relevance of the returned results. However, there are other important factors that one must consider in order to evaluate a search engine properly and thoroughly.

In this work, we propose a formal approach to evaluate and compare search engines. Our philosophy is that the evaluation of search engines should be consistent, reproducible, and unbiased. Over seventy *feature* (e.g., user interface, search criteria,

† This research was supported in part by the Ministry of Education, Culture, Sports, Science and Technology (MEXT) of Japan's Special Coordination Funds for promoting Science and Technology, under the project "Establishment of a Peer-to-Peer Information Sharing Platform for Mobile Computing Environment", and in part by "Priority Assistance for the Formation of Worldwide Renowned Centers of Research - The 21st Century Center of Excellence Program" of the MEXT.

Y. Zhang et al. (Eds.): APWeb 2005, LNCS 3399, pp. 195 – 206, 2005.

etc.) and *performance* (e.g., response time, quality of results, etc.) factors are considered and formulated in a mathematical evaluation model.

A survey has shown that China ranks second in the world in Internet usage. With only 8% of the Chinese population currently online, this projects a huge potential market for the Chinese Internet [5]. This motivates us to evaluate and compare five popular Chinese search engines to illustrate our proposed methodology. Though this case study shows the results of comparing Chinese search engines, our model is general enough to be used in evaluating search engines in other languages.

Web search engines in general, and Chinese search engines in particular, are introduced in Section 2. The selections of search sites and keywords are discussed in Section 3. A formal search engine evaluation model and its parameters are described in Section 4. Observations, analysis, and discussion of the results are made in Section 5. Finally, work in progress and future research directions are presented in Section 6.

2 Web Search Engines

One of the first search engine comparisons was published in 1997 where Kingoff observed that the search engines studied did not have many overlaps in the first page of results [8]. He concluded that the reviewed engines are different in their search focus, and each has its own niche. Since then, there are many search engine comparisons with the majority published on the web [19]. Most of these articles give tabulated qualitative comparisons of the engines under study, with no numerical scoring or ranking given. Many focus on specific aspects of the search and consider only a few evaluation factors. These informal approaches quite often introduce biased subjectivity and produce non-deterministic results. It is our goal to develop a mathematical approach that eliminates subjectivity as much as possible, and to formulate a model that is rigorous and suitable for automation.

2.1 Issues in Chinese Web Search

Due to the lack of white space and the variations in the Chinese spoken and written language, segmentation and indexing are more difficult tasks than that in the English language. Similar conclusions can be made for other Asian languages such as Japanese.

There are many different Chinese character sets in use. BIG5 or *Dawu* (Big Five), the traditional Chinese character set, is used in Taiwan and Hong Kong, while GB or *Guojia Biaozhun* (National Standard) is used to represent simplified Chinese characters in China. Increasingly, new web sites either use GBK, *Guojia Biaozhun Kuozhan* (Extended National Standard), or the multilingual Unicode Standard, both of which have a larger character set that include GB and BIG5. Interested readers should refer to [3] for a comprehensive introduction to Chinese character sets and encodings.

Since there is no white space between words in a sentence, depending on how one reads it or combines the characters, it is possible to interpret the same Chinese sentence in many ways. The effectiveness of word segmentation [7], and therefore the subsequent term extraction process, affect the search engine provider's capability to index its document base in an optimal fashion [10]. Furthermore, the white space problem also occurs at the search keyword level that dictates the relevance of the results, especially for algorithms using similarity measure between the query and document vectors.

2.2 Chinese Search Engine Comparison

There exists only a few informal comparisons on Chinese search engines. The Shanghai Society for Scientific and Technical Information introduced twenty-one Chinese search engines, and compared them based on topic classification, result ranking, hit recentness, page summarization, and coding support [16]. However, no ranking or scoring was given to the compared engines. Though this article was published in 1998, it remains as one of the most complete surveys on Chinese search engines yet. Another article published in the same year in eSAS World introduced twenty-six Chinese search engines, and described each engine's features. The author recommended Openfind, Tianwang, and Yahoo China [11].

The Popular Computer Week magazine published a report on five commonly used search engines in June 2000: Yahoo China, Sohu, Goyoyo, Zhaodaole, and Tonghua [14]. Parameters for comparison included home page features, search options, and keyword entry options. Yahoo China and Sohu were the top-ranked engines.

In August 2003, PC Computing published a comparison of ten search engines (Sina, Sohu, Netease, Chinaren, Wander, Excite China, Yahoo China, Cseek, Tianwang, and Zhaodaole) using various parameters including home page feature, advance search feature, coding support, dead links, total hits, search speed, and search result's relevance, precision, and ranking [13]. Sina was ranked the best search engine. In December 2003, an email survey to Chinese Netizen through iUserSurvey found the top three search engines to be Baidu, Google, and 3721 [4].

In a July 2004 report by the Tsinghua IT Usability Lab, Google, Yahoo China, Baidu, and Zhongsou were compared based on search result's relevancy, recall, and number of dead links [18]. Baidu and Google excelled in this short and simple comparison.

One striking fact from these search engine comparisons and surveys is that they produced a wide range of results recommending different top-ranked search engines. This inconsistency is part of the motivation for our research work. We aim to devise a thorough and complete formal model for search engine evaluation.

3 Selection of Chinese Search Engines and Keywords in Our Study

Currently, there are more than 300 active Chinese search engines. However, most of these engines' databases are relatively small and many are simply powered by the bigger search engines. One of our goals of this work is to provide an overview of the current features and capabilities of the prominent Chinese search engines. We are interested in the most commonly used search sites, as well as sites that are enhanced with attractive features. Therefore, we followed a rigorous process to select the most appropriate and representative engines for our study. After extensive browsing and searching, as well as reviewing the many topic directories, we identified forty-two most commonly referred to web search engines with the affix CN (China, 18 sites), HK (Hong Kong, 11 sites), and TW (Taiwan, 13 sites), including Cseek, Netease, Chinaren, Wander, Excite, Zhogshou, Sina, Sohu, Goyoyo, Zhaodaole, Baidu, Yahoo, Tianwang, and Google.

The list of forty-two search sites was still too large for a thorough and meaningful study. We then further eliminated search engines that are specialized in designated fields such as in consumer electronics; are powered by the same search engine host, for example, popular sites such as Shalala and Yam that use Google's search engine; and are practically inaccessible because they are frequently too busy or too slow. We also discovered that many search sites in Taiwan and Hong Kong are poorly designed and almost unusable due to their long response time and limited capability. Furthermore, most of the sites in these two regions are powered by their equivalent in China, for instance, a search on Google.HK and Google.CN yield almost the same results. We then decided to focus on search engines in China only.

3.1 Selected Search Engines

We finally settled on five search engines (statistics cited as of January 1, 2005):

- Google China (http://www.google.com/intl/zh-CN/): established on September 12, 2000, it has over 8 billion home pages, 880 million images, and 845 million messages, with many search options and features.
- Yahoo Yisou (http://www.yisou.com/): with the current version updated on June 21, 2004, it has over 5 billion web pages, 550 million images, 10 million music pieces, articles available in 38 languages, and many search options and features.
- Zong guo sou suo (http://www.zhongsou.com): founded in September 2002, it claims to have 2.8 billion web page and supports homonym rectification; it is also the first search engine in China to support trade classification.
- Baidu (http://www.baidu.com): founded in 1999, it provides services such as algorithmic search, enterprise search, and pay-for-performance; claiming more than 0.4 billion Chinese web pages, over 50 million images, and over 5 million MP3, it has a large geographic search range including Hong Kong, Taiwan, Macao, Singapore, and some web sites in North America and Europe; it also supports homonym rectification.
- Tianwang (http://e.pku.edu.cn): founded in October 29, 1997, and is very popular among academics, this Peking University site has over 1 billion home pages and can search other Chinese university sites as well as over 1,000 American universities'; it also supports ftp search.

3.2 Selection of Keywords

In order to make the analysis manageable, rare words are often used for the search in an effort to limit the number of hits for testing the capability and effectiveness of the search engines. For examples, 'crumpet' and 'polyphenol' were used in [12], and ten rare words were used in Ljosland's study [9]. In other cases, common words were used to evaluate the coverage of the respective search engines.

3.2.1 Keywords Selected

Two phrases and three of their variations are selected as keywords in this study. As shown in Fig. 1, a phrase of relatively rare occurrence, 'Chinese Search Engine Comparison', is used, an appropriate choice within the context of this work. The second phrase is 'Bird Flu', a hot news item since the beginning of 2004.

(a)	中文搜索引擎比较	A free search on 'Chinese search engine comparison'
(b)	"中文搜索引擎比较"	An exact search of 'Chinese search engine comparison'
(c)	"中文搜索引擎" "比较"	Search using two exact phrases of 'Chinese search engine' and 'comparison'
(d)	禽流感	A free search on 'bird flu'
(e)	"禽流感"	An exact search on 'bird flu'

Fig. 1. Keywords Used in This Study

The three non-exact search variations (a, c, and d) are used to 'fool' the search engines into finding mismatched items, as a preliminary test on their segmentation and retrieval capability. These issues will be discussed in more details in Section 5.1.

4 Evaluation Parameters

As mentioned previously, most existing Chinese search engine comparisons either simply review a few superficial factors, or focus on some parts of the search results, or rate several aspects of the site subjectively. In order to perform a thorough evaluation of the search engines and make meaningful comparisons, we need to explore and review all possible factors from various perspectives. After examining an exhaustive list of possible evaluation parameters, we concluded that the evaluation of a search engine must deal with two logical parts. The first part consists of parameters to evaluate the features and capabilities that enhance the usability of the search engine. The second part includes the various metrics to examine the performance of the search engine including the quality of the results and response time. One can thus evaluate a search engine for its *Feature* part and the *Performance* part, either jointly or separately.

Within each part, collections of related parameters are further classified into subgroups and sub-subgroups, resulting in a hierarchy of evaluation parameters. This hierarchical structure has the advantage of isolating the specific group of evaluation parameters one is interested in, as well as comparing several search engines with a particular focus. Seventy-nine parameters are used in our evaluation model that includes commonly used web metrics such as the ones found in [6].

4.1 Weighed Parameters and Score Equations

A hierarchical structure allows us to rate the search engines at different abstraction levels of details or interest. In general, the model or the score of a collection of parameters can be expressed as

$$\text{Score} = \sum_{i=1}^{X} w_i P_i \qquad (1)$$

Where w_i's are the weights assigned to the X parameters of that group. For example, the total score of a search engine is formulated as

$$w_{feature} * P_{feature} + w_{performance} * P_{performance} \qquad (2)$$

If one feels that performance is more important than the features of a search engine, the weights assigned may be 0.7 and 0.3, respectively. The scores for *Feature* and *Performance*, $P_{feature}$ and $P_{performance}$, in turn, are derived from subsequent weighted scoring equations at lower levels of the evaluation hierarchy. A negative weight can be used to indicate the undesirable impact of a parameter on the total score. For example, the higher the number of dead links (with a negative weight) in the results, the worse the engine is compared to others. The value of some parameters is either a 0 or 1 to indicate whether a feature or capability exists. A range between 0 and 1 is assigned to parameters that have various degrees of quality. The sum of the positive weights assigned to the parameters within a group must be equal to 1. This normalization ensures the consistency of weight distribution among the different groups.

The flexibility of tailoring the scoring system to individual needs makes the proposed evaluation model very attractive to search engine users, subscribers, and providers. As pointed out in a well-referenced workshop position paper [1], specific web search engines are effective only for some types of queries in certain contexts. Using our model and adjusting the weights of the seventy-two parameters, a user will be able to find, empirically, the particular search engine that best suits his/her needs. It should be emphasized that the methodology and the parameters examined in our evaluation model are language independent and can be applied to a wide range of search engines of various languages.

4.2 Feature Parameters

We have classified *Feature* parameters into six major categories as shown in Fig. 2:

1. Home Page Features: This category indicates how user friendly the home page is regarding various help and user selection menus. This group includes a user's evaluation of the home page, the availability and visibility of help links, result language selection, topic directory selection, and advanced search selection.
2. User Preferences: This category includes a choice of the home page language, the availability of safe search filtering, the control of the number of results per page, the choice of displaying the results in a new window, intelligent input correction, setting the search default, having search options within the result page, and news search.

3. Search Options: This category is further divided into the subgroups of search modifier, search field (title, url, links, etc.), search focus selection (web site, web page, directory, etc.), search constraint specification (language, file format, publication date, etc.), and search meta words for focused search (specified sites only, similar pages, geographic regions, etc.).
4. Keyword Entry Options: This category considers the capability of the search engine in stop word interpretation, case sensitivity, exact phrase specification, wildcard allowance, search by pronunciation, and Boolean operators.
5. Database: This category indicates the number of groupings arranged in directories and the total number of pages.
6. Result Features: This category reviews statistics and display type features such as whether there is indication for the total number of hits, the number of pages, and search time, the capability to search within the results, whether the results are ordered and numbered, whether the different file formats are allowed in the returned items, whether pay listing is allowed (a negative weight), web page snap, further search for related pages, and the presence of the hits' date, size, and summarization.

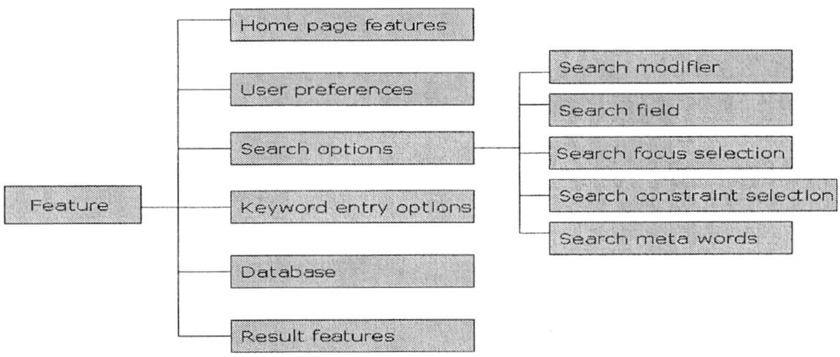

Fig. 2. Feature Parameters

For illustration purpose, we have assigned different weights to the six groups within *Feature*, according to the above order, 0.1, 0.1, 0.3, 0.2, 0.1, 0.2, respectively. We felt that the flexibility of having different search options is the most important factor among the six groups; hence the highest weight of 0.3 was used for that parameter. Equal weights are assigned to the parameters in other groups and subgroups. Table 1 in section 5.1 tabulates the results of the *Feature* group.

4.3 Performance Parameters

Three metrics are considered in *Performance*: the Response Time and the Total Number of Results as indicated on the result page, and the Quality of Results, as shown in Fig.3.

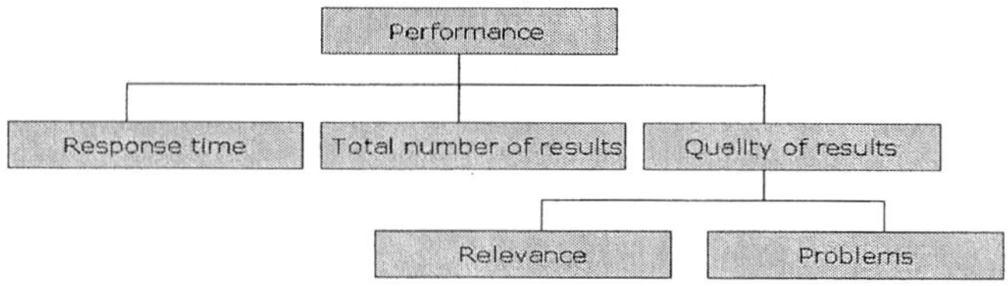

Fig. 3. Performance Parameters

The Quality of Results group consists of the subgroups Problems and Relevance. The Problems subgroup indicates the severity and frequency of problems encountered when one tries to access the search engine or the returned items. This includes the number of times that the search site is down during our experimentation, the number of broken links such as host not found, connection time out, and duplicates. All these parameters within the Problems subgroup carry equal but negative weights.

In order to obtain the Relevance score, we have solicited the assistance of several humans to examine the relevance of the returned items with respect to the keywords. The scores are averaged to eliminate any inherent potential bias and subjectivity in human interpretation.

5 Results, Comments, and Analysis

To collect search statistics, we followed a rigorously designed process based on the averaging principle. For the purpose of illustrating our evaluation methodology in this preliminary study, data were collected four times over a period of two weeks, on two Wednesdays and two Sundays to reflect workday and weekend patterns. On each day, searches were performed at 10am, 9pm, and 1am to examine usage at peak and other times. At each time, three rounds of searches separated by one-half hour were done to eliminate the effect of any burst traffic. All five keywords were used for searches on the five search engines. The top ten results were kept for each search. Through this process, we expect to discover average patterns and the degree of variations on response time, as well as update frequency as indicated in any changes in the number of hits in these thirty-six sets of data. The results show that Google and Yahoo updated most frequently, while Tianwang did not update its database throughout our experimentation period.

5.1 Chinese Language Specific Issues

The results from all five search engines exhibit the peculiarity of the Chinese language. As expected, results of (b) from Fig. 1 are limited while (a) returned items including the ones in (b) and (c). In addition, (a) also returned items with the independent phrases of 'Chinese', 'search', and 'engine comparison', in which engine was interpreted in a machinery sense. All five search engines exhibit this behaviour. Similarly in (d), documents with 'bird' (the first character) and 'flu' (the second and third character together) appeared together and separately when retrieved. This rendered the results in two categories either of which may suit the need of the particular user.

To further examine how each engine handles Chinese phrases, we have performed further experiments using additional keywords as shown in Fig. 4. AIDS is a very specialized word in Chinese and as expected, the free and exact search of AIDS (i) produced similar results. The left-hand-side word in (ii) is used for 'angel' in traditional literature, while the word on the right hand side is its modern English phonetic representation. Both forms are widely used these days. The results obtained, as expected, index the two variations into two distinct categories of documents. Similarly, the two variations of ice cream (iii), both English phonetic representations, resulted in two groups of non-overlapped documents. Finally, in (iv), two sets of documents each referencing a famous author either by his real name or pen name are returned, with some overlaps. These results point to the need of a Chinese synonym database to make the search more effective.

(i)	艾滋病 / "艾滋病"	A free search and an exact search of AIDS
(ii)	天使 / 安琪儿	The two variations of angel
(iii)	冰激凌 / 冰淇淋	The two variations of ice cream
(iv)	鲁迅 / 周树人	The pen name and real name of a famous author

Fig. 4. Additional Keywords

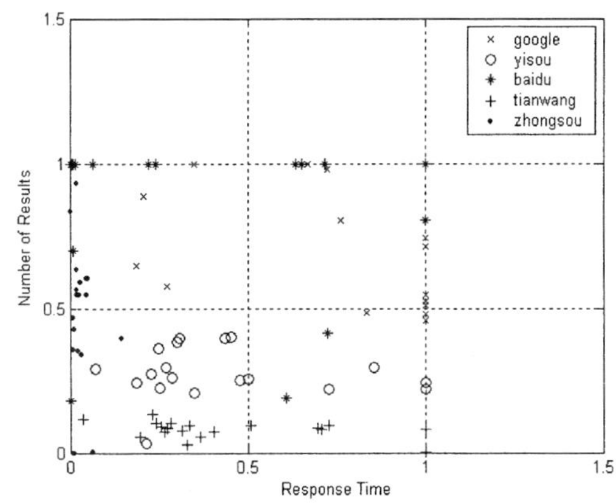

Fig. 5. Response Time versus Number of Results

Fig. 5 shows a plot of the response time versus the number of results of all the keywords used, as indicated in Fig. 1 and 4 in our experiments. For each keyword, the results of all five search engines are normalized to the longest response time and the largest number of returned items, Ideally, a good search engine should locate the largest number of documents in the shortest time. This corresponds to the upper-left quadrant in the figure. For this quantitative measure, Zhongsou and Baidu performed the best. Qualitative performance of these Chinese engines is discussed in Section 5.3.

5.2 Feature Comparison

Assigning the appropriate values for the various parameters in the *Feature* group, it is found that Google has the best features, followed by Yahoo and Baidu, as shown in Table 1.

Table 1. Feature Comparison

		Weight	Parameter value				
			Google	Yahoo	Baidu	Zhong sou	Tianwang
Features group			0.8	0.6	0.6	0.5	0.4
	Home page features	0.1	1.0	1.0	0.8	0.7	0.6
	User preferences	0.1	0.5	0.4	0.4	0.6	0.0
	Search options	0.3	0.9	0.5	0.7	0.4	0.3
	Keyword entry options	0.2	0.7	0.7	0.7	0.6	0.3
	Database	0.1	0.9	0.9	0.0	0.5	0.3
	Result features	0.2	0.6	0.6	0.6	0.5	0.7

5.3 Performance and Overall Comparison

Fig. 6 shows the scores of the components in the *Performance* group. It can be seen that both Google and Yahoo have the best average performance in this category.

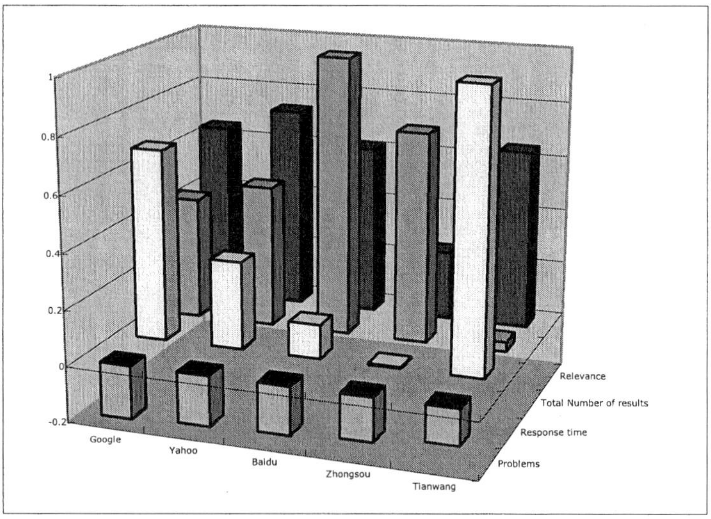

Fig. 6. Performance Score

Fig. 7 shows a comparison of the overall scores of the five engines. Google ranks first as it is evident that it has more good features and equivalent performance as compared to other search engines.

For convenience, we have assigned equal weights to the Problems and the Relevance groups. One can argue that the Relevance of the returned hits is more important than the Problems encountered. In such cases, the weight assigned to Relevance would be higher. This scenario of having a weight of 0.7 for Relevance and 0.3 for Problems is illustrated in Table 2.

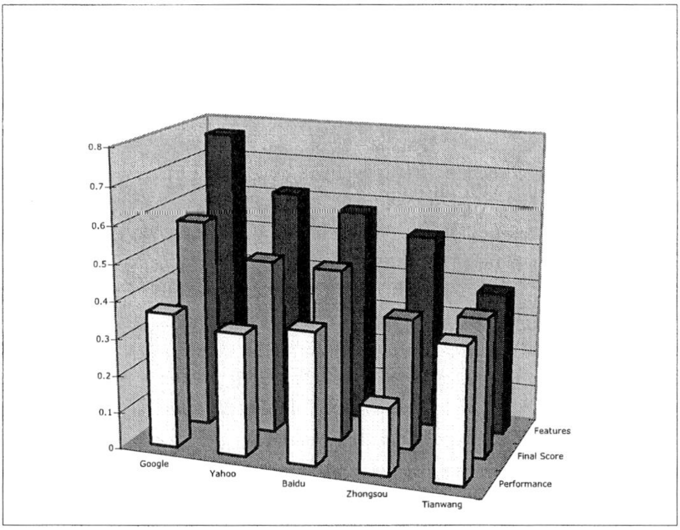

Fig. 7. Overall Comparison of the Search Engines

Table 2. Results with Different Weights for Relevance and Problems

Weight	Value	Google	Yahoo	Baidu	Zhongsou	Tianwang
5-5	Performance	0.3641	0.3314	0.3576	0.1805	0.3636
	Final Score	0.5668	0.4749	0.4691	0.3540	0.3759
7-3	Performance	0.4651	0.441	0.4522	0.2293	0.4569
	Final Score	0.6173	0.5297	0.5164	0.3783	0.4226

6 Current and Future Work

There are a couple of outstanding issues in the proposed methodology. First, humans, being subjective, are involved in the evaluation of the Relevance parameter. Second, as the evaluation process involves humans' input, it cannot be automated. It is an expensive endeavour to rate search engines manually on a regular basis.

In order to eliminate subjectivity and enable automation, the use of a common benchmark or a common list to rate the relevance of the returned results would be appropriate. Since the results from each search engine are already available, a common list can be generated using a data fusion algorithm, such as the ones found in [17]. We are currently focusing on algorithms to merge multiple (possibly multi-lingual) ordered lists into a single ranked list. Once these algorithms are established, the automation process of regularly evaluating search engines according to a user's preference by weight adjustment can proceed.

References

1. Allan, J. et al, "Challenges in Information Retrieval and Language Modeling", Report of a Workshop held at the Center for Intelligent Information Retrieval, University of Massachusetts Amherst, Sep. 2002.
2. Brin, S., Page, L., "The Anatomy of a Large-Scale Hypertextual Web Search Engine", Proceedings of the Seventh International World Wide Web Conference, 1998.
3. Chen, N.-P. et al, "Chinese Mac Character Sets and Encodings", available at (Jan. 1, 2005): http://www.yale.edu/chinesemac/pages/charset_encoding.html
4. Chinese-search-engine.com, "Chinese Search Engine Survey", available at (Sep. 21, 2004): http://chinese-search-engine.com/chinese-search-engine/survey.htm
5. Chinese-search-engine.com, "Marketing China: Simple Facts About China", available at (Sep. 21, 2004): http://chinese-search-engine.com/marketing-china/china-facts.htm
6. Dhyani, D., Ng, W.K. Bhowmick, S.S. "A Survey of Web Metrics," ACM Computing Surveys, vol. 34, no. 4, Dec. 2002, pp. 469-503.
7. Foo, S., Li, H., "Chinese Word Segmentation and Its Effect on Information Retrieval", Information Processing and Management, vol. 40, issue 1, Jan. 2004, pp. 161-190.
8. Kingoff, A., "Comparing Internet Search Engines", IEEE Computer, Apr. 1997, pp. 117-118.
9. Ljosland, M., "A Comparison Between Twenty Web Search Engines on Ten Rare Words", available at (Jan. 1, 2005): www.aitel.hist.no/~mildrid/dring/paper/Comp20.doc
10. Luk, R.W.P. Kwok, K.L., "A Comparison of Chinese Document Indexing Strategies and Retrieval Models", ACM Transactions on Asian Language Information Processing, vol. 1, no. 3, Sep. 2002, pp. 225-268.
11. Ma, L., "An Introduction and Comparison of Chinese Search Site", eSAS World, 139-146, Jul. 1998, (in Chinese) available at (Jan. 1, 2005): http://www.mypcera.com/softxue/txt/s35.htm
12. Notess, G.R., "Search Engine Statistics: Dead Links", Feb. 2000, available at (Jan. 1, 2005): http://www.searchengineshowdown.com/stats/dead.shtml
13. PC Computing, "Comparing the Top Ten Chinese Search Engine", (in Chinese) available at (Jan. 1, 2005): http://www.net345.com/comnet/sousuo--intro.htm
14. Popular Computer Week E-version, "A Report on Commonly Used Search Engines", (in Chinese) available at (Jan. 1, 2005): http://www.ahzx.net/frontpage/CHAP3_7_3.HTML
15. Pokorny, J., "Web searching and Information Retrieval", IEEE Computing in Science and Engineering, Jul./Aug. 2004, pp. 43-48.
16. Shanghai Society for Scientific and Technical Information, "A Research on Chinese Search Engine Comparison", (in Chinese) available at (Jan. 1, 2005): http://www.widewaysearch.com/paper3.htm
17. Si, L., Callan, J., "Using Sampled Data and Regression to Merge Search Engine Results," ACM SIGIR'02, Aug. 11-15, 2002, Finland.
18. Tsinghua University IT Usability Lab, "Search Engine Comparison Report", (in Chinese) available at (Jan. 1, 2005): http://news.ccidnet.com/pub/article/c951_a127264_p1.html
19. Valencia Community College, "Web Search Engines Comparison", available at (Jan. 1, 2005): http://valencia.cc.fl.us/lrcwest/searchchart.html

IglooG: A Distributed Web Crawler Based on Grid Service

Fei Liu, Fan-yuan Ma, Yun-ming Ye, Ming-lu Li, and Jia-di Yu

Department of Computer Science and Engineering, Shanghai Jiaotong University, Shanghai, P. R. China, 200030
{liufei001, my-fy, ymm, li-ml, yujiadi}@sjtu.edu.cn

Abstract. Web crawler is program used to download documents from the web site. This paper presents the design of a distributed web crawler on grid platform. This distributed web crawler is based on our previous work Igloo. Each crawler is deployed as grid service to improve the scalability of the system. Information services in our system are in charge of distributing URLs to balance the loads of the crawlers and are deployed as grid service. Information services are organized as Peer-to-Peer overlay network. According to the ID of crawler and semantic vector of crawl page that is computed by Latent Semantic Indexing, crawler can decide whether transmits the URL to information service or hold itself. We present an implementation of the distributed crawler based on Igloo and simulate the environment of Grid to evaluate the balancing load on the crawlers and crawl speed. Both the theoretical analysis and the experimental results show that our system is a high-performance and reliable system.

1 Introduction

Search engine has played a very important role in the growth of the Web. Web crawler forms an integral part of any search engine. The basic task of a crawler is to fetch pages, parse them to get more URLs, and then fetch these URLs to get even more URLs. In this process crawler can also log these pages or perform several other operations on pages fetched according to the requirements of the search engine. Most of these auxiliary tasks are orthogonal to the design of the crawler itself. The explosive growth of the web has rendered the simple task of crawling the web non-trivial. The architecture of the current crawler [1] [2] is based on a single architecture design. Centralized solutions are known to have problems like link congestion, being single point of failure, and expensive administration.

To address the shortcomings of centralized search engines, there have been several proposals [3, 4] to build decentralized search engines over peer-to-peer networks. Peer to Peer system are massively distributed computing systems with each node communicating directly with one another to distribute tasks or exchange information or accomplish task. The challenge, while using a distributed model such as one described above, is to efficiently distribute the computation tasks avoiding overheads

Y. Zhang et al. (Eds.): APWeb 2005, LNCS 3399, pp. 207 – 216, 2005.

for synchronization and maintenance of consistency. Scalability is also an important issue for such a model to be usable. To improve the quality of service, we adopt the grid service as the distributed environment. Several crawlers can run in one node and the number of the crawler is impacted by the bandwidth and computing ability of the node. The information services are organized with P2P network----CAN [5]. URLs are collected by information service with the semantic vectors of URLs and the ID of the information service. The semantic vectors of URLs are computed with Latent Semantic Indexing (LSI). In this way IglooG can scale up to the entire web and has been used to fetch tens of millions of web documents.

The rest of the paper is organized as follows. Section 2 introduces the related work about crawler. Section 3 introduces the Latent Semantic Indexing. Section 4 proposes the architecture of IglooG. Section 5 describes the experiment and results. We conclude in Section 6 with lessons learned and future work.

2 Related Works

The first crawler, Matthew Gray's Wanderer, was written in the spring of 1993, roughly coinciding with the first release of NCSA Mosaic [6]. Several papers about web crawling were presented at the first two World Wide Web conferences [7, 8, 9]. However, at the time, the web was two to three orders of magnitude smaller than it is today, so those systems did not address the scaling problems inherent in a crawl of today's web. All of the popular search engines use crawlers that must scale up to substantial portions of the web. However, due to the competitive nature of the search engine business, the designs of these crawlers have not been publicly described. There are two notable exceptions: the Google crawler and the Internet Archive crawler. Unfortunately, the descriptions of these crawlers in the literature are too terse to enable reproducibility.

The google search engine is a distributed system that uses multiple machines for crawling [10, 11]. The crawler consists of five functional components running in different processes. A URL server process reads URLs out of a file and forwards them to multiple crawler processes. Each crawler process runs on a different machine, is single-threaded, and uses asynchronous I/O to fetch data from up to 300 web servers in parallel. The crawlers transmit downloaded pages to a single store server process, which compresses the pages and stores them to disk. The pages are then read back from disk by an indexer process, which extracts links from HTML pages and saves them to a different disk file. A URL resolver process reads the link file, derelativizes the URLs contained therein, and saves the absolute URLs to the disk file that is read by the URL server. Typically, three to four crawler machines are used, so the entire system requires between four and eight machines. The internet archive also uses multiple machines to crawl the web [12, 13]. Each crawler process is assigned up to 64 sites to crawl, and no site is assigned to more than one crawler. Each single-threaded crawler process reads a list of seed URLs for its assigned sites from disk into per-site queues, and then uses asynchronous I/O to fetch pages from these queues in parallel. Once a page is downloaded, the crawler extracts the links contained in it. If a link refers to the site of the page it was contained in, it is added to the appropriate site queue; otherwise it is logged to disk. Periodically, a batch process merges these logged "cross-site" URLs into the site-specific seed sets, filtering out duplicates in the process. In the area of extensible web crawlers, Miller and Bharat's SPHINX system [14] provides some of the same customizability features as Mercator. In particular, it provides a mechanism for limiting which pages are crawled, and it allows customized document processing code to be written. However, SPHINX is targeted towards site-specific crawling, and therefore is not designed to be scalable.

3 Latent Semantic Indexing (LSI)

Literal matching schemes such as Vector Space Model (VSM) suffer from synonyms and noise in description. LSI overcomes these problems by using statistically derived conceptual indices instead of terms for retrieval. It uses singular value decomposition (SVD) [15] to transform a high-dimensional term vector into a lower-dimensional semantic vector. Each element of a semantic vector corresponds to the importance of an abstract concept in the description or query.

Let N be the number of description in the collection and d be the number of description containing the given word. The inverse description frequency (IDF) is defined as

$$IDF = \log[\frac{N}{d}] \tag{1}$$

The vector for description Do is constructed as below

$$Do = (T_1 * IDF_1, T_2 * IDF_2, ..., T_n * IDF_n) \tag{2}$$

Where T_i takes a value of 1 or 0 depending on whether or not the word i exists in the description Do. The vectors computed for description are used to form a description matrix S. Suppose the number of returned description is m, the description matrix S is constructed as $S = [S_1, S_2, ..., S_m]$. Based on this description matrix S, singular value decomposition (SVD) of matrix is used to extract relationship pattern between description and define thresholds to find matched services. The algorithm is described as follow. Since S is a real matrix, there exists SVD of $S: S = U_{m\times m} \sum_{m\times n} V^T_{n\times n}$ where U and V are orthogonal matrices. Matrices U and V can be denoted respectively as $U_{m\times m} = [u_1, u_2, ... u_m]_{m\times m}$ and $V_n = [v_1, v_2, ..., v_n]_{n\times n}$, where $u_i (i = 1, ..., m)$ is a m-dimensional vector $u_i = (u_{1,i}, u_{2,i}, ..., u_{m,i})$ and $v_i (i = 1, ..., n)$ is a n-dimensional vector $v_i = (v_{1,i}, v_{2,i}, ... v_{n,i})$. Suppose $rank(S) = r$ and singular values of matrix S are: $\beta_1 \geq \beta_2 \geq ... \geq \beta_r \geq \beta_{r+1} = ... = \beta_n = 0$. For a given threshold ε $(o < \varepsilon \leq 1)$, we choose a parameter k such that $(\beta_k - \beta_{k-1}) / \beta_k \geq \varepsilon$. Then we denote $U_k = [u_1, u_2, \ldots u_k]_{m\times k}$, $V_k = [v_1, v_2, \ldots, v_k]_{n\times k}$, $\sum_k = diag(\beta_1, \beta_2, \ldots \beta_k)$, and $S_k = U_k \sum_k V_k^T$. S_k is the best approximation matrix to S and contains main information among the description. In this algorithm, the descriptions matching queries are measured by the similarity between them. For measuring the descriptions similarity based on S_k, we choose the ith row R_i of the matrix $U_k \sum_k$ as the coordinate vector of description i in a k-dimensional subspace:

$$R_i = (u_{i,1}\beta_1, u_{i,2}\beta_2, \ldots u_{i,k}\beta_k) \quad i = 1, 2, \ldots, m$$

The similarity between description i and query j is defined as:

$$sim(R_i, R_j) = \frac{| R_i . R_j |}{\| R_i \|_2 \| R_j \|_2} \tag{3}$$

4 The Implementation of IglooG

4.1 The Web Crawler Service

We wrap each web crawler as a grid service and deploy it in grid platform. This paper uses crawler of Igloo as single crawler to construct IglooG. First we introduce the architecture of single crawler (Fig. 1).

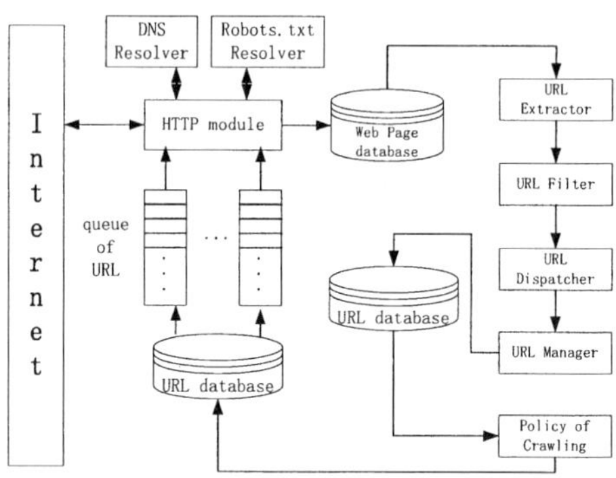

Fig. 1. The structure of single crawler

Each crawler can get IP of host with URL by DNS. Then it downloads the web page through HTTP module if Robot allows access to the URL. URL extractor extracts the URL from the downloaded web page and URL filter check whether the URL accord with the restrictions. Then the crawler uses hash function to compute the hash ID of URL. The crawler inserts the URL into its URL database. Policy of crawling is used to sort the rank of pages to make higher important resource to be crawled more prior. We adopt the PageRank [16] method to evaluate the importance of web page. HTTP module consists of several download threads and each thread has a queue of URL.

4.2 The Information Service

IglooG is designed to use in Grid environment. Information service is in charge of collecting the information about resource and the distribution of URL. Also it adjusts the distribution of URL to make crawlers have good load balance. The system we design is used to deal with large-scale web page download so the number of information service is much. How to organize these information services is challengeable. These information services are regarded as index service in GT3 and is defined as a service that speaks two basic protocols. GRIP [17] is used to access information about resource providers, while the GRRP [17] is used to notify register nodes services of the availability of this information. Each resource has two attributes. One is resource type and the other is the value of the resource. Crawler being a special resource is recorded in information service. The number of URLs in crawling queue and IP of the node the crawler being in are the value of the crawler. Fig. 2 is an example of GRIP data model:

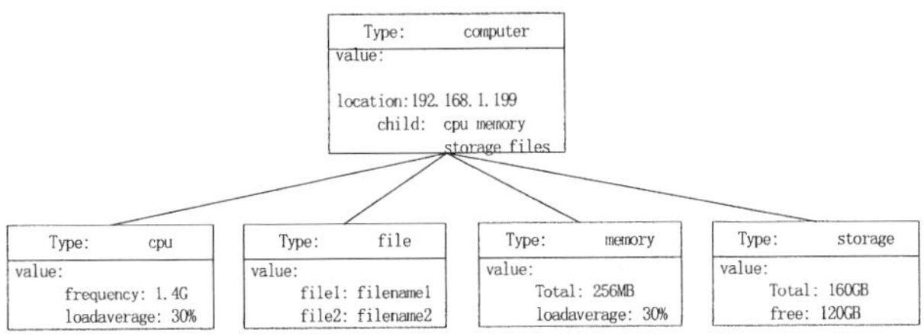

Fig. 2. GRIP data model

We organize these information services in CAN. Our design centers around a virtual 4-dimensional Cartesian coordinate space. At any point in time, the entire coordinate space is dynamically partitioned among all the information services in the system such that every service owns it individual, distinct zone within the overall space. In our system one node can start at most one information service. We assume that IP of node is the identifier of information service in it. We can regard IP as a point in a virtual 4-dimensional Cartesian coordinate space which is defined as $S_a=\{(0,0,0,0),(255,255,255,255)\}$. We assume the 4 axes of S_a are x, y, z, w. The first information service *R1* holds space S_a. When the second information service *R2* joins, S_a is divided into two parts averagely. One parts is controlled by *R1* and the other is held by *R2*. The central point of the space controlled by *R1* is closer to *R1* than the other space. *R1* records the IP of *R2* and the space controlled by *R2* and *R2* records IP of *R1* and the space controlled by *R2*. In this way the neighbor relationship between *R1* and *R2* sets up. After the information service overlay network contains *m* service *[R1, R2, ..., Rm]*, the (m+1)th service joins which split the space controlled by node *Rn {1<=n<=m}* which IP is closest to IP of *Rm+1* into two parts. The one which central point is closer to *Rn* belongs to *Rn* and the other one is held by *Rm+1*. When service *Ry* leaves information service overlay network it notifies its neighbor *Rt* which IP is closest to its. *Rt* will control the space *Rt* held. In this way service left does not affect the function of our system. Each information service sends message periodically to detect its neighbors exists. If *Rt* fails, its neighbor knows its lost after one period. Then the neighbor which IP is closest to *Rt*'s holds the space controlled by *Rt*'s. In this way we construct the information service overlay network.

4.3 The Architecture of IglooG

IglooG uses this pair *(IP, number)* to identify the crawler where *IP* is the IP of the node crawler being in and *number* is a random number that is not used by active crawlers. This pair is added to GRIP data when crawler is registering. Each crawler that joins IglooG must know at least one information service. Then the joining crawler *P1* sends packet containing its GRIP data to the information service *R1* to ask for joining. *R1* checks the IP of *P1*. If the IP of *P1* is in the space controlled by *R1*, *R1* records GRIP data of *P1*. Otherwise *R1* transfer GRIP data to its neighbor which coordinate is closest to the IP of *P1*. Then the neighbor does the same work as *R1* until find an information service which controls the space containing the IP of *P1*. Fig. 3 shows a sample of crawler discovering information service. In Fig. 3 *P1* is the crawler which IP is (162.146.201.148) and it knows the information service *R1* (28.18.36.112). Then *P1* sends its GRIP data to *R1*. *R1* checks IP of *P1* and its space then transfer the GRIP data of *P1* to its neighbor. The neighbor of *R1* does the same as *R1* and Finally the GRIP data is received by *R2*. Then *R2* sends information about itself to *P1* and *P1* regards *R2* as its manage service through recording the information. In this way *P1* registers successfully.

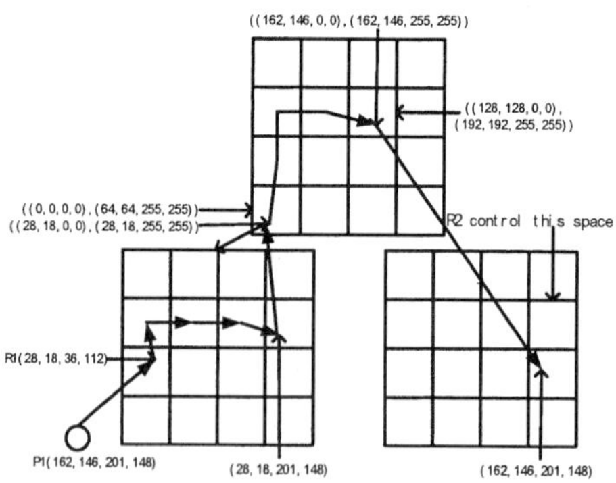

Fig. 3. The process of crawler registering

In this way crawlers are organized by information services. The information services are used to collect URLs and redistribute them to crawlers to balance the load of crawler. The semantic vectors of URLs are generated with LSI. We can set the dimension of semantic vector of URLs to be 4 by adjusting ε in order to resolve match between CAN and semantic vector, where the number of dimension of CAN is 4. After the crawler *c1* download web page and extract URL *u1*, it checks whether the semantic vector of *u1* match the IP of the information service *R1* that manages the crawler. If it does, the crawler inserts *u1* into its own URL database and downloads the web page later. Otherwise it transmits the URL and semantic vector to information service *R1*. We define the semantic vector of *u1* as *v(u1)*. After *R1* receives *u1* and *v(u1)*, it transfers them to its neighbor which coordinate is closest to the *u1*. Then the neighbor does the same work as *R1* until find an information service *R2* that controls the space containing the *u1*. Then *R2* selects a crawler which load is lightest to download *u1*. Fig. 4 shows the architecture of IglooG.

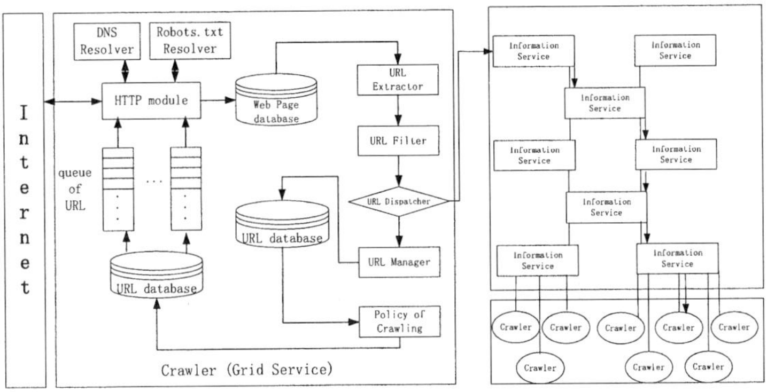

Fig. 4. The architecture of IglooG

5 Experimental Results

We generate 960 computing nodes by GT-ITM models. Then we divide these nodes into seven groups. We implements simulation of CAN. Nodes of one group containing 60 nodes are used as information services and organized by CAN. Each of the other 6 groups of nodes contains 150 nodes and every node runs a crawler. We use seven 1.7GHz Pentium IV machine with 1GB of memory as our experiment hardware. One of these computers is used to run CAN that organizes information services. Each of the other 6 machines run 150 nodes to run crawlers. Seven machines are connected to a 100Mb/s Ethernet LAN that connects to CERNET by a gateway. Igloo is implemented with JAVA that makes it can run in Windows and Linux etc. We choose 20 homepages of Chinese colleges as seed URLs. Owning to the limitation of disk, the web pages downloaded are less than 500 KB and the total crawling of single crawler is less than 1 GB.

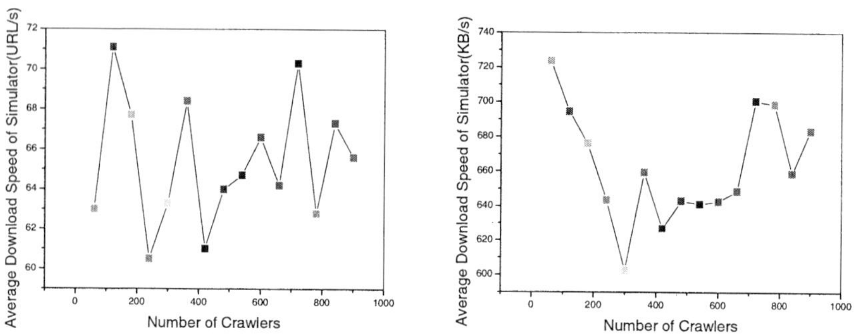

(a)URL/s (b)KB/s

Fig. 5. The average download speed of simulator

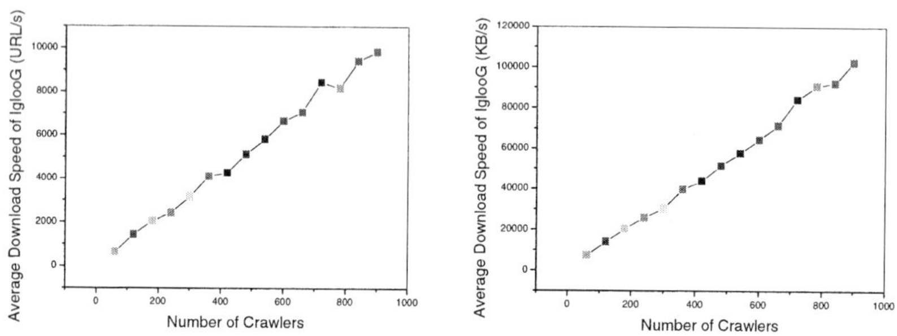

(a)URL/s (b)KB/s

Fig. 6. The average download speed of IglooG

We have experimented 15 times and for each separate experiment we varied the number of participating crawlers from 60 through 900. We run crawlers 24 hours in each experiment. From Fig. 5 we find that the download speed of simulator is at about 66 URL/s and 660KB/s. So the network and web sites we use to crawl are stable. Fig. 6 shows the average download speed of IglooG scales linearly as the number of participating crawlers increase.

6 Conclusions and Future Work

Web crawler is program used to download documents from the web site. This paper presents the design of a distributed web crawler on grid platform. The challenge, while using a distributed model such as one described above, is to efficiently distribute the computation tasks avoiding overheads for synchronization and maintenance of consistency. Scalability is also an important issue for such a model to be usable. To improve the quality of service, we adopt the grid service as the distributed environment. Several crawlers can run in one node and the number of the crawler is impacted by the bandwidth and computing ability of the node. The information services are organized with P2P network URLs are collected by information service with the semantic vectors of URLs and the ID of the information service. The semantic vectors of URLs are computed with Latent Semantic Indexing (LSI). In this way IglooG are load-balanced and can scale up to the entire web and has been used to fetch tens of millions of web documents.

However, there are still some problems to be explored. How to effectively store the web page and construct indices in the distributed environment? We will explore these issues in the future.

Acknowledgements. This paper is supported by 973 project (No.2002CB312002) of China, ChinaGrid Program of MOE of China, and grand project of the Science and Technology Commission of Shanghai Municipality (No. 03dz15026, No. 03dz15027 and No. 03dz15028).

References

1. Sergey Brin, Lawrence Page, Google: The Anatomy of a Large-Scale Hypertextual Web SearchEngine" Proceedings of the 7th International World Wide Web Conference, pages 107-117, April 1998
2. Allan Heydon and Marc Najork, " Mercator: A Scalable, Extensible Web Crawler", *World Wide Web*, 2(4):219–229, 1999
3. J. Li, B. T. Loo, J. Hellerstein, F. Kaashoek, D. Karger, and R. Morrris. On the Feasibility of Peer-to-Peer Web Indexing and Search. In *IPTPS 2003*.
4. C. Tang, Z. Xu, and M. Mahalingam. pSearch: Information retrieval in structured overlays. In *ACM HotNets-I*, October 2002.
5. S. Ratnasamy, P. Francis, M. Handley, R. Karp, and S. Shenker. A scalable -addressable network. In *ACM SIGCOMM'01*, August 2001.
6. Internet Growth and Statistics: Credits and Background. `http://www.mit.edu/people/mkgray/net/background.html`
7. David Eichmann. The RBSE Spider – Balancing Effective Search Against Web Load. In *Proceedings of the First International World Wide Web Conference*, pages 113–120, 1994.
8. Oliver A. McBryan. GENVL andWWWW: Tools for Taming the Web. In *Proceedings of the First International World Wide Web Conference*, pages 79–90, 1994.
9. Brian Pinkerton. FindingWhat PeopleWant: Experiences with theWebCrawler. In *Proceedings of the Second International World Wide Web Conference*, 1994.
10. Sergey Brin and Lawrence Page. The anatomy of a large-scale hypertextualWeb search engine. In *Proceedings of the Seventh InternationalWorld Wide Web Conference*, pages 107–117, April 1998.
11. Google! Search Engine. `http://google.stanford.edu/`
12. Mike Burner. Crawling towards Eternity: Building an archive of the World Wide Web. Web Techniques Magazine, 2(5), May 1997.
13. The Internet Archive. `http://www.archive.org/`

from mobile clients has got lots of concerns of relevant researchers [1-10]. Nevertheless, read-only transaction processing in mobile real-time computing environments, which not only requires consistent data access to database servers but also has time constraints on both data and transactions, has not received adequate attention even though its significance for applications such as stock and traffic information dissemination [6,9,11]. Owing to the inherent limitation of wireless communication network, the bandwidth of the downstream channel from the database server to mobile clients is much larger than that of the upstream channel and in some cases upstream channels even do not exist. Therefore, instead of pull-based data dissemination methods, data broadcast has been widely accepted as an efficient way for mobile clients to get their needed data. When data broadcast is used to propagate frequently updated data to read-only transactions issued from mobile clients, we call it updates dissemination.

To the best of our knowledge, updates dissemination is addressed first in [2] and the authors discuss the tradeoffs between data currency and performance issues. However transaction semantics is not supported and the consistency criterion is relatively relax. Transactional support is introduced in the Datacycle architecture and the serializability is taken as the correctness criterion, while special hardware is needed to detect changes of values read by transactions [12]. Recently two efficient updates dissemination protocols, *the multi-version data broadcast* (MVB) and *the invalidation method* (IR), are proposed in [4,5]. However, the majority of existing updates dissemination protocols do not take the time constraints into account, whereas data dissemination methods referring to real-time characteristics do not support the transactional semantics [6,13]. In this paper, we investigate the problems of disseminating consistent data to read-only transactions with deadlines in mobile real-time computing environments. A novel updates dissemination protocol called *mixed real-time data broadcast* (MRTB) is proposed. In *mixed real-time data broadcast*, a set of new techniques including reducing the length of consistency intervals, immediate updates dissemination policy and on-demand data delivery are incorporated seamlessly. Moreover, an enhanced index structure is designed for read-only transactions to judge precisely when to request the desired data. Simulation results show that the proposed protocol can provide higher data currency and lower miss rate compared with existing updates dissemination protocols and is more appropriate for mobile real-time computing environments.

The rest of the paper is organized as follows. Section 2 presents the preliminaries. Section 3 introduces the details of *mixed real-time data broadcast protocol.* Section 4 presents the performance evaluation of the proposed protocol. Finally, conclusion is made in section 5.

2 Notations and Definitions

We assume that the database is a finite set composed of a number of data items, that is, $DB = \{d_i \mid i = 1, 2, \ldots, n\}$.

Definition 1. The value of data item **d** at time instance τ is called the state of **d** at τ, denoted by $S_\tau(d)$.

Definition 2. The states of all data items in DB at time instance τ is called the state of DB at τ, denoted by $S_\tau(\text{DB}) = \{S_\tau(d_i) \mid i = 1, 2, \ldots, n\}$.

Definition 3. Let $S_{\tau_1}(d)$ and $S_{\tau_2}(d)$ be the states of d at τ_1 and τ_2 respectively. If condition $(\tau_1 < \tau_2) \wedge (S_{\tau_1}(d) \neq S_{\tau_2}(d))$ holds, we say that $S_{\tau_2}(d)$ is more current than $S_{\tau_1}(d)$, denoted by $S_{\tau_2}(d) >_c S_{\tau_1}(d)$.

Definition 4. Let **T** be an read-only transaction that committed at time instance τ_c and $R(\text{T})$ is the read set of **T**. $S^T(d)$ denotes the state of **d** when **T** reads **d**. We say that **T** is consistent if and only if:

$$\exists \tau\, (\tau \leq \tau_c) \wedge (\forall d\, (d \in R(\text{T})) \wedge (S^T(d) \in S_\tau(\text{DB})))$$

T is consistent only if data items in its read set form a subset of a consistent state of DB at time instance τ earlier than τ_c. Guaranteeing the consistency of transactions is essential for many applications such as stock and traffic information dissemination. So we follow strictly the consistency criterion in Def. 4 and do not consider relaxing it to gain the improvement in other performance metrics in this paper.

Definition 5. If **T** is consistent and condition $(d \in R(\text{T})) \wedge (S_{\tau_c}(d) >_c S^T(d))$ holds, we say that **d** is stale for **T**. Let $SR(\text{T})$ be the set of stale data items read by **T**, that is, $SR(\text{T}) = \{d \mid d \in R(\text{T}) \wedge S_{\tau_c}(d) >_c S^T(d)\}$. The staleness of **T**, denoted by ST_T, is defined as $|SR(\text{T})| / |R(\text{T})|$. The system staleness, denoted by SS, is defined as $\sum ST_{T_i} / |\{T_i\}|$, where $\{T_i\}$ is the finite set of read-only transactions in the system during a certain period.

Reading stale data will decrease the usefulness of execution results of transactions. Thus, how to reduce the amount of stale data read by transactions, namely, decreasing *SS*, is one key issue in designing efficient updates dissemination protocols. Smaller *SS* is, transactions will read much more current data items.

Definition 6. The miss rate, denoted by *MR*, is defined as N_{miss}/N_{total}, where N_{miss} and N_{total} are the number of read-only transactions missing their deadlines and the total number of transactions processed in the system respectively.

MR is the other performance metric since missing deadlines is undesirable for applications with constraint on their completion time. In conclusion, the requirements for updates dissemination protocols for read-only transaction processing in mobile real-time computing environments are to reduce *SS* and *MR* on the premise of ensuring the consistency of transactions.

In this paper we follow the assumptions in [4] that the periodic broadcast is adopted, that is, all data items in the database have to be broadcast at least once in each broadcast cycle. Under periodic broadcast, if the waiting time is not of great importance, transactions need not issue explicit data request since all data items definitely appear in the broadcast sooner or later.

Definition 7. Let d^i be the ith data item instance in a broadcast cycle and $\tau(i)$ is the time instance broadcasting d^i. If condition $\forall d^j\, (i \leq j \leq i+k-1) \wedge (S_{\tau(j)}(d^j) \in S_{\tau(i)}(\text{DB})$ holds for d^i to d^{i+k-1}, we say that the *k* data item instances constitute a consistency interval $CI_m^{i,k}$, where *i* is the sequence number of the first item of $CI_m^{i,k}$ in the broadcast cycle, m is the monotonically increasing sequence number of $CI_m^{i,k}$ and k is the length of $CI_m^{i,k}$.

The states of data items in $CI_m^{i,k}$ correspond to $S_{\pi(i)}(DB)$ and then are consistent with each other. Theoretically two successive consistency intervals may be overlapped and their lengths are not necessarily identical, while from the practical point of view, in this paper we only address *qualified* updates dissemination protocols with the following characteristics: 1) the lengths of consistency intervals are constant and 2) the end of one consistency interval is just the beginning of the next one. For simplicity of presentation, in the following sections we use CI_m to represent $CI_m^{i,k}$ and CI^k to denote a set of consistency intervals whose length is equal to k.

3 The Broadcast Protocol

The system model includes two relatively independent parts, the server-side model and the client-side model. The server-side model consists of the database server, the broadcast server and the mobile support station, which are interconnected by the fixed network. We assume the size of each data item is identical and each update is labeled with a time-stamp to indicate when the value is taken. The basic time unit in the system is the time interval for broadcasting a single data item. The broadcast server delivers data through the downstream channel and supports two kinds of broadcast: *broadcast on-schedule* (BOS) and *broadcast on-demand* (BOD). BOS refers to that all data items in the database are propagated according to the chosen scheduling algorithm such as flat broadcast or frequency-based scheduling strategies [6,14], which is aimed at exploiting the channel efficiently. BOD takes the user requirements into consideration and delivers data items on-demand to meet their data requests. The mobile support station is responsible for managing the upstream channel, through which mobile clients may send data requests if the desired data do not appear timely. At the same time, a data requests queue is maintained at the mobile support station.

The client-side model is composed of a large number of mobile clients, from which read-only transactions are generated one at a time. Each read-only transaction consists of a set of ordered read operations and is associated with a deadline on its completion time. In this paper the firm transaction model is adopted, which means that real-time transactions missing their deadlines will be aborted at once while this abortion have no negative effect on the system. If a read-only transaction has finished all read operations without violating the consistency criterion and time constraint, it commits immediately. Otherwise, e.g., an inconsistent read occurs, the read-only transaction will have to be restarted as long as its deadline does not expire. The next run of the transaction can read consistent data item from the local cache directly. Since the functions and behavior of transactions in real-time applications are much more predictable [9], we assume the number of read operations of a read-only transaction can be obtained using certain pre-analysis techniques before its execution.

3.1 Real-Time Data Broadcast

Based on the transaction execution model described above and the definition of *SS*, we can get the following proposition easily.

Proposition 1. Given any *qualified* updates dissemination protocol, for two consistency intervals CI^{k_1} and CI^{k_2}, if $k_1>k_2$ and k_1 can be exactly divided by k_2, *SS* of using CI^{k_2} is necessarily less than that of using CI^{k_1}.
With existing updates dissemination protocols, restarting transactions is the common way to ensure the consistency. To continue their execution, restarted transactions have to wait until the new values of updated data items appear. However, the waiting time depends on particular scheduling algorithms and so is unpredictable, which is quite undesirable for transactions with deadline constraints. To reduce the uncertainty of the waiting time, a new policy is introduced in this paper.

Definition 8. Given any *qualified* updates dissemination protocol, suppose data item **d** is updated during consistency interval CI_m at the server and cannot be broadcast by the chosen scheduling algorithm during the remaining portion of CI_m, the immediate updates dissemination policy (IUDP) delivers the new value of **d** instantly at the beginning of CI_{m+1} without waiting for being scheduled.

By the transaction execution model we can get proposition 2 readily.

Proposition 2. With a particular updates dissemination protocol, using IUDP can provide the new values of updated data items to restarted transactions more timely than the one without IUDP.

MVB seriously affects the data currency mainly due to its long broadcast cycle and the delivery of old versions of data items. To increase data currency, two improvements for MVB are made in the design of *the real-time data broadcast protocol* (RTB: the preliminary version of the proposed protocol). The first improvement is shortening the length of consistency intervals as well as only delivering the latest version of data during each consistency interval. According to proposition 1, appropriate length candidate may be 1/**n**, e.g., half or one third, of the length of the whole broadcast cycle, where **n** is a natural number bigger than 1. This improvement can decrease the probability of reading stale data for read-only transactions dramatically.

In terms of proposition 2, the second improvement is utilizing IUDP to reduce the execution time of restarted read-only transactions. In particular, at the beginning of each consistency interval *the new values* (NV) of updated data during the preceding consistency interval are delivered immediately instead of waiting for being scheduled by the scheduling algorithm. To maintain the consistency, at the beginning of each consistency interval (just before NV) an *invalidation report* (IR) is propagated similar to IM, in which there are the identifiers of data items updated during the preceding consistency interval. Each read-only transaction, say $\mathbf{T_i}$, reads IR periodically and determines to restart or not by judging whether data items in its read set are found in IR. If an inconsistent read occurs, $\mathbf{T_i}$ has to restart to ensure the consistency.

Mobile clients may cache data items of interest locally. In the presence of updates, items in the cache may become stale. There are various approaches to communicating updates to the client caches. Invalidation combined with a form of autoprefetching was shown to perform well in broadcast delivery [4]. Similar to [4], this kind of cache updates policy is used in this paper. In particular, if data items in the cache are found in IR, the new values of such items will be autofetched once they appear in NV. As to the cache replacement policy, the most commonly used one, LRU, is adopted in this paper.

3.2 Mixed Real-Time Data Broadcast

Results presented in [3] indicate that BOD has a better performance in meeting data needs with deadlines compared with pure BOS. Similar research works in [6,12] also show that mixed data broadcast, which combines BOS with BOD, performs better than just using a broadcast policy alone. Though RTB in conjunction with BOD seems to be promising in reducing *the miss rate*, several technical problems still need to be resolved.

The first one is how to allocate restricted bandwidth of the downstream channel between BOS and BOD. Considering the complexity of bandwidth allocation, the ratio of BOD to BOS is fixed in *the mixed real-time data broadcast* (MRTB) and may be adjusted as a system parameter in practice. With respect to the period of BOD, in MRTB it is set the same as that of the consistency interval to simplify the implementation as well as provide much higher data currency.

The second problem is how to determine the time at which read-only transactions send their data requests if necessary. Index techniques are widely used in broadcast organization for mobile clients to locate data of interest precisely [3,8,10] and thus may be a good candidate to solve the second problem. However, existing index techniques assume that the contents of data broadcast is known in advance, which is not suitable for MRTB due to the dynamic change of contents in NV and OD. Therefore, in the following section we will adapt existing index techniques to MRTB by certain enhancements.

Similar to [10], we assume a B-tree structure for the index. For each broadcast cycle, only the contents of BOS, i.e., all data items excluding NV and OD, is used to construct the index, which avoids the difficulty and complexity of index dynamic generation. The whole index consists of a series of index entries and other special attached information. Each index entry consists of a 2-tuple <*K, Pos*>, where *K* is the key value of corresponding data item; *Pos* is the relative position of the data item in BOS. Each data item in data broadcast consists of a 4-tuple <*K, Pos, Offset, Content* >, where *K* is the key value of the data item; for data items not within NV and OD, *Pos* is equal to its relative position in the broadcast schedule and *Offset* is equal to 0; for data items within NV and OD, *Pos* is equal to the *Pos* value of the last data item in the preceding consistency interval and *Offset* is equal to its relative position in NV and OD; *Content* is composed of the other fields of the data item.

To determine the length of NV and OD, the estimation values of *the update rate* at the server, denoted by *UpdateRate*, and the proportion of BOD to BOS, denoted by *Ratio*, are included in the index. *UpdateRate* can be the average of update rates in last several broadcast cycles or other meaningful estimations in terms of practical application scenarios. In addition, the length of BOS, denoted by *N*, is also attached in the index. Based on above index structure and attached information, for any read operation issued by read-only transactions, say $r(\mathrm{d})$, the time elapsed from the read operation begins to the desired data items appears can be got by equation 1 (Note that in this paper time is measured in terms of the time unit for broadcasting a single data item).

$$NODP(\mathrm{d}) = (N + IPos - Pos\text{-}Offset) \text{ MOD } N \times (1 + UpdateRate + Ratio) \quad (1)$$

where *Pos* and *Offset* are the corresponding values of the data item being broadcasted when the read operation begins; *IPos* is the *Pos* value of the needed data item got by index searching. MOD is the modulus operation.

```
Procedure GeneratingBroadcastProgram(Update_Set, k)
Input : Update_Set is the set of identifiers of data updated in the preceding consistency interval
        k is the length of consistency intervals of the choosen updates dissemination protocol
while (true)
/*Each while-loop accomplishes the data dissemination of one consistency interval*/
    Temp = Update_Set;
    Update_Set = φ;
    if (Temp != φ) then
        broadcast invalidation report in terms of data items in Temp;
        broadcast the new values of data items in Temp;
    endif
    broadcast k × Ratio data items according to the data requests queue and EDF scheduling policy;
    broadcast k data items by the broadcast scheduling algorithm;
endwhile
```

Fig. 1. Server-side protocol of MRTB

```
Procedure DataAcquire(d_i, Read_Set)
Input: d_i is the i^th data item needed by the transaction in execution
       Read_Set is the read set of the transaction in execution
if (d_i is in local cache) then
    Add d_i into Read_Set of the transaction that issues the read operation;
else
    Listen to the data broadcast;
    Read current broadcasted data item and get its (Pos, Offset);
    Search the index and locate d_i 's relative position IPos;
    DL(d_i) = (Deadline - Current_Time)/(NoQueries - i +1);
    NODP(d_i) = (N+ IPos -Pos-Offset) MOD N×(1+ UpdateRate + Ratio);
    if ( NODP(d_i) > DL(d_i)) then
        Send a data request to the broadcast server;
    else
        if (it is time to receive IR) then
            if (data items in Read_Set are found in IR) then
                Restart the transaction and re-read data items from local cache and NV;
            endif
        else
            if (d_i appears) then
                Read d_i and add it into Read_Set;
            endif
        endif
    endif
endif
```

Fig. 2. Client-side protocol of MRTB

By comparing *NODP*(d) and d's deadline we will know whether the needed data item may appear in time. However, read-only transactions often have more than one read operations. Thus, the transaction deadline should be assigned to all data items of interest. In MRTB we use the serial assignment policy, i.e., dividing the remaining execution time of a read-only transaction equally among all pending read operations. The deadline of each data item can be determined according to equation 2.

$$DL(d_i) = (Deadline - Current\_Time)/(NoQueries - i + 1) \qquad (2)$$

where $DL(d_i)$ is deadline of the ith data item of a read-only transaction; *Deadline* is the deadline of the read-only transaction; *Current_Time* is the time now; *NoQueries* is the number of read operations of the read-only transaction.

Suppose a read-only transaction initiates a read operation, say $r(d_i)$, if $DL(d_i)$ is bigger than $NODP(d_i)$ the transaction may wait the appearance of the desired data item on the channel. Otherwise, a data request will be generated.

In the mobile support station the data requests are queued and processed according to EDF scheduling policy [12]. The detailed implementation of MRTB protocol is depicted in Fig. 1 and Fig. 2.

4 Performance Evaluation

Our simulation model is similar to the one presented in [4]. There are *NoItems* data items in the database and the broadcast server periodically broadcasts them to a large population of mobile clients. To simplify the analysis and implementation, we evaluate these update dissemination protocols (MVB, IM, RTB and MRTB) combined with the flat scheduling algorithm. The bandwidth proportion of BOD to BOS is *Ratio*. Index is broadcast *NoIndexes* times per broadcast cycle, which is used for read-only transactions to determine the accurate position of needed data items and judge when to send data requests. Update transactions at the server are generated per *UpdateInterval* and their update operations follow a Zipf distribution with parameter θ_u. The update distribution is across the range 1 to *UpdateRange*. The length of consistency intervals is *ConsistencyInterval*. The basic time unit in our simulation is the time used to broadcast a single data item.

The client simulator initiates a read-only transaction per *ThinkInterval*. Each read-only transaction has *NoQueries* read operations. The deadline of read-only transaction is equal to *CurrentTime* + $V \times$*NoQueries*, where *V* is a value randomly selected between *MinLaxity* and *MaxLaxity*. If a read-only transaction has to restart due to inconsistent read, it can continue to execute as long as current time is no larger than its deadline. The read operations of read-only transactions access data items from the range 1 to *ReadRange*. The access probabilities follow a Zipf distribution with a parameter θ_r. The cache size in the client is *CacheSize* and cache replacement policy is LRU. If data items are updated, the corresponding cache entries are invalidated and subsequently autoperfetched. The performance metrics are the miss rate and the system staleness. The main parameters and the baseline values are summarized in Table 1.

Table 1. Parameters and baseline values

Server Parameters				Client Parameters			
NoItems	1000	*UpdateRange*	1000	*ReadRange*	1000	*ThinkInterval*	4
UpdateInterval	40	*ConsistencyInterval*	200	*NoQueries*	4	*MinLaxity*	500
Ratio	0.1	*NoIndexes*	5	*MaxLaxity*	1000	*CacheSize*	125
θ_u	0.9			θ_r	0.9		

Experiment 1: We change *UpdateInterval* to compare the performance metrics of MVB, IM, RTB and MRTB under different update rate. The number of versions for MVB is 2.

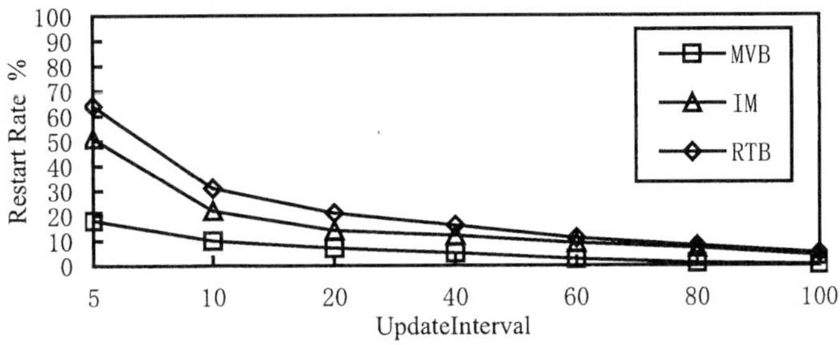

Fig. 3. The restart rate comparison

In Fig.3 the restart rate of several protocols are illustrated. The restart rate of MRTB is not depicted because it is similar to that of RTB. From Fig. 3 we can see that the restart rates of these three protocols all decrease with the reduction of the update rate. RTB has the highest restart rate due to the shortest consistency intervals and strict restart rules. MVB owns the lowest one since it allows transactions to read stale versions of data. Because the number of versions for MVB is 2, there are still probabilities for transactions to restart due to inconsistent read, which is especially obvious when the update rate is high.

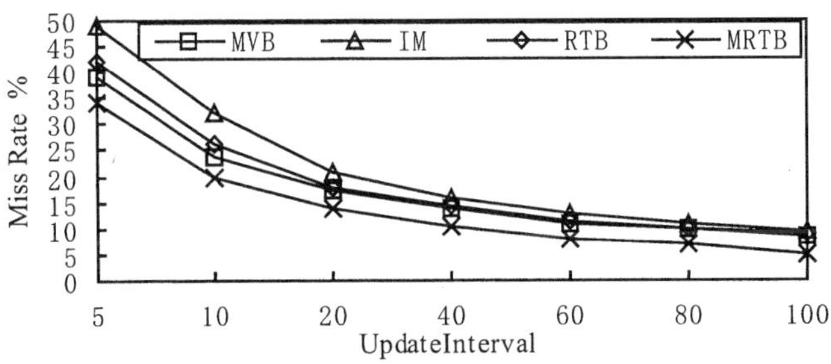

Fig. 4. The miss rate comparison

The miss rates of these four protocols are compared in Fig. 4. IM has the highest one due to its highest restart rate and the lack of IUDP. Although the restart rate of RTB is higher than those of the others, the shortened waiting time of restarted transactions thanks to IUDP leads to its better performance than IM. Compared with MVB, the miss rate of RTB is higher due to its high restart rate when the update rate is high. While with the decrease of the update rate, the difference of the miss rates between RTB and MVB diminishes gradually. Since MRTB can meet more transactions with short deadlines through mixed broadcast policy, it performs best.

The system staleness of MVB, IM and RTB are depicted in Fig.5. This metric of MRTB is not given since it is similar to that of RTB. The system staleness of all three protocols decreases with the reduction of the update rate. MVB has the highest one because it allows transactions to read stale versions of data. Owing to the invalidation method, the metric of IM and RTB is observably better than that of MVB. Compared with IM, RTB has a better performance since the shorter length of consistency intervals further decreases the probability of reading outdated data. Because transactions begins and commits during one consistency interval still may read outdated data, the system staleness of RTB is not equal to 0.

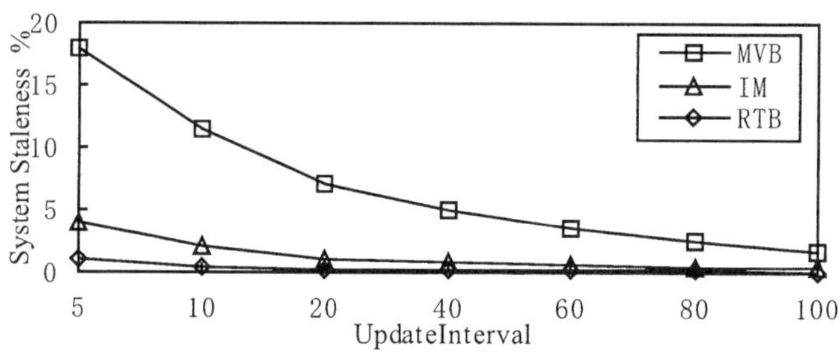

Fig. 5. The system staleness comparison

Experiment 2: In this experiment we change the system workload and the bandwidth ratio of BOD to BOS to observe the variation of performance metrics for RTB and MRTB.

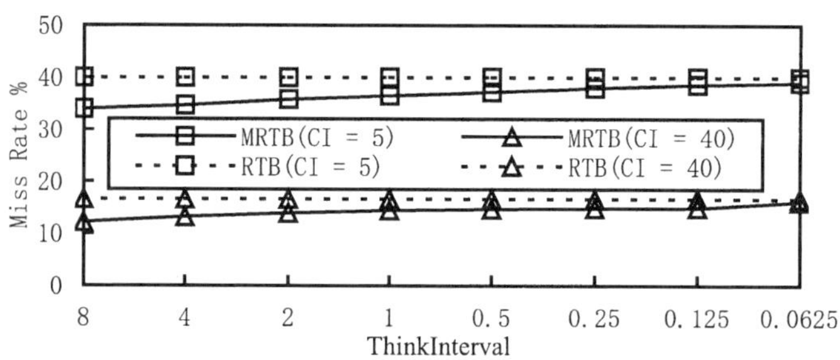

Fig. 6. The miss rate comparison

In Fig.6 the miss rates of RTB and MRTB are illustrated under different values of *ThinkInterval*. As *ThinkInterval* is across the range from 8 to 0.0625, the amount of data needed by read-only transactions changes from 0.5 to 6 times as many as the amount of data broadcast, i.e., the system workload increases by degrees. From Fig.6 we can see that with the increase of the system workload, the miss rate of MRTB increases accordingly due to the limited bandwidth of BOD. But it does not exceed that of RTB under the same update rate.

Fig.7 illustrates the miss rate of MRTB with the variation of *Ratio* under different transaction laxities. From Fig.7 we can see that the miss rate does not constantly decrease with the increase of on-demand bandwidth but ascends slightly after *Ratio* exceeds one critical point. Reason for this phenomenon may be that the increase of bandwidth for BOD results in the longer broadcast cycle, which in turn leads to transactions that can get their needed data through BOS before now have to acquire data from BOD. When the increasing speed of data requests becomes larger than that of bandwidth for BOD, the miss rate may drop instead of increasing constantly. At the same time, the transaction laxities also have an impact on the critical point. The shorter the transaction laxities are, the earlier the critical point emerges.

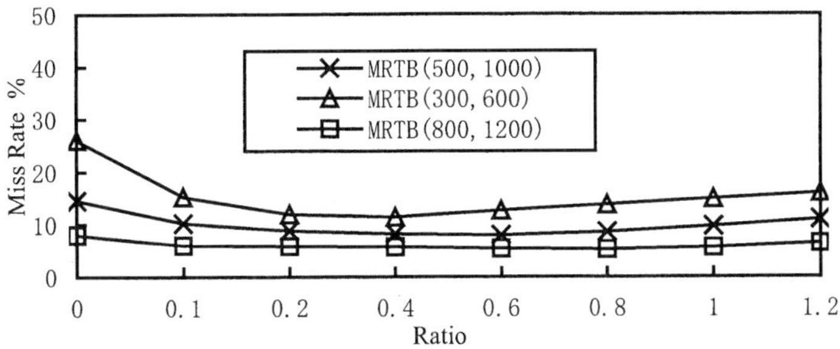

Fig. 7. The miss rate comparison

5 Conclusion and Future Work

Data broadcast has got lots of attentions of relevant researcher due to its scalability and bandwidth effectiveness for disseminating a large volume of data to numerous mobile clients. In this paper, we study the problem of providing consistent data to read-only transactions in real-time data broadcast environment. The main contributions of this paper include the following. First, we formally define the performance objectives based on the detailed analysis of update dissemination protocols for read-only transaction processing in real-time data broadcast environment. Next, a new updates dissemination protocol called *mixed real-time data broadcast* is proposed. Finally, extensive simulation experiments are implemented and numerical results show that MRTB has better performance compared with existing updates dissemination protocols. The future emphasis of our research is the design and evaluation of more flexible and adaptive bandwidth allocation algorithm suitable for the proposed updates dissemination protocol.

Acknowledgements

The work in this paper was partially supported by the National Nature Science Foundation under grant 60203017 and SRF for ROCS, SEM.

References

1. Acharya, S., Franklin, M., Zdonik, S.: Disseminating updates on broadcast disks. Proceedings of the 22nd VLDB Conference, Sep. (1996) 354-365
2. Acharya, S., Franklin, M., Zdonik, S.: Balancing push and pull for data broadcast. Proceedings of ACM SIGMOD, May (1997) 183-194
3. Datta, A., Celik, A., Kim, J., VanderMeer, D.E.: Adaptive broadcast protocol to support power conservant retrieval by mobile users. Proceedings of International Conference on Data Engineering, Sep. (1997) 124-133
4. Pitoura, E., Chrysanthis, P.K.: Multiversion data broadcast. IEEE Transactions on Computers, Oct. (2002) 1224-1230
5. Pitoura, E., Chrysanthis, P.K.: Exploiting versions for handling updates in broadcast disks. Proceedings of Very Large Data Base Conference, Sept. (1999) 114-125
6. Fernandez, J., Ramamritham, K.; Adaptive dissemination of data in real-time asymmetric communication environments. Proceedings of Euromicro Conference on Real-Time Systems, Jun. (1999) 195-203
7. Shanmugasundaram, J., Nithrakashyap, A., Sivasankaran, R., Ramamritham, K.: Efficient concurrency control for broadcast environments. Proceedings of ACM SIGMOD International Conference on Management of Data, Jun. (1999) 85-96
8. Hu, Q., Lee, D.L., Lee, W.C.: A comparison of indexing methods for data broadcast on the air. Proceedings of the 12th International Conference on Information Networking, Jan. (1998) 656-659
9. Lam, K.Y., Kuo, T.W., Tsang, W.H., Law, C.K.: Concurrency control in mobile distributed real-time database systems. Information Systems, vol.25, no.4 (2000) 261-286
10. Imielinski, T., Viswanathan, S., Badrinath, B.R.: Data on air: organization and access. IEEE TKDE, vol.9, no.3 (1994) 353-372
11. Kayan, E., Ulusoy, O.: Real-time transaction management in mobile computing systems. Proceedings of the Sixth International Conference on Database Systems for Advanced Applications, Apr. (1999) 127-134
12. Bowen, T., Gopal, G., Herman, G., Hickey, T., Lee, K., Mansfield, W., Raitz, J.,Weinrib, A.: The datacycle architecture. Comm. ACM, vol. 35, no. 12 (1992) 71-81
13. Xuan, P., Gonzalez, O., Fernandez, J., Ramamritham, K.: Broadcast on demand: efficient and timely dissemination of data in mobile environments. Proceedings of the Third IEEE Real-Time Technology Application Symposium, Jun. (1997) 38-48
14. Lee, G.L., Lo, S.C., Chen, Arbee L.P.: Data allocation on wireless broadcast channels for efficient query processing. IEEE Transaction on Computers, vol.51, no.10 (2002) 1237-1251

Scalable and Fault Tolerant Multiple Tuple Space Architecture for Mobile Agent Communication

Kyungkoo Jun* and Seokhoon Kang

Dept. of Multimedia System Engineering,
University of Incheon, Incheon, Korea
{kjun, hana}@incheon.ac.kr

Abstract. Mobile multi agent based approach has emerged as a new attractive paradigm for the development of large and complex distributed systems. For the efficient communication of mobile agents, architectures employing multiple *tuple spaces* are frequently adopted, but they also introduce complexities related with fault tolerance and replication management. This paper proposes a *federation*, a scalable and fault tolerant multiple tuple spaces architecture. By extending *Adaptive Distributed System level Diagnosis (ADSD)* algorithm, the federation is able to detect and diagnose the failures of its tuple spaces in parallel. We also describe *global tuple*, a new type of tuple allowing the replication without loss of consistency. Finally, we present the numerical performance analysis of the proposed federation scheme.

1 Introduction

Considering the cooperating characteristic of mobile agents, it is obvious that the mobile agent based systems require efficient communication architecture. For this purpose, there have been research efforts about the mobile multi agent communication such as message based middlewares, remote procedure call (RPC) based methods, shared memory etc. Of them, virtual shared memory is frequently adopted because of its simplicity, flexibility, and versatility. Moreover, its model is powerful enough to meet the needs of many coordination challenges.

One of the virtual shared memory implementations used for the mobile multi agent systems is a *tuple space* [1] which behaves like a shared memory where each agent in a system can put or retrieve information to communicate. Particularly, JavaSpace [2], a new realization of the tuple space in Java language, has been developed, and employed as the backbone of the agent communication in many systems.

The scalability and the fault tolerance of multiple tuple space architecture are the main topic of this paper. In the case of a single tuple space, the failure

* This work was supported by the University of Incheon under the 2004 university research fund.

Y. Zhang et al. (Eds.): APWeb 2005, LNCS 3399, pp. 229–240, 2005.

of the tuple space may bring disastrous results such as the system halt and the data loss. Even during the normal operation, the tuple space may turn out to be a bottleneck to the agent communication. To overcome these shortcomings of the single tuple space architecture, there have been research investigations to organize multiple tuple spaces in a system. However, the multiple tuple space architectures introduce other complexities that are not within the scope of the single tuple space, e.g. how to isolate the failures of tuple spaces, how to deal with replicated tuples, etc.

In this paper, we propose a *federation*, a scalable and fault tolerant architecture consisting of multiple tuple spaces. Besides being able to overcome the limitations of the single tuple space architecture, e.g. one–point failure and the bottleneck, the federation is able to detect and isolate the failures of the tuple spaces in it, and keep the consistency among replicated tuples. For the fault detection of the tuple spaces, we extend the Adaptive Distributed System level Diagnosis (ADSD) algorithm [3], which was originally devised for the fault diagnosis in arbitrary networks. For the consistency of duplicated copies of tuples, a *global tuple*, a new tuple type is proposed.

This paper is organized as follows. In Section 2, we provide a brief overview of the tuple space and the ADSD algorithm. We then discuss the fault tolerance capability of the federation as well as the tuple replication schemes in Section 3. Section 4 presents the numerical analysis of the proposed federation, and Section 5 concludes this paper.

2 Tuple Space and Adaptive Distributed System Level Diagnosis Algorithm

2.1 Tuple Space for Agent Communication

Tuple space is a shared and associative virtual memory designed for communication and synchronization of distributed processes [1]. It allows processes to communicate by writing *tuples* into tuple spaces and retrieving them as specified by *templates*. Tuples and templates are ordered sets of typed fields that can be either *actual* or *formal*. An actual field has a specific value, while a formal field represents a set of values. Tuples and templates do not have restrictions on how fields are composed.

The tuple space supports three primitives: *write*, *read*, and *take*. The *write* is to put a tuple into a tuple space; the *read* is to obtain a copy of a tuple that matches a specified template. The *take* is to extract a matched tuple from the tuple space, removing the matched tuple. In the tuple space, associativity is a key concept that enables to retrieve partly matched tuples.

There exist several implementations of the tuple space, e.g. Linda [4], JavaSpaces [2], and TSpaces [5]. These implementations differ in the variety of the extensions they provided. There have been research investigations to extend the tuple space model with multiple tuple spaces. Hierarchical arrangement of tuple spaces has been suggested by [6] [7]. The combination of flat and hierarchical arrangements has been described in [8]. However, these research efforts have not contemplated the issues how the failures of tuple spaces are tolerated and isolated, and how the replicated copies of tuples are controlled to meet the consistency requirement as well as the scalability. These shortcomings of the past research are addressed in this paper.

2.2 Adaptive Distributed System Level Diagnosis Algorithm

This section introduces *Adaptive Distributed System level Diagnosis* (ADSD) algorithm[9] which was developed for detecting and diagnosing faulty nodes in an arbitrary network. In the ADSD algorithm, monitoring of a distributed system which consists of a set of nodes is executed in two separate steps; *detection* and *dissemination*, both of which are executed in a distributed way. First, in the detection step, nodes of a system test neighbor nodes one another periodically and then, in the dissemination step, pass on the test results to other nodes in the system.

The ADSD algorithm represents the testing relationship as a directed graph in which vertices correspond to nodes and directed edges represent testing relationship, i.e. *who tests whom* [9]. The testing results are either *faulty* or *fault-free* and this information is dispersed through a *dissemination tree*, a virtual path which is dynamically formed with the system nodes. The root of this tree is a node that initiates the information dissemination. On receiving the information, nodes determine whether to update their local databases with this information and whether to relay it to next level nodes depending on the recentness of the disseminated information.

Although the conventional ADSD algorithm is superior to traditional centralized schemes in terms of dynamic reconfigurability, parallel processing, and no need of synchronization, it has the limitations in dealing with the complexities introduced by the node failure or join during the dissemination, which will be addressed by the extensions suggested by this paper.

3 Federation of Tuple Spaces

We propose a *federation*, a scalable and fault tolerant multiple tuple space architecture for mobile agent communication. As shown in Figure 1, the federation is a set of tuple spaces which provide mobile agents with the logical view of one large tuple space, mainly enabled by the replication of tuples and the management of failures of tuple spaces.

The federation achieves scalability by replicating *global tuples* to all the tuple spaces in it, thus being able to host a large number of mobile agents. The global tuple is a new type of tuple allowing its replication without loss of consistency. Moreover, with the global tuples, the federation can balance loads on tuple spaces; it can distribute frequently read–accessed tuples to all other tuple spaces by declaring them as global tuples.

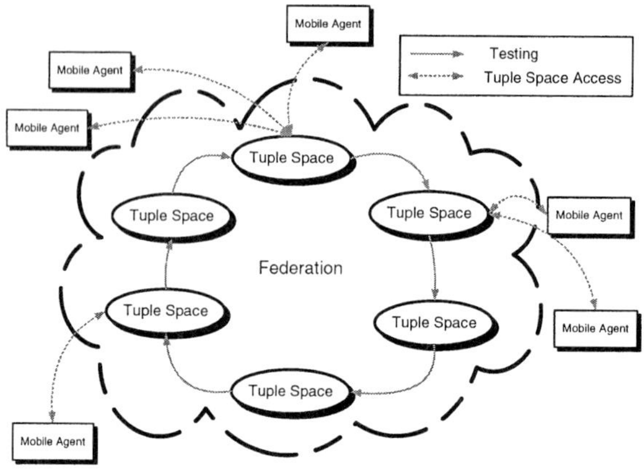

Fig. 1. Federation and its Ring Topology for testing: tuple spaces in a federation test each other

Table 1. Types of Messages of the Federation

Category	Messages	Category	Messages
Monitoring	`test-msg` `test-ack`	Reconfiguration (monitoring)	`request-monitoring` `monitoring--accepted` `monitoring--rejected` `monitoring--stopped`
Dissemination	`info-msg` `info-ack-success` `info-ack-failure`	Reconfiguration (join)	`request-join` `join--accepted` `join--rejected`

The federation is fault tolerant and flexible. For the fault tolerance, tuple spaces diagnose the failures of other tuple spaces by testing one another in a distributed way, and pass on the test results to neighbor tuple spaces without the need of a central observer, thus avoiding the vulnerability to the single point failure. The federation is flexible; tuple spaces can *join* and *leave* the federation at will and at arbitrary moments in time.

Table 1 shows the message types used by the tuple spaces in a federation. The messages are classified, depending on its purpose, into four categories: monitoring, dissemination, reconfiguration for monitoring, and reconfiguration for join. The details of the messages will be discussed in corresponding sections.

We assume that the network connecting the tuple spaces in a federation provides large enough bandwidth to exchange messages among the tuple spaces without unbearable delay. Also, a tuple space can send and receive messages to/from any tuple spaces directly in a federation.

3.1 Fault Tolerance of the Federation

Tuple spaces in a federation test one another periodically to diagnose failures of tuple spaces and share the test results, which are *faulty* or *fault-free*. Based upon these test outcomes, they determine how to manage the federation configuration and replicated tuples. These operations are executed by each tuple space in three discrete steps: *detection*, *dissemination*, and *reconfiguration*. To devise these steps, we modify the ADSD algorithm [3] and also make some extensions so that it can cope with complexities which were not considered in the original work.

Failure Detection. Failure detection in a federation is accomplished by each tuple space; a tuple space periodically tests exactly one other tuple space by sending `test-msg`, and also it is tested by only one another tuple space. It decides the failure by timing out on `test-ack`, a response to the test. The testing relationship among tuple spaces is designed to form a ring. To construct the ring topology, we assign each tuple space with a federation–wide unique identifier which can be also ordered.

Reconfiguration. Whenever a tuple space is removed from, or added to the federation, its ring topology for testing is reconfigured to maintain its circular structure. This reconfiguration process is initiated by an *orphan*, a tuple space with no neighbor tuple space testing it. A tuple space becomes the orphan: i) when the tuple space testing it becomes faulty, resulting in being unable to test, ii) when its tester quits monitoring in order to test another tuple space, and iii) by default, a new or repaired tuple space remains an orphan until it joins the federation successfully.

Once a tuple space becomes or realizes its state as an orphan, it starts the reconfiguration process by which it is able to join the federation. This process is started when the orphans send `request-monitoring` or `request-join` to any of fault–free tuple spaces in the federation; the former message is used by the ones of which tester became faulty or changed its monitoring target, whereas the second one is used by new or repaired tuple spaces.

Upon receiving `request-monitoring` or `request-join`, a tuple space determines whether to allow the join by executing the reconfiguration algorithm. To make this decision, the tuple space compares T_{req}, the identifier of the tuple

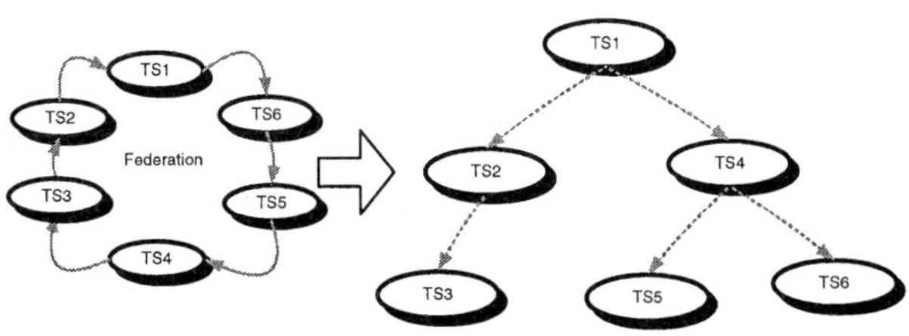

Fig. 2. Binary Tree for Dissemination among Tuple Spaces

space that sent the request with T_{id} and T_{tested}, where T_{id} is its own identifier, T_{tested} is that of the tuple space it is testing at the moment. The order relationship between these identifiers

$$T_{id} < T_{req} < T_{tested}$$

allows the join of the tuple space T_{req}. By this relationship, the ring topology can be maintained after the join of the tuple space T_{req}.

Dissemination. *Dissemination* enables tuple spaces in a federation to share among them the events such as failures, joins, etc. As shown in Figure 2, this dissemination is performed through a *binary tree* representing a virtual channel through which the event is spread to all the tuple spaces. The binary tree is composed dynamically on the spot. The root of the tree becomes the first tuple space that detects an event. The dissemination continues along the binary tree until all terminal nodes receive the event. In Figure 2, the tuple space $TS1$ is the one which has an event to disseminate.

The types of events that initiate the dissemination are as follows: i) failures of tuple spaces, ii) joins of new or repaired tuple spaces, and iii) updates on global tuples, e.g. addition of new global tuples, deletion of existing ones. The global tuples will be discussed later.

Figure 3 shows the procedure of the dynamic composition of the binary tree. At first, a tuple space that initiates the dissemination makes $List_{all}$, a list of all fault–free tuple spaces at the moment. Then it splits $List_{all}$ into two approximately same-size sub–lists, $List_{left}$ and $List_{right}$, corresponding to the left and right sub–trees respectively. From each sub-list, one tuple space is picked as the root of the sub–trees, in this case T_{left} and T_{right}. Then `info-msg` conveying the event information is transmitted only to T_{left} and T_{right}. Of the parameters composing the `info-msg`, there are three parameters related with the dissemination: i) the event, ii) $List_{left}$ or $List_{right}$ depending on whether this message is sent to T_{left} or T_{right}, iii) the list of all fault–free tuple spaces to which this event should be delivered. On receiving the `info-msg`, T_{left} and T_{right} relay the message to others by repeating the above steps except that, in this repetition, $List_{all}$ is replaced by $List_{left}$ in the case of T_{left}, or $List_{right}$ if it is T_{right}.

Local Database Update. On receiving events through the dissemination, tuple spaces determine if it is necessary to update their own *local database* with the events. In the local database, each tuple space keeps the status of other tuple spaces as *entries* each of which represents one corresponding tuple space. An entry is composed of two fields: ID_{ts}, a tuple space identifier and Int_{status}, *status integer*, which has a positive-value and will be discussed shortly. The update is determined if the following two conditions are met: i) the event is about a failure or join and ii) it is not yet reflected on the databases.

The status integers of the entries represent the current status of tuple spaces. Odd values of the status integer represent the fault–free status of an associated tuple space, whereas even values mean the faulty status. The status integer of

```
procedure DISSEMINATION(Event e)
    L_all ⇐ fault–free tuple spaces to which e is relayed
    L_left, L_right ⇐ split L_all
    T_left ⇐ pick a tuple space from L_left,
    T_right ⇐ pick a tuple space from L_right
    Send e To T_left, T_right
    if timeout of acknowledgement from T_left or T_right then
        Spawn new dissemination about failure T_left or T_right.
        if this tuple space is NOT the root of the binary tree then
            Send info-ack-failure To parent
        end if
    else if received info-ack-failure from T_left or T_right then
        if this tuple space is the root of the binary tree then
            restart the dissemination
        else
            Send info-ack-failure To parent
        end if
    else
        if this tuple space is NOT the root of the binary tree then
            Send info-ack-success To parent
        end if
        return
    end if
end procedure
```

Fig. 3. Pseudo Code of Dissemination Algorithm

a tuple space is initialized to 1 when the tuple space joins a federation for the first time, and increments by one whenever the tuple space changes its status: faulty or fault-free. By the ever increasing nature of the status integer, it is also feasible to determine the recentness of events by comparing the status integers, i.e. the event with bigger status integer is more recent than the other.

Figure 4 shows the update procedure of the local database entries on receiving a failure or join event carried by *Msg*, an `info-msg`. Of the fields in the *Msg*, there are two fields, ID_{ts} and Int_{status}, describing this event, the same format as used by the database entries. The update process starts by retrieving from the *Msg*, T_{id} the tuple space identifier stored in the ID_{ts} field. Then a database entry matching T_{id} is searched and, if found, the associated $Status_{db}$ the status integer, is fetched. Finally, by comparing $Status_{db}$ with $Status_{msg}$ a status integer from the *Msg*, the received event is classified into *new*, *same*, or *old* for the update decision of the database.

The events are *new* if the status integer of the event is bigger than that of the corresponding entry, or no database entry matching the event is found. For this new event, tuple spaces update the database entry with the event, or create a new entry if no entry exists. After the update, they continue to relay this event to next level along the binary tree by calling `DISSEMINATE` described in Figure 3.

```
procedure DatabaseUpdate(Msg)
    T_id ⇐ tuple space ID conveyed in the Msg
    if T_id ∈ Database then
        Status_db ⇐ T_id's status integer stored in the local database
        Status_msg ⇐ T_id's status integer conveyed in the Msg
        if Status_db < Status_msg then                    ▷ Msg has new info.
            Update local database With Msg's info.
            Call DISSEMINATION                            ▷ Relay Msg to next level
        else if Status_db = Status_msg then               ▷ Msg has same info.
            Call DISSEMINATION                            ▷ Relay Msg to next level
        else                                              ▷ Msg has old info.
            Discard Msg
        end if
    else
        Add Msg' info. To the local database
    end if
end procedure
```

Fig. 4. Pseudo Code of Local Database Update Algorithm

The events are *same* if the status integer of the event is equal to that of the corresponding entry. With this same event, tuple spaces need not update the entry, however continue to pass on the event to next level by `DISSEMINATE`.

The events are *old* if the status integer of the event is less than that of the matching entry. By this old event, tuple spaces neither update the database entry nor continue the dissemination. They just discard the event without relaying it.

3.2 Extensions to the ADSD Algorithm

The original ADSD algorithm is not able to deal with neither the failures nor joins during the dissemination. In this section, we introduce *late acknowledgement* and *auditor* mechanisms to remedy these drawbacks of the original work.

Late Acknowledgement. It ensures that, once event dissemination is started, all the fault-free tuple spaces along the binary tree receive the events even if some of the tuple spaces fail during the dissemination. Moreover, the late acknowledgement is able to detect these failures by timeout.

The acknowledgement is that a tuple space sends the `info-ack` message to its parent in the binary tree in order to notify that it received an event relayed from the parent. The late acknowledgement is that a tuple space sends this `info-ack` *late*, i.e. after it confirms that its children tuple spaces in the binary tree received the event. This confirmation is accomplished by the `info-ack` from the children. The opposite to the late acknowledgement is *early acknowledgement* by which a tuple space acknowledges its parent without this confirmation, i.e. on receiving an event, it first sends `info-ack` to its parent, and then relays the event to next level children.

To explain the necessity of the late acknowledgement, we first illustrate the problem of the early acknowledgement. In Figure 2, the tuple space $TS1$ begins

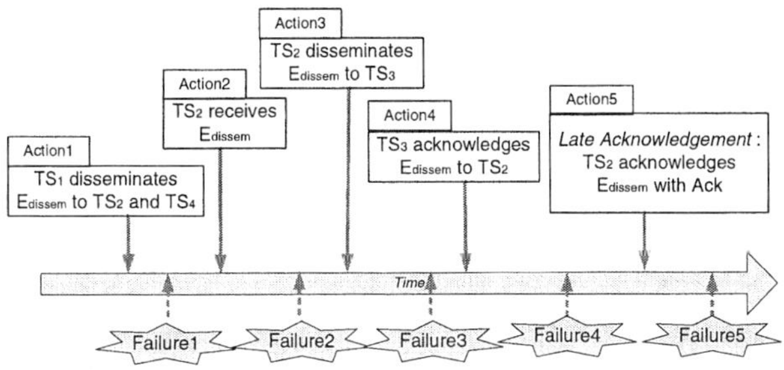

Fig. 5. Time-Space diagram: the late acknowledgement ensures that events are disseminated to all fault–free tuple spaces in a federation

to disseminate an event to two sub–trees each of which consists of $(TS2, TS3)$ and $(TS4, TS5, TS6)$ respectively. With the early acknowledgement, if the tuple space $TS2$ fails at the moment which is after sending `info-ack` to $TS1$ but before relaying the event to $TS3$, this failure leads to the situation where $TS3$ never receives the event, however such inconsistency is never detected.

By the space–time diagram shown in Figure 5, we informally prove that the late acknowledgement is able to prevent this inconsistency. Note that, by using the late acknowledgement in Figure 2, $TS2$ waits until it receives `info-ack` from $TS3$ before sending the acknowledgement to $TS1$. In the diagram, all possible moments at which tuple space $TS2$ may fail are labeled from $Failure_1$ to $Failure_5$.

We now explain how each of the failures is insulated such that it does not incur the inconsistency. First of all, $Failure_1$ does not affect the dissemination because it is prior to the event reception. $Failure_2$ to $Failure_4$ which occur in the middle of the dissemination are also safe because these moments are before tuple space $TS2$ sends `info-ack` to $TS1$, thus $TS1$ is able to notice the dissemination failure by timing out the acknowledgement expected from $TS2$. Finally, $Failure_5$ turns out to be harmless because it is after the completion of the dissemination, i.e. after $TS3$ received the event and acknowledged it.

Auditor. Another inconsistency prevention mechanism is *auditor*, which is devised to ensure the consistency of newly joining tuple spaces. We first illustrate the inconsistency problem that may incur when the auditor mechanism is not in use. In Figure 2, we assume a scenario where a new tuple space TS_{new} asks $TS1$ to allow the join *right after* $TS1$ began to disseminate an event. Then TS_{new} is never able to receive or recognize this event because $TS1$ had no information about the existence of TS_{new} at the moment of building the binary tree for the event dissemination.

The auditor mechanism implemented on each tuple space in a federation works as follows; whenever a tuple space receives an event through the dissemination, it ensures that T_{tested} the tuple space that it is testing at the moment receives the same event. To accomplish this, it searches the identifier of T_{tested} in the third parameter, a list of all fault–free tuple spaces to which the event is intended to be delivered. This list is one of the fields of `info-msg` as described in Figure 3.

The correctness of the auditor mechanism can be informally proved in a similar way to the proof of the late acknowledgement by using a space–time diagram. However, the diagram and the proof are omitted in this paper because of the length restriction.

3.3 Scalability and Fault Tolerance of Tuples

Concerning the consistency problem associated with the tuple replication, we first introduce *global tuples*, a new type of tuples which are allowed to be duplicated, while we use the term *local tuple* for the tuples that are not replicated. Once a tuple is declared as the global tuple, it can be duplicated to all other fault–free tuple spaces in a federation. The duplication proceeds in the same way as the event dissemination; a global tuple is delivered as an event to tuple spaces along the binary tree.

The global tuples are dispersed to not only existing tuple spaces in a federation, but also new tuple spaces. Once joining a federation, these new tuple spaces populate their spaces with the global tuples which are provided by the tuple spaces that permitted their join.

The most critical issue of global tuples is consistency; since global tuples are replicated on multiple tuple spaces, any change on a global tuple should be reflected to all of its copies. We approach this consistency complexity by assigning mobile agents or tuple spaces with *exclusive authority* of modifying global tuples. We classify the global tuples into two subtypes, *agent–exclusive* and *tuplespace–exclusive*, based upon which entity has the exclusive right to modify those tuples. The agent–exclusive tuple is the one that only one associated agent is allowed to modify, whereas the read is allowed to all agents. In a similar way, the tuplespace–exclusive ones can be modified only at a designated tuple space, while read–access is possible at any tuple spaces. The changes on global tuples, either agent–exclusive or tuplespace–exclusive, are disseminated as events to all other tuple spaces in the same way as the dissemination.

Delegation of Exclusiveness. The exclusive authority for tuple modification can be delegated; an agent can become entitled with authority for agent–exclusive tuples, and so does a tuple space with tuplespace–exclusive ones. This delegation capability is necessary not only for the case of failures, but also other cases, e.g. an agent which soon terminates may request that the global tuples authorized to it should be delegated to another agent. Another example is that a tuple space authorized with a large number of global tuples may request the delegation to reduce the load, which is primarily incurred by the modification requests on those tuples.

Delegation of exclusive rights on tuples can be initiated by the request of agents or tuple spaces possessing those authorities. Particularly, for the delegation in the case of failures, one of fault–free agents in a federation is selected to initiate the delegation of exclusive rights owned by the failed agents or tuple spaces.

4 Numerical Analysis of Proposed Federation

We compare the performance of the federation numerically with the corresponding results of a traditional *central observer* scheme in terms of the maximum number of monitoring messages on one tuple space, required time for dissemination, and the maximum elapsed time from fault detection until the completion of its dissemination. The central observer scheme is that all the operations, i.e. detection, dissemination, and reconfiguration, are managed in a centralized way by one designated object, called *central observer.*

Figure 6(a) shows the changes of the maximum number of required monitoring messages per tuple space as the group size increases. In the case of federation, the number of monitoring messages remains as constant regardless of the group size, whereas the central observer needs the maximum $2 * N$ message exchange to monitor all tuple spaces in a group, where N is the group size.

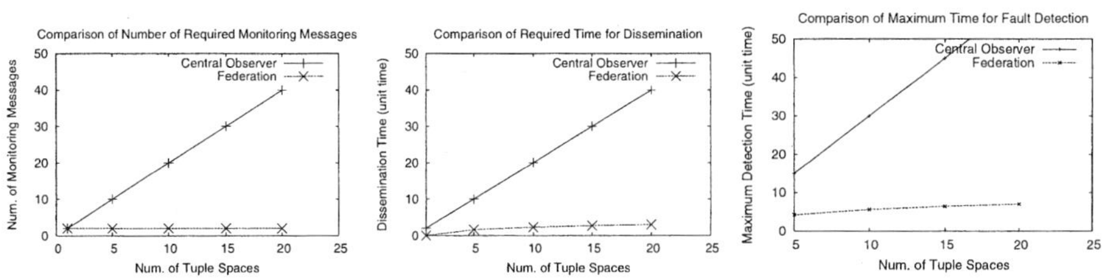

(a) (b) (c)

Fig. 6. Comparison between the federation scheme and the central observer in terms of (a) the number of monitoring messages, (b) the dissemination time, and (c) the maximum detection time

Figure 6(b) shows the changes in the dissemination time as the group size increases. In the case of the federation, the binary tree enables the dissemination to become parallel gradually as it proceeds down the tree, thus the time is logarithmical proportion to the group size. With u the time for one message transmission, and N the group size, the central observer requires the time $2*N*u$ until the dissemination finishes, while the federation needs the time $2 * logN * u$.

Figure 6(c) shows the changes in the maximum elapsed time from failure detection to its completion of the dissemination. Since the central observer tests one tuple space at a time, in the worst case, it can take the time $N * m$ to detect a failure, where m is the monitoring interval. Thus the maximum elapsed time becomes $N * m + 2 * (N - 1) * u$, where $2 * (N - 1) * u$ is the time for dissemination as described above, resulting in the time complexity of $O(n^2)$. In the case of the federation, regardless of the group size, the worst case time for a failure detection becomes the time m and the dissemination takes the time $2 * log(N - 1) * u$, thus the total elapsed time becoming $m + 2 * log(N - 1) * u$, with its time complexity $O(logN)$.

5 Conclusions

This paper proposed the federation, a scalable and fault tolerant architecture consisting of multiple tuple spaces, for the communication of mobile agents. We improved the original ADSD algorithm with the mechanisms such as the late acknowledgement and the auditor; with the former mechanism, failures during the dissemination can be tolerated, whereas the latter one allows tuple spaces to join a federation without the loss of consistency. For the scalability, the federation allows tuples to be replicated to all the tuple spaces in it by the use of the global tuple concept without loss of consistency. The results of the numerical analysis of the proposed federation show that the performance of the federation is superior to the conventional central observer model.

References

1. Carriero, N., Gelernter, D.: Linda in Context. Communications of the ACM **32** (1989) 444–458
2. Microsystems, S.: Javaspace specification (1998)
3. Rangarajan, S., Dahbura, A., Ziegler, E.: A Distributed System-Level Diagnosis Algorithm for Arbitrary Network Topologies. IEEE Transactions on Computers, Special Issue on Fault-Tolerant Computing **44** (1995) 312– 334
4. Gelernter, D.: Communications in Linda. ACM Trans. Programming Languages and Systems **7** (1985) 80–112
5. P. Wycko, S. W. McLaughry, T.J.L., Ford, D.A.: TSpaces. IBM Systems Journal **37** (1998) 454–474
6. Gelernter, D.: Multiple tuple spaces in LindaTSpaces. Lecture Notes in Computer Science **366** (1989) 20–27
7. Hupfer, S.: Melinda: Linda with multiple tuple spaces. Technical Report RR–766, Yale University (1990)
8. Jensen, K.: Towards a Multiple Tuple Space Model. PhD thesis, Aalborg University (1989)
9. Rangarajan, S., Dahbura, A.T., Ziegler, E.A.: A distributed system-level diagnosis algorithm for arbitrary network topologies. IEEE Trans. Comput. **44** (1995) 312–334

LinkNet: A New Approach for Searching in a Large Peer-to-Peer System*

Kunlong Zhang and Shan Wang

School of Information, Renmin University of China, Beijing, China, 100872
zhangkl@ruc.edu.cn, suang@public.bta.net.cn

Abstract. Searching a file by its name is an essential problem of a large peer-to-peer file-sharing system. In this paper, we present a new scalable distributed data structure LinkNet for searching in a large peer-to-peer system. In LinkNet, all elements are stored in a sorted doubly linked list, and one node stores many elements. LinkNet uses virtual link to speed search and enhance fault tolerance. Because LinkNet is based on a sorted list, it benefits operations such as range query, bulk loading of data, and merging of two LinkNets.

1 Introduction

For a large peer-to-peer file-sharing system, searching a file by its name is an essential problem. One initial approach is to setup up a server which maps a file name to its location. Napster ([6]) uses this approach. The problem of this approach is that it uses an unscalable central database to index all files. Another initial approach is that a node broadcasts the search request to all its neighbors when it does not find the file in its local database. Gnutella ([7]) adopts this approach. However this approach doesn't scale well because of its bandwidth consumption and unrelated search in many nodes.

To overcome the scalability problem, several algorithms based on a distributed hash table (DHT) approach are presented ([1], [8], [9], [10], [11]). In these algorithms, each node in the system maintains a small routing table to form an overlay network and each data item is associated with a unique key which is hashed to determine which node it will be stored at. When a search request is received by a node that does not store the search key, the node will use its routing table to routing the request to a neighbor which is closer to the key. Because hashing does not keep the order of the keys, DHT systems do not support range queries efficiently.

Two recent papers [2] [3] try to build a peer-to-peer system on the skip list data structure. The paper [2] describes a distributed data structure called skip graphs. In a skip graph, search, insert and delete operations are done in logarithmic time. Because of no hashing, skip graphs support range queries more efficiently than DHT. Skip

* The work was supported by the National Natural Science Foundation of China under Grant Nos. 60473069, 60496325 and the National High Technology Development 863 Program of China under Grant No. 2003AA4Z3030.

Y. Zhang et al. (Eds.): APWeb 2005, LNCS 3399, pp. 241 – 246, 2005.

graphs also are highly resilient to node failures because they have many redundant links among nodes. The paper [3] describes a distributed data structure called SkipNet which is very similar to skip graphs. One problem of these two data structure is there are a lot of links. With *N* resources in the network, there is a total of O(*N*log*N*) links.

To decrease the number of links, this paper introduces a new scalable distributed data structure LinkNet which is built on the list data structure.

2 LinkNet

To help our discussion, we briefly define some terms first. A peer-to-peer system consists of many **nodes**. Each node has a unique **location**. Typically a node's location is its IP address or domain name. A node stores many data items or **elements**. An element is a file, an object, or one row of a database table. Each element has a **key**. An element is mapped to a **pointer**. A pointer is a pair <*location*, *key*>. Two elements form a **link** if their order is known. If a link is physically stored in main memory or second memory, it is a **physical link**; otherwise it is a **virtual link**.

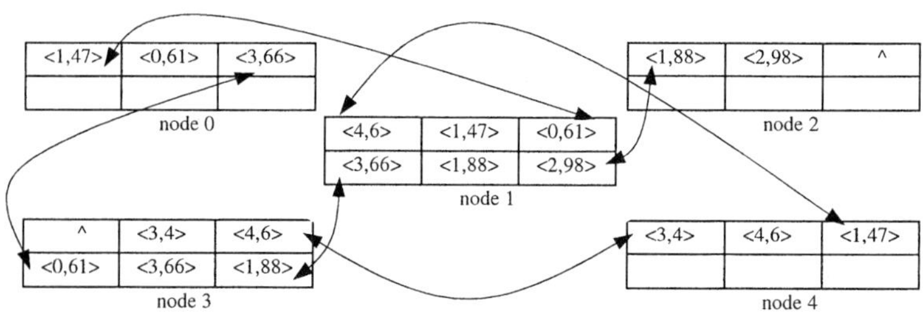

Fig. 1. A network-based sorted doubly linked list

Fig.1 shows a network-based sorted doubly linked list. Search in a network-based sorted doubly linked list is simple and slow. For example, to find key 98 starting from key 4 goes through key 4, 6, 47, 61, 66, 88, 98 and node 3, 4, 1, 0, 3, 1, 2, but the search will only go though key 4, 88, 98 and node 3, 1, 2 if the virtual link <4, 88> is used. For all keys in the same node, one key can share another key's pointers to form virtual links. LinkNet uses virtual links to speed search. Fig.2 shows a list-based LinkNet corresponding to Fig.1. In Fig.2, virtual links are marked by dot lines. The virtual links not only speed search, but also enhance fault tolerance. For example, if node 4 fails, it is still possible to find key 98 starting from key 4.

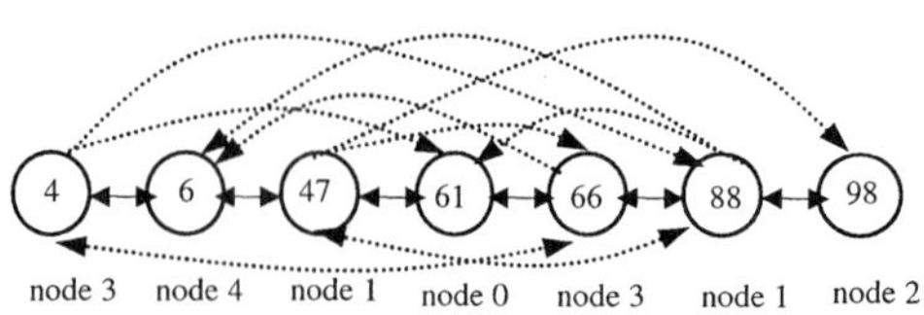

Fig. 2. A list-based LinkNet with 7 keys on 5 nodes

The disadvantage of list-based LinkNet is that its performance depends on the distribution of elements heavily. If each node stores only one element, the list-based LinkNet is degenerated into a network-based sorted doubly linked list. To avoid this problem, skip-list-based LinkNet is built and it is discussed in the next section.

3 Algorithms for LinkNet

In LinkNet, a node can store many elements. These elements are stored in a sorted doubly linked list. A new LinkNet has only two special elements: *header* which is given a key less than any legal key, and *nil* which is given a key greater than any legal key. Each element has a level which is a random number capped at *MaxLevel*. It is not necessary that all elements are capped at the same value of *MaxLevel*. Our approach for concurrent operations is similar to the approach in paper [5], thus we omit the proofs of correctness in this paper.

To describe the operations for LinkNet, we denote node as $\boldsymbol{u}$, $\boldsymbol{v}$ and element as $\boldsymbol{x}, \boldsymbol{y}$. A node has a location ($\boldsymbol{u}$.location). When there is no confusion, the location of a node refers to that node. An element has a key, a location and a level ($\boldsymbol{x}$.key, $\boldsymbol{x}$.location, $\boldsymbol{x}$.level). The successor and the predecessor of element $\boldsymbol{x}$ at level l is denoted as $\boldsymbol{x}$.neighbor[R][l] and $\boldsymbol{x}$.neighbor[L][l]. If $\boldsymbol{x}$.location is equal to $\boldsymbol{u}$.location, the element $\boldsymbol{x}$ is stored on the node $\boldsymbol{u}$; otherwise $\boldsymbol{x}$ is a pointer that points to the element $\boldsymbol{x}$.

The search operation (algorithm 1 in Fig.3) can be started from any node. If no elements are stored on the node, function isEmpty() creates a new LinkNet on this node and returns true. Function chooseSide() is used to decide the search direction. If there is an element whose key equals to the search key, function localSearch() returns that element, otherwise it returns an element which is the nearest element to the search key following the search direction.

The first step of the insert operation (algorithm 2 in Fig.3) is to find the place of new element in the level 1 of LinkNet. The search returns an element $\boldsymbol{y}$ which is the predecessor of the new element $\boldsymbol{x}$ and $\boldsymbol{y}$'s forward pointer points to $\boldsymbol{x}$'s successor. The next step is to insert the new element into a node. A random level generated by function randomLevel() is assigned to the new element. If the random level given to the new element is greater than 1, the new element will be inserted into the LinkNet level by level. The level of the element *header* and *nil* is not less than the level of any element in the LinkNet.

The delete operation (algorithm 4 in Fig.3) is simple. A node can only delete the element stored on it. To delete an element $\boldsymbol{x}$, it is not correct to immediately garbage collect $\boldsymbol{x}$ because other operations may have a pointer to $\boldsymbol{x}$. Instead, function putOnGarbageQueue() is used to put $\boldsymbol{x}$ onto a garbage queue whose element can be taken off any time after the completion of all searches/insertions/deletions that were in progress.

An M elements skip-list-based LinkNet needs expect O(M) space overall. The number of messages exchanged among nodes is used to evaluate the algorithms. For an M elements skip-list-based LinkNet, an operation (i.e. a search, insertion or deletion) takes expected O(log$M$) messages.

Algorithm 1: search for node *u*

```
upon receiving <search, key> from v
  if (u.isEmpty() = true)
    send <retNotFound, header> to v
  else
    side ← u.chooseSide(key)
    send <searchOp, v , key, side> to u

upon receiving <searchOp, startNode, searchKey, side>
  x ← u.localSearch(searchKey, side)
  if (x.location ≠ u.location)
    send <searchOp, startNode, searchKey, side>
          to x.location;
  else if (x.key = searchKey)
    send <retFound, x> to startNode
  else if (side = L)
    send <retNotFound, x.neighbor[L][0]>
          to startNode;
  else
    send <retNotFound, x > to startNode
```

Algorithm 2: insert for node *u*

```
upon receiving <insert, key, value> from v
  send <search, key> to w
  wait until receipt of <retSearchResult, y>
  maxElementLevel ← u.randomLevel()
  x ← u.makeElement(u.location, key, value)
  u.lock(x.level)
  u.insertOp(x, y, 1)
  for level ← 2 to maxElementLevel do
    y ← x.neighbor[L][level-1]
    send <searchNeighbor, u, y, level> to y.location
    wait until receipt of <retSearchResult, y, z>
    u.insertOp(x, y, level)
  u.unlock(x.level)
  send <retInsertSucess> to v

u.insertOp(x, y, level)
  send <getLock, u, y, x, level> to y.location
  wait until receipt of <retLockResult, y, z>
  u.lock(x.neighbor[R][level])
  x.neighbor[L][level] ← y
  x.neighbor[R][level] ← z
  x.level ← level
  send <setPointer, y, R, level, x> to y.location
  wait until receipt of <retSetPointerResult>
  send <setPointer, z, L, level, x> to z.location
  wait until receipt of <retSetPointerResult>
  send <unlock, y, R, level> to y.location
  wait until receipt of <retUnlockResult>
  u.unlock(x.neighbor[R][level])

upon receiving <searchNeighbor, startNode, x, level>
  if (x.level ≥ level)
    send <retFound, x, x.neighbor[R][level]>
          to startNode
  else
    y ← x.neighbor[L][level-1]
    send <searchNeighbor, startNode, y, level)
          to y.location
```

Algorithm 3: Additional operations for node *u*

```
upon receiving <setPointer, x, side, level, y> from v
  x.neighbor[side][level] ← y
  send <retSetPointerSuccess> to v

upon receiving <unlock, x, side, level> from v
  u.unlock(x.neighbor[side][level])
  send <retUnlockSuccess> to v

upon receiving <getLock, startNode, y, x, level>
  z ← y.neighbor[R][level];
  if (z.key < x.key)
    send <getLock, startNode, z, x, level>
          to z.location
  else
    send <getLockOp, startNode, z, x, level>
          to z.location

upon receiving <getLockOp, startNode, y, x, level>
  u.lock(y.neighbor[R][level])
  z ← y.neighbor[R][level];
  if (z.key < x.key)
    u.unlock(y.neighbor[R][level])
    send <getLockOp, startNode, z, x, level>
          to z.location
  else
    send <retLockSuccess, y, z> to startNode
```

Algorithm 4: delete for node *u*

```
upon receiving <delete, key> from v
  x ← u.localSearch(key, u.chooseSide(key))
  if (x.location = u.location and x.key = key)
    maxElementLevel ← x.level
    u.lock(x.level)
    for level ← maxElementLevel down to 1 do
      y ← x.neighbor[L][level]
      send <getLock, u, y, x, level> to y.location
      wait until receipt of <retLockResult, y, z>
      u.lock(x.neighbor[R][level])
      z ← x.neighbor[R][level]
      send <setPointer, y, R, level, z> to y.location
      wait until receipt of <retSetPointerResult>
      send <setPointer, z, L, level, y> to z.location
      wait until receipt of <retSetPointerResult>
      x.level ← level-1
      x.neighbor[L][level] ← z
      x.neighbor[R][level] ← y
      send <unlock, y, R, level> to y.location
      wait until receipt of <retUnlockResult>
      u.unlock(x.neighbor[R][level])
    u.putOnGarbageQue(x)
    u.unlock(x.level)
  send <retDeleteSucess> to v
```

Fig. 3. Algorithms for skip-list-based LinkNet

4 Performance Evaluation

The search algorithm of LinkNet is simulated on a PC. The LinkNet is built with two parameters: one is N, the number of nodes; another is M, the number of keys. The keys are generated by a uniform random number generator. Each node has a random number of keys. The simulation search random keys starting from random selected nodes for 10,000 times to evaluate the search algorithm by the average number of hops. A hop is a message passing from one node to another node.

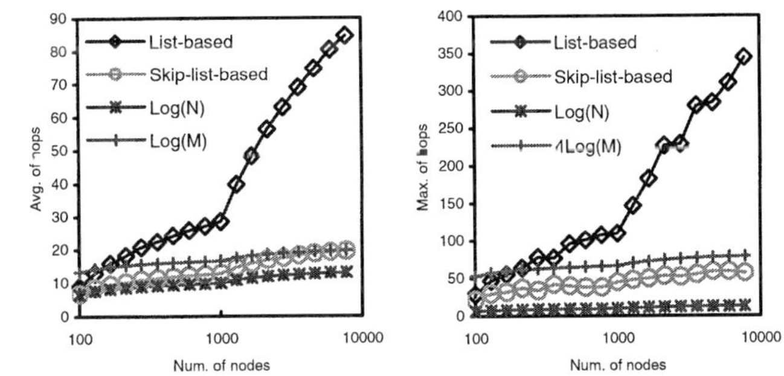

Fig. 4. The number of hops vs. the number of nodes

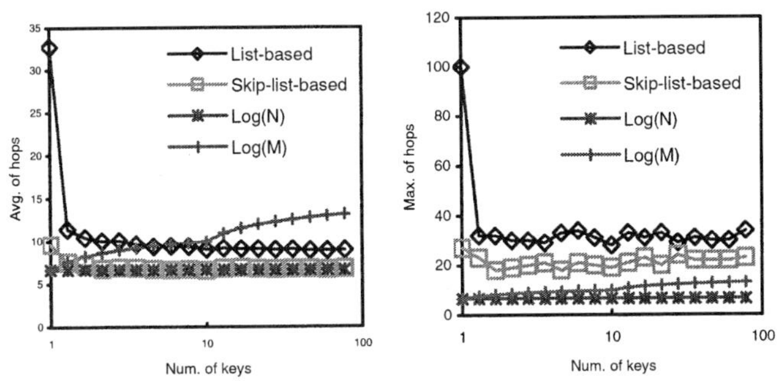

Fig. 5. The number of hops vs. the number of keys

The experiment results are shown in Fig.4 and Fig.5. In Fig.4, each node has average 100 keys. In Fig.5, there are 100 nodes.

The experiment shows that the search performance of list-based LinkNet is worse than that of skip-list-based LinkNet. Fig.4 also shows that when the number of nodes increases and the average number of keys of each node is a constant, the average number of search hops on skip-list-based LinkNet is O(log(M)). Fig.5 also shows that when the average number of keys on each node increases and the number of nodes is a constant, the average number of search hops on skip-list-based LinkNet approaches log(N).

5 Conclusions

We have defined a new scalable distributed data structure LinkNet. By adding virtual links to a skip list, we build a skip-list-based LinkNet. In an N nodes M elements network, the expected total space this data structure takes is $O(M)$, and when M is big enough, the search operation takes expected $O(\log N)$ messages among nodes. Additionally, the virtual links enhance fault tolerance of LinkNet.

Because LinkNet keeps the order of the keys, it provides better support for range query than DHT. LinkNet also benefits many other operations. For example, it is more efficient than DHT to merge two LinkNets, split a LinkNet, and bulk load data into a LinkNet.

Acknowledgments

The work described in this paper was carried out during a visit to database group at school of computing, National University of Singapore. The design presented here is the result of much fruitful discussion with Beng Chin Ooi.

References

1. H. Balakrishnan, M. Frans Kaashoek, D. Karger, R. Morris, and I. Stoica. Looking Up Data in P2P Systems. Communications of the ACM, 46(2), February 2003.
2. J. Aspnes and G. Shah. Skip Graphs. In Proceedings of the 14th Annual ACM-SIAM Symposium on Discrete Algorithms, January 2003.
3. N. J. A. Harvey, M. B. Jones, S. Saroiu, M. Theimer, and A. Wolman. SkipNet: A Scalable Overlay Network with Practical Locality Properties. In Proceedings of the 4th USENIX Symposium on Internet Technologies and Systems (USITS), March 2003.
4. W. Pugh. Skip Lists: A Probabilistic Alternative to Balanced Trees. Communications of the ACM, 33(6):668-676, June 1990.
5. W. Pugh. Concurrent Maintenance of Skip List. Technical Report CS-TR-2222, Department of Computer Science, University of Maryland, June 1990
6. Napster. http://www.napster.com/.
7. Gnutella. http://www.gnutelliums.com/.
8. S. Ratnasamy, P. Francis, M. Handley, R. Karp, and S. Shenker. A Scalable Content-Addressable Network. In Proceedings of the ACM Symposium on Communications Architectures and Protocols (SIGCOMM), San Diego, CA, USA, August 2001.
9. I. Stoica, R. Morris, D. Liben-Nowell, D. Karger, M. Frans Kaashoek, F. Dabek, and H. Balakrishnan. Chord: A Scalable Peer-to-peer Lookup Service for Internet Applications. Tech. Rep. TR-819, MIT LCS, 2001.
10. A. Rowstron and P. Druschel. Pastry: Scalable, distributed object location and routing for large-scale peer-to-peer systems. In Proceedings of the 18th IFIP/ACM International Conference on Distributed Systems Platforms, November 2001.
11. B. Zhao, J. Kubiatowicz, and A. Joseph. Tapestry: An infrastructure for fault-tolerant wide-area location and routing. Tech. Rep. UCB/CSD-01-1141, Computer Science Division, U. C. Berkeley, Apr.2001.

P2P-Based Web Text Information Retrieval*

Shiping Chen[1,2] and Baile Shi[1]

[1] Department of Information Science and Engineering
Fudan University, Shanghai, 200433, China
[2] Network Center
University of Shanghai for Science and Technology, Shanghai, 200093, China
chensp@usst.edu.cn, bshi@fudan.edu.cn

Abstract. This paper proposes a query routing infrastructure that aims at the Web text information retrieval. The routing information is distributed in each query routing node, and needs no central infrastructure, so it can be used in large distributed system to determine which node need to be queried to achieve the function of query routing in semantic network. At the same time, this paper proposes the concept of preference circle, which organizes Web text data sources efficiently , so querying the information for routing become simpler and easier for maintenance, which improves the efficiency of query routing. In addition, we demonstrate the advantages of our system in work load balancing and the completeness of result of query etc.

1 Introduction

When a user gives a query, he hopes that the results can incarnate the present situation and are the best content that he demands in extant results. We have the experience that when we search the name of a sport star on Google, Yahoo and Sohu, it is possible that the first page of the three results is not identical! Here, we hope that it can offer all these 3 pages of contents to select. If the query result and experience of the sport fans can be offered in time to share, the problem is solved. The experiences or query results can be organized well in the P2P network[1][2][3][5][6] and it seems to be a safe shortcut to obtaining the valid information more all-sided and more promptly. The problems left are that how to find your needs and how to organize it on the network.

This paper applies the Chord computing technology for P2P network, and retains its feature of scalability, and also answers the crucial problem in some applications, for example: put forward a catalog services infrastructure for text similarity query; Separat the storage of the routing information from the structural information to reduce the information transfer in the case of node joining or node leaving in P2P network, reduce network transmission cost and obtain a better balance in workload in nodes as well as a better system scalability.

* This research was sponsored by the Shanghai Natural Science Fund, under contract 02ZD14066.

Y. Zhang et al. (Eds.): APWeb 2005, LNCS 3399, pp. 247–252, 2005.

3.1 Query Routing

As one query vector Q is accepted by a routing node, it will process the similarity computing with every center vector FrequentPreference of the relative clusters(See table 1). If the similarity between the vector Q and some FrequentPreference surpasses the threshold, it will obtain the corresponding node address. The system will carry through the distributed Top-N processing in a distributed database environment which has been discussed in previous chapter.

Table. 1. Definition of the query routing information

CharacterItem_ID	CharacterItem Identifier
FrequentPreference	Center vector of preference cluster
SourceNode	Node which preference cluster being stored in

3.2 New Query Routing Information Joins

New query routing information comes from the joining of the new preference cluster. It is the routine procedure of routing information set-up after the node joins the P2P network. The algorithm about how the preference cluster information joins the query routing table is shown as following:

To a preference cluster on the node N, its center vector FP=(t_1, t_2, t_3,..... t_m), m is the number of the character items of the vector.When the preference joins the P2P network service, the steps for routing information setup are as following:

Step1: Compute the identifiers of each character item: t_1->t_1_ID, t_2->t_2_ID, t_3-> t_3_ID, ...t_m->t_m_ID

Step2: Locate the node N_i that is responsible for t_i according to the Successor (ti_ID) algorithm [5] of the Chord ring in the character routing ring.

Step3: The query routing table Query_Router is maintained by N_i. This table is indexed according to CharacterItem_ID. A tuple is added in this table: (t_i_ID,FP,N).

3.3 Dynamic Maintenance of the Query Routing Table

The preference is variable. The center vector of a preference cluster make dynamic adjustment based on the variation of the amount of accessing the text vector in the cluster. In fact, the maintenance of the preference is executed mainly in the preference storage layer(See fig. 1).But this will cause the change of the query routing information in the character routing layer

Suppose that there is a modified center vector of a preference cluster on the node n (due to the space limitation,how it is modified is not discussed in the paper), that is marked as $FP^{(n)}=(t_1^{(n)},t_2^{(n)},.....t_m^{(n)})$. The center vector of the preference cluster before modification is marked as FP=(t_1,t_2,.....t_m). FP is preserved before the relative query routing entries are modified. Compute the identifiers of the character items of $FP^{(n)}$ and FP on the node n. and locate the node on which the routing table corresponding to the character items is. For every corresponding node, the modification of the routing information of it's Query_Router is described by the following algorithm.

It is supposed that F_i={ $t_1^{(n)}$_ID, $t_2^{(n)}$_ID, ...$t_m^{(n)}$_ID},F_j= {t_1_ID, t_2_ID, ...t_m_ID }, r is the located node through any character item t ($t \in F_i \cup F_j$).

Step1: If $t \in F_i \cap F_j$, locate the tuple through ChracterItem_ID = t and SourceNode=n. Replace the attribute of FrequentPreference with $FP^{(n)}$.
Step2: If $t \in F_i - F_j$, add an routing entry which have the content of(t, $FP^{(n)}$, n).
Step3: If $t \in F_j - F_i$, locate the tuple through ChracterItem_ID= t and SouceNode=n and delete this entry.

The advantages of this strategy lie in that the modification of the query routing information does not use the broadcast mode, and thus does not bring about the cost of the network transmission and the cost of the computation in corresponding node owing to a great deal of additions and deletions of the preference content.

4 Experiment

We collect experiment data from three subjects, "Food", "Computer", and "Tourism". The data are collected from tens of web sites. The number of data records returned for each search subject exceeds 6,000. The data records are classified based on the web sites from which they are retrieved, and then stored at 20 peers. After that, we perform vector-based search experiment on the P2P system. At least 30 different vectors are created for each subject. We use two performance metrics to evaluate the proposed system. The first metric measures the accuracy of the search results. Specifically, suppose a query is responded with k data records, among which q records are from the k best-matching records in the whole system. We use q/k to measure the accuracy of the search. The second metric is the search efficiency. Let a be the number of the best matched linkage databases that contains the k best-matching records for a query. Let b be the actual number of such databases that respond to the query. The search efficiency is defined as b/a. In the experiments, there are 20 peer nodes and the number of data records to be returned based on document similarity is k = 20.

Table 2. Results based on the amount of preference cluster(#FP)

# FPs	Accu.	Effi.
1-10	0.99	1.10
11-20	1.00	1.16
21-30	0.99	1.17

Table 2 presents the system accuracy and efficiency measurements with respect to the number of preference clusters. It shows that the system performs very well and the number of preference clusters does not have significant impact on the performance.

Table 3 presents the system performance with respect to the admission threshold. When the admission threshold is increased, the search accuracy slightly degraded, but the efficiency measurement improves. The data records that are deviated from the center vector are not admitted; among them, those that are close to the query vector will be missed.We have performed extensive experiments.Due to the space limitation,most experimental results are omitted.

Table 3. Results based on the admission threshold, the amount of preference cluster in a preference circle is between 10 and 20

#threshold	Accu.	Effi.
Ave.th.+ Ave.th *10%	1.00	1.34
Ave.th+ Ave.th *30%	0.94	1.16
Ave.th+ Ave.th *50%	0.90	1.06

5 Conclusion

In this paper, we offer a new query routing infrastructure for web text information retrieval in the distributed system and the techniques for locating correlative distributed data sources. The important thing is improving the serial computing method in which locating data resources is realized in the Chord algorithm and several refinement algorithms to the parallel computing, By using these methods, the advantage of the P2P network computation is really utilized thoroughly, the load of the nodes is reduced, and the efficiency of the processing information on the nodes has been promoted.

References

1. Gnutella Resources. http: //gnutella. wego. com/
2. Napster. http://www.napster.com
3. Leonidas Galanis,Yuan Wang,Shawn R.Jeffery and David J.DeWitt. Locating Data Sources in Large Distributed Systems. Proceedings of the 29th VLDB Conference, Berlin, Germany,2003.
4. C.Yu,P.Sharma,W.Meng and Y.Qin. Databases Selection for Processing k Nearest Neighbors Queries in Distributed Environments. 1st ACM/IEEE-CS joint conf. On DL,2001.
5. I.Stoica,R.Morris,D.Karger,M.F.Kaashoek,H.Balakrishnan. Chord:A Scalable Peer-to-peer Lookup service for Internet Applications. In Proc.SIGCOMM 2001。
6. S.Ratnasamy,P.Francis, M.Handley, R.Karp, S.Schenker.A Scalable Content-Addressable Network.in Proc. of the 2001 Conference on Applications, Technologies, Architectures, and Protocols for Computer Communications。
7. Clement Yu,George Philip and Weiyi Meng. Distributed Top-N Query Processing with Possibly Uncooperative Local Systems. In Proc. of the 29th VLDB Conference, Berlin ,Germany,2003.

LMIX: A Dynamic XML Index Method Using Line Model

Xuefeng Hao and De Xu

School of Computer Science & Information Technology,
Beijing Jiaotong University, Beijing, China 100044
haoxf123@yahoo.com

Abstract. A new way of indexing XML document is proposed, which supports twig queries and queries with wildcards. An once-over index construction algorithm is also given. According to the Line Model we design, we consider XML document as a line, and every elements of the document as the line's segments. To query an XML document is to identify the corresponding segments. Using a range-based dynamic tree labeling scheme, each segment of the line is given a range. We put all the paths of XML document into a trie, and organize the range sets with B+-trees grouping by the nodes on the trie. Three operations are defined, which enable the range sets on the B+-trees corresponding to different nodes in the trie to operate with each other. The worst-case time complexity of the algorithm we designed for the operations is O(m+n). The final results of twig queries can be got through these operations directly at a speed similar to the simple path query. Through extensive experiments, we compare our method with other popular techniques. In particular, we show that the processing cost and disk I/O of our index method is linearly proportional to the complexity of query and the size of query results. Experimental results demostrate the great performance benefits of our proposed techniques.

1 Introduction

The problem of storing, indexing and querying XML documents has been among the major issues of database research. The semi-structured nature of XML data and the requirements on query flexibilities pose unique challenges to database indexing methods.

XML documents are often modeled as a tree whose nodes are labeled with tags, and queries are formulated to retrieve documents by specifying both their structure and values. In most of the XML query languages, structure of XML documents are typically expressed by simple paths or twig patterns, while values of XML elements are used as part of selection predicates.

In recent years, many XML index methods are proposed. We classify them into the following three categories:

One of the categories is the path index method, such as DataGuides[10] and Index Fabric[9]. Query with a path express has been one of the major focus of research for

Y. Zhang et al. (Eds.): APWeb 2005, LNCS 3399, pp. 253–265, 2005.

indexing and querying XML documents. Path index has a very high efficiency for processing simple path expressions. But it can not well support twig query and query with wildcards. Some refined techniques may be taken, but it often will make the index too big to be efficient in query evaluation.

Another kind of approaches is based on the join operation. A complex path expression is decomposed into a collection of basic path expressions. Atom expressions are found by directly accessing the index structure. All the other forms of expressions involve the expensive join operations. XISS[12] and TwigStack[10] are among this kind of techniques.

ViST[18] and PRIX[16] appeared in recent two years. They transform both the XML documents and query pattern into some kind of sequences. By performing subsequence matching on the set of sequences in the database to find the occurrences of twig pattern. We think this kind of method has the following three drawbacks: i)By transforming the entire XML documents into sequences to form the index structure, the size of this structure could hardly be controlled very well. While the discontinuous substring matching means to search points scattered in this large structure, it will inevitably needs a lot of disk I/O. What's more, unfortunately, the points are scattered, through enlarging the page size could hardly improve the performance. ii)According to Rao *et al.* [16], this kind of methods takes advantage of the frequent occurrences of similar patterns in XML document. From our point of view, on the contrary, we think this character of XML documents forces the algorithm to search more points of the index, and the interim results may be very large, even the final results be manageable. iii) It can not well support unordered twig queries. In order to find unordered matches, extra queries must be taken.

In this paper, we propose LMIX (Line Model for Indexing XML), a dynamic XML index method, which supports twig queries and queries with wildcards. According to the Line Model we design, we consider XML document as a line, and every elements of the document as the line's segments. To query an XML document is to identify the corresponding segments. Using a range-based dynamic tree labeling scheme, each segment of the line is given a range. We put all the paths of XML document into a trie, and organize the range sets with B+-trees grouping by the node on the trie. Three operations are defined, which enable the range sets on the B+-trees corresponding to different nodes (ancestor-descendant, parent-child, sibling or other relationships) in the trie to operate with each other. The final results of twig queries can be got through these operations directly.

In our method, the matched points are clustered in the index structure. We only need to read the clustered blocks as a whole, which greatly decreases the disk I/O, and also allows for disk optimization. We only keep the raw path index, and use defined operations to support twig query. No refined paths are needed and the size of index can be controlled at a proper level. Unlike the traditional join operation, whose worst-case time complexity is O(m*n), our operations are simple and have a worst-case time complexity of O(m+n). (Here and in the following, where concerns time complexity of the operations, m and n stand for the number of elements taking part in the operations.)

The main contributions of this paper are summarized as follows.

- We propose the Line Model (not Linear Model) for querying XML document. According to the model, we consider XML document as a line, and every elements of the document as the line's segments. To query an XML document is to identify the corresponding segments.
- We define three operations and the corresponding algorithms, whose worst-case time complexity is O(m+n).
- The most possible matched points are clustered in the index structure, which greatly decreases the disk I/O needed and allow for further disk optimization.
- Dynamic tree labeling scheme makes our index a dynamic one. An once-over index construction algorithm is given.
- Through algorithm analysis and experiments, we demostrate that the processing cost and disk I/O is linearly proportional to the complexity of the query and the size of query results.

Outline. In section 2, we give the details of our index method. In section 3, we introduce the dynamic tree labeling scheme and give the once-over index construction algorithm. In section 4, we briefly discuss the processing of wildcards in query. Experiments and analysis are presented in section 5. Last, in section 6 we conclude the paper and point out some future researches.

2 Details of LMIX

This section is organized as follows. Section 2.1 introduce the Line Model for querying XML document. In section 2.2 the structure of the trie and B+-tree we using is introduced. In section 2.3 three operations are defined, the corresponding algorithms are given, and a brief comparison between our operations and traditional join operation is also included. In section 2.4 we detail the query processing procedure.

2.1 The Line Model for Querying XML

XML can be viewed as a nested tree structure. If we consider attribute nodes as sub-elements and the value of attributes as text nodes, then we have two kinds of nodes on the XML tree: elements and values.

As shown in Fig.1(a), we consider the XML document as a line, and every elements and values as the line's segments. If we number the elements and values according to the document order, to a well formed XML document, every element and value will get a range, which is a key pair like <LeftPos, RightPos>.

To query an XML document is to identify the corresponding segments. As Fig. 1(c) shown, for example: suppose there is a query "/A/B/E | /A/C", the result of the query would be the ranges of <6,10>,<15,17>, which is marked as the boldface black lines. We call this the Line Model for querying XML documents.

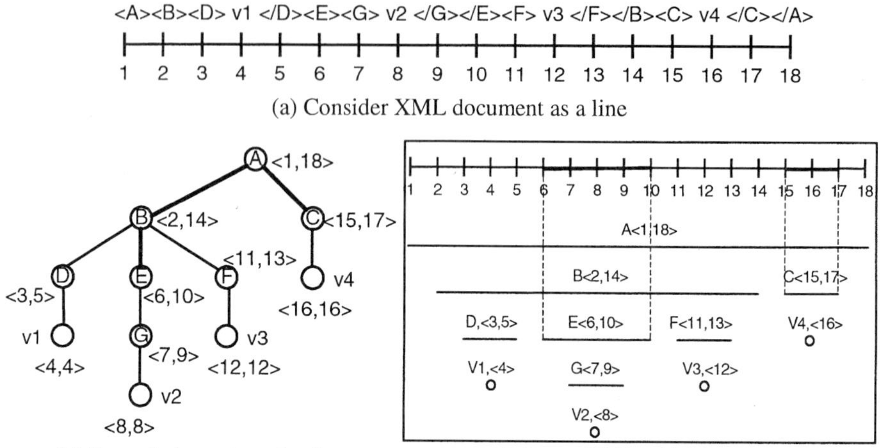

(a) Consider XML document as a line

(b) Ranged elements and values

(c) Query XML with Line Model

Fig. 1. Line model for querying XML

2.2 The Trie and B+-Tree Structure

We put all the paths in XML document into a trie, like Fig.2(a). Every node on the trie stands for a path in the XML document. For the values in the path, such as characters and values of attributes, we change them into some kind of mark, such as 'V'. This will greatly decrease the size of the trie. For every node on the trie, we put all the ranges corresponding to the node into a B+-tree, and store the address of the B+-tree in the trie node. For the element nodes, we put the range sets into B+-tree, using the LeftPos as key and RightPos as data; for the value nodes, we put both the value and their range into B+-tree, using the value as key and range as data.

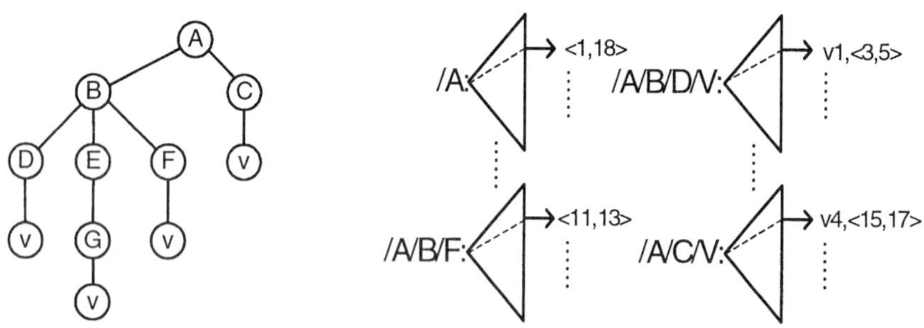

(a) Structure of trie

(b) Elements B+-tree and values B+-tree

Fig. 2. The trie and B+-tree structures

With the techniques mentioned above, the trie structure can be kept in a relatively small size. Generally, we can put the trie structure in memory, while all the B+-trees on the disk.

2.3 Three Operations and the Algorithms

In the following, we'll give the definitions of three operations.

Suppose <l,r> stands for a range of number, and A, B, C are sets composed of <l,r>

Definition 1: Operation CONTAINS:
C=A CONTAINS B, if for any element <l,r> ∈C
1. <l,r> ∈A
2. ∃ <l',r'> ∈B and <l',r'> ⊂ <l,r>.

This operation means choosing all the elements of A, which at least contains one element of B.

Definition 2: Operation CONTAINED:
C=A CONTAINED B, if for any element <l,r> ∈C

1. <l,r> ∈B
2. ∃ <l',r'> ∈A and <l,r> ⊂ <l',r'>.

This operation means choosing all the elements of B, which at least is contained by one element of A.

Definition 3: Operation UNION:
C=A UNION B, if for any element <l,r> ∈C
<l,r> ∈A or <l,r> ∈B.

This operation means merging all the elements of A and B.

Suppose A, B are the range sets on the B+-trees corresponding to different nodes on the trie. According to W3C's definition of a well formed XML document[4], the following theorems can be obvious.

Theorem 1: *For range sets A, B on the B+-trees,*
If A is an ancestor of B on the trie then
Any <l,r> ∈B, there's one and only one <l',r'> ∈A, such that <l, r> ⊂ <l',r'>;
And for all the other <l'',r''> ∈A, <l,r> ∩ <l'',r''>=φ.

This theorem means if A and B have ancestor-descendant relationship, then any element in B is contained by one and only one element of A.

Theorem 2: *For range sets A, B on the B+-trees,*
If A and B has no ancestor-descendant relationship then
Any <l,r> ∈A,<l',r'> ∈B, <l,r> ∩ <l',r'>=φ

This theorem means if A and B have no direct ancestor-descendant relationship, any element in A doesn't intersect with any element in B and vice versa.

With the two theorems, the algorithms for the operations can be very simple and efficient. They are given as follows:

Algorithm 1: CONTAINS
Input: *A <a[i],b[i]>, range set from B+-tree, ordered;*
B <c[i],d[i]>, range set from B+-tree, ordered;
m, the number of elements in A; n, the number of elements in B;

```
Output: C <e[i],f[i]>, range set, ordered; k, the number of elements in C;
Function CONTAINS(a, b, m, c, d, n)
      j=0;k=0;
      for( i=0;i<m;i++)
                 while (c[j]<a[i]) j++; if(j>=n) return ;end while
                 if(d[j]<b[i]) e[k]=a[i]; f[k]=b[i]; k++; end if
                 while(d[j]<b[i] and j<n) j++; end while
      end for
      return ;
end function
```

Algorithm 2: CONTAINED

```
Input: A <a[i],b[i]>, range set from B+-tree, ordered;
      B <c[i],d[i]>, range set from B+-tree, ordered;
      m, the number of elements in A; n, the number of elements in B;
Output: C <e[i],f[i]>, range set, ordered; k, the number of elements in C;
Function CONTAINED(a, b, m, c, d, n)
      j=0; k=0;
      for( i=0;i<m;i++)
         while(c[j]<a[i]) j++; if(j>=n) return; end while
         while(d[j]<b[i] and j<n)<e[k], f[k]>=<c[j],d[j]>; k++; j++; end while
      end for
      return ;
end function
```

Algorithm 3: UNION

```
Input: A <a[i],b[i]>, range set from B+-tree, ordered;
      B <c[i],d[i]>, range set from B+-tree, ordered;
      m, the number of elements in A; n, the number of elements in B;
Output: C <e[i],f[i]>, range set, ordered; k, the number of elements in C;
Function UNION(a, b, m, c, d, n)
      j=0; k=0;
      while(i<m or j<n)
            while(c[j]<a[i] or i>=m)
               <e[k], f[k]>=<c[j],d[j]>; j++; k++;
               if(j>=n)
                  k--;
                  while(i<m) <e[k],f[k]>=<a[i],b[i]>; k++; i++; end while
                  return ;
               end if
            end while
            <e[k],f[k]>=<a[i],b[i]>; k++; i++;
      end while
      return ;
end function
```

We shall briefly compare our operations with the traditional join operation.

- Unlike join, whose worst-case time complexity is O(m*n), our operations is more simple and efficient. It could be proved that the worst-case time complexity of our algorithm is below O(m+n).
- Traditional join uses the structure information during the join, and discard the elements not having correct structure relationships. Our operation use structure information before the operation, all the elements to be operated have the correct structure relationship. This will decrease the number of elements to be evaluated.
- Our operation can be applied to parent-child, ancestor-descendant or sibling nodes. For a twig query, only one operation for a branch is taken. This

minimums the number of operations needed, while traditional join operation does not have this guarantee.

2.4 Query Processing

In this section, we'll detail the procedure of query processing. In Fig.3, we show four kinds of queries in graph form. All the other complex queries can be composed by these four kinds of queries. Now we'll show how these queries can be answered through the three operations we defined.

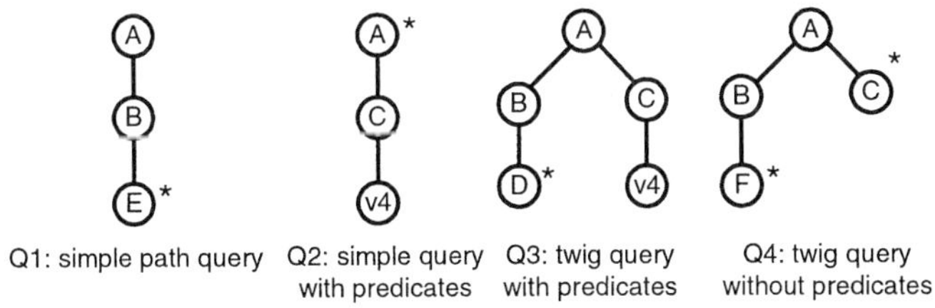

Fig. 3. XML Queries in Graph Form

The path expressions for the queries in Figure 3 can be:

Q1: /A/B/E , E is the output node for Q1;
Q2: /A[./C/text()='v4'] , A is the output node for Q2;
Q3: /A[./C/text()='v4']/B/D , D is the output node for Q3;
Q4: /A/B/F | /A/C , C and F are the output nodes for Q4;

Let S(*path_expression*) denotes the range set on the B+-tree corresponding to the *path_expression*. If *path_expression* ends with a value, then S(*path_expression*) means the range set corresponding to the value on the B+-tree of the *path_expression*. According to our definitions of the operations, we can transform the twig query as follows.

Q1: S(/A/B/E), means the range set on the B+-tree corresponding to path "/A/B/E".

Q2: S(/A) CONTAINS S(/A/C/text()='v4'), means to find the elements among the range set on B+-tree "/A", which contain at least one element of the range set on B+-tree "/A/C/text()='v4' ".

Q3: S(/A) CONTAINS S(/A/C/text()='v4') CONTAINED S(/A/B/D), means the ranges on B+-tree "/A/B/D", which are at least contained by one element of the range set of S(/A) CONTAINS S(/A/C/text()='v4').

Q4: S(/A/B/F) UNION S(/A/C), means all the elements on B+-tree "/A/B/F" and "/A/C".

From the above discussion, we can conclude the query procedures as follows:

1. Using the structure information in the XPath expression, transform the query expression into sets of the three operations. Generally, every branch of the query's tree structure needs one operation. Use CONTAINS to connect the test branch, and

CONTAINED to connect the ancestor-descendant branches and UNION to connect sibling branches.
2. Search the trie, and transform the wildcards in the query to simple path expressions. We'll further discuss the processing of wildcards in section 4.
3. Retrieve the range sets on the corresponding B+-trees, and evaluate the operations.

It should be noticed that some query optimization might be taken here. For example: if S(/A/C/text()='v4') returns one or a few ranges, then we needn't to evaluate other path expressions, but to make a range query on the other B+-tree. This will avoid reading all the ranges in the B+-tree and decrease disk I/O. And the order of operations is very important and might greatly impact the final efficiency. We will do further research on the selection of the operation order in the future. And we also plan to provide an algorithm to automatically execute queries using these three operations.

3 Dynamic Tree Labeling Scheme Makes a Dynamic Index

The purpose of we labeling the XML elements and values is to provide positional representations for them. Each node is labeled with a range <LeftPos, RightPos>, such that the containment property is satisfied. So, we can give the root node a range <1,MAX_INT>, and give the child nodes sub ranges of this maximal range, such that the sub ranges are disjoint and are completely contained in their parent node's ranges. The containment property is recursively satisfied.

Semantic and statistical clues of structured XML data can often assist sub scope allocation. We can get this information through the DTD or schema of XML, or/and through statistical analysis of existing XML documents.

Assume we don't have any information about the document to be indexed, which is a more general condition. For LMIX, we use the following labeling scheme. Fig.4 demonstrates an example of dynamic range allocation. Suppose <L,R> is the range of parent element, and P is the maximum right value of the allocated range within the parent's range, then the range for the next child node will be 1/k of the parent's un-allocated range. More formally, according to the above procedure, for a given node X, with a range of <L,R>, P is the current range, then the range of its next child node would be <P, P+(R-P)/k>. Apparently, the allocation method has a bias that favors nodes inserted earlier. Generally, k is the expected number of child nodes. Here we use an variable instead of a constant value to reflect the fact that different parent nodes may have different number of expected child nodes. k can be changed during the index reconstruction.

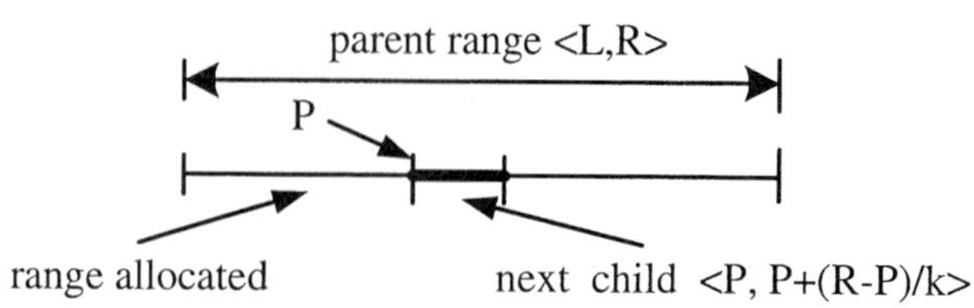

Fig. 4. Dynamic range allocation

On the XML tree, attribute nodes and character nodes are destined to be leaf nodes. Since they won't have any child nodes, we can give them a zero length range such as <range, range>. This will save the ranges of parent nodes.

Using this dynamic tree labeling scheme, we can give the once-over index construction algorithm. It's based on an event-driven SAX parser, and the following is the handle function for the SAX event of StartElement. The handle function for the SAX event of Characters is similar to the handle of attribute values.

Algorithm 4: Once-over index construction

```
Input: XML document to be indexed
      R: the parent element's right value of range
      P: previous sibling's right value of range
Output: the trie and B+-trees
Function StartElement()
      if(there's no trie)  create trie;
      if(there's no corresponding node on the trie) insert current path into the trie;
      if(there's no corresponding B+-tree) create B+-tree, range as key and data;
      allocate range<P,P+(R-P)/k> for the element;
     insert the range into B+-tree, using LeftPos as key, RightPos as data;
     L=P;
      for(the element's every attributes)
         add attribute name to current path;
        if(there's no corresponding node on the trie) insert current path to the trie;
       if(there's no corresponding B+-tree) create B+-tree, range as key and data;
       T=L+1/k'((R-P)/k-(L-P));
       allocate range <L,T>;
       insert the range to B+-tree, using LeftPos as key, RightPos as data;
       add mark 'v' to the current path;
      if(there's no corresponding node on the trie)insert current path into the trie;
  if(there's no corresponding B+-tree)create B+-tree, value as key, range as data;
      allocate range <(L+T)/2,(L+T)/2>to the value;
        insert the range into B+-tree, using the value of attribute as key, and
          <(L+T)/2,(L+T)/2> as data;
        L=T;
      end for
      P=P+(R-P)/k;
end function
```

Since it is an once-over index construction algorithm, the algorithm for updating the index can be very obvious. We just take a query before the update operation to find the corresponding B+-trees, and i) allocate a new range for the new node and insert it into the B+-tree (if insert); ii) find the range corresponding to the node, and delete it from the B+-tree (if delete).

Unfortunately, as the number of nodes in the XML documents increasing, our labeling scheme may experience the problem which is called under-flow when the range gap is used up. When this happens, we will re-allocate the ranges of all the nodes in the XML document according to the statistical characters of the document.

4 Wildcard Processing

We design this index structure on the assumption that most of the XML documents have a structural abstract, such as a DTD or schema, which is relatively smaller to the document itself. We search on the structural abstract instead of the documents or doing complex computation.

To the queries with wildcards, generally we can transform them to the corresponding twig queries without wildcards through searching the in-memory trie structure. It seems inefficient, compared with ViST and PRIX which process wildcards as range query. But, in fact, due to the low disk I/O and low processing cost of every simple query, the total time elapsed is still less than most of the popular techniques.

5 Experimental Results

We implemented LMIX in C++ for XML indexing. The implementation uses the B+-tree API provided by the Berkeley DB Library[17]. For comparison purposes, we also implemented ViST and XISS using the same techniques. We carry out our experiments on a Win2000 Server system with a 1.6GHz Pentium IV processor and 256MB RAM, 80G IDE disk. During the experiment, operating system's cache effects are considered and eliminated carefully. For all the experiment, the buffer pool size was fixed at 200 pages. The page size of 8k was used.

For our experiments, we use the datasets of public XML database DBLP[13], the XML benchmark database XMARK[19]. DBLP is widely used in benchmarking XML index methods. In the version we got, there are totaling 131 MBytes of data. Unlike DBLP, XMARK is a single record with a very large and complicated tree structure. In our experiment, we used a dataset of 116 MBytes. To test the scalability of our index algorithm, we also generated several datasets of different size using xmlgen[19].

Table 1. Sample queries over DBLP and XMARK

Query	Path Expression	Dataset
Q1	/dblp/inproceedings/title	DBLP
Q2	/dblp/article/author[text()=' Xiaoping Li']	DBLP
Q3	/dblp/*/author[text()=' Xiaoping Li']	DBLP
Q4	//author[text()=' Xiaoping Li']	DBLP
Q5	/dblp/article/[key='journals/pami/Lee98']/author	DBLP
Q6	/site//item[location='US']/mail/date[text()='12/15/1999']	XMARK
Q7	/site//person/*/city[text()='Pocatello']	XMARK
Q8	//closed_auction[person='person1']/data[text()='12/15/1999']	XMARK

We tried various kinds of queries on the DBLP and the XMARK datasets, and compared LMIX with the other two index methods. Table 1 list eight queries with ascending complexity. The experimental results of these queries are summarized in Fig.5.

Q1 is a simple path query, and there is no attribute values involved. For this kind of query, LMIX just retrieve the query results from the corresponding B+-tree. We believe LMIX is among the fastest ones in the world. It takes longer for XISS, as it joins the results of two sub queries. An attribute value is involved in path query Q2. To this kind of query, LMIX make a lookups on the B+-tree using the value of attribute as the key, and get the final query results, which involves only 2 pages of disk I/O. Q3 and Q4 use wildcards. LMIX first transform them into expressions without wildcards, this hindered the query performance to some extend, but due to the high efficiency of every single query , the totaling performance is still faster than the other two methods. Q5..Q8 are branching queries. To LMIX, Q5 means three times B+-tree lookups, which involve only 6 pages of disk I/O. Q6,Q7,Q8 with wildcards, the complexity of these kinds of queries depend on the structure of XML documents. When there are wildcards ViST needs to search more points, and performance is not as good as corresponding expressions without wildcards. From the experiment results, we can see that still due to the high speed and low cost of single query, LMIX's performance is similar to ViST, and quite better than XISS.

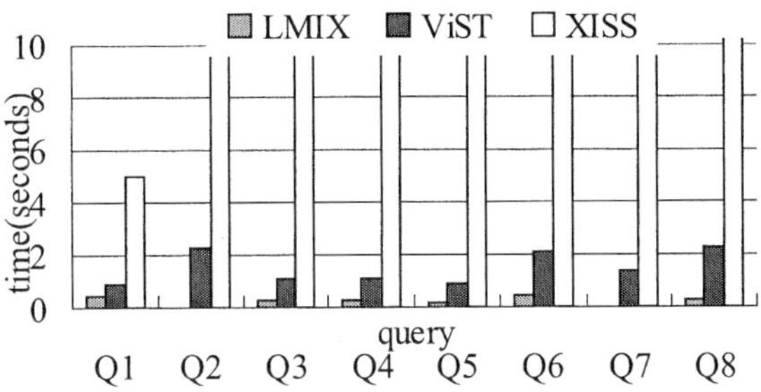

Fig. 5. Comparing LMIX with the other methods

We carried out scalability tests of the proposed algorithms on the datasets generated with xmlgen[19]. The size is 58 MBytes, 131 MBytes, 232 MBytes, 349 MBytes respectively. From Fig.6 and Fig.7, we can see query processing time and disk I/O increase almost linearly as the size of XML data increasing. This result

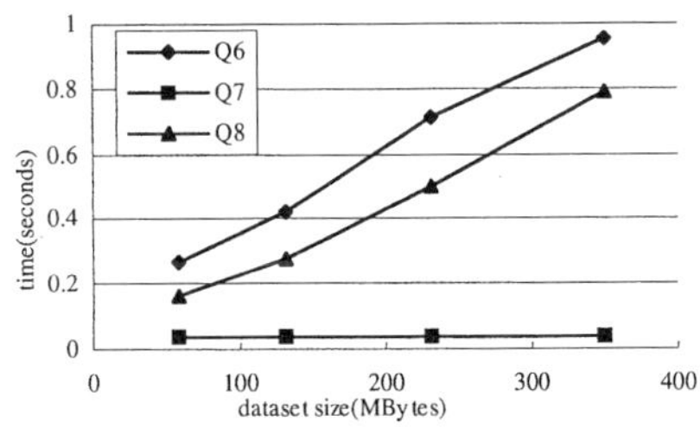

Fig. 6. Elapsed time for datasets

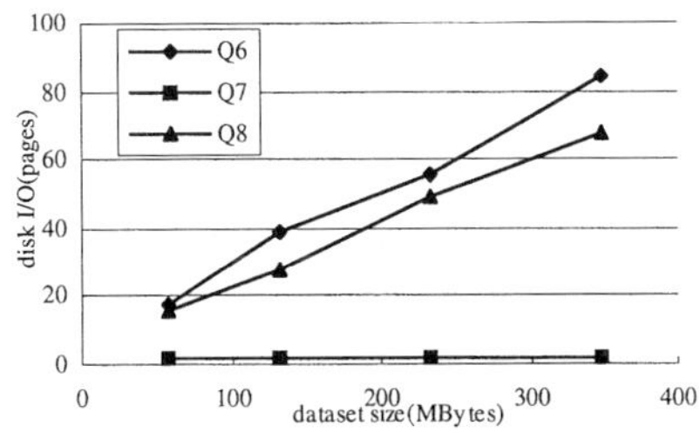

Fig. 7. Disk I/O pages for datasets

shows the linear scalability of our proposed algorithm. To Q7, we used the Optimization techniques mentioned in section 2.4. As the interim result sets are limited to a few ranges, the processing time is almost constant. This shows that the size of query results often has great effects on the query performance.

6 Conclusions and Future Work

In this paper, we proposed a new way of indexing XML document, which supports queries with branches and wildcards. Based on the Line Model we design and the three operations we define, we make our index support twig queries without using expensive join operations. We have shown that the processing cost and disk I/O cost of our index method is linearly propositional to the size of indexed documents and the complexity of XML queries. When interim result is small, the performance is even better. Using a dynamic tree labeling scheme, our index supports index update. And an once-over index construction algorithm is also given. Through experiments, we demostrate the great performance benefits of our proposed techniques.

Since LMIX is an index structure, it does not dictate a particular architecture for the storage manager of the database system. In any case, searching the index proceeds as described, and the returned pointers are interpreted appropriately by the database system. How to improve the efficiency of this procedure has great effects on the query performances. Some clustered storage technique may be used according to the index structure and query patterns in the future.

References

1. S. Abiteboul, P. Buneman, and D. Suciu. Data on the web: from relations to semi-structured data and XML. Morgan Kaufmann Publishers, Los Altos, CA 94022, USA, 1999.
2. A. Berglund, S. Boag, D. Chamberlin, M. F. Fernandez, M. Kay, J. Robie, and J. Simon. XML path language (XPath) 2.0 W3C working draft 16. Technical Report D-xpath20 - 20020816, World Wide Web Consortium, Aug. 2002.
3. S. Boag, D. Chamberlin, M. F. Fernandez, D. Florescu, J. Robie, and J. Simon. XQuery 1.0: An XML Query Language W3C working draft 16. Technical Report WD-xquery-20020816, World Wide Web Consortium, Aug. 2002.
4. T. Bray, J. Paoli, C. M. Sperberg-McQueen, and E. Maler. Extensible markup language (XML) 1.0 second edition W3C recommendation. Technical Report REC-xml-20001006, World Wide Web Consortium, Oct. 2000.
5. N. Bruno, N. Koudas, and D. Srivastava. Holistic twig joins: Optimal XML pattern matching. In Proceedings of the 2002 ACM-SIGMOD Conference, Madison, Wisconsin, June 2002.
6. N. Bruno, L. Gravano, N. Koudas, D. Srivastava. Navigation- vs. Index-Based XML Multi-Query Processing. The 19th Inter. Conference on Data Engineering (ICDE'2003) March 2003.
7. C. Chung, J. Min, and K. Shim. APEX: An adaptive path index for XML data. In ACM SIGMOD, June 2002.
8. Edith Cohen, Haim Kaplan, and Tova Milo. Labeling dynamic XML trees. In PODS, pages 271-281, 2002.

9. Brian F. Cooper, Neal Sample, Michael J. Franklin, Gisli R. Hjaltason, and Moshe Shadmon. A fast index for semistructured data. In VLDB, pages 341-350,September 2001.
10. R. Goldman and J. Widom. DataGuides: Enable query formulation and optimization in semistructured databases. In VLDB, pages 436-445, August 1997.
11. C. Koch. Efficient processing of expressive node-selecting queries on xml data in secondary storage: A tree automata-based approach. In Proc. of VLDB, 2003.
12. Q. Li and B. Moon. Indexing and querying XML data for regular path expressions. In Proceedings of the 27th VLDB Conference, pages 361-370, Rome, Italy, Sept. 2001.
13. Michael Ley. DBLP database web site. http://www.informatik.uni-trier.de/ ley/db, 2000.
14. G. Miklau. UW XML Repository. http://www.cs.washington.edu/research/xmldatasets.
15. T. Milo and D. Suciu. Index structures for path expression. In Proceedings of 7th International Conference on Database Theory (ICDT), pages 277-295, January 1999.
16. P. Rao and B. Moon. PRIX: Indexing And Querying XML Using Prufer Sequences. The 20th Inter. Conference on Data Engineering (ICDE), Boston, MA, U.S.A March 2004.
17. Sleepycat Software, http://www.sleepycat.com. The Berkeley Database (Berkeley DB).
18. H.Wang, S. Park, W. Fan, and P. S. Yu. ViST: A Dynamic Index Method for Querying XML Data by Tree Structures. In Proceedings of the 2003 ACM-SIGMOD Conference, San Diego, CA, June 2003.
19. XMARK: The XML-benchmark project. http://monetdb.cwi.nl/ xml, 2002.

A New Sequential Mining Approach to XML Document Clustering*

Jeong Hee Hwang and Keun Ho Ryu

Database Laboratory, Chungbuk National University, Korea
{jhhwang, khryu}@dblab.chungbuk.ac.kr

Abstract. XML has recently become very popular for representing semi-structured data and a standard for data exchange over the web because of its varied applicability in a number of applications. Therefore, XML documents form an important data mining domain. In this paper, we propose a new XML document clustering technique using sequential pattern mining algorithm. Our approach first extracts the representative structures of frequent patterns from schemaless XML documents by using a sequential pattern mining algorithm. And then, unlike most previous document clustering methods, we apply clustering algorithm for transactional data without a measure of pairwise similarity, considering that an XML document as a transaction and the extracted frequent structures of documents as the items of the transaction. We have experimented our clustering algorithm by comparing it with the previous methods. The experimental results show the effectiveness of the proposed method in performance and in producing clusters with higher cluster cohesion.

1 Introduction

XML(eXtensible Markup Language) is a standard for representing and exchanging information on the Internet. As such, more documents can be represented in XML documents. However, because the size of XML documents is very large and their types vary, it is necessary to provide means to manage XML document collection[1,2,3,4]. Clustering the related XML documents is a potential research topic in integrating a large XML document collection. Several research approaches had tackled the issue.

In [5], a method for clustering the DTDs of XML data source is proposed and it is based on the similarity of structures and semantics of DTDs. This approach produces intermediate DTD in order to integrate DTDs. Although this approach addresses the problem of clustering DTDs, it can't be directly applied to XML documents. Yun Shen et al. [6] propose a clustering technique for schemaless XML documents. And this introduces a decomposition mechanism of a tree model, called macro-path. The similarity matrix for a document collection is constructed by computing the similarity

* This work was supported by University IT Research Center Project in Korea.

Y. Zhang et al. (Eds.): APWeb 2005, LNCS 3399, pp. 266 – 276, 2005.

value among these macro-path sequences from each XML document. Though this approach is similar to our path extraction method, it is different from our clustering approach in that they use hierarchical clustering algorithm to group documents based on similarity matrix which is generated by computing similarity between all the paths of XML documents. In [7], Jong Yoon et al. describe a bitmap indexing technique to cluster the XML documents. In this approach, an XML document is defined as a sequence of ePaths with associated element contents, and a bitmap index is constructed from all the ePaths in the documents. Finally, a bitcube is assembled when element contents of the ePaths are integrated into the bitmap index. Though bitcube can support clustering XML documents, it requires too much space for a large amount of documents. Doucet. et al. [8] address the problem of clustering a homogenous collection of text-based XML documents. In this approach each document is represented by an n-dimensional vector, which is generated by using three difference feature sets in an XML documents; text features only, tag feature only, and text and tags. And it applies k-means algorithm to group XML document by element tags and texts. However, this approach ignores the structural information in XML documents.

And also there are some researches[3,9,10,11] to extract common structures from XML documents. [9] constructs a tree structure from elements in XML documents and estimates semantic similarity of different document by comparing the tree structures. [11] groups trees about the same pairs of labels occurring frequently, and then finds a subset of the frequent trees. But the multi relational tree structure can't be detected, because it is based on the label pairs.

The conventional technique used for the previous XML document clustering approaches[5,6,8] is a hierarchical agglomerative clustering[12], denoted HAC. But it needs in general the number of clusters, and also it is based on a measure of pairwise similarity between documents. Therefore, it is difficult to determine both correct parameter and similarity computation method between XML documents.

In this paper, we propose a new XML clustering technique based on sequential pattern mining, which doesn't need a measure of pairwise similarity between XML documents. We first extract the representative structures of frequent pattern including hierarchy structure information from documents by the sequential pattern mining method. Then, we create document clusters by applying the CLOPE algorithm[13] and the concept of large items[14]. In this step, we consider an XML document as a transaction and the extracted frequent structures from documents as the items of the transaction. The proposed method is useful for document management and retrieval of the similar structure in large amounts of schemaless XML documents.

The remaining of the paper is organized as follows. Section 2 describes the method extracting the representative structure of XML documents. Section 3 defines our clustering criterion, using the notion of large items. Experiment results are shown in section 4. Section 5 concludes the paper.

2 Mining Frequent XML Document Tree Patterns

An XML document can be modeled as a tree T(N, E) where N is a set of nodes and E is a set of edges. Each element is represented as a node in the tree. A path is a sequence of n_1, n_2, .., n_n of nodes. There exists only one path from node n_i to node n_j such that $n_i \neq n_j$. In this paper, the tree model representing XML document is rooted, directed, and node-labeled, and we ignore the order between siblings because we focus on hierarchical path structure of elements in an XML document.

In order to support the clustering of large scale XML document collection, we extract the path information from XML documents, called Mine X_path(*mX_path*). It is similar to [6] but there are some differences in that [6] defines paths considering both attribute node and content node in an XML document. Therefore, any tuple representing paths includes null value if there exists only either attribute node or content node in a path.

We focus on paths of elements with content value, not considering attribute in an XML document because attributes in an XML document doesn't much influence on structure information. Therefore we don't admit null value in representing *mX_path*. We formally define Mine X_path(*mX_path*) as follows.

Definition 1 (Mine *X_path(mX_path)*). Given a node n_i with content value in an XML document tree, *mX_path* of node n_i is defined as a 2-tuple(PrefixPath(n_i), ContentNode(n_i)). An XML document(X_Doc$_i$) consists of many *mX_path* sequences, and the order of *mX_paths* is ignored because we judge structural similarity based on the degree of common structures between XML documents. An *mX_path* sequence is denoted as follows.

$$\text{X\_Doc}_i = \{mX\_path_1, mX\_path_2, ..., mX\_path_n\}$$

where PrefixPath(n_i) is an ordered sequence of tag name from root to node n_{i-1} which includes hierarchical structure. ContentNode(n_i) is a sequence of tag names with content value under the same PrefixPath(n_i) sequence and the order among the content sequence is ignored, but duplicating element names are not omitted. The *mX_paths* extracted from an XML document imply multiple association and level information of elements in an XML document.

Example 1. Figure 1 shows an example of XML document tree. We first construct an element mapping table based on the Figure 1, as shown in Figure 2.

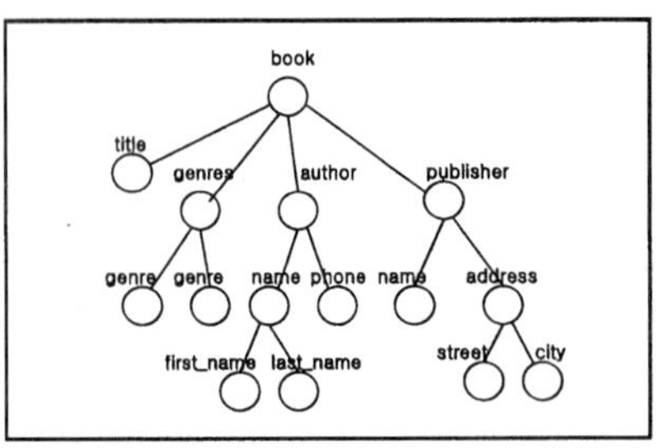

Fig. 1. An example XML document tree

element	rename	element	rename	element	rename
book	1	name	6	address	11
title	2	phone	7	street	12
genres	3	first_name	8	city	13
genre	4	last_name	9		
author	5	publisher	10		

Fig. 2. Element mapping table

We extract *mX_paths* from each XML document tree. And then, to simplify the *mX_path* in each document, we map similar elements on an *mX_path* to the same integer corresponding to the element mapping table of Figure 2, as shown in Figure 3. To consider semantics of element name of *mX_path* in each document, we use WordNet Java API[15] while constructing the element mapping table and determine whether two elements are synonyms.

mX_path	Original paths	Transformed paths
mX_path$_1$	<{book}, {title}>	<{1}, {2}>
mX_path$_2$	<{book/genres}, {genre, genre}>	<{1/3}, {4,4}>
mX_path$_3$	<{book/author/name}, {first_name, last_name}>	<{1/5/6}, {8,9}>
mX_path$_4$	<{book/author}, {phone}>	<{1/5}, {7}>
mX_path$_5$	<{book/publisher}, {name}>	<{1/10}, {6}>
mX_path$_6$	<{book/publisher/address}, {street, city}>	<{1/10/11}, {12,13}>

Fig. 3. Transformed *mX_path* sequence

We finally extract representative structures of each document on the basis of the transformed *mX_path* sequences in Figure 3, using PrefixSpan algorithm [16]. The extraction process of frequent paths consists of two stages. First stage is to extract frequent paths from PrefixPath sequences of the *mX_paths* by PrefixSpan algorithm. Second stage is to find frequent full paths containing ContentNode sequences of the *mX_paths.*

When we find frequent structures from PrefixPath sequences of the *mX_paths*, mX_path$_i$ is regarded as the sequence_id and a PrefixPath sequence of the mX_path is considered to be a sequence. And also we consider each element of PrefixPath as items of the sequence. The complete algorithm is given as follows.

Algorithm mX_path_FrequentSearch
Input: *mX_path* sequences in an XML document (X_Doc$_i$)
the minimum support threshold *min_sup*(the total number of *mX_paths* in a document * minimum_support $\theta(0< \theta \leq 1)$)
Output: the complete set of frequent path Fp_i

1. Find the set of frequent paths Fp_i in the set of *PrefixPath* sequence which is a part of each *mX_path*
   - **call** PrefixSpan algorithm (refer to [16])
2. Find the set of frequent paths Fp_i considering the *ContentNode* of each *mX_path*
   for each *ContentNode* in each *mX_path*
      if the number of *ContentNode* $\geq$ min_sup
         if the number of the same name of *ContentNode* $\geq$ min_sup
            the *mX_path* including *ContentNode* is included in the set of Fp_i
         else
            the only *PrefixPath, mX_path* excluding *ContentNode,* is included in the set of Fp_i

---

After finding the set of frequent paths in each document, we input the frequent paths of length over min_length(the average maximal frequent structure length * length_rate σ (0< σ ≤1)) into clustering algorithm.

Example 2. Consider Figure 3. Assume that min_sup is 2 and length_rate is 0.6. The frequent paths extracted in *PrefixPath* by the first stage of the above algorithms are listed in support descending order(in the form of item : support), such as length_1{1:6, 5:2, 10:2} and length_2{1/5:2, 1/10:2}. And the frequent full path by the second stage considering *ContentNode* of each *mX_path* except for the previous result, is {1/3:2, 1/5/6:2, 1/10/11:2}. After that, we can get the min_length(3 * 0.6 = 2). As a result, we input length_2{1/5, 1/10, 1/3}and length_3{1/5/6, 1/10/11} over min_length for clustering.

3 A New XML Document Clustering Technique

To perform clustering, we assume an XML document as a transaction, the frequent structures extracted from each document as the items of the transaction, and then we perform the document clustering using the notion of large items.

The item set included in all the transaction is defined as $I = \{i_1, i_2, .., i_n\}$, cluster set as $C = \{C_1, C_2, .., C_m\}$, and transaction set represents the document as $T = \{t_1, t_2, t_3, .., t_k\}$. As a criterion to allocate a transaction to appropriate cluster, we define the cluster allocation gain.

Definition 2 (Cluster Allocation Gain). The cluster allocation gain is the sum of the rate of the total occurrences of the individual items in every cluster. The following equation expresses this.

$$Gain(C) = \frac{\sum_{i=1}^{m} G(Ci) \times |Ci(Tr)|}{\sum_{i=1}^{m} |Ci(Tr)|} = \frac{\sum_{i=1}^{m} \frac{T(Ci)}{W(Ci)^2} \times |Ci(Tr)|}{\sum_{i=1}^{m} |Ci(Tr)|}$$

where G is the occurrence rate(H) to individual item(W) in a cluster, H = T (the total occurrence of the individual items) / W (the numbers of the individual items), and $G = T/W^2$. $|C_i(Tr)|$ is the number of transactions included in the cluster C_i.

Gain is a criterion function for cluster allocation of the transaction, and the higher the rate of the common items, the more the cluster allocation gain. Therefore we allocate a transaction to the cluster to be the largest *Gain*. However if we use only the rate of the common items as a criterion of cluster allocation, not considering the individual items like CLOPE, it causes some problems as follows.

Example 3. Assume that transaction $t_4 = \{f, c\}$ is to be inserted, under the condition of the cluster $C_1 = \{a:3, b:3, c:1\}$, $C_2 = \{d:3, e:1, c:3\}$ including three transactions respectively. If t_4 is allocated to C_1 or C_2, *Gain* is $\frac{\frac{9}{4^2} \times 4 + \frac{7}{3^2} \times 3}{7} = 0.654$. Other while if

t_4 is allocated to a new cluster, *Gain* is $\frac{\frac{7}{3^2}\times 3+\frac{7}{3^2}\times 3+\frac{2}{2^2}\times 1}{7}=$ 0.738. Thus, t_4 is allocated to a new cluster by definition 2. As you see in this example, we can get the considerably higher allocation gain about a new cluster, because *Gain* about a new cluster equals W/W^2. Due to this, it causes the production of many clusters over the regular size, so that it may reduce cluster cohesion. In order to improve this problem, we define the large items and the cluster participation as follows.

Definition 3 (Large Items). Item support of cluster C_i is defined as the number of the transactions including item i_j ($j <= n$) in the cluster C_i, about the minimum support determined by the user, θ ($0 < \theta <= 1$). If the number of the transactions including item i_j in cluster C_i is over the item support, $Sup = \theta * |C_i(Tr)|$, the item i_j is the large item in the cluster C_i.

$$C_i(L)i_j = |C_i(Tr)i_{j\in I}| >= Sup$$

where $|C_i(Tr)|$ is the number of the whole transactions in C_i, and $|C_i(Tr)i_{j\in I}|$ is the number of the transactions including the item i_j in the cluster C_i.

Definition 4 (Cluster Participation). It is the rate of the common items about the items of transaction t_k composed of the frequent structure and the large items in the cluster C_j. And it means the probability of transaction t_k to be assigned to cluster C_j. We represent it as follows.

$$P\_Allo(t_k \Rightarrow C_j) = \frac{|t_k| \cap C_j(L)}{|t_k|} \geq \omega_1$$

$$(0 < \omega_1 < 1 : \text{minimum participation})$$

$|t_k|$ is the number of the items of the transaction t_k. In example 3, if there is any cluster that satisfies the given minimum participation about insertion of t4, our approach does not produce a new cluster, but allocate t4 to the existing cluster with maximum participation. Therefore, cluster participation can control the number of cluster. When ω_1 is small, the production of the cluster is suppressed.

The key step is finding the destination cluster for allocating a transaction, which is the most time sensitive part in clustering algorithm. But we can easily find the cluster of the largest *Gain* through calculating the difference operation about current *Gain* as follows.

Definition 5 (Difference Operation). The difference operation is the different *Gain* of the inserted transaction to the existing cluster. We use the inserted difference (*Add_Gain*(Δ^+)) which is formally defined as follows.

$$\begin{aligned} Add\_Gain(\Delta^+) &= New\_Gain(C_i) - Old\_Gain(C_i) \\ &= \frac{T'(Ci)}{W'(Ci)^2}\times(|Ci(Tr)|+1) - \frac{T(Ci)}{W(Ci)^2}\times|Ci(Tr)| \end{aligned} \quad (1)$$

W' is the number of the individual items and T' is the total occurrence number of individual items when the transaction is inserted. We can compute the change value of the current *Gain* by (1) and allocate the transaction to the cluster of the largest *Add_Gain*(Δ^+).

We also reuse the cluster participation(Definition 4) to compute the *Gain* about the only clusters that satisfy the newly given cluster participation ω_2. The XML document clustering algorithm by difference operation is shown in Figure 4(ω_1 and ω_2 can have different value.)

```
■ Insert transaction t
  Extract representative structure using sequence pattern mining;
  while not end of the existing cluster and p_Allo(C) >= ω2   // (ω2=0.2)
     find a cluster(Ci) maximizing add_Gain(C);
     find a cluster(Cj) maximizing p_Allo(C);
     if add_Gain((Ck) > add_Gain(Ci)   // new cluster Ck
        if p_Allo(Cj) >= ω1    // (ω1=0.5) ,  an existing cluster Ci
           allocate t to an existing cluster Cj;
        else allocate t to an new cluster Ck;
     else allocate t to an existing cluster Ci;
```

Fig. 4. XML document clustering algorithm using the difference operation

4 Experimental Results

In order to verify the performance and efficiency of our clustering method, denoted XML_C, we conducted intensive experiments, comparing XML_C with CLOPE and HAC. The data used were 300 schemaless XML documents, selected from 8 topics (i.e., book, club, play, auction, company, department, actor, and movies), taken from the Wisconsin's XML data bank[17]. In the first step of the experiments, in order to extract the representative structure of each document, we set the minimum_support to 0.5 to the number of *mX_paths* of each document and the length_rate to 0.7 to the average maximal frequent structure length. The average maximal length and the number of frequent path structure extracted in each document are 4.3 and 6.2 respectively.

To perform HAC algorithm, we generated the similarity matrix, computing similarity among the decomposed *mX_path* sequences from XML documents in the same manner of [6], and then we grouped XML documents on the basis of the matrix, using hierarchical clustering technique[12].

Figure 5 illustrates the execution time of the algorithms as the number of document increases. The important result in this experiment is that the performance of XML_C is comparable to that of CLOPE, while being much better than HAC. This is because HAC requires much time to calculate the similarities between clusters. On the other hand, XML_C has slightly better performance than CLOPE. It shows that XML_C using cluster participation by the notion of the large item comes into effect on the performance in contrast to CLOPE.

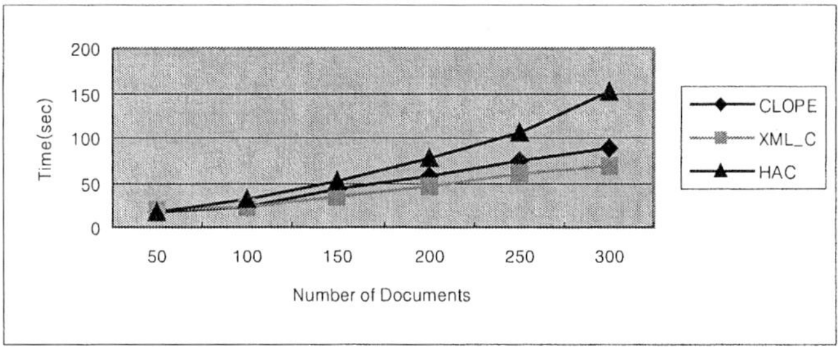

Fig. 5. Execution time

For quality measure of clustering result, we adopted the cluster cohesion and the inter-cluster similarity, and we defined as follows.

The **cluster cohesion(*Coh*(C_i))** is the ratio of the large items to the whole items $T(C_i)$ in the cluster C_i. This is calculated by the following formula, and if it is near 1, it is a good quality cluster.

$$Coh(C_i) = \frac{Ci\,(L)}{T\,(Ci\,)}$$

The **Inter-cluster Similarity(*Sim*(C_i,C_j))** based on the large items is the rate of the common large items of the cluster C_i and C_j. We calculate the inter-cluster similarity by the following formula, and if it is near 0, it is the good clustering.

$$Sim(C_i,C_j) = \frac{L(Ci \cap Cj) \times \dfrac{|\,L(Ci \cap Cj)\,|}{|\,L(Ci + Cj)\,|}}{Ci\,(L) + Cj\,(L)}$$

where $L(C_i \cap C_j)$ is the number of common large items in the cluster C_i and C_j, $|L(C_i \cap C_j)|$ is the total occurrence number of the common large items, and $|L(C_i+C_j)|$ is the total occurrence number of the large items in the cluster C_i and C_j.

To measure *Coh*(C_i) and *Sim*(C_i,C_j), it needs large items in the cluster, but CLOPE and HAC don't use the notion of large item. Therefore, we extract the large items according to the given minimum support from the clustering results in the same manner of XML_C, after running both CLOPE and HAC respectively. The result of the cluster cohesion and the inter-cluster similarity according to the minimum support is shown in Figure 6 and Figure 7.

As we expected, the XML_C exhibits the highest cluster cohesion among these three algorithms in Figure 6. XML_C keeps it well with approximately probability nearly 1. Clearly, it gets better result by considering the distribution of common structures in each cluster during the cluster assignment. On the other hand, the cluster cohesion of HAC has the lowest performance since it does not consider common structures but consider structural similarity. The quality of clustering by similarity depends on the similarity measure.

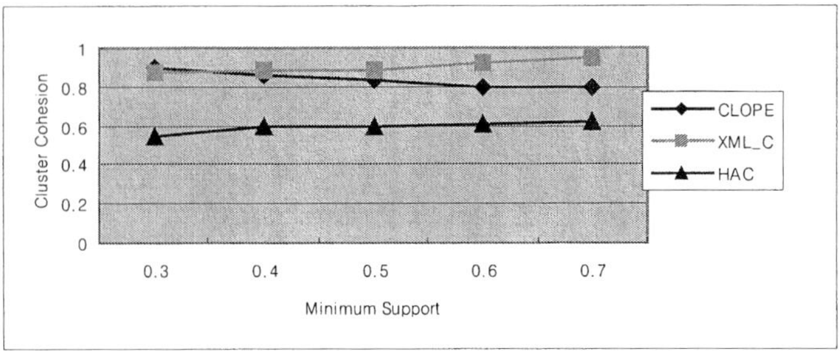

Fig. 6. Cluster cohesion

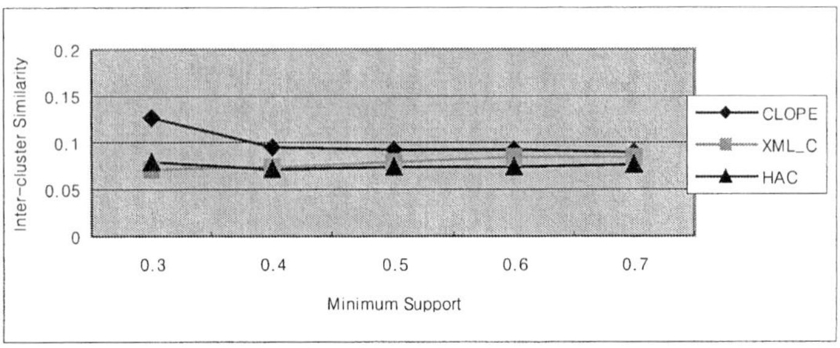

Fig. 7. Inter-cluster similarity

Figure 7 shows inter-cluster similarity measurement, and the performance ranking of three algorithms is HAC > XML_C > CLOPE (">" means better). The explanation here is that HAC produces the smaller number of clusters than XML_C and CLOPE, even if we set the number of cluster similar to that produced by XML_C and CLOPE. This had an effect on the inter-cluster similarity measurement of HAC, with the smallest variation.

By observing both Figure 6 and Figure 7, we can easily realize there exist relations between the number of clusters and inter-cluster similarity, and also between the number of clusters and cluster cohesion. The smaller the number of clusters produces, the smaller inter-cluster similarity we can get. Contrariwise, if the smaller the number of cluster produces, the larger cluster cohesion we can get.

Further more, the bad result of HAC, which both cluster cohesion and inter-cluster similarity are low at the same time, was why it performed clustering by not common structure itself but similarity of structures. On the other hand, the good result of XML_C is due to the global criterion considering both the common structures and individual structures in a cluster together.

In summary, we can determinate that XML_C is better overall at cluster cohesion and inter-cluster similarity. This means that our algorithm groups similar structured XML documents together and gathers dissimilar structured XML documents apart.

5 Conclusion

In this paper, we proposed a new approach to XML document clustering method without using any measure of pairwise similarity. We first extracted the representative structures of XML documents using the sequential pattern mining, which focused on element path including hierarchal element information in the XML document. And then we performed clustering based on similar structure using notion of large items to improve cluster quality and performance, considering that an XML document as a transaction and the extracted frequent structures from documents as the items of the transaction. Our experiments showed that our approach could get the higher cluster cohesion and the lower inter-cluster similarity, taking less time to perform.

Our future works include a way to cluster XML documents by considering both element and content at the same time.

References

[1] Kotasek, P., Zendulka, J.: An XML Framework Proposal for Knowledge Discovery in Database. The Fourth European Conference on Principles and Practice Knowledge Discovery in Databases (2000)

[2] Wang, K., Liu, H.: Discovery Typical Structures of Documents: A Road Map Approach. In ACM SIGIR (1998) 146-154

[3] Widom, J.: Data Management for XML: Research Directions. IEEE Computer Society Technical Commitee on Data Engineering (1999) 44-52

[4] Nayak, R., Witt, R., Tonev, A.: Data Mining and XML Documents. Int. Conf. on Internet Computing (2002) 660-666

[5] Lee, M. L., Yang, L. H., Hsu, W., Yang, X.: XClust: Clustering XML Schemas for Effective Integration. Proc. 11th ACM Int. Conf. on Information and Knowledge Management (2002) 292-299

[6] Shen, Y., Wang, B.: Clustering Schemaless XML Document. Proc. of the 11th Int. Conf. on Cooperative Information System (2003) 767-784

[7] Yoon, J., Raghavan, V., Chakilam, V.: BitCube: Clustering and Statistical Analysis for XML Documents. Proc. of the 13th Int. Conf. on Scientific and Statistical Database Management (2001) 241-254

[8] Doucet, A., Myka, H. A.: Naive Clustering of a Large XML Document Collection. The Proceedings of the 1st INEX, Germany (2002)

[9] Lee, J. W., Lee, K., Kim, W.: Preparation for Semantics-Based XML Mining. IEEE Int. Conf. on Data Mining(ICDM) (2001) 345-352

[10] Asai, T., Abe, K., Kawasoe, S., Arimura, Sakamoto, H.: Efficient Substructure Discovery from Large Semi-structured Data. Proc. of the Second SIAM Int. Conf. on Data Mining (2002) 158-174

[11] Termier, A., Rouster, M. C., Sebag, M.: TreeFinder: A First Step towards XML Data Mining. IEEE Int. Conf. on Data Mining (ICDM) (2002) 450-457

[12] Jain, A.K., Murty, M.N., Flynn, P.J.: Data Clustering: a review. ACM Computing Surveys, Vol. 31 (1999)

[13] Yang, Y., Guan, X., You, J: CLOPE: A Fast and Effective Clustering Algorithm for Transaction Data. Proc. of the 8th ACM SIGKDD Int. Conf on Knowledge Discovery and Data Mining (2002) 682-687

[14] Wang, K., Xu, C.: Clustering Transactions Using Large Items. In Proc. of ACM CIKM-99 (1999) 483-490

[15] http://sourceforge.net/projects/javawn

[16] Pei, J., Han, J., Asi, B. M., Pinto, H.: PrefixSpan: Mining Sequential Pattern Efficiently by Prefix-Projected Pattern Growth. Int. Conf. Data Engineering(ICDE) (2001) 215-224

[17] NIAGARA query engine. http://www.cs.wisc.edu/niagara/data.html.

Labeling Scheme and Structural Joins for Graph-Structured XML Data*

Hongzhi Wang[1,2], Wei Wang[1,3], Xuemin Lin[1,3], and Jianzhong Li[2]

[1] University of New South Wales, Australia
{hongzhiw, weiw, lxue}@cse.unsw.edu.au
[2] Harbin Institute of Technology, Harbin, China
lijz@mail.banner.com.cn
[3] National ICT of Australia, Australia

Abstract. When XML documents are modeled as graphs, many challenging research issues arise. In particular, query processing for graph-structured XML data brings new challenges because traditional structural join methods cannot be directly applied. In this paper, we propose a labeling scheme for graph-structured XML data. With this labeling scheme, the reachability relationship of two nodes can be judged efficiently without accessing other nodes. Based on this labeling scheme, we design efficient structural join algorithms to evaluate reachability queries. Experiments show that our algorithms have high efficiency and good scalability.

1 Introduction

XML has become the *de facto* standard for information representation and exchange over the Internet. XML data has hierarchical nesting structures. Although XML data is often modeled as a tree, IDREFs within the XML document represent additional "referencing" relationships and are essential in some applications, e.g., to avoid redundancy and anomalies. Such XML data could be naturally modeled as a graph.

Query processing of graph-structured XML data brings new challenges:

- One traditional method of processing queries on tree-structured XML data is to encode the nodes of XML data tree with certain labeling scheme and process the query based on structural joins [2]. Under the coding scheme, the structure relationship between any two elements (such as parent-child or ancestor-descendant relationships) can be judged efficiently without accessing other elements. This property is the foundation of all structural join algorithms so far. However, none of the existing XML coding schemes can be applied to graph-structured XML data directly.
- Another query processing methods is based on structural index such as 1-index [14] and F&B index [12]. However, structural indexes of graph-structured XML documents are likely to have a large number of nodes. As

* This work was partially supported by ARC Discovery Grant – DP0346004.

Y. Zhang et al. (Eds.): APWeb 2005, LNCS 3399, pp. 277–289, 2005.

a result, they efficiency could be a problem when there is not enough memory. For example, the number of nodes in F&B index of the standard 100M XMark document, when modeled as a tree, has 0.44M nodes; the number of nodes in F&B index of the same document, when modeled as a graph, has 1.29M nodes [12].

Given the successes of query processing methods based on XML coding schemes and structural joins, in this paper, we adopt a similar approach dealing with query processing tasks for graph-structured XML data. We propose a reachability coding scheme for general digraph, which can be used to assist efficient reachability queries. In this coding scheme, all the strongly connected components of the digraph are contracted to single representative nodes such that the digraph is reduced to a DAG. Then a DAG labeling scheme is applied to the generated the code [15]. Based on the the features of the coding scheme, we design the efficient structural join algorithms, Graph-Merge-Join (GMJ) and its improved version Improved-Graph-Merge-Join (IGMJ). They can be viewed as the natural generalizations of the *tree-merge* and *stack-tree* algorithms [2] for the graph-structured XML data.

The contributions of the paper can be summarized as follows:

- We generalize the coding scheme in [15] and present an effective coding scheme to judge the reachability relationships between nodes in a general digraph.
- We present two efficient structural join algorithms, GMJ and IGMJ, based on the graph coding scheme.
- Our experiments show that our coding scheme is efficient for XMark data. Our two join algorithms outperform 1-index based query processing methods significantly and have good scalabilities.

The reset of the paper is organized as follows: Section 2 introduces some background knowledge and notations used in the paper. Section 3 presents the reachability coding scheme. Structural join algorithms based on the coding scheme are given in Section 4. We present our experiment evaluation results and analysis in Section 5. Related work is described in Section 6. We conclude the paper in Section 7.

2 Preliminaries

In this section, we briefly introduce graph-structured XML data model as well as terms and notations used in this paper.

XML data is often modeled as a labeled tree: elements and attributes are mapped into nodes of graph; directed nesting relationships are mapped into edges in the tree. A feature of XML is that from two elements in XML document, there may be a IDREF representing reference relationships [18]. With this feature, XML data can be modeled as a labeled directed graph (digraph): elements and attributes are mapped into nodes of graph; directed nesting *and* referencing

```
<a id="a1">
<b id="b1">
</b>
<d id ="d1" f="f1"/>
<d id="d2">
<f id="f1">
</d>
<d id="d3" f="f1" c="c1"/>
<c id="c1">
<e id="e1" g="g1" d="d1" d="d2" d="d3">
<e id="e2" g="g1" d="d1" d="d2" d="d3">
<e id="e3" d="d1" d="d2" d="d3">
<g id="g1" f="f1"/>
</e>
</c>
</a>
```

(a) An Example XML Document

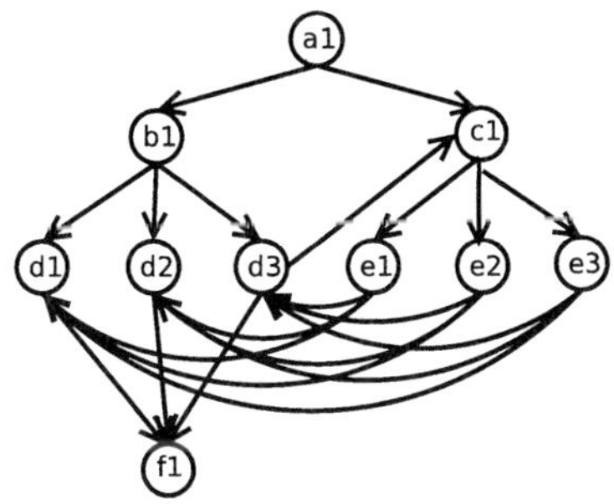

(b) The Corresponding XML Graph

Fig. 1. An Example XML Document and Its XML Graph

relationships are mapped into directed edges in the graph. An example XML document is shown in Fig 1(a). It can be modeled as the digraph shown in Figure 1(b). Note that the graph in Figure 1(b) is not a DAG.

XML query languages, such as XQuery [4], are based on the tree model and allow retrieving part of the XML document by the structural constraints. For example, the XPath query $b//e$ will retrieve all e elements nested within b elements ($//$ represents the ancestor-descendant relationship). In the example XML document in Figure 1(a), the query result is empty. However, when we model XML document as a graph, the ancestor-descendant relationship (as well as parent-child relationship) can be extended based on the notion of reachability. In [12], IDREF edges are represented as $\Rightarrow$ and $\Leftarrow$[1] for the forward and backward edge[2], respectively. Two nodes, u and v belong to a graph G satisfy reachability relationship if and only there is a path from u to v in G (denoted as $u \leadsto v$). Each edge in this path can be either an edge representing nesting relationship or referencing relationship. For example, the query $b \leadsto e$ will return $e1, e2$, and $e3$ for the example XML data graph in Figure 1(b). Such queries are referred to as **reachability queries** in the rest of the paper.

3 The Coding of Graph-Model XML Document

In this section, we describe the coding scheme of graph-structured XML document. We extend the coding scheme for directed acyclic graph (DAG) in [15] to support directed cyclic digraph. Therefore, with this coding, the reachability

[1] **FIXME**
[2] **FIXME**

relationship between two nodes in a general digraph can be judged efficiently without accessing any other node.

3.1 The Coding of DAGs

In this subsection, we encode DAG using the method introduced in [15]. In this coding scheme, each node is assigned a list of intervals. We briefly summarize the encoding method for a DAG G in the following: *First, find an optimal tree-cover* T *of the DAG* D. T *is traversed in a depth-first manner. During the traversal, an interval* $[x, y]$ *is assigned each node* n *of* T*, where* x *is the postorder of* n *in the traversal.* y *is the smallest postorder number of all* n*'s descendants in* T*. Next, examine all the nodes of* D *in the reverse topological order. At each node* n*, copy and merge, if possible, all the intervals of its out-going nodes in* G *to its code.*

The judgement of the reachibility relationship between two nodes a and b is to check whether the postorder of b is contained in one of the intervals of a.

An example of encoding a DAG G is shown as following. The coding of the DAG in Fig 2(a) is the in Fig 2(b). We use *postid* to denote the postorder number of each nodes, which is also the second value of the first interval of its code.

3.2 The Coding of General Graph

We now generalize the above scheme for the case of a directed cyclic graph. We assume that the graph consists of only one connected component with a single root. The root is a node without any incoming edge. Otherwise, we can pick up any root node or add a virtual root node.

The process of coding a general digraph G is sketched as the following steps:

1. Find all Maximal Strongly Connected Components (MSCC) with number of nodes greater than one. A maximal strongly connected component C is a MSCC if and only if there is no strongly connected component (SCC) that contains C in G.
2. Each MSCC of G is contracted to a *representative node*. As a result G is reduced to a DAG G' (the correctness of this step is proved in Theorem 1). Suppose MSCC $S = \{node_0, node_1, \cdots, node_t\}$ in G is contracted in to $node_S$. $node_S$ is the representative node in G'. If a node in G is not contracted, then its corresponding node is itself in G'.
3. G' is encoded using the method introduced in Section 3.1.
4. For each $node_S$ in G', assuming its code is C_s, C_s is assigned to every $node_0, node_1, \cdots, node_t$ in G. It means that all nodes in the same MSCC have the same codes, i.e., the list of intervals and the *postid* number.

For example, a directed cyclic graph G is shown in Figure 1(b). In order to encode G, the first step is to contract all the maximal strongly connected components. In G, there is only one such MSCC, $S = \{d3, c1, e1, e2, e3\}$. By contracting this MSCC, a DAG G' shown in Figure 1(b) is generated. In G', R is the representative node for MSCC S. The interval codes of G' is shown in

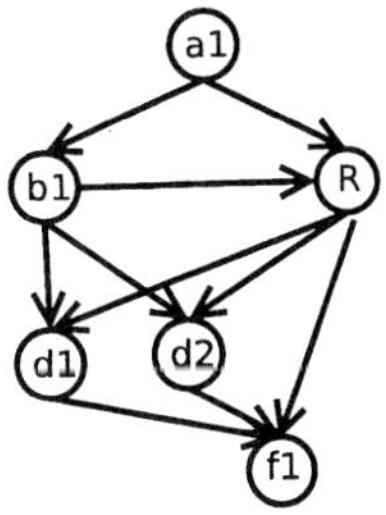

(a) The DAG contracted from Graph XML

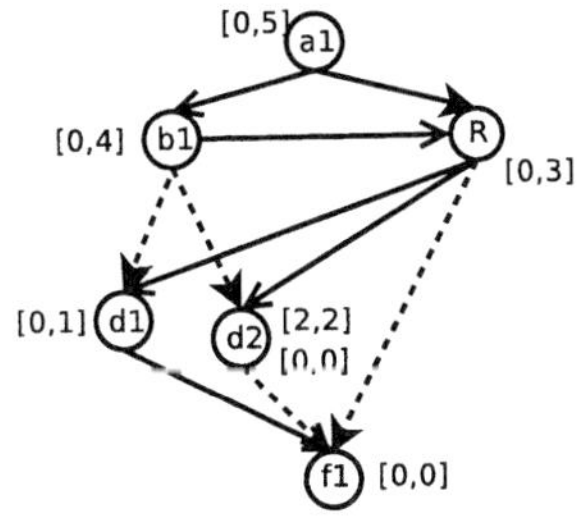

(b) Interval Coding for the DAG

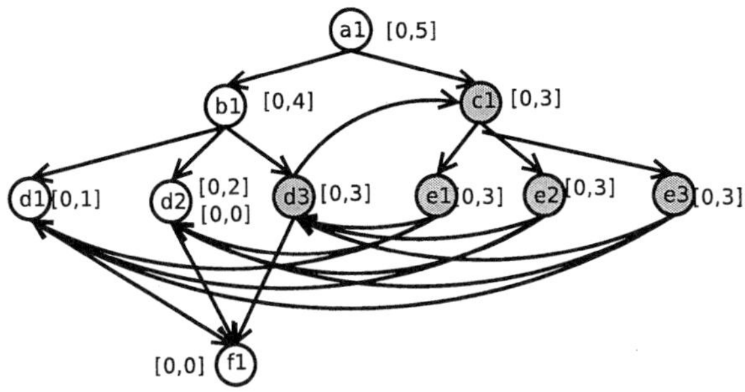

(c) Interval Coding for the XML Graph

Fig. 2. The Coding Scheme

Figure 2(b). At last, the intervals associated with R, i.e., $[0,3]$, is assigned to each node in S in G. As a result, $d3$, $c1$, $e1$, $e2$, $e3$ all have the same interval code $[0,3]$. The interval codes of graph G is shown in Figure 2(c). The *postid* of each node is the second value of its first interval. For example, $d3$.*postid* is 3.

The following theorems ensure the correctness of the encoding method. In the interest of space, we don't show the proofs of the theorems.

Theorem 1. *A directed cyclic graph G is converted to a DAG in the way stated above.*

Theorem 2. *For two nodes a and b of XML graph encoded in steps stated, suppose the $code_a = \{[a_0.x, a_0.y], \ldots, [a_n.x, a_n.y], postid_a\}$ and $code_b = \{[b_0.x, b_0.y], \ldots, [b_m.x, b_m.y], postid_b\}$. $postid_a$ and $postid_b$ are the postorders of a and b in the tree cover T of G' generated from G by contracting MSCCs, respectively. Then $a \rightsquigarrow b$ if and only if $\exists i (0 \leq i \leq n)$ such that $a_i.x \leq postid_b \leq a_i.y$.*

Time Complexity Analysis. The finding of all MSCCs can leverage the DFS-based algorithm in [1], and its time complexity is $O(n)$, where n is the number of the nodes of G. The efficiency of contracting step is $O(n_c)$, where n_c is the total number of nodes belonging to the MSCCs. The complex of encoding a DAG is $O(n')$ [15], where n' is the number of nodes in the DAG. The last step needs $O(n_c)$ time. Since both n_c and n' are smaller than n, the time complexity of encoding method is $O(n)$.

4 Join Algorithms Based on the Labeling Scheme

In this section, we design two join-based algorithms to process reachability query on graph-structured XML data using the labeling scheme presented in Section 3. The structural join algorithms compute the result of reachability query $a \rightsquigarrow d$, where $a \in Alist$ and $d \in Dlist$ are element sets.

4.1 Preprocess of the Input

One difference of the interval labeling scheme of a graph and that of a tree is that there may be more than one interval assigned to a node. The reachability relationship of two nodes a and b can be judged based on Theorem 2. We choose to preprocess the joining nodes by inverting the nodes and their corresponding interval codes. That is, if a node has k intervals, it is treated as k nodes: for Alist, each element has one interval; for Dlist, each element has a *postid* and the *id* of this element. Then both inputs are inverted: for the Alist, the list is sorted on the intervals $[x, y]$ by the ascending order of x and then the descending order of y; for the Dlist, the list is sorted by the ascending order of *postid*. The intuition is to leverage the order in the intervals and *postids* to accelerate join processing.

We note that the same interval will occur more than once in the preprocessed Alist, for one of the following two reasons:

- All the nodes with the same tag in an MSCC have the same codes, hence intervals.
- Even if two nodes does not belong to the same MSCC, there could be some interval associated with both of them. This is because in the third step of the DAG encoding, when considering a node n with multiple children, some intervals of its child will be appended to n. If some added interval of a child c cannot be merged in the existing code of n, c and n with the same tage will have the same interval even if they do not belongs to any MSCC together.

Similar case exists in Dlist as well because all nodes in the same MSCC have the same *postid*.

Inmplementation-wise, in order to decrease the interval set of processing, repeated intervals with different node IDs are merged into one interval with multiple node IDs. Repeated *postids* in Dlist are also merged in a similar way.

For example, before the preprocessing for answering query $d \rightsquigarrow e$ against the XML document shown in Figure 2(c), Alist is $\{d1([0,1]), d2([0,0],[0,2]), d3([0.4])\}$, and Dlist is $\{e1(4), e2(4), e3(4)\}$. The intervals associated with a node is in the brackets following the node. After preproocessing, the Alist becomes $\{[0,4](d3), [0,2](d2), [0,1](d1), [0,0](d2)\}$, the Dlist becomes $\{4(e1, e2, e3)\}$. Preprocessed Alist and Dlist are sorted by the codes (intervals and *postids*, respectively). The nodes corresponds to an interval i (or *postid*) is in the bracket followed the interval (or the *postid*). In Alist, the intervals associated to $d2$ are separated. In Dlist, since $e1, e2, e3$ have the same postid, they are merged into the same *postid*.

4.2 Two Join Algorithms

After preprocessing, a naïve structural algorithm can be obtained by generalizing the sort-merge based structural join algorithm in [2]. One subtlety is that the intervals in the preprocessing Alist might have the same starting or ending values (i.e., x or y). The codes shown in Figure 2(c) is such an example. We present the merge based join algorithm on graph, named *Graph-Merge Join* (GMJ), in Algorithm 1.

Algorithm 1 GMJ(*Alist*,*Dlist*)

```
a = Alist.head()
d = Dlist.head()
while a ≠ NULL ∧ b ≠ NULL do
  while a.x > d.postid ∧ d ≠ NULL do
    d = d.next()
  while a.y < d.postid ∧ a ≠ NULL do
    a = a.next()
  if d ≠ NULL ∧ a ≠ NULL then
    bookmark = a
    while a ≠ NULL ∧ a.x ≤ d.postid ∧ a.y ≥ d.postid do
      Append (a, d) pair to the output
      a = a.next()
    a = bookmark
  d = d.next()
```

For example, assume the two lists (preprocessed) to be joined are:

- Alist: $a1([1,3]), a2([1,1]), a3([3,6]), a4([4,5])$,
- Dlist: $d1(1), d2(4), d3(7)$

In GMJ, the basic idea is to join intervals and *postids* in a sort-merge fashion. Since intervals might be nested, a bookmark is needed to keep track of the current position of intervals while outputting results. In the example, the pointer of Alist, i.e., a, points to $a1$. $d1$ joins $a1$ and $a2$. When processing $d2$, the pointer of Alist moves to $a3$. $d2$ join with $a3$ and $a4$. When processing $d3$, the pointer moves to the tail of Alist, so the algorithm terminates.

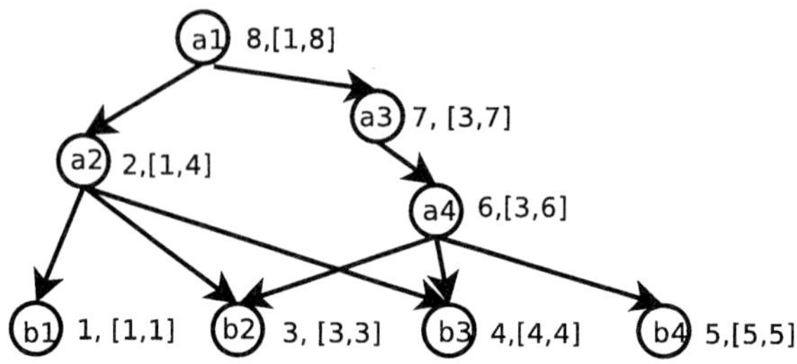

Fig. 3. An Example of Overlapping Code

GMJ suffers the same problem of tree-merge join algorithms in that part of the input might be scanned repeatedly. We note that stack-based structural join algorithm in [2] cannot be directly generalized and work with our coding scheme. This is because that two intervals may be partially overlapped. For an example, a graph and its codes is shown in Figure 3. The intervals assigned to a_2 and a_4 are partially overlapping. As a result, stacks can no longer be used to represent the nesting relationship between intervals in our coding scheme.

Algorithm 2 IGMJ(*Alist*,*Dlist*)

```
a = Alist.head()
d = Dlist.head()
rstree.insert(a)
a = a.next()
while a ≠ NULL ∧ d ≠ NULL do
  if a.x ≤ d.postid then
    rstree.trim(a.x)
    rstree.insert(a)
    a = a.next()
  else
    rstree.trim(d.postid)
    for all element a in rstree do
      Append (a, d) pair to the output
    d = d.next()
```

We design a new algorithm, named *Improved Graph Merge Join* (IGMJ) instead. The basic idea of GRJ is to store the intervals that can be joined in a range search tree (RST for brief). In the tree, the intervals indexed and organized according to their y values. When a new interval a of Alist arrives, it is compared with the current node d of Dlist. If a contains the postorder of d, a is inserted to the tree and all elements in the tree with y value smaller than $a.x$ are deleted (via the *trim*() method). Otherwise, we process current node d in Dlist. All elements in the tree with y value smaller than $d.postid$ are deleted. Then output d with all the a nodes in the tree. The algorithm of IGMJ is shown in Algorithm 2. In this algorithm, *brtree* is a RST that supports the following methods: *insert*(I)

and $trim(v)$. $insert(I)$ will insert an interval I to the BRST; $trim(v)$ will batch delete the intervals in *brtree* whose y values smaller than v.

For example, let's consider running IGMJ on the same example above. x values of $a1$ and $a2$ are smaller than $d1.postid$. At first, $a1$ and $a2$ are inserted into the RST. Then, $(d1, a1)$ and $(d1, a_2)$ are appended to the result list. $a3$ and $a4$ are processed before $d2$[3]. They are inserted to RST. When $a3$ is processed, $a2$ is trimmed from the RST because $a2.y < a3.x$. $a1$ is trimmed from RST when processing $d2$, since $a1.y < d2.postid$. Then, $(a3, d2)$ and $(a4, d2)$ will be appended to the result list. $a3$ and $a4$ are trimmed from RST based on $d3$.

5 Experiments

In this section, we present results and analyses of part of our extensive experiments of the new coding scheme and the structural join algorithms.

5.1 Experimental Setup

All our experiments were performed on a PC with Pentium 1GHz CPU, 256M main memory and 30G IDE hard disk. The OS is Windows 2000 Professional. We implemented the encoding of graph, the Graph-Merge-Join (**GMJ**) and Improved-Graph-Merge-Join (**IGMJ**) using the file system as the storage engine. For comparison, we also implemented a naïve traversal-based query processing algorithm based on the 1-index [14] (**1-index**).

We use the XMark benchmark dataset [16] in our experiments. It is a frequently used dataset and features irregular schema. We measure the performance of different algorithms on the 20M XMark dataset (with scale factor 0.2). It has 351241 nodes and its 1-index has 161679 nodes. We generated other XMark datasets with sizes 10M, 20M, 30M, 40M, and 50M respectively. They are used in the scalability experiment.

We show the set of queries used in the experiments in Table 1. They represent different characteristics in terms of the sizes of Alist, Dlist, and result (based on the 20M XMark dataset).

Table 1. The Query Set

ID	Query	Alist Size	Dlist Size	Result Size
Q1	person$\rightsquigarrow$emph	3158	14222	8032
Q2	site$\rightsquigarrow$item	1	4549	4350
Q3	person$\rightsquigarrow$category	3158	200	199
Q4	people$\rightsquigarrow$privacy	205	1195	1182

[3] **FIXME**

Table 2. The Size of Code

Doc Size	Intervals	Intervals after preprocessing	IPN	IPNJ
11.3M	252284	173702	1.44	0.990
22.8M	503112	346014	1.43	0.985
34.0M	746234	516546	1.40	0.985
45.3M	999784	687596	1.43	0.986
56.2M	1255877	859823	1.44	0.988

5.2 Space Overhead of the Coding

We measure the space overhead of our coding scheme with the following two parameters:

$$IPN = \frac{\text{number of total intervals}}{\text{number of nodes in the XML document}}$$

$$IPNJ = \frac{\text{number of total intervals after preprocessing}}{\text{number of nodes in the XML document}}$$

The former measurement represents the average number of intervals associated to one node. The later measurement represents the average number of intervals associated with one node that will be processed during structural join.

The results of the size of codes are shown in Table 2. IPNJ is small than 1.0. This is because some nodes in the interval sets may share the same interval. It can be observed from the result that even though the average number of intervals of a node is larger than one, the average number of intervals after preprocessing are smaller. This shows that the preprocessing of the Alist and Dlist in join is meaningful by exploiting the sharing of intervals and *postids*, respectively.

5.3 Execution Time

We show in Figure 4(a) the execution time of GMJ, IGMJ, and 1-index for Q1 to Q4 on the 20M XMark dataset. Note that Y-axis is in logarithm scale. Both

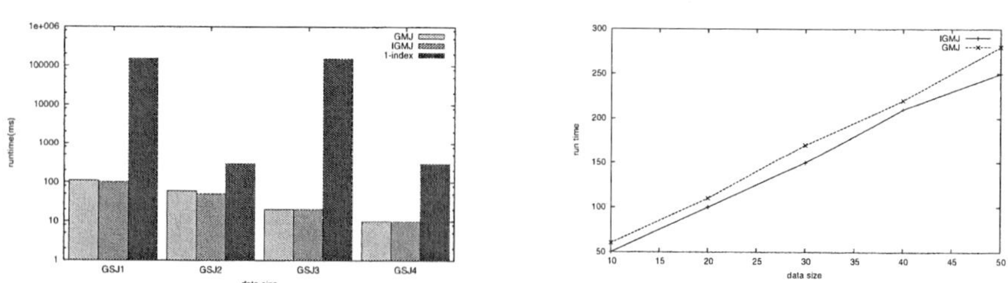

(a) Execution Time

(b) Scalability of IGMJ and GMJ (Q1)

Fig. 4. Experiment Results

GMJ and IGMJ outperform 1-index. This is because there are many nodes in 1-index. During processing the query with form 'a//b', when a node a_1 with tag a is found, all the nodes in the subgraph formed with nodes that are reachable from a_1 need to be traversed. We also found that IGMJ is always faster than GMJ. It is because with the usage of RST, whenever an interval will not join with any d in the Dlist, it will be trimmed from the RST.

5.4 Scalability Experiment

To evaluate the scalability of the new algorithms, We ran Q1 on XMark documents with size ranging from 10M to 50M. The result is shown in Fig 4(b). It can be seen that both algorithms scale linearly with the increase of the data size.

6 Related Work

There are many reachability labeling schemes for trees. Recent work includes [3, 8, 11]. Reachability labeling schema schemes for directed acyclic graphs (DAGs) includes [15, 22]. [6] is a survey of labeling schemes for DAGs and compares several labeling schemes in the context of semantic web applications. [10] presents a reachability coding for a special kind of graph, which is defined as *planar-st* in [17]. Based on this coding, [19] presents a twig query processing method. [17] extends this coding scheme to spherical st-graph. Note that both "planar st" and "spherical st" are strong conditions. To the best of our knowledge, there is no direct generalization of the above two labeling schemes to support general digraph.

[7] presents a 2-hop reachability coding scheme. But the length of the label for a node could be $O(n)$. This might add to much overhead for the query processing for graph-structured XML data.

With efficient coding, XML queries can also be evaluated using the join-based approaches. Structural join is such an operator and its efficient evaluation algorithms have been extensively studied in [2, 21, 13, 8, 5, 9, 20]. They are all based on coding schemes that enable efficient checking of structural relationship of any two nodes in a tree, and thus cannot be applied to the graph-structural XML data directly.

7 Conclusions

In this paper, we present a labeling scheme for graph-structured XML data. With such labelling scheme, the reachability relationship between two nodes in a graph can be judged efficiently. Based on the labeling scheme, we design efficient structural join algorithms for graph-structured XML, GMJ and IGMJ. Our experiments show that the labeling scheme has acceptable size while the proposed structural join algorithms outperform previous algorithms significantly. As one of our future work, we will design efficient index structure based on the labeling scheme to accelerate query processing.

References

1. *Introduction to Algorithms.* MIT Press, Cambridge MA, 1990.
2. Shurug Al-Khalifa, H. V. Jagadish, Jignesh M. Patel, Yuqing Wu, Nick Koudas, and Divesh Srivastava. Structural joins: A primitive for efficient XML query pattern matching. In *Proceedings of the 18th International Conference on Data Engineering (ICDE 2002)*, pages 141–152, 2002.
3. Stephen Alstrup and Theis Rauhe. Small induced-universal graphs and compact implicit graph representations. In *Proceedings of 2002 IEEE Symposium on Foundations of Computer Science (FOCS 2002)*, pages 53–62, Vancouver, BC, Canada, November 2002.
4. Donald D. Chamberlin, Daniela Florescu, and Jonathan Robie. XQuery: A query language for XML. In *W3C Working Draft*, http://www.w3.org/TR/xquery, 2001.
5. Shu-Yao Chien, Zografoula Vagena, Donghui Zhang, Vassilis J. Tsotras, and Carlo Zaniolo. Efficient structural joins on indexed XML documents. In *Proceedings of 28th International Conference on Very Large Data Bases (VLDB 2002)*, pages 263–274, 2002.
6. Vassilis Christophides, Dimitris Plexousakis, Michel Scholl, and Sotirios Tourtounis. On labeling schemes for the semantic web. In *Proceedings of the Twelfth International World Wide Web Conference(WWW2003)*, pages 544–555, Budapest, Hungary, May 2003.
7. Edith Cohen, Eran Halperin, Haim Kaplan, and Uri Zwick. Reachability and distance queries via 2-hop labels. In *Proceedings of the thirteenth annual ACM-SIAM symposium on Discrete algorithms (SODA 2002)*, pages 937–946, San Francisco, CA, USA, January 2002.
8. Torsten Grust. Accelerating XPath location steps. In *Proceedings of the 2002 ACM SIGMOD International Conference on Management of Data (SIGMOD 2002)*, pages 109–120, Hong Kong, China, August 2002.
9. Haifeng Jiang, Hongjun Lu, Wei Wang, and Beng Chin Ooi. XR-Tree: Indexing XML data for efficient structural join. In *Proceedings of the 19th International Conference on Data Engineering (ICDE 2003)*, pages 253–263, 2003.
10. Tiko Kameda. On the vector representation of the reachability in planar directed graphs. *Information Process Letters*, 3(3):78–80, 1975.
11. Haim Kaplan, Tova Milo, and Ronen Shabo. A comparison of labeling schemes for ancestor queries. In *Proceedings of the thirteenth annual ACM-SIAM symposium on Discrete algorithms (SODA 2002)*, pages 954 – 963, San Francisco, CA, USA, January 2002.
12. Raghav Kaushik, Philip Bohannon, Jeffrey F. Naughton, and Henry F. Korth. Covering indexes for branching path queries. In *Proceedings of the 2002 ACM SIGMOD International Conference on Management of Data (SIGMOD 2002)*, pages 133–144, 2002.
13. Quanzhong Li and Bongki Moon. Indexing and querying XML data for regular path expressions. In *Proceedings of 27th International Conference on Very Large Data Base (VLDB 2001)*, pages 361–370, 2001.
14. Tova Milo and Dan Suciu. Index structures for path expressions. In *Proceedings of the 7th International Conference on Database Theory (ICDE 1999)*, pages 277–295, 1999.
15. H. V. Jagadish Rakesh Agrawal, Alexander Borgida. Efficient management of transitive relationships in large data and knowledge bases. In *Proceedings of the 1989 ACM SIGMOD International Conference on Management of Data (SIGMOD 1989)*, pages 253–262, Portland, Oregon, May 1989.

16. Albrecht Schmidt, Florian Waas, Martin L. Kersten, Michael J. Carey, Ioana Manolescu, and Ralph Busse. XMark: A benchmark for XML data management. In *Proceedings of 28th International Conference on Very Large Data Bases (VLDB 2002)*, pages 974–985, 2002.
17. Roberto Tamassia and Ioannis G. Tollis. Dynamic reachability in planar digraphs with one source and one sink. *Theoretical Computer Science*, 119(2):331–343, 1993.
18. C. M. Sperberg-McQueen Franois Yergeau Tim Bray, Jean Paoli. Extensible markup language (xml) 1.0 (third edition). In *W3C Recommendation 04 February 2004*, http://www.w3.org/TR/REC-xml/, 2004.
19. Zografoula Vagena, Mirella Moura Moro, and Vassilis J. Tsotras. Twig query processing over graph-structured xml data. In *Proceedings of the Seventh International Workshop on the Web and Databases(WebDB 2004)*, pages 43–48, 2004.
20. Wei Wang, Haifeng Jiang, Hongjun Lu, and Jeffrey Xu Yu. PBiTree coding and efficient processing of containment joins. In *Proceedings of the 19th International Conference on Data Engineering (ICDE 2003)*, pages 391–402, 2003.
21. Chun Zhang, Jeffrey F. Naughton, David J. DeWitt, Qiong Luo, and Guy M. Lohman. On supporting containment queries in relational database management systems. In *Proceedings of the 2001 ACM SIGMOD International Conference on Management of Data (SIGMOD 2001)*, pages 425–436, 2001.
22. Yoav Zibin and Joseph Gil. Efficient subtyping tests with pq-encoding. In *Proceedings of the 2001 ACM SIGPLAN Conference on Object-Oriented Programming Systems, Languages and Applications (OOPSLA 2001)*, pages 96–107, San Francisco, CA, USA, October 2001.

Constructing Extensible XQuery Mappings for XML Data Sharing

Gang Qian and Yisheng Dong

Department of Computer Science and Engineering, Southeast University, Nanjing 210096, China
{qiangang, ysdong}@seu.edu.cn

Abstract. XQuery has been widely considered as a mapping language for XML-based data sharing systems. Though many recent efforts have been made to provide automated support for constructing such semantic mappings between schemas, in practice it is inevitable for the user to directly construct or maintain the naive yet troublesome mapping expressions. In this paper, we propose the mapping combination framework for incrementally construct so called combined mappings, by starting with simple atomic ones and applying a set of combination operators. Different from the naive expressions, the combined mappings are extensible and maintainable, which gives flexibility and reusability in the process of mapping construction and maintenance, and alleviates the burden on the user in general cases.

1 Introduction

XQuery is a standard query language proposed by W3C [9], and has reached a widespread recognition as a mapping language for many modern XML-based data sharing architectures such as data integration, data exchange and peer-data management systems. However, constructing such semantic mappings is a labor-intensive and error-prone process. Though recent research on *schema matching* (e.g., [7, 3, 2]) and *mapping discovery* [5, 6] has made exciting progress towards semi-automating this process, in practice it is inevitable for the user to directly construct or maintain such mappings, i.e., the naive yet troublesome XQuery expressions.

In this paper we propose a framework for constructing and representing XQuery mapping from source schemas to target schema. In our framework, a global mapping is represented by the combination of atomic mappings and binary operators that recursively combine simpler mappings into more complex mappings. Different from the naive expressions, the combined mappings obtained in this way are extensible and maintainable, which gives flexibility and reusability in the process of mapping construction and maintenance, and alleviates the burden on the user in general cases.

We present the *Nest*, *Join* and *Product* combination operators to connect two atomic or combined mappings (say M_1 and M_2). We say that the resulting combined mapping (say $M_{1,2}$) is extensible, which means that $M_{1,2}$ can be combined again with others, possibly using another combination operator, and it is also able to reset the combination operator of $M_{1,2}$, or recover M_1 and M_2 from it. Thus, the global schema

Y. Zhang et al. (Eds.): APWeb 2005, LNCS 3399, pp. 290–295, 2005.

mappings can be incrementally constructed by continuously applying the combination operators. Further, to maintain such combined mappings, it only needs to adjust the corresponding parts, e.g., the submappings affected by schema evolving, while other parts are reused to the new context.

On the other hand, automated support for constructing the combined mappings can be provided based on the previous works on schema matching (e.g., [7, 3, 2]) and mapping discovery [5, 6]. For example, atomic mappings may be generated in terms of the results of schema matching, and combined mappings may be derived from the cardinality constraints and the semantic relations (called associations in [6]) between schema elements. Due to limited space, we omit the discussion from this paper.

The paper is organized as follows. Section 2 uses a running example to illustrate our framework of mapping combination. Section 3 presents the combination operators in detail. Finally, Section 4 concludes.

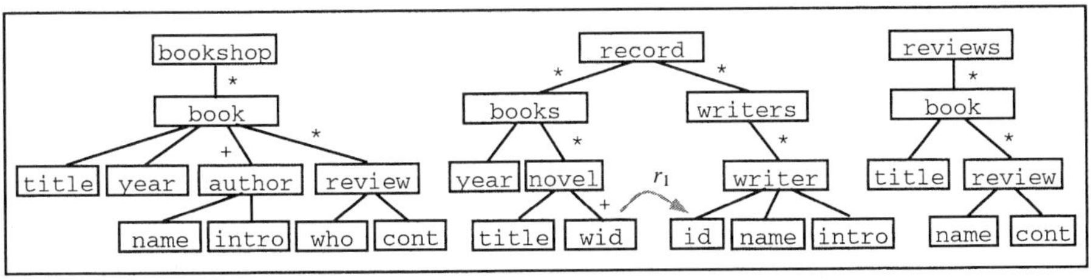

Fig. 1. The target schema T (left), source schema S1 (middle) and S2 (right)

2 The Mapping Combination Framework

Suppose there is an online bookshop that wants to collect data from other sources. Figure 1 shows the nested target schema T of the bookshop and S1 and S2 of its two data sources. We model XML schema as usual with a tree. The nodes correspond to XML elements. The edges represent the parent-child relationships, and have a multiplicity label that takes a value from {?, *, +, ε}, which indicates the cardinality constraint. Every referential relationship is represented as a non-tree edge (e.g., the edge r_1 in S1).

Figure 2 shows a XQuery mapping that defines the data translation from the sources into the target. Note that the target schema element review is optional (constrained by "*"), so even if the novel instance in S1 has no corresponding reviews in S2, the book instance returned will still be valid. Now the shop want to constraint the element review with "+". Accordingly, the above mapping has to be modified to keep it consistent. Yet directly editing the naive XQuery expression is difficult.

To address this problem, we propose to construct and represent the global mapping by the combination of atomic mappings. In our framework, we consider the usual FLWR expression of the XQuery syntax, which is composed of FOR, LET, WHERE and RETURN clauses [9]. The function of the FOR and LET clause is to bind variables, respectively called *F-variables* and *L-variables*. Each F-variable may be specified by an absolute or a relative path expression. For example, in the outermost FOR clause of the above mapping, the F-variable `$bs` is specified by an absolute path (of the element `books`), whereas the specification of `$n` depends on `$bs`. We say that `$bs` is a *prefix F-variable* of `$n`, and `$n` is a suffix F-variable of `$bs`.

```
<bookshop>
FOR $bs IN doc("S1")//books, $n IN $bs//novel
RETURN <book>
    <title>{$n/title/text()}</title>
    <year>{$bs/year/text()}</year>
    FOR $w IN doc("S1")//writer
    WHERE $n/wid=$w/id
    RETURN <author>
              <name>{$w/name/text()}</name>
              <intro>{$w/intro/text()}</intro> </author>
    FOR $b IN doc("S2")//book, $r IN $b//review
    WHERE $n/title=$b/title
    RETURN <review>
              <who>{$r/name/text()}</who>
              <cont>{$r/cont/text()}</cont> </review>
    </book>
</bookshop>
```

Fig. 2. The naive mapping expression formulated using the XQuery query language

Given a mapping, let `$v` be one of the F-variables of the outmost `FOR` clauses. If `$v` has *no* suffix variables in these `FOR` clauses, we say that it is a *primary F-variable* (*PFV*) of the mapping. An atomic mapping satisfies the following constraints: containing no submappings, having only one PFV, and its result pattern (declared by the `RETURN` clause) being one single element. Samples of atomic mappings are given below.

$M_{\texttt{book()}}$: `FOR $n IN doc("S1")//novel RETURN <book></book>`

$M_{\texttt{title}}$: `FOR $t IN doc("S1")//novel/title RETURN <title>{$t/text()}</title>`

$M_{\texttt{year}}$: `FOR $y IN doc("S1")//books/year RETURN <year>{$y/text()}</year>`

We denote the atomic mappings by symbol *M*, which has a subscript in terms of the target schema elements in the result pattern. Note that `book` is complex type in target `T`, so the first atomic mapping above is denoted by $M_{\texttt{book()}}$. More specially, an atomic mapping also allows the prefix F-variables and `WHERE` clause, and functions are also permitted in defining the PFV.

Atomic mappings specify local views of single target schema element. By applying combination operators given in next section, we connect them to form combined mappings, which formulate more complete views. For example, using the *Nest* or *Join* operator, we may connect $M_{\texttt{book()}}$ with $M_{\texttt{title}}$ to get a combined mapping $M_{\texttt{book(title)}}$ (see Section 3). Continuing to combine $M_{\texttt{book(title)}}$ with $M_{\texttt{year}}$, a more complete mapping $M_{\texttt{book(title, year)}}$ is generated.

When there is no confusion, from now on we also use $M_{\texttt{book(...)}}$ to uniformly denote $M_{\texttt{book()}}$, or $M_{\texttt{book(title)}}$, etc. Similarly, we are able to incrementally construct $M_{\texttt{author(...)}}$, $M_{\texttt{review(...)}}$, and the global mapping $M_{\texttt{book(title, year, author, review)}}$, like the one in Figure 2, but now it is extensible and maintainable. For example, the above requirement can be easily satisfied with resetting the combination operator applied between $M_{\texttt{book()}}$ and $M_{\texttt{review(...)}}$.

3 Combination Operators

As shown in the above section, mapping combination is to connect two mappings through a set of combination operators. Driven by the target schema, a combination operator merges the results of two mappings according to the relationship between them. Following from the XQuery standard [6] and the experiences in relational database [1], there are three key ways, i.e., *outerjoin*, *join* and *product*, to connect two mappings. Accordingly, we define them respectively as *Nest*, *Join* and *Product* combination operators.

We use $e(a_1, \ldots, a_i)$ to denote a schema element e that contains $a_1, \ldots$, and a_i subelements (atomic or complex type). The *Nest* and *Join* operators are to connect $M_{\texttt{e(a1, ..., ai-1)}}$ and $M_{\texttt{ai}}$ (or $M_{\texttt{ai(...)}}$, when a_i is complex type), and generate a combined mapping $M_{\texttt{e(a1, ..., ai-1, ai)}}$. They have the following general form.

$$Op(M_{\texttt{e(a1, ..., ai-1)}}, M_{\texttt{ai}}, con)=M_{\texttt{e(a1, ..., ai-1, ai)}}, (i \geq 1)$$

The *Product* operator is to connect $M_{\texttt{e(a1, ..., ai-1)}}$ and $M_{\texttt{e(ai)}}$ and has the form as follows.

$$Merge(M_{\texttt{e(a1, ..., ai-1)}}, M_{\texttt{e(ai)}}, con)=M_{\texttt{e(a1, ..., ai-1, ai)}}, (i \geq 1)$$

As will be seen, the cardinality constraints in the target are satisfied with the operator types, and the source elements (bindings of the F-variables) are related by *con*, the connection condition, which has the form of *path*1=*path*2 in this paper. Finally, the resulting combined mapping $M_{\texttt{e(a1, ..., ai-1, ai)}}$ always nests the instances of a_i within those of e.

Nest Operator. Consider again the mapping in Figure 2. It indicates that for each `$n` binding, there will be a `book` instance returned to the target. However, if there are no corresponding reviews in the source `S2`, the `book` instance will be with no `review` attributes. In other words, there is an outerjoin that connects the outer and inner sub-mappings (i.e., `$n` and `$b` bindings).

We use the *Nest* operator to capture such meanings. Here the resulting combined mapping $M_{\texttt{e(a1, ..., ai-1, ai)}}$ is derived from $M_{\texttt{e(a1, ..., ai-1)}}$ by nesting $M_{\texttt{ai}}$ (or $M_{\texttt{ai(...)}}$) within its `RETURN` clause, with the connection condition *con*. Consider $M_{\texttt{book()}}$ and $M_{\texttt{title}}$. Their PFVs (i.e., `$n` and `$t`) are respectively specified by the schema element `novel` and `title`. To relate `$n` and `$t` bindings, we assign `$n/title=$t` to *con*. The result of *Nest*($M_{\texttt{book()}}$, $M_{\texttt{title}}$, `$n/title=$t`) is as follows.

$M_{\texttt{book(title)}}$:
```
FOR $n IN doc("S1")//novel
RETURN <book>
    FOR $t IN doc("S1")//novel/title
    WHERE $n/title=$t
    RETURN <title>{$t/text()}</title>
    </book>
```

Other combined mappings can be constructed in the same way. In our running example, `title` is mandatory in source `S1`, so the returned `book` instances always contain the attribute. Otherwise, for each `$n` binding, for example, if there was no `$t` bindings satisfying the connection condition, the `book` instance returned would contain *no* `title` attribute.

Join Operator. With the constraints in the schemas of Figure 1, it is valid to apply the *Nest* operator to get the global combined mapping $M_{\texttt{book(title, year, author, review)}}$. However, when the cardinality constraint "*" of `review` in the shop schema is replaced with "+", the mapping should filter out those books with no reviews. The *Nest* operator no more satisfies such requirement. Instead, here a join relationship is needed.

We use the *Join* operator to capture such meanings. To specify the combined mapping $M_{\texttt{e(a1, ..., ai-1, ai)}}$, here a `LET` clause is needed, which binds a L-variable (say `$v`) to the associated sequence (e.g., the results of evaluating $M_{\texttt{ai}}$) as a whole. Then the filter `count($v)>0` is used to guarantee that only when the connection condition *con* is satisfied, can a new instance of *e* be returned. We use the following example to explain it. Suppose the mappings $M_{\texttt{book(title, year, author)}}$ and $M_{\texttt{review(who, cont)}}$ have been obtained by applying the *Nest* operator. We use the *Join* operator to connect them to filter those books with no reviews.

```
FOR $n IN doc("S1")//novel
LET $v :=  FOR $b IN doc("S2")//book, $r IN $b/review
          WHERE $n/title=$b/title
          ......  ......  ......
WHERE count($v)>0
RETURN <book>
       FOR $t IN doc("S1")//novel/title
       ......  ......  ......
       {$v}
       </book>
```

Note that for each `$n` binding, the bindings of the L-variable `$v` are nested as a whole within the corresponding `book` instances. Using the *Join* operator, it is also possible to connect the mappings such as $M_{\texttt{book()}}$ and $M_{\texttt{title}}$, yet the result is same as the *Nest* operator because of the cardinality constraints of the source schema.

Product Operator. The third way to connect mappings is by the product relation. In XML database, it is usual to nest relating author elements within the same book element, whereas in normal relational table one book tuple has one author value. When the target schema is a default XML view over relational database [8], the mappings may need to express product relationship.

We use the *Product* operator to satisfy such requirement. For example, suppose `book-author` is a relational table in target, and `title` and `author` are its two attributes. A `book-author` tuple is determined both by the `novel` and `writer` of `S1`, so two separate atomic mappings are constructed as follows.

$M'_{\texttt{book-author()}}$:

```
FOR $n IN doc("S1")//novel
RETURN <book-author></book-author>
```

$M''_{\texttt{book-author()}}$:

```
FOR $w IN doc("S1")//writer
RETURN <book-author></book-author>
```

Using the *Nest* operator, we combine them with $M_{\texttt{title}}$ and $M_{\texttt{author}}$, respectively. The resulting combined mappings $M'_{\texttt{book-author(title)}}$ and $M''_{\texttt{book-author(author)}}$ are then connected again by the *Product* operator and the following mapping is obtained.

$M_{\text{book-author(title, author)}}$:

```
FOR $n IN doc("S1")//novel
FOR $w IN doc("S1")//writer
WHERE $n/wid=$w/id
RETURN <book-author>
       FOR $t IN doc("S1")//novel/title
       WHERE $n/title=$t
       RETURN <title>{$t/text()}</title>
       FOR $na IN doc("S1")//writer/name
       WHERE $w/name=$na
       RETURN <author>{$na/text()}</author>
       </book-author>
```

The above mapping indicates that for each pair of `$n` and `$w` bindings, as long as there exists a `wid` that equals the corresponding `id`, a flattening `book-author` tuple will be returned. In general, applying the *Product* operator, the resulting combined mapping $M_{e(a1, \ldots, ai-1, ai)}$ is obtained by merging the FOR, LET, WHERE and RETURN clauses of $M_{e(a1, \ldots, ai-1)}$ and $M_{e(ai)}$, respectively.

4 Conclusion

Mapping maintenance is an usual task for the Web-based application. To avoid dealing with the naive yet troublesome mapping expression, this paper described the mapping combination framework for constructing extensible XQuery mappings. In terms of this idea, a set of combination operators including *Nest*, *Join*, and *Product* was presented. Our approach gives the flexibility and reusability in the process of mapping construction and maintenance. We believe that our work is also useful to the problem of managing and visualizing XQuery mappings (or views).

References

1. S. Abiteboul, R. Hull, and V. Vianu: Foundations of Databases. Addison-Wesley. (1995)
2. R. Dhamankar, Y. Lee, A. Doan, A. Halevy, and P. Domingos: iMAP: Discovering Complex Semantic Matches between Database Schemas. In: Proc. of ACM SIGMOD. (2004) 383-394
3. A. Doan, P. Domingos, and A. Halevy: Reconciling schemas of disparate data sources: A machine learning approach. In: Proc. of ACM SIGMOD. (2001) 509-520
4. I. Manolescu, D. Florescu, and D. Kossman: Answering XML Queries on Heterogeneous Data Sources. In: Proc. of VLDB. (2001) 241-250
5. R. Miller, L. Haas, and M. Hernández: Schema Mapping as Query Discovery. In: Proc. of VLDB. (2000) 77-88
6. L. Popa, Y. Velegrakis, R Miller, M. A. Hernandez, and R. Fagin: Translating Web Data. In: Proc. of VLDB. (2002) 598–609
7. E. Rahm and P.A. Bernstein: A survey of approaches to automatic schema matching. VLDB Journal 10 (2001) 334-350
8. J. Shanmugasundaram, J. Kiernan, E. J. Shekita, C. Fan, and J. Funderburk: Querying XML views of relational data. In: Proc. of VLDB. (2001) 261-270
9. XQuery: http://www.w3.org/XML/Query

Towards Secure XML Document with Usage Control

Jinli Cao[1], Lili Sun[2], and Hua Wang[2]

[1] Department of Computer Science & Computer Engineering,
La Trobe University, Melbourne, VIC 3086, Australia
jinli@cs.latrobe.edu.au

[2] Department of Maths & Computing, University of Southern Queensland,
Toowoomba QLD 4350 Australia
(sun, wang)@usq.edu.au

Abstract. XML promoted by the World Wide Web Consortium (W3C) is a de facto standard language for document representation and exchange on the Internet. XML documents may contain private information that cannot be shared by all user communities. Several approaches are designed to protect information in a website. However, these approaches typically are used at file system level, rather than for the data in XML documents that have to be protected from unauthorized access. Usage control has been considered as the next generation access control model with distinguishing properties of decision continuity.

In this paper, we present a usage control model to protect information distributed on the web, which allows the access restrictions directly on structures and documents. The model not only supports complex constraints for XML components, such as elements, attributes and datatypes but also provides a mechanism to build rich reuse relationships between models and documents. Finally, comparisons with related works are analysed.

1 Introduction

XML Web Service is a platform-independent Web application that accepts requests from different systems on the Internet and can involve a range of web technologies such as XML [7], SOAP [6], WSDL[8] and HTTP[14]. XML is used to store and exchange data in the Internet that may include private message of customers. For example, the following XML document displays customer's information.

XML document not only shows the contents of data but also the constraints and relationships between data. In Table 1, the element *customerInfo* includes *cid, name* and *creditCardInfo* sub-elements. The sub-element *cid* is a simple type while sub-elements *name* and *creditCardInfo* are combined with their own sub-elements. An XML document may be generated from various resources with varying security requirements due to its ability to express complex relationship between data. Alternatively, a user may like to limit access to particular parts

Y. Zhang et al. (Eds.): APWeb 2005, LNCS 3399, pp. 296–307, 2005.

Table 1. XML Document Example

```
<?xml version="1.0" encoding="UTF-8"? >
<customerInfo xmlns="http://www.hotel.com/CustomerInfo" gender="Male">
<cid>123-45-6789</cid >
<name>
<firstName> Tony </firstName >
<lastName> Wang ></lastName >
</name >
<creditCardInfo >
<type >Master card </type >
<cardNo >8888888888888888 </cardNo >
<expireDate >12/05 </expireDate >
<nameOnCard > Tony Wang </nameOnCard >
</creditCardInfo >
</customerInfo >
```

of an XML document. In the example above, Tony objects that everyone can read all information on his Mastercard. Another example may happen in an University, when an XML document can consist of information from applications among several faculties and multiple databases. When an internal or external user accesses this document, his/her access permission has to be monitored according to security policies in all these faculties and databases. These examples show that secure XML document is an significant topic.

Several approaches are designed for the security of XML document [12, 13, 22]. But all those approaches have some limitations. Encryption and decryption skills [12] are used in protection of communications between servers and clients rather than dissemination from clients, since these skills focus on the protection of file level but not on a systematic level. Additionally they only manage access requirements from a server side. Both Secure Sockets Layer (SSL) [13] and firewall [22], the recent techniques used on Intranet assume that the computers know XML web services, and firewall can accept only connections coming from those computers which IP addresses are known already. However, IP addresses of users are unknown to services before they connect on the Internet. SSL is applied to encrypt and decrypt messages exchanged between clients and servers. It can protect messages from unauthorized reading while messages are in transition, and also verifies incoming messages whether actually come from the correct sender. However, SSL is not satisfactory in Web service environment, specially in association with XML message used in SOAP - based communications [6]. This is because the SOAP is a specification for performing methods request and was conceived as a message format not bound to any single protocol [10].

There are several security issues that need to be addressed in the application of XML documents. In particular, the following two problems are critical to developing a secure and flexible access control architecture.

Problem 1. Restricting access to XML documents to authorized users;
Problem 2. Protecting XML documents from malicious dissemination.

To address these problems, this paper proposes authorization models which adopt usage control to manage access to XML documents and secure architectures to protect against malicious dissemination. Traditional access control has analyzed authorization decisions on a subject's access to target resources. "Obligations" are requirements that have to be followed by the subject for allowing access resources. "Conditions" are subject and object independent requirements that have to be passed. In today highly dynamic, distributed environment, obligations and conditions of new hosts are decision factors for the management of XML documents.

The remainder of this paper is organized as follows: Section 2 presents the background of XML and usage control. Three decision factors *Authorization, Obligation, Conditions* and Continuity properties *pre* and *ongoing* are introduced in this section. Section 3 shows our proposed authorization models for usage control. It includes *pre-Authorizations, ongoing-Authorizations, pre-Obligations, ongoing-Obligations, pre-Conditions* and *ongoing-Conditions.* Section 4 discusses how to build secure architectures for XML documents by using reference monitors in details. Section 5 compares our work with the previous work on XML document security. The difference between this work from others is presented. Section 6 concludes the paper and outlines our future work.

2 Related Technologies

2.1 XML

XML [7] is a markup language for describing semi-structured information. The XML document is composed of nested elements, each delimited by a pair of start and end tags (e.g. <name> and </name>) or by an empty tag. XML document can be classified into two categories: well-formed and valid. Well-formalization requires XML document to follow some syntax, such as, there is exactly one element that completely contains all other elements, elements may nest but not overlap, etc. Validation requires XML instance to contain specified elements and attributes, following specified datatypes and relationships.

2.2 Usage Control

There are eight components: subjects, subject attributes, objects, object attributes, rights, authorizations, obligations, and conditions in usage control model [20] (see Figure 1). Subjects and objects are familiar concepts from the past thirty years of access control, and are used in their familiar sense in this paper. A right represents access of a subject to an object, such as read or write. The existence of the right is determined when the access is attempted by the subject. The usage decision functions indicated in Figure 1 makes this determination based on subject attributes, object attributes, authorizations, obligations and conditions at the time of usage requests.

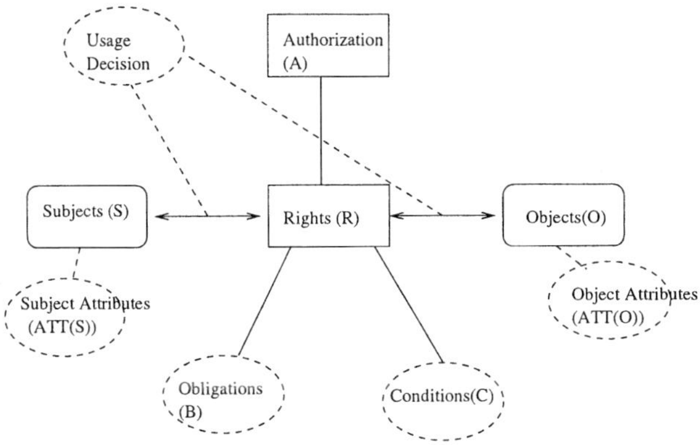

Fig. 1. Components of Model

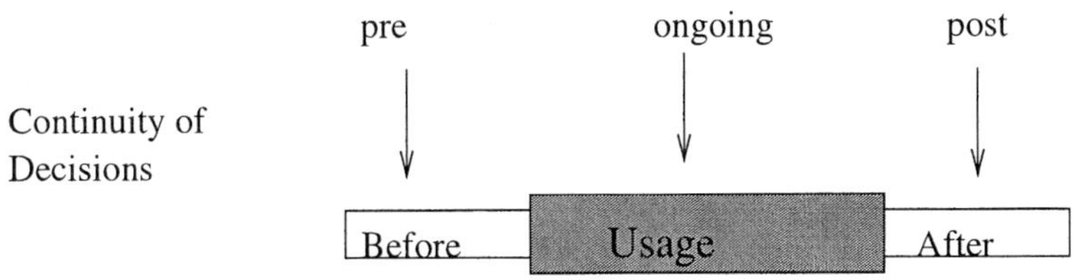

Fig. 2. Continuity Properties

Subject and object attributes can be used during the access decision process. Examples of subject attributes are identities, group names, roles, memberships, credits, etc. Examples of object attributes are security labels, ownerships, classes, access control lists, etc. In an on-line shop a price could be an object attribute, for instance, the book Harry Potter is priced at \$20 for a read right and priced at \$1000 price for a resell right.

Authorizations, obligations and conditions are decision factors used by decision functions to determine whether a subject should be allowed to access an object. Authorizations are based on subject and object attributes and the specific right. Authorization is usually required prior to the access, but in addition it is possible to require ongoing authorization during the access, e.g., a certificate revocation list (CRL) may be periodically checked while the access is in progress. An access is immediately revoked if the relevant certificate appears on the CRL. Authorizations may require updates on subjects and object attributes. These updates can be either 'pre', 'ongoing', or 'post' that are called continuity properties shown in Figure 2.

Conditions are decision factors that depend on environmental and system-oriented requirements. For example, IEEE member can access full papers in the IEEE digital library. They can also include the security status of the system, such as low level, normal, high alert, etc.

As discussed above, continuity is another decision factor as shown in Figure 2. In traditional access control, authorization is assumed to be done before access is allowed (pre). However, it is quite reasonable to extend this for continuous enforcement by evaluating usage requirements throughout usages (ongoing).

3 Authorization Models

We now discuss authorization models for XML documents adopting usage control in this section. Based on three decision factors: authorizations, obligations, and conditions, we develope a family of core models for usage control. By core models, we mean that they focus on the enforcement process and do not include administrative issues. We assume there exists a usage request on an XML target object. Decision-making can be done either before (pre) or during (ongoing) exercise of the requested right. Decision-making after the usage has no influence on the decision of current usage. Based on these criteria, we have 6 possible cases spaces as a core model for usage control: pre-Authorizations, ongoing-Authorizations, pre-Obligations, ongoing-Obligations, pre-Conditions and ongoing-Conditions. Depending on the access requirements on XML documents in real world, it is possible to utilize more than one case.

For simplicity we consider only the pure cases consisting of *Authorizations, Obligations* or *Conditions* alone with *pre* or *ongoing* decisions only. We focus on developing comprehensive usage control models for XML documents. Next we present usage control models (UCM) with different pure cases.

A. UCM_{preA}**:pre-Authorizations Model**
In an UCM_{preA} model, the decision process is performed before access is allowed. The UCM_{preA} model has the following components:

1. $S, XD, XDL, R, R_1, ATT(S), ATT(XD), ATT(XDL)$ and usage decision Boolean functions $preA, preA_1$ on XD, XDL, respectively,
   where S, XD, XDL, R, R_1 represent Subject, XML document, element in XML document and Rights required on XML document and on element (e.g. read, write) respectively. $ATT(S), ATT(XD), ATT(XDL)$ represent attributes of subjects, XML documents and elements in XML document respectively. $preA$ and $preA_1$ are predicates about authorization functions. Fox example, when users log in IEEE website, $preA$, or $preA_1$ is a function on users' account and password (subject attributes), IEEE XML documents and rights (read, write or resell) that is used to check whether users can access the documents with the right or not,
2. $allowed(s, xd, r) \Rightarrow preA(ATT(s), ATT(xd), r)$,
   Where $A \Rightarrow B$ means B is a necessary condition for A. This predicate indicates that if subject s is allowed to access XML document xd with right r then the indicated condition $preA$ must be true.
3. $allowed(s, xdl, r_1) \Rightarrow preA_1(ATT(s), ATT(xdl), r_1)$.
   The $allowed(s, xdl, r_1)$ predicate indicates that if subject s is allowed to access XML document xdl with right r_1 then the decision function $preA_1$ is true.

The UCM_{preA} model provides an authorization method on whether a subject can access XML document or not. The $allowed(s, xdl, r_1)$ predicate shows that subject s can access some part of information in XML document. At this stage, private information in XML document is restricted.

B. UCM_{onA}:ongoing-Authorizations Model

An UCM_{onA} model is used to check ongoing authorizations during access processes. The UCM_{onA} model has the following components:

1. $S, XD, XDL, R, R_1, ATT(S), ATT(XD), ATT(XDL)$ as before, and ongoing usage decision functions onA on XD (XML document) and onA_1 on XDL (XML document elements),
   onA and onA_1 are used to check whether S can continue to access or not.
2. $allowed(s, xd, r) \Rightarrow true$,
   This is a prerequisite for ongoing authorization on xd.
3. $allowed(s, xdl, r_1) \Rightarrow true$,
   This is a prerequisite for ongoing authorization on xdl.
4. $stopped(s, xd, r) \Leftarrow \neg onA(ATT(s), ATT(xd), r)$,
   The access of subject s to xd is terminated if the ongoing authorization onA is failed.
5. $stopped(s, xdl, r_1) \Leftarrow \neg onA_1(ATT(s), ATT(xdl), r_1)$.
   The access of subject s to xdl is terminated if the ongoing authorization onA_1 is failed.

UCM_{onA} introduces the onA, onA_1 predicate instead of $preA$, $preA_1$. *allowed* (s, xd, r) and $allowed(s, xdl, r_1)$ are required to be *true*, otherwise ongoing authorization should not be initiated. Ongoing authorization is active throughout the usage of the requested right, and the onA and onA_1 predicates are repeatedly checked for continuation access. These checks are performed periodically based on time or event. The model does not specify exactly how this should be done. When attributes are changed and requirements are no longer satisfied, *stopped* procedures are performed. We use $stopped(s, xd, r)$ and $stopped(s, xdl, r_1)$ to indicate that rights r and r_1 of subject s on object XML and XML document elements are revoked and the ongoing access terminated. For example, suppose only one user can access customer Mastercard information in an object XML simultaneously. If another user requests access and passed the pre-authorization, the user with the earlier time access is terminated. While this is a case of ongoing authorizations, it is important that the certificate should be evaluated in a *pre* decision.

Based on the length of the paper, other authorization models are omitted. The following algorithm is based on these models and introduces how to manage an XML document access control when a user (subject) applies for accesses to an XML document (target.xml) with right r.

We obtain an authorization method for a XML document and its elements by checking users' (subjects') authorizations, obligations and conditions with continuity properties. The algorithm provides a solution of the problem 1. We analyse security architectures in next section for the problem 2 in which both client and server sides are required to be monitored.

Table 2. Algorithm of XML Access Control

XML-based Algorithm:
Input: Access request: (u, r, target.xml)
Output: target'.xml
Method:
// Verify UCM_preA:
1) **if** $preA(ATT(s), ATT(xd), r) \bigcup preA(ATT(s), ATT(xdl), r_1) = false$
// The process in pre-Authorization is not successful
2) ACCESS denied;
3) **endif**
// Verify UCM_onA:
4) **if** $preA(ATT(s), ATT(xd), r) \bigcup preA(ATT(s), ATT(xdl), r_1) = false$
// The process in pre-Authorization is failed, donot need further verification.
5) Application denied;
6) **endif**
7) $onA(ATT(s), ATT(xd), r) \bigcup onA(ATT(s), ATT(xdl), r_1) = false$
// The process in ongoing-Authorization is not successful
8) ACCESS stopped;
// Verify UCM_preB:
9) **if** $preObfill(s, xd, r) = false$
// Obligations are not fulfilled and pre-Obligation is not passed.
10) ACCESS denied;
11) **endif**
//Verify UCM_onB:
12) **if** $allowed(s, xd, r) = false$
13) Stop verification.
14) **endif**
15) **if** $onObfill(s, xd, r) = false$
// Obligations are not continually fulfilled and on-Obligation is not passed.
16) ACCESS is stopped;
17) **endif**
// Verify UCM_preC:
18) **if** $preC(s, xd, r) = false$
// Conditions are not satisfied and pre-Condition verification is not passed.
19) ACCESS denied;
20) **endif**
//Verify UCM_onC:
21) **if** $allowed(s, xd, r) = false$
22) Stop verification.
23) **endif**
24) **if** $onC(s, xd, r) = false$
// Conditions are not continually satisfied and on-Condition is not passed.
25) ACCESS is stopped;
26) **endif**
27) ACCESS target.xml is permitted;
28) Output target'.xml;

4 XML Security Architecture

In this section, we discuss architecture solutions for XML control based on reference monitors. Reference monitors have been discussed extensively in access control community. Subjects can access XML objects only through the reference monitor since it provides control mechanisms on access XML document and its elements.

4.1 Structure of Reference Monitor

ISO has published a standard for access control framework by using reference monitors [16]. Based on the standard, XML reference monitor consists of Usage Decision Facility (UDF) and Usage Enforcement Facility (UEF) as shown in Figure 3. Each facility includes several functional modules.

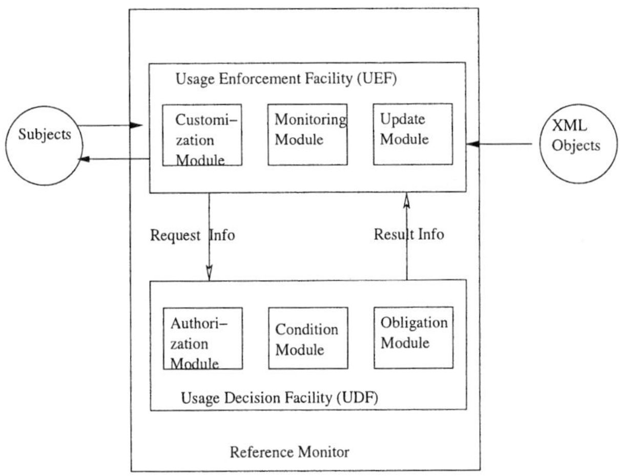

Fig. 3. XML Reference Monitor

UEF includes *Customization, Monitor and Update modules* and UDF includes *authorization, conditions and obligations decision modules.* When a subject sends an access request through *Customization module* to *Authorization module*, *Authorization module* verifies authorization process and checks whether the request is allowed or not. It may return yes or no or metadata information of the authorization result. This metadata information can be used for approved access on XML objects by *Customization module* in UEF. *Condition module* is used to make a decision for whether the conditional requirements are satisfied or not. *Obligation module* is applied to verify whether obligations have been performed or not before or during the requested usage. When any obligation is changed, it must be monitored by *monitor module* and the result has to be resolved by *Update module* in UEF. Applications of these modules rely on object systems requirements.

4.2 Architectures

There are two kinds of reference monitors: Server-side Reference Monitor (SRM), and Client-side Reference Monitor (CRM). Servers provide XML document and clients require access to the XML object. Like a traditional reference monitor, an SRM works in server system environment and manages access to XML objects in the server. On the other hand, a CRM works in the client environment and controls access to XML objects when it works as a server for other clients. For example, the client acts as a server when the XML document is disseminated to other users. SRM and CRM can coexist within a system. For real implementations, both CRM and SRM should be used for better security. We analyse architectures according to reference monitors on server side only (SRM-only), on client side only (CRM-only) and on both server and client sides (SRM & CRM).

SRM-Only Architecture. A system with SRM-only facilitates works on server side only to control subjects access XML objects. In this case an XML object may or may not be stored in client-side. If the XML object is allowed to reside in client-side, it means the saved client copy of the XML object is no longer valid and doesn't have to be controlled. It can be used and changed freely at client-side. For example, an XML on-line bank statement can be saved at a client's local machine for his records and the server (bank) doesn't care how the copy will be used by the client since the bank keeps original account information safe. However if the XML document or some parts of the document has to be protected and controlled centrally, the XML must remain at server-side storage and is not allowed to be stored in client-side. This is the main topics of traditional access control and trust management system.

CRM-Only Architecture. No reference monitor exists on the server-side in a system with CRM-only environment. Rather, a reference monitor exists at the client system for controlling usage of disseminated XML documents. In this environment XML objects can be stored either centrally or locally. The usage of XML saved at the client-side on behalf of a server is still under the control of CRM. Distributed XML documents are associated with certain usage rules and users may need to prove their sufficient credentials to access the document.

SRM and CRM Architecture. With both SRM to CRM, this architecture can provide a comprehensive access control. SRM may be used for distribution related control while CRM can be used for XML document dissemination. For instance, in SRM, XML objects can be pre-customized for distribution. The pre-customized XML objects can be further controlled and customized by CRM. As a result, server can restrict or eliminate unnecessary exposure of XML objects that do not have to be distributed. If a user requests certain XML documents that include some secret information, SRM can pre-customize the requested objects before distribution such that the distributed version of the objects doesn't include any secret information. If the document cannot be disseminated, the CRM at client side can do this work.

The SRM & CRM architecture provides a solution for restricting access to XML documents and protecting XML documents from malicious dissemination.

5 Comparisons

Related work has been done on secure and selective dissemination of XML documents [2] and securing XML Web services [9].

Elisa and Elena [2] proposed an access control system supporting selective distribution of XML document among possible large user communities by using a range of key distribution methods. They demonstrated a formal model of access control policies for XML documents. Policies defined in the model take into account both user profiles, and document contents and structures. An approach based on cryptograph is designed to allow sending the same document to all users, and to enforce the stated access control policies. The approach consists of encrypting different portions of the same document according to different encryption keys, and selectively distributing these keys to the various users. This proposal is different from ours in two aspects. Firstly, it focuses on key distribution methods to protect XML documents. Therefore, it only discussed the management in server side and without any management about how to control the XML document when users get keys. By contrast, our work provides a rich variety of options that can deal with XML documents in both server and user sides. Secondly, users can access XML documents with their keys at any time, even as their properties are updated. There is no ongoing authorization for users in Elisa and Elena's approach. In our scheme, users have to satisfy pre-Authorizations, pre-Obligations and pre-Conditions as well as ongoing-Authorizations, ongoing-Obligations, and ongoing-Conditions.

Securing XML Web services is described by Damiani, Vimercati and Samarati in 2002 [9]. Two experiments are discussed. One is to restrict access to an XML Web service to authorized users. Another one is to protect the integrity and confidentiality of XML messages exchanged in a Web service environment. The authors introduced SOAP highlights, how to use SOAP headers for credential transfer and access control. The main difference between our scheme and the work in [9] is that we focus on a systematic level for XML documents by using usage control model and provide a solution for different kinds of authorizations, whereas the work of [9] is a discussion of providing a secure infrastructure to XML Web services.

6 Conclusions and Future Work

This paper has discussed access models and architectures for XML documents by using usage control. We have analysed not only decision factors in usage control such as authorizations, obligations and conditions, but also the continuity. Different kinds of models are built for XML documents. To protect XML documents from malicious dissemination, we have analysed reference monitors on both server and client sides and obtained several secure architecture solutions. The work in this paper has significantly extended previous work in several aspects, for example, the ongoing continuity for authorizations, obligations and conditions. These methods can be used to control XML documents in a dynamic environment since they provide a robust access control for XML documents and can protect sensitive messages from dissemination. It also begins a new application with usage control.

The future work includes develop algorithms based on the models and architectures proposed in this paper and application of the algorithms in real implementation.

References

1. Arenas M. and Libkin L.: A normal form for XML documents. ACM Transaction on Database System. Vol. 29 (2004) 195–232
2. Bertino E. and Ferrari E.: Secure and selective dissemination of XML documents. ACM Transaction on Information System Security. Vol. 5 (2002) 290–331
3. Bertino E., Castano S., Ferrari E. and Mesiti M.: Specifying and enforcing access control policies for XML document sources. World Wide Web, 3. Baltzer Science Publishers BV (2000) 139–151
4. Bertino E., Castano S. and Ferrari E.: Securing XML documents: the author-X project demonstration. Proceedings of the 2001 ACM SIGMOD international conference on Management of data. Santa Barbara, California, United States (2001) 605
5. Bertino E.,Castano S., Ferrari E. and Mesiti M.: Controlled access and dissemination of XML documents. Proceedings of the second international workshop on Web information and data management. Kansas City, Missouri, United States (1999) 22–27
6. Box D.: Simple Object Access Protocol (SOAP) 1.1. World Wide Web Consortium (W3C). Cambridge, MA, USA (2000) http://www.w3.org/TR/soap
7. Bray T., Paoli J., Sperberg M. and Maler E.: Extensible Markup Language (XML) 1.1 (Second Edition). World Wide Web Consortium (W3C). Cambridge, MA, USA (2000) http://www.w3.org/TR/REC-xml
8. Chinnici R., Gudgin M., Moreau J. and Weerawarana S.: Web Services Description Language (WSDL) 1.2. World Wide Web Consortium (W3C). Cambridge, MA, USA (2002) http://www.w3.org/TR/wsdl12
9. Damiani E., Capitani S. and Samarati P.: Towards Securing XML Web Services. Proc. of the 2002 ACM Workshop on XML Security. Washington, DC, USA (2002)
10. Damiani E., Sabrina D., Paraboschi S. and Samarati P.: Fine grained access control for SOAP E-services. Proceedings of the tenth international conference on World Wide Web. Hong Kong, China (2001) 504–513
11. Damiani E., Vimercati S., Paraboschi S., and Samarati P.: Securing XML Documents. Lecture Notes in Computer Science. Vol. 1777 (2000) 121 – 135
12. Ford W. and Baum M. S.: Secure electronic commerce: Building the Infrastructure for Digital Signatures & Encryption Prentice Hall PTR (1997)
13. Freier A., Karlton P., and Kocher. P.: The SSL Protocol - Version 3.0. http://ftp.nectec.or.th/CIE/Topics/ssldraft/INDEX.HTM (1996)
14. Gettys J., Mogul J., Frystyk H., Masinter L., Leach P., and Berners-Lee T.: Hypertext Transfer Protocol - HTTP/1.1. (1999)
15. Goldschlag D., Reed M., and Syverson P.: Onion routing for anonymous and private Internet connections. Communications of the ACM. Vol. 24 (1999) 39 – 41
16. ISO: Security frameworks for open systems: Access control framework. ISO/IEC 10181-3 (1996)

17. Jajodia S., Samarati P., Subrahmanian V. and Bertino E.: A unified framework for enforcing multiple access control policies. Proceedings of the 1997 ACM SIGMOD international conference on Management of data. Tucson, Arizona, United States (1997) 474–485
18. Kudo M. and Hada S.: XML document security based on provisional authorization. Proceedings of the 7th ACM conference on Computer and communications security. Athens, Greece (2000) 87–96
19. Li Q. and Atluri V.: Concept-level access control for the Semantic Web. Proceedings of the 2003 ACM workshop on XML security. Fairfax, Virginia (2003) 94–103
20. Park J. and Sandhu R.: Towards usage control models: beyond traditional access control. Proceedings of the seventh ACM symposium on Access control models and technologies. Monterey, California, USA (2002) 57–64
21. Sabrina D.: An authorization model for temporal XML documents. Proceedings of the 2002 ACM symposium on Applied computing. Madrid, Spain (2002) 1088–1093.
22. Todd B.: Auditing Firewalls: A Practical Guide. http://www.itsecurity.com/papers/p5.htm (2004)
23. Wang H., Cao J. and Zhang Y.: Formal authorization allocation approaches for permission-role assignments using relational algebra operations. Proceedings of the 14th Australasian Database Conference, Adelaide, Australia (2003) 125–134
24. Wang H., Zhang Y., Cao J., Varadharajan V.: Achieving secure and flexible M-services through tickets. In Benatallah B. and Maamar Z. editor: IEEE Transactions on Systems, Man, and Cybernetics, Part A, Special issue on M-Services. Vol. 33 (2003) 697-708
25. Zhang X., Park J. and Sandhu R.: Schema based XML Security: RBAC Approach. Proceedings of the IFIP WG (2003)

A Comparative Study of Functional Dependencies for XML

Junhu Wang

School of Information Technology,
Griffith University, Gold Coast Campus, Australia
J.Wang@griffith.edu.au

Abstract. Functional dependencies (FDs) have been relatively more intensively studied than other constraints for XML data. Yet there seems to be no consensus on the definition of such dependencies, and all previous definitions capture different types of constraints. In this paper, we survey and compare these XML functional dependencies (XFDs) and propose a new definition of XFD which unifies and generalizes the previous XFDs. We show how our GXFDs can express more constraints and hence can be used to detect more XML data redundancies than those in previous work.

Keywords: Data integrity, XML tree, scheme file, functional dependency.

1 Introduction

Integrity constraints play major roles in ensuring data consistency in traditional database systems. Among them functional dependencies (FDs) are of particular interest because of their ubiquity, simplicity and applications to database design as well as to maintaining data integrity. It is therefore natural to extend the concept of FDs to XML data, and such attempts have been made by several groups of researchers [1, 2, 3, 4, 5, 6, 7, 8, 9].

Due to the structural difference between XML data and relational data, extending FDs to XML is not a trivial task, and not surprisingly, all definitions of FDs for XML so far capture different types of constraints. In this paper, we first survey and compare previous XML functional dependencies (XFDs) in terms of the constraints they express, in particular we show the equivalence of the XFDs in [3] and [5] when there are no null values. We then propose a generalized XFD (GXFD) which is a generalization of the previous XFDs. We show how our GXFDs can be used to express some natural constraints that cannot be captured by previous XFDs, and hence to detect more redundancies in XML data.

The rest of the paper is organized as follows. Section 2 provides preliminary terminology and notations. Section 3 surveys and compares the XFDs in previous work. Section 4 presents our generalized XFDs and shows how they generalize and extend the previous XFDs. Section 5 concludes the paper with a brief discussion about future work.

Y. Zhang et al. (Eds.): APWeb 2005, LNCS 3399, pp. 308–319, 2005.

2 Terminology and Notations

In this section, we introduce the basic definitions, some of which are modified from [9, 3, 10]. We assume the existence of three pairwise disjoint sets $\mathbf{E_1}$, $\mathbf{E_2}$ and $\mathbf{A}$ of *labels*. The labels in $\mathbf{E_1}$, $\mathbf{E_2}$ and $\mathbf{A}$ represent complex element names, simple element names, and attribute names respectively. Let $\mathbf{E} = \mathbf{E_1} \cup \mathbf{E_2}$.

Scheme file. An *(XML) scheme file* is defined to be $\mathcal{S} = (E_1, E_2, A, P, R, r)$ where $E_1 \subseteq \mathbf{E_1}$ is a finite set of *complex element* names; $E_2 \subseteq \mathbf{E_2}$ is a finite set of *simple element* names; $A \subseteq \mathbf{A}$ is a finite set of *attribute names*. P is a mapping from E_1 to element type definitions: $\forall \tau \in E_1$, $P(\tau)$ is a regular expression

$$\alpha = \varepsilon \mid \tau' \mid \alpha|\alpha \mid \alpha, \alpha \mid \alpha^*$$

where ε is the empty sequence, $\tau' \in E_1 \cup E_2$, and "|" , ",", and "*" denote union, concatenation, and the Kleene closure respectively; R is a mapping from E_1 to sets of attributes; for $\tau \in E_1$, either $P(\tau)$ is not ε or $R(\tau)$ is not $\emptyset$; $r \in E_1$ is a distinct element name, which is the only label in E_1 that does not appear in the alphabet of $P(\tau)$ for any $\tau \in E_1$.

XML tree. An *XML tree* is defined to be $T = (V, lab, ele, att, val, root)$, where (1) V is a set of nodes; (2) lab is a mapping from V to $\mathbf{E} \cup \mathbf{A}$ which assigns a label to each node in V; a node $v \in V$ is called a *complex element* node if $lab(v) \in \mathbf{E_1}$, a *simple element* node if $lab(v) \in \mathbf{E_2}$, and an *attribute* node if $lab(v) \in \mathbf{A}$. (3) ele and att are functions from the set of complex elements in V: for every $v \in V$, if $lab(v) \in \mathbf{E_1}$ then $ele(v)$ is a sequence of element nodes, and $att(v)$ is a set of attribute nodes with distinct labels; (4) val is a function that assigns a value to each attribute or simple element. (5) $root$ is the unique root node. (6) If $v' \in ele(v) \cup att(v)$, then we call v' a *child* of v. The parent-child relationships defined by ele and att form a tree rooted at $root$.

Conformity. T is said to *conform* to $\mathcal{S}$ if (1) $lab(root) = r$, (2) lab maps every node in V to $E_1 \cup E_2 \cup A$, and (3) for every complex element node $v \in V$, if $ele(v) = \{v_1, \ldots, v_k\}$, then the sequence $lab(v_1), \ldots, lab(v_k)$ (regarded as a string) is in the language defined by $P(lab(v))$; if $att(v) = \{v'_1, \ldots, v'_m\}$ then $\{lab(v'_1), \ldots, lab(v'_m)\} \subseteq R(lab(v))$.

Fig. 1 shows an example XML scheme file and a conforming XML tree. In the scheme file, complex elements appear to the left of "::=", their type definitions are shown in the parenthesis to the right of "::=", and their attributes (in the set $R(\tau)$) are inside curved braces. We also use the convention that simple elements start with \$, and attributes start with @.

Value equality. Let v_1 and v_2 be nodes in T. We say that v_1 and v_2 are *value equal*, denoted $v_1 =_v v_2$, if $lab(v_1) = lab(v_2)$, and either v_1 and v_2 are both simple elements or attributes and $val(v_1) = val(v_2)$, or v_1 and v_2 are complex elements, and (1) their sequence of child elements are pairwise value equal; (2) for every attribute α of v_1, there is an attribute β of v_2 such that $\alpha =_v \beta$ and vice versa. Clearly if v_1 and v_2 are the same node (denoted $v_1 = v_2$), then $v_1 =_v v_2$.

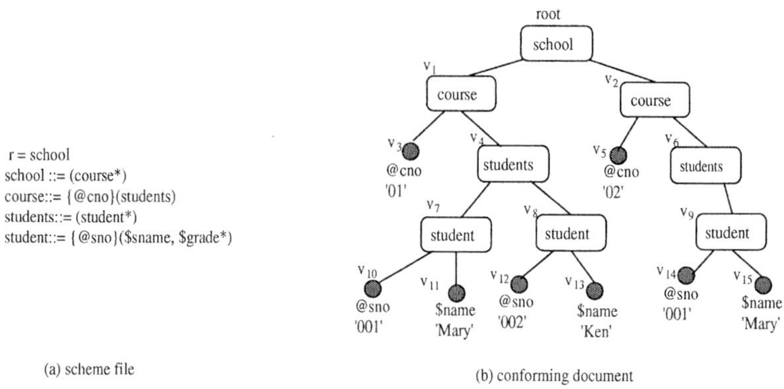

Fig. 1. The Course-Student example

Paths. Let $\mathcal{S} = (E_1, E_2, A, P, R, r)$ be a scheme file. We are interested in the following types of paths in $\mathcal{S}$.

A *simple path* is of the form $l_1.\cdots.l_m$, where $l_i \in E_1$ for $i < m$, $l_m \in E_1 \cup E_2 \cup A$. Furthermore, l_i is in the alphabet of $P(l_{i-1})$ for $i \in [2, m-1]$, l_m is in the alphabet of $P(l_{m-1})$ or in $R(l_{m-1})$, and $l_1 \neq r$. The number of labels in a simple path is called the *length* of the path. The simple path with length 0 is called the *empty path*, denoted ϵ. The simple path is said to be an *absolute path* if l_1 is in alphabet of $P(r)$ or in $R(r)$. The set of all simple paths in $\mathcal{S}$ is denoted $paths(\mathcal{S})$. Also, if $p, q \in paths(\mathcal{S})$, and p is $l_1.\cdots.l_k$ and q is $l_1.\cdots.l_k.l_{k+1}.\cdots.l_{k+m}$, then we say p is a *prefix* of q. A path in $paths(\mathcal{S})$ which is not the prefix of any other paths in $paths(\mathcal{S})$ is called a *full path in $\mathcal{S}$*.

A *downward path* is either a simple path or an expression of the form $l_1.\cdots.l_n$ (where $l_i \in E_1 \cup E_2 \cup A \cup \{\_, \_*\}$ for $i \in [1, n-1]$, $l_n \in E_1 \cup E_2 \cup A$), which can be obtained from another downward path by replacing a label (except the last one) with _, or by replacing a substring (that does not contain the last label) with _∗. In a downward path, the symbol _ represents a wildcard (which can match any label), and _∗ represents the Kleene closure of the wildcard.

An *upward path* is of the form $\Uparrow.\cdots.\Uparrow$. If there are k upward arrows (we require $k \in [1, M]$, where M is the length of the longest simple path in $\mathcal{S}$), we will sometimes abbreviate the path as $\Uparrow^k$.

A *composite path* is of the form $\xi.\rho$, where ξ is an upward path, and ρ is a simple path. An upward path is a special composite path.

A *general path* is a path of the form $p.l_j.\Uparrow^{j-i}$ or $p.l_j.\Uparrow^{j-i}.l'_{i+1}.\cdots.l'_k$, where $p.l_j$ is a downward path, and there exist simple paths $l_i.l_{i+1}.\cdots.l_j$ and $l_i.l'_{i+1}.\cdots.l'_k$ in $\mathcal{S}$.

For a path p, we will use $last(p)$ to denote the last symbol (a label or $\Uparrow$) in p.

Path instances, target set, and target list. Let T be an XML tree conforming to $\mathcal{S}$ and v_0 be a node in T. An *instance of a non-empty downward path* $l_1.\cdots.l_n$ wrt v_0 is a sequence of nodes $v_1, \ldots, v_n$ in T such that for $i \in [1, n]$ (1) if l_i is in $E_1 \cup E_2 \cup A \cup \{\_\}$, then v_i is a child of v_{i-1} and the label of v_i matches

l_i (note that the label of any node matches _); (2) if l_i is _*, then v_i is v_{i-1} or a descendant of v_{i-1}.

An *instance of a composite path* $\Uparrow^k .l_1.\cdots.l_n$ wrt v_0 is a sequence of nodes $n_1, \ldots, n_k, v_1, \ldots, v_n$ in T such that n_1 is the parent of v_0, n_i is the parent of n_{i-1} for $i \in [2, k]$, and v_1 is a child of n_k, v_i is a child of v_{i-1} for $i \in [2, n]$, and the label of v_i matches l_i for $i \in [1, n]$.

If p is a downward or composite path in $\mathcal{S}$, we will use $v_0[p]$ to denote the set

$$\{v_n \mid v_n \text{ is the last node of an instance of } p \textit{ wrt } v_0\},$$

and call it the *target set* of p wrt v_0.

The nodes in $v_0[p]$ can also be put in a certain order, eg, in the order they are visited in a pre-order traversal of T. We call this ordered list of nodes the *target list* of p wrt v_0, denoted $v_0(p)$.

3 Previous XFDs

XFDs have been defined in [1, 2, 3, 4, 5, 6, 7, 8, 9]. The XFDs in all but [8] are *path based*, namely, they are based on the paths in the scheme files and/or trees. Among them, [1],[3], [5, 6] and [4] are based on absolute paths, while [2], [7] and [9] allow for more general paths. The definition in [8] is *subtree based*, that is, it uses subtrees instead of paths in the definition.

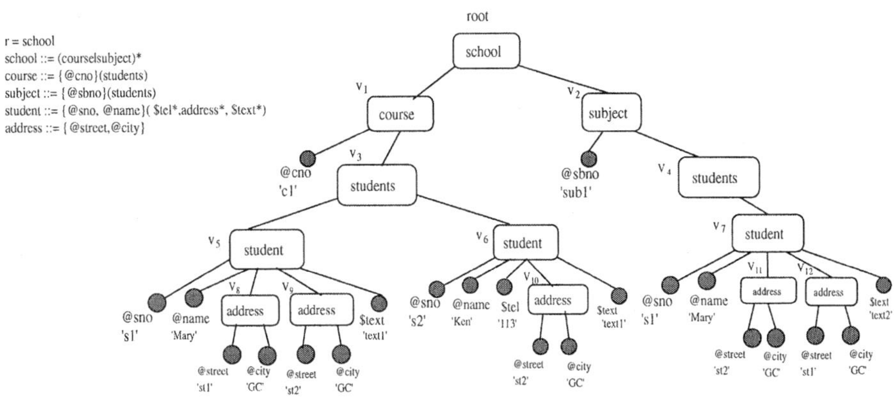

Fig. 2. The Course-Subject-Student example

In what follows, we will use $\text{XFD}_{[i]}$ to denote the XFDs defined in reference [i]. We will also use the following example constraints for the scheme file shown in the up left corner of Fig. 2 in our discussion.

(A) Student number determines student name in the entire tree.
(B) Student number determines the student's set of addresses.

(C) Student number determines the student's (ordered) list of addresses (not satisfied by the tree in Fig. 2).
(D) A student has a single address (i.e., any two addresses are value equal) and the address is determined by the student number (not satisfied by the tree in Fig. 2).
(E) A course always uses the same text.
(F) Any single phone number of a student determines the set of addresses of the student (assuming no students share a phone number).

Due to space limit, we will focus on [3], [5] and [8], and be brief on others.

3.1 XFDs Based on Absolute Paths

The authors of [3], [5] and [6] regard a simple element as having a child node labelled S, under which is attached the value of the element. For example, using their notation the XML tree in Fig. 1 (b) will look like what is in Fig. 3 (b).

XFD$_{[3]}$. An XFD$_{[3]}$ is defined on a DTD which is the same as a scheme file except that there is no explicit distinction between simple and complex elements. However, an element in their DTDs may have a single *text child* labelled S, and these elements are exactly the same as our simple elements (see Fig. 3 (a)). Paths in the DTDs are of the form $r.p$, where p is the same as an absolute path defined in Section 2 except it can end up with the text label S. We will use $\mathcal{P}(D)$ to denote the set of all paths in DTD D as defined in [3].

The definition of XFD$_{[3]}$ uses the concept of *tree-tuples*. In essence, the authors treat a DTD D as a single relation schema, a path in $\mathcal{P}(D)$ as an attribute, and a tree-tuple a tuple in that relation. By definition, a tree-tuple is a mapping from $\mathcal{P}(D)$ to "values": every path which ends with an element name is mapped to a *distinct* node ID or the null value ($\perp$), and every other path is mapped to either a string value or $\perp$. For example, the DTD in Fig. 3 (a) is regarded as a relation schema consisting of the following attributes:

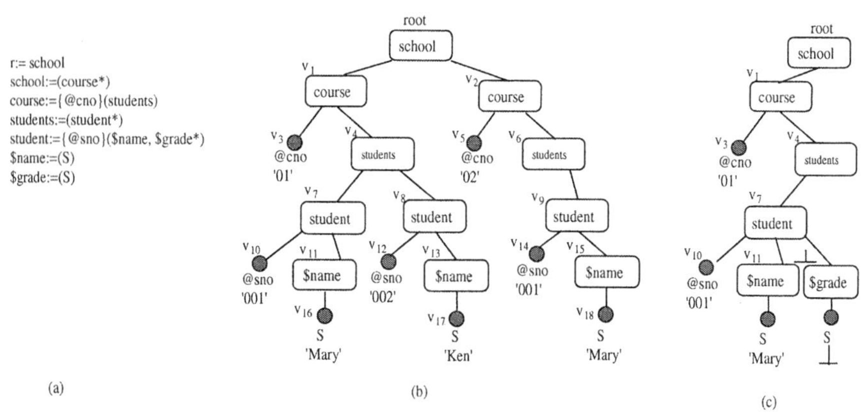

Fig. 3. Notations of [3] (a) A DTD (b) A Conforming XML tree (c) A Maximal Tree-Tuple

school,
school.course,
school.course.@cno,
school.course.students,
school.course.students.student,
school.course.students.student.@sno,
school.course.students.student.$name,
*school.course.students.student.$name.*S,
school.course.students.student.$grade,
*school.course.students.student.$grade.*S.

An example tree-tuple maps the above relation schema to

$(root,\ v_1,\ 01,\ v_4,\ v_7,\ 001,\ v_{11},\ \text{Mary},\ \bot,\ \bot)$,

and the tree-tuple corresponds to a tree, as shown in Fig. 3 (c).

Given an XML tree T conforming to D, a tree-tuple t is considered *subsumed* by T if the tree obtained by removing the null value nodes from t is a subtree of T. A subsumed tree-tuple t is said to be maximal in T if one cannot replace a null value with a non-null value and leave t still subsumed by T. The tree T can then be thought of as consisting of a set of maximal tree-tuples. For example, the XML tree shown in Fig. 3 (b) can be regarded as an instance consisting of the (maximal tree) tuples

$(root,\ v_1,\ 01,\ v_4,\ v_7,\ 001,\ v_{11},\ Mary, \bot, \bot)$,
$(root,\ v_1,\ 01,\ v_4,\ v_8,\ 002,\ v_{13},\ Ken, \bot, \bot)$, and
$(root,\ v_2,\ 02,\ v_6,\ v_9,\ 001,\ v_{15},\ Mary, \bot, \bot)$.

An XFD$_{[3]}$ is defined to be an expression of the form $p_1, p_2, \cdots, p_n \rightarrow q_1, \ldots, q_m$ where $p_i, \ldots, p_n$ and $q_1, \ldots, q_m$ are paths in $\mathcal{P}(D)$. An XML document conforming to D is said to satisfy the XFD if for every two maximal tree-tuples t_1 and t_2, whenever $t_1(p_i)$ is not null and $t_1(p_i) = t_2(p_i)$ for all $i \in [1, n]$, then $t_1(q_j) = t_2(q_j)$ for all $j \in [1, m]$. For example, the XML tree in Fig. 3 (b) satisfies the FD

(i) $p.@sno \rightarrow p.\$name.\mathsf{S}$, but not
(ii) $p.@sno \rightarrow p.\$name$.

where p is the path *school.course.students.student*. Since all null values are considered to be equal, the tree also satisfies

(iii) $p.@sno \rightarrow p.\$grade$.

XFD$_{[5]}$. XFD$_{[5]}$ is defined on a set $\mathcal{P}$ of closed paths, where a path is of the same form as that in [3], and "closed" means that if a path is in the set, then all prefixes of the path is also in the set. This set of paths plays the role of the XML scheme file. An XFD$_{[5]}$ is defined to be an expression of the form $p_1, p_2, \cdots, p_n \rightarrow q$ where $p_1, \ldots, p_n$ and q are paths in $\mathcal{P}$. Satisfaction of the dependency is defined for XML trees that *comform to* $\mathcal{P}$, i.e, all absolute paths in T are paths in $\mathcal{P}$. The satisfaction can be checked as follows.

1. Assign a value $val(v)$ to each node v in T such that if the node is an element, the value is a distinct node ID, otherwise the value is a string value.

2. Extend T as follows: let p be the full path $l_1.\cdots.l_k.l_{k+1}.\cdots.l_{k+m}$ in $\mathcal{S}$. If there is an instance $v_1,\ldots,v_k$ of $l_1.\cdots.l_k$ in T, but there is no path instance $v_{k+1}.\cdots.v_{k+m}$ of $l_{k+1}.\cdots.l_{k+m}$ in T such that v_{k+1} is a child of v_k, then add a path instance $\perp_{k+1}.\cdots.\perp_{k+m}$ under v_k, and assign to these nodes *distinct* null values. The original tree T is said to have *missing nodes*.

3. For $i \in [1,n]$, (1) find the longest common prefix of p_i and q, denoted $pre(p_i,q)$, which always exists and is unique; (2) find $N[pre(p_i,q)]$, which is the set of nodes that can be reached by following $pre(p_i,q)$ from r; (3) for each distinct path instance I of q, find the unique node $x_{I,i}$, which is the common node in I and $N[pre(p_i,q)]$; (4) if $last(p_i)$ (the last label in p_i) is not an element, then find the set $N_{I,i}$ of nodes which are descendants of $x_{I,i}$ and can be reached by following p_i from r. Also find the set $val(N_{I,i})$ of values of the nodes in $N_{I,i}$.

4. If we cannot find two distinct path instances I and J in T, such that for all $i \in [1,n]$, if $last(p_i)$ is an element then $x_{I,i} = x_{J,i}$, otherwise $val(N_{I,i}) \cup val(N_{J,i})$ contains a null value or $val(N_{I,i}) \cap val(N_{J,i}) \neq \emptyset$, but the values of the last nodes of I and J are not equal, then the XFD is satisfied by T.

For example, the XFD (i) can be shown to be satisfied by the XML tree in Fig. 3 (b) as follows: 1. Extend the XML tree by adding a \$grade node under each student node, and a S node under each \$grade node, and assign distinct null values to these nodes. 2. (1) The common prefix pre of the two paths in (i) is $school.course.students.student$, (2) the set $N[pre] = \{v_7, v_8, v_9\}$; (3) for the path instances of the righthand side, $I = r.v_1.v_4.v_7.v_{11}.v_{16}$, $J = r.v_1.v_4.v_8.v_{13}.v_{17}$, and $K = r.v_2.v_6.v_9.v_{15}.v_{18}$, find the nodes $X_I = v_7$, $X_J = v_8$ and $X_K = v_9$; (3) find $N_I = \{v_{10}\}$, $N_J = \{v_{12}\}$ and $N_K = \{v_{14}\}$. 3. The values of v_{10}, v_{12} and v_{14} are not null, and only the values of the nodes in N_I and N_K are equal, but so are the values of last nodes in the corresponding path instances I and K.

Similarly, it can be easily verified that the XFDs (ii) and (iii) are not satisfied by the tree according to [5].

Discussion. As seen above, except for the number of paths on the RHS, the XFDs in [5] and [3] are of the same form. Although the approaches of checking satisfaction of a XFD appear totally different, the actual type of constraints captured by the two are equivalent except for the treatment of null values. In fact, we can prove the following result.

Proposition 1. *Let D be a DTD, and T be an XML tree that conforms to D (so it also conforms to $\mathcal{P}(D)$). Suppose T has no missing nodes. Then every* XFD$_{[5]}$ $p_1,\ldots,p_k \to q$ *over $\mathcal{P}(D)$ is satisfied by T iff the corresponding* XFD$_{[3]}$ *is satisfied by T.*

The major difference between XFD$_{[3]}$ and XFD$_{[5]}$ lies in the treatment of null values. When null values (i.e, missing nodes) exist, the satisfaction of XFD$_{[5]}$

is a stronger condition than that of $\text{XFD}_{[3]}$. For example, in the XML tree of Fig. 3, if we remove both v_{11} and v_{15} (or alternatively, if we remove v_{10}), then the XFD (i) is still considered satisfied by [3], but not by [5].

Another important difference lies in the set of trivial XFDs. Since $\text{XFD}_{[3]}$ is defined for documents conforming to a DTD, while $\text{XFD}_{[5]}$ is defined for documents conforming to a set of closed paths, some trivial XFDs in [3] may be non-trivial in [5]. This is because conforming to a DTD puts more restrictions on XML trees than conforming to the set of paths in the DTD. For example, suppose we have a DTD (in the definition of [3])

```
r:=(a*),   a:=(b,c),   b:=S,  c:=S
```

For documents conforming to the DTD, the XFD $r.a \rightarrow r.a.b$ is trivial because every node labelled with **a** must have exactly one child labelled with **b**. But $r.a \rightarrow r.a.b$ is not trivial for documents conforming to the set of paths $\{r, r.a, r.a.b, r.a.c\}$.

Since $\text{XFD}_{[3]}$ and $\text{XFD}_{[5]}$ consider only absolute paths, and they do not consider the value equality of complex element nodes, they cannot express the constraints (A), (B), (C) and (F) at the beginning of this section.

$\text{XFD}_{[6]}$. $\text{XFD}_{[6]}$ defines *local* XFDs of the form $Q_1 \rightarrow_w Q_2$, where Q_1, Q_2 are sets of paths, and w is a common prefix of the paths in Q_1 and Q_2. The local XFDs are intended by the authors to capture constraints that hold in part of an XML tree determined by w.

$\text{XFD}_{[4]}$. [4] defines XFDs on DTDs, where DTDs and paths are the same as in [3]. XML trees are also defined similarly to that of [3], except a string value is assigned for *every* node (it is not explained what this value will be, however). Value-equality between two nodes v_1 and v_2 is defined in the same way as in [10], except the string values of v_1 and v_2 must also be equal. An $\text{XFD}_{[4]}$ over DTD D is an expression of the form $R(p_1, \ldots, p_n \rightarrow q_1, \ldots, q_m)$ where $R, R.p_i, R.q_j \in \mathcal{P}(D)$ $(i \in [1,n], j \in [1,m])$. A tree T satisfies the XFD if $\forall v_1, v_2 \in root[R]$, $v_1[p_i] \equiv v_2[p_i] (\forall i \in [1,n])$ implies $v_1[q_j] \equiv v_2[q_j] (\forall j \in [1,m])$, where $v_1[p] \equiv v_2[p]$ means there exist $n_1 \in v_1[p]$ and $n_2 \in v_2[p]$ such that n_1 and n_2 are value-equal. Hence the XFDs in [4] cannot express the constraints (A)–(F) (assuming each leaf node is assigned its string value, and other nodes are assigned a common value).

$\text{XFD}_{[1]}$. The authors of [1] made the assumption that, in a scheme file, a label cannot appear in the alphabets of two different complex element names. An XFD is defined to be $X \rightarrow Y$, where X, Y are sets of labels. Because of the assumption in the scheme file, there is a unique path from the root to a label, hence the XFD can be equivalently written as $P_X \rightarrow P_Y$ where P_X (P_Y) is the set of paths corresponding to X (Y). Satisfaction of the XFD is defined for a *set* of XML trees conforming to the scheme file rather than for a single tree. The constraint is said to be satisfied if for any two trees, if they agree on X, they must also agree on Y. Agreements of two trees T_1 and T_2 on a label means the intersection of the two sets of nodes that can be reached by following the unique path, from the roots of T_1 and T_2 respectively, have nodes that are value-equal. Hence the constraints expressed by $\text{XFD}_{[1]}$ are similar to those by $\text{XFD}_{[4]}$.

3.2 XFDs Based on More General Paths

$\text{XFD}_{[2]}$. [2] uses XPaths to define XFDs among a set of XML subtrees. An XFD is defined as an expression $(Q, [e_1, \cdots, e_n \to e_{n+1}])$ where Q is an XPath, and e_i, for $i \in [1, n+1]$, is either an element or an element followed by dot and a set of key attributes of the element. An XML tree is said to satisfy the XFD if for any two subtrees rooted at a node in $root[Q]$, if they agree on the value of $e_1, \cdots, e_n$, then they also agree on the value of e_{n+1}, provided these values exist. For example, for the scheme file in Fig. 2, to say student number determines student name, we can use $(//student, [@sno \to @name])$. While this seems to be more expressive than the XFDs in [3] and [5], it is generally not clear what the "value" of an element means. For example, in Fig. 1 (b), the value of a students node is not defined. Apparently when e_i is an element it must be a simple element so that its value has a meaning. But there is also a strong structural restriction on the elements involved in the XFD: if an element's ancestor appears in the XFD, then so must its parent. This puts restrictions on the expressiveness. For example, to say course number and student number determines student's grade in the course in Fig. 1 (b), we have to use the students node. This will cause trouble because we do not know the "value" of the students nodes.

$\text{XFD}_{[7]}$. The XFDs in [7] are based on simple and downward paths that may contain $\_*$. So the XFDs may express constraints such as (A). However, no set equality or list equality is considered. Therefore the constraints (B), (C) and (F) cannot be captured.

$\text{XFD}_{[9]}$. We defined parameterized XFDs using simple, downward, upward and composite paths in [9]. The ordering of subelements is assumed to be insignificant in [9], and therefore, the conformity of trees to scheme files and the value equality are slightly different from those defined in Section 2. To unify and generalize the XFDs in other previous work, we will use the definitions in Section 2 and describe a modified parameterized XFD in Section 4. The details of $\text{XFD}_{[9]}$ will not be repeated here.

3.3 XFDs Based on Subtrees

$\text{XFD}_{[8]}$. Unlike other previous work that use paths to define XFDs, [8] defines two types of XFDs using *homomorphism, v-subtrees* and *isomorphism* of XML trees. The authors consider slightly different XML scheme files and conforming XML trees from ours. Both a scheme tree and an XML data tree are a labelled tree (we mention only trees although the authors allow more general *rooted graphs*) with each node assigned a *type Ele* or *Att*, and each edge assigned a frequency of either 1 or *. In a scheme tree, no two descendants of a node can have the same type and label. While in a data tree, every leaf node is assigned a value.

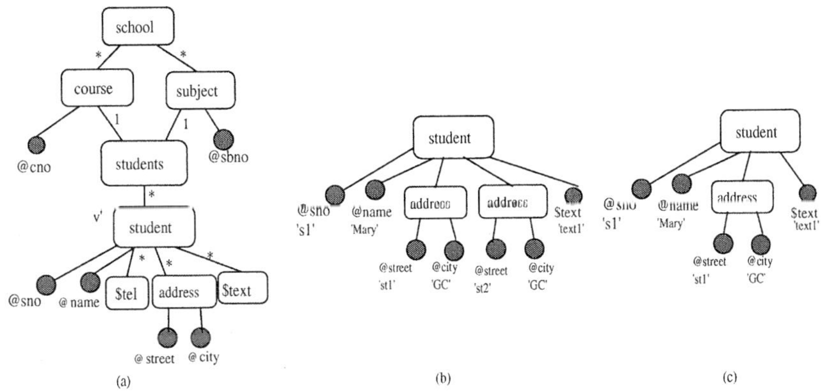

Fig. 4. Notations of [8] for the scheme file and tree in Fig. 2: (a) Schema Graph (b) A pre-image of $\mathcal{T}(v')$ (c) A maximal subcopy of $\mathcal{T}(v')$

A homomorphism between two trees T and G is a mapping ϕ from the nodes of T to the nodes of G such that (1) $\phi(root_T) = root_G$, $label(v) = label(\phi(v))$, $type(v) = type(\phi(v))$ for every node v in T; (2) if (v, v') is an edge in T, then $(\phi(v), \phi(v'))$ is an edge in G. A data tree T *conforms* to a scheme tree G if there is a (unique) homomorphism between them such that the edges in T observe the frequency specified in G. A v-subtree is a subtree which roots at node v and it is determined by the paths from v to a given subset of leaves of the original tree. The isomorphism of two subtrees is a 1-1 mapping between the two sets of nodes which is homomorphic in both directions. Two data trees are equivalent if there is an isomorphism ϕ between them and $value(v) = value(\phi(v))$ for the leaf nodes. An XFD is defined to be of the form $v : X \rightarrow Y$, where v is a node in the schema tree, and X and Y are v-subtrees in the schema tree. Two types of satisfaction by a conforming data tree T (notice the unique homomorphism ϕ between T and G) are defined, and they represent two different types of constraints. The first type is that for every two *pre-images* W_1 and W_2 of the total subtree $\mathcal{T}(v)$ rooted at v, $W_1 \mid_Y$ and $W_2 \mid_Y$ are equivalent whenever $W_1 \mid_X$ and $W_2 \mid_X$ are equivalent. Here a pre-image of $\mathcal{T}(v)$ is a total $\phi^{-1}(v)$-subgraph in T, $W_1 \mid_Y$, for example, is the projection of W_1 on Y, which is the *root*-subtree of W_1 determined by the pre-images of the leaves in Y. The second type is exactly the same as the first type except "pre-images" is replaced with "maximal subcopies". Here a maximal subcopy of $\mathcal{T}(v)$ is a subtree of T which is isomorphic to a *root*-subtree of $\mathcal{T}(v)$, and which is not contained in any other such subtrees. Fig. 4 shows the schema graph corresponding to the scheme file in Fig. 2, a pre-image and a maximal subcopy of $\mathcal{T}(v')$ in the tree shown in Fig. 2. The first type of satisfaction allows us to express some constraints involving set equality, while the second type allows us to express some constraints similar to those in [3]. However, since there are no node equality defined, the XFDs in [8] cannot express the constraint that the student number determines the student node in each course in Fig. 2. Also, since W_1 and W_2 must be both maximal copies or both pre-images, the XFDs cannot express the constraint (F) listed at the beginning of this section. The constraint (C) cannot be expressed either since no ordered lists of nodes are considered.

4 The Generalized XFDs

In this section we provide the definition of generalized XFDs. We need the following types of agreements between two nodes.

Given two nodes v_1 and v_2 and a path p (simple, upward or composite), we are interested in four types of agreements of v_1 and v_2 on p. We say that v_1 and v_2 node-agree or *N-agree* on p if (1) p is a simple path, and $v_1 = v_2$, or (2) p is an upward path, $v_1[p] \neq \emptyset$ and $v_1[p] = v_2[p]$, or (3) p is a composite path, and v_1 and v_2 N-agree on the upward path part of p. We say that v_1 and v_2 list-agree or *L-agree* on p if the nodes in $v_1(p)$ and $v_2(p)$ are pairwise value equal. We say that v_1 and v_2 set-agree or *S-agree* on p if for every node v in $v_1[p]$, there is a node v' in $v_2[p]$ such that $v =_v v'$, and vice versa. We say that v_1 and v_2 intersection-agree or *I-agree* on p if there exist nodes $v \in v_1[p]$ and $v' \in v_2[p]$ such that $v =_v v'$.

For example, in Fig. 2, v_5 and v_7 S-agree on address; v_6 and v_7 I-agree on address; v_5, v_6 N-agree on $\Uparrow$.

We are now ready for the definition of GXFDs.

Definition 1. *Let $\mathcal{S} = (E_1, E_2, A, P, R, r)$ be an XML scheme file. A generalized functional dependency (GXFD) over $\mathcal{S}$ is an expression of the form*

$$Q: \; p_1(c_1), \ldots, p_n(c_n) \;\rightarrow p_{n+1}(c_{n+1})$$

where Q is a downward path, $p_1, p_2, \ldots, p_n$ are simple or composite paths, p_{n+1} is a simple path of length 1 or 0, $Q_i.p_j$ $(i = 1, 2;\ j \in [1, n+1])$ is a general path, and c_i $(i \in [1, n+1])$ is one of N, L, S, and I.

Let T be an XML tree conforming to $\mathcal{S}$. T is said to satisfy *the GXFD if, for any two nodes $v_1, v_2 \in root[Q]$, if $v_1[p_1], \ldots, v_1[p_n]$ are not empty, and v_1, v_2 c_i-agree on p_i (for all $i \in [1, n]$), then $v_1[p_{n+1}]$ and $v_2[p_{n+1}]$ are not empty, and v_1 and v_2 also c_{n+1}-agree on p_{n+1}.*

T is said to strongly satisfy *the GXFD if, for any two nodes $v_1, v_2 \in root[Q]$ the following statement is true: if one of $v_1[p_1], \ldots, v_1[p_n]$, $v_2[p_1], \ldots, v_2[p_n]$ is empty, or v_1, v_2 c_i-agree on p_i (for all $i \in [1, n]$), then $v_1[p_{n+1}]$ and $v_2[p_{n+1}]$ are not empty, and v_1 and v_2 also c_{n+1}-agree on p_{n+1}.*

To simplify the notation, when c_i is omitted we use the following default types of agreement: for the empty path or an upward path, the default is N-agreement; for all other paths, the default is S-agreement. Note that the strong satisfaction implies the weak satisfaction.

Our GXFDs unify and generalize the previous XFDs surveyed earlier, and can express many constraints that cannot be expressed by the previous XFDs. In particular, the strong satisfaction of a special form of the GXFDs is a generalization of $\text{XFD}_{[5]}$, except for some subtle differences when null values exist.

This special form is when the RHS is always ϵ, and the type of agreement on ϵ is S, and for each path p_i on the LHS, the type of agreement is N if $last(p_i)$ is a complex element or $\Uparrow$, and it is I otherwise. For instance, the $\text{XFD}_{[5]}$ (i) in Section 3 for the scheme file in Fig. 1 (b) can be expressed as

$\_ * .student.\$name: \ \Uparrow .@sno(I) \rightarrow \epsilon(S)$.

To demonstrate the expressive power of our GXFDs, the constraints (A) through (F) at the beginning of Section 3 can be expressed as follows.

(A) $\_ * .student: \ @sno \rightarrow @sname$
(B) $\_ * .student: \ @sno \rightarrow address$
(C) $\_ * .student: \ @sno \rightarrow address(L)$
(D) $\_ * .student.address: \ \Uparrow .@sno \rightarrow \epsilon(S)$
(E) $course.students.student.\$text: \ \Uparrow^3 \rightarrow \epsilon(S)$
(F) $\_ * .student: \ \$tel(I) \rightarrow address$.

The XML tree in Fig. 2 strongly satisfies (A), (B), and (E). It satisfies but does not strongly satisfy (F). It does not satisfy (C) and (D).

As a direct application to XML database design, our GXFDs can be used to detect more data redundancies in XML documents.

5 Future Work

The GXFDs will be of practical use only if there are efficient algorithms for their reasoning. We are currently working on such algorithms.

References

1. X. Wu, T.W. Ling, S. Y.Lee, M. L. Lee, and G. Dobbie. NF-SS: A normal form for semistructured schema. *ER Workshop'2001, Lecture Notes in Computer Science*, 2465:292–305, 2002.
2. M. L. Lee, T. W. Ling, and W. L. Low. Designing functional dependencies for XML. *EDBT'2002, Lecture Notes in Computer Science*, 2287:124–141, 2002.
3. M. Arenas and L. Libkin. A normal form for XML documents. *ACM Transactions on Database Systems*, 29:195–232, 2004.
4. Z. Tan, Y. Pang, and B. Shi. Reasoning about functional dependencies for XML. *Journal of Software (in Chinese)*, 14(9):1564–1570, 2003.
5. M. W. Vincent, J. Liu, and C. Liu. Strong functional dependencies and their applicatiopn to normal forms in XML. *ACM Transactions on Database Systems*, 29(3):445–462, 2004.
6. Jixue Liu, Millist Vincent, and Chengfei Liu. Local XML functional dependencies. In *WIDM'03*, pages 23–28.
7. Y. Chen, S. Davidson, C. Hara, and Y. Zheng. RRXS: Redundancy reducing XML storage in relations. In *VLDB conference*, pages 189–200, 2003.
8. S. Hartmann and S. Link. More functional dependencies for XML. In *ADBIS 2003*, pages 355–369, 2003.
9. J. Wang and R. Topor. Removing XML data redundancies using functional and equality-generating dependencies. In *ADC'05*, Jan. 31- Feb. 4 2005.
10. P. Buneman, S. B. Davidson, W. Fan, and C. S. Hara. Keys for XML. *Computer Networks*, 39(5):473–487, 2002.

Checking Multivalued Dependencies in XML*

Jixue Liu[1], Millist Vincent[1], Chengfei Liu[2], and Mukesh Mohania[1]

[1] School of Computer and Information Science, University of South Australia
[2] Faculty of Inf. and Comm. Technologies, Swinburne University of Technology
[3] IBM Research Laboratories, New Delhi, India
{jixue.liu, millist.vincent}@unisa.edu.au
cliu@swin.edu.au
mkmukesh@in.ibm.com

Abstract. Recently, the issues of how to define functional dependencies (XFDs) and multivalued dependencies (XMVDs) in XML have been investigated. In this paper we consider the problem of checking the satisfaction of a set of XMVDs in an XML document. We present an algorithm using extensible hashing to check whether an XML document satisfies a given set of XMVDs. The performance of the algorithm is shown to be linear in relation to the number of tuples of the XML document, a measure which is related to, but not the same as, the size of the XML document.

1 Introduction

XML has recently emerged as a standard for data representation and interchange on the Internet [18, 1]. While providing syntactic flexibility, XML provides little semantic content and as a result several papers have addressed the topic of how to improve the semantic expressiveness of XML. Among the most important of these approaches has been that of defining integrity constraints in XML [7, 6]. Several different classes of integrity constraints for XML have been defined including key constraints [6, 5], path constraints [8], and inclusion constraints [9, 17], and properties such as axiomatization and satisfiability have been investigated for these constraints. Following these, some other types of constraints such as functional dependencies [2, 4, 3, 15, 12, 16], multivalued dependencies (XMVDs) [14], axioms, and normal forms have also been investigated. Once such constraints have been defined, one important issue that arises is to develop efficient methods of checking an XML document for constraint satisfaction, which is the topic of this paper. In this paper we address the problem of developing an efficient algorithm for checking whether an XML document satisfies a set of XMVDs. The problem is addressed in several aspects. Firstly, we propose an algorithm that is based on a modification of the extensible hashing technique. Another key idea of the algorithm is an encryption technique which

* Supported by Australian Research Council Discovery Project DP0559202.

Y. Zhang et al. (Eds.): APWeb 2005, LNCS 3399, pp. 320–332, 2005.

reduces the problem of checking XMVD satisfaction to the problem of checking MVD satisfaction. Secondly, we show that this algorithm scans a document only once and all the information required for XMVD checking can be extracted in this single scan, even when there are multiple XMVDs to be checked. At the same time, we show that the algorithm runs in linear time in relation to the number of tuple of the XML document. The number of tuples of a document is different (though related) to the size of the XML document and is the number of combinations (we call them tuples) of the path values involved in the XMVDs.

2 Preliminary Definitions

In this section we review some preliminary definitions.

Definition 2.1. Assume a countably infinite set $\mathbf{E}$ of element labels (tags), a countable infinite set $\mathbf{A}$ of attribute names and a symbol S indicating text. An **XML tree** is defined to be $T = (V, lab, ele, att, val, v_r)$ where V is a **finite** set of nodes in T; lab is a function from V to $\mathbf{E} \cup \mathbf{A} \cup \{\mathtt{S}\}$; ele is a partial function from V to a sequence of V nodes such that for any $v \in V$, if $ele(v)$ is defined then $lab(v) \in \mathbf{E}$; att is a partial function from $V \times \mathbf{A}$ to V such that for any $v \in V$ and $l \in \mathbf{A}$, if $att(v, l) = v_1$ then $lab(v) \in \mathbf{E}$ and $lab(v_1) = l$; val is a function such that for any node in $v \in V, val(v) = v$ if $lab(v) \in \mathbf{E}$ and $val(v)$ is a string if either $lab(v) = \mathtt{S}$ or $lab(v) \in \mathbf{A}$; v_r is a distinguished node in V called the *root* of T and we define $lab(v_r) = root$. Since node identifiers are unique, a consequence of the definition of val is that if $v_1 \in \mathbf{E}$ and $v_2 \in \mathbf{E}$ and $v_1 \neq v_2$ then $val(v_1) \neq val(v_2)$. We also extend the definition of val to sets of nodes and if $V_1 \subseteq V$, then $val(V_1)$ is the set defined by $val(V_1) = \{val(v) | v \in V_1\}$.

For any $v \in V$, if $ele(v)$ is defined then the nodes in $ele(v)$ are called **subelements** of v. For any $l \in \mathbf{A}$, if $att(v, l) = v_1$ then v_1 is called an **attribute** of v. The set of ancestors of a node v, is denoted by $Ancestor(v)$ and the parent node of v is denoted by $parentV(v)$ where the suffix V means that the parent is a vertex (node). □

Definition 2.2 (path). A **path** is an expression of the form $l_1. \cdots .l_n$, $n \geq 1$, where $l_i \in \mathbf{E} \cup \mathbf{A} \cup \{\mathtt{S}\}$ for all $i, 1 \leq i \leq n$ and $l_1 = root$. If p is the path $l_1. \cdots .l_n$ then $endL(p) = l_n$. □

For instance, if $\mathbf{E} = \{$`root, Dept, Section, Emp`$\}$ and $\mathbf{A} = \{$`Project`$\}$ then `root, root.Dept, root.Dept.Section, root.Dept.Section.Project, root.Section.Emp.S` are all paths.

Definition 2.3. Let p denote the path $l_1. \cdots .l_n$ and the function $parentP(p)$ return the path $l_1. \cdots .l_{n-1}$. Let q denote the path $q_1. \cdots .q_m$. The path p is said to be a **prefix** of the path q, denoted by $p \subseteq q$, if $n \leq m$ and $l_1 = q_1, \ldots, l_n = q_n$. Two paths p and q are equal, denoted by $p = q$, if p is a prefix of q and q is a prefix of p. The path p is said to be a **strict prefix** of q, denoted by $p \subset q$, if p is a prefix of q and $p \neq q$. We also define the intersection of two paths p_1 and

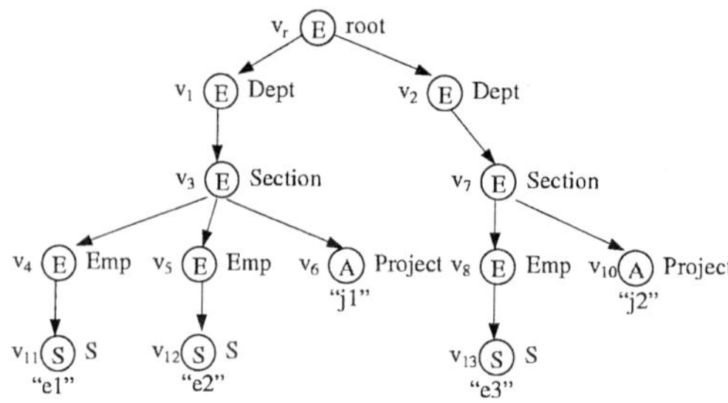

Fig. 1. An XML tree

p_2, denoted by $p_1 \cap p_2$, to be the maximal common prefix of both paths. It is clear that the intersection of two paths is also a path. □

For example, `root.Dept` is a strict prefix of `root.Dept.Emp` and `root.Dept.Section.Emp` $\cap$ `root.Dept.Section.Project` = `root.Dept.Section`.

Definition 2.4. A **path instance** in an XML tree T is a sequence $v_1.\cdots.v_n$ such that $v_1 = v_r$ and for all $v_i, 1 < i \leq n, v_i \in V$ and v_i is a child of v_{i-1}. A path instance $v_1.\cdots.v_n$ is said to be **defined over the path** $l_1.\cdots.l_n$ if for all v_i, $1 \leq i \leq n$, $lab(v_i) = l_i$. Two path instances $v_1.\cdots.v_n$ and $v'_1.\cdots.v'_n$ are said to be **distinct** if $v_i \neq v'_i$ for some i, $1 \leq i \leq n$. The path instance $v_1.\cdots.v_n$ is said to be a **prefix** of $v'_1.\cdots.v'_m$ if $n \leq m$ and $v_i = v'_i$ for all $i, 1 \leq i \leq n$. The path instance $v_1.\cdots.v_n$ is said to be a **strict prefix** of $v'_1.\cdots.v'_m$ if $n < m$ and $v_i = v'_i$ for all $i, 1 \leq i \leq n$. The set of path instances over a path p in a tree T is denoted by $instances(p)$. For a node v, we use $instnodes(v)$ to denote all nodes of the path instance ended at v. □

For example, in Figure 1, $v_r.v_1.v_3$ is a path instance defined over the path `root.Dept.Section` and $v_r.v_1.v_3$ is a strict prefix of $v_r.v_1.v_3.v_4$. $instances($`root.Dept`$) = \{\mathtt{v_r.v_1},\ \mathtt{v_r.v_2}\}$. $instnodes(v_2) = \{v_r,\ v_2\}$.

Definition 2.5. A set P of paths is **consistent** if for any path $p \in P$, if $p_1 \subset p$ then $p_1 \in P$. □

This is natural restriction on the set of paths and any set of paths that is generated from a DTD will be consistent. We now define the notion of an XML tree conforming to a set of paths P.

Definition 2.6. An XML tree T is said to **conform** to a set P of paths if every path instance in T is a path instance over a path in P. □

The next definition is to limit XML trees from having missing information.

Definition 2.7. Let P be a consistent set of paths, let T be an XML tree that conforms to P. Then T is defined to be **complete** if whenever there exist paths p_1 and p_2 in P such that $p_1 \subset p_2$ and there exists a path instance $v_1.\cdots.v_n$ defined over p_1, in T, then there exists a path instance $v'_1.\cdots.v'_m$ defined over p_2 in T such that $v_1.\cdots.v_n$ is a prefix of the instance $v'_1.\cdots.v'_m$. □

For example, if we take P to be {`root`, `root.Dept`, `root.Dept.Section`, `root.Dept.Section.Emp`,
`root.Dept.Section.Project`} then the tree in Figure 1 conforms to P and is complete.

The next function returns all the final nodes of the path instances of a path p in T.

Definition 2.8. Let P be a consistent set of paths, let T be an XML tree that conforms to P . The function *endnodes*(p), where $p \in P$, is the set of nodes defined by $endnodes(p) = \{v|v_1.\cdots.v_n \in instances(p) \wedge v = v_n\}$. □

For example, in Figure 1, *endnodes*(`root.Dept`) $= \{\mathtt{v}_1, \mathtt{v}_2\}$.

The next function returns the end nodes of the path instances of a path p under a given node. It is a restriction to *endnodes*(p).

Definition 2.9. Let P be a consistent set of paths, let T be an XML tree that conforms to P. The function *branEndnodes*(v, p) (meaning branch end nodes), where $v \in V$ and $p \in P$, is the set of nodes in T defined by $branEndnodes(v, p) = \{x|x \in endnodes(p) \wedge v \in instnodes(x)\}$ □

For example in Figure 1 , *branEndnodes*$(v_1,$ `root.Dept.Section.Emp`$) = \{\mathtt{v}_4, \mathtt{v}_5\}$.

We also define a partial ordering on the set of nodes and the set of paths as follows. We use the same symbol for both orderings but this causes no confusion as they are being applied to different sets.

Definition 2.10. The partial ordering $>$ on the set of paths P is defined by $p_1 > p_2$ if p_2 is a strict prefix of p_1, where $p_1 \in P$ and $p_2 \in P$. The partial ordering $>$ on the set of nodes V in an XML tree T is defined by $v_1 > v_2$ iff $v_2 \in Ancestor(v_1)$, where $v_1 \in V$ and $v_2 \in V$. □

3 XMVDs in XML

In this section, we present the XMVD definition and then give two examples.

Definition 3.1. Let P be a consistent set of paths and let T be an XML tree that conforms to P and is complete. An XMVD is a statement of the form $p_1, \cdots, p_k \rightarrow\rightarrow q_1, \cdots, q_m | r_1, \cdots, r_s$ where $p_1, \cdots, p_k$, $q_1, \cdots, q_m$ and $r_1, \cdots, r_s$ are paths in P and $\{p_1, \cdots, p_k\} \cap \{q_1, \cdots, q_m\} \cap \{r_1, \cdots, r_s\} = \phi$. A tree T satisfies $p_1, \cdots, p_k \rightarrow\rightarrow q_1, \cdots, q_m | r_1, \cdots, r_s$ if whenever there exists a q_i, $1 \le i \le m$, and two distinct path instances $v^i_1.\cdots.v^i_n$ and $w^i_1.\cdots.w^i_n$ in $instances(q_i)$ such that:

(i) $val(v^i_n) \neq val(w^i_n)$;
(ii) there exists a $r_j, 1 \le j \le s$, and two nodes z_1, z_2, where $z_1 \in branEndnodes(x_{i_j}, r_j)$ and $z_2 \in branEndnodes(y_{i_j}, r_j)$ such that $val(z_1) \neq val(z_2)$;
(iii) for all $p_l, 1 \le l \le k$, there exists two nodes z_3 and z_4, where $z_3 \in branEndnodes(x_{i_{j_l}}, p_l)$ and $z_4 \in branEndnodes(y_{i_{j_l}}, p_l)$, such that $val(z_3) = val(z_4)$;

then:

(a) there exists a path instance $v_1'^i.\cdots.v_n'^i$ in $instances(q_i)$ such that $val(v_n'^i) = val(v_n^i)$ and there exists a node z_1' in $branEndnodes(x'_{i_j}, r_i)$ such that $val(z_1') = val(z_2)$ and there exists a node z_3' in $branEndnodes(x'_{i_{j_l}}, p_l)$ such that $val(z_3') = val(z_3)$;

(b) there exists a path instance $w_1'^i.\cdots.w_n'^i$ in $instances(q_i)$ such that $val(w_n'^i) = val(w_n^i)$ and there exists a node z_2' in $branEndnodes(y'_{i_j}, r_i)$ such that $val(z_2') = val(z_1)$ and there exists a node z_4' in $branEndnodes(y'_{i_{j_l}}, p_l)$ such that $val(z_4') = val(z_4)$;

where $x_{i_j} = \{v | v \in \{v_1^i, \cdots, v_n^i\} \wedge v \in instnodes(endnodes(r_j \cap q_i))\}$ and $y_{i_j} = \{v | v \in \{w_1^i, \cdots, w_n^i\} \wedge v \in instnodes(endnodes(r_j \cap q_i))\}$ and $x_{i_{j_l}} = \{v | v \in \{v_1^i, \cdots, v_n^i\} \wedge v \in instnodes(endnodes(p_l \cap r_j \cap q_i))\}$ and $y_{i_{j_l}} = \{v | v \in \{w_1^i, \cdots, w_n^i\} \wedge v \in instnodes(endnodes(p_l \cap r_j \cap q_i))\}$ and $x'_{i_j} = \{v | v \in \{v_1'^i, \cdots, v_n'^i\} \wedge v \in instnodes(endnodes(r_j \cap q_i))\}$ and $y'_{i_j} = \{v | v \in \{w_1'^i, \cdots, w_n'^i\} \wedge v \in instnodes(endnodes(r_j \cap q_i))\}$ and $x'_{i_{j_l}} = \{v | v \in \{v_1'^i, \cdots, v_n'^i\} \wedge v \in instnodes(endnodes(p_l \cap r_j \cap q_i))\}$ and $y'_{i_{j_l}} = \{v | v \in \{w_1'^i, \cdots, w_n'^i\} \wedge v \in instnodes(endnodes(p_l \cap r_j \cap q_i))\}$. □

We note that since the path $r^j \cap q^i$ is a prefix of q^i, there exists only one node in $v_1^i.\cdots.v_n^i$ that is also in $branEndnodes(r_j \cap q_i)$ and so x_{i_j} is always defined and is a single node. Similarly for $y_{i_j}, x_{i_{j_l}}, y_{i_{j_l}}, x'_{i_j}, y'_{i_j}, x'_{i_{j_l}}, y'_{i_{j_l}}$. We also note that the definition of an XMVD is symmetrical, i.e. the XMVD $p_1, \cdots, p_k \rightarrow\rightarrow q_1, \cdots, q_m | r_1, \cdots, r_s$ holds if and only if the XMVD $p_1, \cdots, p_k \rightarrow\rightarrow r_1, \cdots, r_s | q_1, \cdots, q_m$ holds. We now illustrate the definition by some examples.

Example 3.1. Consider the XML tree shown in Figure 2 and the XMVD C : `root.A.Course` $\rightarrow\rightarrow$ `root.A.B.Teacher.S`|`root.A.C.Text.S`. Let $v_1^i.\cdots.v_n^i$ be the path instance $v_r.v_{12}.v_2.v_4.v_8$ and let $w_1^i.\cdots.w_n^i$ be the path instance $v_r.v_{12}.v_2.v_5.v_9$. Both path instances are in $instances($`root.A.B.Teacher.S`$)$ and $val(v_8) \neq val(v_9)$. Moreover, $x_{1_1} = v_{12}$, $y_{1_1} = v_{12}$, $x_{1_{1_1}} = v_{12}$ and $y_{1_{1_1}} = v_{12}$. So if we let $z_1 = v_{10}$ and $z_2 = v_{11}$ then $z_1 \in branEndnodes(x_{1_1},$ `root.A.C.Text.C`$)$ and $z_2 \in branEndnodes(y_{1_1},$ `root.A.C.Text.S`$)$. Also if we let $z_3 = v_1$ and $z_4 = v_1$ then $z_3 \in branEendnodes(x_{1_{1_1}},$ `root.A.Course`$)$ and $z_4 \in branEndnodes(y_{1_{1_1}},$ `root.A.Course`$)$ and $val(z_3) = val(z_4)$. Hence conditions (i), (ii) and (iii) of the definition of an XMVD are satisfied. If we let $v_1'^i.\cdots.v_n'^i$ be the path $v_r.v_{12}.v_2.v_4.v_8$ we firstly have that $val(v_n'^i) = val(v_n)$ as required. Also, since the path instances are the same we have that $x_{1_1} = x'_{1_1}$ and $x_{1_{1_1}} = x'_{1_{1_1}}$. So if we let $z_1' = v_{11}$ then $z_1' \in branEndnodes(x'_{1_1},$ `root.A.C.Text.S`$)$ and $val(z_1') = val(z_2)$ and if we let $z_3' = v_1$ then $z_3' \in branEndnodes(x'_{1_{1_1}},$ `root.A.Course`$)$ and $val(z_3') = val(z_3)$. So part (a) of the definition of an XMVD is satisfied. Next if we let $w_1'^i.\cdots.w_n'^i$ be the path $v_r.v_8.v_2.v_5.v_9$ then we firstly have that $val(w_n'^i) = val(w_n)$ since the paths are the same. Also, since the paths are the same we have that $y_{1_1} = y'_{1_1}$ and $y_{1_{1_1}} = y'_{1_{1_1}}$. So if we let $z_2' = v_{10}$ then

$z_2' \in branEndnodes(y'_{1_1}, \texttt{root.A.C.Text.S})$ and $val(z_2') = val(z_1)$ and if we let $z_4' = v_1$ then $z_4' \in branEndnodes(x'_{1_{1_l}}, \texttt{root.A.Course})$ and $val(z_4') = val(z_4)$. Hence part (b) on the definition of an XMVD is satisfied and so T satisfies the XMVD $\mathcal{C}$. □

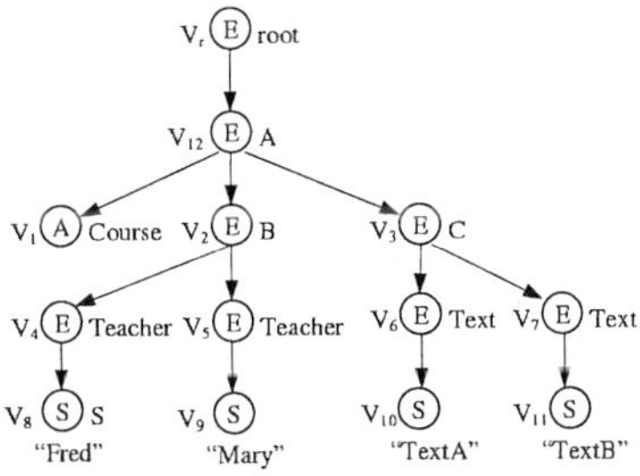

Fig. 2. Satisfaction of XMVD

More example showing the satisfaction and dissatisfaction of XMVDs can be found in [14].

4 Algorithm of Checking XMVD

In this section, we present our algorithm for checking XMVD satisfaction.

Given an XMVD $P \to\to Q|R$, where $P = \{p_1, \cdots p_{n_p}\}$, $Q = \{q_1, \cdots q_{n_q}\}$, and $R = \{r_1, \cdots r_{n_r}\}$, we let $S = \{s'_1, ..., s'_n\} = P \cup Q \cup R$. We call n the **number of paths invovled** in the XMVD. To check this XMVD against a document, we firstly parse the document to extract values for s'_i, $1 \leq i \leq n$. These values are then combined into tuples of the form $< v_1 \cdots v_n >$ where v_i is a value for the path s'_i. Finally, the tuples are used to check the satisfaction of the XMVD. For parsing a document, we need to define a control structure based on the paths involved.

4.1 Defining Parsing Control Structure

We sort $S = P \cup Q \cup R$ by using string sorting and denote the result by $S^o = [s_1, ..., s_n]$. We call the set of end elements of the paths in S^o **prime end elements** and denoted by PE, i.e., $PE = \{endL(s) | s \in S\}$ where $endL()$ is defined in Definition 2.2. Note that S^o being a list can simplify the calculation of all the intersections of path in S^o as shown below. Consider the example in Figure 3 which will be a running example in this section. Let an XMVD be `r.A.C.F` $\to\to$ `r.A.C.D.E|r.A.B`. Then S^o = [`r.A.B`, `r.A.C.D.E`, `r.A.C.F`] and $PE = \{B,\ E,\ F\}$.

Let $H = \{h'_1, \cdots, h'_m\}$ be a set of paths that are the intersections of paths in S^o where $h'_i = s_i \cap s_j$, $(i = 1, \cdots, m)$, $j = i + 1$ and $m = n - 1$. We call

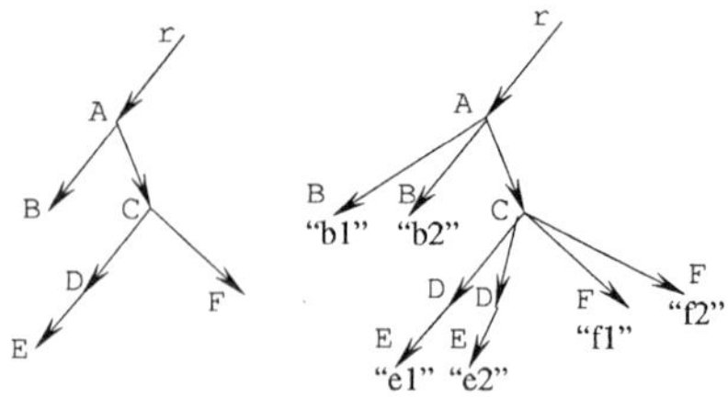

(a) a set of paths (b) the tree presentation of (c)

```
1: <r><A><B>b1</B>
2:          <B>b2</B>
3:          <C><D><E>e1</E></D>
4:             <D><E>e2</E></D>
5:             <F>f1</F>
6:             <F>f2</F>
7:          </C>
8:     </A>
9: </r>
```

(c) an XML document

Fig. 3. a set of paths and an example XML document

the elements ending the paths in H' **intersection end elements** and denote the set by IE. We call both intersection end elements and prime end elements **key end elements** and denote them by KE. In Figure 3, $H = \{\texttt{r.A},\ \texttt{r.A.C}\}$, $IE = \{A,\ C\}$, $KE = \{A,\ C,\ B,\ E,\ F\}$.

Now we define and calculate the contributing elements of intersection elements. Let iE be the intersection end element of a intersection path h,i.e., $iE = endL(h)$. The contributing elements of iE, denoted by $CE(iE)$, are defined to be all key end elements of S^o and H under h but not contributing elements of any other intersection end elements. To calculate the contributing elements, we first sort the paths in H by applying string sorting and put the result in H^o as $[h_1, \cdots, h_m]$. We then follow the following algorithm to calculate contributing elements.

Algorithm 4.1 (calculation of contributing elements)

Inpput: $S^o = [s_1, \cdots, s_n]$ and $H^o = [h_1, \cdots, h_m]$
Do: For $h = h_m, \cdots, h_1$ in order,
  Foreach s in S^o, if s is not marked and if $endL(s)$ is a descendent of h, put $endL(s)$ in $CE(endL(h))$ and mark s.
  Foreach $h_x \in H^o$, if h_x is not marked and if $endL(h_x)$ is a descendent of h, put $endL(h_x)$ in $CE(endL(h))$ and mark h_x.
Output: $CE(endL(h))$ for all $h \in H^o$.

In the running example of Figure 3, the results of applying Algorithm 4.1 are $CE(C) = \{E,\ F\}$ and $CE(A) = \{B,\ C\}$.

4.2 Parsing a Document

We define the function $val(k)$ to mean the value set of a key end element. Note that if k is a prime end element, $val(k)$ will be accumulated if there are multiple presences of the same elements under a same node. If k is an intersection end element, $val(k)$ is a set of tuples generated by the production of the values and/or value sets of contributing elements of k. We call each element of the production **a tuple**. Obviously, $val(k)$ changes as the parsing progresses. We now show some examples of $val(k)$ w.r.t Figure 3. When parsing reaches tag <C> in Line 3, $val(C)$, $val(E)$ and $val(F)$ are all set to empty. When parsing has completed Line

6, $val(E) = \{"e1", "e2"\}$ and $val(F) = \{"f1", "f2"\}$. When parsing of Line 7 is completed, $val(C) = \{<"e1","f1">, <"e1","f2">, <"e2","f1">, <"e2","f2">\}$.

We further define some notation. stk denotes a stack while $stkTop$ is used to refer to the element currently at the top of the stack. For simplicity, we define $e \in X$, where e is an element and X is a path set, to be true if there exists a path $x \in X$ such that $endL(x) = e$. With all these definitions, we present the algorithm that parses a document. Also for simplicity, we use $val(h)$ to mean $val(endL(h))$ where h is a path.

Algorithm 4.2 (parsing documents)

```
Inpput: S^o, H^o, CE, PE, an empty stk, and a document
Do: Foreach element e in the document in the order of presence
      if e ∈ H^o and e closes stkTop, do production of
         the contributing attributes as the following:
         let CE(e) = {e_1,...,e_c}, then
         val(e) = val(e) ∪ {val(e_1) × ··· × val(e_c)}
         Note that some val(e_i) can be sets of tuples while the
         others can be sets of values.
       else if e ∈ H^o
         push e to stk
         reset val(e_1), ···, val(e_c) to empty where
         e_1,···,e_c ∈ CE(e)
       else if e ∈ PE
         read the value v of e and add v to val(e)
         if e is a leaf element, v is the constant string on
            the node.
         if e is an internal node, v is 'null'.
       else
         ignore the element and keep reading
Output: val(h_1) where h_1 is the first element in H^o - the
        shortest intersection path.
```

Note that the algorithm scans the document only once and all tuples are generated for the XMVD.

In the algorithm, the structures S^o, H^o, CE, PE, an empty stk form a structure group. If there are multiple XMVDs to be checked at the same time, we create a structure group for each XMVD. During document parsing, for each element e read from the document, the above algorithm is applied to all structure groups. This means for checking multiple XMVDs, the same document is still scanned once.

4.3 Tuple Attribute Shifting and XMVD Checking

For each tuple t in $val(h_1)$, where h_1 is the first element in H^o - the shortest intersection path, it contains a value for each paths of the XMVD, but the values are in the order of their presence in the document. This order is different from the order of paths in the XMVD. For example in Figure 3, the tuple $<$ $"b1", "e1", "f1"$ $>$ is in val(`root.A`) and the values of the tuple are for the paths `r.A.B`, `r.A.C.D.E`, `r.A.C.F` in order. This order is different from the order of paths in the XMVD: `r.A.B`, `r.A.C.D.E` `r.A.C.F`. We define the operation $shiftAttr()$ to rearrange the order of values of t so that the values for the paths in P are moved to the beginning of t, the values for the paths in Q are moved to the middle of t, and the values for the paths in R are at the end of t. The $shiftAttr()$ operation is applied to every tuple of $val(h_1)$ and the result is denoted by $T_{sa} = shiftAttr(val(h_1))$.

We define a further function $removeDuplicates(T_{sa})$ to remove duplicating tuples in T_{sa} and we denote the returned set as T_{dist}. Thus, the following algorithm checks whether an XML document satisfies an XMVD and this algorithm is one of the main results of our proposal. The basic idea of checking is to group all the tuples for the XMVD so that tuples with the same P value is put into one group. In each group, the number of distinct Q values, $|Q|$, and the number of distinct R values, $|R|$, are calculated. Then if $|Q| \times |R|$ is the same as the number of distinct tuples in the group, the group satisfies the XMVD; otherwise, it violates the XMVD. If all the groups satisfy the XMVD, the document satisfies the XMVD.

Algorithm 4.3 (checking mvd)

```
Inpput: T_dist
Do: violated = 0
    For G be each set of all tuples in T_dist having the same P
      value
      let |G| be the number of tuples in G
      let dist(Q) and dist(R) be the numbers of distinct Q values
         and of distinct R values in G respectively
      if ( |G| != dist(Q) × dist(R) ) then violated ++;
Output: if ( violated == 0 ) return TRUE; otherwise return FLASE.
```

Note that this algorithm assumes that G is the set of all tuples having the same P value. To satisfy this assumption, one has to group tuples in T_{dist} so that tuples with the same P value can be put together. A quick solution to this is not direct as show in the next section and therefore the way of achieving the assumption greatly affects the performance of whole checking algorithm.

5 Implementation and Performance

In this section, we present the performance results of our tests using an adapted hashing implementation. The tests were done on a Pentium 4 computer with 398 MB of main memory. The tests used XMVDs involving 12 paths, 9 paths,

6 paths, and 3 paths respectively. The XML documents used in the tests have random string values of about 15 characters for each path. This means that if there are three paths involved in an XMVD, the length of a tuple is about 45 characters while if there are twelve paths in an XMVD, the length of a tuple is around 180 characters.

In Algorithm 4.3, an assumption is taken that all tuples having the same P value are grouped together. At the same time, in each group, the number of distinct Q values and the number of distinct R values need to be calculated. To obtain these numbers, we choose to use an adapted hashing technique which is based on the standard extensible hashing [11]. In the standard extensible hashing technique, each object to be hashed has a distinct key value. By using a hash function, the key value is mapped to an index to a pointer, pointing to a fixed size basket, in a pointer **directory**. The object with the key value will then be put into the pointed basket. Every time a basket becomes full, the directory space is doubled and the full basket is split into two. In our implementation, we use the digests, integers converted from strings, of P values of tuples as the key values of the standard extensible hashing. Our modification to the standard extensible hashing technique is the following.

The baskets we use are extensible, meaning that the size of each basket is not fixed. We allow only the tuples with the same key value to be put into a basket. We call the key value of the tuples in the basket the **basket key**. Tuples with different keys are said conflicting. If placing a tuple into an existing basket causes a conflict, a new basket is created and the conflicting tuple is put into the new basket. At the same time, the directory is doubled and new hash codes are calculated for both the existing basket key and the new basket key. The doubling process continues until the two hash codes are different. Then the existing and the new baskets are connected to the pointers indexed by the corresponding hash codes in the directory.

Figure 4 shows the directory and a basket. Note that because of directory space doubling, a basket may be referenced by multiple pointers. In the diagram, p stands for the basket key, the three spaces on the right of p are lists storing distinct Q values, distinct R values and distinct Q and R combinations. On top of the lists, three counters are defined. nq stands for the number of distinct Q values, nr the number of distinct R values and nqr the number of distinct Q and R combinations. After hashing is completed, the three counters are used to check the XMVD as required by Algorithm 43. When a new tuple $t =< p, q, r >$, where p, q and r are values for P, Q and R respectively, with the same p value is inserted to a basket, q is checked against all existing values to see if it equals to one of them. If yes, the q value is ignored; otherwise, the q value is appended to the end of the list and the counter is stepped. Similar processes are applied to insert r and the combination $< q, r >$.

We now analyze the performance of hashing. Obviously the calculation of hash codes to find baskets for tuples is linear in relation to the number of tuples.

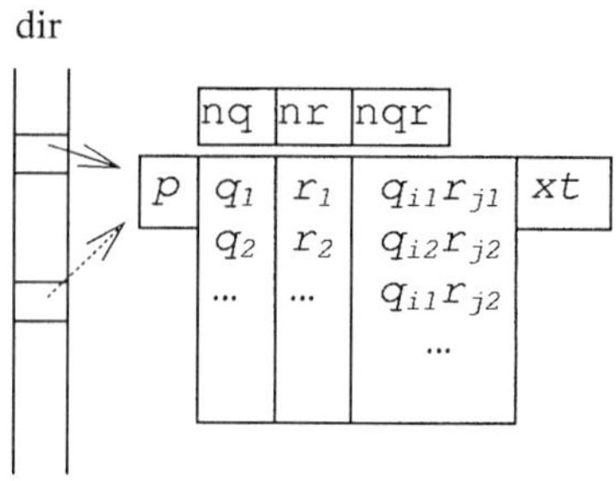

Fig. 4. The structure of a basket and one extension

When a tuple $t =< p, q, r >$ is put into a basket that has already has tuples, then comparisons are needed to see if q, r and the combination $< q, r >$ are already in the lists. The performance of the comparison relates to the number of distinct existing values. Generally, if we need to put n' values into a list that has had m distinct values, then the performance is $O(n' * m)$ comparisons.

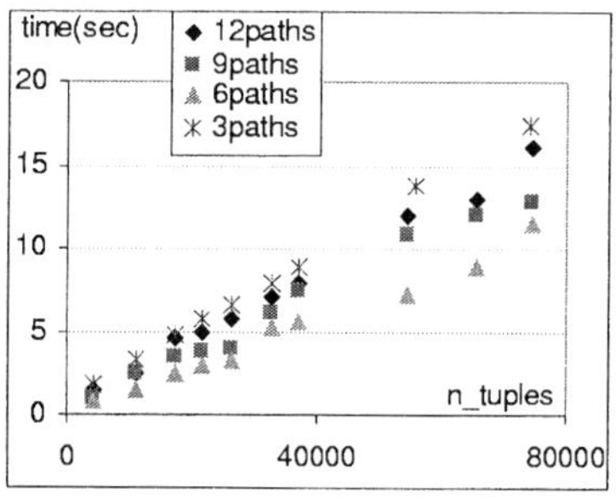

Fig. 5. Performance of hash method

We conducted a number of experiments to observe the performance of the implementation and the results are given in Figure 5. In this experiment we plotted the time taken for checking XMVD satisfaction against the number of tuples in the document, for varying numbers of paths in the XMVD (we used 6, 9, and 12). In the cases of 3 paths and 6 paths, we see that the former has a higher cost. This can be explained because the overall performance contains the time for parsing documents. To have the same number of tuples in the cases of 3 paths and 6 paths, the 3 path case has a much larger file size, about 70 times of that of 6 paths and therefore the parsing time used is much larger in contrast to that of 6 path case. It is the parsing time that makes performance for 3 paths worse than that for 9 or 12 paths.

We also implemented the algorithms in a sorting based approach to compare the performance of this hashing based approach. The result of the sorting implementation and its comparison with the hashing based approach are given in the full version of this paper [10].

6 Conclusions

In this paper we have addressed the problem of developing an efficient algorithm for checking the satisfaction of XMVDs, a new type of XML constraint that has recently been introduced [13, 14]. We have developed an extensible hash based algorithm that requires only one scan of the XML document to check XMVDs. At the same time its running time is linear in the size of the application which is proved to be the number of tuples. The algorithm can check not only the cases where there is only one XMVD, but also the cases involving multiple XMVDs.

References

1. Serge Abiteboul, Peter Buneman, and Dan Suciu. *Data on the Web - From Relations to Semistructured Data and XML.* Morgan Kayfman Publisher, 2000.
2. Marcelo Arenas and Leonid Libkin. A normal form for xml documents. *PODS*, 2002.
3. Marcelo Arenas and Leonid Libkin. An information-theoretic approach to normal forms for relational and xml data. *PODS*, pages 15–26, 2003.
4. Marcelo Arenas and Leonid Libkin. A normal form for xml documents. *ACM Transactions on Database Systems*, 29:195–232, 2004.
5. P. Buneman, S. Davidson W. Fan, C. Hara, and W. Tan. Reasoning about keys for xml. *Information Systems*, 2003.
6. Peter Buneman, Susan Davidson, Wenfei Fan, Carmem Hara, and Wang-Chiew Tan. Keys for xml. *10th WWW Conference*, 2001.
7. Peter Buneman, Wenfei Fan, Jrme Simon, and Scott Weinstein. Constraints for semistructured data and xml. *ACM SIGMOD Record*, 30(1):47–55, 2001.
8. Peter Buneman, Wenfei Fan, and Scott Weinstein. Path constraints in semistructured databases. *JCSS*, 61, 2000.
9. Wenfei Fan and Leonid Libkin. On xml integrity constraints in the presence of dtd's. *PODS*, pages 114–125, 2001.
10. Jixue Liu, Millist Vincent, Chengfei Liu, and Mukesh Mohania. Checking multivalued dependencies in xml. *http://www.cis.unisa.edu.au/ cisjl/publications/ mvdChkAlgo-subm.pdf*, 2005.
11. Raghu Ramakrishnan. *Database Management Systems.* McGraw-Hill Higher Education, 2000.
12. Millist Vincent and Jixue Liu. Functional dependencies for xml. *LNCS 2642 - APWEB*, 2003.
13. Millist Vincent and Jixue Liu. Multivalued dependencies and a 4nf for xml. *LNCS 2681 - Proc. International Conference on Advanced Information Systems Engineering (CAISE)*, pages 14–29, 2003.
14. Millist Vincent and Jixue Liu. Multivalued dependencies in xml. *LNCS 2712 - BNCOD*, pages 4–18, 2003.

15. Millist Vincent, Jixue Liu, and Chengfei Liu. A redundancy free 4nf for xml. *LNCS 2824 - XML Database Symposium (Xsym)*, pages 254–266, 2003.
16. Millist Vincent, Jixue Liu, and Chengfei Liu. Strong functional dependencies and their application to normal forms in xml. *Accepted on 05/Feb/2004 for publication in ACM Transactions on Database Systems*, 29(3):445–462, 2004.
17. Millist Vincent, Michael Schrefl, Jixue Liu, Chengfei Liu, and Solen Dogen. Generalized inclusion dependencies in xml. *APWeb*, 2004.
18. Jennifer Widom. Data management for xml - research directions. *IEEE Data Engineering Bulletin, Special Issue on XML*, 22, 1999.

Making DTD a Truly Powerful Schema Language

Shan Wei[1] and Mengchi Liu[2]

[1] School of Computer Science,
Carleton University, Ottawa, Ontario, Canada K1S 5B6
swei3@connect.carleton.ca

[2] School of Computer Science, Carleton University,
Ottawa, Ontario, Canada K1S 5B6
mengchi@scs.carleton.ca

Abstract. DTD is primarily used XML schema language to structure XML documents via a set of rules. But its too simple to represent XML document structures in a wide spectrum. Thus, many other XML schema languages such as XML Schema and SOX have been proposed to solve this problem. However these XML schema languages are too complicated for nonexperts to comprehend and use. In this paper, we extend DTD with object oriented mechanisms to solve this problem to meet the needs of complex applications and we call the new schema language *Extended DTD*. We describe Extended DTD components including their compositions, properties, constraints and validation rules. Then we come to conclusion.

1 Introduction

In the past few years, XML has emerged as the dominant standard for representing information and exchanging data over the Internet [2]. The Document Type Definition (DTD) [2] determines the structures of XML documents via a set of rules and is the primarily used schema language nowadays [9]. But its too simple to represent complex XML document structures. Many other XML schema languages such as SOX [3], XML schema [5], Schematron [6], DSD [7], XDR [10] have been proposed to solve this problem. Although most of them are more powerful in modeling than DTD, they do not support object oriented features except for XML Schema and SOX [8]. However, XML Schema and SOX are too complicated for nonexperts to comprehend and use [4][11]. In addition, some important features in inheritance such as overriding and blocking, are not supported in SOX and only indirectly supported in XML Schema.

In our point of view, the best way is to improve DTD in its expressiveness and functionality for structure modeling so that it is capable of supporting XML applications with wide spectrum. To achieve this, the most important feature needed to be integrated into DTD is the object orientation. In this paper, we extend DTD systematically with some additional key features to enable pure object oriented modeling and we call the new schema language Extended DTD.

Y. Zhang et al. (Eds.): APWeb 2005, LNCS 3399, pp. 333–338, 2005.

The remainder of this paper is organized as follows: (1) we analyze the requirements of the Extended DTD; (2) we describe the components of Extended DTD including Scope Declaration Component, Element Declaration Component, Attribute Declaration Component, NameSpace Declaration Component, Import/Include Declaration Component; (3) we describe the validity constraints of Extended DTD; Finally, we come to the conclusion.

2 Extended DTD

This section discusses the requirements on Extended DTD and Extended DTD components.

2.1 Requirements and Analysis

There are three tenets in object-oriented design, namely encapsulation, inheritance and polymorphism, which can improve the design, structure and reusability of the application design. To totally emphasize the principles and completely enable object-oriented model design framework, Extended DTD needs to support mechanisms including element type derivation, scope specification, namespace and external schema constructs enclosure.

2.2 Scope Declaration Component

In Extended DTD, scope can be specified at two levels: document level and element level. A scope specified for a document applies for all elements and attributes declared in this document while a scope specified for an element only applies for this element itself.

In Extended DTD, if no scope is specified for the document, the scope should be individually defined for each element and attribute declared in this document. The syntax to declare the scope of a document is:

<scope scopeOfDocument>

This declaration clause specifies the scope of a document to be public or private. For example, the following clause specifies the scope of an Extended DTD document to be public: *<scope public>*. For details on specifying the scope of an element or an attribute, please refer to the subsecitons 2.3 and 2.4 respectively.

2.3 Element Declaration Component

This subsection describes how to declare an XML element type in Extended DTD including the composition of an element declaration and explanation on each component of the declaration.

In Extended DTD, the syntax to declare an element is as follows:

<!ELEMENT elementName scopeOfElement *ISA* superElementName *WITHOUTELEMENT* (withoutElementList) (elementContentModel)>

The elementName is the name of the element which should be an NCName defined in XML-Namespaces [12]. This name belongs to the document namespace declared at the beginning of the document. The scopeOfElement is the scope of the element and can be public or private, which means that the element is exportable or not exportable respectively. The scope of an element is by default public. A public element is exportable while a private element is only available within the document where it is declared. ISA is the keyword to declare the element hierarchy and the superElementName following it is the name of the super-element. Super-element must be an element declared in the same document or in the external construct that is imported or included in this document. The element being declared will inherit from its super-element; WITHOUTELEMENT is the keyword specifying the elements that should be blocked in the inheritance process and withoutElementList is the name list of the elements contained in the parent element content model that should be blocked in the inheritance process. With this mechanism, inheritance with blocking and overriding can be supported. The elementContentModel is the Content model of the element being declared. The constraints, syntax and composition of the elementContentModel property are the same as in DTD.

In Extended DTD, elements are divided into two types: simple element, whose content is a simple character string or empty and without sub-elements in content model, and complex element that contains other elements in its content model or includes one or more attribute values or both at the same time. In Extended DTD, only complex elements can be used for inheritance in which new complex elements can be derived from existing complex elements. The derived complex element will inherit all content model elements and attributes from its base type and the actual content model of this element is its parent's content model with the elements being blocked removed and with its own content model appending to it.

For example, *<!ELEMENT Teacher ISA Person WITHOUTELEMENT (HomePhone) (WorkPhone, Salary, Teaches)>* declares an element *Teacher*, which is a derived type of *Person* with *HomePhone* blocked in the inheritance and *WorkPhone, Salary, Teaches* as its own content model elements. The definition of element *Person* is *<!ELEMENT Person (Name, BirthDate, HomePhone)>* while the actual content model is *(Name, BirthDate, WorkPhone, Salary, Teaches).*

2.4 Attribute Declaration Component

Literally, the attribute declaration is the same as in DTD. All constraints on DTD attribute declaration also apply for Extended DTD attribute declaration. Extended DTD attribute should have the same scope and namespace as the element it belongs to.

2.5 NameSpace Declaration Component

XML namespace specification is defined in one of the W3C Recommendations called Namespaces in XML [12]. DTD doesn't support namespace [14], which makes it incapable of supporting code reuse by enclosing constructs from external schema documents. This is one of the biggest limitations of DTD that make it unsuitable for flexible and modular design of complex XML applications.

In Extended DTD, we integrate the mechanism to support namespace, which is a collection of names that are unique with respect to each other. By doing this, many name conflicts can be avoided. In Extended DTD, names must be unique within a single namespace, but they can be the same in different namespaces without causing any conflict. This will solve the possible name conflict when we enclose an external construct which has the same element or attribute name as in the enclosing document by using different namespaces.

In an Extended DTD document, all the namespaces must be declared at the beginning of the document before the actual schema definition starts. For the syntax to declare a namespace, please refer to the W3C specification Namespaces in XML [12]. For example, *<xmlns = "http://www.university.ca">* declares the default namespace of the XML document is *"http://www.university.ca"* and *<xmlns:e = "http://www.external.com">* declares the name space *e* is *"http://www.external.com"*.

2.6 Import / Include Declaration Component

In order to enable object oriented modular design and construct reuse, Extended DTD needs to provide mechanisms to assemble a whole schema definition from multiple schema documents to allow enclosure of external constructs. The declaration should be at the beginning of the schema document before the actual schema declaration starts and there are two types of enclosure declarations depending on namespaces of the schemas:

- *<include schemaURI>*
  To enclose an external construct with the same namespace as the enclosing schema document. *schemaURI* is the location of an Extended DTD construct. An Extended DTD document can have more than one external constructs included. The included constructs must either have the same namespace as the enclosing document, or have no namespace. In the latter case, the included construct is assigned to the namespace, to which the enclosing document belongs. For the sake of convenience, we call the included document E1, the including document E2. There are some constraints for the include declaration component:
  - E1 must be exportable or the definitions contained in E1 and used by E2 must be exportable;
  - E1 must be a complete Extended DTD document containing element and/or attribute components. E1 must be well formed;
  - If E1 has no namespace declared but E2 has, the schema definition corresponding to E2 must include not only its own declarations, but also all the components contained in E1 with all the absent namespaces replaced with the actual namespace value of E2.
- *<import nameSpace schemaURI>*
  To enclose an external construct with different namespaces than the enclosing schema document. *nameSpace* is the namespace of the external schema

construct being imported in the current document. The *schemaURI* is the location of an external Extended DTD construct. Here we call the included document E1, the enclosing document E2. There are also some constraints for this include declaration component:

- E1 must be exportable or the definitions contained in E1 and used by E2 must be exportable;
- E1 must be a complete Extended DTD document containing element and/or attribute components. E1 must be well formed.

For example,<*include Students.edtd*> declares to enclose an Extended DTD document *Students.edtd* from the same namespace in the current document while <*import "http://www.external.com" ExternalPersons.edtd*> to enclose an Extended DTD document *ExternalPersons.edtd* from a different namespace in the current document.

3 Validation Rules

This section discusses the validity constraints of Extended DTD. The validation of the XML documents against Extended DTD will be based on the validity constraints of DTD [13] with some additional validation rules:

- The element content model in Extended DTD depends not only on its own declaration, but also on the declaration of its parent. For details of element content model construction, please refer to subsection 2.3;
- The Extended DTD supports polymorphism, which means that an element instance in a valid XML document can be substituted with an instance of its subtype and the XML document should still be valid.

4 Conclusion

In this paper, we extend DTD with object orientation supporting mechanisms to make it more expressive and able to express XML document structures in a wide spectrum. First we describe the Extended DTD components including their compositions, properties, constraints. We also discuss the validation rules of XML document against Extended DTD.

Extended DTD supports more object oriented features than other object oriented feature supporting XML schema languages. Table 1 compares four schema languages.

Table 1. Comparison of four XML schema languages

Languages	Element Inheritance	Attribute Inheritance	Overriding	Blocking	Polymorphism
DTD	×	×	×	×	×
XML Schema	√	×	partial	partial	partial
SOX	√	×	×	×	√
Extended DTD	√	√	√	√	√

Extended DTD is simple and straight forward. It is especially easy to use for people who are already familiar with DTD. Also, it is much more expressive and capable to support complex, modular XML application design, which makes it a truly powerful XML schema language.

References

1. Ashley M. Aitken. Object orientation revealed! Internet document. http://www.vuw.ac.nz/acis99/papers/paperaitken-147.pdf, 1999.
2. T. Bray, J. Paoli, C. M. Sperberg-McQueen, and E. Maler(ed.). Extensible markup language (xml) 1.0 (second edition). internet document. http://www.w3.org/tr/rec-xml, October 2000.
3. A. Davidson, M. Fuchs, and M. Hedin. Schema for object-oriented xml 2.0. Internet document. http://www.w3.org/tr/note-sox, July 1999.
4. Bob DuCharme. Converting dtds (and dtd developers) to relax ng schemas. Internet document. http://titanium.dstc.edu.au/papers/er2000.pdf, 2003.
5. D.C. Fallside(ed.). Xml schema part 0: Primer. Internet document. http://www.w3.org/tr/xmlschema-0/, May 2001.
6. R. Jelliffe. Schematron. Internet document. http://www.ascc.net/xml/resource/schematron/, 2000.
7. N. Klarlund, A. Møller, and M. I. Schwartzbach. The dsd schema language. *Automated Software Engineering*, 9(3):285–319, 2002.
8. D. Lee and W.W. Chu. Comparative analysis of six xml schema languages. *ACM SIGMOD Record*, 29(3):117–151, September 2002.
9. Terry Halpin Linda Bird, Andrew Goodchild. Object role modelling and xml-schema. Internet document. http://titanium.dstc.edu.au/papers/er2000.pdf, 2000.
10. Microsoft. Xml schema developer's guide. Internet document. http://msdn.microsoft.com/xml/xmlguide/schema-overview.asp, 2000.
11. Anders Møller and Michael I. Schwartzbach. The xml revolution - technologies for the future web. Internet document. http://www.brics.dk/ amoeller/xml/schemas/index.html, October 2003.
12. W3C. Namespaces in xml. Internet document. http://www.w3.org/tr/rec-xml-names/, 1999.
13. W3C. Extensible markup language (xml) 1.0 (third edition). Internet document. http://www.w3.org/tr/rec-xml/, 2004.
14. Linda Bird Hoylen Sue Zar Zar Tun, Andrew Goodchild. Introduction to xml schema. Internet document. http://titanium.dstc.edu.au/xml/tutorials/xmlschema/intr-to-xmlschema.html, 1999.

An Algebra for Capability Object Interoperability of Heterogeneous Data Integration Systems

Jiuyang Tang, Weiming Zhang, and Weidong Xiao

School of Information System & Management, National University of Defense Technology, Changsha, 410073, Hunan, China
jiuyang_tang@hotmail.com, wmzhang@nudt.edu.cn, wilsonshaw@vip.sina.com

Abstract. In heterogeneous data integration systems, there can be a wide variety of different data sources, which support query interfaces with very varied capabilities. Constrained by the expressiveness of the access interfaces, data integration systems from multiple sources have to cope with different and limited capabilities of the sources. At the same time, several contemporary integration systems export their mediator capabilities in the same way as those of data sources, thus making it hard for them to be integrated by other mediators. In this paper, we propose a capability object conceptual model to capture a rich variety of query-processing capabilities of sources' and outline an algebra to compute the set of mediator-supported queries based on the capability limitations of the sources they integrate. Our work highlights the capability computing approach that enables interoperation among various sources by computing the capability objects associated with them towards scalable application integration. Not only is the process of interoperation semi-automatic and timesaving, but also, often, the end-users have idea of the capabilities of mediator and get a better insight on which queries to submit to the mediator. Finally, we show the properties of the algebraic operators. Query optimization is enabled based on the properties of the algebraic operators.

1 Introduction

With the rapid development of the World Wide Web, the integration of heterogeneous data sources has become a major concern of the database community. The data integration system aims at providing a uniform interface for querying collections of distributed, heterogeneous, and often-dynamic sources and making them work together as a whole. In these systems, a user poses a query on a mediator [1], which computes the answer by accessing the data at the underlying source relations. So the data integration systems have to cope with a wide variety of different data sources with a wide range of query processing capabilities. This introduces interesting capability description challenges, as illustrated by the following example.

Example 1. Consider a source relation *BOOKS* (*author, title, subject*). Users pose queries to the source by filling out search form and cannot retrieve all its data for free. Instead, the only way of retrieving its tuples is by providing an *author* name and

Y. Zhang et al. (Eds.): APWeb 2005, LNCS 3399, pp. 339 – 350, 2005.

subject name, and then retrieving the titles of this author in such subject. Another *BOOKS* source relation admits users searching for books by specifying the *author* or *title* attribute.

Many contemporary integration systems [2-10] have not captured a rich variety of query-processing capabilities of underlying sources and exported mediator capabilities. Therefore, not only is the process of integration manually extremely tedious and time-consuming, but also, often, the end-user does not have any idea of the capabilities of mediator and can't get a better insight on which queries to submit to the mediator.

In this work, we present capability object conceptual model, which is based on the access pattern and content information, making it possible for mediator and base source relations to precisely export their capabilities. This paper is principally concerned with capability object computing approach towards scalable application integration in distributed and heterogeneous resources.

The remainder of the paper is organized as follows. We compare our work with other related work in query-processing capability description in section 2. In section 3 we present our framework for capability object description. We then in section 4 propose capability object algebra and illustrate the computing by example. Section 5 shows the properties of the algebraic operators. Section 6 presents our conclusions.

2 Related Work

In this section, we briefly describe several methods that have been proposed to deal with query-processing capability limitations of a data source in data integration systems.

The usage of binding pattern for discussing diverse capabilities is pioneered in the TSIMMIS system [2]. In TSIMMIS, the source capabilities are expressed as a set of query templates supported by the source. Each attribute in a template can be adorned as bound, free. Since it only has a set of pre-defined query templates that it knows to answer, the integration system can answer a restricted set of queries.

Information Manifold [3] uses capability records to describe query capability limitations of sources. Each source has a capability record that indicates the input attributes of the source local schema, its output attributes, the minimum and maximum number of inputs that must be specified in a query to the source. Since the subset selected is arbitrary, the capability records cannot precisely specify the binding patterns. Therefore, the expressive power of its capabilities describing mechanism is less powerful.

In HERMES [4], the method that explicitly specifies the parameterized calls that are sent to the sources reduces the interface between the integration system and the sources to a limited set of explicitly listed parameterized calls. So it's hard to express source capabilities.

The Garlic system [5] allows for sources to express disjunctive as well as conjunctive condition processing capabilities. But it enforces unique keys for all exported data items, which make it too hard for the data providers.

In DISCO system [6], data is structured in class extents. A wrapper declares the attributes that can be given as input to logical operators (e.g., select, project, join), and the minimal number of attributes for which values are wanted.

The NAIL! system [7] investigates the problem of generating query plans for mediated schemas in the presence of source-capability restrictions. However, NAIL! only considered a limited set of restrictions expressed as attribute adornments, free and bound.

To represent the diverse query capabilities of sources, [8] utilizes an *input-output* relationship *ior* of the form *ior*: *Input* → *Output* or *ior*: *Input* → → *Output*, where the *Input* is a set of bindings for input attributes and the *Output* are the elements that are returned in the answer.

A generic search view mechanism [9] lists all data sources accessing capabilities through attributes, where direct calls are represented as key attributes, search calls are associated with search attributes and hyperlinks are mapped to abstract attributes.

Work in [10] is similar to our approach. Besides the *b*(bound), *f*(free) and *u*(unadorned) adornments, they propose two extra annotations *c*[*s*] and *o*[*s*] for a given attribute in a binding pattern. They define the capabilities of a mediator as the set of queries supported by the mediator on the integrated views it exports. In virtue of the template-computing algorithm, the capabilities of a mediator can be computed from the capabilities of the sources it mediates. Unfortunately, they take the assumption that the same attribute underlying different sources come from the same domain, while our work take into consideration of the content description of attributes. So an important difference is that prior art like [8-10] did not adequately address the role of content descriptions, and this paper extends that work by accounting for content descriptions of data sources in computing mediator capabilities.

3 Capability Object Conceptual Model

Current data integration research makes some simplifying assumptions. The first is that data sources can all be modeled as relational databases. This leads to the formulation of the mediator as integrated views in terms of source views. Data sources are assumed to be able to answer simple relational queries that possibly required binding patterns to be satisfied. Second, we assume that differences in ontologies, vocabularies, and formats used by sources have been resolved through wrappers[11,12], and the difference of the same attribute between the base source and mediator is the former domain is subset of the later.

Our common conceptual model for the internal representation of source capability object is based on the work done by Vidal [13]. In its core, we represent a source capability object by the triple (*OID, R, cp*), where:

- *object id*: uniquely identifies the source capability object.
- *R*: identifies the universal relation (contain base source relations and mediator relations).

- *cp* is a pair (*ior, cd*) called the capability description, where:
  - *ior*: is a pair (*Input, Output*) called the input-output relationship, where *Input* and *Output* are subsets of the attributes of *R*. The *Input* attributes are input restrictions which must be bound. The *Output* attributes require those attributes values projected out when the attributes in *Input* are bound. The input-output relationships typically characterize the limited query capabilities of sources.
  - *cd*: content description is a set of pairs (att_i, dom_i), where att_i is an attribute of *R*, and dom_i is a subset of the domain of this attribute in *R*. A tuple *t* satisfies *cd* iff for every pair (att_i, dom_i) in *cd*, $t.att_i$ is in dom_i. For every attribute att_j in Input, there must be a pair (att_j, dom_j) in *cd*.

Note that any real source may have more than one access pattern, which leads to several capability objects associating to the same source with the same *OID*.

We define the capabilities of a mediator object as the set of queries supported by the mediator object on the integrated objects it exports. The capabilities of a mediator object can be computed from the capabilities of the sources object it mediates.

In the next section, we will briefly define a Capability Object Integration Algebra, which allows us to systematically compose mediator objects from diverse data sources. The capability object integration algebra provides the compositional capability, and thus enhances the scalability of our approach.

4 Capability Object Integration Algebra

In this section, we present an algebra that allows us multiple levels of composition of mediator objects. The problem we are addressing in this paper specially deals with the computation of mediator objects, after the mediator views and their definition in terms of source objects are identified.

The algebra has two unary operators: Select, Project, and two binary operations: Union, Join. Each binary operator takes as operands two capability objects that we want to integrate, and generates a capability object as a result. In our algebra, the two capability objects should come from different sources with different *OID*. Each unitary operator allows us to highlight and select portions of the capability object that are relevant to the condition.

In the description of the algebra below we use the following symbols and definitions.

Let $O = (oid, R, cp)$, $O_1 = (oid_1, R_1, cp_1)$, and $O_2 = (oid_2, R_2, cp_2)$ be three capability objects, where,

$cp = (ior, cd)$, $ior = (Input, Output)$, $cd=\{(att_i, dom_{atti}) \mid att_i \in Att\}$, $cp_1= (ior_1, cd_1)$, $ior_1= (Input_1, Output_1)$, $cd_1= \{(att1_i, dom1_{att1i}) \mid att1_i \in Att_1\}$, $cp_2= (ior_2, cd_2)$, $ior_2= (Input_2, Output_2)$, $cd_2= \{(att2_j, dom2_{att2j}) \mid att2_j \in Att_2\}$, *Att* are attributes set of *cd*, Att_1 are attributes set of cd_1 and Att_2 are attributes set of cd_2.

Definition 1 (Get attributes operation). Let *R* be a relation in capability object *O*(*oid*, *R*, *cp*), we introduce *ATT*(*R*) operation to get all attributes of *R*.

Definition 2 (Sub-attributes projection operation). Let *Att* be attributes set of *cd* in capability object *O(oid, R, cp)*, then $cd|_A=\{(att_k, dom_{attk}) \mid att_k \in A \subseteq Att\}$ denotes the subset of *cd* with the attributes projection on the attributes subset *A*.

Example 2. Let $cd=\{(x, \{0, 1, 2\}), (y, \{True, False\})\}$, $A=\{x\}$, then $cd|_A=\{(x, \{0, 1, 2\})\}$.

Definition 3 (General union operator). The General union operator $\oplus$ on cd_1 and cd_2:

$$cd_1 \oplus cd_2 = cd_1|_{Att1-Att2} \oplus cd_2|_{Att2-Att1} = \{(att_k, dom_{attk}) | ((att_k, dom_{attk}) \in cd_1|_{Att1-Att2}) \cup ((att_k, dom_{attk}) \in cd_2|_{Att2-Att1})\}.$$

Example 3. Let $cd_1=\{(x, \{0, 1, 2\}), (y, \{True, False\})\}$, $cd_2=\{(x, \{0, 3, 4\}), (z, \{Jan, \ldots, Dec\})\}$, then $cd_1 \oplus cd_2=\{(y, \{True, False\}), (z, \{Jan, \ldots, Dec\})\}$.

Definition 4 (General join operator). The General join operator $\ominus$ on cd_1 and cd_2:

$$cd_1 \ominus cd_2 = cd_1|_{Att1 \cap Att2} \ominus cd_2|_{Att1 \cap Att2} = \{(att_k, dom_{attk}) \mid att_k \in Att_1 \cap Att_2, dom_{attk} = dom1_{attk} \cup dom2_{attk}\}.$$

Example 4. Let cd_1 and cd_2 be the same as those in Example 3, then $cd_1 \ominus cd_2=\{(x, \{0, 1, 2, 3, 4\})\}$.

Definition 5 (Absolute join operator). The Absolute join operator $\odot$ on cd_1 and cd_2:

$$cd_1 \odot cd_2 = cd_1|_{Att1 \cap Att2} \odot cd_2|_{Att1 \cap Att2} = \{(att_k, dom_{attk}) \mid att_k \in Att_1 \cap Att_2, dom_{attk} = dom1_{attk} \cap dom2_{attk}\}.$$

Example 5. Let cd_1 and cd_2 be the same as those in Example 3, then $cd_1 \odot cd_2=\{(x, \{0\})\}$.

4.1 Operators for Simple Mediator

As the query capability of a mediator object is affected by the techniques used by the mediator in processing the queries posed to it, we, in this section, make simple query-processing assumption on mediators as in [10]. That is to say, mediator does not apply any post-processing conditions and pass bindings from one join operand to another.

4.1.1 Union

Let O_1 and O_2 be defined as in section 4 and "$R_1 = R_2$" (the two relations have *n* same attribute names and the corresponding attributes come from the same domain), then the union of the two capability objects resulting in a new capability object, which is:

$O = O_1 \cup O_2 = (oid, R, cp)$, where,
$ATT(R) = ATT(R_1) = ATT(R_2)$,
$cp=(ior, cd)$,
$ior=(Input, Output)$,
$Input=\{in_i | in_i \in (Input_1 \cup Input_2)\}$,
$Output=\{out_i | out_i \in (Output_1 \cup Output_2)\}$,
$cd=(cd_1 \oplus cd_2) \cup (cd_1 \ominus cd_2)$.

Note that every object identifier *oid* in capability object is automatically generated by system, and doesn't bear any meaning.

Example 6. Consider a mediator capability object $O(oid, R, cp)$ be defined as the union of three source capability objects $O_1(oid_1, R_1, cp_1)$, $O_2(oid_2, R_2, cp_2)$ and $O_3(oid_3, R_3, cp_3)$. The descriptions of the three source capability objects are as follows:

O_1	$(oid_1, R_1(x, y, z),$ $(\{x\}, \{x, y\}),$ **cp_1** **ior_1** $\{(x, \{0, 1, 2\})\}$ **cd_1** $)$
O_2	$(oid_2, R_2(x, y, z),$ $(\{y\}, \{y, z\}),$ $\{(y, \{True, False\}), (z, \{Jan, ..., June\})\}$ $)$
O_3	$(oid_3, R_3(x, y, z),$ $(\{z\}, \{x, y, z\}),$ $\{(x, \{4, 5\}), (z, \{Jan, ..., Dec\})\}$ $)$

Fig. 1. Descriptions for source capability objects

In Figure 1, source capability object O_1 can return (x, y) tuples set when provided with the values for attribute x.

$ATT(R) = \{x, y, z\}$.

The computing of cp_1 and cp_2 is

$cp_t=((\{x, y\}, \{x, y, z\}), \{(x, \{0, 1, 2\}), (y, \{True, False\}), (z, \{Jan, ..., June\})\})$,

while the computing of cp_t and cp_3 is

$cp = ((\{x, y, z\}, \{x, y, z\}), \{(x, \{0, 1, 2, 4, 5\}), (y, \{True, False\}), (z, \{Jan, ..., Dec\})\})$.

The description of mediator capability object $O(oid, R, cp)$ is:

O	$(oid, R(x, y, z),$ $(\{x, y, z\}, \{x, y, z\}),$ $\{(x, \{0,1,2,4,5\}), (y,\{True, False\}), (z, \{Jan, ..., Dec\})\}$ $)$

Fig. 2. Description for mediator capability object

4.1.2 Join

For simplification, we only discuss natural join in this paper, and other join definitions can be derived by analogy.

The join of the two capability objects O_1 and O_2 resulting in a new capability object, which is expressed as:

$O = O_1 \bowtie O_2 = (oid, R, cp)$, where,
$ATT(R) = ATT(R_1) \cup ATT(R_2)$,
$cp = (ior, cd)$,
$ior = (Input, Output)$,
$Input = \{in_i | in_i \in (Input_1 \cup Input_2)\}$,
$Output = \{out_i | out_i \in (Output_1 \cup Output_2)\}$,
$cd = (cd_1 \oplus cd_2) \cup (cd_1 \odot cd_2)$.

Example 7. Consider a mediator capability object $O(oid, R, cp)$ be defined as the join of three source capability objects $O_1(oid_1, R_1, cp_1)$, $O_2(oid_2, R_2, cp_2)$ and $O_3(oid_3, R_3, cp_3)$, where,

$ATT(R_1) = \{x, y, z\}$, $cp_1 = ((\{x\}, \{y, z\}), \{(x, \{0, 1, 2\}), (z, \{Jan, \ldots, Dec\})\})$,
$ATT(R_2) = \{z, u, v\}$, $cp_2 = ((\{z\}, \{z, u\}), \{(z, \{Jan, \ldots, June\})\})$,
$ATT(R_3) = \{v, w\}$, $cp_3 = ((\{v\}, \{w\}), \{(v, \{True, False\})\})$.
So the mediator capability object $O(oid, R, cp)$ is
$ATT(R) = \{x, y, z, u, v, w\}$, $cp = ((\{x, z, v\}, \{y, z, u, w\}), \{(x, \{0, 1, 2\}), (z, \{Jan, \ldots, June\}), (v, \{True, False\})\})$.

4.1.3 Select

When given selection condition f and capability object $O_1(oid_1, R_1, cp_1)$, mediator can apply the selection condition f on O_1 to gain its capability object, which is expressed as

$\delta [f](O_1) = O(oid, R, cp)$,
where O_1 is defined as in section 4 and f is selection condition in the form of: $att\ \theta\ c, \theta \in \{<, >, :, \geq, =\}$, $att \in Att1$, $c \in const$.
The mediator capability object $O(oid, R, cp)$ is
$ATT(R) = ATT(R_1)$,
$cp = (ior, cd)$,
$ior = (Input, Output)$,
$Input = \{in_i | in_i \in Input_1\}$,
$Output = \{out_i | out_i \in Output_1\}$,
$cd = (cd_1 - cd_1|_{att}) \cup \{(att, dom_{att} \cap f)\}$.

Example 8. Consider a mediator capability object $O(oid, R, cp)$ be defined as the application of condition "x: 3" on source capability objects $O_1(oid_1, R_1, cp_1)$, where,
$ATT(R_1) = \{x, y, z\}$, $cp_1 = ((\{x, y\}, \{y, z\}), \{(x, \{0, 1, 2, 3, 4, 5\}), (y, \{True, False\})\})$,
then
$ATT(R) = \{x, y, z\}$, $cp = ((\{x, y\}, \{y, z\}), \{(x, \{0, 1, 2, 3\}), (y, \{True, False\})\})$.

4.1.4 Projection

When given capability object $O_1(oid_1, R_1, cp_1)$ and attributes set $Att = \{att_1, \cdots, att_k\} \subseteq ATT(R_1)$, the projection on Att of mediator can be expressed as

$\prod[att_1, \cdots, att_k](O_1) = (oid, R, cp)$.

If $Input_1 \not\subset Att$, the mediator has no capability object, because the source can't accept the mediator queries with some required binding attributes absent.

On the other hand, if $Input_1 \subseteq Att$, then only the projected attributes in *Att* remain, while the other attributes in *R*, $Output_1$ *and* cd_1 are left out, where,

$ATT(R) = Att$,
$cp=(ior, cd)$,
$ior = (Input, Output)$,
$Input = \{in_i \mid in_i \in Input_1\}$,
$Output = \{out_i \mid out_i \in (Output_1 \cap Att)\}$,
$cd = cd_1|_{Att}$.

Example 9. Consider a mediator capability object $O(oid, R, cp)$ be defined as the application of projection on $\{x, y, z\}$ on source capability object $O_1(oid_1, R_1, cp_1)$, where,

$ATT(R_1)= \{x, y, z, u\}$, $cp_1= ((\{x, y\}, \{z, u\}), \{(x, \{0, 1, 2\}), (u, \{True, False\})\})$,
So the definition of $O(oid, R, cp)$ is
$ATT(R)= \{x, y, z\}$, $cp= ((\{x, y\}, \{z\}), \{(x, \{0, 1, 2\})\})$.

4.2 Operators for Advanced Query-Processing Techniques in Mediators

In this section, we consider advanced query-processing techniques in mediators, while mediator capability objects support post-processing and passing bindings, which only impact the definition of Join and Selection.

4.2.1 Join

When processing a query on a join view over a set of base views, since some of the output attributes produced from one base-view can be used to bind some input attributes of subsequent base-view queries, the operator is non-commutative.

The join of the two capability objects O_1 and O_2 is expressed as:

$O = O_1 \bowtie O_2 = (oid, R, cp)$, where,
$ATT(R) = ATT(R_1) \cup ATT(R_2)$,
$cp = (ior, cd)$,
$ior = (Input, Output)$,
$Input = \{in_i \mid in_i \in ((Input_1 \cup Input_2) - Output_1)\}$,
$Output = \{out_i \mid out_i \in (Output_1 \cup Output_2)\}$,
$cd = (cd_1 \oplus cd_2) \cup (cd_1 \circledcirc cd_2)$.

Example 10. Consider a mediator capability object $O(oid, R, cp)$ be defined as the join of three source capability objects $O_1(oid_1, R_1, cp_1)$, $O_2(oid_2, R_2, cp_2)$ and $O_3(oid_3, R_3, cp_3)$ as in Example 7.

So the definition of $O(oid, R, cp)$ is

$ATT(R)= \{x, y, z, u, v, w\}$, $cp= ((\{x, v\}, \{y, z, u, w\}), \{(x, \{0, 1, 2\}), (z, \{Jan, ..., June\}), (v, \{True, False\})\})$.

Compared with Example 7, mediator can pass binding attribute value z between O_1 and O_2, which result in the omitting of attribute z in *Input* set in *cp*. That is to say, mediator poses query $R_1(x_1, Y, Z)$ on O_1, then mediator passes every value z_i in returned tuples (y, z) to O_2, invoking query $R_2(z_i, U, V)$. Query $R_3(v, W)$ on O_3 can be executed with query $R_1(x_1, Y, Z)$ on O_1 and O_2 in parallel, while query on O_1 and O_2 must be executed sequentially. With the information of the domain of z in O_1 is $\{Jan, \ldots, Dec\}$ and the domain of z in O_2 is $\{Jan, \ldots, June\}$, we can filter those tuples with z value later than *June* after executing query on O_1, and only pass the concise result to O_2. As is known to all, we can improve query performance by reducing the intermediate results transmission over network.

4.2.2 Select

If there exists post-processing and selection condition f in the form of "$att = c, c \in const$", we can directly deduce the input bind attributes from the selection condition, so we get the definition of $O(oid, R, cp)$ after applying the selection condition as in 4.1.3.

$ATT(R)= ATT(R_1)$,
$cp= (ior, cd)$,
$ior= (Input, Output)$,
$Input=\{in_i | in_i \in (Input_1 - att)\}$,
$Output= \{out_i | out_i \in Output_1\}$,
$cd= (cd_1 - cd_1|_{att}) \cup \{(att, dom_{att} \cap f)\}$.

Example 11. Consider a mediator capability object $O(oid, R, cp)$ be defined as applying selection condition "$x = 3$" on source capability objects $O_1(oid_1, R_1, cp_1)$, whose definition is the same as in Example 8.

So the definition of $O(oid, R, cp)$ is
$ATT(R)= \{x, y, z\}$, cp= $((\{y\}, \{y, z\}), \{(x, \{3\}), (y, \{True, False\})\})$.

5 A Case Study

To verify that our capability object integration algebra makes sense in practice, we explored the Web.

Consider the following three Web sources for bookstores. The Web sources are described in the relational data model. The content description of the multiple Web sources is as follows:

Source S_1: A site with information for all published book in SOUTHCHINA from 1992 to 2004. The site supplies two query forms. In form 1, *title* attribute must be specified and the result of query includes *ISBN*, *publisher*, *publication_date* attributes; while in form 2 *publisher*, *publication_date* attributes must be specified and the result of query includes *title*, *ISBN* attributes. R_1(*title*, *ISBN*, *publisher*, *publication_date*)
Source S_2: A site with information for all published book on computer. Users can get *author* and *abstract* attributes with *title* attribute specified. R_2(*author*, *title*, *subject*, *abstract*)
Source S_3: A site with information for all published book on *computer*, *communication* and *economical management*. Through choosing the book *subject*, users can get the corresponding *author* and *title* attributes. R_3(*author*, *title*, *subject*)

So the derived capability objects descriptions for three web sources are presented in Figure 3, while S_1 contain two capability objects O_1 and O_2.

O_1	(id_1, R_1, ({*title*}, {*ISBN, publisher, publication_date*}), **ior_1** {(*title, String*), (*ISBN, String*), (*publisher, SOUTHCHINAPUBLISHER*), (*publication_date, {1992, ..., 2004}*)} **cd_1**)
O_2	(id_2, R_1, ({*publisher, publication_date*}, {*title, ISBN*}), **ior_2** {(*title, String*), (*ISBN, String*), (*publisher, SOUTHCHINAPUBLISHER*), (*publication_date, {1992, ..., 2004}*)} **cd_2**)
O_3	(id_3, R_2, ({*title*}, {*author, abstract*}), **ior_3** {(*author, String*), (*title, String*), (*subject, {computer}*), (*abstract, String*)} **cd_3**)
O_4	(id_4, R_3, ({*subject*}, {*author, title*}), **ior_4** {(*author, String*), (*title, String*), (*subject, {computer, communication, economical management}*)} **cd_4**)

Fig. 3. Descriptions for capability objects of bookstores

We can build a mediator R on these three Web sources, while the view of R is *R(author, title, subject, ISBN, publisher, publication_date)*.

To apply the capability object integration algebra, we get mediator capability objects O_5 and O_6 in the following operations:

$$O_5 = (\prod[author, title, subject](O_3) \cup O_4) \bowtie O_1$$
$$O_6 = (\prod[author, title, subject](O_3) \cup O_4) \bowtie O_2$$

Suppose mediator capability objects use operators for advanced query-processing techniques (support post-processing and passing bindings), the mediator capability objects O_5 and O_6 are:

O_5	(id_5, R, ({*title, subject*}, {*author, ISBN, publisher, publication_date*}), **ior_5** {(*author, String*), (*title, String*), (*subject, {computer, communication, economical management}*), (*ISBN, String*), (*publisher, SOUTHCHINAPUBLISHER*), (*publication_date, {1992, ..., 2004}*)} **cd_5**)
O_6	(id_6, R, ({*title, subject, publisher, publication_date*}, {*author, title, ISBN*}), **ior_6** {(*author, String*), (*title, String*), (*subject, {computer, communication, economical management}*), (*ISBN, String*), (*publisher, SOUTHCHINAPUBLISHER*), (*publication_date, {1992, ..., 2004}*)} **cd_6**)

Fig. 4. Descriptions for capability objects of mediator in book integration system

Corresponding to mediator capability objects O_5 and O_6, the mediator has two query forms. One form requires the specification of *title* and *subject* attributes, another requires the specification of *title*, *subject*, *publisher* and *publication_date* attributes and the domain of *publisher* attribute is $\{SOUTHCHINAPUBLISHER\}$.

Since end-users have idea of the capabilities of mediator, they get a better insight on which queries to submit to the mediator.

6 Properties of Operators

The challenge for mediator objects is to generate optimal execution plans respecting the limited capabilities of sources. An optimal plan submits the largest possible sub-query to the source based on its specific capability. Typically, this means providing as many input bindings that are supported in the source capability object and projecting out the minimal set of attributes needed by the mediator query.

In obtaining a possibly optimal plan, a mediator object may perform a number of transformations on the operators and identify the best physical implementation for these operators. Typical transformations in this step include commuting operands of binary operators, selecting a join ordering, pushing selections and projections down, etc, to enumerate the space of alternate evaluation plans for a query. These optimizations often depend upon the ability to rearrange operands, which depends upon the properties of the operators.

Some properties that characterize these operators are as follows:

a) the union operator in simple and advanced mediator processing is commutative for the following hold: $O_1 \cup O_2 = O_2 \cup O_1$.

b) the join operator in simple mediator processing is commutative for the following hold: $O_1 \bowtie O_2 = O_2 \bowtie O_1$.

c) the join operator in advanced mediator processing is non-commutative.

These properties have been used to formulate the rules that allow the mediator to perform typical rewriting optimization while making sure that only optimal execution plans are explored. If an operator is commutative the query optimizer can reverse the order of the operands, rearrange operands and design various optimized algorithms that improve the performance of queries tremendously.

7 Conclusion

In data integration systems, data sources exhibit diverse and limited capabilities. It is important to capture the rich variety of query-processing capabilities of sources and describe the capabilities of mediators so that they can be used as easily as base sources are. In some situations, mediator capabilities are manually computed and specified.

In this paper we propose capability object conceptual model to capture a rich variety of query-processing capabilities of sources. Then, we presented a capability object integration algebra that provides the formal basis for composition of capability object. Through computing on capability objects, we can get the mediator capability object. The computing approach supports precise composition of capability objects from multiple diverse sources requiring less manual effort, allows scalable application integration in distributed and heterogeneous resources, helps the end-users get a better insight on which queries to submit to the mediator. Finally, we presented the properties of the algebraic operations that determine whether operands can be rearranged in order to boost performance, which forms the basis for query optimization while composing information from multiple sources.

Acknowledgement

This work is supported by the National Natural Science Foundation of China (Grant No.60172012); the Hunan Provincial Natural Science Foundation of China (Grant No. 03JJY3110).

References

1. Wiederhold, G.: Mediators in the Architecture of Future Information Systems. IEEE Computer Magazine. 25 (1992) 38-49
2. Li, C., Yerneni, R., Vassalos, V., Papakonstantinou, Y., Garcia-Molina, H., Ullman, J., Valiveti, M.: Capability Based Mediation in TSIMMIS. Proceedings of ACM SIGMOD Conference. 27 (1998) 564-566
3. Levy, A.: The Information Manifold Approach to Data Integration. IEEE Intelligent Systems. 13 (1998) 12-16
4. Subrahmanian, V S., Adali, S., Brink, A., Emery, R., Lu, J., Rajput, A., Rogers, T., Ross, R., Ward, C.: Hermes: A Heterogeneous Reasoning and Mediator System. Technical report. University of Maryland (1995)
5. Haas, L., Kossman, D., Wimmers, E., Yang, J.: Optimizing Queries across Diverse Data Sources. VLDB. (1997) 276-285
6. Kapitskaia, O., Tomasic, A., Valduriez, P.: Scaling Heterogeneous Databases and the Design of Disco. INRIA Technical Report. (1997)
7. Morris, K., Ullman, J., Gelder, A.: Design Overview of the NAIL! System. Proceedings on Third International Conference on Logic Programming. London, United Kingdom (1986) 554-568
8. Eckman, B., Lacroix, Z., Raschid, L.: Optimized Seamless Integration of Biomolecular Data. Proceedings of the IEEE 2nd International Symposium on Bioinformatics and Bioengineering Conference. Washington DC (2001) 23-32
9. Lacroix, Z.: Web Data Retrieval and Extraction. Data & Knowledge Engineering. 44 (2003) 347-367
10. Yerneni, R., Li, C., Garcia-Molina, H., Ullman, J.: Computing Capabilities of Mediators. Proceedings of ACM SIGMOD Conference. 28 (1999) 443-454
11. Hakimpour, F., Geppert, A.: Global Schema Generation Using Formal Ontologies. Proceedings of the 21st International Conference on Conceptual Modeling. (2002) 307-321
12. Hakimpour, F., Geppert, A.: Resolving Semantic Heterogeneity in Schema Integration: an Ontology Based Approach. Proceedings of the International Conference on Formal Ontology in Information Systems. USA (2001) 297-308
13. Vidal, M E., Raschid, L.: Websrcmed: A Mediator for Scaling up to Multiple Web Accessible Sources (websources). ftp://www.umiacs.umd.edu/pub/mvidal/websrcmed.ps. (1998)

DartGrid: RDF-Mediated Database Integration and Process Coordination Using Grid as the Platform*

Zhaohui Wu , Huajun Chen, Shuiguang Deng, and Yuxing Mao

College of Computer Science, Zhejiang University, Hangzhou, 310027, China
{wzh, huajunsir, dengsg, maoyx}@zju.edu.cn
http://grid.zju.edu.cn

Abstract. In presence of web, one critical challenge is how to globally publish, seamlessly integrate and transparently locate geographically distributed information resources such as databases, programs, process, etc.. *DartGrid* is an implemented prototype system whose goal is to provide a semantic solution capable of deployment in grid settings. With current implementation of DartGrid, two fundamental resources , data and process, are considered and integrated together to provider semantic-level services. Our approach mainly involve the following notions: a) resource providers are organized as an ontology-based virtual organization; by uniformly defined domain semantics, data and process resources can be both semantically registered to an ontology-based index and seamlessly integrated together to provide high-level service, and, b)we raise the level of interaction with the system to a domain-cognizant model in which data query request and process execution command are specified in the terminology and knowledge of the domain(s), which enable the users to query databases and execute processes at a semantic or knowledge level. We explore the essential and fundamental roles played by semantics, and develop a Semantic Browser with some innovative semantic functionalities such as graphically browsing RDF/OWL ontologies, visually constructing semantic queries and semantically registering the data and process resources.

1 Introduction

In the next evolution step of web, termed semantic web[1], vast amounts of information resources (databases, multimedia, programs, services, processes) will be enriched with uniformed RDF/OWL-based semantics for automatic discovery, seamless communication and dynamic integration. Meanwhile, the Grids[2] is emerging as a building infrastructure that supports coordinated management and sharing of inter-connected hardware and software resources. That also raises the question as to how various web resources can be deployed and integrated in such a

* This work is supported in part by China 973 fundamental research and development project: The research on application of semantic grid on the knowledge sharing and service of Traditional Chinese Medicine; China 211 core project: Network-based Intelligence and Graphics; and Data Grid for Traditional Chinese Medicine, subprogram of the Fundamental Technology and Research Program, China Ministry of Science and Technology.

Y. Zhang et al. (Eds.): APWeb 2005, LNCS 3399, pp. 351 – 363, 2005.

new paradigm where a huge amount of decentralized, independently administrated resources can be involved in the grid-scale sharing cycle.

Built upon Globus toolkit and several semantic web standards, DartGrid is aimed to address above challenges and provide a semantic solution capable of deployment in web-scale for both data integration and process management. With current implementation of DartGrid, we've developed a Database Grid [3] system enabling the user to semantically and dynamically register a database resource to an ontology-based index, query distributed databases using RDF-based queries. We have also developed a DartFlow [4] system enabling the user to easily and conveniently register an applied service at semantic level, doing service discovery and service matchmaking based on semantic concepts. We explore the essential and fundamental roles played by semantics, and develop a Semantic Browser [5] with some innovative semantic functionalities such as graphically browsing RDF/OWL ontologies, visually constructing semantic queries and semantically registering the data and process resources.

This paper is organized as follows: Section 2 introduces on the building architecture of DartGrid, Section 3 elaborates on the implementation of the Semantic Browser, the core components for data management and the process management in DartGrid, Section 4 mentions some related work, and Section 5 gives the summary.

2 Abstract Architecture

Figure 1 displays the layered architecture of DartGrid. Generally, DartGrid can be divided into five layers: resource layer, basic service layer, semantic service layer, collective service layer, and client layer. The main functionality and characteristics of each layer are elaborate on as follows.

2.1 Resource Layer

Two types of resources are considered in DartGrid design; they are data and process resources. These two types of resource are believed to be the most fundamental resources within a virtual organization.

- **Data Resources:** includes database resources, file resource and multimedia resources. With DartGrid, we can access, integrate, and manage these data resources in a semantically meaningful way;
- **Process Resources:** includes e-business processes, e-government processes, e-leaning processes and so on. Process management in DartGrid refers to the management of process lifecycle, including process design, process verification, process execution, process monitoring and process mining.

2.2 Basic Service Layer

At this level, we've built several basic services upon the globus grid services. These services are designed for single data resources and process resources.

– **Basic Services for Data Resources**
  - Database Access Service: supports the typical remote operations on database contents, including retrieval, insertion, deletion of data, and modification of the data schema.
  - Database Information Service: supports the inquiring about the meta information of the database, those meta information include: schema definition, DBMS description, privilege information, statistics information including CPU utilization, available storage space, active session number etc.

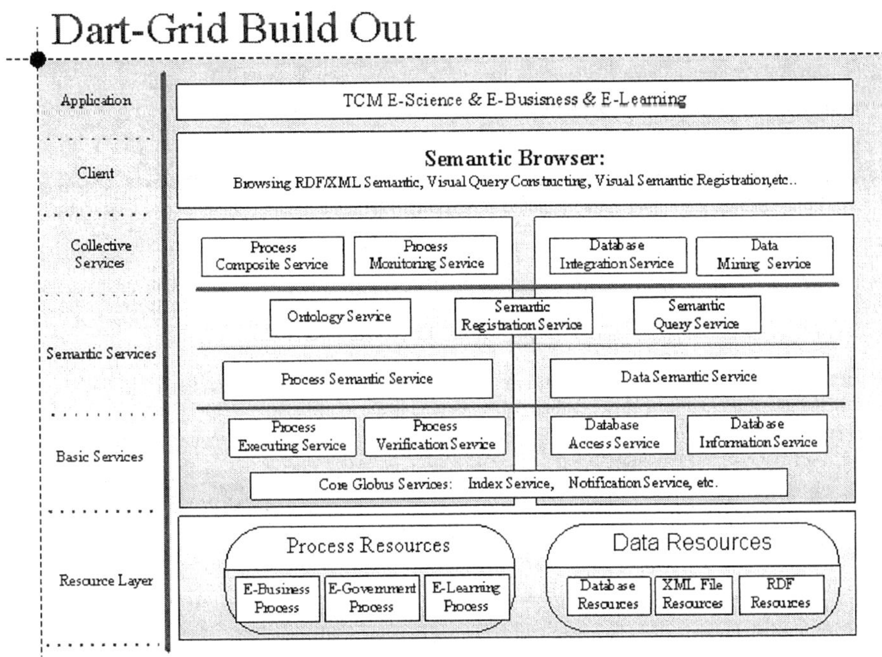

Fig. 1. Abstract Architecture of DartGrid

– **Basic Services for Process Resources**
  - Process Executing Service: supports the basic operations on process execution, such as to start, pause, restart and stop the execution of process instances. It is also responsible for parsing process definitions, generating process instances and invoking outside web services or grid services to execute activities of the processes.
  - Process Verification Service: supports the verification of process definition from both logic aspect and syntax aspect. Before invoking a process execution service to execute a process, the process verification service is usually invoked firstly to ensure the process definition is well-designed.

2.3 Semantic Service Layer

We mainly contribute at this layer. Semantic layer is a layer where ontology-based interaction happens. We argue that in such an open, dynamic, heterogeneous networked environment, semantic is a fundamental issue to achieve the goal of seamless data integration and dynamic process coordination.

- **Data Semantic Service: DSemS**
DSems is used to export source database's relational schema as RDF/OWL semantic description. Typically, local DBA publishes source data semantic of a specific database by DSemS. Others can inquire of this service to fulfill some tasks such as browsing the source semantic, using the source semantic to define semantic queries or do semantic mapping. We've developed a tool to automatically convert relational schema to its corresponding RDF/OWL description.

- **Process Semantic Service: PSemS**
PSemS is used to export processes as OWL-S descriptions. OWL-S is semantic markup language for web service composition. We argue that process composition is the same as service composition in grid environment. This is because all the processes can be implemented based on web service or grid service. Processes are becoming service-oriented. Process designers publish the semantic description of their processes by PSemS. Others can inquire of this service to brows the process semantic, to use the process semantic to define semantic queries or do semantic mapping from the local process description semantic to shared ontologies.

- **Ontology Service: OntoS**
Ontologies could be viewed as mediated schema and are published by OntoS for user to browse RDF/OWL, define semantic queries and do semantic mapping between local data/process semantic to shared ontologies.

- **Semantic Registration Service: SemRS**
Semantic registration establishes the mappings from source data semantic and process semantic to shared ontologies. SemRS maintains the mapping information and provides the service of registering and inquiring about the mapping information. We've developed a visual tool to facilitate the mapping tasks[5].

- **Semantic Query Service: SemQS**
For database resources, SemQS accepts semantic queries, inquires of SemRS to determine which databases are capable of providing the answer, then rewrites the query in terms of relational schema; namely, the semantic queries will be ultimately converted into SQL queries. The results of SQL queries will be wrapped by RDF/OWL semantic again and what SemQS returns is always in RDF/XML format.

For Process Resources, SemQS accepts semantic queries, inquires of SemRS to find out which service compositions or processes are capable of providing the wanted function. The returned result is process definition files both in OWL-S format and its original process definition language format.

2.4 Collective Service Layer

At this level, DartGrid provides some collective services that are built upon the semantic services of lower level.

- **Collective Services for Data Resources:**
  - Data Mining Service: Upon the semantic services, we've developed a data mining service for distributed knowledge discovery and data mining.
  - Database Monitoring Service: This service maintains an entire view of current available database resources and the information about their status. This service also provides some remote control functionalities such as dynamically adding a database resource , remotely start up a database services, and so on.
- **Collective Services for Process Resources:**
  - Process Composite Service: This service is used to compose several component processes into a large scale and multi-functional process. In some cases, more than one component processes can be composed by this service to achieve a larger business goal.
  - Process Monitoring Service: This service maintains an entire view of current running process instances and the information about their status. This service also provides some remote control functionalities such as getting relevant data of process instance, querying the workload of Process Executing Services, retrieving the status of the process instances etc.

2.5 Semantic Browser Client

DartGrid provides end-user with a uniform visual interface, called Semantic Browser [5][6], to interact with various services and manage large-scale resources. Semantic Browser mainly offers the following functionalities:

- Users can browse the RDF/OWL semantics graphically;
- Users can visually construct a semantic query;
- Users can perform semantic mapping from resource schema to RDF/OWL ontologies.

3 Implementation

The principal technical characteristics of DartGrid are highlighted as below:

- We develop it on Globus toolkit, the de facto standard platform to construct Virtual Organization in Grid Computing research area.
- All services are defined according to ggf[†]'s OGSA/WSRF specification;
- We use RDF/OWL[‡] to define the mediated schema, i.e., source data semantic and shared ontologies are both represented by RDF/OWL;

[†] Global Grid Forum: http://www.ggf.org
[‡] RDF: http://www.w3c.org/RDF/

- We use Protégé 2.0 to build the ontologies and HP Jena2 toolkit to store, read, process RDF/OWL data;
- We devise a semantic query language called Q3 [8], and follows the syntax characteristic of N3 [9] , a compact and readable alternative to RDF's XML syntax.

3.1 Semantic Browser

We have implemented a novel semantic-based Grid client, Semantic Browser [5] [6] (see figure 2), which manipulates distributed services and resources at semantic layer and draws out a semantic view [7] for end-users with a series of semantic-based interactions and functionalities. Semantic browser is a lightweight client and accesses the Grid Services of DartGrid to perform high-level tasks.

The Grid entry field, navigator bar and main menu on Semantic Browser, are just similar to those of traditional web browsers; however, there are several new features in Semantic Browser, which distinguish it from others. For various Grid Services, we accordingly develop semantic plug-ins, which are independent and optional functional modules in Semantic Browser. A semantic plug-in usually contains Grid Service stubs and remotely accesses a specific category of Grid Services.

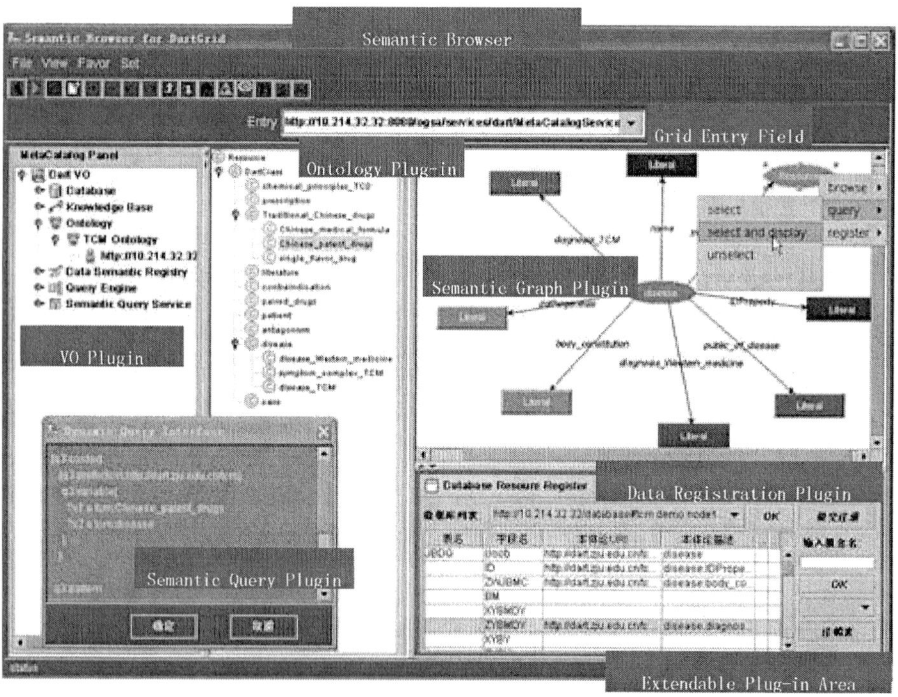

Fig. 2. A screen shot of Semantic Browser

- *VO Plug-in* accesses the core Globus services and dynamically creates an intuitive tree view on various Grid Services delivered in the DartGrid VO. Users can select a needed service simply by clicking a tree node and ask Semantic Browser to access the right service through the GSH. The description about a Grid Service can be viewed by expanding a tree node, which stands for a service instance.

- *Ontology Plug-in* accesses the Ontology Service and provides users with a hierarchical class tree. Users can browse the RDF/OWL semantics graphically just by expanding class tree nodes, which is so called Semantic Browse.
- End-users can use *Data Registration Plug-in* to dynamically register new data resources (DB or KB) with their schema to the ontology during the process of Semantic Browse.
- *Process Registration Plug-in* provides users with the function similar to Data Registration Plug-in for registering Process to be composed into processes dynamically (see Figure 3).
- *Semantic Query Plug-in* generates a dynamic query interface (the floating panel in Figure 2) for users to perform query operations visually [6]. It offers four query operations; they are "select", "select and display", "unselect" and "input constraint", in the querying menu (see Figure 2). When users carry out one of the query operations at a semantic graph node, a corresponding Q3 [8] query string will be automatically constructed in the Q3 query panel. By combining a group of sequential operations, a complete Semantic Query request will be generated. Query results are returned as semantic information and displayed as RDF semantic graphs.

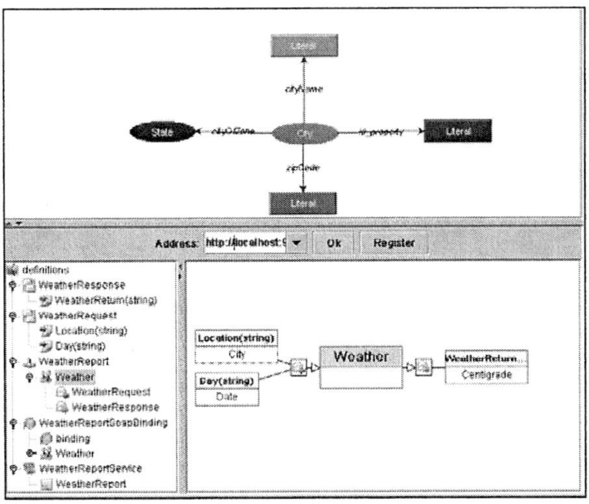

Fig. 3. Process registration plug-in of Semantic Browser

3.2 Data Management in DartGrid

In current implementation of DartGrid, data management here mainly refers to the management of database resources [3]. In the following, we elaborate on two main working processes of DartGid, i.e. semantic registration of a database and semantic query, by two working scenarios from TCM application domain.

3.2.1 Semantic Registration for Database

Typically, a database provider registers his/her database resource to a SemRS for sharing purpose. SemRS maintains a semantic registry functioning as :

1. An ontology-based index for database. It maintains a taxonomy for classifying and enables the automatic discovery of data objects;
2. A global repository maintaining information about the mapping from local database relational schema to shared RDF/OWL ontologies.

The following TCM scenario illustrates how to register a db-resource to SemRS. In this case, a TCM database provider wants to add his compound-medicine (方剂) database resources into the TCM-VO for sharing.

Publish his databases as a Data Service;

Step 1. Visit the data service from Semantic Browser. This will retrieve the data

Step 2. Schema of the databases and display it in the db-registering panel.

Step 3. At the same time, he opens the TCM ontology service and locates the concept compound-medicine in it. Firstly, he maps the concept to the compound-medicine table, and then maps the properties of the concept of compound-medicine to the corresponding column name of the compound-medicine table. This will construct a registration entry in XML format.

Step 4. Before the final submitting, the registration entry will be sent to the ontology service for semantic verification. This will verify that the concepts included in the entry are valid.

3.2.2 Semantic Query Processing in DartGrid

We've design a semantically enriched query language, called Q3[8], for specifying complex queries using RDF/OWL semantic in DartGrid. The following TCM working scenario illustrates how user can semantically query what tcm-compound-medicine could help treat influenza from a TCM database grid.

Step 1. Ontology Browsing: user visits the ontology service of the TCM-VO, and navigates in the TCM-ontologies by semantic browser.

Step 2. Visual Semantic Query Construction: user locates the concept of tcm-compound-medicine(tcm:方剂) in the tcm-ontology; selects its properties he/she want to retrieve, for example, the name property of tcm:方剂 ; by the semantic-link "curedBy" defined in tcm-ontology between the concept *Medicine* and *Disease*, user could easily navigate into the concept *Disease* by just one click; after inputting the "influenza" into the literal slot connected by the arc of "name" property of the concept *Disease*, a whole semantic query is constructed. Simultaneously, the corresponding Q3 query string is displayed in the Q3 display panel. Figure displays the procedure of constructing a semantic query.

Step 3. Semantic Query Parsing: The Q3 query string will be submit to the SemQS for semantic query processing. Firstly, SemQS inquire of SemRS about which databases can provide the answer and the mapping information between the shared ontologies and database schema; secondly, with the mapping information ,SemQS converts the Q3 query to a SQL query plan which will be dispatched to specific databases for data retrieval.

Step 4. Semantic Wrapping: Since the result returned from databases is just a db-record-set without any semantics, the SemQS will convert the record-set into a data stream in RDF/XML format in which all semantics of the concepts such as (方剂) are added. As a result, user could browse the result semantically again.

3.3 Process Management in DartGrid

Process management here refers to the management of serviceflow in DartGrid[4]. It involves the lifecycle management of serviceflow. This includes serviceflow design, serviceflow verification, serviceflow execution, serviceflow monitoring and serviceflow mining. All phases in the lifecycle can be divided into two categories, the build-time phase and the run-time phase.

3.3.1 Process Management in Build-Time Phase

While building a serviceflow, there is some initial work to be done. Component web service or grid service needs to be registered into the service community in DartGrid firstly. Take some for examples, these component services involve weather report service, ticket booking service, stock query service and any other kinds of applied services. To do that, a graphic service registration portal as Figure 3 shows has been implemented for service providers to register their applied services at semantic level. Using this portal, service providers only need to do some mappings between ontology concepts and service elements. Figure 3 shows an example of the registration of a weather report service with two input elements and one output element. Ontology Service Description Language (OSDL)[4] is designed and implemented to store the mapping information between ontology concepts and service elements. Based on the semantic information embodied in those applied services, automatic service discovery and service matchmaking can be easily carried out based on semantic reasoning in DartGrid.

When the service community has been filled with all kinds of applied web service or grid service, process designers can build serviceflows. In order to enhance the flexibility and usability to serviceflow, DartGrid supports both static activity node and dynamic activity node in serviceflow. The former refers to those nodes combined with specific applied services at build-time; and the latter refers to those nodes combined with an OSQL statements. OSQL (Ontology Service Query Language) is designed to specify service query on the service community. Figure 4 illustrates an example of these two kinds of nodes.

After a graphic serviceflow is designed, the corresponding OWL-S file is generated. After that, the Process Verification Service will be invoked to validate the serviceflow from both logic aspect and syntax aspect.

```
<Activity  name=揣 eather Report?
    <Node-Type>Concrete Service Node</Node-Type>
    <WSDL-URL>http://ccnt.zju.edu.cn:8080/axis/Weather.wsdl</WSDL-URL>
    <Operation>WeatherQuery</Operaton>
</Activity>

//-------an OSQL statement for WeatherReport--------
<OSQL name=擮 SQL for a WeatherReport?
    <OntologySpace>
        http://ccnt.zju.edu.cn/Ontology/TouristOntology
    </OntologySpace>
    <InputParts-List>
        <Input-PartCity</Input-Part>
        <Input-PartDate</Input-Part>
    </Input-Parts-List>
    <Output-Parts-List>
        <Output-PartTemperature</Output-Part>
    </Output-Parts-List>
</OSQL>

//------an abstract service node bound with the above OSQL statement --
<Activity  name=揣 eather Report?
    <Node-Type>Abstract Service Node</Node-Type>
    <OSQL-Statement>http://ccnt.zju.edu.cn:8080/axis/Weather.wsdl</OSQL-Statement>
</Activity>
```

Fig. 4. Activity nodes of serviceflow

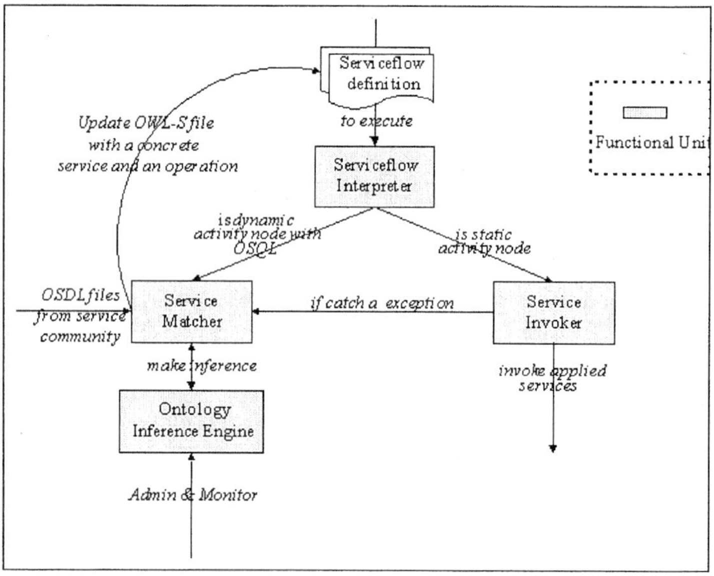

Fig. 5. Process Execution in DartGrid

3.3.2 Process Management in Run-Time Phase

When user invokes the Process Executing Service to start a serviceflow, the serviceflow execution engine (SFEE) will parse the serviceflow definition, generate an instance and start to execute the serviceflow. While in execution, serviceflow execution engine invoke corresponding services for each activity node to perform tasks. The interaction between related components in the Process Execution Service is shown as Figure 5.

- Serviceflow Interpreter is responsible for interpreting serviceflow definition files, generating serviceflow instances and activity instances, making routing decisions.
- Service Matcher is responsible for making service queries in service community in VOs according to OSQL statements, sorting between results, and also responsible for binding the most appropriate concrete service to an activity. It updates the corresponding serviceflow definition according to the binding information.
- Ontology Inference Engine is used to make ontology inference while Service Matcher wants to do service matching. For example, Service Matcher needs Ontology Inference Engine to infer the relationship between two ontology classes. The details about the algorithm used in the inference can be found in [10].
- Service Invoker performs the invoking to concrete services. It sends out the input messages to a target service and gets corresponding responses. It is also responsible for catching and handling exceptions while invoking. If an invoking is overtime before getting any response or an exception is thrown out, the service Invoker will inform the Service Matcher to make a new service binding. After the service matcher returns a new service, it will try to invoke later.

4 Related Work

One of the key goals of DartGrid is to provide a web-scale integration infrastructure for disparate database resources. There are bulks of literatures that are relevant to this issue. The most relevant to our approach, within our investigation scope, are illustrated in Table 1. Among them, OGSA-DAI[§] is a grid-inspired effort aimed to define a standard data service framework ; Piazza[11] focuses more on XML-to-XML

Table 1. Compared to Related Work for Data Management

	Piazza	Edutella	OGSA-DAI	Dart Database Grid
Architecture	P2P	P2P	OGSA / WSRF	OGSA / WSRF
Data Focused	XML Data	RDF Data	Relational Data	Relational Data
Query Language	XQuery	RDF-QEL based on Datalog	SQL	Q3, an OWL-based query language
Mapping Language	a language based on XQuery	RDF-QEL	Not clear	Uses OWL mapping axioms
Registration	Not clear	Provides a registration service	Grid Index Service	Provides a semantic registration service.
Query processing	Query rewriting using XML schema mapping (views)		DQP	Rewriting using mapping axioms, and then using relation schemas.
Security Issues	Not clear	Not clear	GSI	GSI

[§] http://www.ogsadai.org.uk/

mapping including domain mapping and document structure mapping; The focus of Edutella [12] is to provide query and storage services for RDF, but with the ability to use many different underlying stores including database.

The other goal of DartGrid is to management of service-oriented workflow or serviceflow. This issue has allured much attraction both from industry and academy [13-15]. METEOR-S [13] is a project initiated by the Large Scale Distributed Information Systems (LSDIS) Lab at the University of Georgia to build a framework to address the problems of semantic web service description, discovery and composition. SELF-SERV [14] is a platform where web services are declaratively composed and executed in a peer-to-peer environment. A DAML-S based prototype for semi-automatic composition of services is proposed in [15]. The detail comparison between DartGrid and other systems can be found in [4].

5 Summary

The vision of the semantic web and Grid is compelling and will certainly lead to substantial changes in how the web is used. DartGrid is built upon these two innovative technologies, and aimed to provide an integrated solution for both data integration and process management. With current implementation of Dart Database Grid, we have made the following contributions: firstly, we have investigated how semantic web standards and grid technologies can be integrated together to address the challenge of web-scale information sharing; secondly, we have explored the essential and fundamental roles played by semantics in both data integration and process management; thirdly, we've designed and implemented several service for semantic processing including ontology service, semantic registration service, and semantic query service, upon which we have developed a series of grid services enabling database integration, distributed data mining, automatic service discovery and matchmaking, process composition, process execution, process monitoring, etc.

However, web-scale resource management is certainly a big issue, and many big problems remain unsolved. For example, the database grid should deliver nontrivial qualities of service relating to response time, throughput, and performance. With respect to this issue, we plan to employ some grid-inspired scheduling strategies to control and optimize the query processing. We are also planning to develop a complete and integrated management console for database grid and service flow.

References

1. Tim Berners-Lee, James Hendler, Ora Lassila. The Semantic Web. Scientific American May 2001.
2. Ian Foster, Carl Kesselman, and Steven Tuecke. The Anatomy of the Grid: Enabling Scalable Virtual Organizations. Lecture Notes in Computer Science, 2001, Vol. 2150: 1-26.
3. Zhaohui Wu, Huajun Chen, et al. DartGrid: Semantic-based Database Grid. Lecture Notes in Computer Science.v3036, pp. 59 - 66 ,2004.
4. Deng SG, Wu ZH, etc. Management of Serviceflow in a Flexible Way. Proc. of the fifth international conference on web information systems engineering. 2004.

5. Mao YX, Wu ZH, Chen HJ. Semantic Browser: an Intelligent Client for Dart-Grid. LECTURE NOTES IN COMPUTER SCIENCE 3036: 470-473 2004.
6. Mao YX, Wu ZH, Chen HJ. Visual Semantic Query Construction in Dart Database Grid. GRID AND COOPERATIVE COMPUTING, LECTURE NOTES IN COMPUTER SCIENCE 3252: 768-744 2004.
7. Huajun Chen, Zhaohui Wu, Chang Huang, Jiefeng Xu: TCM-Grid: Weaving a Medical Grid for Traditional Chinese Medicine. Lecture Notes in Computer Science, Volume 2659, Jan. 2003.
8. Huajun Chen , Zhaohui Wu and Yuxing Mao: Q3: A Semantic Query Language for Dart Database Grid. Lecture Notes in Computer Science. Volume 3251 / 2004, pp. 372 - 380
9. Tim Berners-Lee & Dan Connolly, Semantic Web Tutorial Using N3: http://www.w3.org/2000/10/swap/doc/ , Tutorial in WWW2003.
10. Lin C, Wu ZH, Deng SG, and Li K. Automatic Service matching and Service Discovery Based on Ontology. LNCS 3252, pp. 99–106, 2004.
11. Alon Y.Halevy, Zachary G. Ives, Peter Mork, Igor Tatarinov: Piazza: Data Management Infrastructure for Semantic Web Applications. Proceeding of The Twelfth International World Wide Web Conference, 2003.
12. Wolfgang Nejdl, Boris Wolf, Changtao Qu, Stefan Decker, Michael Sintek, Ambjor Neve, Mikael Nilsson, Matthias Palmer, Tore Risch. EDUTELLA: a P2P Networking Infrastructure Based on RDF. WWW2002, Honolulu, Hawaii, USA.
13. K. Sivashanmugam, J. A. Miller, A. P. Sheth. Framework for Semantic Web Process composition. International Journal of Electronic Commerce. 2004.
14. B. Benatallah, M.Dumas, Q.Z. Sheng. The SELFSERV Environment for Web Services Composition. IEEE Internet Computing. 17(1):40-48, 2003.
15. E. Sirin, J. Hendler, B. Parsia. Semi-automatic composition of web services using semantic descriptions. Proc. of the International Conference on Enterprise Information Systems, 2002

Collaborative Web Application for Flood Control System of Reservoirs

Chun-tian Cheng[1], K.W. Chau[2], Gang Li[1], and Xiang-Yang Li[1]

[1] Department of Civil Engineering, Dalian University of Technology, Dalian, 116024, P.R. China

[2] Department of Civil and Structural Engineering, Hong Kong Polytechnic University, Hung Hom, Kowloon, Hong Kong

Abstract. Flood control for reservoirs require operations in a dynamic and cooperative manner in order to respond to the changing flood control conditions. There is an increasing emphasis on the collaboration of multiple partners with different backgrounds by sharing data, models and analysis tools in a user-friendly environment, thereby making analysis and evaluation more convenient. One of the key objectives of this paper is to exploit the Web as an infrastructure for running distributed applications that will address reservoir system operation. The web-based flood control system for reservoirs presented in this paper supports the entire decision-making process, including preprocessing the real-data observed data, setting initial conditions, selecting reservoirs constraints, interactively generating alternatives, evaluating alternatives and querying modeling analysis results and recommending alternatives. The system has been implemented in a real flood control management system in China.

1 Introduction

Flood control reservoirs provide an effective means of managing and controlling flood flows by the beneficial reduction of peak runoffs. They result in flood protection afforded at a strategic point on a stream via regulation of reservoir storages. However, a real-time flood control management for reservoirs is very complex due to the following reasons ([1],[3],[5],[11],[18],[19],[20]):

(1) *Multiple participants and multiple purposes.* In general, reservoir flood operation serves for multiple purposes such as flood control, hydropower generation, water supply for irrigation, municipal and industrial use, navigation, water quality improvement, recreation and ecology, and so on. These purposes are often conflicting and require to be balanced. Real-time flood control management usually involves numerous participants such as governments (central, provincial and local), agencies (ministry of water resources, river bureau), interest groups (Water supply companies, hydropower councils), and so on. No single agency is authorized to operate reservoirs as a system for flood control. Flood control decisions are usually a bargaining solution compromised by different parties with conflicting benefits.

Y. Zhang et al. (Eds.): APWeb 2005, LNCS 3399, pp. 364 – 374, 2005.

(2) *Uncertainty and inaccuracies.* These factors include the intrinsic uncertainties in hydrological phenomenon, model assumptions, data or parameter values, result interpretation, as well as objectives in the sense that the values and targets are usually subjective, and the relative emphases on different objectives change with time ([3],[6]). As a result, the group interaction among the affected parties and agencies which are required to contribute ideas and critique the results at each stage are very imperative during reservoir operation simulation.

(3) *Distributed data storages.* Reservoir flood control system involves a large amount of relevant flood management data that is usually maintained by various agencies, each with different levels of complexity ([16]). These data are difficult to be accessed by other agencies before the advent of Internet. Real-time flood control operation requires the latest and dynamic data about the rainfall, level, inflow and outflow distributed among various sites.

(4) *Experience and Knowledge.* Flood control management incorporates the considerations of many political, social, and economic factors that directly affect the severity of floods with respect to damage and available options in limiting this damage. Flood control decisions are difficult to be made based on reservoir operating rule curves that defines the "optimal" strategies because of large numbers of options available for handling a flood situation such as reservoir storages, inflow, social considerations and risk perception and attitudes towards risk. Most decisions depend on the intuitions and experiences of operators after they carefully analyze streamflow data, physical and operational characteristics of the reservoirs, and operational channel capacities for reservoir and downstream points in the system ([14]).

There have been many efforts devoted to establish the decision support system for integrated reservoir flood control since the advent of computers ([8],[9],[10],[11],[12],[13],[15],[17]). However, most of the existing systems, where applications were developed as monolithic entities, are typically single executable program that does not rely on outside resources and cannot access or offer services to other applications in a dynamic and cooperative manner. Especially, they cannot incorporate the experiences and knowledge of experts distributed among the remote areas into the decision process ([2]). This limits rapid decisions where communication and discussions among the multiple agencies are necessary before a final decision will be made. There is an increasing demand for collaborative decision to support geographically dispensed participants in order to allow participants free and fast exchange of data and information. As such, exploiting the Web as the infrastructure for running distributed flood control applications for reservoirs is in time and important.

The objective of this study is to develop a collaborative simulation environment over the Internet and WEB so that participants can share data, models and analysis tools and communicate with each other in different places to server the same flood control problems at the same time. The work presented here is part of a large project to develop a comprehensive management framework that is capable of making flood control decisions for reservoirs by establishing a collaborative platform via Internet and World Wide Web. This paper describes a collaborative environment among multiple agencies and users that acts as an important step before a final decision is made. For the web-based application, J2EE of Sun Microsystems is chosen as the development solutions for the Web-based flood control system, Weblogic 6.0 of BEA as the container provider, and JBuilder 7.0 of Borland as the development tool.

2 Web-Based Flood Control System for Reservoirs

The Web technology is today a convenient and cost-effective tool for information storage, sharing, retrieval and modeling analysis. This new style of application development based on components has become increasingly popular. The proposed web-based application for flood control system of reservoirs is developed to support the

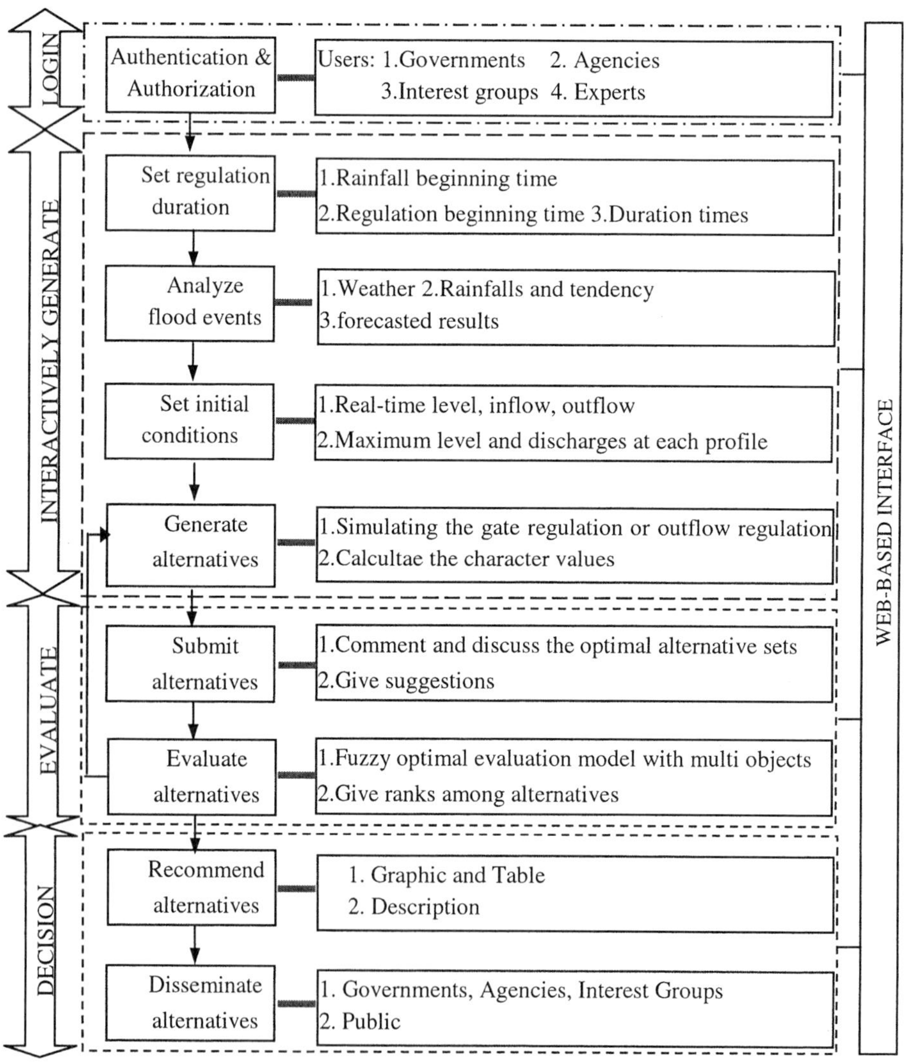

Fig. 1. Conceptural framework of Web-based flood control system for reservoirs

entire decision-making process, including the dissemination of real-time data, the acquisition of flood predictions of reservoirs from different agencies and experts, and the generation of gate control strategies based on modeling analysis. It links with web-enabled database management system in order to determine management responses of different decision-makers and lead to an integrated assessment in a timely manner. It utilizes user-supplied data, user-supplied scenarios, and user-selected manners for on-line and real time web-based decision analysis. Several useful functions are integrated as shown in Fig. 1.

The core of the framework provides dynamic and collaborative interactions among multiple governments, multiple agencies and interests groups as well as experts. Under the web-based form, the agreement discussions are not restricted by geographical location. Access to information about issues being discussed is available from any location that has Web access. The information is also available for the authorized users at any time. More importantly, elite experts from the entire nation will be capable of performing their works and joining in the consultation and discussion with one another to contribute their views. They can freely elicit more detail about issues and problems in hand such as the possibility of rainfalls, the reliability of forecasted models, the special situations, spatial and topological relationships between reservoirs and their downstream flood control points, and so on. The proposed conceptual framework consists of four components: (1) login; (2) interactive generation of alternatives; (3) evaluation of alternatives and (4) recommendation of alternative.

2.1 *Login*

Flood control decisions for reservoirs were often made on an hourly or even shorter timescale based on real-time flood forecasts and hydrologic data readily available. The demand for rapid processing of information and selecting the alternatives of flood control under urgent constraints of reservoirs requires a dynamic operating environment for emergency planners or managers or experts who bear legal responsibility for the protection of life and property. This system is designed to assist specific users who are responsible for handing real-time large-scale flooding events and for simulating essential operational actions. Thus, authentication and authorization are provided in order to effectively manage the cooperative system. The cooperative partners include (1) governments who are responsible for the final decisions under the authority of the specific level flood events, (2) agencies who are responsible for bargaining the conflicts among the interests groups based on legal regulations, (3) interest groups who supply their concerns and opinions, and (4) experts who are invited to join and discuss the important flood events and located usually at remote locations. They will give their suggestions based on their experiences and knowledge at any time and anywhere.

2.2 Interactive Generation of Alternatives

The goal of using web-based flood control system for reservoirs is to determine a set of feasible alternatives for group users. It is vital for group users to understand what is happening and what results they can obtain in terms of the selected flood forecasting conditions and setting of possible flood control strategies. During the development of a modeling system for flood control operation, one of core aspects of the implementation is appropriate user interfaces where flood control decisions are highly dependent onl

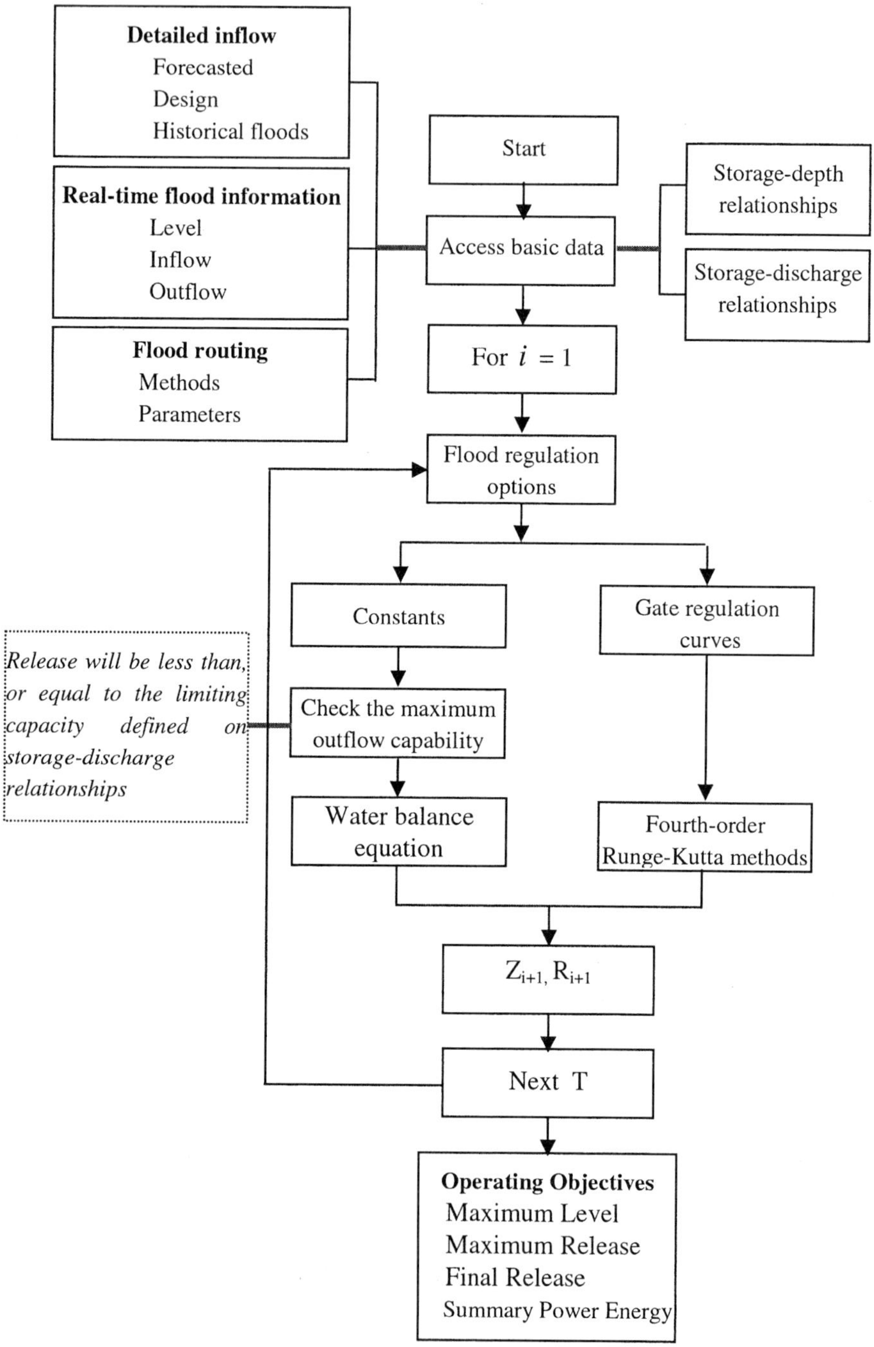

Fig. 2. Basic structure of interactive generation of alternatives

rapid response to the transient change of practical flood conditions and the capability of simulating intuitions and experience of operators. Simple and convenient interfaces for interactive generation of alternatives are greatly desired. A procedure for generation of a flood control operation alternative in an interactive manner is represented in Fig. 2.

Simulating flood control alternatives first require accessing real-time and dynamic information about rainfalls, inflow, and current reservoir system conditions by the related agencies and personals. One obvious advantage over traditional monolithic entities is the capacity of accessing basic information related to flood control decision via web and Internet and therefore a great impact on the flood control management is produced. The system supplies three options of reservoir inflow, (1) forecasted floods based on rainfall-runoff modeling analysis that come from experts and agencies, (2) design floods and (3) historical floods. Each option responds to a scenario and possible emphasis on simulating alternatives. The user can simulate different alternatives by selecting various forecasted flood results which may be from oneself or other, or by picking design floods and historical floods for comparison with specific floods. After an inflow process has been selected, the next step is to set the observed status including the level, inflow and outflow at the current stage. For reservoir system, the observed values are a sheet table that considers the flow routing from upper reservoir to associated downstream ones.

Dynamic simulation of flood operation requires building feasible and efficient interfaces in order to respond to changing flood conditions. The system supplies transient analysis function to respond to the users' input of simulating flood operation strategies when control strategies are changed on screen. The system integrates multiple analysis modules in order to deal with the limiting capacity defined on storage-discharge relationships when a constant operation strategy input is entered, and to calculate the reservoir routing under a spillway gate status. A simulation alternative is constituted of a series of constant or gate regulation or their mixtures ([2]). The mass balance equation for reservoir routing ([7]) is used to determine the change of flood control storage at the reservoir.

When the outflow is represented with a constant outflow, the mass balance equation is

$$S_{t+1} = S_t - (I_t - R_t - EL_t)\Delta t \tag{1}$$

where S_t ,I_t, R_t, EL_t are respectively the reservoir storage, inflow, outflow and evaporation at time t, with unit of S_t in m^3, and units of I_t, R_t, EL_t in m^3/s. EL_t is usually neglected and is only considered for runoff calculation procedure during flooding events. Δt is the time interval between time t and t+1, with unit in s.

When outflow is represented with opening status of the gates, reservoir routing ([7]) is needed. Equation 2 is a simplified formulation developed here.

$$S_{t+1} = S_t + \frac{1}{6}[k_1 + 2(k_2 + k_3) + k_4)] \tag{2}$$

It is noted that the resulting equation is obtained from Taylor's expansion with fourth order (refers to[7]). The coefficients are

$$\begin{aligned}
k_1 &= h_{t+1}[I_{t+1} - R(Z(S_t))] \\
k_2 &= h_{t+1}[I_{t+1} - R(Z(S_t + k_1 / 2))] \\
k_3 &= h_{t+1}[I_{t+1} - R(Z(S_t + k_2 / 2))] \\
k_4 &= h_{t+1}[I_{t+1} - R(Z(S_t + k_3))]
\end{aligned} \tag{3}$$

where k_1, k_2, k_3, k_4 = coefficients, with units in m^3; h_{t+1} = time interval between time $t - 1$ and t; Z() is the functional relationship between storage S_t and level Z_t. When S_t is given, Z_t is obtained by using the interpolation method. R() is the functional relationship between level Z_t and outflow R_t. When Z_t is given, R_t is obtained by using the interpolation method.

For each alternative, equation (1) or equation (3) will be used and repeated at each time interval within the decision interval. Accordingly, some key flood control indexes such as the maximum level of reservoir, the maximum outflow and the maximum discharge of downstream flood control points will be listed and alerted when specific values are reached. The user can adjust a series of combinations at one or more time intervals during the exploration of solutions. After an interactive procedure, the on-line analysis results can be displayed at client side in tables and graphs or their mixtures. Furthermore, they can be saved as a new alternative if the user obtains an acceptable result. All users can implement the application over WEB and Internet. The interactive procedure is active and without any time and spatial constraints. Their results will become part of the simulation results.

2.3 Evaluation of Alternatives

Generally, a large group of users result in complexity, potential conflicts and high transaction costs before a solution can be found that allows a consensus to be reached. It assumes that each user is capable of accurate representation of his or her goals and preferences through these alternatives that are generated by the aforementioned methods. Their results should include their knowledge and experiences. Based on these assumptions and considerations, this system unitizes the fuzzy iteration method of reservoir flood operation developed by Cheng and Chau ([4]) to evaluate the alternatives and to rank them. Two key equations are

$$w_i = \left[\sum_{k=1}^{m} \frac{\sum_{j=1}^{n} \left\{ [u_j (g_i - r_{ij})]^2 + [(1-u_j)(r_{ij} - b_i)]^2 \right\}}{\sum_{j=1}^{n} \left\{ [u_j (g_k - r_{kj})]^2 + [(1-u_j)(r_{kj} - b_k)]^2 \right\}} \right]^{-1} \tag{4}$$

and

$$u_j = \left[1 + \frac{\sum_{i=1}^{m} [w_i (g_i - r_{ij})]^2}{\sum_{i=1}^{m} [w_i (r_{ij} - b_i)]^2} \right]^{-1} \quad (5)$$

where m and n are the total number of objectives and the total number of alternatives. $i=1,2,...,m$; $j=1,2,...,n$. w_i and u_j denote the weight of ith objective and the membership degree of alternative j. g_i and b_i are the ith objective values corresponding to the ideal alternative G and the non-ideal alternative B. Only the fundamental principles of the methodology have been mentioned here. For more details, the reader may refer to Cheng and Chau ([4]). Equations (4) and (5) imply that experience and knowledge of users are duly incorporated in selected alternatives and the rank represents the group opinions. The system integrates the evaluation method for ranking alternatives provided by group users.

2.4 Recommendation of Alternative

Evaluation provides the initial agreement results that concentrate the opinions of associating partners and experts. Criteria assessing alternatives and final results are transparent to the all users. From the assessment results, users can know the emphasis of flood control operation at the current interval based on the weight of each objective and the rank of alternatives determined by equations (4) and (5). For the evaluation results, users can submit their opinions and revise their alternatives with the additional information, such as BBS and memos included in the associated alternatives through the web-based interface. In addition, feedback and appeals routines will be provided to all authorized users to exchange opinions and comments in order to moderate the results of assessment. Final recommended alternative will be a bargaining solution among group users and it is real-timely updated and disseminated.

3 Development Solutions for Web-Based Application on Reservoir Flood Control

3.1 Toolkit

Web-based flood control system for reservoirs is a complicated Web application. Large-scale databases and on-line modeling analysis are its two main characteristics. It is not a difficult task to develop the web-based application not only for a data-oriented but also a task-oriented under the latest information technologies, such as Java servlets, JSP, EJB. The system adopts J2EE as the development tool for this project and ORACLE databases as DBMS. The application system includes three basic components: (1) applets and application clients at the client side, (2) servlets at Web server and (3) EJB at application server. On the front line of the Web site are the Web Servers that act as the presentation layer. Web Servers dynamically format content as

HTML or JSP to be displayed by Web browsers. All the business logic of the system resides in the Application Server tier. Application Servers receive requests from Web Servers, look up information in databases and process the requests. The processed information is then passed back to the Web Servers where it is formatted and displayed. Complicated middleware services such as resource pooling, networking, security, multithreading, clustering and distributed computing are provided in the Application Server. Examples of such Application Server products are BEA's WebLogic, iPlanet's iPlanet Application Server, IBM's WebSphere. All these products can also act as Web Server at the same time. The relational database management system is the repository of the entire system. All input data, historical records, middle calculation procedure and results output are stored in the database.

3.2 Database Tables Design

Flood control management data consist of a variety of data sets, each of which is used for specific purposes. These data can be categorized into: (1) real-time data, such as the observed levels of control points and rainfalls of rain gauges; (2) historical record data; (3) attribute data about the topography, imagery, infrastructure, environment, hydro-meteorology, and so on; and, (4) modeling analysis results. The first three types of data are generally unique and fixed so that no specific design is given. But for the last one, a specific layout is necessary to support the communication on web and Internet.

(a)

AltsProcess
AlrsID
ReservoirID
HourlyTime
Inflow
Outflow
Level
Volume
SpillGates

(b)

AltsAttribs
AlrsID
ReservoirID
FloodsNo
UserName
SelectedInflowAlts
InitialLevel
Objective1
Objective2
Objective3
Objective4
Memo

Fig. 3. The design table of simulation alternative (a) The process of flood control operation alternative; (b)The objective values of flood control operation alternatives

The web-based application involves multiple users, whose modeling analysis is identified during discussion and evaluation. Fig. 3 depicts design tables of flood control operation alternatives. Figure 3(a) represents the simulating process determined by interactive interfaces, including the inflow, outflow, level, volume, and spillway status. Figure 3(b) shows the details of the simulation alternative, including the username, initial level, objective values for this simulation, memos such as judgment and analysis about future floods, decision emphasis explanation, and so on, which supply a discussion and communication outlet with other parties. The output is transferred to the user interface to facilitate queries by users. This output allows users to evaluate the flood control strategies and gather the opinions for flood control operation.

3.3 Interactive Interfaces

Web technology is used by group members as a medium to share data, information, and knowledge. Java applets and JSP are used in this project for developing the client side user interfaces, servicing for data input, setting reservoirs initial conditions, selecting operation constraints, interactively generating alternatives, evaluating alternatives, displaying outflow by tables and graphs, querying modeling analysis results and recommending alternatives. All interfaces in the current project are developed in Chinese version and the version translation and readjustment takes a lot of time. Owing to limited space, interfaces are not included in this paper. Interested readers can refer to the Chinese site (http://202.118.74.192:7001/dalian), where a prototype system is supplied and has been applied to the flood control management system that consists of nine reservoirs in Dalian region, Liaoning Province, China.

4 Conclusions

The flood control operation for reservoirs should be undertaken in a dynamic and cooperative manner in order to respond to the changing flood control conditions. There is an ever-increasing need for the continuous collaboration among geographically distributed agencies and personals with different backgrounds by sharing data, models and analysis tools in a user-friendly environment, thereby making analysis and evaluation more convenient. The web-based flood control system for reservoirs presented in this paper supports the entire decision-making process, including preprocessing the real-data observed data, setting initial conditions, selecting reservoirs constraints, interactively generating alternatives, evaluating alternatives and querying modeling analysis results and recommending alternatives. The system has been implemented in a real flood control management system in China and run within an Internet-based environment, accessible by authorized users without geographical constraints.

Acknowledgments

This research was supported by "The Teaching and Research Award Program for Outstanding Young Teachers in Higher Education Institutions of Ministry of Education, P.R.C" (No.200026), the National Natural Science Foundation of China (No. 50479055), and the Central Research Grant of Hong Kong Polytechnic University (G-T592).

References

1. Chang, L.C., Chang, F.J., 2001. Intelligent control for modeling of real-time reservoir operation. *Hydrological Process*, 15, 1621-1634
2. Cheng, C.T., Chau, K.W., 2004. Flood control management system for reservoirs. *Environmental modeling & Software*, 19(12), 1141-1150
3. Cheng, C.T., Chau, K.W., 2002. Three-person multi-objective conflict decision in reservoir flood control. *European Journal of Operational Research*, 142 (3),625-631
4. Cheng, C.T., Chau, K.W., 2001. Fuzzy iteration methodology for reservoir flood control operation. *Journal of the American Water Resources Association*, 37(5), 1381-1388
5. Cheng, C.T., 1999. Fuzzy optimal model for the flood control system of upper and middle reaches of the Yangtze River. *Hydrological Sciences Journal* 44(4),573~582
6. Dubrovin, T., Jolma, A., Turunen, E., 2002. Fuzzy model for real-time reservoir operation. *Journal of Water Resources Planning and Management*, 128(1), 66-73
7. Fenton, J.D., 1992. Reservoir routing. *Hydrological Sciences Journal*, 37(3), 233~246
8. Ford, D.T, 2001. Flood-warning decision-support system for Sacramento, California. *Journal of Water Resources Planning and Management*, 127(4), 254-260
9. Ford, D.T, Killen, J.R, 1995. Pc-based decision-support system for trinity river, Texas. *Journal of Water Resources Planning and Management*, 121 (5): 375-381
10. Huang, W.C., Yang, F.T., 1999. A handy decision support system for reservoir operation in Taiwan. *Journal of the American Water Resources Association*, 35 (5): 1101-1112
11. Mcmahon, G.F, 1989. Real-time flood management model for highland lake system – discussion. *Journal of Water Resources Planning and Management,* 115 (1),125-127
12. Miller, B.A, Whitlock, A, Hughes, R.C, 1996. Flood management - The TVA experience. *Water International*, 21 (3), 119-130
13. Robillard, P.D., Walter, M.F., Allee D.J., 1979. Computer-based methodology for analysis of nonstructural flood management alternatives. *Water Resources Bulletin,* 15 (5): 1430-1443.
14. Russell, S.O., Campbell, P.F., 1996. Reservoir operating rules with fuzzy programming, *Journal of water resources planning and management*, 122(3), 165-170
15. Shim, K.C., Fontane, D.G., Labadie, J.W., 2002. Spatial decision support system for integrated river basin flood control. *Journal of Water Resources Planning and Management*, 128(3), 190-201
16. Simonovic S.P., 2002. Two new non-structural measures for sustainable management of floods. *Water International*, 27(1), 38-46
17. Unver, O., Mays, L.W., Lansey, K., 1987. Real-time flood management model for highland lake system. *Journal of Water Resources Planning and Management*, 113 (5), 620-638
18. Wurbs R.A., 1993. Reservoir system simulation and optimization models. *Journal of water resources planning and management*, 119(4), 455-472
19. Yeh, W.W.G., 1985. Reservoir management and operations models: a state -of -the -art review. *Water Resources Research*, 21(12): 1797-1818
20. Yakowitz, S., 1982. Dynamic programming application in water resources. *Water Resources Research*, 18(40), 673-696

IWWS: A Reliability-Based WWW Collaborative Recommender System

Haoyang Che[1], Jiacai Zhang[2] , Shengquan Yu [2] , and Jun Gu[3]

[1] Institute of Software, The Chinese Academy of Sciences,
100080, Beijing, China
chehy@hotmail.com

[2] College of Information Science, Beijing Normal University,
100875, Beijing, China

[3] Department of Computer Science,
Science & Technology University of Hong Kong

Abstract. Recommender systems using collaborative filtering are a popular technique for reducing information overload and finding products. In this paper, we present a reliability-based WWW collaborative recommender system IWWS (Intelligent Web Wizard System), mainly aiming to attack so-called "Matchmaker" problem in collaborative filtering. The "Matchmaker" problem stems from false assumptions that users are counted only by their similarity and high similarity means good advisers. In order to find good advisers for every user, we construct a matchmaker's reliability mode based on the algorithm deriving from Hits, and apply it in IWWS. Comparative experimental results also show that IWWS contrastively improves performance.

1 Introduction

The Web is structured as a hypermedia system, in which documents are linked to one another, and users surf from one document to another along hypermedia links that appear relevant to their interests [1]. Browsing the Web is much like visiting a museum, but visitors find it difficult to locate the relevant documents on the Web, which is provided by individuals and institutions scattered throughout the world

The common ways of finding information on the Web is through query-based search engines or designing an effective and efficient classification scheme. Some web sites today build intelligent recommender systems that can automatically recommend the documents according to the interests of each individual visitor [2][3]. There are three prevalent approaches to build recommender systems: Collaborative Filtering (CF), Content-based (CB) recommendation and Content-based Collaborative Filtering (CBCF). Recommender systems help to overcome information overload by providing personalized suggestions based on the history of a user's likes and dislikes [4].

The content-based approach to recommendation has its roots in the information retrieval (IR) community, and employs many of the same techniques [3]. CB methods can uniquely characterize each user, but CF still has some key advantages over them [4][5]. The collaborative approach to recommendation is very different. Instead of

Y. Zhang et al. (Eds.): APWeb 2005, LNCS 3399, pp. 375–380, 2005.

recommending items that are similar to items a user has liked in the past, it recommends items other similar users have liked. Instead of computing the similarity of the items, it computes the similarity of the users. As suggested by Malone, collaborative filtering takes advantage of social interactions between people to create a filter [6]. A further motivation for collaborative filtering comes from the following observation made by Hill [7].

CF exploits similarities between the tastes of different users to recommend (or advise against) items without analysis of the items at all, and recommendations for a user are made solely on the basis of similarities to other users. We can see that CF embodies the idea of Human-Machine Integration. The basic idea of CF is [8]: (1) the system maintains a user-item matrix, and every row of this matrix is a user profile (a record of the user's interests in specific items, positive as well as negative). (2) It compares this profile with other user profiles, and weighs each profile for its degree of similarity with the user's profile. The metric used to determine similarity can change. (3) Finally, it considers a set of the most similar profiles, and uses information contained in them to recommend (or advise against) items to the user.

CF System has been used fairly successfully to build recommender systems in various domains [1][2][8]. However they suffer from some fundamental problems, one of which is the "Matchmaker" problem.

The remainder of the paper is organized as follows. Section 2 introduces the "Matchmaker" problem and we migrate the Hits algorithm [9] from Hyperlink analysis to Collaborative Filtering for measuring user reliability in section 3. In section 4 we describe in detail our implementation method of the CF advisor, and present our informal experimental results in section 5; finally in section 6, we conclude with some future extensions to our work.

2 "Matchmaker" Problem

The "Matchmaker" problem involved in CF put simply is, some users have big correlation efficient based on the user-item matrix, but these users can't recommend authoritative web pages. In other words, these users are not reliable.

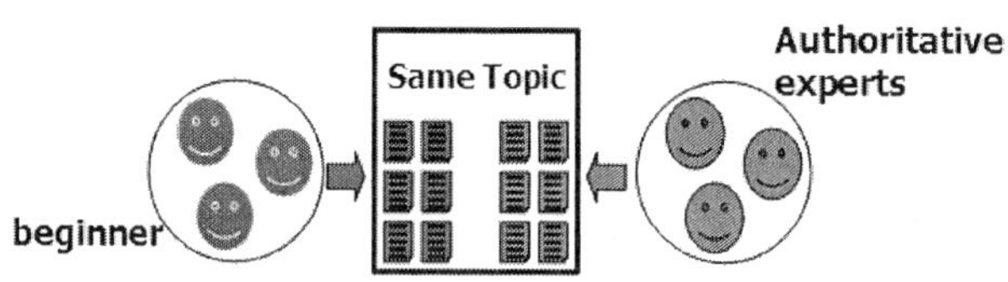

Fig. 1. "Matchmaker" Problem

This problem is a big trouble for those beginners who are new to the field contained in a web site. Beginners maybe visit a lot of introduction web pages, while experts maybe visit those authoritative and professional web pages instead of these introduction web pages. So similar users for a beginner are still beginners, and IWWS recommends web pages based on these similar beginners. In fact, beginners need recommendation from experts, and IWWS should recommend authoritative web pages to users.

Therefore, IWWS need to weigh those reliable advisors. Then the next problem is how IWWS distinguish reliable advisors from trite advisors?

3 Our Method

CF system relies on the fact that people's tastes are not randomly distributed, and performs well when the taste of a user is similar to the taste of his advisors in one group. The advisors are chosen based on their similarity to the active user, the similarity between two users is computed using the Pearson correlation coefficient in IWWS [4].

This issue resembles the distillation of broad search topics within search engines, and researchers have developed a set of algorithmic tools for extracting information from the link structures to address this issue. Hits algorithm [9] formulate of the notion of authority, based on the relationship between a set of relevant authoritative pages and the set of "hub pages" that join them together in the link structure.

We start describing the Hits algorithm with the explanation of hub pages, which have links to multiple relevant authoritative pages. Hubs and authorities exhibit what could be called a mutually reinforcing relationship: a good hub is a page that points to many good authorities; a good authority is a page that is pointed to by many good hubs [9].

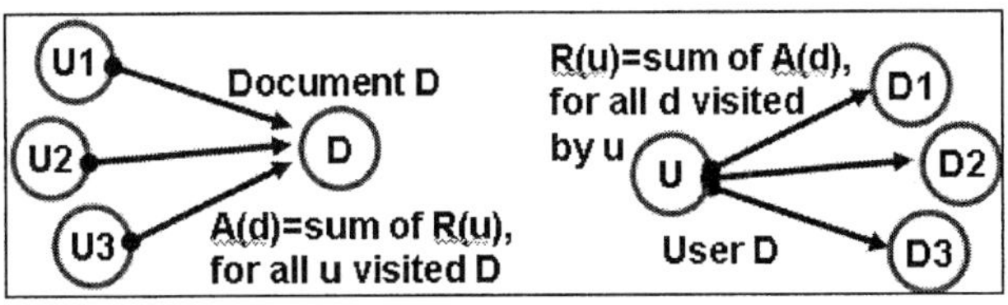

Fig. 2. The Basic Operations

With an eye to select those reliable advisor, we associate a non-negative authority weight A with each document and a non-negative reliability weight R with each advisor, and we maintain the invariant that the weights of each type are normalized so their squares sum to 1. The following iterative algorithm makes use of the relationship between reliabilities and authorities via an iterative algorithm that maintains and updates numerical weights for each user and each document:

$$R^{(a)} = \sum_{b:\ a\ \text{visited}\ b} A^{(b)} \tag{1}$$

$$A^{(b)} = \sum_{a:\ a\ \text{visited}\ b} R^{(a)} \tag{2}$$

Numerically, it's naturally to express the mutually reinforcing relationship between advisors and web documents: if an advisor recommends many good web documents with large A-value, he/she should receive a large R-value; and if document b is recommended by many a good advisor with a large R-value, it should receive a large A-value.

4 Implementation and Experimental Results

We have partly implemented IWWS, a web site wizard tool based on the framework described below. Here we will discuss those implementation-specific issues during our development. The right-top part of the framework performs the kernel activities.

IWWS analyzes the web site log files to construct user-page matrix, from which we can compute the reliability of every user who recommends authoritative pages for active visitors.

CF always uses neighborhood-based algorithms, where a subset of users are chosen based on their similarity to the active user, and a weighted combination of their ratings is used to produce predictions for the active user [4]. In order to weigh those reliable neighborhoods, we compute the predictions as follows:

$$P_i^r = \sum_{k=1}^{30} C^{(k,r)} R^k P_i^k \tag{3}$$

Where Pir is the prediction for the active user r for item i; Rk is the reliability for user k; and C(r,k) is the similarity between users r and k. IWWS uses a neighborhood size of 30 [4].

Our experiment was performed on a Question-and-Answer part of the website, where students asked questions and their teacher would answer these questions. Many students may ask similar questions. If others also asked the same question, he may just browse the answer, or he may submit the question. The website contained 331 questions and their corresponding answers on Oct.29 2002.

A key point during the construction of extended referential user-item matrix of our experiments is detailed access to logs for users' surfing behaviors. Totally, 3,835 users had visited the Q&A part between Oct. 22 2002 and Oct.27 2002, 484 of them had visited 6 or more pages. We construct the initial referential user-item matrix from these 484 users.

The referential users' reliabilities will converge to fixed points if iterate the operations (1) and (2) with an arbitrarily large values. But we just need to sort the referential users, and 20 iterations are sufficient for the order based on referential users' reliability is stable.

The performance measurement method used in IR is somewhat problematic in our experiment. Since our domain is the Web, we can't rely on a standardized collection, and there is no query involved in the use of our system, the concept of relevance is inappropriate [10]. We use a new performance measurement method derived from NDPM (Normalized Distance based Performance Measure) [11]. NDPM differs between ideal recommendation and system's recommendation for the user. Lower number of NDPM denotes that the algorithm provides better performance of recommendation. We focus on the probability of web pages recommended by IWWS containing the page actually visited by active users, who don't know IWWS run on the web server in our experiment. IWWS starts to recommend web page for a user as soon as he visits 4 or more pages.

We compare the web site logs from Oct.28 2002 to Oct.30 2002 with the recommendation of IWWS. IWWS recommends pages for the surfing users 492 time every round, with the recommended pages varying every round. Figure 5 shows the comparative results with pure collaborative recommendation. As the recommended pages increases every time, these approaches would more likely recommend the web pages users visited actually, and the differences among these approaches decrease, i.e. IWWS improves on sort of recommended pages.

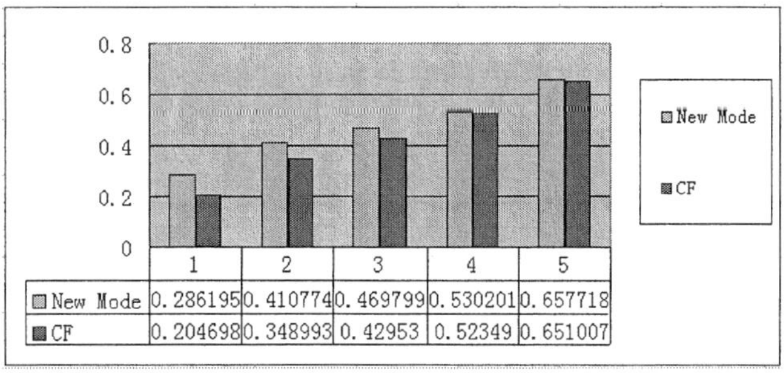

	1	2	3	4	5
New Mode	0.286195	0.410774	0.469799	0.530201	0.657718
CF	0.204698	0.348993	0.42953	0.52349	0.651007

Fig. 3. Comparative experimental results w represents the web pages recommended

5 Conclusions and Future Work

In this paper, we present a novel method to incorporate Hits algorithm into collaborative filtering, which significantly improves the prediction quality of recommender systems. The comparative results also exhibits that IWWS sorts the web pages recommended for users out considerately.

This paper opens the door to a wide range of future work. Here, we list two of our ongoing work. First, we are creating a hybrid recommender system by combining both collaborative and content-based filtering. Both pure CF or CB approaches are special cases of hybrid CBCF scheme. If the content analysis component returns just a unique identifier rather than extracting any features, it will degenerate into pure collaborative recommendation; if there is only a single user, it will degenerate into pure content-based recommendation [3].

Second, we are looking for a way to rearrange the organization of web sites, thus IWWS will act as an effective device for users to surf from one page to another without returning to the directory every time. This domain needs further research both in theory and technology.

Acknowledgement

This research is partly supported by the National Grand Fundamental Research 973 Program of China under Grant No.G1998030410.

References

1. Resnick,P, Iacovou,N, Sushak,M, Bergstrom,P and Reidl,J. GroupLens: An open architecture for collaborative filtering of netnews. Proceedings of 1994 Computer Supported Coorperative Work Conference, New York:ACM, 1994
2. Prem Melville and Raymond J.Mooney and Ramandass Nagarajan, Content-boosted Collaborative Filtering for Improved Recommendations, Proceedings of the Eighteenth National Conference on Artificial Intelligence (AAAI-2002), pp.187-192, Edmonton, Canada, July 2002
3. Marko Balabanovic and Yoav Shoham. Fab:Content-based, Collaborative recommendation. Communications of the ACM, 40(3):66-72, March 1997
4. Herlocker,J, Konstan,J, Borchers,A. and Riedl,J. An algorithmic framework for performing collaborative filtering, In SIGIR'99: Proceedings of the 22nd Annual International ACM SIGIR Conference on Research and Development in Information Retrieval, 230-237, 1999
5. http://www-2.cs.cmu.edu/~dmaltz/main-report/node9.html
6. Malone, T. W.; Grant, K.R.; Turback, F.A.; ``The Information Lens: An Intelligent system for Information Sharing in Organizations," *Human Factors in Computing Systems, CHI'86 Conference Proceedings (Boston, MA),* ACM: New York, 1986, pp. 1-8
7. Hill, William, Hollan, James, Wrobleski, Dave, McCandless, Tim. "Edit Wear and Read Wear," Human factors in computing systems: Striking a balance. Proceedings of the 9th annual conference. SIGCHI '92 Proceedings (Monterey, CA), Addison-Wesley, 1992, pp. 3-9
8. Upendra Shardanand and Pettie Maes. Social information filtering: Algorithms for automating "word of mouth". Proceedings of CHI'95-Human Factors in Computing Systems, 210-217, Denver, CO, USA, May 1995
9. Jon M.Kleinberg. Authoritative Sources in a Hyperlinked Environment. Proceedings of the ACM-SIAM Symposium on Discrete Algorithms, 1998
10. Balabanovic, M. An adaptive web page recommendation service. In Proceedings of the 1st International Conference on Autonomous Agents (Marina del Rey, Calif., Feb.1997)
11. Y. Yao. Measuring retrieval effectiveness based on user preference of documents. J. of the American Society for Information Science, 46(2):133-145,1995

Transforming Non-covering Dimensions in OLAP*

Zehai Li, Jigui Sun, Jun Zhao, and Haihong Yu

College of Computer Science and Technology, Jilin University,
130012 Changchun, China
lizh@email.jlu.edu.cn,
{jgsun,zhli,yuhh}@jlu.edu.cn

Abstract. OLAP (On-Line Analytical Processing) systems are used to support decision-making processes by providing agile analytical operations on large amounts of data. Usually, the operations require dimensions to be onto and covering; however, in real-world applications, many dimensions fail to meet the requirements, which can be non-covering, non-onto or self-into. In this paper, we will mainly concern the transforming of non-covering dimensions; we first define four different types of non-covering dimensions, and then devise several algorithms to transform them into covering ones respectively. The algorithms are of low computational complexity and can provide full support for transforming various non-covering dimensions into covering ones correctly.

1 Introduction

According to OLAP council, a dimension is defined as "a structural attribute of a cube that is a list of members, all of which are of a similar type in the user's perception of the data."[1], and a dimension usually includes one or more hierarchies [2]. OLAP systems are used to support decision-making processes by providing analytical operations on large amounts of data. Since dimensions are formally defined based on the everywhere-defined mapping between two levels in previous multidimensional models [4,5,6]; nowadays, many commercial OLAP systems require dimensions to be onto and covering so as to ensure proper pre-aggregations and queries associated with dimension hierarchies. However, in real-world applications, many dimensions fail to meet the requirements and they could be self-into, non-onto or non-covering [3].

There are two ways to deal with these "irregular" dimensions. One way is to provide an effective multidimensional model to support these dimensions, and also the cubes with irregular dimensions and the OLAP operations on them. The models can be found in [7,8,9]. However, they are very complex and great efforts are needed to develop practical OLAP systems based on them. Another way is to devise some algorithms to transform irregular dimensions into well-formed ones that can be used in most multidimensional models. Moreover, this way seems more practical than the former. Therefore, we will mainly concern the transforming algorithms for irregular dimensions in this paper, especially those for non-covering dimensions.

---

* Supported by National Natural Science Foundation of China (No. 60073039,60273080).

Y. Zhang et al. (Eds.): APWeb 2005, LNCS 3399, pp. 381 – 393, 2005.

Recently, some research work [3,10,11] has been done to solve the problem. In [3], Pedersen proposed several algorithms to transform irregular dimensions into well-formed structures by adding some marked elements to the domains of certain levels. However, the MakeCovering algorithm for transforming non-covering dimensions is too simple. If we use the algorithm to transform every non-covering dimension in the same way, then errors may occur in the resulting dimension; for instance, the transformed dimensions may become confusing to the experts, or incorrect aggregation results may be gotten. We will discuss them in the following sections. In [10], Tapio proposed a new formal form for OLAP cube design, and some decomposition algorithms to produce normalized OLAP cube schemata, and then it could control the structural sparsity resulting from inter-dimensional functional dependencies. However, the normalization algorithms are mainly used to control the sparsity that is mostly caused by non-normalized relationships between dimensions and facts; moreover, Tapio could not concern the possible non-normalization caused by the complex inner structure of a dimension; therefore, there are no further discussions in their work about the normalization of irregular dimensions. In [11], Jensen proposed a data model to accommodate spatial values that exhibit partial containment relationships in dimensions, especially in some spatial dimensions. In addition, he offered some algorithms for transforming the dimension hierarchies with partial containment relationships into simple hierarchies. However, these algorithms are merely the extended versions of those in [3] so as to deal with the partial containment relationships between the elements that need to be duplicated or moved. There are no further extensions to consider the four cases mentioned in this paper. Therefore, like those in [3], these algorithms would cause the same problems discussed above when transforming irregular dimensions.

In this paper, based on the dimension model in our previous work [9], we first present the formal definitions of onto, non-onto, covering, non-covering, self-onto and self-into dimensions; and it is the first time that self-into dimensions are mentioned. After carefully analyzing of the problems related with non-covering dimensions we have met in real-world applications, we define four types of non-covering dimensions that need to be transformed in different ways. Furthermore, we propose several algorithms to transform the four types of non-covering dimensions respectively. The algorithms are more powerful in dealing with irregular dimensions than those in previous work [3,10,11]. Moreover, they are of low computational complexity and can certainly provide full support for transforming the four types of non-covering dimensions into covering ones correctly.

The rest of the paper is organized as follows. Several irregular dimensions are formally defined in section 2. Section 3 mainly defines four types of non-covering dimensions. In section 4, we propose some algorithms for transforming the four types of non-covering dimensions. Section 5 presents case study and defines a calling priority order for the algorithms we proposed. Finally, section 6 concludes the paper.

2 Basic Concepts

In [9], we proposed a new multidimensional model, which can support both standard dimensions and irregular dimensions. In this section, based on the dimension model, we will present the formal definitions of onto, covering, self-onto, non-onto, non-covering and self-into dimensions. Especially, self-into dimensions

First, we review some basic concepts stated in [9]. Given a dimension d=(D, $\prec'$), where D={l_1, ...l_k, l_{k+1}} is the set of levels, the partial order $\prec'$ is called the aggregation relationship (AR) on D. The domain of d is defined as: dom(d)= $\bigcup_{1\le i\le k+1}$ dom(l_i), and the partial order $\le$ is called the element aggregation relationship (EAR) on dom(d). Let h=(H, $\prec'$) be a hierarchy of dimension d, where H a totally ordered subset of D, Parent(l_i) denote the set of all parent levels of l_i, and Child(l_i) denote the set of all child levels of l_i.

As stated in [3], OLAP systems use a technique known as *pre-aggregation* to improve query performance. Moreover, summarizability is necessary for the use of pre-aggregated results. With summarizability, we can organize the pre-aggregated results in a reasonable dependency order, so that we can effectively perform analyzing operations, like drill-down and roll-up, on them. Furthermore, in most multidimensional models, summarizability needs the mappings between levels to be covering, onto and self-onto. These concepts and their counter-parts are given below.

Definition 1. Given a hierarchy h of dimension d=(D, $\prec'$), let l_1, l_2 be two levels of h such that $l_1 \prec' l_2$; we say that the mapping from l_1 to l_2 is *onto* iff for each $e_2 \in$ dom(l_2), there is at least one element $e_1 \in$ dom(l_1) such that $e_1 \le e_2$. Otherwise, it is *non-onto*.

Definition 2. Given a hierarchy h of dimension d=(D, $\prec'$), let l_1, l_2, l_3 be three levels of h such that $l_1 \prec' l_2$ and $l_2 \prec' l_3$; we say that the mapping from l_2 to l_3 is *covering* w.r.t. l_1 iff for any elements $e_1 \in$ dom(l_1), $e_3 \in$ dom(l_3), if $e_1 \le e_3$ then there is an element $e_2 \in$ dom(l_2) such that $e_1 \le e_2$ and $e_2 \le e_3$. Otherwise, it is *non-covering* w.r.t. l_1.

Definition 3. Given a hierarchy h of dimension d=(D, $\prec'$), let l_1 be a level of h; for each element $a \in$ dom(l_1), if there is no element $b \in$ dom(l_1)-{a} such that $a \le b$ or $b \le a$, then we say that h is *self-onto* in level l_1; otherwise, h is *self-into* in l_1.

Given a dimension d=(D, $\prec'$) and three levels: l_1, l_2 and l_3 such that d is self-into in level l_2 and $l_1 \prec' l_2$, $l_2 \prec' l_3$, let b_1, b_2 are two elements of dom(l_2) such that $b_1 \neq b_2$ and $b_1 \le b_2$. Then there may be three different cases for the self-into mapping: (1) b_1 has no children in dom(l_1) and no direct parents in dom(l_3), (2) b_1 has some children in dom(l_1) but has no direct parents in dom(l_3), (3) there is an element $c_1 \in$ dom(l_3) such that $b_1 \le c_1$. The three cases lead to *three types of self-into dimensions*. In addition, for the third case, $b_1 \le c_1$ must be concluded from $b_1 \le b_2$ and $b_2 \le c_1$ according to the specification of the dimension model in [9]. In the three types, the first one is the simplest, and other two types are much complex when being transformed into self-onto mappings. Since we mainly concern the transforming of non-covering dimensions here, *we assume that the self-into mappings in this paper are of the first type.*

3 Four Types of Non-covering Dimensions

This section will present four different types of non-covering dimensions, along with some figures to illustrate the differences in their structures.

According to our experiences from real-world applications, we find that there are four different types of non-covering dimensions, which need to be transformed into covering ones in different ways. We will mainly discuss these non-covering dimensions here, and call them type A, B, C and D respectively; we distinguish them mainly depending on the different cases of the mapping between two adjacent levels.

Fig.1 shows the schema structure of a non-covering dimension, in which the mapping from l_2 to l_3 is non-covering w.r.t. l_1. We will define the four types according to the different cases of the mapping between l_2 and l_3.

Type A. If the non-covering mapping between l_2 and l_3 is also everywhere defined and onto, then the dimension is of type A. For instance, the depot dimension in fig. 2 is of type A because "Shunyi depot" in dom(GrainDepot) directly belongs to "Central Grain Company" in dom(ParentCompany) without passing by any element in dom(SubCompany), and each sub-company belongs to "Central Grain Company".

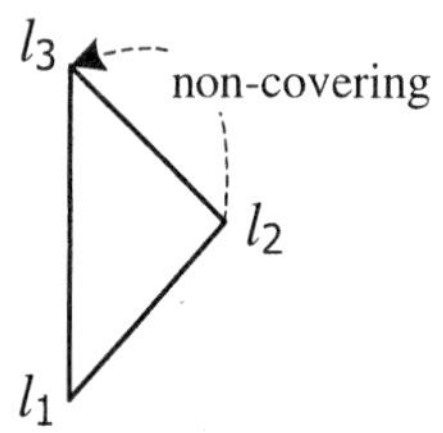

Fig. 1. Non-covering dimension

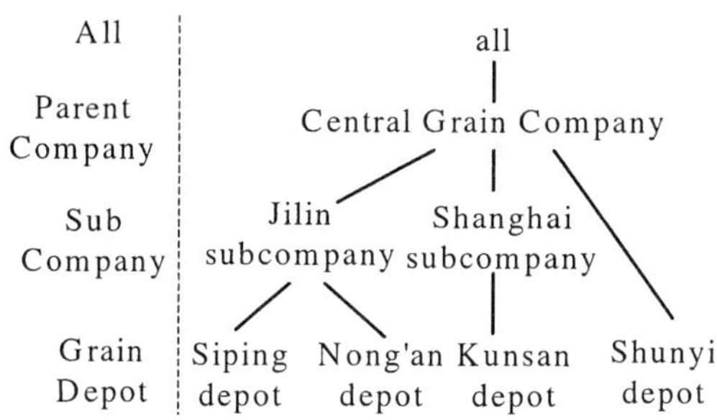

Fig. 2. Partial structure depot dimension

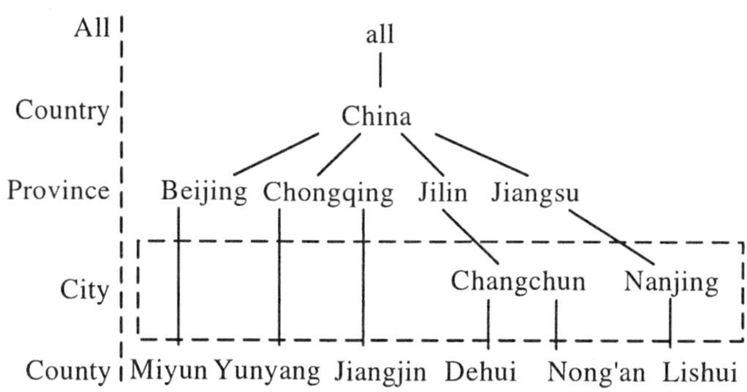

Fig. 3. Partial structure of location dimension

Type B. If the non-covering mapping between l_2 and l_3 is also non-onto and everywhere defined, then the dimension is of type B. This means that there is at least one element in dom(l_3), which has direct children in dom(l_1) and has no children in dom(l_2). For example, the location dimension in fig.3 is of type B, because "Beijing" in dom(Province) has no children in dom(City), while it has a child "Miyun" in dom(County).

Type C. If the non-covering mapping is also non-onto and not everywhere defined (i.e. partial), then the dimension is of type C. There are two cases for the partial mapping: (1) there may be another level l_4 satisfying that the mapping from l_3 to l_4 is non-covering w.r.t l_2, (2) the dimension may be self into in l_3. The two cases mean that there is at least one element in dom(l_3), which has no children in dom(l_2) but has some in dom(l_1); and there is at least one element in dom(l_2), which has no parent in dom(l_3) but has one in dom(l_4). Furthermore, we treat the second case as *type D*.

4 Transforming Algorithms

In this section, we will devise some algorithms to transform irregular dimensions, especially non-covering dimensions, into well-formed dimensions that can be used in most multidimensional models. Moreover, these algorithms are much powerful in dealing with various non-covering dimensions by overcoming the deficiencies of the algorithms proposed by Pedersen in [3].

As stated in section 1, the MakeCovering algorithm proposed by Pedersen is too simple. If we use the same algorithm to transform the four types of non-covering dimensions, then errors might occur in the resulting dimensions. For example, the depot dimension in fig.2 is a non-covering dimension of type A, and the location dimension in fig. 3 is of type B. Now, we execute the MakeCovering algorithm on them respectively. For the location dimension, "Beijing", "Chongqing" are duplicated and added to dom(County) after being marked with "L2-", and the resulting dimension is still acceptable. Whereas, for the depot dimension, "Central Grain Company" is added to dom(SubCompany) after being marked with "L1-", and then the transformed depot dimension becomes confusing to analyzers because they think that sub-companies cannot be ranked together and compared with their parent company. Furthermore, this transformation can lead to error aggregations, e.g., the element "Central Grain Company" will be aggregated twice with different resulting values. However, if only "Shunyi depot" is duplicated and added to dom(SubCompany) after being marked with "L3-", then the resulting dimension will become acceptable. Therefore, we should employ different algorithms to transform the four types of non-covering dimensions respectively.

From the discussions above, we could know that the MakeCovering algorithm is only suitable to transform the non-covering dimensions of type B. Moreover, algorithm MakeCovering could only deal with the dimensions in which the non-covering mappings are between adjacent levels; thus, we have to improve the algorithm to support those dimensions of type B, in which non-covering mappings are between non-adjacent levels.

The MakeCoveringB algorithm is the improved version of MakeCovering, and it is shown in fig.4. In the algorithm, D is the dimension to be transformed, l_x is a child level, l_m is a parent level, l_n is an ancestor level of l_m and it is still a parent level of l_x. The algorithm works as follows. Given the arguments: dimension D and level l_x (initially the level *Atomic* [9]), for each parent level l_m of l_x, it further looks for another parent level l_n that is "bigger" than l_m. If l_n exists and the mapping from l_m to l_n is non-covering w.r.t. l_x, then those elements in dom(l_n) which cause the non-covering mapping are found out and put in the set L in lines 6 and 7. In line 8, algorithm AdjustMappingB is called with the arguments: D, l_x, l_n and L to adjust the domains of the levels between l_x and l_n along the corresponding mappings with the elements in L. However, the elements in L cannot be copied to the domains of other levels without being marked. Here we follow the marking method in [3], and use the prefix "Li-" to mark the elements, where "i" denotes the rank of the level in the dimension hierarchy.

After AdjustMappingB is executed, the marked elements in dom(l_m) are linked to those elements in dom(l_x) that are originally related with the original elements in dom(l_n); and then the originally linked pairs in F are removed from the mapping σ_{xn} in line 11. Line 12 is the recursive call of the algorithm to fix each non-covering mapping higher up in the dimension D.

```
(1)  Procedure MakeCoveringB(D,l_x)
(2)  for each l_m∈Parent(l_x) do
(3)   begin
(4)     for each l_n∈D where l_m≺'l_n and l_n∈Parent(l_x) do
(5)       begin
(6)         F=σ_xn−σ_xm·σ_mn
(7)         L={n|(x,n)∈F}
(8)         AdjustMappingB(D,l_x,l_n,L)
(9)         σ_xm =σ_xm∪{(x,Mark(n))|(x,n)∈F}
(10)        σ_xn=σ_xn−F
(11)       end
(12)    MakeCoveringB(D, l_m)
(13) end
```

Fig. 4. Algorithm MakeCoveringB

```
Procedure AdjustMappingB(D,l_p,l_top,L)
for each l_q in Parent(l_p) where l_q≺'l_top do
 begin
   if l_q= l_top then
     σ_pq=σ_pq∪{(Mark(n),n)|for any n∈L}
   else
     begin
       dom(l_q)=dom(l_q)∪{Mark(n)|n∈L}
       σ_pq=σ_pq∪{(Mark(n),Mark(n))| for any n∈L}
     end
   AdjustMappingB(D,l_q,l_top,L)
 end
```

Fig. 5. Algorithm AdjustMappingB

Algorithm AdjustMappingB is shown in fig.5, where L contains the elements to be duplicated, l_p is the least level and l_{top} is the greatest level to be adjusted. For each parent level l_q of l_p that is "smaller" than or equal to l_{top}, if l_q=l_{top} then we need only to link every marked element "Mark(n)" in dom(l_p) to the corresponding element "n" in dom(l_q); otherwise, the marked elements are first added to dom(l_q), and then they are linked to the corresponding marked elements in dom(l_p). Line 11 contains a recursive call to the algorithm on l_q to process every level between l_p and l_{top}.

In the two algorithms above, operations on sets are standard relational algebra operators. The worst case of multiplication is $o(n^2)$, where n is the maximum size of the mappings between any pair of levels. Given two mappings σ_{xy} and σ_{yz}, if their elements are ordered in the same sequence by the elements in dom(y), then the complexity becomes $o(n \log n)$. Similarly, the subtraction and the union between two sets can also be evaluated in time $o(n \log n)$.

Since the number of elements that need to be marked is much fewer than n, we suppose that the operation Mark() can be performed in time $o(1)$. Moreover, MakeCoveringB is recursively called at most once for each mapping between any two levels. Therefore, if we leave alone self-mappings, then the number of recursive calls would be m(m-1)/2; otherwise, it is m(m+1)/2, where m is the number of levels. In algorithm AdjustMappingB, the maximum number of the recursive calls is m(m-1)/2, but normally it is m. Then the worst-case complexity of AdjustMappingB is $o(m^2 n \log n)$, and the normal case is $o(mn \log n)$. Therefore, for MakeCoveringB, the worst case is $o(m^4 n \log n)$ and the normal case is $o(m^3 n \log n)$.

The correctness argument for algorithm MakeCoveringB has two aspects: (1) each mapping in the resulting dimension should be covering upon termination, (2) the algorithm should only perform the transformations that are semantically correct, i.e., we should get the same results when computing aggregated values with the new dimension as with the old one. The correctness follows from Theorem 1, 2 and 3.

Theorem 1. Algorithm AdjustMappingB terminates and the original aggregation semantics will not be changed in the resulting dimension.

Proof: By induction in the height of the dimension. (1) If the height is 1, then the algorithm does nothing to the dimension and the theorem is obviously true. (2) Suppose the theorem holds true for the dimensions with height n. (3) Consider the dimensions with height n+1. For termination, l_p has finite number of parent levels and all operations in the loop but the recursive call will terminate; the recursive call on l_q will perform the algorithm on a sub-dimension with height n, then according to the induction hypothesis, the algorithm must terminate. As to the aggregation semantics, in the loop, after the marked elements are added to dom(l_q), they are linked to the corresponding elements in dom(l_p), and other links are kept untouched; this means that the original aggregation relationships among elements are inherited by the resulting dimension. Moreover, the recursive call will perform the algorithm on a sub-dimension with height n. Therefore, the statement holds true for the transformations by the induction hypothesis.

Theorem 2. Algorithm MakeCoveringB terminates and the resulting dimension is covering.

Proof: By induction in the height of the dimension (similar to theorem 1, omitted).

Theorem 3. Let $d_1=(D_1, \prec'_1)$ be the resulting dimension after executing MakeCoveringB on dimension $d=(D, \prec')$, $\leq_1$ be the EAR of d_1, and $\leq$ be the EAR of d; then the following holds true: for any $e_1, e_2 \in D$, $e_1 \leq_1 e_2 \Leftrightarrow e_1 \leq e_2$.

Proof: By induction in the height of the dimension (similar to theorem 1, omitted).

Theorem 3 ensures that the aggregation paths in dimension d are kept unchanged in the resulting dimension d_1. Therefore, for each aggregation query Q on d, an aggregation query Q_1 on d_1 can be found, such that $Q \subseteq Q_1$.

For the non-covering dimensions of type A, we provide another algorithm named MakeCoveringA shown in fig.6, which works as follows. Given the arguments: dimension D and level l_x (initially the level *Atomic*), for each parent level l_m of l_x, it further looks for another parent level l_n that is "bigger" than l_m. If the mapping from l_m to l_n is non-covering w.r.t l_x, then the elements in dom(l_x) which cause the non-covering mapping are found out and put into the set L in lines 6 and 7. Line 8 calls algorithm AdjustMappingA by passing the arguments: D, l_x, l_n and F.

AdjustMappingA is shown in fig.7. In the algorithm, if l_q is not equal to l_{top}, then AdjustMappingA adds the elements, which are extracted from F and belong to dom(l_x), to the domain of the level l_q between l_x and l_n; moreover, they are linked to the corresponding elements in the domain of the child level l_p. Otherwise, the pairs in F are marked and added to the mapping σ_{pq} to establish the links between the marked elements in dom(l_p) and the corresponding marked elements in dom(l_q).

After AdjustMappingA is executed, the marked elements in dom(l_m) are linked to those original elements in dom(l_x), and then the originally linked pairs in F are removed from the mapping σ_{xn} in line 11. In line 12, the algorithm is called recursively to fix each non-covering mapping higher up in the dimension D.

```
(1)  Procedure MakeCoveringA(D,l_x)
(2)  for each l_m∈Parent(l_x) do
(3)     begin
(4)      for each l_n∈D where l_m≺'l_n and l_n∈ Parent(l_x) do
(5)        begin
(6)           F=σ_xn-σ_m·σ_mn
(7)           L={x| (x,n)∈ F}
(8)           AdjustMappingA(D, l_x, l_n,F)
(9)           σ_xm =σ_xm∪{(x,Mark(x))|for every x∈ L}
(10)          σ_xn=σ_xn-F
(11)       end
(12)     MakeCoveringA(D, l_m)
(13)    end
```

Fig. 6. Algorithm MakeCoveringA

Following previous reasoning and analyses, the worst-case complexity of algorithm AdjustMappingA is $o(m^2 n \log n)$, and the normal case is $o(mn \log n)$, where n is the maximum size of the mappings between any pair of levels and m is the number of levels. For algorithm MakeCoveringA, the worst-case complexity is $O(m^4 n \log n)$ and the normal case (also the usual case) is $O(m^3 n \log n)$.

The theorems related with the correctness of algorithms AdjustMappingA and MakeCoveringA are given below. Moreover, the proofs are similar to that of theorems 1 and we omit them here.

```
Procedure AdjustMappingA(D,l_p,l_top,F)
L={x|(x,n)∈F}
for each l_q in Parent(l_p) where l_q≺'l_top do
  begin
   if l_q= l_top then
      σ_pq=σ_pq∪{(Mark(x), n)|for every (x,n)∈F}
   else
      begin
        dom(l_q)=dom(l_q) ∪ {Mark(x)|x∈L}
        σ_pq=σ_pq∪{(Mark(x),Mark(x))| for every x∈L}
      end
   AdjustMappingA(D,l_q,l_top,F)
  end
```

Fig. 7. Algorithm AdjustMappingA

Theorem 4. Algorithm AdjustMappingA terminates and the original aggregation semantics will not be changed in the resulting dimension.

Theorem 5. Algorithm MakeCoveringA terminates and the resulting dimension is covering.

Theorem 6. Let $d_1=(D_1, \prec'_1)$ be the resulting dimension after executing MakeCoveringA on dimension $d=(D, \prec')$, $\leq_1$ be the EAR of d_1, and $\leq$ be the EAR of d; then the following holds true: for any $e_1, e_2 \in D$, $e_1 \leq_1 e_2 \Leftrightarrow e_1 \leq e_2$.

For the non-covering dimension of type C stated in previous section, we could first call algorithm MakeCoveringA to transform the non-covering mapping between l_2 and l_3. If the non-covering mapping between l_3 and l_4 is also non-onto, then the dimension can be transformed into covering one just by MakeCoveringA; otherwise, if the non-covering mapping between l_3 and l_4 is onto, then the MakeCoveringB algorithm should also be called.

For a dimension of type D, we should call algorithms MakeSelfOnto, MakeOnto [3] and MakeCoveringA or MakeCoveringB to transform it into a covering one, but the calling sequence is pending; we will discuss this problem in the next section.

The MakeSelfOnto algorithm is shown in fig.8, and it works as follows. From line 4 to line 7, the elements in $dom(l_x)$ that cause the self-into mapping are found out, and then they are put into the set Q; while the set H contains the corresponding pairs in the self-into mapping. In line 8 and line 9, the elements in Q are added to $dom(l_n)$ after being marked, and they are removed from $dom(l_x)$. In line 11 and line 12, the pairs in H are added to the mapping between l_n and l_x after x is marked, and then they are subtracted from the self-into mapping on dom(l_x). Line 15 is the recursive call to the algorithm on l_n. The set V is used to ensure that the algorithm would not process one level twice. If l_n is *Atomic*, then nothing needs to be done after the elements are added into dom(l_n); otherwise, the mappings between the child levels and l_n would become non-onto, and then need to be transformed by algorithm MakeOnto. Therefore, given a self-into dimension, after MakeSelfOnto is first executed on it, algorithm MakeOnto must be called immediately to deal with the non-onto mappings that might be caused by the marked elements in the domains of the lower levels.

```
(1) Procedure MakeSelfOnto(D,l_x,V)
(2) for each l_n∈Child(l_x) do
(3)   begin
(4)     F={(x,y)|(x,y)∈σ_xx and x•y}
(5)     P={x|(x,y)∈F}
(6)     L={x|(n,x)∈σ_nx }
(7)     Q=P-L
(8)     H={(x,y)| (x,y)∈F and x∈Q}
(9)     dom(l_n)=dom(l_n)∪{Mark(x)|x∈Q}
(10)    dom(l_x)=dom(l_x)-Q
(11)    σ_xx=σ_xx-H
(12)    σ_nx = σ_nx∪{(Mark(x),y)| for any (x, y)∈H }
(13)    V=V∪{l_x}
(14)    if l_n∉V then
(15)       MakeSelfOnto(D, l_n, V)
(16) end
```

Fig. 8. Algorithm MakeSelfOnto

Following the analyses of algorithm AdjustMappingB, the overall complexity of algorithm MakeSelfOnto is $o(mn\log n)$ because the set V ensures that the algorithm would transform each level once at most. The following theorems ensure the correctness of algorithm MakeSelfOnto. Their proofs are also omitted here.

Theorem 7. Algorithm MakeSelfOnto terminates and the resulting dimension is self-onto.

Theorem 8. Let d_1=(D_1, $\prec'_1$) be the resulting dimension after executing MakeSelfOnto on dimension d=(D, $\prec'$), $\leq_1$ be the EAR of d_1, and $\leq$ be the EAR of d; then the following holds true: for any e_1, e_2∈ D, $e_1 \leq_1 e_2 \Leftrightarrow e_1 \leq e_2$.

For a non-covering dimension of type C, we could know from previous analyses that MakeCoveringA should be called first; then, it depends on the transformed mappings' types whether MakeCoveringB should still be called in turn. Therefore, according to previous analyses of the two algorithms, the worst case for transforming the dimension is in time $o(m^4 n\log n)$, and the normal case is $o(m^3 n\log n)$.

For a non-covering dimension of type D, MakeSelfOnto, MakeOnto and MakeCoveringA (or MakeCoveringB) should be called. Following the complexity analyses of these algorithms, we could conclude that the worst case for transforming the dimension is also in time $o(m^4 n \log n)$, and the normal case is $o(m^3 n \log n)$.

5 Case Study

In this section, we will take a non-covering dimension of type D as example to explain the correctness of the algorithms we proposed; furthermore, we intend to define a calling priority order for the algorithms. The dimensions of type A and type B have been illustrated in section 3. The dimensions of Type C are similar to those of type D in transforming processes.

We will investigate the location dimension in fig.9 in detail, and the algorithms proposed in previous section are employed to transform the dimension into a covering one. In addition to the theorems in section 4, the resulting dimension further verifies the correctness and effectiveness of these algorithms.

According to the definition in section 3, we know that the location dimension is of type D. Moreover, according to the analyses in previous section, we should call algorithms MakeSelfOnto and MakeOnto to transform the dimension into a self-onto and onto dimension, and then only one of the MakeCoveringA and MakeCoveringB algorithms should be executed to transform the dimension into a covering one.

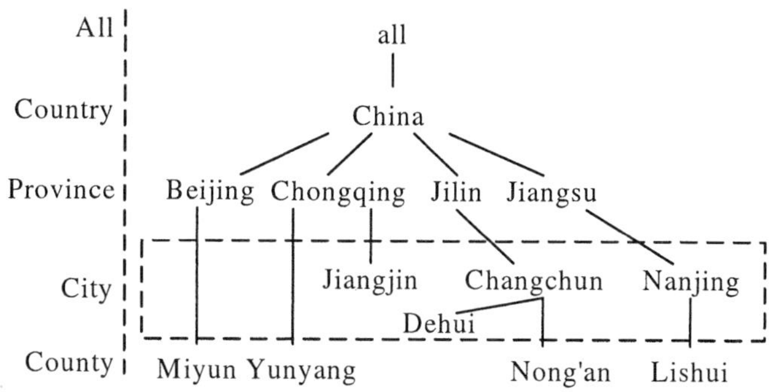

Fig. 9. Another structure of location dimension

In these algorithms, MakeSelfOnto should be called first to transform the self-into mapping on level City, because it might cause non-onto mappings. Without any restriction, the rest algorithms can be called in various sequences, which would lead to different transformed results. There are three likely feasible calling sequences: {MakeSelfOnto, MakeOnto, MakeCoveringA}, {MakeSelfOnto, MakeCoveringB, MakeOnto} and {MakeSelfOnto, MakeCoveringA, MakeOnto}. If the algorithms are executed in the first sequence, then "L2-Beijing" and "L4-Yunyang" will be added to dom(City), while "Chongqing" is kept unprocessed. Obviously, the resulting dimension is unacceptable due to the different treatment of the two municipalities. If they are executed in the second sequence, then "Chongqing" will be added to dom(City) after being marked, and thus it is in the same level as its child "Jiangjin'; this would lead to two different aggregation results on "Chongqing". Therefore, this resulting dimension is also unacceptable. If we execute these algorithms in the third sequence, then "L4-Miyun" and "L4-Yunyang" will be added to dom(City), "L3-Jiangjin" is added to dom(County), "Dehui" is removed from dom(City) and "L3-Dehui" is added to dom(County). These processes seem reasonable and do not cause error aggregation results; therefore, the resulting dimension of the third calling sequence is acceptable.

Given the sequence: MakeSelfOnto, MakeCoveringA, MakeCoveringB, Make-Onto, based on the example and the discussion in previous section, we could conclude that the priority decreases gradually along the sequence. Now, as to the location dimension in fig.9, the calling sequence of the algorithms can be easily obtained according to this priority order.

6 Conclusions

In this paper, we first formally defined several types of irregular dimensions based on the dimension model in [9]; especially, we mainly analyzed the characteristics of the four types of non-covering dimensions, which are never mentioned in previous work and need to be transformed into covering ones in different ways. Then, we extended the MakeCovering algorithm proposed by Pedersen to algorithm MakeCoveringB so as to deal with much complex non-covering hierarchies; moreover, we proposed two new algorithms: MakeCoveringA and MakeSelfOnto. Along with the MakeOnto algorithm, they can correctly transform the four types of non-covering dimensions into covering ones in proper combinations. Furthermore, we defined a calling priority order for them; along the sequence: MakeSelfOnto, MakeOnto, MakeCoveringB, MakeCoveringA, the priority decreases gradually.

As stated in section 2, there are still other two types of self-into dimensions. We will investigate them further in future work, and we also plan to propose an algorithm to identify the four types of non-covering dimensions and call the four algorithms to transform them automatically.

References

1. OLAP Council, The OLAP glossary, The OLAP Council, http://www.olapcouncil.org/ research/glossary.htm, 1997.
2. P.Elaheh, R.Maurizio. Characterization of Hierarchies and Some Operators in OLAP Environment. In *Proc. of the 2nd ACM Int. Workshop on Data Warehousing and OLAP*, pages 54-59, ACM Press, November 1999.
3. T.B.Pedersen, C.S.Jensen, C.E.Dyreson. Extending Practical Pre-Aggregation in On-Line Analytical Processing. In *Proc. of the 25th VLDB Conf.*, pages 663-674, Morgan Kaufmann Publishers, 1999.
4. A.Datta, H.Thomas. The cube data model: a conceptual model and algebra for on-line analytical processing in data warehouses. Decision Support Systems, 27(3): 289-301, 1999.
5. T.B.Nguyen, A.M.Tjoa, R.Wagner. An Object Oriented Multidimensional Data Model for OLAP, In *Proc. of the 1st Int. Conf. on Web-Age Information Management*, pages 69-82, Springer-Verlag press, 2000.

6. W.Lehner, J.Albrecht, H.Wedekind. Normal Forms for Multidimensional Databases. In *Proc. of 10th Int. Conf. on Statistical and Scientific Database Management*, pages 63-72, IEEE Computer Society press, 1998.
7. H.V.Jagadish, L.V.S.Lakshmanan, D.Srivastava. What can Hierarchies do for Data Warehouses?. In *Proc. of the 25th VLDB Conf.*, pages 530-541, Morgan Kaufmann Publishers, 1999.
8. T.B.Pedersen, C.S.Jensen, C.E.Dyreson. A foundation for capturing and querying complex multidimensional data. Information System, 26(5): 383-423, 2001.
9. Z.H.Li, J.G.Sun, H.H.Yu. Activating Irregular dimensions in OLAP. In *Proc. of Int. Conf. on Computational Method 2004*, Springer-Verlag press, to appear.
10. N.Tapio, N.Jyrki, T.Peter. Normalising OLAP cubes for controlling sparsity. Data & Knowledge Engineering, 46: 317–343, 2003.
11. C.S.Jensen, A.Kligys, T.B.Pedersen and I.Timko. Multidimensional data modeling for location-based services. The VLDB Journal, 1(13): 1-21, 2004.

Mining Frequent Trees Based on Topology Projection

Ma Haibing, Wang Chen, Li Ronglu, Liu Yong, and Hu Yunfa

Computer and Information Technology Department,
Fudan University 200433, Shanghai, China
martin0721@163.com

Abstract. Methods for mining frequent trees are widely used in domains like bioinformatics, web-mining, chemical compound structure mining, and so on. In this paper, we present TG, an efficient pattern growth algorithm for mining frequent embedded suttees in a forest of rooted, labeled, and ordered trees. It uses rightmost path expansion scheme to construct complete pattern growth space, and creates a projected database for every grow point of the pattern ready to grow. Then, the problem is transformed from mining frequent trees to finding frequent nodes in the projected database. We conduct detailed experiments to test its performance and scalability and find that TG outperforms TreeMiner, one of the fastest methods proposed before, by a factor of 4 to 15.

1 Introduction

Frequent patterns mining is an important problem in data mining domain. It involves mining transactions, sequences, trees and graphs. Methods for mining frequent trees are widely used in domains like bioinformatics, web-mining, chemical compound structure mining, and so on. For instance, in web usage mining, it can be used to mine user access patterns from web logs and mine useful information from hyperlinks, and it can also be used to mine common tree structures from XML documents. In bioinformatics, researches can find important topology from known RNA structure and use this information to analyses new RNA structure.

Frequent tree discovery has been studied popularly in recent years. Most of them are reminiscent of the level-wise Apriori [1,2] approach: Wang and Liu developed an algorithm to mine frequent subtrees in XML documents [3]; Asai presented FREQT method for mining frequent labeled ordered trees [7]; Chi proposed FreeTreeMiner algorithm for mining free unordered trees[4]. An apriori heuristic is used to reduce the number of candidate patterns: every sub-pattern of a frequent pattern is also frequent. Whereas, as indicated in previous itemset mining [5], if there are many complex patterns, there can be a huge number of candidates need to be generated and tested, which degrades performance dramatically. Furthermore, their work deals with traditional induced subtrees.

Zaki and Asai respectively proposed a very useful rightmost expansion schema to generated candidate tree patterns [6,7]. In [6], Zaki presented two algorithms, TreeMiner and PatternMatcher, for mining embedded subtrees from ordered labeled trees. PatternMatcher is a level-wise algorithm similar to Apriori. TreeMiner performs

Y. Zhang et al. (Eds.): APWeb 2005, LNCS 3399, pp. 394–404, 2005.

depth-first search for frequent subtrees, and uses a vertical representation of trees, scope-list, for fast support counting. TreeMiner is the fastest method among the published method to mine embedded subtrees. Whereas, using intersection of scope-list to count support is still a bottleneck of this method.

Researches have indicate that depth-first search based, pattern growth method, such as FP-growth [5], H-mine [8], for frequent itemset mining, and PrefixSpan [9] for sequential pattern mining, be very efficient for mining frequent patterns. Our previous work also found that method based on static IS+-tree [10] was more efficient than that based on dynamic created FP-trees. Then, with combination of pattern growth method and static projection approach, is it possible to obtain a more efficient algorithm for mining frequent tree patterns?

In this paper, we systematically study the problem of frequent tree pattern mining and develop a novel and efficient algorithm, TG to tackle this problem. The key contributions of our work are as follows:

(1) We introduce array-based method to represent trees and forest in order to random access trees and their nodes.
(2) The rightmost path expansion method is assimilated in our approach to form the complete pattern growth space.
(3) We develop a framework to form the projected database systemically at every possible growing point for a frequent tree. Then, the problem is transformed from mining frequent trees to finding frequent nodes in the projected database.
(4) We design and implement a novel method, TG, for frequent embedded subtrees.

We contrast TG with TreeMiner and experimental results show that TG outperforms TreeMiner by a factor of 4-15 while the mining results are the same.

2 Problem Statements

A *tree* is denoted as $T<r, N, B>$, where (1) N is the set of labeled nodes, with labels taken from a label set, L; (2) $r \in N$, is the unique root; (3) B is the set of branches, each branch $b=<u_1, u_2> \in B$, is an ordered pair, with $u_1, u_2 \in N$, where u_1 is the parent of u_2, and u_2 the child of u_1. If the order of children matters, the tree is called an *ordered tree*. For brevity, we use $T(r)$ or T denoting a labeled tree rooted at r. the *size* of T is the number of nodes in T, denoted as $|T|$. A collection of trees is a forest. A database D is just a forest. When r is not unique, it's a *free tree*, which we do not deal with in this paper.

A path P is a set of connected branches of $T(r)$, denoted as $<u_1,u_2,\ldots, u_k>$, with $<u_i, u_{i+1}> \in B$. The *level* of a node v is the length of the path from r to v, denoted as l_v. Any node u on the path from r to v is an ancestor of v, and v the descendant u. Each node has a *node order* number, according to its position in the pre-order traversal of the tree. If the last node of $T(r)$ is w according to its node order, the path from r to w is called the *rightmost path* of $T(r)$. The *scope interval* of a node u is a piece of interval $[l, r]$, i.e., l is the node order of its first child, and r is the node order of its last descendant. That is, the scope of node u contains all its descendants. The concepts of rightmost path and the scope interval play an important role in constructing topology projection.

Given a tree $T(r, N, B)$, tree $S(r_s, N_s, B_s)$ is called an *embedded subtree* of T, and denoted as $S \prec T$, if (1) $N_s \subset N$; (2) for any branch $(u, v) \in B_s$ in S, there exists a path $< r,\ldots,u,\ldots,v>$ in T, ie., u is an ancestor of v in T. We say that T *contains* S. if u and v must keep parent-child relation in T, then S is a *induced subtree* of T. It's a special case of embedded subtrees. A tree with k nodes denoted as a k-tree. Usually, S is a pattern we are looking for, and T is a tree in D. For any node $u \in N_s$ in S, there must exists a mapping node $u' \in N$ in T. All the mapping nodes of S in T are called an *occurrence* of S in T.

Given a tree database D, the *support* of a tree T is the number of trees in D such that T contains S, i.e., $SUP(S) = |\{T \mid T \in D,\ S \prec T\}|$. Let $\lambda_T(S)$ denotes the number of occurrences of S in T, then, the *weighted support* is the total occurrences of S in D. i.e., $SUP_w(S) = \sum_{T \in D} \lambda_T(S)$. The *relative support* means the percentage of the number of trees contains S over the total number of trees in D. i.e., $sup(S)=SUP(S)/D$. The *relative weighted support* means the percentage of the number of all occurrences of S over the total number of trees in D. i.e., $sup_w(S)=SUP_w(S)/D$.

Definition 1 (Frequent tree). Given a minimum support threshold ε, a tree S is called a frequent tree pattern if $sup(S) \geq \varepsilon$, or for some other users, $sup_w(S) \geq \varepsilon$.

3 Pattern Growth Based on Rightmost Path Projection

Pattern growth method first used in frequent itemset mining [5]. The core of pattern growth method is transforming the problem from mining frequent patterns to finding frequent 1-patterns in projected database. In itemset mining, as there does not exist repetitive item in one transaction, adding one item on an itemset pattern can only generate a unique new pattern. Whereas, a tree can has many nodes with same label, and tree's topology makes it have many possible growing points, and adding one node at different growing point will generate different trees. Thus, it is a non-trivial work to determine a correct and efficient pattern growth framework to mining frequent trees.

There are three obstacles of using pattern growth method for mining frequent trees: Firstly, how to denote trees and their collection to be in favor of pattern growth method? Secondly, how to form a complete and non-redundant pattern growth space? Thirdly, how to grow a frequent k-tree pattern into frequent $(k+1)$-tree patterns?

3.1 Topology Encodings of Trees and ForestAccess the Springer

There are two schemes to construct projected database. One is to reallocate space dynamically for it,, where there are no useless nodes in it. The other is that the projected database shares the same space with original database, called static projection. Our previous study shows that the later is more efficient both for space and time [10]. TG adopts static projection method. Since array has the good property of random access, a array-based topology encoding method of trees and forest is presented in this paper.

Definition 2 (Topology Sequence). Given a tree $T(r)$, a label sequence can be constructed by arrange the node label in node order. We refer to a label sequence added with extra level information as topology sequence. Let the last node of $T(r)$ is w, then the topology sequence of $T(r)$ is, $top(T)$=<rl_r,…ul_u,…wl_w>. We refer to ul_u as a *tuple* of $top(T)$.

Property 1 (Rightmost Path). Let $top(T)$ refer to the topology sequence of $T(r)$, and the last node of $T(r)$ is w, its level l_w. The parent node of w is u, its level l_u. Then u is the nearest node located at the left-hand of w with $l_u=l_w-1$. By analogy, this procedure goes ahead step by step until we reach the root node r. Then <r,…u,…w> is the rightmost path of $T(r)$.

Lemma 1 (The uniqueness of topology sequence). Given a tree$T_1(r_1,N_1,B_1)$ and a tree $T_2(r_2,N_2,B_2)$, they are isomorphic if and only if there exists a order-keeping mapping function $f: N_1 \rightarrow N_2$, for each node $u \in N_1$, having $u = f(u)$ and $l_u = l_{f(u)}$.

Example 1. Figure 1 shows a database D used throughout the paper as a sample database. The labels of each tree taken from a set $L=\{A,B,C,D\}$. We use n_i to denote the node with order i. Then, $top(T_1)$=<B0A1C1D2>, the scope of <B0> is <A1C1D2>. $top(T_2)$=<B0A1B2D2B1C1>, the scope of <A1> is <B2D2>. Suppose there be a subtree S, $top(S)$ =<B0B1D1>, then S occurs in T_2 and T_3. The occurrence of S in T_2 is $(n_0n_2n_3)$, in $T3$ is $(n_3n_5n_6)$. If sup=2, then S is a frequent subtree in D.

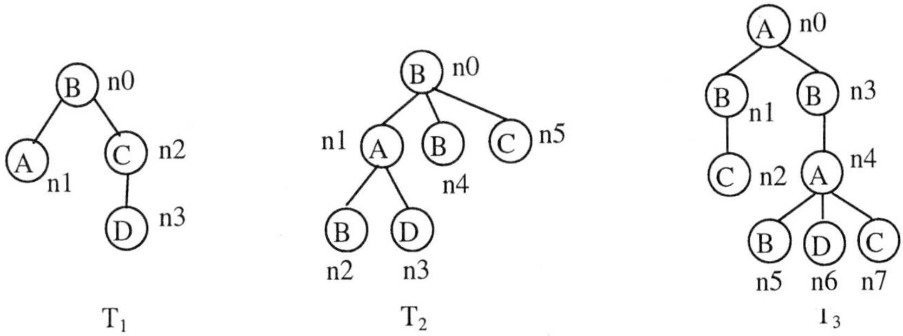

Fig. 1. Sample Database D

As scope interval plays important role in constructing projection, it was added into the denotation of a node, in order to be computed once and used everywhere. For scope interval $[l, r]$ of node u, value l is implied by the position of u, that is, if u is the ith node, the $l=i+1$. Thus, we can only record r.

Definition 2 (Topology Encoding). The definition of topology encoding is as follows:

(1) Each node of a tree consists of three fields: *label*, *level*, and *scope* (equal to r).
(2) A tree is an array of nodes. The subscription associated with a node implies its node order in the tree.
(3) A forest is an array of trees.

3.2 Construct Pattern Growth Space Using Rightmost Path Expansion Users

Zaki and Asai respectively developed this method to construct the complete enumeration search space [6,7]. The method adds new nodes only on the nodes of the rightmost path of a tree. They had proved that the enumeration space is complete and non-redundant. Whereas, in [6,7], the rightmost path expansion method is used to generate candidate patterns. Totally different with that, we use rightmost path expansion approach to construct the complete pattern growth space. i.e., a frequent (*k*-1)-subtree can grow into a frequent *k*-subtree only by adding on the nodes of its rightmost path.

Definition 4 (Growing point). Suppose $S(r_s)$ is a frequent (*k*-1)-subtree and $k>1$. Let *w* is its last node, and the rightmost path $p=<r_s,\ldots,u,\ldots,w>$, $u\in N_s$, its length is $|p|$. Let function $p(i)$ return the *i*th node of p (i=0…$|p|$-1). Let $T(r)$ is a *k*-subtree that is obtained by adding a child node at $p(i)$ on $S(r_s)$. Then, when $i=|p|-1$, i.e., $p(i)=w$, $p(i)$ is called *downward growing point*; when $0\leq i<|p|-1$, $p(i)$ is called *rightward growing point*. The number of growing point is, $g=|p|$.

Lemma 2 (The completeness of pattern growth space). Suppose $T(r)$ is a frequent *k*-subtree (*k*>1), then, there must exist a unique (*k*-1)-subtree $S(r_s)$, that $T(r)$ is obtained by adding child node on some node of its rightmost path of $S(r_s)$.

Proof: we use an induction on the size *n* of $T(r)$. The base is n=1, that is, $T(r)$ is 1-subtree constructed by frequent nodes in *D*. When n=2, it's obvious that $T(r)$ is obtained by downward growing of some frequent 1-subtree. Suppose when $n=k-1$, the lemma holds. For the induction, when $n=k$, by pre-order traversing $T(r)$, we get the last node, *w*. Then, constrained by node order of $T(r)$, *w* must be a child node added on some node of the rightmost path of a (*k*-1)-subtree, otherwise, *w* can't be the last node of $T(r)$. On the other hand, if $T(r)$ is a frequent *k*-subtree, by removing its last node, we can get that unique frequent (*k*-1)-subtree.

3.3 Pattern Growth Framework Based on Topology Projection

Definition 5 (Projection and projected database). Suppose $S(r_s)$ be a frequent subtree, $T(r)\in D$, and $S(r_s)\prec T(r)$. Suppose *w* be the last node of $S(r_s)$, and its mapping node on $T(r)$ be *w'*, that is, $w'=f(w)$, and *w'* be the *n*th node of $T(r)$. Let the rightmost path of $S(r_s)$ is *p*. Then:

(1) For downward growing point *w*, the projection at w of $S(r_s)$ on $T(r)$ is determined by the scope of *w'*, that is, all the nodes located in interval [n+1, *w'.scope*] of $T(r)$.
(2) For some rightward growing point, let it be *u*, and its child node on *p* be *v*, and their respective mapping node be *u'* and *v'* on $T(r)$. Then, the projection at *u* is determined by the scope of *u'* and *v'*, that is, the nodes located at interval [*v'.scope*+1, *u'.scope*] of $T(r)$.

The set of all pieces of projections at growing point $p(i)$ forms the projected database at $p(i)$ of $S(r_s)$.

Example 2. In figure 2, suppose the pattern ready to grow be *P*=<B0A1>. Its occurrences in T_1, T_2 and T_3 are respectively (n_0n_1), (n_0n_1) and (n_3n_4). Then, *P* can downward grow into <B0A1X2>, and rightward grow into <B0A1X1>, where X denotes any possible label. Based on the definition of topology projection, the projected database of the former one is the parts under the line in T_2 and T_3. The projected database of the later one is the parts under the arc in T_1 and T_2.

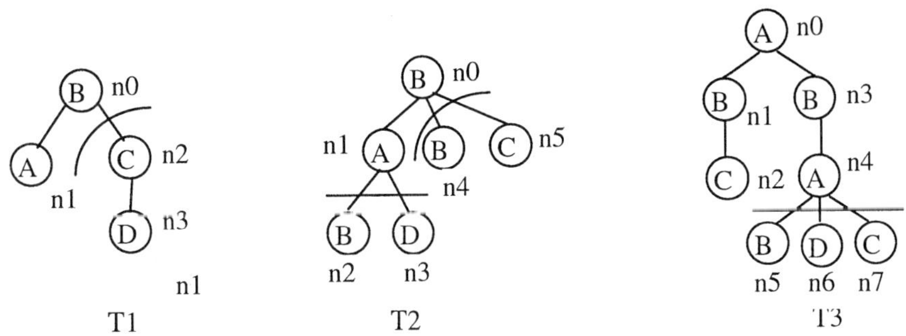

Fig. 2. Projected Dtabase of <B0A1>

Whereas, how to handle the cases where a subtree S has multiple occurrences in some T tree in D? The key to handle repetitive labels in projected database is: when the projected database is scanned and the support is counted, the labels are counted once if their tree ID is the same. However, the algorithm should record every occurrence of it in order to project it later; otherwise, information of some pattern may be lost. The case of weighted support is an easier context where each associated counter is just simply accumulated when meets a label.

Definition 6 (A framework of Pattern Growth) For a (k-1)-subtree pattern $S(r_s)$ ready to grow, its rightmost path p is first determined based on its topology structure; for each growing point $p(i)$ on p, each projection of $p(i)$ is determined by occurrences of $S(r_s)$; then, all pieces of projection form the projected database at $p(i)$. The problem of mining frequent subtree is then transformed to finding frequent nodes in the projected database at $p(i)$ of $S(r_s)$. Let the number of all frequent nodes in projected database be m, if each of them is added at $p(i)$ and become its child node, then $S(r_s)$ grow into m number of k-subtree pattern at $p(i)$. This process can be conduct recursively. It's the **framework of frequent subtree pattern growth based on topology projection**.

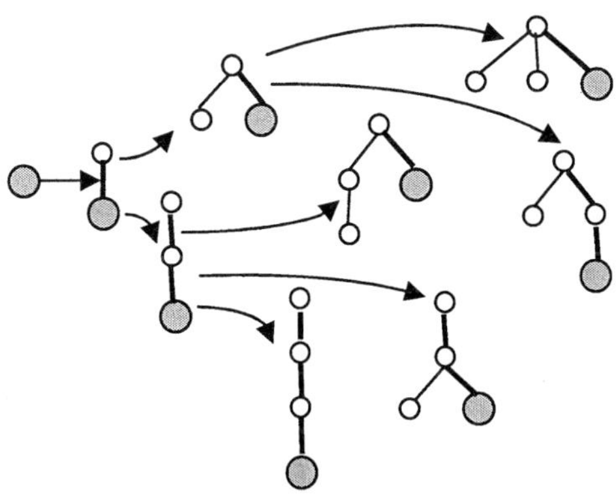

Fig. 3. Framework of Pattern Growth

The basic idea of pattern growth framework is illustrated as figure 3. Thick lines refer to the rightmost path. Circles with shadow denote projected database. Pattern growth is started with frequent nodes in *D*, which form frequent 1-subtrees. Adding all frequent nodes to the growing point of a frequent (*k*-1)-subtree can form multiple frequent *k*-subtrees.

4 Pattern Growth Algorithm Based on Topology Projection

TG Algorithm tries to use pattern growth method to mine frequent embedded subtrees in pattern growth space.

It's clear that in order to get the projected database at any growing point of a frequent tree ready to grow, the algorithm should record following information: (1) the position and scope of any node of any tree in the forest; (2) the support and topology structure of a pattern and a list of all its occurrence.

The first kind of information is recorded in topology encodings of trees and forest. The second kind of information is recorded in a concise structure called header table. The entries in the header table record all frequent nodes and their (weighted) supports in the projected database, pointing the lists of their occurrence by link. For example, in sample database *D*, let *sup* =2. At beginning, the pattern ready to grow is ϕ , its head table is just like figure 5-(a). It includes four frequent nodes.

<ΦX0>

Entry	Occurrence list
A: 3, 4	{(T_1, n_1), (T_2, n_1), (T_3, n_0), (T_3, n_4)}
B: 3, 7	{(T_1, n_0), (T_2, n_0), (T_2, n_2), (T_2, n_4), (T_3, n_1), (T_3, n_3), (T_3,n_6)}
C: 3, 4	{(T_1, n_2), (T_2, n_3), (T_3, n_2), (T_3, n_7)}
D: 3, 4	{(T_1, n_3), (T_2, n_3), (T_3, n_6)}

(a) the header table about <ΦX0>

<B0B1X1>

Entry	Occurrence list
C: 2, 3	{(T_2, $n_0\,n_2\,n_5$), (T_2, $n_0\,n_4\,n_5$), (T_3, $n_3\,n_5\,n_7$)}
D: 2, 2	{(T_2, $n_0\,n_2\,n_3$), (T_3, $n_3\,n_5\,n_6$)}

(b) the header table about <B0B1X1>

Fig. 4. Header Table

For each frequent (*k*-1)-subtree *S* ready to grow, the algorithm first determines its rightmost path *p* based on its topology structure. Then it creates a header table for every growing point *p*(*i*) on *p*. Figure 4-(b) is the header table of <B0B1> at rightward growing point <B1>. From the occurrence list of <B0B1>, the projected database at <B0> can be induced. The algorithm uses two-scan strategy to fill this header table. In the first scan, the supports are counted, and all frequent nodes are found and are filled in each entry. In the second scan, the useless nodes are filtered through the entries of header table. At the same time, the occurrence list of each entry is filled. In the end, each entry in the header table is added at the grow point of <B0B1> and become the rightmost node of a new frequent pattern which ready to grow.

The header table structure can be more concise. Since in the recursive procedure of algorithm, only the rightmost path of a tree plays role, the algorithm can only record the mapping nodes on the rightmost path.

Based on above analyse, we presents algorithm TG.

```
Algorithm: TG (D, •)
Input: Database D; the minimum support•
Output: All frequent subtrees in D
Steps:
begin
     minsup=•*|D|;
     F1=scan D, accumulating sup(or supw), getting all
     frequent nodes;
     Forest=topology encodings after removing non-frequent
     nodes from D;
     header=create header table of •, filling each entry and
     its link using F1;
     TreeGrow (header);
end
Function: TreeGrow (header)
begin
     for each entry in header, do:
               P=the corresponding pattern;
          Put out P•
               for each growing point of P, do:
                  determine the projected database through the
                  occurrence list of P;
                  F1=scan the projected database, accumulating
                  sup(or supw), finding frequent nodes;
                  newHeader= create a header table, filling
                  each entry and its link using F1;
                  TreeGrow (newHeader)•
          end
     end
end
```

The completeness of algorithm TG can be proved. It is omitted for limited space.

5 Experimental Result

In this section, we compare the performance of TG with TreeMiner. All experiments are performed on a 466-MHz Celeron PC with 256 megabytes main memory, running on Windows XP. All programs are written in C++ with STL and compiled by visual C++ .net. We get the source code from the author of TreeMiner. After trivially modified, we recompiled it by visual C++ .net.

5.1 Synthetic Datasets

We wrote a synthetic data generation program to output all the test data. There are 5 parameters for adjustment: the number of the labels, (*S*); the probability threshold of one node in the tree to generate children, (*P*); the data size of synthetic trees, (*N*); the average height of synthetic trees, (*H*), and the maximum fanout of nodes, (*F*). The actual height of each tree is determined by the Gaussian distribution having the average of H, and the standard deviation of 1. The default parameters are: S = 100, p = 0.5, L = 10, N = 10000, H = 8, F = 6. In order to compare with TreeMiner, the format of original dataset is the same as [5]. The algorithm transforms it to topology sequence encodings after reading it.

5.2 Performance Comparison

Figure 5 shows the experimental result, TreeMiner called TM for short. Except for figure 5-(f), Y axes figures have been processed as logarithm.

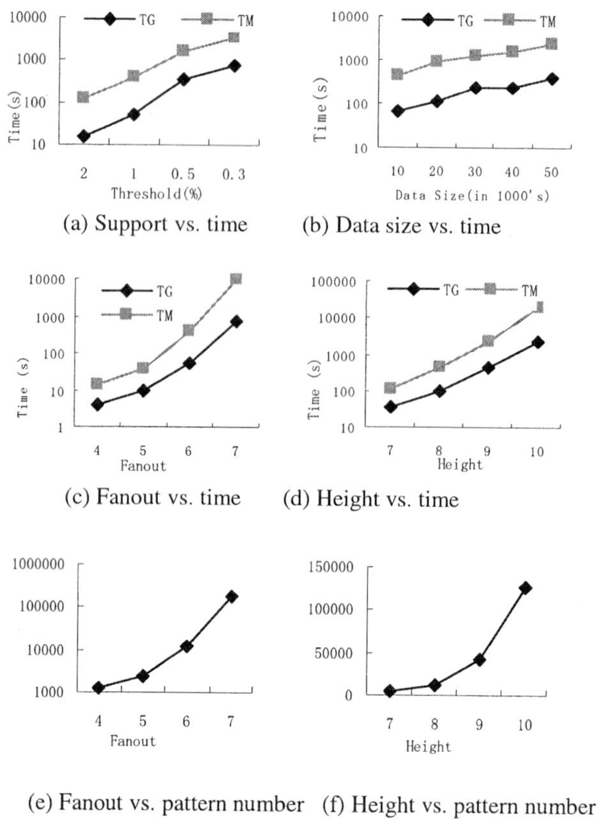

(a) Support vs. time (b) Data size vs. time

(c) Fanout vs. time (d) Height vs. time

(e) Fanout vs. pattern number (f) Height vs. pattern number

Fig. 5. Performance Comparison

At first, we consider the performance variance with descending minimum support of the two algorithms. Figure 5(a) shows the result, where $\mathcal{E}$ is set from 0.02 to 0.003, and all other parameters are set to default value. In this case, TG is about 5 to 8 times faster than TreeMiner.

Figure 5(b) shows how the algorithms scale with increasing number of trees in the database D, which changes from 10,000 to 50,000 trees, with other parameter in default value and ε with 0.01. The running time of both algorithms increases linearly, though TG continues to be 5 to 10 times faster than TreeMiner.

Figure 5(c) and figure 5(d) show how the algorithm performs with variant tree size. With increasing maximal fanout or average height of tree, the size of tree becomes larger and larger, and the found patterns become more complex. First, we scale the fanout from 4 to 7, ε with 0.01 and other parameter in default value, as shows in figure 5(c). In the beginning, both algorithms have good performance. With the growth of fanout, the performance margin between them becomes wider and wider. When F=7, TG is 15 times faster than TreeMiner. If we vary the average height of trees with other parameters in default value, as figure 5(d) shows, we get similar result. When H=9, TG is 10 times faster than TreeMiner. It's outstanding that when the fanout changes from 6 to 7, or the average height changes from 8 to 9, the running time goes up sharply. Comparing the numbers of frequent patterns at those cases, as figure 5(e) and figure 5 (f) show, we found that the numbers increase sharply from 12081 to 170688, and from 41971 to 126018, and most of them are very complex. Thus we expect that TG will outperform TreeMiner by a wider and wider margin if the tree size becomes larger.

5.3 Result Analysis

These experiments clearly indicate the superiority of pattern growth method based on topology projection for mining frequent trees, especially as patterns become long and complex. There exist three main reasons for this: Firstly, array-based representation of tree and forest supports random access any node and any tree, which is in favour of determining the static projected database; Secondly, the search space is non-redundant; Thirdly, the process of scanning projected is just simply operation like counting or recording position, which greatly reduces the complexity of the algorithm.

Note that both TG and TREEMINER are memory-based mining method. TG needs transform the original database into topology encodings, which are static structures and should be read into memory. In addition, it has an extra spending on header table. Header table is a dynamic structure, whose size is proportion to search depth, that is, the size of the pattern. TREEMINER should create a scope list for each node, which is a static data structure, and its size is as much as a copy of database. In addition, in the process of depth-first search, it generates dynamic scope list for candidate patterns, just like header table. Experimental results show that the two algorithms spend similar amount of memory.

6 Conclusions

We present a efficient pattern growth algorithm based on topology projection for mining frequent embedded subtrees. Experimental results show it is efficient both for space and time.

Whereas, when potential frequent tree patterns are very complex, the users are often confused by the significant magnitudes of complete set of frequent patterns. One solution is to mine frequent maximal trees or frequent closed trees. A tree pattern M is called maximal if there does not exist a super set *M'* of *M*, that *M'* is also frequent. A tree pattern *C* is called closed if there does not exist a super set *C'* of *C*, that has same support. All frequent patterns can be deduced from max mal frequent patterns, and frequent closed patterns have same power as complete frequent patterns. The number of maximal or closed patterns can be orders of magnitude smaller. It's a challenge to mine maximal or closed embedded subtree patterns. Method form mining frequent has been successfully used in classifying XML documents [14]. Yan has adopted frequent structure-based approach for graph index and query, which achieves good performance [15]. It's a better stimulation for us to extend tree mining method for indexing and querying XML document.

Acknowledgements. We would like to express our thanks to Mr. Zaki for his sending us the source code of TreeMiner.

References

1. R Agrawal, T Imielinski, A Swami. Mining association rules between sets of items in large databases. The 1993 ACM2SIGMOD,Washington, 1993
2. R Agrawal, R Srikant. Fast algorithms for mining association rules. The 1994 VLDB, Santiago, Chile, 1994
3. K. Wang and H. Liu. Schema discovery for semistructured data. In KDD'97, Newport Beach, CA.
4. Y. Chi, Y. Yang, and .R.R. Muntx. Index and mining free trees. In Proc. of the 2003 IEEE Int. Conf. on Data Mining, 2003
5. J. Han, et al. Mining frequent patterns without candidate generation. In SIGMOD' 00, Dallas, TX.
6. M.J. Zaki. Efficiently mining frequent trees in a forest. In KDD'02, Edmonton, Alberta, Canada.
7. T. Asia, et al. Efficient substructure discovery from large semi-structured data. In Proc. 2002 SIAM Int. Conf. Data Mining, Arlington, VA.
8. J. Pei, et al. H-Mine: Hyper-structure mining of frequent patterns in large databases. In ICDM'01, San Jose, CA.
9. J. Pei, et al. PrefixSpan: Mining sequential patterns efficiently by prefix-projected pattern growth. In ICDE'01, Heidelberg, Germany.
10. HaiBing Ma. Jin Zhang. Ying Jie-Fan. Yun Fa-Hu.. Mining frequent patterns based on IS+-tree. In ICMLC 2004, Shang Hai,China.
11. L. Dehaspe, et al. Finding frequent substructures in chemical compounds. In KDD'98, New York, NY.
12. T. Miyahara, et al. Discovery of frequent tree structured patterns in semistructured web documents. In PAKDD'01, Hong Kong, China.
13. X. Yan and J. Han. gspan: Graph-based substructure pattern mining. In Proceedings of the 2002 IEEE International Conference on Data Mining (ICDM 2002), 9-12 December 2002, Maebashi City, Japan.
14. M. J. Zaki and C. C. Aggarwal. XRules: An effective structural classifier for XML data. In Proc. of the 2003 Int. Conf. Knowledge Discovery and Data Mining, 2003.
15. X.Yan, S. Yu and J. Han. Graph Index: A Frequent Structure-based Approach. In SIGMOD 2004, Paris, Fance.

Mining Quantitative Associations in Large Database*

Chenyong Hu[1], Yongji Wang[1], Benyu Zhang[2], Qiang Yang[3], Qing Wang[1], Jinhui Zhou[1], Ran He[1], and Yun Yan[4]

[1] Lab for Internet Software Technologies, Institute of Software, Chinese Academy of Sciences, Beijing
{huchenyong, ywang, wq, jinhui, heran}@itechs.iscas.ac.cn
[2] Microsoft Research Asia, Beijing, P.R. China
byzhang@microsoft.com
[3] Department of Computer Science, Hong Kong University of Science and Technology,
qyang@cs.ust.hk
[4] LMAM, Department of Information Science, School of Mathematical Science, Peking University, Beijing
yanjun@math.pku.edu.cn

Abstract. Association Rule Mining algorithms operate on a data matrix to derive association rule, discarding the quantities of the items, which contains valuable information. In order to make full use of the knowledge inherent in the quantities of the items, an extension named Ratio Rules [6] is proposed to capture the quantitative association. However, the approach, which is addressed in [6], is mainly based on Principle Component Analysis (PCA) and as a result, it cannot guarantee that the ratio coefficient is non-negative. This may lead to serious problems in the association rules' application. In this paper, a new method, called Principal Non-negative Sparse Coding (PNSC), is provided for learning the associations between itemsets in the form of Ratio Rules. Experiments on several datasets illustrate that the proposed method performs well for the purpose of discovering latent associations between itemsets in large datasets.

1 Introduction

In recent years, due to the increasing popularity of dealing with a large number of data in various fields, association rule as a central issue has received considerable interest in data mining. The problem of Association Rule Mining (ARM) in large transactional databases was introduced in [1, 5], Its basic idea is to discover important and interesting associations among the data items such that the presence of some items in a transaction will imply the presence of other items in the same transaction. The form of such association is as follows:

$$\{bread, milk\} => butter\ (80\%)$$

* Supported by the National Natural Science Foundation of China under Grant No.60373053, 60273026;the hundred Talents of the Chinese Academy of Sciences; the National High-Tech Research and Development Plan of China (863)under Grant No. 2002AA116080.

Y. Zhang et al. (Eds.): APWeb 2005, LNCS 3399, pp. 405 – 416, 2005.

The above form means that customers who buy "bread" and "milk" are likely to buy butter with 80% confidence. Inspired by work [1], several fast algorithms based on the level-wise Apriori framework[2]and partitioning [9] are proposed to remedy the performance bottleneck of Apriori. In addition, several novel mining techniques, such as parallel algorithms [10, 19], uncertain algorithm [4, 11] and other techniques[8, 12, 17], also received much attention lately.

Most of the prevalent approaches assume that the transactions only carry Boolean information and ignore the valuable knowledge inherent in the quantities of the items. To find the association rules, the Boolean approach assumes that all we need to know is whether an item is contained in a transaction or not. Thus, Boolean association rules have the advantages that they are easy to interpret. However, the major drawback is that a given data matrix V (with e.g. amounts spent per customer per product) is converted to a binary matrix by treating non-zero amounts as plain "1"s. This approach simplifies the data mining algorithms but tends to lose lots of valuable information.

In fact, considering that the quantities of the items in many datasets contain valuable information for us, it is necessary to provide a definition of association rules when the datasets contain quantitative attributes. Several efficient algorithms for mining quantitative association rules have been proposed in the past [3,6,16]. A notable algorithm is the work [6], where they provided a stronger set of rules as *Ratio Rules*. A rule under this framework is expressed in the following form:

$$bread : milk : butter = a : b : c$$
$$(a,b,c \text{ is arbitrary numerical values})$$

This rule states that for each a amount spent on bread, a customer normally spends a b amount on milk and c amount on butter. Given such a definition, Ratio Rules allow quantitative information to be expressed in many practical applications, including forecasting such as *"if a customer spends \$ a on bread, how much will s/he spend on butter?"* and "what-if" scenarios such as *"we expect the demand for bread, how much butter should we stock up on?"*.

Principal Component Analysis (PCA) is often used in data mining applications to discover the eigen-vectors of a dataset. Ratio Rules [6] can represent the quantitative associations between items as the principal *eigen-vectors* of a data matrix, where the values *a, b* and *c* in the example above correspond to the projections of the eigenvector in the space defined by bread, milk and butter. Because PCA factorization requires only the orthogonality in matrix factorization, the ratio coefficient of rule (element of *eigen-vector*) can be either positive or negative. An example of Ratio Rules, which contains a negative value, is

$$Shoe : Coat : Hat = 1 : \text{-}2 : \text{-}5$$

Obviously, this rule loses the intuitive appeal of associations between items when containing negative values, because a customer's spending should always be positive (there is no consideration of profit here). In this paper, we present a method to address this problem.

Our method amounts to a novel application of non-negative matrix factorization (NMF) [7]. Like PCA, the NMF is aimed at learning latent components; unlike PCA, the NMF imposes the non-negativity constraints in the matrix factorization to ensure that all principle components are positive. However, we cannot directly apply NMF for our purpose; we observe that although all the coefficients of the latent components learned by NMF are non-negative, it is still difficult to explain that these latent components represent the latent association between items in a quantifiable dataset. We need to provide a bridge to bring NMF closer to association rules.

In this work, we propose a novel method called *Principal Non-negative Sparse Coding (PNSC),* for learning the latent components. Furthermore, we extend the definition of Ratio Rules with all the ratio coefficients constrained to be non-negative. An example of such a rule according to this definition would be:

$$bread : milk : butter = 1:2:5$$

This rule implies that the customer who spends $ 1 on bread tends to buy $ 2 of milk and $ 5 of butter. We will illustrate that the Ratio Rules by PNSC can also support a variety of important tasks such as forecasting and answering "what-if" scenarios.

The rest of the paper is organized as follows: Section 2 reviews the related work. Section 3 describes the problem and the intuition behind the Ratio Rules. Section 4 introduces Principal Non-negative Sparse Coding (PNSC) and compares it with PCA. Section 5 presents the experimental results. Section 6 concludes the paper.

2 Related Work

Association rule algorithms find rules of the form $X \Rightarrow Y$ where X and Y are disjoint sets of items. The data used in the notable Apriori algorithms [1] is market basket data that is naturally binary (two-valued), that we refer to here as Boolean. Either an item has been purchased by a customer and is in his/her market basket, indicated by a value of 1 (true), or it has not, indicated by a value of 0 (false). Although Although finding association rules in two-valued categorical data has been well researched, Problems occur when trying to find these types of rules in data with pure numeric (quantitative) or mixed numeric and categorical (qualitative) values. Srikant et al. extended the traditional definition to include quantitative data, and proposed quantitative association rules [16]. A notable algorithm is proposed in [6], where a type of quantitative rules known as Ratio Rules are introduced. In the framework of Ratio Rules, Principal Component Analysis (PCA) is used to discover the latent associations, and the *eigen-vectors* are used to represent the associations between items. Following lists the simple example for these types of association rules:

Boolean association rules[15, 18]:

$$\{bread, milk\} => butter \ (80\%)$$

Quantitative association rules [16]:

$$\langle bread : [2-5] \rangle => \langle butter : [1-2] \rangle$$

Ratio Rules [6]:

$$bread : milk : butter = a : b : c$$

$$(a, b, c \text{ is arbitrary value.})$$

In the Ratio Rules listed above, *a*, *b* and *c* are used to denote relative coefficient of the corresponding items, that is the association among such items can be represented as $a:b:c$. The method in [6] is based on the Principal Component Analysis (PCA), where each Ratio Rule corresponds to a *eigen-vector* found by the PCA. Because PCA factorization requires only the orthogonality in matrix factorization, the ratio coefficient of rule can be of arbitrary numerical values. Obvious it is not interpretable in the context of association rules.

3 Problem Definition

The problem that we tackle is as follows. Given a large set of N customers and M products organized in a $N \times M$ matrix V where each row corresponds to a customer transaction (e.g., market basket databases), and the entity v_{ij} gives the dollar amount spent by customers on the products. The goal is to find all Ratio Rules of the form:

$$v_1 : v_2 : v_3 : \ldots : v_M \quad (v_i \geq 0)$$

The above form means that there are some latent components, which represent the non-negative associations between the items of the dataset V. That is, customers who buy the items will spend *v1, v2, ...* respectively on each itemset with sufficient frequency.

Fig1. (a) lists a large set of N customers and M $(M = 2)$ products organized in a $N \times M$ matrix V. Each row vector of the matrix can be thought of as a M-dimensional point. Fig 1. (b) lists such 2-points distribution in graphical form. Here we assume that the dataset is made up of two clusters. Each cluster corresponds to a latent component that implies the association between items in the dataset. Given this set of N points, the goal is to capture the latent components, which represent the associations between items. We list two Ratio Rules discovered by PCA[6] in Fig.2 (a), where one contains negative values:

$$bread : butter = \text{-}0.77 : 0.64$$

According to the above definition of Ratio Rules, negative association between items ("bread" and "butter") does not make sense. However, the PCA does not prevent this from happening. Furthermore, the Ratio Rules which tend to represent the association between items often do not give the latent associations behind the distribution of these points. In Fig 1.(b), it is obvious that Ratio Rules found by PCA are deviated with the latent associations between items.

In fact, from Fig.1 (b) we find that the latent associations are not mutually orthogonal, while the method by PCA imposes the orthogonality constraint on these Ratio Rules. Therefore, Ratio Rules found by the PCA cannot truly reflect the latent associations among the items correctly. Compared to Fig.2 (a), Fig 2(b) illustrates the Ratio Rules captured by our proposed PNSC in this work. Surprisingly, each rule could be treated as an association between items in the two clusters respectively. Furthermore, our method guarantees that all the values of Ratio Rules is positive. For example:

$$bread : butter = 0.21 : 0.79$$
$$bread : butter = 0.64 : 0.36$$

From Fig.2 (b), we can find that the customers of one cluster mainly depend on the first rule where their relative spending amounts between bread and butter are closely to the ratio (0.21:0.79). Furthermore, customers of another cluster are related by the ratio (0.64:0.36). In addition, in this work, a *support* measurement is designed to illustrate the importance of each rule for the entire dataset.

	bread ($)	*butter ($)*
T_1	2.50	4.39
T_2	3.91	8.44
T_3	3.99	11.56
T_4	3.65	8.20
T_5	4.99	15.58
T_6	4.64	14.05
T_7	6.92	24.69
T_8	2.75	4.08
T_9	6.14	3.67
T_{10}	4.24	1.64
T_{11}	4.32	2.32
...	...	...
Tn	4.36	2.55

(a) Data matrix with 2-dimension in table form

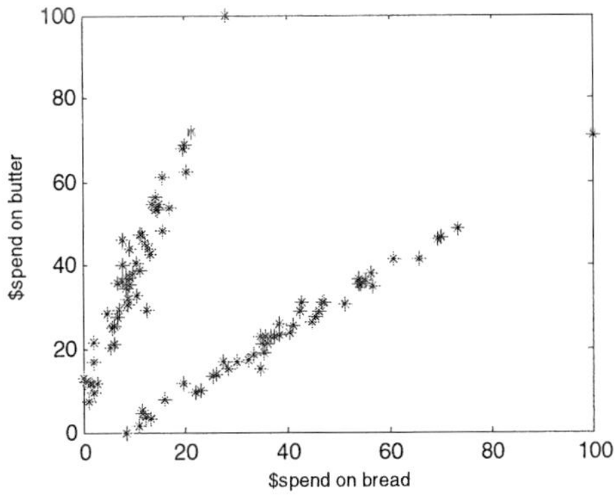

(b) Data matrix with 2-dimension in graphical form

Fig. 1. Data matrix with 2-dimension in table form and in graphical form

4 Principal Non-negative Sparse Coding (PNSC)

Let a set of N M-dimension training records be given as a $M \times N$ matrix V , with each column consisting of the M non-negative attribute values of records. Denote a set of $P \ll M$ basis components by a $M \times P$ matrix W , where each record can be represented as a ratio combination of the basis components using the approximate factorization:

$$V \approx WH \tag{1}$$

where H is a $P \times N$ coefficients matrix, and the entities of H are the coefficients of corresponding basis components.

Korn et.al [6] applies the Principal Component Analysis (PCA) in matrix factorization. PCA factorization requires that the basis components that are the columns of W are orthogonal and the rows of H are mutually orthogonal. One major problem with PCA is that the basis vectors have both positive and negative components, and the data is represented as linear combinations of these vectors with positive and negative coefficients. In many applications, the negative components contradict physical realities. For example, in representing the associations between items, anomalies such as the following can happen, which is clearly not desirable:

$$bread : butter = 1 : \text{-}2.$$

4.1 Non-negative Matrix Factorization

To address this philosophical problem, a method called NMF [7] is proposed as a procedure for matrix factorization which imposes non-negative instead of orthogonal constraint in learning basis component. The element values of component vector, as well as coefficients, are all non-negative, i.e. the entries of W and H are all non-negative.

In contrast to PCA, NMF uses the Euclidean distance of a matrix V from another matrix Y , defined as

$$\|V - Y\|^2 = \sum_{i,j} (v_{ij} - y_{ij})^2 \tag{2}$$

As the measurement of fitness for factorizing V into $WH \triangleq Y = [Y_{ij}]$, a NMF factorization is defined as

$$\min_{W,H} \|V - WH\|^2 \quad s.t\ W, H \geq 0, \sum_i w_{ij} = 1\ \forall j \tag{3}$$

where $W, H \geq 0$ means that all entries of W and H are non-negative. The above optimization can be done by multiplicative update rules [7].

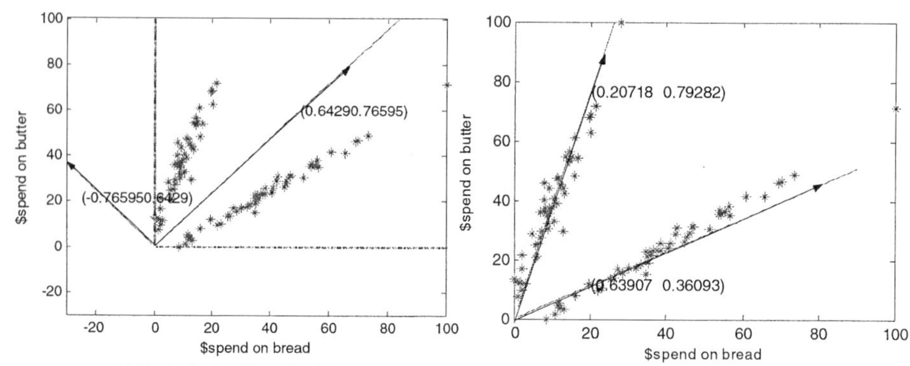

(a) Ratio Rules identified by PCA (b) Ratio Rules identified by PNSC

Fig. 2. Latent associations discovered by PCA and PNSC

4.2 Non-negative Sparse Coding (NNSC)

Although NMF is successful in matrix factorization, the NMF model as defined by the constrained minimization of Equation (2) does not impose the sparse constraints. Therefore, it can hardly yield a factorization, which reveals local sparse features. The sparsity implies that the projection coefficients over all training records have probability densities, which are highly peaked at zero and have heavy tails. This basically means that any given training record can be represented using only a few significantly non-zero latent coefficients. Related sparse coding is proposed in the work of [13] for matrix factorization.

Considering both the non-negativity constraints and the sparseness are important for learning latent component, Non-Negative Sparse Coding (NNSC) is provided in [14], Here, we briefly the algorithm NNSC in [14] which combines the non-negativity and sparseness constraints in a matrix factorization.

Definition 1. *Non-negative sparse coding (NNSC) of a non-negative data matrix* V *(i.e.*$\forall ij: v_{ij} \geq 0$*) is given by the minimization of*

$$C(W,H) = \frac{1}{2}\|V - WH\|^2 + \lambda \sum_{ij} H_{ij} \tag{4}$$

subject to the constraints $\forall ij: w_{ij}, h_{ij} \geq 0$ *and* $\forall i: \|w_i\| = 1$

As for estimating the hidden components *H*, the author [14] developed a multiplicative algorithm by iterating the following update rule:

$$H^{t+1} = H^t .* (W^T V) ./ (W^T W H^t + \lambda) \tag{5}$$

where .* and ./ denote element multiplication and division. After H is updated, basis matrix W can be updated by the following three steps:

1. $W' = W^t - \mu(W^t H - V)H^T$ (6)
2. Any negative values in W' are set to zero
3. Rescale each column of W' to unit norm, and then set $W^{t+1} = W'$.

In [14], the authors have proved that the objective function is non-increasing under the above iterative updating rules, and the convergence of the iteration is guaranteed.

4.3 Principal Non-negative Sparse Coding (PNSC)

When a dataset V is decomposed with W and H, the column vectors of W make up a new basis components space, and each column value of H represent the corresponding projection on the new basis component space. In other words, every row coefficient of H is the affection fact of a corresponding column basis for the whole dataset. As a whole, the sum of every row vector of H represents the importance of corresponding base for the whole dataset. Therefore, we define a *support* measurement after normalizing every column of H :

$$h_{kl} = h_{kl} \Big/ \sum_k h_{kl} \tag{7}$$

Definition 2. For every rule (column vector) of W, we define a support measurement:

$$support(w_i) = \sum_j h_{ij} \Big/ \sum_{ij} h_{ij} \tag{8}$$

where $rule(w_i)$ *denotes the column of* W

$support(w_i) \in [0,1]$, *and* $\sum_i support(w_i) = 1$

Consequently, we can measure the importance of each rule for the entire dataset by their *support* values. The high value of *support* implies more importance of such rule is given by for the whole dataset V .

In order to select the principal k rules as Ratio Rules to denote the associations among items of the dataset, firstly, we rank the whole rules in descending by the *support* value of each rule. And then, we retain the first k principal rules as Ratio Rules because they are more important than the other rules for the entire dataset. About the selection of k value, a simple method is taken such as:

$$\min_k \left(\frac{\sum_{i=1}^{k} support(w_i)}{\sum_{i=1}^{M} support(w_i)} > threshold \right) \tag{9}$$

From above form (9), the Ratio Rules are obtained effectively according that the sum of the k *support* values of the Ratio Rules covers *threshold (i.e.90%)* of the grand total *support* values.

5 Experiments

Experiments are performed on synthetic and real datasets to illustrate that the proposed method is effective in mining Ratio Rules between items on quantitative matrix.

Synthetic Dataset:
We have applied both the PNSC and the PCA to a dataset that consists of two clusters, which contains 25 Gaussian distribution points on a x-y plane (generated with μ =[3;5], σ =[1,1.2;1.2,2]) and 50 points on y-z plain. (generated with μ =[3;5], σ =[2,1.6;1.6,2]) (Fig.3).

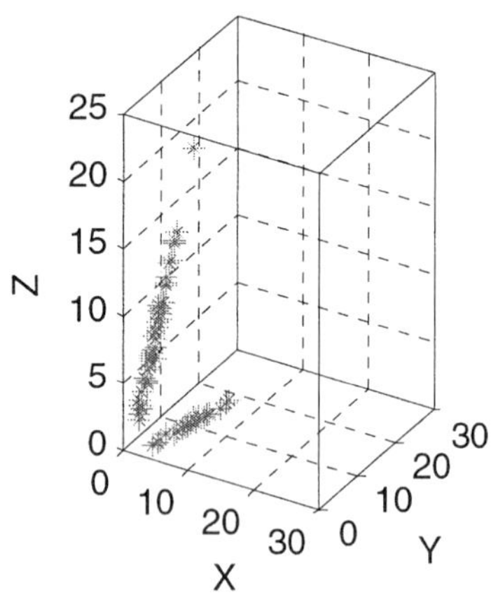

Fig. 3. Two clusters (25 Gaussian distribution points on x-y plain and 50 points on y-z plain)

Table 1. Rules Based on PNSC

PNSC	RR_1	RR_2	RR_3
(X)	0.000	0.696	0.020
(Y)	0.493	0.304	0.980
(Z)	0.507	0.000	0.000
$Sum(w_i)$	49.88	21.636	3.488
$Support(w_i)$	0.665	0.289	0.046

Table 2. Rules Based on PCA

CA	RR_1	RR_2
(X)	-0.518	0.720
(Y)	-0.765	-0.148
(Z)	-0.383	-0.678

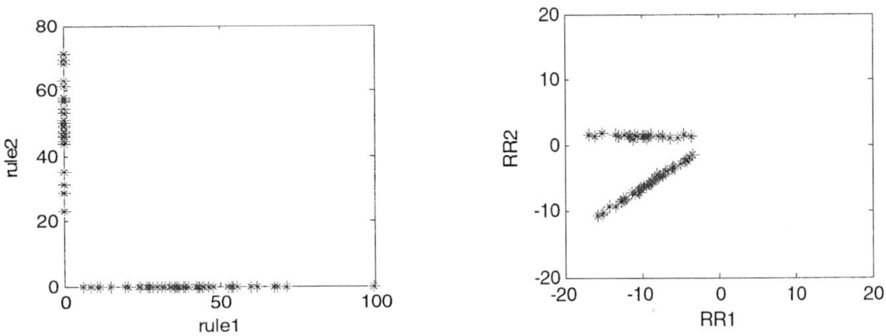

(a) PNSC (b) PCA

Fig. 4. Data projection in PNSC and PCA subspace

Ratio Rules on PNSC:

Table 1.lists all rules (columns of W) and corresponding *support* values. According to the *support* measurement of rule we rank rules: $RR_1 > RR_2 > RR_3$. Since $support(w_1) + support(w_2) = 0.9535 > 90\%$ Thus, the Ratio Rules, which illustrate the association between items, are:

$$rule_1 :: \quad X:Y:Z \;\; => 0:0.493:0.507 \qquad (0.6650)$$
$$rule_2 :: \quad X:Y:Z \;\; => 0.696:0.304:0 \qquad (0.2885)$$
where X,Y,Z represents the items (columns of matrix)

In addition, Fig.4 (a) indicates all the data projection in PNSC subspace possess the sparse property. That is, every record can be well represented using only a few significant non-zero latent coefficients. For example, 2/3 records (the cluster with distribution on y-z plain) mostly depend on $rule_1$ and others on $rule_2$. Therefore, the corresponding *support* value (0.665) of $rule_1$ is consistent with intuition.

Ratio Rules on PCA:

According to the method by PCA, we retain two corresponding *eigen-vectors* as Ratio Rules in Table 2. From Table 2, we find some entities of Ratio Rule to contain negative values, which cannot be explained intuitively the association between such items. Furthermore, in the work [6], no measurement is given to rank the importance of Ratio Rules for the input dataset, thus we can not separate those Ratio Rules that are more important for the entire dataset. In addition, from Fig.4 (b), the projection of a dataset in a PCA space does not have the sparsity features, which are the features of PNSC instead.

Real Dataset: NBA (459×11)
This dataset comes from the basketball statistics from the dataset obtained from the 1997-1998 season, including minutes played, Point per Game, Assist per Game, etc. The reason why we select this dataset is that it can give an intuitive meaning of such latent associations. Table 3 presents the first three Ratio Rules (RR_1, RR_2, RR_3) by the PNSC. Based on a general knowledge of basketball and through examination of these rules, we conjecture the RR_1 represents the agility of a player, which gives the Ratio of Assists per Game and Steals, is $0.21{:}0.22 \approx 1{:}1$. It means that the average player who possesses once of assist per game will be also steal the ball once. RR_2 shows the number

Table 3. Relative values of Ratio Rules by PNSC from NBA

Field	RR_1	RR_2	RR_3
Games			0.450
Minute			0.013
Points Per Game			0.010
Rebound Per Game		0.12	
Assists per Game	0.21		
Steals	0.22		
Block Shots			
Total Rebound			
Fouls		0.26	
Field Goals			
3Points			

Table 4. Relative values of Ratio Rules by PCA from NBA

field	RR_1	RR_2	RR_3
Games			-0.586
Minute		0.280	0.332
Points Per Game			0.389
Rebound Per Game		-0.374	
Assists per Game	0.167		
Steals	0.229		
Block Shots			
Total Rebound			
Fouls		-0.320	
Field Goals			
3Points			

of rebounds per game is correlated with Fouls time in a $0.12 : 0.26 \approx 1:2.17$ ratio, and this Ratio Rule can be interpreted with the following: an average player who makes better in rebound usually are easy to make more fouls per game. In this case, the traditional method cannot give such ratio information behind the dataset. In addition, in the Table 4, we list the results according to the method by PCA and we will find some entities of Ratio Rule to contain negative values (such as RR_2). Obviously, this rule lacks the intuition to explain the association that a player who adds 0.28 minute of play time will obtain (-0.374) rebound per game and (-0.320) times of fouls.

6 Conclusions

In this paper, we have defined the Principal Non-negative Sparse Coding (PNSC) as a combination of sparse coding with the constraints of non-negative matrix factorization. Based on PNSC algorithm, an extension of association rules is provided for learning latent components in large database. Although this approach is a special case of NMF in fact, experimental results illustrate that our approach is more suitable for learning quantifiable associations between items.

Acknowledgments

We are very grateful to the anonymous reviewers and editor. Their many helpful and constructive comments and suggestions helped us significantly improve this work.

References

[1] Agrawal, R., Imielinski, T. and Swami, A.N., Mining association rules between sets of items in large databases. In Proceedings of the 1993 ACM SIGMOD, (Washington, 1993), 207-216.

[2] Agrawal, R. and Srikant, R., Fast algorithms for mining association rules. In Proceedings of VLDB'94, (Santiago,Chile, 1994), 487 - 499.

[3] Aumann, Y. and Lindell, Y., A statistical theory for quantitative association rules. In Proceedings of KDD, (1999), 261-270.

[4] Guan, J.W., Bell, D.A. and Liu, D.Y., The Rough Set Approach to Association Rule Mining. In Proceedings of the Third IEEE International Conference on Data Mining, (Melbourne, Florida, 2003) 529- 532.

[5] Han, J. and Fu, Y., Discovery of Multiple-Level Association Rules from Large Databases. In Proceedings of the VLDB95, (1995), 420--431.

[6] Korn, F., Labrinidis, A., Kotidis, Y. and Faloutsos, C., Quantifiable Data Mining Using Principal Component Analysis. In Proceedings of VLDB, (1998), 582-593.

[7] Lee, D.D. and Seung, H.S., Algorithms for nonnegative matrix factorization. In Proceedings of the Advances in Neural Information Processing Systems 13, (Cambridge, 2001), MIT Press, 556-- 562.

[8] Li, W., Han, J. and Pe, J., CMAR: Accurate and Efficient Classification Based on Multiple Class-Association Rules. In Proceedings of the 2001 Int. Conf. on Data Mining (ICDM'01), (San Jose, CA, 2001) 369--376.

[9] Lin, J. and Dunham, M.H., Mining association rules: Anti-skew algorithms. In Proceedings of the Intl. Conf. on Data Engineering, 1998, 486--493,

[10] Otey, M.E, Wang,C, Parthasarathy, S, etc, Mining Frequent Itemsets in Distributed and Dynamic Databases. In Proceedings of the ICDM 2003, (2003), 617-620.

[11] Kaya,M and Alhajj, R, Facilitating Fuzzy Association Rules Mining by Using Multi-Objective Genetic Algorithms for Automated Clustering. In Proceedings of the ICDM 2003, (2003), 561-564.

[12] Ng, E.K.K., Fu, A.W.-C. and Wang, K., Mining Association Rules from Stars. In Proceedings of the 2nd IEEE Intl. Conf. on Data Mining, (Maebashi, Japan,, 2002), 322-329.

[13] Olshausen, B.A. and Field, D.J. Emergence of simple-cell receptive field properties by learning a sparse code for natural images. Nature 381. 607--609,1996.

[14] Patrik O. Hoyer. Non-negative sparse coding. In Proc. IEEE Workshop on Neural Networks for Signal Processing, Martigny, Switzerland, 2002

[15] Schuster, A., Wolff, R. and Trock, D., A High-Performance Distributed Algorithm for Mining Association Rules. In Proceedings of the ICDM 2003, (2003), 291-298.

[16] Srikant, r. and Agrawal, R., Mining quantitative association rules in large relational tables. In Proceedings of the the 1996 ACM SIGMOD international conference on Management of data, 1996, 1-12

[17] Wang, H., Perng, C.S., Ma, S. and Yu, P.S., Mining Associations by Pattern Structure in Large Relational Tables. In Proceedings of the 2nd IEEE Intl. Conf. on Data Mining, (Maebashi, Japan, 2002), 482-489.

[18] Wolff, R. and Schuster, A., Association Rule Mining in Peer-to-Peer Systems. In Proceedings of the ICDM 2003, (2003), 291-298.

[19] Zaki, M.J., Parthasarathy, S., Ogihara, M. and Li, W. New parallel algorithms for fast discovery of association rules. Data Mining and Knowledge Discovery: An International Journal, 4(1):343--373, December 1997.

A Fast Algorithm for Mining Share-Frequent Itemsets

Yu-Chiang Li[1], Jieh-Shan Yeh[2], and Chin-Chen Chang[1,3]

[1] Department of Computer Science and Information Engineering,
National Chung Cheng University, Chiayi 621, Taiwan
{lyc, ccc}@cs.ccu.edu.tw
[2] Department of Computer Science and Information Management,
Providence University, Taichung 433, Taiwan
jsyeh@pu.edu.tw
[3] Department of Computer Science and Information Engineering,
Feng Chia University, Taichung 407, Taiwan

Abstract. Itemset share has been proposed as a measure of the importance of itemsets for mining association rules. The value of the itemset share can provide useful information such as total profit or total customer purchased quantity associated with an itemset in database. The discovery of share-frequent itemsets does not have the downward closure property. Existing algorithms for discovering share-frequent itemsets are inefficient or do not find all share-frequent itemsets. Therefore, this study proposes a novel Fast Share Measure (FSM) algorithm to efficiently generate all share-frequent itemsets. Instead of the downward closure property, FSM satisfies the level closure property. Simulation results reveal that the performance of the FSM algorithm is superior to the ZSP algorithm two to three orders of magnitude between 0.2% and 2% minimum share thresholds.

1 Introduction

Recent developments in information science have a surprisingly rapid accumulation of data. Accordingly, efficiently managing massive bodies of data, rapidly discovering useful information, and making effective decisions based on data are crucial [10]. Newly developed data mining or knowledge discovery techniques have made routine the once impossible task of gathering hidden but potentially useful information from data in a large database or in a data warehouse. Such techniques have been widely applied in numerous areas, and have come to represent an important field of research.

Mining association rules is the main task of various data mining techniques. Agrawal *et al.* first introduced the problem, and developed an Apriori algorithm to generate all significant association rules for the retail organization in the context of bar code data analysis [2, 3]. The mining of association rules includes two-step process (1) finding all *frequent itemsets*, and (2) using these frequent itemsets to derive the association rules. Restated, the corresponding association rules can be straightforwardly derived from the frequent itemsets. Therefore, the first step is critical in mining associations. As the amount of data increase, the design of efficient algorithm becomes increasingly urgent. Various methods have been proposed to speed up the mining process, such as Apriori and subsequent Apriori-like algorithms [2, 3, 7, 8, 16] and pattern-growth methods [1, 11, 12, 15, 17].

Y. Zhang et al. (Eds.): APWeb 2005, LNCS 3399, pp. 417 – 428, 2005.

Given a database of customer transactions, the goal of data analysis is to discover the buying patterns of customers. Such information hints that how to group the products in store layout or product packets to promote these goods. Each product is regarded as an *item*. An *itemset* is a group of items bought together in a transaction. The *support* value of an itemsets is the typical measure to address the importance of an itemset in a transaction database [2]. An itemset is referred as frequent itemsets when the occurrence count of the itemsets in a database is above a threshold value. However, the support measure only considers the number of transactions in which the itemset was purchased. The exact purchased number of products is not analyzed. Therefore, the support count method does not measure in terms of the profit or cost of an itemset. In 1997, Carter *et al.* presented a share-confidence framework to provide useful information about numerical values associated with transaction items and addressed the problem of mining characterized association rules from itemsets [9]. Recently, several searches about share measure have been proposed to efficiently extract share-frequent (SH-frequent) itemsets with infrequent subsets [4, 5, 6, 13, 14].

An SH-frequent itemset usually includes some infrequent subsets. Consequently, the downward closure property cannot be applied to discover all share-frequent itemsets. Existing algorithms are either inefficient or do not discover complete share-frequent itemsets. Accordingly, this study proposes an efficient Fast Share Measure (FSM) algorithm to discover all SH-Frequent itemset. Instead of the downward closure property, FSM employs the level closure property to rapidly reduce the number of candidate itemsets. The inequality of level closure property guarantees all supersets of the pruned itemsets must be infrequent. This study focuses on the technique to discover all SH-frequent itemsets efficiently.

The rest of this paper is organized as follows. Section 2 introduces the review of support-confidence and share-confidence frameworks. Section 3 explains the level closure property and the proposed fast share measure (FSM) algorithm. FSM applies the level closure property to efficiently prune useless candidates. Section 4 provides experimental results and evaluates the performance of the proposed algorithm. Finally, we conclude in Section 5 with a summary of our work.

2 Reviews of Support and Share Measures

2.1 The Support-Confidence Framework

In 1993, Agrawal *et al.* first presented a model to define the problem of mining association rules [2, 3]. Given a transaction database, the mining of association rules is to discover the important rules that apply to items. Let $I = \{i_1, i_2, \ldots, i_m\}$ be a set of literals, called items. Let X be a set of items $X \subseteq I$, which is called an itemset. Let $DB = \{T_1, T_2, \ldots, T_n\}$ be the transaction database, where each transaction $T \in DB$, $T \subseteq I$, $1 \le q \le n$. Each transaction is associated with a unique identifier, called *TID*. An itemset X is contained in T if and only if $X \subseteq T$. An association rule is an implication of the form $X \Rightarrow Y$, where $X \subseteq I$, $Y \subseteq I$ and $X \bigcap Y = \phi$ (For example, $I=\{ABCDE\}$, $X=\{AE\}$, $Y=\{BD\}$). An association rule $X \Rightarrow Y$ has two characteristic values, called *support* and *confidence*. The support of an itemset X, denoted as support(X), is the percentage of transactions in *DB* containing *X*. If the itemset $X \cup Y$ appears in *s*% transactions of *DB*, the support of the rule $X \Rightarrow Y$ is *s*%. This is taken to be the probability, $Pr(X \cup Y)$. The rule $X \Rightarrow Y$ has confidence *c*% in *DB* if *c*% is the percentage of transactions in *DB* containing *X* that also contain *Y*. This is taken to the conditional probability, $Pr(Y|X)$. The mathematical expression of confidence is confidence($X \Rightarrow Y$) = support($X \cup Y$)/support(X). The problem of mining association rules is to discover all rules whose support and confidence satisfy the user-specified minimum support (*minSup*) and minimum confidence (*minConf*) requirements, respectively. An itemset is called a *frequent* itemset when its support is greater than or equal to the *minSup* threshold.

Given a user-specified *minSup*, Apriori employs the characteristic of the downward closure to discover the frequent itemsets by filtering some infrequent itemsets beforehand. The downward closure property is that any subset of a frequent itemset must be frequent; otherwise the itemset is infrequent. The process makes multiple passes over the database. In each pass, Apriori collects a candidate set of frequent itemsets. The algorithm scans the entire transaction database to count the number of the occurrences of each candidate *k*-itemset (which is an itemset with *k* items), and then determines the frequent itemsets. Candidate *k*-itemsets are established from two arbitrary frequent (*k*-1)-itemsets, whose first *k* - 2 items are identical. If $k \geq 3$, Apriori applies the downward closure property to reduce the number of candidates. The process is repeated until no candidate can be generated.

Example 2.1. Consider the example database with eight transactions in Table 1 and the minimum support threshold is 36%. Let C_k be the set of candidate *k*-itemsets and F_k be the set of frequent *k*-itemsets. In the first pass, Apriori scans the database to count the support value of each item of C_1. In Figure 1, four 1-itemsets $\{B\}$, $\{C\}$, $\{D\}$ and $\{E\}$ satisfy the minimum support requirement and are added to F_1. Then, each frequent 1-itemset joins with each other to form C_2. In the second pass, Apriori scan the database second time to examine which itemsets of C_2 are frequent. C_3 is generated from F_2 as follows. Figure 1 displays two frequent itemsets of F_2 with the same first item, such as $\{BC\}$ and $\{BD\}$. Then, Apriori checks the 2-itemset $\{CD\}$, which is a subset of $\{BCD\}$ to determine whether $\{CD\}$ is frequent. If $\{CD\}$ is not frequent, then $\{BCD\}$ must be infrequent. Since $\{CD\}$ is in F_2, all the subsets of $\{BCD\}$ are frequent. Hence, $\{BCD\}$ is a candidate 3-itemset. The algorithm stops when no candidate 4-itemset can be generated from F_3. In each pass, Apriori scans the database once. Consequently, Apriori scans the database *k* times.

2.2 The Share-Confidence Framework

In 1997, Hilderman *et al.* first introduced the share-confidence framework, which is an alternative measure of the importance of itemsets [9]. The local measure value of an itemset *X* is the total count of each distinct item in the itemset in each transaction, which contains *X*. The share value is of an itemset *X* is known as the ratio of the local measure value to the total measure value in *DB*. Each item has a numerical attribute in each transaction. The value of the numerical attribute of an item i_p in a transaction T_q is called the *transaction measure value*, denoted as $tmv(i_p, T_q)$. For Table 1 example, *tmv*(*F*, *T02*) = 4. The type of the numerical attribute can be an integer type, such as the purchased quantity of customers in a transaction, or a real type such as profit margin, unit cost, or total revenue. The other notations and definitions of share measure are described as follows [6].

Table 1. Example of a transaction database with counting

TID	Transaction	Count
T01	{A, B, C, D, E, G, H}	{1, 1, 1, 1, 1, 1, 1}
T02	{F, H}	{4, 3}
T03	{B, C, D}	{4, 3, 3}
T04	{C, E}	{4, 1}
T05	{B, D}	{3, 2}
T06	{B, C, D}	{3, 2, 1}
T07	{B, C, D, E}	{3, 4, 1, 2}
T08	{A, F, G}	{4, 1, 1}

Pass 1

Scan *DB* ==>

C_1	Support
{A}	2
{B}	5
{C}	5
{D}	5
{E}	3
{F}	2
{G}	2
{H}	2

==>

F_1	Support
{B}	5
{C}	5
{D}	5
{E}	3

Pass 2

$F_1 \infty F_1$ ==>

C_2
{BC}
{BD}
{BE}
{CD}
{CE}
{DE}

Scan *DB* ==>

C_2	Support
{BC}	4
{BD}	5
{BE}	2
{CD}	4
{CE}	3
{DE}	2

==>

F_2	Support
{BC}	4
{BD}	5
{CD}	4

Pass 3

$F_2 \infty F_2$ & Prune ==>

C_3
{BCD}

Scan *DB* ==>

C_3	Support
{BCD}	4

==>

F_3	Support
{BCD}	4

Fig. 1. Application of Apriori algorithm

Definition 2.1. Each *k*-itemset $X \subseteq I$ has an associated transaction set $db_X = \{T_q \in DB \mid X \subseteq T_q\}$. In other words, db_X is a set of transactions containing itemset *X*.

Definition 2.2. The *global measure value* $gmv(i_p)$ of an item i_p is the sum of $tmv(i_p, T_q)$, where $T_q \in DB$. In other words, $gmv(i_p) = \sum_{T_q \in DB} tmv(i_p, T_q)$.

Definition 2.3. The *total measure value TMV* of all items is the sum of the *global measure value* of each item i_p. In other words, $TMV = \sum_{p=1}^{m} gmv(i_p)$, where m is the number of all distinct items.

Definition 2.4. The *local measure value* $lmv(i_p, X)$ of an item i_p in an itemset X is the sum of the transaction measure values of the item i_p in all transactions that contain X. In other words, $lmv(i_p, X) = \sum_{T_q \in db_x} tmv(i_p, T_q)$. Similarly, the local measure value $lmv(X)$ of an itemset X is the sum of the local measure values of each item i_p in X. In other words $lmv(X) = \sum_{i_p \in X} lmv(i_p, X)$.

Definition 2.5. The *item share* of an item i_p in X, denoted as $SH(i_p, X)$, is the ratio of the local measure value of i_p to the total measure value. In other words, $SH(i_p, X) = \frac{lmv(i_p, X)}{TMV}$. Similarly, the *itemset share* of an itemset X, denoted as $SH(X)$, is the ratio of the local measure value of X to the total measure value. In other words, $SH(X) = \frac{lmv(X)}{TMV}$.

Definition 2.6. A k-itemset X is *share-frequent* (SH-frequent) if $SH(X)$ is greater than a pre-defined minimum threshold (*minShare*) $s\%$.

Example 2.2. Consider the same transaction database as in Table 1 with a minimum share threshold of 36%. As shown in Table1, the column Count lists the corresponding count of each item in a transaction. The global measure value and the item share of each item are listed in Table 2, where $TMV = 56$. The local measure value of $\{B\}$ in the itemset $\{B, C, D\}$ is $lmv(B, \{BCD\}) = 1 + 4 + 3 + 3 = 11$. $SH(\{BCD\}) = lmv(\{BCD\})/TMV = (lmv(B, \{BCD\}) + lmv(C, \{BCD\}) + lmv(D, \{BCD\}))/56$. Then, $SH(\{BCD\}) = (11 + 10 + 6)/56 = 0.482 > 36\%$. Therefore, $\{B, C, D\}$ is SH-frequent. Table 3 enumerates all SH-frequent itemsets.

Table 2. Occurrence count (global measure value) and itemset share of each 1-itemset

Item	A	B	C	D	E	F	G	H	Total
$gmv(i_p)$	5	14	14	8	4	5	2	4	56
$SH(i_p)$	8.9%	25%	25%	14.3%	7.1%	8.9%	3.6%	7.1%	100%

Table 3. All SH-frequent itemsets of the sample database

SH-frequent itemset	BC	BD	BCD
$lmv(X)$	21	22	27
$SH(X)$	37.5%	39.3%	48.2%

3 Fast Share Measure (FSM) Algorithm

The Apriori-like algorithms employ the downward closure property to discover efficiently frequent itemsets based on the support measure. All (k-1)-itemsets of a candidate k-itemset are frequent itemsets, otherwise, the k-itemset can be pruned. Therefore, the characteristic of downward closure can be used to reduce the number of candidates and speed up the process. However, an SH-frequent itemset could include some infrequent subsets. It does not satisfy the downward closure property. Obviously, the exhaustive search method can find all SH-frequent itemsets, but has an exponential running time. Barber and Hamilton presented the ZP (zero pruning) algorithm and the ZSP (zero subset pruning) algorithm to improve the performance [6]. However, the two algorithms only prune the candidate itemsets whose local measure values are exactly zero. There is no efficient algorithm to discover all SH-frequent itemsets up to now. Consequently, this study develops a fast share measure (FSM) algorithm to find all SH-frequent itemsets efficiently.

3.1 Level Closure Property

The notations and definitions of FSM are described as follows.

Definition 3.1. The maximum length of all transactions in DB is denoted as ML. That is, $ML = \max(|T_q| \mid T_q \in DB)$.

Definition 3.2. Let MV be the *maximum transaction measure value* of all items in DB. That is, $MV = \max(tmv(i_p, T_q) \mid i_p \in T_q, \text{ and } T_q \in DB)$.

Definition 3.3. Let X be an itemset, which is a subset of X', the local measure value of X on X', denoted as $lmv(X, X')$, is the sum of the local measure values of each item i_p in X' in DB, where i_p in X. That is, $lmv(X, X') = \sum_{i_p \in X} lmv(i_p, X')$.

If $X = X'$, then $lmv(X, X') = lmv(X)$. The local measure values of itemsets have some characteristics, which are described as follows.

Lemma 3.1. Let X, X' and X'' be itemsets, where $X \subseteq X' \subseteq X''$, then
(1) $lmv(X, X'') \leq lmv(X', X'')$. Especially, when $X' = X''$, $lmv(X, X') \leq lmv(X')$.
(2) $lmv(X, X') \geq lmv(X, X'')$. Especially, when $X = X'$, $lmv(X) \geq lmv(X, X'')$.

Proof.
(1) Since $X \subseteq X'$, for arbitrary item i_p in X, i_p is also in X'. $lmv(X, X'') = \sum_{i_p \in X} lmv(i_p, X'') \leq \sum_{i_p \in X'} lmv(i_p, X'') = lmv(X', X'')$.

(2) Since $X' \subseteq X''$, $db_{X'} \supseteq db_{X''}$. For arbitrary item i_p in X, $lmv(i_p, X') \geq lmv(i_p, X'')$. Therefore, $lmv(X, X') \geq lmv(X, X'')$. Q.E.D

Lemma 3.2. Let X be a *k-itemset*, then $|db_X| \times k \leq lmv(X) \leq |db_X| \times k \times MV$.

Proof. By Definition 2.4, $lmv(X) = \sum_{i_p \in X} lmv(i_p, X) = \sum_{i_p \in X} \sum_{T_q \in db_x} tmv(i_p, T_q)$. For each item i_p and transaction T_q, $1 \leq tmv(i_p, T_q) \leq MV$. Therefore, $|db_X| \times k \leq lmv(X) \leq |db_X| \times k \times MV$. Q.E.D

Theorem 3.1. Given a *minShare* and a k-itemset X, if $lmv(X) + (lmv(X)/k) \times MV < minShare \times TMV$, all supersets of X with length $k + 1$ are infrequent.

Proof. For arbitrary superset X' of X with length $k + 1$, says $X' = X \cup \{i_p\}$. By Definition 3.3, $lmv(X') = lmv(X', X') = lmv(X, X') + lmv(i_p, X')$. First, by Lemma 3.1, we have $lmv(X, X') \leq lmv(X)$. Second, by Lemma 3.2 on X', $lmv(i_p, X') \leq |db_{X'}| \times MV$. Since $db_{X'}$ is a subset of db_X, $|db_{X'}| \leq |db_X|$. So, $lmv(i_p, X') \leq |db_X| \times MV \leq (lmv(X)/k) \times MV$, by Lemma 3.1 on X. Now, we have $lmv(X') \leq lmv(X) + (lmv(X)/k) \times MV$. If the inequality $lmv(X) + (lmv(X)/k) \times MV < minShare \times TMV$ holds, $lmv(X') < minShare \times TMV$. That is, $SH(X') = lmv(X')/TMV < minShare$. X' is infrequent. Theorem is proofed. Q.E.D

Theorem 3.2. Given a *minShare*, a k-itemset X and a positive integer k', if $lmv(X) + (lmv(X)/k) \times MV \times k' < minShare \times TMV$, all supersets of X with length less than or equal to $k + k'$ are infrequent.

Proof. Let X' be an arbitrary superset of X with length $k + i$, where $1 \leq i \leq k'$. Let $Y = X' - X$. Clearly, the size of Y is i. With the same argument in Theorem 3.1, we have

(1) $lmv(X') = lmv(X', X') = lmv(X, X') + lmv(Y, X')$.
(2) $lmv(X, X') \leq lmv(X)$.
(3) $lmv(Y, X') \leq |db_{X'}| \times i \times MV \leq (lmv(X)/k) \times MV \times i \leq (lmv(X)/k) \times MV \times k'$.

So, $lmv(X') \leq lmv(X) + (lmv(X)/k) \times MV \times k'$. If the inequality $lmv(X) + (lmv(X)/k) \times MV \times k' < minShare \times TMV$ holds, $lmv(X') < minShare \times TMV$. That is, $SH(X') = lmv(X') / TMV < minShare$. X' is infrequent. Q.E.D

Corollary 3.1. Given a *minShare* and a k-itemset X, if $lmv(X) + (lmv(X)/k) \times MV \times (ML - k) < minShare \times TMV$, all supersets of X are infrequent.

Proof. Since the maximum length of all transactions in DB is ML, $lmv(X') = 0$ for any superpset X' of X with length greater than ML. Definitely, X' is infrequent. For arbitrary superset X' of X with length less than or equal to ML, if the inequality $lmv(X) + (lmv(X)/k) \times MV \times (ML - k) < minShare \times TMV$ holds, by Theorem 3.2, X' is infrequent. Corollary is proofed. Q.E.D

Definition 3.4. The characteristic of Theorem 3.1, Theorem 3.2 and Corollary 3.1 is called the *level closure property*. For a given integer k', let CF be a critical function, defined as $CF(X) = lmv(X) + (lmv(X)/k) \times MV \times L$, where $L = \min\{ML-k, k'\}$.

Theorem 3.2 guarantees if $CF(X) < minShare \times TMV$ holds, no superset of X with length $\leq k + k'$ is SH-frequent. The level closure property can be applied to prune candidates whose supersets are not SH-frequent with length $\leq k + k'$, but it cannot ensure the SH-frequency of the supersets with length greater than $k + k'$. Accordingly, Corollary 3.1 modifies the level closure property of Theorem 3.2 and assures that all supersets of X are not SH-frequent if $CF(X) < minShare \times TMV$.

3.2 Fast Share Measure (FSM) Algorithm

The FSM algorithm is a level-wise and a multiple passes algorithm. In the k-th pass, let C_k be the candidate set, RC_k be the remainder candidates after checking the critical function *CF*, and F_k be the SH-frequent set. Like Apriori, each single item is a candidate. In the first pass, FSM scans the database to count the local measure value of each item. Each candidate 1-itemset X is pruned when $CF(X) < minShare \times TMV$. In next each pass, FSM joins arbitrary two candidates in $RC_{k\text{-}1}$, whose first k-2 items are identical. The k subsets with length (k - 1) of each k-itemset in C_k are in $RC_{k\text{-}1}$; otherwise the k-itemset can be pruned. After C_k is produced, delete the $RC_{k\text{-}1}$. Next, for each itemset X in C_k, if the itemset share $lmv(X)/TMV$ is higher than *minShare*, X is added to F_k; if $CF(X)$ is greater than *minShare,* the superset of X could be SH-frequesnt, so X is added to RC_k. The process is repeated until no candidate can be generated.

The pseudo code of FSM is described as follows.

Algorithm. FSM(k')

Input: (1) *DB*: a transaction database with counts, (2) *minShare*: minimum share threshold, and (3) k': the parameter of critical function (Definition 3.4)

Output: All SH-frequent itemsets

Procedure:

```
k:=1; F_1:=∅; C_1:=I;
foreach T∈ DB { // scan DB
     count the local measure value of each item; }
foreach i_p∈ C_1    {
     if lmv(i_p) ≥ minShare× TMV {
          F_1:= F_1+i_p; }
     elseif CF(i_p)<minShare× TMV {
          C_1:= C_1-i_p;   }
}
RC_1:=C_1;
for k:=2 to h {
     foreach X_p, X_q ∈ RC_{k-1} {
          C_k :=Apriori-join(X_p, X_q); }
     foreach T∈ DB { // scan DB
          count each candidate's local measure value; }
     foreach X∈ C_k     {
          if lmv(X) ≥ minShare× TMV {
               F_k:= F_k+X; }
          elseif CF(X) <minShare× TMV {
               C_k:= C_k-X;    }    }
     RC_k:= C_k;
}
return F
```

4 Experimental Results

The performance of FSM was compared with that of ZSP using a 1.5GHz Pentium IV PC with 1GB of main memory, running Windows XP Professional. All algorithms were coded using Visual C++ 6.0, and applied to process the synthetic dataset. The whole SH-frequent itemsets were output to main memory to reduce the effect of disk writing.

The IBM synthetic dataset was generated using a synthetic data generator [18]. The VC++ version of the data generator was obtained from [19]. Table 4 lists the parameters of the synthetic data generation program.

Table 4. Parameters

x	Mean size of the transactions
y	Mean size of the maximal potentially frequent itemsets
z	Number of transactions in *DB*
n	Number of items

The notation Tx.Iy.Dz.Nn denotes a dataset with given parameters x, y, z and n. To simulate the characteristic of the count in each item in each transaction, the count of each item in each transaction is randomly generated between 1 to m, with the proportion of 1 equal 50%. The notation of the dataset becomes Tx.Iy.Dz.Nn.Sm.

Figures 2 plots the performance curves associated with the two algorithms applied to T4.I2.D100k.N50.S10. The x-axis represents the several distinct *minShare* thresholds between 0.2% and 2%, and the y-axis represents the running time. Note that Fig. 2 uses a logarithmic scale for y-axis. *FSM*(1), *FSM*(2), *FSM*(3) and *FSM*(*ML*-1) are special cases of the FSM algorithm with different parameter k', respectively. The lower *minShare* threshold results in the longer running time of FSM. In the low *minShare* (0.2%) scenario, *FSM*(*ML*-1) outperforms the ZSP algorithm two orders of magnitude. Contract to the high *minShare* (2%) scenario, *FSM*(*ML* – 1) outperforms ZSP more than three orders of magnitude. *FSM*(*ML* – 1) always outperforms ZSP and discovers all SH-frequent itemsets. In Fig. 2, *FSM*(1) is always the fastest. Although it could loss some SH-frequent itemsets while the parameter k' of FSM is set less than *ML* – 1, the output set of SH-frequent itemsets is identical with that of ZSP using T4.I2.D100k.N50.S10 with *minShare* = 0.8% as listed in Table 5. The number of C_k, RC_k and F_k and the total running time of ZSP and FSM algorithms are also listed in Table 5. ZSP only prunes the itemsets with $SH(X) = 0$. Therefore, ZSP terminates the process at pass *ML*. The value of *ML* of T4.I2.D100k.N50.S10 is 14. Contrast to *FSM*(1), *FSM*(2), *FSM*(3) and *FSM*(*ML*-1), their processes terminate at pass 5, 6, 6 and 6, respectively. In a very low *minShare* (0.005%) scenario, *FSM*(1), *FSM*(2) and *FSM*(3) lose some SH-frequent itemsets using the dataset. In the scenario, *FSM*(*ML* - 1) discovers all SH-frequent itemset.

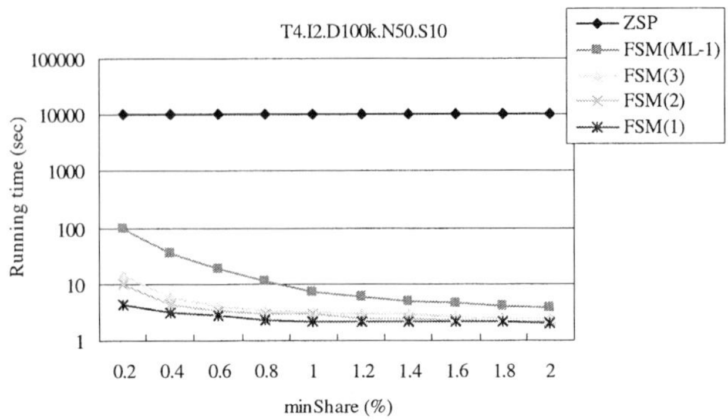

Fig. 2. Comparison of running time using T4.I2.D100k.N50.S10

Table 5. Comparison of the number of candidate set and SH-frequent set (F_k) in each pass using T4.I2.D100k.N50.S10 with *minShare* = 0.8% (*ML*=14)

Pass (*k*) \ Method		ZSP	FSM(1)	FSM(2)	FSM(3)	FSM(*ML*-1)
k=1	C_k	50	50	50	50	50
	RC_k	50	49	49	49	50
	F_k	32	32	32	32	32
k=2	C_k	1225	1176	1176	1176	1225
	RC_k	1219	570	754	845	1085
	F_k	119	119	119	119	119
k=3	C_k	19327	4256	7062	8865	14886
	RC_k	17217	868	1685	2410	5951
	F_k	65	65	65	65	65
k=4	C_k	165077	1725	3233	5568	24243
	RC_k	107397	232	644	1236	6117
	F_k	9	9	9	9	9
k=5	C_k	406374	81	258	717	6309
	RC_k	266776	5	40	109	1199
	F_k	0	0	0	0	0
k=6	C_k	369341	0	1	4	287
	RC_k	310096	0	0	0	37
	F_k	0	0	0	0	0
$k \geq 7$	C_k	365975	0	0	0	0
	RC_k	359471	0	0	0	0
	F_k	0	0	0	0	0
Time(sec)		10349.9	2.30	2.98	3.31	11.24

Figure 3 presents the scalability with the number of transactions of *DB*. The *x*-axis represents the several distinct *DB* sizes between 100k and 1000k, and the *y*-axis represents the running time. Figure 3 uses a logarithmic scale for *y*-axis. Consider *minShare* = 0.8%, the running time linearly increases with the growth of the *DB* size. The running time of ZSP exceeds 10^5 seconds when $|DB| \geq 600$k.

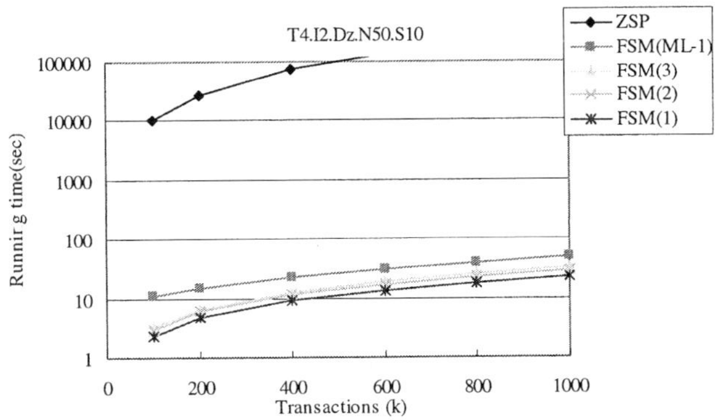

Fig. 3. Scalability with the transaction number of *DB*

5 Conclusions

Data mining techniques have been applied extensively across many areas, and data mining has become an important research field. Mining frequent itemsets in a transaction database plays an important role for mining association rules. Itemset share has been proposed to measure the importance of itemsets for mining association rules. Developing an efficient approach for discovering complete SH-frequent itemsets is very useful in solving numerous mining problems. However, share-frequent itemsets do not satisfy the downward closure property. To solve the problem and develop an efficient method for fast generating all SH-frequent itemsets, this study proposes the level closure property. The inequality of level closure property guarantees all supersets of the pruned itemsets must be infrequent. Consequently, the developed FSM algorithm, which implements the level closure property, can efficiently decrease the number of itemsets to be counted. Experiments indicate that FSM outperforms ZSP several orders of magnitude. In the future, the authors will consider the development of superior algorithms to improve the performance of discovering all SH-frequent itemsets.

References

1. R. C. Agarwal, C. C. Aggarwal, and V. V. V. Prasad: A Tree Projection Algorithm for Generation of Frequent Itemsets. Journal of Parallel and Distributed Computing **61** (2001) 350-361
2. R. Agrawal, T. Imielinski, and A. Swami: Mining Association Rules between Sets of Items in Large Databases. In: Proc. 1993 ACM SIGMOD Intl. Conf. on Management of Data, Washington, D.C., (1993) 207-216
3. R. Agrawal and R. Srikant: Fast Algorithms for Mining Association Rules. In Proc. 20th Intl. Conf. on Very Large Data Bases, Santiago, Chile (1994) 487-499
4. B. Barber and H. J. Hamilton: Algorithms for Mining Share Frequent Itemsets Containing Infrequent Subsets. In: D. A. Zighed, H. J. Komorowski, J. M. Zytkow (eds.): Principles of Data Mining and Knowledge Discovery. Lecture Notes in Computer Sciences, Vol. 1910. Springer-Verlag, Berlin Heidelberg New York (2000) 316-324

5. B. Barber and H. J. Hamilton: Parametric Algorithm for Mining Share Frequent Itemsets. Journal of Intelligent Information Systems **16** (2001) 277-293
6. B. Barber and H. J. Hamilton: Extracting Share Frequent Itemsets with Infrequent Subsets. Data Mining and Knowledge Discovery **7** (2003) 153-185
7. S. Brin, R. Motwani, J. D. Ullman, and S. Tsur: Dynamic Itemset Counting and Implication Rules for Market Basket Data. In: Proc. 1997 ACM SIGMOD Intl. Conf. on Management of Data, Tucson, AZ (1997) 255-264
8. F. Berzal, J. C. Cubero, N. Marín, and J. M. Serrano: TBAR: An Efficient Method for Association Rule Mining in Relational Databases. Data & Knowledge Engineering **37** (2001) 47-64
9. C. L. Carter, H. J. Hamilton, and N. Cercone: Share Based Measures for Itemsets. In: H. J. Komorowski, J. M. Zytkow (eds.): Principles of Data Mining and Knowledge Discovery. Lecture Notes in Computer Science, Vol. 1263. Springer-Verlag, Berlin Heidelberg New York (1997) 14-24
10. M. S. Chen, J. Han, and P. S. Yu: Data Mining: An Overview from a Database Perspective. IEEE Trans. Knowledge Data Engineering **8** (1996) 866-883
11. G. Grahne and J. Zhu: Efficient using Prefix-Tree in Mining Frequent Itemsets. In: Proc. IEEE ICDM Workshop on Frequent Itemset Mining Implementations, Melbourne, FL (2003)
12. J. Han, J. Pei, Y. Yin, and R. Mao: Mining Frequent Patterns without Candidate Generation: A Frequent Pattern Tree Approach. Data Mining and Knowledge Discovery **8** (2004):53-87
13. R. J. Hilderman: Predicting Itemset Sales Profiles with Share Measures and Repeat-Buying Theory. In: J. Liu, Y. M. Cheung, H. Yin (eds.): Intelligent Data Engineering and Automated Learning. Lecture Notes in Computer Science, Vol. 2690. Springer-Verlag, Berlin Heidelberg New York (2003) 789-795
14. R. J. Hilderman, C. L. Carter, H. J. Hamilton, and N. Cercone: Mining Association Rules from Market Basket Data using Share Measures and Characterized Itemsets," Intl. Journal of Artificial Intelligence Tools **7** (1998) 189-220
15. J. Liu, Y. Pan, K. Wang, and J. Han: Mining Frequent Item Sets by Opportunistic Projection. In: Proc. 8th ACM-SIGKDD Intl. Conf. on Knowledge Discovery and Dada Mining, Alberta, Canada (2002) 229-238
16. J. S. Park, M. S. Chen, and P. S. Yu: An Effective Hash-Based Algorithm for Mining Association Rules. In: Proc. 1995 ACM-SIGMOD Intl. Conf. on Management of Data, San Jose, CA (1995) 175-186
17. J. Pei, J. Han, H. Lu, S. Nishio, S. Tang, and D. Yang: H-Mine: Hyper-Structure Mining of Frequent Patterns in Large Databases. In: Proc. 2001 IEEE Intl. Conf. on Data Mining, San Jose, CA (2001) 441-448
18. http://alme1.almaden.ibm.com/software/quest/Resources/datasets/syndata.html
19. http://www.cse.cuhk.edu.hk/~kdd/data/IBM_VC++.zip

CORE: A Search and Browsing Tool for Semantic Instances of Web Sites

Myo-Myo Naing[1], Ee-Peng Lim[1], and Roger H.L. Chiang[2]

[1] Centre for Advanced Information Systems,
School of Computer Engineering, Nanyang Technological University,
Nanyang Avenue, N4-B3C-13, Singapore 639798, Singapore
mmnaing@pmail.ntu.edu.sg, aseplim@ntu.edu.sg

[2] Information Systems Department, College of Business,
University of Cincinnati, OHIO 45221-0211, USA
roger.chiang@uc.edu

Abstract. Web pages from a web site can often be associated with some semantic concepts, and relationships can exist between pairs of web pages. By deriving these concepts and relationship instances, web pages can be searched, browsed or even reorganized based on their associated concepts and relationships. In this paper, we present a search and browsing tool, CORE, for concept and relationship instances which are derived using some web classification and link chain extraction techniques. CORE assists users to quickly search and navigate the concept and relationship instances using a single user interface.

1 Introduction

The goal of recent research on Semantic Web is to enhance the accessibility of the current Web by providing semantics information about Web pages so that applications and users can easily process the Web page content [7]. To achieve this goal, one of the important tasks is to derive knowledge about the web pages and the relationship between the web pages. Once such kind of knowledge is derived, search engines and browsers are able to access web pages of different categories and their semantic relationships so as to support more complex user queries. In order to meet the above requirement, web pages from web sites need to be classified into categories.

An ontology consists of concepts and relationships between the concepts. Web pages can be associated with concepts while pairs of web pages can be associated with relationships between concepts. For example, web pages from a movie web site can be associated with concepts such as *Movie*, *Actor*, *Director*, *Producer*, etc.. These web pages are therefore instances of different concepts. Relationships between concepts such as *Actor-of(Movie,Actor)* and *DirectedBy(Movie,Director)* can have instances relating pairs of web pages. When concepts and relationships are associated with web pages, new semantic approaches to access web sites can be supported [7]. For example, web pages can

Y. Zhang et al. (Eds.): APWeb 2005, LNCS 3399, pp. 429–440, 2005.

be queried by their concept labels, or can be navigated using the relationship labels as some guidances.

Automatic assignment of concept labels to web pages has been studied extensively [6, 4]. On the other hand, automatic assignment of relationship labels is relatively new problem. In our research, we investigated the learning of link chain pattern for pairs of web pages [3]. For example, at the Yahoo! Movies Web Site[1], determining the relationships between the instances of the *Actor-of(Movie, Actor)* relationship can be found by traversing from movie web pages to the actor web pages following the links with some specific anchor text.

The semantically labelled web pages enable a new approach (sometimes known as the ontology approach) to access a web site. For example, instead of plain keyword queries, web page queries can be augmented with concept labels. Web pages can also be browsed via their relationships instead of physical links. The main objective of this research is to develop a tool known as CORE (CORE) to allow users to access a web site using the ontology approach. An integrated search and browsing interface is provided. CORE treats web pages as concept instances and its search module can support not only keyword queries on web pages of user specified concepts, but also complex queries involving web pages connected by some relationships. CORE's browser module allows web pages of user specified concepts to be browsed and virtual links are provided to traverse to other related web pages.

The rest of the paper is organised as follows. In Section 2, we review some related works. The system architecture of searching and browsing tool CORE is presented in Section 3. Section 4 gives the definition of *link chain* and brief description of *link chain* extraction method that was used to find the relationship instances. A few use case scenarios of using CORE are given in Section 5. We finally conclude the paper and highlight the future research directions in Section 6.

2 Related Work

This section reviews three research projects closely related to CORE.

Magpie [1] is a semantic Web browsing tool that allows users to view concept and relationship instances embedded in the Web pages of a Web site. Each concept instance is represented by a name and a set of attribute values, and each relationship instance is represented by a pair of concept instances. Magpie assumes that the concept and relationship instances are pre-defined in a database. These concept and relationship instances will be highlighted in those Web pages containing their names. No search capability is provided in Magpie.

MnM project [8], similar to CORE, is a tool for browsing and annotating Web pages. It adopts a knowledge base definition that consists of classes (similar to concepts in CORE) and each class has one or more attribute slots. Relationships between Web pages however are not captured. MnM can learn extraction

[1] http://movies.yahoo.com/

patterns from annotated attribute slots from a Web page and apply them to annotate other Web pages. Both the manually and automatically annotated attribute slots can be viewed in the MnM browser. Since MnM deals with mainly text based Web pages, the extraction patterns involves text matching only. There is no search module provided by MnM.

CREAM [5] supports manual annotation of Web pages (e.g., home page of a PhD student) as concept instances, text fragments (e.g., name, postal address, email address) in these pages as concept attributes, and pairs of Web pages as relationship instances, in order to facilitate navigation and queries on the Web pages. When browsing Web pages, the attribute instances and anchor text of links to related concept instances will be highlighted.

Compared to the above three projects, CORE provides both browsing and search facilities, and allows users to browse any search results. The concept instances in CORE are Web pages, and relationship instances are pairs of Web pages such that the pages representing source concept instances are connected to the pages representing target concept instances. The target concept instances of currently browsed Web pages can be reached by mouse hovering the highlighted anchor texts.

3 System Architecture

The system architecture of CORE is shown in Figure 1. It mainly consists of a search and a browsing server application, web page classification module, link chain extraction module and a knowledge repository.

Server Application. There are two main application components, namely:

- **Search Component.** The search component accepts user queries and communicates with the knowledge repository in order to derive the query results. Both *concept queries* and *relationship queries* are supported as defined below:

  Definition 1. ***Concept Query***
  Let site, C, and K be a Website, a concept label and a set of keywords respectively.
  $CQ(site, C, K) = \{w \mid w \in site, w \text{ is an instance of } C \text{ and } w \text{ contains } k\ \forall k \in K\}$

  For example:
  CQ("http://movies.yahoo.com", "*Actor*", {"*Harry*"}) returns Web pages that are *Actor* instances and that contain "Harry".

  Definition 2. ***Relationship Query***
  Let site, $R(C_1, C_2)$, K_1 and K_2 be a Website, a relationship from C_1 to C_2, two sets of keywords respectively.
  $RQ(site, R(C_1,C_2),K_1,K_2) = \{ (w_1,w_2) \mid w_1,w_2 \in site \text{ and } (w_1,w_2) \text{ is an instance of } R(C_1,C_2) \text{ where } w_1 \text{ contains } k_1\ \forall k_1 \in K_1 \text{ and } w_2 \text{ contains } k_2\ \forall k_2 \in K_2 \}$

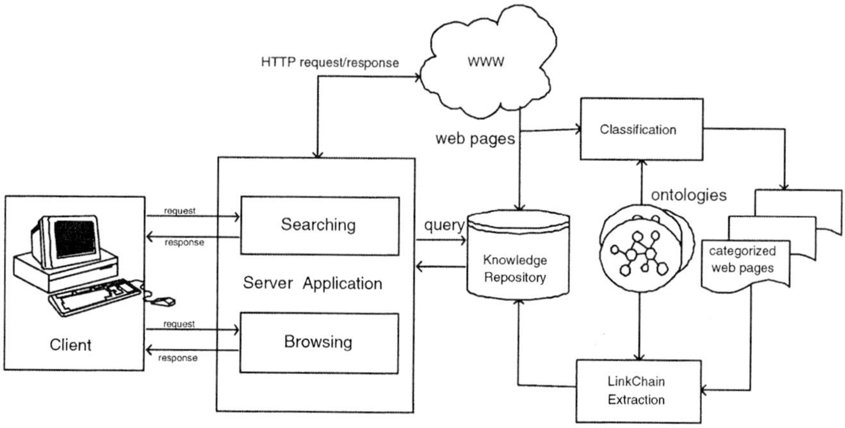

Fig. 1. Overall architecture of CORE

For example:
RQ("http://movies.yahoo.com", *Actor-of(Movie,Actor)*,{"big"},{"Harry"}) returns pairs of Web pages each consists of a *Movie* instance that contains "big", and an *Actor* instance that contains "Harry".

The search component requires Web pages from each Website to be classified and their relationships to be extracted using the Web page classification module and link chain extraction module respectively.

We use Jakarta Lucene[2] text search tool as the core indexing and search engine in our search component. Since Lucene only handles term indexing and simple keyword search. Additional query evaluation procedures have been developed to examine the concept and relationship labels of web pages.

- **Browsing Component**
  The browsing component allows users to browse any instance (Web page) in the search results or by simply entering the URL of a Web page. If the Web page to be browsed has been classified, its concept label(s) and associated relationships will be displayed in the page information frame. Note that more than one concept label may be assigned to a Web page. For example, the director of a movie may also be a producer of the other movie. Similarly, a Web page can be the source concept instance of more than one relationship. The browsing component also allows users to view Web pages augmented with highlighted anchor text strings that lead to related target pages in terms of a particular relationship. The highlighted anchor texts are parts of link chains originating from the currently viewed Web pages.

Web Page Classification Module. The web page classification module assigns concept labels to web pages from a given web site. It assumes that each

[2] http://jakarta.apache.org/lucene/docs/index.html

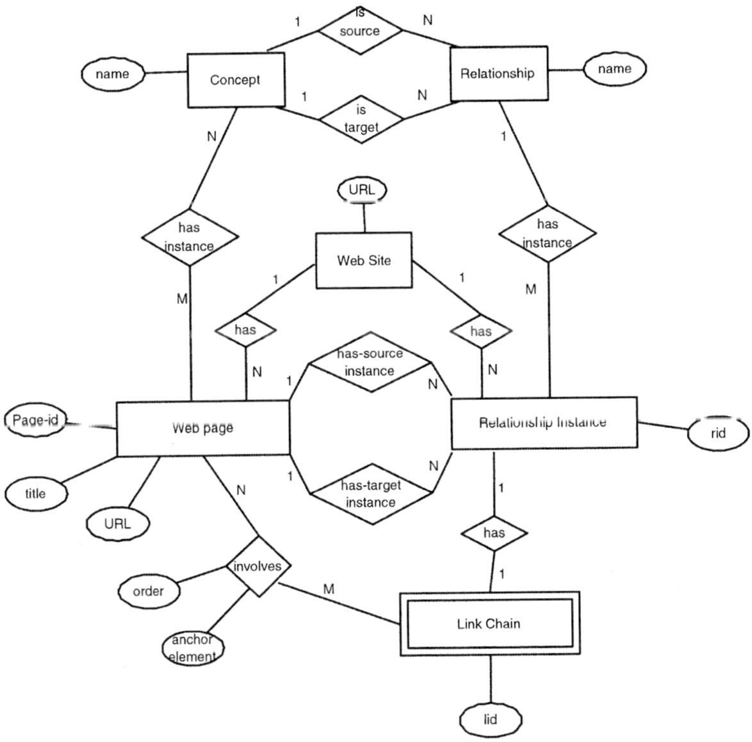

Fig. 2. ER diagram of Knowledge Repository

web site can be associated with some semantic domain and the concepts relevant to the domain will be used to label the web pages. For example, in the movies domain, the relevant concepts are *Actor*, *Movie*, *Director*, etc.. It is not necessary for CORE to classify every web page as some of them could not be assigned any concept labels and others will be labelled during the link chain extraction process as they are identified as target concept instances of some relationship instances. The current version of CORE uses URL features to classify web pages as the web sites are well structured. Web pages from two web sites, Yahoo! Movies web site[3] and DBLP web site[4], have been categorized under seven concepts. They are *Movie*, *Actor*, *Director*, *Producer* and *Writer* for the Yahoo! movie web site and *Journal* and *Author* for the DBLP web site.

Link Chain Extraction Module. Link chain extraction module extracts *link chains* from some given web pages that constitute the source concept instances. A link chain is a series of links from a source web page to a target web page such that a relationship exists between the two web pages. The link chain ex-

[3] http://movies.yahoo.com/
[4] http://www.informatik.uni-trier.de/~ley/db/journals/

traction module is designed to learn the extraction patterns of link chains from some training examples and apply them to other source web pages. The formal definition of *link chain* and extraction of link chain information will be described in Section 4.

Knowledge Repository. The knowledge repository maintains information about the ontology concepts and relationships, their instances, the link chain information of relationships, and Web pages. The ER diagram describing the content of knowledge repository is shown in Figure 2. At the top of Figure 2, the ontology concepts and relationships are modelled. The lower portion of the figure depicts the instance-level knowledge about the Web site. We apply one-to-one association between link chains and relationship instances.

CORE has been fully implemented in Java running on a Tomcat application server. It uses Microsoft Access as its underlying database system. The graphical user interface is implemented using Java Server Page(JSP) in J2EE platform.

4 Extraction of Link Chains

In this section, we give the definition of link chain and describe briefly our link chain extraction method.

4.1 Link Chain

Suppose (w_s, w_t) is an instance of a relationship $R(C_s, C_t)$. We define the link chain of (w_s, w_t) as follows:

Definition 3. (Link Chain)
The **link chain** *of* (w_s, w_t) *with respect to* $R(C_s, C_t)$ *is a list of* **chain elements** *denoted by* $((w_1, l_1), (w_2, l_2) \ldots, (w_n, l_n))$ *such that (i)* $w_1 = w_s$*; (ii)* l_i *is an anchor element in* w_i*; (iii)* $l_n.target = w_t.url$*; and (iv)* $\forall 1 \leq i < n, l_i.target = w_{i+1}.url$.

In the above definition, the target of an anchor element, $l_i.target$, refers to its *href* attribute.

For example, Figure 3 depicts a relationship instance of *Actor-of(Movie, Actor)* that involves an intermediate page (w_2)(that contains the list of cast and credits). The link chain of the relationship instance, (w_1, w_3), with respect to *Actor-of(Movie, Actor)* is $((w_1, l_1), (w_2, l_2))$.

As shown in Figure 3, the link chain $((w_1, l_1), (w_2, l_2))$ connecting from movie home page(w_1) to actor's home page(w_3) represents an essential piece of information about the *Actor-of(Movie, Actor)* relationship instance. It allows us to know which anchor elements in the chain of web pages leads us from the source web page to the target web page of a *Actor-of* relationship instance.

When a web site is well structured or is generated from some backend database, the link chains of instances of the same relationship can share very

Fig. 3. An *Actor-of* (*Movie,Actor*) relationship instance, (w_1, w_3), and its link chain

similar pattern in the way their anchors elements are embedded in the source and intermediate web pages. By learning this pattern, one can extract *all* instances of the relationship from the web site automatically. This is extremely useful in applications where only selected web pages are to downloaded from a structured web site and they can only be located by traversing from source web pages which are instances of some given concept.

4.2 Learning of Link Chain Extraction Patterns

In our research, we define a link chain extraction pattern to be a set of rules on the page paths leading to the chain elements of the link chains. Within a web page containing a chain element, a page path consists of a series of HTML segments (also known as page segments) one nested within another with the chain element being the innermost page segment. The extraction pattern therefore includes a hierarchy of extraction rules to identify these segments and extract the relevant chain element.

Formally, we can define link chain extraction pattern as follows:

Definition 4. (Link Chain Extraction Pattern)
The **link chain pattern** *of* $R(C_s, C_t)$ *is a series of* **page path patterns** *denoted by* $(pp_1, pp_2, ..., pp_n)$ *such that each* pp_i *represents the page path of web page containing the i-th chain elements. Each page path* pp_i *is a list of page segment nodes where each node is assigned one or more extraction rule.*

Definition 5. (Extraction Rule)
Each extraction rule of a page segment node is set of text predicates to determine the page segment from a given web page corresponding to the node.

The text predicates used in CORE include matching of literal strings, token types, and regular expressions.

In the current implementation, we assume that page path patterns are specified by expert users. To learn extraction rules associated with the page segment nodes, a sequential covering [2] based method has been developed. The learning method requires some link chains to be given as training examples. Detailed description of these algorithms will be reported in an extended version of [3].

Based on our experiments that involved over 1000 movie source pages from Yahoo! movie, our link chain extraction method was able to extract link chains of a few pre-defined relationships with high precision and good recall using less than 15 training examples.

5 Scenario of Searching and Browsing the Semantic Instances

In this section, we describe some usage scenarios of CORE and highlight its unique features.

5.1 Searching Scenarios

We describe the usage scenarios for querying concept and relationship instances as follows.

Concept Query
Consider a movie enthusiast gathering information about movies and related information such as actors, directors, etc.. Suppose he/she wants to search his/her favourite actor at Yahoo! Movie web site. He/she however does not recall the full name of the actor except the first name "Harry". When Google[5] search engine is given the query string "Harry site:.movies.yahoo.com" which specifies "Harry" as the search term and "movies.yahoo.com" as the web site to be searched, the results returned consist of mainly the home pages of movies containing "Harry" in their titles, e.g., "Harry Potter and the Prisoner of Azkaban", "Harry Potter and the Chamber of Secrets", etc.. In this example, Google actually fails to return any actor page in the top 10.

Unlike Google, CORE allows the user to use the concept query facility and select *Actor* as the concept to be queried. The search term "Harry" can now be specified against the web pages that are instances of the *Actor* concept. As expected, the results returned will consists of actor pages only as shown in Figure 4(a).

[5] http://www.google.com

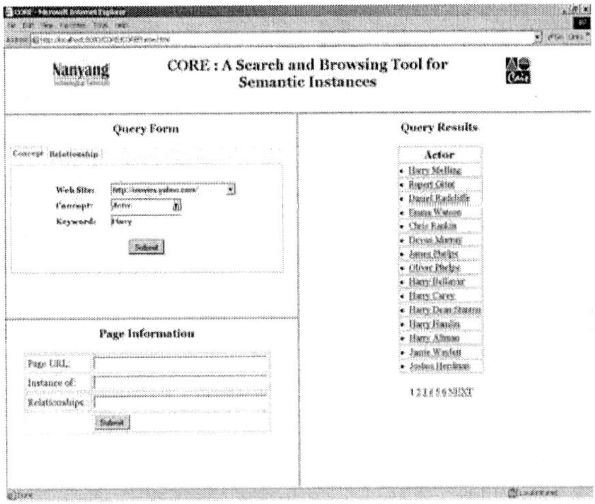

(a)

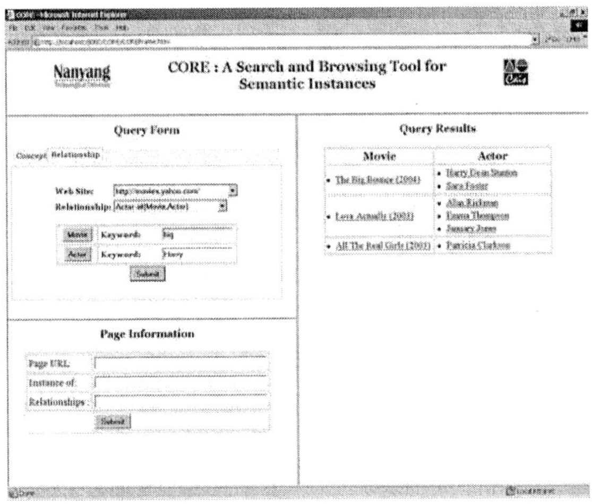

(b)

Fig. 4. (a) Results of querying *Actor* concept instances using search term "Harry" (b) Results of querying *Actor-of* relationship instances using search term "big" for the *Movie* concept instances and search term "Harry" for the *Actor* concept instances

Relationship Query

Suppose now the user wants to find a specific movie which involves his/her favourite actor. Unfortunately, he/she only remembers that the movie title includes the word "big" and the actor's name includes "Harry".

Again, when such a query is posed to Google in a query string "big Harry site:.movies.yahoo.com" where the search terms "big" and "Harry" are included, the results fail to match the user requirement. The query results will even be more unexpected when the query string "movie + give + actor + harry site:.movies.yahoo.com" is used.

Using CORE, the user can formulate a relationship query that involves *Actor-of(Movie, Actor)* relationship. Appropriate search terms can be specified against the source and target concepts. In this example scenario, the user can input "big" as the search term for the *Movie* concept and "Harry" as the search term for the *Actor* concept. CORE will return pairs of instances (web pages) of the *Actor-of* relationship that satisfy the relationship query. The query results are shown in Figure 4(b).

The left column of the result table displays the *Movie* concept instances and the right column displays the related *Actor* concept instances. Note that when the same source web page have multiple related target web pages that satisfy the relationship query, the results have the same source page will be merged together showing the source page only once.

5.2 Browsing Scenario

The traditional Web browsers are not aware of the semantics of web pages. They are not equipped with the ability to display semantic information and to support browsing based on the concept and relationship labels. Users therefore have to decide which web pages to visit by examining the anchor elements linking to the pages. Due to the limited information provided by the anchor text and intermediate web pages to be traversed before reaching the wanted web pages, the users are likely to commit errors in the choice of web pages to be browsed next and waste some of their time and efforts.

For example, starting from a movie home page, a user may want to navigate to its actor home page. The user can directly reach the actor home pages only if there are some anchor elements (i.e, with the names of the actors as anchor text) available within the movie home page. If there is no direct link from the movie page to the actor page, the user will not know which anchor element should be traversed in order to reach the desired actor page.

To rectify the above problem, CORE allows a semantic-based selection of web pages for browsing, and the navigation of relationship instances.

Let us assume that a user has browsed the movie page "The Big Bounce(2004)" from the relationship query result as shown in Figure 5. In the figure, the URL, concept label and relevant relationships of the selected movie web page are automatically displayed in the page information frame while the page is displayed in another browser window.

Suppose the user wishes to see the web page of some actor who appeared in "The Big Bounce(2004)", he/she can select the *Actor-of* relationship in the page information frame. Upon selection, the anchor element (i.e., "Cast and Credits") that leads to actor web pages will immediately be highlighted. Moreover, as the user moves the mouse over the highlighted anchor text, virtual links that lead to actors' web pages will appear in the browser window. These virtual links display the names of actors in the movie as shown in Figure 5(a). The user can now choose any of the actor web pages to browse without going astrayed.

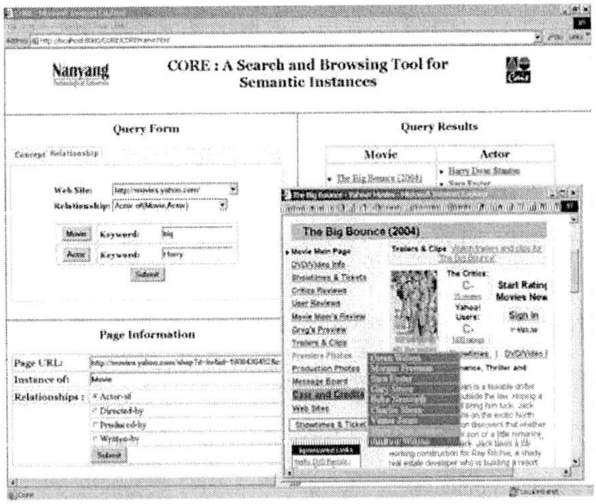

(a)

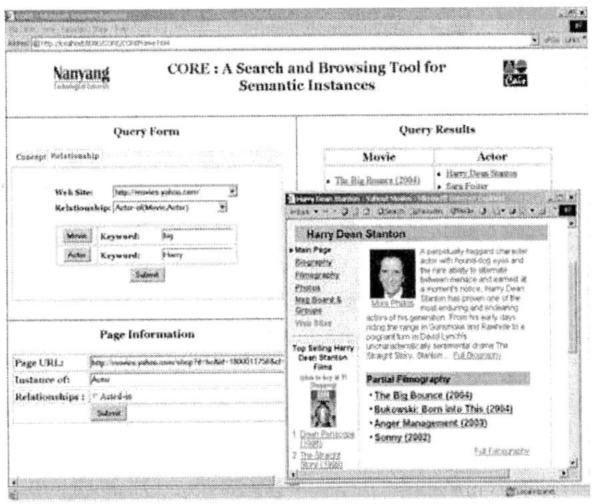

(b)

Fig. 5. (a)Browsing Movie home page with highlighted anchor texts for Actor-of relationship (b)Browsing Actor's home page by directly clicking the Actor-of relationship instance listed in the Movie source page

Suppose the user chooses to visit the web page of actor "Harry Dean Stanton" as shown in Figure 5(b). The web page is loaded into the browser window and the page information panel is updated accordingly including a new set of relationships relevant to actors. In this way, user can minimise errors in the web site navigation.

6 Summary

Knowledge about the concept labels of web pages from a web site and the relationships among the pages is crucial in realizing the goal of the Semantic Web. In this paper, we introduce an integrated search and browsing tool CORE for searching and browsing web pages that are concept instances and their relationships.

CORE has been implemented and it includes modules for assigning concept labels to web pages, learning link chain extraction patterns and using them to determine the relationships among web pages. A new web search model has been introduced to support both concept and relationship queries. We also highlight a few example scenarios where CORE can be used to enhance web site searching and browsing.

References

1. J. Domingue, M. Dzbor, and E. Motta. Magpie: Supporting Browsing and Navigation on the Semantic Web. In *Proceedings of the 9th International Conference on Intelligent User Interface (IUI'2004)*, pages 191–197, Funchal, Madeira, Portugal, January 2004.
2. Tom Mitchell. *Machine Learning.* McGraw Hill, 1997.
3. M. M. Naing, E.-P. Lim, and D. H.-L. Goh. On Extracting Link Information of Relationship Instances from a Web Site. In *Proceedings of the International Conference on Web Services-Europe 2003*, pages 213–226, Erfurt, Germany, September 2003.
4. X. Peng and B. Choi. Automatic Web Page Classification in a Dynamic and Hierarchical Way . In *Proceedings of IEEE International Conference on Data Mining*, pages 386–393, Maebashi City, Japan, December 2002.
5. S. H. Steffen. CREAM - Creating Relational Metadata with a Component-based, Ontology-driven annotation Framework. In *Proceedings of 1st International Conference on Knowledge Capture*, pages 76–83, Victoria, BC, Canada, 2001.
6. A. Sun, E.-P. Lim, and W.-K. Ng. Web classification using support vector machine. In *Proceedings of the 4th International Workshop on Web Information and Data Management (WIDM 2002)*, pages 96–99, Virginia, USA, November 2002.
7. T. B.-Lee and J. Hendler and O. Lassila. The Semantic Web. *Scientific American*, 284(5):35–43, 2001.
8. M. Vargas-Vera, E. Motta, J. Domingue, M. Lanzoni, A. Stutt, and F. Ciravegna. MnM: Ontology Driven Semi-Automatic and Automatic Support for Semantic Markup. In *Proceedings of the 13th International Conference on Knowledge Engineering and Management(ECAW 02)*, pages 379–391, Siguenza, Spain, October, 2002.

An LOD Model for Graph Visualization and Its Application in Web Navigation

Shixia Liu[1], Yue Pan[1], Liping Yang[1], and Wenyin Liu[2]

[1] IBM China Research Lab,
2/F, HaoHai Building, No. 7,
5th Street, ShangDi, Beijing 100085, PRC
{liusx, panyue, yanglip}@cn.ibm.com
[2] Department of Computer Science,
City University of Hong Kong,
83 Tat Chee Avenue, Kowloon, Hong Kong
csliuwy@cityu.edu.hk

Abstract. This paper presents a new method for visualizing and navigating huge graphs. The main feature of this method is that it applies Level-Of-Detail (LOD) strategy to graph visualization and navigation, and allows the user to navigate the graph in real time. First, the algorithm calculates the weight for each vertex by an improved link analysis method. Second, representative vertices with higher weights are selected. Third, a wavefront algorithm is utilized to cluster neighboring vertices for each representative vertex. This step produces several clusters characterized by the representative vertices. Then steps two and three are repeated in each cluster to form an LOD tree. Finally, we use a force-directed method to draw the sub-graph under the non-leaf node of the LOD tree. Based on the proposed method, we develop a graph visualization and navigation system—DynamicViewer. We then demonstrate its application in Web navigation. With DynamicViewer, the user can have an overview of the Web and then browse individual information on demand. The experiment results show that DynamicViewer enhances the ability to provide the right information to the user.

1 Introduction

Graph is one important data type. We are surrounded by graphs of all kinds: social network, knowledge network, computer network, economic network, and so on. With web pages considered as the vertices and the hyperlinks between them as edges, the Web can be regarded as the most popular graph. As the amount of information on the Web increases exponentially, it becomes increasingly difficult for users to find information and increasingly easy for users to be overloaded with information.

Because of the web's exponential growth, tools that help users browse and search this vast information space are now essential. Visualization is a powerful tool to help finding the relations and trends of the data. Applying visualization technology to the Web can help to find the important pages and the connectivity of the Web. Thus a better way to present the information on the Web is by drawing a nice picture, i.e., a

Y. Zhang et al. (Eds.): APWeb 2005, LNCS 3399, pp. 441 – 452, 2005.

graph which represents the Web. Drawing such a graph enables people to deal with information by taking advantage of our innate visual perception capabilities.

The size of the graph to view is a key issue in graph visualization [12]. The Web often consists of thousands of vertices or more, which severely limits the usefulness of the traditional graph visualization methods. Huge graphs pose several difficult problems. First, if the number of elements is large, it can compromise performance or even reach the limits of today's graphics hardware. Second, even if it is possible to place and display all the elements, the issue of readability or usability arises, because it will become impossible to discern between vertices and edges. Thus it is important to study the graph visualization methods for efficiently browsing and navigating huge graphs.

However, most existing methods aim at getting a final and stable graph layout and pay little attention to huge graph navigation. In this paper, we present a method to visualize and navigate a huge graph such as Web. With this method, a user can have an overview of the graph and then view individual information on demand. The main feature of this method is that it applies LOD strategy to graph visualization and navigation, and allows users to navigate the graph in real time and then explore further knowledge about their interests.

2 Related Work

Over the past two decades, much effort has gone into the area of two dimensional graph drawing [1, 2, 12, 16]. The most commonly used methods are based on physical analogies [16]. The main idea of this kind of methods is that they treat the graph as a system of interacting physical objects and assume that energy-minimal states of suitably defined systems correspond to readable and informative layouts. Force-directed method is a well-known physical analogy technique for drawing general undirected graphs [4, 5, 12, 14, 22]. Many models and algorithms have been proposed for it. The spring embedder proposed by Eades [4] is one of the earliest examples. In this model, vertices are physical objects (steel rings) and edges are springs connecting them. The vertices are given initial positions, usually random, and the system is released so that the springs move the vertices to a minimal energy state. Since then, this method has gradually been revisited and improved [3, 5, 7, 13, 14].

In the force-directed method, each iterative process involves a visit of all pairs of vertices in the graph and the quality of the layout depends on the number of full iterations. Therefore a general problem with this method is that it is only applicable to relatively small graphs. Most of later research efforts have been focused on drawing huge graphs efficiently [8, 10, 18].

Although a lot of graph layout algorithms have been proposed to deal with large graphs, no layout algorithm alone can overcome the problems raised by the large size of the graphs. Thus, navigation and interaction facilities are essential in information visualization. By the efforts of graphics researchers, many such facilities have been proposed. The techniques in this aspect can be classified into two main categories: focus+context [6, 24] and zooming[9, 23, 25].

Based on the above techniques, many methods have been proposed to visualize and navigate the structure of the Web. Natto [26] visualizes a number of Web pages by drawing such a vertex/edge graph that is initially distributed on a flat horizontal plane. Then the user may select nodes and raise them vertically to de-occlude the structure. Narcissus [11] also produces a graph-like representation. Occlusion is automatically reduced through the metaphor of attractive and repulsive forces. An alternative approach is to construct a hyperbolic space that supports "focus+context" exploration of hyper-text structure [20]. However, most of these methods try to display all the information on the Web in one screen, which severely limited their usaget is therefore important to find a new way to navigate the Web.

3 Visualization and Navigation of the Huge Graph

Here, a new approach is developed to construct an LOD model for browsing and navigating huge graphs. The LOD model organizes a complex graph into several levels. The main feature of this approach is that it combines link analysis technique with wavefront algorithm to facilitate the graph visualization and navigation. In the following sub-sections, we describe the proposed graph visualization method in detail.

3.1 Construction of an LOD Tree

The key of LOD construction lies in finding representative vertices for each level of the LOD tree and discovering clusters for each representative vertex. The representative vertex of a cluster is the vertex which conceptually represents all the vertices in the cluster. We begin the construction process of the LOD model with selecting a representative vertex for each cluster. The main task of this step is to calculate weights for all vertices, and then select several representative vertices for the input graph according to their weights. Next, the graph is divided into several clusters (subgraphs) according to the representative vertices.

3.1.1 Selection of Representative Vertices

In this section, we propose a novel vertex ranking method to measure the importance of the vertices in a graph, which is based on the link analysis technique [17, 19] in web information retrieval.

The basic principle of link analysis is to rank pages by citation popularity. High quality web pages are those pointed to by many other pages or those pointing to many high quality pages. Web pages that are pointed to by many other web pages are authorities, which provide the best source of information on a given topic. While web pages that point to many high quality pages are hubs, which provide collections of links to authorities. Hubs and authorities exhibit what could be called a mutually reinforcing relationship: a good hub is a page that points to many good authorities; a good authority is a page that is pointed to by many good hubs. Thus, with each page p, we associate a non-negative authority weight $x^{<p>}$ and a non-negative hub weight $y^{<p>}$. Without loss of generality, we assume that $\sum(x^{<p>})^2=1$, $\sum(y^{<p>})^2=1$. We view the pages with larger x-values and y-values as being better authorities and hubs respectively.

Numerically, it is natural to express the mutually reinforcing relationship between hubs and authorities as follows [17]: if p points to many pages with large x-values, it should receive a large y-value; and if p is pointed to by many pages with large y-values, it should receive a large x-value. This motivates the definition of two operations on weights, which we denote by Γ and Ω. Given $\{x^{<p>}\}$, $\{y^{<p>}\}$, the Γ operation updates the x-weights as follows.

$$x^{<p>} \leftarrow \sum_{q:(q,p)\in E} y^{<q>} \tag{1}$$

Here, we view the collection of hyperlinked pages as a directed graph $G = (V, E)$: the vertex in the vertex set V correspond to the Web page, and the directed edge (p,q) in the edge set E indicates the presence of a link from p to q.

The Ω operation updates the y-weights as follows.

$$y^{<p>} \leftarrow \sum_{q:(p,q)\in E} x^{<q>} \tag{2}$$

In calculating the weight of a vertex p, the HITS algorithm [17] only considers the vertices which directly connect to p (to or from). However, Miller et al. [19] have found certain tree-like web structure can lead the HITS algorithm to return arbitrary or non-intuitive results. Based on this observation, they modified the Kleinberg's HITS algorithm. The basic idea of the modified algorithm is as follows: when measuring the authority or hub importance of a vertex p, they extended the graph distance between vertices p and q from 1 to r (r>1). The graph distance between a pair of vertices is the length of the shortest path between them in the graph G. Our vertex ranking algorithm adopts the basic idea of the modified HITS algorithm proposed by Miller et al. [19].

We first introduce some preliminary definitions which are useful for subsequent discussions.

Definition 1 (directed-graph-distance (q, p)). The shortest directed path from vertex q to vertex p in the graph is termed as the directed-graph-distance between q and p.

Definition 2 (r-in-set (p)). The vertices whose directed-graph-distances to p are less than or equal to r are defined as the r-in-set of p.

Definition 3 (r-out-set (p)). The vertices to which the directed-graph-distances from p are less than or equal to r are defined as the r-out-set of p.

Based on these definitions, the traditional link analysis method is modified. We use the vertices in the r-in-set of p to measure its authority importance; similarly, we use the vertices in r-out-set of p to measure its hub importance. Thus, equations (1) and (2) can be rewritten as

$$x^{<p>} \leftarrow \sum_{q\in \text{r-}in\text{-set}(p)} y^{<q>} / r^{<q,p>} \quad r^{<q,p>} \le r, \text{for any } q \in \text{r - }in\text{ - set}(p) \tag{3}$$

$$y^{<p>} \leftarrow \sum_{q\in \text{r-out-set}(p)} x^{<q>} / r^{<p,q>} \quad r^{<p,q>} \le r, \text{for any } q \in \text{r - out - set}(p) \tag{4}$$

where, $r^{<q,p>}$ is the directed-graph-distance(q, p) between q and p.

Compared with the traditional link analysis method, the modified equations accelerate the convergence of iterations for calculating vertex weight. The comparison between these two methods is illustrated by the example in Fig. 1 (see Section 4).

The modified link analysis algorithm is used to calculate the *x*-weight and *y*-weight for each vertex, and equation (5) is used to calculate the weight of each vertex. We then select representative vertices for the LOD model according to these weights. Vertices with higher weights will be the representative vertices in the higher level of LOD model.

$$w_p = ((1-\alpha)\ x^{<p>} + \alpha\ y^{<p>}) \cdot w_{pd} \cdot \tilde{w}_{pe} \qquad 0 \le \alpha \le 1 \tag{5}$$

where, w_{pd} is the semantic weight of the vertex, which indicates its semantic importance to the Web. $\tilde{w}_{pe}$ is the average of the semantic weights of the edges directly connected to the given vertex, including the edges which are from or to this vertex. In our program, w_{pd} and $\tilde{w}_{pe}$ are determined manually by the user.

3.1.2 Clustering

After selecting representative vertices, a clustering process is applied to group vertices around each of the representative vertices. Here, the wavefront algorithm [21] is utilized to group vertices around each representative vertex. The principle of the wavefront algorithm can be viewed as exploring the graph in waves that expand outward from a given vertex *n*, much as waves expand from a pebble thrown into a pond. The wavefront algorithm is a breadth-first search algorithm. It starts out from some initial vertices in the graph and iterates to find all of vertices reachable from these initial vertices by using breadth-first search.

Based on this algorithm, the LOD model can be constructed by the following steps. First, we divide a set of vertices into a certain number of clusters based on the above clustering algorithms. The vertices in each cluster form a sub-graph. Next for each cluster, we repeat the above operation until the number of vertex of each sub-graph falls below a given threshold. And finally, a hierarchy is yielded from the repeated clustering process and it can be navigated as a tree, with each cluster represented as a node in the tree. The cluster vertices under each non-leaf node of the LOD tree form a cluster graph. We will discuss the layout of such a graph in the next section.

3.2 Graph Layout

3.2.1 Initial Placement of the Whole Graph

To provide an overview of the graph structure to the user, we present a structure-based method for quickly generating an initial placement of the whole graph. Our method is based on the intelligent placement method adopted by the GRIP system [7]. The idea behind the initial placement method in GRIP is that each vertex *v* is placed "close" to its optimal position as determined by the graph distance from *v* to several already placed vertices. The intuition of this method is that if the vertices are placed close to their optimal positions from the very beginning, then the refinement stages need only a few iterations of a local force-directed method to reach a minimal energy state.

GRIP adopts two simple strategies for the initial placement. The first strategy, "simple barycenter" starts with setting the initial position of a new vertex *t* at the barycenter (*u*+ *v*+ *w*)/3 of *u*, *v*, and *w*, the three vertices closest to *t* that have already been placed. This is followed by a force-directed modification of the position vector of t with the energy function calculated at the three vertices u, v, w. One major limitation of this method is that some vertices may overlap after initial placement.

In this section, we propose a structure-based method for quickly generating an initial placement of the whole graph. We have successfully overcome the limitation in the above method by utilizing a subdivision strategy. Our method first divides the original placement region into a finite number of sub-regions. The number of the sub-regions is calculated by

$$k = |V| / C \tag{6}$$

where C is a constant, it is the maximum number of vertices which a sub-region contains. In our program, C is set to 100.

Next, three vertices with the highest weights are placed. Here, the vertex with the highest weight is placed on the center of the placement region. The other two vertices are placed according to their graph distances to the first one. Then our method finds an unprocessed vertex t which has the maximum degree in the sub-graph formed by t and the vertices that are already placed. In a graph, the degree of a vertex is the number of edges incident to it. The new vertex t is placed at the barycenter $(u+ v+ w)/3$ of u, v, and w, the three vertices closest to t that are already placed. And finally, a local force-directed method is applied to reach a minimal energy state. Here, instead of applying the local force-directed method at the three closest points to t, we apply it to the sub-region in which vertex t lies. This greatly reduces vertex overlap.

3.2.2 Layout of a Cluster Graph

In this section, we describe a force-directed method for positioning the cluster vertices in each cluster graph. Our graph layout algorithm is based on Fruchterman-Reingold method [5]. For each vertex v in V, we first compute its local Fruchterman-Reingold force vector by

$$\vec{F}_{FR}(v) = \sum_{u \in Adj(v)} \frac{\text{dist}_{R^n}(u,v)^2}{\text{edgeLength}^2}(u-v) + \sum_{u \in V(G_L)} s\frac{\text{edgeLength}^2}{\text{dist}_{R^n}(u,v)^2}(v-u) \tag{7}$$

where, $\text{dist}_{\mathbf{R}^n}(u,v)$ is the Euclidean distance between u and v, edgeLength is the unit edge length, Adj(v) is the set of vertices adjacent to v, and s is a small scaling factor which is set to 0.05 in our program, just as in GRIP system [7], $V(G_L)$ is the vertex set of the cluster graph in which the vertex v lies. In equation (7), the first item indicates the sum of attractive forces to v, and the second item is the sum of repulsive forces to v.

Next, our method calculates vertex-edge repulsion force vector by equation (8)

$$F_{VE}(v,e) = \sum_{e} \frac{\text{edgeLength}^2}{\text{dist}_{R^n}(u,v)^2} - 1)(v-p) \tag{8}$$

where e is an edge which does not incident to v and p is the projection of v onto e.

Finally, the boundary repulsion force vector is calculated by the equation (9). Here, instead of using a step function to simulate the repulsion forces exerted by the boundaries of the placement region, we propose to use a linear function to simulate such repulsion forces. The equation (9) indicates that the boundary repulsion force of a vertex is proportional to the vector which starts from the center point of the placement region and end with this vertex.

$$F_{BR}(v,e) = \frac{\text{edgeLength}^2}{4}(Norm(v_c) - Norm(v)) \tag{9}$$

where Norm(v) normalizes v by dividing its x-component and y-component by the width and height of the placement region respectively. v_c is the center point of the placement region.

In this algorithm, the local temperature heat[v] of v is a scaling factor of the displacement vector for vertex v. We adopt the same algorithm as in GRIP [7] for determining the local temperature.

4 Implementation and Evaluation

4.1 System Design

Based on the proposed method, we developed a graph visualization system—DynamicViewer. Its novelty is in the use of different views: global view, detail view and text view, together to help a user navigate the Web. The first view, global view, is responsible for giving an overview of the graph being displayed. In order to improve the efficiency of graph drawing, the graph layout algorithm adopted for this view is the one described in Section 3.2.1. The second view, detail view, focuses on displaying the detail sub-graph. A force-directed method described in Section 3.2.2 is utilized to draw the sub-graph for this view. The third view, text view displays additional textual information in response to mouse move in detail view or global view.

4.2 Experimental Results

A number of examples have been tested to demonstrate various cases that could be handled by our method.

First, to evaluate the performance of our representative vertex selection method, we compare it with the traditional link analysis method [17] using the example in Fig. 1. In this example, vertex A is actually the most important vertex since it is the root node of the tree. However, the traditional link analysis method found vertex F being the most important one after performing 38 iterations. As a comparison, our method converged after iterating only 19 times. It recognized vertex A being the most important one. Tables 1-2 show some intermediate results of the two iteration processes. In these two tables, the weight value whose font is italic bold is the largest one at each iteration. From these two tables, we can conclude that the results generated by the improved method are more reasonable than the ones generated by the traditional method. This is because the improved method recognized vertices A, B, F, C, G, and H being the important ones; while the traditional method found vertices F, I, J, K, and L being the important ones. Furthermore, our comprehensive study on other 10 real examples shows similar improvement (see Table 3).

Next, we demonstrate the distinction between our initial layout method (Section 3.2.1) and GRIP's method by a simple graph with 46 vertices (see Fig. 2). Fig. 2(a) shows an initial layout generated by GRIP, and Fig. 2(b) gives our initial layout result. Compared with the initial layout algorithm adopted in GRIP, our approach avoids the drawbacks of vertex overlap by utilizing a subdivision strategy. Moreover, our method distributes the vertices more evenly.

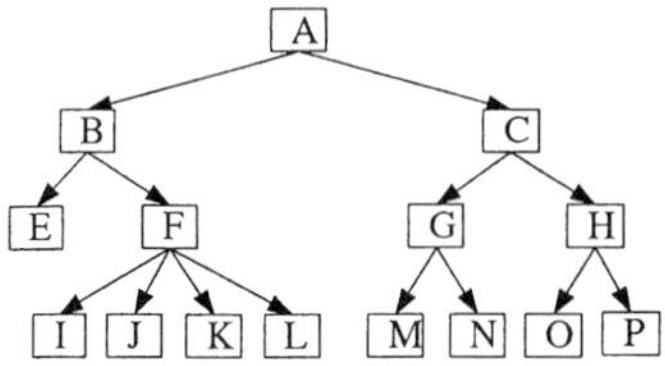

Fig. 1. An example

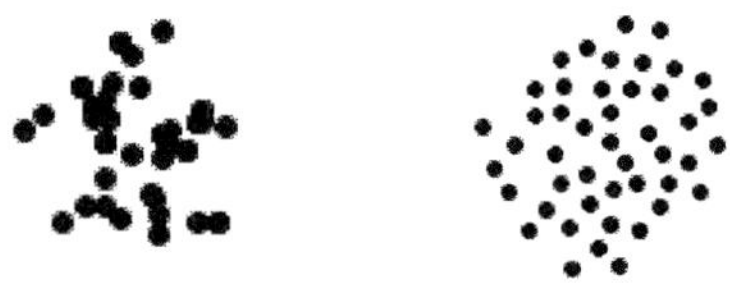

(a) GRIP (b) Our algorithm

Fig. 2. Comparing the layout results

Theoretically, information on the Web can be regarded as a graph. It is therefore feasible to apply graph visualization and navigation technology to the Web. In the following part of this section, we will illustrate the application of DynamicViewer in Web navigation. Here the Web also includes the Semantic Web since it is an extension of the current Web.

Fig. 3 illustrates the construction process of LOD model by an example of Semantic Web. It is a repository that contains RDF data and schema information about art and museum (e.g., museum web sites, web pages with exhibited artifacts). This example is taken and adapted from [15]. Fig. 3(a) is the original graph with 46 vertices. Fig. 3(b) shows the graph corresponding to the first level of the LOD tree, the representative vertex of this cluster is “ExtResource”. After clicking “painting” in the graph of the first level, we obtain a sub-graph at the second level (see Fig. 3(c)). Then in the sub-graph shown in Fig. 3(c), we click the vertex “abraham.jpg” and then obtain a sub-graph at the third level (see Fig. 3(d)).

Fig. 4 shows an example of how DynamicViewer helps the Web user to find the information he needs. This web graph was produced by submitting query words “Lotus Workplace” to the search engine on the home page of IBM Corp (http://www.ibm.com). With this query, 74,774 results were acquired. Next, the first 100 search results were analyzed and a graph representing these results was formed. Finally, an LOD model was constructed for this graph. In DynamicViewer, pages with higher connectivity will be in the higher level of the LOD tree, and thus will be displayed to the user first. Thus DynamicViewer enhances the ability to provide the right information to the user. Fig. 4(a) shows the graph corresponding to the first level of the LOD tree, the representative vertex of this cluster is “IBM Lotus Software-Products”. This graph gives an overview of 9 Lotus products; while the first page of the search result only contains 6 Lotus products. After clicking “IBM Lotus Software-QuickPlace” in the graph of the first level, we obtain a sub-graph at the second level (see Fig. 4(b)). This graph illustrates the relationship between “QuickPlace” and other Lotus products. Compared with traditional browsing tools of search engines, DynamicViewer provides an overview of the search result to the user, which enhances his or her understanding of the knowledge structures, thus promotes further exploration. In addition, traditional search engine organizes the search results with a linear model, and the user has to click the "Next" button to find new information. It does not provide the navigation cue for next page since next page is marked by “Next” only. While our method provide navigation cues before going to the next graph since each vertex has a hover text to describe it. This text information can help the user to find the right navigation path. Thus this can reduce the number of clicks.

Table 1. The intermediate results of the traditional link analysis method [17] on the example of Fig. 1

Step	Weight of each vertex							
	A	...	F	I	J	K	L	...
1	0.166667	...	*0.466964*	0.133631	0.133631	0.133631	0.133631	...
...	...	...	...	...	...	...	...	...
22	0.000244	...	*0.500122*	0.250000	0.250000	0.250000	0.250000	...
...	...	...	......	...	...	...	...	...
37	0.000001	...	*0.500001*	0.250000	0.250000	0.250000	0.250000	...
38	0.000001	...	*0.500000*	0.250000	0.250000	0.250000	0.250000	...

Table 2. The intermediate results of our improved link analysis method on the example of Fig. 1 (r=3)

Step	Weight of each vertex							
	A	B	C	E	F	G	H	...
1	*0.395994*	0.241234	0.241234	0.109556	0.240680	0.175118	0.175118	...
2	*0.374747*	0.288806	0.288806	0.131428	0.285297	0.208363	0.208363	...
...	...	...	...	...	...	...	...	...
18	*0.384202*	0.295436	0.267787	0.133160	0.285732	0.189180	0.189180	...
19	*0.384201*	0.295442	0.267779	0.133161	0.285739	0.189175	0.189175	...

Table 3. Comparison between traditional link analysis method and our method based on 10 examples

Method	Average iterations (times)	Precision
Traditional method	42.6	20%
Our method	26.2	100%

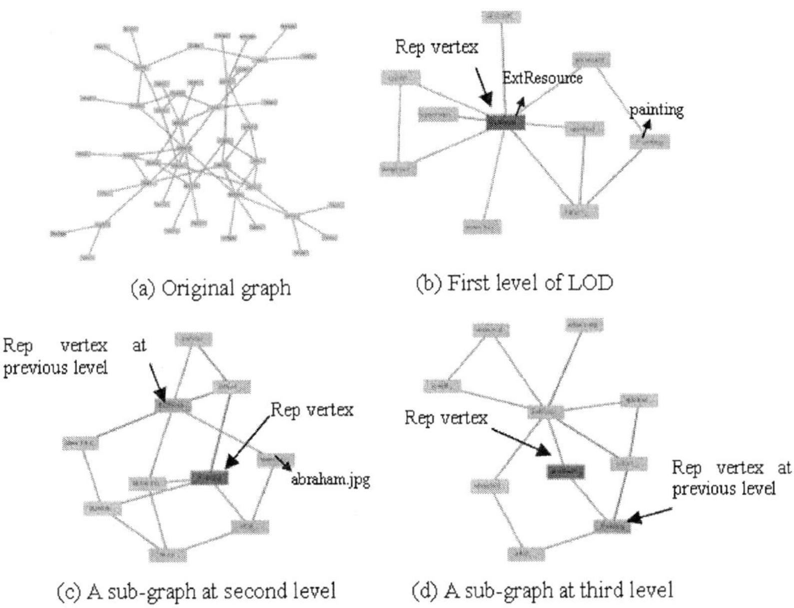

(a) Original graph (b) First level of LOD

(c) A sub-graph at second level (d) A sub-graph at third level

Fig. 3. LOD model of a graph with 46 vertices

The final example is intended to demonstrate the distinction between our method and the ratio cut method proposed by Roxborough et al [25]. The result is shown in Fig. 5. Comparatively, our method does not display all vertices in one cluster. Instead, it only displays the representative vertex of each cluster (see Fig. 5(b)). In our method, more details are shown when clicking a particular vertex in the detail view or selecting several vertices in the global view. Our approach avoids the drawbacks of displaying all vertices by selecting a representative vertex for each cluster.

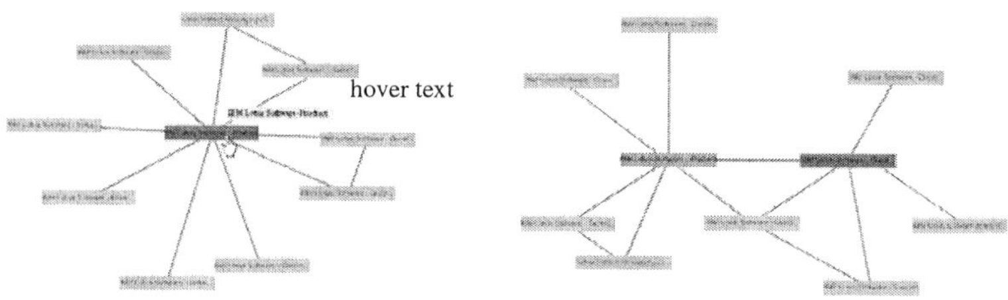

(a) First level of LOD (b) Second level of LOD

Fig. 4. LOD model of the search result from the homepage of IBM Corp

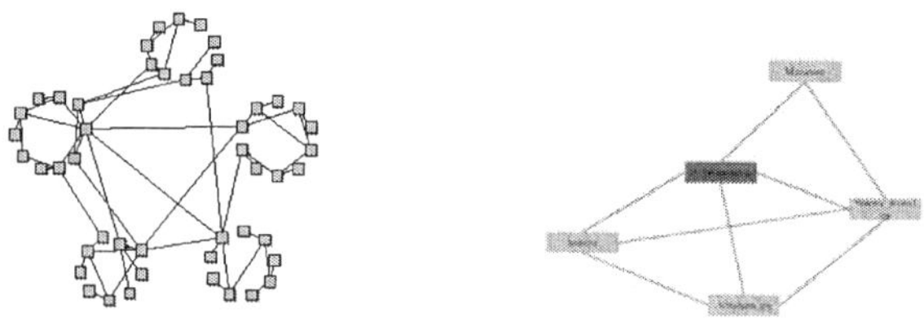

(a) Roxborough's method (b) Our method

Fig. 5. A comparison illustrating the viewability of our approach

5 Conclusion

We propose a new method for visualizing and navigating huge graphs. The main feature of this method is that it applies LOD strategy to graph visualization and navigation, and allows the user to navigate a huge graph in real time. To provide a friendly interactive system in which the user can retain context while viewing individual information on demand, we apply link analysis and wavefront algorithms to graph visualization and navigation.

The development of a prototype visualization system—DynamicViewer, is presented in this paper. In this system, three views, global view, detail view, and text view, are provided to facilitate the navigation and exploration of the huge graph. Moreover, we demonstrate its application in Web navigation.

We regard the work presented as an initial step and there are improvements to be made as well as many directions to pursue. The future work will be focused on improving the usability and reliability of the LOD model. Semantic information embedded in the Web should be fully exploited to improve the clustering results. In addition, we should study user experience in navigating Web and provide a more friendly interaction mechanism.

Acknowledgements

We would like to thank our colleagues, Dr. Zhong Su, Dr. Li Zhang, Dr. Li Ma, and Dr. Zhaoming Qiu for their helpful discussions and thoughtful criticisms. My colleague, Dr. Chen Zhao, gave us valuable comments to UI design. Special thanks go to Dr. Ivan Herman from W3C for many constructive suggestions.

References

1. Battista GD, Eades P, Tamassia R, Tollis I. Algorithms for drawing graphs: an annotated bibliography. Computational Geometry. Vol. 4, No. 5 (1994) 235-282
2. Battista GD, Eades P, Tamassia R, Tollis I. Graph drawing. New Jersey: Prentice-Hall (1999)
3. Davidson R, Harel D. Drawing graph nicely using simulated annealing. ACM Transaction on Graphics. Vol. 15, No. 4 (1996) 301-331
4. Eades P. A heuristic for graph drawing. Congressus Numerantium. (1984) 149-160
5. Fruchterman TMJ, Reingold EM. Graph drawing by force-directed placement. Software – practice & Experience, Vol. 2, No. 11 (1991) 1129-1164
6. Furnas GW. Generalized fisheye views. Proceedings of the ACM SIGCHI'86 Conference on Human Factors in Computing Systems, Boston, Massachussetts, ACM Press. (986) 15-22
7. Gajer P, Kobourov S. GRIP: Graph drawing with intelligent placement. Journal of Graph Algorithms and Applications. Vol. 6, No. 3 (2002) 203-224
8. Hadany R, Harel D. A multi-scale method for drawing graphs Nicely. Discrete Applied Mathematics. Vol. 113, No. 1 (2001) 3-21
9. Ham FV, Wetering H, Wijk J. Interactive visualization of state transition systems. IEEE Transactions on Visualization and Computer Graphics. Vol. 8, No. 3 (2002) 1-11
10. Harel D, Koren Y. A fast multi-scale method for drawing large graphs. Proceedings of 8th International Symposium on Graph Drawing (GD'00), Lecture Notes in Computer Science, Vol. 1984, Springer Verlag. (2000) 183-196
11. Hendley RJ, Drew NS, Wood A, Beale R. Narcissus: Visualizing Information. in Proceedings of the 1995 Information Visualization Symposium, Atlanta, GA. (1995) 90-96
12. Herman I, Melancon G, Marshall MS. Graph visualization and navigation in information visualization: a survey. IEEE Transactions on Visualization and Computer Graphics. Vol. 6, No. 1 (2000) 24-43
13. Huang ML, Eades P. A fully animated interactive system for clustering and navigating huge graphs. Proceedings of the 6th International Symposium on Graph Drawing, Springer LNCS 1547. (1998) 374-383
14. Kamada T, Kawai S. An algorithm for drawing general undirected graphs. Information Processing letters. Vol. 31, No. 1 (1989) 7-15
15. Karvounarakis G, Christophides V, Plexousakis D, Alexaki S. Querying RDF descriptions for community Web portals. Proceedings of the French National Conference on Databases (BDA'01). Agadir, Maroc. (2001) 133-144
16. Kaufmann M, Wagner D. Drawing graphs: methods and models. New York: Springer-Verlag. (2001)

17. Kleinberg JM. Authoritative sources in a hyperlinked environment. Journal of the ACM (JACM). Vol. 46, No. 5 (, 1999) 604-632
18. Koren Y, Carmel L, Harel D. ACE: A fast multiscale eigenvector computation for drawing huge graphs. Proceedings of IEEE Information Visualization. (2002) 137-144
19. Miller JC, Rae G, Schaefer F. Modifications of Kleinberg's HITS algorithm using matrix exponentiation and web log records. SIGIR'01, September 9-12, 2001, New Orleans, Louisiana, USA. (2001) 444-445
20. Munzner T, Burchard P. "Visualizing the Structure of the World Wide Web in 3D Hyperbolic Space" in Proceedings of VRML '95, San Diego, CA. (1995) 33-38
21. Qadah GZ. The wavefront and δ-wavefront algorithms: a comparative study. International Phoenix Conference on Computers and Communications. (1991) 799-805
22. Quinn N, Breur M. A force directed component placement procedure for printed circuit boards. IEEE Transactions of Circuits and Systems. Vol. 26, No. 6 (1979) 377-388
23. Risch JS, Rex DB, Dowson ST, Walters TB, May RA, Moon BD. The STARLIGHT information visualization system. Proceedings of the IEEE Conference on Information Visualization. (1997) 42-49
24. Robertson GG, Markinlay JD, Card SK. Cone tree: animated 3D visualizations of hierarchical information. Proceedings of the ACM SIGCHI'91 Conference on Human Factors in Computing Systems. (1991) 189-194
25. Roxborough T, Sen A. Graph clustering using multiway ratio cut. Proceedings of the Symposium on Graph Drawing (GD'97), Springer Verlag.(1998) 291-296.
26. Shiozawa H, Matsushita Y. WWW visualization giving meanings to interactive manipulations. in Advances in Human Factors/Ergonomics 21B (HCI International 97), San Francisco, CA. (1997) 791-794

Automatic Runtime Validation and Correction of the Navigational Design of Web Sites

Sven Casteleyn[1], Irene Garrigós[2], and Olga De Troyer[1]

[1] Vrije Universiteit Brussel, Department of Computer Science, WISE, Pleinlaan 2, 1050 Brussel, Belgium
{Sven.Casteleyn, Olga.DeTroyer}@vub.ac.be
[2] Universidad de Alicante, IWAD, Campus de San Vicente del Raspeig, Apartado 99 03080 Alicante, Spain
igarrigos@dlsi.ua.es

Abstract. Essential to an audience driven website design philosophy is the organization of information and functionality according to the requirements of the different audience classes. However, at design time, it is often difficult to correctly assess the different needs and requirements of the different prospective users of a website. This may result in a non-optimal navigation structure, which will decrease the usability of the website. In this paper, we describe how to correct, at run-time and automatically, possible flaws in the design resulting from incomplete requirement assessment, using adaptive behavior. By observing the browsing behavior of the users, the requirements for the different users are validated and the website is adapted according to adaptation specifications made by the designer. These specifications express when and how the website needs to be adapted and are expressed using an Adaptation Specification Language. The work is presented in the context of an audience driven design method but we also elaborate shortly on the applicability of the technique in general.

1 Introduction

In the beginning of the World Wide Web (WWW), when web sites consisted of one single page with hyperlinks, or a small amount of linked pages, the necessity for a well thought-out, structured design was not important: complexity was well manageable for web designers and the resulting site was easy to grasp for its visitors. However, as the WWW aged, and web sites became large, professional applications, offering both static and dynamic, rapidly changing information and functionality, maintenance and usability problems with ad hoc designed sites became apparent [16]. Visitors failed in making a mental model of the website, experienced difficulties in locating the information they were looking for and felt 'lost in hyperspace'.

Quite recently, we see that companies and organizations, in an attempt to better facilitate the user in finding information relevant for him/her, use a so called Audience Driven approach [6]. In this approach, the designer takes into account the target audiences of the web site, and creates the main structure of the site according to the information and functionality required by these different target audiences. Concretely,

Y. Zhang et al. (Eds.): APWeb 2005, LNCS 3399, pp. 453 – 463, 2005.

for the visitors this results in different links on the homepage, each representing a different navigation path (also called *audience track*) for a different type of visitor. Examples of leading companies and organizations applying an audience driven approach include[1]: HP (http://www.hp.com/), Sun Microsystems (http://www.sun.com/), IBM (http://www.ibm.com/us/), AIG (http://www.aig.com/GW2001/home/), NASA (http://www.nasa.gov/), Dell (http://www.dell.com/), several universities (Oxford University: http://www.ox.ac.uk/ and others),…

Although the audience driven design philosophy significantly reduces the amount of information the visitor needs to plough through, it also has as drawback that possibly some information needed is not available in the audience track chosen by the user. This is a direct result of the fact that the assessment of requirements by a designer (at design time) is reflected in the final navigation structure of the site, i.e. incorrectly assessed requirements result in information/functionality being in a wrong navigation track. More specifically, some relevant information may be missing in a certain audience track but present in another, while other information present in that audience track may be superfluous.

Indeed, for web designers it is very difficult, if not impossible, to correctly assess the exact requirements relevant or irrelevant for a certain user: it is often difficult or impossible to access the targeted web visitors and perform standard requirement engineering techniques. In this paper, we tackle this (requirement-) problem by describing how to identify missing or superfluous requirements for audience classes (section 4 and 5). Based on this identification, correction of the structure and navigation of the web site can be done automatically, at runtime (section 6). Note however that the specification of when, what and how to adapt is done at design time. This effectively gives the designer the means to anticipate possible requirement/design problems, and specify during the design how to correct for them if they are detected (at runtime). Preliminary results on this topic can be found in [3]. The work will be presented in the framework of the Web Site Design Method (WSDM), explained in section 3. Section 2 gives an overview of related work.

2 Related Work

Using adaptation to better tailor a web site to the users exists in the adaptive hypermedia community (e.g. [18] and others). In this community, most of the work is done in the context of learning and user assistant applications. In these systems, the user is 'guided' towards a certain goal (mostly a *learning* goal), by (adaptively) constructing the pages tailored to his knowledge (which is e.g. gathered by analyzing browsing behavior). This approach is fundamentally different from the one taken in this paper: the navigation space is conditionally specified during design and the actual navigation space for a user is generated based on the profile of the user. The navigation space is in fact personalized. Our goal is different. We do not want to personalize the navigation space; we only want to improve it using adaptive techniques. The adaptation is done after the (statically) designed navigation space has been used, and this usage data has been analyzed (note that the adaptation *is* specified during design).

[1] At the time of writing this paper.

Web design methods that have support for adaptation include WebML[4], Hera[10], UWE[14] and OOH[11]. However, these methods focus on personalization (e.g. content personalization) or/and customization towards different devices or context. They do not evaluate and alter an existing navigation space (after it has been deployed), as described in this paper.

WebML does describe a quality evaluation framework that exploits conceptual knowledge when analyzing web access logs [15]. The framework supports web usage analysis (e.g. access analysis of data schema entities at instance level) and web usage mining (e.g. finding data that is accessed together, navigation sequences). But there is no provision for (automatic) adaptation based upon this analysis.

3 WSDM Overview

Given the fact that WSDM has been sufficiently specified in the literature [1] [2] [7] [8], we will only provide a short overview and go into deeper detail only where necessary for the context of this paper.

The general design cycle for WSDM can be summarized as follows. In the mission statement, the purpose and the subject of the web site is expressed and the target audience is identified. Based on the mission statement, an audience modeling phase is performed, consisting of an audience classification and an audience characterization. During audience classification, the different audience classes based upon the informational and functional requirements of the potential visitors are identified and classified into an audience class hierarchy. During audience characterization, the relevant characteristics for the different audience classes are described.

The next phase, the Conceptual Design, consists of two sub-phases: task modeling and navigation design. During task modeling, for each requirement of the different audience classes, a task is defined. Consequently, the task is elaborated and decomposed in elementary tasks using ConcurTaskTree ([7] describes how). In this way, a task model is specified for each requirement. In parallel, for each elementary requirement, a tiny conceptual schema, called a chunk, is specified, formally describing the information or functionality needed to fulfill the requirement. These chunks are modeled using ORM [12] with some extensions to express functionality.

During navigational design, the conceptual navigation model for the website is constructed. It consists of a graph of nodes, connected by means of links. Every node contains information that logically belongs together, in the form of (information or functional) chunks. A node can contain zero or more chunks (a node without chunks represents a kind of *hub*, presenting a choice of navigation possibilities to the user). In WSDM, the navigation model is obtained in two steps. First, the audience class hierarchy from the audience modeling phase is used to obtain the basic structure of the navigational model, by creating one navigation track (a so called *audience track)* for every audience class [1]. Such an audience track can be thought of as a "sub-site", where all and only the information/functionality relevant for that particular audience class can be found. Secondly, the internal structure of each audience track is derived from the task models of the task modeling phase, elaborating the requirements of each audience track.

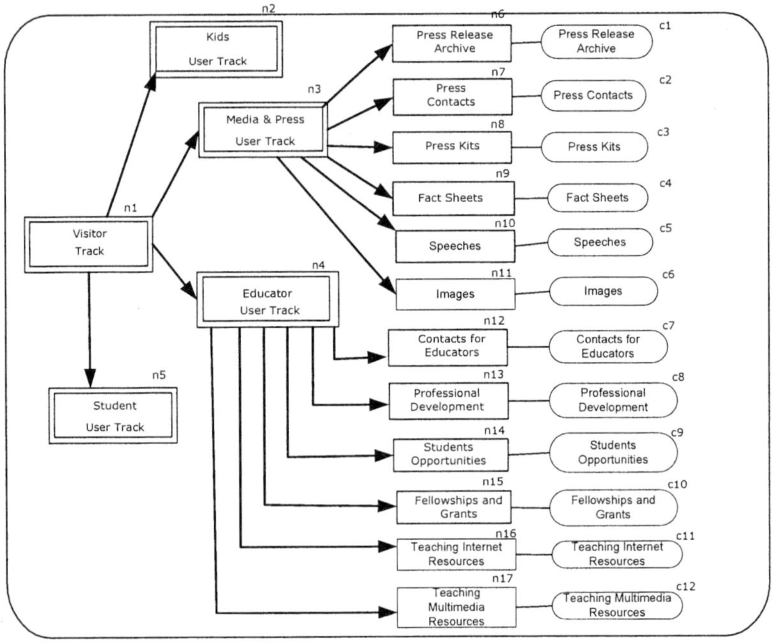

Fig. 1. Simplified Navigational Model for (part of) the NASA website

It is only in the next phase, the implementation design, that the conceptual nodes from the navigational model are actually mapped on pages, and that layout and presentation is specified. Finally, the last phase, the actual implementation, is a mapping of the previous phases onto the chosen implementation platform.

A (simplified) example of a Navigational Model of an audience driven website is given in figure 1. The example is the NASA website (http://www.nasa.gov/) and shows the main structure of the website and the navigation structure for both the Media & Press User Track and the Educator User Track. The other tracks are not elaborated to not overload the figure. Nodes are represented by rectangles, chunks by rounded rectangles, links by arrows and the connections between chunks and nodes by lines. A double lined rectangle is used for the root of a track or the root of the web site (in this example the node 'Visitor Track' is the root of the web site).

4 Missing or Superfluous Information

As already explained in the introduction, the aim in this paper is 1) to detect missing or superfluous requirements for a certain audience class by investigating the access to information offered in the corresponding audience track, and 2) to adaptively alter the structure of the site to correct for detected problems. In this section, we will describe the data necessary to be able to identify missing or superfluous requirements. In the next section, we will describe how to use this data to detect flaws, and in section 6, we will give possible solutions to correct the flaw.

From now on, the requirements originally assigned (by the designer) to an audience class will be called *native* requirements; all other requirements will be called *foreign* requirements (for that particular audience class).

According to the audience driven philosophy, a user should find *all* the information and functionality he needs in his particular audience track. Consequently, if a user leaves his audience track, to look for information elsewhere, then the information he is visiting outside of his audience track might be information that is actually missing in his own audience track. If a significant amount of users of the same audience class do this, then we have a good indication that that information is actually relevant for this audience class.

When a user does not leave his audience track, still some problems with the information in the track are possible. Some information in the track might be accessed very few times (compared to the other information), suggesting the information does not belong there in the first place. Note that identifying information that is accessed few times does not necessarily imply that information is superfluous. We will discuss this in more detail in section 5.

Thus, to identify missing/superfluous information, the following steps are identified:

1. Determine the audience class of the current user
2. Track which information the user visits, both in and outside his audience track
3. Analyze the accumulated data to determine if the information within the audience track is relevant, or if visits to information/functionality outside the audience track are significant

Because an audience driven design has been used, the first step is simple: when a user enters the web site, he is presented with a choice of different audience tracks (i.e. subsites), each representing the information/functionality for a certain type of user. By selecting one of these tracks, the current user effectively identifies the role in which he is currently visiting the website, and thus reveals his/her audience class.

In the second step, we store data about which information a user visits. As we want to keep track of which information is visited outside a particular audience track, and relate this information to the frequency of visits inside the track, we need to store the number of visits to each piece of information (chunk) relative to each audience class. This data can be conveniently stored in a matrix, which we will call the *information access matrix.* Rows of the matrix represent the different elementary requirements R_i (track-able in the website by their corresponding chunk C_i), while the columns represent the different audience classes. An example is given in the next section.

In pseudo code, the algorithm to populate the matrix is as follows:

WHEN session.start **THEN** Determine Audience Class A_j by observing first click(s)
    WHILE browsing **DO: IF** currentNodeVisited has chunk(s) C_i connected
        THEN FOREACH (R_i) **:** M(i,j)++
    END
END

Note how the connection between the requirements (line 3) and their corresponding chunks (line 2) is exploited. Over time[2], the matrix contains a good summary of the

[2] An exact estimate the (first) evaluation time of the matrix is not the subject of this paper; suffices to say a significant amount of visitors needs to have visited the site.

amount of accesses to the different chunks for each audience class. In the next section, we will give an example of an information access matrix, and we will describe how the matrix can be used to identify missing or superfluous information in an audience track.

5 Method for Identifying Missing or Superfluous Information

5.1 Identifying Missing Information

To determine if the amount of accesses from a certain audience class to information outside the audience track is significant, we can use known statistical techniques. In statistics, the problem of determining if a certain value *fits well* in a given relatively small sample data set is solved using basic statistical measures for central tendency (e.g. mean, median, ..) and standard measures of spread (e.g. variance, standard deviation, median absolute deviation, ..).

As our dataset (and its distribution) is unpredictable and we do not want our calculations influenced by (a few) extreme values (e.g. nodes that are highly popular), we choose median, a robust central tendency (i.e. not influenced by extremes in our data set). As a measure of spread the median absolute deviation (MAD) is chosen, as this measure is less influenced by outliers (compared to other measures) and has robustness of validity (i.e. the underlying distribution doesn't influence reliability too much). The following formula is used to calculate absolute median deviation:

- $MAD = median\ (|x_i - x_m|)$

where x_i is each of the values of the data set, and x_m is the median of the data set.

As the spread denotes how far, on average, the values of the dataset are removed from the middle value, we can conclude that most of the values of the dataset lie within the distance of the spread from the middle value (for more exact estimates of how much elements of the data set lie within this interval, we refer to [5]). Consequently, external values *fit well* in the given dataset, if they lie within that range.

Applied to the problem of finding information outside the audience track of a particular audience class that is actually relevant for that particular audience class, we adopt the following method:

For a given audience class/track:

1. Calculate median and MAD for the set of number of accesses to information resulted from *native* requirements and calculate the threshold (median – MAD)
2. For all information resulting from *foreign* requirements, verify if the amount of accesses is greater than the calculated threshold. If this is the case, we have an indication that that particular information is relevant to the audience class under investigation

Note that only the lower limit of the range is used as information resulting from a foreign requirement track that is accessed more than (median + MAD) is off course also relevant for the current audience class.

To clarify this method, let's consider the (simplified) example of the NASA web site that was introduced in section 3 (see figure 1). The information access matrix for this example is shown in figure 2. In the columns we have the two audience classes considered in this example (Media & Press and Educators) and in the rows we have the different requirements that resulted in information chunks on this web site. As explained, each cell in the matrix denotes the number of visits to some information by a certain audience class. For example, cell (1,1) shows that members of the audience track "Media & Press" have accessed 52 times the information resulting from requirement R1 "*Press Release Archive*".

Note that the first six requirements in the matrix are native for the *Media & Press* track, and the last six ones are native to the *Educator* track. As we were unable to obtain the *real* access information for the NASA website, we have used here fictitious data.[3]

Lets now analyze the accesses to the native information of the Educators audience track (R7 … R12), and determine if accesses to foreign information (R1 .. R6) were significant compared to these accesses. Calculating median and MAD we obtain:

Data set (ordered): 10 15 20 30 50 56 ; **Median:** 25 ; **MAD:** 12.5

		Media & Press	Educators
R1	Press Release Archive	**52**	**40**
R2	Press Contacts	**49**	**4**
R3	Press Kits	**31**	**10**
R4	Fact Sheets	**16**	**5**
R5	Speeches	**40**	**5**
R6	Images	**38**	**12**
R7	Contacts for educators	**0**	**56**
R8	Professional development	**5**	**50**
R9	Student opportunities	**1**	**30**
R10	Fellowships and grants	**0**	**10**
R11	Teaching Internet Resources	**3**	**20**
R12	Teaching Multimedia Resources	**2**	**15**

Fig. 2. Information Access Matrix

The threshold that is the lower limit to decide if foreign information is relevant for the current audience track is median – MAD = 25 – 12.5 = 12.5. The information of the *Media & Press* track with a number of accesses greater then this threshold is determined to be relevant for the *Educator* audience track. This is the case for the *Press Release Archive* information (40 accesses). We can thus conclude that this information should somehow be included in the Media & Press track (how and where this information is added is the subject of the next section).

5.2 Identifying Superfluous Information

As for identifying missing information, we also use statistical techniques to determine when information is superfluous. In statistics, the problem of finding an outlier in a

[3] Experiments are being performed at the author's university web site with real access data.

data set is generally seen as hard, especially when the dataset is small, and accurate information about it (e.g. distribution) is missing. Consequently, most existing tests are not usable here because they only work on large datasets (e.g. Rosner's Test [17] and others [5], [13]), and those that were usable for small data sets gave poor results (e.g. Dixon's test [9] and others).

However, for our purposes, detecting *significantly low* values (but not per se outliers as they are defined in statistics) in our dataset is already sufficient. To identify these *low* values, we will use a double strategy: we will look for values which lay both *far* from their (bigger) neighbor, and also lay far from the middle value of the dataset.

To determine which value lies far from its neighbor, we take the ordered dataset, and calculate the distances between each 2 consecutive values. These distances give us a new dataset, for which we calculate mean and standard deviation[4] (= std). Calculating the interval [(mean–std) (mean+std)] gives us the range in which most of the distances (i.e. 50% for normally distributed data) lie. Distances above the (mean+std) are thus relatively big, compared to the other distances, and we have identified two points which are relatively far from each other.

To determine which point lies *far* from the middle value, we apply the same technique as in the previous section: values below the threshold (median–MAD) can be labeled as being *far* from the middle value.

Let's consider the NASA website example from the previous subsection, and apply the technique described above to identify possible superfluous information in the Media & Press track:

Data set (ordered): 16 31 38 40 49 52	Data set of distances: 15 7 2 9 3
Median: 39 ; MAD: 9	Mean: 7.2 ; Std.: 4.7
Lower limit: 39 – 9 = 30	Upper limit: 7.2 + 4.7 = 11.9

The distance between the first and the second element of the original dataset is 15, which is bigger than the threshold 11.9. Therefore, we can conclude that the first element lies significantly *far* from the next element. As this first element, namely 16 in the original dataset, lies below the threshold of 30, we can also conclude that it lies *far* from the middle. With both tests positive, we conclude that the value 16 is indeed significantly low compared to the other values: the information related to the requirement 'Fact Sheets' is detected as (possibly) superfluous for the audience class Media & Press. The concentrated reader will note that, in case the detected value is not the first value of the data set (as in this example), then also all smaller values are marked as superfluous, as they obviously are also significantly low compared to other values.

6 Adaptation of the Web Site Structure

Having identified missing or superfluous information in a certain audience track, the structure of the web site can be adapted (automatically) to reflect the detected defi-

[4] As this time, we want to detect high distances, we use mean and standard deviation, as they are more affected by the presence of extreme low or high values.

ciencies. To leave the control over the web site structure to the designer, we allow the designer to specify at design time how the structure of the web site should be adapted when such deficiencies are detected. For this, the Adaptation Specification Language (ASL) [2] can be used, which is defined upon the navigational model to allow specifying (at design time) possible adaptive changes to the structure of the site (at run time). Due to space restrictions, we have simplified ASL notation in this paper to reflect the basic idea.

6.1 Adaptively Correcting Missing Information

There are several ways to anticipate the fact that information present in some audience track is apparently missing in a certain audience track. The designer might duplicate the information in the place it is missing; provide a link to the existing information from where it is missing; or totally re-arrange the structure of the site so that all interested users can access the information.

The approach taken in this paper consists of "duplicating" the information, and offering a link to the information at the root of the audience track. Although more suitable adaptations can be chosen, we think that the ratio effort/benefit is certainly the highest for this adaptation.

Let W be a web site, with a set of Audience Classes A={A_1, ..., A_n} with associated Audience Tracks T={T_{A1}, ..., T_{An}} and MR_{Ai} the set of nodes containing information detected to be missing from the audience track T_{Ai}. We can express the adaptation explained above as follows:

(1) **Foreach** *AudienceClass* **in** A
(2) **Foreach** *node* **not in** NodesOfAudienceTrack(*AudienceClass*):
(3) **if** *node* **in** $MR_{AudienceClass}$ **then** addLink(root($T_{AudienceClass}$), duplicate(*node*))

In words, this rule iterates over all audience classes (line 1). Within each audience class, for each node outside the audience track of that audience class (line 2) it is checked if that node contains *missing* information (line 3). If this is the case, the node is duplicated (along with all chunks connected to it) and a link from the root of the audience class under investigation to the duplicated node is added (then-part line 3).

6.2 Adaptively Correcting Superfluous Information

As mentioned in section 4, information identified as superfluous in a certain audience track does not necessarily need to be removed. Although visited only few times, it might still be valuable for (a small amount of) visitors (think of 'how to get there' information for a research lab: only a minority of users will actually want to go to the lab, yet the information is invaluable on the website). Thus, we see the detection of superfluous information rather as an alert to the web master, rather than something that requires (automatic) adaptation. If the web master indeed decides the information is not needed in that track, he can remove it. However, an (automatic) adaptation that may be useful for the designer to specify, is re-arranging the links so that a link to information detected as superfluous appears last.

(1) **Foreach** *AudienceClass* **in** A:
(2) **Foreach** *node* **in** NodesOfAudienceTrack(*AudienceClass*):
(3) **if** *node* **in** $SR_{AudienceClass}$ **then**
(4) **foreach** *link* **with** target(*link*) = *node*: reorder(*link*, last)

In words, the rule iterates over all audience classes (line 1). For each node within the audience class (line 2), it is checked if the node has been detected to contain superfluous information (line 3). If this is the case, then each link to this node (line 4) will be re-ordered so it appears last in the originating node (end line 4).

7 Applicability Beyond the Audience Driven Approach

The technique, described in this paper, to validate requirements by detecting missing or superfluous information in a certain audience track, can also be applied to web sites not following the audience driven philosophy. The key requirement for the applicability of the approach is the existence of a collection of information belonging logically together (in our case, the requirements for an audience class). Information in such a collection can be tested to be superfluous, and information external (to this collection) can be tested to be missing. Two example applications are given below.

In a data driven web site, where the navigation structure is determined by the available data, the main navigation structure (e.g. the main navigation options from the homepage) is usually topical. The technique described in this paper could be used to determine relevant data outside a certain topic group, and possibly adaptively alter the navigation structure to cluster related topic groups or to provide a link within the topic group to the (external) relevant data.

In e-commerce, product categories can be considered as sets of related items, and thus the technique described in this paper could be used to determine which products from other categories could be of interest to a user browsing a particular category. E.g. if a user is leaving a product category, briefly browses outside the category, and consequently returns, this may indicate that the information visited outside the category may also be relevant for the current category. Consequently, the navigation structure could be adaptively altered to include a link to the categories in question.

8 Conclusion

In this paper, in the context of WSDM, we show how to validate the requirements of the different users by detecting two types of flaws in an audience driven web site. These flaws are 1) information put wrongly in a certain track (superfluous information), and 2) information missing in a certain track but present in another (missing information). The automatic detection is done using statistical techniques, performed on the web access log. Furthermore, this paper describes how the existing navigation structure can be (automatically) adapted to remedy for detected flaws: at design time, the designer can specify (using the Adaptive Specification Language) the adaptive actions that should be taken in case such situations are detected at run time. By doing so, the structure of the web site will better reflect the audience driven design philosophy, and the site will be better tailored to the needs of the different audience classes. Finally, the paper elaborates on the use of this technique outside the scope of audience driven web design.

References

1. Casteleyn, S., De Troyer, O.: Structuring Web Sites Using Audience Class Hierarchies, In Proceedings of DASWIS 2001 workshop (ER conference), Yokohama, Japan (2001)
2. Casteleyn, S., De Troyer, O., Brockmans, S.: Design Time Support for Adaptive Behaviour in Web Sites, In Proceedings of the 18th ACM Symposium on Applied Computing, Melbourne, USA (2003)
3. Casteleyn, S., Garrigós, I., De Troyer, O.: Using Adaptive Techniques to Validate and Correct an Audience Driven Design of Web Sites, In Proceedings of ICWE'04 (2004)
4. Ceri S., Fraternali P., and Bongio A: Web Modeling Language (WebML): a modeling language for designing Web sites, In WWW9 Conference, First ICSE Workshop on Web Engineering, International Conference on Software Engineering (2000)
5. DeGroot, M..H.: Probability and Statistics. Addison-Wesley, Reading, Massachusetts (1989)
6. De Troyer, O.: Audience-driven web design, In Information modelling in the new millennium, Ed. Matt Rossi & Keng Siau, IDEA GroupPublishing, ISBN 1-878289-77-2 (2001)
7. De Troyer, O. ,Casteleyn, S.: Modeling Complex Processes for Web Applications using WSDM, In Proceedings of the IWWOST2003 workshop, Oviedo, Spain (2003)
8. De Troyer, O. ,Leune, C.: WSDM: A User-Centered Design Method for Web Sites, In Computer Networks and ISDN systems, Proceedings of the 7th International World Wide Web Conference, Elsevier (1998) 85 – 94
9. Dixon, W. J.: Analysis of extreme values. Ann Math Statist, 21 (1950) 488 - 506
10. Frasincar, F., Houben G., and Vdovjak R.: Specification Framework for Engineering Adaptive Web Applications, In Proceedings of the WWW Conference, Honolulu, USA (2002)
11. Garrigós, I., Gómez, J. and Cachero, C.: Modelling Dynamic Personalization in Web Applications, In Proceedings of ICWE'03, LNCS 2722 (2003) 472 - 475
12. Halpin, T.: Information Modeling and Relational Databases: From Conceptual Analysis to Logical Design, 1 st Edition. Morgan Kaufmann Publishers, San Francisco, USA (2001)
13. Hawkins D.: Identification of Outliers, Chapman and Hall (1980)
14. Koch, N.: Software Engineering for Adaptive Hypermedia Systems, Reference Model, Modeling Techniques and Development Process, PhD Thesis, Verlag UNI-DRUCK, ISBN 3-87821-318-2 (2001)
15. Lanzi, P.L., Matera, M., Maurino, A.: A Framework for Exploiting Conceptual Modeling in the Evaluation of Web Application Quality. In Proceedings of ICWE2004, Munich (2004)
16. Nielsen, J.: Finding usability problems through heuristic evaluation. Proceedings of the SIGCHI conference on Human Factors and Computer Systems. Monterey, California, United States ISBN:0-89791-513-5 (1992) 373 – 380
17. Rosner, B.: On the detection of many outliers. Technometrics, 17, pp. 221-227.(1975)
18. Wu., H., Houben, G.J., De Bra, P.: AHAM: A Reference Model to Support Adaptive Hypermedia Authoring, In Proc. of the Zesde Interdisciplinaire Conferentie Informatiewetenschap, Antwerp (1998) 77 - 88

Summarizing Spatial Relations - A Hybrid Histogram*

Qing Liu[1,2], Xuemin Lin[1,2], and Yidong Yuan[1,2]

[1] University of New South Wales, Australia
[2] National ICT Australia
{qingl, lxue, yyidong}@cse.unsw.edu.au

Abstract. Summarizing topological relations is fundamental to many spatial applications including spatial query optimization. In this paper, we examine the selectivity estimation for range window query to summarize the four important topological relations: contains, contained, overlap, and disjoint. We propose a novel *hybrid histogram* method which uses the concept of Min-skew partition in conjunction with Euler histogram approach. It can effectively model object spatial distribution. Our extensive experiments against both synthetic and real world datasets demonstrated that our hybrid histogram techniques improve the accuracy of the existing techniques by about one order of magnitude while retaining the cost efficiency.

1 Introduction

For range query in the spatial databases, users are looking for data objects whose geometries lie inside or overlap a query window. In many applications, however, users are more interested in summarized information instead of objects' individual properties . Especially with the availability of a huge collection of on-line spatial data [1, 2, 3] (e.g. large digital libraries/archives), it becomes extremely important to support *interactive* queries by *query preview* [4, 1]. These applications require systems to provide a fast summarized spatial characteristics information. Summarizing spatial datasets is also a key to spatial query process optimization.

In this paper, we investigate the selectivity estimation problem of summarizing topological relations between rectangular objects and window query. Several techniques have been proposed for estimating the selectivity [5, 6]. Technique based on histogram to approximate data distributions is widely used by current database systems [7]. Histogram-based techniques can be classified into two categories: 1) *data partition techniques* and 2) *cell density techniques* [8]. The Min-skew algorithm [9] and the SQ-histogram technique [10] belong to the first category. They group "similar" objects together into one bucket for estimating the number of *disjoint* and *non-disjoint* objects with respect to window query.

* This project was supported by ARC Discovery Grant DP0346004.

Y. Zhang et al. (Eds.): APWeb 2005, LNCS 3399, pp. 464–476, 2005.

Techniques based on cell density [4, 11, 3, 8] propose to divide the object space evenly into a number of disjoint cells, and record object density information in each cell. Cumulative density based approach [11] and Euler histogram [4] can provide the exact solutions against the *aligned* window query (to be defined in Section 2) for non-disjoint and disjoint topological relations only. Euler-Approx [3] and Multiscale Histogram [8] substantially extended the Euler histogram techniques for summarizing the 4 important binary topological relations: "*contains*", "*contained*", "*overlap*", and "*disjoint*" (to be defined in Section 2) against the aligned window query.

In this paper, we will focus on these 4 relations against aligned window query. Specifically, we developed a novel hybrid histogram method that combines Min-skew technique with Euler histogram approach. By combining these two techniques together, this hybrid histogram may lead to more accurate solution for aligned window query. We evaluate our new techniques by both synthetic and real world datasets. Our experiment results demonstrated that the hybrid histogram may improve the accuracy of the existing techniques by about one order of magnitude while retaining the cost efficiency.

The rest of the paper is organized as follows. In Section 2, we provide preliminaries and related work. Section 3 presents our hybrid histogram construction algorithm, query algorithm and analysis of this structure. Section 4 evaluates the proposed methods through extensive experiments with synthetic and real datasets, and Section 5 concludes the paper with direction for future work.

2 Preliminary

In this section, we give a brief overview of Min-skew algorithm [9], Euler histogram [4], Euler-Approx algorithm [3] and Multiscale Histogram [8]. These techniques are closely related to our work in this paper. First we introduce the middle-resolution topological relations.

A binary topological relation between two objects, P and Q, is based upon the comparison of P's *interior*, *boundary*, *exterior* with Q's interior, boundary,

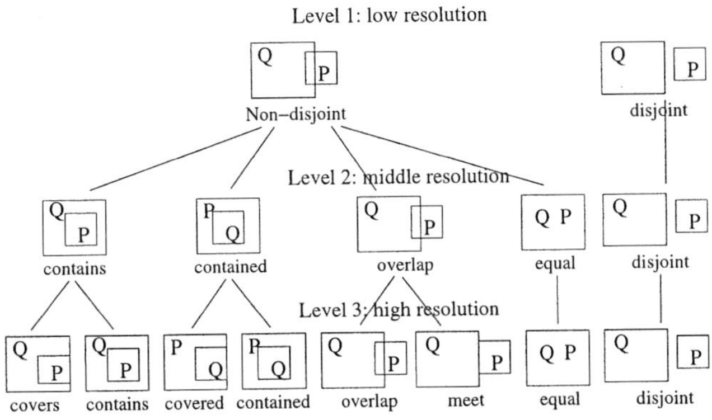

Fig. 1. Topological Relations between Two Objects

and exterior [12]. It can be classified into 8 high-resolution topological relations according to the 9-intersection model [12], and can be also classified into the middle-resolution topological relations by removing the intersections involving the object boundaries [13, 3] (Figure 1).

Aligned window query means the query window contains whole cells but not part of the cells.

2.1 Min-Skew Algorithm

Acharya, Poosala, and Ramaswamy proposed a partitioning scheme to build histograms for spatial data called Min-skew partition [9]. It is regarded as the winner among several other histogram techniques. The technique uses a uniform grid that covers the whole space and their spatial densities as input. Initially one bucket represents the whole space. The algorithm iteratively splits a bucket into two until the histogram has the required number of buckets B. The algorithm tries to minimize the spatial-skew, defined as the variance of the number of objects in the grid cells constituting the bucket, at each step.

2.2 Euler Histogram

To construct an Euler histogram [4], the whole space is first divided evenly into $n_1 \times n_2$ disjoint cells. For each node, edge and cell, a bucket would be allocated respectively. So the total space required is $(2n_1 - 1) \times (2n_2 - 1)$. For every object insertion, an update is needed for all the nodes, edges and cells that the object intersects: the value of relevant cell and node is increased by 1 and the value of relevant edge is decreased by 1. Figure 2(a) gives an example of an Euler histogram for a dataset with only one object.

Table 1 lists the symbols that will be used frequently throughout the paper. Given Q, we can get P_i by summing up all the bucket values inside Q. By Euler formula, we have:

$$N_{nds} = P_i \tag{1}$$

$$N_{nds} + N_{ds} = |S| \tag{2}$$

Equation (1) and equation (2) yield the exact solution for low-resolution relations N_{nds} and N_{ds}. In Figure 2(b) for example, given Q (shadow area), $N_{nds} = P_i = 2 - 1 + 3 = 4$, $N_{ds} = |S| - N_{nds} = 5 - 4 = 1$, which means there are 4 objects (cs, cd, it, cr) non-disjoint with Q and 1 object (ds) disjoints with Q.

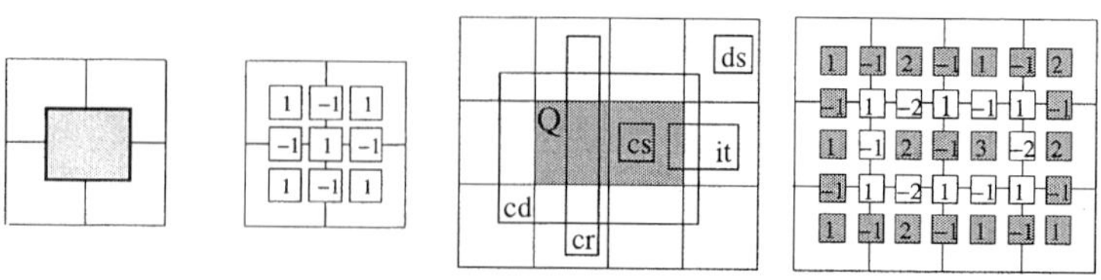

(a) Euler histogram for one object (b) Compute Pi and Pe

Fig. 2. Euler Histogram and Query Method

Table 1. Frequent Symbols

Q	aligned window query
$\|S\|$	the total number of objects in dataset
P_i	the summation of all the bucket values inside Q
P_e	the summation of all the bucket values outside Q
N_{ds}	the number of objects that disjoint with Q
N_{nds}	the number of objects that non-disjoint with Q
N_{cs}	the number of objects that Q contains
N_{cd}	the number of objects by which Q is contained
N_{ov}	the number of objects that overlap Q
N_{it}	the number of objects that intersect Q
N_{cr}	the number of objects that crossover Q

2.3 Euler-Approx Algorithm

Sun, Agrawal and El Abbadi [3] proposed to use the histogram information outside query window, P_e, to solve middle-resolution relations: contains, contained, overlap and disjoint. The equal relation is merged into contains relation. It is shown the overlap relation has to be separated into two classes: intersect relation and crossover relation. This is because an object with intersect relation contributes 1 to the outside of query and an object with crossover relation contributes 2 to the outside of query (see Figure 2(b) object *it* and *cr* for example). So we have to deal with crossover and intersect relation respectively, and then sum them up to get overlap relation. In the rest of paper, the 5 relations represent contains, contained, intersect, crossover and disjoint relations. Again, by Euler formula, we have:

$$N_{cs} + N_{it} + N_{cr} + N_{cd} = P_i \tag{3}$$

$$N_{ds} + N_{it} + 2 \times N_{cr} = P_e \tag{4}$$

$$N_{cs} + N_{it} + N_{cr} + N_{cd} + N_{ds} = |S| \tag{5}$$

For example, in Figure 2(b), $P_i = 4$. This 4 comes from the object *cs*, *cd*, *cr*, and *it*. We can also have $P_e = 4$. This 4 comes from the object *ds*, *it*, and *cr* which contributes 2 to P_e.

The information in one Euler histogram is not enough to determine all the above 5 relations. To solve these 5 relations with only 3 exact equations, Sun et. al proposed three query algorithms: Simple-Euler, Euler-Approximate and Multi-resolution Euler Approximate. All algorithms are based on assumptions $N_{cd} = 0$ and/or $N_{cr} = 0$ (see [3] for details).

2.4 Multiscale Histogram

Lin et. al proposed a multiscale framework [8] which can provide exact solution for many real applications. The framework contains two parts: exact algorithm ($MESA$) and approximate algorithm ($MAPA$). In $MESA$, it is proved that if all the objects involved in one Euler histogram have at most four adjacent scales $(w, h), (w + 1, h), (w, h + 1), (w + 1, h + 1)$, the exact results can be obtained. So objects with adjacent scales are grouped together and one Euler histogram is constructed for each group. When storage space is limited to k, MAPA will build $k - 1$ exact histograms and 1 approximate histogram.

For an Euler histogram with a resolution $n_1 \times n_2$, the storage space required is $O(n_1 \times n_2)$. Both Euler-Approx and Multiscale Histogram run in constant time with the *prefix-sum* technique [14].

3 EM Histogram

In this section, we introduce the hybrid histogram technique. The histogram captures information not only about the location of the data objects, but also about their sizes. These information are essential to the accuracy of 5 relations estimation. We call this hybrid histogram *EM histogram*. It takes advantages both from **E**uler histogram and **M**in-skew partition to achieve high accuracy as well as efficiency. We first identify our motivation.

Our study shows, despite different techniques have their own attractive aspects, they also have their own limited applicability due to this unique problem. Min-skew provides a good location estimation. But to approximate the objects within a bucket, all objects are presented by an average size object. Obviously this solution could not be applied for our problem because it is very unlikely all the objects in one bucket only have one relation with respect to a given query. Multiscale Histogram could provide a very accurate estimation if most of objects are involved in the exact histograms. But usually the histogram space is limited. If given 1 histogram space, no accurate result can be obtained for any objects. So estimation accuracy for using only 1 histogram is a critical component to solve the 5 relations problem. Motivated by these, next we present our EM histogram.

3.1 Histogram Construction

EM histogram includes two parts: Min-skew-like partition and Euler histogram. The construction method for Euler histogram is exactly the same as that in Section 2.2. For Min-skew-like partition, given a regular $n_1 \times n_2$ cells and object scale range, we partition the objects based on the location of their bottom-left corners as well as their scale information. So instead of only minimizing the location variance sum in Min-skew partition, Min-skew-like partition aims at minimizing the location as well as scale variance sum of all the buckets.

It generates B rectangular buckets whose edges are aligned with the cell boundaries. In each bucket, the distribution of object location and scale are almost uniform. Then the location uniform model is applied locally in each bucket. The scale uniform model could not be applied directly. But with this uniform model, the accuracy of estimation can be improved a lot in each bucket. Each bucket b records the following information:

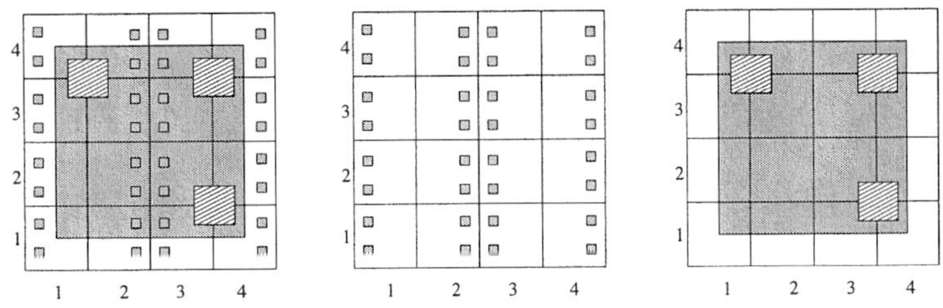

Fig. 3. Skewed Scale Distribution

- the spatial extent b_l.MBR $[(minX, maxX), (minY, maxY)]$ $(1 \leq l \leq B)$
- the scale matrix b_l.Matrix of the objects involved in the bucket $[(width_1, height_1)\ objNum_1, \ldots.., (width_n, height_n)\ objNum_n]$ $(1 \leq l \leq B)$

Figure 3 gives an example for skewed scale data distribution with 2 buckets. The overall location distribution of this dataset is uniform. So by the Min-skew-like partition, 2 buckets are obtained. In bucket 1 (Figure 3(b)), b_1.MBR is [(1, 4), (1, 4)], b_1.Matrix is [(1, 1) 32]. In bucket 2 (Figure 3(c)), b_2.MBR is [(1, 4), (1, 4)], b_2.Matrix is [(2, 2) 3, (4, 4) 1].

3.2 Querying EM Histogram

By Section 2.2, we have equation (3), (4) and (5) based on the Euler histogram. Next we will use the Min-skew-like partition to get 2 more equations to solve 5 relations: contains(cs), contained(cd), intersect(it), crossover(cr) and disjoint(ds).

Given a query Q and a bucket, we estimate its selectivity with respect to 5 relations based on the bucket scale matrix information. The basic idea is by the scales of objects and a given query, the objects in each bucket can be separated into 5 groups. In each group, a mean object will be calculated to represent the objects in that group. Then probabilistic method is applied to estimating the 5 relations. Details can be explained in 3 steps:

Step 1. For each bucket, Q divides the objects into five groups according to object scale $O_{w,h}$ and query scale $Q_{i,j}$. In each group, we know exactly how many objects may contribute to the specific relations.

Group A. $w \leq i$ and $h \leq j$ - at most 3 relations: cs, it and ds.
Group B. $w \geq i + 2$ and $h \geq j + 2$ - at most 3 relations: cd, it and ds.
Group C. $w \leq i$ and $h \geq j + 2$ - at most 3 relations: cr, it and ds.
Group D. $w \geq i + 2$ and $h \leq j$ - at most 3 relations: cr, it and ds.
Group E. $w = i + 1$ or $h = j + 1$ - at most 2 relations: it and ds.

In the example of Figure 3(c), there are 2 kinds of objects in this bucket. A query window with scale (3, 3) separates the scale matrix into five groups: A, B, C, D, E. Objects with (2, 2) scale belong to group A. So these objects will only contribute contains, intersect or disjoint relation to Q. No object belongs to group B, C, D which indicates no object contributes to contained

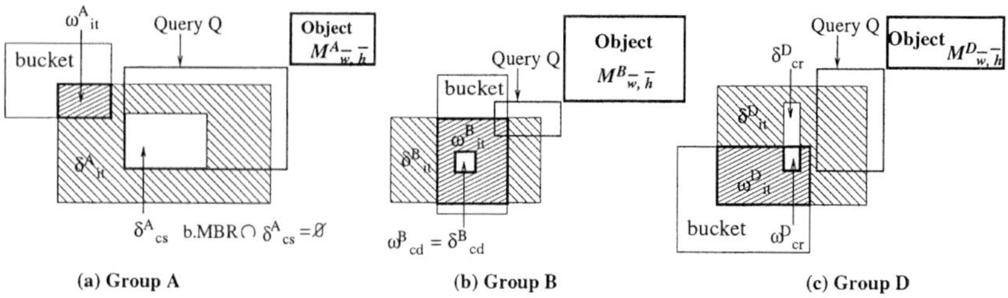

Fig. 4. Possible Area regards to Different Relations in Group A, B, D

(crossover) relation. The objects with (4, 4) scale belong to group E. So they may only contribute to intersect and disjoint relation.

Step 2. Calculate a mean object $M^g_{\bar{w},\bar{h}}$ $(g \in \{A, B, C, D, E\})$ for each group. To make the computation more efficient, we use 5 mean objects $M^g_{\bar{w},\bar{h}}$ to represent all the objects in 5 groups respectively. The number of $M^g_{\bar{w},\bar{h}}$ (m_g) can be calculated by adding up all the objects with scales belonging to group g.

Step 3. Estimate the number of objects with respect to the 5 relations using probabilistic approach based on the mean object. Each mean object has 3 or 2 relations with respect to the query window $Q_{i,j}$. The occurring probabilities against the 3 or 2 relations can be calculated based on each mean object $M^g_{\bar{w},\bar{h}}$ by applying the location uniform model in each bucket.

In Figure 4, δs show the rectangular areas used by the mean object bottom-left corner regards to different relations for group A, B and D respectively. The rectangular areas for group C is similar to group D and for group E, it is similar to group A without the white area δ^A_{cs}. $\delta^g_{relation}$ $(g \in \{A, B, C, D, E\}$, $relation \in \{cs, cd, cr, it, ds\})$ denotes the possible area covered by the objects $M^g_{\bar{w},\bar{h}}$ that will contribute to relation $relation$ in group g with respect to Q. For example, in Figure 4(a) δ^A_{cs} means if the mean object $M^A_{\bar{w},\bar{h}}$ has cs relation with Q, its bottom left corner should locate in this δ^A_{cs} area. So compared with other bucket estimation method, we would not compute the intersection area between bucket and query window, but between bucket and $\delta^g_{relation}$. Even there is no intersection between bucket and query window, the objects in this bucket may still contribute to some relations (eg. contained, crossover or intersect) to Q (see Figure 4(a, c) for example). N_{ds} can be computed directly from equation (3) and (5). We would not compute it using probability approach. There are 2 possible cases between $b.MBR$ and $\delta^g_{relation}$:

- case 1: $b.MBR \cap \delta^g_{relation} = \emptyset \quad (relation \in \{cs, cd, cr, it\})$
- case 2: $b.MBR \cap \delta^g_{relation} = \omega^g_{relation} \quad (relation \in \{cs, cd, cr, it\})$

In case 1, there is no object that will contribute to relation *relation* in this group. For example in Figure 4(a), $b.MBR \cap \delta_{cs}^{A} = \emptyset$, so all the objects in this bucket will not contribute to cs relation with respect to Q.

In case 2, the selectivity $\rho_{relation}^{g}$ that objects in the g group contribute to relation *relation* can be calculated by the ratio of $\omega_{relation}^{g}$ to the total area $b.MBR$. The number of objects which contribute to a specific relation in each group is $m_g \times \rho_{relation}^{g}$. The summations of the results from 5 groups with respect to 5 relations form the results of this bucket.

By summing up the estimation of different relations ($\alpha_{cr}, \beta_{it}, \gamma_{cs}, \mu_{cd}$) from each bucket, 2 more equations can be obtained:

$$N_{cs} : N_{cd} = \gamma_{cs} : \mu_{cd} \tag{6}$$

$$N_{cr} : N_{it} = \alpha_{cr} : \beta_{it} \tag{7}$$

Together with equation (3), (4) and (5), five relations $N_{cs}, N_{cd}, N_{cr}, N_{it}, N_{ds}$ can be solved.

3.3 EM Maintenance

If an object is updated, EM histogram may be also updated. First, for an insertion or deletion, the value of relevant node, cell and edge should be updated. Because Euler histogram is constructed in a cumulative fashion, an efficient update technique, Δ tree [15], can be applied. Second, based on the object's spatial location and scale, the scale matrix information in the corresponding bucket will also be updated.

3.4 EM Performance Analysis

The storage space required by Euler histogram is $(2n_1 - 1)(2n_2 - 1)$. And the space for buckets is Bn_1n_2 in the worst case (B is the number of buckets). The total actual storage space required by EM histogram can be calculated as $(2n_1 - 1)(2n_2 - 1) + Bn_1n_2$. But in practice, by our extensive experiments, it takes much smaller space than that in theory. This would be shown in our experiment part.

Because we can also represent the scale matrix information in each bucket by applying prefix-sum techniques, querying each bucket runs in constant time. The time for querying B buckets is $O(B)$. And we know an Euler histogram can be queried in constant time, so the total time for querying EM histogram is $O(B)$.

4 Performance Evaluation

This section experimentally evaluates the proposed methods. All the experiments were performed on Pentinum IV 1.80GHz CPU with 512 Mbytes memory.

The objective of this study is to show by taking advantages of Euler histogram and Min-skew-like techniques, EM histogram provides an accurate and efficient method for spatial selectivity estimation for middle-resolution topological relations, especially for non-uniform distribution dataset. In the first part of experiments, we will show the importance that we integrate Min-skew-like partition technique into our EM histogram. In the second part of experiment, we will show the importance of Euler histogram. And cost comparison will be examined in the third part. We evaluate the accuracy of the following techniques:

- EM Histogram
- Euler-Approx [3]
- Multiscale Histogram [8]
- Pure-Minskew Method: it is used to show the advantages of Euler histogram. In Pure-Minskew method, only bucket information is recorded without any Euler information. The spatial space and object scale space are partitioned by Min-skew algorithm. In each bucket, the bucket spatial extent as well as object scale matrix are maintained. For previous Min-skew algorithm, only 1 average scale information is recorded. Modified in this way, the Pure-Minskew method can also be used to answer the query for middle-resolution relations.

Datasets. In our experiment, both real-world and synthetic datasets are used. To do a fair comparison with Euler-Approx and Multiscale histogram regarding accuracy, we adopt the 360×180 resolution to evaluate the accuracy of our algorithms, as this resolution was used in [3] and [8] to provide the experiment results. The 360×180 grid is a simulation of the earth resolution by the longitude and latitude. Below are the datasets used.

- **Ca_road** consists of the $2,851,627$ California road segments obtained from the US Census TIGER [16] dataset. We normalized the dataset into the 360×180 grid.
- **Zipf** is a synthetic dataset with one million square objects. Both the side length and the spatial location of the object follow a Zipf distribution.

Query Sets. We adopt the same query setting in [8]. This is because this setting simulates various user query patterns. Query windows are divided into 2 classes, small and non-small. A query window in small class has a scale such that the width and height are both smaller than 5, while a query window in non-small class has either height between 6 and 20 or width between 6 to 20. We randomly generate 3 different sets of windows, T_1, T_2, and T_3, each of which has $100,000$ query windows.

In T_1, 20% of the $100,000$ query windows are in the small class. In T_2, 40% of the query windows are in the small class, while in T_3, 80% of the query windows are in the small class.

Error Metrics. We adopt average relative error for N_{cs}, N_{cd} and N_{ov} where $N_{ov} = N_{it} + N_{cr}$.

4.1 The Advantages of Min-Skew-Like Partition

To prove the advantages of Min-skew-like partition, in this part, we evaluate the performance of EM histogram in comparison with Euler-Approx and Multiscale Histogram.

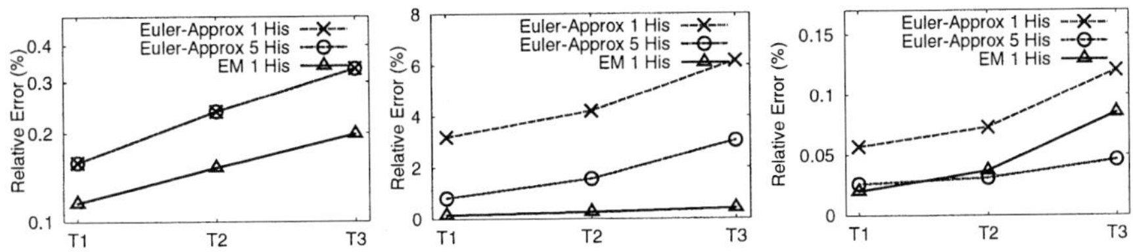

(a) Nov (b) Ncs (c) Ncd

Fig. 5. Performance Comparison for Real Dataset: Ca_road

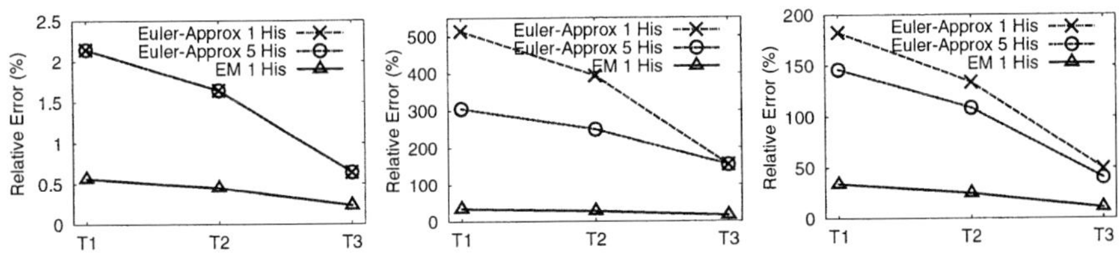

(a) Nov (b) Ncs (c) Ncd

Fig. 6. Performance Comparison for Synthetic Dataset: Zipf

First we compare the performance between EM histogram and Euler-Approx. Both algorithms can calculate the N_{ds} accurately. Figure 5 shows the experiment results for Ca_road dataset. Because the location distribution is not quite skew, the performance with different number of buckets of EM is quite similar. By Figure 5, we can see even using 1 bucket, EM histogram has a better result than that of Euler-Approx using 5 histograms in most cases.

Figure 6 shows the experiment results for synthetic dataset Zipf using different query set. 100 buckets are allocated to EM histogram. Again, even using 1 histogram, the EM still outperforms the Euler-Approx with 5 histograms. The performance difference between 2 algorithms is quite large compared with that of Ca_road dataset. This is because when the dataset follows non-uniform distribution, the assumptions made by Euler-Approx would be fail. On the other hand, EM histogram uses only a few buckets to capture the skew data distribution and local uniformity assumption is applied only in each bucket. Another problem of Euler-Approx shown in [8] is the accuracy of N_{ov} is fixed regardless of the number of histograms used (see Figure 5(a), 6(a)).

In fact, Multiscale histogram is a special case of EM histogram if $k = 1$ (the number of Euler histograms) and $B = 1$ (the number of buckets). On the other hand, we can also treat EM histogram as a solution for the last histogram in Multiscale histogram techniques. So for Ca_road dataset, the performance of EM (Figure 5) is also the performance of Multiscale histogram. Figure 7 for $B = 1$ is the experiment result of Multiscale histogram for dataset Zipf. We can see EM always outperforms Multiscale histogram.

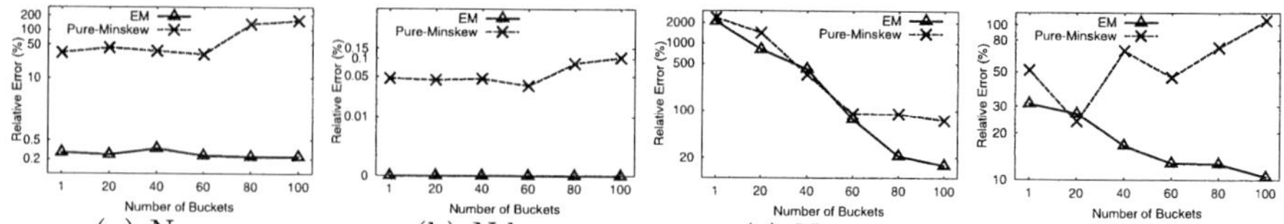

(a) Nov (b) Nds (c) Ncs (d) Ncd

Fig. 7. Synthetic Data: Zipf

With Min-skew-like partition technique, EM histogram can capture the features of data objects accurately which are the critical information for the estimation accuracy.

4.2 The Advantages of Euler Histogram

To prove the advantages of Euler histogram, in this part, we evaluate the performance of EM histogram in comparison with Pure-Minskew method in which no Euler information is provided.

Figure 7 shows the experiment results of T_3 query set against the different number of buckets The results for T_1 and T_2 query set are similar to T_3 query set. With the increase of number of buckets, the N_{cs} and N_{cd} calculated by EM histogram are improved quickly. The N_{ov} with low relative error is not changed too much. We can always get the exact results for N_{ds} from EM histogram by using equation (3) and (5).

The accuracy of N_{cs} by Pure-Minskew method is increased with the increase of number of buckets. But it is interesting to note the performance of N_{cd} and N_{ov} are decreased. Another major concern about Pure-Minskew is, even the performance could be improved with the increase of number of buckets, a big number of buckets means more buckets have to be accessed in the on-line phase, which slows down the query performance.

With Euler histogram, EM histogram could use only a relative few number of buckets to accurately estimate the underlying data distribution. It is especially noteworthy for the on-line case. Pure-Minskew could not be a solution for selectivity estimation of middle-resolution relations.

4.3 Cost Evaluation

Storage Space. In theory, the storage space required is $(2n_1 - 1)(2n_2 - 1) + Bn_1n_2$. By our experiment, the space required for every 100 buckets is about 2.5KB (0.18% of one Euler histogram space) both for Ca_road dataset and Zipf dataset. So the storage space required for EM histogram is slight higher than those of the other 2 algorithms when using 1 Euler histogram. But from the experiments, we can see this is worthwile especially for non-uniform data. And more, 1 EM histogram even outperforms 5 Euler-Approx histogram in most cases but with much less space.

Histogram Construction Time. We evaluate the time to construct the EM histogram. The time costs for constructing 1 Euler histogram are similar to the Euler-Approx and Multiscale algorithms, about 40 to 41 seconds. For EM histogram, extra time is required to build buckets. With the resolution 360 × 180 spatial resolution, the time cost is about 43 seconds to build 100 buckets. The histogram construction time will be decreased with the decrease of spatial resolution.

Query Time. As analyzed in Section 3.4, the time for querying EM histogram is $O(B)$ (B is the number of buckets), which is irrelevant to the size of the Euler histogram and the underlying dataset. By our experiment, for every 10,000 window queries, it takes about 1 seconds for querying EM histogram with 100 buckets.

5 Conclusion and Remarks

In this paper, we investigate the problem of summarizing the spatial middle-resolution topological relations: contains, contained, overlap and disjoint. Spatial datasets could be various both in location distribution and scale distribution. A novel hybrid histogram technique, EM histogram, is presented as an accurate and effective tool to solve the problem. EM histogram use the concept of Min-skew partition in conjunction with Euler histogram approach. Our experiment results demonstrated that our approach may greatly improve the accuracy of existing techniques while retaining the costs efficiency.

As a possible future study, we will investigate the problem of non-aligned window query and explore other related research topics.

References

1. Greene, S., Tanin, E., Plaisant, C., Shneiderman, B., Olsen, L., Major, G., Johns, S.: The end of zero queries: Query preview for nasa's global change master directory. International Journal of Digital Libraries (1999) 70–90
2. Szalay, A., Kunzst, P., Thakar, A., Gray, J., Slutz, D., Brunner, R.: Designing and mining multi-terabyte astronomy archieves: The sloan digital sky survey. In: SIGMOD. (2000) 451–462
3. Sun, C., Agrawal, D., Abbadi, A.E.: Exploring spatial datasets with histograms. In: ICDE. (2002) 93–102
4. Beigel, R., Tanin, E.: The geometry of browsing. In: Proceedings of the Latin Ameriacn symposium on Theoretical Informatics,1998,Brazil. (1998) 331–340
5. Papadias, D., Kalnis, P., Zhang, J., Tao, Y.: Efficient OLAP operations in spatial data warehouses. In: SSTD. (2001) 443–459
6. Papadias, D., Tao, Y., Kalnis, P., Zhang, J.: Indexing spatial-temporal data warehouses. In: ICDE. (2002)
7. Poosala, V., Ioannidis, Y.E., Haas, P., Shekita, E.: Improved histograms for selectivity estimation of range predicates. In: SIGMOD. (1996) 294–305
8. Lin, X., Liu, Q., Yuan, Y., Zhou, X.: Multiscale histograms: Summarizing topological relations in large spatial datasets. In: VLDB. (2003) 814–825
9. Acharya, S., Poosala, V., Ranmaswamy, S.: Selectivity estimation in spatial databases. In: SIGMOD. (1999) 13–24

10. Aboulnaga, A., Naughton, J.F.: Accurate estimation of the cost of spatial selections. In: ICDE. (2000) 123–134
11. Jin, J., An, N., Sivasubramaniam, A.: Analyzing range queries on spatial data. In: ICDE. (2000) 525–534
12. Egenhofer, M.J., Herring, J.R.: Categorizing binary topological relations between regions, lines, and points in geographic databases. In Egenhofer, M.J., Mark, D.M., Herring, J.R., eds.: The 9-Intersection: Formalism and Its Use for Natural-Language Spatial Predicates. National Center for Geographic Information and Analysis, Report 94-1. (1994) 13–17
13. Grigni, M., Papadias, D., Papadimitriou, C.: Topological inference. In: IJCAI. (1995) 901–907
14. Ho, C.T., Agrawal, R., Megiddo, N., Srikant, R.: Range queries in olap data cubes. In: SIGMOD. (1997) 73–88
15. Chun, S.J., Chung, C.W., Lee, J.H., Lee, S.L.: Dynamic update cube for range-sum queries. In: VLDB. (2001) 814–825
16. TIGER: Tiger/line files. Technical report, U.S.Census Bureau, Washington, DC (2000)

Providing Geographic-Multidimensional Decision Support over the Web

Joel da Silva, Valéria C. Times, Robson N. Fidalgo, and Roberto S.M. Barros

Center for Informatics – Federal University of Pernambuco, P. O. Box 7851
Cidade Universitária, Recife – PE, Brazil, 50.732-970
{js, vct, rdnf, roberto}@cin.ufpe.br

Abstract. For the last years, many researchers have been addressing their efforts to try to solve the problem regarding the integration between analytic and geographic processing systems. The main goal is to provide users with a system capable of processing both geographic and multidimensional data by abstracting the complexity of separately querying and analyzing these data in a decision making process. However, this integration may not be fully achieved yet or may be built by using proprietary technologies. This paper presents a service integration model for supporting analytic and/or geographic requests over the Web. This model has been implemented by a Web Service, named GMLA WS, which is strongly based on standardized technologies such as Web Services, Java and XML. The GMLA WS query results are displayed using a Web browser as maps and/or tables for helping users in their decision making.

1 Introduction

Several researchers from the Information Technology community have thoroughly investigated the problem of integrating the analytic and geographic processing [29-33]. However, much of this work does no more than proposing an operator for the system interface. Moreover, this is an arduous task and deserves some special attention. The main idea is to develop an open and extensible system with the analysis capabilities available in these two technologies. Thus, a geographic processing system [5-8] could take the advantage of the facilities implemented by an analytic tool [1,16], while the latter would receive a considerable gain in aggregating some spatial treatment for the geographic dimension.

According to this, members from the project GOLAPA (Geographic Online Analytic Processing Architecture) [17,18], have been studying a way of providing users with an abstraction of the complexity involved in querying analytic and geographic data for decision support [34,35]. The work presented in this paper is part of the GOLAPA project and aims to integrate the analytic and geographic services for decision support over the Web. This article presents the GMLA Web Service, which provides operations for performing analytic and/or geographic analysis over a geographic-multidimensional data source. The remainder of this paper is organized as follows. The second section presents a summary of the main related work. The third section outlines the XML and Web services technologies together with a view of

Y. Zhang et al. (Eds.): APWeb 2005, LNCS 3399, pp. 477–488, 2005.

some other related standards. In the four section, the integration model namely ISAG is presented. In the section five, some details concerning the GMLA Web Service implementation are given. The section six shows an application of the GMLA Web Service, with some experimental results. Finally, some conclusions regarding this investigation are given in the section seven.

2 Related Work

A lot of research about the integration of analytic and geographic processing has been found in literature [48-56], but just the following studies have showed to be more relevant to the work given in this paper: MapCube [29], GeoMiner [30], GOAL [31, 57] and SIGOLAP [32, 33].

MapCube is an operator used to perform aggregation and visualization of geographic data and may be seen as a metaphor for an album of maps. MapCube is based on the Cube [58] operator and performs all combinations of aggregation for each data of each Data Warehouse (DW) dimension. The main difference between these two operators is the presentation of their results. The Cube operator just presents its results in a tabular view, whereas the MapCube operator shows the results as both tables and maps.

GeoMiner is a project aiming at the mining of geographic data and is composed by three basic modules. However, just two modules of them can be considered as related work: the module for geo-cubes construction and the one for geographic OLAP. In [59, 60], Han *et al.* proposed two algorithms for the efficient construction of geographic data cubes: Pointer Intersection and Object Connection. These algorithms provide a means of building analytic and spatial cubes based on the selective materialization of a geographic dataset. The specified criteria were: 1) the geo-dataset access frequency, 2) its storage cost and 3) the support for building other derivatives geographic cubes.

Geographical Information On-Line Analysis (GOAL) is a project that aims to accomplish the integration between DW / On-Line Analytical Processing (OLAP) and Geographical Information Systems (GIS). To achieve this, Kouba et al. [31,57] have implemented an architecture where the main component used to manage this task is the Integration Module (IM). For the case study presented in [57] the software GT Media98 and ArcView were used together with the MSOLAP server as the OLAP component. Because these tools have different interfaces for communication, the IM has to be adjusted to offer the appropriate support for each new software component. While the communication with ArcView was achieved by using Avenue scripts (the native language of ArcView) and Delphi libraries, the communication with MSOLAP was done by implementing an OLE DB for OLAP provider [61] with Visual C++.

SIGOLAP aims to provide the integration between GIS and OLAP by a three tier architecture, which is based on a mediation approach. The implemented case study demonstrates this architecture by using the following technologies: MSOLAP Server; MSAccess and AutoDesk Mapguide Server; SQL Server and Visual Basic, and, Visual Basic Script.

With regard to the work discussed above, we shall now conclude that: the MapCube approach, just provides multidimensional analytic processing over geographic data without considering the GIS operators (e.g. distance and adjacency). However, despite using proprietary technologies and as a result, preventing them from being multi-platform based approaches and from providing extensibility and data interchange capabilities, the reminding work discussed above, namely GeoMiner, GOAL and SIGOLAP do integrate SIG and OLAP functionalities. This lack of platform independence can be seen as a motivation for the work given in this paper.

3 XML and Web Services

This paper presents a XML (eXtensible Markup Language) based approach to provide users with analytic and geographic processing over the Web. The main goal is to provide an environment for decision making that abstracts the complexity involved in simultaneously querying multidimensional and/or geographic data. To overcome the limitations cited in the previous section, we use the Web Services technology, because it is strongly based on XML, and thus, allows us to easily integrate systems with distinct functionalities. Using the Web Services and XML technologies, we have obtained an open and platform independent solution for the analytic and geographic processing integration.

The development of the XML [20] has been recognized as an important issue in the Information Technology research area. XML has become a standard for data publication and data interchange over the Web. It is an extensible language that allows new standards to be specified from it, and thus, enables the development of new technologies to be operated in conformity with it. Another technology that has been developed from XML is Web Services [9]. These compose a distributed computational architecture based on auto-descriptive services that can be published, located and executed through the Web, and that publish interfaces and connections that are both defined and described in XML.

In this paper, both the XML and Web Service technologies are considered as essential for the processing, interchange and visualization of the analytic and geographic data over the Web. XML for Analysis (XMLA) [13], Web Feature Service (WFS) [15] and Geography Markup Language (GML) [14] are mainly standardized and key technologies, that can be used in the development of Web Services for geographic-multidimensional processing.

XML For Analysis (XMLA) is one of the open technologies that is available to enable the OLAP [1] processing over the Web. It is a XML API based on SOAP[11] that has been created as an initiative of the Microsoft Corporation [23] and Hyperion Solutions Corporation [24] to provide an open access for multidimensional databases. This standardized access enables a non-proprietary communication between client applications and OLAP data servers through the Internet. XMLA implementation is based on the Web Services architecture and the description of its service is defined in terms of a WSDL document. XMLA provides two methods for managing their functionality: *Execute* and *Discover*. These enable the access to both data and metadata stored in a multidimensional OLAP Server. As these methods are invoked through SOAP, the input and output are XML documents.

The two most important XML based technologies that makes the provision for the geographic data processing over the Web are GML [14] and WFS [15]. GML is the OpenGIS [27] XML Schema for interchanging and storing the descriptive and geometric properties of geo-referenced data. GML is based on the abstract model [26] of the OpenGIS consortium and its last stabilized version (i.e. 2.1.2) supports vector geo-data only. Although the GML 3.0 has recently been launched already, this is still under industry evaluation, and for this reason, we have decided to use GML 2.1.2 which is an evaluated and stabilized version.

WFS [15] is the OpenGIS Specification for providing some interfaces for the description of operations used to manipulate geographic features (coded in GML) in a distributed environment through the HTTP protocol. The geographic features are spatial objects that must at least contain one geometric property and may have one or more descriptive properties. Operations for data manipulation include abilities to create, erase, change, obtain or search features based on spatial restrictions (e.g. adjacency and distance) and on non-spatial criteria (e.g. population >= 800.000 and gender = "M"). The recovery of both data and metadata stored in a geographic database is achieved by the use of the following WFS operations: *GetCapabilities*, *DescribeFeatureType* and *GetFeature*. The spatial, logic, arithmetic and comparison operators, which may be used in a WFS request are described in [25].

Based on XMLA and GML, we have specified the GMLA [17] according to the XML Schema [22] syntax. Thus, GMLA imports, extends, and integrates the original XML Schemas. With GMLA, the data that had been previously described by two distinct schemas, can now be described and semantically integrated by just one schema. This resulting schema is then used by the GMLA Web Service to describe and validate the geographic-multidimensional data.

The technologies discussed in this section have fundamentally contributed for the integration of the analytic and geographic processing. Using them helped in the development of the GMLA Request Schema, of the integration model and of the GMLA Web Service. These are described in the following sections.

4 The Model ISAG

Before developing the integration model and the GMLA Web Service for the analytic and geographic services integration, the GMLA Request Schema [37,63] was defined. This XML schema is responsible for the validation of requests that are processed by the GMLA Web Service and, consequently, for the prevention of syntactic errors. The GMLA Request Schema integrates the request syntax of the XMLA and WFS services and was defined to support the following three query types: MD (Multidimensional), GEO (Geographic) and GEOMD (Geographic-Multidimensional).

A query of type MD just contains analytic parameters allowing the execution of a multidimensional expression [28] or a metadata request. When this query type is submitted to the GMLA WS, it delegates this request to the XMLA analytic service that will process the corresponding result. On the other hand, a request of type GEO just contains geographic parameters, making the GMLA WS to activate the WFS service to produce the needed result. Finally, a GEOMD request contains both analytic and geographic parameters, and in this case, both services (i.e. XMLA and WFS) are processed to obtain a solution satisfying the query. In addition, a GEOMD request can be further classified as follows: 1) Mapping GEOMD, where an analytic request is sent to the GMLA WS and analytic data are displayed on a map, and 2) Integration

GEOMD, where analytic and spatial restrictions are specified and used in the request processing. The GMLA Request Schema can be downloaded from http://www.cin.ufpe.br/~golapa/schemas, while some query examples can be downloaded from http://www.cin.ufpe.br/~golapa/gmlaws/requests.

In software engineering methodologies, models [36] are used to simplify and graphically indicate the main concepts, activities, processes and/or data involved in the development of a system. In using models, some aspects pertinent to the implementation can be abstracted, enabling a better understanding of the main processes that compose a system.

After specifying the GMLA Request Schema, which defines the supported operations types, the services integration model named ISAG [37] was specified. This model was specified in UML [36] and defines an activities group to enable the integration of the analytic and geographic processing.

In figure 1, the highest abstraction level of the ISAG model is given. The activities of this model are sequentially performed and each execution result is used by the following activity in the sequence, until the processing is completed and the final state is reached. Each model activity has some sub activities, which need to be performed so that the main activity is concluded.

The ISAG model takes into account the existence of a metadata source, which contains information about which analytic data have a geographic correspondence, and about how to recover these correspondences. These are very useful for requests needing to either integrate or map the final query results. Data with geographic correspondences are considered here as those analytic data which are associated with some information that represent their geometry.

The first activity of the ISAG model shown in figure 1 is *Receive Request*. Then, the activity *Verify Request Type* is performed which classifies the request according to the query types defined by the GMLA Request Schema (i.e. MD, GEO or GEOMD). The next activity is *Extract Request Parameters*, which extracts some information from the analytic and/or geographic parameters found in the user request. Following this, these parameters are validated by the activity *Validate Request Parameters*. Next, the analytic and/or geographic services are asked to produce the query results. Following this, for a request of type MD, the activity *Request MD Service* solves the query and returns its response. Finally, for a GEO request, the next activity to be executed is the *Query GEO Service* which recovers the geographic information satisfying the query.

If the request type is GEOMD, the next activity to be executed is the *Request MD Service*. Then, the activity *Query Metadata* is performed. For a mapping GEOMD, the metadata source is used to identify which analytic data have geographic correspondences and how to recover these correspondences. After doing this, in the activity *Build GEO Request*, the GEO query that recovers all geographic correspondences of the analytic members involved in the request is formulated. In the activity *Map Results*, the resulting document is built, which contains the analytic data together with their corresponding geographic correspondences. If the request is of type integration GEOMD, after querying the metadata source, the next activity is the *Query GEO Service*, which recovers all geographic features satisfying the request. Then, in the activity *Integrate Results*, the response document is built, which just contains the geographic and analytic data that satisfy the spatial operators found in the user request.

The integration model outlined in this section has been implemented by the GMLA Web Service that will be presented in the next sections.

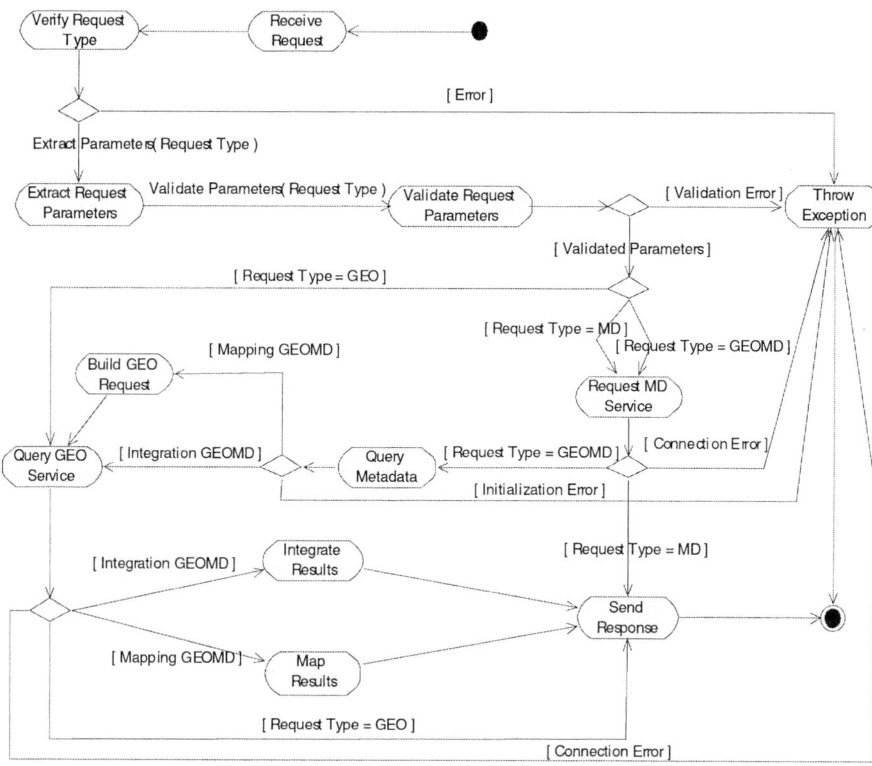

Fig. 1. The ISAG Model diagram

5 GMLA Web Service – GMLA WS

The main components of the GMLA Web Service (i.e. GMLA WS) architecture proposed here are displayed in figure 2. The GMLA WS enables the integration of the analytic service (i.e. XMLA) and geographic service (i.e. WFS), both discussed in the third section of this paper. This integration provides users with the capability of executing their geographic-multidimensional requests.

This enables users to query and analyze geographic and/or multidimensional data stored in a Geographic Data Warehouse (GDW) [19,40-42]. A GDW schema is similar to the traditional Data Warehouse schemas (e.g. star schema) [1-4]. However, the geometries of the geographic data are stored in the GDW as well.

The metadata source (METADATA) plays an important role in the integration of the XMLA and WFS services. The integration metadata are accessed by the GMLA

WS whenever a GEOMD request is received. Thus, the GMLA WS can find out if the analytic data have some geographic correspondences. The metadata source implemen tation has been based on the MOF (MetaObject Facility) [38] specification, by the OMG (Object Management Group) [39] and on the metamodels GAM (Geographical and Analytical Metamodel) and GeoMDM (Geographical Multidimensional Metamodel) presented in [62].

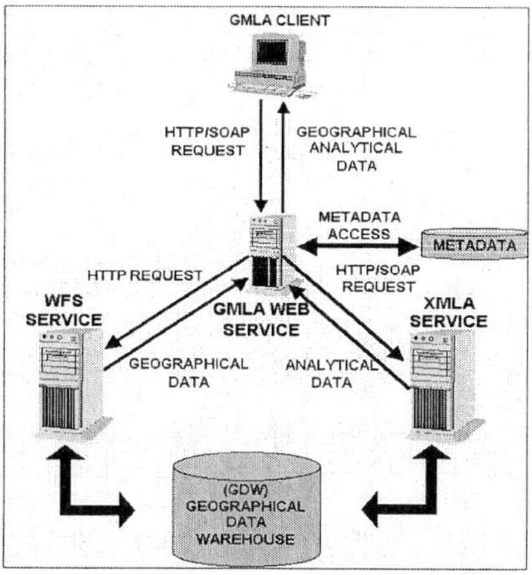

Fig. 2. GMLA WS architecture

The GMLA WS implementation has been based on the Web Services architecture [9]. Thus, the GMLA WS provides a WSDL [21] document with the service description and available operations, allowing a client application to be implemented regardless of the chosen operating system or programming language.

The GMLA WS is both a client and a server. It can be seen as a client because it may access two other services (i.e. XMLA and WFS), and as a server, because a WSDL interface is provided to allow other applications to be developed.

The communication between the GMLA WS and the XMLA is based on the Web Services standard, and made by sending and receiving information coded in a SOAP envelope. On the other hand, the communication between the GMLA WS and the WFS service is achieved by sending and receiving HTTP [12] requests, instead of using the SOAP protocol due to the WFS do not operate according to the Web Services standard.

The GMLA CLIENT component is responsible for formulating the requests according to the GMLA Request Schema, sending these requests to the GMLA WS and then, after obtaining the response document, for graphically displaying the results.

When a client application sends a request to the GMLA WS, this is executed and a XML document is returned as the final result. The structure of this document is defined and validated by the GMLA Schema [17].

6 A GMLA WS Application

To illustrate an application for the GMLA WS, the processing of a GEOMD query is demonstrated having both analytic and geographic requests. In this example, the idea is to visualize the total of the product sales, classifying by the product category and grouping the results by country, states and cities. The key issue in this request is that users wish to graphically visualize the result on a map. Then, a query of type *mapping GEOMD* will be sent to the GMLA WS containing the proper request parameters.

After having received the request parameters sent by the client application, the GMLA WS performs the multidimensional request, which will result in a collection of product categories, together with their total of sales organized by country, states and cities. This processing is performed by the multidimensional service XMLA.

Following this, the GMLA WS identifies the resulting elements of the multidimensional request that have geographic correspondences, so that the needed information is displayed on a map. This is done by using the GMLA WS metadata source. Accessing this metadata allows the system to elaborate a request that will be sent to the WFS geographic service to recover all the geographic features that are involved in the corresponding query.

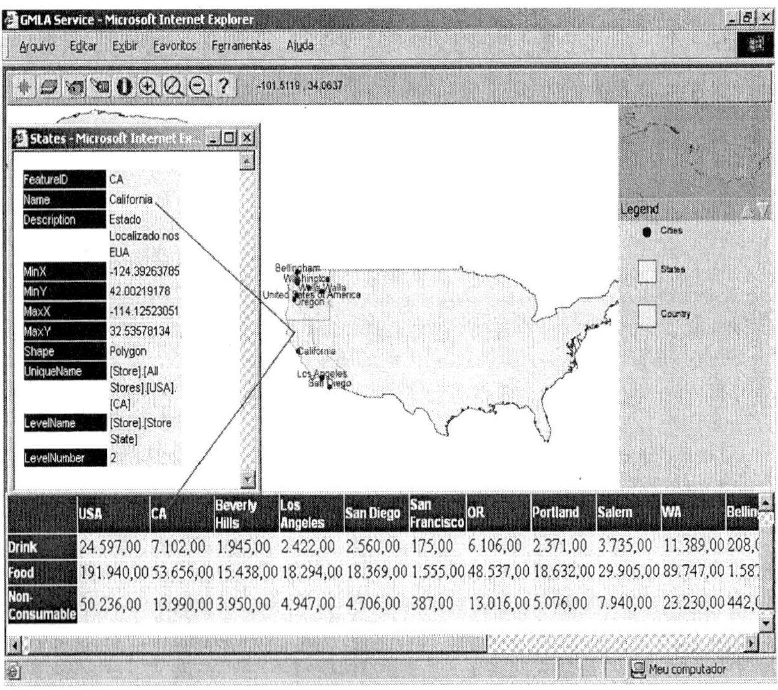

Fig. 4. Graphic visualization of a GEOMD request result

After having received the response from the WFS geographic service, the GMLA WS builds a XML document containing the integration of the multidimensional and geographic data, creates a SOAP envelope and then, returns it to the client application that had previously sent the request. Next, the client application receives the SOAP envelope and graphically shows the result. Then, the geographic data of the resulting document are transformed by the GMLA CLIENT to the Scalable Vector Graphics format (SVG) [43], showing them as a map. The multidimensional data are also submitted to a XSLT processing [47] and visualized in the HTML format. The figure 4 demonstrates this query processing result, where a table with the multidimensional data is given at the bottom, and a map showing the elements involved in the request that have geographic correspondences is given at the top. The final graphic result can be visualized in a Web browser with a SVG Plugin [44]. For this case study, the Internet Explorer [45] was used.

As can be seen in the legend given above, in the right side of the browser screen (figure 4), the geographic data are organized in three themes: 1) Country, 2) States and 3) Cities. In these themes, all members showed in the multidimensional data table given at the bottom of the browser screen are displayed. To manipulate the data found in these themes, the operations available in the toolbar, located at the top of the web browser screen and above the map, may be used. These available operations include zoom in, zoom out, pan operator, label insertion and exclusion, and presentation of detailed information about each geographic feature found in the map. The interface component that is responsible for graphically showing the geographic data coded the in SVG format is an adaptation of the GeoClient Component of the GeoServer Project [46].

Any other request type that satisfies the GMLA Request Schema (see section 4) can be sent to the GMLA WS to be processed. However, this processing has not been shown here for the sake of simplicity and limitation of space.

7 Conclusions

The integration between analytic and geographic processing as a single tool provides a wider context for decision support. This is so because it aggregates: the capability of quickly analyzing a large volume of data and the power of visualizing data on maps and running spatial queries.

The work presented in this paper is part of the GOLAPA project, which is concerned with the development of a service layer, making a set of operations available for the geographic-multidimensional processing. Due to the use of open and extensible technologies, the solutions discussed in this paper are independent from the GOLAPA, and as a result, they may be applied to any other projects aiming at integrating analytic and geographic processing.

The proposed integration model defines a set of activities that are performed for integrating the tools provided by the analytic and geographic services used in the query and analysis of geographic-multidimensional data. The model is based on three request types defined by GMLA Request Schema, which integrates the syntax of both XMLA and WFS services. Also, this model takes into account the use of a metadata source to provide information about the relationships existing between the analytic and geographic data.

The implementation of the integration model was achieved by specifying and developing a Web Service namely GMLA WS. This integrates both the XMLA and WFS services to make operations available for the processing of analytic and/or geographic requests. This system prototype provides an environment that abstracts the complexity found in the joint use of analytic and spatial operators found in decision support queries. Moreover, the GMLA WS provides the visualization of both the analytic and/or geographic information on maps and/or tables, through the use of a simple Web browser. Finally, for implementing the system prototype, technologies such as Web Services, GML, SVG, MOF, Java and XML were used to provide an extensible and platform independent solution.

References

1. S. Chaudhuri, U. Dayal. Decision support, Data Warehouse, and OLAP, Tutorials of the Twenty-Second international Conf. On Very Large Data Base, 1996.
2. W. H. Inmon. Building the Data Warehouse. 2nd edition. John Wiley & Sons, 1997.
3. R.Kimball. The Data Warehouse Toolkit., John Wiley&Sons, Inc, 1996.
4. R. Kimball, L. Reeves, M. Ross, and W. Thornthwaite. The Data Warehouse Lifecycle Toolkit. Wiley, 1998.
5. G. Câmara, et al. Anatomia de Sistemas de Informação Geográfica. 10ª Escola de computação, http://www.dpi.inpe.br/geopro/livros/anatomia.pdf, 1996.
6. N. Chrisman. Exploring Geographic Information Systems. John Wiley and Sons, 1996.
7. P. A. Longley, et al. Geographical Information Systems: Principles, Techiniques, Applications and Managemente. 2nd Edition, John Wiley and Sons, 1999.
8. M. F. Goodchild. Geographical Data Modeling. Computers & Geosciences. 1992.
9. W3C, Web Service Official Home Page, (http://www.w3.org/TR/2002/WD-ws-arch-20021114/).
10. UDDI, UDDI official home page, last visit on 2003, (http://www.uddi.org/).
11. W3C, SOAP official home page, last visit on 2003 (http://www.w3.org/TR/2002/CR-soap12-part0-20021219/).
12. W3C, HTTP official home page, last visit on 2003 (http://www.w3.org/Protocols/).
13. XMLA.org, XML For Analysis Specification, Version 1.1, Microsoft Corporation & Hyperion Solutions Corporation. 2002.
14. OpenGIS® Geography Markup Language (GML) Implementation Specification, version 2.1.2, 2002.
15. OpenGIS© Web Feature Service Implementation Specification, Version: 1.0.0., 2002.
16. E. Thomsen. OLAP Solutions - Building Multidimensional Information Systems. John Wiley, 1997.
17. R. N. Fidalgo, J. Silva, V. C. Times, F. F. Souza, R. S. M. Barros. GMLA: A XML Schema for Integration and Exchange of Multidimensional-Geographical Data. GEOINFO 2003, (http://www.geoinfo.info/Anais/geoinfo2003-48.pdf).
18. R. N. Fidalgo, V. C. Times, F.F. Souza - GOLAPA: Uma Arquitetura Aberta e Extensível para Integração entre SIG e OLAP. In Proc. GeoInfo 2001, 2001.
19. Fidalgo R. N., Times, V. C., Silva, J., Souza, F.F.:GeoDWFrame: A Framework for Guiding the Design of Geographical Dimensional Schemas. Proc. Int. Conf. on Data Warehousing and Knowledge Discovery (DaWaK), 2004.
20. W3C, XML official home page, 2003, (http://www.w3.org/XML).

21. W3C, WSDL official home page, last visit on 2003 (http://www.w3.org/TR/2001/NOTE-wsdl-20010315).
22. W3C, XML Schema official home page, last visit on 2003 (http://www.w3.org/).
23. Microsoft Corporation Official Home Page (www.microsoft.com).
24. Hyperion Solutions Corporation Official Home Page (www.hyperion.com).
25. OpenGIS© Filter Encoding Implementation Specification, (http://www.opengis.org/techno /specs/02-059.pdf).
26. OpenGis. The Abstract OpenGIS Specification. OpenGIS Document Nunber 99-100. Jun., 1999.
27. OpenGis Official Home Page (www.opengis.org).
28. Introduction to Multidimensional Expressions - MDX (http://msdn.microsoft.com/ library/default.asp?url=/library/en-us/dnolap/html/intromdx.asp).
29. S. Shekhar, et al. Map Cube: A Visualization Tool for Spatial Data Warehouse. 2000 (http://www.cs. umn.edu /Research/shashi-group/Mapcube/mapcube.html)
30. J. Han, K. et al. GeoMiner: a system prototype for spatial data mining. Proc. ACM SIGMOD, 1997.
31. GOAL Project official home page. Last visit on 2003 (http://krizik.felk.cvut.cz/goal/).
32. A.C. Ferreira, et al. An Architecture for Spatial and Dimensional Analysis Integration. In Proc. of World Multiconference on Systemics, Cibernetics and Informatics (SCI 2001), 2001.
33. A.C. Ferreira. Um Modelo para Suporte à Integração de Analises Multidimensionais e Espaciais. Dissertação de Mestrado - UFRJ, 2002.
34. Daniel J. Power, Decision Support Systems Web Tour, http://dssresources.com/tour/index.html, 2002.
35. Daniel J. Power, What is a Decision Support Systems?, http://dssresources.com/papers/ whatisadss/index.html, 1998.
36. G. Booch, J. Rumbaugh, and I. Jacobson. The Unified Modeling Language User Guide. Addison-Wesley, 1999.
37. J. Silva, Integrando Serviços Analíticos e Geográficos para Suporte à Decisão na Web. MSc. Thesis – Universidade Federal de Pernambuco (UFPE), Brazil, 2004.
38. OMG - Object Management Group. MetaObject Facility (MOF) Specification 1.4. Especificação, 2002.
39. Object Management Group Home Page, (www.omg.org).
40. H. B. Zghal, S. Faïz, H. B. Ghézala, Exploration Techniques of the Spatial Data Warehouses: Overview and Application to Incendiary Domain, IEEE International Conference on Computer Systems and Applications (AICCSA'01), 2001.
41. T.Barclay, R. D. Slutz. J. Gray, TerraServer: A Spatial Data Warehouse. Proceedings of the 2000 ACM-SIGMOD Conference, 2000.
42. R. N. Fidalgo, Integração de Processamento Analítico com Sistemas de Informações Geográficas para Suporte à Decisão em Ambientes de Data Warehouse Geográfico, Phd Proposal, Universidade Federal de Pernambuco (UFPE), 2003
43. W3C Scalable Vector Graphics (SVG). http://www.w3.org/Graphics/SVG/.
44. Adobe SVGviewer, (http://www.adobe.com/svg).
45. Microsoft Internet Explorer Official Home Page, (http://www.microsoft.com/windows/ie/ default.asp).
46. The GeoServer Project, (http://geoserver.sourceforge.net/html/index.php).
47. World Wide Web Consortium, XSL Transformations (XSLT), http://www.w3.org/ TR/xslt.

48. F. Ferri, E. Pourabbas, M. Rafanelli, F.L. Ricci, Extending Geographic Databases for a Query Language to Support Queries Involving Statistical Data, International Conference on Scientific and Statistical Database Management (SSDBM'00), 2000.
49. E. Pourabbas, M. Rafanelli, A Pictorial Query Language for Querying Geographic Databases Using Positional and OLAP Operators, SIGMOD Record, Vol. 31, N° 2, June 2002.
50. D. Papadias, Y. Tao, P. Kalnis, J. Zhang, Indexing Spatio-Temporal Data Warehouses, IEEE International Conference on Data Engineering (ICDE), 2002.
51. L. Zhang, Y. Li, F. Rao, X. Yu, Y. Chen, D. Liu, An Approach to Enabling Spatial OLAP by Aggregating on Spatial Hierarchy, International Conference on Data Warehousing and Knowledge Discovery (DaWaK), 2003.
52. J. Han, K. Koperski, N. Stefanovic, Object-Based Selective Materialization for Efficient Implementation of Spatial Data Cubes, IEEE Transactions on Knowledge and Data Engineering, 2000.
53. T. B. Pedersen, N. Tryfona, Pre-aggregation in Spatial Data Warehouses, International Symposium on Spatial and Temporal Databases, 2001.
54. S. Prasher, X. Zhou, Multiresolution Amalgamation: Dynamic Spatial Data Cube Generation, Australian Database Conference (ADC2004), 2004.
55. L. Zhang, Y. Li, F. Rao, X. Yu, Y. Chen, Spatial Hierarchy and OLAP-Favored Search in Spatial Data Warehouse, ACM Sixth International Workshop on Data Warehousing and OLAP, 2003.
56. D. Papadias, P. Kalnis, J. Zhang, Y.Tao, Efficient OLAP Operations in Spatial Data Warehouses, International Symposium on Spatial and Temporal Databases, (SSTD), 2001.
57. Z. Kouba, K. Matousek, P. Miksovsky. On Data Warehouse and GIS integration. International Conference on Database and Expert Systems Applications (DEXA), 2000.
58. J. Gray, et al. Data cube: A relational aggregation operator generalizing group-by, cross-tab, and sub-totals. In Proc. 12th ICDE, 1996.
59. J. Han, et al. Selective materialization: An efficient method for spatial data cube construction. In PAKDD, 1998.
60. N. Stefanovic. Design and implementation of on-line analytical processing (*OLAP*) of spatial data. M.Sc. Thesis, Simon Fraser University, Canada, 1997.
61. Microsoft OLE DB 2.0. Program Reference and Data Access SDK, Microsoft Press, 1998.
62. Fidalgo R. N., Times, V. C., Silva, J., Souza, F.F., Salgado, A.C.:Providing Multidimensional and Geographical Integration Based on a GDW and Metamodels. Proc. Brazilian Symposium on Databases (SBBD). 2004.
63. Silva, J., Times, V. C., Fidalgo R. N., Barros, R. S. M., Towards a Web Service for Geographic and Multidimensional Processing. VI Brazilian Symposium on GeoInformatics, Campos do Jordão, SP, 2004.

Spatial Selectivity Estimation Using Compressed Histogram Information*

Jeong Hee Chi, Sang Ho Kim, and Keun Ho Ryu

Database Laboratory, Chungbuk National University, Korea
{jhchi, kimsh, khryu}@dblab.chungbuk.ac.kr

Abstract. Selectivity estimation for spatial query is very important process in finding the most efficient execution plan. Many works have been performed to estimate accurate selectivity. However, the existing works require a large amount of memory to retain accurate selectivity, and these works can not get good results in little memory environments such as mobile-based small database. In order to solve this problem, we propose a new technique called MW histogram which is able to compress summary data and get reasonable results. The proposed method is based on the spatial partitioning algorithm of MinSkew histogram and wavelet transformation. The experimental results showed that the MW histogram has lower relative error than MinSkew histogram and gets a good selectivity in little memory.

1 Introduction

Most of database management systems (DBMS) use summary data for efficient processing of a query. The summary data consists of paired attribute values and frequencies, which implicitly represent the data distribution for attribute value of records stored in the database. With the recent dramatic increase in the scale of the database, the significance of the summary data has further intensified.

Especially, for estimating selectivity of spatial query, the summary data can be generated by histogram methods using spatial partitioning, graphic theory, dimension transformations, and trees. Among these methods, the spatial histogram is the simplest method, which preserves the buckets produced by spatial partitioning to be adjusted under any circumstances. Various histograms that have thus far been proposed in the field display the variety of performance according to bucket partitioning methods and the information kept within the buckets[1,3,6,8].

Also recent advancements in computing and mobile technology make it possible to provide information services on the user's position and geography using small size database, thus the importance, in practical as well as in theoretical aspects, of selectivity estimation method for small database is on the increase. However, the existing methods are capable of producing good selectivity estimation only when sufficient

* This research was supported by University IT Research Center Project in Korea.

Y. Zhang et al. (Eds.): APWeb 2005, LNCS 3399, pp. 489–494, 2005.

memory space is available. If such methods are used in given small memory capacity, good selectivity cannot be obtained.

In this paper we propose a compressed histogram called MW histogram that yields a good selectivity estimation using a small space. This method exploits the spatial properties which allocate more buckets to place with more spatial distribution, and ensure each bucket to have uniform density. The proposed histogram method is designed to maintain summary data using a small space that results from compression of these partitioned buckets.

The rest of this paper is organized as follows. In the next section we summarize related work. The proposed structure of MW Histogram is presented in section 3. In section 4 we describe the strengths and weakness of the proposed method through experiments. Finally, we draw conclusions and give a future work in Section 5.

2 Related Work

Selectivity estimation is a well-studied problem for traditional data types such as integers. Histograms are the most widely used form for doing selectivity estimation in relational database systems. Many different histograms have been proposed in the literature and some have been deployed in commercial DBMSs. In case of selectivity estimation in spatial databases, some techniques for range queries have been proposed in the literature[2,4,5,7].

In [2], Acharya et. al. proposed the MinSkew algorithm. The MinSkew algorithm starts with a density histogram of the dataset, which effectively transforms region objects to point data. The density histogram is further split into more buckets until the given bucket count is reached or the sum of the variance in each bucket cannot be reduced by additional splitting. In result, the MinSkew algorithm constructs a spatial histogram to minimize the spatial-skew of spatial objects. The CD (Cumulative Density) histogram is proposed in [5,7]. Typically when building a histogram for region objects, an object may be counted multiple times if it spans across several buckets. The CD algorithm address this problem by keeping four sub-histogram and store the number of corresponding corner points that fall in the buckets, so even if a rectangle spans several buckets, it is counted exactly once in each sub-histogram. The Euler Histogram is proposed in [4]. The mathematical foundation of the Euler Histogram is based on Euler's Formula in graph theory. As in the CD Histogram, Euler Histogram also addresses the multiple-count problem.

Though these techniques are efficient methods to estimate selectivity in spatial databases, these techniques require a large amount of memory for better accuracy.

To compress the summary information in conventional databases, in [1] Matias et al. introduce a new type of histograms, called wavelet-based histograms, based upon multidimensional wavelet decomposition. Wavelet decomposition is performed on the underlying data distribution, and most significant wavelet coefficients are chosen to compose the histogram. In other words, the data points are compressed into a set of numbers via a sophisticated multi-resolution transformation. Those coefficients constitute the final histogram.

3 MW Histogram

For estimating the selectivity for spatial query using small memory space, the proposed MW histogram is constructed by through the spatial partitioning and wavelet transformation stage.

3.1 Spatial Partitioning

The partitioning of space is conducted by using spatial density and spatial skew. Spatial density refers to an elementary function *h* among the partitioning function *MF*, and presents the number of the objects that intersect certain grid cell $c_{i,j}$. Spatial skewness corresponds to a weight function *g*, and is computed by the statistical processing of grid cell in a given domain. Thus, the partitioning function *MF* can be defined as a combination of the following functions (*MF–f-g-h*).

$$h(c_{i,j}) = f_{i,j} = count(intersect(c_{i,j}, ST)) \tag{1}$$

$$g(B_k) = s_k = \frac{(f_{i,j} - \bar{f})^2}{|B_k|} \tag{2}$$

$$f(A) = MAX(s_k) \tag{3}$$

(*i,j*: grid cell index included in *k*th bucket B_k, *ST*: the total data distribution, $0 \le k \le b$)

This partitioning function *MF* makes the spatial skewness of each partitioned bucket as small as possible. Fig.1 shows the process of the spatial split.

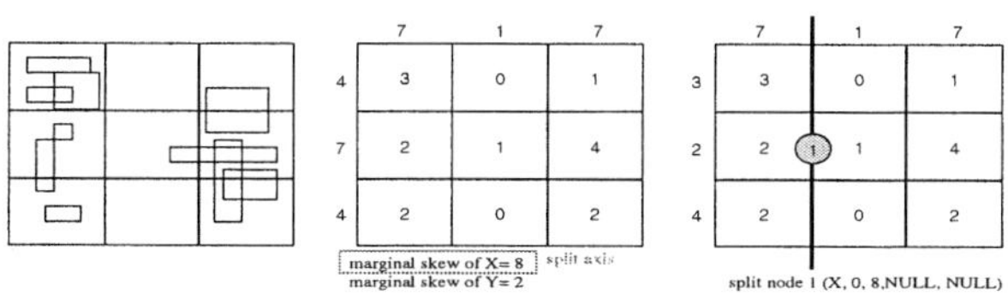

Fig. 1. Process of Spatial Split

First, the spatial frequency inside the grid cell is obtained using the function h. Second, compute the axis skew by applying function g to each axis after calculating cumulative spatial frequency abstracted in each axis. Third, choose the bucket and axis that has the maximum skew using the elementary function h, and then partition until the skew of the divided bucket is at its lowest level. Finally, generate split node 1 possessing the partitioning information and extrapolate into the binary split tree. Following these steps, repeat the process until a desired number of buckets is generated.

3.2 Wavelet Transformation

If all process of the split terminate, generate the gird cell with elementary resolution r, and establish the value of each grid cell after applying the summary function *TF*. The summary function will produce the output value, counting the number of objects with the center of the spatial object included in lattice $c_{i,j}$. Summary function is defined as follows:

$$TF(c_{i,j}) = count(contain(c_{i,j}, centroid(ST))) \tag{4}$$

Next step is to wavelet transform the grid that exists inside the domain that each bucket occupies. In this process, one dimensional wavelet transformation is applied in MW histogram.

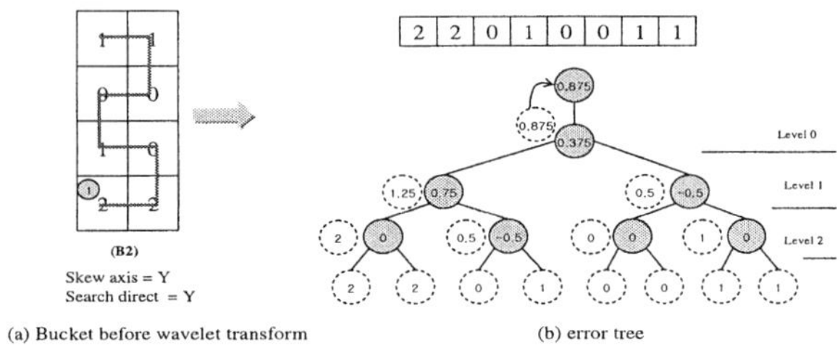

Fig. 2. Wavelet Transform

First procedure is to transform two dimensional grid of a bucket into one dimensional grid. This process is accomplished using a space-filling order method. When the values of the adjacent domain are similar, wavelets generate a lot of coefficients close to 0, increasing the compression effects further. As shown in Fig.2, the search direction is in the same direction of the split axis of the parent split node. Since the similar values in the direction of the split axis will be distributed more likely, it can be said to be an efficient compression method because it has many coefficients with automatic 0 values. Fig 2(b) is an error tree for wavelet transformation of single bucket. Second procedure is to shrink wavelet coefficients. In order to choose wavelet coefficients retained, we use a deterministic threshold with simple computations, while effectively minimizing the total error. The number of wavelet coefficients preserved in each bucket has to be properly allocated in order to store histogram in a limited storage space. When the number of buckets needed is determined using Equation 5, the wavelet coefficients that are maintained on average can be found. However, if all buckets preserve average number of wavelet coefficients, it may generate much error, because the skewness of each bucket is different, and the size of the occupied space is also different, a number of coefficients excepts those with 0 are quite different. For buckets with large occupied space size and high spatial skewness, average square error of the removed wavelet coefficients increases. Thus, if a given query intersects with this bucket space, the selectivity error rate increases. On the other hand, a bucket that occupies small space and has skewness close to 0 results in wasting of the storage space. Thus, we set differently the number of the coefficients preserved in each bucket. If the skewness is close to 0, the spatial frequency of grid cell becomes consistent. Therefore, even if we use the least number of coefficients, a low error occur. The preserved number of the coefficients $|W_{Ai}|$ is determined by the following equation (*coeff_size* is the total number of preserved coefficients):

$$|W_{Ai}| = \frac{B_i.skew \times |B_i|}{\sum B_i.skew \times |B_i|} \times coeff\_size \tag{5}$$

4 Experimental Results

In this section, we compare MW histogram with MinSkew histogram and use the 11,000 building data in JoongGu, Seoul, Korea as the experimental data. Also we changed storage space to 60~720 units as an experimental parameter, and the size of the query to 5%~20% of the total space. Finally, to evaluate the relationship between the number of buckets and the number of wavelets, we produced MW histogram with the required number of buckets and the size of the storage space. MW0~MW2 is a histogram that makes preserved number of the buckets be {0.3, 0.5, 0.7} * M/6, where M is the size of total storage space. In order to experiment the validity of the proposed method, we compared MinSkew histogram with 360 storage space with MW histogram, MW0~MW2 with 180 storage space.

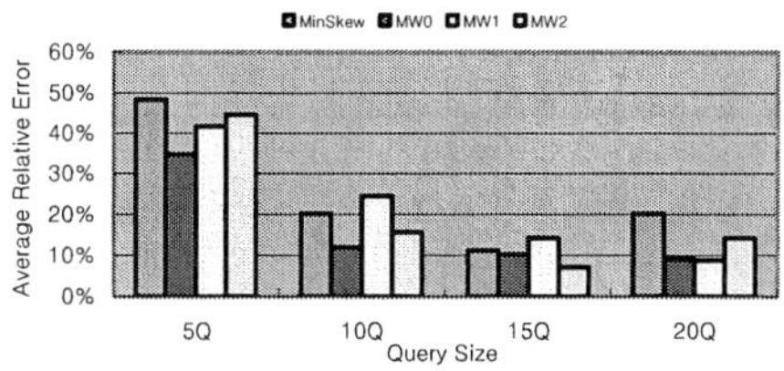

Fig. 3. Average Relative Error according to Query Size

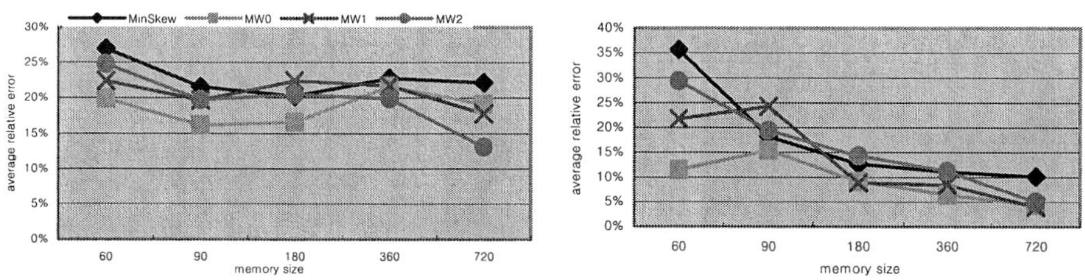

(a) 5% query

(b) 20% query

Fig. 4. Average relative error according to memory size

As shown in Fig.4, MW0~MW2 has relatively lower than or similar to MinSkew histogram despite the storage space being half the size. We can see that the size of the relative error to the large size of the query is similar in MW0 through the experimental results. Also, in case of MW1, the larger the query, the lesser the relative error. On the other hand, MW2 has higher error than MW0 and MW1 in 20% of query. The smaller size of the query is included relatively easily in larger domain, and thus the probability of false counting is high, resulting in higher error. But, MW0, in which preserved wavelet coefficient is big, reduces the probability of false counting because it stores efficiently as compressing the distribution information inside each bucket into wavelet summary data. The big size query includes completely one bucket, or most buckets, so that it can get more accurate selectivity. This result implies that the designed MW histogram can solve the problem of distributional skewness in a relatively large bucket space, even in the case where the spatial domain is big, or the restriction to the storage space is severe.

Fig.4 (a) and (b) show the average relative error of MW0~MW2 according to the storage space in 5% and 20% query. In Fig.4 (a), since the intersecting number of buckets with query is small, there is little effect on the size of storage space. This result demonstrates that MW histogram can maintain more information even with small storage space. The relative error curve in 20% query of Fig.4 (b) shows a big change as the size of the storage space increases. Especially, MW histogram in 60 storage space has lower error than the relative error of the MinSkew histogram. MW0, in which the number of wavelet coefficients preserved per bucket are big, has lower error than other histogram. That is, the bigger the number of preserved wavelet coefficients, the better selectivity we can get even with small storage space.

5 Conclusions

Selectivity estimation is used in query optimization and decision of optimal access path cardinally. The existing works for spatial selectivity estimation have been focused on obtaining high accuracy and fast response time. However, they require very large memory space to maintain high accuracy of selectivity if spatial domain is also large. Therefore, we proposed a new method called MW histogram that could get reasonable selectivity with small memory size. Based on our experimental analysis, we showed that the proposed technique can obtain maximum compression effects and reasonable selectivity simultaneously.

In the future, we need to analyze our histogram to improve much experimental evaluation. We also will extend our histogram to do work easily about dynamic insertion.

References

1. 1.Yossi Matias, Jeffrey Scott Vitter, Min Wang, "Wavelet-Based Histograms for Selectivity Estimation", In Proc. ACM SIGMOD Int. Conf. on Management of Data(1998), pp.448-459.
2. 2.Swarup Acharya, Viswanath Poosala, Sridhar Ramaswamy, "Selectivity estimation in spatial databases", In Proc. ACM SIGMOD Int. Conf. on Management of Data(1999), pp.13-24.
3. 3.L. Getoor, B. Taskar, D. Koller, "Selectivity estimation using probabilistic models", In Proc. ACM SIGMOD Int. Conf. on Management of Data(2001), pp.461-473
4. 4.C. Sun, D. Agrawal, A. El Abbadi, "Selectivity for spatial joins with geometric selections", Proc. of EDBT(2002), pp.609-626
5. 5.Jeong Hee Chi, Sang Ho Kim, Keun Ho Ryu, "Selectivity Estimation using the Generalized Cumulative Density Histogram", Asian Symposium on Geographic Information System from Computer Science & Engineering View 2th(ASGIS 2004), pp.201-207
6. 6.Minos G., Phillip B.G., "Wavelet Synopses with Error Guarantees", ACM SIGMOD(2002), Madison, Wisconsin, USA, pp.476-487.
7. 7.Jin, N. An, A. Sivasubramaniam, "Analyzing Range Queries on Spatial Data", In Proceedings of the IEEE International Conference on Data Engineering(ICDE 2000), pp. 525-534
8. 8.Ning An, Zhen-Yu Yang, Sivasubramaniam A., "Selectivity estimation for spatial joins", In Proceedings of the IEEE International Conference on Data Engineering(ICDE 2001), pp.175-196

Representation and Manipulation of Geospatial Objects with Indeterminate Extents*

Vu Thi Hong Nhan, Sang Ho Kim, and Keun Ho Ryu

Database Laboratory,
Chungbuk National University, Korea
{nhanvth, kimsh, khryu}@dblab.chungbuk.ac.kr

Abstract. A spatiotemporal database system manages data of geospatial objects whose geometry change over time and vagueness is their inherent nature. In this paper, we concentrate on the applications dealing with objects whose extents are indeterminate and change constantly. To support geographic information systems (GIS) in representing and handing such objects efficiently, we propose a fuzzy spatiotemporal data model called FSTDM based on fuzzy set theory. Also, we introduce algorithms for proceeding queries depending on whether the predicate is fuzzy spatial, temporal, or fuzzy spatiotemporal (FST). This work is applicable to many applications handling time-varying geospatial data, including global change (as in climate or land cover change), social (demographic, health, etc.) applications.

1 Introduction

Most of phenomena existing in the world are dynamic and vagueness is their inherent feature. In GIS community, models for vague objects[3, 5, 7] do not include the time dimension of objects. Besides that, spatiotemporal data models (STDM) have also been introduced to deal with time-varying spatial objects, but they do not accommodate fuzzy aspect of objects[2, 6, 12]. For the purpose of this paper, we concentrate on spatial fuzziness that captures the property of many spatial objects with no sharp boundaries, called fuzzy objects and applications dealing with objects that change their extents over time. We propose an FSTDM, outcome of the aggregation of spatial, temporal and fuzzy components into a single framework, based on fuzzy set theory. We also introduce algorithms for proceeding queries on FST data. This work is applicable to the applications including change (as in climate or land cover change), or social (demographic, health, ect.) applications.

The rest of this paper is organized as follows: Data models for crisp objects are reviewed in the next section. Section 3 presents an FSTDM followed by the integration method of fuzzy spatial and temporal operations. In section 5, the experimental result is displayed. Conclusions and future work are given in section 6.

* This research was supported by University IT Research Center Project in Korea.

Y. Zhang et al. (Eds.): APWeb 2005, LNCS 3399, pp. 495–500, 2005.

2 Related Work

This section summarizes several STDM and models for geospatial objects with vague boundaries. Definitions for fuzzy regions and their fuzzy spatial topological relationship are given.

2.1 STDM and Models for Geospatial Objects with Indeterminate Boundaries

So far STDM for crisp objects have been received many attentions[2, 6, 12]. Query languages are the subjects of the related researches. ST query language extensions need developing in parallel with the independent spatial[8] and temporal[9] query language development[12]. At present, there are several approaches available to represent vague objects. Among them, exact model transfers the type system for spatial objects with sharp boundaries to that for objects with unclear boundaries[3]. Because this model treats a vague boundary as a thick one finer distinction between points lying within it cannot be made[11]. The view of vague regions in 5] is coarse and restricted, the original gradation in the membership values of the points of the boundary gets lost[7].

2.2 Definition of Fuzzy Regions and Fuzzy Spatial Relationship

Fuzzy regions defined based on fuzzy set theory take the view of a collection of nested crisp α-cut regions[11]. Let $\mu_F{:}X\times Y\rightarrow [0,1]$ be the membership function of a fuzzy region F. An α-cut region F_α for $\alpha\in[0,1]$, is defined as $F_\alpha=\{(x,y)\in \mathrm{IR}^2|\mu_F(x,y)\geq \alpha\}$. Therefore F is described as $F=\{F_{\alpha i}|1\leq i\leq \Lambda_F\}$ with $\alpha_i>\alpha_{i+1}\Rightarrow F_{\alpha i}\subseteq F_{\alpha i+1}$ for $1\leq i\leq|\Lambda_F|-1$ and Λ_F is the level set $\alpha\in[0,1]$ representing distinct α-cuts of F.

Let $\pi_f(P,S)$ be the value representing the topological relations between two fuzzy regions P and S. It is determined by the following formula:

$$\pi_f(P,S)=\sum_{i=1}^{N}\sum_{j=1}^{N}(\alpha_i-\alpha_{i+1})(\alpha_j-\alpha_{j+1})\pi_{cr}(P_{\alpha i},S_{\alpha j}) \tag{1}$$

where N is the number of α-cut regions; $\pi_{cr}(P_{\alpha i},S_{\alpha j})$ is the predicate between two crisp α-cut regions $P_{\alpha i}$, $S_{\alpha j}$ calculated by 9-IM in [4]. Its value should belong to the interval [0,1]. With that way, a set of eight fuzzy predicates between two fuzzy regions T_f={*disjoint*$_f$, *meet*$_f$, *overlap*$_f$, *covers*$_f$, *coveredBy*$_f$, *equal*$_f$, *inside*$_f$, *contains*$_f$ } is obtained.

3 The Fuzzy Spatiotemporal Data Model

Following is the description of the data model. We examine the two-dimensional geographic space and linear time.

The data model can be viewed as a hierarchy of data. Map at the top level is a library of space-time cubes, called *thematic* layers. Each thematic layer consists of a set of space-time cubes, called *lexical* layers. Each lexical layer accommodates the degree of the membership value of each individual space-time location in the lexical layer characterizing a theme.

Regions extracted from field observation data. Due to the vagueness of object class definition, for each individual location P_{ij} a membership function value vector vector $[L(P_{ij},C_1),L(P_{ij},C_2),\ldots,L(P_{ij},C_n)]^T$ $(0\leq L(P_{ij},C_k)\leq 1)$ after classification is generated. Here $L(P_{ij},C_k)$ represents the membership function value of individual location P_{ij} belonging to class C_k, n is the total number of the classes. Objects may have fuzzy transition zones, that is, in the transition zone an individual zone location might belong to multiple objects. The change of natural phenomena is a gradual continuous process. Thus regions which may have been *shifted*, *expanded*, or *shrunk* at different time points should be linked to form lifetime of the objects. An object that appears at a specific moment represents a *new* object, and disappears at some moment represents a *disappearing* object. They can be *merged* or *split*.

The design of FSTDB is based on the integration of independent researches on spatial and temporal databases. In term of spatial databases, whenever a new object instance is inserted into a database, the old one should be deleted. It does not support the ability of managing the historical information about geospatial objects that have been changed with temporal evolution. In view of temporal databases, it is extremely hard to manage directly spatial objects without any modification.

Definition 1. FSTDB Scheme
The feature relation FR_i' and feature history relation FR_i" for the thematic layer i^{th}, describe a vector of spatial data <*fid*, *density*, $f_1,\ldots,f_n$, Geo_i> with *fid* is object discriminator; *density* indicates the number of α-cuts, $f_1,\ldots,f_n$ are geometric elements describing spatial extents of the objects; Geo_i indicates the actual shape and size of the objects. An attribute history relation AR_i" for i^{th} layer represents an attribute vector of non-spatial attribute <*fid* ,A_i, *VT*, *prev*> where A_i is an attribute vector for the fuzzy spatial object *fid* of the ith layer <*fid*, a_1 ,a_2,...a_m>, a valid time vector VT=(VT_s,VT_e) denotes the beginning and ending time of valid time, and *prev* is a historical pointer of a feature in an attribute history relation. The attribute relation AR_i' for the ith layer is described by an attribute vector of non-spatial data <A_i, VT_s, *prev*>. A merge relation MR_i describes a historical pointer vector of merged objects <*fid*, *hid*, *VT*> in which *hid* denotes the historical pointer of the object determined by *fid* in the feature history relation. The merge relation MR_i stores only history information of spatial objects in which merge operation occurs.

4 Fuzzy Spatiotemporal Operators

The idea of FST operators is the unification of fuzzy spatial operators and temporal operators. Temporal predicates including *before, equal, meets, overlaps, during, starts, finishes* and their semantics introduced in [1]. Given two valid time intervals VT_1=<*VTs*,*VTe*> and VT_2=<*begin*,*end*>, and a given predicate *Top* the function `Temporal_Operator(VTs, VTe, begin, end, Top)` verifies if VT_1 and VT_2 has the relation *Top*.

Since fuzzy spatial predicates are embedded into query languages via the qualitative linguistic descriptions of fuzzy topological relations. For example, depending on the value generated by $contains_f$, we can distinguish *not contain, somewhat contain,* and *completely contain*, where *not, somewhat, quite, completely* are called *fuzzy quantifiers*. Each fuzzy quantifier is represented by an appropriate fuzzy set with a membership function. We need to define a classification for them: **Create** Fquantifier(*not, somewhat, quite, completely*); Then activate it: **Set** Fquantifier;

Given two fuzzy regions *P* and *S* the function `FS_Operator()` verifies if they satisfy a given quantified fuzzy spatial predicate *Fq.Sop* composed of a fuzzy quantifier *Fq* and a spatial predicate *Sop* using equation 1.

```
Function Boolean FS_Operator(P,S,Fq,Sop)
  Begin
    result=0; temp=0;
    for(i=1;i<N;i++)//N is the number of α-cuts
    for (j=1;j<N;j++)
      - Identify α-cut regions P_αi and S_αj and check if
        they satisfy Sop using semantics of spatial
        operators between simple crisp regions in[4]
      - If the determined value crisprel= true then
         temp+=(alp_j-alp_j+1)*crisprel;
      result +=(alp_i-alp_i+1)*temp;
    If (result coincides the value defined for Fq in
    Fquantifier) then return 'False'; Else return
   'True'
End.
```

With those pretreatments we are ready to define FST_Operator() as below which are used in 'where' clause of query statements.

```
Function Boolean FST_Operator(P, S, Top, Fq.Sop)
  Begin
    Get time period of P&S (VTs,VTe) and
    (begin,end)respectively
    Invoke Temporal_Operator(VTs,VTe,begin,end,Top)
    If Temporal_Operator()is True
    Return FS_Operator(P,S,Fq.Sop); Else return False;
End.
```

5 Experiment and Evaluation

We now implement an FSTDB scheme by extending valid time and fuzziness in GIS and new operators.

5.1 Experimental Results

Assume we have two relations: Pollution keeps information about factors causing pollution sources. The blurred geometry of polluted zones are considered as fuzzy region. LandUse stores information about the use of land areas and vague spatial extents. The valid time is used to represent the lifespan of objects.

We define values for fuzzy quantifiers as Fquantifer{*not*(0,0.05), *somewhat*(0.05,0.5), *quite*(0.5,0.8), *completely*(0.8,1)}.

An FST query can be "Search regions are quite in polluted area caused by the Cement Factory during 1990-2000". The result displayed in figure 1(b) consists all regions retrieve from LandUse satisfying temporally *overlap* the time period '1990-2000' and spatially *quite overlap* the Cement Factory.

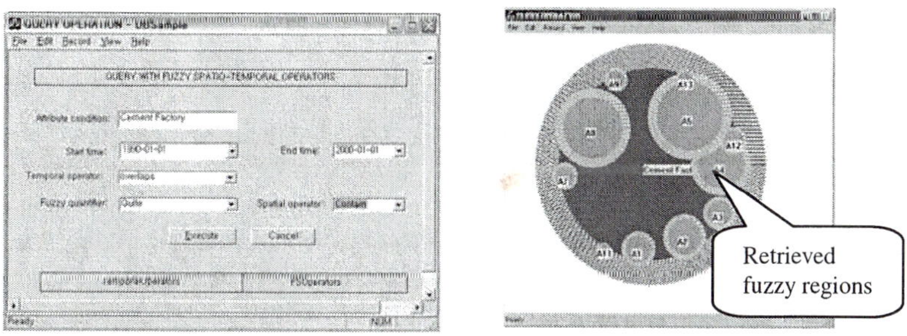

(a) An identify operation with fuzzy spatial and temporal conditions

(b) Result of query operation with fuzzy spatial and temporal conditions

Fig. 1. FST query

5.2 Comparison of Our Model to Previous Works

Here, we compare our model to the prior models using criteria time semantics, query capability, and database scheme shown in table 1. The previous models address temporal, spatial, and ST query operations, but do not support fuzzy spatial types. An FST framework introduced in [10] only reasons the ST concepts with respect to fuzzy characteristic of spatial objects. It defines no operators to support queries on FST data. Our work inherits nearly all the advantages of the previous works. With the definition of FSTDB scheme and the new operators our work is directly applicable to the management of time-varying information of fuzzy spatial objects

Table 1. Comparison of FSTDM and previous models

ST models	Database scheme	Time semantics		Query Capability		
		Valid time	Transaction time	Temporal queries	Fuzzy queries	FST queries
[12] Kim, D.H.	STDB	√	√	√		
[2] Claramunt, C.	ST framework	√	√	√		
[6] Peuquet, D.J.	ESTDM	√				
[10] Stefanakis, E.	FST framework	√		√		
FSTDM	FSTDB	√		√	√	√

6 Conclusions and Future Work

In this paper, we concentrated on the applications handling objects whose extents are vague and change over time. We introduced an FSTDM based on fuzzy set theory.

Moreover, we introduced and implemented operators to help process queries relating to whether the predicate is fuzzy spatial, temporal, or both. Our research is feasible to use in applications dealing with time-varying geospatial data, including global change, social applications. We are creating a richer set of operators and investigating a suitable indexing method to efficiently retrieve fuzzy spatial objects.

References

1. Allen, F.J.: Maintaining Knowledge About Temporal Intervals. Communication of the ACM 26, (1983) 832-843.
2. Claramun, C., Theriault, M.: Managing Time in GIS: An Event-Oriented Approach. Recent Advances in Temporal Databases, Springer-Verlag (1995) 23-42.
3. Clementini, E., Felice, P.D.: A Spatial Model for Complex Objects with a Broad Boundary Supporting Queries on Uncertain Data. DKE, Vol.37. (2001) 285-305.
4. Enhofer, M.J., Franzosa, R.: Point-set Topological Spatial Relations. Int J Geographical Information Systems, Vol.3. (1991) 161-174.
5. Erwig, M., Schneider, M.: Vague Regions. 5th. Int.Sym. on Advances in Spatial Databases, Springer-Verlag, LNCS , (1997) 298-320.
6. Peuquet, D.J., Wentz, E.A.: An Approach for Time-base Analysis of Spatiotemporal Data. Advances in GIS Research Proceedings (1996) 489-504.
7. Schneider, M.: A Design of Topological Predicates for Complex Crisp and Fuzzy Regions. Int.Conf. on Conceptual Modeling (1997) 103-116.
8. Egenhofer, M.: Spatial SQL: A Query and Representation Language. IEEE Transactions on Knowledge and Data Engineering, Vol.6, pp.86-96, 1994.
9. Snodgrass, R.T.: The TSQL2 Temporal Query Language. Kluwer Acadamic Publisher (1995) 123-152.
10. Stefanakis, E.: A Unified Framework for Fuzzy Spatiotemporal Representation and Reasoning. Proceeding of the 20th Int.Conf Beijing China (2001) 6-10.
11. Zhan, F.B.: Approximate Analysis of Topological Relations between Geographic Regions with Indeterminate Boundaries, Soft Computing, Vol.2. (1998) 28-34.
12. Kim, D.H., Ryu, K.H., Kim, H.S.: A Spatiotemporal Database Model and Query Language. Journal of Systems and Software, Vol.55. (2000) 129-149.

A Pattern Restore Method for Restoring Missing Patterns in Server Side Clickstream Data

I-Hsien Ting, Chris Kimble, and Daniel Kudenko

Department of Computer Science, The University of York
Heslington, York YO10 5DD, United Kingdom
{derrick, kimble, kudenko}@cs.york.ac.uk

Abstract. When analyzing patterns in server side data, it becomes quickly apparent that some of the data originating from the client is lost, mainly due to the caching of web pages. Missing data is a very important issue when using server side data to analyze a user's browsing behavior, since the quality of the browsing patterns that can be identified depends on the quality of the data. In this paper, we present a series of experiments to demonstrate the extent of the data loss in different browsing environments and illustrate the difference this makes in the resulting browsing patterns when visualized as footstep graphs. We propose an algorithm, called the ***P**attern **R**estore **M**ethod* (PRM), for restoring some of the data that has been lost and evaluate the efficiency and accuracy of this algorithm.

1 Introduction

Clickstream data is a principle resource for the analysis of user's browsing behavior on a website. The process of analyzing clickstream data and taking actions as a result of that analysis can be viewed as a circular process (see Figure 1) [7]. There are many open problems in this process. For example, the data integrity problem between the first step and the second step, the problem of measuring the "interestingness" of a pattern between the second and the third step, the problem of assessing the significance of a pattern between the third step and the fourth step, and the final problem of how to close the loop.

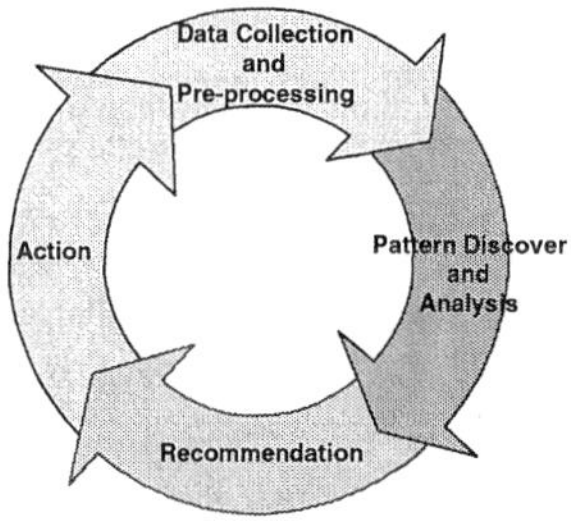

Fig. 1. The process of web usage mining for E-commerce [Adopted form 7]

The quality of the pattern discovery and analysis step depends on the quality of the data that is produced after the data pre-processing step [1]. Missing data in server side

Y. Zhang et al. (Eds.): APWeb 2005, LNCS 3399, pp. 501 – 512, 2005.

logs is a common problem in this respect. For example, clickstream data can be lost due to the use of the “back” button in the browser, which does not show in the server side clickstream data. Consequently, some of the user’s browsing patterns may be misinterpreted due to the missing data.

In this paper, we describe a series of experiments that show how clickstream data is lost at the server side. We examine the effects of different browsers, different ISPs and different proxy servers and propose a pattern restoration method (PRM) to overcome the caching problem caused by use of the browser’s "back" button.

The structure of this paper is as follows. Some related literature is discussed in section 2. Section 3 briefly describes the concept of a footstep graph, the experiment design and results. Section 4 describes the concept and the process of the PRM algorithm in detail and section 5 evaluates the efficiency and accuracy of the PRM algorithm. Section 6 concludes the paper.

2 Data Pre-processing for Web Usage Mining

In web usage mining, there are three main sources of usage data. These are client side data, intermediate data and server side data [8]. Client side data is normally collected by installing an agent in the client user’s computer or using embedded script in the web page. No data is lost in this process and the data is complete [5].

However, server side data is the most common source of data for web mining, as it is easy to collect. Unfortunately, raw server side data contains much noise and is usually incomplete [6]. Therefore, research has focused on pre-processing server side data to improve it’s quality. The pre-processing is an essential step but one that consumes a large proportion of the processing time in web usage mining [4]. Colley et al. [3] have developed a series of steps for data pre-processing for web usage mining. These include data cleaning, user identification, session identification and data formatting.

In recent years, the use of "bots" (search engine robots and web crawlers) has become widespread and a single bot can visit a website many times. However, these visits do not represent “real” users and are simply seen as noise in the server logs. Therefore, some systems try to find and delete these requests as an initial step in pre-processing [10]. In addition to this noise, incomplete information is also a problem when mining server side data. In [2], two problems that cause the loss of information in server side clickstream data have been pointed out.

The first is that there may be data missing in the server side data due to a frame-based website. Such a website may cause errors in user browsing time measurements, because every page of the framesets is treated as a single page and an independent request in the server side data. This problem has been solved by Spiliopoulou et al., who use a referrer-based heuristic algorithm to reconstruct the incomplete session record [9]. Others have used the web site structure to reconstruct incomplete session data [1].

The second is the problem caused by web page caching, e.g. when the “back” function of a browser is used. When the "back button" is used, the browser does not send a request to the server and consequently the user’s browsing behavior is not recorded in server's logs. However, the user’s backward browsing is important information for web usage mining, and this kind of missing data problem will affect the quality of any patterns discovered.

3 The Missing Data Problem in Server Side Clickstream Data

In this paper, we propose a method for restoring this lost data by using referrer information from the clickstream data and website structure. However, first we present the results of a series of experiments to investigate the missing data problem. In order to visualize the user's browsing behavior, we use footstep graphs [11]. A footstep graph is based on a simple x-y plot: the x-axis in this graph denotes time and the y-axis represents the nodes (i.e. pages) on the user's browsing route. Horizontal distance in this graph represents the time between two nodes, and changes in the vertical axis indicate a transition from one node to another node (See figure 2). An *Upstairs* pattern in the footstep graph is found when the user only moves forward. A *Mountain* pattern occurs when a *Downstairs* pattern follows an *Upstairs* pattern. A *Valley* pattern occurs after the user goes back to a page they visited and then goes to another new page. A *Fingers* pattern in a footstep graph indicates that a user is in a browsing loop.

3.1 Design of an Experiment to Find the Scope of the Missing Data Problem

The goal of the experiment is to look at the difference between browsing patterns as they appear at the client and server side in order to identify what data is lost in different user browsing environments. Three different browsing environments were chosen for the experiments using different browsers, ISPs and proxy servers. Additionally, four browsing routes representing the *Upstairs* (figure 2a), *Mountain* (figure 2c), *Fingers* (figure 2e) and *Valley* pattern (figure 2g) were used.

Three widely used browsers were chosen for the experiments: Microsoft Internet Explorer, Netscape Navigator and Opera. Different users, using different ISPs to access the web site, were asked to follow a predetermined browsing route. The tests were repeated using different proxy server settings.

3.2 The Results

3.2.1 Using Different Browsers

The main purpose of this test is to see if there is any difference in the server side data when different browsers are used to browse a predetermined route. We used the default setting for the cache and did not set a proxy server in this part of the experiment.

Internet Explorer & Netscape Navigator. Internet Explorer & Netscape Navigator both use the same default cache setting. The default setting is that when the user uses the backward and forward function, the browser does not sent the request to the server but use the cached webpage. Thus, server side data is lost if the user clicks the backward and forward buttons. Figure2 shows the results of this experiment. There is no difference between the Upstairs patterns in the client side and server side data when using Internet Explorer and Netscape Navigator (See (a) and (b) in the figure2), but data for all other patterns are lost due to caching.

Opera. Opera browser does not send a request to the website server when the user opens a web page that has been browsed within the last five minutes. Thus, much of the server side information is lost. For example, figure 3b should be a Mountain pattern, but there is no server side data because all of the web pages had been requested before. Figure 3c has been affected in the same way.

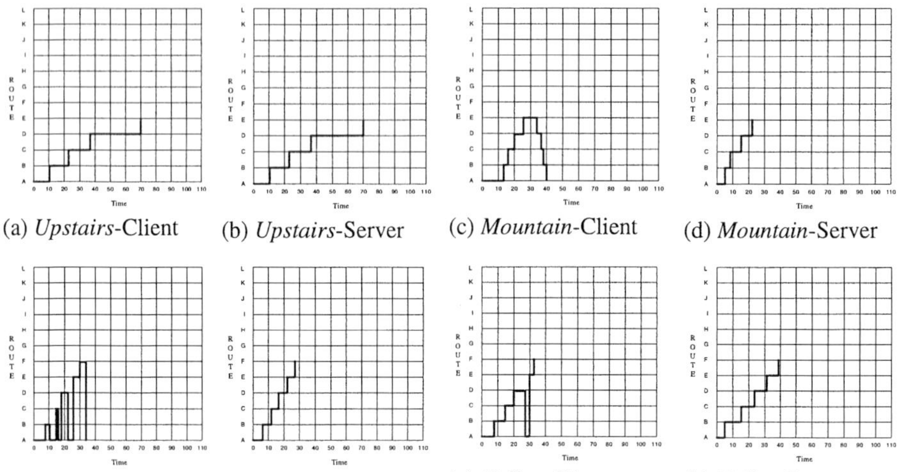

(a) *Upstairs*-Client (b) *Upstairs*-Server (c) *Mountain*-Client (d) *Mountain*-Server

(e) *Fingers*-Client (f) *Fingers*-Server (g) *Valley*-Client (h) *Valley*-Server

Fig. 2. Browsing patterns when using Internet Explorer and Netscape Navigator

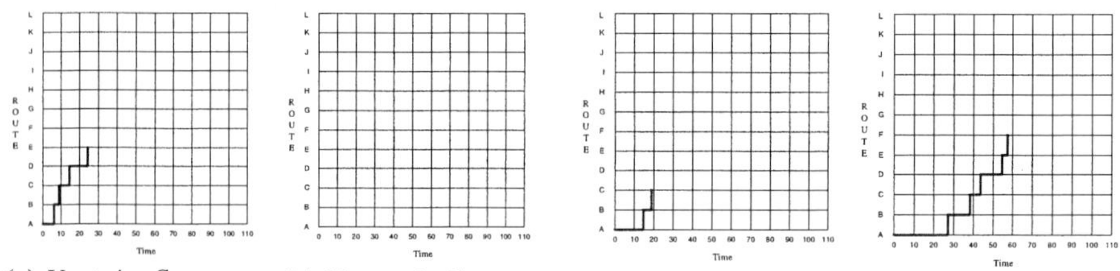

(a) *Upstairs*-Server (b) *Mountain*-Server (c) *Fingers*-Server (d) *Valley*-Server

Fig. 3. Server side browsing patterns when using Opera

3.2.2 Using Different ISPs

The second test investigated the server side patterns formed by using different ISPs. Again, users were asked to follow a pre-defined route through a given web site. Here only Internet Explorer or Netscape Navigator, without proxy server settings, were used. The commercial ISPs used in this experiment (Onetel, Hinet, SeedNet, BT and AOL) did not cache the experimental web pages and all of these ISPs created the expected patterns in server side data. However, some server side data was lost when using Loughborough University as an ISP as Loughborough appeared to cache web pages that had been browsed before. In this case, the user's browsing pattern at the server side appeared similar to the pattern produced by the Opera browser.

3.2.3 Using Different Proxy Servers

In the third set of experiments, we tested the impact of different proxy settings. The server side image of the user's browsing pattern depends on the proxy server's type. If the proxy server caches web pages for the user but does not send a request to the website server, some server side clickstream records will be lost and the server side pattern will be similar to the pattern when using the Opera browser. If the proxy server still sends a request to the website server, the server side pattern will suffer no losses.

4 The Pattern Restore Method (PRM) Algorithm

Having identified the potential scope of the problem, we now turn to a possible solution. Below we describe a method to restore the lost data that we call the pattern restore method (PRM). The basic idea behind the PRM algorithm is to use referrer information and the web site structure to restore the lost data. The PRM algorithm has two phases, the details of which are presented below.

4.1 The First Phase of the PRM Algorithm

4.1.1 The Process and Algorithm of the First Phase PRM Algorithm

Before we discuss the PRM algorithm, the general description of a clickstream format after pattern restoration is defined as:

C_i: [U_i, T_i, L_i, R_i, Mark]
C_i: C_i denotes the ith clickstream in one user session
U_i: Ui denotes the IP address of ith clickstream in one user session (In our example, we use the IP address to identify the session. Therefore, all the U_i in one session are the same)
T_i: T_i denotes the timestamp of ith clickstream in one user session
L_i: L_i denotes the requested URL of ith clickstream in one user session.
R_i: R_i denotes the referrer information of the ith clickstream in one user session
Mark: Mark is used to distinguish original from restored clickstream data.

The first phase of the PRM algorithm uses the referrer information to restore the missing clickstream data. First, the algorithm checks the first clickstream record in a session to check if it has any referrer information. If it does, and if the referrer belongs to the current site, some clickstream data must have been lost and needs to be restored. The restoration rule uses the referrer information of the first record as the URL of a new record. The referrer information of this new record is set to a null value, the time stamp is set to a suitable time (in this case 5 seconds earlier than the first record) and the record is marked as "Restored". The general description of the restored clickstream record in this step is **$C_{1'}$ [U_1, T_1-5, R_1, -, Mark]**. Figure 4 shows an example of original clickstream data in a session and Figure 5 shows the restored data for the same session.

(1) 61.59.121.221, 16:02:54, http://www-users.cs.york.ac.uk/~kimble/research/ research. .html, http://www-users.cs.york.ac.uk/~kimble/
(2) 61.59.121.221, 16:03:00, http://www-users.cs.york.ac.uk/~kimble/teaching/teach.html, http://www-users.cs.york.ac.uk/~kimble/

Fig. 4. The clickstream data before the first phase of the PRM algorithm

(1) 61.59.121.221, 16:02:49, http://www-users.cs.york.ac.uk/~kimble/, -, Restored
(2) 61.59.121.221, 16:02:54, http://www-sers.cs.york.ac.uk/~kimble/research/research.html, http://www-users.cs.york.ac.uk/~kimble/
(3) 61.59.121.221, 16:03:00, http://www-users.cs.york.ac.uk/~kimble/teaching/teach.html, http://www-users.cs.york.ac.uk/~kimble/

Fig. 5. The clickstream data after the first step of the first phase of the PRM algorithm

The next step of the first phase of the PRM algorithm compares the referrer URL in each clickstream record with the target URL from the previous record. If they are the same (such as record 1 and 2 in figure 5), it means that the user moved directly from one URL (e.g. record 1 in figure 5) to another (e.g. record 2 in figure 5). Thus, it is assumed that there is no missing data and no need to perform pattern restoration. However, if the target and referrer are different, it means that some data must have been lost before the current record (e.g. between record 2 and 3 in figure 5).

In this case, the algorithm will restore a record using the information in the current record. The IP address of the restored record is set to the same as the current record and the timestamp is set to be midway between the time between the current record and the previous record (i.e. midway between the times of record 2 and 3 in figure 5). The target URL of the restored record is taken from the referrer of the current record and the referrer of the restored record is set to null. Finally, the marker of this record is set to "Restored". The general description of the restored clickstream record in this step is **$C_{i'}$ [U_1, $(T_{i-1}+T_i)/2$, R_i, -, Mark]**.

(1) 61.59.121.221, 16:02:49, http://www-users.cs.york.ac.uk/~kimble/, -, Restored
(2) 61.59.121.221, 16:02:54, http://www- sers.cs.york.ac.uk/~kimble/research/research.html, http://www-users.cs.york.ac.uk/~kimble/, **Original**
(3) 61.59.121.221, 16:02:57, http://www-users.cs.york.ac.uk/~kimble, -, Restored
(4) 61.59.121.221, 16:03:00, http://www-users.cs.york.ac.uk/~kimble/teaching/teach.html, http://www-users.cs.york.ac.uk/~kimble/, **Original**

Fig. 6. The clickstream data after the second step of the first phase of the PRM algorithm

Record (3) in figure 6 is an example of a restored record created by comparing records (2) and (3) in figure 5. The algorithm will continue until the last record in a session has been processed. The pseudo code of the first phase of the PRM algorithm is given in figure 7.

```
IF R1 is not null then
        IF R1 belongs to website THEN Restore C1' [U1, T1-5, R1, -, Mark]
END IF
FOR i=2 to n
        IF Li-1 ≠ Ri THEN Restore Ci' [U1, (Ti-1+Ti)/2, Ri, -, Mark]
END FOR
```

Fig. 7. The pseudo code of the first phase of the PRM algorithm

4.1.2 Server Side Browsing Patterns After the First Phase of the PRM Algorithm

After the first phase of the PRM algorithm, *Fingers* patterns and *Valley* patterns have been restored. Figure 8(a) shows an example of a *Fingers* pattern recorded in a client side; Figure 8(b) shows the corresponding pattern in the server side log. The pattern now looks like an *Upstairs* pattern because data from pages browsed using the back function has been lost. Figure 8(c) shows the restored pattern after the first phase of the PRM algorithm has been run. Figures 9(a) to 9(c) show a similar restoration process with a *Valley* pattern.

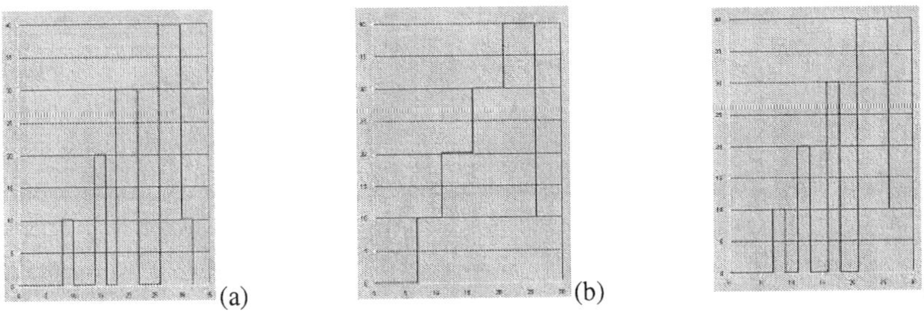

(a) (b) (c)

Fig. 8. (a) The *Fingers* pattern in client side data (b) The *Fingers* pattern appears as an *Upstairs* pattern in server side data (c) The restored *Fingers* pattern from the server side data

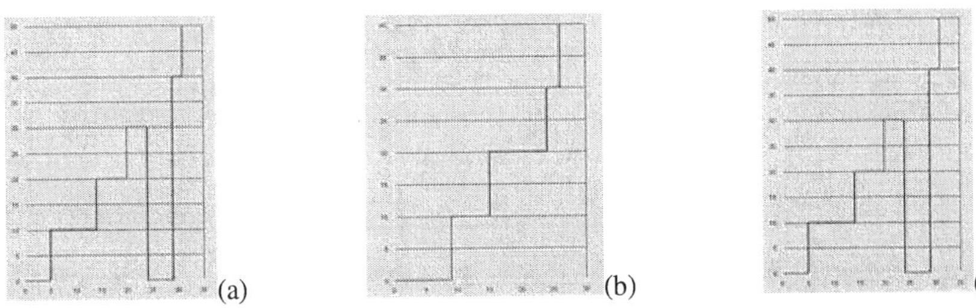

(a) (b) (c)

Fig. 9. (a) The *Valley* pattern in client side data (b) The *Valley* pattern appears as an *Upstairs* pattern in server side data (c) The restored *Valley* pattern from the server side data

Although the algorithm works with *Fingers* and *Valley* patterns, *Mountain* patterns cannot be restored using this method. Figure 10(a) shows a *Mountain* pattern in the client side data and the Figure 10(b) shows the corresponding pattern in server side data. The data lost by backward browsing cannot be restored and the pattern after the first phase of the PRM algorithm looks the same as in figure 10(b).

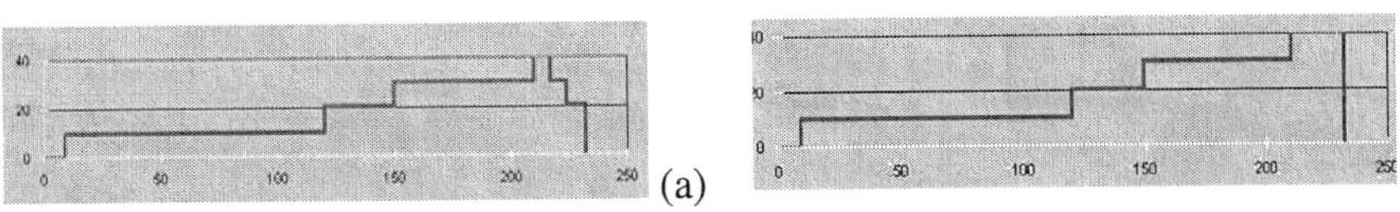

(a) (b)

Fig. 10. (a) The *Mountain* pattern in client side data (b) The *Mountain* pattern as it appears in the server side data and/or after the first phase of the PRM algorithm

4.2 The Second Phase of the PRM Algorithm

4.2.1 The Process and Algorithm of the Second Phase of the PRM Algorithm

As described above, the *Downstairs* part of *Mountain* patterns cannot be restored by the first phase of the PRM algorithm. Therefore, a second phase is needed to replace the missing data. The second phase of the PRM algorithm uses information from the website's link structure to insert the "most probable" browsing path of the user. To do this, a list of pages and the link structure for the site must be maintained.

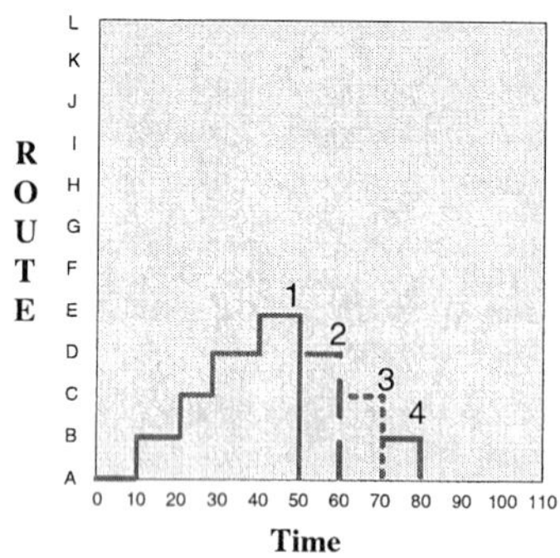

Fig. 11. An example of the second phase of the PRM algorithm

Figure 11 shows a simple example of how this algorithm works; the *Downstairs* part of *Mountain* pattern begins at node E. Firstly, the algorithm will check the link structure of node E. If node E has a direct link to node A, then the restored pattern

```
FOR i=2 to n
IF R_i ≠ L_{i-1} THEN
        IF L_{i-1} has link to L_i THEN
                Restore C_i [U_i, T_i, L_i, L_{i-1}, Mark]
        ELSE
                FOR j=1 to m
                IF L_{i-1-j} ≠ L_i THEN
                        IF L_{i-1-j} has link to L_{i-1-j+1} and has link to L_i THEN
                                k=k+1, Restore C_i^k [U_i, T_i, L_{i-1-j}, L_{i-1-j+1}, Mark]
                                Restore C_i [U_i, T_i, L_i, L_i^k, Mark]
                                Exit for
                        ELSE IF L_{i-1-j} has link to L_{i-1-j+1} THEN
                                k=k+1, Restore C_i^k [U_i, T_i, L_{i-1-j}, L_{i-1-j+1}, Mark]
                        END IF
                END IF
                END FOR
                FOR all restored clickstream k=1 to p T_i^k=(T_i-T_{i-1})/p
        END IF
END IF
```

Fig. 12. The pseudo code of the second phase of the PRM algorithm will look like pattern 1 in figure 11. If node E does not have a direct link to node A, it means some data must have been lost. In this case, the algorithm will search back from the nodes before node E to find the closest node that has a direct link to it. For example, the closest node to node E in figure 11 is node D, which has a direct link to node E. The algorithm then checks the link structure of node D. If there are direct links to node A, node D will be restored and the pattern is shown as 2 in figure 11. The algorithm will continue to loop until it finds a node that has a direct link to node A or the node is equal to A.

The pseudo code for the second phase of the PRM algorithm is shown as figure 12. Here, m denotes the total records before the current record, and k is used to count the total number of restored records in a single restoration session.

4.2.2 The User's Browsing Pattern After the Second Phase of the PRM Algorithm

After the second phase of the PRM algorithm, some of the lost clickstream data can be restored. For example, figure 13(a) shows how a *Mountain* pattern appears in the server side logs; figure 13(b) shows the restored *Mountain* pattern.

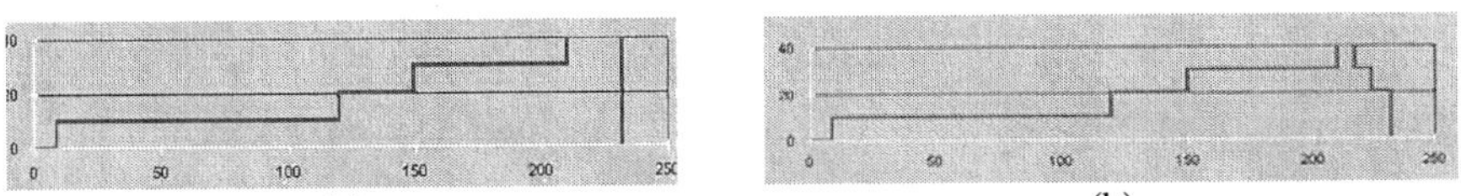

(a) (b)

Fig. 13. (a) The original *Mountain* pattern as it appears in the server side data (b) The restored *Mountain* pattern after the second phase of the PRM algorithm

Unfortunately, there is a weakness of the second phase of the PRM algorithm: when attempting to restore a *Valley* pattern, some errors may occur.

Figure 14(a) shows how a *Valley* pattern appears in the server side log. After the second phase of the PRM algorithm, the pattern becomes that shown in figure 14(b). However, the original pattern was as shown in figure 14(c), not figure 14(b).

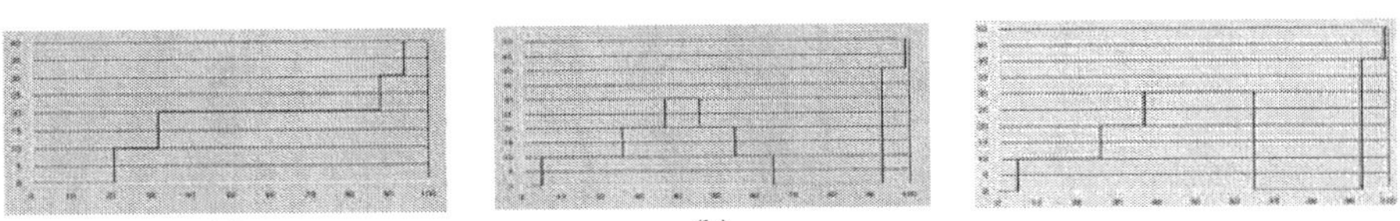

(a) (b) (c)

Fig. 14. (a) The server side data (b) The restored *Valley* pattern (c) The original *Valley* pattern

5 Evaluation of the PRM Algorithm

To evaluate the performance of the PRM algorithm, we tested the processing time of the PRM algorithm under different restoration rates (i.e. the number of restored records / total number of records after restoration) and the restoration accuracy under different user's browsing patterns. The evaluation was performed under Windows XP operation system, 512Mb RAM, 2.4 GHz Intel Pentium 4 CPU.

5.1 The Evaluation of the Processing Time of the PRM Algorithm

The tested number of original records ranged from 10 records (about 2 Kbytes file size) to 51200 (About 30 Mbytes file size). The results are shown in figure 15.

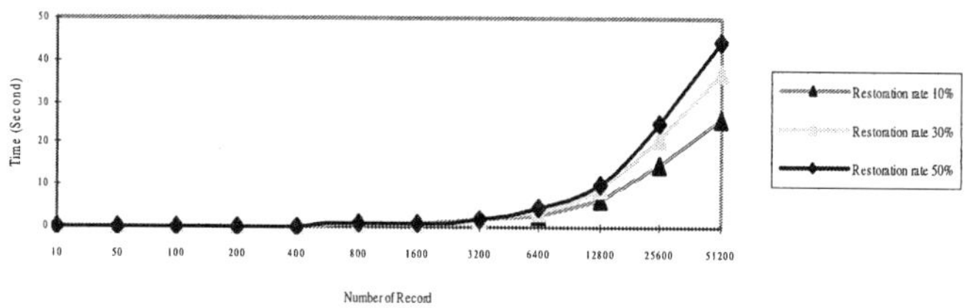

Fig. 15. Processing time of the first phase of the PRM algorithm

This shows that the rate of increase in processing time is similar under different restoration rates. When running the first phase of the PRM algorithm to process 51200 records, the processing time for 10% restoration rate is about 26 seconds; for 30% it is about 36 seconds and for 50% it is about 44 second. The processing time needed is not particularly high, even when given a large amount of data.

The same testing method is also be used to evaluate the second phase of the PRM algorithm; the results are shown in figure16. Here, the processing time with a restoration rate of 10 % is quite low and does not increase very much as the number of records processed increases.

When the restoration rate has reached 30%, the time / number of records slope has increased substantially. The reason for this is that the second phase of the algorithm needs to check the site structure. When the restoration rate and record number increases, the algorithm needs to check the structure table many times. Thus, the processing time increases as the restoration rate and the number of records increases.

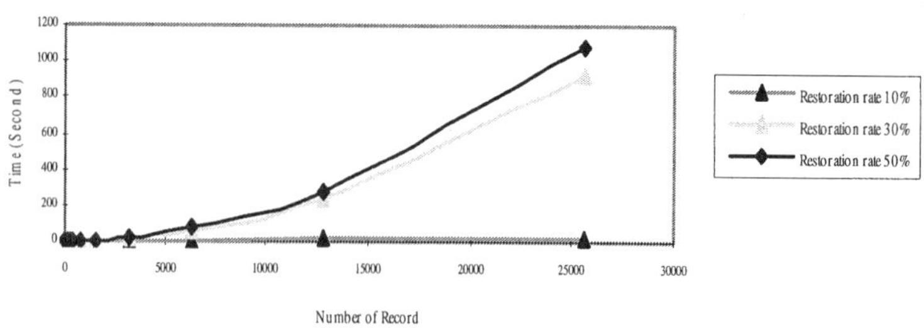

Fig. 16. The evaluation of processing time of the second phase of the PRM algorithm

5.2 The Evaluation of the Accuracy of the PRM Algorithm

In order to evaluate the accuracy of the algorithm, we designed ten different browsing routes that produced different *Fingers*, *Valley* and *Mountain* patterns, run the PRM algorithm on each of the resultant sets of server side data, and compared the result to the original pattern.

Table 1. The accuracy of restoration of the first phase of the PRM algorithm under different user's browsing pattern

	Finger			*Valley*			*Mountain*		
Route	Correct	Error	Rate	Correct	Error	Rate	Correct	Error	Rate
1	9	0	1	9	0	1	5	4	0.556
2	10	0	1	10	1	0.909	5	4	0.556
3	7	1	0.875	9	0	1	5	4	0.556
4	7	0	1	9	0	1	6	4	0.600
5	8	1	0.889	7	1	0.875	6	3	0.667
6	9	0	1	6	1	0.857	7	4	0.636
7	11	1	0.917	8	0	1	5	5	0.500
8	8	0	1	9	0	1	5	4	0.556
9	9	0	1	7	0	1	4	4	0.500
10	11	0	1	10	0	1	6	2	0.750
Avg.			0.968			0.964			0.587

Table 1, shows the restoration accuracy of the first phase of the PRM algorithm when restoring *Fingers*, *Valley* and *Mountain* patterns. Although the restoration accuracy for the *Fingers* and *Valley* is high, restoring *Mountain* patterns is only about 60% accurate, as the first phase of the PRM algorithm cannot deal with the *Downstairs* part of *Mountain* patterns.

Table 2. The accuracy of restoration of the second phase of the PRM algorithm under different user's browsing pattern

	Fingers			*Valley*			*Mountain*		
Route	Correct	Error	Rate	Correct	Error	Rate	Correct	Error	Rate
1	9	1	0.900	7	2	0.778	8	1	0.889
2	10	0	1	8	3	0.727	9	0	1
3	6	2	0.750	7	2	0.778	7	2	0.778
4	7	0	1	9	2	0.818	9	1	0.900
5	7	0	1	8	3	0.727	8	1	0.889
6	9	0	1	7	2	0.778	11	0	1
7	10	0	1	8	2	0.800	8	2	0.800
8	8	1	0.889	9	3	0.750	7	2	0.778
9	9	0	1	7	2	0.778	6	2	0.750
10	11	0	1	10	3	0.769	8	0	1
Avg.			0.954			0.770			0.878

In table 2, the restoration accuracy rate of *Mountain* patterns has been increased by about 30%, but the restoration accuracy rate of *Valley* patterns has been decreased by about 20%. The reason for this is that the second phase of the PRM algorithm can deal with the *Downstairs* part of the *Mountain* pattern but some *Valley* patterns are now restored as *Mountain* patterns (see figure 14).

6 Conclusion

This paper describes a series of experiments to examine the differences between clickstream data on the client side and on the server side. We found that due to caching, some data is lost. We subsequently developed and evaluated an algorithm for restoring the lost data. The evaluation showed that the algorithm could restore most of the lost patterns. Although not perfect, we believe that the method we describe can be used as the last part of the data pre-processing step in web mining. Consequently, we believe that by using the PRM algorithm the accuracy of the pattern discovery can be increased.

References

1. Berendt, B., Mobasher, B., Nakagawa, M. and Spiliopoulou, M.: The Impact of Site Structure and User Environment on Session Reconstruction in Web Usage Analysis. Proceedings of the WebKDD 2002 Workshop, Edmonton, Alberta, Canada, July (2002) 159-179
2. Clickstream Technologies Plc.: Technical White Paper: A clickstream Though-leadership Paper, http://www.clickstream.com/docs/cswhitepaper.pdf (Access date: 6 September 2004)
3. Cooley, R., Mobasher, B. and Srivastava, J.: Data Preparation for Mining World Wide Web Browsing Patterns, Knowledge and Information System, Vol. 1, No. 1 (1999) 5-32
4. Eirinaki, M. and Vazirgiannis, M.: Web Mining for Web Personalization, ACM Transactions on Internet Technology, Vol. 3, No. 1 (2003) 1-27
5. Fenstermacher, K. D. and Ginsburg, M.: Mining Client-Side Activity for Personalization, Proceedings of the Fourth Workshop on Advanced Issues in Electronic Commerce and Web Information Systems, Newport Beach, California, USA, June (2002) 26-28
6. Kohavi, R.: Mining E-commerce Data: The Good, the Bad, and the Ugly, Proceedings of the KDD 01 Conference, San Francisco, CA, USA (2001) 8-13
7. Lee, J., Podlaseck, M., Schonberg, E., Hoch, R.: Visualization and analysis of clickstream data of online stores for understanding web merchandising, Journal of data mining and knowledge discovery, Vol.5 (2001) 59-84
8. Pierrakos, D., Paliouras, G., Papatheodorou, C. and Spyropoulos, C. D.: Web Usage Mining as a Tool for Personalization: A Survey, User Modeling and User-Adapted Interaction, Vol. 13 (2003) 311-372
9. Spiliopoulou, M., Mobasher, B., Berendt, B. and Nakagawa, M.: A Framework for the Evaluation of Session Reconstruction Heuristics in Web Usage Analysis, INFORMS Journal of Computing, Special Issue on Mining Web-Based Data for E-Business Applications, Vol. 15, Issue. 2 (2003) 171-190
10. Tan, P. N., and Kumar, V.: Discovery of the Web Robot Sessions Based on their Navigational Patterns, Data Mining and Knowledge Discovery, Vol. 6 (2002) 9-35
11. Ting, I. H., Kimble, C., Kudenko, D.: Visualizing and Classifying the Pattern of User's Browsing Behavior for Website Design Recommendation, Proceedings of First International Workshop on Knowledge Discovery in Data Stream (ECML/PKDD '04), Pisa, Italy, 20-24 September (2004) 101-102

Tree Structure Based Data Gathering for Maximum Lifetime in Wireless Sensor Networks

Qing Zhang, Zhipeng Xie, Weiwei Sun, and Baile Shi

Department of Computing and Information Technology, Fudan University
qzhang79@yahoo.com
{xiezp, wwsun, bshi}@fudan.edu.cn

Abstract. Wireless sensor networks are envisioned to be promising in gathering useful information from areas of interest. Due to the limited battery power of sensors, one critical issue in designing a wireless sensor network is to maximize its lifetime. Many efforts have been made to deal with this problem. However, most existing algorithms are not well optimized. In this paper, we investigate the maximum lifetime data gathering problem formally. We adopt tree structure as the basic routing scheme for our analysis, and propose a near optimal maximum lifetime data gathering and aggregation algorithm MLDGA. MLDGA tries to minimize the total energy consumption in each round as well as maximize the lifetime of a routing tree used in the round. Comparing with existing algorithms which are only efficient in some specified conditions, the simulation results show that our algorithm performs well regardless of the base station location and the initial battery energy levels of sensors.

1 Introduction

Wireless sensor networks have received increasing interest in recent years [1, 10]. A wireless sensor network usually consists of a large number of small, inexpensive, limited-battery-powered sensors. The sensors can be densely deployed to monitor the environment and collect useful information on their surroundings. During the lifetime of network, the collected information is periodically gathered and transmitted to a base station for further processing.

To gather more information, one of the key challenge in designing a sensor network is to increase the network lifetime. In [3], Chang and Tassiulas proposed a maximum lifetime routing algorithms by treating the data transmission process as a maximum flow problem which meets the flow conservation principle. Nowadays data aggregation has emerged as a particularly useful paradigm for wireless routing in sensor networks to reduce the energy consumption [2, 6]. The idea is to combine the data from different sensors enroute to eliminate redundant transmission. This paradigm greatly reduces the amount of data transmitted and thus saves energy. Several protocols, such as LEACH [4] and PEGASIS [8], used data aggregation to minimize the energy consumed by sensors and increase the network lifetime accordingly. Further, Lindsey et al proposed PEDAP-PA [9],

Y. Zhang et al. (Eds.): APWeb 2005, LNCS 3399, pp. 513–522, 2005.

a tree based routing algorithm, which tries to improve the network lifetime. It achieves a good performance comparing with LEACH and PEGASIS in terms of lifetime. However, these algorithms are not well optimized.

In this paper, we investigate the maximum lifetime data gathering and aggregation problem formally. Tree structure is used as the basic routing scheme for our analysis since it is the minimal graph structure supporting the network connectivity. After giving some analysis, we propose a new near optimal maximum lifetime data gathering and aggregation algorithm MLDGA. MLDGA tries to construct a maximum lifetime routing tree for each data gathering round while the tree is energy-efficient. The experimental results show that MLDGA succeeds in achieving longer lifetime and better network utility than several other existing algorithms in various conditions.

The rest of the paper is organized as follows. Section 2 reviews some related works. Section 3 presents the maximum lifetime data gathering problem and gives some definitions used in this paper. Section 4 investigates the problem and proposed a near optimal algorithm MLDGA. In section 5, we conduct experiments to compare our algorithm with other known algorithms. We conclude our work in section 6.

2 Related Work

Several efficient data gathering routing algorithms have been proposed in the recent years.

LEACH, a cluster-based distributed routing protocol, was described in [4]. In LEACH, each cluster-head collects data from sensors in its cluster, fuses the data, then sends the result to the base station. LEACH utilizes randomized rotation of cluster-heads to evenly distribute the energy load among sensors in the network. Simulation results show that LEACH achieves as much as a factor of 8 reduction in energy dissipation comparing with direct transmission [4].

In PEGASIS [8], sensors are formed by chain. Each sensor communicates only with a close neighbor, and takes turns transmitting to the base station to prevent the failure of network. Only one node is designated to communicate with the base station, consequently the energy dissipation is significantly reduced. PEGASIS achieves better lifetime than LEACH about 100 to 200% [8].

In [9], the authors proposed two tree based protocols PEDAP and PEDAP-PA. The basic idea is to minimize the total energy expended in a round of communication while balance the energy consumption among sensors. In PEDAP, the weights of edges are the transmission cost between two connected sensors. In PEDAP-PA, the weight of edges is the ratio of the transmission cost between two connected nodes to the remaining energy of the sending node. PEDAP prolongs the lifetime of the last node death while PEDAP-PA provides a good lifetime for the first node death. Simulation results show that these two algorithms perform better than LEACH and PEGASIS both in systems that the base station is far away from and inside the field [9].

3 Problem Statement and Definitions

In this section, we present some background information about the maximum lifetime data gathering and aggregation problem, and give some definitions which will be used in the following paper.

3.1 Problem Statement

We consider a wireless sensor network consisting of a group of sensors and a base station which are randomly distributed over a region. The locations of sensors and the base station are fixed. The base station knows the locations of all sensors apriori, which can be obtained by manually entering coordinates or by using GPS-equipped sensors. A sensor can transmit data to any other sensor, and can communicate directly with the base station. The sensors periodically monitor their vicinity and generate monitoring data. The data from sensors are gathered at each time unit and sent to the base station for further processing. The time unit is called *round*. We assume that each sensor has limited battery energy and the action of transmitting or receiving data will consume its battery power. Our problem is to find a routing scheme to deliver data from all sensors to the base station, which can maximize the lifetime of the sensor network. In the process, data aggregation can be used to reduce the number of messages in the network.

Our energy model for sensors is based on the first order radio model described in [4]. In this model, the radio dissipates $E_{elec} = 50nJ/bit$ to run the transmitter or receiver circuitry, and $E_{amp} = 100pJ/bit/m^2$ for the transmit amplifier. Therefore, the energy expended to transit a k-bit message to a distance d is:

$$E_{Tx}(k, d) = E_{elec} \times k + E_{amp} \times k \times d^2, \tag{1}$$

while the energy expended to receive this message is:

$$E_{Rx}(k) = E_{elec} \times k, \tag{2}$$

which is a constant for a fixed-size message.

We treat the time when the first node dies as the lifetime of the network. [9] mentioned two different definitions for lifetime: In applications that the cooperation of all sensors working together is important, lifetime is defined as the time when the first node is drained of its energy; In applications that adjacent sensors record identical data, lifetime is defined as the time when a specified percentage of the sensors die. In this paper, we focus on the applications that need the cooperation of all sensors, and we adopt the first type of definition. Put it another way, we try to maximize the time when the first node dies.

3.2 Definitions

We can view a sensor network as a directed graph $G = (N, A)$, where:

- N is a set of all sensors and the base station in network. Each sensor is labelled with a node $ID \in \{1, 2, \ldots, |N|\}$, the base station is labelled with ID 0;
- A is a set of directed edges connecting two sensors, i.e. $A = \{(i, j)\}$.

We denote the weight of edge $(i, j) \in A$ as w_{ij} ($w_{ij} \neq w_{ji}$).

Definition 1. *For a sensor network $G = (N, A)$, $T = (N, A')$ is a rooted directed spanning tree of G, where A' is a subset of A (i.e. $A' \subset A$) and T is rooted at the base station (i.e. root[T] = 0). we call T a* routing tree *for network G.*

The tree structure can be used as a basic routing scheme for data gathering in sensor networks. It can be seen that a spanning tree is the minimal graph structure supporting the network connectivity. In the tree-based routing scheme, for each sensor i, we can find a directed path from i to the base station, and the path does not contain a cycle. In section 2, we have reviewed three types of routing scheme: cluster-based, chain-based and tree-based routing scheme. In fact, cluster-based and chain-based routing scheme can be viewed as a special case of the tree structure based routing scheme. Therefore, we base our discussion on the tree structure in the following paper.

Definition 2. *We define the* lifetime of a sensor i *as the duration of the time when i is alive, and denote it as l_i. We also define the* lifetime of a edge (i, j) *in tree T as the duration of the time when i and j are alive, and denote it as l_{ij}. For a edge (i, j) in tree T, we have $l_{ij} = \min\{l_i, l_j\}$.*

Here, we also introduce some notations used in the following paper. For a sensor i in routing tree T, the residual battery energy level of a sensor i at round t is denoted as $R_i(t)$, the transmit power of i is denoted as $E^i_{Tx}(T)$, the number of sensors sending data to i is denoted as $n_i(T)$. Then the receive power of sensor i is $n_i(T) \times E_{Rx}$. The tree with minimum total energy consumption is denoted as T^o,

$$T^o = \underset{T \subset G(N,A)}{\arg min} \sum_{i=1}^{|N|} \left(E^i_{Tx}(T) + n_i(T) \times E_{Rx}\right). \tag{3}$$

4 Maximum Lifetime Data Gathering and Aggregation

In this section, we investigate the maximum lifetime data gathering and aggregation problem in sensor networks. Based on tree structure routing scheme, we propose an algorithm MLDGA for the problem.

By using tree-based routing scheme, the maximum lifetime data gathering problem can be described formally as following: For a sensor network $G = (N, A)$, find a series of routing trees $\{T(t)\}$ of G, where $T(t)$ is the routing tree for G at round t. When data is gathered through these routing trees, the lifetime of the network G can be maximized.

Definition 3. *For a sensor network $G = (N, A)$, let the series of routing trees used by G be $\Gamma = \{T(t)\}$. Then the network lifetime of G is*

$$L(\Gamma) = L(T(1), T(2), T(3), \ldots) = \min_{i \in N}\{l_i\}, \tag{4}$$

where l_i is the maximum value which satisfies

$$\sum_{\tau=1}^{l_i} \left(E_{Tx}^i (T(\tau)) + n_i (T(\tau)) \times E_{Rx}\right) \leq R_i (0) . \tag{5}$$

The optimum network lifetime L^o of G is defined as

$$L^o = \max_{\Gamma \in \Gamma^*} \{L(\Gamma)\} , \tag{6}$$

where Γ^* is the set of all possible routing tree series for G.

We have following theorem for the optimum network lifetime L^o.

Theorem 1. *For a sensor network G, its optimal network lifetime L^o is upper bounded by*

$$L_U^o = \frac{\sum_{i=1}^{|N|} R_i (0)}{\sum_{i=1}^{|N|} \left(E_{Tx}^i(T^o) + n_i(T^o) \times E_{Rx}\right)}, \tag{7}$$

i.e. $L^o \leq L_U^o$.

Proof. We cannot spend more energy than the total energy of G, which is $\sum_{i=1}^{|N|} R_i (0)$. In every round, at least $\sum_{i=1}^{|N|} \left(E_{Tx}^i(T^o) + n_i(T^o) \times E_{Rx}\right)$ amount of power should be spent no matter what kind of tree we use. Therefore, the network lifetime cannot exceed L_U^o.

Here we present two strategies to deal with the maximum lifetime data gathering problem. (1) Try to minimize the total energy consumption of a routing tree in each round. From theorem 1, we know that if the total energy consumed in a round is minimized, we will have more energy to be used in the following data gathering process, thus the lifetime of the network can be increased. (2) Try to maximize the lifetime of a routing tree constructed in a round. By maximizing the lifetime of a routing tree used in a round, we will have a cumulative effect to improve the lifetime of the network.

Integrating the two strategies discussed above, we propose a new maximum lifetime data gathering and aggregation algorithm MLDGA. In each round, MLDGA constructs a routing tree for this round. We describe the tree construction process of MLDGA by presenting an example.

Step 1: Initialize variables. Figure 1(a) shows a five-node sensor network. The base station is location in (2, -100), which is labelled by 0. The current energy

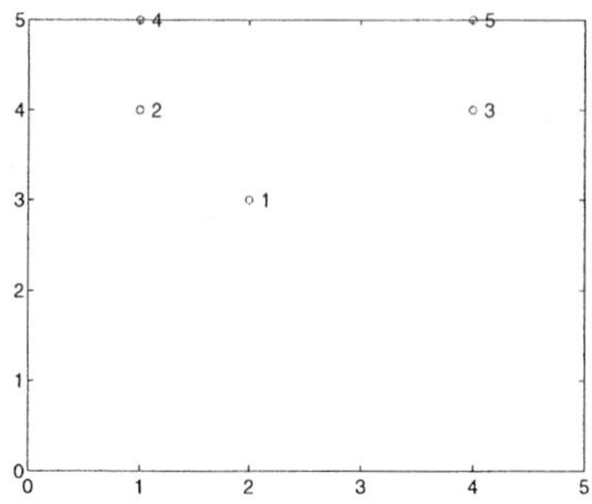

(a) Step 1: A five-node sensor network

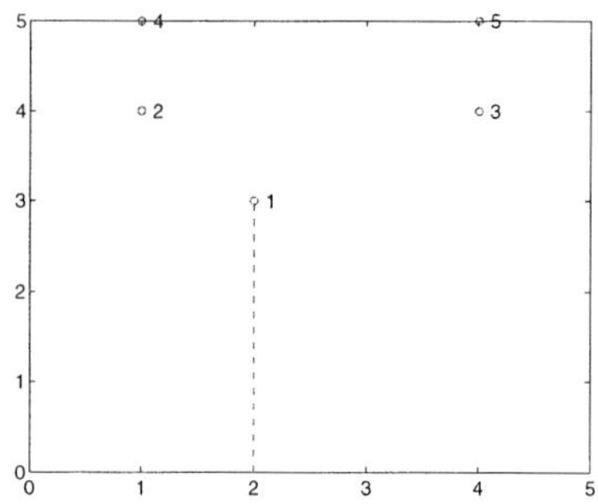

(b) Step 2(1): $1 \rightarrow 0$

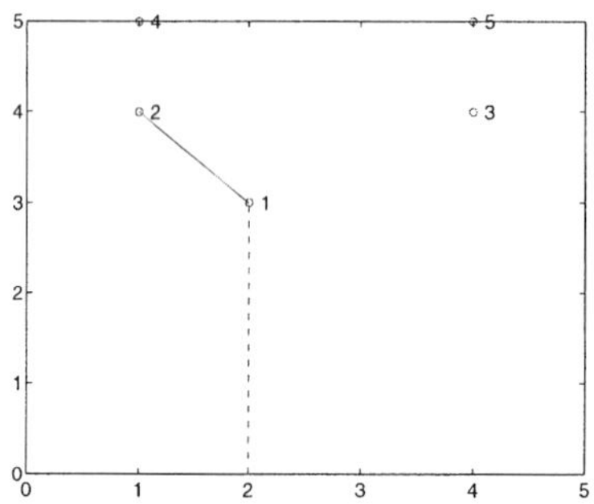

(c) Step 2(2): $2 \rightarrow 1$

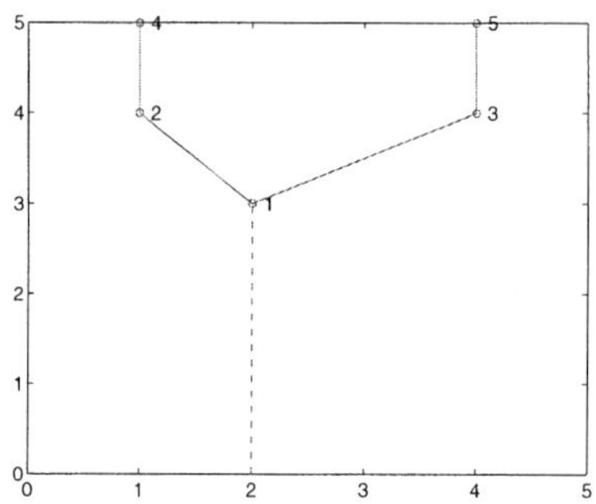

(d) Final tree

Fig. 1. Example of routing tree construction in a round using MLDGA

level of 1 is 0.12J, and the current energy levels of 2, 3, 4, 5 are 0.01J. Each sensor sends 2000-bit message to the base station in a round. We use tree structure T_0 to represent the sub-routing-tree that has been built for G at a round, use S to represent the sensors that have already been selected as part of T_0 (includes the base station), and use U to represent the sensors that have not been inserted into T_0 ($U = N - S$). S is initialized to the base station, and U is initialized to all the sensors. In Fig. 1(a), $S = \{0\}$ and $U = \{1, 2, 3, 4, 5\}$.

Step 2: Determine which edge can be added to T_0. For each node i in U and each node j in S, we compute the edge weight $w_{ij}(t)$ between i and j at round t, and add the edge with maximum weight to T_0. We define the edge weight $w_{ij}(t)$ as the ratio of the edge lifetime ($l_{ij} = \min\{l_i, l_j\}$) to the transmission cost between i and j. The lifetime of a node is related to its residual battery power, transmission cost and receive cost. Since the routing tree has not been constructed and the tree is dynamic, we cannot determine the lifetime of a node until the death of the node. Therefore, we have to make an estimation to the lifetime of a node, and give an estimation to the weight of an edge accordingly.

(1) If j is the base station, we treat the lifetime of base station as ∞ and make

$$w'_{ij}(t) = \frac{\min\{l'_i(t), \infty\}}{E^i_{Tx}(k, d_{ij})} = \frac{1}{E^i_{Tx}(k, d_{ij})} \times \frac{R_i(t)}{E^i_{Tx}(k, d_{ij})}. \quad (8)$$

as the estimation to edge weight $w_{ij}(t)$. In Fig. 1(b), $E^1_{Tx}(2000, d_{10}) \approx 0.00218$, $l'_1 \approx 55$ and $w'_{10} \approx 25220$. w'_{10} is the maximum weight among w'_{20}, w'_{30}, w'_{40} and w'_{50}. We add edge (1, 0) to T_0. The base station is located far from the boundary of figure, so we use the dotted line to denote the edge between 1 and 0 in Fig. 1(b). Set S and U are changed correspondingly. $S = \{0, 1\}$ and $U = \{2, 3, 4, 5\}$.

(2) If j is not the base station, we make

$$\begin{aligned} w'_{ij}(t) &= \frac{\min\{l'_i(t), l'_j(t)\}}{E^i_{Tx}(k, d_{ij})} \\ &= \frac{1}{E^i_{Tx}(k, d_{ij})} \times \min\left\{\frac{R_i(t)}{E^i_{Tx}(k, d_{ij})}, \frac{R_j(t)}{E^j_{Tx}(T_0) + (n_j(T_0) + 1) \times E_{Rx}}\right\}. \end{aligned} \quad (9)$$

as the estimation to edge weight $w_{ij}(t)$. In Fig. 1(c), $E^2_{Tx}(2000, d_{21}) \approx 0.0001$, $l'_2 \approx 99.6$, $l'_1 \approx 52.6$ and $w'_{21} \approx 517928.3$. w'_{21} is the maximum weight among w'_{20}, w'_{21}, w'_{30}, w'_{31}, w'_{40}, w'_{41}, w'_{50}, and w'_{51}. We add edge (2, 1) to T_0. S and U are changed correspondingly. $U = \{3, 4, 5\}$ and $S = \{0, 1, 2\}$.

Continue: The procedure is continued until all sensors in U have been added to S. Figure 1(d) shows the final tree. The routing tree T for G in current round is constructed ($T_0 = T$).

From the definition of edge weight, we can get following two points that fit our strategies about the maximum lifetime data gathering problem:

- If the transmission cost between the sending sensor i and the receiving sensor j is low, the edge weight w_{ij} tends to be high. Thus the sensor i has high possibility to be added to T_0 and connects to j. It meets the strategy to minimize the total energy consumption in each round;
- If the lifetime of edge (i, j) is high, the edge weight w_{ij} tends to be high. Here we adopt a heuristic greedy strategy that the higher the weight of an edge, the higher the possibility of the edge being added to T_0. It meets the strategy to maximize the lifetime of a routing tree constructed in a round.

The tree construction process of MLDGA is similar to Prim's algorithm essentially. It inserts a sensor into the tree based on the maximal weight edge one at a time until all sensors are included in the tree. In [9], the authors used Prim's algorithm to construct a minimal spanning tree. The edge weight of PEDAP-PA relates to the transmission cost and the remaining energy of sending node, which only considers the effect of the sending node and keeps unchanged during the construction of routing tree at a round. However, our definition of edge weight considers not only the transmission cost of sending node, but also the combined effect of sending node and receiving node, which can be got from the definition of edge lifetime ($l_{ij} = \min\{l_i, l_j\}$). We think our definition of edge weight better reflects the essence of maximum lifetime data gathering problem, and can achieve a longer lifetime comparing with other existing algorithms, which is confirmed by experiments.

5 Experiments

In this section, we conducted experiments to evaluate performance of our algorithm. We compared MLDGA with several other different data gathering algorithms: LEACH, PEGASIS, PEDAP and PEDAP-PA. We tried to investigate the effect of base station location and the effect of initial energy level to these algorithms by considering two metrics: the round when the first node dies (RFND) and the round when the last node dies (RLND). RFND is considered in the first place since it meets our definition of network lifetime. For a sensor network, we try to maximize RFND and also expect to prolong RLND.

The basic setting of our experiments is described as following. 100 sensors were randomly distributed over a region of 50m×50m. Each sensor had an initial energy level of 0.5J or uniform distribution between 0.2J and 0.8J. The base station was located far away from the field (at point (0, -100)) or in the center of the field (at point (25, 25)). In each round, a sensor sent a 2000-bit message to the base station. The base station computed a routing scheme to deliver data in each round.

5.1 Effect of Base Station Location

We investigate the effect of base station location first. [9] mentioned that PEDAP-PA performs well both in systems that the base station is far away from the field and the base station is in the center of the field, while LEACH and PEGASIS

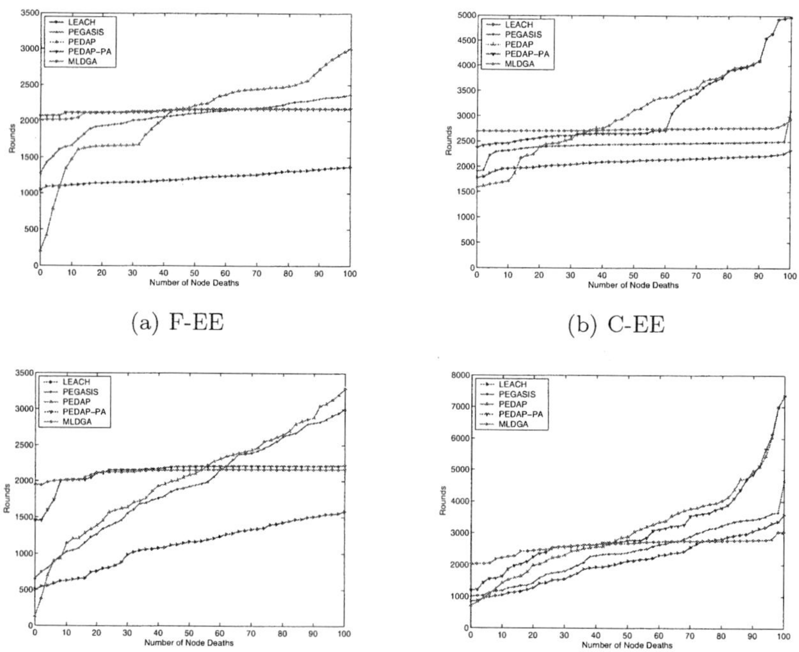

(a) F-EE (b) C-EE

(c) F-UE (d) C-UE

Fig. 2. Timings of node deaths

perform poor when the base station is inside the field because they do not take the cost of sending data to base station into account. So we examined the effect of base station location to our algorithm.

Figure 2(a) presents the situation that the base station was located far away from the field and all sensors had equal initial energy levels (F-EE). It can be observed from Fig. 2(a) that both MLDGA and PEDAP-PA achieve a good RFND comparing with other algorithms. PEDAP provides a good RLND but has a bad RFND, since it constructs a minimum energy consuming routing tree for each round of communication but pays no attention to balance the load among sensors. PEGASIS provides both a good RFND and a good RLND. However, MLDGA and PEDAP-PA further improves the RFND about 60% comparing with PEGASIS.

Figure 2(b) presents the situation that the base station was located in the center of the field and the sensors had equal initial energy levels (C-EE). It can be seen from Fig. 2(b) that MLDGA also achieves a good RFND. It is the best one which achieves the longest RFND in all algorithms.

From Fig. 2(a) and 2(b), we can conclude that MLDGA has a good RFND (i.e. lifetime) regardless of the base station location. It distributes the load evenly among sensors and tries to minimize the total energy consumed in a round, so it achieves a good RFND and a RLND near to RFND.

5.2 Effect of Initial Energy Level

To check the ability of balancing the load among sensors further, we investigate the situations when the sensors have unequal initial energy levels. We distributed the initial energy levels of all sensors between 0.2J and 0.8J uniformly. The average energy level of a sensor is 0.5J, which is the same as Fig. 2(a) and 2(b).

Figure 2(c) presents the situation that the base station was located far away from the field and the sensors had unequal initial energy levels (F-UE). Comparing with Fig. 2(a), we see from Fig. 2(c) that the RFNDs of all algorithms decrease significantly except MLDGA. It means that MLDGA is robust to balance the energy consumption among sensors even the initial energy levels of all sensors are different greatly. MLDGA improves the RFND about 35% comparing with PEDAP-PA, and about 200% comparing with PEGASIS.

Figure 2(d) presents the situation that the base station was located in the center of the field and the sensors had unequal initial energy levels (C-UE). Again, MLDGA is the best one which achieves the longest RFND in all algorithms. It improves the RFND about 70% comparing with PEDAP-PA, and about 100% comparing with PEGASIS.

From Fig. 2(c) and 2(d), we can conclude that MLDGA has a good RFND (i.e. lifetime) regardless of the initial energy levels of all sensors. Its abilities to distribute the load evenly among sensors and to minimize the total energy consumed in a round are further confirmed because it achieves a good RFND and a RLND near to RFND even when all sensors have unequal initial energy levels.

6 Conclusion

In this paper, we investigated the maximum lifetime data gathering and aggregation problem in wireless sensor networks. We convert this problem into a problem that: finding a series of routing trees for a sensor network so that the network lifetime can be maximized when data is gathered through these trees. After giving some analysis, we proposed a near optimal algorithm MLDGA to construct the series of routing trees. In MLDGA, the edge weight is estimated as the ratio of the edge lifetime to the remaining energy of sending node, which meets the requirement to construct an energy-efficient maximum lifetime routing tree for each data gathering round. We conducted experiments to evaluate the performance of MLDGA. The experimental results show that MLDGA achieves a good lifetime performance and a good network utility performance regardless of the base station location and the initial battery levels of sensors.

References

1. I. F. Akyildiz, W. Su, Y. Sankarasubramaniam, and E. Cayirci. Wireless sensor networks: a survey, *Computer Networks*, Vol. 38, No. 4, 2002.
2. J. Considine, F. Li, G. Kollios, and J. Byers. Approximate aggregation techniques for sensor databases. In *Proceedings of International Conference on Data Engineering (ICDE)*, Mar. 2004.
3. J. H. Chang and L. Tassiulas. Energy Conserving Routing in Wireless Ad-hoc Networks, in *Proceedings of IEEE INFOCOM*, March 2000.
4. W. R. Heinzelman, A. Chandrakasan, and H. Balakrishnan. Energy-Efficient Communication Protocol for Wireless Microsensor Networks, in *Proceedings of 33rd Annual Hawaii International Conference on System Sciences*, 2000.
5. I. Kang and R. Poovendran. Maximizing Network Lifetime of Broadcast over Wireless Stationary Ad Hoc Networks, *ACM/Kluwer MONET Special Issue on Energy Constraints and Lifetime Performance in Wireless Sensor Networks*, 2004.
6. B. Krishnamachari, D. Estrin, S. Wicker. Modelling Data-Centric Routing in Wireless Sensor Networks, in *Proceedings of IEEE INFOCOM*, 2002.
7. J. M. Kahn, R. H. Katz and K. S. J. Pister. Next Century Challenges: Mobile Networking for Smart Dust, in *Proceedings of 5th Annual ACM/IEEE International Conference on Mobile Computing and Networking (MobiCom 99)*, August 1999.
8. S. Lindsey and C. S. Raghavendra. Pegasis: Power-Efficient Gathering in Sensor Information Systems, in *IEEE Aerospace Conference*, March 2002.
9. H. O. Tan and I. Korpeoglu. Power Efficient Data Gathering and Aggregation in Wireless Sensor Networks, *SIGMOD Record*, Vol. 32, No. 4, December 2003.
10. M. Tubaishat and S. Madria. Sensor Networks: An Overview, *IEEE Potentials*, Vol. 22, April 2003.

Processing Frequent Items over Distributed Data Streams

Dongdong Zhang[1], Jianzhong Li[1,2], Weiping Wang[1],
Longjiang Guo[1,2], and Chunyu Ai[2]

[1] School of Computer Science and Technology,
Harbin Institute of Technology, China
[2] School of Computer Science and Technology,
Heilongjiang University, China
{zddhit, lijzh, wpwang, guolongjiang,
cyai}@hit.edu.cn

Abstract. To improve the availability of communication bandwidth in distributed data stream systems, communication overhead should be reduced as much as possible under the constraint of the precision of queries. In this paper, a new approach is proposed to transfer data streams in distributed data stream systems. By transferring the estimated occurrence times of frequent items, instead of raw frequent items, communication overhead can be saved greatly. Meanwhile, in order to guarantee the precision of queries, the difference between the estimated and true occurrence times of each frequent item is also sent to the central stream processor. We present the algorithm of processing frequent items over distributed data streams and give the method of supporting aggregate queries over the preprocessed frequent items.

1 Introduction

The technique of processing distributed data stream has attracted the researchers in the database community [1,2,3]. In distributed data stream systems, the distributed remote data source nodes produce and collect data, and transfer them to the central stream processor node in the form of stream. Meanwhile, the central stream processor node receives users' queries and returns answers to users. The available communication bandwidth is a bottleneck resource [1]. Especially in the application of sensor networks, the battery energy, which sensors use to transmit the data, is also a bottleneck resource [4]. So, one research issue in distributed data stream systems is how to reduce the transferred data volume as much as possible under the constraint of the precision of queries, in order to save the communication cost or the electric energy.

At present, there are some kinds of methods to reduce communication cost [1,4,5] in distributed data system systems. However, these work can't extensively support queries in real time with a good precision guarantee. Note that the frequent items in data streams occupy most of the communication cost. We propose to transfer the estimated occurrence times of frequent items, instead of the raw frequent items, in distributed data stream systems for the purpose of saving communication overhead. Meanwhile, in

Y. Zhang et al. (Eds.): APWeb 2005, LNCS 3399, pp. 523–529, 2005.

order to guarantee the precision of queries, the difference between the estimated and true occurrence times of each frequent item is also sent to the central stream processor. Thus, our method can not only overcome the drawback of the previous methods and guarantee the precision of queries, but also reduce the communication overhead.

2 Problem Description

2.1 Model of Distributed Data Stream Systems

Figure 1 illustrates the model of distributed data stream system. All kinds of processor nodes consist of the central stream processor node, relay nodes and remote data source nodes. Remote data source nodes produce and collect data, and transmit raw data to the relay nodes. Relay nodes preprocess the received raw data and transmit it to the central stream processor node. The central stream processor node takes charge of user's queries and returns the answers. The controller on the central stream processor node is responsible for sending the registered requirement and precision of queries to the relay nodes.

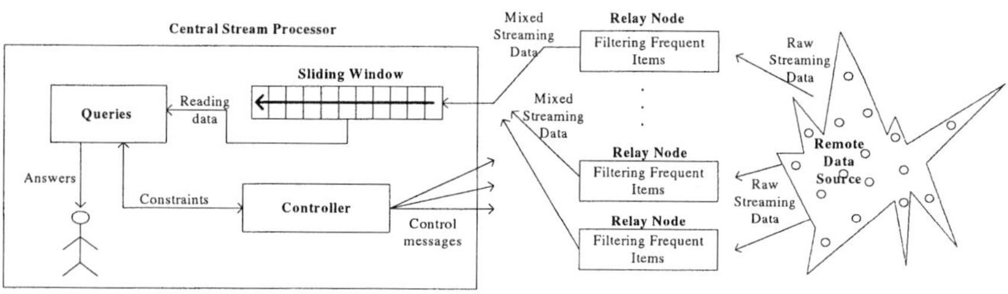

Fig. 1. Model of distributed data stream systems

2.2 Frequent Items

The data stream from the remote data source nodes can be denoted as an unlimited multiset with the form of $<r, t>$, where r denotes an item and t denotes its timestamp (i.e. time order) which is determined by the time when r enters the data stream system or when the remote data source produces r [6]. Suppose the items in data streams form into a series $r_1, \ldots, r_n$, and $F(r_i)$ denotes the occurrence times of the item r_i in data streams. Given a real number λ, where $0 \leq \lambda \leq 1$, if $F(r_i) \geq \lambda \times n$ holds, r_i is called as a *frequent item* in data stream and λ is the *support-degree* of frequent items.

Definition 1. Suppose r is a frequent item, the triple (r, T_v, *Count*) is called as the *derived-body* of r, where $T_v=[t_b, t_e]$ is the *lifetime* of r and we denote $|T_v|$ as $t_e - t_b$. Derived-body is divided into two classes, named as *forecast-body* and *correct-body* respectively. When the derived-body is a forecast-body (denoted by *Prb*), *Count* means the estimated occurrence times of r within T_v. When the derived-body is a correct-body (denoted by *Crb*), *Count* means the difference between the estimated and true occurrence times of r within T_v.

Definition 2. A unit doublet (*Qid*, T_v) is called as a *Querying-metadata*, denoted by *MoQ*, where *Qid* identifies the query and $T_v=[t_b , t_e]$ is the querying time interval.

Each registered query, especially for motoring queries, can specify a querying time interval, which can be represented by querying-metadata. The controller on the central processor node collects querying-metadata based on the requirement of registered queries and sends it to relay nodes. Meanwhile, in order to control the progress of generating derived-bodies of frequent items in data streams, each relay node maintains a *querying-metadata series* as $MoQ_1,\ldots,MoQ_n$, where $MoQ_i.T_v.t_e \le MoQ_j.T_v.t_e$ and $i<j$ hold.

2.3 FDI Structure

Each relay node maintains a data structure about frequent data items (denoted by FDI) described as in Figure 2, which preserves the corresponding information of the frequent items who will occur within the future period of time T_p. The information includes the raw frequent item r, the estimated occurrence times $r.f_e$ of r within T_p, and the true occurrence times $r.f_r$ of r within T_p, where T_p is defined as the *lifetime* of FDI and $r.f_e$ is the approximate estimated value of $r.f_r$. We use *TopK* to denote the set of all frequent items in FDI.

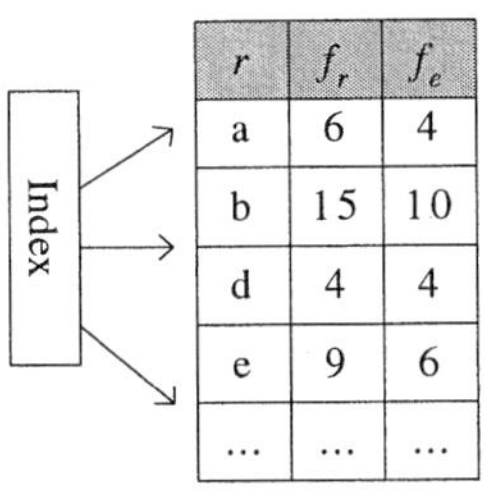

Fig. 2. Example of FDI structure

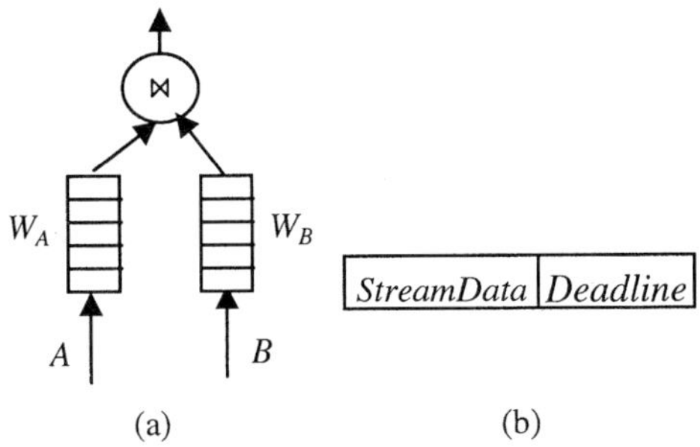

Fig. 3. Structure of join operator

Information of frequent items in FDI structure is maintained as follows. Initially, for each frequent items r in FDI, the value of $r.fr$ is set to zero. When the relay node receives a raw item s from remote data source nodes, it will examine whether $s \in TopK$ holds. If it holds, the value of $s.f_r$ in FDI is increased by one.

2.4 Research Issue

Based on the model of distributed data stream systems in Figure 1, the research issue in this paper is how relay nodes generate derived-bodies of frequent items in data streams, so as to filter raw frequent items and reduce the communication cost under the constraint of precision of queries. Meanwhile, the method for processing derived-bodies on the central stream processor node also needs to be studied.

3 Processing Data Streams on Relay Nodes

3.1 Determining Frequent Items

In distributed data stream systems, reducing the volume of transferred frequent items can decrease the communication overhead greatly. Therefore, frequent items in data streams need to be determined firstly. In our work, we can adopt one of the well-known algorithm of finding frequent items over data streams such as *Lossy Counting* algorithm [7], *Majority* algorithm [8] and *hCount* algorithm [9], which we refer to as *FFDS* algorithm. During the time interval T_h, suppose *FFDS* algorithm outputs the set of frequent items over data streams as $TopK=\{k \mid F(k)\geq\lambda\times N \wedge k\in D\}$ with the support-degree λ, where T_h is the *valid-statistical-interval* of *FFDS* algorithm and N is total occurrence times of all items within T_h.

3.2 Processing Frequent Items

3.2.1 Generating Forecast-Bodies

In fact, the forecast-bodies are the compressed form of frequent items in data streams. So, transferring forecast-bodies, instead of the raw frequent items, can reduce the communication cost. Forecast-bodies should be generated and transmitted at the beginning of their lifetime. Otherwise, it will cause the delay for querying frequent items on the central stream processor. Concretely, forecast-bodies of frequent items should be generated at the end time of the first querying requirement in querying-metadata series (mentioned in Section 2.2). Following is the algorithm of generating forecast-bodies of frequent items.

Algorithm 1: Generate-Prb

(1) Delete all entries in FDI structure, obtain frequent items using *FFDS* algorithm and preserve them in FDI structure;
(2) For any frequent item k in FDI structure, set $k.f_r=F(k)$ and $k.f_e=0$, where $F(k)$ is the occurrence times of the frequent item k computed by *FFDS* algorithm;
(3) Determine the lifetime T_p of FDI structure, where $T_p.t_b=Now$, $T_p.t_e=MoQ_1.T_v.t_e$ (i.e. the end time of the first querying requirement in querying-metadata series) and *Now* denotes the current system clock;
(4) For any frequent item k in *TopK*, generate and transmit the forecast-body $Prb_k=(k, T_v, Count)$ of k, where $Prb_k.T_v=T_p$, $Pdb_k.Count=|Prb_k.T_v|\times F(k)/|T_h|$, T_h is the valid-statistical-interval of *FFDS* algorithm and $F(k)$ is the occurrence times of k computed by *FFDS* algorithm within T_h;

Based on Generate-Prb algorithm, it is obvious that the lifetime of FDI structure ranges from the time of generating forecast-bodies to the end time of the first querying requirement in querying-metadata series. In fact, generating forecast-bodies is the process of estimating the occurrence times of frequent items within the lifetime of FDI.

3.2.2 Processing Data During Lifetime of FDI

After generating the forecast-bodies of frequent times, relay nodes continue to deal with the arriving raw data and reduce the volume of data transferred to the central stream processor as much as possible. Meanwhile, relay nodes also prepare to generate the next round forecast-bodies of frequent items. During this process, there are some variables needed to be computed respectively, including the true occurrence times of total frequent items (denoted by C_f), the occurrence times of all items (denoted by C_r), the summation of frequent items (denoted by S_f) and the summation of all items (denoted by S_r). The algorithm of dealing with data during the lifetime T_p of FDI on relay nodes can be described as follows.

Algorithm 2: Processing-within-Tp

(1) Initialize the parameters used in *FFDS* algorithm, set the valid-statistical-interval T_h of *FFDS* algorithm to be T_p;
(2) Initialize the variables, let C_f=0, C_r=0, S_f=0 and S_r=0;
(3) WHILE (there is a new item *r* arriving and $Now \leq Tp.t_e$ holds)
(4) Invoke *FFDS* algorithm with the input *r* ;
(5) IF ($r \in TopK$) $r.f_r$++, C_f++, S_f+=*r* ;
(6) ELSE transmit *r* to the central stream processor; /* *r* is a non-frequent item.*/
(7) C_r++, S_r+=*r* ;

Relay nodes filter raw frequent items in data streams and only transmit the non-frequent items to the central stream processor. Thus, the communication overhead is reduced greatly. Meanwhile, relay nodes take the new arrival of raw data as the input of *FFDS* algorithm, i.e. predicting the future frequent items based on the newest historical data, which can enhance the performance of algorithms.

3.2.3 Generating Correct-Bodies

As the characters of data streams fluctuate continuously, the deviation will exist between the estimated occurrence times in forecast-bodies and the true occurrence time of frequent items. To guarantee the precision of queries on the central stream processor node, relay nodes should also transmit the correct-bodies of frequent items to correct the content of transferred forecast-bodies. Correct-bodies should be generated and transmitted before the next round forecast-bodies are generated, i.e. the end time of the lifetime of FDI. Note that, the time of generating the correct-body of frequent item *k* is the deadline of forecast-body of *k*.

Following is the algorithm of generating correct-bodies.

Algorithm 3: Generate-Crb

(1) FOR (each frequent item *k* in *TopK*)
(2) Generate the correct-body $Crb_k=(k,T_v,Count)$ of *k*, where $Crb_k.T_v=T_p$, $Crb_k.Count=k.f_r-k.f_e$ and T_p is the lifetime of FDI ;
(3) Transmit the correct-body Crb_k of *k* to the central stream processor;
(4) Delete MoQ_1 from the querying-metadata series;

3.3 Algorithm of Processing Data Streams on Relay Nodes

The algorithm of processing data streams on relay nodes is given as follows.

Algorithm 4: RelayNode-Processing

(1) As data continuously arrives, use *FFDS* algorithm to make statistical analysis;
(2) WHILE (querying-metadata series is not null)

(3) Invoke Generate-Prb algorithm;
(4) Invoke Processing-within-Tp algorithm;
(5) Invoke Generate-Crb algorithm;

For each repetition in RelayNode-Processing algorithm, correct-bodies generated by step (5) are corresponding to the forecast-bodies produced by step (3).

4 Processing Data on Central Stream Processor Node

In this paper, we mainly focus on aggregate queries over distributed data streams. In aggregate queries plans, the input data flows through several middle operators and finally arrives aggregate operators (such as SUM, COUNT and so on) that will output the querying results. In this section, we will discuss how operators in query plans process derived-bodies and skip the simple case of project and select operators.

4.1 Join Operators

At present, most of join algorithms over data streams are based on sliding windows. The join process over sliding windows is separated into three phases [10]: expiring, inserting, probing and joining. Suppose T is the valid time interval span of sliding windows and *Now* denotes the current system clock. The structure of a join operator is shown in Figure 3(a), where A and B are two different data streams, W_A and W_B are the sliding windows over A and B respectively. Figure 3(b) illustrates the data structure of sliding windows, where the column *StreamData* preserves the data coming from data streams and the column *Deadline* (denoted by *Dl*) preserves the deadline of data in sliding windows.

Expiring: The condition of expiring the data in sliding windows is $Dl<Now$. The time complexity of expiring the old data is $O(n)$ and n is total number of data in sliding windows.

Inserting: When a new data r arrives, r is inserted into *StreamData* of sliding windows. If r is a derived-body, set *Deadline* of r to be $r.T_v.t_e+T$. Otherwise (i.e. r is a raw data), set *Deadline* of r to be $r.Timestamp+T$. The time complexity is $O(1)$.

Probing and joining: When a new data r arrives from A (or B), data s in B (or A) satisfying the join condition should be probed and joined with r. Then, the join-result is yielded. Due to space limitation, we skip the content of processing $r \bowtie s$, which has been completely discussed in our full paper [11].

4.2 Aggregate Operators

It is straightforward for aggregate operators to process derived-bodies. When handling derived-bodies, aggregate operators directly regard them as many same items. Suppose $db=(k,T_v,C)$ is a derived-body, $aggV$ and $aggV'$ respectively denote the aggregate results before after processing db. So, we have:

(1) $aggV'_{\text{COUNT}} = aggV_{\text{COUNT}}+C$. (2) $aggV'_{\text{SUM}} = aggV_{\text{SUM}}+ k \times C$.
(3) $aggV'_{\text{AVG}} = aggV'_{\text{SUM}} / aggV'_{\text{COUNT}}$. (4) $aggV'_{\text{MAX}} = \max\{ aggV_{\text{MAX}}, k \}$.
(5) $aggV'_{\text{MIN}} = \min\{ aggV_{\text{MIN}}, k \}$.

5 Summary

In this paper, a new method is proposed to transfer data streams in distributed data stream systems. Replacing frequent items with derived-bodies, not only the transferred data size is reduced greatly, but also the precision of queries can be guaranteed.

References

1. C. Olston, J. Jiang, and J. Widom. Adaptive Filters for Continuous Queries over Distributed Data Streams. SIGMOD, 2003.
2. M. Cherniack, H. Balakrishnan, M. Balazinska. Scalable Distributed Stream Processing. In Proc. 1st Biennial Conf. On Innovative Data Syst. Res (CIDR), 2003.
3. B. Babcock and Chris Olston. Distributed Top-K Monitoring. SIGMOD, 2003.
4. Y. Yao, J. Gehrke. Query Processing for Sensor Networks. CIDR, 2003.
5. I. Lazaridis, S. Mehrotra. Capturing Sensor-Generated Time Series with Quality Guarantees. ICDE, 2003.
6. A. Araru, S. Babu, J. Widom. An Abstract Semantics and Concrete Language for Continuous Queries over Streams and Relations. Technical Report, Stanford University Database Group. Nov. 2002. Available at http://dbpubs.stanford.edu/pub/2002-57.
7. G. Manku, R. Motwani. Approximate frequency counts over data streams. In Proceedings of the Twenty-Eighth International Conference on Very Large Data Bases (2002).
8. G. Manku, R. Motwani. Approximate frequency counts over data streams. In Proceedings of the Twenty-Eighth International Conference on Very Large Data Bases (2002).
9. R. M. Karp, S. Shenker, C.H. Papadimitriou. A simple algorithm for finding frequent elements in streams and bags. ACM Trans. Database Syst. 28, 1 (2003), 51-55.
10. C. Jin, W. Qian, C.Sha, J. X. Yu, A. Zhou. Dynamically Maintaining Frequent Items Over Data Stream. CIKM, 2003.
11. D. D. Zhang, J. Z. Li, W. P. Wang. Processing frequent items over distributed data streams. Technical report. 2004.

Distinct Estimate of Set Expressions over Sliding Windows

Cheqing Jin and Aoying Zhou

Dept. of Computer Science and Engineering, Fudan University, China
{cqjin, ayzhou}@fudan.edu.cn

Abstract. Recently, lots of work focus on devising one-pass algorithms for processing and querying multiple data streams, such as network monitoring, sensor networks, .etc. Estimating the cardinality of set expressions over streams is perhaps one of the most fundamental problems. Unfortunately, no solution has been devised for this issue over sliding windows. In this paper, we propose a space-efficient algorithmic solution to estimate the cardinality of set expression over sliding windows. Our probabilistic method is based on a new hash based synopsis, termed *improved 2-level hash sketch*. A thorough experimental evaluation has demonstrated that our methods can solve the problem efficiently.

1 Introduction

A data stream is an ordered sequence of items that arrive in timely manner. Motivation applications include financial applications, stock tickers, sensor networks and telecom call records, etc. The volume of a stream is unbounded and the rate of a stream is rapid. Lots of applications prefer to sliding window model where only a collection of latest N elements are considered. Distributed processing is another key topic in stream applications. In distributed environments, each stream is observed and summarized by its party and the resulting synopses are then collected at a central site, where queries over the entire collection of streams can be processed [8].

One of the most fundamental problems over data stream is estimating the cardinalities of set expressions over multiple streams. Assume three streams of IP addresses (A, B, C) are seen at routers R_1, R_2 and R_3. A network manager may want to know the number of distinct IP addresses rising at either R_1 or R_2 but not R_3. It is equally estimating the number of distinct elements for $(A \cap B - C)$. In [7], Ganguly et al. devised an algorithm to estimate the cardinalities of set expressions. Unfortunately, their method is lack of ability to handle sliding window situations.

In this paper, we propose an algorithmic solution to estimate the cardinality of set expressions over sliding windows. Based on a hash based synopsis data structure, termed *improved 2-level hash sketch*, our algorithm can provide low-error, high-confidence estimates with small memory space. We will firstly describe *improved 2-level hash sketch* in Section 2, followed which, a novel solution is presented in Section 3.

Y. Zhang et al. (Eds.): APWeb 2005, LNCS 3399, pp. 530–535, 2005.

Problem Definition

Let $\{\cdots, a_{t-2}, a_{t-1}, a_t, \cdots\}$ be a stream of data elements, where a_t represents the data element observed at time t, $a_t \in [1..u]$. In sliding window model, at any time t, only last N elements, $a_{t-(N-1)}, a_{t-(N-2)}, \cdots, a_t$, are considered. Let A^N and B^N denote two itemsets, each containing N latest elements in streams A and B. Three set operators are defined as follows. (1) (*Union*) Operator $A \cup B$ returns an itemset containing all items in A^N and B^N. The frequency of each item is the sum of each item in A^N and B^N respectively. (2) (*Difference*) Operator $A - B$ returns an itemset containing all items in A^N but not in B^N. The frequency of an item is equal to the frequency of the item in A^N. (3) (*Intersect*) Operator $A \cap B$ returns an itemset containing all items in A^N and B^N at the same time. The frequency of an item is the sum of the frequency of the item in A^N and B^N.

Let $E = (((S_1 \mathtt{op}_1 S_2) \mathtt{op}_2 S_3) \cdots S_k)$ denote an arbitrary set expression, where $S_1, \cdots, S_k$ are k input streams and $\mathtt{op_i}$ is a set operator defined above. The goal of the query is to estimate the cardinality of an itemset generated by expression E and a predefined window size N.

Related Work

Recently, many researches have focused on processing data streams[2]. Several literatures are done for sliding window model[5][11]. Estimating the cardinality of a stream is a basic problem, which has been widely studied including the algorithm by Flajolet and Martin [6] and its variant[1].

There are still a few literatures on distinct queries over multiple streams. In [8], Gibbons .et al considered the problem on the union of streams, followed which, in [9], Gibbons extended their work to meet sliding windows. The method of Minwise Independent Permutations (MIP)[3][10] can estimate the result cardinality of set operators. Ganguly et al.[7] proposed another solution, which can query set-expressions over update streams. Their recent work[4] focuses on estimating cardinality of set expressions in distributed applications with a goal to minimize transmission costs. Notice that neither of above work [3][4][7][10] has considered the sliding window model.

2 Improved 2-Level Hash Sketch

An *improved 2-level hash sketch*, as shown in Fig. 1, is in fact an improvement upon *2-level hash sketch* (please refer to [7] for detailed information) in two aspects. Firstly, it contains a *time level*, which does not appear in *2-level hash sketch*. Secondly, each counter in second-level only occupies 1 bit, not $\log N$ bits. Three kinds of hash functions are applied in an *improved 2-level hash sketch* including one first-level hash function h ($h : [M] \rightarrow [M^k]$), s second-level hash functions, $g_1, \cdots, g_s$ ($g : [M] \rightarrow [2]$) and one LSB operator ($\mathtt{LSB} : [M] \rightarrow [\log M]$ and $\mathtt{Pr}[\mathtt{LSB}(j) = l] = \frac{1}{2^{l+1}}$).

Conceptually, a 3-dimension array, $X.bits[i_1, i_2, i_3]$ can be used to present counters in the first- and second- levels of sketch X. Additionally, $X.time[i_1].Prev$

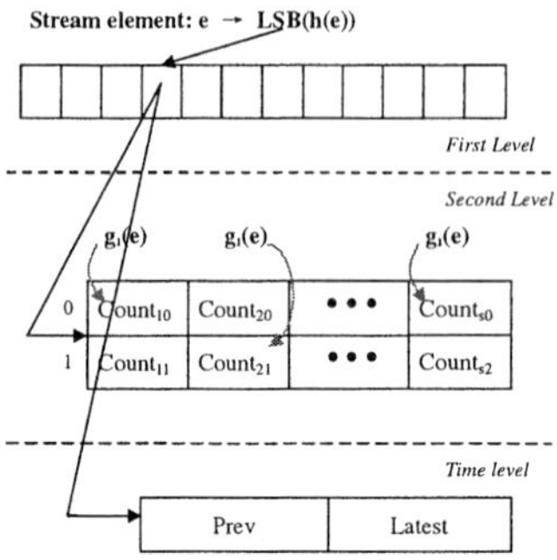

Fig. 1. *Improved 2-level hash sketch*

```
Algorithm   Maintain(X, e, t)
pos ← LSB(h(e)); b ← true;
for i=1 to s do
   b ← (b and (X.bits[pos, i, g_i(e)] = 1));
end for
if b = false then
   X.time[pos].Prev ← X.time[pos].Latest;
   for i = 1 to s do
      X.bits[pos,i,g_i(e)] ← 1;
      X.bits[pos,i,1 − g_i(e)] ← 0;
   end for
end if
X.time[pos].LatestTuple ← t;
```

Fig. 2. Algorithm to process an incoming tuple

and $X.time[i_1].Latest$ are used to represent counters in *time level.* Field *Latest* represents the time when the latest tuple is mapped to the bucket. Field *Prev* represents the time for the latest different tuple. Algorithm `Maintain`(X, e, t)(Fig. 2) demonstrates the way to process an element e arriving at time t. Detailed descriptions are omitted due to lack of enough space.

For the reason that an *improved 2-level hash sketch* is just an enhanced version of a *2-level hash sketch*, it also owns six elementary properties of the latter. We list them here. Assume X_A, X_B are sketches for streams A and B. (1) `SingletonBucket`(X_A, i, t, N) checks if only one item in the window mapped to the ith first-level bucket of X_A; (2) `EmptyBucket`(X_A, i, t, N) checks if no element in the window mapped to the ith first-level bucket of X_A. (3) `IdenticalSingletonBucket`$(X_A,\ X_B, i, t, N)$ checks if one identical element is mapped to the ith first-level bucket of X_A and X_B at the same time; (4) `SingletonUnionBucket`$(X_A,\ X_B, i, t, N)$ checks if there is only one element in $A \cup B$ mapped to the ith first level bucket of X_A and X_B; (5) `AtomicDifference` (X_A, X_B, i, t, N) checks whether there is one element in $A - B$ mapped to the ith first-level bucket of X_A and X_B. It is worth noting that `AtomicDifference` returns 1 when ((**not** `EmptyBucket`(X_A, i, t, N)) **and** `EmptyBucket`(X_B, i, t, N)) is equal to **true**. (6) `AtomicIntersection`(X_A, X_B, i, t, N) checks whether there is one element in $A \cap B$ mapped to the ith first-level bucket. It returns 1 when ((**not** `EmptyBucket`(X_A, i, t, N)) **and not** `EmptyBucket`(X_B, i, t, N)) = **true**.

3 Algorithms for Distinct Estimating

In this section, we will introduce our solutions. Firstly, three algorithms, termed `WinUnion`, `WinDiff` and `WinIntersect`, are presented to estimate the cardinality of three basic set operators, such as *union*, *difference* and *intersection*. We then claim that our algorithms can be extended to cope with a general set expression.

All of our three methods require r independent improved 2-level hash sketch synopses built over streams A and B, denoted as $\{X_A^i\}$, $\{X_B^i\}$. Notice that X_A^i and X_B^i share same hash functions for $1 \le i \le r$. Algorithm `WinUnion` can

Algorithm 1 `WinUnion(`$\{X_A^i\},\{X_B^i\}$`, t, N)`

1: $f \leftarrow (1+\epsilon)r/8; j \leftarrow 0$;
2: **while** (**true**) **do**
3: count $\leftarrow$ 0;
4: **for** $i = 1$ **to** r **do**
5: **if** (**not** `EmptyBucket`(X_A, j, t, N) **or not** `EmptyBucket`(X_B, j, t, N)) **then**
6: count $\leftarrow$ count + 1;
7: **end if**
8: **end for**
9: **if** count $\leq f$ **then**
10: **break**;
11: **else**
12: j $\leftarrow$ j + 1;
13: **end if**
14: **end while**
15: $p \leftarrow$ count / r; $R \leftarrow 2^{j+1}$;
16: **return** $(\frac{\log(1-p)}{\log(1-1/R)})$

Algorithm 2 `WinDiff(`$\{X_A^i\},\{X_B^i\}$`, u,` ϵ`, t, N)`

1: sum$\leftarrow$ 0;count$\leftarrow$ 0
2: **for** $i = 1$ **to** r **do**
3: index $\leftarrow \lceil\log(\frac{2\cdot u}{1-\epsilon})\rceil$; atm $\leftarrow$ `AtomicDifference`$(X_A^i,\ X_B^i, index, t, N)$;
4: **if** atm $\neq$ **noEstimate then**
5: sum $\leftarrow$ sum + atm; count $\leftarrow$ count+1;
6: **end if**
7: **end for**
8: **return** (sum $\times$ u / count);

estimate the cardinality of $A \cup B$. Algorithm `WinDiff` can estimate the cardinality of $A - B$ by following steps. Firstly, an estimate for $|A \cup B|$ is calculated through `WinUnion` as input variable u. Then, calculate $|A - B|/|A \cup B|$ to estimate $|A - B|$. Notice that ϵ is an error parameter for Algorithm `WinDiff`; Algorithm `WinIntersect` can estimate the cardinality of $A \cap B$. we omit the algorithm description because it is similar to `WinDiff` except that at Line 3, `AtomicDifference` is replaced by `AtomicIntersection`.

Analysis. In [7], by using *2-level hash sketch*, Ganguly et al. have given out three algorithms, SetUnionEstimator, SetDifferenceEstimator and SetIntersectionEstimator, to estimate three set operators, including *union*, *difference* and *intersection*. Our new algorithms are similar to them except that the basic data structure changes to be *improved 2-level hash sketch*. Remember that *improved 2-level hash sketch* is in fact an extension of *2-level hash sketch*, our three algorithms can become an (ϵ, δ)-algorithms when given same number of first- and second- level buckets. And, For the reason that a second-level counter only occupies 1 bits in an *improved 2-level hash sketch*, the space requirement of our algorithms are reported in Theorem 1.

Theorem 1. *Algorithms* `WinUnion`,`WinDiff` *and* `WinIntersect` *can return an* (ϵ, δ)*-estimate for the cardinality of* set union $A \cup B$, set difference $A - B$ *and* set intersection $A \cap B$ *over sliding windows by using* improved 2-level hash sketch *synopses with a storage requirement of* $O(\frac{\log(1/\delta)}{\epsilon^2} \log M \log N)$, $O(\frac{\log(1/\delta)|A \cup B|}{\epsilon^2 |A-B|} \log M (\log(\frac{\log(1/\delta)M}{\epsilon^2 \delta}) + \log N))$, *and* $O(\frac{\log(1/\delta)|A \cup B|}{\epsilon^2 |A \cap B|} \log M (\log(\frac{\log(1/\delta)M}{\epsilon^2 \delta}) + \log N))$ *respectively.*

Extended to General Set Expression. Algorithms `WinUnion`, `WinDiff` and `WinIntersect` are devised to estimate the cardinality of single set operator, including *union*, *difference*, and *intersection* over sliding windows. These algorithms can be extended to estimate the cardinality of a general set-expression $E = (((A_1 \texttt{op}_1 A_2) \texttt{op}_2 A_3) \cdots A_n$ by following two steps. Firstly, estimate $| \cup_i A_i|$ by using `WinUnion` with the **if**-condition at Line 5 changed to: **not** `EmptyBucket` (X_{A_1}, j, t, N) **or** $\cdots$ **or** **not** `EmptyBucket`(X_{A_n}, j, t, N). Secondly, estimate $|E|/|\cup_i A_i|$ in a way similar to `WinDiff`. Remember that `WinDiff` identifies a witness of $A - B$ by `AtomicDifference`. we can also identify a witness of E by checking a condition integrated with `AtomicDifference`, `AtomicIntersection` and `WinUnion`. For example, assume $E = ((A - B) \cap C) \cup D$. A witness is found iff expression ((((**not** `EmptyBucket`(X_A, i, t, N)) **and** `EmptyBucket`(X_B, i, t, N)) **and** (**not** `EmptyBucket`(X_C, i, t, N))) **or** (**not** `EmptyBucket`(X_D, i, t, N))) returns true.

4 Experimental Study

We report experimental results here. All codes were written in C and implemented at a 2.8GHz PC with 1G memory. Our experiments are done upon a synthetic dataset following zipfian distribution with $z = 0.8$. The dataset contains 1,000,000 elements each in a range of $[1, \cdots, 2^{20}]$. The first half and the rest are simulated as stream A and B respectively. The size of sliding window N is set to 50,000 elements. Fig. 3 shows the true values of $|A \cup B|$, $|A - B|$, $|B - A|$ and $|A \cap B|$ at time points N, $2N$, $\cdots$, $10N$. We can observe that $|A \cap B|$ is far smaller than $|A - B|$ and $|B - A|$.

Let $\hat{e}$ denote an estimate for the cardinality of an expression E. The error of the estimate can be defined as the ratio $|\hat{e} - |E||/|E|$. According to Theorem 1, the error is greatly influenced by the number of *improved 2-level hash sketch*

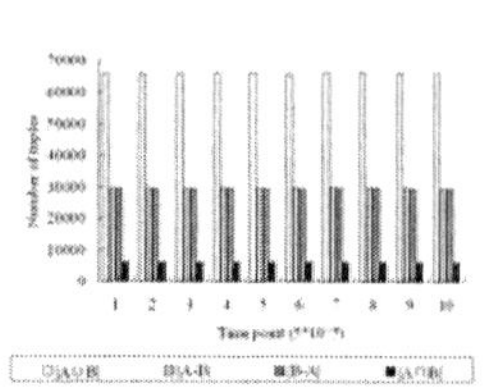

Fig. 3. Real cardinality of set operators

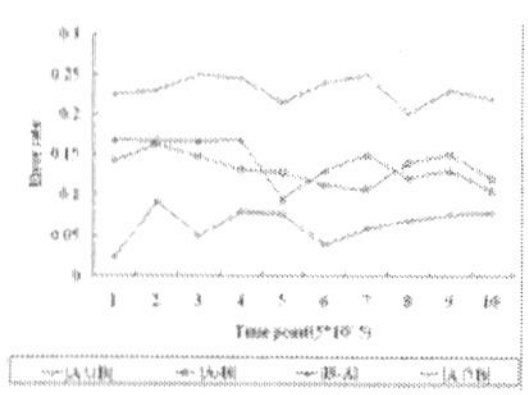

Fig. 4. Error changes with 500 synopses

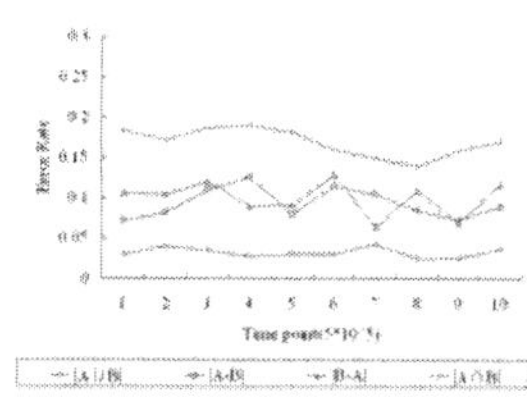

Fig. 5. Error changes with 1,000 synopses

synopses. Fig. 4 and 5 demonstrate the error change with 500 and 1000 *improved 2-level hash sketch* synopses respectively. Although both settings are far smaller than the theoretic boundaries, the errors of all set operators are below 25%. The errors are greatly reduced when the number of synopses is doubled. The estimate for $|A \cup B|$ owns smallest error, while the estimate for $|A \cap B|$ owns largest error. It is because that $|A \cap B| < |A \cup B|$.

5 Conclusion

Estimating the cardinality of set expressions defined over multiple streams is perhaps one of the most fundamental problems over data stream. Earlier work focused solely on the unbounded model(all tuples in a stream are considered). Sliding window model is very important when only latest N tuples of a stream are considered. In this paper, we have restudied previous work and devise a probabilistic space-efficient algorithmic solution to estimate the cardinality of set expressions over sliding windows. Our experimental results evaluate the correctness of algorithms.

References

1. N. Alon, Y. Matias, and M. Szegedy. The space complexity of approximating the frequency moments. In *Proc. of ACM STOC*, 1996.
2. B. Babcock, S. Babu, M. Datar, R. Motwani, and J. Widom. Models and issues in data stream systems. In *Proc. of ACM SIGACT-SIGMOD Symp. on Principles of Database Systems*, 2002.
3. A. Z. Broder, M. Charikar, A. M. Frieze, and M. Mitzenmacher. Min-wise independent permutations. In *Proc. of STOC*, 1998.
4. A. Das, S. Ganguly, M. Garofalakis, and R. Rastogi. Distributed set-expression cardinality estimation. In *Proc. of VLDB*, 2004.
5. M. Datar, A. Gionis, P. Indyk, and R. Motwani. Maintaining stream statistics over sliding windows. In *Proc. of SODA*, 2002.
6. P. Flajolet and G. N. Martin. Probabilistic counting algorithms for data base applications. *Journal of Computer and System Sciences*, 31:182–209, 1985.
7. S. Ganguly, M. Garofalakis, and R. Rastogi. Processing set expressions over continuous update streams. In *Proc. of SIGMOD*, 2003.
8. P. B. Gibbons and S. Tirthapura. Estimating simple functions on the union of data streams. In *Proc. of SPAA*, 2001.
9. P. B. Gibbons and S. Tirthapura. Distributed streams algorithms for sliding windows. In *Proc. of SPAA*, 2002.
10. P. Indyk. A small approximately min-wise independent family of hash functions. In *Proc. of SODA*, 1999.
11. Y. Zhu and D. Shasha. Statstream: Statistical monitoring of thousands of data streams in real time. In *Proc. of VLDB*, 2002.

An Extended Planning Mechanism to Increase Web Service Utilization[1]

Ji-Hyeon Kim, Yun Jin, Yeo-Jung Kim, and Ji-Hoon Kang[2]

Dept. of Computer Science,
Chungnam National University,
220 Gung-Dong, Yuseong-Gu, Daejeon, 305-764
South Korea
jhkim10@kopec.co.kr
{wkim, innias, jhkang}@cs.cnu.ac.kr

Abstract. An essential problem of automatic Web service planning is, how to compose the services together with minimal human effort. Most composition mechanism depends on relevant feedback method to ask the user to change the request or to accept insufficient services when there is no available services for the user (agent)'s request. This paper focuses on the point that even though there is no available autonomous services that satisfy the user's request, the planner tries to find out a way that can satisfy the request through extended service planning with available services. The extended service planning mechanism consists of two parts. First, if the request is not entitled to receive a service, the planner tries to find the complement services for the request so that the request can get the desired service. Secondly, if the request is partially satisfied by a service, then the planner tries to find the complement service that can complete the requester's service requirement. The extended service planning mechanism is based on the service matching cases between service request of user (agent) and the service description of provider that are described in semantic service ontology, e.g., DAML-S Service Profile Ontology. The service matching cases are derived from the Plugin match and the non-Plugin match with the in-/out-part parameters. This paper presents a new mechanism for extended service planning process that can enhance autonomous semantic Web service.

1 Introduction

Unlike the domain specific dedicated legacy system service, the benefit of a Web service is that it can be found and utilized dynamically among agents in a Web environment. There are several key issues to smoothing the Web service mechanism in a more lively way. One of them is to have well standardized Web service descriptions [4] and to have well explored service finding and planning technologies. The second is focused on the development of the capabilities for rich service discovery and service planning which is done by the service planning agent.

---

[1] This work was partly supported by Software Research Center of CNU.

[2] He is a corresponding author.

Y. Zhang et al. (Eds.): APWeb 2005, LNCS 3399, pp. 536–547, 2005.

The rich service discovery implies the service planning agent support as much as it can for the part of human being, especially in case of the complex service environment without much interference of human decision. Most service matching algorithms feed back to human effort at the end of service finding when there is no complete satisfied service. If there is no satisfied service the system feed back the service request to user for a modification of the request or to select one out of a set of candidate services that partially satisfy the original request of the user (agent). The user feed back mechanism is a good design for service accuracy and completeness, but the point is that the service planning agent must do its best to solve the problem with its own effort before resorting to the service requester.

We define two problem domains, one is how to do service planning for complex service request, and another is how to maximize automation of service planning without human interaction.

This paper suggests an automated service composition with logically valid paths. The approach is based on in/out-part concept and concept restriction. Section 2 presents the service matching cases of Plugin match and Non-Plugin match with further solution strategy. Section 3 presents service planning service grounding. Section 4 presents the related work with the conclusion following.

2 Service Matchmaking

The extended matching/planning processes for each matched case are based on the Exact, Plugin [9][14] and non-Plugin match. The Exact match is subsumed by Plugin match, so every match case converges to Plugin and non-Plugin match. The matching is done on in-/out-parts, which corresponds to the concept in Description Logic (DL)[20].

2.1 Definition of Matching Type

To explain the matching types, we introduces the terms of Requester (R), Requester's Service (RS), Provider (P) and Provider's Service (PS).

Definition 1. Concept-Spectrum (ConS)
A set of concepts that compose the in-part or out-part in conjunctive form.

Definition 2. Concept-Depth (ConD)
The set of concepts with range restriction that compose the in-part or out-part in conjunctive form. It can be specified as follows:

- ConD of PS's in-part : A set of PS's in-part concepts that also exists in RS's in-part. Each concept in this ConD has range restriction in either in-part, or in both in-part of PS and RS.
- ConD of PS's out-part : A set of PS's out-part concepts that also exists in RS's out-part. Each concept in this ConD has range restriction in either out-part, or in both out-part of PS and RS.

- ConD of RS's in-part : A set of RS's in-part concepts that also exists in PS's in-part. Each concept in this ConD has range restriction in either in-part, or in both in-part of PS and RS.
- ConD of RS's out-part : A set of RS's out-part concepts that also exists in PS's out-part. Each concept in this ConD has range restriction in either out-part, or in both out-part of PS and RS.

ConD is more specific case of ConS with restriction. If there are RS.in-part = (Painter:Europe, Time:1880-1990), PS.in-part = (Painter:Italy, Time: 1880-1990), then the ConS of RS's in-part is (Painter, Time) and the ConD of RS.in-part is (Europe(Painter), 1880-1990(Time)). In this case every concept in RS's in-part must have a corresponding concept of PS's in-part by definition.

Definition 3. Services R Sand PS is Exact Matching if,
(For in-part)
ConS of RS.in-part(c) = ConS of PS.in-part(c) and ConD of RS.in-part(c) = ConD of PS.in-part(c)
(For out-part)
ConS of RS.out-part(c) = ConS of PS.out-part(c) and ConD of RS.out-part(c) = ConD of PS.out-part(c)

The Plugin match(PS Plugin match to RS) is the case when all requests in demand are available in provider's supply, i.e., RS is satisfied by PS. The definition the Plugin match [14] can be expressed as,

$\text{Match}_{\text{plugin}}(\text{RS,PS}) = (\text{RS}_{\text{pre}} \Rightarrow \text{PS}_{\text{pre}}) \wedge (\text{PS}_{\text{post}} \Rightarrow \text{RS}_{\text{post}})$

Definition 4. Services RS and PS is Plugin Matching if,
(For in-part)
ConS of RS.in-part(c) $\supseteq$ ConS of PS.in-part(c) and ConD of RS.in-part(c) $\subseteq$ ConD of PS.in-part(c)
(For out-part)
ConS of RS.out-part(c) $\subseteq$ ConS of PS.out-part(c) and ConD of RS.out-part(c) $\subseteq$ ConD of PS.out-part(c)

The non-Plugin match(PS Plugin match to RS) is the case when not all requests in demand are available in provider's supply, i.e., RS is not satisfied by PS.

Definition 5 Service RS and PS is non-Plugin Matching if,
(For in-part)
~(ConS of RS.in-part(c) $\supseteq$ ConS of PS.in-part(c)) or ~(ConD of RS.in-part(c) $\subseteq$ ConD of PS.in-part(c))
(For out-part)
~(ConS of RS.out-part(c) $\subseteq$ ConS of PS.out-part(c)) or ~(ConD of RS.out-part(c) $\subseteq$ ConD of PS.out-part(c))

2.2 Matching Cases

For explanatory convenience, we introduce the concept tables. Each column describes a concept where the top most field denotes the name of the concept and the other fields denote the concept restrictions. There are four types of matching cases as described below.

Type-A, PluginC (Plugin match without Concept Restriction)

(1) Match-1: In-PluginC (in-part PluginC)

- Condition : ConS of RS.in-part(c) $\supseteq$ ConS of PS.in-part(c)
- Result: Satisfied.
- Solution: Return the matched service.
- Consideration: False Positive (Maybe finds surplus not wanted answer)

(Example)
RS.in-part: (Picture, Genre, Museum, Time)
PS.in-part: (Picture, Genre, Museum)

(2) Match-2 : Out-PluginC (out-part PluginC)

- Condition : ConS of RS.out-part(c) $\subseteq$ ConS of PS.out-part(c)
- Result: Satisfied.
- Solution : Return the matched service.

Type-B, PluginCR (Plugin match with Concept Restriction)

(3) Match-3 : In-PluginCR (in-part Plugin match for Concept Restriction)

- Condition : ConD of RS.in-part(c) $\subseteq$ ConD of PS.in-part(c) .AND.
  ConS of RS.in-part(c) $\supseteq$ ConS of PS.in-part(c)
- Result: Satisfied.
- Solution: Return the matched service.

(4) Match-4 : Out-PluginCR (out-part Plugin match for Concept Restriction)

- Condition : ConD of RS.out-part(c) $\supseteq$ ConD of PS.out-part(c) .AND.
  ConS of RS.out-part(c) $\subseteq$ ConS of PS.out-part(c)
- Result: Satisfied.
- Solution: Return the matched service.
- Consideration: False Negative (Maybe can't find a result that should be done).

Type-C, nPluginC (no Plugin match without Concept Restriction)
Some concepts in request are not satisfied by provider's service.

(5) Match-5.: In-nPluginC (in-part non Plugin match for Concept)

- Condition : ~(ConS of RS.in-part(c) $\supseteq$ ConS of PS.in-part(c))
- Result: Need to be expanded.
- Solution: Find a service that gets RS's in-part as in-part and provides the out-part
  which is not in RS's in-part but in PS's in-part.

(6) Match-6 : Out-nPluginC (out-part non Plugin match for Concept)

- Condition : ~(ConS of RS.out-part(c) $\subseteq$ ConS of PS.out-part(c))
- Result: Need to be expanded.
- Solution: Find a service that gets RS's in-part as in-part and returns RS's not covered concept (e.g.,Genre) as out-part.

(Example)
RS.out-part: (Museum ∩.location.West, Title ∩.(< stringsize 30), Genre)
PS.out-part: (Museum ∩.location.West, Title ∩.(< stringsize 30))

Type-D, nPluginCR (no Plugin match with Concept Restriction)
Some concepts in request are not satisfied by provider's service considering the concept restriction.

(7) Match-7: in-PluginCR (out-part non Plugin match for Concept Restriction)
• Condition:

Case 7A : ((ConD of RS.in-part(c) $\subseteq$ ConD of PS.in-part(c)) .AND.
~(ConS of RS.in-part(c) $\supseteq$ ConS of PS.in-part(c))), or
Case 7B : (~(ConD of RS.in-part(c) $\subseteq$ ConD of PS.in-part(c)) .AND.
(ConS of RS.in-part(c) $\supseteq$ ConS of PS.in-part(c))), or
Case 7C : (~(ConD of RS.in-part(c) $\subseteq$ ConD of PS.in-part(c)) .AND.
~(ConS of RS.in-part(c) $\supseteq$ ConS of PS.in-part(c)))

(Match-7-1) (In-nPluginCR) (concept conflict cases for 7B and 7C)

- Result: Can't get the service.
- Solution: No solution, return Fail.

(Example)

RS.in-part: (Painter ∩.nationality.Italy, Time ∩.($\geq$ year 1880)
∩.($\leq$ year 1900))
PS.in-part: (Painter ∩.nationality.France, Time ∩.($\geq$ year 1880)
∩.($\leq$ year 1900))

(Match-7-2) (In-nPluginCR) (non concept conflict case for 7A)

- Result: Need to be expanded.
- Solution: Find a service that gets RS's in-part as in-part and provides the out-part
which is not in RS's in-part but in PS's in-part.

(Match-7-3) (In-nPluginCR) (non concept conflict case for 7B)

- Result: Satisfied.
- Solution: Return the matched service.
- Consideration: False Positive (Maybe finds surplus not wanted answer)

(Match-7-4) (In-nPluginCR) (non concept conflict case for 7C)

- Result: Need to be expanded.
- Solution: Find a service that gets RS's in-part as in-part and provides the out-part
  which is not in RS's in-part but in PS's in-part.
- Consideration: False Positive (Maybe finds surplus not wanted answer)

(8) Match-8: Out-nPluginCR (out-part non Plugin match for Concept Restriction)

- Condition:

<u>Case 8A</u> : ((ConD of RS.out-part(c) $\supseteq$ ConD of PS.out-part(c) .AND.
~(ConS of RS.out-part(c) $\subseteq$ ConS of PS.out-part(c))), or

<u>Case 8B</u> : (~(ConD of RS.out-part(c) $\supseteq$ ConD of PS.out-part(c)) .AND.
(ConS of RS.out-part(c) $\subseteq$ ConS of PS.out-part(c))), or

<u>Case 8C</u> : (~(ConD of RS.out-part(c) $\supseteq$ ConD of PS.out-part(c)) .AND.
~(ConS of RS.out-part(c) $\subseteq$ ConS of PS.out-part(c)))

(Match-8-1) (Out-nPluginCR) (concept conflict cases for 8B and 8C)

- Result: Can't get the service.
- Solution: No solution, return Fail.

(Match-8-2) (Out-nPluginCR) (non concept conflict case for 8A)

- Result: Need to be expanded.
- Solution: Find a service that gets RS's in-part as in-part and returns RS's not covered concept as out-part.
- Effect: False Negative

(Example)

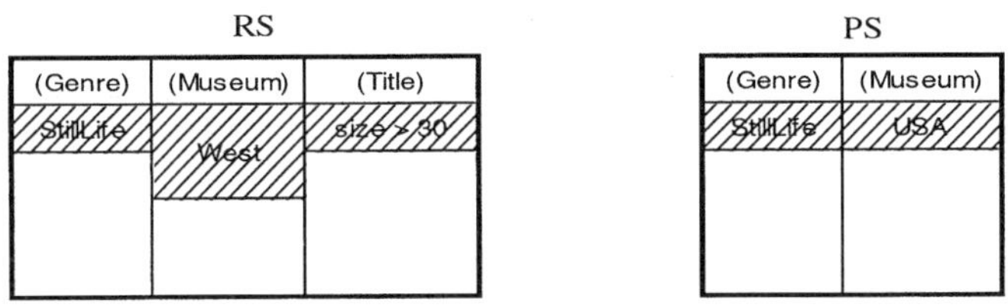

RS.out-part: (Museum∩.location. West, Title ∩.(< stringsize 30),
Genre ∩.genre.StillLife).

PS.out-part: (Museum∩.location.USA, Genre ∩.genre.StillLife))

(Match-8-3) (Out-nPluginCR) (non concept conflict case for 8B)

- Result: Satisfied
- Solution: Return the matched service.
- Consideration: False Positive

(Match-8-4) (Out-nPluginCR) (non concept conflict case for 8C)

- Result: Need to be expanded.
- Solution: Find a service that gets RS's in-part as in-part and returns RS's not covered concept as out-part.
- Consideration: False Positive

3 Service Planning and Grounding

3.1 Planning Description

This planning phase is done at the abstract layer based on matching cases. The services found in this phase are composed with link and order information that defines the sequence of operation and service precedence. To get the service results that the user requested, the services composed in this phase should be realized through the corresponding Web service providers. The successful services composition in the planning phase doesn't guarantee the successful service result. That's because the service planning only ensures the service availability, not the service result itself. For example, Even if the request for an Airplane ticket matched a proper service, the service result is dependent to the requester's in-part data, e.g., flight time. If there is no available airline at the requested time, the service provider returns null result.

(Explanatory Example A)
The service expansion we suggest here has the purpose to derive the extended service set to satisfy the user (agent)'s request as much as possible. For example, let's consider the following P and R's service definition.

Web Service Requester(R):
 RS1= (in-part:Painter/out-part:Picture,Genre)
Web service provider 1(P1):
 PS1=(in-part:Painter,Nationality/out-part:Picture)
Web service provider 2(P2):
 PS2=(in-part:Painter/out-part:Nationality)
 PS3=(in-part:Painter,Picture/out-part:Genre)

In here, there is no direct matching Web service for the request RS1. To get the Picture, the in-part of PS1 must be satisfied by the in-part of RS1. Because RS1 has no in-part of Nationality, it should search other service, which returns Nationality as out-part with Painter in-part that is the only one RS1 can support. This service expansion process is self-complement processing because it is the pre-processing to be entitled to get the PS1 service. Fortunately another Web service provider (P2) registered a service PS2 that return Nationality with Painter in-part. Now RS1 get the Nationality information from PS2 and can receive PS1 service. Until now the original RS1 is not satisfied because the Genre. To obtain the Genre information for RS1, the planning agent must use PS3 service, which returns Genre information. Now, the planning agent must have Painter and Picture to receive the service from PS3. The RS1 has the Painter intrinsically, and the agent can obtain the Picture from PS1, so it can obtain the Genre information from PS3. From the extended service planning as described here, the user's request of RS1 can be satisfied.

As we can see here, the in-part service expansion is, naturally, self-complementing which means the additional in-part required by currently matched service is derived as out-part from existing in-part information through a service. The out-part expansion is to find out a complementing service which receives existing in-part and returns the out-part that current service can't cover.

3.2 Planning Tree Generation

The planning algorithm omitted here for space limitation generates a planning tree with the planning domain described above.

The planning tree consists of Reference service, Current service and New service. The Reference service is a target service that should be satisfied by service providers. At starting point, a Reference service is selected from the request service set that is derived from a user's request and the planning tree for the selected Reference is generated. The planning agent finds the matched service for the Reference service and selects most appropriate service (Current) from the matched candidate services. In **Fig. 1**, the generated planning tree for the Planning Example A, the service S1(Painter,Nationality/Picture) is selected as a Current service for the Reference service RS1. The unselected candidate Current services will be pushed into a stack for next use in case the selected Current service is proved unsolvable. If the in-/out-part match type of Current service and Reference service is falling into match cases 1,2,3,4, the Planning Tree generation will be completed with success. But if not the cases, the planning agent defines new service goals(New) to complement the Current service. The new goals are generated according to the Actions regarding to the match types. In **Fig. 1**, the new goals "Painter/Nationality", "Painter/Genre" for the Current service S1 are generated according to the Action 5 and 6 for the match cases of 5 and 6 respectively. At this time each generated New service becomes the Reference service and does recursively the planning steps for the Reference service. If all leaf nodes of the generated Planning Tree are Null, the planning is finished successfully. The planning is failed if one of the leaf nodes of generated Planning Tree is Fail.

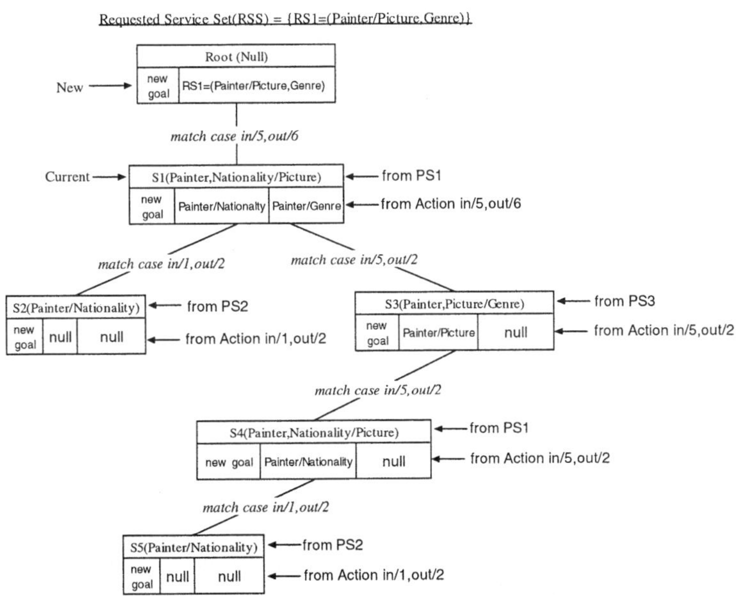

Fig. 1. Planning example for Explanatory Example A

3.3 Service Grounding

The planned service set must be grounded to get the real data from service provider. The service grounding is done using WSDL in SOAP protocol.

(Explanatory Example B)
Fig. 1 shows the generated PSS with the service execution sequence "S2-S1-S5-S4-S3" for the RS1 with the provider's services of PS1, PS2 and PS3(see Explanatory Example A). It takes 188msec. for this planning tree generation with our planning agent that is supported by RACER [22] for subsumption relation check among concepts.

If the RS1 is "find Pictures and Genres with Painters of Vincent Van Gogh, Claude Monet and Pablo Picasso" with the following grounding service results of PS1, PS2 and PS3, the final answer for RS1 is:

{(Vincent Van Gogh/Sunflowers 1888,Stilllife),
(Vincent Van Gogh/Olive Grove,Landscape),
(Claude Monet/Le Vieux Guitariste,Portrait)}

PS2(in-part:Painter/out-part:Nationality) returns the following information.
{(Vincent Van Gogh/Netherlands),
(Claude Monet/France),
(Pablo Picasso/Spain)}

PS1(in-part:Painter,Nationality/out-part:Picture) returns the following information.
{(Vincent Van Gogh,Netherlands/Sunflowers 1888),
(Vincent Van Gogh,Netherlands/Olive Grove),
(Claude Monet,France/Le Vieux Guitariste),
(Claude Monet,France/White and Purple Water Lilies),
Claude Monet,France/Nymphaeas, Effect du Soir)}

PS3(in-part:Painter,Picture/out-part:Genre) returns the following information.
{(Vincent Van Gogh,Sunflowers 1888/Stilllife),
(Vincent Van Gogh,Olive Grove/Landscape),
(Claude Monet,Le Vieux Guitariste/Portrait)}

4 Related Work

Sheshagiri[2] describes the service composition planner that uses STRIP-style[1] services. In his approach the requester must specify the complex service in detailed atomic service level that results in a large burden on the requester contrary to our approach that requires only an abstract level description of complex service.
Sirin[18] presents Web service pipelining through input/output matching. His service pipelining concept looks similar to our service composition, but his service pipelining is based on the user's selection among the candidate services of exact and generic matching contrary to our full automatic composition and he even doesn't consider the cases of non-Plugin match.

Zaremski[13][14] suggests the signature matching and specification matching for software library and components. His matching definition is based on logic expression of in-/out-part parameters but does not have the in-/out-part constraints as we have. Sycara [9][11] proposed a matching process of matchmaker in Web environment. Among his five filter matching processes, the Signature and Constraints Filter is closely related to our work. While his approach end with fail or success in service finding after tried to find a Plugin match, our approach tries to maximize the chance of success before returning fail with autonomous extended service composition according to each match type even though there is no Plugin match services.

The Web service matchmaking and discovery [7][8][10] for Grid environment is suggested. Even they use input/output constraints for service matchmaking, they still don't consider the automated service planning in case that there is no directly satisfiable service.

WSDL [4] based matching processes are proposed by [12][15][21]. Wang [12] presents a Web service matching algorithm with WSDL specification through multi step processes of data type comparison, service message comparison, service operation comparison based on input/output. His approach has no extended match processing when the request is not fully satisfied, as we suggested in this paper. Medjahed [15] proposes an ontology based framework for the automatic composition of Web services. He presents a technique to generate composite services from high-level declarative description. His experienced composition similar to case based reasoning [19] but does not consider the extended matching process as we proposed. Sudhir Agarwal [21] provides a framework, OntoMat-Service, to embed the process of Web service discovery, composition and invocation. It assumes that the service provider describes its service through WSDL. The framework supports the semi-automatic composition and invocation of Web services contrary to our full automatic approach. P. Traverso [16] proposes an automated composition of Web services into executable processes without considering extended planning to satisfy the in-part requirement of the found service for execution. Horrocks [17] describes the DAML+OIL constructor and axioms in DL syntax. The main idea is to consider a conjunctive query as a directed graph. Our approach also assumes the query as conjunctive as he does with the difference that we do the extended matching process for the request.

5 Conclusion

The paper presents an extended service planning mechanism to increase the Web service utilization through the extended Web service planning. The suggested mechanism can increase the automatic Web service planning possibility significantly. The planning is done on the requested service set that is generated from user's triple information. The proposed planning algorithm doesn't consider the timing requirements. The planning time can be shortened by, for example, limiting the planning tree depth. It can happen that several candidate services are available for a Reference service and the service selection is very important in this case because it can impact service planning time. It is important to select really available service as a Current service from the candidate services, and the selection algorithm should be considered more in the future.

The vocabulary and concept standardization is necessary for enriched service semantics. There are so many kinds of terms in the Web and it is difficult to select a proper term that the counter part can understand. An elaborated concept ontology for the known designated service domain is required for an efficient service matchmaking between requesters and providers.

References

1. Fikes, R., Nilsson, N.: STRIPS: A New Approach to the Application of Theorem Proving to Problem Solving. Artificial Intelligence, 2(3/4), 1971.
2. Sheshagiri, M., desJardins, M., Finin, T.: A Planner for Composing Service Described in DAML-S, ICAPS 2003, Workshop on Planning for Web Services,10 June 2003, Trento, Italy.
3. Web Services Architecture: W3C Working Draft 8 August 2003, http://www.w3.org/TR/ws-arch/.
4. Web Services Description Language (WSDL) 1.1: W3C Note 15 March 2001, http://www.w3.org/TR/wsdl.
5. UDDI Version 3.0.1: UDDI Spec Technical Committee Specification, 14 October 2003, http://uddi.org/pubs/uddi-v3.0.1-20031014.htm.
6. SOAP Version 1.2 Part 1: Messaging Framework,W3C Recommendation 24 June 2003, http://www.w3.org/TR/soap12-part1/.
7. Hoschek, W.: The Web Service Discovery Architecture, In Proc. of the Int'l. IEEE/ACM Supercomputing Conference (SC 2002), Baltimore, USA, November 2002. IEEE Computer Society Press.
8. Ludwig, S.-A., van Snaten, P.: A Grid Service Discovery Matchmaker based on Ontology Description. In *Proc.* EuroWeb 2002 Conference*, Oxford, UK*, December 2002.
9. Sycara, K., Widoff, S., Klusch, M., Lu, J.: LARKS: Dynamic Matchmaking Among Heterogeneous Software Agents in Cyberspace. Journal on Autonomous Agents and Multi-Agent Systems, 4(4), 2001.
10. Foster, I., Kesslman, C., Nick, J., Tuecke, S.: The Physiology of the Grid: An Open Grid Services Architecture for Distributed Systems Integration, January 2002.
11. Sycara, K., Klusch, M., Widoff, S., Lu, J.: Dynamic Service Matchmaking Among Agents in Open Information Environments. In *Journal ACM SIGMOD Record (Special Issue on Semantic Interoperability in Global Information Systems)*, A. Ouksel, A. Sheth (Eds.), Vol. 28, No. 1, March 1999, pp. 47-53.
12. Wang, Y., Stroulia, E.: Flexible Interface Matching for Web-Service Discovery, Fourth International Conference on Web Information Systems Engineering, December 10-12 2003, Roma, Italy.
13. Zaremski, A.M., Wing, J.M.: Signature Matching, a Tool for Using Software Libraries, *ACM Transactions on Software Engineering and Methodology (TOSEM)*, Vol. 4, No. 2, April 1995.
14. Zaremski, A.M., Wing, J.M.: Specification Matching of Software Components, *3rd ACM SIGSOFT Symposium on the Foundations of Software Engineering*, October 1995.
15. Medjahed, B., Bouguettaya, A., Elmagarmid, A.-K.: Composing Web services on the Semantic Web. VLDB J. 12(4): 333-351 (2003).
16. P. Traverso, M. Pistore: Automated Composition of Semantic Web Services into Executable Processes *Third International Semantic Web Conference (ISWC2004),* November 9-11, 2004, Hiroshima, Japan.
17. Fikes, R.; Hayes, P.; Horrocks, I.: DQL - A Query Language for the Semantic Web. Knowledge Systems Laboratory, Stanford, 2002.

18. Sirin, E., Hendler, J., Parsia, B.: Semi-automatic composition of web services using semantic descriptions. In *Web Services: Modeling, Architecture and Infrastructure workshop at ICEIS2003*, Nantes, France, 2003.
19. Aamodt, A., Plaza, E.: Case-Based Reasoning: Foundational Issues, Methodological Variations, and System Approached. AI Communications(1994). ISO Press, Vol.7:1,pp.39-59.
20. Baader, F., Calvanese, D., McGuinness, D., Nardi, D., Patel-Schneider, P.: The Description Logic Handbook, Theory, Implementation and Applications, Published January 2003.
21. Agarwal, S., Handschuh, S., Staab, S.: Surfing the Service Web. Second International Semantic Web Conference, Springer, LNCS, 2870, pages: 211-226, OCT 2003.
22. Volker Haarslev, Ralf Möller : Description of the RACER System and its Applications, Proceedings International Workshop on Description Logics(DL-2001), August 2001.

Web Services Based Cross-Organizational Business Process Management

Guoqi Feng[1, 2], Chengen Wang[3], and Haiyue Li[2, 4]

[1] Postgraduate School, Chinese Academy of Sciences, Beijing 100086
[2] Shenyang Institute of Automation, Chinese Academy of Sciences, Shenyang 110016
[3] Information Science and Engineering College, Northeastern University, Shenyang 110004, China
[4] Heilongjiang Institute of Science and Technology, Harbin 150027, China
gqi@sia.cn
http://www.sia.ac.cn

Abstract. Fierce market competition nowadays forces enterprises integrating processes internal or across organizational boundaries, which makes distributed business process management (BPM) difficult with existing technologies. Web services are rapidly emerging as important building blocks for business integration. This paper discusses the application of web services in BPM context. The relationship between web services and BPM are described and t e implementation steps of deploying web service oriented BPM are discussed. A two-level web services selection approach based on six selection criteria are proposed and discussed. An example of web services for credit card authentication in order entry process is illustrated to show the application of web services in BPM context.

1 Introduction

Fierce market competition nowadays forces enterprises integrating internal or external processes. The advancement of communication technologies and network computing make it easier for enterprises to organize their manufacturing or service processes. Since it is difficult for enterprises to produce complete products or services in isolated facilities, and with the support of existing advanced network and communication technologies, they would form alliances and integrate their services to share knowledge, skills, and resources in offering a value-added service. Therefore, business processes take place in an open distributed environment of heterogeneous and autonomous nodes.

BPM enables enterprises to automate and integrate the disparate internal and external corporate business processes. It can be categorized into two kinds according to the processes spans: the first type is BPM for enterprise application integration (EAI) that enables companies to achieve integration of internal systems; and the other type is BPM for business-to-business integration (B2Bi) which focuses on how business partners can refine their business processes so that the applications supporting them can be seamlessly integrated.

Y. Zhang et al. (Eds.): APWeb 2005, LNCS 3399, pp. 548 – 559, 2005.

A whole new set of tools has arisen to facilitate the integration and automation of business processes, including graphical process modeling tools, middleware technologies such as CORBA, integration brokers, business process management systems and B2B servers. However, until recently the investment required by organizations to integrate the IT systems both inside their organization and across the firewall has been very high. This is mainly because the different proprietary interfaces and data format used by each application.

Web services technology promise to change this by replacing proprietary interfaces and data formats with low-cost, ubiquitously supported standards for interfaces and data that work as well as across the firewall as within it [1, 2]. The freely flow of applications and services can interact and negotiate among themselves without having a specialist to key in data and commands over a browser interface. The web services technologies can therefore streamlines inter-business processes by creating an open, distributed systems environment (EAI), and allow the possibility of significantly reducing the cost of integrating disparate heterogeneous business systems (B2Bi).

The rest of this paper is organized as follows. The next section explores the relationship between web services and BPM and gives a simple literature review of related works; Section 3 discusses the implementing steps of deploying web services based BPM system; Section 4 proposed the two-level selection approach based on the six criteria defined and discusses the detailer implement process according to three of the criterion; In section 5 a simple example of web services application is given. And concluding remarks are given in the last section.

2 Web Services Enabled BPM

BPM is dealing with the reality that business processes are complex, dynamic and intertwined throughout an organization or beyond the firewall to its partners and customers. By automating and streamlining the unique and routine processes that power the enterprise, BPM offsets the administrative burden of the organization and creates an environment where processes can be leveraged for strategic value.

Web services based on SOA framework provide a suitable technical foundation for making business processes accessible within or across enterprises boundaries. Web services are seen as an important infrastructure to foster business processes by composing individual Web services to represent complex processes, which can even span multiple organizations. META Group describes the latest move to integrated BPM suites as offering significant business value as organizations transition their application portfolios into service-orientated architectures and Web services.

The relationship between business process and web services is very important, but is not often explained very clearly. In [4], the authors have discussed the relationship between web services and business processes from a specific viewpoint. Roughly speaking, web services can be used as implementations of activities within a business process, and that business processes in turn can be externalized as web services. The business processes that can be built based on this simple observation range from simplex to complex. More generally, we can view the relationship from the following several aspects.

- The services don't define what process you can implement; rather, the business processes define what services you used.
- A business process description (or flow model) can be published as a web service, it becomes impossible to distinguish whether an invoked service is an atomic service or a service composed with business process.
- The interaction between services is what creates the implementation of the business processes. Multiple services in a business process can come from different organizations.
- Individual services can be composed into a process flow that itself can be described as a service using the same web services standards.
- A business comprised of hundreds of discrete web services isn't particularly efficient. What is more interesting is the composition of multiple web services into a coherent business process that meets business requirements. In order for this composition to occur, a way of composing atomic, fine-grained web services into coarse-grained business services is needed.

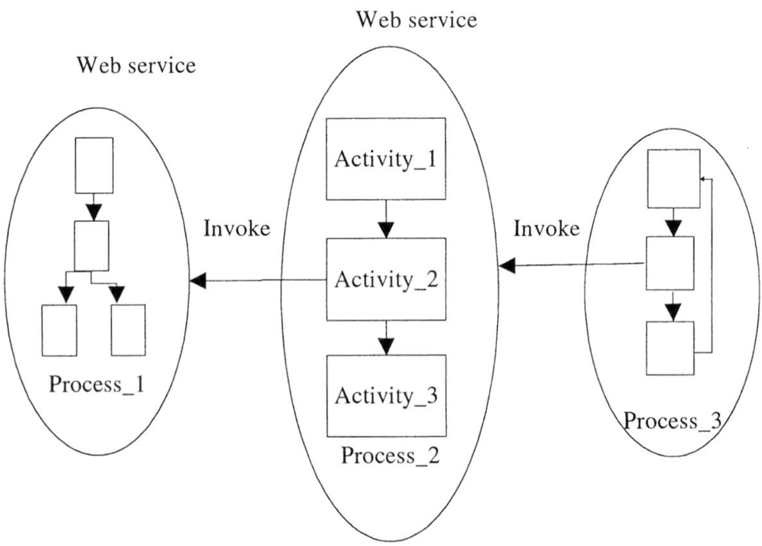

Fig. 1. Relations between Web services and business process

The relations between web services and business processes could be approximately sketched with Fig. 1. From the figure we can see that activity_2 of Process_2 in an enterprise is implemented by a web service, which in fact is another process (Process_1) within the enterprise or from some other enterprise. While the process Process_2 itself can also be treated as a web service that could be invoked by a third process (Process_3).

Driven by web services, BPM offers a prime opportunity to create new types of business solutions that were impossible before. Web services could offer the key to unleashing the power of BPM. They enhance its benefits by providing lower integration costs, accelerating the time to market, through shorter implementation cycles, and increasing the ability to adapt.

Although BPM poses difficulties with both soft (such as human resistance and behavioral issues) and hard elements (such as technology, tools, and techniques), web services can alleviate some of the complexities [3].

In [1], the authors proposed a web service based framework for business integration, which enables the composition of pre-defined canonical web services for developing business integration solutions more efficiently and reliably than existing approaches. Wombacher and Mahleko have highlighted the challenges that inhibit the use of web services to support ad-hoc business processes and how these challenges might be overcome [10]. Estrem examines economic, technical, and organizational contexts that will influence the ability of manufacturing-related enterprises to deploy advanced information architectures based on web services to support the complex business processes needed to collaborate with suppliers, customers, and other stakeholders in virtual enterprise environments [6]. In [7] the authors propose a methodology which provides a framework for identifying web services from business processes and principles in web services design which covers both functional perspectives such as coupling and cohesion, and non-functional perspectives such as provision, billing, pricing and metering. And in [11], the authors propose a technique for automatic reconciliation of the web Service interfaces involved in inter-organisational business processes. Reference [8] presents the seven dominant principles of good web services design. The principles are based on 15 years of software technology evolution, combined with practical experience from today's deployed web services applications. And it also describes effective web services architecture for business process management. Based on the study of e-business standards and research of relevant literatures, Chen has identified several factors that affect the adoption and diffusion of web services for e-business standards [9].

3 Implement Solutions

Building BPM solutions that leverage web services is the result of methodical approaches. The opportunity is certainly there, and by creating a solid roadmap that identifies and overcomes the challenges, companies can reap the reward.

Drawn from the practices, the deployment of web service oriented BPM can be partitioned into four sequential steps, which are outlined as follows.

3.1 Defining Strategic Objectives

Business processes are collections of activities with common objectives and human activities are primarily driven by goals. A clear understanding of organization goals is essential to the selection of alternative activities and serves as a guide of choosing among the alternatives while implementing the goals [5]. Therefore, far before the deployment of BPM project, business process objectives must be clearly determined which will contribute much to the efficient description of the business operations. It is the fundamental step.

In order to elicit process goals various techniques can be applied, e.g. interviewing staff working in different areas and management-level, field of stakeholders' needs, analyzing internal and external complaints, or monitoring competitors. Following the elicitation, goals should be decomposed and the relationships among subgoals should be clearly outlined.

3.2 Business Process Modeling and Implementation Description

Business process is a network of activities, performed by enterprise actors (roles element) that are equipped with resources to reach certain enterprise goals, and the executions of activities are under the control of business rules. A business process can be formalized as

$$P = \{A | G, R_o, \mathrm{R}_e, R_u\}$$

in which G, R_o, R_e, R_u represents the goals, roles, resources and rules corresponding to the activities in A. Detail information about the process elements may refer to [5].

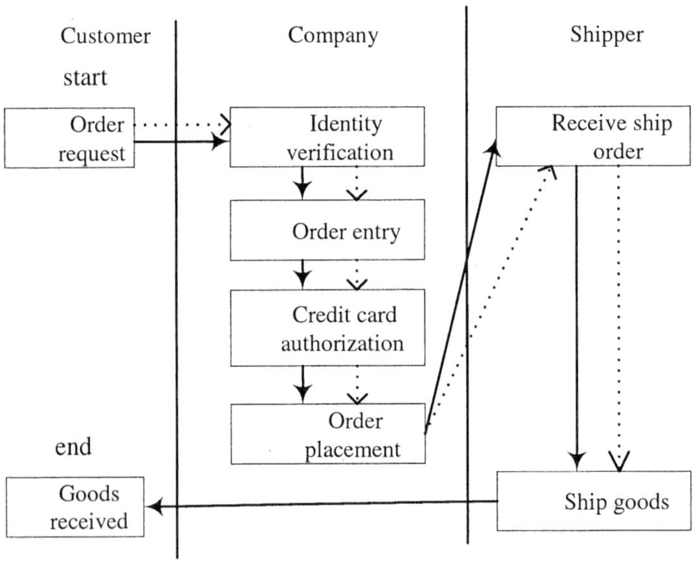

Fig. 2. A Busines process

From the point of implementation, business process should be described to define the operations and performers. Fig. 2. is a simplified process about purchase request. Rectangles represent process activities, the solid line and dotted line represents control flow and information flow in the process respectively.

WSFL (Web Services Flow Language) is an XML language for the description of Web Services compositions. It covers both public and private processes. Fig. 3. is the corresponding WSFL services composition that defines the above process named as totalSupplyFlow. In this example, the flow model imposes "sequencing constraints" for the execution of operations of the totalSupply service provider type.

```
<flowModel name="totalSupplyFlow" serviceProviderType="totalSupply">

<serviceProvider name="customer" type="customer"/>
<serviceProvider name="company" type="company" />
<serviceProvider name="shipper" type="shipper" />
<activity name="orderRequest">
 <performedBy serviceProvider="customer"/>
 <implement>
 <export>
 <target  portType="totalSupplyPT" operation="orderRequest"/>
 </export>
 </implement>
 </activity>
        ...
<controlLink source="orderRequest" target="identityVerification"/>
...
<dataLink source="orderRequest" target="identityVerification">
<map sourceMessage="purchaseOrder" targetMessage="purchaseOrder"/>
</dataLink>
...
</flowModel>
```

Fig. 3. WSFL definition for process flow

3.3 Role Allocation

Following the modeling of the business process, the responsibilities associated with each of the activities should be identified. In other words, each of the activities should be allocated to specific roles that implementing it, i.e. human beings, software applications or web services within or across the enterprises. It is the core step in deploying web service enabled BPM projects. In this stage, the providers of each web services that responsible for the execution of the business process activities should be defined; it is the most critical step to deploy web services based BPM systems.

Roles allocation among persons mainly according to the operation costs. Define weak-deduction symbol "$\triangleright$", and $A \triangleright B$ means that if A is true, then B should be true.

$$(\exists o_1)(\exists o_2)\text{competent}(o_1, a, r) \wedge \text{competent}(o_2, a, r) \wedge$$
$$Large(cost(o_1, a, r), cost(o_2, a, r)) \triangleright Take(o_2, a, r)$$

This formula shows that both actor o_1 and o_2 are capable of taking role r in activity a, but the operation cost of o_1 is higher than that of o_2, therefore o_2 should be selected to take the role r. However in practice, more flexible allocation strategies may be adopted considering the interests and skills of the staff and some other factors.

Before allocate web services to be responsible for the activity execution, enterprises must carry out a strategic analysis about the projects to balance the advantages and disadvantages of adopting web services, measure the costs, potential impacts and the benefits for the enterprises. Even if web services-based plan is established, specific web services should be selected from multiple similar web services provided by different providers, which is an optimal problem involving various parameters and will be detailed in the next section.

3.4 Business Process Execution

Executing the business process modeled in stage 2, during the operations, related resources are used to carry out the activities. In this stage, web services defined to execute the tasks are banded and invoked. Fig.4. is a simple SOAP request to a identify verification services for customer identity affirmation.

```
<SOAP - ENV:Envelope
xmlns :SOAP - ENV =" http://schemas.xmlsoap .org/soap/envelope/ "
SOAP - ENV: encodingStyle ="http://schemas.
xmlsoap .org/soap/encoding/">
<SOAP - ENV:Body>
<CustMana: IdentityVeri xmlns : CustMana ="Some -URI">
< CustomerInfo >
< CustomerID >C0100</ CustomerID >
< Password >birthdaydate</ Password >
</ CustomerInfo >
</ CustMana: IdentityVeri >
</SOAP - ENV:Body>
</SOAP - ENV:Envelope>
```

Fig. 4. SOAP request message

4 Web Services Selection

Before deployment the web based BPM systems, companies need to understand the benefits and potential impacts of web services on the enterprise, and the selection of web services is a pivotal part of it that will be more difficult than traditional product selections. The difficulty lies in complex web services selection criteria and web services compositions problems if needed. Some researchers have explored the selection of web services from different aspects. Benatallah and his fellows have discussed the selection of web services for composition based on the criteria of execution cost, execution time, and location of provider hosts [12, 13]. Tang and Cheng analyzed the optimal location and pricing of web services from the view of web services intermediary, whose selection criteria can contribute to the companies for making selection decisions [14]. Web services selection bears some similarities with supplier selection problem in supply chain management domain, from which we can draw some ideas to construct the selection method. However, since web services different from the common products and its web based characteristics makes its different selection criteria.

4.1 Selection Criteria Definition

In this paper, we adopt a two-level web services selection method that based upon six selection criteria.

Six web services selection criteria are defined as

Criteria = (*Function*, Price, *Location*, *Integration*, Re*putation*), in which each criteria means:

Function: The functions of the web services provided, it can be measured with satisfaction degree of the companies, Satisfactio*nDegree*= x, $x \in [0,1]$;

Price: Purchase price of the web services, it is a fix value for specific web services;

Location: The physical address of the web services provider, which impacts the service transport time and represented as network latency. Since the data flow amount on the network is fluky so the latency time could not be looked as a fixed function of the physical distance, it can reference the average transport time for simplicity.

Integration: The costs of integrating multiple individual web services, this criteria may give some support for selecting multiple elementary web services from different providers or selecting one composition web services from an intermediary;

Reliability: It is the probability that whether the web services could successfully process the requested transactions within expected time. It relies on the software and hardware configurations of the service-side server and even the network transport facility status, such as bandwidth. In quantitative analysis, it can be defined as the ratio of successful delivery times to all the invocations times.

Reputation: It is the trustiness of that the enterprises feel about the services. It can be got from the services' past users' evaluations, simply for example, the average of all the evaluations.

In practice, enterprise may assign different priorities to each criterion according to specific requirements, for example, for time-sensitive business, the execution time (location) and reliability will be granted relatively higher values.

4.2 Selection Approach

Based on the above criteria, we can adopt a two-level selection approach for web services selection.

(1) Function search: Take a rough-grain search of the UDDI service registry center using keywords about web services functions. Far above all the other criteria, the functions that the web services must full fill the enterprise's business function requirements.

(2) Criteria constraints selection: The search results of step1) will be a set of multiple services from different providers that need a further filter. In this step, a fine-grain selection operation is executed based on the remainder five criteria and the priorities that the enterprise defined. One by one with the criteria constraints selection, the result set will become smaller and smaller, and the enterprise will eventually get the right web services until the criteria with lowest priority constraints selection is performed.

When a enterprise needs to import multiple services to efficiently implement the business process management task, more complex computation will be need in step(2) about the integration cost that will taka a relative big part of the total costs. Following, we take function, cost and location as the selection criteria to give a relatively detailer illustration of the above approach.

Service provider's location is an import factor should be considered when deploying a BPMS composing multiple isolate web services (or services compositions). Maximizing the number of services provided by the same provider will decrease the interactions between different providers and the data exchange between host where the services resident. Based on this fact, we define the following selection guidelines concerning the location factor:

(a) Firstly, considering the host where the current running services resident, which will avoid data exchange between services of heterogeneous locations;

(b) Secondly, considering the host where the user agent is currently resident, which will implement the local invocation and reduce the data exchange;

(c) Once the searches of (a) and (b) are failed, considering the other hosts.

Following, we take function, location and execution cost as major criteria in the selection to discuss the detail selection procedure.

Define the distributed business process includes n isolated procedural web services (services compositions), $BP = (WS_1, WS_2 ... WS_i ... WS_n)$ (i=1,..,n), the execution sequence of the services is $WS_1 > WS_2 > ... > WS_i > ... > WS_n$. Therefore, the selection process can be carried out according to the following approach.

(1) Function selection: As described above, as for each WS_i (i=1,..,n), select the service providers, which form the corresponding sets, WSP_i (i=1,..,n);

(2) Criteria constraints selection: As for the first web services WS_1 in the business process, select the cheapest provider from WSP_1 according to the total execution cost, which may including the actual execution cost, costs brought by the network transport and delay,etc. (Itself is a complex problem in the network computation domain and will not be detailed here.) Once the first web services provider is identified, the subsequencing services providers will be determined according to the execution costs and providers' location. In this paper, we define the priority of location is higher than that of the execution costs. Therefore, as for each of the WS_i (i=2,…,n), perform the compare process according to the three guidelines described above to select the candidate providers, and then according to the second criteria, i.e., execution cost to determine the final service provider WSP_i .

After the successful performs of the two level selections, the final proper web services providers will be selected and scheduled to implement the distributed business process management. However, as for different industries will have different business requirements, which leads to the industries will value the criterion differently and assign different priorities to each of them. Accordingly, it will lead to different selection guidelines and approaches.

5 An Illustrating Example

For a large manufacturing company, the requirements for electronic payment have been widely used in many areas, such as ERP, SCM and CRM. However, credit card authorization remains a problem that baffling the enterprises. Because the credit card companies wouldn't going to distribute authority for credit card authorization among every vendor who wishes to support credit card purchases. Considering the function of credit card authorization involves many technical and other factors that are difficult to implement, and in scenarios where such interactions over a global network are necessary to do business, the most promising solution, i.e. web services are adopted to resolve this problem.

In the following example, the business process of order entry comprises a third-party web service for credit card authentication, as shown with Fig.5.

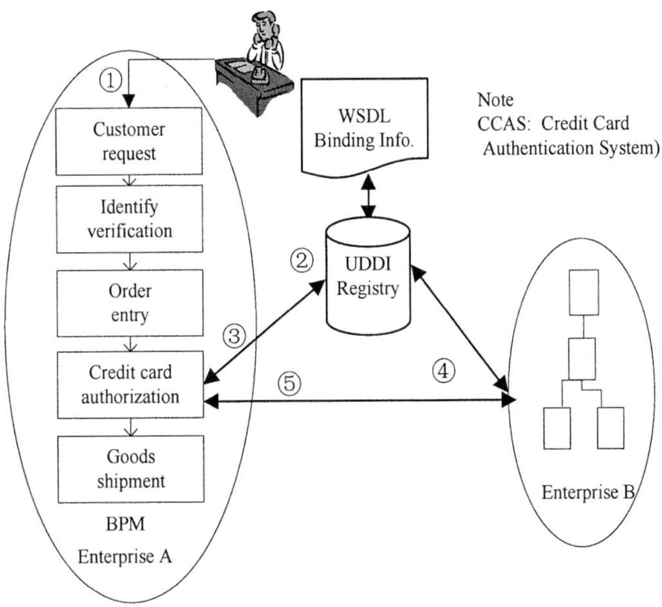

Fig. 5. An example of Web Service Applied in BPM

The detailed implementation steps are described as following:

Through the procurement portal, the customer request for goods. A series of operations are carried out to verify customer information, which belongs to the traditional business processes executions.

Enterprise A's BPMS gets information about Enterprise B's Web service (credit card authentication) by doing a lookup in the private UDDI registry.

Service registry returns the matched URLs of WSDL files to the BPM system of enterprise A. In fact, step (2) and (3) are carried out prior to the custom request, so that step (1) will directly jumps to (4) except that the web services of credit card authentication has no longer been provided by Enterprise B.

Enterprise A's BPMS invokes the CCAS of enterprise B to authenticate the customer's credit card;

Enterprise B's CCAS receives the Web service request and sends the credit card validation response back to enterprise A. And some subsequent operations are carried out to complete the whole order entry process.

To enhance the efficiency and implement software reuse, the update of ERP, CRM and SCM systems caused by the new order entry can also be implemented as internal web services, which was not presented in the figure.

6 Conclusions

In this paper we have discussed the relationships between web services and BPM and some relevant problems in implementation. Web services and business process management both promise to impact profoundly the way that organizations use the Internet to conduct business internally and with partners, suppliers and customers. BPM and web services help re-establish enterprises' control over IT. New innovations including, web services and grid technology, will combine with BPM to allow users to quickly, easily and even invisibly use technology resources of all kinds to support their requirements. However, much works need to do to deployment a successful web services based BPM system, such as the right selection of web services provider. From the point view of web services, some technical challenges, such as lack of security controls at the protocol level and lack of transaction management capabilities, must also be addressed.

Acknowledgment

The authors would like to acknowledge the Chinese Hi-Tech R&D program under the Grant (2002AA414420) for supporting this research.

References

1. Ying Huang, J.Y.Chung, A web services-based framework for business integration solutions, Electronic Commerce Research and Applications, Vol.2, 2003, pp.15-26
2. K. Gottschalk, S. Graham, H. Kreger, and J. Snell , Introduction to Web services architecture, IBM system journal, Vol. 41, No.2, 2002, pp.170-177
3. Gunjan Samtani & Dimple Sadhwani, Business Process Management & Web Services, Web Services Journal, http://www.sys-con.com/webservices
4. F.Leymann, D.Roller, M.-T.Schmidt, Web services and business process management, IBM systems Journal, Vol.41, No.2, 2002, pp.198-211
5. Guoqi Feng, Chengen Wang, a formal business process modeling method, Proceedings of the Seventh world conference on Integrated Design process technology, 2003 Dec.3-5, Austin, Texas, America, pp.708-713
6. William A. Estrem, An evaluation framework for deploying Web Services in the next generation manufacturing enterprise, Robotics and Computer Integrated Manufacturing Vol.19, pp.509–519, 2003

7. Mike P.Papazoglou, Jian Yang, Design methodology for web services and business processes, Lecture notes in computer science, Vol.2444, 2002, pp.54-64
8. Mark Palmer, the Seven Principles of Web Services Business Process Management, Web Services Journal, http://www.sys-con.com/webservices
9. Minder Chen, Factors affecting the adoption and diffusion of XML and web services standards for e-business systems, International Journal of Human-Computer Studies, Vol.58, 2003, pp.259-279
10. Andreas Wombacher, Bendick Mahleko, Ad-Hoc Business Processes in Web Services, 2003 Symposium on Applications and the Internet Workshops (SAINT'03 Workshops), January 27 - 31, 2003 Orlando, Florida
11. G.Piccinelli, W. Emmerich, C. Zirpins, K. Schütt, Web Service Interfaces for Inter-organisational Business Processes-An Infrastructure for Automated Reconciliation, Proceedings of the Sixth International enterprise distributed object computing Conference, 2002
12. L. Zeng, B. Benatallah, M. Duams, J. Kalagnanam, Q. Sheng Quality Driven Web Service Composition, The 12th International World Wide Web Conference, 20-24 May, 2003, Budapest, Hungary
13. Z. Maamar, Q.Z. Sheng, B. Benatallah, Selection of Web Services for Composition Using Location of Provider Hosts Criterion, Ubiqitous Mobile Information and Collabration Systems (UMICS 2003), Held in conjunction with CAiSE'03. 16-17 June 2003, Austria.
14. Q.C. Tang, H.K. Cheng, Optimal location and pricing of Web services intermediary, Decision Support System, In press

Conversations for Web Services Composition

Zakaria Maamar[1], Soraya Kouadri Mostéfaoui[2], and Djamal Benslimane[3]

[1]Zayed University, U.A.E
zakaria.maamar@zu.ac.ae
[2]University of Fribourg, Switzerland
kouadris@acm.org
[3]Lyon 1 University, France
djamal.benslimane@liris.cnrs.fr

Abstract. This paper presents how conversations are integrated into Web services composition. While much of the recent work on Web services has focussed on low-level standards for publishing, discovering, and triggering them, this paper promotes Web services to the level of active components. Such components engage in conversations, make decisions, and adjust their behavior according to the context of the situations in which they participate. Conversations between Web services are specified with state chart diagrams enhanced with context-awareness mechanisms.

Keywords: Web service, conversation, composition, context.

1 Introduction

Web services are nowadays emerging as a major technology for deploying automated interactions between distributed and heterogeneous systems. While much of the work on Web services (also called services in the rest of this paper) to date has focussed on low-level standards for publishing, discovering, and invoking them [14], we aim at promoting Web services to the level of active components by using *conversations*. A conversation is a consistent exchange of messages between participants that are engaged in joint operations and hence, have common interests. A conversation either succeeds or fails. When a conversation succeeds, this means that the expectations out of the conversation are reached (e.g., action implemented). When a conversation fails, this means that the conversation faced technical difficulties (e.g., communication medium disconnected) or didn't achieve what was expected (e.g., action requested not-implemented).

Conversations have been the object of multiple investigations in various research fields [7]. In this paper we discuss conversations from a Web services perspective. In order to engage in a conversation, Web services have to be leveraged from the level of passive components, which only respond to triggers, to the level of active components, which make decisions in order to adjust their behavior to their surrounding environment. Sensing, collecting, and refining the features of an environment result in defining its *context*. Context is the information that characterizes the interactions between humans, applications, and the surrounding environment [5]. Huhns backs the importance of leveraging Web services and

Y. Zhang et al. (Eds.): APWeb 2005, LNCS 3399, pp. 560–571, 2005.

suggests using *software agents* [8]. Indeed Web services, unlike software agents, are not designed to use and reconcile ontologies. Moreover software agents are inherently communicative, whereas Web services remain passive until triggered.

While some authors agree on the necessity of leveraging Web services [8], others already identify some similarities between Web services and software agents [6]. Web services advertise their capabilities, search for other services, and invoke other services without prior notice. This kind of behavior bears many similarities to software agents. A service accepts requests (i.e., sense) and returns responses (i.e., action) [6]. In addition once a service is invoked it performs tasks with or without further inputs (i.e., autonomy). Despite these similarities, the aforementioned behavior is mainly hard-coded in the service and consequently, limits the service in its actions. Web services should "talk" to each other so that they can discover their capabilities, reveal their constraints, decide on the actions to take, and coordinate their actions.

Web services composition is a very active area of R&D. However, *very little* has been achieved to date regarding the seamless integration of conversations into composition approaches of Web services. In particular, several obstacles still hinder this integration including (i) Web services are dealt with as passive components rather than active components that can be embedded with context-awareness mechanisms, (ii) existing approaches for service composition typically facilitate orchestration only, while neglecting contextual information on services, and (iii) lack of support techniques for modeling and specifying conversations between Web services. In this paper **the focus is on the conversations happening among a group of Web services, which are called to constitute composite services**. The rest of this paper is organized as follows. Section 2 discusses the rationale of using conversations in Web services. Section 3 presents the context-aware conversation approach for composing Web services. Section 4 provides some examples on specifying conversations between Web services. Section 5 overviews the status of the implementation work and concludes the paper.

2 Conversations and Web Services

Ardissono et al. observe that current standards of Web services are integrated into systems featured by simple interactions [2]. Simple because the interactions are based on question-answer communication-patterns (e.g., announce/confirm). However there are multiple situations such as negotiation, that require more than two turns of interaction (e.g., propose/counter-propose/accept$\oplus$reject$\oplus$counter-propose/..., $\oplus$ stands for exclusive or). The participants in these situations have to engage in conversations before they reach an agreement. In addition Benatallah et al. notice that despite the growing interest in Web services, several issues remain to be addressed before Web services can provide the same benefits as traditional integration middleware do [3]. Benatallah et al.'s suggestion to enhance Web services is to develop a conversational metamodel. Yi and Kochut also note that as the range of Web services-based applications expands, complex conversation protocols are required [15]. Participants in these protocols exchange a series of messages that comply with synchronization rules. Last but not least, the Web Services Conversation Language (WSCL) is an initiative, which promotes the adoption of conversations in Web services [4]. WSCL describes the structure of documents that a Web service expects receiving and producing, and the order in which the exchange of documents is expected occurring. In this paper **we focus on the conversations that take place among Web services, which are requested to enroll in a composite service as components**. These Web services might have different providers and have to engage in conversations in order to agree on what to exchange, how to exchange, when to exchange, and what to expect out of an exchange.

2.1 Stages of Web Services Composition

To assess the progress of the conversations during Web services composition, we decompose this progress into three stages: pre-composition, composition, and post-composition.

Pre-Composition Stage. Because similar Web services exist on the Internet, it is important to search for and identify the services that satisfy user-defined selection criteria (e.g., execution cost/time).Conversations in this stage are about the following aspects:

- Identification aspect: use search mechanisms (e.g., UDDI registries) to identify Web services. In this paper, we assume that the Web services are already specified and advertised.
- Invitation aspect: invite Web services to participate in a composition. The rationale of service invitation is discussed in [11].
- Compatibility aspect: check if the Web services can exchange meaningful information because of the data-heterogeneity issue that may raise. Semantic compatibility between Web services is discussed in [12, 13].

Composition Stage. It aims at completing the details that finalize a composition. These details are related to the nature of exchange (e.g., representative, directive) in which the Web services will be involved with peers, with whom to exchange after invitation acceptance, and what to exchange after a positive compatibility check. Conversations in this stage are about the following aspects:

- Execution aspect: details sent out to Web services on the execution procedures (normal and exceptional cases, execution locations, etc.). The conversations that are related to this aspect are given in Section 4.
- Interaction aspect: details sent out to Web services on the invocation procedures, outcomes expected, and types of (un)successful interactions.

Post-Composition Stage. It consists of executing the specification of the composite service (we combine service and state chart diagrams for this specification [10]) by invoking the respective component Web services. Conversations in this stage are about the following aspects:

- Monitoring aspect: progress acquisition of the status of the Web services.
- Exception handling aspect: corrective strategies to Web services in case of unforeseen situations during specification or failures to be fixed.

2.2 Building Blocks of a Conversation

Pre-composition, composition, and post-composition stages have each focussed on specific conversational aspects that occur during Web services composition. Because of the variety and complexity of these aspects, we decided on (i) associating each aspect with a *conversation session* and (ii) encoding a conversation session as a *course of actions*.

To handle the multiple conversation sessions, we use *Conversation Schemas* (CSs) for describing these sessions and their respective courses of actions. A conversation schema is a specification of the exchange of messages that is expected to happen between participants. This exchange depends on several factors including the application domain, current context, and current status of a chronology. For example, a conversation schema describes both the side-effects and corrective actions of a conversation that is misunderstood.

We decompose a conversation schema into two parts: *argument* and *policy*. The argument part is made up of the following arguments: sender, receiver, category, conversation object, and condition of activation. Category corresponds to a conversation aspect as listed in Section 2.1. Conversation object is the topic of exchange (e.g., invitation to participate). Finally, condition of activation is the data elements that are checked before the status of a conversation changes (i.e., conversation takes on a new state). The policy part manages the dynamic aspect of a conversation such as status changes, admissible turns, and timeouts.

First of all, the initiator of a conversation downloads a CS from the library of conversation schemas (Fig. 2) according to the following elements: (i) current composition stage, and (ii) progress in this stage with regard to the active aspect. Next, the initiator instantiates the conversation object (i.e., gives a value) and checks the activation condition before it sends a message to a receiver. Upon reception of the conversation object, the receiver adopts one of the following options: (i) accept the conversation object and take actions based on the conversation object's content by triggering for example a service; (ii) change the conversation object and submit this conversation object to the initiator by changing for example the triggering time of a service; and (iii) reject the conversation object and either submit a new conversation object to the initiator or ignore the initiator (this one conforms to a time-out constraint).

Modeling conversations is a complex process as several requirements need to be satisfied. Some of these requirements include [9]: (i) conversation models should be task-oriented, (ii) conversation models should be associated with a semantics, (iii) conversation models must provide communication abstractions, and (iv) conversation models should be reusable and extendable. In this paper, we specify a conversation schema with state charts. In addition to satisfying some of the aforementioned requirements such as (i) and (iv), encoding the flow of conversations using state charts has several benefits. First, state charts have a formal semantics, which is essential for reasoning over the content of conversations. Second, state charts support modeling admissible turns and decision makings during conversations. Finally, state charts offer most of the control-flow constructs that can be found in real conversations (e.g., branching, looping).

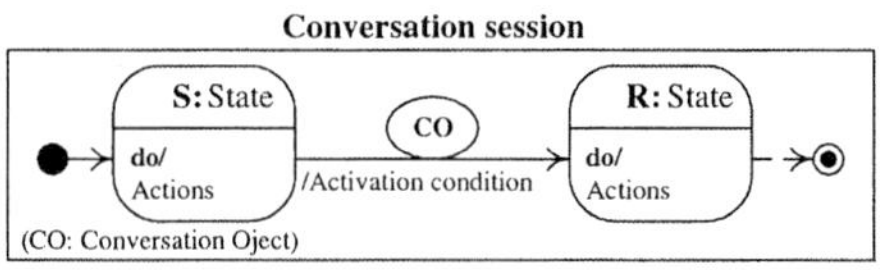

Fig. 1. Conversation schema illustrated with a state chart

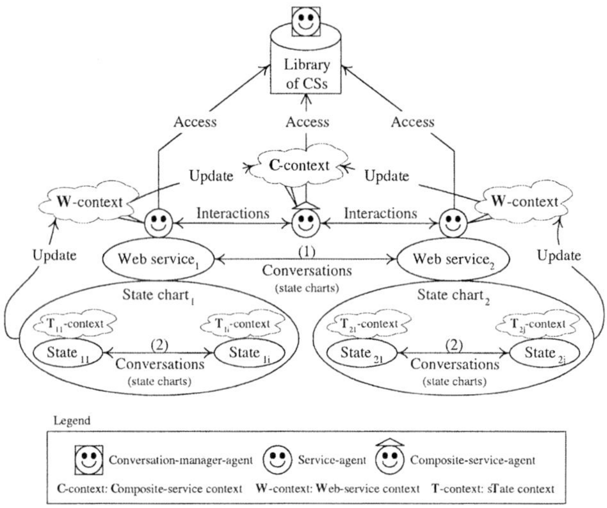

Fig. 2. Context-aware conversation approach for composing Web services

Fig. 1 depicts the mapping of the arguments of a conversation schema into the concepts of a state chart. This mapping is as follows:

- Name of states has an **S/R** (sender/receiver) label. These states track the progress of a conversation.
- Name of transitions has an activation condition and a conversation object.
- Actions of states implement the information that conversation objects carry.
- A complete state chart corresponds to a conversation schema of a conversation session. Examples of developing such schemas are given in Section 4.

3 Context-Aware Conversation Approach

3.1 Overview

To assess the progress of a composition of Web services so that relevant conversation schemas are downloaded from the library of conversation schemas (Fig. 2), the use of awareness mechanisms is required. These mechanisms ensure that the status of a Web service is known and reflected in its $\mathcal{W}$-context (context of $\mathcal{W}$eb service). Using $\mathcal{W}$-context, it is possible to know if a Web service is (i) part of a composition, (ii) under execution, or (iii) invited to participate in a composition.

Besides $\mathcal{W}$-context, it will be shown in the rest of the paper that several types of context are adopted. These types are decomposed into those associated with services and those associated with conversations.

In the previous paragraphs we strengthened the benefits of the combination (software agent, Web service). Agents track Web services in order to update their respective $\mathcal{W}$-contexts. The tracking concerns the composition in which a service takes part, the current state of a service, and the type of conversation that a service has initiated during the composition. Fig. 2 presents the context-aware conversation approach for Web services composition. The features of this approach are as follows.

A) Three types of agents are set up: conversation-manager-agent, composite-service-agent, and service-agent.

A conversation-manager-agent runs on top of the library of conversation schemas. It updates the library when a new specification of a conversation schema is ready (e.g, updates done by designer). Plus the conversation-manager-agent responds to the requests of downloading conversation schemas that come from composite-service-agents and service-agents.

A composite-service-agent triggers and monitors the deployment of the specification of a composite service (to keep Fig. 2 clear, the specification repository is not represented). This monitoring is reflected in its $\mathcal{C}$-context (context of $\mathcal{C}$omposite-service). In addition, the composite-service-agent interacts with service-agents when it comes to inviting services for composition or informing services of the changes of the specification of a composite service.

A service-agent gets a Web service ready for composition, tracks its execution through its state chart, and updates its $\mathcal{W}$-context.

B) Besides the state charts of the conversation schemas (Fig. 1), additional state charts are associated with Web services so that their tracking can happen (Fig. 2). The states of a Web service are reflected in its $\mathcal{W}$-context. Interesting to note that the transitions in the state chart of a service are *context-based* and *conversation-oriented* (see (2) in Fig. 2). However these conversations are less complex than the conversations that involve Web services (see (1) in Fig. 2). Therefore, each state of a Web service is associated with a $\mathcal{T}$-context (context of Web-service s$\mathcal{T}$ate). In Fig. 2, $\mathcal{T}_{1i}$-context corresponds to the context of state$_{1i}$ of Web service$_1$.

C) A library of conversation schemas to store the specifications of conversation schemas (Fig. 2). The library is a resource from which composite-service-agents and service-agents download conversation schemas after interaction with the conversation-manager-agent.

Fig. 2 depicts three levels of abstraction: Web-service state ($\mathcal{T}$-context), Web service ($\mathcal{W}$-context), and composite service ($\mathcal{C}$-context). State context is fine grained, whereas the composite-service context is coarse grained. Details of the context of a state are used for updating the context of a Web service. In addition details of the context of a Web service are used for updating the context of composite services. The update operations are illustrated in Section 3.4.

3.2 Operation

The operation of the context-aware conversation approach consists of four steps. The *context awareness* step is about the mechanisms that track the changes of the states of a Web service (e.g., from committed to executed state). In case a change of state happens, the $\mathcal{T}$-context of the current and previous states of the Web service are updated. The *context acquisition* step is about the mechanisms that collect information from the $\mathcal{T}$-contexts of a Web service so that these details are submitted to the $\mathcal{W}$-context of the Web service for update needs. In addition the update is propagated to the $\mathcal{C}$-context of the composite service. The *context assessment* step is about the mechanisms that refine the information obtained from the *context acquisition* step. The purpose is to assess the contexts so that decisions are made on (i) the conversation session to enter and (ii) the conversation schema to download. Finally the *conversation session deployment* step is about the actions that are executed such as downloading a conversation schema after assessing the appropriate contexts.

In Fig. 2 the conversations occur in two separate locations. In the first location (see (1) in Fig. 2), the conversations concern the component Web services of a composite service. These conversations are specified using the conversation schemas of Fig. 1. In the second location (see (2) in Fig. 2), the conversations concern the states of the Web services. It should be noted that the state chart of a conversation schema is primarily aimed at supporting the interactions between the state charts of Web services. The distinction between states of services and states of conversations gives better flexibility for managing the aspects that each type of state chart is concerned about. The state chart of a service focusses on the changes that apply to the service such as availability and commitment, whereas the state chart of a conversation focusses on the changes that apply to the conversation such as formulation and response.

Because of both types of state (those associated with services and those associated with conversations), we deemed appropriate annotating each state of conversation with a context that we refer to as $\mathcal{S}$-context (context of conversation $\mathcal{S}$tate). The rationale of $\mathcal{S}$-contexts of the states of conversations is similar to the rationale of $\mathcal{T}$-contexts of the states of services. Moreover to track the progress of a conversation, a context that we denote by $\mathcal{V}$-context (context of a con$\mathcal{V}$ersation), is used. This is similar to the $\mathcal{W}$-context of a Web service.

3.3 Structure of Contexts

The $\mathcal{T}$-context of a service state has these parameters:

- *Label*: corresponds to the name of the service state.
- *Status (confirmed/not-confirmed)*: informs if the current state of the service is confirmed or not-confirmed. We recall that state charts of services are conversation-oriented, which means that the states need to be confirmed or not-confirmed.
- *Transition in/Previous state*: illustrates the pre-arguments in terms of transition and state that have brought the service from a previous state to the current state (the previous state may be null in case of no predecessor).

- *Transition out/Next state*: illustrates the post-arguments in terms of transition and state that will take the service from the current state to a next state (the next state may be null in case of no successor).
- *Regular actions*: illustrates the operations to execute in the current state in order to take the service from the current state to a next state. The execution of these operations relies on the transition out/next state parameter. As previously discussed, a positive confirmation from the next state means updating status parameter of this current state (i.e., confirmed as value).
- *Compensation actions*: illustrates the operations to execute in the current state to bring back the service from the current state to a previous state. This execution relies on transition in/previous state parameter. Due to the negative confirmation that originates from this current state, status parameter of the previous state is updated (i.e., not-confirmed as value).
- *Time*: illustrates the period of time in which the service has been in the current state whether that state was confirmed or not-confirmed.
- *Date*: identifies the time of updating the parameters above.

The $\mathcal{W}$-context of a Web service is built upon the $\mathcal{T}$-contexts of its respective states and has these parameters (not detailed): label, status, previous states, current active state, potential next state, time, and date.

The $\mathcal{C}$-context of a composite service is built upon the $\mathcal{W}$-contexts of its component services and has these parameters (not detailed): label, previous services, current active services, next potential services, time, and date.

The $\mathcal{S}$-context of a conversation state has these parameters:

- *Label*: corresponds to the name of the current conversation state.
- *Transition in/Previous state*: illustrates the pre-arguments in terms of transition and state that have brought the conversation from the previous state to the current state (the previous state may be null in case of no predecessor).
- *Transition out/Next state*: illustrates the post-arguments in terms of transition and state that will take the conversation from the current state to the next state (the next state may be null in case of no successor).
- *Regular actions*: illustrates the operations to execute in the current state in order to take the conversation from the current state to a next state. The execution of these operations relies on transition out/next state parameter.
- *Compensation actions*: illustrates the operations to execute in the current state in order to bring back the conversation to a previous state. This execution relies on transition in/previous state parameter.
- *Time*: illustrates the period of time in which the conversation has been in the current state.
- *Date*: identifies the time of updating the parameters above.

We recall that the states in a conversation's state chart are not conversation-oriented, which is in opposition with the states in a service's state chart.

The $\mathcal{V}$-context of a conversation is built upon the $\mathcal{S}$-contexts of its respective states and has these parameters (not detailed): label, conversation session, conversation schema, participants, previous states, current active state, potential next state, time, and date.

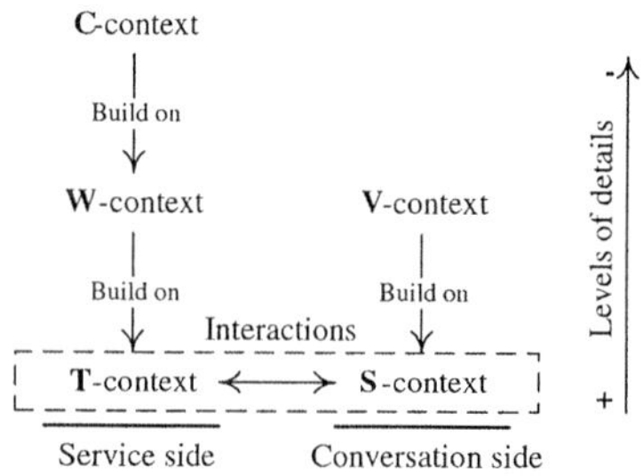

Fig. 3. Types of connection between contexts

3.4 Interactions Between Contexts

Fig. 3 shows how the different contexts are devised and inter-connected. The figure is divided into two parts: service and conversation. In addition two types of connection exist: *vertical* and *horizontal*. In the service part the vertical connections involve $\mathcal{C}$-context, $\mathcal{W}$-context, and $\mathcal{T}$-context. In the conversation part the vertical connections involve $\mathcal{V}$-context and $\mathcal{S}$-context. Regarding the horizontal connections, which are the most interesting to our context-aware conversation approach, they involve the $\mathcal{T}$-context of the service part and the $\mathcal{S}$-context of the conversation part. The link between both contexts corresponds to *previous state* and *next state* parameters of the $\mathcal{S}$-context of a conversation. These parameters can receive as value the value of *label* parameter of the $\mathcal{T}$-context of a service[1]. Indeed the previous state of the current state of a conversation can be the state of a service. Plus the next state of a conversation can be the state of a service.

The previous section has detailed the structure of each context. The five contexts are inter-related and thus, engage in interactions for information exchange and update purposes (Fig. 3, vertical and horizontal connections). For instance the contexts of states update the contexts of services. In the context-aware conversation approach, interactions between contexts are encoded as *control tuples* stored in a *control tuple* space [1]. A control tuple is a rule of the form Event-Condition-Action (`E[C]|A`) where:

- `E` is an event. For example, **modified($\mathcal{T}$-context t, WebService ws)** means that the context state of a Web service was modified. Thus, actions need to be executed after checking the appropriate condition (Table 1).
- `C` is a conjunction of conditions on the parameters of contexts. These parameters are explained per type of context in Section 3.3. For instance a control tuple's condition can be dependent on the value assigned to *conversation session* parameter of $\mathcal{V}$-context.
- `A` is an execution action. For example, **update($\mathcal{W}$-context w, WebService ws)** means that a Web service needs to update its context based on the information it has collected from the contexts of states (Table 1).

[1] $\mathcal{S}$-context.Value(previous state/next state) $\leftarrow$ $\mathcal{T}$-context.Value(label).

Table 1. Some events and actions in the context-aware conversation approach

Event & Description
- **modified($\mathcal{T}$-context t, WebService ws)**: $\mathcal{T}$-context t of Web service ws is modified.
- **accepted(WebService ws, CompositeService cs)**: Web service ws accepts the invitation of Composite service cs.
Action & Description
- **update($\mathcal{S}$-context s, Conversation c)**: $\mathcal{S}$-context s of conversation c to be updated.
- **fire(TransitionConversation trc, ConversationState cst)**: Transition conversation trc to be fired so conversation state cst can be entered.

Example: **modified($\mathcal{T}$-context t, WebService ws)[status** == "*confirmed*"]|**update($\mathcal{W}$-context w, WebService ws)** means that if the $\mathcal{T}$-context t of a state of the Web service ws is modified and the status of this state is *confirmed*, thus the $\mathcal{W}$-context w of this Web service needs to be updated after collecting information from this $\mathcal{T}$-context t.

4 Example of Developing a Conversation Schema

In Section 2.1 we decomposed the composition of Web services into three stages. Each stage has different aspects, which characterize the conversations that occur. In the following we provide an example of how a conversation schema is developed. This consists of devising two state charts, one for conversations and one for the services that participate in these conversations. Prior to description, the following comments are made on both types of state chart:

- State labels are annotated with S/R (sender/receiver). If there is no annotation, the state identifies the communication network.
- Transitions connect the states together. Two types of transition exist. Those connecting the states of the same chart are represented with regular lines, and those connecting the states of distinct charts are represented with dashed lines. Ovals anchored to transitions correspond to conversation objects.

Fig. 4 is the state chart of the conversation schema that is devised for the composition stage with a focus on the execution aspect. The submission of the details of an execution occurs from a composite service to a component service. There are two service states seen from a sender perspective (one state identifies the sender service namely scheduling) and a receiver perspective (one state identifies the receiver service namely analysis). In addition, there are three conversation states seen from a sender perspective (one state identifies the sender service namely preparation), a receiver perspective (one state identifies the receiver service namely reception), and a network perspective (one state identifies the network namely transmission from the sender to the receiver).

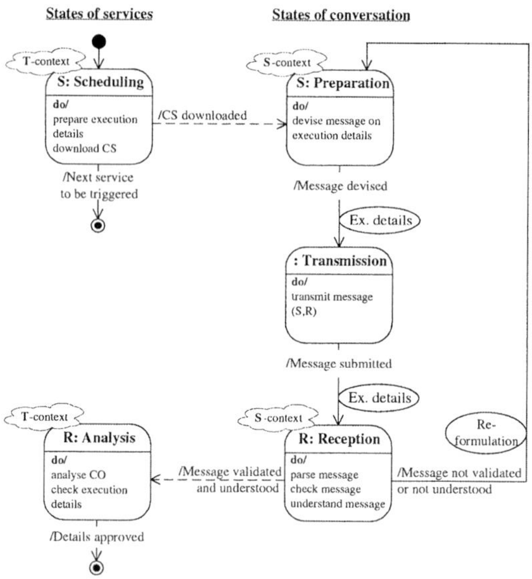

Fig. 4. State chart of a conversation schema with a focus on execution

5 Implementation and Conclusion

As a first step of validating the approach of Fig. 2, we have developed a *conversation and Web services composition-manager*, using Borland JBuilder Enterprise Edition version 9.0 (www.borland.com/jbuilder/enterprise/index.html).

The manager integrates a set of tools, which allow for instance Web services' providers and users to create, compose, and execute services based on the different contexts. WSDL is used for Web services specification and UDDI is used for Web services announcement and discovery. Details of contexts and conversation sessions are structured as XML files. A dedicated XML editor is developed in order to create, validate, test, and monitor the different XML files. The validation of these files is based on two XML schemas (conversations.xsd and context.xds). In addition, the conversation manager offers an editor for describing the state charts of conversation sessions and composite services. The graphical editor provides means for directly manipulating conversations and service chart diagrams, states, and transitions graphically using drag and drop operations. All changes are reflected in real time into the corresponding conversation and context details, in the same way all modifications of the conversation or context details files are directly reflected into the graphical representation of the state chart.

In this paper, we presented our approach for integrating conversations into Web services composition. We mainly focussed on modeling these conversations using state charts, which in fact connect the state charts of the services that participate in these conversations. Both services and conversations have been contextualized to ensure that the actions of services and the progress of conversations consider the features of their surrounding environments. We promoted the idea that Web services have to engage in conversations in order to decide whether to join a composition process, what states to take with regard to the outcome of a conversation, and what actions to perform within these states.

References

1. S. Ahuja, N. Carriero, and D. Gelernter. Linda and Friends. *Computer*, 19(8), August 1986.
2. L. Ardissono, A. Goy, and G. Petrone. Enabling Conversations with Web Services. In *Proceedings of the Second International Joint Conference on Autonomous Agents & Multi-Agent Systems (AAMAS'2003)*, Melbourne, Australia, 2003.
3. B. Benatallah, F. Casati, and F. Toumani. Web Service Conversation Modeling, A Cornerstone for E-Business Automation. *IEEE Internet Computing*, 8(1), January/February 2004.
4. D. Beringer, H. Kuno, and M. Lemon. Using wscl in a uddi registry 1.02. http://www.uddi.org/pubs/wsclBPforUDDI_5_16_011.doc, 2001. UDDI Working Draft Best Pratices Document, Hewlett-Packard Company.
5. P. Brézillon. Focusing on Context in Human-Centered Computing. *IEEE Intelligent Systems*, 18(3), May/June 2003.
6. B. Burg. Agents in the World of Active Web Services. In *Proceedings of Second Kyoto Meeting on Digital Cities*, Kyoto, Japan, 2001.
7. B. Chaib-draa and F. Dignum. Trends in Agent Communication Language. *Computational Intelligence*, 18(2), 2002.
8. M. Huhns. Agents as Web Services. *IEEE Internet Computing*, 6(4), July/August 2002.
9. F. Lin and D. H. Norrie. Schema-based Conversation Modeling for Agent-oriented Manufacturing Systems. *Computers in Industry*, 46(3), October 2001.
10. Z. Maamar, B. Benatallah, and W. Mansoor. Service Chart Diagrams - Description & Application. In *Proceedings of The Alternate Tracks of The Twelfth International World Wide Web Conference (WWW'2003)*, Budapest, Hungary, 2003.
11. Z. Maamar, S. Kouadri Mostéfaoui, and H. Yahyaoui. Towards an Agent-based and Context-oriented Approach for Web Services Composition. *IEEE Transactions on Knowledge and Data Engineering*, 2005 (forthcoming).
12. Z. Maamar, N. C. Narendra, and W. J. van den Heuvel. Towards an Ontology-based Approach for Specifying Contexts of Web Services. In *Proceedings of The Montreal Conference on e-Technologies (MCETECH'2005)*, Montreal, Canada, 2005.
13. B. Medjahed, A. Bouguettaya, and A. Elmagarmid. Composing Web Services on the Semantic Web. *The VLDB Journal, Special Issue on the Semantic Web, Springer Verlag*, 12(4), 2003.
14. A. Tsalgatidou and T. Pilioura. An Overview of Standards and Related Technology in Web services. *Distributed and Parallel Databases, Kluwer Academic Publishers*, 12(3), 2002.
15. X. Yi and K. J. Kochut. Process Composition of Web Services with Complex Conversation Protocols: A Colored Petri Nets Based Approach. In *Proceedings of The Design, Analysis, and Simulation of Distributed Systems Symposium (DASD'2004)*, Arlington, Virginia, USA, 2004.

A Framework of Web Service Composition for Distributed XML Query Evaluation*

Kun Yue[1], Weiyi Liu[1], and Aoying Zhou[2]

[1] Department of Computer Science and Engineering, School of Information Science and Engineering, Yunnan University, 2 North of Cuihu Road, 650091 Kunming, China
kyue@ynu.edu.cn

[2] Department of Computer Science and Engineering, Fudan University, 220 Handan Road, 200433 Shanghai, China

Abstract. The generic architecture of Web services provides the Web data processing with a distributed and standardized infrastructure. It is indispensable to evaluate the composite services, e.g., the complex query evaluation on multiple data sources on the Web. In this paper, we propose a mediator framework as a middleware of Web service composition for distributed XML query processing on the heterogeneous data sources, regarding the system of the respective data source and the query processor as provider. In addition, lazy service processing as the optimization is proposed. Preliminary experiments and performance studies show our framework and the corresponding techniques are practical and efficient.

1 Introduction

The basic architecture of Web services lay out the primary Web service components including Provider, Broker and Requester, including such a series of standard protocols as XML, SOAP, WSDL, UDDI, etc. In Web service environments, legacy components can be efficiently managed in line with the Web based requirement while transparent to the requesters. Motivated by real applications, Web services related research issues are carried out increasingly, and Web service composition is one of most important aspects [1].

RDB and XML documents are two representative data sources. Moreover, XML is also the standard of Web data representation, transformation and exchange. There are many query languages and corresponding processors for XML data, such as *Quilt* language and *Kweelt* processor. Publishing relational data as XML, and transforming one XML to another are the most frequent and critical facets of XML-based query processing. By far, the generic publishing strategy and some optimizations are presented in [2]. The method of DTD-directed XML publishing and the DTD-conforming XML to XML transformation are proposed in [3] and [4] respectively. However, the complex query evaluation and the corresponding optimizations that concern both publishing and transformation are more challenging than those of the simple ones. In order to make facilitated the distributed query service reuse and integration, it is indispensable to provide standard interfaces that can be advertised on the Web and can be requested by the applications based on http protocol.

* This work is supported by the National Natural Science Foundation of China (No. 60263006), and Natural Science Foundation of Yunnan Province (No. 2002F0011M).

Y. Zhang et al. (Eds.): APWeb 2005, LNCS 3399, pp. 572–578, 2005.

Data integration systems typically consist of data sources and the mediators or warehouses that carry out some data processing and exchange w.r.t. a schema [5, 6, 7, 8]. It is natural that Web services are used as uniform wrappers for heterogeneous data sources, but also provide generic means to apply various transformations on the retrieved data. The generic architecture for XML data exchange has been the subject of increasing attention [9]. The architecture of Web service composition in P2P environments is presented in [10, 11]. In particular, SELF-SERV is specific application oriented for the definition of composition flow [10, 11]. And the concrete data processing in Web service environment is carried out in AXML [12], but the composition on queries is not concerned in that just the relationship among service calls is considered by lazy XML query evaluation [13]. Therefore, service composition of query processing or data retrieving on the distributed and heterogeneous data sources is the significant research issue based on above motivations and related work.

In this paper, we propose a framework of Web Service composition for query evaluation on distributed data sources. Regarding query as service, the method of Web-Service-customized complex XML query evaluation is proposed centered at concrete data processing, including composition and the corresponding optimizations. Generally, the central contributions of this paper can be summarized as follows:

- We propose a generic framework and concrete methods for RDB and XML query processing in information integration under Web service environment.
- We exploit the composite service of distributed XML query, and make full use of the existing query related techniques to enable the effective service composition adopting RDB publishing and XML transformation as the elementary services.
- We correspondingly propose the optimizations and present the preliminary experiments.

The remainder of the paper is organized as follows: Section 2 presents the basic structure of our framework, and the definitions and description of services. Then the optimization method is presented in Section 3. The experimental results and performance analysis are described in Section 4. Finally, we conclude and discuss the future work in Section 5.

2 From Elementary Service to Composite Service

Based on the classical mediator model [6] and Web Service architecture w.r.t. distributed queries, the "mediator" will be taken place by "Composite Service Evaluator", which distributes the service requests to "RDB Wrapper" and "XML Wrapper", integrate the

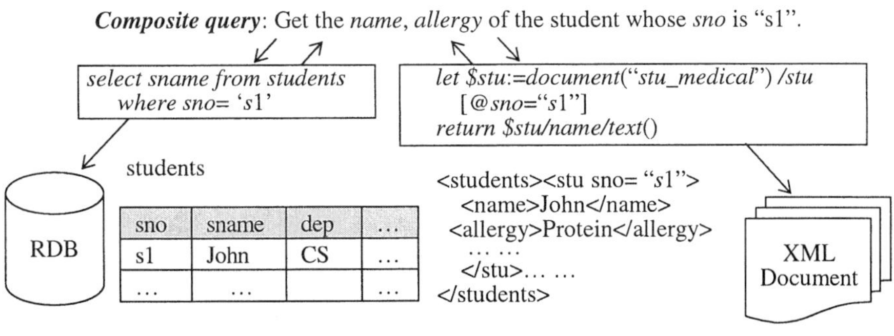

Fig. 1. A Composite Query on RDB and XML data sources

results. The concrete elementary services are *publishing* and *transformation* [3, 4]. Fig. 1 gives a motivating example of a composite query service on RDB and XML.

2.1 Description of Elementary Service and Composite Service

Definition1 (Elementary Service).
(1) An elementary service is a query invocation that just concerns one data source, either RDB or XML document. The registry information of an elementary service is (*URL*, *DSN*, *interface*), where *DSN* is the data source name, i.e., RDB name or XML document name including relational schema or XML DTD; *interface* accepts query statements.
(2) An elementary service returns the XML document by *publishing* the retrieved relational data or *transforming* the source XML by executing SQL or Quilt statements.

Definition 2 (Elementary Service Function). Suppose that *DSN* and *URL* can identify a data source uniquely, the elementary service can be uniformly expressed as the following declarative function of *S-Query*(*URL*, *DSN*, *query_statememt*).

For example, the elementary services on RDB and XML can be given as follows.

*Q*1: *Get the information of the dep. that the student whose sno is* "*s*1" *belongs to.*
*S-Query*1("10.11.3.41","*education*","*select dno, dname, dean, … from departments where dno in select dep from students where sno='s*1'")
*Q*2: *Get the medical information of the student whose sno is* "*s*1".
*S-Query*2("10.11.3.42", "*stu_medical*", "*let $stu:=document stu_medical*")/*stu*[@*sno*="*s*1"] *return $stu*")

As for the services and the procedures of service execution, there are three critical problems. First, what is the structure that publishing or transformation should conform to? Second, how does RDB wrapper or XML wrapper get the supervising structure to satisfy the composite query request? Third, how to tackle the more general cases that combine publishing and transformation? First of all, the composite query structure is defined.

Definition 3 (Composite Query Structure Tree). A composite query structure is a tree that the query result, in XML format, should conform to, denoted by *CQST*. For simplicity, we consider the tree structure not to be a graph. Similar to DTD, $CQST=<r, V, E>$, where r is the root, V is the node set, and $E=\{c|c=(v_1, v_2)$, is an edge from v_1 to v_2, $v_1\in V$, $v_2\in V\}$. $L\subset V$ is the set of leaf nodes in *CQST*.

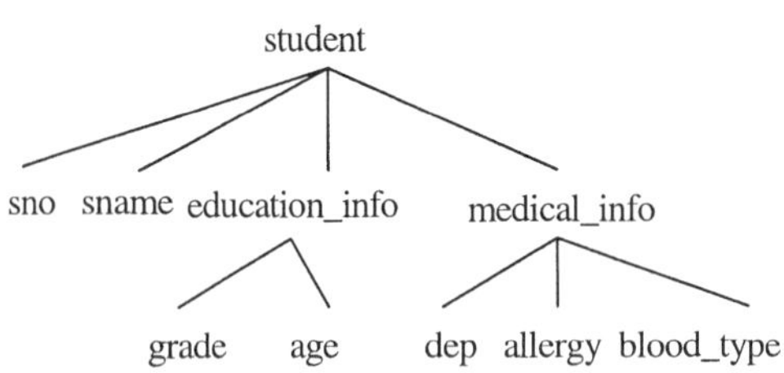

Fig. 2. An example composite query structure tree

grade→get(grade, education_info) ⇒ *S-Query*("10.11.3.41", "*education*", "*select grade from students where sno ='s*1'")

age→get(age, education_info) ⇒ *S-Query*("10.11.3.42","*stu_medical*", "*let $stu:=document*("*stu_medical*")/*stu* [@*sno*="*s*1"] *return $stu/age/text*()")

Fig. 3. Two query productions

Definitions 4 (Query Production in *CQST*). Supervised by *CQST* structure, in order to retrieve the required data, each leaf node $l \in L$ is attached to a query invocation, and the production on l is defined as $l \rightarrow get(l, pn)$, where pn is the parent node of l and $pn \in V$, i.e., $\exists c \in E$, such that $c=(pn, l)$. The actual service invocation on l is *S- Query* function as Definition 3. That is, $l \rightarrow get(l, pn) \Rightarrow$ *S-Query*(*URL*, *DSN*, *query_statement*).

CQST describes the orders and procedures for the composite query service execution, in which the query productions attached to the leaf nodes, define the concrete and respective operations to fill the hierarchical *CQST* step by step. Taking Fig. 1 as the example, Fig. 2 and Fig. 3 show a composite query structure tree and some query productions respectively.

2.2 Composite Logic Guided Query Service Evaluation

CQST gives the service composition logic and the pre-defined structure, so that the evaluation of composite query services can be simplified as the execution of *publishing* and *transformation* mentioned above. For instance, in Fig. 2, "*grade*" information can be returned by adding a tag "*grade*" to the retrieved relational data as the XML fragment:

<grade>grade 2**</grade>**.

As for "*age*", the XML wrapper revises the received *query_statement* parameter by adding some desired tag of the XML fragment:

<age> *let $stu:=document("stu_medical")/stu[@sno="s1"] return $stu/age/text()* **<age>**.

Following, the next procedure is to construct the result subtree guided by *CQST* bottom-up. Definition 5 gives the description of combination referring to the ideas in [9].

Definition 5 (XML Fragment Combination). Suppose the two fragments are $frag_1$ and $frag_2$, and the corresponding query productions are $l_1 \rightarrow get(l_1, pn_1)$, $l_2 \rightarrow get(l_2, pn_2)$ respectively, if $pn_1 = pn_2 = pn$, then $frag_1$ and $frag_2$ should be combined into one subtree as the child of *Pn* by executing the operation of $combine(XMLfragment_1, XMLfragment_2)$.

There are various cases of *transfer* and *combine*. The first case is that the fragment on RDB spot is transferred to XML spot, and the *combine* is carried out on XML spot to generate the result. The second case is that the fragment on XML spot is transferred to RDB spot, and the *combine* operation is done on RDB spot. The third case is that both fragments on RDB spot and XML spot are transferred to the client, and then combined. As for these alternatives, we choose the optimal one according to their median total execution costs.

Thus, not only these techniques can be extended to process nested and aggregation queries across the RDB and XML wrappers, but also the composite service can be invocated as a virtual elementary service to generate more complex query services.

3 Lazy Query Service Processing as Optimization

In *CQST*, for a set of query productions with the same parent node, the frequent initializations on RDB or XML are equivalent and carried out repeatedly if they are processed one by one in immediate mode. However, the lazy query processing on the leaf nodes in *CQST* can be done in bulk mode by partitioning the continuous query productions into some sections. The queries in one section will have the same parent node and the same selected data source. *Lazy-Process* algorithm is invoked during the pre-order traversal of *CQST*, shown in Algorithm 1, in which the inputs are *CQST* and the set of query productions, $\{l_i \rightarrow get(l_i, pn_i) \Rightarrow S\text{-}Query(URL, DSN, query\_statement)\}$.

Algorithm 1: Lazy-Process
{ $\mathfrak{R}$ to denote the queue of query productions}
{*source*() to represent the data source}
1. l_0 is the first leaf node when traversal, $\mathfrak{R} := \mathfrak{R} + (l_0 \rightarrow get(l_0, pn_0))$, i:=0, i:=i+1
2. for the leaf nodes in *CQST* do
3.   if $pn_i = pn_{i-1}$ and $source(l_i) = source(l_{i-1})$ then
4. $\mathfrak{R} := \mathfrak{R} + (l_i \rightarrow get(l_i, pn_i))$
5.   else
6.   Bulk-Evaluate ($\mathfrak{R}$), $\mathfrak{R} := \mathfrak{R} + (l_i \rightarrow get(l_i, pn_i))$
7.   end if
8. i:=i+1
9. end for

Algorithm 2: Bulk-Evaluate
Input: Query Production Set $\mathfrak{R}$
1. Initialize the date source (all productions in $\mathfrak{R}$ have the same data source)
2. if $\mathfrak{R} \neq \Phi$ then
3.   reconstruct query function for all productions in $\mathfrak{R}$
4.   execute the query statement
5. end if
6. $\mathfrak{R} := \Phi$

For example, the "*allergy*" and "*blood_type*" nodes in *CQST* of Fig. 2 are attached to the query productions of "*allergy*→*get*(*allergy*, *medical_info*)" and "*blood_type*→ *get*(*blood_type*, *medical_info*)". They have the same parent node of "*medical_info*" and the same data source of "*stu_medical*", so the lazy optimization is feasible to be performed.

4 Experimental Results

In this section, we present the experimental results and the performance studies of our framework, and especially for the lazy processing of query services. Our experiments were conducted on the machine with a 1.4GHZ P4 processor, 512M of main memory, running the operating system of Windows XP Home Edition. Our codes were written in JAVA, and JDBC-ODBC is used to communicate with DB2 (UDB 7.0). The size of the buffer pool is 30M. The artificial data set is used including the XML document conforming to a specific DTD, and the relational data of specific relational schemas, which is similar to those in Fig. 1. The XML query structure tree for the composite service result in Fig. 2 is used.

In the experiments, we take the number of "*student*" entities as the size of RDB and XML data source. At the same time, we take the node number of the result XML document, evaluated conforming to the pre-defined *CQST*, as the size of query service workload.

The costs of the lazy query service processing and the immediate version are given and compared. The query productions are processed one by one in immediate mode, while processed in bulk manner in lazy mode, in which a section of queries are processed in each pass. Fig. 4 gives the comparison of the two strategies w.r.t the same size of service workload It is clear that the lazy strategy is much better than the immediate one until the data source is very large. Following, as for immediate and lazy modes, we carried out the experiments on the same data source of 1000 "*student*" entities, to give the comparison with the increase of the sizes of query service workloads as the measure of the desired evaluation results. It can be seen from Fig. 5 that the lazy method is more scalable for the size-increasing services compared to the immediate one, and it can improve the performance of composite service execution by an order of magnitude.

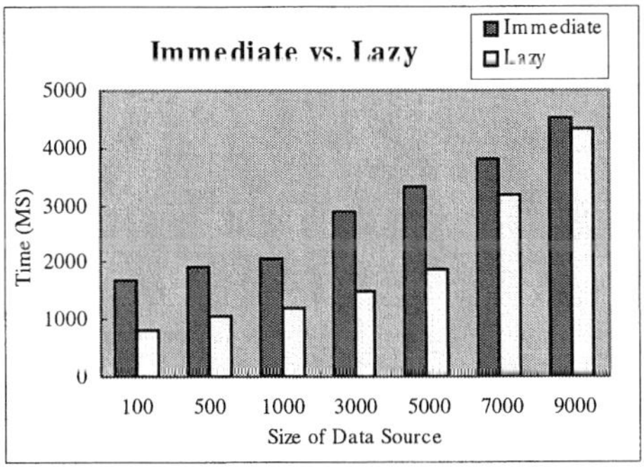

Fig. 4. Immediate vs. Lazy (Different Sizes of Data Sources)

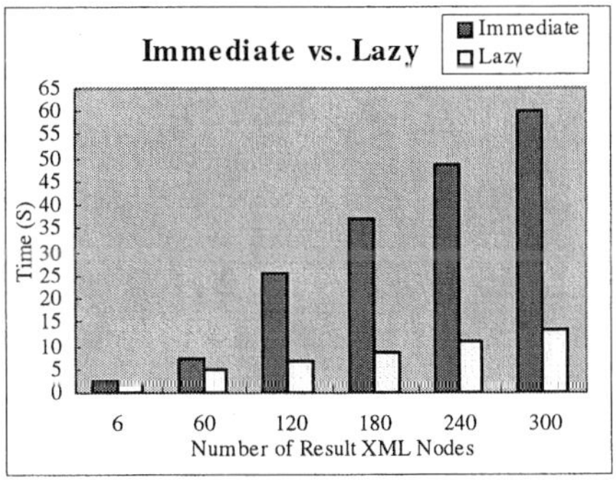

Fig. 5. Immediate vs. Lazy (Different Sizes of Results)

In addition, we also perform the experiments for cost based data source selection, and *combine* and *transfer* alternative strategies that are mentioned in Section 2. However, it will not be described here for space limitation.

5 Conclusion and Future Work

In this paper, we propose a middleware framework of Web service Composition for distributed XML query evaluation based on the mediator architecture and the corresponding composite query service evaluation strategies. As well, this paper arouses some interesting research issues from the inherent point of Web Services, such as cache and materialization mechanisms to improve the query service evaluation. Then, if the semantics are considered in service processing, some heuristic approaches can be used as the optimization to exclude some useless retrieval. As well, statistics based methods can be used in the discovery of Web service semantics, and automatic composition, including the real application development. Most of these issues are out current or future work.

References

1. Yue, K., Wang, X., Zhou, A.: The Underlying Techniques for Web Services: A Survey. Journal of Software. 3(2004) 428–442
2. Shanmugasundaram, J., Shekita, E., Barr, R., Carey, M., Lindsay, B., Pirahesh, H., Reinwald, B.: Efficiently Publishing Relational Data as XML Documents. In: VLDB. (2000) 65–76
3. Benedikt, M., Chan, C., Fan, W., Rastogi, R., Zheng, S., Zhou, A.: DTD-directed Publishing with Attribute Translation Grammars. In: VLDB. (2002) 838–849

4. Zhou, A., Wang, Q., Guo, Z., Gong, X., Zheng, S., Wu, H., Xiao, J., Yue, K., Fan, W.: TREX: DTD-Conforming XML to XML Transformations. In: SIGMOD. (2003) 670
5. Papakonstantinou, Y., Vassalos, V.: Query Rewriting for Semistructured Data. In: SIGMOD. (1999) 455–466
6. Wiederhold, G.: Mediators in the Architecture of Future Information Systems. In: IEEE Computer C-24. 1 (1992) 38–49
7. H. Garcia-Molina, Y. Papakonstantinon, D. Quass, A. Rajaraman, Y. Sagiv, V. Vassalos, J. Ullman, J. Widom. The TSIMMIS Approach to Mediation: Data Models and Languages. Journal of Intelligent Information Systems. 8 (1997) 117–132
8. A. Halevy, Z. Ives, D. Suciu, I. Tatarinov. Schema Mediation in Peer Data Management Systems. In: ICDE. (2003) 505–516
9. Amer-Yahia, S., Kotidis, Y.: A Web-Services Architecture for Efficient XML Data Exchange. In: ICDE. (2004) 523–534
10. Sheng, Q. Z., Benatallah, B., Dumas, M., Oi-Yan Mak, E.: SELF-SERV: A Platform for Rapid Composition of Web Services in a Peer-to-Peer Environment. In: VLDB. (2002)
11. Benetallah, B., Dumas, M., Sheng, Q., Ngu, A.: Declarative Composition and Peer-to-Peer Provisioning of Dynamic Services. In: ICDE. (2002) 297–308
12. Abiteboul, S., Benjelloun, O., Manolescu, I., Milo, T., Weber, R.: Active XML: Peer-to-Peer Data and Web Services Integration. In: VLDB. (2002)
13. Abiteboul, S., Benjelloun, O., Cautis, B., Manolescu, I., Milo, T., Preda, N.: Lazy Query Evaluation for Active XML. In: SIGMOD. (2004) 227–238

An Agent-Based Compositional Framework

R. Anane[1], Y. Li[2,*], C.-F. Tsai[3], K.-M. Chao[1], and M. Younas[1]

[1] DSM Research Group, School of MIS, Coventry University, UK
{r.anane, k.chao, m.younas}@coventry.ac.uk
[2] Software School, Fudan University, Shanghai, P.R. China
liys@fudan.edu.cn
[3] Department of IM, Aletheia University, Taiwan
tsai@email.au.edu.tw

Abstract. Web services requirements for means of automating the coordination of distributed heterogeneous applications have been addressed by a two-pronged initiative. One has been driven by process management technologies, represented by the compositional language BPEL4WS, and the other by the Semantic Web technologies, represented by ontologies and agents. The framework presented in this paper integrates agent technology with BPEL4WS, to enable two levels of coordination, namely local and centralised coordination through composition, and wider, distributed coordination by means of negotiation between agents. This framework takes advantage of the efficient management of processes in BPEL4WS and of the flexibility and versatility of agents. A design and run-time environment, called SOA, has been developed to evaluate the feasibility of the framework.

1 Introduction

The execution of distributed applications, in general, and Web services, in particular, requires coordination. In the process management approaches, this has seen the development of compositional languages for workflow management, such as BPEL4WS. The underlying models are relatively efficient and their behaviour is predictable. Interactions take place in a well-defined and stable environment, with clearly specified components; coordination is by workflow management. They implement a static binding policy, and operate at the syntactic level. In Semantic Web technologies, on the other hand, the aim is to go beyond mere interoperation towards increased automation. Of importance in this context is the creation of semantically rich entities that can display intelligent behaviour and engage in meaningful negotiation [1].

These two forms of coordination, namely workflow management and negotiation, are complementary and can be successfully integrated by adding semantics to the composition process of Web services [2]. One key feature of this work of integration is the dynamic discovery and utilisation of Web services. As an example of integration, wrappers were used to make Web services behave like agents [3]. The

* Corresponding author.

Y. Zhang et al. (Eds.): APWeb 2005, LNCS 3399, pp. 579–584, 2005.

work presented in this paper is concerned with the development of a framework based on a symbiotic relationship between agents and Web services, within a BPEL4WS platform. The aim is to reconcile the two forms of coordination, so that Web services can be composed, discovered dynamically, reasoned upon and executed efficiently by workflow management.

The rest of the paper is organised as follows. Section 2 defines the main issues in Web service composition. Section 3 gives an introduction to Semantic Web technologies and agents. Section 4 presents a conceptual view of the proposed framework. Section 5 deals with the implementation of the system. Section 6 puts the framework in context, and Section 7 concludes the paper.

2 Web Services and BPEL4WS Composition

One consequence of the decoupling of ownership of software from its use in Web services is that the binding of services can be performed dynamically. Web services are further enhanced by the introduction of formalisms for composing them into new Web services, which can be discovered and invoked in response to user requirements [4]. BPEL4WS is a workflow-based composition language for describing interactions of Web services as business processes [5]. A new composite Web service can be generated from the aggregation of other Web services. Its interface can be described as a set of WSDL *PortTypes*, in the same manner as for atomic Web services.

BPEL4WS and its engine, BPWS4J, offer predicable behaviour and performance. BPEL4WS has, however, some limitations, in particular its centralised workflow enactment and the fact that Web services must be known and defined *a priori* [6]. The main criticism levelled at these technologies is that they operate at the syntactic level, are implementation focused and require human intervention at various stages [7]. In contrast, the Semantic Web technologies underline the fact that the drive towards more automation and meaningful interaction between Web services requires greater semantic content in the descriptions.

3 Semantic Web Technologies and Agents

The semantic gap between XML-based constructs and agents can be bridged by use of Semantic Web technologies, such as OWL-S [8]. The aim of the Semantic Web initiative is to provide technologies that will enable heterogeneous systems to collaborate in the execution of an activity. For Web services description, the introduction of OWL-S is a significant factor in matching service providers and service requestors [9]. OWL-S is an ontology for providing richer Web service description, and has three components:

1. ServiceProfile: describes what the service does, its inputs and outputs and its preconditions and effects (IOPE); this is equivalent to UDDI content.
2. ServiceModel: describes how the service works (control and dataflow in its use). This is similar to BPEL4WS.
3. ServiceGrounding: describes how the service is implemented and provides a mapping from OWL-S to WSDL.

Agents are suitable for highly dynamic environments and operate at a conceptual level. BDI agents [10] are particularly apt at exploiting the semantically rich environment defined by OWL-S ontologies [11]. These agents hold beliefs (B), have goals (D) and use Intentions/plans (I) to achieve their goals. An agent can be generated from an OWL-S structures. The ServiceProfile in OWL-S maps to an agent's beliefs (B). The ServiceModel is mapped to a set of intentions associated with plans (I). Preconditions and effects from the ServiceProfile will translate into conditions and effects for the BDI plan. The desire (D) is specified by additional functionality in conjunction with the specification of the ServiceProfile. In essence, the ServiceProfile and the ServiceModel in OWL-S provide the semantics, while the Service Grounding is used to generate the interface signatures.

4 A BPELWS Compositional Framework with Agents

The framework is defined at two levels: the specification of compositions and enactment of the process. The first level concerns the composition process and introduces virtual Web services (VWS) as potential partners, alongside ordinary, concrete Web services. Virtual Web services decouple the composition process from the binding of Web services. A virtual Web service specifies its input and output requirements and associates itself with a nominal *PortType*; its is used in the composition in the same manner as an ordinary Web service. Composition within this framework involves incorporating concrete Web services when known and statically bound, and virtual Web services when unknown and to be dynamically bound.

The second level is identified with the binding of the VWS, and therefore with the enactment of the BPEL4WS process. This requires a mechanism for implementing late or dynamic binding. This form of binding is performed by an agent, which operates on the high-level semantics provided by OWL-S. At design time, two stages are required in order to generate an agent. A VWS, mainly identified by its input/output (I/O), is first augmented with richer semantics provided by OWL-S; the VWS is now endowed with IOPE properties. A BDI agent is subsequently generated from the OWL-S description. The agent obtains the semantic description and combines it with its reasoning mechanism. Once the agent is created from the OWL-S structures it acts as a proxy for the VWS; the OWL-S description is kept for documentation and reasoning purposes. The role of this agent is akin to that of a broker, since it takes requests from a VWS, performs the necessary matchmaking tasks, and then invokes the corresponding Web service on behalf of the VWS.

5 Implementation

The implementation involves the provision of an appropriate structure for the VWS, a mechanism for generating an agent from an OWL-S description and a specification of the interaction between the virtual Web service and the agent. A VWS includes operators that trigger events in the agent when it receives the request from the BPWS4J engine, or forwards an input to BPWS4J when the agent relays the required input from other agents or Web services. The VWS contains only interfaces to agents.

In order to facilitate the process of creating service-oriented agents, a template agent was designed, with two elementary functions: one for listening to events triggered by a VWS, and the other one for passing the response from other agents to the VWS. The required input and output must be explicitly described in the agent. The template agent also includes a number of generic coordination protocols such as contract net, English auction, reverse auction etc. A matchmaking mechanism is required for discovering appropriate Web services, according to syntactic signatures and semantic requirements of the composition process. The auction coordination protocol is used to coordinate the selection process.

We have implemented a system with a flexible GUI, in order to support the architectural framework presented above. The system, SOA (Service-Oriented Agent) 1.2 studio [12] includes a template for creating VWS and a template for creating agents (see Figure 1). A GUI was designed so that users can describe semantics of Web services and incorporate OWL-S descriptions. JAXRPC 1.3 and Tomcat are used to support the Web services. For composition the IBM BPWS4J 2.1 engine and BPEL4WS Editor Eclipse plug-in provide an environment for creating and interpreting workflows.

Agent technology was incorporated by means of two components. JADE agent is used for reasoning and communication, while OWL JessKB [13] provides the reasoning capability over OWL-S profiles in the agent. Once the users specify the required information, the studio allows the generation and compilation of code to take place in the same environment. Figure 1 show a GUI provided by SOA for inputting the ServiceProfile information in OWL-S. The user can also specify the ServiceGrounding profile, which can be stored as a project; essential Java code can then be generated, compiled and executed. The SOA creates agents and deploys them, as shown in Figure 2.

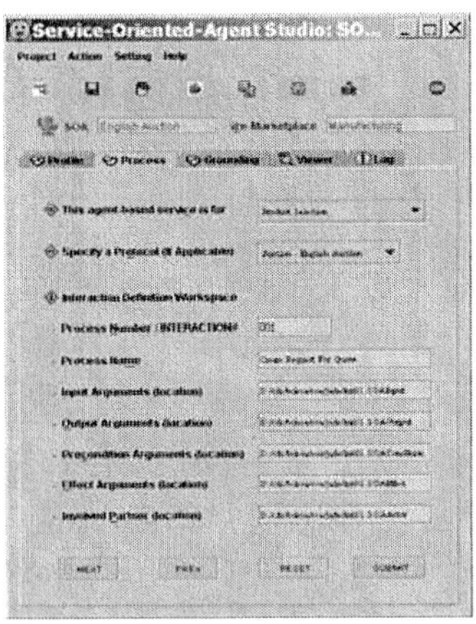

Fig. 1. Model and Profiles in SOA

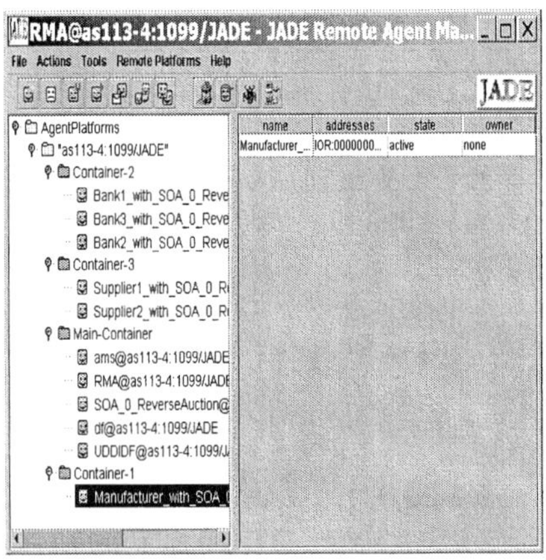

Fig. 2. Agent Platform in SOA

Since the proposed system is to provide an integrated environment for developing agent-based Web services, usability, as a criterion for evaluation, acquires special significance. Users can take advantage of the templates that the system provides for the creation of agents and their coordination. They can easily enhance Web services with semantics through a user friendly GUI. The system combines input from users and templates and generates the necessary code. This can reduce design time and ensure consistency.

6 The Framework in Context

In this section an attempt is made at putting the proposed framework in context, by considering two approaches to composition. In [6], the rationale is to move away from the rigidity of workflow enactment of BPEL4WS/BPWS4J to the decentralised and flexible mode of coordination of multi-agent systems. The work is aimed at producing a multi-agent enactment from BPEL4WS composition. This approach offers flexibility and can lead to the optimised use of resources. Its main drawback, however, is the added complexity entailed by a transition from one domain of execution to another. Closer to the work described in this paper is the model presented in [14] where BPEL4WS is enhanced by Semantic Web technologies as a means of overcoming the limitations of BPWS4J. BPEL4WS is extended with a Semantic Discovery Service (SDS), which acts as a proxy between BPWS4J and the potential partners to be located and selected dynamically. All requests to previously selected partners are directed to the SDS, which implements a late-binding policy. This model preserves the original BPEL4WS structure.

Although our work is less ambitious in scope, the model we propose offers more flexibility and customisation because each virtual Web service is associated with an agent. The decentralisation of the discovery process makes the system more reliable and avoids the single point of failure of the SDS. These features may, however, be costly in computational and in storage terms, not least because of the duplication of resources. The model may require a heavier human intervention than the SDS-based model, because of the semantic enrichment. Both models maintain, however, the original composition structure. The approach promoted by the framework allows for an incremental development of composition and combines the predictability of BPEL4WS enactment with the versatility of Semantic Web technologies.

7 Conclusion

The requirement for the provision of mechanisms to support a two-level mode of coordination has led to the development of a hybrid system that capitalises on the efficiency afforded by compositional BPEL4WS platform and on the versatility of Semantic Web and agent technologies. This was achieved by enhancing Web services through a symbiotic relationship with agent technology. This has allowed, on one hand, for the implementation of dynamic binding of Web services and incorporation into BPWS4J, and for Web services to engage, through its manifestation as an agent, in autonomous behaviour and active negotiation. The system is operational and work is currently carried out on further enhancement and integration of agent technology.

References

1. Chen, J-H, Chao, K-M, Godwin, N., Soo, V-W.: Combining Cooperative and Non-Cooperative Automated Negotiations. Information Systems Frontiers, Kluwer Academic Publisher (2005) (to appear)
2. Sirin, E., Parsia, B., Hendler, J.: Filtering and selecting Semantic Web Services with Interactive Composition Techniques, IEEE Intelligent Systems (July/August 2004) 42-49
3. Knoblock, C., Minton, S., Ambie, J. L., Muslea, M., Oh J., Frank, M: Mixed-initiative, multi-source information assistants, In: Proceedings of the World Wide Web Conference, ACM press, New York, NY (2001) 697-707
4. Limthanmaphon, B., Zhang, Y.: Web Service Composition with Case-Based Reasoning. In: 14th Australasian Database Conference (ADC 2003), Adelaide, South Australia (February 2003) 201-208
5. Khalaf, R., Mukhi, N. , Weerawarana, S.: Service-oriented Composition in BPEL4WS. [Online]. Available: http://www2003.org/cdrom/papers/alternate/P768/choreo_html/ p768-khalaf.htm (2003)
6. Vidal, J. M., Buhler, P., Stahl, C.: Multiagent Systems with Workflows. IEEE Internet Computing (January/February 2004) 76-82
7. Richards, D., van, Spunter S., Brazier, F.M.T., Sabou M.: Composing Web Services using and Agent Factory. In: AAMAS Workshop on Web Services and Agent-Based Engineering (2003) 57-66
8. Huhns, M. N.: Agents as Web Services. IEEE Internet Computing (July/August 2002) 93-95
9. Richards, D., Sabou, M., van, Splunter, S., Brazier, F.M.T.: Artificial Intelligence: a Promised Land for Web Services. In: Proceedings of The 8th Australian and New Zealand Intelligent Information Systems Conference (ANZIIS2003) Macquarie University, Sydney, Australia (December 2003) 205-210
10. Rao, S. A., Georgeff, M. P.: BDI Agents: From Theory to Practice. In: Conference Proceedings of 1st international conference on multiple agent system (1995) 312-319
11. Hendler, J.: Agents and the Semantic Web. IEEE Intelligent Systems (March/April 2001) 30-37
12. Li, Y., Ghenniwa, H. H., Shen, W.: Agent-based Web Services Framework and Development Environment. Journal of Computational Intelligence (2004)
13. Joseph, B., Kopena, William, C. Regli: DAMLJessKB: A Tool For Reasoning With The Semantic Web. In: 2nd International Semantic Web Conference (ISWC2003), Sanibel Island, Florida, USA (October 20-23 2003)
14. Mandell, D. J., McIlraith, S.: The Bottom-Up Approach to Web Service Interoperation. International Semant Web Conference (2003) 227-241

Integrating Web Services into Ontology-Based Web Portal

Jian Zhou, Yong Yu, Lei Zhang, Chenxi Lin, and Yin Yang

APEX Data and Knowledge Management Lab,
Department of Computer Science and Engineering,
Shanghai JiaoTong University, 200030, China
{priest, yyu, zhanglei, linchenxi, yini}@apex.sjtu.edu.cn

Abstract. With the explosive emerged Web services, the Web becomes a world of information and applications. So portals whose goal is presenting a structured view onto the Web should provide users with a single point access to multiple types of not only information but also services. Recently, many systems have been developed using ontology-driven approaches to automatically generate and manage Web portals. However, all of them lack the integration of Web services. In this paper, we describe SPortS, an OWL-DL(Web Ontology Language-Description Logics) based portal generation system that integrates semantic Web services into generated portals at the presentation level, the data level and the function level. We present the portal generation process, the query decomposition and the service recommendation algorithms through which semantic Web services are integrated tightly into the generated portal.

1 Introduction

Currently Web portals which try to weave loosely pieces of Web into a structured view for a special interested group of people have received much attention. Leading industry companies like Microsoft[1] and IBM[2] have developed products for automatically generating and maintaining portals. They provide an extensible framework that lets information and services be easily plugged in and allows the end user personalize and organize their own view of the portal. However the lack of semantics makes the generated portals difficult to be processed by machines.

In order to solve the problems mentioned above, a lot of research has gone into ontology-based Web portal generation and maintenance. SEAL[1] provides a general framework for developing semantic portals. Numerous tools such as KAON portal[2], ODESeW[3], OntoWeaver[4], and OntoWebber[5] have been developed to help design, generate and maintain ontology-based Web portals. However, these systems lack the integration of Web services which may provide more dynamic information and richer functionalities.

[1] see http://www.microsoft.com/sharepoint/

[2] see http://www-106.ibm.com/developerworks/Websphere/zones/portal/proddoc.html

Y. Zhang et al. (Eds.): APWeb 2005, LNCS 3399, pp. 585–596, 2005.

In this paper, we propose a novel approach to combine semantics and services into a portal. A software framework called SPortS(**S**emantic + **Port**al + **S**ervice) has been designed and implemented to automatically generate service-integrated Web portals based on declarative specifications. The generated portals can provide users and computer agents with convenient access to everything they need to get their tasks done.

The major features of the system are the following:

- Based on the common OWL-DL[6] formalism, semantic Web services[7] and domain knowledge are processed and presented uniformly in our system.
- By decomposing complex queries until they can be answered using available Web services and domain knowledge, we unified the two information sources. The result is that, besides domain knowledge, information providing services which serve as an important extension can also transparently feed information to the portal.
- Through capturing recently visited concepts to form a semantic context, SPortS can dynamically recommend services that users may be interested in under the current context. In this way, not only the portal's functionalities are greatly enriched by these services but also the portal's contextual knowledge is exploited to help users act in the portal.
- In order for other programs and agents on the Semantic Web to visit the portal, SPortS exposes itself as Web services.
- SPortS uses OWL-DL as the underlying knowledge representation formalism. Compared with RDFS, OWL-DL is more expressive in describing the constraints on and relationships among ontologies. Meanwhile, unlike OWL-FULL, OWL-DL is decidable and computationally complete with support from many existing DL(Description Logics) reasoners (e.g. FaCT[8] and Racer[9]).

The rest of the paper is organized as follows. Firstly, we give an overview of the SPortS system in section 2. By explaining the Web portal generation and presentation process, section 3 shows how Web services are integrated in the presentation level. Then in section 4, we describe the query decomposition algorithm that integrates information from both Web services and domain knowledge. This explains how data level integration with Web services is achieved. Section 5 describes the dynamic context-sensitive recommendation of Web services in the generated portal. By recommending services to the user, the generated portal integrates the functions of the services. Finally, we discuss related work in section 6 and conclude the paper in section 7.

2 Overview of the SPortS System

In the design of the SPortS architecture(Fig.1), the main objective is to integrate Web services at the presentation level, the data level, and the function level. Among them, the data level plays a central role of driving the integration on the other two levels. In SPortS, data is stored in four knowledge bases which are all based on the OWL-DL formalism.

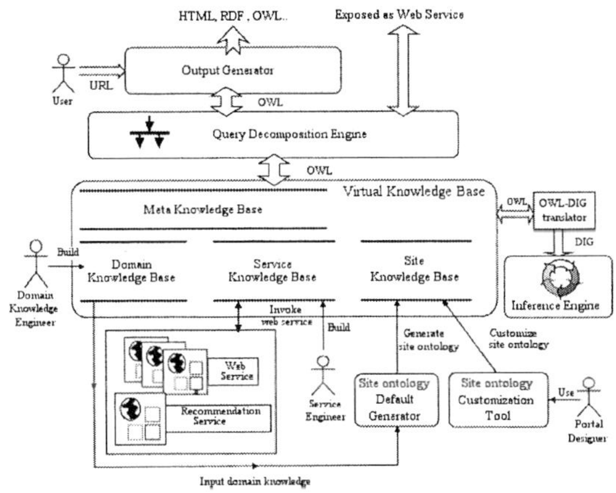

Fig. 1. SPortS architecture

Domain Knowledge Base stores the domain classes, properties, and individuals. It serves as the primary knowledge source for the portal.

Service Knowledge Base stores OWL-S[3] descriptions of all available semantic Web services. Through this knowledge base, SPortS can retrieve services' specifications to render or invoke them.

Site Knowledge Base contains the site ontology used to model the portal at a conceptual level and stores the declarative specification of the portal as the instance of the site ontology.

Meta Knowledge Base is designed to enable us to directly manipulate classes and properties in other knowledge bases as individuals. This capability is necessary in a semantic portal system because of the need to show and process both classes and individuals at the same time.

The four knowledge bases are grouped into a virtual knowledge base with a unified ontology. Queries issued to the virtual knowledge base can be expressed in the unified ontology without caring how knowledge from different knowledge bases and services are composed to answer them. This task is actually accomplished by the Query Decomposition Engine. In this way, information from different sources are integrated and can be accessed transparently.

The major task of the portal creation process is to prepare the four knowledge bases. The domain knowledge engineer builds the domain knowledge base from which the default site knowledge base is automatically generated by *the site ontology default generator*. After that, the portal designer uses a WYSIWYG tool to design the content, layout and navigational structure of the portal by changing the site knowledge base. At the same time, the service engineer is responsible for populating the service knowledge base with available semantic Web services.

[3] http://www.daml.org/services/owl-s/1.0/

Then there will be a running daemon called Output Generator which dynamically constructs a Web page for the user's request according to the virtual knowledge base. The construction process will be described in Section 3. The Query Decomposition Engine which is utilized by Output Generator to provide all data in the Web page is discussed in Section 4. Decomposed queries that can be answered by a single knowledge bases are ultimately processed with the help of the inference engine.

When a user browses Web pages in the portal, the Recommendation Service intelligently analyzes context knowledge and recommends services that the user may be interested in. The recommended service can be presented in the portal for invocation, which achieves function level integration. Section 3.2 and Section 5 will give more details about this process.

Recall that all Web pages are created on the fly based on the virtual knowledge base. So the change to the virtual knowledge base will simultaneously be reflected in the generated Web pages. It means that the maintenance work will only consist of updating the virtual knowledge base. This can greatly reduce the resources (manpower, money) for maintaining and editing the portal.

3 Portal Generation and Service Presentation

3.1 Site Ontology and Portal Generation

The site ontology is designed to model Web portals at a conceptual level. As shown in Fig.2, the site ontology includes the following core classes: *Web page*, *container*, *class binding* and *navigation rule.*

The class *Web Page* models the static view of the portal as a tree of containers. It has a property *hasRootContainer* which specifies the entry point of the recursive construction process. In this paper, we use our lab's internal portal, Apex-Lab-Portal, as an example. Fig.3 shows a Web page of the portal and the tree structure of its containers.

The class *Container* models the structure unit of Web pages. Container has two sub classes *Atomic container* and *Composite container.*

- Atomic Container are mainly used to present the concrete information. It has a property *hasParameter* which specifies a query over the virtual knowledge base. The answer to the query then compose the atomic container. Currently, queries can only be expressed in the form of OWL-DL

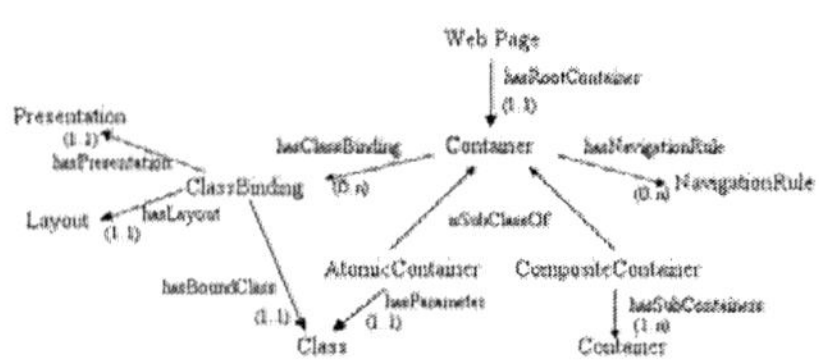

Fig. 2. Overview of the Site Ontology

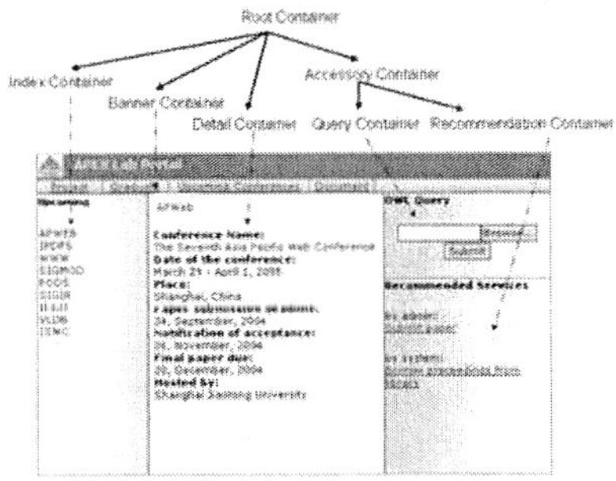

Fig. 3. A Web page of the Apex-Lab-Portal example

class descriptions. Hence, the content of an atomic container is the set of all individuals of the query class.

- Composite Container are mainly used to group and layout basic containers which will be described by the property *hasSubContainer*.

The class *Class Binding* models what properties of and how the individuals are displayed. Every class binding is attached to some containers and has a bound class. When an individual i in an atomic container O is to be presented, i must use a class binding B whose bound class C satisfies $i \in C$ and B must be attached to O or O's ancestors. For example, in Fig.3, the class binding of the DetailContainer determines that the names, date, place, etc. of the conference are displayed. Class binding has another two properties *hasLayout* and *hasPresentation* which will be described as follows:

- A presentation is actually a piece of program that completely handles the rendering of the individual. So the portal designer can customize the presentation for specific set of individuals. In this way, SPortS can present semantic Web services. We further discuss this issue in Section3.2.
- Layout models the algorithms which arrange the properties of the displayed individual and the values of these properties are presented recursively until a presentation can fully handle them.

The class *NavigationRule* models the navigational structure of the portal. Recall that a Web page is modelled as a tree of containers. Thus the navigation from one page to another is modelled as a tree transformation that replaces a subtree with another one. A rule will be triggered when an item satisfying specific conditions is clicked.

3.2 Presentation of Semantic Web Services

Based on the common OWL-DL formalism, semantic Web services and domain knowledge are processed and presented uniformly in our system. In this subsection, we show in detail how Web services are presented in exactly the same manner using the mechanism mentioned above.

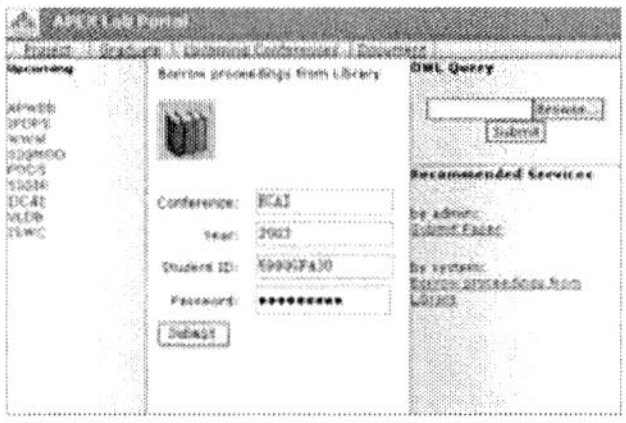

Fig. 4. Detailed View of the Borrow-Proceeding Service

In Fig.3, there is a RecommendationContainer that lists dynamically recommended Web services. The OWL-DL class description of its content is RecommendedService, whose individuals are retrieved by the Query Decomposition Engine (ref. Section 4) via the Recommendation Service (ref. Section 5). When the "Borrow proceedings from library" service link is clicked, a navigation rule which replaces the content of the DetailContainer with the clicked individual is activated. Fig.4 illustrates the result page.

We developed two specific presentations, ServiceInputPresentation and ServiceResultPresentation, to act as the proxy between the user and the Web service provider. The ServiceInputPresentation will generate a specific form according to every service's Input in service knowledge base. Then the user can input service parameters by filling the form. After the form is submitted, a navigation rule is activated to use the ServiceResultPresentation to capture the input, invoke the Web service and display the result in a uniform way.

In the future, the integration of Web services at presentation level can be more fantastic. There are some attempts to develop a standard for Web Services for Remote Portlets (WSRP)[10]. Its aim is to enable reuse of services at the presentation layer. So when it is being widely used, every WSRP-compliant Web service can be fully integrated into our portal without loss of even presentation details.

4 Query Decomposition on Virtual Knowledge Base

The primary motivation for designing the Query Decomposition Engine is to provide SPortS with the ability to get data from the virtual knowledge base without knowing whether it comes from domain knowledge bases or Web services. Then the data level integration which is at the core of the SPortS system can be achieved.

4.1 Problem Definition

Until now, there is no standard for how to query DL knowledge bases. In [11], a DL query language is proposed. However, just as [11] has stated, how to efficiently retrieve answer sets for the proposed query language is still an open problem. Besides, [11] showed that by *rolling up* role terms, many queries can be transformed into the form of a DL class expression. Then in order to make our system work, we formalize queries as OWL-DL class expressions in the unified ontology of the virtual knowledge base.

An information providing service's query answering capability can be described as the combination of its input/output class descriptions. Each input of a service will have an *input class description* to constrain its type. We simplify the output as another class of individuals, which is described as an output class O. Moreover, we require that the output class be constructed by inputs and constants with OWL-DL constructors. The O is called *output class description* which records the functional relationship between the output and the inputs.

By the formalization above, the problem then can be described as how to compose all services to retrieve all individuals of the query's class expression. In this sense, it is actually a problem of semantic composition of information providing services as we described in [12].

But besides normal services, there are also other information sources in the SPortS. The domain knowledge base with the support of a DL reasoning engine can answer any complex queries about it alone. So its capabilities can't be easily be described by OWL-DL class expressions. However, it can be dealt with separately in the query decomposition algorithm. Whenever a query (or part of a query) is going to be decomposed, it is first checked against domain knowledge base to see whether it can be answered entirely . It will be further decomposed if the domain knowledge base cannot handle it alone. In the following, we thus focus on how normal information providing services are described and composed.

4.2 Basic Ideas

In this subsection, we give a brief description of the query decomposition algorithm. A more complete and detailed description of the the algorithm and some discussion are available in [12].

Queries and capabilities of information providing services are expressed as OWL-DL class expressions. Therefore, in theory, the query decomposition algorithm needs to find a semantically-equivalent logic combination of several OWL-DL class expressions for a given OWL-DL query class. It is tightly related to the problem of DL query rewriting on views[13][14] . Currently in SPortS, we attack the problem through decomposing the query's syntax tree with regard to its semantics.

Any OWL-DL class expression can be parsed into a syntax tree. According to the OWL-DL abstract syntax definition in [6], the tree has 6 basic elements shown in Fig. 5. Note that in the figure union ($\sqcup$) is not regarded as a basic element of the syntax tree. Actually with the application of the De Morgan Law $A \sqcup B = \neg(\neg A \sqcap \neg B)$, all union operations can be normalized into intersection and complement operations. Furthermore, we normalize the query expressions and service output class descriptions so that no intersection operations contain intersection class operands (e.g. $(A \sqcap B) \sqcap C$ is normalized to $A \sqcap B \sqcap C$), and no complement operations contain complement class operands (i.e. $\neg(\neg A)$ is normalized to A).

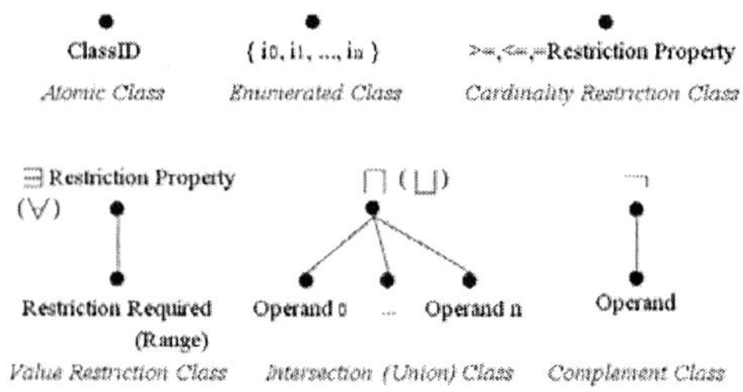

Fig. 5. OWL-DL Syntax Tree Elements

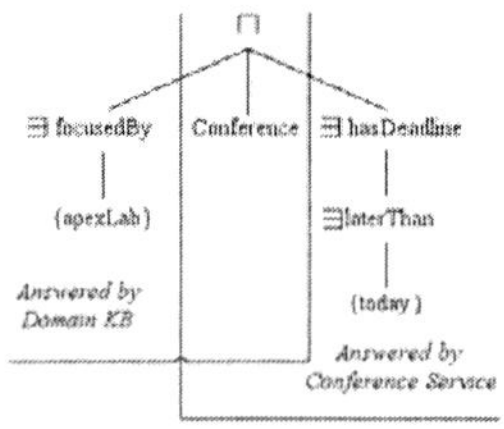

Fig. 6. Syntax Tree of Query

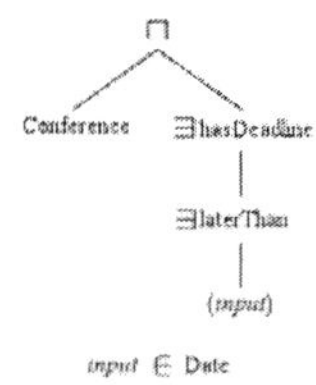

Fig. 7. Syntax Tree of Service Output

We will illustrate our basic ideas by our Apex-Lab-Portal example. In order to show a list of upcoming conferences focused by our lab in the IndexContainer, the query Q_A in the Apex-Lab-Portal example can be expressed as formula:

$$\exists\,\text{focusedBy}.\{\text{apexLab}\}\sqcap\text{Conference}\sqcap\exists\,\text{hasDeadline}.\,(\exists\,\text{laterThan}.\{\text{today}\}) \quad (1)$$

It can be parsed as a syntax tree shown in Fig.6. In the example, there is a service which has the capability to return a list of conferences whose paper submission deadlines are later than an input date. The input class description of the service's capability is the class Date. The output class description O is:

$$\text{Conference}\sqcap\exists\,\text{hasDeadline}.\,(\exists\,\text{laterThan}.\{\mathit{input}\}) \quad (2)$$

and its syntax tree is shown in Fig.7.

In addition, the Apex-Lab-Portal's domain knowledge base knows what conferences are focused by the lab. That is, the class

$$\exists\,\text{focusedBy}.\{\text{apexLab}\}\sqcap\text{Conference} \quad (3)$$

can be answered by the domain knowledge base. We can see that the intersection ($\sqcap$) of (2) and (3) is equivalent to (1) – the query Q_A. It is more clear seen on the Fig.6. (3) is the central-left part of the tree and (2) is the central-right part of the tree. The query is then equivalent to the intersection of the two parts. This example shows how the information providing service S_A and the domain knowledge base is composed together to answer a query. This idea can be seen as a horizontal decomposition. On the other hand, we also need a vertical decomposition method, i.e. query result of a sub-tree may be used as input to feed another service.

5 Recommendation of Services

In Web portals, especially E-Commerce portals, world changing services may play a pivotal role because they can perform real world (business) transactions. Many current semantic portals are limited to only presenting domain knowledge. Adding world changing services will greatly enrich the portal's functionality and help user act based on contextual knowledge. However, simply listing all available services on the portal is far from an appropriate integration method. Users may be overloaded with lots of irrelevant or uninteresting services. SPortS solves the problem by listing only those services that are contextually relevant. The function is provided by another information providing service – Recommendation Service.

Intuitively, the semantic context that determines which service is relevant includes the concepts/classes that the user recently visits. For instance, in our running Apex-Lab-Portal example, when the user clicks a conference link to show its details, he/she is probably interested in those services that involve related concepts, such as conferences, papers, proceedings, etc at that moment. However, with time, the user may gradually shift his/her focus to other concepts in the portal during his/her visit and the list of relevant services should change accordingly. We simulate this process by assigning temperatures to concepts that reflect their degrees of the user's attention. "Hotter" concepts receive more visits and the temperature will be dropped if it is not visited by the user for a while.

In SPortS, the semantic context is constructed based on an un-directional graph $G = (V, E)$ where V is the set of all the classes in the unified ontology of the virtual knowledge base and the edges in E are the semantic relations between classes. The graph can be obtained by converting the OWL-DL descriptions of the virtual knowledge base into an RDF graph. Currently in SPortS, we obtain the graph using a special algorithm that analyzes the OWL-DL class descriptions. For each vertex $c \in V$, a temperature $t(c)$ is assigned and for each edge $r \in E$ a thermal conduction factor $d(r)$ is assigned. All $t(c)$ are initialized to 0 and $d(r)$ are initialized according to the semantic types of r. For a path p consisting of edges $r_0, r_1, \ldots r_n$ in the graph, its thermal conduction factor $d(p) = \prod_{i=0}^{n} d(r_i)$. To measure the mutual influences between any pair of vertices c_1 and c_2, we define the maximum thermal conduction factor between them as $md(c_1, c_2) = max\{d(p) \,|\, p \text{ connects } c_1 \text{ and } c_2\}$ and we define $md(c, c) = 1$ for any c. Whenever a user visits some concepts by browsing a Web page, the following procedure is used to update the temperatures of concepts:

```
void update_temperature () {
  let C be the set of the currently visited concepts;
  let G = (V, E) be the entire graph;
  for each v ∈ V, t(v) = α * t(v); // α is a cooling coefficient.
  for each c ∈ C do
    for each v ∈ V do
      t(v) = t(v) + Δ * md(c, v); // Δ is the temperature increment.
  for all v ∈ V normalize t(v) into the range of 0..1;
}
```

The semantic context then consists of all the concepts and their current temperatures. Based on this context, the relevance value of a semantic Web service s is calculated as

$$rel(s) = \frac{t(c_0) + t(c_1) + \ldots + t(c_{n-1})}{n}$$

where c_i is the concept in the OWL-S description of s. The services are then ranked according to the relevance values $rel(s)$ and recommended to the user. In addition to the dynamic recommendation, SPortS also supports static recommendation that always recommends specific services for certain concepts. System administrators can utilize this feature to enforce business policies on service recommendation.

6 Related Work

Recently, a great variety of technologies and systems have been developed to achieve the goal of automatic semantic Web portal generation. Similar to SPortS, they use ontologies to model a data-intensive Web site at a conceptual level. As a result, the portal designer can focus on the conceptual structure of the target portal and domain knowledge, independently of its realization.

SEAL[1] proposed a generic architecture for developing, constructing and maintaining semantic portals, and extended the semantic modules to include a large diversity of intelligent means for accessing the Web site, like semantic ranking, machine accessing, etc.

ODESeW[3] is an ontology-based application designed on the top of WebODE[15] ontology engineering platform that automatically generates and manages a knowledge portal. It provides functions for content provision, content visualization, and content search and querying. It also provides an easy-to-use tool suite for the administration of the generated knowledge portals.

The OntoWebber[5] is a tool that was used to build the Semantic Web Community Portal as part of the OntoAgents project. It takes the sources from ontologies in RDF or semi-structured data like HTML with corresponding data translators.

IIPS[16] is another ontology based portal generating system. Similar to SPortS, It defines a site ontology to model the navigational structure and the compositional structure of a data-intensive Web site on the basis of pre-existing site modelling approaches. It provides explicit mapping mechanisms, which make it possible to generate quickly site implementations from the conceptual model. OntoWeaver[4] extends IIPS by proposing and introducing a customization framework into the ontology-based Web modelling approach to the design and maintenance of Web applications.

The fundamental difference between the SPortS approach and previous approaches is that SPortS tightly integrates semantic Web services, both information providing services and world changing services, into generated portals. Semantic portals generated by previous approaches are mostly limited to only presenting and editing domain knowledge. By integrating information providing services into the portal, more dynamic and up-to-date information from services can be combined with domain knowledge to serve the users. By adding services to the generated portal and recommending them according to semantic contexts, the portal's functionality is greatly enriched and the user can act on the contextual knowledge in the portal.

7 Conclusion and Future Work

In this paper, we have presented SPortS, an OWL-DL based semantic portal system that integrates semantic Web services into generated portals at the presentation level, the data level, and the function level. At the presentation level, semantic Web services can be uniformly presented as first class citizens with domain knowledge. At the data level, knowledge from information providing services can be retrieved and composed together with domain knowledge to answer complex queries. In this way, potentially broader and more up-to-date information from services can be synthesized. At the function level, the recommendation of services greatly enriches the generated portal's functionality and can help users act in the portal based on contextual knowledge.

Currently, the SPortS prototype system is limited in the following aspects. At the presentation level, the generated portal can only display Web services in a uniform way, so for those services which serve as desktop-applications, SPortS can only integrate their functions without presentation details. The WSRP standard can be used to solve this problem. At the data level, due to the lack of an appropriate OWL query language and the difficulties in decomposing queries, we cannot fully utilize the information to answer more queries with better results. At the function level, the portal personalization is not yet designed in the current prototype. For example, the semantic context used by the service recommendation does not include any personalization information. Our future work will be focused on these aspects.

References

1. Maedche, A., Staab, S., Stojanovic, N., Studer, R., Sure, Y.: SEAL – a framework for developing semantic web portals. In: Proceedings of the 18th British National Conference on Databases. Volume 2097 of LNCS. (2001) 1–22
2. R.Volz, D.Oberle, B.Motik, S.Staab: KAON server - a semantic web management system. In: Proceedings of the 12th International Conference on World Wide Web (WWW2003). Alternate Tracks - Practice and Experience, Budapest, Hungary (2003)
3. Corcho, O., Gómez-Pérez, A., López-Cima, A., López-García, V., Suárez-Figueroa, M.: ODESeW: automatic generation of knowledge portals for intranets and extranets. In: Proceedings of 2nd International Semantic Web Conference. Volume 2870 of LNCS., Springer (2003)

4. Lei, Y., Motta, E., Domingue, J.: Design of customized web applications with OntoWeaver. In: Proceedings of the international conference on knowledge capture (KCAP03), ACM Press (2003) 54–61
5. Jin, Y., Decker, S., Wiederhold, G.: OntoWebber: model-driven ontology-based web site management. In: Proceedings of SWWS'01, The first Semantic Web Working Symposium, Stanford University, California, USA, July 30 - August 1, 2001. (2001)
6. F.Patel-Schneider, P., Hayes, P., Horrocks, I.: OWL Web Ontology Language semantics and abstract syntax. W3C Recommendation, W3C (2004) http://www.w3.org/TR/owl-semantics/.
7. McIlraith, S., Son, T., Zeng, H.: Semantic web services. IEEE Intelligent Systems (Special issus on the Semantic Web) **16** (2001) 46–53
8. Horrocks, I.: The FaCT system. In: Tableaux98. (1998) 307–312
9. Haarslev, V., Moller, R.: Racer system description. In: Proceedings of the First International Joint Conference on Automated Reasoning, Springer-Verlag (2001) 701–706
10. Kropp, A., Leue, C., Thompson, R.: Web services for remote portlets specification. Oasis specification, OASIS (2003) http://www.oasis-open.org/committees/download.php/3343/oasis-200304-wsrp-specification-1.0.pdf.
11. Horrocks, I., Tessaris, S.: Querying the Semantic Web: A formal approach. In: Proceedings of the 1st International Semantic Web Conference (ISWC2002). LNCS 2342 (2002) 177–191
12. Lin, C., Yu, Y., Yang, Y., Zhang, L., Zhou, J.: Towards composing information providing services. In: Proceedings of the 2004 IEEE International Conference on Services Computing, IEEE Computer Society Press (2004) to appear.
13. Beeri, C., Levy, A.Y., Rousset, M.C.: Rewriting queries using views in description logics. In: Proceedings of PODS-97. (1997) 99–108
14. Goasdoue, F., Rousset, M.C.: Rewriting conjunctive queries using views in description logics with existential restrictions. In: Proceedings of the 2000 International Workshop on Description Logics. (2000) 113–122
15. Corcho, O., López, M.F., Pérez, A.G., Vicente, O.: WebODE: An integrated workbench for ontology representation, reasoning, and exchange. In: Proceedings of EKAW 2002. LNCS 2473 (2002) 138–153
16. Lei, Y., Motta, E., Domingue, J.: An ontology-driven approach to Web site generation and maintenance. Lecture Notes in Computer Science **2473** (2002) 219–234

Knowledge-Level Management of Web Information

Seung Yeol Yoo and Achim Hoffmann

School of Computer Science and Engineering University of New South Wales,
Sydney 2052, NSW, Australia
{syy, achim}@cse.unsw.edu.au

Abstract. We present a knowledge-rich software agent, **ContextExplicator**, which mediates between the Web and the user's information or knowledge needs. It provides a method for incremental knowledge-level management (i.e., knowledge discovery, acquisition and representation) for heterogeneous information in the Web.

In ContextExplicator, the incremental knowledge management works through iterative negotiations with the human user:

1. Automatic Word-Sense[1] Disambiguation and Induction. General knowledge (e.g., from a lexicon) and previously discovered knowledge support the sense-disambiguation & sense-induction of a word in the given documents, resulting in an improved and refined organization of previously discovered knowledge,
2. Interactive Specialization of Query Criteria. At a given moment, the user can reduce certain semantic ambiguities of previously discovered knowledge by selecting one of the context-words which are suggested by ContextExplicator to discriminate between sets of retrieved documents. The selected context-word is also used to direct the discovery of new knowledge in the given documents, and
3. Visualization of the Discovered Knowledge. The discovered knowledge is represented in a conceptual lattice. Each lattice-node represents a single word-sense or a conjunction of senses of multiple words. To each node the respectively identified documents are associated. Each web-document is multi-classified into relevant word-sense clusters (lattice nodes), according to the occurrences of specific word-senses in the respective web-document. As a conceptual lattice allows the user to navigate the word-sense clusters and the classified web-documents with multi-level abstractions (i.e., super-/sub-lattice nodes), it provides a flexible scheme for managing knowledge and web-documents in a scalable way.

1 Introduction

The Web provides virtually unlimited, but poorly organized information resources for a user's information or knowledge needs, resulting in information overload. Thus, the next-generation Web requires a knowledge-rich software agent which can

[1] In this paper, "term(s)" and "word(s)" are used interchangeably.

Y. Zhang et al. (Eds.): APWeb 2005, LNCS 3399, pp. 597–608, 2005.

practically mediate between the Web (i.e. web-documents containing knowledge) and a user (i.e., the user's query-intentions; the semantics which can be referred to by the conjunction of the relevant senses of relevant words).

In this paper, we introduce such a software agent (ContextExplicator), which incrementally supports knowledge management through iterative negotiations with a human user: 1) *Automatic Word-Sense Disambiguation and Induction.* It incrementally discovers knowledge in the given web-documents. For example, knowledge might be represented by some words in a web-document, thus ContextExplicator aims to disambiguate, induce and combine conjunctively the senses of those words, 2) *Interactive Specialization of Query Criteria.* It allows to incrementally narrow the search for web-documents by suggesting useful context-words occurring in the given web-documents, and by acquiring the user's selections. A selected context-word reflects the user's knowledge needs, and works to direct further knowledge discovery, and 3) *Visualization of Discovered Knowledge.* It visualizes the inherent lattice structure of co-occurred word-senses in the given web-documents, and classifies the given web-documents into relevant word-sense clusters. The heart of ContextExplicator is that newly added context-words and their selected word-senses can be used to incrementally articulate the user's information needs.

The rest of the paper is organized as follows. In Section 2, we briefly review related works. Section 3 describes our approach. We present an empirical evaluation along with an example of the system output in Section 4. Section 5 provides discussion and conclusion.

2 Related Works

The first step for managing heterogeneous information at the knowledge-level is to conceptually classify the available documents. To identify documents relevant to a given concept many approaches, including ours, utilize the context-similarities (i.e., the similarity between two sets of information-items which respectively surround information) as follows:

The Frequencies of Co-occurred Neighborhood Terms: In this approach, the context of a term is defined as the neighborhood terms of the term, in the given documents. It compares the context-similarity of a term in two different documents by calculating the frequencies of commonly co-occurred neighborhood terms. However, such approaches (e.g., information categorization [1], information retrieval [6]) did not address the problem of "how to incrementally discover knowledge in heterogeneous information sources, in a scalable way".

One suggested way to support an incremental knowledge discovery is to use a clustering method based on the co-occurrence frequencies among terms without considering their meanings in the given documents. For example, Context Vectors [2], [3], [9] and Latent Semantic Indexing [5] extract co-occurring terms and transform their associations into a decomposed vector model. The associations among terms can transitively be expanded through commonly co-occurred terms.

However, this results in the following two problems. Firstly, in a document, if "Travel" occurs with "Agent" and "Agent" occurs with "Automobile", then "Travel" and "Automobile" are considered as having some relationship. Let us assume that the document has some information about "a travel broker who also works for a car rental service". "Agent" means "a broker (person)", and "Automobile" means "car". In another document, "Agent" occurs with "Automobile". Let us assume that the document has information about "coolant for car radiator". "Agent" means "a kind of substance" in that document. In this situation, using only the co-occurrence frequencies based on the same word-form (e.g., "Agent") can cause critical problems to recognize the real meaning of words in the given documents. Secondly, it can also give lower priority to really important context-words to explicate the knowledge in documents, because it does not consider a user's knowledge needs. For example, in the first document above, the meaning "a broker (person)" of "Agent" should be constrained by the context-word "Travel" rather than "Automobile", to be distinguished from the sense "a kind of substance" of "Agent" in the second document. However, in the above case, higher priority will be assigned to "Automobile" as the context-word of "Agent" than to "Travel", because "Agent" and "Automobile" have co-occurred more frequently.

The Occurrence of Predefined Concepts: This approach constrains the possible contexts of commonly shared terms by predefined conceptual descriptions (such as an ontology; it reflects a particular point of view with respect to a given specific-domain, with concepts and inter-relationships). It measures the context-similarities of a term in the given documents, by calculating the degree of mapping between predefined contexts (e.g., context-words such as synonyms) in the conceptual description and the occurred terms in the given documents. For example, the usage of pre-defined word-senses (concepts) for information retrieval or indexing is also motivated by [4], [7], [8], [10], [11].

3 Our Approach

In this paper, our aim is to propose a practical knowledge-level management approach for heterogeneous information in the Web, which overcomes the mentioned problems. In addition, our approach mediates between the Web and a user's knowledge needs. In other words, it is a problem of not only identifying documents about certain selected word-senses or their conjunctions, but also facilitating the construction of conceptual structures incrementally evolving in parallel as a reflection of the user's information needs. Figure 1 shows the user interface of our system ContextExplicator.

3.1 The Evolution of the Conceptual Structure

Our system, ContextExplicator, constrains the possible contexts of terms by predefined, generic sense-descriptions (using WordNet 2.0 [12] which provides a generic point of view that can be used in any domains, as well as different

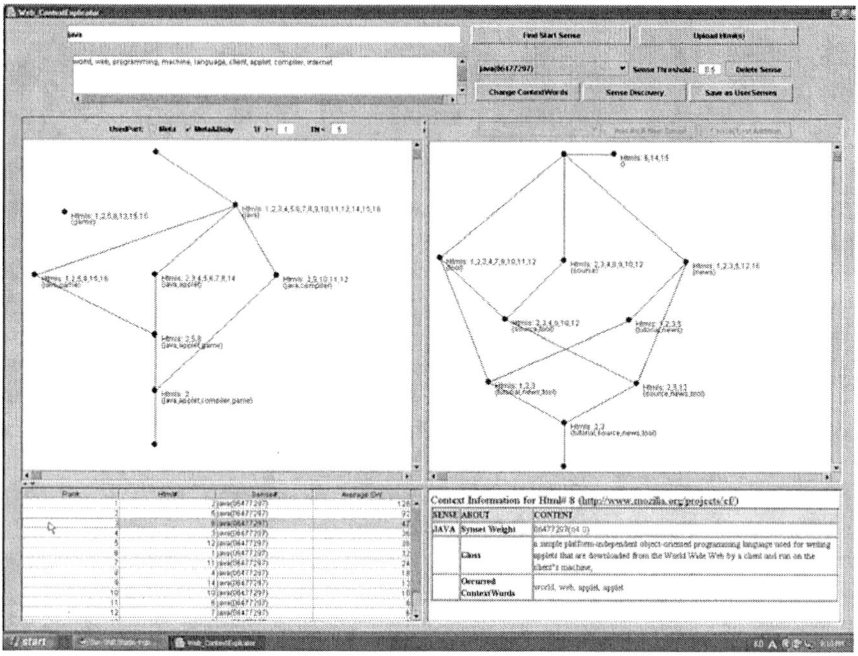

Fig. 1. User Interface of Our System ContextExplicator

word-senses and lexical relationships). However such generic sense-descriptions are frequently too general to cover more specific relevant word-senses and lexical relationships in specific domains. Thus ContextExplicator incrementally specializes the relevant word-senses and clusters them in a conceptual lattice structure, according to the user's decisions on alternative specializations of word-senses on the knowledge previously discovered. As such sense-specializations are based on the contents of documents, which are clustered in the conceptual lattice. The details are explained with Figure 2 in Section 4.

3.2 Conceptual Lattice

A critical issue for visualizing information in a lattice structure is the problem of scalability. Our solution is to reasonably minimize the amount of information which would be shown to the user at one time, by separating it into two different abstraction levels: Sense Disambiguated Neighborhood Terms and Sense Ambiguous Neighborhood Terms. (In Figure 1, they appear in the top left and top right sub-windows, showing the visualized conceptual lattices, respectively. In Figure 2, they are represented with solid and dashed lines, respectively.)

Sense Disambiguated Neighborhood Terms: At a higher abstraction level, ContextExplicator visualizes a conceptual lattice by clustering incrementally disambiguated word-senses and by classifying the given web-documents into relevant word-sense clusters.

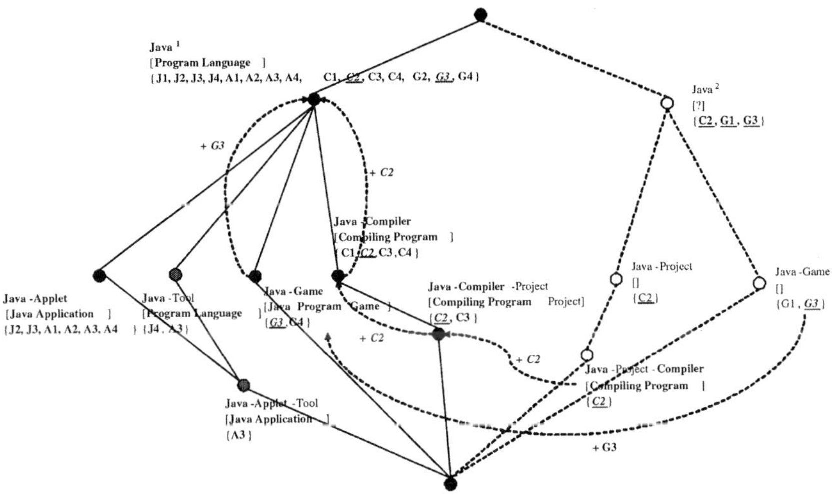

Fig. 2. An example evolution of a Conceptual Lattice, based on the discovered senses and their relationships from the documents in Table 1. The arrowed, dashed lines illustrate the automatic propagations of newly discovered context-information (Details are in Section 4.4). More relevant concepts of other words can be incrementally disambiguated and integrated into the Conceptual Lattice, as the user's information needs

Word-senses and word-sense clusters (rather than terms and term clusters) are utilized for the conceptual descriptions of the classified documents, it provides the following advantages: Firstly, a word-sense has its own context-words (i.e., keywords describing the word-sense; extracted from a synset having synonyms, definition and gloss, in WordNet), it can increase the recall performance to access relevant web-documents. Secondly, a word-sense can also increase precision by reducing the problem of polysemy by disambiguating the senses of words with the co-occurred context-words in the given web-document. Thirdly, as this conceptual lattice allows the user to navigate the word-sense clusters and the classified web-documents with multi-level abstractions (i.e., super-/sub-lattice nodes), it provides a flexible scheme for managing knowledge and web-documents in a scalable way.

To a word-sense cluster belong correspondingly classified documents. Each classified document contains more specific context information which can further specialize the word-sense cluster. A user can decide 1) if further context specialization is necessary for their information needs, and 2) if and only if 1), which word-sense cluster will be used. ContextExplicator provides some keywords based on the selected word-sense cluster as below.

Sense Ambiguous Neighborhood Terms: At a lower abstraction level, ContextExplicator constructs a conceptual lattice which consists of keywords extracted from the documents which are classified into a word-sense cluster in the conceptual lattice constructed with previously sense-disambiguated neighborhood terms. Although such keywords are not sense-disambiguated yet, they are constrained by the specific senses in a word-sense cluster and by the classified documents to those specific senses.

4 Experimental Results

In this experimental evaluation, we show that our approach can construct a semantically reasonable meaning structure (i.e., conceptual lattice), with given html documents and a user's query criteria about the term "java". See Figure 2.

4.1 Test Documents

We collected 16 html documents (in Table 1) classified by Yahoo!. Yahoo! is a directory system generated by human experts. In Yahoo!, they are classified at a parent-category (Directory > Computers and Internet > Programming and Development > Languages > Java) and its three child-categories (> applets), (> compilers) and (> games). From each category, we collected four top-ranked documents (J1∼J4, A1∼A4, C1∼C4, and G1∼G4). Table 1 shows the details of those documents. For example, the document J1 is classified into the parent-category (...>Java). Referring to the document J1, it represents its URL (e.g., " http://java.sun.com/") and the summary about the document (e.g., "featuring developer resources, ... support, news, and more") in Yahoo!

The category information in the Yahoo (i.e., created categories and their labels, connections between categories, and document classification) can be used as a gold standard to evaluate the concept lattice generated by ContextExplicator.

We notice that only the html-based free-texts, without any category information, are given to ContextExplicator to construct a conceptual lattice (e.g., Figure 2) for the given documents. As all documents are closely related to the sense "programming language" of "java", it might be a difficult task to construct a conceptual lattice which shows both their contextual distinctions and semantic consistencies. For example, document set A composed of two very similar topics are relatively much harder to be classified into two subsets, compared to document set B containing two very distinctive topics.

For the simplification of this case study, we used very few documents. However with even more documents, our approach would not lose the advantages, as discussed in Subsection 3.1, because the basic unit of our knowledge representation is the sense, and the increase rate of new senses might be much lower than that of new documents or the terms in them.

4.2 Sense Disambiguation

The construction of a conceptual lattice starts with the sense disambiguation of a term (Currently, the term is limited to use only a *content-word*. A content-word is a noun which has more than one sense in WordNet). Trying to disambiguate several terms at one time is an inefficient way to discover a few matched contexts (i.e., sense-combinations indicating subtopics which exist in both the user's query-intentions and in the documents given) from huge candidate sense-

Table 1. The information about test data set. ($Ji_{[1,4]}$, $Ai_{[1,4]}$, $Ci_{[1,4]}$, and $Gi_{[1,4]}$) represent aliases for documents in each Category. $J2^*$ is also classified into the Child 1 category (`..>Java>Applets`)

Category: Parent (...>Java)	
J1	http://java.sun.com/; featuring developer resources, community, documentations, support, news, and more
*J2**	http://javaboutique.internet.com/; collection of applets for web pages
J3	http://www.freewarejava.com/; offers Java applets, tutorials, references, books
J4	http://www.microsoft.com/mscorp/java/; news, articles, downloads, FAQs, and security info
Category: Child 1 (...>Java>Applets)	
A1	http://java.sun.com/applets/; resources, archives, and more
A2	http://science.nasa.gov/RealTime/JTrack/; a Java applet which tracks dozens of satellites including the Space Shuttle, Mir, COBE, UARS, and Hubble right in your browser
A3	http://www.buttontool.com/; create Java applets buttons without programming
A4	http://www.mud.de/se/jta/
Category: Child 2 (...>Java>Compilers)	
C1	http://www.mozilla.org/projects/ef/
C2	http://www.rr.iij4u.or.jp/ kkojima/glass.html; a classical static compiler implemented as a .class (java bytecode) frontend of gcc
C3	http://compose.labri.fr/; a Java environment that includes a compiler from Java bytecode to C and a Java interpreter
C4	http://pizzacompiler.sourceforge.net/; small, fast and free compiler for an important superset of the Java programming language
Category: Child 3 (...>Java>Games)	
G1	http://tournaments.playsite.com/playsite/index.jsp; play networked games against live opponents
G2	http://www.kurumi.com/roads/signmaker/signmaker.html; make your own freeway sign
G3	http://www.ichess.com/
G4	http://www.javagame.net/

combinations. Thus, ContextExplicator follows one way which incrementally specializes previously disambiguated senses. For example, if the user inputs 3 query-terms having 3 senses at one time, the number of possible sense-combinations is $({}_3C_1+{}_3C_2+{}_3C_3)^3 = 729$. However, when the user sequentially selects sense(s) for each term, the number of possible combinations is $3*({}_3C_1+{}_3C_2+{}_3C_3) = 21$. This number 21 can also be reduced by using only incrementally sense-disambiguated senses (in the given web-documents) for each term, and combining them. With ContextExplicator, the input-order of terms are independent to classify the documents given, as long as the user selects the same word-sense(s) for each term.

In Figure 2, the first query-term is "java", the sense of "java" in each document is disambiguated with respect to the three senses ("programming language", "land", and "coffee") taken from WordNet. As the result, it constructs one sense node "$Java^1$" (where the document set A (J1,J2,...C4,G2,G4) is classified into the sense "Programming Language") and one *dummy sense node* "$Java^2$" (where, a document set B (C2,G1,G3) failed to be sense disambiguated for the given query-term). The occurred senses' weights in the document set B are not greater than a sense-selection threshold-value (In this example, we selected "0.5" as the threshold-value. See Algorithms for details). The precision of this first sense disambiguation of the term "java" over the given whole documents is 81%. We can see the identified sense "programming language" is inherited to its child word-senses clusters (e.g., Java-Applet, Java-Compiler).

Algorithm. In the following, we consider a set D of html-documents $d \in D$. Furthermore, we consider a term t and their respective primitive senses $s_1, ..., s_n \in WS(t)$ as provided by WordNet, where the function $WS(t)$ provides us with the set of senses of t in WordNet. For each primitive sense s_i, a set $CTS(s_i)$ of context-words is extracted from WordNet, which we use as indicators (context) for a particular sense, if they are collocated with the original term t. The sense disambiguation algorithm is as follows:

1. Input a term t (i.e., a content-word).
2. Obtain the senses $s_1, ..., s_n \in WS(t)$ in WordNet.
3. We denote the set of context-words as extracted content-words from a particular sense s_i by $CTS(s_i)$ in WordNet. Form the set

$$CT = \bigcup_{s_i \in WS(t)} CTS(s_i) \tag{1}$$

   of all context-words for all senses $s_1, ..., s_n$.
4. For each document d and each context-word $t \in CT$, determine the occurrence frequency for each of the following parts of the html-document: meta-data(e.g., title, description, keywords, emphasized terms) and body.
5. Let the term weight $tw(t)$ of the term t be defined as followed:

$$tw(t) = \frac{|WS(t)|}{|\{s_i | t \in CTS(s_i)\}|} \tag{2}$$

   i.e. the total number of all senses, divided by the number of senses which have t as context-word. The unique context-words of a sense are more likely to contextualize the sense than are common context-words.
   Let s_{id} be the sense weight of a document d for sense s_i as followed:

$$s_{id} = \sum_{t \in CTS(s_i)} tw(t) \times freq(t, d) \tag{3}$$

   where $freq(t, d)$ is the frequency of term t occurring in the document d.
6. Classify all documents according to their used senses as followed:
   If the normalized sense weight $\frac{s_{id}}{\sum_{j=1}^{n} s_{jd}}$ of a d is greater than an adjustable threshold θ $(0 < \theta \leq 1)$, d is classified into sense s_i. When the senses (in the definition of WordNet) themselves are too general (or many) to distinguish each other, the lower threshold value is proper for the sense disambiguation.
7. Assign each document d, classified into sense s_i, to all relevant sense clusters whose all senses are disambiguated as coexisting in the document d. At this moment, we do not explain the context transport algorithm (See Subsection

4.4; a newly sense disambiguated term can be joined as a new context-word of previously disambiguated terms, and it could affect on the sense disambiguation results of those terms).

4.3 The Selection of Representative Context-Words

The user might expect to subclassify the document set A into more specific sense(s) than the sense $Java^1$, and/or want to discover new sense(s) to which the unclassified document set B can be assigned. For such purposes, ContextExplicator recommends some candidate representative context-words (i.e., sense ambiguous neighborhood terms, in Subsection 3.2) for each sense-cluster, existing in the documents classified into respective sense cluster. The efficiency measure of a candidate representative context-word is based on how it can support the construction of a conceptual lattice which satisfying following three principles:

1) *Maximizing the topical commonality* among the intentions of the authors who wrote the documents. For example, each sub-sense clusters (e.g., "Applet", "Game", and "Compiler") of the sense $Java^1$ has sub-classified the documents set A according to the shared senses among documents in A.

2) *Maximizing the semantic relevancies* between the sense of a representative context-word, and some previously discovered sense clusters. It can direct the sub-classification of the documents classified into a sense cluster to the meaning reinforcement of the sense cluster. For example, the sense "java application that uses the client's web browser to provide a user interface" of a representative context-word "applet" has reinforced the previously discovered sense $Java^1$ (i.e., "programming language"), by providing a positive context-word "web" (A positive context-word exists only in a sense of a term, compared with the other senses (e.g., "island" and "coffee") of the term). As the result, the sense cluster "Java-Applet" becomes a newly induced sense combining two primitive senses "programming language" and "java application that uses the client's web browser to provide a user interface". It makes it possible to overcome the problem of generic sense-descriptions, discussed in Subsection 3.1.

3) *Minimizing the semantic obscureness* between the sense of a selected representative context-word and a sense cluster which contains the representative context-word. For example, it should not weaken the sense $Java^1$ "programming language" by selecting a negative context-word "drink" (A negative context-word exists only in the other senses (e.g., "island" or"coffee") of a term, which are not conjuncted in the sense-cluster) which can cause obscureness of the previously disambiguated sense $Java^1$ "programming language".

Algorithm. The selection algorithm of representative context-words in a selected sense cluster S_{ni} is as following:

1. Let CS_{ni} be the set of component senses of S_{ni} ($cs_1, ..., cs_m \in CS(S_{ni})$). If S_{ni} is a compound sense, it entails several component senses (primitive senses and/or compound senses). Let $D_{S_{ni}} = \{d_1, d_2, ..., d_d\}$ be the set of documents classified to S_{ni} through the sense disambiguation algorithm in Subsection 4.2.

2. If $CS(S_{ni}) \neq \emptyset$ (S_{ni} is not a dummy sense node) and $D_{S_{ni}} \neq \emptyset$, find the most representative context-words $K = \{r_1, r_2, ..., r_r\}$ of $D_{S_{ni}}$ as followed:
   Firstly, find a set of candidate representative context-words CR_1: We denote two sets of context-words CR_{11} and CR_{12} as extracted content-words by $CTS(s')$ and $CTS(s'')$, respectively, from WordNet. Form the set

$$CR_1 = CR_{11} \setminus CR_{12} \tag{4}$$

   where $CR_{11} = \bigcup_{s' \in CS(S_{ni})} CTS(s')$ and $CR_{12} = \bigcup_{s'' \in CS(-S_{ni})} CTS(s'')$. CR_1 satisfies the second principle *Maximizing the semantic relevancies* and third principle *Minimizing the semantic obscureness*. $-S_{ni}$ represents all component senses occurring in the other sense clusters that are not hierarchically connected in a conceptual lattice. The function $CTS(*)$ removes the content-words, previously sense-disambiguated, in DW for CR_{11} & CR_{12}.
   Secondly, find a set of candidate representative context-words CR_2: CR_2 is extracted from meta-data parts and the body parts in $D_{S_{ni}}$.
   Thirdly, find representative context-words RCT: Form the set

$$RCT = CR_2 \setminus CR_{12} \tag{5}$$

   It removes CR_{12} to follow the third principle *Minimizing the semantic obscureness*. With the set $RCT = \{r_1, r_2, ..., r_k\}$, the representative context-words are ranked by the following rules:
   1) The context-words in CR_1 have the highest priorities according to 2) and 3) below.
   2) The priorities are given in order of context-words which occur in both the meta-data part and the body part, and which occur in the meta-data part in document d.
   3) If a context-word r_m, occurring in RCT but not selected in above step 1), occurs only in the body part of d, then give following weight value

$$r_m = argmax_{r_m \in N} \sum_{d \in D_{S_{ni}}} \log(freq(r_m, d)) \tag{6}$$

   4) If more documents share a context-word achieved in step 2) or 3), then give next priority to that context-word.
3. If $CS(S_{ni}) = \emptyset$ (S_{ni} is a dummy sense node) and $D_{S_{ni}} \neq \emptyset$, find the most representative context-words $RCT = \{r_1, r_2, ..., r_r\}$ of $D_{S_{ni}}$ by applying the priority ranking rules, as mentioned above, to all content-words in $D_{S_{ni}}$.

4.4 The Automatic Propagation of Newly Discovered Context-Information

ContextExplicator can automatically choose the most representative context-words (RCT) and utilize them to further specialize the clustering of the given documents, by following the principles and algorithms mentioned above. However we believe that ContextExplicator should allow the user to verify the provided

RCT for their query-intentions, and control further knowledge management procedures (i.e. knowledge discovery, query refinement, and visualization of the discovered knowledge). In this respect, one of our interests is "how can we ensure the order-independence of selected context-words?" For example, the unclassified document set B might be changed according to what word is targeted for the sense disambiguation, at first time. For example, the document $\underline{C2}$ in document set B can be classified to one sense, if they are sense disambiguated about word "compiler" rather than "java". It implies that the start word "java" can eliminate some possibilities where some documents can contribute the structure of conceptual lattice and/or the classifications of documents.

ContextExplicator covers this issue by automatically propagating the context-information of newly disambiguated word-senses to previously disambiguated senses. For example, in Figure 2, ContextExplicator recommends the representative context-words $\{applet, compiler, free, game, menu, navigation, news, source, tool, tutorial, utility, ...\}$, ranked according to their occurrence frequencies, for further specialization of the sense $Java^1$. When a user selects a context-word "compiler", ContextExplicator disambiguates the sense of word "compiler" in documents $(C1, \underline{C2}, C3, C4)$ as "compiling program". As this shares one unique context-word "program" with the sense "Programming Language" of "java", the word-sense "compiler"is propagated to become a new context-word of the sense $Java^1$. Thus, the word "java" in $\underline{C2}$ can be disambiguated as "Programming Language". As the result, the previously unclassified document $\underline{C2}$ can be classified into the sense "Programming Language", and be merged with document set A (J1,J2,...,C4,G2, G4). It means that documents can contribute to the knowledge construction processes (i.e., Subsection 4.2 and 4.3), while the result is independent of the order of selection of the context-words. Figure 2 shows more procedures performed with other context-words (e.g., "Applet" and "Game").

4.5 Advantages Compared to Traditional Directory Structures

When we compare the constructed conceptual lattice, at this stage, with the directory structure of Yahoo!, several advantages can be recognized: 1) it finds more specific senses for documents satisfying the user's knowledge needs: e.g., "J2" and "J3" are classified into more specialized sense "Java-Applet" than "Java". In Yahoo!, only "J2" is classified into the "Java-Applet" sense. The target senses can be created by the user's knowledge needs rather than limited to the decisions of search-indexing experts, 2) it can increase the performance of word-sense disambiguation, through the propagation of newly discovered context-information. E.g. the automatic propagation of two disambiguated senses of "compiler" and "game" increased the sense-disambiguation performance of word "java" from "81%" to "93%", and 3) it automatically tracks the sense relationships among incrementally disambiguated word-senses, and makes it possible for the user to recognize newly appearing sense relationships. For instance, when "Java-Applet" is specialized into "Java-Applet-Tool", it automatically generates a new sense "Java-Tool" and sense-relationship with "Java-Tool".

5 Discussion and Conclusion

In this paper, we presented a software agent, ContextExplicator, which mediates between the Web and the user's information needs. It provides a method for incremental knowledge management (i.e., knowledge discovery, acquisition and representation) for heterogeneous information in the Web. The experimental results indicate that our approach can yield new high quality senses and their relationships, and are comparable to human-crafted senses as found in the Yahoo! directory. Thus, we find our initial experimental results very encouraging. The novelty of our approach lies in extracting context-words and exploiting the sense disambiguation and induction over those words, in the process of automatic document categorization. It makes it possible to overcome the problems associated with generic sense-descriptions of words. In addition, ContextExplicator propagates the context-information of newly disambiguated word-senses to previously disambiguated senses. This results in improved word-sense disambiguation.

In our future work, we will introduce a segmentation process which divides a document into topic-based segments. Topically relevant segments may use a given term in the same sense against the other segments. We will then apply the presented approach of sense disambiguation and document categorization on the topic-based segments basis. We expect better results from that which will hopefully lead to even more sophisticated word-sense disambiguation/induction performances.

References

1. J. Barwise and J. Seligman. *The rights and wrongs of natural regularity.* Ridgeview, 1994.
2. H. Billhardt, D. Borrajo, and V. Maojo. A context vector model for information retrieval. *JASIST*, 53(3):236–249, 2002.
3. P. Bollmann-Sdorra and V. V. Raghavan. On the necessity of term dependence in a query space for weighted retrieval. *JASIS*, 49(13):1161–1168, 1998.
4. M. P. O. Christopher Stokoe and J. Tait. Word sense disambiguation in information retrieval revisited. In *the Proceedings of the 26th SIGIR Conference*, pages 159 – 166. ACM, 2003.
5. S. Deerwester, S. T. Dumais, G. W. Furnas, T. K. Landauer, and R. Harshman. Indexing by latent semantic analysis. *JASIS*, 41(6):391–407, 1990.
6. W. Fan, M. D. Gordon, and P. Pathak. Discovery of context-specific ranking functions for effective information retrieval using genetic programming. *IEEE Transactions on Knowledge and Data Engineering*, 16(4):523–527, 2004.
7. A. W. B. Joyce Yue Chai. The use of word sense disambiguation in an information extraction system. In *AAAI/IAAI 1998*, pages 850–855. AAAI / MIT, 1999.
8. R. Mihalcea and D. Moldovan. Semantic indexing using wordnet senses. In *ACL Workshop*. ACL, 2000.
9. A. Rungsawang. Dsir: the first trec-7 attempt. In *Proceedings of the Seventh Text REtrieval Conference (TREC 1998)*, pages 366–372. National Institute of Standards and Technology (NIST), 1998.
10. M. Sanderson. Retrieving with good sense. *Information Retrieval*, 2(1):49–69, 2000.
11. E. M. Voorhees. Using wordnet to disambiguate word senses for text retrieval. In *the Proceedings of the 20th SIGIR Conference*, pages 171–180. ACM, 1993.
12. Wordnet, 2004. http://www.cogsci.princeton.edu/~wn/.

Ontology Construction for Semantic Web: A Role-Based Collaborative Development Method

Man Li[1], Dazhi Wang[2], Xiaoyong Du[1], and Shan Wang[1]

[1] School of Information, Renmin University of China, Beijing 100872, China
{liman1, duyong, swang}@ruc.edu.cn
[2] Chengdu Institute of Computer Application, Chinese Academy of Sciences, Chengdu 610041, China
wdzfortune@126.com

Abstract. Ontologies are often seen as basic building blocks for the semantic web, as they provide a shared and reusable piece of knowledge about a specific domain. With the rapid development of semantic web, the scale and complexity of ontologies grow fast. The construction of large-scale ontologies will involve collaborative efforts of multiple developers. However, collaborative construction of ontologies is a complicated task. This paper discusses the challenging issues in collaborative ontology development, gives an overview of the related technologies and proposes a practical role-based collaborative development method, named RCDM. According to it, a pyramidal taxonomy of roles is adopted to divide ontology developers into different roles. Developers serving as different roles work collaboratively to construct a large-scale ontology, and a weighted statistical algorithm is adopted to solve conflicts led by different opinions. Compared with existing methods, RCDM is more suitable to large-scale ontology development, and does well in developers management, concurrency control, and conflicts resolution. It integrates wisdoms of different kinds of developers, no matter whether they are domain experts or not.

1 Introduction

Semantic web is designed as the next-generation web. It augments the current web by adding machine understandable content to web resources, providing extra information on content, and enabling agents acting on behalf of humans to reason with the information obtained[1, 2]. Ontologies are often seen as basic building blocks for the semantic web, as they provide a shared and reusable piece of knowledge about a specific domain. With the rapid development of semantic web, the scale and complexity of ontologies grow fast. The construction of large-scale ontologies will involve efforts of multiple developers. The collaborative construction of ontologies is a complicated task, and the main challenges are: i) how to avoid interference of different developers' works; ii) how to arbitrate among different (even opposing) opinions of developers.

Nowadays, several ontology development tools claim that they support concurrent operations of multiple developers on the same ontology. KAON[3, 4] is

Y. Zhang et al. (Eds.): APWeb 2005, LNCS 3399, pp. 609–619, 2005.

the representative one among them. It resolves concurrence and conflict problems by transaction and locking. It adopts a client-server system structure. An engineer server runs as a server, and user can connect to the engineering server through a client panel. Different users operate concurrently the same ontology on the engineering server. This is really a good approach to make a collaborative development environment, but there are some limitations. First, there is no distinction of roles. Ordinary developers can operate the ontology just as the domain experts, which may induce errors or conflicts. Second, the concurrence degree is low because of the (tree-) locking on the ontology. If too many people operate concurrently, the system may be inefficient. Third, the workspace is public for every developer. If developers have different opinions, the latter operation will overwrite the former without discussion.

Some other researchers proposed that ontologies development just as the software code does. Tool for managing versions of software code, such as CVS[5], is a good choice for software engineers to participate in dynamic collaborative projects. Naturally, collaborative development of dynamic ontologies requires tools that are similar to software-version tools[6]. Therefore, they suggest that ontology developers can use the storage, archival, and checkout mechanisms of tools like CVS, and only need to improve the approach of comparing versions of ontologies. However, in CVS, every user must do check-in after he finishes his own work. After check-in, a new version is created in server, and the new version need be merged with the baseline version. In this way, the system record every version of the ontologies, and user can easily find out his operation or contribution done before, but there are still problems. First, the operation such as check-in and check-out is boring and time consuming. Second, the system mechanism is based on the comparison of file content. It does not support ontology stored in database. However database is more suitable for large-scale data. Third, there is still not distinction of roles in this kind of system.

This paper proposes an effective role-based collaborative development method named RCDM. In RCDM, different developers serving as different roles work concurrently with different ontology views and different privileges, and a semi-automatic conflicts resolution mechanism is adopted to resolve conflicts problem led by different opinions. The method allows more developers to involve in the development process and ensures the correctness and agreement of ontologies. It has been proven by practice that RCDM is realistic and effective.

This paper is organized as follows. Section 2 explains RCDM in detail. Section 3 gives the implementation of RCDM and especially discusses the ontology views control and conflicts resolution problem. Section 4 analyzes the related tools, and compares them with ours. Section 5 draws the conclusion.

2 RCDM

Ontologies reflect the consensus in some domain. Ontologies may be large or small. Small ontologies may be constructed by a few developers, but the construction of large-scale ontologies is labor-intensive and time-consuming. The

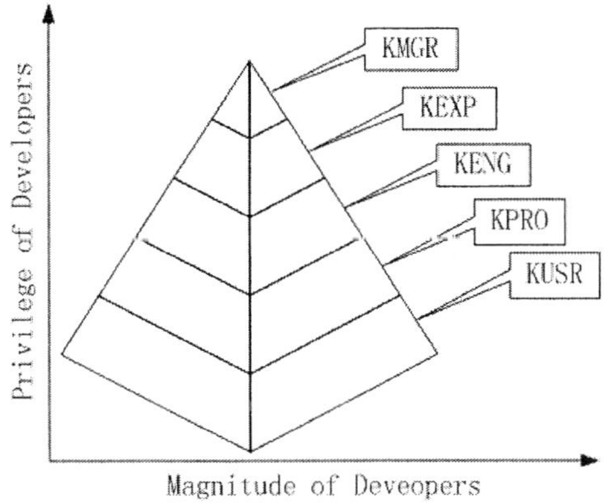

Fig. 1. Pyramidal taxonomy of roles

challenge of constructing a large-scale ontology is how to harmonize different developers with different knowledge backgrounds to work together. Previous tools do not take developers' backgrounds into account. It treats every developer without difference. However, it is not proper that every developer is permitted to modify the ontology at will. Otherwise confusion will be incurred. Although not every developer is permitted to modify ontology freely, we believe that he should have right to bring forward proposals. Therefore we solve the problem by limiting his privilege and providing limiting views for them.

According to our viewpoint, developers are divided by roles, and roles are distinguished by privileges in the process of ontology construction and the magnitude of developers who can act as the role. The more privileges have the role, the less magnitude has developers who can act as the role. All the roles form a pyramidal developer structure. Here, we divide developers into five kinds of roles, which are KMGR (Knowledge Manager), KEXP (Knowledge Expert), KENG (Knowledge Engineer), KPRO (Knowledge Proposer) and KUSR (Knowledge User). The five kinds of roles form a pyramidal structure, which is shown in figure 1.

KMGR is on the peak of the pyramid, because he is the authority of the domain. He has the most privileges and the highest credibility. His task is to manage the whole ontology. So he can modify the ontology at will and every developer' work is visible to him. Confronted with conflicts, KMGR is the final arbitrator.

KEXP is the knowledge expert of the domain. His main task is to adjust the structure of the ontology. Ontology is dynamic and evolves with time, so it is necessary to adjust the existing structure continually. However, the modification of structure is a complicated task and may influence many parts of ontology. To ensure the consistency of ontology, in our method, KEXP' work will not take effect until it has been confirmed by KMGR.

KENG and KPRO cannot modify the ontology structure. Their task is to enrich the ontology, so they can only add objects to the ontology. The difference

Table 1. Roles comparison

ROLE	ADD	DELETE	MODIFY	QUERY	VALIDATE
KMGR	Yes	Yes	Yes	All	Yes
KEXP	Yes	Yes	Yes	Base&Self	No
KENG	Yes	No	No	Base&Self	Yes
KPRO	Yes	No	No	Base&Self	No
KUSR	No	No	No	Base	No

between KENG and KPRO is that KENG's work will take effect at once but KPRO's work will not. It means that KENG has more credibility than KPRO. KPRO is only the proposer of some new knowledge.

KUSR is at the bottom of the pyramid. There are a large number of KUSR in the web. He is the user of ontology, so he has only the privilege of browsing and querying the ontology.

There are four kinds of operations during construction of ontology, and they are query, addition, deletion and modification. According to RCDM, different roles have different privileges for the operations. The privilege of roles is shown in Table 1. The first column (ROLE) is the name of role. The second column (ADD) shows whether the role is allowed to add objects to the ontology. The third column (DELETE) indicates whether the role is allowed to delete existing objects in the ontology. The fourth column (MODIFY) indicates whether the role is allowed to modify existing objects in the ontology. The fifth column (QUERY) indicates the area accessed by the role. There are three values: *All*, *Base*, and *Self*. *All* indicates the role can access all objects in the ontology. *Base* indicates the role can access the objects having been confirmed by KMGR in the ontology. *Self* indicates the role can access objects created by himself in the ontology. The last column (VALIDATE) explains whether the role's operations (add, delete or modify) would take effect directly after he committed his work.

From the analysis above, it can be seen that the pyramidal role-based collaborative development method contributes to ontology construction at the following aspects.

- Multi-role make developer management more easily by classifying developers according to the pyramidal taxonomy and by providing different privileges and views for them.
- The method allows more people to participate in the ontology construction. According to the method, the construction of ontology does not completely depend on domain experts. Developers with less domain knowledge can contribute to ontology construction too.
- It assures the authority and consensus of ontology because more developers are involved in the development process and proper concurrency control and conflicts resolution strategies are adopted.

3 Implementation

This chapter presents our implementation of RCDM in detail and discusses the important mechanism such as views control and conflicts resolution.

3.1 System Framework

The system framework based on RCDM is shown in figure 2.

As shown in figure 2, the system architecture consists of three layers which are storage layer, management layer and interface layer. As for storage layer, our system support relational database and file system. Relational database is the backbone of collaborative development. In the management layer, the import and export module are responsible for importing ontology from OWL or RDF files and exporting ontology stored in database to OWL or RDF files. The file access module is used to access the ontology described by OWL or RDF files. User management module, query processing module,view control module, concurrency control module, conflict resolution module and version control module are used to ensure collaborative work of multiple developers. The views control and conflicts resolution will be discussed in detail in the rest part of this chapter.In the interface layer, the system provides application APIs for other applications to access the ontologies and GUI for users to access the ontologies.

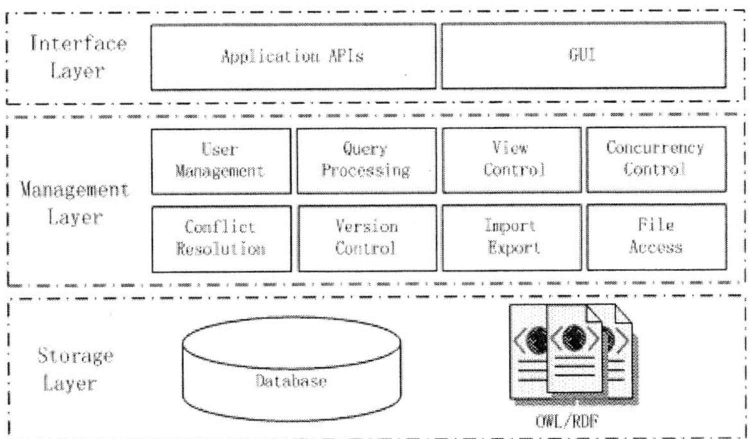

Fig. 2. System framework overview

3.2 Views Control

In our system, operations of KEXP and KPRO will not take effect until KMGR confirms them. The objects waiting for confirmation will not be visible to others, so different developers may have different ontology views. Here we use *object* to represent element in ontology, which is different from object in RDF model. Object here may be delegation of a concept, a property, an instance, or any element in ontology. Objects set of ontology is denoted as O. For object O_i ($O_i \in O$),we define $Creator(O_i)$ as the creator of object O_i, $Delete(O_i)$ as developers set in which developers ever delete object O_i and $Status(O_i)$ as the status of object O_i. The value of $Status(O_i)$ can be *valid*, *added* or *deleted*.

- *valid*: it means that the object has been validated by KMGR or has been created without controversy, so correctness of the objects with *valid* tag can be ensured.
- *added*: it means that the object is added by KEXP or KPRO and has not been confirmed by KMGR yet.
- *deleted*: it means that the object was deleted by KEXP and the operation has not been confirmed by KMGR yet.

According to the status of the objects and the operations of developers, the system provides different views for different developers. Suppose the whole developers set is D, for developer D_i ($D_i \in D$), we define $Role(D_i)$ as the role of D_i and $View(D_i)$ as objects that developer D_i can access. $View(D_i)$ is a subset of O. For the five kinds of developers in our system, the principle of composing views of different developers is as following:

- $Role(D_i) = \text{KMGR}$:
  $View(D_i) = \{O_j \mid O_j \in O\}$

- $Role(D_i) = \text{KEXP}$ or $Role(D_i) = \text{KENG}$ or $Role(D_i) = \text{KPRO}$:
  $View(D_i) = \{O_j \mid Status(O_j) = valid \vee (Status(O_j) = added \wedge Creator(O_j) = Di) \vee (Status(O_j) = deleted \wedge D_i \notin Delete(O_j)), O_j \in O\}$

- $Role(D_i) = \text{KUSR}$:
  $View(D_i) = \{O_j \mid Status(O_j) = valid \vee (Status(O_j) = deleted \wedge D_i \notin Delete(O_j)), O_j \in O\}$

The object with *deleted* status was deleted by some KEXP and had not been validated by KMGR. So the object with *deleted* status should be accessible for all others developers. According to our principle, all the objects accessed by KUSR is *valid* and each KEXP cannot modify the objects added by other KEXP or KPRO and had not been confirmed by KMGR.

3.3 Conflicts Resolution

Different developers will have different (even opposing) opinions during the process of ontology construction. When KMGR begin solving conflict, it is difficult to judge whether the object is preferable to be accepted or deleted. In our system, the operations of KEXP or KPRO will not take effect until they are confirmed by KMGR, but the operations express their opinions on the corresponding object. So we give the following rule:

- The operation that deletes object O_i is regarded as opposing the object O_i.
- The operation that creates object O_i is regarded as supporting the object O_i.
- The operation that creates objects *related to* object O_i is regarded as supporting the object O_i.
- The operation that deletes objects *related to* object O_i is regarded as supporting the object O_i, when the deleting operation is not induced by deleting O_i.

Here, if there is some relation between two objects in a ontology, we call one object is *related to* the other. For example, object 'student' is a class and the object 'name' is a property. If 'name' is a property of 'student' in a ontology, we call 'name' is *related to* 'student' or 'student' is *related to* 'name'.

According to RCDM, different developers have different role, which means they have different credibility. So we proposal a weighted statistical algorithm. Here, weight is the reflection of developer's credibility. The weight value is related to each role and the developer acting as a role has the corresponding weight value. To formally describe the algorithm, some functions are defined as following.

- $Status(O_i)$: status of object O_i, $O_i \in O$.
- $Creator(O_i)$: creator of object O_i, $O_i \in O$.
- $Delete(O_i)$: developers set in which developers ever delete object O_i, $O_i \in O$.
- $Related(O_i)$: objects that are related to object O_i, $O_i \in O$.
- $CreatorR(O_i)$: developers who create the objects which are related to object O_i, $O_i \in O$.
- $DeleteR(O_i)$: developers who delete the objects which are related to object O_i, $O_i \in O$.
- $SD(O_i)$: developers that support object O_i, $O_i \in O$.
- $OD(O_i)$: developers that oppose object O_i, $O_i \in O$.
- $Role(D_i)$: the role that developer D_i acting as, $D_i \in D$.
- $Weight(Role(D_i))$: the weight value of developer D_i, $D_i \in D$.
- $Support(O_i)$: supporting value of object O_i, $O_i \in O$.
- $Oppose(O_i)$: opposing value of object O_i, $O_i \in O$.

The algorithm to compute the supporting value of an object is shown in Algorithm 1.

Algorithm 1. Supporting Value Computation.
Input: object O_x, $O_x \in O$
Output: $Support(O_x)$

1. Get the creator of object O_x:
   $Creator(O_x)$;
2. Get deleting developers of O_x:
   $Delete(O_x)$;
3. Get the related objects of object O_x:
   $Related(O_x)$;
4. if $Related(O_x) = \phi$ then $SD(O_x) = \{Creator(O_x)\}$ goto 8;

5. Get all creating developers of $Related(O_x)$:
   $CreatorR(O_x) = \bigcup_{O_i \in Related(O_x)} Creator(O_i)$;
6. Get all deleting developers of $Related(O_x)$:
   $DeleteR(O_x) = \bigcup_{O_i \in Related(O_x)} Delete(O_i)$;
7. Get supporting developers set $SD(O_x)$:
   $SD(O_x) = Creator(O_x) \bigcup CreatorR(O_x) \bigcup DeleteR(O_x) - Delete(O_x)$;
8. Get the supporting value of object O_x:
   $Support(O_x) = \sum_{D_i \in SD(D_x)} Weight(Role(D_i))$

The algorithm to compute the opposing value of an object is shown in Algorithm 2.

Algorithm 2. Opposing Value Computation
Input: object O_x,$O_x \in O$
Output: $Oppose(O_x)$

1. Find users who ever delete object O_x:
   $Delete(O_x)$;
2. Get opposing developers set $OD(O_x)$:
   $OD(O_x) = Delete(O_x)$;
3. Get the opposing value of object O_x:
   $Oppose(O_x) = \sum_{D_i \in OD(D_x)} Weight(Role(D_i))$

$Support(O_x)$ and $Oppose(O_x)$ are important factors during the arbitration process of KMGR. For object O_x , $Support(O_x)$ reflects the supporting degree of the developers and $Oppose(O_x)$ reflects the opposing degree of the developers. However, KMGR should not make decision only based on $Support(O_x)$ and $Oppose(O_x)$. His own opinion is an important factor too.

4 Analysis and Comparison

A good overview, viz. a comparative study of existing tools up to 1999, is given in[7]. Naturally, it could not fully consider the more recent developments. Here we focus on the latest tools and that supporting collaborative construction for ontologies.

Ontolingua[8] is developed by Stanford University. It supports for collaborative development of consensus ontologies by access control of user and group and multi-user sessions. The Ontolingua Server uses the notion of users and groups that are typical in most multi-user file systems. As with file systems, access to ontologies such as read and write, is controlled by the ontology owner giving access to specific groups. This mechanism supports both access protection as well as collaboration across groups of people who are defined within the ontology development environment. The server provides supports for simultaneous work through group sessions. When a user opens a session, she may assign a group ownership to it. This enables any other members of that group to join the session and work simultaneously on the same set of ontologies. A notification mechanism informs each user of the changes that other users have made.

Inspired by the Ontolingua system, Ontosaurus[9] combines support for collaboration with reasoning and allows individuals to add to an ontology only when consistency is retained within the ontology as a whole. In Ontosaurus, changes can only be made by an individual user if they are consistent with the rest of the ontology. This is made possible due to the reasoning capabilities built-in to the LOOM representation language and prevents inconsistent ontologies from being built. Due to the simple "state-less" HTML interaction, it has several limitations. E.g. does a server not maintain any state information about users, i.e. clients, nor is it possible for a server to initiate an interaction on its own, e.g. alerting users to simultaneous changes by others.

OntoEdit[10], developed by Karlsruhe University, is a collaborative ontology development environment for the Semantic Web. To ensure safe development conditions, OntoEdit employed a locking and transaction protocol. It adopts the strategy of locking a complete subtree of the concept hierarchy. After the subtrees have been locked no conflicts can arise anymore. This (tree-) locking information is distributed to all other clients and visually indicated in the GUI. KAON, as the successor of OntoEdit, adopts similar concurrent controlling strategy.

WebODE[11] is developed by Technical University of Madrid. It covers and gives support to most of the activities involved in the ontology development process proposed by METHONTOLOGY. It offers inference services and an axiom manager (providing functionalities such as an axiom library, axiom patterns and axiom parsing and verification), but the very brief mentioning of these functionalities is too short to assess precisely. About collaboration, it is said that this is supported at the knowledge level, but how this is achieved remains open.

Other tools, such as Protégé [12] developed by Stanford University and OilEd[13] in the context of the European IST On-To-Knowledge project, offer sophisticated support for ontology engineering, but lack sophisticated support for collaborative ontology engineering.

The comparison between our system and previous tools is shown in Table 2. It lists eight tools, Ontolingua, Ontosaurus, OntoEdit, KAON, WebODE, Protégé, OilEd and our cooperative ontology development environment (abbr. CODE). The column Developer, Ontology Storage, Collaboration Control, and Conflicts Resolution show the corresponding tool's developer, ontology storage mode, collaboration control strategy, and conflicts resolution method in turn. The last column User Demand indicates the developers demanded on condition that ontology validity is ensured.

From Table 2, we can see that our CODE has the following advantages. i) It make developers management more easily by adopting the pyramidal taxonomy of developers. ii) It has good conflicts resolution method by using the weighted statistical algorithm. iii) It integrates wisdoms of different kinds of developers, no matter whether they are domain expert or not.

Table 2. Comparison of ontology construction tools

Tool	Developer	Ontology Storage	Collaboration Control	Conflicts Resolution	User Demand
Ontolingua	Stanford University	Files	User and Group Access Control & Multi-user Sessions	Session& Communication	Domain Expert
Ontosaurus	University of South California	Files	User and Group Access Control & Multi-user Sessions	Session& Communication	Domain Expert
OntoEdit	Karlsruhe University	Files&DBMS	Locking & Transaction Protocol	Session& Communication	Domain Expert
KAON	Karlsruhe University	Files&DBMS	Locking & Transaction Protocol	Session& Communication	Domain Expert
WebODE	Technical University of Madrid	DBMS	Group Access Control	Session& Communication	Domain Expert
Protégé	Stanford University	Files&DBMS	None	None	Domain Expert
OilEd	University of Manchester	Files	None	None	Domain Expert
CODE	Renmin University of China	Files&DBMS	RCDM	KMGR& Weighted statistical algorithm	KMGR KEXP KENG KPRO

5 Conclusion

This paper discusses the challenging issues in constructing large-scale ontology and proposes a practical collaborative ontology development method. The method allows more developers to involve in the ontology development process, so that the constructed ontology may reach a better coverage of a specific domain of interest.

Acknowledgements

The work was supported by the National Science Foundation of China (Grant No. 604963205) and 211 project. Thanks to graduate students Yan Wang and Yiyu Zhao for their work to the system realization.

References

1. Tim Berners-Lee, T., Fischetti, M.:Weaving the Web. Harper San Francisco, USA. 1999
2. Tim Berners-Lee, James Hendler, Ora Lassila, The Semantic Web, Scientific American, May 2001
3. Raphael Volz, Daniel Oberle, Steffen Staab, Boris Motik. KAON SERVER - A Semantic Web Management System. Alternate Track Proceedings of the Twelfth International World Wide Web Conference, WWW2003, Budapest, Hungary, 20-24 May 2003, ACM, 2003
4. E. Bozsak, Marc Ehrig, Siegfried Handschuh, Andreas Hotho, Alexander Maedche, Boris Motik, Daniel Oberle, Christoph Schmitz, Steffen Staab, Ljiljana Stojanovic, Nenad Stojanovic, Rudi Studer, Gerd Stumme, York Sure, Julien Tane, Raphael Volz, Valentin Zacharias. KAON - Towards a large scale Semantic Web. E-Commerce and Web Technologies, Third International Conference, EC-Web 2002, Aix-en-Provence, France, September 2-6, 2002, Proceedings, Kurt Bauknecht and A. Min Tjoa and Gerald Quirchmayr, Springer, Lecture Notes in Computer Science, 2455, pages: 304-313, 2002
5. Fogel, K., and Bar, M. Open Source development with CVS. The Coriolis Group, 2nd edition. 2001
6. Noy N F, Musen M A. PromptDiff: A Fixed-Point Algorithm for Comparing Ontology Versions. In: The Eighteenth National Conf. Artificial Intelligence (AAAI-02), Edmonton, Alberta, Aug. 2002
7. A. J. Duineveld, R. Stoter, M. R. Weiden, B. Kenepa, and V. R. Benjamins. WonderTools? A comparative study of ontological engineering tools. In Proc. of the Twelfth Workshop on Knowledge Acquisition, Modeling and Management. Banff, Alberta, Canada. October 16-21, 1999
8. A. Farquhar, R. Fickas, and J.Rice. The Ontolingua Server: A tool for collaborative ontology construction. In proceedings of the 10th Banff Knowledge Acquisition for Knowledge Based System Workshop (KAW'95), Banff, Canada, November 1996
9. B. Swartout, R. Patil, K. Knight, and T. Russ. Toward distributed use of large-scale ontologies. In Proceedings of the 10th Knowledge Acquisition Workshop (KAW'96), Banff, Canada, November 1996
10. Y. Sure, M. Erdmann, J. Angele, S. Staab, R. Studer, and D. Wenke. OntoEdit: Collaborative Ontology Engineering for the Semantic Web. In International Semantic Web Conference 2002 (ISWC 2002), Sardinia, Italia, 2002
11. J. C. Arprez, O. Corcho, M. Fernandez-Lopez, and A. Gomez-Perez. WebODE: a scalable workbench for ontological engineering. In Proceedings of the First International Conference on Knowledge Capture (K-CAP) October 21-23, 2001, Victoria, B.C., Canada, pp. 6-13, 2001
12. N. Fridman Noy, R. Fergerson, and M. Musen. The knowledge model of Protg-2000: Combining interoperability and flexibility. In proceedings of EKAW 2000, LNCS 1937, PAGES 17-32. Springer, 2000
13. S. Bechhofer, I. Horrocks, C. Goblen and R. Stevens. OilEd: a reason-able ontology editor for the Semantic Web. In Joint German/Austrian conference on Artificial Intelligence (KI'01), Lecture Notes in Artificial Intelligence, vol. 2174, Springer, Berlin, 2001, pp.396-408

Ontology-Based Matchmaking in e-Marketplace with Web Services

Li Li, Yun Yang, and Baolin Wu

Faculty of Information and Communication Technologies,
Swinburne University of Technology,
PO Box 218, Hawthorn, Melbourne, Australia 3122
{lli, yyang, bwu}@it.swin.edu.au

Abstract. The proliferation of Internet technology and globalisation of business environment give rise to the advent of virtual e-marketplace among complementary organisations. With significant computational resources available online, it is hardly to imagine that individual organisations will reinvent the wheel by themselves but ignore those standards-based available services. Ontology-based matchmaking in e-marketplace with Web services is a process of finding a particular Web service to fill a specific role. In this paper, firstly, a general e-business conducting phase is described. Then a novel mechanism with embedded matchmaking components is presented to facilitate finding specific services. A Web services repository and a Web services description as essential parts are discussed. Finally, Web services described in DAML-S along with domain ontologies in DAML are illustrated in a case study.

1 Introduction

With significant computational resources available online, organisations do not need to reinvent the wheel but instead to discover and composite those particular standards-based services according to their requirements through new technologies. Owing to more and more businesses increasingly relying on collaboration, huge profit and non-profit organisations are aware of the great potential to achieve greater productivity and efficiency of Web services. Web services, as defined by W3C, are "a key component of the emerging, loosely coupled, Web-based computing architecture". Through Web services, companies are enabled to find one another on the Internet by UDDI (Universal Description, Discovery, and Integration) standard which defines a protocol for directory services that contain Web service descriptions. UDDI, WSDL (Web Services description language), and SOAP (a lightweight protocol for transport) are important steps into the direction of a Web populated by services. Of course, XML is the basis of offering the "what" description of the data. Likewise BPEL4WS, WSCI, BPML and more and more Web services related standards and specifications or recommendations are available or will be available to illustrate this new trend in both industry and academia.

Y. Zhang et al. (Eds.): APWeb 2005, LNCS 3399, pp. 620–631, 2005.

Consortia and organisations such as W3C, OASIS and BPMI.org are looking to work out a series of standards/specifications/protocols to provide models/languages to deploy Web services. But if we look at the existing specifications generally, it is not too hard to get the idea that for business areas which are dynamic and non-deterministic and most importantly which require human participation, a real solution is still far away. Just as BPEL4WS replaced WSFL and XLANG in late 2002, BPML later became a superset of BPEL4WS.

Currently, one of the most challenging problems that Web-services-enabled e-marketplaces face is the lack of appropriate mechanisms to find the prospective services on behalf of participants by considering constraints. In an e-marketplace such as a `car service centre` (a real scenario in the following sections), the agent may possess certain capability to make a decision by himself/herself upon a customer request (i.e. query). Currently, there are no specifications to address agent's capability from an organisational aspect. Decision making in a partnership which is driven by a task in a business process would allow considering partners' roles and their capabilities in decision making in the business.

AI and agent technology [6] offer a high potential for decision making in distributed environments. In particular, ontologies [5] providing participants with unambiguous domain knowledge and relationships pave the way to smooth communications between parties, especially in e-marketplace. And ontologies and ontology-based approaches [9] have been recognised having great benefits in many areas such as e-commerce, knowledge and content management and the newly emerging field like Semantic Web. Advantages of ontology-based approaches include reusability, extensibility, evolution and justification, etc. [14]. Also multi-agent systems (MAS) which definitely increase the synergy by individual collaborations, is a sound way in modelling business processes. Of course solutions of constraint problems in AI are obviously one of the great benefits to matchmaking in e-marketplaces. That is why in this paper we investigate matchmaking in e-marketplaces from the AI perspective.

This paper will focus on finding prospective partners to fill specified roles in an e-marketplace by studying agents' decision making pre-, current- and post-actions within a decision making cycle. By doing so, an agent can take advantages of collaboration with others to accomplish a task without losing his/her own flexibility either in external or internal activities. Agents may interact with the Web service in a manner prescribed by its definition, using XML based messages conveyed by Internet protocols.

To comply with the above requirements, our approach is summarised as follows: (1) to develop domain ontologies by using DAML, e.g. car ontology, car part ontology and others if required; and (2) to develop a decision making mechanism to assist locating the most suitable services of Web services. The work here is driven by two factors. One is the intrinsic business conducting phase, which indicates how a business is running, that is exemplified with internal relations which most of the time are isolated from external observers. Another is interactions between participants with exchanging messages to determine a subsequent process dedicated to the task. The former addresses the basic flow in doing business upon receiving XML-based messages from a sender, while the latter emphasises collaboration between two or more parties. Our contribution lies in the service search and decision making mechanisms embedded in the roles of the parties to help them make appropriate selections in e-marketplace formation.

It is worth noting that basic infrastructures such as HTML, WSDL, UDDI and SOAP are the foundations of this paper. DAML-S is also available to enable describing agents' profile in services. Additionally, XQuery is available to make up a basic query. The baseline is XML. Every example in this paper is based on XML.

This paper is organised as follows. The next section addresses preliminary knowledge. The basic business conducting phase and XQuery language will be introduced. Section 3 describes interactions between partners in e-marketplace. Section 4 proposes a five stage decision making cycle for agents to find the most suitable partners in forming an e-marketplace dedicated to a task and based on Web services. Section 5 illustrates the five-stage decision making mechanism with a case study - a `car service centre`. Section 6 is about related work. Finally, Section 7 concludes our work and identifies potential further work.

2 Preliminary Knowledge

As mentioned in the introduction, we assume the basic infrastructures are available to enable businesses to list them on the Internet (UDDI), to exchange structured information in a decentralised, distributed environment (SOAP), to extend description messages regardless of what message formats or network protocols are used to communicate (WSDL). All of them are based on the baseline XML. However, XML itself provides no semantics for its tags. Even if one creates a program that assigns similar semantics to a particular tag, because the semantics is not part of the XML specification, an assertion still cannot be made for an application. Surprisingly, an ontology described in DAML-S enables reasoning about implicit assertions [1]. That is the reason why we use DAML-S[1] to describe an ontology creation and its application in matchmaking. Additionally, in contrast to WSDL which provides a communication level description of the messages and protocols used by Web services, DAML-S [1] is interested in developing semantic markup that will sit at the application level above WSDL, and describing what a service can do, not just how it does. That is, we assume that Web services are described, presented, and populated by appropriate languages and protocols in the Internet. Bearing these in mind, we are going to describe a general business conducting phase in the next subsection. In the following, we do not distinguish terms between agents, roles, parties, partners and participants but care about meanings in certain circumstance. We treat them the same in the context of agent technology and Web service technology.

---

[1] Although corresponding equivalent ontology element in DAML+OIL can be found in OWL (http://www.w3.org/2004/OWL/), generally, available HTML and documentation files (http://www.daml.org/services/daml-s/0.9/) refer to the DAML+OIL files. So we use DAML-S instead of OWL-S in this paper.

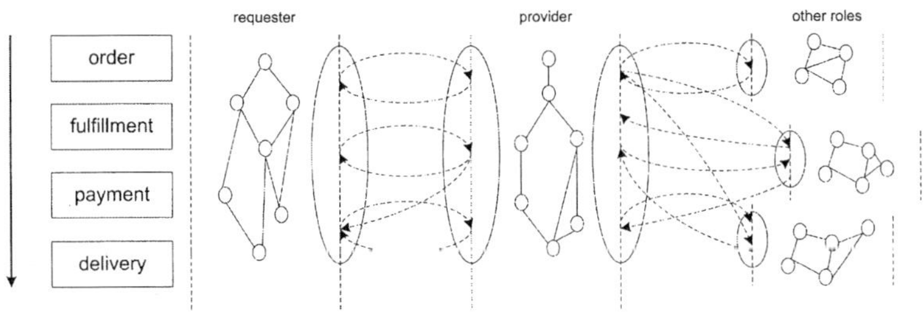

Fig. 1. Diagram of roles' interaction to achieve a goal

2.1 Basic Business Conducting Phase

Generally speaking, a business flows from one stage to another if requirements are met. Intuitively, four phases are encompassed in Figure 1 (on the far left). First is the `order` stage. A requester sends a provider a request with the descriptions of a specific task. Then several rounds of message exchange lead to the next stage, i.e. the `fulfillment` stage. In this stage, both the requester and the provider intend to fulfill their own subtasks in parallel. Before that, the prospective provider and the requester may negotiate mutual terms and conditions. As for the requester, he/she might need to check his/her credit limit, whereas for the provider, he/she must get everything in the order ready if these two parties can reach an agreement in terms of goals, deadlines, and exception scenario. `payment` comes next, after everything has been done. Finally it is the `delivery` stage. In this stage, `delivery` is arranged. There are other stages such as pre-purchase and post-purchase (CRM) which also need to be taken into account in businesses. What we mentioned here is the basic blueprint of doing business. Every stage actually consists of many sub-processes. If we look into the `payment` stage, it is clear that some kinds of payment such as Direct debit, Pay by Phone, Pay by Web, Pay in Person and Pay by Mail are available now and may request authorisation from a third party service (like IBM SET-compliant software) rather than direct payment between the requester and the provider. But our research concentrates on combining different Web service technologies for agents to make a decision in an e-marketplace. We focus on these four stages by viewing accomplishing a task as a flow of tasks to meet the requirements.

2.2 Query in Web Services

In XQuery, a query shown below is expressed in a FLWOR expression to return required services. Mostly, this simple query structure is adapted to query services on the Internet by extending its grammar and is eventually associated with temporal logic in some ways [13, 4]. We identify a set of relations which represent agents possessing some properties for further inferencing. We do not distinguish terms such as role and service for the reason that every role's function is to provide service(s).

```
for $x in doc("catalog.xml")/vehicle/car
where $x/year>2001
order by $x/price
return $x
```

In this paper, the basic form of a query, which consists of two parts, namely `requirement` and `goal` are as follows:

```
<Qreq>
<requirement>
<!-- FLWOR expression goes here-->
</requirement>
<goal>
<!-- goal goes here-->
</goal>
</Qreq>
```

Bearing this background knowledge in mind, we will discuss interactions between two parties in more detail next.

3 Interactions Between Parties

Business aims vary from domain to domain. Intuitively, the purpose of business is to get something (no matter whether the product is tangible or intangible) by collaboration to maintain the efficient low operation cost and minimise the total investment. More and more businesses which increasingly rely on collaboration now, are greatly supported by Web technologies. What we would like to convey in Figure 1 is how two parties achieve their goals by interacting with each other in e-marketplaces. On the far left of Figure 1 is the blueprint of conducting any business. The rest of the diagram shows interactions taking place not only between the requester and the provider, but between the provider and other roles as well.

- Vertical dashed lines separate the roles of different parties, like swimming lanes represent each role
- Other dashed lines represent external relations between two parties, while solid lines within the lanes show internal relations
- Small circles represent processes and the process flow (in solid lines) stands for a business process for that role dedicated to a task at that time
- Solid ellipses represent services (showing interactions between two parties)
- Arrowed lines represent directions of message flow

Interactions may take place more than once in an e-marketplace to achieve a goal. We concentrate on the following messages between roles in which Request and Answer may iterate many times until they reach a failure or success state: (1) Request - to ask something such as query for flights, query for price, etc. as well as to address something bound with some constraints which may change from time to time; (2) Inform - to inform something; (3) Answer - to provide alternative solutions; (4) Accept/Reject - to show the results of communications.

We adopt a very simple notation to describe the basic form of an interaction. The basic form of an interaction in BNF is as follows:

```
interaction::= <interExp>* <accept|reject>|<inform>*}
interExp::= <request> <answer>}
```

where the `interExp` expression consists of a series of rounds of `request` and `answer` with every agent making a proposal at every round, followed by a mandatory `accept` or `reject` or `inform` which may iterate many times, where "*" specifies the cardinality of the actions repeated once or more. Other specifics without any qualifiers occur only once.

The XML-like informal description for interactions is as follows:

```
<rdf:RDF xmlns:rdf="http://www.w3.org/1999/02/22-rdf-syntax-ns#">
<action>
<requester name="carCentre" type="request" role="sender">
<content ID=""> <!--detailed content goes here--> </content>
<reference rdf:resource="http://www.swin.edu.au/process/interaction" />
</requester>
<provider name="engineSupplier" type="answer" role="receiver">
<content ID=""> <!--detailed content goes here--> </content>
<reference rdf:resource="http://www.swin.edu.au/process/interaction" />
</provider>
</action>
</rdf:RDF>
```

After getting enough information about services, agent `car service centre` decides which one(s) its partners will be for a specified task in an e-marketplace. Next we will discuss how to make a decision in this regard.

4 Matchmaking in e-Marketplace

One of the greatest challenging in e-marketplace today is how to find suitable partners to meet certain requirements, for example, quality, locality, time, and cost. through Web services. In doing so, firstly, they should know what they are going to achieve. The subsequent sections address this in detail.

4.1 Decision Making Cycle

Figure 2 represents the life cycle of decision making in an e-marketplace. Participants involved in the task will take part in collaboration to obtain information for further actions to achieve the task with the following steps:

Step 1: **Problem Recognition.** This step is to be aware of problems which come out of interactions (like a customer requires a certain price range). The problems change all the time, so the agent needs to consider each of them and generate a query according to relevant constraints.

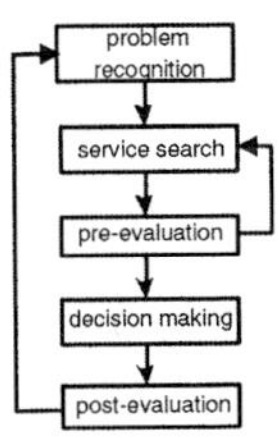

Fig. 2. Life cycle of decision making

Step 2: **Service Search.** With each generated query, this step selects services meeting basic constraints. All selected services with names, phone numbers, fax numbers, postal addresses, emails, URLs, etc. go through the next step for evaluation.
Step 3: **Pre-evaluation.** Selected services are options for the requester. What he/she is interested in is the most suitable one(s). Exact matching is desirable but is unusual in e-marketplaces, so filtering method is a necessity. Step 3 considers all selected services according to given criteria by using AI approaches. However, in most cases, the agent must estimate by his/her knowledge if there is no existing assertions or facts. Sometimes, the process will go back to step 2 to search again if the selected services did not well fit in the e-marketplace.
Step 4: **Decision Making.** This step is about commitment of actions. Agents must make sure that the selected services meet all requirements before this step. This step leads to activities such as payment and delivery to be fulfilled subsequently.
Step 5: **Post-evaluation.** Post-evaluation takes place by looking a step ahead in the business process to evaluate the total cost, total time consumption and response time, etc. in the direction of completing the task by deploying the service based on activities which have taken place so far. Intuitively, any feedback from this step will affect subsequent "`problem recognition`" step by adjusting matching conditions, if that is possible. Of course, unlike data manipulation in databases, some business transactions cannot be rolled back. In this case, feedback from this step is considered for further reference.

4.2 Functionality

Because not all services are likely to be discovered just by matching between the requester's query and the provider's profile (from where extraction items are generated), some other mechanisms are needed to guide further filtering to locate prospective providers if needed. Decision making is such a kind of mechanism to assist in making a decision in partnership formation in e-marketplaces. With our understanding, this mechanism is embedded in each role (agent) although we did not show that in Figure 3 for simplicity.

5 Case Study

We use a real world scenario of a car service centre to illustrate how agents collaborate with each other, and what the main issues are in decision making. The interaction process between all parties is illustrated in Figure 3. Actually, Figure 3 is a special case of Figure 1 with detailed names such as "`customer`" replacing "`requester`", "`car centre`"(simplicity for "car service centre" in Figure 3) replacing "`provider`" and detailed part suppliers replacing "`other roles`" in Figure 1. Basically, only two roles (`customer` and `car centre`) are involved if the work is a simple task. But mostly, `car centre` needs to look for other agents such as parts suppliers over the Internet. In this example, we assume the agents (`car centre`) are only required to consider decision making constraints like time

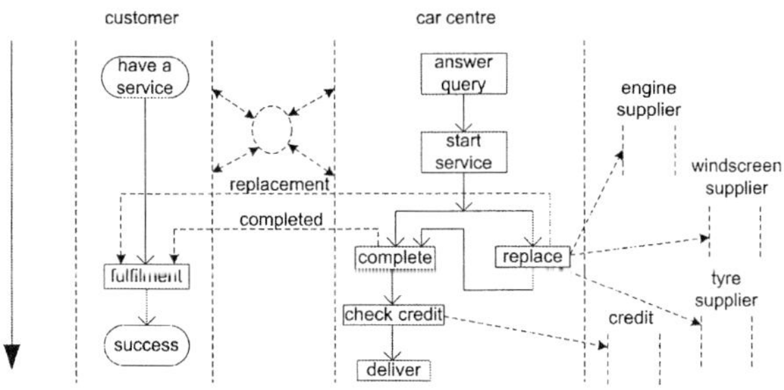

Fig. 3. Interaction diagram

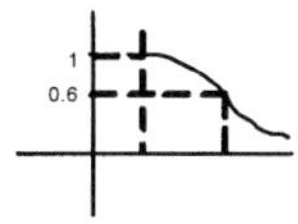

Fig. 4. Expectation function

and cost. But we omit their detailed calculations in this section due to the space limit. The process starts when the `customer` sends a request like "would like to have a service". `car centre` replies (most time they give a quote about the service for a specified kind of car). `customer` takes available quotes with other information such as location, time, etc. into account to select the quote (i.e. a specific car centre) which satisfies him/her. He/she then sends `car centre` an `accept` message. All message exchanges are shown in Figure 3 with a dashed line circle in the second column. The arrowed lines represents message sending and receiving. After `car centre` gets the message, it starts the service. When the car service is completed successfully, `car centre` sends a message to inform `customer` and continues subsequent activities such as `check credit` and arranges delivery (`deliver`) if they are applicable. If a replacement is needed, `car centre` sends another message and waits for `customer` reply. A series of sending and receiving messages (shown by the dashed line circle in the second column in Figure 3) are needed to reach another agreement until an `accept` message can be issued. Then `car centre` will start to search the Internet (unless `car centre` has relevant information in its local repository) to locate related parties (`engine suppliers`, `windscreen suppliers`, `tyre suppliers`, etc.) through Web services. `Request-Answer` may be repeated many times until agreements have been reached by the two parties. The `car centre` will then contact the `customer` again to notify any adjustments. This communication about the service goes on and on until it is completed (`complete`). `check credit` and `deliver` can then continue. Figure 3 focuses on how an e-marketplace is formed to accomplish a task (providing parts for a car) based on interactions between `car centre`, and `customer` in a Web service environment.

5.1 Ontology

As mentioned earlier in this paper, ontology plays an important role in e-marketplaces with Web services. The term is not only used for describing domain knowledge, but also for definitions of processes, and partner relationships. A simple ontology (about a car) is presented below to illustrate this. The following simple XML description shows that `car` is a subclass of `vehicle`, whereas `sedan` is a subclass of `car`.

```
<rdf:RDF
    xmlns:rdf="http://www.w3.org/1999/02/22-rdf-syntax-ns#"
    xmlns:ont="http://www.swin.edu.au/process/ontology"
    xmlns:daml="http://www.daml.org/2001/03/daml+oil">
    <!--imported resources go here-->
    <ont:entry rdf:ID="Vehicle">
        <ont:label>vehicle</ont:label>
    </ont:entry>
    <ont:entry rdf:ID="Car">
        <ont:label>Car</ont:label>
        <ont:subClassOf rdf:resource="http://www.swin.edu.au/process/ontology/vehicle" />
    </ont:entry>
    <ont:entry rdf:ID="Sedan">
        <ont:label>Sedan</ont:label>
        <ont:subClassOf rdf:resource="http://www.swin.edu.au/process/ontology/vehicle/car" />
    </ont:entry>
    <!--other car categories go here-->
</rdf:RDF>
```

5.2 Decision Making

Decision making is crucial in almost every phase of the decision making cycle. Sometimes people are unconscious of its presence due to the very small effort needed for making a decision. However in an e-marketplace, (let us take the above example for instance) every effort must be made to ensure prospective partners are selected carefully. `customer` at first even needs to make a decision on which `car centre` to choose by taking cost, time, location, trustworthiness, etc. into consideration.

In light of the decision making cycle, after problem recognition, a query is generated according to requirements. An example of a query is given below:

```
<request
xmlns="http://www.swin.edu.au/process/models"
xmlns:part="http://www.swin.edu.au/process/models/car/parts"
xmlns:customer="http://www.swin.edu.au/process/carcentre/customer"
xmlns:car-centre="http://www.swin.edu.au/process/carcentre">
    <requirement>
    {
    FOR $x in doc("catalog.xml")/vehicle/car
    <!-- condition goes here-->
    LET $v1 as customer:lowprice
    RETURN $v1
    LET $v2 as customer:highprice
    RETURN $v2
    WHERE
    { [$v1&lt;price&lt;$v2] AND [brand in SET {...}] AND [quality="high"] AND [...] }
    ORDER BY {<!-- sorting item goes here-->}
    LET $info:=(carcentre_name, address, service_time>)
    RETURN
    <car-centre:Display> {$info}</car-centre:Display>
    RETURN
    {
    <part:Name> {$pN} </part:Name>
    <part:Quantity> {$pQ} </part:Quantity>
    <part:Brand> {$pB}</part:Brand>
    <part:Type> {$pT}</part:Type>
    <!-- other return items go here-->
    }
    </requirement>
    <goal> <!-- the goal goes here--> </goal>
</request>
```

Then service `search` starts to search services on the Internet. After that, the `pre-evaluation` phase begins, for example, for a windscreen replacement scenario. The agent (`car centre`) must make a decision on which services are the best ones to meet `customer` requirements. Suppose there are many services (all of them are `windscreen supplier` services) meeting the conditions after previous filtering but still with slight differences. At this stage, we may turn to defining a utility function like $(\sum_{j=1}^{n} w_i \cdot att_j)$, where w_j ($w_j \in (0,1)$) is the element of weight vector corresponding to attribute att_j. Again, expectation functions combining with user's expectation and `car centre` agent's experiences (described in a curve in Figure 4) are used to assist filtering unexpected services.

Finally, the average weighted values decide the suitable services which meet the customer requirements. After `pre-evaluation`, `decision making` occurs which deals with the commitment of the business actions including `payment`, `delivery`, etc. For the next step, `post-evaluation`, the mechanism looks a step ahead by putting the windscreen replacement service into the process to see if all the conditions have been met. This step calculates all measures, including the total cost, time consumption and response time. In short, matchmaking in the car centre case study proceeds 5 steps according to Figure 2 to select prospective services and briefly measure run-time characteristics such as total cost and time consumption. Matchmaking is a great help to select partners during Web-enabled e-marketplaces.

6 Related Work

As discussed in paper [8], one of the most challenging problems today is to locate suitable services from Web services. Much work has been done from the semantic perspective [2, 10, 11] but with different emphasises. In paper [1], DAML-S, as a service description language, provides a semantics based view of Web services, particular the DAML-S profile to advertise the functionalities that organisations offer to the community. Paolucci et al. [12] claim that the locations of Web services should be based on the semantic match between a declarative description of the service being sought, and a description of the service being offered. Paper [15] introduces a language for describing the matchmaking process by using five different filters based on a domain specific ontology. In their papers [3, 7], a process ontology is developed to improve precision of key word based querying. In paper [13], a Web service request language is developed on the basis of XML and AI planning technique. Its purpose is to allow users to associate goals with a service request. In contrast to the semantic approaches presented above, paper [16] bases matchmaking on finite state automata. The approach in the paper discusses service discovery by using business process descriptions rather than individual message passing. Unfortunately, its business process description is unable to catch dynamic features of a real business process. In addition, its computations are complex and need to be further addressed.

The approach in our paper is inspired by the work from the semantic point of view where ontologies are the foundations of communications. We believe this approach is applicable in e-marketplaces whenever different parties communicate with one another. But our approach is different from semantically-oriented methods described above in that we believe decision making embedded in the roles of the different parties is desirable as they carry out a task to help filter unsuitable services in service discovery.

7 Conclusions

In this paper, our general focus has been on developing a decision making mechanism in e-marketplaces with Web services. In order to tackle partnership formation in e-marketplaces, we have discussed ontologies which are the foundation of communication on the Internet. Furthermore, we have presented an interaction diagram to illustrate what basic elements should be encompassed. Additionally, we have addressed query generation based on `problem recognition` including interactions of parties. The query is later used in `service search` on the Internet. Consequently, the query plays an important role in decision making to provide assistance for the subsequent `pre-evaluation`, `decision making`, and `post-evaluation` phases. The novelty of this approach lies in the service search, based on the generated query and decision making mechanisms embedded in the roles of the parties to help them make appropriate selections in e-marketplace formation. Most work presented is about investigating e-marketplaces at the formation level. We have developed several ontologies for different domains. Experimental systems for generating queries and extracting query related items from the service profile are under construction. In this paper, we have only addressed interactions between two parties, presumably in a way that is compatible. In most cases in e-marketplaces, however, interactions are not totally direct but indirect. The mobility of interaction is open for future investigation. Also, at the e-marketplace implementation level, error handling is another big challenge which needs to be addressed.

Acknowledgements

Work reported in this paper is partly supported by Swinburne Vice Chancellor's Strategic Research Initiative Grant 2002-2004 for project "Internet-based e-business ventures". It is also partly supported by the National Natural Science Foundation of China under grant No. 60273026 and grant No. 60273043.

References

1. Anupriya, A., Burstein, M., Hobbs, J. R., Lassila, O., Martin, D., McDermott, D., McIlraith, S. A., Srini, N., Paolucci, M., Payne, T. R., and Sycara, K., "DAML-S: Web Service Description for the Semantic Web," In: Proceeding of the First International Semantic Web Conference (ISWC), Sardinia, Italy, 2002.
2. Berbers-Lee, T., Hendler, J., and Lassila, O., The Semantic Web, Scientific America, 284(5), pp.34-43, 2001.

3. Bernstein, A., and Klein, M., "Discovering Services: Towards High-Precision Service Retrieval," In: Proceedings of CAiSE International Workshop, Web Services, E-Business, and the Semantic Web (WES), LNCS 2512, pp. 260-275. Springer, 2002.
4. Emerson. A. E., "Temporal and Modal Logic," In: Handbook of Theoretical Computer Science, Volume B: Formal Models and Semantics(J. Van Leeuwen, editor), Elsevier, 1990.
5. Gruber, T. R., Toward Principles for the Design of Ontologies Used for Knowledge Sharing, KSL-93-04, Knowledge Systems Laboratory, Stanford University. http://ksl-web.stanford.edu/.
6. Hendler, J., Agents and the Semantic Web, IEEE Intelligent Systems, Special Issue on the Semantic Web, 16(2), pp. 30-37, March/April, 2001.
7. Klein, M., and Bernstein, A., "Searching for Services on the Semantic Web Using Process Ontologies," In: Proceedings of 1st Semantic Web Working Symposium (SWWS-1), Stanford, 2001.
8. Koehler, J. and Srivastava, B., "Web Service Composition: Current Solutions and Open Problems," ICAPS 2003 Workshop on Planning for Web Services, Trento, Italy, pp. 28-35, 2003.
9. Li, L., Wu, B., and Yang, Y., "An Ontology-Oriented Approach for Virtual Enterprises," In: Proceedings of the 6th Asia-Pacific Web Conference (APWeb 2004), P.R. China., LNCS 3007, pp. 834-843, Springer, April 2004.
10. McIlraith, S., and Martin, D., Bringing Semantics to Web Services, IEEE Intelligent Systems, 18(1), pp. 90-93, January/February, 2003.
11. McIlraith, S., Son, T. C., and Zeng, H., Semantic Web Services, IEEE Intelligent Systems, Special Issue on the Semantic Web, 16(2), pp. 45-53, March/April, 2001.
12. Paolucci, M., Kawamura, T., Payne, T. R., and Sycara, K., "Semantic Matching of Web Services Capabilities," In: Proceedings of the First International Semantic Web Conference (ISWC), Sardinia, Italy, 2002.
13. Papazoglou, M. P., Aiello, M., Pistore, M., and Yang, J., XSRL: A Request Language for Web Services, 2002. http://eprints.biblio.unitn.it/archive/00000232/01/79.pdf.
14. Stojanovic, L., Schneider, J., et al., The Role of Ontologies in Autonomic Computing Systems, article, IBM Systems Journal, 43(3), August 2004.
15. Sycara, P. K., Klusch, M., Widoff, S., and Lu, J., Dynamic Service Matchmaking among Agents in Open Information Environments. SIGMOD Record, 28(1), pp. 47-53, 1999.
16. Wombacher, A., Fankhauser, P., Mahleko, B., and Neuhold, E., "Matchmaking for Business Processes based on Choreographies," In: Proceedings of the 2004 IEEE International Conference on e-Technology, e-Commerce and e-Service (EEE'04), 0-7695-2073-1/04.

An Empirical Study on the Change of Web Pages†

Sung Jin Kim[1] and Sang Ho Lee[2]

[1] School of Computer Science and Engineering,
Seoul National University, Seoul, Korea
sjkim@oopsla.snu.ac.kr
[2] School of Computing, Soongsil University, Seoul, Korea
shlee@comp.ssu.ac.kr

Abstract. As web pages are created, destroyed, and updated dynamically, web databases should be frequently updated to keep web pages up-to-date. Understanding the change behavior of web pages certainly helps the administrators manage their web databases. This paper introduces a number of metrics representing various change behavior of the web pages. We have monitored approximately 1.8 million to three million URLs at two-day intervals for 100 days. Using the metrics we propose, we analyze the collected URLs and web pages. In addition, we propose a method that computes the probability that a page will be downloaded on the next crawls.

1 Introduction

Web search services can create web databases (a collection of web pages) that enable users to retrieve web pages internally. Proxy servers, meta-search engines, and web browsers tend to maintain web databases to cache web pages internally, providing users web pages without downloading the same pages repeatedly. As web pages are created, modified, and destroyed dynamically, users are likely to see out-of-date pages instead of seeing up-to-date ones. Administrators should frequently update web databases to keep the databases fresh. Understanding the change behavior of web pages certainly helps the administrators manage their web databases.

A number of studies have investigated the evolution of web pages [1, 2, 3, 4, 6, 8]. In Cho and Garcia-Molina [2, 3], 720,000 pages were crawled daily for four months. They found that pages in the "com" domain changed more frequently than those in other domains, that about 40% of all web pages changed in a week, and that it took about 50 days for half of all the pages to change. Fetterly et al. [6] attempted to download 151 million pages 11 times over 11 weeks. They found that the average interval of the page change varies widely across top-level domains, and that large pages change more often than small ones do. Ntoulas et al. [8] picked 154 sites in the five top-ranked pages in each topical category of the Google directory. They crawled about 4.4 million pages from the sites weekly for one year. They found that every week 8% of downloaded pages were new, and that 25% of all crawled links were new.

† This work was supported by Korea Research Foundation Grant. (KRF-2004-D00172).

Y. Zhang et al. (Eds.): APWeb 2005, LNCS 3399, pp. 632–642, 2005.

Previous studies have not taken into account various factors worthy of investigation. First, although web pages are created daily, the page creation phenomenon draws little attention in research communities. To our best knowledge, only Ntoulas et al. [9] studied the page creation phenomenon. Second, there is no research that considers downloading issues of URLs. In the real world, we cannot always download a page with a given URL. An approach that makes a distinction between URLs and successfully downloaded pages (possibly in a single page basis) is recommended. Third, even though previous researchers computed the average change intervals of web pages in one way or another, there has been no technical attempt to investigate what portion of all the web pages change at uniform rates and what portion of them do not.

Our research is motivated to answer the limitations of previous research. In this paper, we introduce a number of metrics, including the download rate, the modification rate, and the coefficient of age variation to represent the change behavior of web pages. These metrics take into account not only the unsuccessful download states of web pages, but also the creation of new URLs and new web pages. From the 34,000 Korean sites we selected, we have monitored approximately 1.8 million to 3 million URLs at two-day intervals for 100 days. Using the metrics we propose, we analyze the collected URLs and web pages. This paper presents our findings from the analysis. Also, we propose a method that computes the probability that a page will be successfully downloaded in the next crawls. Our experiment shows that the method estimates the probability well.

The paper is organized as follows. Besides this introduction, we define a number of metrics to represent the changes of web pages in section 2. Section 3 analyzes the collected URLs and web pages. Section 4 proposes a formula that predicts the change behavior of the web pages. Section 5 contains the closing remarks.

2 New Metrics

In this section, we define metrics that show the change behavior of web pages. We are going to use an illustrative example (see Fig. 1) to explain these metrics. There are 16 crawls with six URLs. In each crawl, the web robot [7] starts off by placing an initial set of URLs in a queue that stores URLs to be visited. From this queue, the robot gets a URL, downloads a page, extracts (detects) any URLs in the downloaded page, and puts the new URLs in the queue. This process is repeated until either there are no URLs in the queue or the robot visits a predetermined number of pages.

A dash symbol ("-") in Fig. 1 means that there is no download attempt since the corresponding URL is not available at that point. A black circle ("•") means that we fail to download a web page. The content of a downloaded page is denoted as a circled character (here ⓐ, ⓑ, etc.). For example, on the first crawl where four URLs (A, B, E, and F) are available, we can download two pages from URL A and B successfully, and we denote the contents of the downloaded pages as ⓐ and ⓑ, respectively.

URL	Crawl number															
	1	2	3	4	5	6	7	8	9	10	11	12	13	14	15	16
A	ⓐ	ⓑ	ⓒ	ⓓ	ⓔ	ⓕ	ⓖ	ⓗ	ⓘ	ⓙ	ⓚ	ⓛ	ⓜ	ⓝ	ⓞ	ⓟ
B	ⓠ	ⓠ	ⓠ	ⓠ	ⓠ	ⓠ	ⓠ	ⓠ	ⓠ	ⓠ	ⓠ	ⓠ	-	-	-	-
C	-	-	-	-	ⓡ	●	ⓢ	-	●	-	-	-	-	-	-	-
D	-	-	ⓣ	ⓣ	-	●	ⓤ	ⓤ	●	-	●	●	-	-	-	-
E	●	ⓥ	-	●	ⓥ	ⓥ	ⓦ	ⓦ	-	ⓧ	●	ⓧ	ⓧ	-	-	ⓧ
F	●	●	●	●	●	●	●	●	●	●	●	●	●	●	●	●

Fig. 1. Crawling example

Definition 1: *The first detection number* and *the last detection number* are crawl numbers on which a URL is detected first and last, respectively. The *detection rate* of a URL is a value produced by the following equation:

$$\frac{\textit{the number of detections}}{\textit{the last detection number} - \textit{the first detection number} + 1}$$

For example, URL C is detected at the 5th, 6th, 7th, and 9th crawls. The detection rate of URL C is 4/(9-5+1)=0.8. The more frequently a URL is detected between the first and last detections, the higher the detection rate value becomes. The low detection rate value means that a URL has not been detected frequently since first detected. Because the URLs with low detection rates are not informative enough to be studied, we should analyze the change behavior of web pages with URLs whose detection rates are higher than a given threshold.

Definition 2: The *download rate* of a URL is a value computed by the following equation:

$$\frac{\textit{the number of successful downlaods}}{\textit{the number of download requests}}$$

For example, URL D is detected eight times, and the page for URL D is downloaded at the 3rd, 4th, 7th and 8th crawls. The download rate of URL D is (4/8)=0.5. A download rate value shows how consistently a web page is downloaded.

Definition 3: The *download recall* of a URL is a value computed by the following equation:

$$\frac{\textit{the number of download requests}}{\textit{the total number of crawls}}$$

For example, since there are 8 attempts to download a page with URL D in 16 crawls, the download recall of URL D is (8/16)=0.5. Suppose a URL is detected only once and a page with the URL is downloaded successfully. Then, even though the download rate of the URL becomes 1.00, we cannot accept this number for granted because there is only one download attempt in 16 crawls. We should consider the URLs whose download recalls are higher than a given threshold.

Definition 4: Suppose that a page with URL u is downloaded on crawl number i, and that there is at least one download success with URL u prior to crawl number i. The *current content* of URL u on crawl number i is defined as the content of a page that is downloaded on crawl number i. The *previous content* of URL u on crawl number i is defined as the content of the page of URL u that is successfully downloaded latest prior to crawl number i. If the current and previous contents of URL u on crawl number i are different from each other, the page of URL u is defined to be *modified* on crawl number i.

For example, the current content of URL E on the 10th crawl is ⓧ and the previous content is ⓦ. The page for URL E is modified on the 10th crawl. On the 12th crawl, the current and previous contents are of the same as ⓧ. We say that the page is not modified on the 12th crawl.

Definition 5: The *modification rate* of a page is a value computed by the following equation:

$$\frac{\textit{the number of modifications}}{\textit{the number of successful downloads} - 1}$$

Definition 6: The *modification recall* of a page is a value computed by the following equation:

$$\frac{\textit{the number of successful downloads} - 1}{\textit{the total number of crawls} - 1}$$

For example, the page corresponding to URL E is downloaded nine times, which implies that eight comparisons take place. The page is modified twice on the 7th and 10th crawls. The modification rate and modification recall of the page are computed as (2/(9-1)) = 0.25 and (8/15)=0.53, respectively.

The modification rate represents how frequently a web page changes in terms of the page contents. Because the content of a first page cannot be compared, we do not consider the first one in the modification rate computation. This is why the denominator of the modification rate computation is (*the number of successful downloads* – 1). As before, we also should analyze the modification rates of the pages whose modification recalls are higher than a given threshold.

Definition 7: Suppose we have a page with content c that is successfully downloaded with URL u. Let i and j ($i \leq j$) be the first and last crawl numbers on which the content c of the page of URL u is successfully downloaded, respectively. If there is no crawl number k ($i < k < j$) on which other content, different to the content c, of the page of URL u is successfully downloaded, then the *content age* of the page is defined to be $(j - i + 1)$.

Definition 8: The *coefficient of age variation* of a URL is a value computed by the following equation:

$$\frac{\textit{the standard deviation of content ages}}{\textit{the average of content ages}}$$

Definition 9: The *variation recall* of a URL is a value computed by the following equation:

$$\frac{\textit{the number of modifications}}{\textit{the total number of crawls} \; - \; 1}$$

For example, consider URL E. The content ages for URL E are 5 on the 6th crawl, 2 on the 8th crawl, and 7 on the 16th crawl, respectively. The content age represents how long a page keeps its content unchanged. The average of the content ages is (5+2+7) / 3 = 4.7. The standard deviation of the content ages is 2.52. Consequently, the coefficient of age variation of URL E is (2.52/4.7) = 0.54. The coefficient of age variation represents how regularly a page is modified. If a web page with URL *u* is modified regularly, the content ages of *u* become more or less uniform, and the standard deviation of the content ages becomes small. As before, we need to compute the coefficients of age variation for URLs whose variation recalls are higher than a given threshold.

3 Analyzing the Change of the Web Pages

3.1 Experimental Setups

In order to diminish possible bias toward sites we were monitoring, we chose sites from two separate categories: famous sites and random sites. The famous sites are composed of the top 4,000 sites offered by RankServ (http://www.rankserv.com/), which ranks all Korean sites in terms of popularity, as of November 2003. The random sites are composed of the 30,000 sites that were randomly selected from 1.2 million Korean sites we crawled in October 2003. A single site could belong to both the categories.

The crawling process works out as follows. We hold a list of URLs of the root pages of all the monitored sites. Our robot visits all the URLs in the list periodically, and visits a predetermined number of pages that are reachable from the root pages in a breadth-first fashion. As web pages are created and destroyed dynamically, the crawled pages are different on each visit. This scheme is superior to one that simply tracks a fixed set of pages on each visit, since the latter one would not capture new pages.

The robot was allowed to crawl at most 3,000 pages for each site. The maximum depth (i.e., the number of hops from a root page) was limited to nine. The robot was not allowed to crawl URLs containing a question symbol ('?') because these URLs mean the pages are not static. The page comparison was made character by character. All the characters on a page including the tags were compared with ones on other pages, to see if the pages are of the same.

When a web server receives a URL to serve, the web server often responds with a page with a different URL instead of the received URL. This is called redirection, which allows a page to be accessed with different URLs. When the redirection takes place, we consider that we failed to download a page with an original URL. In this case, we also tried to crawl a new page with the redirected URL.

3.2 Experimental Results

In this subsection, we analyze the change behavior of the web pages and describe our findings. Fig. 2 shows the number of the detected URLs, downloaded pages, and accumulated URLs for each crawl. The robot detected approximately 0.8 million URLs and downloaded 0.62 million pages (about 78% of the 0.8 million URLs) from the famous sites. From the random sites, the robot detected one million URLs and downloaded 0.83 million pages (about 83%). After all the 50 crawls, we accumulated 1.32 million URLs from the famous sites and 1.69 million URLs from the random sites.

In both set of the sites, 1.3% of the detected URLs on each crawl were new ones (they were not detected on the previous crawls). After 50 crawls (during 100 days), 40% of the accumulated URLs, which is much greater than expected, were not detected on the first crawl. On a weekly basis, about 5% of URLs detected were new in our experiment. These figures imply that any approaches to indexing, searching, and maintaining web databases should consider newly generated URLs (and pages) in an appropriate way. It should be emphasized that new web pages or URLs are created dynamically in the real world.

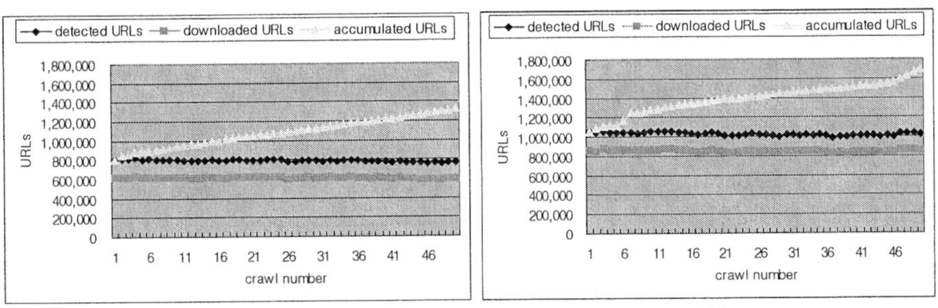

(a) (b)

Fig. 2. Results of crawls

Fig. 3 shows the distribution of detection rates for all the accumulated URLs. 90% of the detection rates were 0.9 or more. For exactly 9 URLs out of 10 URLs, we were able to detect them repeatedly (exactly speaking, 9 or 10 detections in 10 crawls). Simply speaking, once a URL is detected, it continues to be detected. We also learned that there were few URLs with the detection rates less than 0.9, which implies that a URL is hardly detected again once it ceases to be detected. From here, we are going to analyze the change behavior of web pages with URLs whose detection rates are higher than 0.9, because URLs with the low detection rates are simply unstable.

Fig. 4 shows the distribution of the download rates for the accumulated URLs (1.93 million URLs from both set of the sites) satisfying the condition that the download recall is at least 0.2 and the detection rate is 0.9 or more. The download rates of 19% of all the URLs were zero, which means that approximately one out of five URLs with detection rates at least 0.9 was not downloadable.

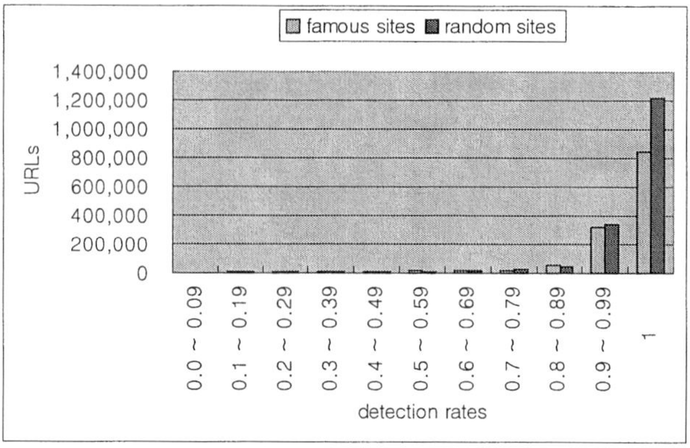

Fig. 3. Distribution of detection rates

The download rates of 80% of the URLs were 0.9 or above. What Fig. 4 implies is two-fold. First, if the first download of a URL is successful, the URL continues to be downloadable (precisely speaking, at least 9 out of 10 download attempts are successful). Second, if the first download of a URL fails, all the subsequent downloads are very likely to be unsuccessful.

When a robot has failed to download a web page with a URL several times, some administrators may have an expectation that the page will be downloaded someday. They may keep the URL and request the page later, in a hope that the page is restored, or the network condition is back to normal, etc. Fig. 4 says that it is virtually meaningless to keep and request such a page.

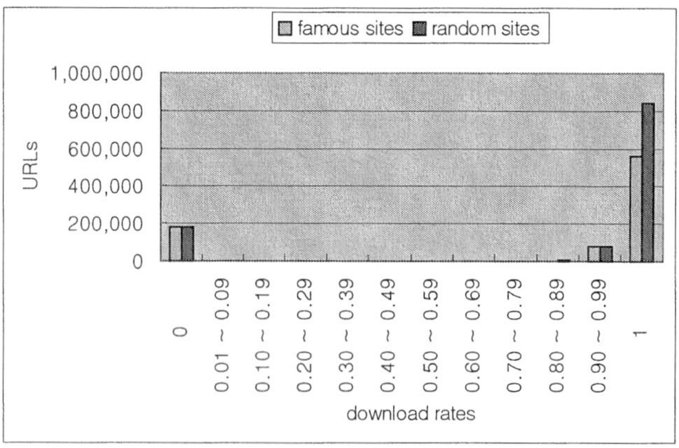

Fig. 4. Distribution of download rates

Fig. 5 represents the distribution of the modification rates of the pages in which the modification recalls were at least 0.2 and the detection rates were at least 0.9. 73% of the pages were never modified (i.e., their modification rates were zero) during our experiment. Roughly speaking, the figure means that if pages are downloaded in a row, at least 73% contents of them are the same as before. The rest 27% of the URLs were changed at least once. 47% of the modification rates of the rest were less than 0.1, and 18% of them were one (modified at every crawl). Less than 5% of all the pages change on each crawl. Recalling that we visited a site every other day, we do not know how many times the pages change in our visiting interval. We also learned that most of the pages were not frequently modified and a small number of pages were modified very frequently.

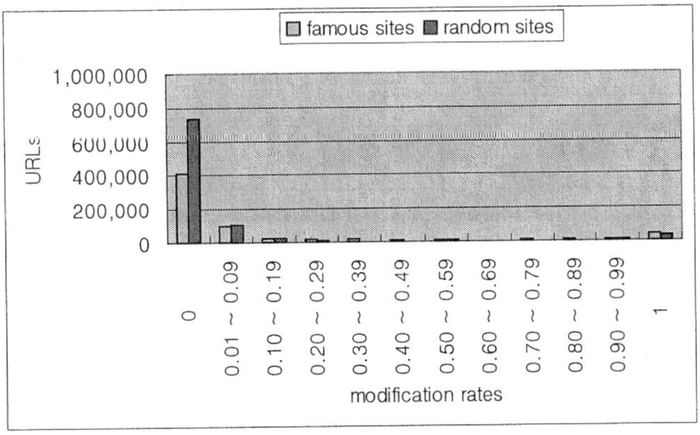

Fig. 5. Distribution of modification rates

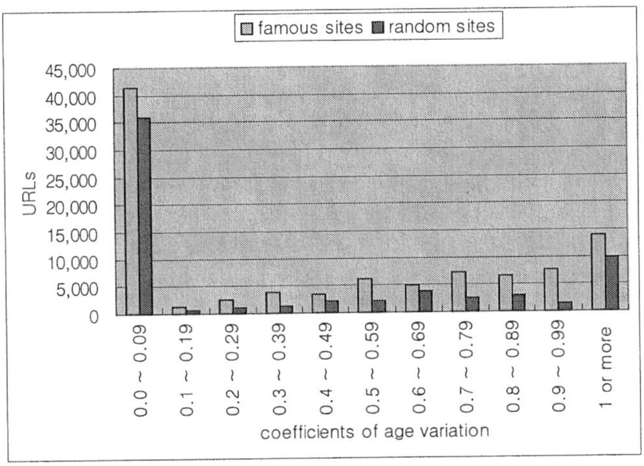

Fig. 6. Distribution of coefficients of age variation

Fig. 6 represents the distribution of coefficients of age variation for the URLs whose variation recalls were at least 0.2 and detection rates were 0.9 or more. We regarded URLs whose coefficients of age variation were less than 0.2, as having a modification cycle. In our experiments, 43% URLs of the famous sites had modification cycles and 57% URLs did not. 58% URLs of the random sites had modification cycles and 42% URLs did not. These results show clearly that we cannot assume that web pages are modified with fixed cycles.

4 Estimating the Change of Web Pages

This section presents a method that estimates the probability that a page will be downloaded in the next crawls. The approach postulates that the future change behavior of web pages is strongly related to the past one.

Table 1. Distribution of download rates

Download rate	Number of URLs	Percent of URLs
0	181,770	22.01%
0.01 ~ 0.09	489	0.06%
0.10 ~ 0.19	323	0.04%
0.20 ~ 0.29	461	0.06%
0.30 ~ 0.39	356	0.04%
0.40 ~ 0.49	396	0.05%
0.50 ~ 0.59	557	0.07%
0.60 ~ 0.69	575	0.07%
0.70 ~ 0.79	761	0.09%
0.80 ~ 0.89	2,725	0.33%
0.90 ~ 0.99	78,734	9.53%
1	558,842	67.66%
Total	825,989	100.00%

As a first step, we create a table that shows the distribution of download rates of URLs. An instance of the table is Table 1 that shows the distribution of download rates of URLs that were monitored for 100 days at two-day intervals in our experiment. We calculate the download rates to the two places of decimals. Based on Table 1, we estimate the probability of successful downloading of a web page.

Let $P(DR(x))$ of a URL denote the probability that a download rate value of the URL is x, where x is rounded into two decimals. Using Table 1, we can compute P(DR(x)) easily. For instance, P(DR(0)), the probability that the download rate of a page is 0, is 22.01%, and P(DR(1)) is 67.66%. In Table 1, we assume that instances are distributed uniformly in the intervals. Hence, we compute P(DR(x)) by dividing the percent corresponding to x by 9 when $0.01 \leq x \leq 0.09$, or 10 when $0.10 \leq x \leq 0.99$. For instance, P(DR(0.55)) is 0.07%/10 = 0.007%.

Let $P({}_{Y=a,N=b}DR_{Y=c,N=d})$ of a URL denote the probability that a page that was downloaded a times for $(a+b)$ download attempts will be downloaded c times for $(c+d)$ download attempts. Before computing the probability, we have two preconditions. First, the sum of a, b, c, and d should be less than or equal to the total number of crawls (50 in this paper). Second, intervals of $(a+b)$ and $(c+d)$ download attempts are the same as those of the monitoring interval (2 days in this paper). The probability is computed by the following formula:

$$P(_{Y=a,N=b}DR_{Y=c,N=d}) = \frac{P\left(DR\left(\frac{a+c}{a+b+c+d}\right)\right)}{\sum_{i=0}^{c+d} P\left(DR\left(\frac{a+i}{a+b+c+d}\right)\right)}$$

An experiment was done to see how well the formula works. First, we selected 581,608 URLs that were detected five times in the 46th to 50th crawl in the famous sites. Second, we have attempted to download pages with the selected URLs five times for 10 days at a two-day interval. With the number of successful downloads in the five past crawls, we estimate the number of successful downloads in the five future crawls. There are all the six cases such that a page will be downloaded 0, 1, 2, 3, 4, and 5 times, respectively, i.e., $P(_{Y=a,N=(5-a)}DR_{Y=0,N=5})$, $P(_{Y=a,N=(5-a)}DR_{Y=1,N=4})$, …, and $P(_{Y=a,N=(5-a)}DR_{Y=5,N=0})$, where a is the number of successful downloads. We estimated how many pages belonged to each case, and investigated how many pages actually did. Over 581,608 URLs, 715 URLs (323, 86, 39, 64, 175, and 92, respectively, in each case) wrongly estimated is very trivial.

5 Closing Remarks

We have defined a number of new metrics (including the download rate, the modification rate, and the coefficient of age variation) that shows the change behavior of web pages, and we have monitored 34,000 sites at two-day intervals for 100 days. Following are what we have learned in our experiment. First, 1.3% of the URLs detected at a crawl were not detected at the previous crawls (new pages are created at a rapid rate). Second, if the first download of a URL succeeds, at least 9 out of 10 next download attempts are to be successful. Third, the 73% web pages that were downloaded successfully at least 10 times were unmodified and the less than 5% web pages were modified on each crawl. Lastly, a large portion of the pages that were modified at least 10 times did not follow a fixed change interval. After observing the change behavior of the web pages, we presented the method estimating the change behavior in terms of downloading issues.

To our best knowledge, this is the first experiment that considers downloading issues in a single page basis. We believe that the findings in our experiment will help web administrators maintain web databases fresh (such as which pages to re-crawl, the interval of re-crawling, the order of pages to re-crawl, and so on).

A good change model for a web page can help us keep web databases fresh efficiently. As the future work, we are going to improve the change model of web pages. A more intensive experiment on the change model of web pages is currently under way. In particular, we are working on how significantly recent states of web pages affect the future change behavior.

References

1. Brewington, B., Cybenko, G.: How Dynamic is the Web? the 9th World Wide Web Conference (2000) 257-276
2. Cho, J., Garcia-Molina, H.: The Evolution of the Web and Implications for an Incremental Crawler. the 26th VLDB Conference (2000) 200-209

3. Cho, J., Garcia-Molina, H.: Synchronizing a Database to Improve Freshness. the 26th SIGMOD Conference (2000) 117-128
4. Douglis, F., Feldmann, A., Krishnamurthy, B.: Rate of Change and Other Metrics: a Live Study of the World Wide Web. the 1st USENIX Symposium on Internetworking Technologies and System (1997) 147-158
5. Edwards, G., McCurley, K., Tomlin, J.: Adaptive Model from Optimizing Performance of an Incremental Web Crawler. the 10th World Wide Web Conference (2001) 106-113
6. Fetterly, D., Manasse, M., Najork, M., Wiener, J. L.: A large-scale study of the evolution of web pages. the 12th World Wide Web conference (2003) 669-678
7. Kim, S. J., Lee, S. H.: Implementation of a Web Robot and Statistics on the Korean Web. the 2nd Human.Society@Internet Conference (2003) 341-350
8. Lawrence, S., Giles, C. L.: Searching the World Wide Web. Science, Vol. 280. No. 5360 (1998) 98-100
9. Lawrence, S., Giles, C. L.: Accessibility of Information on the Web. Nature, Vol. 400. No. 6740 (1999) 107-109
10. Ntoulas, A., Cho, J., Olston, C.: What's New on the Web? The Evolution of the Web from a Search Engine Perspective. the 13th World Wide Web Conference (2004) 1-12
11. Wills, C., Mikhailov, M.: Towards a Better Understanding of Web Resources and Server Responses for Improved Caching. the 8th World Wide Web Conference (1999) 1231-1243

Using XML in Version Management of Chemical Process Models

Heidi Rose, Chiou Peng Lam and Huaizhong Li

School of Computer and Information Science,
Edith Cowan University
2 Bradford St, Mount Lawley, Perth WA 6060, Australia
heidir@student.ecu.edu.au, c.lam@ecu.edu.au,
and h.li@ecu.edu.au

Abstract. Process modeling develops models of chemical engineering systems to promote better understanding and allow simulated investigation. Currently, there are no standards for process models, and no tool that addresses all phases of development. Model knowledge is frequently lost in this conversion, due to improper documentation of models, and the lack of systematic management mechanisms to manage all the models concerned. The ability to reuse models or model parts would greatly reduce the resources required for model development. This paper presents a strategy and framework for reuse that is facilitated through the documentation, control and information management of the model development process. This is accomplished through the application of Software Configuration Management strategies, and increases portability of information encapsulated by using XML based models. Incorporated in this is the automatic determination of versions, variants and revisions of models to assist modelers in tracking the evolution of model instances.

1 Introduction

Process modeling is the task of developing models of chemical process engineering systems, for the better understanding and simulated investigation of a system. The benefits of modeling and simulation include simplification of complex systems for understanding, safer representation of dangerous systems, and to reduce expensive experimentation.

Currently, the process modeling systems which are available from a wide range of sources do not adhere to a set of standards for interoperability between tools. Each system or tool uses different modeling languages for their development, implementing their own set of semantics and modeling representation techniques.

Present process modeling packages utilize their own modeling techniques and proprietary model representations without the ability to facilitate reuse of these models, let alone facilitating the reuse of models from other packages. This is a significant issue, hampering process design and modeling practices. In considering mechanisms for reuse in process modeling, a number of aspects can be considered. The focus for this paper is on the documentation, control and information

Y. Zhang et al. (Eds.): APWeb 2005, LNCS 3399, pp. 643–654, 2005.

management of the model development process. This is to be accomplished through the application of Software Configuration Management (SCM) strategies and XML technologies.

In the following section we describe current approaches for process modeling, their limitations and the motivation behind our work. We then describe our framework for supporting model reuse, and the techniques used to automatically identify versions. Section 5 outlines example test scenarios and their results from our test suite. The paper concludes with a summary of our observations and summarizes future work on the framework.

2 Background and Motivation

Presently the status of process modeling involves the solving of very large systems of equations (10,000 – 100,000) as part of the process models. However, existing limitations include a lack of mechanisms to handle the following:

1. Modeling complexity [1] [14];
2. Reuse parts of models, out of and sometimes even within their original context [4] [12] [15];
3. Documenting information/decisions during the design phase [1] [19];
4. Controlling and documenting the history of the various versions being built in a modeling project [1] [4] [12]; and
5. Support for team effort in model development [4] [12].

Recent developments in modeling and simulation environments have attempted to address limitation 1 by applying object-orientated concepts to the design of the tools (example packages include ASCEND [1], Modelica [9], SMILE [10], Aspen Plus [3], n-dim [1], Ptolemy II [8], SpeedUp [14], and MODKIT [4]). However, there have been limited advancements with regard to the second, third and fourth limitations.

The development of process models from scratch is still costly, time consuming and error prone. The ability to reuse models or model parts would greatly reduce the resources required for model development. However, there currently exists no universally applied standard for developing models or the model semantics. In order to have the reuse capability, it is necessary to overcome these three limitations – an objective that a number of systems are attempting [1].

With regard to limitation 5, the authors have found no existing software tools that can completely support team efforts in process model development. One of the aims of the recent CAPE-OPEN project signifies an initial effort towards addressing this specific limitation [12], although its overall objectives also deal with the other limitations listed. Global CAPE-OPEN commenced in June 1999.

2.1 Software Engineering Applied to Process Modeling

The application of processes and tools utilized in the software engineering profession would address a number of the limitations detailed above. Some works have already taken this approach. Examples include PhD studies involved in the N-dim [1] and ASCEND [17] projects by Allen and Thomas, and a recent dissertation by Thommi

Karhela [13] outlining a software architecture for process modeling using XML. Thomas's [17] studies involved the successful integration of ASCEND with N-dim, which supports information management and collaboration. This facilitates possible reuse through revision-management, a significant issue when considering team based model development. Allen's [1] study focused primarily on exploring methods for facilitating reuse, applying the software engineering component based concept of information sharing. Important ideas were discussed, with the project aiming to develop an Open Conceptual Framework to implement: dynamic configuration within set model structures; methods and documentation bound to models; and generalized equation based modeling.

Karhela [13] outlined a set of requirements for process modeling regarding the reuse of models. An architecture which allows the sharing of models, facilitating model customisation and co-use between different process tools were identified as the key requirements. Secondary to this (from our consideration), was the need for a flexible, fast run-time connection between process simulators and a virtual Distributed Control System (DCS).

Both requirements outlined where achieved to varying extents. A repository was implemented to facilitate sharing and co-use. In addition to this, the configuration was implemented in XML with component descriptions to allow for easy model customisation and co-use [13]. The secondary requirement outlined was addressed through the implementation of component technology and OLE.

While this work provided a significant step in facilitating re-use of process models, a number of limitations exist in the approach. The repository, while allowing a centralised storage location of process and proprietary library models, doesn't support the evolution of models developed by modelers. There are no versioning capabilities other than the noted history mechanism [13], and no method for storing the different states of the process models (i.e. variants). Although some component technology is implemented, no intelligent selection means are offered.

Research is also currently being carried out by the Process Systems Engineering Group at Aachen University headed by Professor Wolfgang Marquardt concerning computer-aided modeling and process design [2][3]. Their investigations are currently attempting to address the following topics:

- integrated information models for data and documents;
- comparisons of data models in chemical engineering [15]; and
- tool integration and modeling frameworks [2] [3] [11].

As a part of the research being done of particular interest here is the work by Schopfer et al. [15] involving the development of a co-ordination system for process simulators (Cheops) where a centralized model repository (Rome) has an important role [13]. The primary idea is to develop and deploy unit operation models using Rome [11], executing the models based on different modeling schemes utilizing Cheops. The models can be exported from Rome into textual or binary representations of a compliant software component. Rome provides its functionality for other tools via CORBA [11]. This functionality includes manipulation of the neutral model representation or retrieval of information about the model implementation. Rome has also a web user interface known as RomeWWW. These studies have provided significant advantages to process modeling, proving that Software Engineering principles can contribute to the efficiency of process modeling.

2.2 XML in Process Modeling

Extensible Mark-up Langauge (XML) has quickly become the standard for the interchange for information. XML instance documents are text that can be read and edited easily on any platform, and thus suits the presentation of structural data. With a XML based data model, different modeling and simulation tools can be integrated, and easily used on the Internet. Process models described in XML would increase the portability of information encapsulated within models.

There have been two noted applications of XML to process modeling thus far. The first is by the Aachen Research Group previously noted through their development of an XML based data model CapeML [18]. CapeML is based on CAPE-OPEN work aiming to facilitate standards for Process Modeling. CapeML is outlined in [18]. The second is the Logical data model by Karhela [13] for use in the modeling repository Gallery. The data model for Gallery is specified using XML and referred to as GML. When server clients are communicating with Gallery they are sending and receiving parts of this data model. The current GML is described as a UML class diagram in [13].

These works have both aimed at assisting model openness and reuse. The use of XML is central to this openness and is already being applied to Process Modeling. Clearly a set schema or DTD for process models needs to be universally adopted to aid the possibility of standardizing process data models through XML. Regardless of this, any process methods or techniques developed to assist reuse will have the ability to be applied to any XML Instance. This premise is the basis of the work outlined here.

2.3 Software Configuration Management Theory

Software configuration management provides for complete product life cycle management [20]. There are seven operational aspects involved in SCM [6] [7] [16]: Identification, control, audit, status accounting, management of the SCM process, software release management and delivery, and team work. As an initial step, our focus is on providing identification and control for process models. Given the lack of any of the above mechanisms currently for process modeling, this is considered a significant step in aiding reuse.

The functionalities of SCM can be implemented in various ways. The various techniques and concepts which have been applied are often deeply intertwined, with concepts often pertaining to more than one area. More recently, the approach has been to divide the concepts into *product space* and *version space* [6] [19]. The product space is used to describe the structure and storage of the product, and the version space is used to define the items to be versioned and the approaches to be applied. The product space outlines the objects and relationships that are to be managed by the system, at what level the versioning is to be applied, and how the objects and relationships are to be stored [19]. In the application to process modeling, the objects are clearly the models and the level of versioning is dependent on the versioning strategy to be applied by the company or institution. Any other aspects are outside the scope of this paper.

Central to the concept of versions is the specification of the version space. A *version* is an object at a particular time during its evolution [6]. As the object changes many *versions* of it are created. These different versions can be stored for many reasons, including to track the evolution of an object, to support previous product releases, as well as to allow development to go back to a previous version if a new line isn't successful. Versioning is therefore concerned with managing all these different versions and how they relate to each other. A version space identifies the objects to be versioned, version identification and organization strategies and defines operations for retrieving existing versions and constructing new versions. There are four key concepts involved in version space specifications. These concepts are *State* and *Change-based* versioning, which are concerned with the evolution of the objects, and *Extensional* and *Intensional* versioning which are concerned with how the versions are reconstructed and stored [6] [16]. Their combination results in vastly different systems with different capabilities. These four concepts are outlined as follows.

2.3.1 State-Based Versioning

Version models which focus on the state of versioned items are called *state-based*. In state-based versioning, versions are described in terms of revisions and variants. The difference between these terms can be classified with respect to the intent of the evolution used in the development of the version as outlined below [6] [19]:

1. a **revision** is a version which permanently or temporarily supersedes one of it's predecessor(s) (i.e. it is a direct replacement of a previous version); and
2. a **variant** is created with the intension of co-existing with alternative versions (i.e. alternative implementations of a system with respect with respect to operating system or system specifications)..

Therefore, instead of performing modifications by overwriting, old versions are retained to support maintenance of software already delivered to customers as well as to recover from erroneous updates, etc.

2.3.2 Change-Based Versioning

Changes provide an alternative way of characterising versions [1]. In *change-based* models, a version is described in terms of changes applied to some baseline. A *baseline* is a software item that has been formally designated and fixed at a specific time during development. The term has also been used to refer to a version that has been agreed upon. In this situation, changes are assigned *change identifiers* (CID), and additional attributes to characterise the reasons and the nature of the change.

Change-based versioning requires that changes made between one version and another be stored. This is done through the application of *deltas*. All versions of a particular versioned object share some common aspects, and vary with respect to other specific parts. The differences between two versions are called a *delta* [6] [19]. These differences are stored and are used to either construct new versions (by merging them with a baseline version) or indicate the changes made between versions.

2.3.3 Extensional Versioning

Extensional versioning supports retrieval of versions that have been previously constructed [6] [16] [19]. A versioned item can be considered as a set of explicit versions V = {v_1, …, v_n} [6]. Here all versions are explicit and have been checked in once before with each version being typically identified by some unique version number (flat such as 1, 2, .., or hierarchical such as 1.1, 1.2, 1.2.1, …). A user interacting with the SCM system retrieves some version v_i, performs some changes on the retrieved version and submits the changed version as a new version v_{i+1} into the object base. To ensure safe retrieval of previously constructed versions, versions can be immutable. In many systems all versions are made immutable when they are checked into the object base. This is generally done through explicit operations which freeze mutable versions. Furthermore, immutability may be imposed selectively i.e. by distinguishing between mutable and immutable attributes.

2.3.4 Intensional Versioning

Intensional versioning supports flexible, automatic construction of consistent versions in a large version space [6] [19]. The term 'potential versions' is used when describing intensional versioning, emphasizing that versions may not have been constructed explicitly before when using this technique [20].

Intensional versioning involves the construction of versions by the application of rules (which satisfy a set of requirements) from property based descriptions [16]. Therefore, intensional versioning is driven by global version rules which may be either stored in the versioned object base or submitted as part of a query.

3 Outline of Framework

Figure 1 depicts a UML representation of the framework of a future modeling design support environment. A prototype of such an environment with partial functionality has been implemented and evaluated with the results included in this paper.

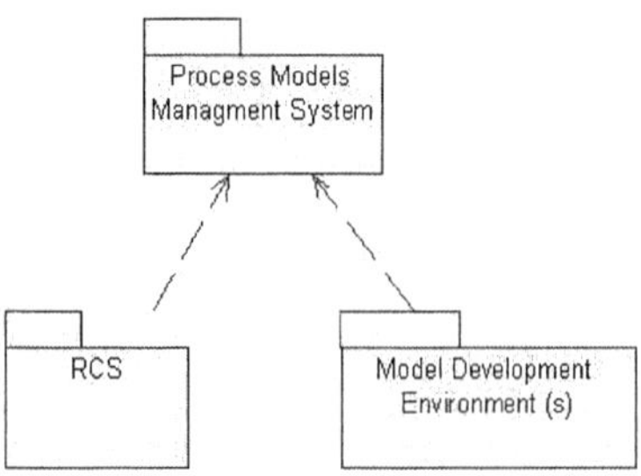

Fig. 1. UML Representation of Framework

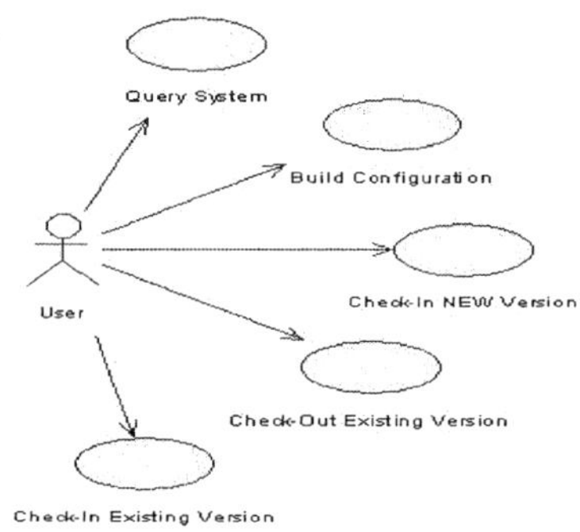

Fig. 2. Framework Use-Case Scenarios

The environment consists of three independent yet integrated tools. It consists of two existing tools, a model development environment employed in industrial practice and RCS, a basic software versioning tool. The third tool, the Process Models Management System (PMMS) acts as a central access point for all the model developers and any users during the model development and design lifecycle. Tool integration such as this will remain a considerable issue for chemical engineering operating companies, despite the effort of major vendors to integrate their own tools with each other and those of selected collaborating partners. End users need to customize their design support environments by integrating additional tools and databases provided by other vendors or in-house development groups in order to differentiate their technology from that of their competitors. Additionally, in order to support the whole development process, different packages are often required as no one package (or group of packages) offered by one vendor successfully addresses all aspects of design.

The framework supports this integration requirement by supporting the use of different design environments. This is facilitated by using XML based process data models and the openness of their text based structure. Any development environment that outputs an XML instance document can be implemented in the environment. In using XML based models as a tool independent representation, any process model development environment that develops XML based models can be integrated into the framework in a 'plug-and-play' manner. The focus of this paper is the PMMS and its interaction with RCS. Further details regarding model development environments (MDE) and their use are outside the scope of this paper.

The aim is for the framework to completely support the versioning of process modeling through all current techniques previously outlined (state-based or change-based, intensional or extensional versioning). The following sections outline the versioning approach of the prototype environment. Intensional versioning has not been implemented here but the framework included aspects allowing the introduction of this technique at a later stage. RCS was integrated with the PMMS over other systems due to its simplicity and ease of use for text-based files. Choosing a more complicated SCM system would reduce the chances of process modelers successfully utilising the system. The overhead required is significantly less in using a simple versioning system (such as RCS) rather than a fully fledged SCM system as used by software developers. Additionally, many of the functionalities offered do not necessarily apply. The user has the following scenarios available to them from the framework as diagrammatically represented in Figure 3. GUIs from the prototype Process Model Management System are representative of the use cases outlined. Figure 3 is the main GUI for the system. Due to space requirements no others have been included.

In Check-In Models and Comparing Models a delta is created. The delta contains the differences involved in changing the original model to create the altered model. This is further detailed in the next section. The current implementation uses the delta to determine the version type and allows the user to store the delta if desired. This supports change-based strategies and change requests and ultimately will allow for intensional versioning. The framework thus presently supports state-based and change-based versioning with extensional versioning. This results in all models (or delta representations of models) being explicitly enumerated and have been previously constructed.

The scenarios involving New Models involve directly invoking propriety tools. Create New Models involves invoking the chosen model development environment (MDE) to develop a completely new model. The framework allows the user to choose from a number of MDEs that have been integrated (plug-and-play) into the framework. Check-In New Model scenario entails passing the model directly from the MDE to RCS for management and storage. Confirmation that no model like it has been previously checked-in is sought before the system allows the model to be checked-in.

Check-Out of Existing Models is a direct interaction with RCS with the concerned model explicitly located and its status in RCS changed. Comparing Models involves the comparison of two models for the identification of changes and differences between the models. The identified differences are stored in a delta file at the developer's discretion. The model is not checked-in in this instance. This is the difference between this scenario and the Check-In Existing Model scenario. If the model (on comparison) is deemed a revision or a variant, this information is added to the model and the model (or delta) is passed to RCS for Check-In. Depending on the users chosen implementation, the Check-In Existing scenario either passes the created delta file or the whole altered file to RCS for management.

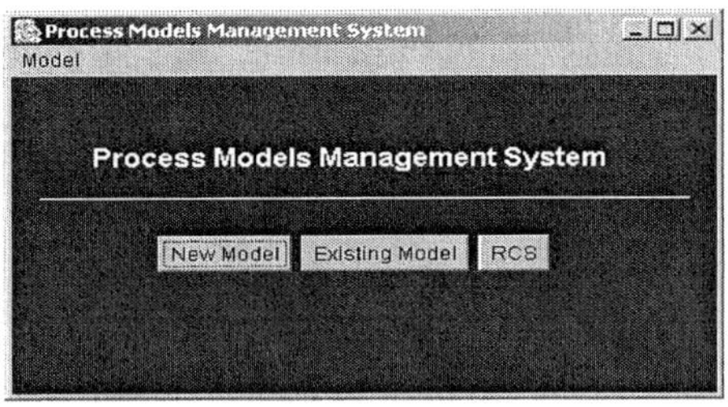

Fig. 3. Main GUI of the Prototype PMMS

4 Automatic Identification of Versions

Fundamental to the versioning system in PMMS is the identification of models as either *revisions* or *variants*. Due to the complicated mathematical nature of models, this automatic detection assists the modelers in providing the differences in an external document, saving them the time in manually comparing models. It could also be used to compare library models to identify the model more suited to an application. This detection facility provides several key additional advantages in facilitating reuse:

(1) It assists the modelers in indicating the level of changes made;
(2) It allows the identification of the evolution of the model;
(3) It prevents the storing of insignificant model changes; and
(4) It allows the reuse of models through 'template' use of previous models to develop new models.

In order to illustrate what is involved in automatic determination, a manual example has been outlined. The example, a continuous stirred tank reactor (CSTR), contains a set of mathematical equations which typically represent various mass and energy balances used to model the system. The CSTR is a standard component extensively used in the modeling of process systems. The steady-state of a CSTR is achieved when:

$$\frac{dC_d}{dt} = 0 \quad \text{and} \quad \frac{dT}{dt} = 0\text{, that is} \tag{1}$$

$$f_1\ (C_A, T) = 0 = \frac{F}{V}(C_{Af} - C_A) - k_0 \exp\left(\frac{-\Delta E}{rT}\right)C_A \tag{2}$$

$$f_2(C_A, T) = 0 = \frac{F}{V}(T_f - T) + \left(\frac{-\Delta H}{\rho c_p}\right)k_0 \exp\left(\frac{-\Delta E}{rT}\right)C_A - \frac{UA}{V\rho c_p}(T - T_j) \tag{3}$$

To solve these two equations for the steady states of the two variables C_A and T, all parameters and initial values must be specified. Given these numerical values, the application of for example Newton's methods can be used to solve for the steady-state values of C_A and T. In simulations any changes that are made to any of the parameter values or set points result in a ***variant*** of the model which represents the same system operating at different operating conditions, as the model structure is still the same. If more equations are used, for example, due to linearisation or additional dynamic modeling for mass balances or energy balances, the structure of the model is significantly changed. This therefore is a ***revision.***

The analysis of the created delta file is based on whether the model operating conditions or the model structure has been changed. If operating conditions (e.g. parameters or set points) are changed then it is a variant from a process modeling view point, otherwise it is a revision. Current analysis is based on the delta XML created using XyDiff [5]. Research is currently being carried out to intelligently create a semantic delta.

5 Scenarios and Results

In order to test the system and prove the validity of the analysis technique, three scenarios were devised and implemented. These scenarios where a modification, a insertion/deletion, and finally a scenario were no changes where made. All examples used the CapeML example available from [18] as the base (original) model file as outlined below in Figure 4.

5.1 Modification Scenario

The first scenario used to test the PMMS automatic versioning identification, involved a modification to the original model file. This modification involved the changing of two parameter values (see lines 5 and 33 of Figure 6). Line 5s modification was to a attribute value, to change the upperbound from 200 to 250 in the altered file. Line 33s modification was to change the value here from 8.3144 in the original model, to 16.6288. These changes are outlined in Figure 5.

```
<?xml version="1.0" encoding="UTF-8"?>
<CapeModelTypes xmlns="http://www.lfpt.rwth-aachen.de/CapeML">
<VariableType name="Temperature" myID="temperature" lowerBound="0.0"
upperBound="1000.0" unit="K"/>
<VariableType name="Volume" myID="volume" lowerBound="0.0"
upperBound="1E8" unit="m3"/>
<VariableType name="Pressure" myID="pressure" lowerBound="0.0"
upperBound="200" unit="bar"/>
<VariableType name="AmountMoles" myID="amount_moles" lowerBound="0.0"
upperBound="1E500" unit="mol"/>
<ModelType myID="M-1" name="GasPhase">
<VariableDefinition myID="V-1" xlink:href="#id(temperature)" name="T"/>
<VariableDefinition myID="V-2" xlink:href="#id(pressure)" name="p"/>
<VariableDefinition myID="V-3" xlink:href="#id(volume)" name="V"/>
<VariableDefinition myID="V-4" xlink:href="#id(amount_moles)" name="n"/>
<Equation>
<BalancedEquation myID="E-1">
<Expression>
<Term> <Factor> <VariableOccurrence xlink:href="#id(V-2)"/>
</Factor>
<Factor mul.op="MUL"><VariableOccurrence xlink:href="#id(V-3)"/
</Factor>
</Term>
</Expression>
<Expression>
<Term><Factor><VariableOccurrence xlink:href="#id(V-1)"/>
</Factor>
<Factor mul.op="MUL"><VariableOccurrence xlink:href="#id(V-4)"/>
</Factor>
<Factor mul.op="MUL"><Number value="8.3144"/>
</Factor>
</Term>
</Expression>
</BalancedEquation>
</Equation>
</ModelType>
</CapeModelTypes>
```

Fig. 4. CapeML based Example

```
(8)  upperBound="200" unit="bar"/>
(30) <Factor mul.op="MUL"><Number value="16.6288"/>
```

Fig. 5. Change 1 of CapeML example

```
(24) <Term><Factor><VariableOccurrence xlink:href="#id(V-1)"/>
(25) </Factor>
```

Fig. 6. Change 2 of CapeML example

From here, the models where passed through PMMS where a delta file was produced. From the analysis of the delta file the system produced the following output window with the resulting classification. As can be clearly seen in Figure 7 the system successfully identified the version to be a variant.

5.2 Insert / Delete Scenario

The second scenario used to test the PMMS automatic versioning identification capabilities involved the insertion of equation details and the deletion of a model equation block from the original model file. This alteration involved the creation of an additional model factor and the deletion of the second expression (lines 25-33) from the original model. The inserted lines can be clearly seen in Figure 6 which indicates the changes made to create the second file used in this instance.

Both models where then passed through PMMS where the corresponding delta file was produced. From the analysis of the delta file the system produced the following output window with the resulting classification. Figure 8 indicates that the system successfully identified the version to be a revision.

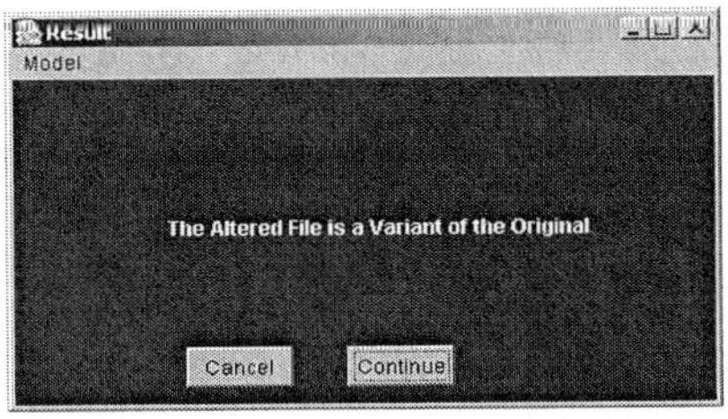

Fig. 7. Result from Modification example

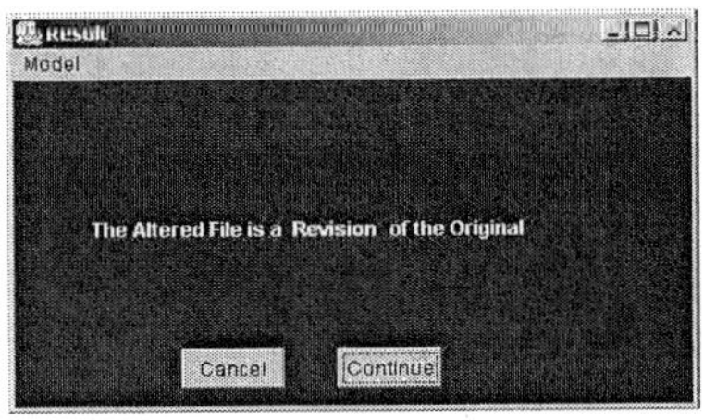

Fig. 8. Result from Insert/Deletion example

5.3 No Changes Scenario

The final scenario used to test the PMMS versioning classification involved putting the same file into the system twice, ensuring that the contents are identical. Both models where then passed through PMMS and a delta file was produced. From the analysis of the delta file the system correctly produced a SAME classification of the files. The system then only offers the user the 'Cancel' option as the change is not significant and will not allow the user to check-in the file to RCS.

6 Conclusions

In this paper, we have described a framework for supporting reuse of process models. In the current phase of development the Process Models Management System was created as the central access point for the framework. Additionally the PMMS automatically identifies version types prior to management in RCS. This prototype system was tested using three scenarios which all returned successful results. Research is currently being carried out to intelligently create a semantic delta therefore making the identification technique intelligent. The intention is for the framework to assist in the reuse of process modeling by tracking the evolution of models and allowing template-based re-use of previous models. Future work for the framework aims to continue with seeking SCM and information management techniques that will aid reuse in process modeling, including the application of intensional versioning and component based techniques.

References

[1] Allen, B. A. 1997a, *A More Reusable Modeling System*, PhD Thesis, Chemical Engineering, Carnegie Mellon University, Carnegie-Mellon University, Pittsburgh, PA.

[2] Bayer, B., Schneider, R. and Marquardt, W. 2002, 'Issues in Developing Open Software Environments for Chemical Engineering', *6th Int. Conf. on Work with Display Units,* Berchtesgadenm Germany, ER-GONOMIC Institut fur Arbeitis - und Sozialforschung.

[3] Becker, S., Hasse, T., Westfechtel, B. and Wilhelms, J. 2002, 'Integration Tools Supporting Cooperative Development Processes in Chemical Engineering' *Integrated Design and Process Technology (IDPT),* Society for Design and Process Science .

[4] Bogusch, R., Lohmann, B. and Marquardt, M. 1999, 'Computer-Aided Process Modelling with MODKIT', *Computers & Chemical Engineering,* 25.

[5] Cobéna, G., Abiteboul, S. and Marian, A. 2002, *XyDiff: tools for detecting changes in XML documents.* Available: http://www-rocq.inria.fr/~cobena/XyDiffWeb/

[6] Conradi, R. & Westfechtel, B. 1998, 'Version Management of Software Configuration Management', *ACM Computing Surveys,* vol. 30, No. 2, June.

[7] Dart, S. 1991, 'Concepts in Configuration Management Systems', *Proceedings of the Third International Workshop on Software Configuration Management,* ACM SIGSOFT.

[8] Davis, J., Hylands, C., Janneck, J., Lee, E. A., Liu, J., Liu, X., Neuendoffer, S., Sachs, S., Stewart, M., Vissers, K., Whitaker, P. and Xiong, Y. 2001, *Overview of the Ptolemy Project*, Dept.Elect. Engg. & Comp. Sci., University of California, California.

[9] Elmqvist, H. and Mattsson, S. E. 1997, 'Modelica - The Next Generation Modelling Language An International Effort', *Proc. 1st World Congress on System Simulation,* Singapore.

[10] Ernst, T., Jahnichen, S. and Klose, M. 1997, 'The Architecture of the Smile/M Simulation Environment', *Proceedings of the 15th IMACS world congress on Scientific Computation, Modelling and Applied Mathematics,* Berlin, Wissenschaft und Technik Verlag.

[11] Hackenberg, J, Krobb, C, Schopfer, G, von Wedel, L, Wyes, W., and Marquardt, W. 2000, 'A Repository-based Environment for Lifecycle Modeling and Simulation', *JSPS Int. Workshop on Safety-Assured Operation and Concurrent Engineering*, Yokohama.

[12] Jarke, M., Koller, J., Marquardt, W., Wedel, L. v. and Brauschweig, B. 1999, *CAPE-OPEN: Experiences from a Standardization Effort in Chemical Industries*, Lehrstuhl fur Prozebtechnik

[13] Karhela, T 2002, *A Software Architecture for Configuration and Usage of Process Simulation Models,* PhD Thesis, VTT Industrial Systems, ISBN 951-38-6011-6.

[14] Pantelides, C. C. 1998, 'SpeedUp - Recent Advances in Process Simulation', *Computer Chemical Engineering,* 12**,** 745-755.

[15] Schopfer, G., von Wedel, L., and Marquardt, W. 2000. 'An Environment Architecture to Support Modelling and Simulation in the Process Design Lifecycle', *Proceedings of AIChe Annual Meeting 2000,* Los Angeles, 12-17.11.2000.

[16] Syrjanen, T. 1999, *A Rule-Based Formal Model for Software Configuration,* Helsinki University of Technology, Available: http://citeseer.nj.nec.com/472460.html

[17] Thomas, M. E. 1996, *Tool and Information Management in Engineering Design*, PhD Thesis, Chemical Engineering, Carnegie Mellon University.

[18] von Wedel, L. 2002, *CapeML - A Model Exchenge Language for Chemical Process Modeling*, Aachen University, Germany.

[19] Westfechtel, W., Munch, B.P., and Conradi, R. 2001, 'A Layered Architecture for Uniform Version Management', *IEEE Transactions on Software Engineering,* Vol. 27, No. 12, December.

[20] Zeller, A. 1997, *Configuration Management with Version Sets - A Unified Software Versioning Model and it's Applications*, PhD Thesis, Technische Universitat Braunschweig.

An Algorithm for Enumerating SCCs in Web Graph*

Jie Han[1], Yong Yu[2], Guowei Liu[1], and Guirong Xue[1]

Department of Computer Science and Engineering,
Shanghai Jiao Tong University, Shanghai 200240, China
{micro_j, gwliu, grxue}@sjtu.edu.cn
yyu@cs.sjtu.edu.cn

Abstract. The pages and their hyperlinks of the World-Wide Web can be viewed as nodes and edges of a directed graph, i.e. the Web Graph. To study the connectivity and structure of the graph, strongly connected component (SCC) analysis is important. When the graph contains hundreds of millions of nodes and billions of edges, it's difficult to use traditional algorithm because of the intractability for both time and space. In this paper, we investigate some properties of web graph, and propose a feasible algorithm for enumerating its SCCs.

1 Introduction

The web pages and the hyperlinks between them form a huge directed graph. The nodes of the graph represent web pages while the directed edges represent the hyperlinks. Exploitation of the information in this graph is helpful for the improvement of some classic algorithms in web search, topic classification and cyber-community enumeration.

Connectivity analysis is an important part of the research on web graph. Enumerating SCCs is the most common way when studying the connectivity of web graph. Some algorithms are available in O(n+e) time when enumerating SCCs in a directed graph. But, because of the large scale of the web graph, we can hardly load the full graph into the main memory. Thus, we cannot use these algorithms directly.

In this paper, we first review some traditional algorithms for enumerating SCCs in a general directed graph (Section 2). Then, we will describe some special properties of web graph. With these helpful properties, we propose an algorithm to enumerate SCCs in this graph. In this algorithm, to take advantage of main memory, we split the original graph into parts which are smaller enough, decompose them one by one and finally merge them together (Section 3). Finally, we discuss our detailed implementation of this algorithm on the web graph in China. The algorithm ends in a week while we can hardly apply the traditional algorithm on this web graph as it may run for years (Section 4).

* This project is supported by National Foundation of Natural Science of China(No. 60473122).

Y. Zhang et al. (Eds.): APWeb 2005, LNCS 3399, pp. 655 – 667, 2005.

2 Related Work

The web graph contains billions of nodes and grows exponentially with time. Interesting properties are found in this graph such as the power law distribution and the bow-tie structure.

In the prior observations from Broder and Kumar [1], the web is depicted as a bow-tie in Figure 1.

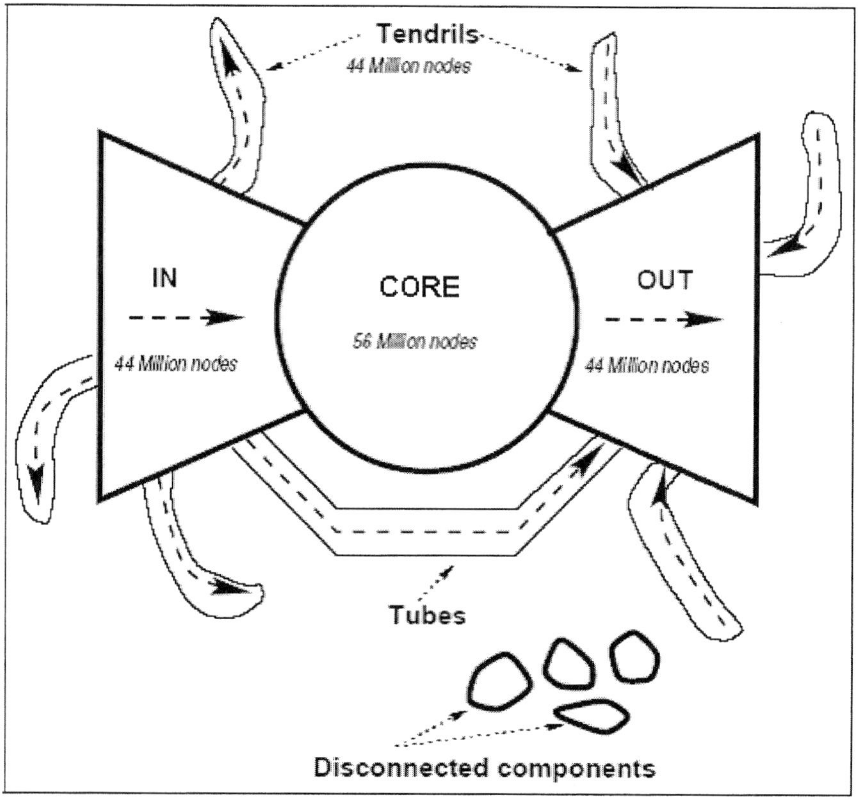

Fig. 1. The web as a bowtie [1]

The web graph is divided into several parts according to Figure 1. The core of the figure, CORE, represents the maximum strongly connected component of the graph. The left side of the bowtie, named IN, represents the pages from which at least a path exists to some nodes in CORE. The right side of the bowtie, named OUT, represents the pages which can be reached from some nodes in CORE. The TENDRILS contains pages that are reachable from IN, or that can reach OUT, without passages through CORE. IN can be viewed as the set of new pages that link to their interesting pages but not yet been discovered by CORE, while OUT can be viewed as some well known pages whose links point to internal pages only. As for TENDRILS, The web has not yet discovered these pages, and these pages do not link to better-known regions. The deeper analysis of Figure 1 reveals the connectivity of the web graph. If pages u and v are randomly chosen, the probability that there exists a path from u to v is only 1/4.

In order to compute the structure of the web graph, enumerating SCCs in web graph is necessary.

Tarjan presented an algorithm to decompose a directed graph into strongly connected components in O(n+e) [2] , where n denotes the number of nodes and e denotes the number of edges. The algorithm was composed of two interleaved depth-first searches (DFS). Firstly, a DFS traverses all the nodes and constructs a depth-first forest. Then, a stack is used in the second DFS to find the root of each SCC and all the descendents of the root including the root itself are in the same SCC.

However, the most famous algorithm to decompose a directed graph into strongly connected components is Sharir's algorithm [3][4]. His elegant algorithm finds all SCCs in a directed graph in O(n+e) time. In the algorithm, two DFSs are performed. Firstly, use DFS to find all nodes in the graph, and compute f(u) where f(u) denotes the order when the DFS algorithm finds node u. Compute G^T, the transpose of the original graph G. Then, DFS again on G^T in the order of decreasing f(u). Each tree in the forest output by the second DFS denotes a strongly connected component.

Lisa.K.Fleischer brought up a parallel algorithm in year 2000 [5]. The main idea of the algorithm is as follows:

DCSC (G):

1) Choose a random node v in the graph G.
2) For v, compute the predecessors Pred(G,v) and descendents Desc(G,v). The predecessors denote the nodes which can reach v while the descendents denote the nodes which v can reach.
3) Output the SCC: Pred(G， v)∩Desc (G, v) ∪ {v}.
4) DCSC(Pred(G, v)\SCC)
5) DCSC (Desc(G, v)\SCC)
6) DCSC(G\(Pred(G, v) ∪ Desc(G, v)))

The algorithm divides the graph into three sub-graphs after outputting each SCC and decomposes the three sub-graphs recursively. As for finding the predecessors and descendents of a node, both DFS and BFS (broad-first search) work well. The algorithm works efficiently in multiprocessor system.

3 The Split-Merge Algorithm

The algorithms of SCC enumeration described in section 2 require traversing the graph, which is sometimes not applicable to the web graph. Generally speaking, web graph consists of several hundreds of millions of nodes and several billions of edges. Although machines with 8GB main memory are popular in many organizations involved in web graph research and powerful algorithms of web graph compression [6] are available, sometimes it's still impossible to load the entire graph into main memory. Therefore, link information will be loaded from hard disk to main memory back and forth when traversing the graph. The time cost on I/O is unaffordable. So it's infeasible to enumerate SCCs in the web graph in a straightforward way.

3.1 The Basic Idea

The principal difficulty of the problem is the large scale of web graph. Were the graph smaller, it should be easier to find all SCCs. If we split the graph into several parts, the scale of each part will be much smaller. Thus, we get a rough idea of split-merge as follows:
The split-merge algorithm:

1) Classify the nodes of graph G into n groups. Build a sub-graph with each group of nodes and the links among them.
2) Decompose each sub-graph into SCCs. If the sub-graph is small enough, use any algorithm for enumerating SCCs. Otherwise, recursively apply the split-merge algorithm.
3) Assume each SCC in a sub-graph is a node, and eliminate the duplicated links between them. We obtain the contracted graph G', a graph composed of all the SCCs.
4) Decompose the contracted graph G' into SCCs. If the G' is small enough, use any algorithm of enumerating SCCs. Otherwise, recursively apply the split-merge algorithm.
5) Merge the SCCs from sub-graphs with the help of the decomposition of G'.

For instance, look at the directed graph in Figure 2.

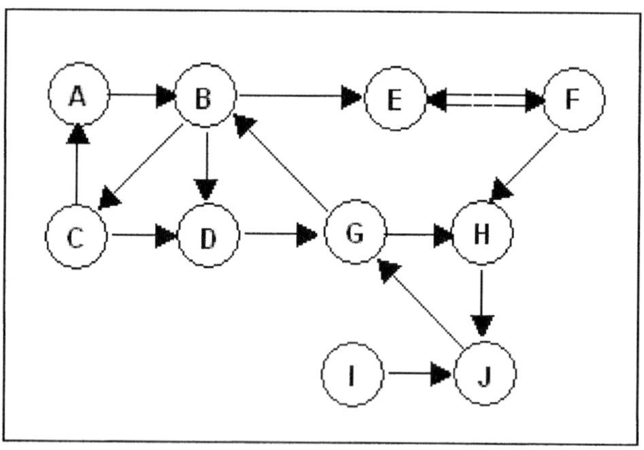

Fig. 2(a). An directed graph G'

The directed graph G consists of 10 nodes and 15 edges (Figure 2(a)). We split the graph into three sub-graphs (Figure 2(b)). Thus, the largest sub-graph only contains 4 nodes and 5 edges. The sub-graph in box 1 can be decomposed as (A, B, C) and (D).

The sub-graph in box 2 can be decomposed as (E, F). And the sub-graph in box 3 can be decomposed as (G, H, J) and (I). After each sub-graph is decomposed, we can contract the graph as G' (Figure 2(C)). G' only contains 5 nodes and 6 edges and can be decomposed as ((A, B, C), (E, F), (G, H, J), (D)) and (I). By merging the result from Figure 2(c) and Figure 2(b), we can enumerate all the SCCs in the original graph

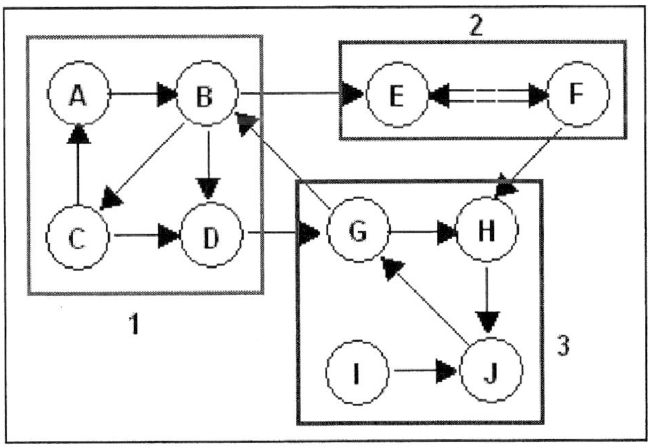

Fig. 2(b). Split the graph G into three sub-graphs

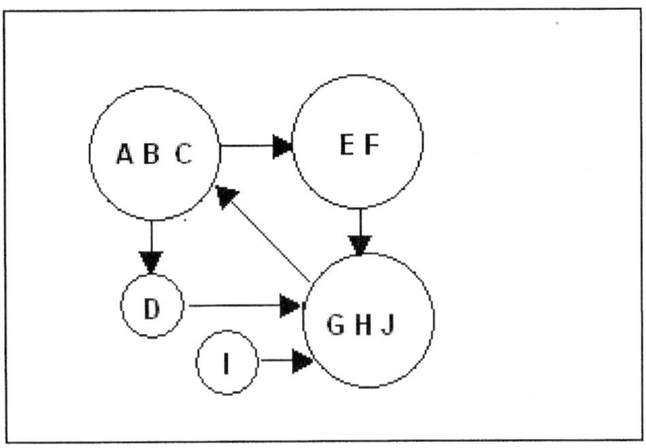

Fig. 2(c). The contracted graph G'

G: (A, B, C, E, F, G, H, J, D) and (I). In this example, we can see that the scale of both sub-graphs and the contracted graph G' are much smaller than that of the original graph G. If we split the web graph into sub-graphs, it's possible to load one entire sub-graph into main memory when decomposing. Thus, the extra cost of split and merge seems to be affordable compared with swapping edges between hard disk and main memory back and forth.

However, the basic split-merge algorithm does not always work on a general directed graph. Have a look at Figure 3.

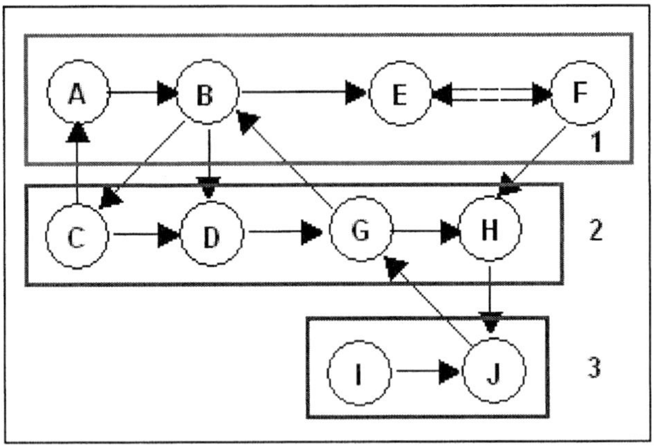

Fig. 3(a). Another way to split graph G

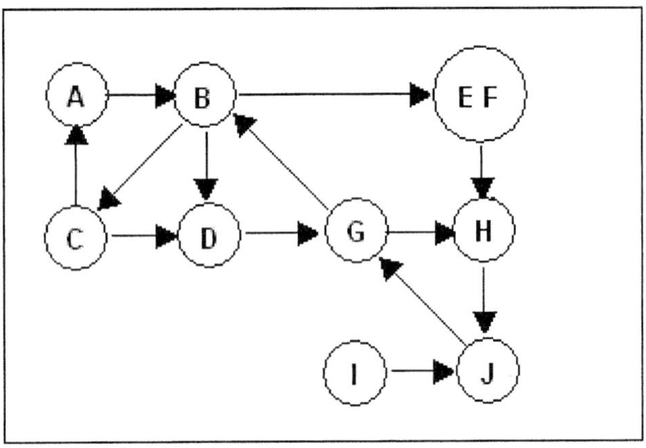

Fig. 3(b). The scale of the contracted graph G' is only a bit smaller

Figure 3 illustrate another way to split the original graph G. But this time, the basic split-merge algorithm doesn't work because of the awful split. The scale of G' is only a bit smaller. Thus, we should split the graph G' again. The only result of this round of split and contraction is that E and F are in the same SCC. In contrast with the cost of split and contraction, these kinds of split are just waste of time. If we always split the graph in this way, the cost of split and contraction will make the algorithm endless.

Now, what remains is to find a way to split the web graph appropriately. However, it seems to be difficult to do the job well if only the link information is concerned. So we take advantage of some special properties of the potential relationship between pages and sites in the web graph.

3.2 Pages and Sites

The web graph contains not only link information, but also URL information. Taking advantage of URL information will make the problem easy.

On the web, each html page belongs to its owner site. For example, the page with URL http://apex.sjtu.edu.cn/home.zh-cn.gb.htm belongs to the site http://apex.sjtu.edu.cn. In the web graph, a large portion of links are between two pages from a same site. In our observation on the web graph in China, more than two thirds of the links are pointed to a local page within the same site, while only about one third links are remote which is across different sites. Further, for most sites, a homepage is provided to guide the user to the pages they want. The homepage points to the most important pages and those pages also link back to the homepage. In conclusion, pages in the same site connected tightly with each other. If we group the pages according to their owner sites, the split will not be too bad.

3.3 Clustering the Sites

If we regard each site as a group of nodes and thus split the web graph, each sub-graph will be small enough to fit into main memory. But when we decompose all the sub-graphs and contract the graph G', we feel unsure whether G' can be wholly

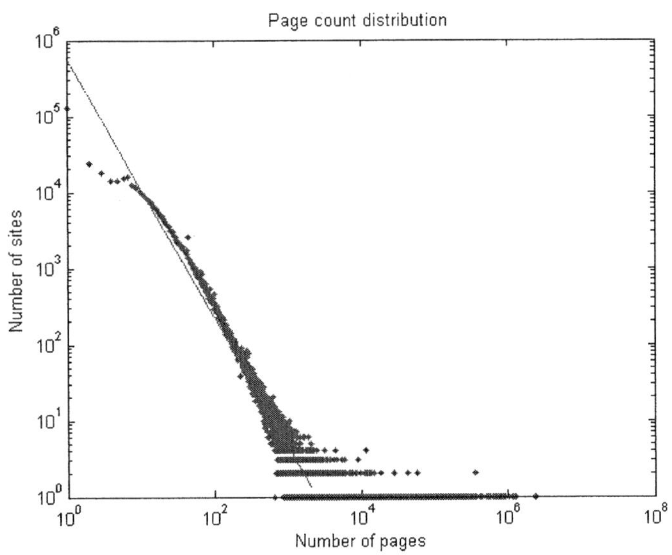

Fig. 4. The power law distribution of page count

loaded into main memory. As a fact, the number of pages in a site follows a power law: the number of sites which contain x pages is proportional to $1/x^k$ with some $k > 1$. In our observation on the web graph in China, the exponent k is about 1.74. Under this distribution, the richest 10% sites possess more than 90% pages while 90% sites contain only less than 10% pages. Figure 4 exhibits the power law.

Most sites contain only several tens of pages. If we regard these sites as a sub-graph, the small scale of sub-graph will make the effect of split unsatisfactory because we can only get a little information in many small sub-graphs. If we cluster the sites and regard pages in each cluster of sites as a sub-graph, the effect will be better.

Algorithms of graph partitioning [7] are available, but most of them demand extra properties of the graph, which seems not applicable to site graph. Also, some of the algorithms requires at least O(nm), which is still too large to applied to site graph.

Here we propose three easier clustering methods which demand affordable time respectively.

Random Assignment

The easiest way to cluster the sites is random assignment. In this way, sites are clustered in a random way and little link information is considered. Each sub-graph is composed of pages in several random-chosen sites. The advantage of random assignment is we can control the size of each cluster in order to be fit into memory.

The disadvantage of random assignment is obvious. Sometimes the sites in a cluster are irrelevant, and the connectivity among these sites is poor. The effect is as the same as they are not clustered. To avoid this situation, we may find another way to cluster the sites.

Site Graph SCC

If we want high quality of the clusters, naïve random assignment is not a good idea. Here, we introduce a method following the idea of hierarchical clustering.

As a fact, sites and links among them also forms a directed graph. We refer this graph as the site graph. In this graph, nodes represent sites and edges represent links. Both the nodes and the edges of this directed graph are weighted. The weight of the node denotes the number of pages which the site possesses and the weight of edges denotes the number of real hyperlinks across the pages of two sites.

If we regard each SCC of site graph as a cluster of site, the internal connectivity of each cluster could be high. Sites in the same component can reach each other by directed hyperlinks between their pages.

In our recommendation, most well-connected sites can be clustered into the same sub-graph. We ignore the edges with small weight in the site graph and decompose it into SCCs, and regard each component as a well connected cluster of sites.

While we can get well-connected sub-graphs by using site graph SCC, we can not control the size of each sub-graph precisely. So how to compromise between the quality of the sub-graphs and the size of them is a problem. In section 4 we will discuss our detailed implementation of this work.

Hierarchical Site SCC

Each of the two methods we just mentioned considers only one of the two factors, the quality of the blocks and the sizes of the blocks. Here we introduce another method which takes both these factors into account.

In the second method, the threshold of the edges is fixed in each step. Here we break this rule. We gradually increase the threshold of the edges, starting from 0.

When the threshold gets higher, small components will be detached from the core. Then we fill the current cluster with those detached components. Once the size of the current cluster is estimated to reach the memory limit, we begin to construct another cluster. This procedure is stopped when the remained graph is estimated to be smaller than the memory limit.

This method will somehow decrease the equality of the blocks because it may clusters irrelevant sites into one cluster. However, it has the benefit of full utilization of memory.

3.4 Efficiency

As a result, the cost of the split-merge algorithm is affordable if the graph is split properly. The cost of each step of the algorithm is as follow.

Split: Splitting the graph requires one extra copy of the full graph each time. It may cost several hours to several days depending on the size of the graph. (As the web graph is very large, even to read the whole graph from hard disk to memory costs several hours.)

Decompose Sub-graphs/G': Decomposing sub-graphs (or G') can be finished in O(n+e) time in all assuming that we use the algorithm from Sharir. n denotes the number of nodes and e denotes the number of edges in the graph. As a fact, each edge in the original graph G will be visited at most once in one sub-graph or in one contracted graph G'. It may cost a few days in total depending on the size of the whole graph.

Contract the Graph: Graph contraction requires at most one full-graph copy. In fact, only a small portion of edges will be copied if the split is appropriate.

Merge the SCCs: The cost of merging SCCs is O(nlog(n)). When we got the SCC information M1 from sub-graphs and the SCC information M2 from G', we can sort the information in M1. Then we can output each component in M2 using binary-search in M1. So the total cost of this algorithm is O(nlog(n)). It takes only a few hours to merge SCCs and we can ignore the cost in contrast with those in other steps.

To sum up, the extra cost of split-merge algorithm only depends on how many times we need to split the graph. Such costs only come from the IO operation during the process of split and graph contraction. If we just split the graph a few times, such cost is affordable. Also, no extra cost of traversing on the graph is required, which assure us that there will be no redundant computing on SCC information.

Further, optimizations are still available. For example, eliminating the nodes with zero out-degree (or in-degree) is a good advice if the final G' is a bit larger.

4 Experiments and Results

In this section, we will discuss our detailed implementation of enumerating SCCs in the web graph in China. The data is from the crawl offered by Peking University's

Sky Net (http://e.pku.edu.cn) search engine in May 2003. In our data set, the graph contains around 140 millions of nodes and 4.3 billions of edges. Our machine is Xeon 2GHz*4 /4GB SDRAM /150GB*7 HDD RAID5 /Windows2003, and our compiler is gcc version 2.95.3 for windows. Some of the main memory is assigned to system processes and the other processes. In our real implementation, about 2.1G main memory is available to us.

4.1 Traditional Algorithm

First we built a program using traditional algorithm directly. The main program visited the edges in the graph by cache. Here, hit rate of the cache is crucial for the performance. Unfortunately, the hit rate is very low. Only around a hundred of edges are visited per second. So it could take several years to finish the work. Furthermore, increasing the hit rate slightly will not change a lot, and we find it hard to increase the hit rate a lot because of the large scale of the graph.

4.2 The Split-Merge Algorithm

Then we tried the split-merge algorithm. First we split the graph into 100 sub-graphs. In order to group nodes of the giant web graph, we built a site graph. The site graph contains about 470 kilos of nodes and 18 millions of edges. In this graph, we find that the sum of the weight from the edges which link nodes to themselves is around two thirds of total weight of the graph. It assured us that the connectivity of each site is good.

To cluster the sites, we set a "threshold" for the site graph, and the edges with weights less than the "threshold" were ignored. Then we listed all the strongly connected components with at least three sites. Each component was viewed as a cluster of sites. Unclassified sites were viewed as a temporary cluster. The pages of each cluster and hyperlinks between them constructed a sub-graph. And also, we recorded the hyperlink across two clusters which were useful when contracting the graph. In the first round, the threshold was set to 1000. Thus, 1249 sites were classified into 99 clusters, and other 469 kilos of sites are still unclassified. Most classified sites were famous ones and have more pages than the unclassified sites, and most of the unclassified sites were very small sites. Some of the clusters were just parts of a big famous site. For example, a cluster was constructed of sites such as http://edu.china.com, http://business.china.com, http://news.china.com, http://sports.china.com, http:// finance.china.com, etc. In fact, they all belong to http://china.com.

We then built a sub-graph for each cluster, and also for the unclassified site. Unfortunately, two of these sub-graphs were still too large to load into memory. One was the biggest cluster of sites. The other was the sub-graph of unclassified sites. They owned around 25% and 70% of total pages respectively. We thus recursively applied split-merge algorithm to them. This time, we used the random assignment to split these two sub-graphs.

After all the SCCs in each sub-graph had been found, we get the final G'. As a fact, the G' contained only less than 46 millions of edges. At last, we decomposed the G' and merge the SCCs of each sub-graphs with the help of the decomposition of G'.

4.3 Efficiency

Let's analyze the total time cost of this implementation. Building the site graph required one scan of the full graph, one scan of URL table and I/O operation of copying the edges of the site graph. In our implementation, we split the graph twice, so the I/O cost of split and contraction of the graph was less than four copies of the full graph. As a fact, a copy of the full graph took less than one day. And thus the cost of I/O was less than five days. The decomposition of all sub-graph and the G' requires two scans of full graph in main memory and one loading of the full graph in total, which took a bit more than one day and a half. Merging SCCs was very fast. It only took less than six hours in total. The other cost in the algorithm like decomposing of the site graph was not listed here, but they can be ignored in contrast with those we have listed. To sum up, the total time cost of this run took only less than a full week.

4.4 Result

Here we just exhibit our result briefly. Figure 5 is the bowtie structure of our data set of web graph in China.

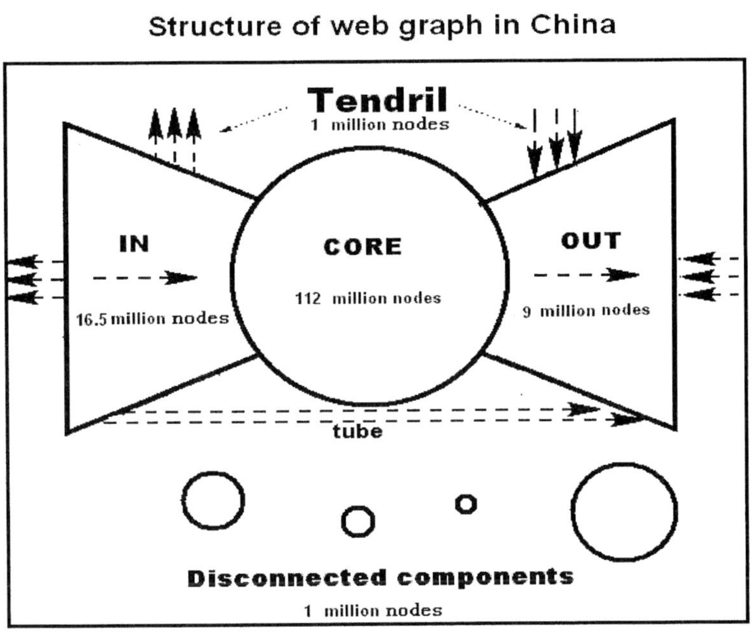

Fig. 5. The bowtie structure of web graph in China

The graph shows that around 80% of web pages are in the maximum SCC in the web graph. And, if pages u and v are randomly chosen, the probability that there exists a path from u to v is around 4/5 according to this structure. It's much different from the structure in Figure 1. This difference may be caused by the difference of culture, different styles that people create html pages or some reasons else. The size of the SCC follows a power law with the exponent around 2.3. Figure 6 shows the distribution.

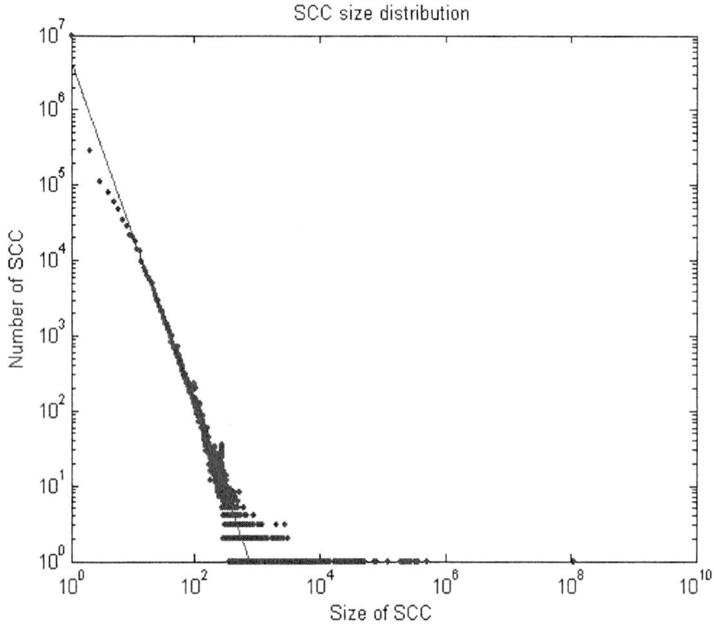

Fig. 6. Distribution of the size of SCC

5 Conclusions

In this paper, with a basic idea of split-merge, we take advantage of some useful properties of the graph and find a feasible method to enumerate strongly connected components. Then we analyzed our detailed implementation. The algorithm is applied on the web graph in China, and the task is accomplished in an affordable time.

In our solution, site graph played an important role. Actually, the site graph can be viewed as a folded version of web graph. In the future work, we will make further observation on this graph, find more potential relationship between sites and pages, and try to predict some properties on the web graph with the analysis on the site graph.

References

1. Andrei Broder, Ravi Kumar, Farzin Maghoul, Prabhakar Raghavan, Sridhar Rajagopalan, Raymie Stata, Andrew Tomkins, and Janet Wiener, Graph structure in the web. Computer Networks (Amsterdam, Netherlands: 1999).
2. R. Tarjan, Depth first search and linear graph algorithms. SIAM J. Comput.1(1972) 146-160.

3. M.Sharir,A strong-connectivity algorithm and its application in data flow analysis. Computers and Mathematics with Applications 7 (1981),67-72.
4. Alfred V.Aho, John E.Hopcroft, and Jeffrey D.Ullman. Data Structure and Algorithms. Addison-Wesley, 1983.
5. Lisa K. Fleischer, Bruce Hendrickson, and Ali Pinar, On identifying strongly connected components in parallel. Lecture Notes in Computer Science, 2000.
6. Micah Adler and Michael Mitzenmacher , Towards compressing Web Graphs. Data Compression Conference, 2001.
7. A. Capocci, V. Servedio, G. Caldarelli, and F. Colaiori, Detecting communities structure in networks. Third Workshop on Algorithms and Models for the Web-Graph, 2004

China Web Graph Measurements and Evolution*

Guowei Liu, Yong Yu, Jie Han, and Guirong Xue

Computer Science & Engineering Department,
Shanghai Jiaotong University,
Shanghai, China
{gwliu, yyu, micro_j, grxue}@sjtu.edu.cn

Abstract. With the huge number of Web pages on the World Wide Web, there are many characteristics that should be analyzed in the Web mining fields. As a subset of the global Web graph, China Web graph shows many different properties compared with the global Web graph from the structure to the evolution of the Web. In this paper, we indicate to study the China Web graph both on its static and dynamic nature, and then to analyze the similarity and difference between the global Web graph and China Web graph. A number of measurements and properties of the China Web graph are reported both on the Web page level and Web site level. Finally the evolution of the China Web graph will be represented from several aspects.

1 Introduction

The Web can be represented by a directed graph where nodes stand for Web pages, and edges stand for hyperlinks among pages. There are about five more billions of nodes and edges on the today's Web graph. Furthermore, the Web graph appears to grow exponentially as time goes by. Since the authors of the Web pages are with different background, culture, interest and education, they create, annotate and exploit the Web pages and hyperlinks in a variative way, which leads the Web graph structure to be a complex network. Research on structure of the Web graph could exploit the inherent useful information for link analysis and Web search.

As a subset of the global Web graph, China Web graph shows many different properties compared with the global Web graph from the structure to the evolution of the Web. The research on China Web graph will be useful for understanding the evolution process of China Web graph, predicting the scale of the Web, improving the performance of Chinese Web page search engine, and processing Chinese Web information.

In this paper, we study the China Web graph both on its static and dynamic nature, and then analyze the similarity and difference between the global Web

* This project is supported by National Foundation of Natural Science of China (No.60473122).

Y. Zhang et al. (Eds.): APWeb 2005, LNCS 3399, pp. 668–679, 2005.

graph and China Web graph. We verify power law distributions in China Web graph from several aspects. With our SCC algorithm, we outline the macro structure of the China Web both on Web graph level and site graph level. We also study the evolution of the China Web graph from the evolving of Web pages, link structure and the popularity of the pages.

The rest of the paper is organized as follows. In Section 2, we introduce the previous study work on the global Web graph and some regional Web graph. In Section 3, we describe our research result from a static snapshot of China Web graph. In Section 4, we present the studies on the evolution on China Web graph from several aspects. Finally we conclude in Section 5.

2 Related Work

In the area of Web graph analysis, [2] estimated the diameter of the Web. [8] [5] reported in-degree and out-degree distributions of the global Web graph following the power law distributions, and they also analyzed the structure of the global Web graph. [3] focused the study on the Web site level of the global Web, measured the weighted degree sequences of the global site graph. [4] focused the study on the African Web, showing that the African Web graph appears different properties from the global Web graph. The maximal strongly connected component of the African Web graph is much bigger than the global Web graph and it points to lots of small strongly connected components. The work [7] is similar to ours, however, they just inferred the structure of the China Web graph by the structure properties of the global Web graph, making the result inadequate.

In the area of Web evolution, [10] performed experiments to study the evolution of the Web from a search engine perspective. [6] study the popularity evolution of Web pages.

3 China Web Graph Measurements

In this section we first show the results on China Web graph measurements. Then we do experiments to validate the power law distribution phenomenon in China Web from several aspects. Finally we analyze the macro structure of the China Web graph and the China site graph.

3.1 Datasets

In the experiment, we use the China Web graph dataset crawled by Peking University Sky Net search engine in May, 2003. The size of the raw data is nearly 300G, which contains hyperlinks from the source page to the destination page. Before the experiments, we preprocess the raw data to create the China Web graph and China site graph. After preprocessing, the invalid URLs are removed, each URL is assigned a unique ID. Finally the China Web graph is created, which contains 140 million pages and 4.3 billion links. Furthermore, we construct site graph as follows: each Web page belongs to a site, then the site connectivity also

Table 1. Domain Distribution

Domain	China	Global
.com	71.3%	41.0%
.net	20.2%	4.1%
.org	3.9%	15.7%
.edu	3.0%	16.5%
.gov	1.5%	18.7%
.mil	0.1%	2.9%

be represented as a directed graph, where sites are represented as nodes, edges are represented as connections between the sites. Also the directed graph is a weighted graph where the weight of the edges is the number of hyperlinks among sites. We create such a China site graph with 479 kilo nodes and 18 million edges.

3.2 Domain Distribution

The domain number distribution presents differently from the global Web, from Table 1 we can notice .com accounts for most of the domain number and the .gov and .mil accounts for little. The statistic data indicates the development of World-Wide Web in China is not in balance, the World-Wide Web is used mostly for commerce in China and e-government needs to be further developed.

3.3 Power Law Distributions

Previous work observed that various properties of the Web graph follow a power law distribution, which is defined on positive integers, with the probability of the value i being in proportion to $1/i^{\beta}$ for some constant $\beta > 0$.

Degree Distributions. [11] shows that the fraction of Web pages with in-degree i is roughly proportional to $1/i^2$. [1] reports an exponent of 2.1 for the in-degree distribution and they also show that the fraction of Web pages with out-degree i is roughly proportional to $1/i^{2.45}$. In a recent paper [5] reported an in-degree exponent of 2.1 and an out-degree exponent of 2.72. The study on African Web [4] gives further evidence to the power law distribution, the in-degree of African Web pages with a exponent of 1.92. A previous research on China Web [7] also shows an in-degree distribution with an exponent 1.86.

[3] shows that the fraction of sites of the site graph with weighted in-degree i is (roughly) proportional to $1/i^{1.62}$ and the fraction of sites of the site graph with weighted out-degree i is (roughly) proportional to $1/i^{1.67}$.

Our experiments on the China Web degree distributions also testify the power law distribution in China Web. Our experiments are carried both on China Web graph and China site graph.

Fig 1 and 2 are log-log plots of the in-degree distribution and out-degree distribution of the China Web graph. Derived from the slope of the line providing the best fit to the data in the figures, in-degree and out-degree distribution with the exponent $\beta = 2.05$ and $\beta = 2.62$ respectively. Fig 3 and 4 show the weighted

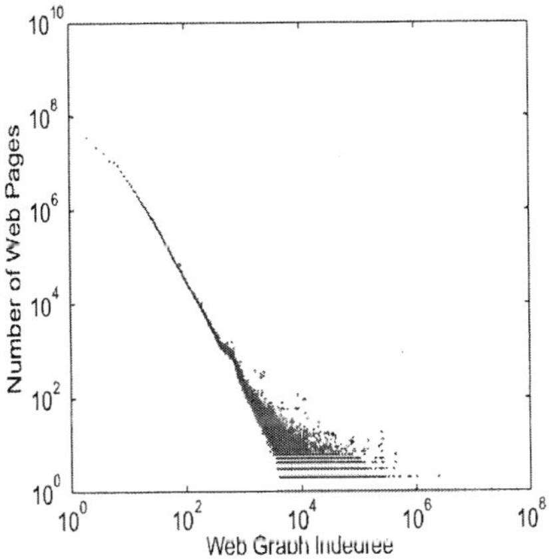

Fig. 1. China Web graph In-degree distribution

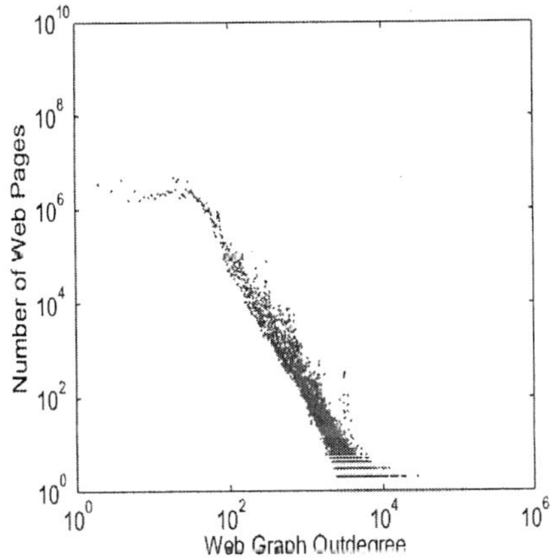

Fig. 2. China Web graph Out-degree distribution

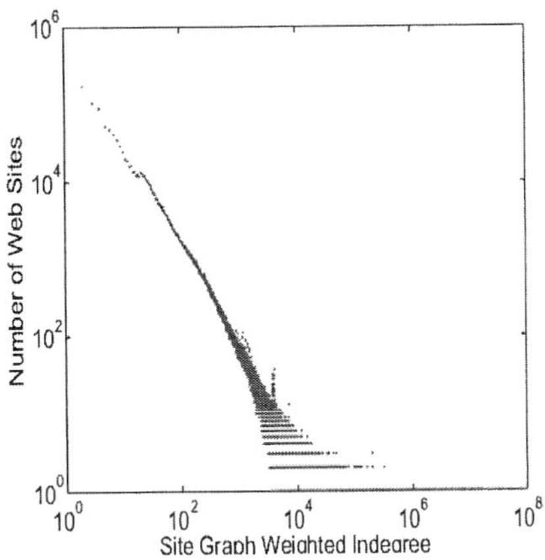

Fig. 3. China site graph weighted In-degree distribution

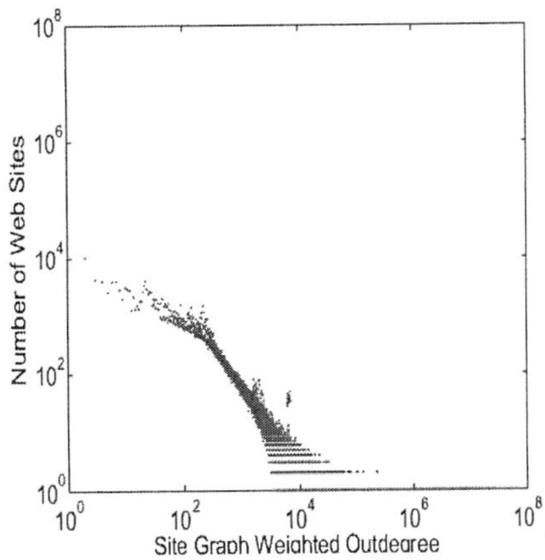

Fig. 4. China site graph weighted Out-degree distribution

in-degree and weighted out-degree distribution of the China site graph with the exponent $\beta = 1.4$ and $\beta = 1.5$.

The power law distribution of the degree sequence appears to be a very robust property of the Web despite its dynamic characteristics.

Page Number Distributions in Web Sites. We count the Web pages in every Web site and surprisingly observe that the number of Web pages in Web sites also follows power law distribution with the exponent $\beta = 1.74$. This is another evidence that the Power Law distribution is a common phenomenon in Web graph. Fig 5 shows the distribution.

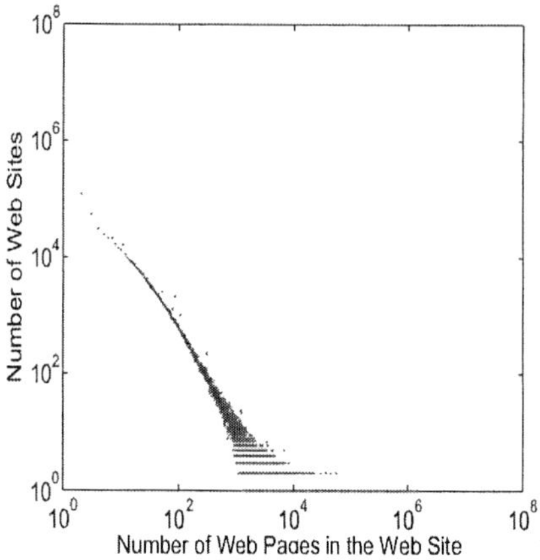

Fig. 5. The number of pages in Web sites follows a power law distribution

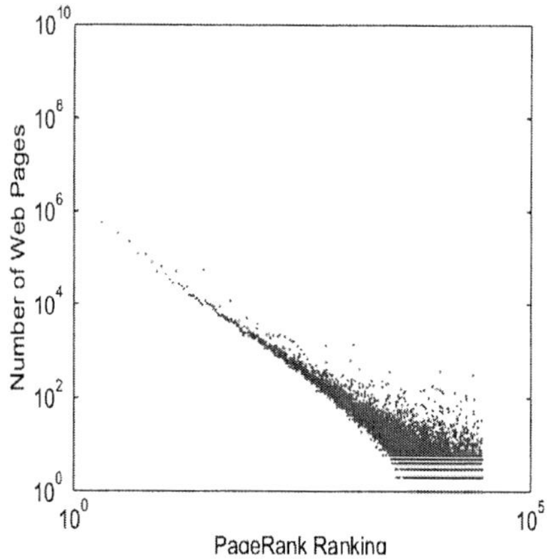

Fig. 6. PageRank Zipf Distribution

PageRank Value Distribution. The PageRank algorithm is carried out on the China Web graph. As PageRank value is continuous, we discretized the PageRank value by equal-width binning with the bin size 0.005. We found that the pagerank values also follow a power law distribution. Fig 6 shows the distribution.

Connected Components. A strongly-connected component is a set of pages such that for all pairs of pages (u, v) in the set, there exists a directed path from u to v. Previous studies note that the number of components, either weak or strong, of a given size also follow a power law distribution [9].

Our study shows that the number of components in China Web graph also exhibits a power law distribution with exponent β roughly 2.3. Fig 7 shows the distribution.

3.4 Connectivity of the China Web

The graph structure of the China Web presents some differences from that of the global Web graph.

The graph structure of the global Web graph presents a picture that we refer to as a bow-tie [9]. This research is based on the crawl of Web pages in May 1999, which contains over 200 million pages and 1.5 billion links. The core of the figure, SCC, represents the largest strongly connected component of the graph. SCC contains 56 million pages. The left side of the bow-tie, named IN, represents the pages from which at least a path exists to some nodes in SCC. The right side of the bow-tie, named OUT, represents the pages which can be reached from some nodes in SCC. Both IN and OUT contain around 44 million pages respectively. IN can be viewed as the set of new pages that link to their interesting pages but not yet been discovered by SCC, while OUT can be viewed as some well

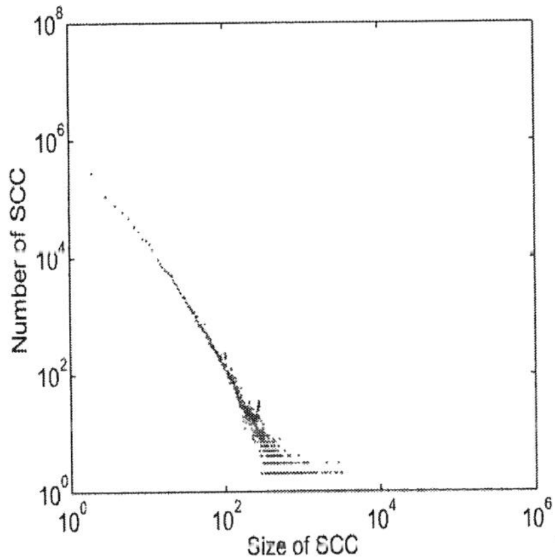

Fig. 7. The sizes of the strongly connected components follow a power law distribution

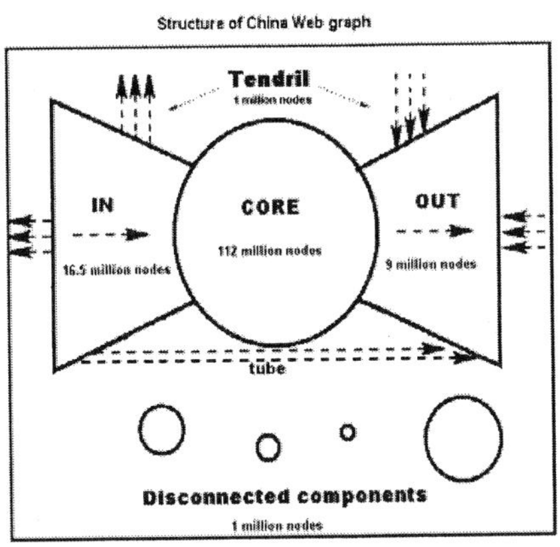

Fig. 8. Web Graph Macro Structure

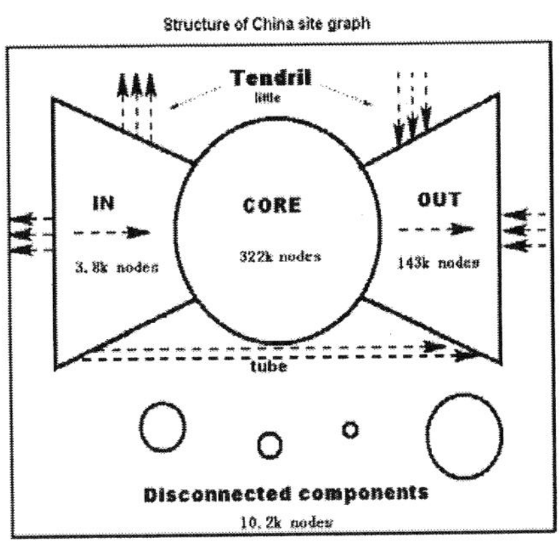

Fig. 9. Site Graph Macro Structure

known pages whose links point only internally. The TENDRILS contains pages that are reachable from IN, or that can reach OUT, without passages through SCC. The Web has not yet discovered these pages, and these pages do not link to better-known regions. TENDRILS include a surprisingly significant part of the pages, around 44 million.

The graph structure of the China Web presents some difference from the global Web. Fig 8 depicts the structure of China Web Graph. The China Web graph contains 140 million pages and 4.3 billion links. The SCC contains 112 million pages, the IN contains 16.5 million pages, the OUT contains 9 million pages, the TENDRILS and the disconnected components contain around 1 million pages respectively. The graph shows that around 80% Web pages are in the maximum SCC and if pages u and v are randomly chosen, the probability that there exists a path from u to v is around 4/5 according to this structure.

The graph structure of the China Web on a site level is depicted in Fig 9. The site graph totally contains 479 kilo Web sites, as we can notice in the figure that the number of sites in SCC accounts for about 2/3 of all the Web sites, indicating that most of the Web sites in China are connected to each other. The small fraction number of sites in IN implies that most of the Web sites in China are known by people and linked to by Web pages in other Web sites.

4 China Web Graph Evolution

In this section we show our experiment results in China Web evolution.

4.1 Data Collection

In order to study the evolution of China Web graph, we have collected the temporal data from China Web, obtained a Web graph data sample periodically. Due to the limitation of the band width and storage, it is impossible for us to download the whole China Web graph each time, so we attempt to get a representative subgraph of the China Web graph as the dataset of our study. In our experiments, we select 150 Chinese Web sites, and crawl the Web pages from their home pages once a week, from May 2004 until June 2004, for a total 6 weeks.

In order to make our experiment results more accurate, the representative subgraph of the China Web graph to be selected should meet the following four characteristics: (1)covering a multitude of topics; (2)following domain distributions; (3)with higher PageRank value; (4)can be accessed by existing network resource.

4.2 Weekly Birth Rate of Pages

We first examine how many new Web pages are created every week. New Web page refers to the one which has not been downloaded before. We use the URL of a page as its identity, so if new URL emerged, we consider that a new page is created. The fraction of the new Web page represents the "weekly birth rate" of Web pages.

Fig 10 shows the weekly birth rate of Web pages. The line in the middle of the graph gives the average of all the values, representing the "average weekly birth rate" of the pages. From the graph we can observe that the average weekly birth rate is about 9.8%, which is a little higher than the value 8%, the average weekly birth rate of global Web graph [10]. That is, 9.8% of pages downloaded in a weekly crawl had not been downloaded in any previous crawl.

4.3 Birth and Replacement of Pages

In this experiment, we study how many new pages are created and how many disappear over time.

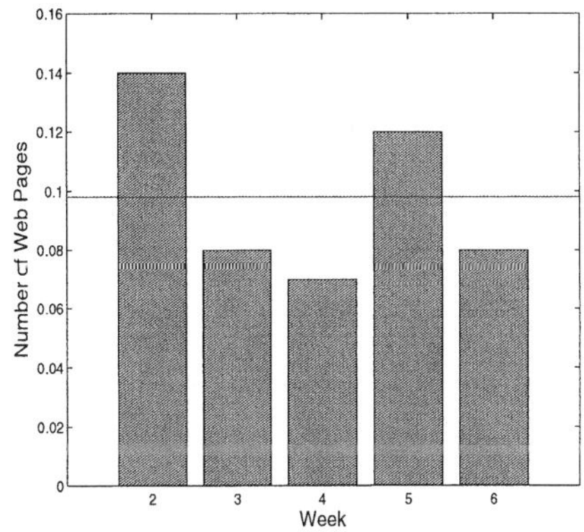

Fig. 10. Fraction of new pages between successive snapshots

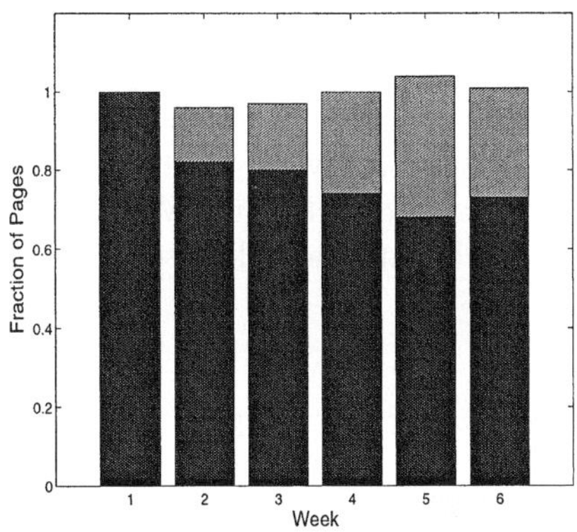

Fig. 11. Fraction of pages from the first crawl still existing after n weeks (dark bars) and new pages (light bars)

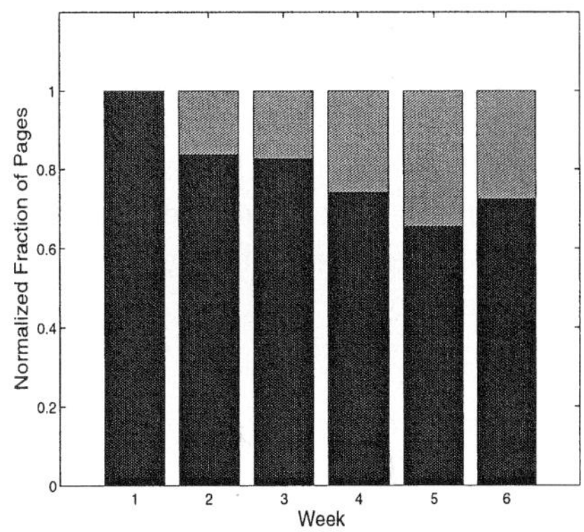

Fig. 12. Normalized fraction of pages from the first crawl still existing after n weeks(dark bars) and new pages (light bars)

Fig 11 shows the experiment. The horizontal axis of this graph plots the week and the vertical axis shows the number of pages that we crawled during the given week. The bars are normalized such that the number of pages in the first is one. The dark bars represent the number of first week pages that were still available in the given week. The light bars represent the number of pages that exist in the given week but did not exist in the first week. For example, the number of pages in the second week in the 96% of the first week, and 82% of them already exist in the first week. The fluctuations in weekly crawl sizes are primarily due to the temporarily unavailable of the Web sites and the unreliable of the network connection. The normalized version of Fig 11 is shown in Fig 12.

4.4 Link Structure Evolution

Link structure is useful information in measuring the importance of Web pages. Link analysis algorithms such as PageRank and HITS play an important role in the performance of search engine. In order to keep up with the changing importance of Web pages, it is important for search engines to capture the Web link structure accurately. In this experiment, we study how many links remain unchanged and how many new links are created.

Fig 13 shows the experiment result. The horizontal axis represents the week and the vertical axis represents the number of links in the given week. We normalize the vertical axis so that the number of links in the first week is 1. The height of every bar shows the total number of links in each snapshot relative to the first week. The dark-bottom portion represents the number of first-week links that still remain in the given week. The grey portion shows the number of new links in those pages that exist both in the first week and the given week. The white portion shows the number of links in those new pages that exist in the given week but not exist in the first week. Fig 14 shows a normalized figure where the total number of links in every snapshot is one. From the figure, we can notice that the link structure of the Web is more dynamic than the pages. On average there are 24.7% new links created every week. This result is a little greater than that of link structure evolution of global Web graph [10]. The dynamic of the link structure is an important characteristic of the Web graph, which implies that search engine may need to recalculate the link-based ranking value frequently.

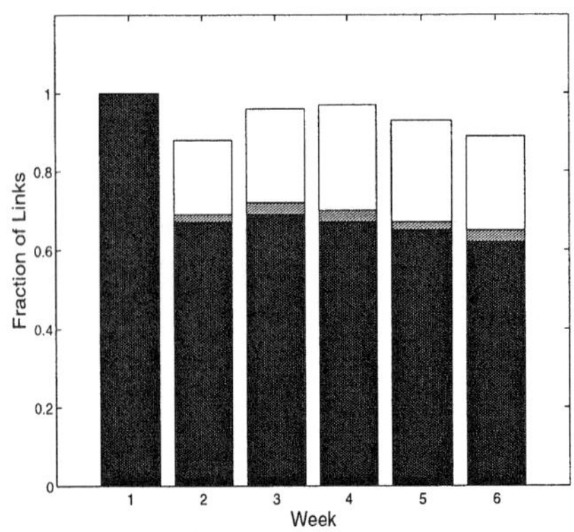

Fig. 13. Fraction of links from the first weekly snapshot still existing after n weeks (dark/bottom portion of the bars), new links from existing pages (grey/middle) and new links from new pages (white/top)

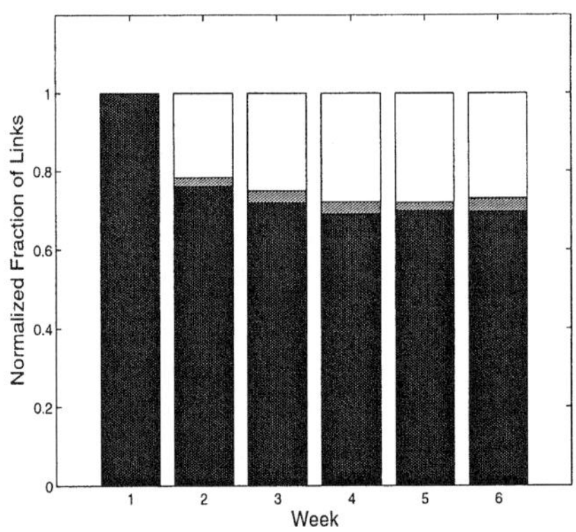

Fig. 14. Normalized fraction of links from the first weekly snapshot still existing after n weeks (dark/bottom portion of the bars), new links from existing pages (grey/middle) and new links from new pages (white/top)

4.5 Page Popularity Evolution

In this experiment, we study the evolution of the page popularity. We will use two methods to estimate the popularity of a page: one is the number of all incoming links of the page, i.e., In-Links; the other is the PageRank value of the page. We compare the two Web graphs at week one and week six.

We first take the In-Links as the measure of the popularity. Fig 15 shows the relationship between the absolute increase of In-Links and the popularity of the first week. We sort the pages by their popularity and then divide them into ten groups of the same size. The horizontal axis represents the ten groups ordered by their popularity, with the right side corresponding to the most popular groups. The vertical axis represents the sum of absolute increase of In-Links in all pages in the group. The height of the bars represents the sum of absolute increase of all pages in the given group. For example, the height of the bar marked 80 represents the sum of absolute increase of the pages ranking from 70% to 80%. We can notice from the figure that it is only the popular pages that become more popular over time. In Fig 16 we show more details of the top 10% group. We further divide the top group into 5 subgroups and plot their popularity increase. We can see that the most popular pages obtain more new incoming links than others.

We use PageRank value of the page as the popularity, and similarly plot the relationship between the absolute increase of PageRank and the popularity in Fig 17. From the figure, we can see that the pages in the 70%-100% group increase their popularity, while the pages in the 20%-50% group actually decrease their popularity. The detailed view for the top 20% group is shown in Fig 18.

The experiment results shows the "rich-get-richer" phenomenon mentioned in [6] also appears in China Web.

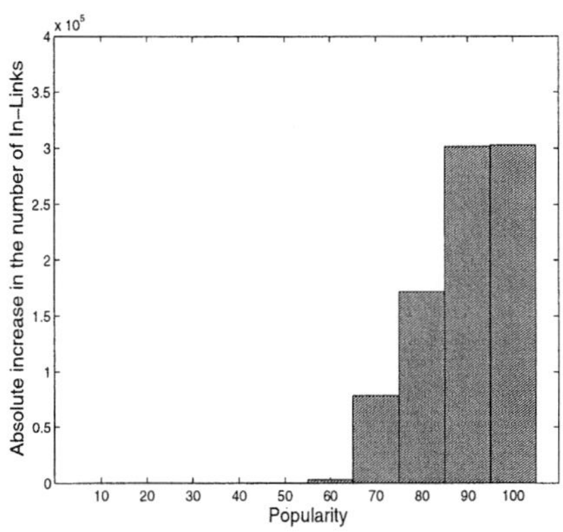

Fig. 15. The popularity on the X axis and the absolute change in the values of the incoming links on the Y axis

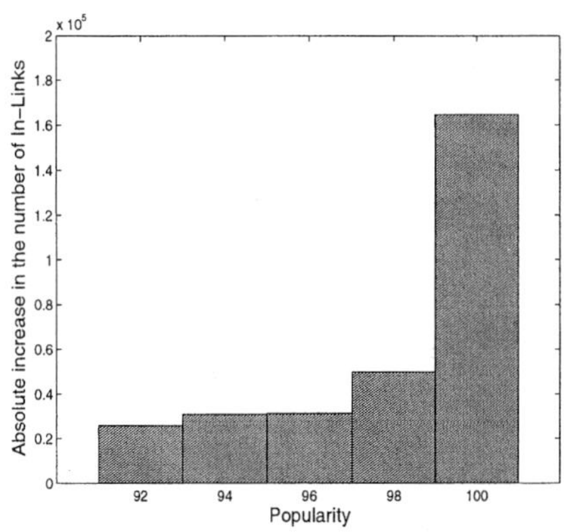

Fig. 16. The popularity on the X axis and the absolute change in the values of the incoming links on the Y axis for the top 10% most popular pages

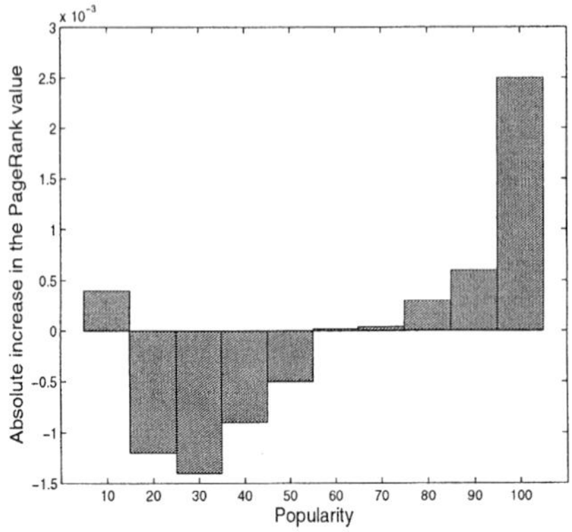

Fig. 17. The popularity on the X axis and the absolute change in the values of the PageRank on the Y axis

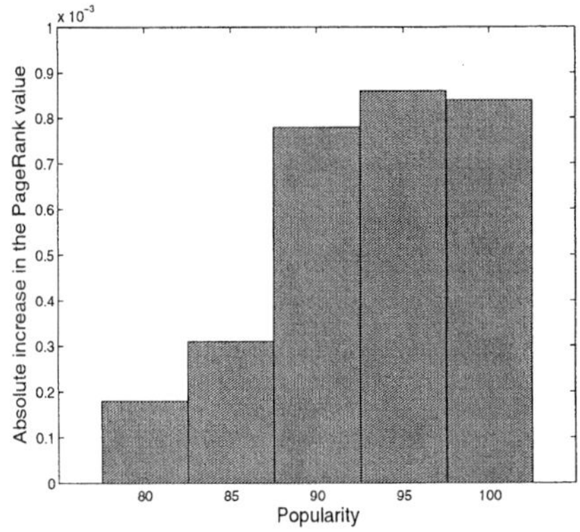

Fig. 18. The popularity on the X axis and the absolute change in the values of the PageRank on the Y axis for the top 20% most popular pages

5 Conclusions and Future Work

In this paper, we have thoroughly studied the China Web both on its static and dynamic characteristics. The result shows that the China Web graph have many differences from global Web graph from the structure to the evolution of the Web. Additionally, we also analyze the nature of China site graph. As a future work, we plan to study the random model of China Web graph and to understand how the Web is created by the editors.

References

1. A.Barabasi and R.Albert. Emergence of scaling in random networks. 1999.
2. R. Albert, H. Jeong, and A.-L. Barabasi. Diameter of the world wide web. *Nature*, 401(6749), 1999.
3. K. Bharat, B.-W. Chang, M. R. Henzinger, and M. Ruhl. Who links to whom: Mining linkage between web sites. In *ICDM*, pages 51–58, 2001.
4. P. Boldi, B. Codenotti, M. Santini, and S. Vigna. Structural properties of the african web. 2002.
5. A. Broder, R. Kumar, F. Maghoul, P. Raghavan, S. Rajagopalan, R. Stata, A. Tomkins, and J. Wiener. Graph structure in the web: experiments and models. In *In Proceedings of the Ninth International World–Wide Web Conference, Amsterdam, The Netherlands.*, 2000.
6. J. Cho and S. Roy. Impact of search engines on page popularity. In *Proceedings of the 13th international conference on World Wide Web*, pages 20–29. ACM Press, 2004.
7. Y. Hongfei and L. Xiaoming. On the structure of chinese web 2002. In *Journal of Computer Research and Development*, 2002.

8. J. M. Kleinberg, R. Kumar, P. Raghavan, S. Rajagopalan, and A. S. Tomkins. The Web as a graph: Measurements, models and methods. *Lecture Notes in Computer Science*, 1627:1–??, 1999.
9. R. Kumar, P. Raghavan, S. Rajagopalan, D. Sivakumar, A. Tomkins, and E. Upfal. The Web as a graph. In *Proc. 19th ACM SIGACT-SIGMOD-AIGART Symp. Principles of Database Systems, PODS*, pages 1–10. ACM Press, 15–17 2000.
10. A. Ntoulas, J. Cho, and C. Olston. What's new on the web? the evolution of the web from a search engine perspective. In *Proceedings of the Thirteenth International World Wide Web Conference*, pages 1–12, New York, New York, May 2004.
11. R.Kumar, P.Raghavan, S.Rajagopalan, and A.Tomkins. Trawling the web for cyber communities. 1999.

PODWIS: A Personalized Tool for Ontology Development in Domain Specific Web Information System[1]

Lv-an Tang, Hongyan Li[2], Zhiyong Pan, Shaohua Tan, Baojun Qiu, Shiwei Tang, and Jianjun Wang

National Laboratory on Machine Perception,
School of Electronics Engineering and Computer Science,
Peking University, Beijing, 100871, P.R. China
{Tangla, Lihy, Panzj, Tan, Qbj}@cis.pku.edu.cn
tsw@pku.edu.cn
Wangjj@cis.pku.edu.cn

Abstract. Complex structure and varying requirements increase the difficulties in developing domain specific Web Information Systems. People appeal to a smart tool to customize Web Information Systems automatically. To achieve that goal, this article makes following contributions: (1) Proposes the concept of Web Information System ontology to express the integrated domain semantics and maintain their relationships as a hierarchal structure; (2) Implements the Personalized tool for Ontology Development in domain specific Web Information System(PODWIS) with algorithms for (a) leaning the user's behaviors while building the ontology, (b) mining the repeated contents and composing reusable components, (c) guiding developer's work efficiently with high quality; (3)Designs two different self-learning strategies: online learning and offline learning to meet different situations; (4) Gives a semi-automatic tool to generate the personalized information system(includes user interface, operations and database access) based on ontology; (5)Shows the feasibility of this technique in practical application.

Keywords: Web Information System, Data Mining, Ontology, Reuse, Personalization.

1 Introduction

The concept of Web Information System (WIS) was proposed in 1998[1]: Different from existing information presentation systems, WIS is featured with client logic, operational integration, high level knowledge-management and decision-supporting.

---

[1] This work was supported by National Key Fundamental Research and Development Plan (973) of China under grant G1999032705 and the Natural Science Foundation of China(NSFC) under grant number 60473072.

[2] LI Hongyan is the associate author.

Y. Zhang et al. (Eds.): APWeb 2005, LNCS 3399, pp. 680–694, 2005.

When WIS is applied in a particular domain, it becomes domain specific, such as ERP or Hospital Information Systems. Researchers have got fruitful results in this Realm. However, as Tomas Isakowitz pointed out[1], the huge amount of data and various requirements from different users make the development of WIS very difficult: WIS development needs both domain knowledge and computer skills, the combination of these two essentials is quite troublesome. Researchers tried to find solution from traditional approaches and many methods were proposed, but they do not satisfy the expected goals[2].

Some rough ideas borrowed from ontology for building information system can be found in reference [3,4]. The advantages of using ontology in domain specific WIS development are as following:

- Clear specification: It helps confirm the user's requirements and disciplines in applications.
- High reliability: Its formalization makes the auto-examination of information consistency.
- Good Reusability: It is highly reusable, hence can turn to the shared components.

However, there are few works about ontology on WIS yet, the complexity of WIS leads special difficulties in WIS ontology building:[4]

- It lacks convenient tools for the domain experts who may not be proficient in computer.
- Extracting the various relationships from resources is a challenging task.
- Manually constructing WIS ontology is time-consuming, labor-intensive and error-prone.
- Ontology can be represented as conceptual graph, description logic, web standards, or a simple hierarchy. But not all of them are suitable for WIS application.

To solve these problems, we propose and implement a tool named *Personalized tool for Ontology Development in domain specific Web Information System* (PODWIS) with following features:

- Visualization: provides graphical views as "What you see is what you get" in ontology building.
- Reusability: discovers the frequent resources and composes them to a reusable component in order to improve efficiency and quality.
- Personalization: A large project is always developed by a group of developers, PODWIS keep the behavior's features for different users.

The rest of the paper is organized as follows: Section 2 presents the background and some related works. Section 3 gives some concepts about Domain Specific Web Information System's ontology (WIS ontology). Section 4 gives the algorithm of PODWIS, Section 5 gives a case study of PODWIS' application, at last Section 6 draws the conclusion.

2 Related Works

Reference [5] gives a definition of Information System ontology: The IS ontology is designed for at least one specific and practical application, it depicts the structure of a specific domain of objects, and it accounts for the intended meaning of a formal vocabulary or protocols that are employed by the agents of the domain under investigation.

There is no standard language for IS ontology description yet. The World Wide Web Consortium (W3C) suggests RDF[6], DAML+OIL[7] and OWL[8] to be the standards for ontology description language. However, as the WIS ontology is a combination of the knowledge in application domains and the concepts in IS engineering, the above languages do not fit for WIS ontology. To precisely define the conceptions in domain and explicitly specify the hierarchy of WIS, we implement a new ontology description language—*Web Information System Ontology Markup Language* (WISO-ML) based on XML.

Researchers have proposed many ontology generating tools. The AIFB have developed various tools to support ontology generation that include OntoEdit[9]and Text-To-Onto[10].Kietz, Maedche and Volz[3] adopted AIFB's method to build an insurance ontology from a corporate Intranet. Relations between concepts were learned by analyzing the corporate Intranet documents based on a multi-strategy learning algorithm. Similar to the analyses in reference [4], generating WIS ontology in these manners is plagued with several challenges and problems such as:

- The automatically constructed ontology can be too prolific and deficient at the same time. Excessively prolific ontology could hinder domain expert's browsing and correction.
- It is not easy to reuse the data and operations of WIS by these methods.
- Without considering personalization and agility, the refinement of the ontology is a trickle issue.

3 Features of WIS Ontology

Our WIS ontology is featured with the idea partially borrowed from reference [11]:

- Top-level ontology describes very general concepts.
- Domain ontology describes the vocabulary related to a generic domain.
- Task ontology describes a task or activity, such as data operation (inserting, deleting and modifying) or make a query from the data source.
- Application ontology describes concepts depending on both a particular domain and a task, and is usually a specialization of them. In WIS this ontology is created from the combination of the above ontologies. They represent the user requirements regarding a specific application.

WIS ontology aims to help generate web pages and operation code considering compatibility, portability and integration, our *WIS Ontology Markup Language*

(WISO-ML) is based on XML Schema so that the WIS ontology can be parsed conveniently by other tools through XML interface.

Now we derive the formal concepts of WIS ontology from examples in the Web Health Resource Planning System (WHRP) developed by department of Intelligence Science and Technology of Peking University.

Example 1. The web page of patient admission in WHRP as Fig.1 This web page contains two parts: Patient Information and Admission Information, which is composed by admitting doctor and some other items. It illustrates that the relations and structures of WIS are very complex, so we define WIS ontology step by step.

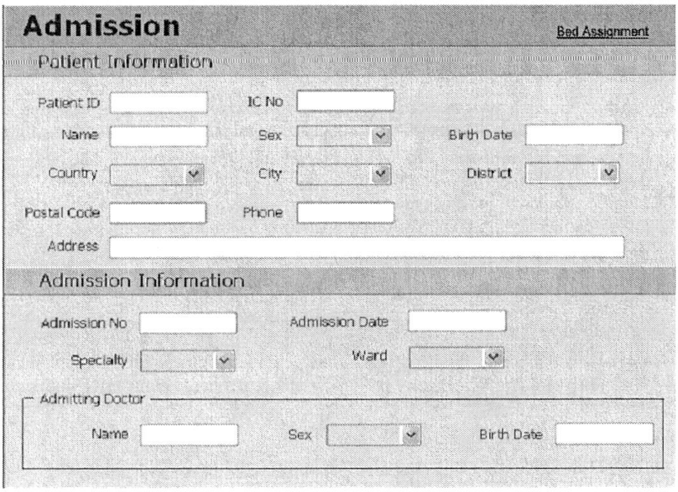

Fig. 1. The Page of Patient Admission

Definition 1. The basic item *I* is a 5-tuples, *I=<ItemName, ItemType, Constrains, DisplayInfo, Fields>*, where *ItemName* is the name of the basic item, *ItemType* is the type of the item, *DisplayInfo* is a set of display features used for the generation of web pages, *Constrains* is a set of constraints used for the input value verify, and *Fields* is a mapping of the items from web page to database.

All items in a page are distinguished by ItemName. ItemType could be the usual page elements such as textfield, droplist,, etc. DisplayInfo includes tags,and formats such as size, color and location.

Definition 2. A component *C* is a 4-tuples, *C=<ComName, Elements, Operations, AddTag >*, where *ComName* is the name of the component, *Elements* is a set of elements used for establishing the component, *Operations* is a set of operations defined on the component, and *AddTag* is a possible tag used for the comment of the component.

Note that, components in WIS should be distinguished by names, *Elements* reflects architecture, which only contains components and basic items. *AddTag* records the style of the components.

The above definition shows that a component could be applied to represent a whole interface page, or a part of another component. Respectively, it is called *Page Component* or *Child Component*.

Example 2. Figure 2 illustrates the hierarchy of page component 'Admission' which represents the web page in figure 1. Component's structure is denoted by a pedigree-tree whose root is component's name, the elements of the component become children nodes: the child components are the inter-nodes and the basic items are the leaf-nodes. WIS ontology can be represented by a forest of component-tree.

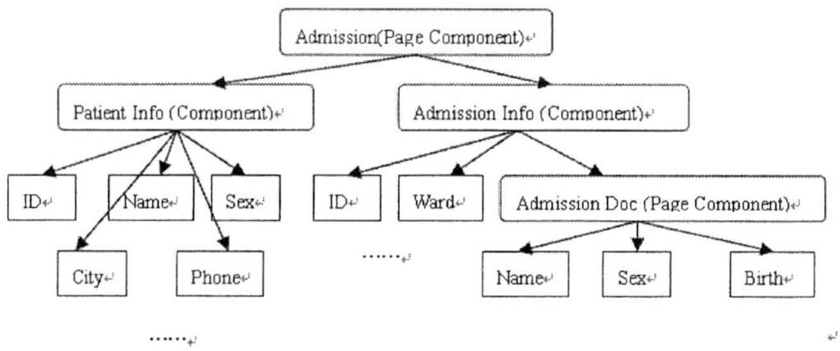

Fig. 2. The Hierarchy of 'Patient Admission' in WHRP

From Example 2 and the intuition of the pedigree-tree, we have the following Observations:

Observation 1. WIS ontology usually contains hundreds of Page Components, which are divided to several groups according to different requirements. In each group there are dozens of components, they bears resemblance to each other on contents, layouts, operations, etc.

As figure 3 shows, there are 335 page components of WIS ontology in WHRP, the child component 'Patient Information' appears in nearly 200 pages and the child component 'Doctor Information' appears in over 120 pages.

Observation 2. Beyond the similarity of components is a deep level knowledge of WIS ontology. Because of the particularity of task, the knowledge can be preserved by simple relations.

Observation 3. To describe the WIS ontology in tree structure, it is enough to keep it in binary relation {Node, subNode}.

These observations are satisfied in most practices, thus they are basic assumptions in this paper.

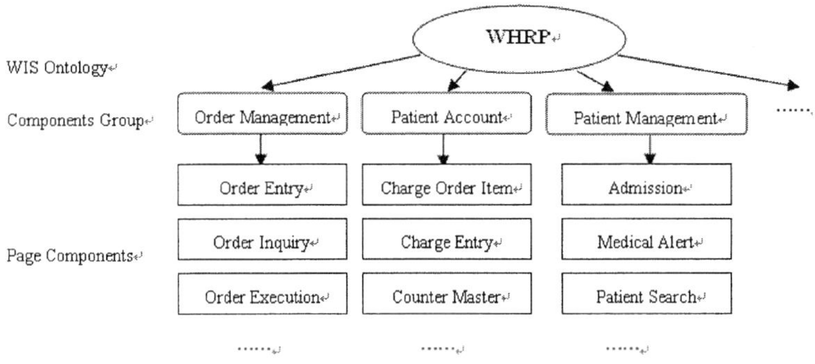

Fig. 3. The Hierarchy of WHRP's ontology

In this paper, relationship is a multi-predication. It denotes the connections among several conceptions. There are four usual relations in ontology building[12]: part-of, kind-of, instance-of, attribute-of. In WIS ontology there are mainly two relations: part-of and attribute-of. By Assumption 3, the relation 'attribute-of' can be replaced by 'part-of'. For example, the basic item 'Patient Name' is an attribute of component 'Patient Information', and it is also a part of the component. Frankly, Partof (ComName, PartName) means the item or component distinguished by PartName is a part of the component distinguished by ComName. Formally, we have:

Definition 3. Given a WIS ontology, let C be the set of component's names of the current system, I be the set of basic items names of the system, $P=C \cup I$, a subset of T X P is said to be a part-of relation.

According to Assumption 2 and 3, each complex nesting relation can be decomposed to several simple part-of relations, so the whole WIS ontology can also be built by these binary relations.

As mentioned in Assumption 1, there are many frequent child components in WIS ontology. Constructing them one by one is a time-consuming and err-prone work. If we can extract them out and make the whole component to be one item just like a text field, it must save a lot of time. However, the operation needs some programming skills, which cannot be finished by domain users. On the other hand, the components are filled with domain semantics, the system cannot provide these services before action. To solve this problem we make a trade-off by asking domain users to construct a small set of page components and learn to auto-generate the often-repeated child components.

Problem Specification. Giving a user defined threshold t and the WIS ontology, which is composed by the forest of Page Components, discover a Child Component C so that: for each element A satisfying Partof(C,A), the count(Partof(T,A))>= t, and for each existing component B satisfying Partof(B,C), the count(part of(B,C))<t;

Definition 4. The Component T satisfying the condition in above Problem Specification is called *the Max Frequent Child Component* (MFCC).

4 The Algorithms for WIS Ontology Personalization

The procedure to mine Max Frequent Child Component (MFCC) is a continuous work through the whole ontology building process. PODWIS provides 3 editor panels and a component palette, at first there are only basic items in the palette, when the users submit preliminary works, PODWIS starts a module based on data-mining to learn the users' behaviors and save the results in database, then generates the MFCC with a user defined threshold. While starting PODWIS the next time, users can find MFCC in the component palette and build ontology in personalized style under their guidance.

4.1 The Resource Content and Relationship Extraction Algorithm

The resources of our WIS ontology are stored in the format of *WIS Ontology Markup Language*(WISO-ML), which is an extension of XML as shown in the figure 2.

By Assumption 2 and 3, user's actions in building WIS ontology can be stored in a relation database, and the conceptual schema of the resource stored in database is shown as Figure 4:

To meet different needs, we designed two self-learning strategies: online learning and offline learning. The main difference between them is the time at which to fill the field 'Frequency' in the view. In fact the main time-consuming work is counting the frequency, so we make a trigger to check the system idle state and start the self-learning module in free time. But if the users want to generate MFCC immediately, we also design an online algorithm to meet these emergent needs.

1	ComName	VARCHAR	2	PartName	VARCHAR
3	PartType	SHORT INT	4	User	VARCHAR
5	DateTime	DATETIME	6	Frequency	SHORT INT
7	SourcePage	VARCHAR	8	...	...

Fig. 4. The Conceptual Schema of the Resource

The idea of Offline Resource Relationship Extraction Algorithm (ORREA) is scanning WIS ontology while keeping mark in stack. The detail is as following:

Algorithm 1. The Offline Resource Relationship Extraction Algorithm (ORREA):
Input: a file descript by WISO-ML, named PageCom;
Output: a user behavior dataset, named UserBehaviorData
Interior variables: a variable denotes the WISO-ML element, named Part;

Initialize the stack;
For each line of the file PageCom, do
{ if the line contains "<" then Push the current XML element in stack;
  if the line contains "</" then

5. {Pop stack top to variable Part;
6. Create a new record in UserBehaviorData;
7. Set the record's field "PartName" to Part.name and field "PartType" to Part.type;
8. Set the record's field "User" to the current user's name;
9. Set the record's field "DateTime" to the current date and time;
10. Read the top element of the stack to variable Part;
11. Set the record's field "ComName" to Part.name;}
12. } Return UserBehaviorData;

Proposition 1. Let n be the length of Page Component File, the complexity of Algorithm 1 is O(n).

Proof. This Algorithm scans the Page Component file once, so the time complexity is O(n);

Note. As Page Component File is in restricted format, the parsing procedure is simpler than that on general XML files.

A trigger in our system is designed to check the system idle state and to start the learning module to mine the frequency of the tuples with the same value in field 'ComName', 'PartName' , 'PartType' and 'User', the algorithm is as following:

Algorithm 2. oFfline Frequency Mining (FFM)

Input: a user behavior dataset without the behavior frequency, named OldDataSet;
Output: a user behavior dataset with the behavior frequency, named NewDataSet;
Interior variables: two variables denote the record of user behavior, named r1, r2; the scan pointer i;

1. Scan the records in OldDataSet , i is the scan pointer, for each record do
2. { Read the current record to variable r1;
3. Scan the records in OldDataSet from the i-th line, for each record do
4. { Read the current record to variable r2;
5. if r2 is the same as r1, then
6. {r1.frequency++; delete the current record in OldDataSet; }
7. write r1 to NewDataSet; }
8. } Return NewDataSet

Proposition 2. Let n be the size of the behavior dataset,

(1) The complexity of Algorithm 2 is $O(n^2)$ without index.
(2) The complexity of Algorithm 2 is O(n*log(n)) with index.

Proof. For each i-th tuple, the algorithm needs to compare it with other n-i tuples, in the worst case, it needs to compare n(n+1)/2 times totally. Thus the time complexity is $O(n^2)$.

In the case with index, the index search spent time log(n) for each one from n tuples, thus the total time complexity can be evaluated by n*log(n).

The online learning policy is to count the same tuples while extracting the relationship from WIS ontology, the algorithm is a mixture of the above 2. We do not present the algorithm's detail here because of the page limitation.

Proposition 3. Let n be the length of Page Component, m be the size of the user behavior dataset,

(1) The complexity of Algorithm 3 is O(m*n) without index.
(2) The complexity of Algorithm 3 is O(n*log(m)) with index

Proof. The proof is similar to Proposition 2 and omitted here because of the page limitation.

The above 3 propositions show that the online learning strategy is good at the beginning, when the size of user behavior data is small, algorithm 3 generates MFCC in time. Then user behavior data gets larger and online learning becomes time-consuming, it is better to choose offline policy.

4.2 MFCC (the Max Frequent Child Component) Generation Algorithm

After extraction and learning, the relationship of WIS ontology is stored in database. It is the time to mine the MFCC of a specified user as following:

Algorithm 4. MFCC Generating:
Input: the original user behavior dataset, named OriginalDataSet;
the name of the current user; the threshold of the frequency;
Output: the MFCC files descript by WISO-ML

```
{ Get_valid_dataset;      //Procedure 1
Get_names _of_MFCC;  // Procedure 2
Generate_ MFCC;       // Procedure 3:}
```

The three procedures are explained in the following:

Procedure 1. Get_Valid_Dataset
Input: the original user behavior dataset, named OriginalDataSet;
the name of the current user; the threshold of the frequency;
Output: the valid user behavior dataset ValidDataSet;
Interior variables: a variable denotes the record of user behavior, named r1;

```
For each record in OriginalDataSet do
{ Read the current record to variable r1;
 if r1.user==current user's name and r1. frequency > threshold
Write r1 to ValidDataSet;}
Return ValidDataSet
```

The above Procedure 1 is simple and self-explainary.

Procedure 2. Get_names_of_MFCC
Input: the valid user behavior dataset ValidDataSet;
Output : a list of the names of MFCC□named MFCCNames;
Interior variables: the string array denotes the component's names set, named ComNameSet;
the string array denotes the part's names set, named PartNameSet;

```
1.  For each record in ValidDataSet do
2.  { if ComNameSet does not include value in the field "ComName" of current
    record
    then
3.      add the value in the field "ComName" to ComNameSet;
4.   if PartNameSet does not include value in the field "PartName" of current
    record then
5.      add the value in the field "PartName" to PartNameSet;}
6.  For each string in ComNameSet do
7.  {if PartNameSet does not include the current string then
8.     add the string to the list MFCCNames;}
9.  Return MFCCNames
```

Because there may be a series of MFCC in WIS ontology, thus it firstly needs to confirm the names of these MFCC, the definition of MFCC shows that in the valid dataset of user behavior, MFCC are in the top of the hierarchy, thus the {MFCC's name}={ComName}- {PartName};

Procedure 3. Generate_MFCC

Input: the valid user behavior dataset ValidDataSet;
the list of the names of MFCC□named MFCCNames;

Output: the MFCC files descript by WISO-ML

Interior variables: a string denotes the component's name, named SearchString;
a variable denotes the record of user behavior, named r1;
a boolean variable denote whether the records are same, named IsSame;

```
1.   For each string in MFCCNames do
2.   {Create a WISO-ML descript file, named by the string;
3.    Write the string to the file in WISO-ML;
4.    Read the string to SearchString;  Initialize the stack;
5.    For each record in ValidDataSet
6.     if the field "ComName" is the same as SearchString then
7.    { Read the current record to variable r1;;
8.      if r1.PartType== "Component" then
9.       {Push r1.ComName to stack;
10.       Write r1.PartName to the file in WISO-ML;
11.       Read r1.PartName to SearchString;}
12.     else then
13.        Write r1.PartName and r1.PartType to the file in WISO-ML;
14.        Delete the current record from ValidDataSet;
15.        If there is no record in ValidDataSet whose field "ComName" is the
           same as
           SearchString, and the stack is not empty then
16.          {Read the top string of the stack to SearchString;
17.           Pop the stack;}  }  }
18.     Return MFCC files
```

Procedure 3 generates MFCC files by their names. For each MFCC, PODWIS searches in valid user behavior dataset, if the type of the result record is 'component', it means this MFCC contains child components, the child components will be pushed in stack until all their elements are constructed. At last, the MFCC is built from bottom to top.

Proposition 4. Let n be the size of the original user behavior dataset, m be the size of the valid user behavior dataset, the complexity of Algorithm 4 is O(m*log(m)).

Proof. Procedure 1 scans the original dataset once, so the time complexity is O(n); Procedure 2 scans the valid dataset twice, which consumes O(m) time; In procedure 3, for each MFCC, it needs to search through the valid dataset, in the worst case, it consumes O(m) time. By creating an index, the time cost is O(log*m*). Thus procedure 3 needs O(*m**log(*m*)) time.

Mostly, m and n has the same magnitude, so time complexity of Algorithm 4 is O(*m**log(*m*)).

The proposition 3 shows that the speed of WIS ontology personalization algorithm is acceptable.

5 The Application of PODWIS

As PODWIS is a new exploration on WIS ontology generation, there is seldom similar existing algorithm to be compared with. Thus our experiment is combined with practical applications. The results show that PODWIS works with good quality and acceptable speed.

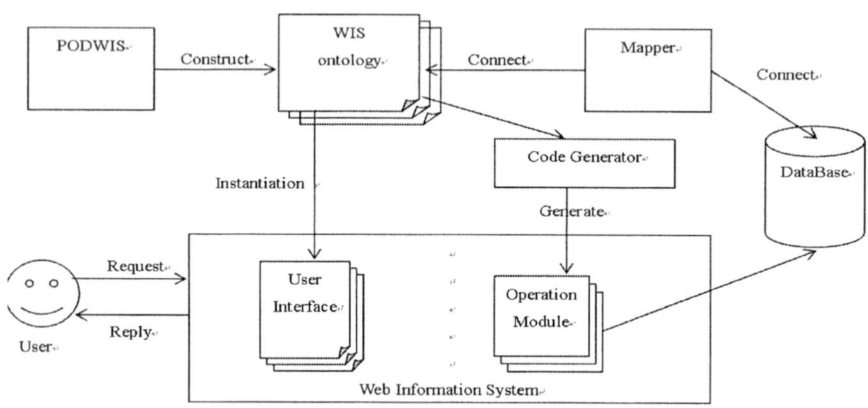

Fig. 5. Automatic Generation of WIS Based on ontology

The Department of Intelligence Science and Technology of Peking University has rich experiences in developing WIS. In order to implement the automatic process of user interface and operations in WIS, a ontology-based approach is adopted in project WISE (Web Information System Environment)[13][14],the key points are:

- With the aid of PODWIS, domain experts build WIS ontology to describe the domain knowledge and user requirements.
- By making page component instances in WIS ontology, the user interfaces are generated automatically.
- According to the WIS ontology, WISE Mapper implements database access and business process control.
- By switching code transformation rules, WISE Code Generator can generate the code of operation modules and the developer may add other functions to complete the work.

Consequently a WIS is generated semi-automatically from the user's view as shown in Figure 5.

5.1 Ontology Building

To be one part of the Web Information System Environment (WISE), PODWIS has been implemented on the eclipse platform. Just as we have mentioned, PODWIS is based on a MVC structure and provides 3 different editor panels as shown in Figure 6. The non-professional user can use the tool easily to personalize WIS ontology.

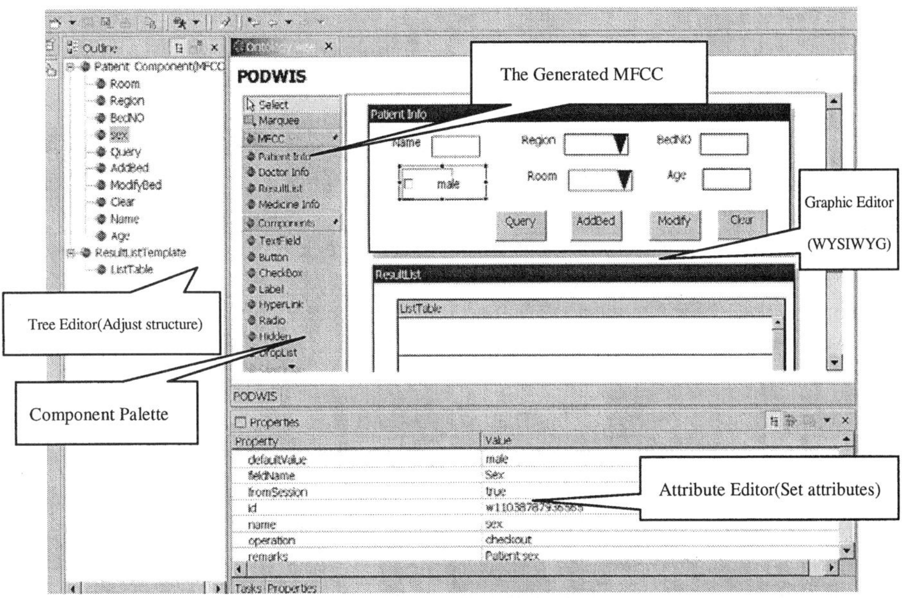

Fig. 6. The Main Interface of PODWIS

5.2 User Interaction Pages Generation and Operation Code Processing

With aid of the WIS ontology, the user interaction pages can easily be generated: The basic items directly maps to the display elements on the web pages. The web forms can be built by accessing the hierarchy structure of the components. The generation will not be totally automatic, because WIS ontology does not contain much information about the style of the web pages. A basic web form can be generated according to WIS ontology's structure and user can adjust the default layout of the pages. The layouts and the styles can be stored in cascading style sheets (CSS) apart from the ontology files.

A mapping strategy is adopted to bridge the gap between the web pages and database. We first map the basic items to data source. Then the operations on web pages, like SELECT, INSERT, UPDATE, DELETE, can be mapped to concrete operations on data sources. The operation mapping method can be used as a part of an automatic WIS construction framework to generate the operation processing code, business logic developers may adjust automatic generated code or write other functions to complete the code module. The details of these techniques are presented in reference [13].

5.3 Application in WHRP

PODWIS and WISE currently are used in developing a web-based hospital information system–WHRP, and they do a good job. There are totally 227 JSP pages and 108 HTML pages in WHRP, which are all generated from the corresponding page components in WHRP's ontology, and the system was required to provide multi-views and support multi-formats. Using PODWIS and WISE solved the following problems:

- Acquire the requirements: The doctors used PDOMIS to construct the ontology of WHRP so as to provide a precise requirements and system structure.
- Multi-view output: WHRP need to output a page component in many formats such as the HTML page for browsing and PDF page for printing, but the ontology building on PODWIS was not affected, even they didn't need to know the existence of different views.
- Shorten developing period: Use WISE to generate the user interfaces and operations based on WIS ontology, and the system developers complete the other functions. Totally about 55% codes are generated and reused, the developing period is shortened greatly while the system is easier to be maintained.

6 Summary and Future Work

Automatic developing WIS based on ontology is a new approach in WIS engineering. In order to customize the WIS ontology smartly, we have proposed a tool named *Personalized tool for Ontology Development in domain specific Web Information System* (PODWIS), the main contributions include:

- Learning the user behavior modes during ontology building, mining frequent resources and composing them to reusable components in order to guide developer's work efficiently with high quality.

- Four Algorithm for WIS ontology personalization, namely, the Offline Resource Relationship Extraction Algorithm (ORREA), Offline Frequency Mining(FFM), Online Frequency Mining(OFM), MFCC Generating.
- Four propositions about the algorithms.
- Auto-generating the domain specific web information system (includes user interface, operations and database access) based on ontology.
- Demonstrating the feasibility of this technique via practical application.

The research on the personalized tool for ontology development on WIS is just beginning, there is much more work to be done, such as the control of different user roles, the expression to complex conditions for operations on web pages and the support of dynamic ontology refinements, etc.

Acknowledgments

Several people have contributed to the project and this paper, they are: YANG Dongqing (Peking University), XUE Ming (IBM China), YAN Bo (CAS), TAN Yongsheng (PKU Third Hospital), YING Ying, LI Meimei, etc. We would like to thank for their helpful discussions, and 3 anonymous reviewers for their comments.

References

1. Tomas Isakowitz, Michael Bieber, Fabio Vitali: Web Information Systems. Communications of the ACM, Page: 78 - 80, Vol 41(7), ACM Press, July 1998.
2. Piero Fraternali: Tools and Approaches for Developing Data-Intensive Web Application. ACM Computing Surveys, September 1999, Vol.31,No.3;
3. Kietz, J.U., Maedche, A. and Volz, R.: Extracting a Domain-Specific Ontology Learning from a Corporate Intranet. Second "Learning Language In Logic" Workshop. Lisbon, Portugal, September 13-14, 2000.
4. Ding, Y., & Foo, S.: Ontology research and development. Journal of Information Science, Vol 28(5), 375-388, 2002.
5. Gloria L. ZWiga: Ontology: Its Transformation From Philosophy to Information Systems. FOIS01, October 17-19,2001, Ogunquit, Maine, USA.
6. Dan Brickly and R.V. Guha. W3C Candidate Recommendation, Resource Description Framework (RDF) Schemas, http://www.w3.org/TR/rdf-schema/, 2000.3
7. http://www.daml.org/
8. http://www.w3.org/2004/OWL/
9. Y. Sure, M. Erdmann, J. Angele, S. Staab, R. Studer, and D. Wenke: OntoEdit: Collaborative Ontology Engineering for the Semantic Web. In International Semantic Web Conference 2002 (ISWC 2002), Sardinia, Italia, 2002.
10. Maedche, A. & Staab, S.: Mining Ontologies from Text. In Dieng, R. & Corby,O. (Eds). EKAW-2000 - 12th International Conference on Knowledge Engineering and Knowledge Management. October 2-6, 2000, Juan-les-Pins, France. LNAI, Springer.
11. Guarino,N: Semantic Mathing: Formal Ontological Distinctions for Information Organization, Extraction and Integration. Information Extraction: A Multidisciplinary Approach to an Emerging Information Technology, SCIE—1997.Frascati, Italy pp139-170

12. Gomez-Perez, A., Juristo, N. & Pazos, J. : Evaluation and assessment of knowledge sharing technology. In. Mars, N.J. (Ed.). Towards very large knowledge bases– Knowledge building and knowledge sharing (pp. 289-296). IOS Press: Amsterdam.1995
13. Xue Ming, Li Hongyan: Managing User Interaction Forms On Web Pages: A Component-base approach. Journal (Naturals Science) Of Peking University, Vol. 40(5), May 2004
14. Wang Jianjun, Li Hongyan, Tang Lv-An, Ying Ying and Xue Ming: Components Reuse and Dynamic Schema Modification Strategy Based on Template Models. In Computer Science 31(10.Supp), 470-474, 2004.

A Structured Approach to Personalize Websites Using the OO-H Personalization Framework*

Irene Garrigós[1], Sven Casteleyn[2], and Jaime Gómez[1]

[1] Universidad de Alicante, IWAD, Campus de San Vicente del Raspeig,
Apartado 99 03080 Alicante, Spain
{igarrigos, jgomez}@dlsi.ua.es

[2] Vrije Universiteit Brussel, Department of Computer Science,
WISE, Pleinlaan 2, 1050 Brussel, Belgium
Sven.Casteleyn@vub.ac.be

Abstract. Most current web engineering approaches don't have clear criteria for personalization, nor a clear strategy that designers can use to classify users and formulate a personalization strategy for the web site at design time. In this paper, we present a structured approach to personalize websites based on three criteria: characteristics, user requirements and context. The users are classified into groups of users (profile groups) based on these criteria. For each group, a personalization strategy is defined by attaching personalization rules to its profile group. The work is presented in the context of the OO-H method which' personalization framework can be instantiated by the web designer, and connected to any OO-H based site to empower it with personalization support. Finally, we introduce a tool that allows designers to specify and generate the personalizable client-side of a web application based on this approach.

1 Introduction

Nowadays, web sites are complex applications, offering both static and rapidly changing information and functionality. When implemented at hoc, this leads to enormous usability and maintenance problems [9] for web designers.

Introduction of web design methods and methodologies [10] [1] [7] have provided some solutions for designers (design support, help in determining consistent structuring, easier maintenance) and for visitors (better tailored content, easier navigation). In order to better tailor the site to one particular user, or a group of users, some methods provide personalization support (see next section for an overview). However, approaches vary widely both on how and what they personalize, and most of the approaches do not provide an underlying CAWE[1] tool to support the personalization. The lack of such tools causes the personalization to be implemented in an ad hoc manner.

---

* This paper has been supported by Ministerio de Educacion y Ciencia with the METASIGN project ref. Code TIN2004-00779.

[1] Computed Aided Web Engineering.

Y. Zhang et al. (Eds.): APWeb 2005, LNCS 3399, pp. 695–706, 2005.

In this paper, we tackle the problems described above by providing support for defining personalization during web site design cycle and by offering the designer a method and a tool to specify the adaptation of the client-side of a web application (i.e. personalize). We present a structured approach to personalize websites based on three criteria of a user profile: user characteristics, user requirements and user context. A *user profile* can be defined as a set of data representing the significant features of the user. User profiling is becoming more and more important in adaptive web applications, due for example to the heterogeneous devices used to access the World Wide Web. In our approach, users are classified into user groups[2], called profile groups, based on the values of the defined criteria in their user profiles. The profile groups are defined by means of profile rules. For each group, a personalization strategy is specified by attaching personalization rules to its profile group. In this way, the OO-H (Object Oriented Hypermedia) method allows personalization of the content and the navigation of the website, both for single users, and groups of users.

The paper is structured as follows. In the next section, related work is studied. The paper continues describing in section 3 the general criteria for personalization showing, by means of a running example, how to categorize each criterion. The criteria are embedded into a personalization framework in the context of the Web Design Method OO-H [5] [6] that is presented in section 4. We continue in section 5, explaining how personalization relates to navigation in OO-H Section 6 shows how the personalization strategy for our running example is described using the Personalization Rule Modeling Language, and how it is connected to navigation. Finally, section 7 sketches some conclusions and further work.

2 Related Work

There are other methods (besides OO-H) that also allow personalization on the basis of the user profile information. Some of them permit adaptation for users with some common user profile data (e.g. groups of users). But, existing methods supporting profiling don't consider the attachment of users to profile groups, although groups are implicitly defined (i.e. users with the same user profile information). In OO-H, the total user base can be partitioned (on the basis of user profile information) into groups. The advantage of explicitly defining these user groups is that for each user only the personalization rules attached to her/his profile group(s) are considered (i.e. the system has not to check the rest of the personalization rules). Next we explain how other methods use the profile information to personalize.

WUML [7], in the context of ubiquitous computing, has personalization based on context. The authors propose an object oriented framework (which consists out of four models) that can be extended by the designer. The context and profile models provide detailed information about the environment of an application and trigger the actual customization as soon as the environment changes. Context represents current

[2] A group can be composed (only) by one user, and a user can belong to one or more profile groups.

and historical information about the environment of the application which is automatically monitored. Profiles cover more stable information which is explicitly given by a designer or a user (e.g. user preferences) or is transparently acquired by the system itself (e.g. usage statistics).

In the OOHDM approach [10] user roles are considered, those users roles are (only) static profile groups (defined at design time and cannot be dynamically changed). Different web applications can be built for different user profiles reusing a conceptual schema. The navigation model is built as a view over a conceptual model, thus allowing the construction of different models according to different user profiles. OOHDM also supports dynamic customization. In the navigation model, node contents and structure can be customized and links and indexes can be personalized. Only one of the six different kinds of navigational contexts supported allows to capture dynamic user preferences. In the interface model different layouts can be defined according to user preferences or selected devices.

In the Hera methodology [4], two kinds of adaptation are considered: adaptation with respect to devices capabilities and user preferences stored in a profile (adaptability, i.e. personalization defined at design time), and adaptation based on user navigation history stored in a User Model during browsing (adaptivity, i.e. personalization performed while the user is browsing the application). To model the adaptability in the Hera methodology, the Composite Capability / Preference Profile (CC/PP) [9] offers a framework to model profiles that characterize device capabilities and user preferences. In Hera static adaptation (i.e. adaptability) is applied to users belonging to a profile, (e.g. users with a wap phone). To add adaptivity functionality to Hera the authors use the AHA (Adaptive Hypermedia Architecture) system [3].

None of these methods provide the designer with a structured user model based on (all) the features of the user (characteristics, context, requirements), nor do they offer the designer a high level language to personalize based upon these criteria[3]. And most importantly, none of these methods provides a rigid, industrially tested CAWE tool supporting the proposed (personalization) design.

3 Criteria for Personalization

In this section, we will explain the different criteria upon which a personalization strategy can be built. We will concentrate here on the user-specific features (user profile information) rather than on domain-specific features. The former ones are features independent from the domain and dependent only on the user, the latter ones consist of features specific for the domain (e.g. history of buys in e-commerce sites). We have classified these user-specific features distinguishing between user characteristics, user requirements, and context.

We first elaborate on these features and the role they may play in personalization. For this purpose we have modelled a simplified version of the Fnac web site (http://www.fnac.com, online shop of spare time cultural products) and we have added

[3] Implicitly, our approach also includes support for behaviour by means of acting upon events, see section 3.2.

personalization based on the criteria defined in this paper. Now we will explain the different criteria upon which can be personalized by means of this running example. The next sections will cover personalization itself for the case study defined here.

3.1 User Characteristics

User characteristics (such as age or language) may be relevant for the structure, content or presentation of the web site. Designers might try to exploit the user' characteristics to adapt the site to either arrive at a better usability and/or have a greater benefit for the company. Examples include: adapting the font size for users with low vision; avoiding the use of specific colors in case of color blindness; etc.

In our case study we will show or not show some products depending on the user's age. (E.g. we will "censure" some books, dvds... for non-adults users). The user's age is considered as a relevant characteristic of the user and we will define a profile group based on this characteristic. The designer then can specify a personalization strategy over the defined group of users (e.g. users whose age is less than 18).

3.2 User Requirements

Every user comes to a web site for specific reasons, and with specific goals. He is looking for some specific information or functionality and he expects to find it on the web site, i.e. the user has *user requirements*. A good web site design method starts out with specifying the user requirements, elaborating these requirements further and specifying the information or functionality needed to fulfil the requirements at a conceptual level (e.g. using modelling techniques such as UML, ER, ORM, ...). Next, these conceptual representations are translated into actual web pages, using some presentation and layout mapping.

As an example of personalization based on (fulfilling) user requirements, we can consider adding a link to information relevant for a certain user, even though it was not originally assessed as a requirement for this particular user.

Continuing the running example, we will consider the (fine-grained) requirements browseBooks, browseMusic, browseDvd... (rather then the course-grained requirement "browse products"). In section 4 (and 6) we will define as an example a profile for the users interested in books by specifying the requirement of this type of users (browseBooks). A personalization strategy will be applied over this group of users: if the user is interested in books, we offer him new books that have arrived on the front page.

3.3 User Context

The variety of devices that can access the web gets larger every day, and the particularities of the different devices may influence the way we want to structure or present information for/to the visitor, or even which information we offer. In other words, information concerning the context of the current session of the user will be relevant to consider for personalization.

In the OO-H framework four kinds of context are considered: LocationContext (ubiquity of the user), NetworkContext (e.g. latency, speed, bandwidth ...), DeviceContext (e..g. PC, PDA, WAP ...), and TimeContext (date and local time of the connection). In the Fnac example we consider a type of context personalization based on the device context of the user. We will define a profile for users who are browsing the website using a small display device (in the example we consider PDA, mobile phone and MP3 player). The personalization strategy for this group of users consists of not showing any pictures associated to products, since resolution of the PDA, MP3 player and mobile phone screen does not allow images to be displayed conveniently, and big images would also hinder convenient navigation.

Now that we have defined the different (user related) criteria considered for personalization[4], we will explain the (general) OO-H framework, and see how the different criteria are represented within the OO-H personalization framework.

4 The OO-H Personalization Framework: General Overview

The OO-H (Object Oriented Hypermedia) Method is a generic model, based on the object oriented paradigm that provides the designer with the semantics and notation necessary for the development of web-based interfaces. Figure 1 shows the package view of the whole approach. Web design modelling is achieved by means of the two complementary views, namely (1) the Navigational Access Diagram (navigation package), that enriches a standard UML class diagram (structure package) with navigation and interaction properties, and (2) the Abstract Presentation Diagram (presentation package) that gathers the concepts related both to structure of the site and specific presentation details respectively.

The OO-H also supports dynamic personalization (a preliminary version was described in [5]), allowing the designer to better tailor the site to the particularities and needs of the individual user. This is done by means of a personalization framework that is a part of the model. That framework can be instantiated by the web designer, and connected to any OO-H based site to empower it with personalization support for (individual) users. The goal of the personalization framework is twofold: (1) provide the designer with the means of gathering and storing all information needed to personalize the site, and (2) provide the designer with the means of specifying the personalization policy for the different users (adapting structure, content, layout and/or presentation). According these goals, the framework can be divided in two parts: (1) *The user model* and (2) *The personalization model*. We now discuss both parts in more detail and indicate how they are related.

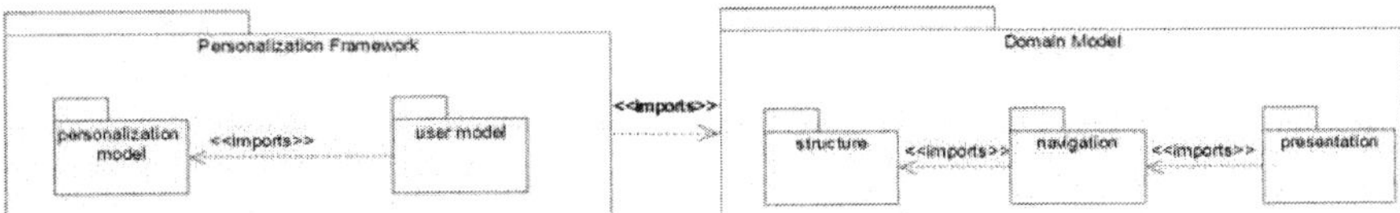

Fig. 1. OO-H package view

[4] Although here, all examples of profile groups are based on one type of criterion, we can also define profiles combining different types of criteria (e.g. a profile defined by a characteristic and a context)

4.1 The User Model

In the user model, all the knowledge about the user is stored. It will contain information on the three criteria explained in the previous section as well as information related to the browsing behaviour of the user.

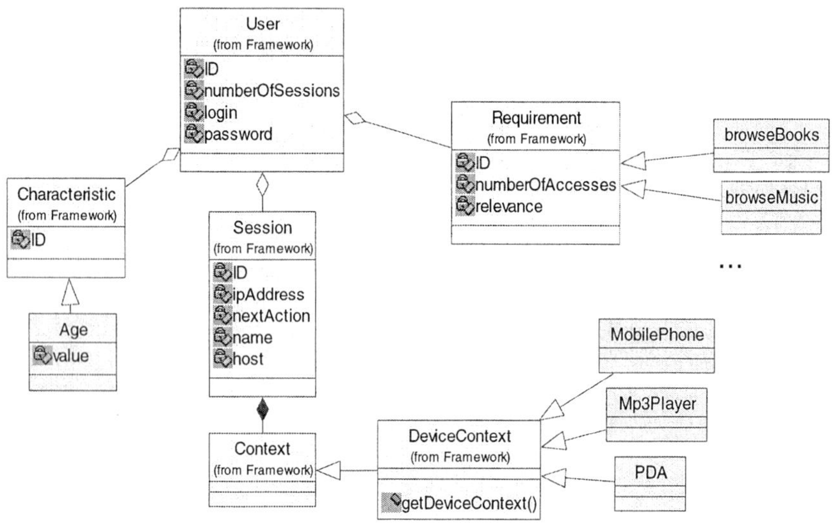

Fig. 2. User Model for the FNAC system

Figure 2 shows the relevant part of the user model for the running example presented in section 3 (some attributes and methods not directly relevant for this example have been omitted). The figure shows some classes that belong to the framework package, marked with the text 'from Framework'. Those classes constitute the skeleton to adapt the generic OO-H user model to the concrete personalization requirements. In our example, the designer needs to capture information regarding the user's age. Following the criteria presented in the previous section this information can be classified as a user characteristic. That is why the class *Age* inherits from the predefined characteristic class of the user model. In the same way, the other relevant information for fulfilling the personalization requirements are captured by means of inheritance relations with the proper classes from the user model (e.g. PDA, MP3Player and MobilePhone inheriting from DeviceContext and browseBooks and browseMusic from Requirement).

4.2 The Personalization Model

The personalization model allows the designer to define a collection of rules that can be used to define a personalization strategy for a user or group of users. The rules are Event-Condition-Action [2] rules: they are triggered by a certain event (e.g. a browsing action, the start of a session) and if a certain condition is fulfilled (for example "categoryMovie="drama""), the associated action is performed. For satisfying a personalization requirement we have to define where and what information is acquired to obtain the required knowledge to personalize (acquisition rule) and define the personalization in terms of the effects this personalization causes in the system (personalization rules). We also have profile rules to classify the users using the acquired information.

In the following table we have summarized for the different personalization requirements of our case study the different rules that should be defined.

Personalization requirement	**Acquisition rule**	**Profile rule**	**Personalization rule**
Adult users can see some products that are not shown to minors *(type: characteristic)*	Not defined. The user's age is acquired in an explicit way (e.g using a form)	If the user's age is less than 18 we attach the user to the profile group "Minors".	If the user belongs to the "Minors" profile, products with 18+ rated material are omitted
Users with the requirement "browse Books" will see the newest books in home page *(type: requirement)*	Not defined. The user's requirements are acquired in an explicit way (e.g using a form)	If the user has the requirement browseBooks, attach the user to the profile group "browseBooks"	If the user belongs to the profile "browseBooks" show the new books in the home page.
Users with small screen-devices will not be shown product images. *(type: context)*	Capture the device context when the user enters the application	If device context is PDA, Mobile Phone or MP3 Player, attach the user to the profile group "smallScreen".	If the user belongs to the profile "smallScreen" don't show images of products

As an example to better understand this table, consider the last row. It expresses that we'd like to support users browsing with a small screen device, by not showing them images not to overload their (small) screen. An acquisition rule is used to capture the deviceContext of a user starting a session (column 2). Based on the kind of device that is detected, the user is or is not attached to the profile group smallScreen by means of a profile rule (column 3). Finally, if the user is a smallScreen user, a personalization rule expresses that images are not shown.

The rules described in this table needed for our running example will be defined using an efficient, simple and easy to learn language defined in OO-H. The purpose of this language is to help the web designers to define all the rules required to implement a personalization strategy. This language is called PRML (*Personalization Rule Modelling Language*). The basic structure of a rule defined with this language is the following:

When *event* **do**
        If *condition* **then** *action* **endIf**
endWhen

As we have said the different type of rules in OO-H are Event-Condition-Action [2] rules. In this basic structure we define the event that triggers the rule, the condition to be checked and the action to be performed. The rules defined for the running example are shown in next section and we will also show how to connect users and their personalization strategy.

5 Navigation and Personalization in OO-H

Having explained the OO-H personalization framework (user and personalization model) and its use, we will now describe how a personalization strategy is specified and how exactly it relates to the OO-H Navigation Access Diagram (NAD).

A NAD is a conceptual model that provides the necessary constructs to represent how a web site visitor navigates through and accesses the information/services of the application. Moreover, it shows which events trigger the different rules and which type of criteria is being satisfied to fulfil the personalization requirements.

Figure 3 shows the NAD for the running example. The starting point (*entry point* element) is the home page where information about product *categories* (navigational class) and *novelties* (navigational class) is presented. That information is shown in the context of the home page because their corresponding links "view categories" and "view novelties" are shown in origin (*origin* property). When the user selects a category (*view categories* link), the set of products that belongs to that category is shown in a new page (*destination* property). The information shown about a product is name, *price*, *picture* and *description* (attributes of *product* navigation class). The service *BuyProduct* can be invoked by means of the service link Buy.

Personalization is embedded in a NAD by means of events, which are generated by the user throughout a browsing session. The types of events are: *Start event* that is associated with the entrance of the user in the system (activation of *Entry point link*). *Navigation event* that implies the activation of any navigation link (e.g. view categories,). *Method Invocation event* that implies the invocation of a method defined in our system (in fig. 3 we can see one of this type of link: "Buy")[5].

When a user enters the website (*Entry Point Link*) the Start event is launched. At this point, we attach the user to user profile(s) (by means of profile rules; see next section for examples). Obviously, to be able to attach a user to a user profile, some information about the user is needed. The required information is gathered by means of acquisition rules triggered also by the Start event (in our example the rule to get the device context) but with a higher priority than the profile rules (i.e. they are executed first). Information that cannot be gathered automatically is asked to the user at first visit by means of a form. Once a user is attached to a profile(s) only the personalization rules attached to that (those) profile(s) are considered (as far as the current user is concerned). The personalization and acquisition rules attached to a profile will be triggered by certain browsing event (Start, Navigation or MethodInvocation) generated by the user during his session. In our example all the personalization rules are triggered by Navigation events (activation of navigational links). In this way one NAD has different executions for different users (as they will be attached to different user

[5] A 4th event not associated with any type of link, the init event, will be explained shortly.

profiles). The whole set of rules associated to a NAD is stored in a PRML file. In the next section, we show the PRML file for our running example.

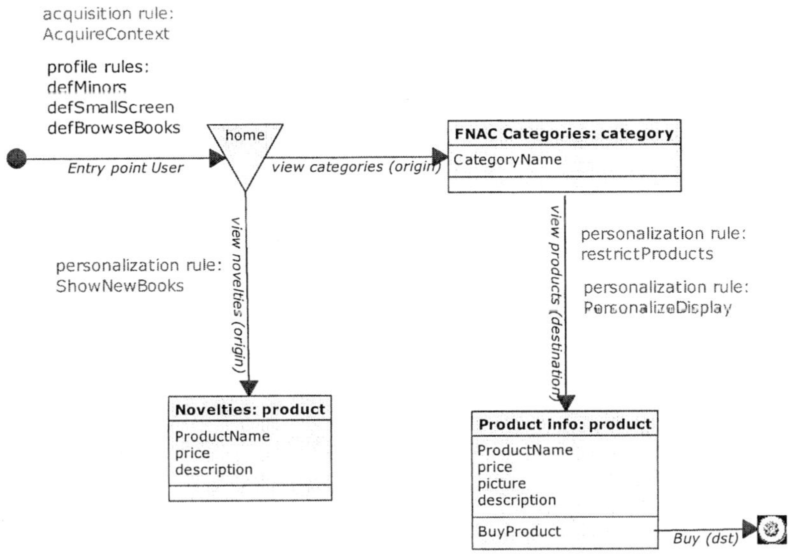

Fig. 3. (Simplified) NAD for the Fnac example

6 Personalizing the NAD Using a PRML File

All that remains now is to show the content of the PRML configuration file for our running example[6] (the rules needed in this example are described in the table in section 4.2). We can see how the structure of this file follows the organization of the personalization model in OO-H. This file has four big sections.

- The **acquisition rule section** defines the rules needed to gather the required information to classify the user into user groups. In our example we have an acquisition rule to capture the device from which the user is connecting to the website (device context). This rule gets the device context using a method defined in the personalization framework.
- The **profile rule section** contains the profile rules. The profile rules for this example, defining "Minors", "BrowseBooks" and "smallScreen", are all triggered by the *Start* event. When a user enters the system (i.e. starts a session), s/he is attached to the profile group(s) s/he belong to (based on the profile condition).
- The **personalization rule section** contains the personalization rules which describe the effect of personalization in the website. In our example, we have

[6] Some attributes of the rules have been omitted for simplicity reasons.

three personalization rules. All of them are triggered by *Navigation* events, but of course other events could also trigger personalization rules.

- *The first rule* is triggered by the activation of the link *"ViewProducts"*. Each product in the site has an attribute *"allowedFromAge"*, denoting the required age to view the product. On basis of this attribute, we will only show products allowed from age greater than 18 (i.e. the action changes the property *Visible* [7] of the Product class to *false*).
- *The second rule* personalizes the website by omitting pictures to be shown. It is triggered by the *Navigation* event of activating the "*ViewProducts*" link. The action of not showing images (of products) is achieved by setting the property *Visible* of the picture attribute to *false.*
- *The third rule* is triggered when the user consults the new products activating the link *"ViewNovelties"*. It specifies that the category of products to be shown should be 'books'. The other condition checks that the selected products are "new"[8], checking the date of addition of the product to the website.

▪ Finally, every PRML configuration file has an ***Init* section**. The deployment of the website causes the rule engine to be set up with all rules, and the launch of an INIT event). Upon this INIT event, user profiles are defined and personalization rules are associated to them. In this way we specify a personalization strategy for the defined user profiles. The acquisition rule and the profile rules are attached to the special profile OOH:all (i.e. applied to all users).

```
# ACQUISITION SECTION
#RULE:"AcquireContext" priority="high"
When start do
DeviceContext=getDeviceContext()
endWhen

# PROFILE SECTION
#RULE:"defMinors"
priority:"medium"
When start do
   If (charHasValue (Age,<,18))
  then
   AttachUserToPGroup("Minors")
 endIf
endWhen
```

```
#RULE:"defSmallScreen"
priority:"medium"
When start do
 If   (deviceContext="PDA"   or
deviceContext="MP3"          or
deviceContext="WAP") then

AttachUserToPGroup("smallScreen")
   endIf
 endWhen
```

```
#RULE:"defBrowseBooks" priority:"medium"
When start do
 If (userhasReq ("brosweBooks")) then
  AttachUserToPGroup("browseBooks")
 endIf
endWhen
```

[7] In OO-H, every class and attribute has a *visible* property, denoting if it should or shouldn't be shown

[8] We consider products new if they have been added at most one week ago.

```
# PERSONALIZATION SECTION
# RULE:"restrictProducts"
When Navigation.ViewProducts do
   If
   (Products.allowedFromAge>18)
 then
         Product.Visible=false
    endIf
endWhen

# RULE:"PersonalizeDisplay"
When Navigation.ViewProducts do
    Product.picture.Visible=false
endWhen

# RULE:"ShowNewBooks"
When Navigation.ViewNovelties do
  If (Products.category='Books' and
  Products.dateOfAddition=currentDate-week) then
      Select(name, description, price) in Products
  endIf
endWhen

# INIT SECTION
When init do
      AttachRuleToPGroup("AcquireContext", "OOH:all")
      AttachRuleToPGroup("defMinors", "OOH:all")
      AttachRuleToPGroup ("defSmallScreen", "OOH:all")
      AttachRuleToPGroup("defBrowseBooks", "OOH:all")
      AttachRuleToPGroup("restrictProducts", "Minors")
      AttachRuleToPGroup("ShowNewBooks", "browseBooks")
      AttachRuleToPGroup("PersonalizeDisplay", "smallScreen")
endWhen
```

We have introduced the presented approach in the context of a CAWE tool to design web applications called VisualWADE [6] (developed by the web engineering research group of the University of Alicante) that follow the OO-H design method presented in section 4. We have extended VisualWADE with new properties in the OO-H personalization framework to be able to gather the needed information to personalize web applications based on the criteria presented in section 3. Also we have incorporated a PRML parser to specify the acquisition rules, profile rules and personalization rules. The NAD and the PRML can be compiled by means of an advanced model compiler that was presented in [6]. The compilation process produces an XML default presentation that fulfils the conceptual specification.

7 Conclusions and Future Work

In this paper, we have presented a personalization framework for (general) personalization support during the web site design process, in the scope of the OO-H method. We have focused on the user model of the framework, and distinguished three different criteria upon which personalization support can be built: characteristics, user requirements and context. Based upon these three features, personalization rules can be defined. By means of a running example, we have shown how these rules can be specified using PRML, a high level language easy to use by web designers. Finally, we have discussed the VisualWade tool that supports generating websites with personalization based on an OO-H design. Future work includes elaborating personalization based upon a fourth criterion: behavior.

Although support for limited behavior based personalization is already present in our framework (i.e. based on browsing events), we intent to extend this capability, so that more complex navigation patterns can give rise to personalization.

References

1. Ceri S., Fraternali P., and Bongio A: "Web Modeling Language (WebML): a modeling language for designing Web sites", WWW9 Conf, 2000.
2. Dayal U.: "Active Database Management Systems", In Proc. 3rd Int. Conf on Data and Knowledge Bases, pp 150–169, 1988.
3. De Bra, P., Aerts, A., Houben, G.J., Wu, H: Making General-Purpose Adaptive Hypermedia Work. In Proc. WebNet World Conf on the WWW and Internet, AACE pp 117-123, 2000.
4. Franciscar, F., Houben G.J.:"Hypermedia Presentation adaptation on the Semantic Web", Adaptive Hypermedia and Adaptive Web-Based Systems, Second International Conf, AH 2002, Vol. 2347, LNCS, Springer, pp 133-142, 2002.
5. Garrigós, I., Gómez, J. and Cachero, C.: "Modelling Dynamic Personalization in Web Applications", 3rd International Conf on Web Engineering (ICWE), LNCS 2722, pp 472-475. Springer-Verlag, 2003.
6. Gómez, J., Cachero, C., and Pastor, O.: "Conceptual Modelling of Device-Independent Web Applications", IEEE Multimedia Special Issue on Web Engineering, pp 26–39, 2001.
7. Kappel, G., Retschitzegger, W., Poll, W., & Schwinger, W. "Modeling Ubiquitous Web Applications - The WUML Approach". In: Proc. of the International Workshop on Data Semantics in Web Information Systems,2001.
8. Klyne, G., Reynolds, F., Woodrow, C., Ohto, H.: Composite Capability/Preference Profiles (CC/PP): Structure and Vocabularies. W3C(2001), http://www.w3.org/TR/CCPP-struct.vocab
9. Nielsen, J.:Finding usability problems through heuristic evaluation.. In Proc. of the SIGCHI Conf on Human factors in computing systems.Monterey, California, United States pp: 373 – 380. 1992.
10. Schwabe, D. and Rossi, G. A Conference Review System with OOHDM. In First Internacional Workshop on Web-Oriented Software Technology, 2001.

Using Probabilistic Latent Semantic Analysis for Personalized Web Search

Chenxi Lin[1], Gui-Rong Xue[1], Hua-Jun Zeng[2], and Yong Yu[1]

[1] Apex Data and Knowledge Management Lab,
Department of Computer Science and Engineering,
Shanghai JiaoTong University, Shanghai, 200030, P.R. China.
{linchenxi, grxue, yyu}@apex.sjtu.edu.cn
[2] Microsoft Research Asia,
49 Zhichun Road, Beijing, 100080, P.R. China
hjzeng@microsoft.com

Abstract. Web users use search engine to find useful information on the Internet. However current web search engines return answer to a query independent of specific user information need. Since web users with similar web behaviors tend to acquire similar information when they submit a same query, these unseen factors can be used to improve search result. In this paper we present an approach that mines these unseen factors from web logs to personalized web search. Our approach is based on probabilistic latent semantic analysis, a model based technique that is used to analyze co-occurrence data. Experimental results on real data collected by MSN search engine show the improvements over traditional web search.

1 Introduction

Search engines, such as Google, Yahoo! and MSN, have been the major tools to help users find useful information on the Internet. However current search technologies work in "one size fits all" fashion with results ordered by web site popularity rather than user interests. Since different users may have different information need, it is essential to personalize web search as well as better the service.

Many methods are proposed to study user's interests and build user profiles based on user's search history. These methods focus on analyzing content of the queries and web pages, but in some case there are no suitable descriptors such as keywords, topics, genres, etc. that can be used to accurately describe interests. According to [1], web users usually exhibit different types of behaviors depending on their information needs. Thus, web users with similar web behaviors tend to acquire similar information when they submit a same query to search engine. [2] conducted experiments to verify the effectiveness of several profile construction approaches and the results showed that the user profile constructed based on modified collaborative filtering achieved better retrieval accuracy. The collaborative filtering technique used in [2] is based on nearest neighbor regression or so-called memory-based techniques. These memory-

Y. Zhang et al. (Eds.): APWeb 2005, LNCS 3399, pp. 707–717, 2005.

based methods are simple and intuitive on a conceptual level while avoiding the complications of a potentially expensive model-building stage. However, there are a number of severe shortcomings as Hofmann point out in [3]: (i) The accuracy obtained by memory-based methods maybe suboptimal. (ii) Since no explicit statistical model is constructed, nothing is really learned form the available user profiles and very little general insight is gained. (iii) Memory-based methods do not scale well in terms of their resource requirements (memory and computing time). Especially, in web search tasks, the data set are always very large and the online response should be in a very short time. (iv) Actual user profiles have to be kept for prediction, potentially raising privacy issues.

Users' previous web behaviors and other personal information can be used to identify the users' information needs. In this paper, we indicate to analyze clickthrough data to personalize Web search. Clickthrough data is a kind of search log that could be collected by search engine implicitly without any participation of users. It logs for each query the query submitter and the web pages clicked by her. This process is different from those approaches based on user effort, such as providing relevance feedback or registering interest and demographic information. Through analysis of the clickthrough data, we could consider a single user's behavior characteristic and take similar users' interests into account, so as to identify the user's search intention and thus improve the search results.

To address the shortcomings of the memory-based methods mentioned above, we use a model-based technique called *Probabilistic Latent Semantic Analysis* (PLSA) [4]. A three-way learning and prediction model is proposed to deal with the triple relationship between users, queries and web pages on the usage data. The advantages of our method are as follows:

- The algorithm could compress the data into a compact model to automatically identify user search intention.
- The preference predictions could be computed in constant time so as to reduce online response time.
- The huge user profile data does not need to be kept.
- The experimental results also show that our proposed algorithm could achieve higher prediction accuracies on real data set collected by MSN search engine.

This paper is organized as follows. In Section 2, we introduce related work about personalized web search and probability latent semantic analysis. In Section 3, we present our model and show how to perform personalized web search based on the model. Our experiments and interpretation of the result is given in Section 4. Finally, we conclude this paper in Section 5.

2 Related Work

2.1 Personalized Web Search

[5] first proposed personalized PageRank and suggested to modify the global PageRank algorithm, which computes a universal notion of importance of a Web page. [6] used personalized PageRank scores to enable "topic sensitive" web searches.

Because no experiments based on a user's context, this approach actually cannot satisfy different information needs by different users.

Several approaches are proposed to construct user profiles by content of queries and web pages. [7] used ontology to model a user's interests, which are studied from user's browsed web pages. To distinguish long-term and short-term interests, [8] focused on using user's search history rather than browsing history to construct user profiles. Furthermore [9] mapped a query to a set of categories and [10] clustered words into a user interest hierarchy. All these methods are built on the fundamental assumption that users' interests or information needs can be formulated in term of intrinsic features of the information sought. In some case keywords, topics, genres and other descriptors are not able to describe information needs accurately.

[2] considered the unseen factors of the relationship between the web users behaviors and information needs and constructs user profiles through a memory-based collaborative filtering approach. Nevertheless it could not avoid the shortcoming listed in Sec.1.

2.2 Probabilistic Latent Semantic Analysis

Latent semantic analysis (LSA) [11] stems from linear algebra and performs a Singular Value Decomposition. It is mostly used in automatic indexing and information retrieval [12]. The key idea is to map high-dimensional count vectors to a lower dimensional representation in a so-called *latent semantic space*. Although LSA has proven to be a valuable analysis tool with a wide range of applications, its theoretical foundation remains to a large extent unsatisfactory and incomplete.

Hofmann presented a statistical view on LSA which leads a new model, *Probabilistic Latent Semantics Analysis* (PLSA) [4] [13], and provided a probabilistic approach for the discover of latent variables which is more flexible and has a more solid statistical foundation than the standard LSA. The basic of PLSA is a latent class statistical mixture model named aspect model. It is assumed that there exist a set of hidden factors underlying the co-occurrences among two sets of objects. That means the occurrences of two sets of objects are independent when the latent variables are given. PLSA uses *Expectation-Maximization* (EM) algorithm [14] to estimate the probability values which measure the relationship between the hidden factors and the two sets of objects.

Because of its flexibility, PLSA has been used successfully in a variety of application domain, including information retrieval [15], text learning [16] [17], and co-citation analysis [18] [19]. Furthermore, web usage mining can also be based on PLSA. [1] presented a framework to use PLSA for discovery and analysis of web navigational patterns, while it did not refer how to use PLSA to improve personalized web search. In our paper we present the approach and give an experimental evaluation.

3 Using PLSA to Predict

3.1 Prediction Problem Description

As we described in Sec.1, clickthrough data is collected by search engines without any participations of users. When a user submits a query to a search engine, the search engine returns search results corresponding to the query. Based on the search results, the users may select the web pages which are related to their information need. Search engines could record the behaviors as the clickthrough data. The users, queries and web pages are collected as a co-occurrence triple in the web log. There are two kinds of data we should deal with differently. One is the queries the user has submitted several days ago, the search engine can easily to calculate which page is most frequent and rank it to the top one for the user. We experiment the real data from MSN search engine. If selected pages are not new pages, in other words they occurred in any search tasks in the past 20 days, more than 70% precision are reached of the top ones. The other is the queries that the user never submitted. Then the problem is: Given the clickthrough data, which page should be recommended to the user as the top results. Formally, given a set T that contains all previous (u,q,p) triples, a mapping function $f: U*Q \rightarrow P$ should be learned. The input of the function is any pair (u,q) where for any p', the triple $(u,q,p') \notin T$. The output is the page which is predicted the most possible needed page by the user. More generally, the top k pages will be interested as the recommendation problem.

3.2 Model Specification

The starting point for PLSA is a latent class statistical mixture model which has been called aspect model. This model is a latent semantic class model for co-occurrence data which associates an unobserved class variable $z \in Z\{z_1, z_2, \cdots z_k\}$ with each observation. These unobserved classes stand by the hidden factors underlying the co-occurrence among the observed sets of objects. Therefore this model well capture unseen factor that lead to the fact that web users exhibit different types of behavior depending on their information needs. At the same time it well characterizes the hidden semantic relationship among users, queries as well as users, queries and web pages. Therefore, in our web search scenario, an observation is a triple (u,q,p) corresponding an event that a user u submits a query q to a search engine, and selects a page p from the results. In the context of web search, users $u \in U\{u_1, u_2, \cdots u_n\}$, queries $q \in Q\{q_1, q_2, \cdots q_m\}$, together with web pages $p \in P\{p_1, p_2, \cdots p_l\}$, form triple relationship (u,q,p). The relationships are associated with the latent variables $z \in Z\{z_1, z_2, \cdots z_k\}$. The mixture model depends on a conditional independence assumption, namely each set of observed objects are independent conditioned on the state of the associated latent variable. Conceptually, the latent variables are search intentions. According to the assumption, users, queries and web pages are independent when given search intentions. It means that a user u and a query q determine a latent search intention z, and latent variables in turn "generated" web page p. Fig.1 depicts the model as a Bayesian network.

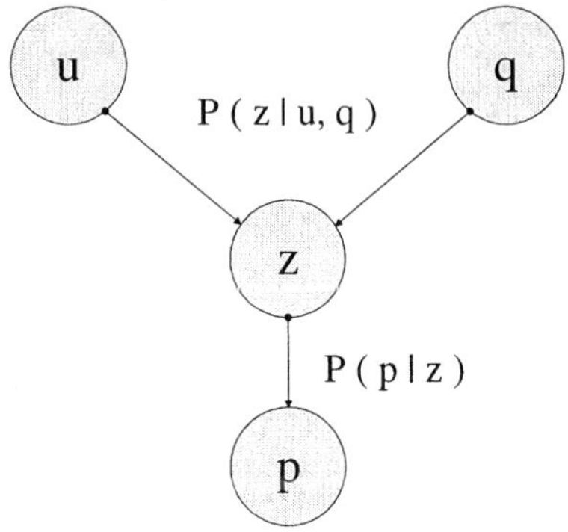

Fig. 1. Graphical representation of the three-way aspect model

Therefore, the joint our model is defined as follows:

$$P(u,q,p) = P(u,q)P(p \mid u,q) , \tag{1}$$

$$P(p \mid u,q) = \sum_{z \in Z} P(p \mid z)P(z \mid u,q) . \tag{2}$$

Reversing the arc from users and queries to latent search intentions, we can get an equivalent symmetric specification:

$$P(u,q,p) = \sum_{z \in Z} P(z)P(u \mid z)P(q \mid z)P(p \mid z) . \tag{3}$$

3.3 Model Fitting with the EM Algorithm

PLSA uses the *Expectation-Maximization* (EM) [14] algorithm to estimate the probability value which measure the relationships between the hidden factors and the sets of objects. According to Formula (3), in order to explain a set of observation (u,q,p) , we need to estimate the parameters $P(z)$, $P(u \mid z)$, $P(q \mid z)$ and $P(p \mid z)$, while maximizing following likelihood. The algorithm alternates two steps:

- An expectation (E) step, where posterior probabilities are computed for the latent variable, based on the current estimates of the parameters;
- A maximization (M) step, where parameters are re-estimated to maximize the expectation of the complete data likelihood.

Let $n(u,q,p)$ be the number of times user u selects page p of query q . Given training data, the log likelihood L of the data is:

$$L = \sum_{u,q,p} n(u,q,p) \log P(u,q,p) . \tag{4}$$

In the E-step, we compute:

$$P(z \mid u,q,p)=\frac{P(z)P(u \mid z)P(q \mid z)P(p \mid z)}{\sum_{z'\in Z}P(z')P(u \mid z')P(q \mid z')P(p \mid z')}, \tag{5}$$

In the M-step, the formulae are:

$$\begin{aligned} P(z) &= \frac{\sum_{u,q,p} n(u,q,p)P(z \mid u,q,p)}{\sum_{z'\in Z}\sum_{u,q,p} n(u,q,p)P(z' \mid u,q,p)} \\ &= \frac{\sum_{u,q,p} n(u,q,p)P(z \mid u,q,p)}{\sum_{u,q,p} n(u,q,p)} \end{aligned} \tag{6}$$

$$P(u \mid z)=\frac{\sum_{q,p} n(u,q,p)P(z \mid u,q,p)}{\sum_{u',q,p} n(u',q,p)P(z \mid u',q,p)} \tag{7}$$

$$P(q \mid z)=\frac{\sum_{u,p} n(u,q,p)P(z \mid u,q,p)}{\sum_{u,q',p} n(u,q',p)P(z \mid u,q',p)} \tag{8}$$

$$P(p \mid z)=\frac{\sum_{u,q} n(u,q,p)P(z \mid u,q,p)}{\sum_{u,q,p'} n(u,q,p')P(z \mid u,q,p')} \tag{9}$$

Iterating these two steps monotonically increases the log-likelihood of the observed data until a local maximum optimal solution is reached.

3.4 Prediction in Practice

Theoretically in our model, prediction is provided to users according to:

$$P(p \mid u,q)=\frac{\sum_{z\in Z} n(u,q,p)P(z \mid u,q,p)}{\sum_{p'}\sum_{z\in Z} n(u,q,p')P(z \mid u,q,p')}. \tag{10}$$

In practice, we cluster the web users, queries and web pages before using PLSA in order to: (1) overcoming the overfitting problem with sparse data, (2) reduce the memory and offline time cost with large data set. We make assumption that each user is belong to exactly one group of users, so as each query and web page. Hence we have mapping functions $c(u) \in C = \{c_1, c_2, \cdots c_h\}$, $d(q) \in D = \{d_1, d_2, \cdots d_i\}$ and $e(p) \in E = \{e_1, e_2, \cdots e_j\}$. Then the cluster algorithm partitions U into h groups, Q into i groups and P into j groups. The algorithm also give the probability values $P(u \mid c(u))$, $P(q \mid d(q))$ and $P(p \mid e(p))$. After the processing, we use PLSA to calculate the probability values which measure the relationships between C, D, E and Z, so in practice we predict the probability for a given (u, q, p) as follows:

$$P(p \mid u, q) = P(e(p) \mid c(u), d(q)) P(p \mid e(p)). \tag{11}$$

4 Experimental Evaluation

4.1 Dataset

In our experiments, we use web log data collected by MSN search engine in December 2003. We select those users who use MSN search engine more 25 days in the month in order that the data is not too sparse. Then we randomly select about 100,000 queries submitted to the search engine by the users and 200,000 web pages they selected to browse from the results given by the search engine. In order to evaluate different scenarios, we design two data sets as following:

First, since our approach could show higher performance on the situation that the pairs of user and query do not occur in the training set, we divide the data set by random selecting pairs of user and query. In our experiment, 85% pairs of user and query are selected as training set and the left as testing data, so we get 290,000 data records in training set and 78,000 data records in testing set. This data set is referred as the first data set in our experiment.

Second, we divide the data according to the time series in the log. We use all the data in the first 20 days as training data, while the testing data is from those of later 5 days. If some queries or web pages are in the testing data but not in the training data, without content-based techniques they are impossible to be predicted. So we remove these data in the testing set. Finally we get a training set with 340,000 data records and a testing set with 6,000 data records. We refer to this data set as the second data set in our experiment.

4.2 Evaluation Metric

From the view of the user, the effectiveness of our method is evaluated by the precision of the predictions. Given a triple (u, q, p) in the test set, we first get the predicted list P based on u and q. Then we sort all the $p' \in P$ according to the probability $P(p' \mid u, q)$ in the descending order, and get the rank of p in the sorted list. For each rank $r > 0$, we calculate the number of triples that exactly rank the r th as $N(r)$. Let $M(r) = \sum_{1 \le i \le r} N(i)$, and $S(r) = M(r)/G$ where G stands by the number of triple in the whole test set. Thus $S(r)$ stands for the precision of the method when predicting the top r web pages.

4.3 Baseline Method

We have implemented a baseline method to calibrate the achieved results. The method is based on cluster technique. We use the relationship between the users, queries and web pages to cluster the users and the queries. Then we calculate the times of each page is occurred with every user group and query group in the training set and give the prediction. Let $n(c(u), d(q), p) = \sum_{u,q} n(u, q, p)$ for any $(u, q, p) \in T$. So for a given (u, q, p), the probability is predicted as follows:

$$P(p \mid u, q) = \frac{n(c(u), d(q), p)}{\sum_{p'} n(c(u), d(q), p')} \tag{12}$$

4.4 Experimental Results

As we know, the number of cluster is difficult to decide. In our experiment, we tried several times to tune the parameters in order to get higher performance of clustering. We finally cluster the users into 1000 groups, the queries into 1500 groups and the web pages 2000 groups. Meanwhile, that the EM algorithm will get a local optimization after 30-60 iterations.

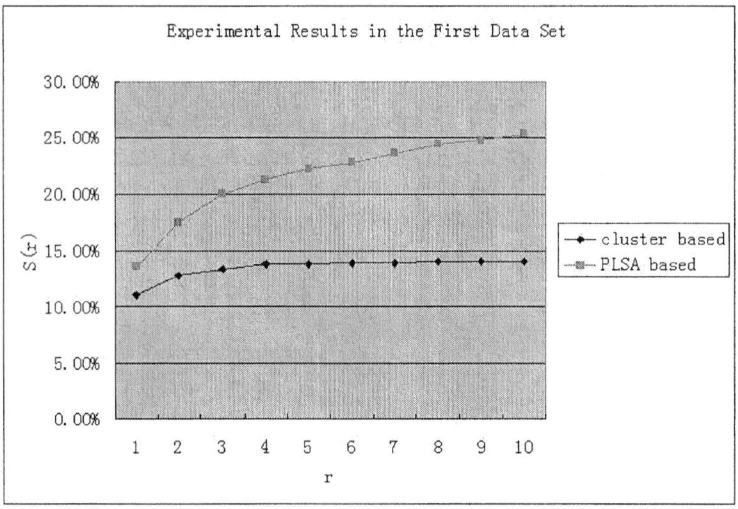

Fig. 2.

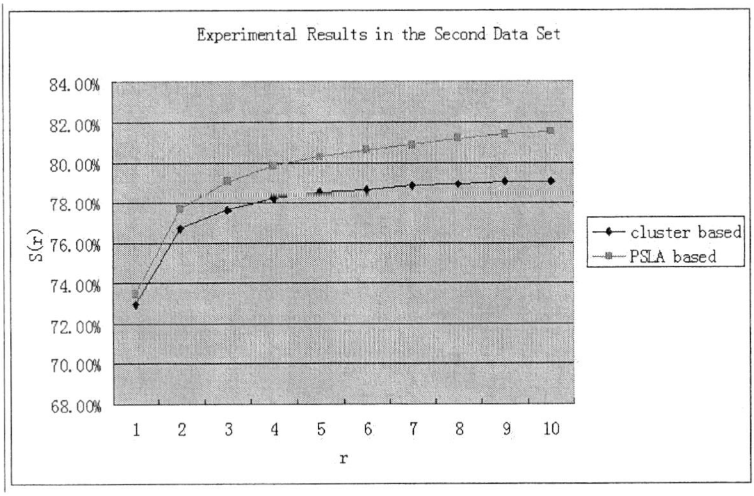

Fig. 3.

Fig.2 shows the results on the first data set. As shown in the figure, our method gets a better performance on the queries that the user never submitted. The top 5th precision has been increased to 22.23% over the cluster-based method. The result shows that our model has strong ability of prediction. Without any direct information about the user and the submitted query, the results of the prediction based on the statistics are not very good. As illustrated in Fig.3, our method also outperforms the baseline method on the second data set.

4.5 Computational Complexity

In the web search scenario, because of the amount of data is always large, the computational complexity is one of the crucial factors for a successful algorithm. One has to distinguish between the offline and online computational complexity. The former accounts for computations that can be performed before hand, that is, before actual predictions for specific users have to be made. In contrast, the latter deals with those computations that can only be performed in real-time during the interaction with a specific user. Therefore the online computational complexity is more important here. PLSA algorithm has an online computational complexity of $O(|Z|)$. The detail complexity analysis of PLSA could be found in [20].

5 Conclusions

In this paper, we present an approach to perform better personalized web search based on PLSA. We consider the latent semantic relationship between users, queries and web pages by a three-way aspect model and use the proposed algorithm to deal with the sparsity problem. Meanwhile, the model could character the users' search intention. An effective algorithm is proposed to learn the model and compute the preference prediction. The results on the real clickthrough data show that our proposed algorithm could achieve higher prediction accuracies than the baseline work. In the future, we consider integrating the content and the link information into the algorithm and doing the better prediction.

References

1. X. Jin and Y. Zhou and B. Mobasher: Web Usage Mining based on Probabilistic Latent Semantic Analysis In: Proceedings of the ACM SIGKDD Conference on Knowledge Discovery and Data Mining (KDD'04), Seattle (2004)
2. Sugiyama, K., Hatano, K., Yoshikawa, M.: Adaptive web search based on user profile constructed without any effort from users. In: Proceedings of the 13th international conference on World Wide Web, ACM Press (2004) 675-684
3. Hofmann, T.: Collaborative Filtering via Gaussian Probabilistic Latent Semantic Analysis. In: Proceedings of the 26th annual international ACM SIGIR conference on Research and development in information retrieval, ACM Press (2003) 259-266
4. Hofmann, T.: Probabilistic Latent Semantic Analysis. In: Proceedings of Uncertainty in Artificial Intelligence, UAI'99, Stockholm (1999)
5. Page, L., Brin, S., Motwani, R., Winograd, T.: The pagerank citation ranking: Bringing order to the web. Technical report, Stanford Digital Library Technologies Project (1998)
6. T. H. Haveliwali.: Topic-Sensitive PangeRank. In: Proceedings of the 11th International World Wide Web Conference (WWW2002), pages 517-526, 2002.
7. Pretschner A., Gauch S.: Ontology based personalized search. In: ICTAI. (1999) 391-398
8. Micro Speretta, Susan Gauch: Personalizing Search Based on User Search Histories. In: Thirteenth International Conference on Information and Knowledge Management (CIKM 2004).
9. Liu, F., Yu, C., Meng, W.: Personalized web search by mapping user queries to categories. In: Proceedings of the eleventh international conference on Information and knowledge management, ACM Press (2002) 558-565
10. Kim H. R., Chan P. K.: Learning implicit user interest hierarchy for context in personalization. In: Proceedings of the 8th international conference on Intelligent User Interfaces, ACM Press (2003) 101-108
11. Deerwester, S., Dumais, S., Landauer, T., Furnas, G., Harshman, R.: (indexing by latent semantic analysis)
12. Berry, M., Dumais, S., G.OBien: Using linear algebra for intelligent information retrieval. (1995)
13. Hofmann, T.: Unsupervised learning by probabilistic latent semantic analysis. Machine Learning 42 (2001) 177-196
14. Dempster, A.P., Laird, N.M., Rubin, D.B.: (Maximum likelihood from incomplete data via the EM algorithm)
15. Hofmann, T.: Probabilistic Latent Semantic Indexing. In: Proceedings of the 22nd Annual ACM Conference on Research and Development in Information Retrieval, Berkeley, California (1999) 50-57
16. T. Brants, F. Chen, I.T.: topic-based document segmentation with probabilistic latent semantic analysis. In: Proceedings of Eleventh International Conference on Information and Knowledge Management. (2002)

17. E. Gaussier, C. Goutte, K.P.F.C.: a hierarchical model for clustering and categorising documents. In: 24th BCS-IRSG European Colloquium on IR Research.(2002)
18. Cohn, D., Chang, H.: Learning to probabilistically identify authoritative documents. In: Proceedings of the Seventeenth International Conference on Machine Learning, Morgan Kaufmann Publishers Inc. (2000) 167-174
19. Cohn, D., Hofmann, T.: The missing link - A probabilistic model of document content and hypertext connectivity. In Leen, T.K., Dietterich, T.G., Tresp, V., eds.: Advances in Neural Information Processing Systems 13, MIT Press (2001) 430-436
20. Hofmann, T.: Latent semantic models for collaborative filtering. ACM Trans. Inf. Syst. 22 (2004) 89-115

Resource Management and Scheduling for High Performance Computing Application Based on WSRF

Chuliang Weng, Minglu Li, and Xinda Lu

Department of Computer Science and Engineering, Shanghai Jiao Tong University, Shanghai, 200030, People's Republic of China
{weng-cl, li-ml, lu-xd}@cs.sjtu.edu.cn

Abstract. In this paper, we challenge the issue of resource management and scheduling in the grid context, which is compliant with WS-Resource Framework. Firstly, we focus on the high performance application, and model the large-scale scientific computing problem that can be decomposed into multiple sub-problems, which evolves to be represented by a DAG. Then, a hierarchical infrastructure for resource management in the grid context is proposed in accordance with the specifications of WS-Resource Framework. Thirdly, we discuss the scheduling issue in the presented scenario and present a modification of the DLS algorithm. At last we analyze the presented modified algorithm with simulation experiments.

1 Introduction

Advances in networking technology and computational infrastructure make it possible to construct large-scale high-performance distributed computing environments, or computational grids [1]. A grid system is a distributed collection of computer and storage resources maintained to serve the need of some community or virtual organization (VO) [2]. Resources in the grid are organized as resource domains that are individual and autonomous administrative domains, which usually are in the range of Local Area Network. The choice of strategies used to schedule jobs in such environments will depend on the target application. Grid computing can be used for the deployment and solution of problems involving large-scale equation systems such as they are appearing in finite element analysis of solids and structures as well as fluid dynamics.

With the development of Grid computing and Web service, the WS-Resource Framework (WSRF) [3] was presented by a team from IBM and Globus Alliance, which was introduced as an attempt to re-factor many of concepts in OGSI [4] to be more consistent with current Web service [5]. The central theme of WSRF is the manipulation of state, and the argument is that there is great value in the canonical referencing and/or manipulation of state. The difference between OGSI and WSRF is that WSRF requires no modification to Web service tooling; while the problem with OGSI is that it is not a pure subset or constraining of Web service. For example, OGSI required a modification to the Web Service Description Language (WSDL) that was

Y. Zhang et al. (Eds.): APWeb 2005, LNCS 3399, pp. 718–729, 2005.

eventually called Grid-WSDL. This meant that special tools were needed to parse and process Grid-WSDL for these Grid services and that commercial and non-commercial WSDL tools could not be used. Currently, the significant research challenge for this community is to determine the extent to which WSRF and WS-Notification adds value above the Web service approach.

The core of the WS-Resource Framework (WSRF) is the WS-Resource, "the component from the composition of a Web service and a stateful resource" [6] described by an XML document (with known schema) that is associated with the Web service's portTypes and addressed by a WS-Addressing endpoint reference [7]. WSRF is based on the OGSI specification and can be thought of as expressing the OGSI concepts in terms that are more compatible with today's Web service standards. In fact, OGSI did not really support interacting with these base Web services and instead only interacted with Grid services, while WSRF fully supports interacting with these base Web services.

In this paper, we introduce a resource management infrastructure for the computational grid based on the WS-Resource Framework, and present a scheduling strategy for assigning jobs in the grid context.

The paper is organized as follows. In Section 2, we discuss the related works. In Section 3, we introduce the application mode derived from the practical scientific applications. In Section 4, we propose a hierarchical infrastructure for resource management based on WS-Resource Framework. In Section 5, we present a modification of the DLS algorithm in the grid environment. Section 6 focuses on the performance evaluation with simulations, and experimental results are presented in this section. At last, we conclude this paper in Section 7.

2 Related Works

There are many research efforts focusing on the issue of resource management and scheduling in the grid context. In the previous research works for grid computing, paper [8] introduce an architecture for resource management in traditional computational grids, and paper [9] describe the resource management portions of the Legion metacomputing system, which is based on the object-oriented concept. The Grid Architecture for Computational Economy (GRACE) [10] is presented, which mainly focus on incorporating an economic model into a grid system with existing middlewares, such as Globus and Legion. An agent-based resource management system [11] is proposed for grid computing, which uses a hierarchy of homogenous agents for both service advertisement and discovery, and integrates these with a performance prediction based scheduler. There are also many other related research works for resource management in the grid environment such as [12][13][14]. These presented models or architectures have a common characteristic, that is, resources in the grid are organized by the hierarchical means, which facilitates the scalability of the system. And the virtualization of resources is the trend for managing resources in the grid context.

In this paper, we proposed a resource management architecture for computational grids, which is compliant with the specifications of the WS-Resource Framework, and inherits the merit of the research works of the predecessors. In addition, we present a modified algorithm for scheduling issue in the grid context, which is based on the work found in [15].

3 Application Model

Many large-scale high performance scientific applications are available today that were written well before Grid computing appeared. Sometimes, it needs to integrate some legacy code programs together for solving a large-scale scientific or engineering problem. How to integrate these legacy code programs into service-oriented grid architectures with the smallest possible effort and best performance is a crucial point in more widespread industrial take-up of grid technology.

Considering the characteristic of WAN (wide area network), it is not suitable to schedule jobs among different distributed control domains, which need frequent communication with each other. In this paper we focus on computational grids, which provide the computational platform for high performance computing applications. There are different kinds of computers in a computational grid, and the variety includes different computation architectures, different operating systems and different compile environments, etc. Furthermore, some scientific computing problems need specific scientific and engineering library, which is owned by the specified control domain. So we argue that the computational grid is suitable for one kind of the scientific computing problem that can be divided into multiple sub-problems, which can be solved with these legacy scientific or engineering applications with the small communication frequency.

A series of large-scale sub-problems derived from one scientific computing problem could be solved in parallel by deploying them to the grid context. However, these sub-problems are generally dependent on each other, and we assume that the dependence among the solving of these sub-problems derived from the same scientific computing problem is that the output of one sub-problem is the input of the other sub-problem of the same scientific computing problem.

Solving a large-scale scientific computing problem can be represented by a set of computational tasks, which solving a set of sub-problems derived from the scientific computing problem. Formally, these tasks can be organized using a directed acyclic graph (DAG), $G=(V, E)$, where the set of vertices $V=\{v_1, v_2, \ldots, v_n\}$ represents the tasks to be executed for solving the corresponding sub-problems, and the set of weighted, directed edges E represents communications between tasks, which can be divided into two classes, one class represents transferring the large data file and the other class is the message for transferring parameters. $e_{ij}=(v_i, v_j) \in E$ indicates communication from task v_i to v_j, and $|e_{ij}|$ represents the volume of data sent between these two tasks.

In the following, we use the term "task" or "job" to represent the sub-problem derived from the scientific computing problem, which are executed respectively on the distributed resources as corresponding specific computational application instances in the computational grid.

4 Hierarchical Infrastructure for Resource Management

In this section, we focus on the resource management infrastructure for high performance computing based on the WS-Resource Framework, which is shown as Fig. 1. For facilitating the application scheduling in the grid context, there are three components in the middleware infrastructure. In the following, we will discuss the three parts respectively.

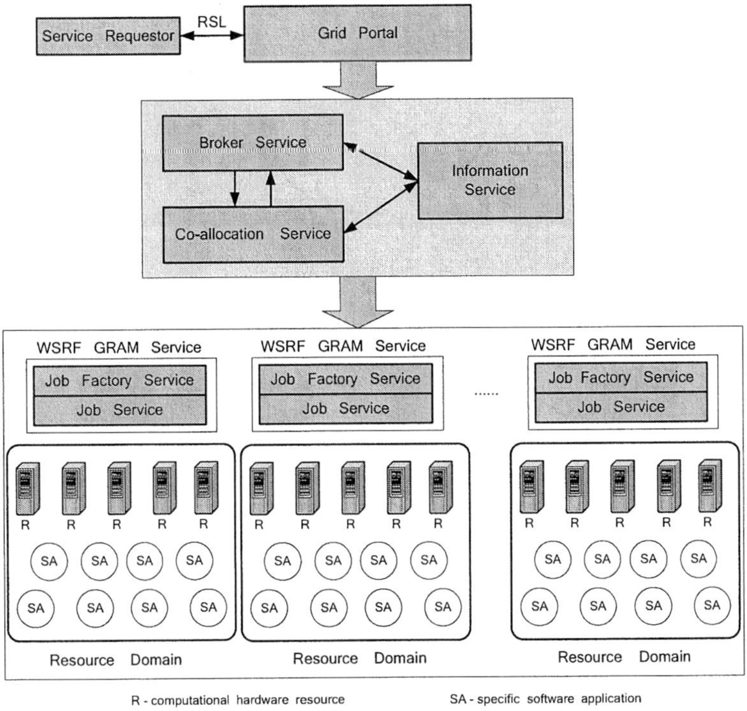

Fig. 1. Hierarchical infrastructure for resource management based on WSRF

4.1 Grid Portal

One component is the grid portal, by which the end users can easily query the service information such as computing power, scientific and engineering library, system load, etc, and initialize the parameters, invoke the computational service, monitor the median computational result, and download the final computational result, and so on.

Grid Portals provide well-suited interfaces for grid end users to co-schedule the large-scale application on the grid system. Generally, end users use a simple graphical or Web interface to supply application specific parameters and simple execution configuration data. Ideally, end users have little knowledge about actual grid protocols and WS-Resource, etc. In the other hand, the specific applications are developed by researchers who have little or no experience with building distributed applications. Ideally, end users can conveniently solve the large-scale scientific computing problem with the multiple specific applications through the grid platform. Many engineering experiences show that end users are best severed by Grid Portals, which are web severs that allow users to configure or run a class of applications. The server is then given the task of authenticating the user with the Grid and invoking the needed Web services required to launch the user's applications.

4.2 Global Resource Management

After the customized request of end users sent to the global middleware that implements the global resource management and scheduling in the grid environment, it will be analyzed and decomposed in accordance with the characteristic of the request. In this paper, we assume that the end user's request for solving a large-scale scientific computing problem can be decomposed into a set of sub-problems that are dependent on each other.

One component of the global middleware is the broker service, which resolves the request outputted by grid portal and generally adopts different decomposition strategies for different problems. For example, the integration simulation for an airplane can be decomposed into multiple sub-application models, such as tail plane, airframe, aerofoil, vertical tail, etc. For analyzing the dynamic characteristic of new designed airplane model, airplane designers can set the parameters by the grid portals and initialize the simulation scenario, and then it is broker services that decompose the problem into multiple sub-problems, and at last solving the sub-problems come down to solving a series of tasks of solving large-scale dynamics equation systems. The decomposition strategy is dependent on the specific application type, and correspondingly the strategy for problem decomposition varies from one application type to the other application type.

As described above, a large-scale scientific computing problem can be decomposed and evolved into a series of computational tasks, which can be denoted as a DAG. Then, it is the co-allocation service that retrieves the service real-time information from the information center, and decide how to assign the multiple computational tasks to distributed computational Web service with effective scheduling strategies. In section 5, we will propose a scheduling strategy for resource assignment in the grid.

4.3 Local Resource Management

If a scientific or engineering computational problem can be decomposed into multiple sub-problems, the sub-problems can be solved across distributed computational resources with the benefit of the grid computing. In the WS-Resource Framework, these distributed application instances created for solving corresponding sub-problems, are treated as stateful resources and can be manipulated by Web services in order to form WS-Resources [6].

One of key ideas in the WS-Resource Framework is that the service is separated from the state, that is, service is static and stateless, and resource is dynamic and stateful. To create a new stateful service, besides the stateless Web service providing the function, a WS-Resource factory is required, which also is a Web service to create the instance of a stateful resource. Therefore for managing the local computational resources, there are two kinds of Web services, and we name them as JobFactoryService and JobManageService, which are illustrated as Fig. 2.

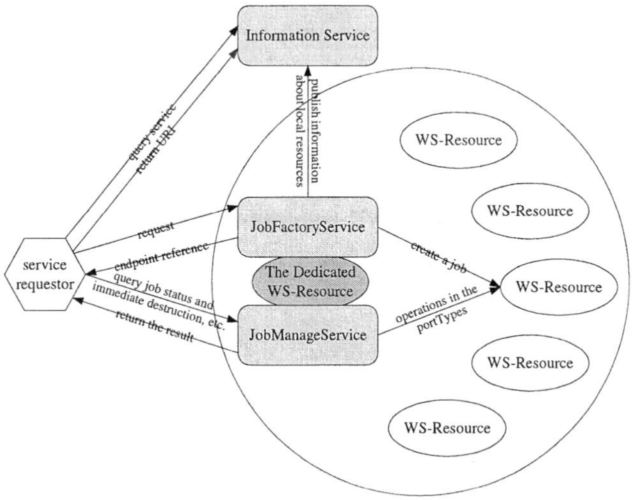

Fig. 2. Local resource management based on WSRF

JobFactoryService is a Web service that creates all jobs for all requests, and functions as a WS-Resource factory. The created jobs are also modeled as WS-Resources, and the state of jobs are represented by WS-Resource Properties and are identified by endpoint references (EPR), which are returned to the service requestor. For publishing information of local computational resources, there is a Dedicated WS-Resource that is utilized to model the physical resources so that JobFactoryService can release not only its specific functions but also the information of computational resources, which is very useful for scheduling jobs across multiple distributed computational resources.

JobManageService is also a Web service that manages all jobs created by JobFactoryService corresponding to user requests, and encapsulates the jobs as WS-Resource. It is JobManageService that publish information about jobs submitted to back-end scheduling system, and the information is represented by the resource properties of the corresponding WS-Resource, which include job state, stdout location, stderr location, etc. JobManageService also has all the operations defined in the portTypes such as WS-ResourceProperties [16], WS-ResourceLifetime [17], WS-BaseNotification[18], which are executed by the Dedicated WS-Resource.

4.4 Physical Computational Resource Management

In the WS-Resource Framework, not only tasks created for solving sub-problems can be modeled as WS-Resources, but also physical computational resources in the grid are modeled as WS-Resource. It is the Dedicated WS-Resource that defined in the section 4.3 as illustrated in Fig. 3, which is associated with JobFactoryService to model physical resources in the local domain and publish the information about the physical computational resources. The information is very important for co-allocation service to determine how to assign tasks in the grid context. Through the grid portal, end users can conveniently query the information about physical resources such as CPU speed, memory capacity, system load, etc.

Physical computational resources include hardware such as high performance computers, high-speed network, large capability storage, and software such as specific applications and legacy code programs. All these resources are modeled as WS-Resource in the WS-Resource Framework. Then the WS-Resource in the specified local resource domain performs the computational function differing from WS-Resources in other resource domains. Then one sub-problem derived from a large-scale scientific problem can be solved only in some particular resource domains with corresponding specific WS-Resources instead of all resource domains, which is vital to the resource scheduling strategy. Although the specific application or legacy code program can be executed in parallel in the range of one resource domain, this problem is beyond the scope of the paper.

5 Scheduling Strategy

In this section, we focus on the scheduling algorithm, which is used to assign tasks derived from one large-scale scientific computing problem in the grid context.

5.1 Conceptual Model for Resource Scheduling

Generally, the scientific computing problems discussed in the paper are computation-intensive rather than communication-intensive, and each specific software application is limited to executing one copy at a time, which also is common characteristic of many scientific computing softwares. Correspondingly, the WS-Resource modeling one specific software application only executes one task at a time, which also is modeled by one WS-Resource. We assume this WS-Resource modeling the specific software application is associated with one dedicated computational hardware resource for simplicity. The computational grid consists of a set of heterogeneous WS-Resources, which can be represented by the set $R=\{R_1,R_2,...,R_m\}$. The computational cost function, $C:V\times R\rightarrow \mathbf{R}$, represents the cost of each task on each available WS-Resource. The cost of executing task v_i on WS-Resource R_j can be denoted by $C(v_i,R_j)$. For a particular task that cannot be executed on a given WS-Resource, the function will be infinity. Then, the concept model for resource scheduling in the grid context is illustrated as Fig. 3.

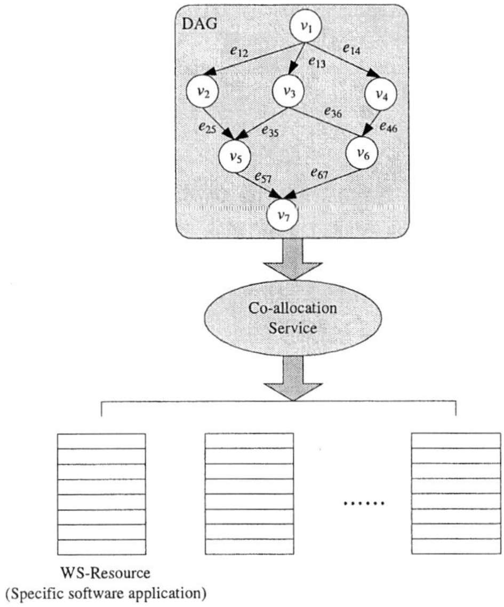

Fig. 3. Conceptual model for resource scheduling

5.2 Scheduling Strategy

For scheduling tasks in one large-scale computing problem effectively, we present a modification of DLS algorithm, which will be described in details as follows.

As with nearly all list scheduling algorithms, the DLS algorithm operates by assigning a priority to each task in that graph, and the priority is called a level. And the priority is used to choose among the set of tasks, which are ready to be scheduled at that time. The DLS algorithm differs from previous algorithms in that the level of a task depends upon the tasks that have already been assigned, and the dynamic level, denoted as $DL(v_i, R_j, \sum(t))$, reflects how well task v_i and WS-Resource R_j are matched at state $\sum(t)$, where $\sum(t)$ encompasses both the state of the WS-Resources and the state of the communication resources at time t. The dynamic level can be defined to be

$$DL(v_i, R_j, \sum(t)) = SL(v_i) - \max(t_d(v_i, R_j), t_a(R_j)) + \Delta(v_i, R_j) \quad (1)$$

Where t is current time. The first term of the expression is the static level of the task, and is defined as the largest sum of execution times along any directed path from v_i to an endnode of the graph, overall endnodes of the graph, and it is the static information for one problem solution. $t_d(v_i, R_j)$ denotes the earliest time that all data required by task v_i is available at state $\sum(t)$, and $t_a(R_j)$ denotes the time at which WS-Resource R_j will be idle. $\Delta(v_i, R_j)$ accounts for the varying processing capability, and it is defined as:

$$\Delta(v_i, R_j) = \bar{C}(v_i) - C(v_i, R_j) \tag{2}$$

Where $\bar{C}(v_i)$ denotes the median execution time of a task v_i over all the WS-Resources. If the actual median is infinite, the median value will be substituted with the largest finite execution time.

In equation (1), the value of the three items determines the dynamic level of a task in the DAG. However, one task can only be scheduled to some specific WS-Resources in the grid context, which is different from the situation where a majority of tasks can be scheduled to all processors in paper [15], and the value of a majority of *DLs* is negative infinite, and cannot be solved even with the "generalized" dynamic level. So the modification of DLS algorithm is proposed as follows.

$$MDL(v_i, R_{j|j\in A(v_i)}, \sum(t)) = SL(v_i) - \max(t_d(v_i, R_j), t_a(R_j)) + \Delta(v_i, R_j) \tag{3}$$

$A(v_i)$ denotes the set of the available WS-Resources that can execute task v_i. And $SL(v_i)$ is defined as the largest sum of execution times along any available directed path from v_i to the end of the graph, and $\bar{C}(v_i)$ in $\Delta(v_i, R_j)$ denotes the median execution time of a task v_i over all available WS-Resources. With this dynamic level definition, scheduling a task in the graph, is equivalent to finding the ready task and the WS-Resource in order to maximize the MDL. The other merit of this strategy is that both tasks and WS-Resources are chosen at the same time, which is superior to independently selecting either tasks or WS-Resources.

6 Experiments and Results

For testing the performance of the presented scheduling algorithm, we perform a series of simulation experiments with a custom, event-based simulator. Our scheduling goal is to minimize the makespan [19], or the scheduling length for a large-scale scientific computing problem. We define *the task-WSR ratio* as the number of available WS-Resources for one task divided by the total of all WS-Resources, and examine the effect of the task-WSR ratio on the performance of the presented algorithm.

In the first situation, the total of WS-Resources are 8, and one large-scale scientific computing problem can be decomposed into 32 tasks. The size of tasks is uniformly distributed in the range [10000, 50000], and the communication volume between tasks is uniformly distributed in the range [0, 500], the processing capability of WS-Resources is uniformly distributed in the range [100, 500], the communication speed is uniformly distributed in the range [10, 50]. The experimental results are the average value of the 1000 simulation runs where one task can be executed randomly on relative WS-Resources, and the experimental result is illustrated as Fig. 4(a).

The second situation is the same as the first situation except that the size of tasks is uniformly distributed in the range [1000, 5000], and the experimental result is illustrated as Fig. 4(b).

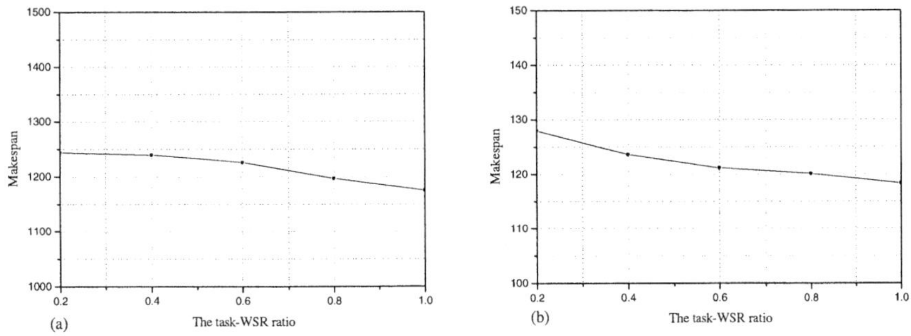

Fig. 4. The results of the first situation and the second situation

According to the Fig. 4 (a) and (b), the makespan reduces as the task-WSR ratio increases, and the experimental result indicates that when the number of available WS-Resources for executing one task increases, the total execution time of all tasks in one large-scale scientific computing problem would decrease. However, it is noted that when the number of available WS-Resources for executing one task decreases, the performance of the algorithm does not deteriorate quickly, the performance loss is about 8% compared to the situation that one task can be executed on all WS-Resources.

So we can conclude that the modified algorithm is suitable for scheduling multiple sub-problems derived from one large-scale scientific computing problem in the grid context, where these sub-problems just can be assigned to some particular WS-Resources instead of all WS-Resources, which is described in this paper.

7 Conclusions

In this paper, we focus on resource management and scheduling for high performance computing application, which is based on the WS-Resource Framework. We firstly abstract the concrete implementation in a particular large-scale scientific computing problem and generally model theses kinds of scientific computational problems as DAGs. Then we propose a hierarchical infrastructure for resource management in the grid context, which is compliant with the WS-Resource Framework. Based on the application model and resource management model, we expand the existed DAG scheduling algorithm for grid computing, and propose a modified scheduling algorithm in the grid context, and test the performance of the presented scheduling algorithm. Experimental results indicate that the proposed algorithm is suitable for the grid scenario.

In the further, we will work on utilizing the presented hierarchical infrastructure and the scheduling strategy to organize CFD Grid Application Platform [20] and manage distributed computational resources in the grid environment.

Acknowledgements

This research was supported by the National 863 Program of China (No.2004AA104340 and No.2004AA104280), the National Natural Science Foundation of China (No. 60173031 and No. 60473092), ChinaGrid Program of MOE of China, and the grand project (No.03dz15027) of the Science and Technology Commission of Shanghai Municipality.

References

[1] Foster, I., Kesselman, C. (eds.): The GRID: Blueprint for a New Computing Infrastructure. Morgan Kaufmann, San Francisco, USA, 1998.

[2] Foster, I., Kesselman, C., Tuecke, S.: The Anatomy of the Grid: Enabling Scalable Virtual Organizations. The International Journal of Supercomputer Applications, 15(3): 200-222, 2001.

[3] Czajkowski, K., Ferguson, D., Foster, I., Frey, J., Graham, S., Sedukhin, I., Snelling, D., Tuecke, S., Vambenepe, W.: The WS-Resource Framework, 2004. http://www-106.ibm.com/developerworks/library/wsresource/ws-wsrf.pdf

[4] Tuecke, S., Czajkowski, K., Foster, I., Frey, J., Graham, S., Kesselman, C., Maguire, T., Sandholm, T., Vanderbilt, P., Snelling, D.: Open Grid Services Infrastructure (OGSI) Version 1.0. Global Grid Forum, GFD-R-P.15, Version as of June 27, 2003.

[5] Czajkowski, K., Ferguson, D., Foster, I., Frey, J., Graham, S., Snelling, D., Tuecke, S.: From Open Grid Services Infrastructure to Web Services Resource Framework: Refactoring and Evolution, 2004. http://www-106.ibm.com/developerworks/library/ws-resource/gr-ogsitowsrf.html

[6] Foster, I., Frey, J., Graham, S., Tuecke, S., Czajkowski, K., Ferguson, D., Leymann, F., Nally, M., Sedukhin, I., Snelling, D., Storey, T., Vambenepe, W., Weerawarana, S.: Modeling Stateful Resources with Web Services, 2004. http://www.ibm.com/developerworks/library/ws-resource/ws-modelingresources.pdf

[7] IBM, BEA, and Microsoft: WS-Addressing, 2004. http://msdn.microsoft.com/webservices/default.aspx?pull=/library/en-us/dnglobspec/html/ws-addressing.asp

[8] Foster, I., Kesselman, C.: The Globus Project: A Status Report. Future Generation Computer Systems 15(5): 606-621, 1999.

[9] Chapin, S., Katramatos, D., Karpovich, J., and Grimshaw, A.: Resource Management in Legion. Future Generation Computer Systems, 15(5): 583-594, 1999.

[10] Buyya, R.: Economic-based Distributed Resource Management and Scheduling for Grid Computing. PhD Dissertation, Monash University, 2002.

[11] Cao, J., Jarvis, S., Saini, S., Kerbyson, D., Nudd, G.: ARMS: An Agent-based Resource Management System for Grid Computing. Scientific Programming, 10(2): 135-148, 2002.

[12] Lee, Y., Yoon, C.: An Unified Resource Management Framework for a Large Scale Globus Based Grid Testbed. In: Proceedings of the International Conference on Parallel and Distributed Processing Techniques and Applications, Las Vegas, USA, Jun 2003, pp. 57-63

[13] Kumar, R., Talwar, V., Basu, S.: A Resource Management Framework for Interactive Grids. Concurrency Computation Practice and Experience, 16(5): 489-501, 2004.

[14] Zheng, R., Li, S., Jin, H.: Grid Resource Management and Scheduling Model. Journal of Huazhong University of Science and Technology (In Chinese), 29(12): 87-89, 2001.
[15] Sih, G., Lee, E.: A Compile-time Scheduling Heuristic for Interconnection-constrained Heterogeneous Processor Architectures. IEEE Transactions on Parallel and Distributed Systems, 4(2): 175-187, 1993.
[16] Graham, S., Czajkowski, K., Ferguson, D., Foster, I., Frey, J., Leymann, F., Maguire, T., Nagaratnam, N., Nally, M., Storey, T., Sedukhin, I., Snelling, D., Tuecke, S., Vambenepe, W., Weerawarana, S.: WS-ResourceProperties, 2004. http://www.ibm.com/developerworks/ library/ws-resource/ws-resourceproperties.pdf
[17] Frey, J., Czajkowski, K., Ferguson, D., Foster, I., Leymann, F., Maguire, T., Nagaratnam, N., Nally, M., Storey, T., Sedukhin, I., Snelling, D., Tuecke, S., Vambenepe, W., Weerawarana, S.: WS-ResourceLifetime, 2004. http://www.ibm.com/developerworks/library/ws-resource/ws-resourcelifetime.pdf
[18] Graham, S., Niblett, P., Chappell, D., Lewis, A., Nagaratnam, N., Parikh, J., Patil, S., Samdarshi, S., Sedukhin, I., Snelling, D., Tuecke, S., Vambenepe, W., Weihl, B.: WS-BaseNotification, 2004. ftp://www6.software.ibm.com/software/developer/library/ws-notification/WS-BaseN.pdf
[19] Pinedo, M.: Scheduling: Theory, Algorithms, and Systems. Prentice Hall, Englewood Cliffs, USA, 1995.
[20] CFD Grid Application Platform. http://grid.sjtu.edu.cn:7080/grid/en/index.htm

Multiresolution Query Optimization in an Online Environment

Kai Xu[1] and Xiaofang Zhou[2]

[1] IMAGEN group, National ICT Australia, Sydney, Australia
kai.xu@nicta.com.au

[2] School of ITEE, The University of Queensland, Brisbane, Australia
zxf@itee.uq.edu.au

Abstract. Multiresolution (or multi-scale) techniques make it possible for Web-based GIS applications to access large dataset. The performance of such systems relies on data transmission over network and multiresolution query processing. In the literature the latter has received little research attention so far, and the existing methods are not capable of processing large dataset. In this paper, we aim to improve multiresolution query processing in an online environment. A cost model for such query is proposed first, followed by three strategies for its optimization. Significant theoretical improvement can be observed when comparing against available methods. Application of these strategies is also discussed, and similar performance enhancement can be expected if implemented in online GIS applications.

1 Introduction

Internet provides a revolutionary way to access geographical data. Significant efforts, such as Microsoft's TerraServer [1] and NASA's "World Wind" project [2], have been put into the development of core technologies of web-base GIS. It is more accessible than ever before with increasing data availability, client processing power and network bandwidth. However, the large size of terrain data remains a major challenge. The size of a data repository, such as the Digital Elevation Model of America (available from U.S. Geological Survey [3]), is measured in terabyte. The size of accessible dataset is increasing quickly as the data collection continues. The "Shuttle Radar Topography Mission" by NASA [4] is collecting the data of most land on earth.

Applications based on such dataset require excessive resources. However, the resolution can be unnecessarily high in many cases. Figure 1(a) shows an small terrain model with only 10,000 triangles, but the top-right part already appears to be unnecessarily dense. *Multiresolution* (or *multi-scale*) techniques are introduced to address this problem [5]. The intuition is to construct a simplified terrain approximation (*mesh*) as the substitute of the original model with guaranteed accuracy according to application requirements. Therefore, the resource requirement can be significantly reduced without sacrificing necessary quality. A

Y. Zhang et al. (Eds.): APWeb 2005, LNCS 3399, pp. 730–741, 2005.

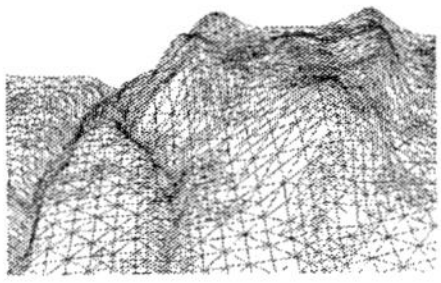

(a) 10,000 triangles

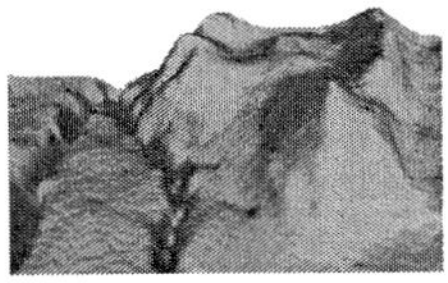

(b) 10,000 triangles with texture

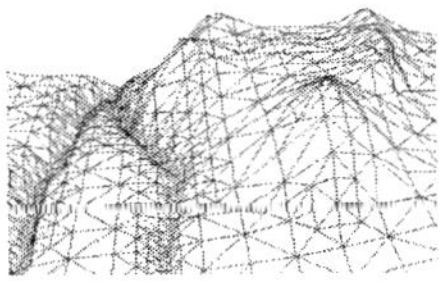

(c) 1,000 triangles

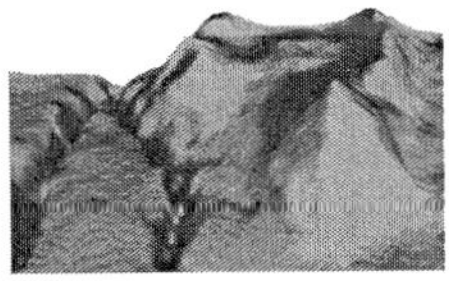

(d) 1,000 triangles with texture

Fig. 1. Terrain at multiple resolutions

simplified terrain with 1,000 triangles is shown in Figure 1(c). For visualization purpose, the difference is hardly noticeable after texture is applied (Figure 1(b) and 1(d)).

Constructing a mesh directly from the original model is expensive, it involves the data of the original model, which is usually extremely large, and intermediate data generated during simplification. The possible benefit of using a mesh can be overcomed by its expensive construction. In order to reduce the cost, we need to represent it as a *Multiresolution Triangular Mesh (MTM)* - a terrain representation that supports the reconstruction of meshes with variable resolutions with acceptable overhead. The fact that terrain data can be used at any resolution and that data of different resolutions may be used together to construct a single mesh means that it is not feasible to pre-generate terrain data at a fixed number of resolutions. Instead, most MTM methods adopt a tree-like data structure, and each node stores a lower resolution approximation of its child nodes data. The construction of a mesh starts from the root, which contains the least detailed data, and refines this coarse mesh progressively by replacing it with the data stored at its children nodes until the desired resolution is achieved (details are provided in Section 2). Since the data with low resolution is substantially less than the original terrain model, such MTM can significantly reduces the mesh construction cost. Such structure also can provide large number of possible meshes and mesh with changing resolution, because the initial coarse mesh can be refined to any resolution available and each part can have different resolutions.

The ability to reduce data amount, and thus resource requirement, makes it possible to perform visualization and analysis on large dataset in an online environment. Recently, a number of work has been published for visualizing large terrain over network [6, 7, 8, 9, 10, 11]. These methods focus on "compressing MTM", i.e., using compact MTM data structure to reduce the amount of data transfer. However, none of them considers the role of database system. There are also signification research attention on multiresolution terrain database [12, 13, 14, 15, 16, 17]. These methods employ various *multiresolution access methods* to improve the performance of *multiresolution query*, i.e., efficiently identify and retrieve data required for mesh construction. Unfortunately these methods do not take into account any constrains imposed by network environment.

We think multiresolution query processing, which mainly performed at the server end, is a critical to the performance of online GIS applications. Such query is quite resource intensive because it involves large amount of data. Large number of simultaneous queries can easily exceed server capacity. Since the available bandwidth is increasing much faster than that of server processing power, it is possible that the query processing will replace the bandwidth as the bottleneck of online GIS applications.

In this paper, we aim to improve multiresolution query processing in an online environment. We started with examining existing work, and a cost model for current multiresolution query processing is proposed. An optimal cost, which serves as a bound for possible improvement, is derived from this framework. Three optimization strategies are proposed to address different problems identified from performance analysis. The details of these strategies are discussed when applying them to existing methods, which also confirms the feasibility of our strategies in real applications.

The remainder of this paper is organized as follows. In Section 2 we provide an brief overview on multiresolution query processing. The cost model is introduced in Section 3. In Section 4, the optimal cost is derived, followed by three optimization strategies, whose application to existing methods is also included. The paper is concluded in Section 5.

2 Multiresolution Query Processing

A multiresolution query retrieves a mesh within given area with required resolution, i.e., it can be specified by two parameters: the *Level Of Detail (LOD) condition* and the *Region Of Interest (ROI) condition*. For a mesh polygon t, the LOD condition returns a value $e(t)$, which is the required LOD value for polygon t. In a mesh m, we denote the resolution of a polygon t as $l(t)$. We say t is *LOD feasible* with respect to e if $l(t) \geq e(t)$. A LOD feasible polygon implies it is detailed enough for current application, and no further refinement is required. There are two types of LOD conditions: *uniform LOD*, where $e(t)$ is a constant, i.e., the LOD of every polygon t is at least a constant value; or *variable LOD*, where $e(t)$ is a function of polygon attribute(s). An example is that a LOD condition can be a function of the distance from the viewpoint, i.e., the further away from the viewpoint the less LOD value.

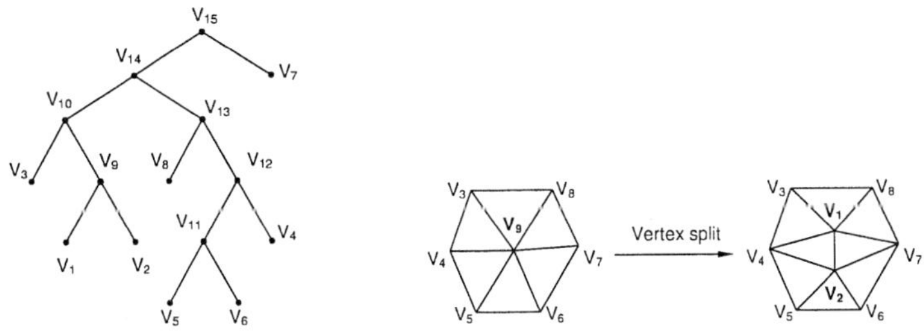

(a) Tree structure of progressive meshes

(b) Vertex split

Fig. 2. Progressive Meshes

While the LOD condition defines mesh resolution, the ROI condition defines mesh location, size and shape. It is specified by a collection of two-dimensional spatial objects (points, lines and/or polygons). Given a ROI condition r, a polygon t is *ROI feasible* if its two-dimensional projection $P(t)$ has at least one point in common with r, i.e., $r \cap P(t) \neq \emptyset$. For multiresolution query, a polygon that is not ROI feasible means it is irrelevant. Therefore, only the polygons that are ROI feasible are checked against the LOD condition; whereas the LOD of polygons that are not ROI feasible can be arbitrarily low.

Given LOD and ROI conditions, a *multiresolution query* returns a mesh with minimal number of polygons that satisfies both. Formally, given a MTM M a *multiresolution query* $Q(M, r, e)$ returns a mesh m from M that satisfies both the ROI condition r and the LOD condition e with minimal number of polygons. A multiresolution query is a *uniform-LOD query* if its LOD condition is a constant; a *variable-LOD query* if its LOD condition is a function of polygon attribute(s).

Here we use the *progressive meshes* [18], one of the most popular MTMs, to explain multiresolution query processing. The structure of a progressive meshes is an unbalanced binary tree (Figure 2(a)). The fundamental step in mesh construction is *vertex split*, i.e., one point is replaced by its two children (Figure 2(b)). To answer a multiresolution query, a mesh that contains the root only is created first; then it is refined by applying vertex split progressively following the tree structure, until both the ROI and LOD conditions are met. In the progressive meshes, each node has the following information:

$$(ID, x, y, z, l, parent, child1, child2, wing1, wing2, MBR)$$

where ID is the unique ID of the point, (x, y, z) is the three-dimensional coordinates, l is the LOD, $parent$, $child1$, $child2$ are the IDs of its parent, left and right child node, $wing1$ and $wing2$ are the IDs of the left and the right point connecting to both children, and MBR is the minimal bounding rectangle that encloses this node and all its descendants. The *wing points* (i.e., $wing1$ and $wing2$) are essential to form a correct triangulation after vertex split (v_4 and v_7 for v_9 in

Figure 2(b)). The MBR is for identifying ancestors of ROI feasible nodes. Due to the progressive refinement process of mesh construction, all ancestor nodes are necessary if a point exists in the final mesh. While this point is ROI feasible, some of its ancestor nodes may not. With MBR, all such nodes can be identified because their MBR intersects with ROI. The fact that the necessity of every node (except the root) depends on its predecessor makes it difficult to retrieve all necessary data together. In fact, the data for every vertex split (two child nodes) has to be fetched individually. Therefore, the data fetch of a multiresolution query is composed of many retrievals with every small amount, which makes it intrinsically inefficient for query processing.

3 Cost Model for Multiresolution Query

The I/O cost of a multiresolution query $Q(M, r, e)$ has two major components: the cost of retrieving the index and the cost of retrieving data. In other words, the total I/O cost $D(Q)$ of a multiresolution query $Q(M, r, e)$ is the sum of index retrieving cost C_i and data retrieving cost C_d:

$$D(Q) = C_i + C_d \tag{1}$$

The cost of index retrieving depends on two factors: the average cost of one index scan i_0 and the number of index scans N_s. The value of i_0 depends on the indexing method used, while the value of N_s is decided by the query processing method. The total cost of index retrieving (C_i) is the product of i_0 and N_s:

$$C_i = i_0 \times N_s \tag{2}$$

Ideally, data retrieval costs (C_d) should only include the cost of retrieving data necessary for multiresolution query. However, in many cases redundant data is also retrieved during query processing (this is further explained in the next section). Therefore, the value of C_d is the sum of the cost of retrieving necessary data C_n and unnecessary data C_u:

$$C_d = C_n + C_u \tag{3}$$

Combining previous equations, we have a cost model for multiresolution query:

$$D(Q) = i_0 \times N_s + C_n + C_u \tag{4}$$

Based on the discussion in last section, the I/O cost of multiresolution query on the progressive meshes is:

$$D_p(Q) = i_0 \times N_s + C_n \tag{5}$$

Here $C_u = 0$ because it only retrieves required data. Without any caching strategy, the number of index scan (N_s) depends on the number of retrievals (N_r), i.e., one index scan is required for each retrieval:

$$N_s = N_r \tag{6}$$

As mentioned, each retrieval fetches two child nodes; all data is fetched this way, except the root, which is retrieved by itself at the very beginning. Therefore, given the total number of nodes needed (N_p), the number of retrieval (N_r) is:

$$N_r = (N_p + 1) \ / \ 2 \tag{7}$$

The cost of necessary data retrieval (C_n) is determined by the number of retrievals (N_r) and the number of disk page access in each retrieval (N_d), i.e.,

$$C_n = N_r \times N_d \times t_0 \tag{8}$$

where t_0 is the cost of retrieving one disk page. Since there are two nodes involved in each refinement and each node has little associated data, it is unlikely that the data for one refinement exceeds disk-page size. If we assume nodes for one refinement are always stored together in one disk page (can be achieved by clustering progressive meshes nodes on disk), the number of disk page access for each retrieval (N_d) is one, i.e.,

$$N_d = 1 \tag{9}$$

Combining Equation 5, 6, 7, 8 and 9, the I/O cost of multiresolution query on the progressive meshes is:

$$D_p(Q) = (i_0 + t_0) \times (N_p + 1) \ / \ 2 \tag{10}$$

The discussion so far is based on progressive meshes, now we extend the cost model to more general multiresolution query, where a node can have more than two children. If each internal node has F child nodes, the number of retrievals (N_r) is now:

$$N_r = (N_p - 1) \ / \ F + 1 \tag{11}$$

Therefore, the total cost of index scan C_i is

$$C_i = i_0 \times N_s = i_0 \times N_r = i_0 \times [(N_p - 1) \ / \ F + 1] \tag{12}$$

Similarly, the cost of necessary data retrieval C_n is:

$$C_n = N_r \times N_d \times t_0 = [(N_p - 1) \ / \ F + 1] \times t_0 \tag{13}$$

Combine Equation 12 and 13, the total cost $D(Q)$ is:

$$D(Q) = C_i + C_n = (i_0 + t_0) \times [(N_p - 1) \ / \ F + 1] \tag{14}$$

The cost model for general multiresolution query (Equation 14) has a configuration similar to that for the progressive meshes (Equation 10):

1. The total cost of is proportional to the number of required nodes (N_p) since the value of other variables (F, i_0 and t_0) are decided by either the MTM (F) or the database system (i_0 and t_0).
2. The cost of index scan accounts for a large portion of total cost. From Equation 14 we can say that the number of index scan is the same as the number of disk page retrieved (both are $(N_p - 1) \ / \ F + 1$), but the cost of the former (i_0) is much larger than that of the latter because the indexing structure size is several-order larger than disk page size.

These observations lead to our strategies for multiresolution query optimization.

4 Multiresolution Query Optimization

There are several possible approaches to reduce the cost of multiresolution query processing. For simplicity, we use the cost model for the progressive meshes instead of the general one since they share similar structure. From Equation 10, we know that the cost of index scan and data retrieval are $i_0 \times N_m$ and $t_0 \times N_m$ respectively. We think neither of them is optimal. In ideal case, one index scan should identify necessary data, i.e.,

$$min(C_i) = i_0 \tag{15}$$

Regarding data retrieval cost, the optimal case is that all required data is stored continuously on the disk, i.e. it can be as small as:

$$min(C_d) = \lceil N_p \ / \ B \rceil \times t_0 \tag{16}$$

where B is the number of points each disk page can hold. Therefore, the optimal I/O cost of a multiresolution query is:

$$min(D(Q)) = min(C_i) + min(C_d) = i_0 + \lceil N_p \ / \ B \rceil \times t_0 \tag{17}$$

Comparing the minimal cost and the cost of current processing method (Equation 10), we can say that there is significant gap between the two, in other words, considerable potential for improvement.

4.1 Optimization Strategy 1 - Reducing Retrieval Number

Our first strategy aims to decrease the number of index scan to reduce total cost. A possible solution is to retrieve all necessary data before mesh construction, which can avoid data fetch during mesh construction and thus reduce index scan numbers. Moreover, it has the potential to improve data retrieval efficiency since all data is fetched together instead of bit by bit during construction. With this strategy, it possible to complete data retrieval with one index scan, which is the optimal value as shown in Equation 17. However, there are a few challenges:

1. It is difficult to identify the spatial extent. Among the data needed by a multiresolution query, nodes that appear in the mesh are within the ROI, but their ancestors may not be. A naive method to encode each node as a MBR enclosing all its decedents in an index will cause severe overlapping in the indexing structure, because the nodes in the upper part of MTM have large MBRs covering many nodes. This can significantly degrade the search performance of multiresolution access method. Another possible solution is to enlarge the ROI by some extent to include such ancestor nodes. However, it is difficult to estimate the extent of enlargement, and this also introduces redundant data;
2. It is difficult to identify the LOD interval. The requirement to support variable-LOD mesh implies that mesh LOD can be a function of spatial location. It is well known that such a function condition can not be handled efficiently in a database systems. A naive solution is to retrieve all data at the most detailed level, which inevitably includes redundant data.

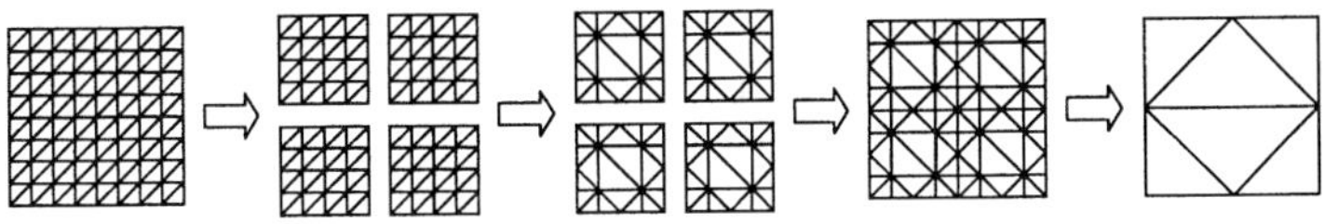

Fig. 3. Secondary-storage PM

The existence of these challenges results in possible redundant data fetch (C_u), i.e., unnecessary data may also be retrieved in order to include all required data. However, the overall performance can be better if the amount of redundant data is acceptable. The I/O cost of this strategy methods can be described as:

$$D_1(Q) = i'_0 + C_n + C_u \tag{18}$$

where

1. The value of i'_0 varies depends on the multiresolution access method used, but it should be much smaller than the previous index scan cost ($N_m \times i_0$);
2. It is difficult for the value of C_n to be as small as the optimal value ($\lceil N_p / B \rceil$) because it is impossible to have all necessary data always stores continuously on the disk for different queries;
3. As a side effect, such method may incur unnecessary data retrieval. In some cases such cost (C_u) is comparable to that of necessary data.

To further illustrate our approach, we apply them to existing work. Since there is no method that exactly implements our strategy, we choose similar approach to illustrate the idea. The secondary-storage progressive meshes [12] is one of the first attempts to employ multiresolution access method in MTM. It builds a two-dimensional quadtree [19] into the progressive meshes (Figure 3). The bottom-up construction starts by dividing the terrain into blocks, which serves as the leaf level of quadtree. Every four simplified blocks are merged to form larger blocks (serve as the internal nodes of quadtree), which are further simplified. This process repeats until only one block is left. The LOD-R-tree [13] and the HDoV-tree [15] adopt a similar approach, but they adopt a R-tree instead. For these methods, a multiresolution query is translated into a range query whose query window is the ROI. During processing, it traverses down the index tree from the root, retrieves nodes that intersects with ROI, and stops at the level where the resolution is sufficient. The performance improvement reported in the test results of these methods confirms that reducing retrieval number can considerably improve overall performance even if it may introduce some redundant data. It is reasonable to expect similar enhancement if applied in an online environment.

4.2 Optimization Strategy 2 - Balancing Retrieval Number and Redundant Data

Besides the difficulty of identifying data extent, there is another factor that contribute to redundant data fetch, the "boundary effect": the boundary of ROI intersects with some data blocks (nodes of index tree); these blocks need to be retrieved because they contain required data; but they also includes unnecessary data outside ROI. The boundary-effect is inevitable since it is unusual that the query window matches the data block perfectly. However, its negative impact can be reduced by using smaller data block. Most spatial access methods use one disk page, which is the minimal possible value, as the block size to reduce redundant data. However, the block size of previous methods that are based on MTM partitioning can not be small: extra edges are generated at the block edge when partitioning; it will introduce too many edges if the block size is very small. The fact that boundary-effect happens at every level when traversing down the MTM tree worsens the problem.

For this problem, we propose our second optimization strategy: balancing retrieval number and redundant data. This strategy retrieves most data before mesh construction and leaves the rest during construction if this can reduce redundant data. Obvious candidates are those nodes that are outside ROI but still necessary. Excluding such nodes also makes it possible to applying well-studied spatial access methods, which incurs a much less boundary effect, directly to MTM because MBR was a major hurdle but it is no longer needed.

Similar idea appears in a multiresolution access method, the LOD-quadtree, recently proposed by Xu [16]. A MTM is indexed in a x-y-LOD space using a modified three-dimensional quadtree. Multiresolution query is translated into a three-dimensional range query that retrieves nodes within ROI and whose resolution is between minimal LOD (the root) and the LOD conditions. The LOD-quadtree treats every node in a MTM as a point, and extra queries are needed during mesh construction to find missing nodes. The cost of this strategy can be modeled as:

$$D_2(Q) = i_0 \times N'_s + C_n + C_u \tag{19}$$

Experiment results show that the number of index scan (N'_s) is usually small, and the value of C_u is much less than that of previous methods (first strategy), thus even better performance in most cases. We think the reason is that this method achieves a better balance between number of index scan and amount of redundant data: current query processing method, which retrieves all data during mesh construction, is one end; whereas our first strategy, which fetches all data before mesh construction, is the opposite end; the second strategy is somewhere in between and manages to ease the problems of both. The ability to use spatial access method also helps to reduce boundary effect.

4.3 Optimization Strategy 3 - Integrating MTM and Query Processing

The cost of the second strategy (Equation 19) is considerably better than that of current processing method (Equation 10), but still not close to the optimal cost (Equation 17). It is rather difficult to further reduce the cost because of the two challenges inherited in MTM (mentioned in first strategy). Therefore, our third optimization strategy takes a different perspective and try to integrate MTM and query processing, i.e., including query processing information in MTM node, to preclude the inherent problems. For instance, the progressive refinement of mesh construction is well known for not suitable to query processing, if this can be avoided totally, it can significantly reduce processing cost.

Our strategy can be better explained with a recent work, the direct mesh [17], by Xu *et al.* . It encodes topological data in every node of a MTM, which makes it possible to start mesh construction from the level specified by the LOD condition. This avoids fetching any ancestor nodes and substantially reduces the amount of data required, and thus I/O cost. To avoid introducing too much topological data, direct mesh only encodes relations among nodes with "similar" LOD, which means it can not solve the problem completely for variable-LOD query, which may have nodes whose LOD changes dramatically. The cost of this strategy can be modeled as:

$$D_3(Q) = i_0 + C_n + C_u \tag{20}$$

where

$$C_u \begin{cases} = 0, & \text{uniform-LOD query} \quad (21) \\ > 0, & \text{variable-LOD query} \quad (22) \end{cases}$$

For uniform-LOD query, the direct mesh only retrieves nodes that appear in the mesh, and the total cost is:

$$D(Q) = i_0 + C_n \approx i_0 + \lceil N_m \ / \ B \rceil \times t_0 \tag{23}$$

This is very close to the optimal value, or even better in some case because the number of nodes here (N_m) is much less than that in Equation 17 (N_p) because the ancestors are no longer needed. However, this does not mean that Equation 17 is not optimal. The reason is that the direct mesh breaks the assumption that all the ancestors of mesh nodes are also required. According to the test results of the direct mesh, the cost of this strategy significantly outperforms others for both uniform- and variable-LOD queries.

Due to the scope of this paper, we only optimize multiresolution query processing qualitatively rather than quantitatively, which requires more detailed examination of specific indexing structure. In many cases this is essentially range query based on spatial access methods. The cost of such queries have been well studied in the literature. Interested reader please refer to [20, 21, 22] for range query on Quadtree family and [23, 24, 25] for range query on R-tree family.

5 Conclusions

In this paper, we proposed a cost model for multiresolution query processing in an online environment and three strategies for its optimization, among them

1. Reducing retrieval number is an effective method to reduce the total I/O cost, but it also introduces redundant data;
2. Balancing retrieval number and redundant data seems to a more sensible approach in many cases. The ability of utilizing existing spatial access method also helps to ease boundary effect;
3. The limitation of MTM, especially the progressive refinement routine of mesh construction, is a major hurdle of query performance. Integrating query processing information in MTM is a potential solution, and it has surprisingly good performance.

We think there is no simple best strategy among the three. Adopting which one should be based on the specific application. Our optimization strategies are proposed based on theoretical analysis. Their feasibility in practice is confirmed by applying them to existing methods. It is reasonable to expect that they can significantly improve performance if employed to real online GIS applications.

References

1. Barclay, T., Gray, J., Slutz, D.: Microsoft terraserver: a spatial data warehouse. In: ACM SIGMOD international conference on Management of data, Dallas, Texas, United States, ACM Press (2000) 307–318
2. NASA: World Wind project (2004) http://learn.arc.nasa.gov/worldwind/.
3. U.S. Geological Survey: Earth Resources Observation Systems (EROS) Data Center (2004) http://edc.usgs.gov/.
4. Rabus, B.and Eineder, M.R.A., Bamler, R.: The shuttle radar topography mission - a new class of digital elevation models acquired by spaceborne radar. ISPRS Journal of Photogrammetry and Remote Sensing **57** (2003) 241–262
5. Garland, M.: Multiresolution modeling: Survey and future opportunities. In: Eurographics'99, Aire-la-Ville (CH) (1999) 111–131
6. Danovaro, E., De Floriani, L., Magillo, P., Puppo, E.: Compressing multiresolution triangle meshes. In: Advances in Spatial and Temporal Databases. 7th International Symposium SSTD 2001, Springer Verlag (2001) 345–364
7. Aasgaard, R., Sevaldrud, T.: Distributed handling of level of detail surfaces with binary triangle trees. In: 8th Scandinavian Research Conference on Geographical Information Science, Norway (2001) 45–58
8. Gerstner, T.: Multiresolution visualization and compression of global topographic data. GeoInformatica, to appear (2001)
9. DeCoro, C., Pajarola, R.: Xfastmesh: fast view-dependent meshing from external memory. In: Conference on Visualization, Boston, Massachusetts, IEEE Computer Society (2002) 363 – 370
10. Lindstrom, P.: Out-of-core construction and visualization of multiresolution surfaces. In: Symposium on Interactive 3D graphics, Monterey, California, ACM Press (2003) 93 – 102

11. Wartell, Z., Kang, E., Wasilewski, T., Ribarsky, W., Faust, N.: Rendering vector data over global, multi-resolution 3d terrain. In: symposium on data visualisation, Grenoble, France (2003) 213 – 222
12. Hoppe, H.: Smooth view-dependent level-of-detail control and its application to terrain rendering. In: IEEE Visualization '98, Research Triangle Park, NC, USA (1998) 35–42
13. Kofler, M., Gervautz, M., Gruber, M.: R-trees for organizing and visualizing 3D GIS database. Journal of Visualization and Computer Animation (2000) 129–143
14. Shou, L., Chionh, C., Ruan, Y., Huang, Z., Tan, K.L.: Walking through a very large virtual environment in real-time. In: 27th International Conference on Very Large Data Base, Roma, Italy (2001) 401–410
15. Shou, L., Huang, Z., Tan, K.L.: HDoV-tree: The structure, the storage, the speed. In: 19th International Conference on Data Engineering (ICDE) 2003, Bangalore, India (2003) 557–568
16. Xu, K.: Database support for multiresolution terrain visualization. In: The 14th Australian Database Conference, ADC 2003, Adelaide, Australia, Australian Computer Society (2003) 153–160
17. Xu, K., Zhou, X., Lin, X.: Direct mesh: a multiresolution approach to terrain visualisation. In: ICDE. (2004) 766–777
18. Hoppe, H.: Progressive meshes. In: 23rd International Conference on Computer Graphics and Interactive Techniques (SIGGRAPH'96), New Orleans, LA, USA, ACM press (1996) 99–108
19. Samet, H.: The quadtree and related hierarchical data structure. ACM Computing Surveys **16** (1984) 187–260
20. Aref, W.G., Samet, H.: Efficient window block retrieval in quadtree-based spatial databases. GeoInformatica **1** (1997) 59–91
21. Faloutsos, C., Jagadish, H., Manolopoulos, Y.: Analysis of the n-dimensional quadtree decomposition for arbitrary hyperrectangles. IEEE Transactions on Knowledge and Data Engineering **9** (1997) 373–383
22. Aboulnaga, A., Aref, W.G.: Window query processing in linear quadtrees. Distributed and Parallel Databases **10** (2001) 111–126
23. Theodoridis, Y., Sellis, T.: A model for the prediction of R-tree performance. In: 15th ACM SIGACT-SIGMOD-SIGART Symposium on Principles of Database Systems, Montreal, Canada, ACM Press (1996) 161–171
24. Proietti, G., Faloutsos, C.: I/O complexity for range queries on region data stored using an R-tree. In: 15th International Conference on Data Engineering, Sydney, Australia, IEEE Computer Society (1999) 628–635
25. Jin, J., An, N., Sivasubramaniam, A.: Analyzing range queries on spatial data. In: 16th International Conference on Data Engineering, San Diego, California (2000) 525–534

A Comparison of Advance Resource Reservation Bidding Strategies in Sequential Ascending Auctions

Zhixing Huang and Yuhui Qiu

Computer and Information Science Faculty,
Southwest China Normal University
{huangzx, yhqiu}@swnu.edu.cn

Abstract. Grid Computing is a newly emerging technology that enables users to share a large number of computing resources distributed over a network. Due to that the grid computational resources are not storable, the advance reservation of these resources are necessary for users to request resources from multiple scheduling systems at a specific time. In this paper, we use auction-based scheduling method for resource reservation. We propose a variant version of traditional ascending auction for automatic resource reservation and introduce two novel heuristic strategies to guide agents on participating actions. We also compare our bidding strategies with several other different bidding strategies for the computational resource reservation in different scenarios. The results of experiments show that our heuristic bidding strategies outperforms those methods in those cases.

1 Introduction

Grid Computing is a newly emerging technology that enables users to share a large number of computing resources distributed over a network. Computational grid applications use high-performance, distributed resources such as computers, networks, databases and instruments. The Grid is a highly dynamic environment with servers coming on-line, going off-line, and with continuously varying demands from the clients. Since grid resources are not storable, thus that capacity not used today can be put aside for future use. So the advance reservation of these resources are needed for users to request resources from multiple scheduling systems at a specific time and thus gain simultaneous access to enough resources for their application. As be defined in [2], an Advance Reservation is a possibly limited or restricted delegation of a particular resource capability over a demand time interval, obtained by the requestor from the resource owner through a negotiation process [8]. Example resource capabilities: number of processors, amount of memory, disk space, software licences, network bandwidth, etc. Moreover, the works of advance reservations, started within the GGF (Global Grid Forum) to support advance reservations, are currently being added in some test-bed of grid toolkit, such as the Nimrod-G

Y. Zhang et al. (Eds.): APWeb 2005, LNCS 3399, pp. 742–752, 2005.

[3], Portable Batch System (PBS) and the Maui scheduler, however the study of the dynamic of the advance reservations through software agents participating in multiple overly auction-based scheduling systems has seldom been made.

In this paper, we investigate a market-based approach for automatic resource reservation through software agent participating multiple overlapping English auctions. Auction-based method fill three important needs. First, they respect the natural autonomy and private information within a distributed system. Secondly, they can provide incentives for agents to reveal truthful information (indirectly, via bids) about their values for different schedules. Thirdly, an economic basis for resource sharing can provide flexibility, efficiency, scalability and feedback for budget and investment decisions [1]. We also introduce and evaluate the performance two novel heuristic bidding strategies, compared with several other different bidding strategies for computational resource reservation in scheduling systems . Although, in this paper, only CPU resources are considered here this approach may be generalized to other resources such as network and storage.

The remainder of this paper is structured as follows. In Section 2, we give a brief review of the related works about our research. In Section 3, the definition and the states of advance reservation used in this paper are given, and the model of advance reservation by multiple English is discussed. In Section 4, we demonstrate the empirical evaluation of our heuristic algorithm against a number of strategies that have been proposed in the literature. Finally, in Section 5 we present the conclusions and future work.

2 Related Works

As online auctions are increasingly being used to trade goods and services [6], in order to make effective decisions, users need to monitor many different auctions. And the researcher begin to pay more attention to how to use agent to participate in multiple overlapping auctions. Anthony [4] developed a heuristic decision-making framework that an autonomous agent can exploit to tackle the problem of bidding across multiple auctions with varying start and end times and with vary protocols (including English, Dutch and Vickrey). Byde [11][12] studied simulations of populations of agents for purchasing similar goods by participating in sequences of overlapping English auctions, using three different bidding algorithms. Minghua He [5] introduced a bidding strategy for obtaining goods in multiple overlapping English auctions. The strategy uses fuzzy sets to express trade-offs between multi-attributes goods and exploits neuro-fuzzy techniques to predict the expected closing prices of the auctions and to adapt the agent's bidding strategy it reflects the type of environment in which it is situated. The works about bidding multiple auctions as mentioned above are not consider the deliver time of the service and how to bid the reservations.

Wellman [9] proposed an (single) auction-based method for a factory-scheduling problem, in which agents compete for periods of time on shared machine. However, in this study the service units are restricted to be discrete and the service is provided by the signal owner. It's quite different from the reality of grid environment.

In the next section, we will present the model of auction-based resource reservation.

3 The Model

In this section, we specifically consider the case of bidding in multiple overlapping English auctions and the state of advance reservation is simplified.

3.1 The State of Advance Reservation

As be noted in GRAAP-WG [2], the state of advance reservation has nine different states. For simplicity, in this paper we only consider the following three most important states:

- Requested: A user has requested a set of resources for a reservation. If the reservation accepted, it goes to being booked. Otherwise, it becomes declined.
- Declined: The reservation is not successfully allocated for some reason.
- Booked: A reservation has been made, and will be honored by the scheduler. From here, the reservation can become active.

That is, the booked reservation can not be altered or be cancelled.

3.2 Multiple Ascending Auction

Now, we present a new variant of ascending auction protocol which is different from the standard ascending auction [9] for the general continuous resource reservation protocol. In detail, we consider a multiple English auction market, where each auction is given a start and an active bidding lasting time that may overlap with other auctions. We assume that English auctions work according to the following principles:

1) The auctions proceed in **rounds**. Each auction administrate the price of the service. We don't assume that the different auctions' rounds are synchronized, that is, all auctions move from one round to the next simultaneously.

2) In each round, after all the user agents propose their bids, the service provider will select the highest bidding agent as the active one, and then it will update its current price. If there are more than one highest bidding, the service provider randomly selects one as the *active* agent. If the request of the user agent is declined, the agent is *inactive*. If the agent i's bidding to the service provider j and is active in the last l_j round, the agent i will win this auction and the request of resource reservation is booked. The service provider will reset the

service price to its' *reserve* price, and update the start time of the next service, and then a new auction **turn** will begin.

3) In each round, the user agent considers bidding if and only if it is not holding an active bid in an auction or it has not already obtained the service. If user agent i is inactive, the user agent will choose the service provider which it will request to and then decide whether or not to propose the next bid in this server. As we note below, each service provider has its reserve price, and the valid bids to the service provider j must be increased by λ_j.

Though simultaneous ascending auction protocol does not include announcements of bidder identities, the task size of the active agent will be announced by the auctioneer, and the number of user agents remaining in the system can be known by everyone.

3.3 Service Provider

Suppose there are R service providers willing to provide computation service, the services of the providers are homogenous. The services are reserved through auctions, and each service provider runs one auction independently.

Suppose each service provider owns a computation pool with the capacity c_j, and computation service can be started at time s_j. Each service provider has its lowest price r_j for providing service (also call reserve price) and the minimal increase of the price λ_j in the auction. If one agent's bid to the service provider j is the highest bid in the last l_j rounds, the agent i will win this auction and the request of resource reservation is booked. As we have mentioned before, the agent's task size and the service's new start time are announced by provider and can be known by all the user agents. We also call the service provider server later on.

Note that there may exist two kinds of pricing methods for the service in auctions. One is the price for executing a job, and the other is the price of one computation unit. In this paper, we adopt the latter.

3.4 User Agent

Next we are to describe the user agent. Suppose there are N user agents, each agent with one task to fulfill before the deadline. Furthermore, we assume that agent i has a budget m_i, the size of the task of agent i is t_i and the deadline of the task d_i. The information of agents' task size , deadline and budget are private information, and the distributions of these information are all unknown to the agents.

Suppose the current price of the service j is p_j, so the cost of user agent is:

$$b_{ij} = \frac{t_i p_j}{c_j}; \tag{1}$$

And, if the agent i's task running on server j starts at s_{ij}, the end time of the task is

$$e_{ij} = s_{ij} + \frac{t_i}{c_j} \tag{2}$$

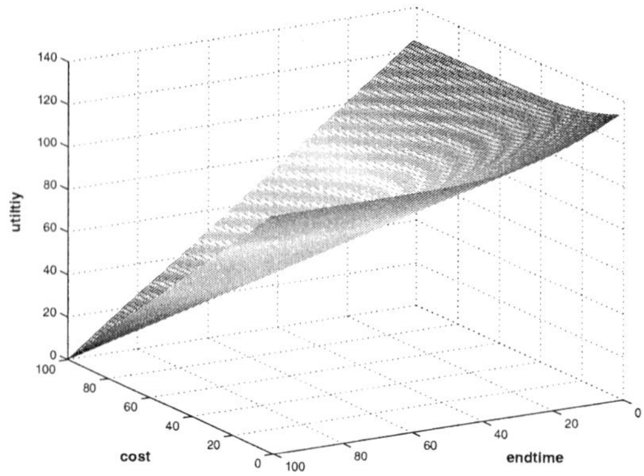

Fig. 1. the CES utility function, where $A_i = 1$, $\rho = 6$, $\delta_1 = 4$, $\delta_2 = 2$ $deadline = 100$, $budget = 100$

The utility of agent is related to the cost of fulfilling the task and the task's end time. In this paper, we use a constant elasticity of substitution (CES) function to present user agent's utility u_{ij}. If $d_i \geq e_{ij}$ and $m_i \geq b_{ij}$,

$$u_{ij} = A_i(\delta_{i2}(d_i - e_{ij})^{\rho_i} + \delta_{i2}(m_i - b_{ij})^{\rho_i})^{1/\rho_i} \tag{3}$$

otherwise, $u_{ij} = 0$. So the agents must make trade-offs between the task finish time and the cost of the execution.

In the next section, we will propose a novel heuristic bidding strategy to resource advance reservation.

3.5 Heuristic Bidding Strategy

An English auction is one in which a single good is on offer and the auctioneer starts with his reserve price (minimum acceptable) and solicits successively higher (public) bids from the bidders and the last bidder remaining in the auctions will be the winner. In contrast to the stand-alone English auction, there is no dominant strategy that can be exploited in the multiple auction context [12]. Moreover, our analysis is from the standard noncooperative perspective, which assumes that agents do not directly coordinate their bidding.

A key component of the successful strategy is able to make predictions about the likely closing prices of the various auctions, so that the agent can determine whether is should place a bid at current moment or whether is should be delay because better deals may subsequently become available. So before we propose our heuristic algorithm, we firstly make a distinction between the bidding strategies. If the agent's strategy can predict the prices of the next k turns of the auctions, we call the strategy level k strategy. And more specifically, if the agent takes into consideration all the future turns of the auctions, we call this strategy level $*$ strategy.

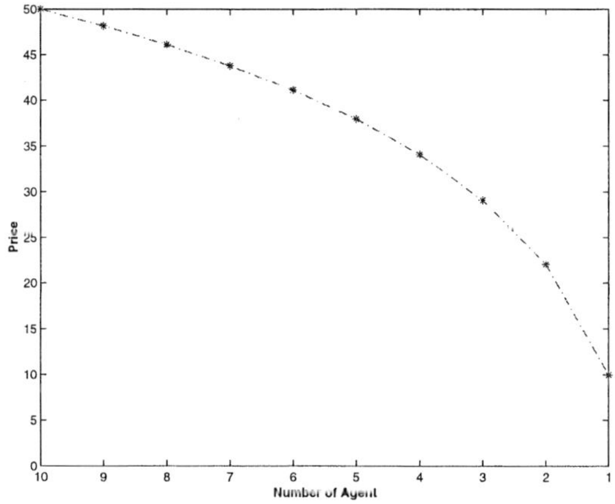

Fig. 2. The predication of the price, where the number of user agents is 10, the current price of the service is 50 and the reserve price of this server is assumed to be 10

We use the following equation to predicate the closing price of the next k turn in the same server.

$$p_j(t_k) = r_j + \frac{(p_j(t) - r_j) * lg(n(t_k))}{lg(n(t))} \tag{4}$$

In this equation, $p_j(t)$ is the current price and $n(t)$ is the current number of agent who are participating in the auctions at the current time t. Moreover, $p_j(t_k)$ is the predication of the price on server j and $n(t_k)$ is the number of agents remaining in the system at the time of t_k, $n(t_k) \in [1, n(t) - 1]$. As is shown in Figure 2, we can see that if there is only one user agent in the system, the price of the service on server j will fall down to the server's reserve price. But as the number of agents increases, the competition of the service becomes severe, and the price of the service will increase.

We specially consider the following heuristic bidding strategies:

Greedy(1) strategy: unless the agent is active in some auction, based on Equation 4, the agent decides to bid in whichever auction currently has the highest evaluation, or decides not to bid if there exists a higher expected evaluation in the next turn than the current highest evaluation.

For example, suppose the number of agents currently in the system is n and the current auction will be closed soon. If we want to predict the likely closing price p'_j of the service j in the next turn, conservatively, we say the number of active agent remaining in the system will be $n-1$, so $p'_j = r_j + (p_j - r_j) * lg(n-1)/lg(n)$. Through comparing the utilities of the current turn and the utilities of the next turn using Equation 3 and Equation 4, the agents can make decisions on when and which auction they will bid to.

Greedy(*) strategy: If the agent knows the average size of agents' tasks, it can use the following equation to predicate its task end time.

$$e_{ij} = s_j + \frac{t_j}{c_j} + \bar{t} * \left\lceil \frac{\bar{t} * (n(t_k) - 1)}{\sum c_j} \right\rceil \tag{5}$$

For $n(t_k) \in [1, n(t) - 1]$, based on Equation 3 and Equation 4, the agent can predicate the maximum utility by comparing different utilities. Unless the agent is active in some auction, the agent decides to bid in whichever auction currently with the highest evaluation, or decides not to bid if there exists a higher expected evaluation in future turns than the current highest evaluation. It indicates in the complex scenarios that the highest level of the strategy is not certainly with the best performance.

4 Experiment Analysis

This section evaluates our heuristic agent by comparing it in a variety of environments, with other agents using bidding strategies proposed in the literature.

4.1 Evaluation Criterion

Since most of the extant multi-auction bidding strategies are concerned solely with price, we have to extend them to dealing with bidding for resource reservation that is characterized by multiple attributes. In all cases, the agents use the CES utility function specified in Section 3 in order to make trade-offs between price and service time. The satisfaction of the user agent is defined as follows:

$$\theta_i = \frac{u_i}{A_i(\delta_{i2} {d_i}^{\rho} + \delta_{i2} {m_i}^{\rho})^{1/\rho}} \tag{6}$$

The average satisfaction of the user agents of type i is:

$$\Theta_i = \frac{1}{N_i} \sum_{i=1}^{N_i} \theta_i \tag{7}$$

N_i is the number of type i agents.

4.2 Experimental Setup

If we only consider the current turn of each auction, there were three most significant strategies has been proposed in this literature [11][12]. The specific benchmark strategies we used are:

- *Fix Auction* strategy: randomly select at the beginning of a game the auctions in which bids will be placed and then bid in these auctions only. The agent continues bidding in this auction until its' satisfaction is negative, then it will switch to another auction.

- *Greedy* strategy: unless the agent is active in some auction, bid in whichever auction currently has the highest evaluation.
- *Fix Threshold* strategy: randomly assign an evaluation threshold $\theta \in [0, 1]$ for satisfaction degree. Then bid in a randomly selected auction until the good is procured or *theta* is reached. In the latter case, switch to another random auction until all of them close.

Obviously, the strategies we mention above are all level 0 strategies. And if we consider not only the current turn of each auction, but also the future turns of each auction, we can use the following level 1 strategy and level $*$ strategy. In the following section, we compare the performance of difference strategies.

4.3 Results

In this section we present the results of simulations of our model while considering a variety of parameters. We compare the performance of the strategies in single and multi Service Provide environments and evaluate the bidding strategies in both homogeneous and heterogenous environments. In each case, at least 100 simulations of advance resource reservation are played among agents. Note that in following tables (i) indicating the level of the strategy.

Case 1: Single Service Provider and the homogenous Agents
In this case, all the agents are of the same type, that is, in each simulation each agent use the same bidding strategies. We assume that $\delta_{i1} = \delta_{i2} = 1$, $A_i = 1$, ρ_i=2, $l_j = 10$, $\lambda_j = 1$, $\theta = 0.5$, the agent's task size is normally distributed between $[100, 200]$. Agents' deadline, cost, and the capacity of server are independent and normally distributed in $[100, 200]$. The average satisfactions of the agents are demonstrated in Table 1 when the total number of agents N is 10, 20, or 30.

Case 2: Single Service Provider and Agents are heterogenous
In this case, heterogenous agents are competed the resource in the games. The parameters of simulation keep the same as those of case 1 when the agents are homogenous, except that the agent adopt different bidding strategy, and each type of agents accounts for 25 percent. The results of the experiments are demonstrated in Table 2 when the total number of agents is 10, 20, or 30.

Table 1. Agents are homogenous

Algorithm	$N = 10$	$N = 20$	$N = 30$
Fixed(0)	0.7345	0.6534	0.6431
Greedy(0)	0.7316	0.6561	0.6450
Threshold(0)	0.7068	0.6778	0.6487
Greedy(1)	0.9616	0.9122	0.6609
Greedy($*$)	0.9737	0.9674	0.9237

Table 2. Agents are heterogenous

Strategy	$N = 10$	$N = 20$	$N = 30$
Fixed(0)	0.6538	0.6721	0.6308
Greedy(0)	0.7013	0.6677	0.6390
Threshold(0)	0.6730	0.6738	0.6418
Greedy(1)	0.7500	0.6858	0.6516
Greedy(∗)	0.8778	0.7766	0.7423

Case 3: Multiple Service Providers and the Agents are homogenous. In this case, the agents can bid to multiple service providers and all the agents use the same bidding strategies. we assume also that $\delta_{i1} = \delta_{i2} = 1$, $A_i = 1$, ρ_i=2, $l_i = 10$, $\lambda_j = 1$. The agent's task size is normally distributed between $[100, 200]$. Agents' deadline, cost, and the capacity of servers are independent and normally distributed in $[100, 200]$. However, we assume that the number of service providers is 3, 5 or 7 in simulations. The experimental results are showed in Table 3 when the total number of agents is 20.

Case 4: Multiple Service Providers and the Agents are heterogenous. In this case, we assume also that $\delta_{i1} = \delta_{i2} = 1$, $A_i = 1$, ρ_i=2, $l_i = 10$, $\lambda_j = 1$. The agent's task size is normally distributed between $[100, 200]$. Agents' deadline, cost, and the capacity of servers are independent and normally distributed in $[100, 200]$, In Table 4 shows the result of experiments when the number of service providers is 3, 5 or 7 and the total number of agents is 20 with each type of agents accounting for 25 percent.

Table 3. Agents are homogenous

Strategy	$R = 3$	$R = 5$	$R = 7$
Fixed(0)	0.7001	0.7584	0.8029
Greedy(0)	0.7163	0.7695	0.8118
Threshold(0)	0.7176	0.7470	0.8406
Greedy(1)	0.9735	0.9839	0.9869
Greedy(∗)	0.9681	0.9790	0.9813

Table 4. Agents are heterogenous

Strategy	$R = 3$	$R = 5$	$R = 7$
Fixed(0)	0.7618	0.8317	0.8712
Greedy(0)	0.7600	0.8635	0.9195
Threshold(0)	0.7398	0.8533	0.9216
Greedy(1)	0.8495	0.9394	0.9782
Greedy(∗)	0.8336	0.9370	0.9682

The above experiments show that our two heuristic strategies outperform the other three strategies in these four cases. One interesting result of our simulations is that the *Greedy(∗)* strategy performs much better than other methods in single service provider cases, however it gains slightly lower scores than the *Greedy(1)* strategy in multiple service providers ones.

5 Conclusion and Future Work

In this paper, we develop a novel resource reservation framework based on multiple overlaying and sequential ascending auctions. We also introduce a novel heuristic strategy to guide agents on which auction they should bid to, when to bid, and how much they should bid in multiple overlapping Ascending English auctions. Through comparing our bidding strategies with several other different bidding strategies for the computational resource reservations in single provider and multiple service providers scenarios when agents are homogenous or when agents are heterogenous, we show that our heuristic bidding strategies outperforms other methods in all those cases.

In current work, we assume that our agents have little prior information about the system, and since the auctions don't close simultaneously, it is difficult to predict the remaining active agents in the system except the next turn, so their bidding strategies are quite myopic. We believe that a more effective decision mechanism needs to use the explicit probability distribution over possible agent's task size, agent's budget, and the predication of each auction's closing time. And the different price predication functions and bidding strategies also need to be investigated.

References

1. G.Cheloitis, C.Kneyon and R. Buyya: 10 Lessons from Finance for Commercial Sharing of IT Resources, *Peer-to-Peer Computing: The Evolution of a Disruptive Technology*, IRM Press, Hershey, PA, USA, 2004.
2. Advance Reservation State of the Art: Grid Resource Allocation Agreement Protocol Working Group, *URL http://www.fz-juelich.de/zam/RD/coop/ggf/*graap/graap-wg.html.
3. Rajkumar Buyya, David Abramson, Jonathan Giddy and Heinz Stockinger: Economic models for resource management and scheduling in Grid computing, *The Journal of Concurrency and Computation*, Volume 14, Issue 13-15, Wiley Press, USA, 2002.
4. P. Anthony, N. R. Jennings: Developing a Bidding Agent for Multiple Heterogeneous Auctions, *ACM Trans on Internet Technology* 3 (3) 185-217. 2003.
5. M. He, N. R. Jennings and A. Prugel-Bennett: An adaptive bidding agent for multiple English auctions: A neuro-fuzzy approach. *Proc. IEEE Conf. on Fuzzy Systems*, Budapest, Hungary. 2004.
6. M. He, N. R. Jennings, and H. F. Leung: On agent-mediated electronic commerce. IEEE Transaction on Kowledge and Data Engineering, 2003.

7. P. Vytelingum, R. K. Dash, E. David and N. R. Jennings: A risk-based bidding strategy for continuous double auctions", *Proc. 16th European Conference on Artificial Intelligence*, Valencia, Spain. 2004.
8. W. Smith, I. Froster, V. Taylor: Scheduling with Advanced Reservations, *Proc. of the IPDPS Conference*, May, 2000.
9. Michal P. Wellman, William E. Walsh, Peter R. Wurman and Jeffrey K. Mackie-Mason: Auction protocols for decentralized scheduling. *Game and Economic Behavior.* 2001.
10. Aram Galstyan, Karl Czajkowski, and Kristina Lerman: Resource Allocation in the Grid Using Reinforcement Learning. *Proc. of the International Conference on Autonomous Agents and Multi-Agent Systems AAMAS-03*, New York, NY. 2003.
11. A. Byde: A comparison among bidding algorihms for multiple auctions. Technical report, HP Research Labs. 2001.
12. A. Byde, C. Preist, and N.R.Jennings: Decision Procedures for Multiple Auctions. *Proc. of the first International Joint Conference on Autonomous Agents and Multi-Agents System*, Pages 613-620, 2002.
13. R. Min and M. Maheswaran: Scheduling Advance Reservation with Priorities in Grid Computing Systems. *Thirteenth IASTED International Conference on Parallel and Distributed Computing Systems(PDCS'01)*, Pages 172-176, Aug, 2000.

An Efficient Web Page Allocation on a Server Using Adaptive Neural Networks

You-wei Yuan[1,2], La-mei Yan[1], and Qing-ping Guo[2]

[1] Department of Computer science and technology, ZhuZhou Institute of technology, ZhuZhou, HuNan, 412008, China
[2] School of Computer Science and Technology, Wuhan University of Technology, Wuhan, 430063, China
y.yw@163.com

Abstract. In this paper, we present a novel application of connectionist neural modeling to map web page requests to web server cache to maximize hit ratio and at the same time balance the conflicting request of distributing the web requests equally among web caches. In particular, we describe and present a new learning algorithm for a fast Web page allocation on a server using self-organizing properties of neural network. We present a prefetching scheme in which we apply our clustering technique to group users and then prefetch their requests according to the prototype vector of each group. Our prefetching scheme has prediction accuracy as high as 98.18%. A detailed experimental analysis is presented in this paper.

Keywords: World Wide Web, Self-Organization, Neural networks, refetching.

1 Introduction

The increasing popularity of the World Wide Web has resulted in large bandwidth demands which translate into high latencies perceived by Web users. To tackle this latency problem, multiple copies of documents are distributed geographically and placed in caches at optimal locations. [5] The performance of Web servers is limited by several factors. In satisfying a request, the requested data is often copied several times across layers of software, for example between the file system and the application and again during transmission to the operating system kernel, and often again at the device driver level. [3] Other overheads, such as operating system scheduler and interrupt processing, can add further inefficiencies.

In this paper, we present a novel application of connectionist neural modeling to map web page requests to web server cache to maximize hit ratio and at the same time balance the conflicting request of distributing the web requests equally among web caches. In particular, we describe and present a new neural network-learning algorithm for a fast Web page allocation on a server using self-organizing properties of neural network.

The paper is organized as follows. In Section 2 we describe the conceptual framework and formulation of the problem. The routing configuration of the web

Y. Zhang et al. (Eds.): APWeb 2005, LNCS 3399, pp. 753 – 758, 2005.

page requests based on neural networks is described in Section 3. Our Mathematical formulation using competitive learning is described in Section 4. We show the experimental results in section 5 and conclude in section 6.

2 Conceptual Framework and Formulation of the Problem

A new model to ensure high performance of a web server using neural networks is proposed in this paper. One technique for improving performance at web sites is to cache data at the client site so as to provide fewer overloads to the server. However this approach is limited by the cache capacity and is very inefficient for serving dynamic web objects because copies of data may have to go through several layers of software and file system, require intermediate processing, object fetches from cache, and then again be passed through operating system layers of the client machine. To handle increasing web traffic we propose a technique to assign web objects to the server cache at the router level. This router may be one of the servers or a dedicated machine to act as a server.

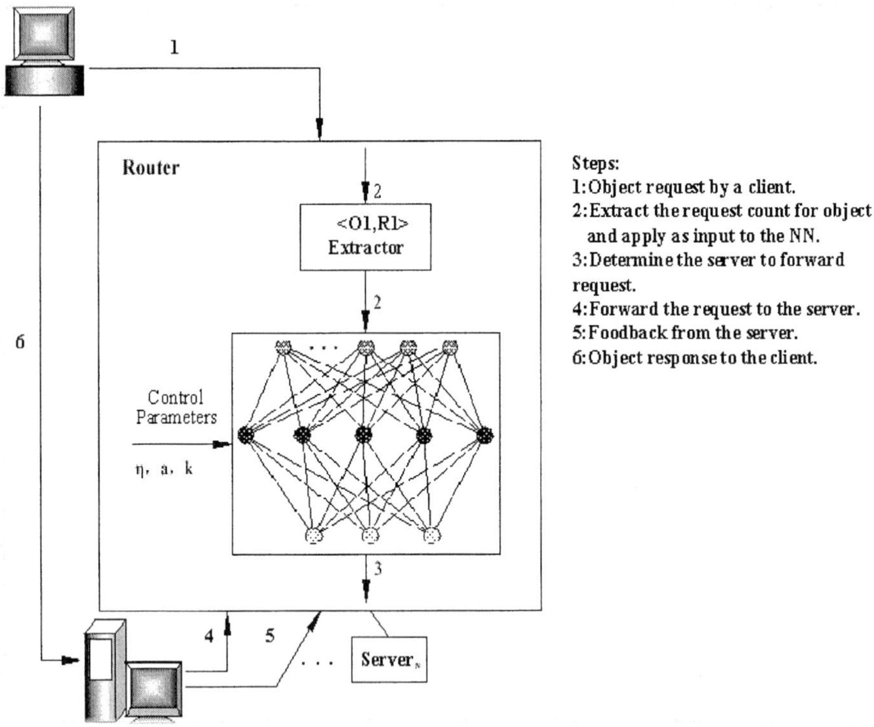

Fig. 1. A Conceptual Framework of our model

Figure 1 presents a conceptual framework of the proposed model. The object id, and request count of the most frequently accessed objects are in the router's memory.

The actual objects reside in the server's cache. This approach is also related to Kohonen's elf-organizing feature map [5] technique, which facilitates mapping from higher to lower dimensional spaces so that the relationships among the inputs are mapped onto high reliable outputs.

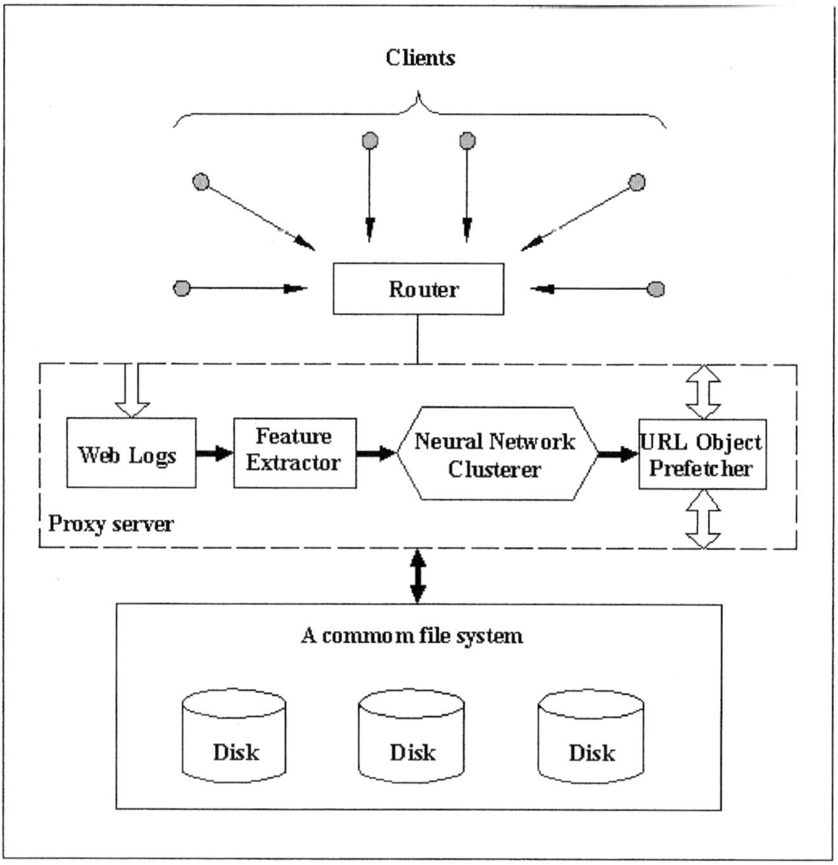

Fig. 2. Architecture of our clustering and prefetching scheme

3 The Routing Configuration of the Web Page Requests Based on Neural Networks

We describe and present a new neural network-learning algorithm for a fast Web page allocation on a server using self-organizing properties of neural network. Our perfetching scheme predicts future requests according to the prototype vector of each cluster. The overall architecture of our clustering and prefetching technique is illustrated in Figure 2.

Each client's request is recorded in the proxy server's Web log file. The feature vector of each client is the input to our offline neural networks based clusterer. The prefetcher requests all URL objects represented by the prototype vector, and the proxy server responds to the clients with prefetched URL objects.

4 Mathematical Formulation Using Competitive Learning

Application of the artificial neural networks, constructed on the basis of model E, for further analysis is the second stage of this investigation. Since it is impossible to introduce all 89 variables into ANN experiments, the input layer contains only the significant, according to the regression analysis, variables. Thus, the set of input variables is different for each country. Two types of ANN models are constructed:

The simple neuron with linear activation function GLRM [3],

$$y^0 = b_1^0 + \sum_{L\in\beta^0} b_L^0 ly^0(L) + \sum_{L\in\beta^1} b_L^1 ly^1(L) + \ldots + \sum_{l\in\beta^5} b_L^5 ly^5(L) \tag{1}$$

Where,

$\beta^0, \beta^1, \ldots, \beta^5$ -are the sets of L indices defining significant variables,

b_1^0 -the intercept (bias),

b_L^j -are parameter estimates (j=0, 1, … , 5; L=1, 2,…, 15).

Multilayer perceptron (MLP) with one hidden layer containing two MLP (2) or five MLP (5) units with the logistic activation function for the hidden layer and linear activation function for the output layer. Elements in the hidden layer are estimated on the basis of the following relation:

$$h_n = f[c_{n1}^0 + \sum_{L\in\beta^0} c_{nL}^0 l\tilde{y}^0(L) + \sum_{L\in\beta^1} c_{nL}^1 l\tilde{y}^1(L) + \ldots + \sum_{L\in\beta^5} c_{nL}^5 l\tilde{y}^5(L)] \tag{2}$$

for n = 1, 2 or n = 1, 2... 5,
Where,
f - the logistic function,

$l\tilde{y}^j(L)$ - standardized variables $ly^j(L)$,

c_{n1}^0 - the intercept - bias of the n-th unit in the hidden layer (n= 1, 2 or n = 1, 2... 5),

c_{nL}^j - are weights estimated for the n-th unit in the hidden layer standing by L-th variable from the j-the country (j = 0, 1... 5; L = 1, 2... 15).

The output layer consists of one variable $ly^0(1)$ that is estimated according to the following relation:

$$ly^0(1) = d_0 + \sum_{n=1}^{H} d_n h_n \tag{3}$$

Where,

d_0 - the intercept - bias estimated for the output variable $ly^0(1)$,

d_n - are the estimated weights standing by n-th (n = 1... H) unit in the hidden layer,

H - number of elements in the hidden layers of the ANN.

5 Experimental Results

In this section, we present the results of our work. We discuss the performance of our algorithm for clustering. We compare performance of our algorithm with that of the K-Means clustering algorithm. As can be seen from figure 3, our neural network (NN) competitive learning algorithm performs much better as compared to Round Robin schemes (also RR2) [2]when input pages follow a Pareto distribution. As the number of input objects increase, our algorithm achieves a hit ratio close to 0.993, whereas the round robin schemes never achieved a hit ratio of more than 0.3.

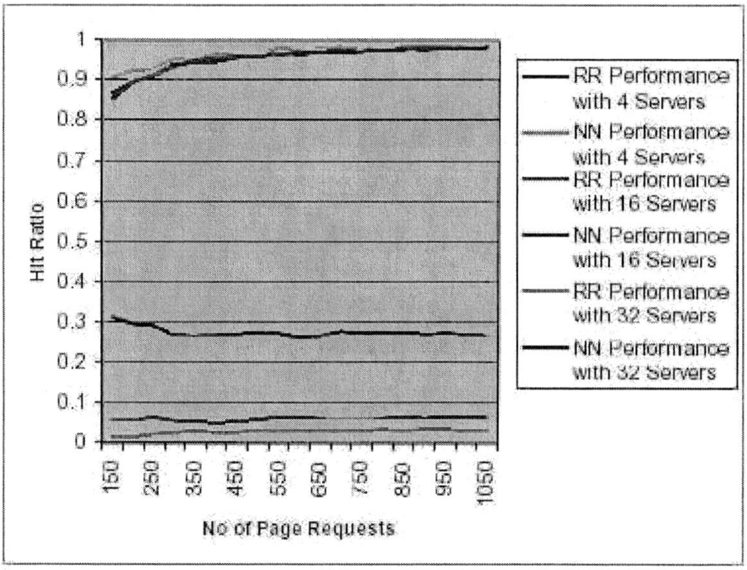

Fig. 3. Performance of page placement algorithm using competitive learning (Neural Network) versus Round Robin Algorithms (for Non-Uniform Input Data Distribution)

6 Conclusion

In this paper, we present a novel application of connectionist neural modeling to map web page requests to web server cache to maximize hit ratio and at the same time balance the conflicting request of distributing the web requests equally among web caches. Using our prefetching scheme, were able to obtain prediction accuracy as high as 98.18 %.

In summary, we have presented a novel approach using a competitive model of neural network for fast allocation of web pages and balancing the load between various servers. Our algorithm has ability to learn the arrival distribution of Web requests and adapts itself to the load and the changing characteristics of web requests. Simulation results show an order of magnitude improvement over some existing techniques.

Acknowledgements

The work was supported by NSFC (Grant No: 60173046). And also supported by the science foundation of Hunan province ministry of finance and education. (No.04C717)

References

[1] M. Beck, T. Moore, "The Internet2 Distributed Storage Infrastructure Project: An architecture for Internet content channels," Proc. Of 3rd Workshop on WWW Caching, Manchester, England, June 1998.
[2] Phoha V., "Image Recovery and Segmentation Using Competitive Learning in a Computational Network," Ph.D. Dissertation 1992, Texas Tech University, Lubbock, Texas, 1992.
[3] V. Paxson and S. Floyd, "Wide-area traffic: The failure of Poisson modeling," IEEE/ACM Transactions on Networking, 3(3):226-244, June 1995.
[4] A. Iyengar and J. Challenger. Improving Web Server Performance by Caching Dynamic Data. In Proceedings of the USENIX Symposium on Internet Technologies and Systems, December 1997.
[5] T. Kohonen, "Self-Organization and Associative Memory", 3rd ed. Berlin: Springer-Verlag, 1989.
[6] M. E. Crovella and A. Bestavros, "Self-Similarity in World Wide Web Traffic: Evidence and Possible Causes," IEEE/ACM Transactions on Networking Vol. 5, Number 6, pp 835-846, December 1997.
[7] V. Cardellini, M. Colajanni, and P. Yu, "DNS Dispatching Algorithms with State Estimators for Scalable Web-server Clusters," World Wide Web Journal, Baltzer Science, Vol. 2, No. 2, July 1999.
[8] V. Cardellini, M. Colajanni, and P. Yu, "Dynamic Load Balancing on Web-server Systems," IEEE Internet Computing, Vol. 3, No. 3, pp. 28-39, May-June 1999.

An Implementation of the Client-Based Distributed Web Caching System

Jong Ho Park and Kil To Chong

Electronics and Information Engineering,
Chonbuk National University, Chonju, 561756, South Korea
{jhpark, kitchong}@chonbuk.ac.kr

Abstract. A distributed web caching system can supply fast and stable transmission of information to the user avoiding a congested network section, storing and supplying the content that the user requested to cache by distributing and sharing a cache like a proxy server. It is located near the user. This paper proposes a simple client-based distributed web caching system (2HRCS) that can assign an object and control the load by using the direct connection of a client to the shared caches without the help of the Additional-DNS. In addition, this paper investigates the hash routing schemes such as CARP (Cache Array Routing Protocol) and GHS (Global Hosting System) which are shared web cache protocols. They need the Additional-DNS for the load balancing. The proposed system in this study makes the existing system simpler by removing the Additional-DNS and reducing the DNS query delay time for all objects. Moreover, the overhead of DNS can be lowered by reducing the general use of the DNS query through the direct object assignment for the client browser. A hash routing scheme system and the proposed system are compared in terms of the average delay time according to the object sizes.

1 Introduction

A method that transmits information by using the web these days is recognized as a new medium for media and has an explosive increase of the Internet users. The bottleneck of networks or the exceeding requests for a server will be a major factor for the increase of delay and possibility of failure. In order to solve these problems, some study for the reducing the total delay time has been performed by avoiding the bottleneck of network, distributing the requests that are concentrated to a single web server through the installed cache, which will be installed near the user's client, and supplying the copied information of the original servers to the clients. These studies are classified into the two categories. The one uses the communication method according to the object assignment and searching method between the shared caches [4-7], and the other one applies a hash function [8-11][1][3] which is called a hash routing method. The communication methods assign a single configured cache due to the characteristics of the client in the system. Thus, it is not able to use the storing space effectively because the requested objects may exist between the shared caches by this assignment. In addition, if there is no object requested by the clients in the cache,

Y. Zhang et al. (Eds.): APWeb 2005, LNCS 3399, pp. 759–770, 2005.

the absence of the object can be verified by applying a request for all of the shared caches. Then, the object is stored in the cache from the original server and transmitted to the client at the same time. It will include a delay time for an inquiry and lower the performance of a distributed web caching system and waste the resources of the network. On the other hand, the hash routing methods have been proposed to solve these problems. The Consistent Hashing [3] used in GHS (Global Hosting System) [2] by Akamai and CARP (Cache Array Routing Protocol) designed by Microsoft [1] have been used in recent years as a representative methods for applying a hash function even though they have different ways in their applications.

In the case of CARP, however, it can control the loads in the shared caches by using DNS [14]. In addition, it can be considered in order to control the load by controlling the value of TTL (Time To Live) of DNS [14] and optimizing the assignment of objects of the caches [22]. Similarly, the Consistent Hashing requires DNS essentially to assign an object and control the loads. In the case of adding or using DNS by the necessity in a distributed web caching system by this way, it will be noted by an Additional-DNS in the main body hereafter. This may be operated as an average web environment that uses DNS all the time to find an object in DNS and has a DNS delay time (Of course, the total time is very small.), the waiting time for the response of an inquiry between the DNSs in order to find an object. Therefore, if CARP [1] and Consistent Hashing [3] have a complex domain delegation for DNS due to the system that becomes a huge scale, the system becomes complex so that the DNS delay time may increase.

If a client can be changed to find a cache directly, the use of DNS will be reduced in the existing web environments. Moreover, it is possible to configure a simple system that doesn't require an installation of the Additional-DNS in the present distributed web caching system (CARP or GHS). This will reduce the DNS delay time that is included in the total delay time in order to bring an object by using the existing distributed web caching system. Consequently, it can improve the performance of a distributed web caching system. Then, the loads of DNS can be reduced in the present network system. This paper develops a simple client-based distributed caching system. It doesn't require an Additional-DNS for CARP [1] and Consistent Hashing [3]. This system doesn't lower its performance compared with the present hash routing scheme when it proved through a implementation to the Heterogeneous Cache System that is similar to an actual environment.

Following the introduction, chapter 2 presents the configurations of a shared cache protocol and its problems. Chapter 3 includes the configurations and contents of the developed client-based distributed web caching system. Chapter 4 describes the experimental setup and the results. Finally, Chapter 5 describes the conclusions of this study.

2 Shared Cache Protocols

According to the use of the object allocation methods which assign an object to caches and search the location in shared caches. The shared cache protocols can

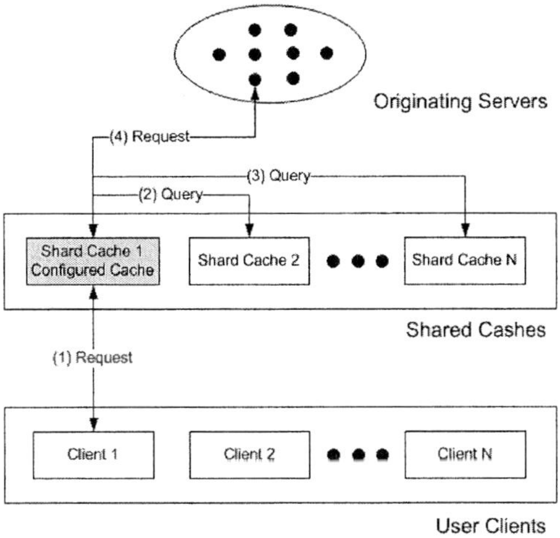

Fig. 1. ICP System

be classified with the communication methods using ICP and the Hash Routing methods. It has been developed by complementing the demerits of each method. This ICP [8] is a kind of distributed web caching method to solve the problems arise in a single cache with multiple users, such as the processing speed, storing capacity, and number of connected users. As shown in Figure 1, a system that basically uses the ICP will communicate between the shared caches by steps (2) and (3) if the configured cache is the Shared Cache 1 when the first Client 1 requests an inquiry to the original server by using the UDP/IP to search an object. In the worst-case scenario, it should communicate with N-1 caches and then requests an object by connecting the original server by step (4) in which the configured cache stores the object and transmits to the Client 1 at the same time. Therefore, the ICP method has a delay time inherently due to the communication to search an object in the shared caches result in waste the bandwidth of the network due to the excess of the ICP communication if the objects do not exist in the cache. Moreover, it has a demerit that wastes the whole storing spaces of the caches because the requested objects are duplicated in the each shared cache.

A number of methods [8-11][1][3] propose the Hash Routing methods to solve these problems only by using ICP through hashing the URL of an object that the client wants to find with a basic hash function. These methods are expressed by the Hash Routing Protocol. According to the main factors for the assignment of an object in the system, it can be classified into tree types which are Client-type, Cache-type and DNS-type. In the Client-type system, a client will assign and take an object by connecting the cache directly through a hash function. In the Cache-type system, a cache will assign and take an object by using a hash function, which is configured in the client. In the DNS-type system, a client will assign and take an object by using a DNS, which is requested by the client.

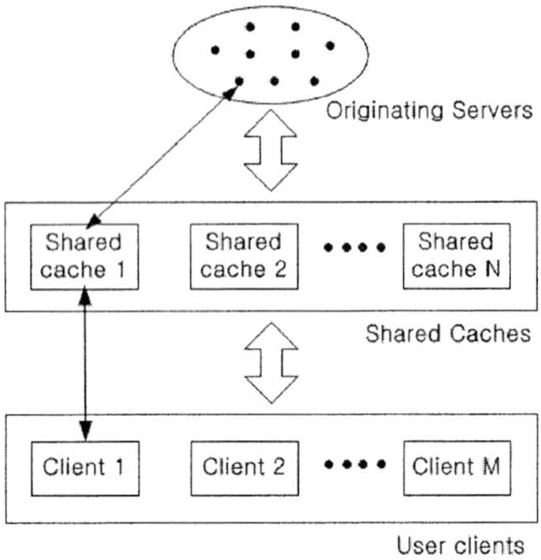

Fig. 2. System configuration for the Client-type system

On the other hand, the hash routing methods can also be classified into the Simple Hash Routing [8-11] and Robust Hash Routing methods [1][3]. A method applying a simple hash routing in the ICP [8-11] uses a basic hash function is expressed by equation (1) in a distributed cash environment, where u is the URL [13], $h(u)$ is a hash function that is able to form a fixed hash value, such as MD4 and MD5, and p is the number of caches.

$$h(u) = f(u)\ mod\ p \tag{1}$$

Therefore, it is possible to know where the hashed values of u , are to be located. In addition, the duplication of the objects can be reduced by configuring the system that directly connects to each cache. However, this method will reassign all of the URLs and assign the objects to the cache when a cache is added or removed. Therefore, it presents a problem because the errors or faults for the requests of the user are increased and will lead to the lowering of the hit ratio. In order to solve these problems, the CARP [1] and the Consistent Hashing [3] use a different Robust Hash Routing methods[10][3].

The Client-type system among the hash routing methods has an ideal configuration, assuming that each client has the same hash functions for allocating an object to the shared caches. If the client already know the IP Address of each shared cache, the system can be configured as shown in Figure 2. The Client 1 can find which IP address of the shared cache is for the object's URL through the hash function. Therefore, it is possible to take the object from the Shared Cache 1 that is to be assigned an object when the cache is connected. If the cache has no object to be taken from it, the Shared Cache 1 stores an object by taking it from the original server and transmits it to the Client 1 at the same time. The configuration of the Client-type system can be setup by modifying the browser. However, it is actually hard to change the browser so that the system will be configured as a similar the Client-type system to the Cache-type system

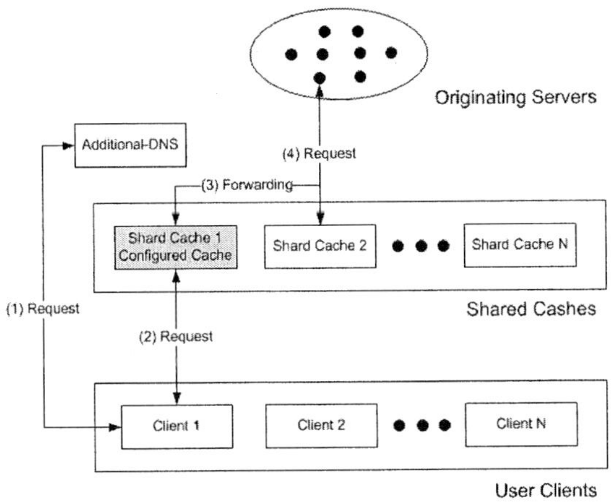

Fig. 3. System configuration for the Cache-type system (CARP)

or the DNS-type system as presented in Figures 3 and 4 respectively. Actually, the system configuration of the CARP [1] is the Cache-type system, and the Consistent Hashing [3] system is the DNS-type system. The CARP [1] is configured as shown in Figure 3 in which the clients use the Robust Hashing [10]. In this case, the Client 1 brings the IP address of the shared cache 1(Configured Cache) which assigned by step (1) and then requests and gets the objects in step (2). While it waits for receiving of the object, the Configured Cache hashes the URL of u and cache domain name of c for the numbers of N and makes each pair of $h(u, c_1), h(u, c_2), \cdots, h(u, c_N)$. If a Configured Cache gets Shared Cache 2 through taking a high score value of these pairs, it requests an object for the Shared Cache 2 and gets the object in step (3). During the step (3), Shared Cache 2 immediately forwards the object to the Configured Cache if there is a proper object. Otherwise, the Shared Cache 2 requests the object to the Originating Server. At this time, it saves the object obtained from Originating Server in step (4) and forwards this to Configured Cache(Shared Cache 1) at the same time in step (3). Finally, the Configured Cache transmits the object to Client 1 without the duplication of the object in step (2).

The CARP [1] can be extended to the Heterogeneous system because each cache can be assigned to the cache by considering the probability of the hash value of the URL for the different capacities of each shared cache in their hash function. However, the protection of the load concentration for a particular cache using Round Robin method [14] of an Additional-DNS which assigns a domain name of configured cache to N IP Addresses of each shared cache doesn't reduce the present use of DNS and DNS delay time caused by the DNS for the clients. The system of the Consistent Hashing [3] used in the GHS [2] is configured as shown in Figure 4 in which the clients use the hash value to be taken by the use of a simple hash function for the URL of an object. Then, it makes a virtual domain name that has a hash value to assign the URL to N virtual cache

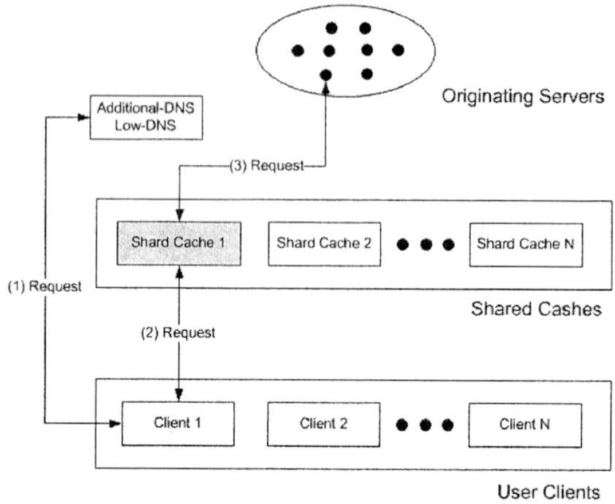

Fig. 4. System configuration for the form of DNS (Consistent Hashing for GHS)

names. For instance, a URL like v101.cnn.com can be produced. The Low Level DNS periodically reassigns the IP address of both the virtual domain name and shared cache through the DNS-Helper which is an assistant program to consider the load for each cache, the addition and the disappearance of the shared cache in this system. Thus, it is possible for the Client 1 to get the IP Address of real shared cache for the URL of the object. For step (1) presented in Figure 4, the Client 1 brings the IP address of the virtual domain name related to the URL of an object from the Low Level DNS (Additional-DNS), that is, an IP address of the Shared Cache 1 that is to be assigned for the object. Next, it requests the URL of the object for the Shared Cache 1 in step (2). If a requested object doesn't exist in the Shared Cache 1, the Shared Cache 1 brings the object from the Originating Server, transmits it to the Client 1 and stores it at the same time in step(2) and (3). After that, if there is a request for the same object, the stored object in the Shared Cache 1 will be transmitted immediately. The Consistent Hashing [3] is required to use existing DNS same as CARP [1] and has a DNS delay time of the Additional-DNS. Moreover, if this system expand in scale, the DNS Delay time will be increased and a problem may exist for managing the Additional-DNS.

3 Development of a Client-Based Distributed Web Caching System

A client-based distributed web caching system proposed in [23] is configured as a type of Single-tier which is a hybrid robust hash routing client system (hereafter, this will be expressed as the 2HRCS). Each client is configured to include the Consistent Hashing algorithm [3]. However, a load control algorithm is excluded and used which a cache load control algorithm. From the system configuration shown in Figure 5, it shows that the system is simplified by excluding the Additional-DNS, the same as the CARP [1] presented in Figure 3 and the Consistent Hashing [3] illustrated in Figure 4. The main elements of the system are CP Helper, Proxy Helper, and client.

The CP Helper periodically stores the information of each cache in the CP(Contents Provider). The information has load and Hot page in each cache and is transmitted by CP Helper to the multi-client. The multi-client uses it to assign an object to the each cache when each client connects to the CP at the first request for a page. The Proxy Helper is a program module that generates

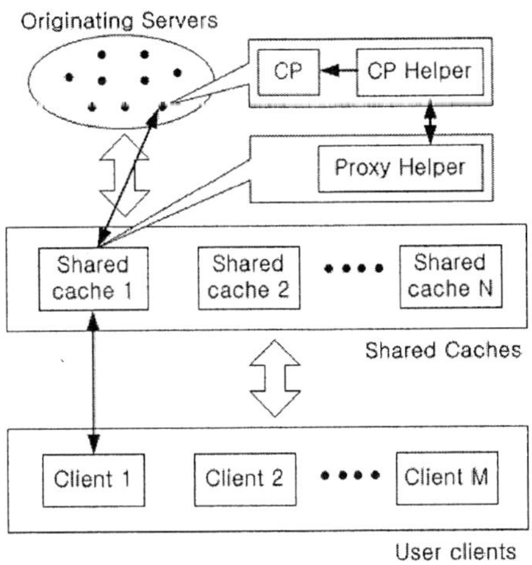

Fig. 5. System configuration of proposed system(2HRCS)

the information of each shared cache. The information will be obtained from the log files of the each cache. Also it assigns the maximum number of request that each proxy can handle. The Proxy Helper is programmed by C&C++ language for the TCP/IP communication and PERL script is used for the log file analysis. The proxy helper is triggered by the CP Helper. When CP Helper requests information to the Proxy Helper, the Proxy Helper provides the Hot Pages and load conditions to the CP helper after analysis of the log files. The Hot Page is a popular page. The page will be assigned as a Hot Page when its request exceeds 30% of the total request of cache in 3 minutes.

The redirecting client browser is produced using the HTTP 1.1 [12]. In addition, it can receive a simple HTML source from a CP server and be implemented by using a TCP/IP communication to receive the information of caches from the CP Helper at the same time. The client uses the existing DNS when it finds the IP address of the first CP server. It can be defined by the self-installed hash function (Consistent Hashing method) and load control algorithm without an Additional-DNS for assigning the URL of an object included in the HTML source brought by the CP. Therefore, the client doesn't use the DNS except

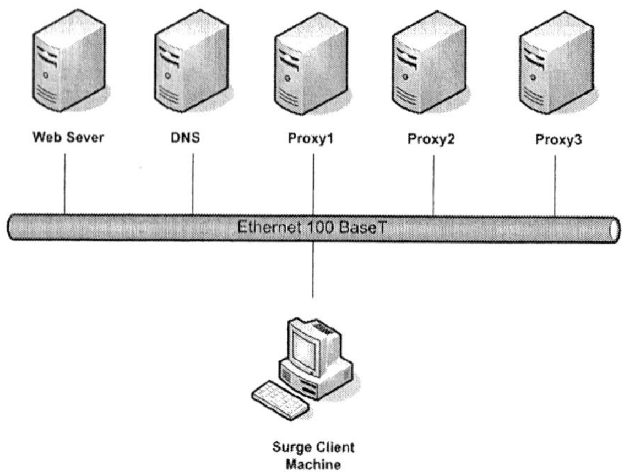

Fig. 6. Architecture of experimental system

for the request to get an IP address which corresponds to the name of the CP. It reduces the use of general DNS, minimizes the DNS delay time and doesn't need the Additional-DNS. The clients receive the load information of the shared caches and the Hot Page (Hot Virtual Name) whenever they connect to the CP server and have an algorithm to control the load by controlling the assignment of the virtual name to the actual caches according to the levels of the load. The 2HRCS has a simple load control algorithm that distributes the assignment of Hot page to the shared cache with most lower load. It's possible to distribute the number of requests based on the cache information updated periodically. If the load information of ith cache denotes α_i, we assume it is $\alpha_i = \frac{r_i}{R_i}$ where R_i is the maximum number of requests that can processed by the ith cache in given period and r_i is the number of present requests processed by the ith cache in the same period. If each shared cache has a same capacity or not in the system, it is able to control the load of each shared cache since it can control the value of R_i.

Therefore, the 2HRCS has a merit because each client can control the load of each shared cache which has a different capacity without using a complex calculation. The information of each shared cache is downloaded from the CP Helper when it connects to the CP Helper. Consequently, the proposed system is simplified and improved by removing the Additional-DNS.

4 Implementation

4.1 Configurations of a Experimental System

The existing Surge [15] developed by Boston University is modified for the investigation of the proposed system. The MD4 [16] in the Surge is used to produce a hash value for the object's URL. Each client thread in the Surge takes the

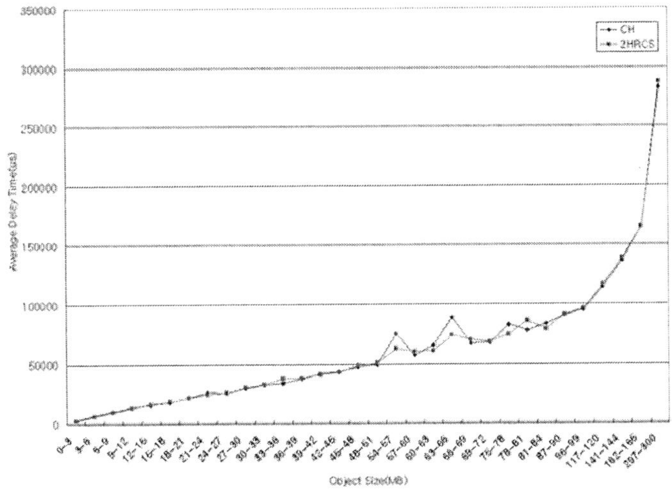

Fig. 7. Average delay time of a single object

role of a client and brings the cache information of every shared cache from the CP Helper located in the CP Server in every 30 seconds. The cache information has IP Addresses, the load and Hot Pages of each shared cache. In addition, the Surge produces more than 1000 virtual caches through the modulo calculation, it is similarly as in the Consistent Hashing [3] method, and stores the hash values of the IP addresses of the actual caches by using a binary tree. Moreover, by using 10-copied caches of virtual caches, the distribution of the virtual caches is improved.

After that, the Surge searches the IP address of the real cache that is related to the name of virtual cache that existed in the binary tree by using the hash values of the URL. Then it requests the object to the cache and receives the object. Moreover, the Surge can control the variables of the Zipf's law to produce the requests by considering the characteristics of the cache [17-19]. If all pages are requested to a certain server, the numbers required for a single file can be expressed by $p = \alpha\gamma^{\beta}$ where α is a constant, the ranking is expressed by $\gamma = \frac{Events_{Doc}}{Events_{Total}}$. In addition, the value of β can be set lower than 1 when a cache was loaded when it is assumed to be 1 for the web server. In this experiment, the value of β was defined by 0.75. This makes it possible to increase the requests for a certain object and creates the Hot Spot in the given time. The Surge is installed on the Intel Pentium III 500Mhzx2 computer which uses Linux Redhat 7.2 Kernel version 2.4.7 for the Operating System.

The CP server is configured to supply the contents based on Linux Redhat 7.2 Kernel version 2.4.7 operating system by installing the Apache release 1.3 [21] in a Pentium III 800Mhz computer. The CP Helper is installed to the CP server. For configuration of the shared cache servers, the Squid release 2.3 [20] is installed to three Intel Pentium II machines with the same OS. The Proxy Helper is installed to each shared cache server.

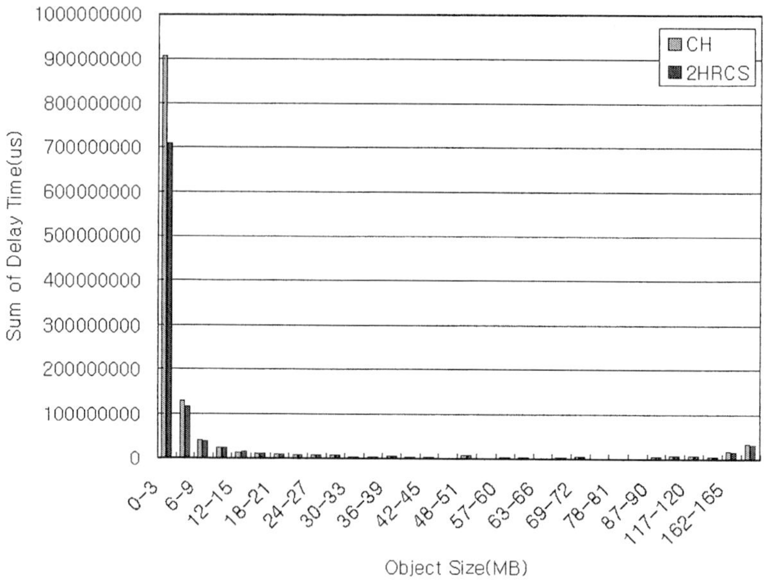

Fig. 8. The total delay time of the request occurred in each interval of object

The Proxy Helper, which has been developed to analyze the Squid log file, is installed in each shared cache server. When it was requested for the information of cache from CP Helper, it transmits the cache information including the analyzed load information and also Hot Pages in every 2 minutes.

Therefore, the request period is to be defined as 30 seconds that are lower than 2 minutes, the cache information will be overlapped for 90 seconds.

Then, the load control is possible depends on the load information in each shared cache. The experimental system is configured to compare the consistent hashing with 2HRCS on the private network in Figure 6.

4.2 Implementation Results

In this experiment, the shared cache has different capacity of handling the requests. The average delay time of the Consistent Hashing and the proposed 2HRCS are presented in Figure 7 and Figure 8. The experiment has been performed by applying 300,000 requests for 50 minutes with 5,000 different files. The files were produced by Surge generation program. This experiment was performed for five times. Figure 7 presented the average delay time of each service with respect to the object size for the hash routing scheme (CARP, GHS) and the proposed scheme (2HRCS). Although it looks almost same for each one, the proposed system shows a little better than the Consistent Hashing system for the local area network. In order to show a more certain difference, the total delay time of the request occurred in each interval of object size has been presented in Figure 8. it shows that the proposed scheme completes the service with smaller delay time.

5 Conclusions

This paper examines the problems of the existent distributed web caching system and simplifies it to the Client-type system by removing the Additional-DNS that is an element of the CARP and Consistent Hashing through the modification of the client browser. By implanting the proposed system into the real local network, the proper operation of system was verified. Furthermore, the performance of the proposed system is better than the consistent hashing scheme in the aspect of the service delay time. In conclusion, the advantage of the proposed scheme is the simplicity of the system and the shorter delay time of service.

Acknowledgements. The authors thank KEPCO R-2004-B-120 and RRC (KOSEF) R-12-1998-026-02003 for their financial support.

References

1. V. Valloppillil and K. Ross.: Cache array routing protocol v1.1. Internet Draft, http://www.globecom.net/ietf/draft/draft-vinod-carp-v1-03.html (1998)
2. Leighton, *et al.*: Global hosting system. US Patent, 6,108,703, http://www.delphion.com/cgi-bin/viewpat.cmd/US06108703_ (2000)
3. D. Karger, *et al.*: Web caching with consistent hashing. In Proceedings of the 8th International World Wide Web Conference (1999)
4. A. Chankhunthod, *et al.*: Hierarchical internet object cache. In USENIX (1996)
5. R. Malpani, *et al.*: Making world wide web caching servers cooperate. In forth International World Wide Web Conference (1995) 107-110
6. S. A. Gadde, *et al.*: A taste of crispy squid. In Workshop on Internet Server Performance, http://www.cs.duke.edu/ari/cisi/crisp (1998)
7. L. Fan, *et al.*: Summary Cache:a scalable wide-area web-cache sharing protocol. Technical Report 1361, Computer science dept., University of wisconsin (1998)
8. D. Wessels and K. Claffy: Internet cache protocol version 2. Internet draft, http://icp.ircache.net/rfc2187.txt (1997)
9. V. Valloppillil and J. Cohen: Hierarchical HTTP routing protocol. Internet Draft, http://icp.ircache.net/draft-vinod-icp-traffic-dist-00.txt (1997)
10. D. G. Thaler and C. V. Ravishankar: Using named-based mappings to increase hit rates. To appear in IEEE/ACM Transactions on Networking (1997)
11. Super proxy script: How to make distributed proxy servers by URL hashing. White Paper, http://naragw.sharp.co.jp/sps/ (1996)
12. R. Fielding, *et al.*: Hypertext transfer protocol - HTTP/1.1. RFC 2616, http://www.faqs.org/rfcs/rfc2616.html (1999)
13. T. Berners-Lee, *et al.*: Uniform Resource Locators (URL). RFC 1738, Network Working Group (1994)
14. P. Albitz and C. Liu: DNS and BIND(4th edition). O'Reilly & Associates, Inc., April (2001)
15. P. Barford and M.E. Crovella: Generating representative web workloads for network and server performance evaluation. In Proceedings of ACM SIGMETRICS Conference (1998) 151–160
16. R. Rivest: The MD4 Message-Digest Algorithm. RFC 1320, Network Working Group (1992)

17. A. Mahanti and C. Williamson: Web proxy workload characterization. Technical report, Department of Computer Science, University of saskatchewan (1999)
18. C. Cunha, *et al.*: Characteristics of WWW client-based traces. Technical report BU-CS-95-010, Department of Computer Science, Boston University (1995)
19. M. Arlitt, *et al.*: Workload characterization of a web proxy in a cable modem environment. HP Labs Technical report HPL-1999-48 (1999)
20. D. Wessels: Squid Web Proxy Cache. http://www.squid-cache.org
21. R. McCool: The Apache Software Foundation. http://www.apache.org
22. X. Tang and S. T. Chanson: Optimal Hash Routing for Web Proxies. In Proceedings of the 21st IEEE International Conference on Distributed Computing Systems (ICDCS) (2001) 191–198
23. Jong Ho Park and Kil To Chong: A Simple Client-Based Hybrid Robust Hash Routing Web Caching System(2HRCS). LNCS 3007, The 6th Asia Pacific Web Conference (APWeb'04) (2004) 467–472

Anycast-Based Cooperative Proxy Caching

Jinglun Shi[1], Weiping Liu[1], Tsui Kc[2], and Jiming Liu[2]

[1] Department of Electronic Engineering, Jinan University, 510632 Guangzhou, China
{jlshi, wpliu}@jnu.edu.cn
[2] Department of Computer Science, Hong Kong Baptist University, Kowloon Tong, Hong Kong
{TsuiKC, jiming}@comp.hkbu.edu.hk

Abstract. As one of the most popular applications currently running on the Internet, the World Wide Web is of an exponential growth in size, which results in the network congestion and server overloading. Web caching as an important technique aims at reducing network traffic, server load, and user-perceived retrieval delays by replicating popular contents on proxy caches. In our paper, we develop an anycast-based cooperative web proxy caching mechanism. It puts response time, hop counts, self-organized load balancing, adaption, and self-configuration as primary concerns. In our scheme, anycast is used to bring a server "nearest" to a client to improve overall performance, all proxies in a local network consists an anycast group. The object placement and replacement problems are formulated as an optimization problem and the solution is obtained by using an anycast-based cooperative proxy caching algorithm. Some simulation experiments have been conduced to evaluate the proposed scheme in terms of a wide range of performance metrics. Analytical and experimental results show that our algorithm outperforms some existing algorithms in response time, hop counts.

1 Introduction

It is well known that the size of the Internet is increasing everyday. This can be measured in terms of the number of web pages added, the number of people connected, and the number of web servers put online. All these factors together contribute to a single phenomenon – traffic on the Internet is getting heavier and heavier. Two of the major problems that the web users are suffering from are the network congestion and server overloading. One of the solutions to alleviate this problem is to store some frequently referenced web objects in proxy servers so the need to retrieve the same object from its host web site is reduced [3]. The Internet traffic is expected to reduce and the response to user request is expected to improve. Proxy severs help lower the demand on bandwidth and improve request turn around time by storing up the frequently referenced web objects in their local caches. However, the cache still has a physical capacity limit and objects in the cache need to be stored in the cache. A single proxy cache is always a bottleneck; a limit has to be set for the number of clients a proxy can serve [17, 14]. An efficiency lower bound (i.e. the proxy system is ought to

Y. Zhang et al. (Eds.): APWeb 2005, LNCS 3399, pp. 771 – 782, 2005.

be at least as efficient as using direct contact with the remote servers) should also be enforced. With the increasing demand for information from the Internet, multiple proxy servers in one site are common. As suggested in [20, 21], a group of caches cooperating with each other in terms of serving each others' requests and making storage decisions result in a powerful paradigm to improve cache effectiveness. Cooperative proxies provide an effective way to use such information. These cooperative proxies usually share the knowledge about their cached data and allow fast document fetching through request forwarding. Cooperating caches have three separate functions: discovery, dissemination, and delivery of cache objects [8]. Discovery refers to how a proxy locates cached objects. Dissemination is the process of selecting and storing objects in the caches. Delivery defines how objects make their ways from the web server or a remote proxy cache to the requesting proxy [9, 25]. In this paper, we use an anycast-based architecture and develop and anycast-based cooperative web proxy caching algorithm. In our scheme, we mainly pay attention to the following issues:

1. Load balancing: Since requests tend to target at a small part of the entire collection of documents, frequently requested documents should be replicated to avoid bottlenecks. Documents and their replicas should be placed in such a manner that most of the time the load of the participating server nodes is equalized according to their capability.
2. Self-configuration of cache groups: In order for the infrastructure of web caches to be both scalable and robust, the organization of web caches must be self-configuration, for several reasons. Manual configuration does not scale, as evidenced in the SQUID system [1]; Manual configuration tends to be error-prune. Self-configuration capability enables cache groups to dynamically adjust themselves according to the changing conditions in network topology, traffic load, and users' demands, thus achieve the goals of both robustness and efficiency.
3. Response time: As an important performance for the user, response time is reduced in our scheme by the anycast-based scheme. In our algorithm, the request documents tend to the nearest proxy, which can efficiently save the response time.

Together with the increasing number of proxy, there are some proxies in a local network, which provides a base to apply the anycast. To apply the anycast routing, the simplest method could be to have all web servers and cache servers joined into a single anycast group. The nearest cache or origin server with the page will be the first one to hear the request and respond. However, one fatal flaw of this method is that it does not scale. In this paper, we design a scalable infrastructure to make the anycast apply possible and easy. Another challenge in building the anycast-based proxy caching system is that, generally speaking, we do not know beforehand which pages would be interesting to users, or where the interested parties may be located, or when they may fetch the pages. Following the basic principles in the Internet architecture design, we propose to build a cooperative caching system. For the clients, the documents requested trends to be located in the nearest proxy in the anycast group. Sometime the placement may be change, but the system can adaptive these changes quickly. In our scheme, the object placement and replacement problems [18] are formulated as an optimization problem and the solution is obtained by using our replace algorithm based on the anycast mechanism. The rest of the paper is organized as follows. Section 2 provides a brief review of existing cooperative proxy systems and the concept of anycast. Section 3 presents our based design, the related formulation and ACPA algorithm. Section 4 evaluates the performance of our scheme and algorithm. Finally, section 5 concludes the paper and discusses the future directions.

2 Related Work

As we know, proxy severs help to lower the demand on bandwidth and improve request turnaround time by storing up the frequently referenced web objects in their local caches [11]. There are a lot of researchers agree that the browser and local proxy caching improve performance [10, 16], but there is considerable debate about the fundamental structure and mechanisms for cooperative proxies [23]. Existing cooperative proxy systems can be organized in hierarchical and distributed manners. The hierarchical approach is based on the Internet Caching Protocol (ICP) [6] with a fixed hierarchy. A page not in the local cache of a proxy server is first requested from neighboring proxies on the save hierarchy level. Root proxy in the hierarchy will be queried if request objects are not resolved locally and they continue to climb the hierarchy until the request objects are found. This often leads to a bottleneck situation at the main root server. Most operational proxy cache hierarchies use a three-level hierarchy with a top level consisting of dedicated regional or national caches. These caches predominately use software descended from the Harvest project[2], one popular variant being the freely available Squid proxy cache. In the United States, the National Laboratory for Applied Network Research operates a global cache hierarchy composed of eight parent caches that service tens of proxies each. Organization of caches in these systems is static and usually configured manually. The distributed approach is usually based on a hashing algorithm like the Cache Array Routing Protocol (CARP)[26], which divides the URLs space among an array of loosely coupled caches and lets each cache store only the documents whose URLs are hashed to it. Each requested page is mapped to exactly one proxy in the proxy array in a hashing system and will either be resolved by the local cache or requested from the origin server. Hashing-based allocations can be widely regarded as the ideal way to find cached web pages, due to the fact that their location is predefined. Their major drawbacks are inflexibility and poor adaptability. The third approach organizes proxies into multicast groups. The Adaptive Web Caching (AWC) design of Zhang et al. [15] uses IP multicast to automatically configure cache groups. Proxies are self-organizing and form a tight mesh of overlapping multicast group and adapt as necessary to changing conditions. Queries are sent to a multicast address, so clients need not be manually reconfigured every time a member joins or leaves the group. Proxies are partitioned into groups and objects are returned from the origin Web Server through a path of overlapping groups. Consequently, AWC delivery may require multiple remote network transfers, just as in a cache hierarchy. This paper does not explicitly model a multicast group organization, although the concept of using multicast groups to dynamically maintain the proxy cooperation group could be applied to either a hierarchy or a mesh organization [4, 24].

In our paper, we design an anycast-based cooperative proxy. Anycast is a network service whereby receivers that share the same characteristics are assigned the same anycast address [5, 19]. A sender interested in contacting a receiver with those characteristics sends its packet to the anycast address and the routers conspire to deliver the packet to the receiver nearest the sender, where nearest is defined according to the routing system measure of distance. Anycast was first introduced in the RFC 1546 [19] as a method for discovering services in the Internet and for providing host auto-configuration. Now it has been defined as a standard service under IPv6 [22]. Using anycast communication services may considerably simplify some applications. For example, it is much easier for a client to find a best server when there are a multiple available services for one kind of service in the network. In the Figure 1, *P1*, *P2* and *P3* are in the same anycast group. If sender1 sends a packet to the anycast address, the network delivers it to the nearest receiver *P2*, if sender2 and sender3 send packet to the anycast address, the network delivers it to receiver *P1*. But the relations between senders and receivers are not fixed, which will be dynamic according to the network environments. It provides us an adaptive infrastructure to put objects into the nearest proxy and get the high efficiency and load balancing.

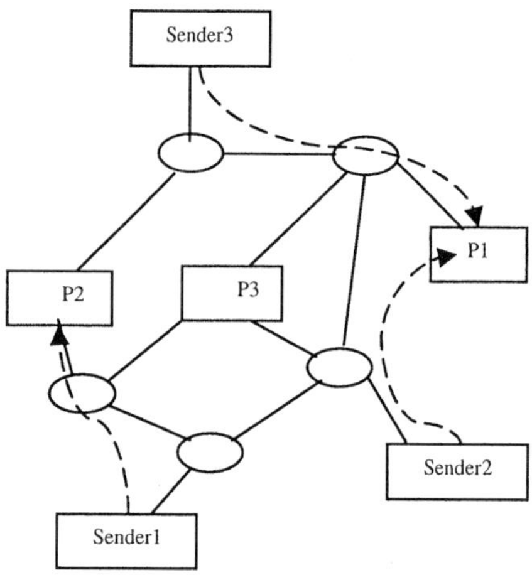

Fig. 1. Architecture of Anycast

3 Formulation and ACPA

We model the network as a graph $G=(V,E)$, where V is the set of nodes (routers) in the networks, each associated with a cache, and E is the set of networks links. The anycast group is defined as G', where $G' = (V', E')$. Clients issue requests for web objects maintained by content server. Each web object is served by exactly one server. Usually, the client and the server of a request are not located at the same site and there are a lot more clients than servers. For each object O, a nonnegative cost $C(u, v, O)$ is associated with each link *(u, v)*. It represents the cost of sending a request for object *O* and the associated response over link *(u, v)*. If a request travels through multiple network links before obtaining the target object, the access cost of the request is simply the sum of the corresponding costs on all these links. The term "cost" in our analysis is used in a general sense. It can be interpreted as different performance measures such as network latency, bandwidth requirement, and processing cost at the cache, or a combination of these measures. It is known that most web objects are relatively static, i.e. the access frequency is much higher than the update frequency. We shall assume the objects stored in the caches are up-to-date [7]. After the request reaches object proxy, the target object is sent along the same path back to the client. Routing paths form all nodes to a given server are represented by a tree topology. For simplicity, symmetric routing is assumed in our analytical model. However, since this assumption may not be valid in some situation, we have also modified the proposed coordinated caching scheme to handle routing asymmetry and studied its performance by simulation experiments. To reduce the cost of future accesses to object *O*, a copy of *O* can dynamically placed in some of caches along the path as *O* is being sent to the client. The issues to be investigated include:

1) Which nodes should *O* be placed (object placement problem).
2) Which objects should be removed from a cache if there if not enough free space (object replace problem.

3.1 Placement Problem

The object placement problem is trivial if cache size are infinite, in which case, objects can be stored in every cache to minimize total access cost. However, due to limited cache space, one or more objects may need to be removed from the cache when a new object is inserted. Removing an object increases its access cost (referred to as cost loss), while inserting an object decreases its access cost (referred to as cost saving). The object placement problem for anycast-based proxy cacheing is further complicated by cacheing dependencies, i.e., a placement decision at one node in the network affects the performance gain of cacheing an object nodes. The optimal locations to cache an object depend on the cost losses and cost saving at all the nodes along the routing path. Our objective is to minimize the total access cost of all objects in the network by anycast scheme. We start by computing the cost saving and the cost loss of cacheing an object at individual nodes. We introduce two cost functions: the link and processing cost functions. The link cost function is denoted by $c(v,v^{'}) = \sum_{(u_1,u_2)\in PATH(v,v^{'})} C(u_1,u_2,size(O))$, where the v is the source node, $v^{'}$ is the proxy or origin server which have the document requested. The processing cost function is denoted by $c_p(v^{'})$. The total cost function is then defined as the sum of these two costs:

$$f(v,v^{'},size(O)) = c(v,v') + c_p(v^{'}) \quad (1)$$

Where

$$c(v,v') = \sum_{(u_1,u_2)\in PATH(v,v')} C(u_1,u_2,size(O)) \tag{2}$$

$$c_P(v') = size(O)/p_{v'}(t) \tag{3}$$

$p_{v'}(t)$ is associated with the processing capability of v' in time t.

In the anycast-based view, the $c(v,v')$ can divided into two parts: $c(v,u)$ and $c(u,v')$, where u is the nearest proxy among the cooperative proxies to v.

$$c(v,u) = \sum_{(u_1,u_2)\in PATH(v,u)} C(u_1,u_2,size(O)) \tag{4}$$

The cost $c(u,v')$ is the cost from u to v', which belongs to the cost between two nodes in the cooperative proxies (the anycast group), and

$$c(u,v') = \sum_{(u_1,u_2)\in PATH(u,v')} C(u_1,u_2,size(O)) \tag{5}$$

Thus, we obtain (6) from (1),(2),(3),(4) and (5).

$$f(v,v',size(O)) = \sum_{(u_1,u_2)\in PATH(v,u)} C(u_1,u_2,size(O)) + \sum_{(u_1,u_2)\in PATH(u,v')} C(u_1,u_2,size(O)) + size(O)/p_{v'}(t) \tag{6}$$

Our objective is to place object O in a proxy u that minimizes the cost $c(v, u)$ and $c(u,v')$, thereby minimizes the total cost $f(v,v',size(O))$. So if the object O is requested from the source node v next time, the total cost is:

$$f(v,u,size(O)) = \sum_{(u_1,u_2)\in PATH(v,u)} C(u_1,u_2,size(O)) + size(O)/p_u(t) \tag{7}$$

Compare (6) with (7), we obtain the cost saved: $\Delta cost(u,v',O)$

Where

$$\Delta cost(u,v',O) = \sum_{(u_1,u_2)\in PATH(u,v')} C(u_1,u_2,size(O)) + size(O)/p_{v'}(t) - size(O)/p_u(t) \tag{8}$$

To calculate $\Delta cost(u,v',O)$, we add a variable $S(h\ ,O)$ to replace $\sum_{(u_1,u_2)\in PATH(u,v')} C(u_1,u_2,size(O))$. Here h means hop counts from u to v'. So our placement problem is solved according to the following policies:

If $S(h,O)+size(O)/p_{v'}(t)-size(O)/p_u(t)\geq 0$, then place object O in proxy u.

If $S(h,O)+size(O)/p_{v'}(t)-size(O)/p_u(t)\leq 0$, then do not place object O in proxy u.

3.2 Replacement Problem

In the anycast view, a requested object should be placed in the nearest proxy in the anycast group. In this way, cost of refunded is minimized in the next time. In Fig.1, we can see that the requested document move from the proxy which have the document to the nearest proxy. As the cache is getting full, we need to decide what to be replaced in the proxy, cache if it is full, which belongs to the object replacement problem bound. From our experiments, if we do not deal with replicates, the cooperative proxies will be low efficient, for the replicates will fill in the cooperative proxies.

We adopt the cost saving table to replace it. In each cooperative proxy, a cost saving table is used to record the frequently requested object's average cost. For each proxy, it is a nearest proxy to some document requested. For a document O, its average cost in the node v' can be defined as:

$$c_{v'}(O)=\frac{\sum_{i=1}^{n} f_i \times \sum_{(u_1,u_2)\in PATH(v_i,v')} C(u_1,u_2,O)}{\sum_{i=1}^{n} f_i} \tag{9}$$

Now there are two different cost between the nearest proxy u and v' if we migrate the object O from v' to u. Here we define them as:
Cost saving for object O in node u, *costsaving(size(O))*:

$$\begin{aligned}\cos tsaving(size(O)) = &\sum_{(u_1,u_2)\in PATH(v,u)} C(u_1,u_2,size(O)) \\ &+ \sum_{(u_1,u_2)\in PATH(u,v')} C(u_1,u_2,size(O)) + size(O)/p_u(t)\end{aligned} \tag{10}$$

Cost loss for object O in node v':

$$\cos tloss(size(O)) = c_{v'}(O) + size(O)/p_{v'}(t) \tag{11}$$

We estimate $p_i(t)$, $i\in anycastgroup$, by the delay time of the probe messages that a proxy sends to others.

- If *costsaving(size(O))>costloss(size(O))*, the proxy will send the object to other anycast member, and delete the object from its cache.
- If *costsaving(size(O))<=costloss(size(O))*, the proxy just send the object to other anycast member.

Table 1 shows steps of the anycast-based cooperative proxy algorithm (ACPA):

Table 1. ACPA Algorithm

```
1) Initialization
   Randomly generate network topology;
   Total number of nodes (routers) : 10;
   Number of routers in anycast group: 3;
   Number of network links: 13;
   Average request rate at each router: U(1,9) per second;
2) Start the simulation
For each request, send to the nearest proxy u in the anycast group
  If u.findobject(object) then
     u.update(object);
     u.sent(object);
  Else communicate with other anycast member
    If anycast.findobject(object) then
       { anycast.replace(object);
       anycast.send(object,u);}
    Else communicate with the original server
    End If
  End If
3) Replacement Algorithm
  For each proxy in anycast group
  If Proxy.findobject(object)
     If Proxy.nearestproxy(destination)
        Proxy.update(object);
     Else Proxy.replace(object);
  End If
Else Proxy.anycastcommunicate(object);
End If
        Method replacement (object)
  If costsaving(size(O))<costloss(size(O))
     Proxy.delete(object);
     Proxy.send(object.u);
  Else Proxy.send(object,u);
  End If
        Method update(object)
If(!Proxy.cachefull())V Proxy.cost(object)>Proxy.costMax)
     {Proxy.costtable.update(object);
     Proxy.time.update(object);
     Proxy.frequent.update(object);}
  End If
End
4) Placement algorithm
     For each document
  Proxy1=Document.findnearestproxy(document);
  Method placement(object,proxy1);
  If proxy.nearestproxy(object)
```

Table 1. (Continued)

```
            Proxy.update(object);
            Else If Proxy.cost(object)>=Proxy1.cost(object)
           {Proxy.delete(object);
           Proxy1.add(object);}
        End If
      End If
    End
```

The ACPA algorithm is based on our formulation. The ACPA algorithm simply selects the nearest proxy in the anycast group according to cost for each document. In the ACPA, by the "nearest" characteristics, client can get the documents with minimum cost. In Table 1, the first part presents a function for initializing the network topology and the anycast group. From this we can see that each proxy has two major tasks, one is update the objects, and other is to communicate with other anycast member or the original server. The second part shows those actions of proxy in anycast group. The third and fourth parts provide the replacement and the placement functions.

4 Performance Results

This section provides a quantitative description of the potential improvement when ACPA is used. And the simulation results show that our scheme can reduce hop counts, decrease the average delay time.

4.1 Simulation Environment

In Figure 2, we can get the network topology used in the experiments. The network topology is randomly generated using the Georgia Tech ITM topology generator [12], which generates topologies that resemble typical networks. Following is the topology used for our experiment.

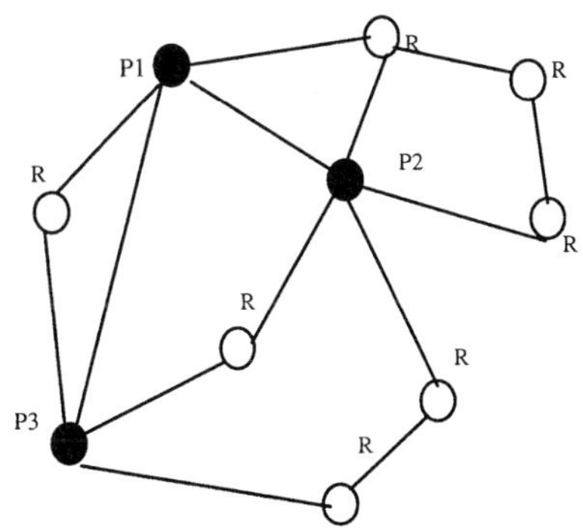

Fig. 2. Topology of Network

Here to simple the experiment, we just simulate a metropolitan area network (MAN) with ten routers. From the Figure 2, we can get that the network consists of ten nodes (routers), and there are three nodes acting as proxy group. The three nodes have the same anycast address and are in the same local area.

4.2 Simulation Results

In our simulations, assignment in each routers follows a Zipf-like distribution, that is, a parametric distribution where the probability of selecting the ith item is proportional to $1/i^{(1-x)}$, in our experiments $x=0.2$. In Figure 3, the performance shows the average response time of ACPA and CARP when Zipf parameter $x=0.2$. The average response time of ACPA is 1.073s/req, and CARP is 1.115s/req. From the figure, we can get that the time of CARP in high value is longer than that of ACPA. At the same time, we can see that ACPA can quickly come down from the high value.

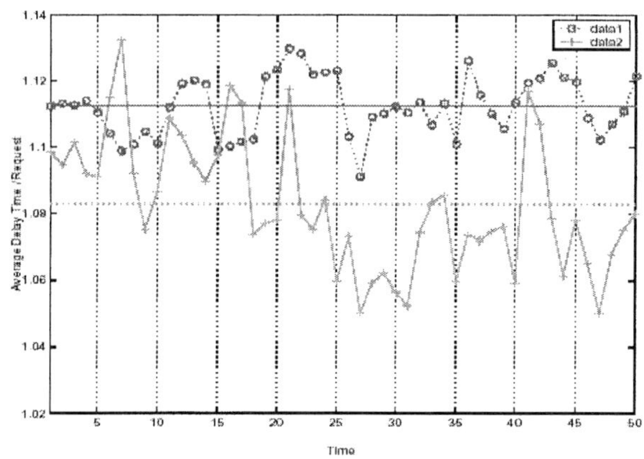

Fig. 3. The Average Delay Time

Figure 4 illustrates the average hop distance of Zipf-like distribution. From the figure, we can get that ACPA performs well than CARP in the hop counts. These results also show that CARP represents a average hop counts for using a hash function based upon

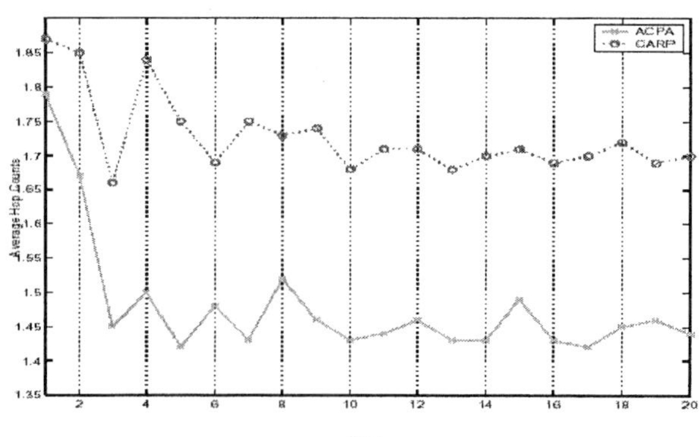

Fig. 4. The Hop Counts

the "array membership list" and URL to provide the exact cache location of an object. But ACPA is an adaptive algorithm where the client gets the object from the nearest proxy. In table 2 and 3, we count t-test result of twenty experiments with average delay time and hop counts. From the t-test, we can also get that ACPA performs better than CARP.

Table 2. T-test Result about Delay Time with Zipf-like Distribution

Title	ACPA		CARP
Delay Time	1.069		1.109
Std	0.006		0.009
t-value		16.098	
P(x>t)		<0.0001	

Table 3. T-test Result about Hop Counts with Zipf-like Distribution

Title	ACPA		CARP
Hop Counts	1.51		1.75
Std	0.047		0.063
t-value		13.750	
P(x>t)		<0.0001	

5 Conclusion

In this paper, we propose a new scheme which employs anycast-based cooperative proxies. It puts response time, hop counts and load balancing as primary concerns. In our formulation, we integrate the anycast conception with the cooperative proxies group. Each object can get from the nearest anycast member. In our paper, we solve the placement and replacement problems as an optimization problem and the solution is obtained by using our ACPA algorithm. From the analytical and simulation results, we can get that anycast-based proxy cooperation could reduce the average response time and the hop counts efficiently. In our simulation, we just provide the experiments on response time and hop counts. In the future research, we will consider to design some experiments for the adaption, load balancing and stability.

References

[1] Squid internet objects cache. Available online at http://squid.nlanr.net/.

[2] C. M. A.Chankhunthod, P.Danzig and K.Worrell. A hierarchical inter- net object cache. In In Proc. of the 1996 USENIX Annual Technical Conf., San Diego, CA, Jan. 1996.

[3] J. C.Aggarwal and P.S.Yu. Caching on the World Wide Web. IEEE Transactions on Knowledge and data engineering, 11(1), Jan. 1999.

[4] K. T. H. V. D. R. K. S. Datta, A.; Dutta. A proxy-based approach for dynamic content acceleration on the www. Advanced Issues of E- Commerce and Web-Based Information Systems, pages 159 -164, June 2002.

[5] D.Johnson and S.Deering. Rfc 2526: Reserved ipv6 subnet anycast address. Technical report, March 1999.
[6] D.Wessels and K.Clay. Rfc 2186: Internet cache protocol (icp), version 2. Technical report, The Internet Engineer Taskforce, Sep. 1997.
[7] Dykes and Robbins. Limitations and benefits of cooperative proxy caching. IEEE Selected Areas in Communications, 20:1290 -1304, Sep. 2002.
[8] S. Dykes and K. Robbins. A viability analysis of coopertive proxy caching. Volume 3, pages 1205-1214. IEEE Infocom 2001, Apr. 2001.
[9] C. P. A. J. B. A. Fan, L. Summary cache: A scalable wide-area web cache sharing protocol. IEEE/ACM Transactions on Networking, pages 281-293, 2000.
[10] [J.E.Pitkow. Summary of www characterizations. Computer Networks and ISDN Systems, 30(5):551-558, 1998.
[11] J. Z. K. L. Y. G. Z. Jin and J. Ma. Architecture and development of dis-tributed www caching proxy. In Electrical and Computer Engineering, volume 3, pages 1467 -1471, May 2002.
[12] M. K.Calvert and E.W.Zegura. Modeling internet topology. IEEE Communications, Jun. 1997.
[13] M. K.C.Tsui and J.Liu. Distributed proxy server management: A self- organized approach. Kluwer Academic Publishers, March 2003.
[14] J. X. B. L. D. L. Lee;. Placement problems for transparent data replica-tion proxy services. Selected Areas in Communications, IEEE Journal on, 20:1383 {1398, Sep. 2002.
[15] K. A. R. S. L.Zhang, S.Michel and V.Jocobson. Adaptive web caching: towards a new global caching architecture. In Proc. of 3rd International Caching Workshop, 1998.
[16] G. S. M.Abrams, C.R.Standridge and E.A.Fox. Caching proxies: Limi- tations and potentials. In Proc.of the 4th Int'l World-Wide Web, pages 119-133, Dec. 1995.
[17] V. Murta, C.D. Almeida. Characterizing response time of www caching proxy servers. Workload Characterization: Methodology and Case Studies, pages 69 -75, Nov. 1998.
[18] K. K. D. Park. Least popularity-per-byte replacement algorithm for a proxy cache. In Parallel and Distributed Systems, 2001. ICPADS 2001. Proceedings. Eighth International Conference on, pages 780 -787, June 2001.
[19] C. Partridge and W. Milliken. Rfc 1546: host anycasting service. Technical report, November 1993.
[20] P.Krishnan and B.Sugla. Utility of cooperating web proxy caches. Computer Networks and ISDN Systems, pages 195-203, April 1998.
[21] M. S. Raunak. A survey of cooperative raunak. Technical report, Technical report, Dec. 1999.
[22] R.Hinden and S.Deering. Rfc 2373: ip version 6 addressing architecture. Technical report, July 1998.
[23] C. S.G.Dykes and S.Das. Taxonomy and design analysis for distributed web caching. In Proc. of the IEEE Hawaii Int'l. Conf. on System Sci- ence, Maui, HI, Jan 1999.
[24] A. H. N. Srbljic, S. Milanovic. Performance tuning of large-scale distributed www caches. In Electrotechnical Conference, 2000. MELECON 2000. 10th Mediterranean, volume 1, pages 93-96, May 2000.
[25] M. H. S. Tian-Cheng Hu; Ikeda, Y., Nakazawa. A study on the content distribution of cooperative proxy caching using total cost-aware scheme. In Computer Networks and Mobile Computing, 2003. ICCNMC 2003. 2003 International Conference on, pages 266 -273, Oct. 2003.
[26] V.Valloppillil and K.W.Ross. Cache array routing protocol. In draft- vinod-carp-v1-03.txt.

Semantic Caching for Web-Based Spatial Applications

Sai Sun and Xiaofang Zhou

School of Information Technology and Electrical Engineering,
The University of Queensland, Australia
{sunsai, zxf}@itee.uq.edu.au

Abstract. Client-side caching of spatial data is an important yet very much under investigated issue. Effective caching of vector spatial data has the potential to greatly improve the performance of spatial applications in the Web and wireless environments. In this paper, we study the problem of semantic spatial caching, focusing on effective organization of spatial data and spatial query trimming to take advantage of cached data. Semantic caching for spatial data is a much more complex problem than semantic caching for aspatial data. Several novel ideas are proposed in this paper for spatial applications. A number of typical spatial application scenarios are used to generate spatial query sequences. An extensive experimental performance study is conducted based on these scenarios using real spatial data. We demonstrate a significant performance improvement using our ideas.

1 Introduction

Geographic applications have been used extensively in the Web environment, providing online customized digital maps and supporting map-based queries. However, the overall potential of these applications has yet to be achieved due to the conflict between large size and high complexity of spatial data and relative low transmission speed of the Internet [14]. The conflict is even more serious in the mobile environment which suffers from low bandwidth and low-quality communications (such as frequent network disconnections). Caching pertinent and frequently queried data on the client side is an effective method to improve system performance, since it can reduce network traffic, shorten the response time and lead to better scalability by reusing local resources [4]. Client-side semantic data caching has great potential in spatial database systems. It is enabled by improved processing capacity on the client-side. About ten years ago, clients are still low-end workstations. Caching is only done on the server side aiming to avoid disk traffic in typical commercial relational databases [6]. However, with rapid growth of client-side processing capacity, complex processing required for spatial caching can now be done at an acceptable speed on the client side. Spatial queries are usually related to each other semantically. Statistical analysis shows that spatial queries submitted by a client in a limited time interval have

Y. Zhang et al. (Eds.): APWeb 2005, LNCS 3399, pp. 783–794, 2005.

great semantic correlation. Users of 'location-aware' websites usually interact with a map to zoom in or out and pan on the client side by clicking on spatial objects to request further information. Progressive queries of multiresolution spatial databases, which are used extensively for decision support systems, data mining and interactive systems, usually begin with a general scope of parameters that are iteratively refined in both location and precision until a final satisfactory result is obtained. Semantic caching of highly correlated spatial data on the client side is helpful to improve spatial query response time. Table 1 shows a sample of a typical set of queries submitted by a client. Query 0 begins from a large query scope (query window size 49% = 70%*70%) and low resolution level (Resolution 13). Query 1, 2 and 3 keep zooming in (Refining window as well as increasing resolution level). To Query 3, the query window area is 4% of the whole map and resolution level is 22. Query 4 pans the query window.

Table 1. A typical set of queries in Web-Applicaton

QueryID	Query Window (x, y, width, height)	Query Resolution
0	0.1, 0.1, 0.7, 0.7	13
1	0.36, 0.13, 0.5, 0.5	15
2	0.42, 0.19, 0.4, 0.4	18
3	0.47, 0.28, 0.2, 0.2	22
4	0.53, 0.31, 0.2, 0.2	22

Compared with standard data, spatial data have some notable properties. Spatial data tend to be very large and have complex structures; this makes data organization a significant factor to consider. A good organization method should compress and cluster data reasonably as it can reduce the size of the storage and also the time of accessing database, and increase the utilization of client cache. In this paper, we explore different spatial data organization strategies based on single resolution, multi-representation and multi-resolution ideas. We propose a new data organization method named *Bit_Map* which balances data between the opaque and the fragment ways and allows multi-resolution data access. Our experiments shows that *Bit_Map* is more flexible and needs less data than *SDO_GEOMETRY* — the method used in Oracle DBMS, as well as The multi-representation one. It is especially suitable for semantic caching as it also maximizes data reuse.

In this paper, we investigate the problem of multi-resolution spatial query trimming which is much more complex than aspatial query trimming. We focus on *Window Query* because it is the basic geometric selection and can be served as building blocks for more complex spatial operations. We also discuss about caching coalescence and propose three schemes (reconstruction scheme, fragment scheme1 and fragment scheme2). Our experiments show that the performance of fragment scheme1 is better than or comparable to the other two schemes in all scenarios.

The remainder of this paper is organized as follows. In section 2, we analyze problems combining with related works. Our approach is introduced in section 3. Section 4 describes experiments and provides experiment results. We conclude this paper in section 5.

2 Background

2.1 Semantic Cache

Past research on semantic caching focuses mainly on relational database. It includes: a) query folding [9], [5], which check the satisfiability, equivalence or implication relationship between a query and a given set of data, then further decide whether the query is rewriteable according to given data and how to rewrite. Note that not all queries can be rewritten. In fact, most research in semantic caching is just based on simple query such as 'select object from table where $x > a$ and $x < b$'. b) caching coherency strategy, which is used to ensure that cached data are consistent with those stored in server [1]. c) caching coalescence strategy, which decides how to re-organize cache regions after new data are fetched from database. d) caching replacement policy [4], [2].

Recently, semantic caching in mobile computing environment has received more attention [10], [12], [3], [8], [13]. Most of them focus on location-dependent information services (LDIS) and take the movement of mobile client and the valid region of data into account. Till now, in our best literature review, we have not found any work done to solve the above issues we discussed in Section 1.

2.2 Data Organization

In traditional spatial systems, spatial data are organized based on geometry. Here all information of a spatial object is stored as one record in a database. Consequently geometry elements are opaque to applications and only one resolution level is available to be accessed - the highest level. The advantage of this technique is that the information of the exact geometry can be accessed directly and no extra step of reconstruction is needed. However, to solve the Query 0 in Table 1, 49% data of the whole digital map need to be accessed from database. If local cache is large enough to save the result, no data need to be fetched to answer Query 1 to Query 4. However, usually local cache can not provide such a large space and data have to be abandoned which causes a great waste. Another problem of this model is that the response time of Query 0 is dispensable long. If users finally find the following queries need not be executed, too many unnecessary data had been fetched. One improvement is to use multiple representations of spatial objects. Previous work in this area aims to exploit the benefit of essentially pre-computing of a query result. An object can have up to n representations, denoted as $O_1, O_2, \ldots, O_n$. Each representation contains all vertexes of an equal or lower resolution level. Thus all points in O_i also exist in $O_{(i+1)}$. A representation with a maximum resolution n contains all data of the lower resolutions. The multi-representation technique is, intuitively, superior in terms of data retrieval speed for single queries. However the total replication scheme of multi-representation defeats the purpose of progressively iterating queries as data in different resolutions are not associated, so duplicated data at a low resolution will be retrieved again when a higher resolution is required. Thus, this model can not well utilize the benefit of cache. Our proposed Bit_Map scheme solves this problem by only storing additional information for every resolution level except the base level. Every representation at higher resolution δ than the base level need to be constructed by combining data of base level and additional information equal to or less the than δ. Therefore, to execute queries in table 1, data of base level and additional information equal to or less than Resolution 13 will be accessed from database to answer Query 0. In the following queries, only additional data in the refined area need to be fetched from database and combined with cached data for construction. The disadvantage of this model is that extra time jis needed for reconstruction. However, noticing that transmission usually cost much more time than CPU computing, the extra time can be ignored.

3 Our Approach

In this section, we introduce our approaches. We focus on three issues, 1) Data Organization, 2) Window Query trimming, 3) Caching Re-organization.

Figure 1 is a three-layer client-server architecture. The client maintains a semantic cache C locally, which begins from empty. When users submit a request, the client formulate a window query Q according to the request, then process query trimming based on Q and C. If C can not fully answer Q, missing data will be fetched from database via web server. Then the client re-organize local cache. Finally, the result of the query is rendered to the user. Additional refinement may be processed in web server and client side.

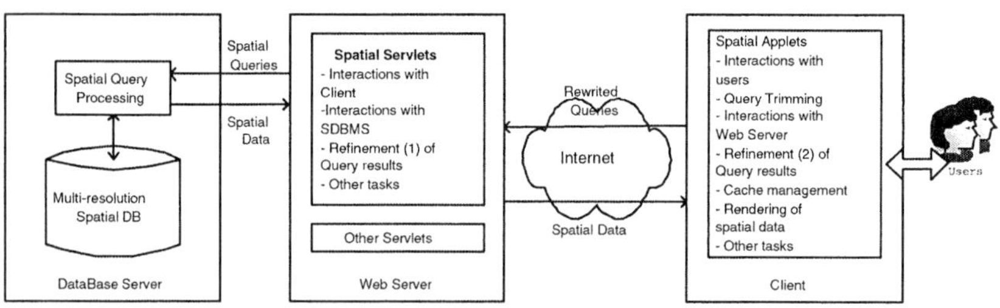

Fig. 1. System Architecture

3.1 Our Database Organization – *Bit_Map*

An object at lower resolution can be considered as an approximation of the object at higher resolution, which still maintains important features of this object but its data complexity is simpler and it needs less storage. We use z-ordering to fragment spatial objects into series of resolutions. Z-ordering is a method using a space filling curve to transfer two dimensional data into one dimensional data. Starting from the fixed map size, space is iteratively decomposed into four same-size subspaces, named as Peano cells. Each Peano cell is labelled with a unique number that defines its position in the total z-order, which is called z-value of this Peano cell [7], as shown in Figure 2(a). Because the decomposition and encoding is iterative, each child Peano cell's z-value contains its father Peano cell's z-value as a prefix. The longer a z-value is, the smaller the Peano cell is. When a z-value is long enough(usually 22-28 digits), the Peano cell is small enough to represent a point. Thus, we can use Peano cells to represent spatial objects at different resolution [11]. Figure 2(b) shows an approximation at lower resolution. With additional information, we can extend shadowy Peano cells in Figure 2(b) to smaller Peano cells in Figure 2(c) with more details and achieve an approximation at higher resolution.

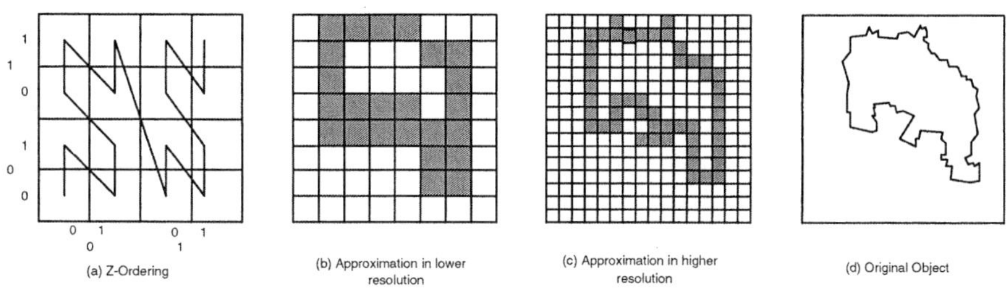

Fig. 2. Using Z-ordering to fragment spatial objects into series of resolutions

Bit_Map scheme chooses a certain resolution level as the base level. Each geometry point at the base level is stored as a variable array. For higher levels, additional information is provided to extend the approximation to the finer polygon with more details. Thus we use relation $R(ObjectID, BLData, AData, Delta)$ to describe Bit_Map, where $BLData$ stores the approximations at the base level; $AData$ stores the additional information to reconstruct data at higher resolution, $Delta$ denotes the resolution of data. A spatial object i will have n tuples as $(i, bldate, \emptyset, bl)$, $(i, \emptyset, a_1data, a_1)$, ..., $(i, \emptyset, a_{(n-1)}data, a_{(n-1)})$ in R. To an arbitrary O_δ, all data with resolution level equal to or less than δ need to be fetched to reconstruct the spatial object O at resolution δ. Figure 3 is an example about the data in Bit_Map. At base level bl, we have a point '12002330' and it expands to two new points in level a_1 ('120023302' and '120023303'). '120023302' further expands to three new points in level a_2. They are '1200233020', '1200233022' and '1200233023'. Note that if the change in the number of points between adjacent resolution levels is small, several continuous levels can be integrated into a single level. Bit_map provides a reasonable, natural method to cluster points to different resolution levels. Because this method uses the common prefix to construct data iteratively, the reduplication between points is well avoided. In our experiments, data stored with this method occupy 21.501MB, whereas data

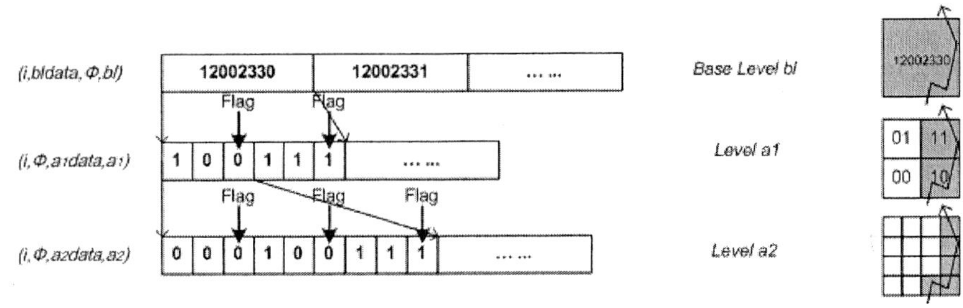

Fig. 3. Bit Map

stored as geometry class of Oracle 9i need 33.438MB. If data is stored by multi-representation technology, same series of resolutions need 152.313MB.

The algorithm to create $R(ObjectID, BLData, AData, Delta)$ is:

1)Choose a proper z-value length (n) as the highest resolution level, and encode spatial objects at this level as $Z(ObjectID, PointID, z, delta)$, where z is the z-value for the point, $delta$ is the resolution value given to the vertex, which is calculated as the number of digits of the longest common prefix between the two end points of the line.

2)Choose resolution bl as base resolution level and constructing $BLData$ at resolution bl. To a spatial object o, using the following SQL to choose points:

select $substring(z, 1, bl)$
from Z
where $ObjectID = o$ *and* $delta \leq bl$
order by $PointID$

Thus, the $BLData$ of o is $(o, bldata, \emptyset, bl)$, where $bldata$ is the digital sequence of $substring(z, 1, bl)$.

3)Constructing $AData$ at resolution a_i.

select $substring(z, a_i - 1, a_i)$
from Z
where $ObjectID = o$ *and* $delta = a_i$
order by $PointID$

The collection of $substring(z, a_i - 1, a_i)$ is the additional information $a_i data$. Because it is impossible to estimate the exact number of how many Peano cell at a_i will be extended from its father Peano cell at a_{i-1}, we add a binary bit to flag it (0 - the next Peano cell is extended from the same father Peano cell; 1 - the end of extension in the same father Peano cell and the next cell is extended from a different father Peano cell). Thus, the $ADATA$ is $(i, \emptyset, a_1 data, a_1)$, ..., $(i, \emptyset, a_{(n-1)} data, a_{(n-1)})$.

3.2 Query Trimming

In this study, we focus on *Window Query*, the most common query in spatial database. Dealing with more complex spatial queries is an important direction

Table 2. Multi-resolution Window Query trimming

	W_S Disjoint W_Q	W_S contains W_Q	W_Q contains W_S	W_S intersects W_Q
$\delta_1^S > \delta_2^Q$ or $\delta_2^S < \delta_1^Q$	P:$\emptyset$ R:$\langle W_Q, \delta_1^Q, \delta_2^Q \rangle$	P:$\emptyset$ R:$\langle W_Q, \delta_1^Q, \delta_2^Q \rangle$	P:$\emptyset$ R:$\langle W_Q, \delta_1^Q, \delta_2^Q \rangle$	P:$\emptyset$ R:$\langle W_Q, \delta_1^Q, \delta_2^Q \rangle$
$\delta_1^S \leq \delta_1^Q$ and $\delta_2^S \geq \delta_2^Q$	P:$\emptyset$ R:$\langle W_Q, \delta_1^Q, \delta_2^Q \rangle$	P:$\langle W_Q, \delta_1^Q, \delta_2^Q \rangle$ R: $\emptyset$	P:$\langle W_S, \delta_1^Q, \delta_2^Q \rangle$ R:$\langle W_Q \bigcap \neg W_S, \delta_1^Q, \delta_2^Q \rangle$	P:$\langle W_Q \bigcap W_S, \delta_1^Q, \delta_2^Q \rangle$ R:$\langle W_Q \bigcap \neg W_S, \delta_1^Q, \delta_2^Q \rangle$
$\delta_1^S > \delta_1^Q$ and $\delta_2^S < \delta_2^Q$	P:$\emptyset$ R:$\langle W_Q, \delta_1^Q, \delta_2^Q \rangle$	P:$\langle W_Q, \delta_1^S, \delta_2^S \rangle$ R:$\langle W_Q, \delta_1^Q, \delta_1^S - 1 \rangle$ +$\langle W_Q, \delta_2^S + 1, \delta_2^Q \rangle$	P:$\langle W_S, \delta_1^S, \delta_2^S \rangle$ R:$\langle W_S, \delta_1^Q, \delta_1^S - 1 \rangle$ +$\langle W_S, \delta_2^S + 1, \delta_2^Q \rangle$ +$\langle W_Q \bigcap \neg W_S, \delta_1^Q, \delta_2^Q \rangle$	P:$\langle W_Q \bigcap W_S, \delta_1^S, \delta_2^S \rangle$ R:$\langle W_Q \bigcap W_S, \delta_1^Q, \delta_1^S - 1 \rangle$ +$\langle W_Q \bigcap W_S, \delta_2^S + 1, \delta_2^Q \rangle$ +$\langle W_Q \bigcap \neg W_S, \delta_1^Q, \delta_2^Q \rangle$
$\delta_1^S \leq \delta_1^Q$ and $\delta_2^S < \delta_2^Q$	P:$\emptyset$ R:$\langle W_Q, \delta_1^Q, \delta_2^Q \rangle$	P:$\langle W_Q, \delta_1^Q, \delta_2^S \rangle$ R:$\langle W_Q, \delta_2^S + 1, \delta_2^Q \rangle$	P:$\langle W_S, \delta_1^Q, \delta_2^S \rangle$ R:$\langle W_S, \delta_2^S + 1, \delta_2^Q \rangle$ +$\langle W_Q \bigcap \neg W_S, \delta_1^Q, \delta_2^Q \rangle$	P:$\langle W_Q \bigcap W_S, \delta_1^Q, \delta_2^S \rangle$ R:$\langle W_Q \bigcap W_S, \delta_2^S + 1, \delta_2^Q \rangle$ +$\langle W_Q \bigcap \neg W_S, \delta_1^Q, \delta_2^Q \rangle$
$\delta_1^S > \delta_1^Q$ and $\delta_2^S \geq \delta_2^Q$	P:$\emptyset$ R:$\langle W_Q, \delta_1^Q, \delta_2^Q \rangle$	P:$\langle W_Q, \delta_1^S, \delta_2^Q \rangle$ R:$\langle W_Q, \delta_1^Q, \delta_1^S - 1 \rangle$	P:$\langle W_S, \delta_1^S, \delta_2^Q \rangle$ R:$\langle W_S, \delta_1^Q, \delta_1^S - 1 \rangle$ +$\langle W_Q \bigcap \neg W_S, \delta_1^Q, \delta_2^Q \rangle$	P:$\langle W_Q \bigcap W_S, \delta_1^S, \delta_2^Q \rangle$ R:$\langle W_Q \bigcap W_S, \delta_1^Q, \delta_1^S - 1 \rangle$ +$\langle W_Q \bigcap \neg W_S, \delta_1^Q, \delta_2^Q \rangle$

of our future research. A window query Q of a multi-resolution spatial relation R, described as $Q\langle W_Q, \delta \rangle$, finds all objects at resolution level δ with at least one point in common with window W_Q. Under the above data organization scheme Bit_Map, we can define the following constraint formula to describe a semantic region or a general query:

Definition 1. *Given a spatial relation R(ObjectID, BLData, AData, Delta), a constraint formula, denoted as* $\langle W, \delta_1, \delta_2 \rangle$ ($\delta_1 \leq \delta_2$ *and* $\delta_1 \geq bl$)*, describes the data (at resolution* δ_1 *to* δ_2*) of spatial objects intersecting window* W *on* R*. When* $\delta_1 = bl$*, it describes the data answering the window query* $\langle W, \delta_2 \rangle$*.*

For a general query $Q\langle W_Q, \delta_1^Q, \delta_2^Q \rangle$ and a semantic region $S\langle W_S, \delta_1^S, \delta_2^S \rangle$, Table 2 gives a conclusion of query trimming, where P denotes Probe query and R denotes Remainder Query.

3.3 Caching Re-organization

After missing data is transmitted to client, data will be reconstructed for rendering and cache need to be re-organized. In this section, we propose three re-organizing schemes in client cache.

Reconstruction Scheme. As the name suggests, local cache stores reconstructed data. This scheme can avoid repeated reconstruction, but because reconstruction always companies with decompression, this method needs more storage. As shown in Figure 4(a), given three semantic regions S_A, S_B, S_C in cache, δ_1 of S_A, S_B, S_C is 12; δ_2 of S_A, S_B, S_C are 13, 22, 16 respectively; the query is 'to find all polygons intersect window W at resolution level 16'. After executing this query, A and C are decomposed into two parts, *Part 1* is the intersection with Q and *Part2* the difference from Q. Part 1 of A, C, all data of

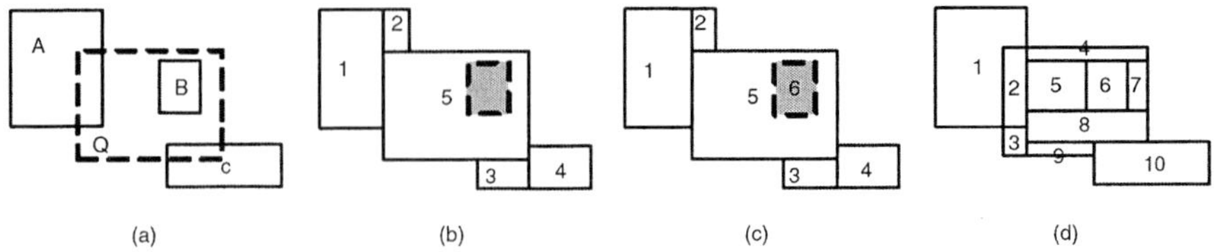

Fig. 4. Three schemes of client cache

B and ship data are coalesced together as the data of new region. Figure 4(b) shows the regions after Q. Note that δ_2 of S_B is larger than δ_2^Q, data in shadow area is at higher resolution than query needed. After repetitious queries, data in regions may be much more than necessary.

Fragment Scheme 1. In this scheme, data are organized according to Bit Map. The coalescence method is same as reconstruction scheme. The disadvantage of this scheme is that data may be reconstructed duplicately. But it avoids the two problem of reconstruct scheme. Figure 4(c) shows the regions after query. Note region B is divided into two parts in this scheme, data of resolution 12 - 16 and data of resolution 17 - 22. The latter part of data forms Region 6.

Fragment Scheme 2. In this scheme, data are still organized according to Bit Map. But the coalescence method is different. In this scheme, existing regions are not changed. Query window is divided according to difference between existing regions as figure 4(d). This scheme may create numerous too small regions which is easy to cause volatile of accessing database.

4 Experiments and Results

In this section, we investigate the performance of various cache strategies on spatial queries. The data used for experiments are from California SEQUOIA polygon dataset. It contains 20,137 objects which are composed of 2,635,065 points. We have produced tests on various aspects of cache scheme to check the efficiency of semantic caching for web-based spatial applications and to determine the most efficient semantic caching scheme. These aspects include: 1) size of cache in client side; 2) three different data organizations, SR (single resolution), MP (multirepresentation), BM (our proposed method); 3) For BM, three different re-organizing schemes in client side as discussed in Section 3.3. The primary measurement we use is the amount of transmission as it affects the response time dominantly for spatial query. Other measurements such as time of accessing database, time of data processing are also used. Note that data processing include query trimming, cache region management and data refinement etc. The results of each test are obtained by running 30 groups of queries. Each group begins with an empty cache and performs a window query with the following actions in succession: zoom in, zoom in, zoom in, pan, pan, pan, zoom out, pan, zoom out, pan, zoom in, zoom in, pan, pan, pan. The location of the first window and the

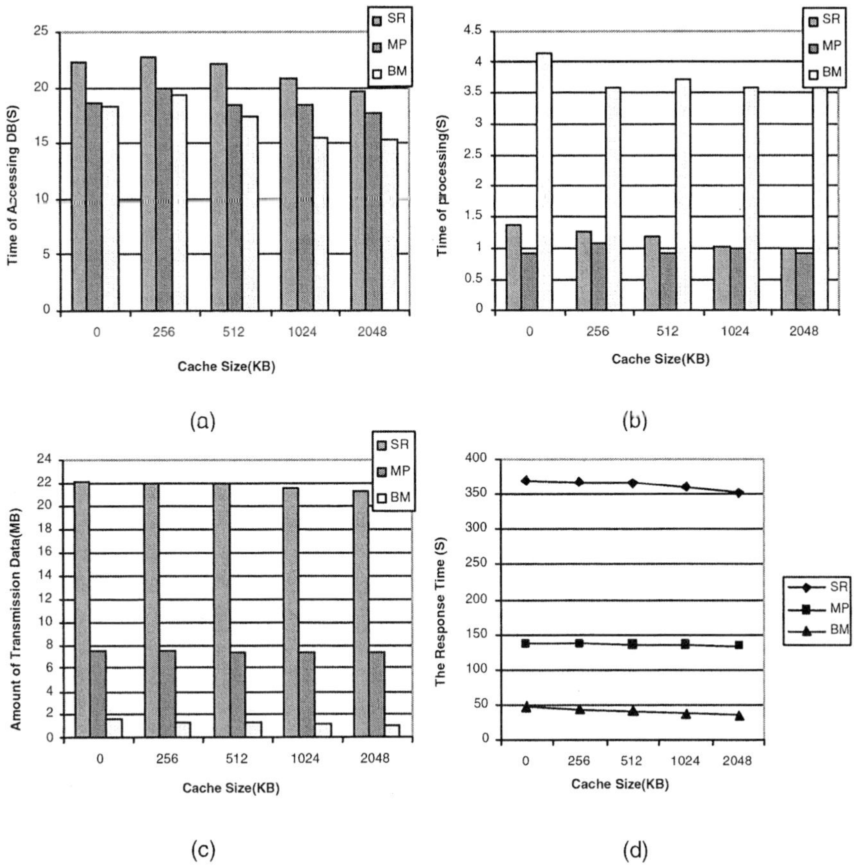

Fig. 5. Comparing SR, MP and BM

extent of zoom in, zoom out, pan is randomly generated. The area of the largest query window is 36% of the whole map, the smallest query window is 0.5%.

4.1 Three Different Data Organizations

We first study the performance of the three data organizations in database: *SR* (Single Resolution), *MP* (Multi-representation) and *BM* (Bit Map). In our experiments, data stored in *SR* require 33.438MB for storage and 152.313MB in *MP*, 21.501M in *BM*. All data in client cache are organized as polygons. The y-axis of figures in Figure 5 (a), (b), (c) and (d) are the time of accessing database, the time of processing data, the amount of transmission and the total response time respectively; the x-axes of the figures are the size of cache (0 means no cache). From figure 5(a) we can see that our proposed data model *BM* always has the least database accessing time, about 20% lower than that of *SR* and *MP* takes less time than *SR*. However, the difference of data accessing

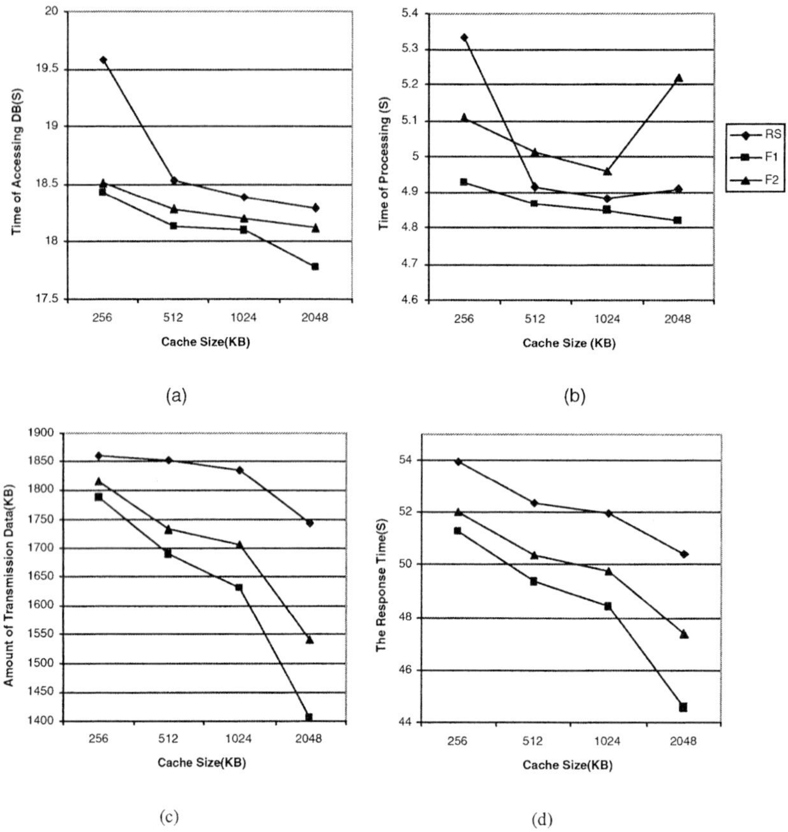

Fig. 6. Different schemes under BM

time between three data models is not so significant compared to the amount of data transmitted. Figure 5(b) demonstrates the time cost for data processing in client side. BM spends more time than SR and MP in data processing because it needs extra time for reconstruction. But data processing time has little effect on the whole performance as it is much less than the time cost for accessing database, which is nearly 10 times of the processing time. The most significant difference is the amount of data transmitted. Spatial data is more complex than aspatial data, there needs at least 20 MB data transmission in only 16 queries for SR. As SR always accesses data at the highest resolution, the amount is far more than other models. The amount of data transmitted for BM is the lest because it avoid the repeat farthest. Figure 5(d) shows the total response time with a quite high transmission speed at 512Kbps on the internet. Compared to Figure 5(c), we can see that the trend of three models are very similar in the amount of data transmission and total response time. That is because data transmission is the most time consuming stage for spatial queries which occupies around 95% of the total response time for SR, 80% for MP and 60% for BM respectively even in such a high transmission speed. Moreover, with limited transmission speed, the effect of other factor except the size of data transmission can even be ignored. Compared to two other kinds of data organization, BM achieves a great performance for spatial web-application.

4.2 Different Caching Schemes Under BM

We have also studied the performance of different caching schemes under BM which includes RS (reconstruction scheme), $F1$ (Fragment Scheme 1) and $F2$ (Fragment Scheme 2). From figure 6 we can see that $F1$ is the best scheme under various cache size with the least time of database accessing and the least amount of data transmission. Data processing only takes one fourth of the time of database accessing which is similar as in Figure 5. The total response time is mainly affected by the time of data transmission and the time of database access. To sum up, $F1$ is the best scheme for the whole performance with the least response time while RS is the worst. The response time for all curves tends to decrease with the cache size increasing. Moreover, data accessing becomes more important and has influence on the overall performance of all schemes under BM because of the minimum size of data transmission.

5 Conclusion

In this paper, we have investigated the effect of semantic caching on the performance of web based spatial applications. We have focused on three problems: data organization, query trimming and caching re-organization. By comparing three major measurements: database accessing time, data processing time and the amount of data transmission for three different data models under various client cache sizes, we found that with limited network transmission speed (less than 512Kbps), the amount of data transmission is the most dominant factor that affects the response time. Among the three models, BM outperforms the other two by a significant margin, which further improves with the cache size increasing. In order to achieve the optimal caching strategy, we have also constructed three different schemes for BM and tested their performance. Experimental results demonstrated that scheme $F1$ performs better than RS and $F2$ under various cache sizes.

Acknowledgment: The work reported in this paper has been partially supported by grant DP0345710 from the Australian Research Council. We thank Sham Prasher and David Horgan for many helps received from them during this project.

References

1. J. Cai, K.-L. Tan, and B. C. Ooi. On incremental cache coherency schemes in mobile computing environments. In *ICDE*, 1997.

2. B. Y. Chan, A. Si, and H. V. Leong. Cache management for mobile databases: Design and evaluation. In *ICDE*, 1998.
3. X. Chen, Y. Chen, and F. Rao. An efficient spatial publish/subscribe system for intelligent location-based services. In *2nd International Workshop on Distributed Event-Based Systems*, 2003.
4. S. Dar, M. J. Franklin, B. Jonsson, D. Srivastava, and M. Tan. Semantic data caching and replacement. In *VLDB*, 1996.
5. J. Gryz. Query folding with inclusion dependencies. In *ICDE*, 1998.
6. A. M. Keller and J. Basu. A predicate-based caching scheme for client-server database architectures. *The VLDB Journal*, 5(1):35–47, 1996.
7. J. Orenstein and T.H.Merrett. A class of data structures for associative searching. In *PODS*, pages 181–190, 1984.
8. W.-C. Peng and M.-S. Chen. Mining user moving patterns for personal data allocation in a mobile computing system. In *Proceedings of the 29th International Conference on Parallel Processing*, 2000.
9. X. Qian. Query folding. In *ICDE*, 1996.
10. Q. Ren and M. H. Dunham. Using semantic caching to manage location dependent data in mobile computing. In *Proceedings of the 6th annual International Conference on Mobile Computing and Networking*, pages 210 – 221, 2000.
11. S. Sun, S. Prasher, and X. Zhou. A scaleless data model for direct and progressive spatial query processing. In *The First International Workshop on Conceptual Modeling for GIS*, 2004.
12. J. F. Yao and M. H. Dunham. Caching management of mobile dbms. *Integrated Computer-Aided Engineering*, 8(2):151–169, 2001.
13. B. Zheng, J. Xu, and D. L. Lee. Cache invalidation and replacement strategies for location-dependent data in mobile environment. *IEEE Transactions on Computers*, 51(10):1141–1153, 2002.
14. X. Zhou, S. Prasher, S. Sun, and K. Xu. Multiresolution spatial databases: Making web-based spatial applications faster. In *Proceedings of Asia-Pacific Web Conference 2004*, pages 36–47, 2004.

Neural Network Hot Spot Prediction Algorithm for Shared Web Caching System

Jong Ho Park[1], Sung Chil Jung[2], Changlei Zhang[1], and Kil To Chong[1]

[1] Electronics and Information Engineering,
Chonbuk National University, Chonju, 561756, South Korea
{jhpark, zhangchanglei, kitchong}@chonbuk.ac.kr
[2] Research Engineer Commercial Vehicle Chassis Engineering Team,
R&D Division for Hyundai Motor Co. & Kia Motors Corp.
sungchil_jung@hotmail.com

Abstract. There are innumerable objects found on the Web. Both the popular objects that are requested frequently by the users and unpopular objects that are rarely requested exist. Hot spots are produced whenever huge numbers of objects are requested by the users. Often this situation produces excessive load on the cache server and original server, resulting in the system becoming a swamped state. Many problems arise, such as server refusals or slow operations. In this paper, a neural network prediction algorithm is suggested in order to solve the problems caused by the hot spot. The hot spot would be requested in the near future is prefetched to the proxy servers after the prediction of the hot spot; then the fast response for the users' requests and a higher efficiency for the proxy server can be achieved. The hot spots are obtained by analyzing the access logs file. A simulator is developed to validate the performance of the suggested algorithm, through which the hit rate improvement and the request among the shared proxy servers are load-balanced.

1 Introduction

A lot of objects on the Web present important information for users. Some of the objects are frequently requested by users, but there are huge numbers of objects that are rarely requested. Generally, a request pattern of web documents followed Zipf's law [1-3]. A frequently requested object by users is called a 'hot spot'. It forms 90% of the total amounts of request by the 10% of hot spots that hold a high rank for Web server [2] and forms 70% of the total requests by the 25 $\sim$ 40% of hot spots that hold a high rank in the case of a Proxy server [3]. These hot spots will cause problems. That is, a server that is requested by sudden huge hot spots not only transfers information within a short time to users, but it also will make the functions of the server perfectly stop due to a huge amount of traffic.

In order to solve these problems, a proxy-cache is used in which caching plays an important role in an effective and efficiency transmission of data in the Internet. The cache can quickly supply a cached object to users even though an excessive load will be applied to the original server, and network lies in a very congested state. In the case of requesting a cached object, it will reduce

Y. Zhang et al. (Eds.): APWeb 2005, LNCS 3399, pp. 795–806, 2005.

consumption of the source of server and amount of works in server or network so that it give a favor for all the users.

A consistent hashing method [8] that is used to map URL (Uniform Resource Locator) in the shared proxies in a distributed web caching uses a hash routing method. This method improves the existing hashing methods [4] that largely affected by the increase or decrease of the proxy and maps URL without any effects from the increase or decrease of the proxy.

An internal cache communication protocol has a various kind, such as the ICP, CARP, and so on. The squid server uses the CARP [5] to make a load balancing. There are many studies [6] proposed to use a DNS (Domain Name Server) to make a load balancing. However, the load balancing is not considered in the previously investigated results of the studies for the shared proxies from the viewpoint of hot spot.

A replication method is proposed to replicate the hot spot to other shared proxies using an adaptive controlled replication method [7] applied by a hash routing in the results of studies in recent years. At this time, it is divided into two spaces, such as a space that will store hot spots from other proxies, and another space that will store the objects, which are assigned to its own cache.

In this process, it is considered that controlling the space that will store hot spots replicated from other proxies to its own cache will maximize the efficiency of a proxy. However, there are some problems that the traffic increased by the increment in the amount of objects brought by the replication and some replicated objects will be thrown away because of no requests.

This study configures a distributed caching system based on a consistent hashing algorithm. This will supply directly the request objects by requesting for the cache that is stored by using a hash routing. The characteristic of the proposed method performs a prefetch by estimating whether a hot spot will be required in the future. A prediction model using a neural network that is useful to build a time series modeling is obtained after analyzing the request patterns of the proxy access log files and estimates hot spots that will occur in the future. For the estimated hot spots, it is possible to improve the system performance by applying a prefetch to the proxy that has a low level load using the load information for each proxy as follows.

- *It makes short the service time for the request of hot spot by prefetching hot spots to the proxy.*
- *The efficiency of the proxy will increase by distributing hot spots to the shared proxy.*
- *The quality of service will increase due to the increase in the hit rate for the request of users.*

2 Configurations of the Simulator

2.1 Network System

A caching system proposed in this paper adopted a Global Hosting System (GHS) [9] and was applied by round-robin DNS method. A global hosting system is presented in Figure 1 and the processes for the response are as follows. First of all, let us assumed that users already know the IP of the Content Provider (CP). If a user requests a web page to the CP using process 1, the CP will provide a text that is included in HTML. In addition, it will supply an embedded object like images or media files that are included in other documents using a proxy that is located near the user. That is, if a user requests an HTML page, the CP will send a page that includes the embedded object URLs instead of a typical page. At this time, a user creates a new embedded object URL by hashing the embedded object URLs that are received by using a script and connects to the local DNS through process 2 in order to find the proxy IP that includes the new embedded object URLs. The upper level DNS decides the locations of users in network through process 3. In addition, it makes a connection to the lower level DNS that is located near the user by using a function of the domain delegation. Here, the lower level DNS provides the proxy IP address where the embedded objects are mapped by using a consistent hashing method through process 4. In addition, the embedded objects will be requested by connecting the proxy IP address that is provided in process 5. If the requested materials exist, the proxy will supply the embedded objects. Otherwise, the proxy server requests the embedded objects again to the server through process 6. Furthermore, the proxy server supplies it to the user and stores it in its own cache.

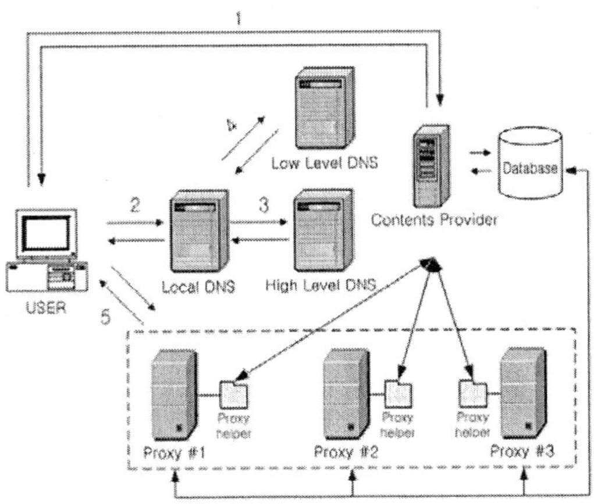

Fig. 1. Verification results of the neural network

The method proposed in this paper estimates hot spots in advance and applies the load balancing using the round-robin method to each proxy for the estimated hot spots. A global hosting system (GHS) has a drawback in which a certain proxy will be swamped because of requests for a certain proxy due to hot spots. However, this study introduces a process for analyzing the dynamic characteristic of hot spots and for estimating in advance through process 6 presented in Figure 1. At this time, the prefetch will be performed according to priority of the low load proxy using the load information for each proxy that were obtained from the proxyhelper of the shared proxy.

2.2 Computer Simulation

A simulator was configured to simulate the system proposed in the previous section using the PERL language. The simulator was built by using a modular method to make an easy modification and management. The performance test for a web caching system will be operated by the various settings, such as the numbers of proxies, memory size of the queue, and processing time. A cache policy for the memory that is related to the storing space of the proxy [13] is applied by the LRU (Least Recently Used) method. A service policy for the proxy server will follow the FIFO scheme. The processing speed of the proxy can be controlled by the option of *process_time* in the program, and it means the time used to process a single object. Moreover, the parameter of *process_time* used in the program is also applied to present the time to process single data. That is, the parameter of *real_process_time* can be produced by applying the calculations in which the total objects that are requested for a constant period of time are divided by the time required. In the case of *process_time* > *real_process_time*, there is no miss because the performance of the proxy can sufficiently handle the requested services. However, in the case of *process_time* < *real_process_time*, a miss exists because the request is not processed by the time delay. Moreover, if the data that is stored in a queue of the proxy is requested, it will be processed as a hit. Otherwise, it will be recorded as a miss.

For the simulation process, first of all, the options are set in the execution file of Test. The hashing is performed by the MD5 [10] for the objects that come from the Web module. In addition, the hashed objects will be stored in the selected proxy using a consistent hashing. The load conditions for each proxy will be checked by the proxyhelper every 30 minutes in order to perform the load distribution for the request of the shared proxy.

The subroutine of run in the Virtual module plays a role in the main function and processes all objects. First, the Dns module hashes the objects using the MD5 and assigns it to the 1000 virtual caches that are charged by each proxy. Then, the proxy ID of the hashed object will be decided. If the requested object is a hot spot, the load balancing will be performed. Moreover, in the case of an object that is not a hot spot is requested, the assignment is achieved by the virtual caches that are hashed by the MD5.

2.3 Prefetch Method

The load information of the shared proxies will be collected by the proxyhelper presented in Figure 1 in order to prefetch the estimated hot spots to the shared proxies using a neural network model. At this time, the original server decides how many proxies will be used and which proxies will be used to prefetch the hot spots. Although the numbers of proxies are decided by the optimal method, various numbers of the proxies are decided through several additional simulations to analyze the system proposed in this study. In addition, the issue that which proxy is to be used to prefetch is solved by the order of the proxy that has a low load using the load information of each proxy.

3 Collection of the Test Data

An experimental data produced by analyzing the access logs file from the NASA server. Let us consider the analyzing method of the access logs file, producing an experimental data and its characteristics that are used in the prediction process of hot spots.

3.1 Analyzing the Access Logs Files from the NASA Server

The access logs file records all processes performed by the server. If user contacts to the server, all related information for the work are stored in an access logs file. That is, if a user requests a particular web page, the server will access all objects that are related to the web pages. In addition, all the processes to handle the requested objects will be stored in the access logs file not only the web pages that the users requested, but also the image files, linked data, and various other information. Therefore, it becomes an important information that shows the objective of the site visiting based on the data, which includes the numbers of requested data, contact times, numbers of the visitors, and routes of the visiting through the analyzing of the access logs file. Moreover, it stores the request for the processes of the server and its success or failure. In the case of failure, the information to solve the problem is stored in it.

The access logs file from the NASA server used in this study has recorded the information as follows.

in24.inetnebr.com - - [01/Aug/1995:00:00:01 -0400] "GET /shuttle/missions/ sts-68/news/sts-68-mcc-05.txt HTTP/1.0" 200 1839.

The record shown above consists of seven kinds of information, such as host, verification, user approval, time, request HTTP, state code, and amounts of transmission by the order of its record. This study extracts the request time and HTTP among the information of the log files and uses it as a data to estimate hot spots.

3.2 Producing an Experimental Data

A pattern for the request of the extracted data is verified by analyzing the access logs file from the NASA server follows Zipf's law. However, the results are not suited to the objective of this study that will improve the performance of the system for the state in which hot spots increase rapidly because the amount of the request for hot spots is very low. Therefore, this study produces a proper experimental data for the characteristics of this study using the Surge program [11] as a load generator that was developed in Boston University. Although the production of data was achieved by the same amount of the requested amount in the period of time request for the access logs file of the NASA server, the experimental data was produced by the execution of the Surge program to request much higher than that of the general request of data for the amount of requests for hot spots.

4 Hot Spot Prediction Neural Network Modeling

A hot spot prediction can be performed by analyzing some objects that have a high frequency of requests in the access logs file of a particular proxy. A prediction for the future request will be processed by using the existing amount of requests for hot spots from the information obtained from the objects being analyzed. A time series method using a multilayer perceptron neural network is applied as a prediction method.

This study applies the Levenberg-Marquardt method [12] as a learning method to minimize the sum of the square of error. This learning method has a merit that it converges faster than that of the Backpropagation method, which uses a gradient descent method, due to the use of a second-order method. This paper selects 4 nodes for the input layer, 8 nodes for the hidden layer, and 1 node for the output layer for the neural network model. In addition, the gradient of the activation function was applied by the value of 2. The learning was performed by scaling the values of $0.01 \sim 0.99$ for all pattern inputs.

The upper one shown in Figure 2 presents the results of the learning of experimental data and lower one shows the error values for each input pattern. Figure 3 presents the results of the requested amounts of hot spots and actual requested amounts of hot spots using the neural network. This process shows the results of the verification stage of a neural network modeling, and the data used in this process was not used in the learning process. The amounts of the requests presented in the figures are the converted values of the amounts of the

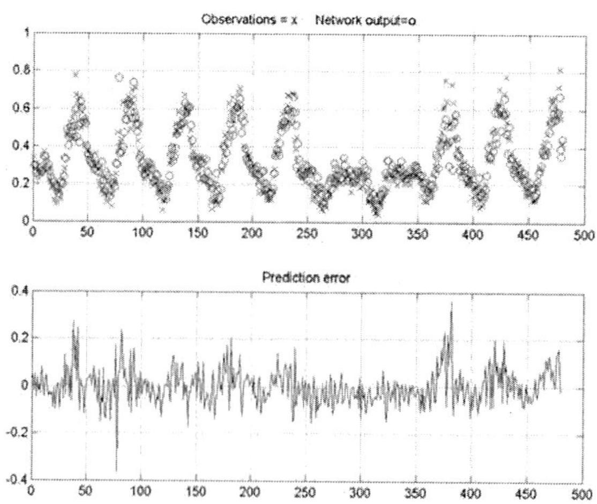

Fig. 2. Results of the learning of the neural network and modeling errors

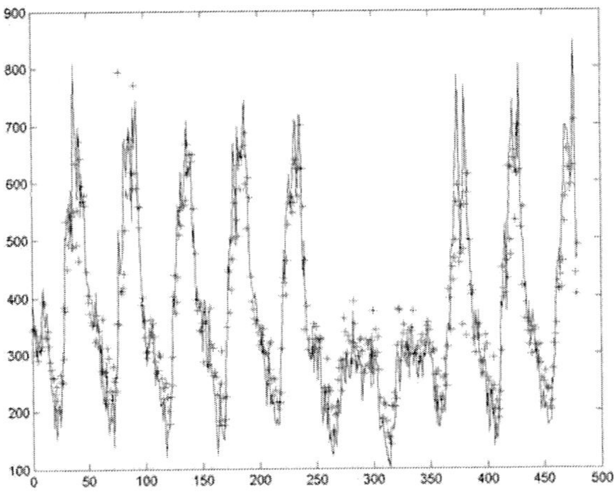

Fig. 3. Verification results of the neural network

requests for the output of the neural network that was previously scaled. The solid line shown in the figures presents the amounts of the request, the values marked by + are the amounts of the request for the predicted hot spots by using the neural network. The error rate between the two requests is 8.7%. It can be seen that the neural network modeling is good for considering the characteristics of the system.

5 Simulation for the Performance Evaluation

The prediction of hot spots will be performed by using the neural network prediction model as previously produced in Chapter 4. In addition, this paper compares the prefetching method that distributes the expected hot spots to the web caches in advance for the load distribution method proposed in this study with the existing consistent hashing method through a computer simulation. The simulator that was configured in Chapter 2 will be used to the simulation. In addition, the configurations for a load balancing and various web caching are also investigated.

5.1 Performance Evaluation for the Load Balancing

For the performance evaluation, this study compares the round-robin method using a DNS, which is based on the consistent hashing method, and the load balancing method using a hot spot prediction proposed in this paper. Figure 4 illustrates the standard deviation for the loads that are requested by the proxies when the loads are distributed to several shared proxies. Moreover, the numbers of hot spots that are to be distributed and numbers of proxies that are to be prefetched are considered as the parameters in the simulation. For the distribution of hot spots, the tests were performed by various methods of the distributed prefetch in which the largest numbers of requests for hot spots were applied to multiple proxy servers that have the smallest load, and more than one hot spot was also applied to multiple proxy servers. As shown in the figure, the x-axis means the various methods used in the test, that is, it presents numbers of simulations by using a particular distribution method. The y-axis presents the standard deviation of load that is applied to the proxy. That is, the simulation was performed using various distribution methods for the 14 different cases as

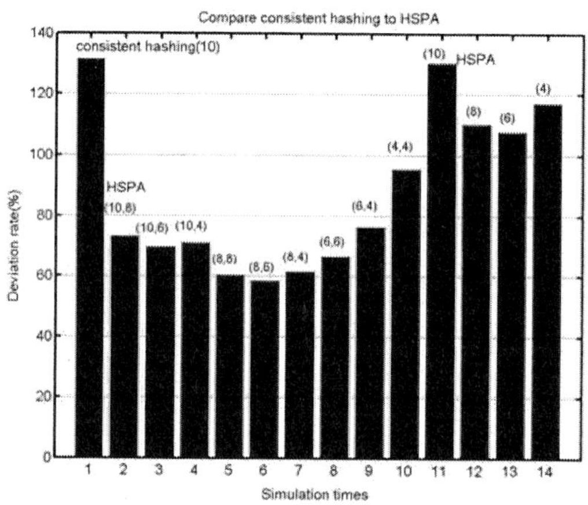

Fig. 4. Deviations for the request applied to the distribution proxy

presented in the figure. As presented in the graph, the consistent hashing (10) means that hot spots are distributed to 10 proxies in the consistent hashing method, and HSPA (10,10) means that the two hot spots that have the highest frequency are distributed to each of the 10 proxies respectively using the HSPA algorithm. That is, a hot spot that has the highest frequency will be distributed to 10 proxies and that has the second highest frequency will also be applied to another 10 proxies. In this paper, a hot spot that has the highest frequency will be expressed by HS(1) and the second one will be expressed by HS(2). From the results of the simulation, it can be seen that the load distribution will be performed more smoothly up to two hot spots than that of one hot spot. In addition, in the case of the distribution for two hot spots, it shows the highest performance in the load distribution that the HS(1) is applied to 8 proxies and HS(2) applied to 6 proxies. In the case of the distribution of multiple hot spots, therefore, it can be seen that the performance of the whole system will be affected according to the methods of the combination between numbers of the distributed proxies and hot spots.

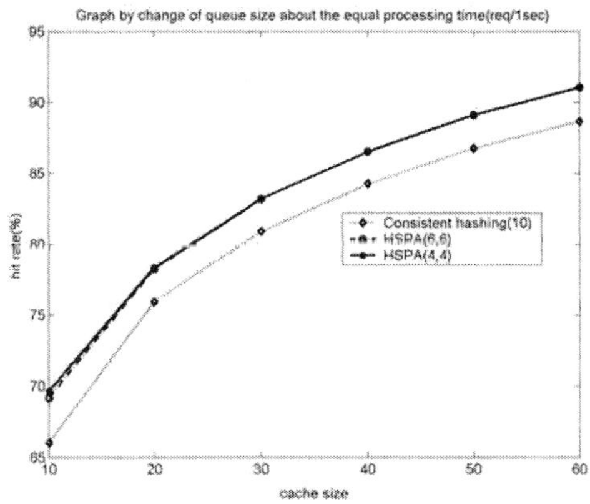

Fig. 5. Hit rates for the fast processing speed of the proxy (req/1 sec)

5.2 Performance Evaluation for the Hit Rate

A comparison for the performances of the load balancing for the consistent hashing method and HSPA method was presented in the previous section. In order to examine the performance of the hit rate that is important for the performance of a web caching system, a test was applied to the two hot spots by combining various processing speeds of the server and cache sizes. The tests were applied to the proxies that have 1 second and 12 seconds respectively for the time required to process for one request. Figures 5 and 6 present the results of the distribution of the 10 proxies using the existing consistent hashing method and the suggested method of the hit rates according to the processing speed and load information of each proxy for the distribution of the two hot spots.

Figure 5 presents the simulation results for the proxy server that has 1 second for the time required to process for one request by the distribution of 10 proxies using the consistent hashing method and of 6 or 4 proxies using the proposed HSPA method. As a result, it is verified that the distribution of two hot spots for the shared proxies shows a higher hit rate than that of the load balancing method by the distribution of one hot spot. Moreover, it can be seen that the HSPA method shows the increase in the hit rate on the average compared with the consistent hashing method. From the results of various tests, the highest hit rate of the distributed fetch can be produced by the 6 proxies for the HS(1) and the same proxies for the HS(2).

Figure 6 presents the simulation results for the proxy server that has 12 seconds for the time required to process for one request by the distribution of 10 proxies using the consistent hashing method and of 8 proxies using the proposed HSPA method. In this test, it presents the highest hit rate of the distributed patch in the case of the 8 proxies for the HS(1) and the same proxies for the HS(2). The HSPA method proposed in this study shows a higher hit rate than that of the consistent hashing method.

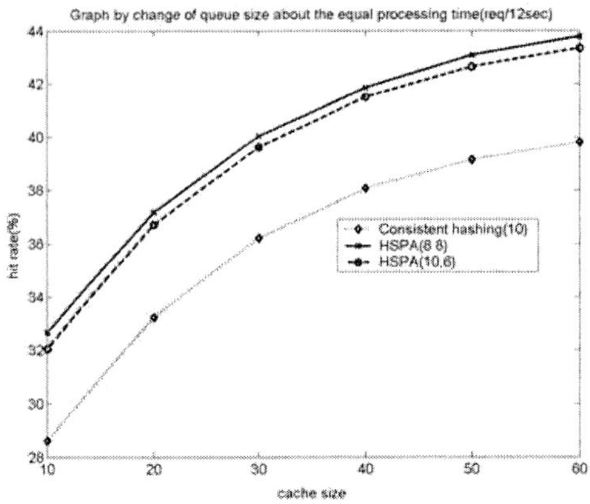

Fig. 6. Hit rates for the slow processing speed of the proxy (req/12 secs)

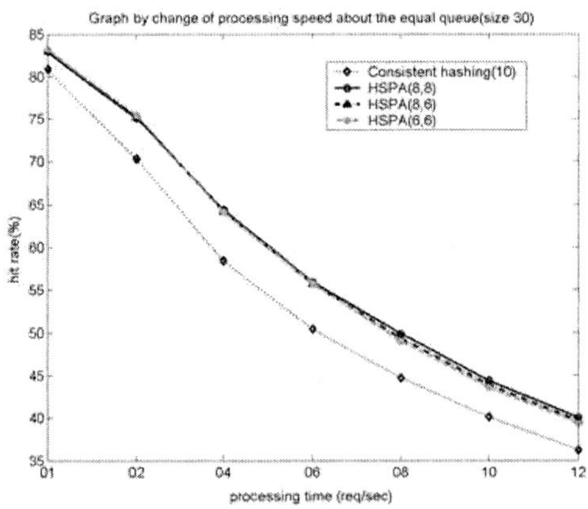

Fig. 7. Hit rates for the same queue size of the distributed proxy

Figure 7 shows the hit rates for the test that was applied to the same queue size of the distribution proxy. The load distribution was applied to two hot spots in which the HS(1) that was distributed by 4 proxy servers and HS(2) that was also distributed by 4 proxy servers. A server that has the fast processing speed in the HSPA method shows the highest hit rate. For the slow processing speed, the highest hit rate can be obtained by the distribution of 8 proxies for HS(1) and HS(2) respectively.

It can be seen that the optimal numbers of the proxies obtained by the test can be verified by the overall characteristics for the distributed web caching system. That is, numbers of the distributed proxies will decrease in the case of the small amount of work and fast processing speed. On the other hand, in the case of the large amount of work and slow processing speed, hot spots will be distributed to several proxies.

6 Conclusions

This paper investigated the problems that are caused by hot spots in a distributed web caching system and proposed the HSPA method that increases the performance of the load balancing and hit rate in a distributed web proxy system. The HSPA method produces a prediction model, which will predict hot spots possibly requested in the future. In addition, it will distribute a congestion of the request that will be caused by the expected hot spots in the future to the present proxy that has a low load by the prefetch using a prediction model. In order to verify the performance of the method proposed in this study, a test that includes a neural network modeling, configuration of the simulator system, consisting of the request data, load balancing, and performance of the hit rate was applied. Moreover, the consistent hashing algorithm used in the present method was implemented to compare the performance of the proposed system.

It can be verified that the load balancing of the HSPA algorithms proposed by the load balancing test was better than that of the consistent hashing algorithm. For the test of the hit rate, in addition, it was investigated that the HSPA algorithm proposed by this study was better than the existing method by comparing the consistent hashing method in which the queue size that is the capacity of a processing speed and memory storage in the performance of a proxy server was decided differently. As a result, a hot spot prediction algorithm proposed in this study will increase the hit rate and application of the shared proxies for the distribution system.

Acknowledgements. The authors thank KEPCO R-2004-B-120 and RRC (KOSEF) R-12-1998-026-02003 for their financial support.

References

1. M. Arlitt and C. Williamson: Web Server Workload Characterization: The Search for Invariants., ACM SIGMETRICS 96, (1996).
2. Lee Breslau *et al.*: Web Caching and Zipf-like Distributions: Evidence and Implications., IEEE INFOCOM, (1999).
3. Yantai Shu *et al.*: Intelligent Proxy Techniques in Plasma physics Laboratories., Real Time Conference, 1999. Santa Fe 1999. 11th IEEE NPSS, 14-18 June (1999), 338-341.
4. K.W. Ross: Hash-routing for collections of shared web caches, IEEE Network Magazine, (1997), 34-44.
5. O. Pearson: Squid: A user's guide., available at http://www.squid-cache.org/, (2000).
6. M. Colajanni, P.S. Yu, and D. Dias: Analysis of task assignment policies in scalable distributed web-server system., vol. 9, no. 6. IEEE Trans. on Parallel and Distributed Systems, (1998), 585-600.
7. Kun-Lung Wu, Philps S. Yu: Replication for Load Balancing and Hot-Spot Relief on Proxy Web Caches with Hash Routing., 2003 Kluwer Academic Publishers, vol.13. Distributed and Parallel Databases, (2003), 203-220.

8. David Karger *et al*: Web Caching with Consistent Hashing., In Proceedings of the 8th International World Wide Web Conference, (1999).
9. Leighton *et al.*: Global hosting system., united states patent & trademark office, august 22, (2000).
10. R. Rivest: The MD5 Message-Digest Algorithm., RFC 1321, Network Working Group, April (1992).
11. P. Barford and M.E. Crovella: Generating representative web workloads for network and server performance evaluation., In Proceedings of ACM SIGMETRICS Conference, (1998), 151-160.
12. Saini, L.M., Soni, M.K: Artificial neural network based peak load forecasting using Levenberg-Marquardt and quasi-Newton methods., Generation, vol.149. Transmission and Distribution, IEE Proceedings, Sept. (2002), 578-584.
13. Woei-Luen Shyu and Cheng-Shong Wu it et al.: Efficiency analyses on routing cache replacement algorithms., Communications, vol.4. ICC 2002. IEEE International Conference, (2002), 2232-2236.

A Common Application-Centric QoS Model for Selecting Optimal Grid Services[1]

Derong Shen, Ge Yu, Tiezheng Nie, and Zhibin Zhao

Dept. of Computer, Northeastern University, Shenyang, 110004, China
{Shendr, yuge}@mail.neu.edu.cn

Abstract. Application-centric QoS (AQoS) model is needed for evaluating semantic equivalent Grid Services in an application-oriented service Grid. Previous related researches on QoS mainly are for resource allocation in computing Grids or for evaluating Web Services. Their approaches are not suitable for evaluating Grid Services and no common AQoS models are defined. According to the characteristics of Grid Services, an AQoS model named as GS_AQoS for Grid Services is proposed, which consists of evaluation factors, evaluation modes and constraints. By analyzing the differences between AQoS for Grid Services and ordinary QoS for Web Services, factors suitable for GS_AQoS are defined, and three types of evaluation modes summarized on applications' needs are addressed in detail. At last, a Grid Services for manufacturing parts is used as an example, by simulation experiments, the availability of GS_AQoS is verified, and some suggestions are given.

1 Introduction

Grid Services [1](GSs) are Web services following the OGSA specification, and the Service Grid is a service system for providing more powerful services for customers by integrating Grid Services. With Service Grid technology developing, a challenge for Service Grid is how to provide services with better performance to customers. Currently, related researches on QoS are for resource allocation in Grid system [2-8] or for Web services [9-17], the former focus on the infrastructure such as CPU, memory, network bandwidth, and typically are the study on resource allocation-centric QoS, the latter focuses on the study of application-centric QoS. For simplification, in this paper, we denote them as Resource QoS(RQoS) and Application QoS(AQoS) respectively. RQoS is usually discussed in Grid computing, but it is not suitable for Grid Services with service-oriented property, while, even though the QoS of Web Services and the QoS of Grid Services are typically AQoS, But the QoS of Web Services is not suitable completely to evaluate the QoS of Grid Services since their supporting technologies are not the same.

---

[1] This research is supported by the National High-Tech Development Program (2003AA414210), the National Science Foundation (60173051).

Y. Zhang et al. (Eds.): APWeb 2005, LNCS 3399, pp. 807 – 819, 2005.

In [9-17], the QoS of Web Services focus on AQoS, and based on these researches, a QoS model [9] is proposed for evaluating semantic equivalent Web Services, and the availability of the QoS is verified. But the supporting technology of stateless Web Services is not the same as that of stateful Grid Services. The researches [2-5] on QoS in computing Grid typically are GARA [3], GARA discusses the resource reservation based on capability of network, processors and storage devices, and gives some guidance to related researches, but it does not discuss how to coordinate resources belonged to different owners. To overcome shortage of GARA, Rashid Al-Ali[6-8] in Cardiff University discussed the presentation schema of QoS, the process for coordinating resources and the SLA[18] of resources further, and their typical framework are G-QoSM, in which, its architecture, how to coordinate and discover resources are addressed and RQoS are focused on. GM-QoS[11] is presented by Shang Hai University based on AQoS, it only discusses the AQoS model suitable for manufacturing grids and is not a common AQoS model.

This paper focuses on AQoS and proposed a common AQoS model named GS_QoS for evaluating Grid Services. The formal definition of GS_AQoS is given and the evaluation factors and the evaluation modes are addressed in detail. At last, in order to validate the availability of GS_AQoS and recommend some usable suggestions, some simulation experiments are made.

2 Design of GS_AQoS Model

In general, a model consists of structural constitutions, behaviors and constraints. According to the characteristics of Grid Services, GS_AQoS model also includes three parts: (1) factors for evaluating Grid Services and their formulas. (2) Evaluation modes supporting for applications' needs, namely evaluation algorithms provided based on evaluation factors. (3) Constraints on evaluation factors. Based on the three parts included in GS_AQoS model, the formal definition of GS_AQoS is given in the followings.

Definition 1. GS_AQoS={FN,OP,CS}, where,

(1) $FN=\{fn_i(a_i,b_i)|a_i \in A \wedge b_i \in B \wedge 1 \le i \le n\}$, where FN represents the set of evaluation factors and their formulas, $A=\{a_1,a_2,\ldots,a_n\}$ represents the set of evaluation factors, $B=\{b_1,b_2,\ldots,b_n\}$ represents the set of business entities providing the information of A. $fn_i(a_i,b_i)$ represents the definition rules about a_i, its formula is unique given according to b_i, but there may be some differences among different domains.

(2) $OP=\{op_1,op_2,\ldots,op_m\}$ represents the set of evaluation modes provided for customers in a application. For example, *OP={AQoS_relation_sort, AQoS_value_range, AQoS_value_Integration}*, which is described in section 2.2.

(3) $CS=\{cs_1,cs_2,\ldots,cs_m\}$ represents the constraints on evaluation factors in GS_AQoS.

According to the definition of GS_AQoS above, it's XML scheme is described as Fig.1, where, AQoS_Attribute is used to describe the evaluation factors, and BusinessEntity is used to describe the business entity that provides basic information of factors, AQoS_SLA represents the evaluation modes provided, each evaluation mode has its relevant evaluation algorithm. Since the definition rules of evaluation factors are transparent to users, they are not included in the XML scheme of GS_AQoS. The information provided by customers following the XML schema is stored in Shunsaku Data Manager developed by FUJITSU.

Next, we will address the formulas of evaluation factors and the evaluation modes in GS_AQoS.

```
<xsd:schema xmlns:xsd="http://www.w3.org/2001/XMLSchema">
        <xsd:element name="GS_AQoS" type="AQoS_Type"/>
        <xsd:element name="AQoS_Attribte">
            <xsd: complexType>
                <xsd: sequence>
                <xsd:element name="AttributeName" type="string">
                <xsd:element name="Description" type="string">
                <xsd:element name="AttributeValue" type="string">
                <xsd:element name="ValueUnit" type="string">
                <xsd:element name="Direction" type="string">
                <xsd:element name=" BusinessEntity" type="string"/>
                </ xsd: sequence>
            </xsd: complexType>
      <xsd:element name="AQoS_SLA" type="string"/>
</xsd: schema >
```

Fig. 1. The XML Scheme of GS_AQoS

2.1 Evaluation Factors in GS_AQoS

The evaluation factors belonged to GS_AQoS of different domains may be more different. Nevertheless, some common features can be summarized. In order to designate the evaluation factors in GS_AQoS for evaluating Grid Services efficiently, by discussing the difference between Grid Services and Web Services as well as the difference between computing grids and service grids, we give the following discussions:(1) Network bandwidth cannot be given a guarantee in current Internet environment, and existing researches are all restricted in private networks. But in the future, for the Internet supporting Ipv6, network bandwidth will play an important role in GS_AQoS. (2) Service-oriented Grid Services needs limited or little information to be transferred, so in stable network environment, the transmitting cost can be omitted, especially for non just-in-time Grid Services. (3) According to Grid Services, users always care much for the total responding time and the result of Grid Services, so the major factors for allocating resource in computing grids, such as CPU process capability and storage capability, are not considered as important evaluation factors of GS_AQoS. (4) Grid Services provide flexible information exchange mechanism, selecting broker can allocate an available Grid Service based on the information subscribed. So, Reliability that is much more important in QoS of Web Services is not included in GS_AQoS of Grid Services. (5) The Reputation is not needed since grid system provides services for customers transparently.

Based on the discussions above, it is sure that the factors of GS_AQoS for evaluating Grid Services at least include Price and Responding Time, and Fidelity can be considered as their supplement. While, other factors should be designated on special domain's demand.

Usually, Price is provided by service provider, and Responding Time and Fidelity are calculated by monitor broker for giving creditability to customers, of course, it can be given by service provider also. Here, Price, Responding Time and Fidelity are described as following:

Responding Time(T_i^p and T_i). Responding Time is the interval from the start time of a request sent to the time responding results returned, T_i^p represents the information with unique value provided by service provider, and T_i is provided by monitor broker and denoted as:

$$T_i=(\sum_{j=1}^{n} T_i^j)/n \tag{1}$$

Where, T_i^j is the Responding Time of GS_i invoked for the *jth* time, *n* is the total invoked number of GS_i invoked, when Fidelity is higher, T_i^p can be used as the information of Responding Time.

Price(*P*). Service provider provides Price.

Fidelity(*F*). Fidelity represents the promise given by service provider, which is usually monitored by monitor broker, the faith is broken if the real Responding Time exceeds that promised by service provider, in order to keep consistent linear trend with other factors, it is denoted as:

$$F=No/n \tag{2}$$

Where, *n* is the total invoked number, and *No* is the times that the faith is broken.

2.2 Evaluation Modes in GS_AQoS

According to customers' requirements, the modes for selecting Grid Services are summarized as three types: (1) one factor is emphasized. (2) The ranges of values are satisfied. (3) Integrated performance is emphasized. Therefore, in GS_AQoS model, corresponding three types of modes are provided, namely AQoS_relation_sort, AQoS_value_range and AQoS_value_integration. Customers can apply one of them to select Grid Services with better performance, which is named as the best set of Grid Services, abbreviated as GS_Best. Let GS_S=$\{GS_1, GS_2,\ldots,GS_n\}$ represents the set of Grid Services, $n>1$. $A=\{a_1,a_2,\ldots,a_m\}$ represents the set of evaluation factors in GS_AQoS, a_i^j is the value of *jth* evaluation factor of GS_i. $M_{AQoS}=\begin{bmatrix} a_1^1 & a_1^2 & \cdots & a_1^m \\ a_2^1 & a_2^2 & \cdots & a_2^m \\ \cdots & \cdots & \cdots & \cdots \\ a_n^1 & a_n^2 & \cdots & a_n^m \end{bmatrix}$ is the matrix made up of factors' values of GSs. In the followings, we will give the definitions of GS_Best according to these three evaluation modes respectively.

(1) AQoS_relation_sort Mode. Suppose the most important factor a_k is given by customers, then selecting broker selects Grid Services with optimal a_k, denoted as:

Definition 2. Let $A_k=\{a_1^k,\ldots, a_n^k\}$, then GS_Best=$\{GS_i | a_i^k = Best(A_k) \wedge GS_i \in GS\_S\}$. Where, $m>1$, $n>1$, $t<m$, $Best(A_k)$ represents that the optimal a_i^k is selected from A_k, and the GS_Best is the set of Grid Services with optimal a_k. For example, if a_k is Price, then $Best(A_k)=Min(A_k)$, and GS_Best is the set of Grid Services with lower Price.

(2) AQoS_value_range Mode. GS_AQoS information of Grid Services selected will be in the range of values of that needed by customers, denoted as:

Definition 3. GS_Best=$\{GS_i | \ a_i^j \in [L_i^j,U_i^j] \wedge \ j=1..m \wedge GS_i \in GS\_S\}$. Where, 1<i<n, $[L_i^j,U_i^j]$ represents the range of value of factor a_j of GS_i, where L_i^j is the lowest threshold, and U_i^j is the upper threshold. If the value of a factor is lower then U_i^j, then L_i^j is assigned to 0, while, if the value of a factor is higher then L_i^j, then ∞ is assigned to U_i^j.

(3) AQoS_value_integration Mode. Space vector distance is adopted to evaluate the integrated performance of Grid Services.

Firstly, evaluation factors are defined as the dimensions of space vector distance, and a threshold point is developed based on customers' demand on Grid Services. Secondly, in order to improve the capability of processing, a subset of all the semantic equivalent Grid Services are produced by simple predicates such as "larger than" or "less than". Thirdly, each Grid Service in the subset will produce an AQoS point based on their GS_AQoS information. Fourthly, the space vector distances between the AQoS points and the threshold point are calculated respectively for ordering the semantic equivalent Grid Services by their performance, and the higher the distance of a Grid Service is, the better its integrated performance is. But before calculating the distance, all of the values of factors should be converted into the same range of quantity, to do this, the following approach is adopted: First, Let $P_t=(a_t^1,a_t^2,\ldots,a_t^n)$ represents the threshold point based on the customers' requirements, then mapping the $(a_t^1,a_t^2,\ldots,a_t^n)$ into $(1,1,\ldots,1,1)$, second, let $P_i=(a_i^1,a_i^2,\ldots,a_i^n)$ be the AQoS point of GS_i, and $m_i=1/a_t^j$, then $a_i^j=a_i^j * m_i$. So, the formal definition is denoted as following:

Definition 4. Suppose, D_i is the space distance between P_t and P_i, then $D_i = \sqrt{\sum_{j=1}^{n}((a_i^j - a_t^j)w_j)^2}$, where, w_j is the weight of *jth* dimension, a_i^j and a_t^j are the factor values in range of the same quantity. Let D=$\{D_1, D_2,\ldots,D_n\}$, then GS_Best=$\{GS_i | D_i \in Max(D) \wedge GS_i \in GS\_S\}$.

In GS_AQoS application, two steps are adopted, (1) based on the modes discussed above, GS_Best are obtained first, (2) according to the criteria of load balance, the best resource is reserved based on RQoS efficiently.

In the following, we will give some simulation experiments based on GS_AQoS instance to verify availability and efficiency of GS_AQoS model.

3 Validation of GS_AQoS Model

In this section, we present the simulation experiments to evaluate the proposed approach. First, we will give the experiment scenario, and then some tests are done and deduce some conclusions.

3.1 Scenario

GS_AQoS model is applied in e-SGS prototype[19]. The processing of jobs are: (1) Local Broker receives jobs integrated by multi-Grid Services, and (2) sends the jobs' requirements to Selecting Broker, then (3) optimal Grid services are selected based on AQoS and RQoS models and put them into a Services list. (4) Engine Broker finishes the execution process of the job based on the Services lists and records the running information about the Grid Services invoked. Here, a manufacturing grid as an instance is used to validate GS_AQoS model, the integrated job is shown in Fig.2, in which, a GS_AQoS named GS_MAQoS suitable for GS_2 is as a sample to do the simulation experiments. The experiment results can be extended to the multi-Grid Services in an integrated job yet, to evaluate the Integrated Performance of job instances.

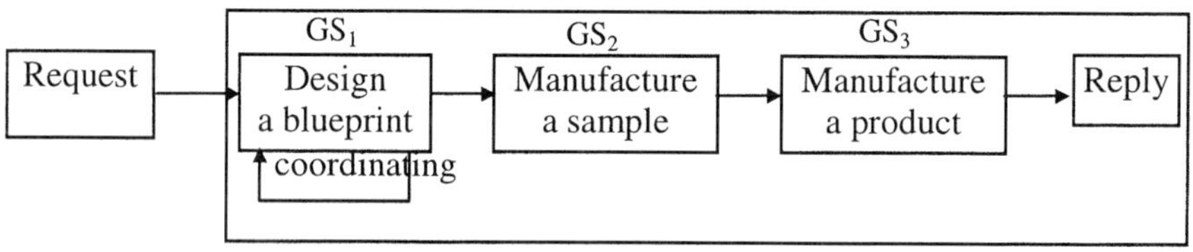

Fig. 2. A Manufacturing Process Flow

Suppose there are 10 semantic equivalent Grid Services to GS_2, and service providers have provided GS_MAQoS information namely Price(P), Quality(Q), Responding Time(T) and Fidelity(F), where, P and Q are provided by service providers, T and F are given by monitor broker. The definition rules of P, T, F and the evaluation modes are the same as those definitions above, and the constraints are empty. Q is a given evaluation factor provided by service provider for the manufacturing grid to describe the tolerance of the parts manufactured by GS_2. In the sample of GS_2, of course, monitor broker can collect it. Suppose, the 10 semantic equivalent Grid Services are all satisfying the function requirements of GS_2, and based on their GS_MAQoS information we will do some tests, in which, suitable Grid Services are selected based on the evaluation modes provided in GS_AQoS and the average Price($\overline{P}$), average Quality($\overline{Q}$), average Responding Time($\overline{T}$), average Fidelity($\overline{F}$) and Integrated Performance($\overline{I}$) of these selected Grid Services are calculated. At last, by comparing the results of experiments, we can deduce some recommended conclusions.

First, the basic information of evaluation factors in GS_MAQoS will be simulated.

3.2 Simulation Information

The information of evaluation factors is the basis of applying GS_AQoS. Here, we only simulate Responding Time and Fidelity since service providers give Price and Quality. The basic information is simulated by means of the Responding Time and Fidelity provided by service providers. Suppose T_i^P and F_i^P are respectively the Responding Time and Fidelity of GS_i given by service providers, the simulation information is shown in Table 1.

Table 1. Factor values of 10 semantic equivalent GSs

	Q	*P*	*T*	*F*
GS_1	0.1	150	4	0.03
GS_2	0.2	200	3.2	0
GS_3	0.1	100	6	0
GS_4	0.2	300	5.6	0.04
GS_5	0.15	100	3	0.02
GS_6	0.1	500	5	0
GS_7	0.1	500	2	0.12
GS_8	0.15	200	6.4	0
GS_9	0.1	200	3	0
GS_{10}	0.2	200	4.2	0.1

3.3 Testing Results

Let $P=\{ P_1, P_2, \ldots, P_{10} \}$, $Q=\{ Q_1, Q_2, \ldots, Q_{10}\}$, $T=\{T_1, T_2, \ldots, T_{10} \}$, $F=\{F_1, F_2, \ldots, F_{10} \}$ are respectively the information set of Price, Quality, Responding Time and Fidelity about the 10 semantic equivalent Grid Services. Next, we will do some experiments according to the three algorithms corresponding to the three evaluation modes in GS_AQoS. In AQoS_value_range, the random approach is adopted to select Grid Services from the set of Grid Services satisfying the application's constraints, while AQoS_relation_sort and AQoS_value_integration are to select suitable Grid Services on customers' demand. In the experimentation, for simplification, RQoS(*GS_Best*)=Random(*GS_Best*), namely one of Grid Services is selected at random from GS_Best. Their detail is given as following:

(1) Testing 1. AQoS_relation_sort is used for selecting Grid Services. Let GS_P, GS_Q, GS_T and GS_F represent respectively the GS_Best with *P* emphasized, that with *Q* emphasized, that with *T* emphasized and that with *F* emphasized. Then, RQoS function is impacted on the Grid Services in GS_Best to select the best Grid Service. The processes of selecting Grid Services about the Price emphasized and the Quality emphasized are represented as following:

- Price emphasized: Let $\overline{p}$ = Min(P), GS_P ={GS_i| P_i= $\overline{p}$ ∧GS_i ∈ GS_S}, then
  Do While $j<100$ {
  If GS_i = RQoS(GS_P) then $P^j = P_i$, $Q^j = Q_i$, $T^j = T_i$, $F^j = F_i$, $j=j+1$}.
- Quality emphasized: Let $\overline{Q}$ = Min(Q), GS_Q={GS_i|Q_i= $\overline{Q}$ ∧ GS_i ∈ GS_S }, then
  Do While $j<100$ {
  If GS_i = RQoS (GS_Q) then $P^j = P_i$, $Q^j = Q_i$, $T^j = T_i$, $F^j = F_i$, $j=j+1$}.

And both the Responding Time emphasized and the Fidelity emphasized are the same as those above and omitted due to space limit.

According to the information obtained, $\overline{p}$, $\overline{Q}$, $\overline{T}$, $\overline{F}$ of selected Grid Services are denoted as:

$$\overline{P}=\sum_{j=1}^{n}(P^j)/n,\ \overline{Q}=\sum_{j=1}^{n}(Q^j)/n,\ \overline{T}=\sum_{j=1}^{n}(T^j)/n,\ \overline{F}=\sum_{j=1}^{n}(F^j)/n,\ \text{where, } n=100.$$

(2) Testing 2. AQoS_relation_sort is used, Grid Services are selected at random based on the basic information of the 10 semantic equivalent Grid Services directly, which is denoted as:

Let GS_Best={GS_1, GS_2,…,GS_{10}}, then
Do While j<100 {
If GS_i = RQoS (GS_S) then $P^j = P_i$, $Q^j = Q_i$, $T^j = T_i$, $F^j = F_i$, $j=j+1$}.

And then $\overline{P}$, $\overline{Q}$, $\overline{T}$, $\overline{F}$ of selected Grid Services are calculated as the same as those in Testing1.

(3) Testing 3. Space vector distance is adopted to evaluate the AQoS of Grid Services, here, several measures with various weights are applied in AQoS_value_integration, and the factors with higher weights are more important than those with lower weights. The experiments are planed as following:

- Weights of *0.7, 0.1,0.1,0.1* are assigned to the factors of *P, Q,T, F*.
- Weights of *0.6, 0.2,0.1,0.1* are assigned to the factors of *P, Q,T, F*.
- Weights of *0.5, 0.2,0.2,0.1* are assigned to the factors of *P, Q,T, F*.
- Weights of *0.4, 0.2,0.2,0.2* are assigned to the factors of *P, Q,T, F*.
- Average weights are assigned to these factors, namely all the weights are *0.25*.

Based on these plans given above, corresponding space vector distances are calculated, and the Grid Service with bigger distance is selected, then $\overline{P}$, $\overline{Q}$, $\overline{T}$, $\overline{F}$ of the selected Grid Service are obtained, denoted as following:

$$D_i=\sqrt{\sum_{j=1}^{n}((a_j^i-a_j^t)w_j)^2}\ ,\ \text{and let } D=\{D_1, D_2,\ldots,D_{10}\},$$

if D_i=Max(D) then $\overline{P}=P_i$, $\overline{Q}=Q_i$, $\overline{T}=T_i$, $\overline{F}=F_i$.

At last, based on $\overline{P}$, $\overline{Q}$, $\overline{T}$ and $\overline{F}$, then $\overline{I}$ is defined as:

$$\overline{I}=(\overline{T}+\overline{Q}+\overline{F})/3\overline{P} \tag{5}$$

The Grid Service with lower value of $\overline{I}$ will have better performance than those with higher values.

3.4 Testing Results and Analyzing

Suppose the constraints of a requester for a Grid Service are: *Q* is lower than *0.25* μm, *P* is lower than *600* yuan, *T* is lower than 8 day, *F* is lower than *0.3*, and their units are the same as those simulated, then the *10* semantic equivalent Grid Services in Table 1 are all satisfying customers' constrains. The *P*, *Q*, *T* and *F* in Table 2 are the values in range of [*0,1*], and *DEQ*,*DEP*,*DET* and *DEF* represent the space vector distances of *P* emphasized, that of *Q* emphasized, that of *T* emphasized, and that of *F* emphasized respectively, the weight of the factor emphasized is assigned to *0.7*, and others weights are *0.1*. Next, based on the information in Table 2 and the given three algorithms in GS_AQoS, the cases of Grid Services selected are addressed as following:

- In AQoS_relation_sort, firstly, Best_GS, namely *GS_P*, *GS_Q*, *GS_T* and *GS_F*, which are obtained based on a factor emphasized on customer's demand respectively. Then, one of Grid Services is selected from GS_Best at random. For example, if *Q* is emphasized, then a GS will be selected among GS_1, GS_3, GS_6, GS_7, GS_9.
- In AQoS_value_range, Grid Services are selected at random, simply denoted *RDM*.
- In AQoS_value_integration, vector similarity distance technology is used for selecting Grid service with the biggest distance. For example, the distance of GS_3 is the biggest for *Q* emphasized, and GS_5 for *P* emphasized, etc. The Grid Services selected by AQoS_relation_sort and AQoS_value_integration are shaped in Table 2.

Table 2. Vector distances of GSs calculated by AQoS_value_integration

	Q	*P*	*T*	*F*	*DEQ*	*DEP*	*DET*	*DEF*
GS_1	0.4	0.25	0.5	0.1	0.4389	0.5384	0.3739	0.6392
GS_2	0.8	0.33	0.4	0	0.1941	0.4837	0.4374	0.7060
GS_3	0.4	0.17	0.75	0	0.4404	0.5931	0.2261	0.7079
GS_4	0.8	0.5	0.7	0.133	0.1747	0.3624	0.2335	0.6100
GS_5	0.6	0.17	0.375	0.06	0.3131	0.5932	0.4569	0.6673
GS_6	0.4	0.83	0.625	0	0.4337	0.1708	0.2877	0.7038
GS_7	0.4	0.83	0.25	0.4	0.4312	0.1643	0.5321	0.4312
GS_8	0.6	0.33	0.8	0	0.3054	0.4816	0.1889	0.7046
GS_9	0.4	0.33	0.375	0	0.4414	0.4873	0.4577	0.7085
GS_{10}	0.8	0.33	0.525	0.33	0.1756	0.4766	0.3463	0.4766

Based on the basic information of Grid Services selected, $\overline{P}$, $\overline{Q}$, $\overline{T}$, $\overline{F}$ and $\overline{I}$ of them are calculated, while, if more than one Grid Services are included in

GS_Best, $\overline{Q}$, $\overline{P}$, $\overline{T}$, $\overline{F}$ and $\overline{I}$ are calculated statistically, such as *EQ*, *EP*, *EF* and *RDM*, which are shown in Table 3.

To discuss further, the following measures are taken:

- Let unique Grid Service be selected by using AQoS_relation_sort, then the results are the same as those by using AQoS_value_integration. For example, if the information of Grid Services in Table 1 are modified as following: the *Q* of GS_1 is changed into *0.075*, and the *P* of GS_3 is changed into *150*, then GS_1 is selected for *Q* emphasized, and GS_5 is selected for *P* emphasized.
- The weights in AQoS_value_integration are changed as following: (1) If average weights are assigned, only GS_9 is selected, shown in Table 4, and we can learn that the vector distance of GS_9 is the biggest one and the value of $\overline{I}$ of it is lower than *0.1*. (2) If the weights are assigned to *0.6, 0.2, 0.1, 0.1*, or *0.5, 0.2, 0.2, 0.1*,or *0.7, 0.1, 0.1, 0.1* respectively, the results that the Grid Services are selected are all the same, namely GS_1, GS_5, GS_7, GS_9 are selected Grid Services. When the weights are set *0.4, 0.2,0.2,0.2*, the Grid Services selected are changed as GS_1, GS_5, GS_9 and GS_9, the results table is omitted due to space limit.

Table 3. The $\overline{Q}$, $\overline{P}$, $\overline{T}$, $\overline{F}$ and $\overline{I}$ of GSs selected by three types of evaluation modes

	$\overline{Q}$	$\overline{P}$	$\overline{T}$	$\overline{F}$	$\overline{I}$
GS_P	*0.504*	*0.17*	*0.555*	*0.0312*	*0.0618*
GS_Q	*0.4*	*0.4902*	*0.4925*	*0.102*	*0.1625*
GS_T	*0.4*	*0.83*	*0.25*	*0.4*	*0.2905*
GS_F	*0.514*	*0.3996*	*0.59*	*0*	*0.1471*
RDM	*0.572*	*0.3921*	*0.5298*	*0.10543*	*0.1578*
DEP(GS_5)	*0.6*	*0.17*	*0.375*	*0.06*	*0.0587*
DEQ(GS_3)	*0.4*	*0.17*	*0.75*	*0*	*0.0652*
DET(GS_7)	*0.4*	*0.83*	*0.25*	*0.4*	*0.2905*
DEF(GS_9)	*0.4*	*0.33*	*0.375*	*0*	*0.0853*

Table 4. The vector distances of GSs with average weights by AQoS_value_integration

	Q	*P*	*T*	*F*	*I*	*DEQ*	*DEP*	*DET*	*DEF*
GS_1	*0.3*	*0.25*	*0.5*	*0.1*	*0.075*	*0.3634*	*0.3634*	*0.3634*	*0.3634*
GS_2	*0.8*	*0.33*	*0.4*	*0*	*0.132*	*0.33994*	*0.33994*	*0.33994*	*0.33994*
GS_3	*0.4*	*0.25*	*0.75*	*0.06*	*0.100833*	*0.34174*	*0.34174*	*0.34174*	*0.34174*
GS_4	*0.8*	*0.5*	*0.7*	*0.133*	*0.272167*	*0.26594*	*0.26594*	*0.26594*	*0.26594*
GS_5	*0.6*	*0.17*	*0.375*	*0.06*	*0.05865*	*0.36424*	*0.36424*	*0.36424*	*0.36424*
GS_6	*0.4*	*0.83*	*0.625*	*0*	*0.283583*	*0.30914*	*0.30914*	*0.30914*	*0.30914*
GS_7	*0.4*	*0.83*	*0.25*	*0.4*	*0.2905*	*0.28624*	*0.28624*	*0.28624*	*0.28624*
GS_8	*0.6*	*0.33*	*0.8*	*0*	*0.154*	*0.32104*	*0.32104*	*0.32104*	*0.32104*
GS_9	*0.4*	*0.33*	*0.375*	*0*	*0.08525*	*0.3704*	*0.3704*	*0.3704*	*0.3704*
GS_{10}	*0.8*	*0.33*	*0.525*	*0.33*	*0.18205*	*0.26964*	*0.26964*	*0.26964*	*0.26964*

Now, based on the information above, we calculate the statistic performance values ($\overline{P}$,$\overline{Q}$,$\overline{T}$,$\overline{F}$,$\overline{I}$) about selected Grid Services by using three different evaluation modes, which are shown in Fig.3. Where, AQoS_value_integration1 represents AQoS_value_integration with weights of *0.7,0.1,0.1,0.1* and AQoS_value_integration2 represents the AQoS_value_integration with average weights, coordinate x represents five groups of experiments, namely average Price, average Quality, average Responding Time, average Fidelity, and average Integrated Performance about Grid Services selected by using different evaluation modes, For example, group 1 represents the results of average Price about the Grid Services selected by using different evaluation modes, group 2 represents the results of average Quality and so on.

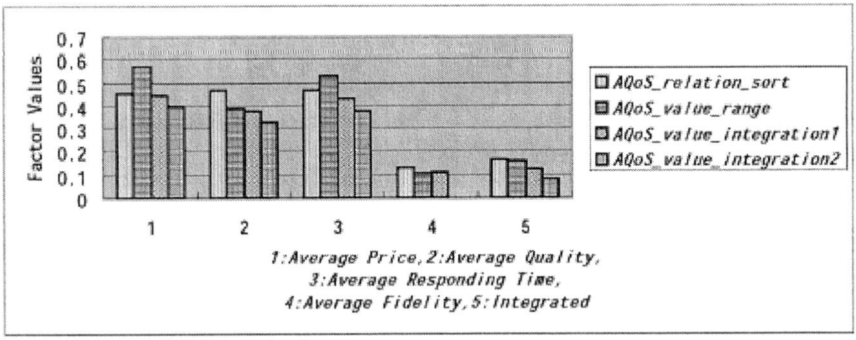

Fig. 3. Performance comparisons among GSs selected by using different evaluation modes

Based on these testing results above, it is obvious that GS_AQoS model is efficient and we can summarize the following suggestions. (1) AQoS_value_range is suitable for customers selecting Grid services at random. (2) AQoS_relation_sort is suitable if one factor is emphasized on customers' demand. (3) AQoS_value_integration is suitable for selecting Grid services with integrated performance, but average weights are suggested to embody the advantage of AQoS_value_integration, otherwise, the conclusion is the same as those by using AQoS_relation_sort. (4) It concludes that the Grid Services selected by AQoS_value_integration with average weights have the best performance. (5) AQoS_relation_sort and AQoS_value_range are simple to use but with some limitation for their applications, while AQoS_value_integration mode is flexible for its applications and with more advantages with it, such as the Grid Services selected with better integrated performance can obtained easily on their demand.

4 Conclusions

The AQoS Model for evaluating Grid Services is the need for selecting Grid services on customers'demand. In this paper, according to the characteristics of Grid Services, a common AQoS model (GS_QoS) is proposed, which is application-centric, and provides three types of flexible evaluation modes for customers' selection. By simulation experiments, GS_AQoS model shows:

- Not only common but also personality is represented in GS_AQoS model.
- The common GS_AQoS XML schema as a common profile template is provided for service providers and service requesters to describe the GS_AQoS information of Grid Services so as to simplify the process of Grid Services matching.
- It can raise the efficiency and utility of resources reservation since the number of Grid Services can be reduced by using the GS_AQoS.
- The quality of Grid Services described by two parts such as RQoS and AQoS make the function RQoS() more flexible, they can be set independently to embody the personality of Grid Services.
- It can help to improve both the total performance of jobs and that of single Grid Service on customers' demand.

In the next step, we will study the integration of RQoS and AQoS for Grid services and the QoS of jobs, as well as the coordination of resources in the execution of a job.

References

1. Foster I., Kesselman C.: Grid services for distributed system integration. IEEE Computer,35(6)(2002)37~46
2. Wang X., Luo J. Architecture of Grid Resource Allocation Management Based on QoS GCC 2003, LNCS 3033 (2004) 81–88.
3. Foster I., Kesselman C., Lee C.: A Distributed Resource Management Architecture that Supports Advance Reservation and Co-Allocation, In Proceedings of the International-Workshop on QoS (1999) 27-36
4. Foster I., Markus Fidler C.: End-to-End Quality of Service for High-End Applications. www.globus.org/research/papers/e2e.pdf (2001)
5. Rashid Al-Ali, Gregor von Laszewski.: QoS Support for High-Performance Scientific Grid Applications. proceeding of ccgrid04 (2004)
6. Al-Ali R., Hafid A., Rana O.: QoS Adaptation in Service-Oriented Grids.In Proceedings of the 1st International Workshop on Middleware for Grid Computing (MGC2003) at ACM/IFIP/USENIX Middleware 2003. Rio de Janeiro, Brazil (2003)
7. Al-Ali R., Rana O., Walker D.: GQoSM: Grid Service Discovery using QoS Properties. Computing and Informatics Journal, Special Issue on Grid Computing, 21(4) (2002) 363–382
8. Al-Ali R., Amin K., von Laszeswski G. An OGSA-Based Quality of Service ramework. In Proceedings of the Second International Workshop on Grid and Cooperative Computing (GCC2003), Shanghai, China (2003)
9. Shen D.R., Yu G. Modeling QoS for Semantic equivalent Web Services. WAIM04, LNCS 3129 (2004) 478-4888
10. Zeng L. Z., Benatallah B.. Quality Driven Web Services Composition. WWW2003. Budapest, Hungary (2003)
11. Shi Z., Yu T. MG-QoS: QoS-Based Resource Discovery in Manufacturing Grid. GCC 2003, LNCS 3033 (2004) 500-506
12. Sumra R, Arulazi D. Quality of Service for Web Services-Demystification, Limitation, and Best Practices. http://www.developer.com/services (2003)
13. Sheth A.,Cardoso J.: QoS for Service-oriented Middleware. In proceedings of the Conference on Systemics,Cybernetics and Informatics.Orlando, FL (2002)

14. Chandrasekaran S., Silver G.: Web service technologies and their synergy with simulation. In Proc. of the 2002 Winter Simulation Conference (2002).
15. Fengjin W., Zhoufeng Z.: A Dynamic Matching and Binding Mechanism for Business Services Integration. In Proc. of the EDCIS (2002).
16. Cardoso J., Bussler C.: Semantic Web Services and Processes: Semantic Composition and Quality of Service.On the Move to Meaningful Internet Computing and Ubiquitous Computer 2002.Irvine CA (2002).
17. Cardoso J., Miller J.: Modeling Quality of Service for Workflows and Web Service Processes, The International Journal on Very Large Data Bases. Springer Verlag, Berlin-Heidelberg (2003).
18. Dan D., Davis R.: Web services on demand: WSLA-driven automated management. IBM Systems Journal, Vol 43(1) (2004) 136-157.
19. Shen D.R., Yu G.: Study on Service Grid Technologies Supporting Enterprises Business Agile Integration. Computer Science, Vol.31(6) (2004)82-85.

Temporal Dependency for Dynamic Verification of Fixed-Date Constraints in Grid Workflow Systems

Jinjun Chen and Yun Yang

CICEC – Centre for Internet Computing and E-Commerce,
Faculty of Information and Communication Technologies,
Swinburne University of Technology,
PO Box 218, Hawthorn, Melbourne, Australia 3122
{jchen, yyang}@it.swin.edu.au

Abstract. Grid workflow systems aim to support large-scale complex e-science and e-business processes. Due to the complexity of these kinds of processes, to control the execution of them in terms of time in the grid workflow execution environments, multiple fixed-date temporal constraints often need to be set simultaneously. Hence the dependency problem between them must be considered and emphasised, which affects the verification effectiveness and efficiency of the fixed-date temporal constraints. However, current relevant workflow verification works do not take into consideration this dependency. Therefore, in this paper, we explore it in depth and analyse its impact on the verification of the fixed-date temporal constraints. Furthermore, based on the temporal dependency, we develop some new temporal verification methods and algorithms. The comparison and evaluation show that these new methods and algorithms make the verification more effective and efficient. All these analyses, new methods and algorithms further strengthen the grid workflow time management.

1 Introduction

Grid workflow systems which are evoking a high degree of interest aim to support modeling, redesign and execution of large-scale sophisticated e-science and e-business processes [2, 3, 9, 10, 11, 12]. In Open Grid Services Architecture (OGSA), a grid workflow can be defined as the automation of a Grid process, in whole or part, during which documents, information or data are passed from one grid service to another for action, according to a set of procedural rules [2, 11, 12]. A grid service can be seen as a Web service with additional grid-oriented features [11, 12]. Conceptually, a grid workflow is a collection of activities, and the dependencies between activities which define their execution orders and form four basic control structures: sequential, parallel, selective and iterative. These activities are implemented and executed by corresponding grid services. The whole work process of grid workflow systems can be divided into three stages: build-time stage, run-time instantiation stage and run-time execution stage. At the build-time stage, grid workflow specifications are defined by some grid workflow definition languages such as Grid Services Flow Language (GSFL), Service Workflow Language (SWFL) and Grid Workflow Execution Language (GWEL) [2, 3, 11, 12]. At the instantiation stage, grid workflow in-

Y. Zhang et al. (Eds.): APWeb 2005, LNCS 3399, pp. 820 – 831, 2005.

stances are created, and especially grid services specified in the build-time definition documents are discovered. This could include an instantiation service that is a high-level grid service and responsible for finding factories on the Grid, downloading them to the local system and instantiating them [2, 3, 12]. At the execution stage, the grid workflow instances are executed, and the execution is coordinated between grid services by a grid workflow engine which itself is a high-level grid service, hence automatically grid aware [2, 3, 12].

To control the temporal correctness of the grid workflow execution, some temporal constraints mainly including upper bound, lower bound and fixed-date constraints must be set when a grid workflow is defined at build time [4, 5, 7, 21] and the temporal verification is carried out at the different stages. Currently, some relevant temporal verification works have been done. In [17, 18, 19], the authors propose some algorithms to adjust activity deadlines and estimate the escalations and assign the predictive deadlines. [7] uses the modified Critical Path Method (CPM) to calculate temporal constraints and is one of the very few projects that considers temporal constraint reasoning at both build-time and run-time. [15, 16] present a method for dynamic verification of absolute and relative deadline constraints. However, these works and some others such as [1, 8, 13, 14, 20] do not take into consideration the dependency between temporal constraints. Although [4, 5] address the temporal dependency, they do not discuss it for fixed-date constraints, only for upper bound and lower bound constraints. In grid workflow systems, due to the complexity of large-scale sophisticated e-science and e-business processes, multiple fixed-date temporal constraints need to be set simultaneously. Hence the dependency between them must also be considered. Therefore, in this paper, we analyse this dependency and its impact on the temporal verification in depth, and furthermore, we develop some new temporal verification methods and algorithms. The comparison and evaluation show that these methods and algorithms can achieve better verification effectiveness and efficiency.

The remainder of the paper is organised as follows. Section 2 describes some preliminaries. Section 3 discusses the dependency between fixed-date constraints. Section 4 describes the build-time fixed-date constraint verification considering the dependency. Section 5 discusses how to conduct the fixed-date constraint verification more efficiently based on the temporal dependency at the run-time instantiation and execution stages. Section 6 shows the benefits of our work through a comparison and evaluation. Section 7 concludes our contributions and points out the future work.

2 Preliminaries

Based on directed graph, a grid workflow can be represented by a grid workflow graph, where nodes correspond to activities and edges correspond to dependencies between activities, called flows. Here, we assume that execution dependencies between activities form an acyclic graph and the grid workflow is well structured. Because we only consider the time attributes, we can treat activities and flows in the same way. Therefore, for convenience, in the remainder of this paper, we will use term "activity" to refer to the real activity and the flow and we will not distinguish them if not explicitly mentioned. We denote i^{th} activity of a grid workflow as a_i, the expected time the grid workflow specification will come into effect as *Cie(w)*. Only from *Cie(w)*, the corresponding grid workflow instances can be enacted. For each a_i, we denote the minimum duration, maximum duration, start time at run-time, end time at run-time, run-time real completion duration as $d(a_i)$, $D(a_i)$, $S(a_i)$, $E(a_i)$, $Rcd(a_i)$ respectively [4, 5, 15, 16, 17, 18, 19]. If there is a fixed-date constraint at a_i, we denote it as $fd(a_i)$. If there is a path from a_i to a_j ($j \geq i$), we denote the maximum duration, the minimum duration and the run-time real completion duration between them as $D(a_i, a_j)$, $d(a_i, a_j)$ and $Rcd(a_i, a_j)$ respectively [4, 5, 15, 16]. For convenience of our discussion, in the remainder of this paper, we consider one execution path in the grid workflow and assume all activities which we will address are on this execution path. For every other execution path, the discussion is very similar. In addition, we assume that the activity numbering on the path is $1,2,3,\ldots,i,i+1,i+2,\ldots,i+(j-i-1),j,j+1,j+2,\ldots$. For the computation of $D(a_i, a_j)$ and $d(a_i, a_j)$, if there are no parallel or selective structures between a_i and a_j, we can use the following two formulas to compute them.

$$D(a_i, a_j) = \sum_{k=i}^{j} D(a_k) \tag{1}$$

$$d(a_i, a_j) = \sum_{k=i}^{j} d(a_k) \tag{2}$$

If there are parallel or selective structures between a_i and a_j, for each structure, we use the largest of the maximum durations of all branches as the maximum duration of the structure, and use the largest of the minimum durations of all branches as the minimum duration of the structure. Then, if we see each structure as an activity in terms of time, we are still able to use (1) and (2) to compute $D(a_i, a_j)$ and $d(a_i, a_j)$.

According to the above denotations, we have: $D(a_i,a_i)=D(a_i)$, $d(a_i,a_i)=d(a_i)$, $Rcd(a_i,a_j)=E(a_j)-S(a_i)$, $Rcd(a_i,a_i)=Rcd(a_i)$. Also, we define: $D(a_m,a_i)=0(m>i)$, $d(a_m,a_i)=0(m>i)$, $Rcd(a_m,a_i)=0(m>i)$. Normally, $d(a_i) \leq Rcd(a_i) \leq D(a_i)$, $d(a_i,a_j) \leq Rcd(a_i,a_j) \leq D(a_i, a_j)$.

The temporal verification is conducted stage by stage, from build-time stage, to run-time instantiation stage, and finally to run-time execution stage. At each stage, we can take it for granted that the temporal verification at previous stages is consistent. In addition, at the execution stage, we only conduct the temporal verification at some selected checkpoints because normally it is unnecessary to do so at each activity point [5, 15, 16]. Similarly, at checkpoint a_i, we can take it for granted that all fixed-date constraints before the execution of a_i are consistent. If at a certain stage or at a point, one of fixed-date constraints is violated, we may take some time adjustment measures to make it consistent.

In terms of the consistency of fixed-date constraints, based on [7, 15, 16], we give the following definitions which are easy to understand. So, we do not explain them.

Definition 1. The fixed-date constraint at activity a_i is consistent at the build-time stage if and only if $D(a_1, a_i) \leq fd(a_i)- Cie(w)$.

Definition 2. The fixed-date constraint at activity a_i is consistent at the instantiation stage if and only if $D(a_1, a_i) \leq fd(a_i)-S(a_1)$.

Definition 3. The fixed-date constraint at activity a_i is consistent at checkpoint a_p which is either before or at a_i ($p \leq i$) at the execution stage if and only if $Rcd(a_1, a_p)+D(a_{p+1}, a_i) \leq fd(a_i)-S(a_1)$.

Definition 4. The fixed-date constraint at activity a_i is consistent at a checkpoint after a_i at the execution stage if and only if $Rcd(a_1, a_i) \leq fd(a_i)\text{-}S(a_1)$.

3 Temporal Dependency Between Fixed-Date Constraints

Because all fixed-date constraints have the same start point, i.e. start activity a_1, and are nested one after another, based on Allen's interval logic [6, 22], we can conclude that there are two types of basic relationships between fixed-date constraints, as depicted in Figure 1 and Figure 2 respectively. Figure 2 is the extension of Figure 1.

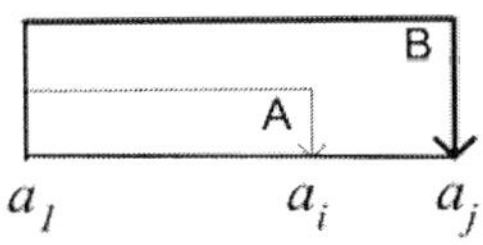

Fig. 1. Nested fixed-date constraints A and B

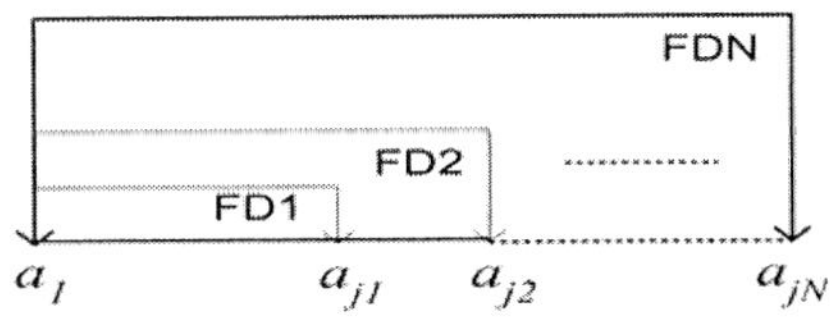

Fig. 2. Multiple nested fixed-date constraints

In Figure 1, if $fd(B) \leq fd(A)$, then, if B is consistent, A must be consistent. If B is not consistent, even if A is consistent, we need to adjust the setting of B, which inevitably addresses A because A is included in B, and results in the necessity of re-verification of A. So, the current setting of A is unnecessary. Therefore, in Figure 1, we have $fd(A)<fd(B)$. Now, we consider a more complicated situation. Based on Definition 1 and the above discussion, if A and B are consistent and necessary, we have:

$$fd(A) < fd(B);\quad D(a_1, a_i) \leq fd(A)\text{- } Cie(w);\ D(a_1, a_j) \leq fd(B)\text{- } Cie(w)$$

Considering a grid workflow where $fd(A)\text{-}Cie(w)=9.5$, $fd(B)\text{-}Cie(w)=11$, $D(a_1, a_i)=8$ and $D(a_1, a_j)=10$. Obviously, the above three inequations hold. In addition, we have: $fd(A)\text{-}Cie(w)+D(a_{i+1}, a_j)=fd(A)\text{-}Cie(w)+D(a_1, a_j)\text{-}D(a_1, a_i)=9.5+10\text{-}8=11.5$. Clearly, 11.5 is more than 11, which means: $fd(A)\text{-}Cie(w)+D(a_{i+1}, a_j) > fd(B)\text{-}Cie(w)$. In this situation, at the build-time stage, if B is consistent, we have: $fd(A)\text{-}Cie(w)+D(a_{i+1}, a_j) > fd(B)\text{-}Cie(w) \geq D(a_1, a_i)+D(a_{i+1}, a_j)$. Therefore, we have: $fd(A)\text{-}Cie(w)>D(a_1, a_i)$. According to Definition 1, A is consistent. Similar to the situation where $fd(B) \leq fd(A)$, if B is not consistent, even if A is consistent, when we adjust the setting of B, we inevitably address the setting of A and need to re-verify the consistency of A. Therefore, the current setting of A is unnecessary. So, for the necessity of the existence of fixed-date constraints, in Figure 1, we have: $fd(A)\text{-}Cie(w)+D(a_{i+1}, a_j) \leq fd(B)\text{-}Cie(w)$, namely, $D(a_{i+1}, a_j) \leq fd(B)\text{-}fd(A)$.

In addition, in Figure 1, if A and B are consistent, according to Definition 1, we have:

$$D(a_1, a_i) \leq fd(A)\text{- } Cie(w) \tag{3}$$

$$D(a_1, a_j) \leq fd(B)\text{- } Cie(w) \tag{4}$$

Then, if we omit the dependency between them, at the execution stage, we face the following problem. At point a_i, to ensure fixed-date constraint B at a_j is consistent, according to Definition 3, we must make sure that the following inequation holds:

$$Rcd(a_1, a_i) + D(a_{i+1}, a_j) \leq fd(B) - S(a_1) \tag{5}$$

Considering an extreme case where $E(a_i)$ is equal to $fd(A)$, then, we have: $Rcd(a_1, a_i) = fd(A) - S(a_1)$. If we apply this equation to (5), we can deduce that we must ensure:

$$D(a_{i+1}, a_j) \leq fd(B) - fd(A) \tag{6}$$

The problem is that we cannot derive (6) from (3) and (4) that we only have. In fact, (6) may or may not hold.

In overall terms, we can see that we must consider the dependency and we have:

Definition 5. In Figure 1, the dependency between fixed-date constraints A and B is consistent if and only if $D(a_{i+1}, a_j) \leq fd(B) - fd(A)$.

Definition 5 ensures the consistency of the dependency between two fixed-date constraints. However, we still need to consider the dependency between multiple ones, as shown in Figure 2. The following theorem solves this problem.

Theorem 1. In Figure 2, if the dependency between any two adjacent fixed-date constraints is consistent, the dependency between any two non-adjacent fixed-date constraints must also be consistent.

Proof: For simplicity, we consider the fixed-date constraints respectively at a_{j1}, a_{j2} and a_{j3} $(j3>j2>j1)$. Suppose that the dependency between a_{j1} and a_{j2} is consistent and the dependency between a_{j2} and a_{j3} is consistent, according to Definition 5, we have:

$$D(a_{j1+1}, a_{j2}) \leq fd(a_{j2}) - fd(a_{j1}) \tag{7}$$

$$D(a_{j2+1}, a_{j3}) \leq fd(a_{j3}) - fd(a_{j2}) \tag{8}$$

Now we prove that the dependency between a_{j1} and a_{j3} is also consistent. That is to say, the consistency is transitive. In fact, if we add (7) and (8) together, we can derive:

$$D(a_{j1+1}, a_{j3}) \leq fd(a_{j3}) - fd(a_{j1}) \tag{9}$$

According to Definition 5, (9) means that the dependency between a_{j1} and a_{j3} is consistent. So, Theorem 1 holds.

4 Build-Time Verification of Fixed-Date Temporal Constraints

At the build-time stage, according to Section 3, for the effectiveness of the temporal verification, in addition to the verification of fixed-date temporal constraints themselves, we still need to verify their temporal dependency.

For each fixed-date constraint, say at a_i, we compute $D(a_1, a_i)$. Then, we compare it with $fd(a_i) - Cie(w)$. If $D(a_1, a_i) \leq fd(a_i) - Cie(w)$, the fixed-date constraint at a_i is consistent. Otherwise, it is violated. In addition, we still need to verify the dependency between fixed-date constraints. Based on Definition 5 and Theorem 1, we only need to consider the dependency between any two adjacent fixed-date constraints. Taking

Figure 1 as an example, to verify the consistency of the dependency between A and B at a_i and a_j respectively, firstly, we need to compute $D(a_{i+1}, a_j)$. Then, we compare it with the difference between $fd(A)$ and $fd(B)$. If $D(a_{i+1}, a_j)$ is less than or equal to the difference, according to Definition 5, the dependency is consistent. Otherwise, the dependency is not consistent.

Based on the above discussion, we can further derive Algorithm 1 for build-time verification.

```
symbol definitions:
    SetFD: a set of all fixed-date constraints;
end definitions
Algorithm 1: build-time temporal verification of fixed-date temporal constraints
             whose dependency is like the situation in Figure 2
Input: SetFD, Cie(w), maximum durations of all activities involved in fixed-date con-
       straints in SetFD;
Output: consistent or inconsistent report for fixed-date constraints and their temporal
        dependency;
Set a copy of SetFD to CopyOfSetFD;
while (SetFD not empty) do
        Pop up a fixed-date constraint from SetFD, say at a_i ;
        Compute D(a_1, a_i);
        if ( (fd(a_i)-Cie(w))< D(a_1, a_i) ) then
           Output 'fixed-date constraint at a_i is inconsistent'
        else
           Output 'fixed-date constraint at a_i is consistent'
        end if
end while
while (CopyOfSetFD not empty)
        Pop up current two adjacent fixed-date constraints from CopyOfSetFD, say at a_i
           and a_j respectively;
        Compute D(a_{i+1}, a_j);
        if (D(a_{i+1}, a_j) > (fd(a_j)-fd(a_i)) ) then
           Output 'fixed-date constraint dependency between a_i and a_j is inconsistent'
        else
           Output 'fixed-date constraint dependency between a_i and a_j is consistent'
        end if
end while
```

Algorithm 1. Build-time temporal verification algorithm for fixed-date constraints and their temporal dependency

5 Run-Time Verification of Fixed-Date Temporal Constraints

5.1 Instantiation Stage Verification

At the instantiation stage, grid workflow instances are enacted and we can get absolute start times. For a specific grid workflow instance, because its absolute start time may be different from the build-time expected time $Cie(w)$, the build-time consistency of the fixed-date constraints cannot ensure that they are still consistent at the instantiation stage. Therefore, we need to re-verify them. For each fixed-date constraint, say at a_i, we compute $D(a_1, a_i)$. Then, we compare it with the difference between $fd(a_i)$ and $S(a_1)$. If $D(a_1, a_i)$ is bigger, according to Definition 2, the fixed-date constraint at a_i is inconsistent. Otherwise, it is consistent. In terms of the dependency between fixed-date constraints, according to Definition 5, it has nothing to do with the absolute start time and the build-time expected time. Hence, we need not re-verify it.

5.2 Execution Stage Verification

In this section, we will see that based on the temporal dependency discussed in Section 3, we can conduct the temporal verification more efficiently. According to Definitions 3 and 4, actually, we only need to consider those fixed-date temporal constraints which include the checkpoints [5, 15, 16].

Regarding the temporal verification of fixed-date temporal constraints in Figure 1, we have:

Theorem 2. In Figure 1, given the build-time consistency of the temporal dependency between fixed-date constraints, at checkpoint a_p between a_1 and a_i, if A is consistent, B must be consistent.

Proof: Because A is consistent, according to Definition 3, we have:

$$Rcd(a_1, a_p)+D(a_{p+1}, a_i) \leq fd(A)\text{-}S(a_1) \tag{10}$$

In addition, according to the build-time consistency of the temporal dependency between fixed-date constraints, we have:

$$D(a_{i+1}, a_j) \leq fd(B)\text{-}fd(A) \tag{11}$$

If we add (10) and (11) together, we have: $Rcd(a_1, a_p)+D(a_{p+1}, a_i)+ D(a_{i+1}, a_j) \leq fd(A)\text{-}S(a_1)+fd(B)\text{-}fd(A)$, namely, $Rcd(a_1, a_p)+D(a_{p+1}, a_j) \leq fd(B)\text{-}S(a_1)$. According to Definition 3, the fixed-date temporal constraint B at a_j is consistent. So, Theorem 2 holds.

Accordingly, regarding the temporal verification in Figure 2, we have:

Theorem 3. In Figure 2, given the build-time consistency of the temporal dependency between fixed-date constraints, when the execution of a grid workflow instance reaches a checkpoint at activity a_p, if a fixed-date constraint at an activity after a_p is consistent, any fixed-date constraint after this consistent fixed-date constraint must also be consistent.

Proof: Suppose each of a_{jk} and a_{jl} has a fixed-date constraint ($jl>jk>p$) and at checkpoint a_p, the fixed-date constraint at a_{jk} is consistent. Now, we prove that the fixed-date constraint at a_{jl} must be consistent. Because the fixed-date constraint at a_{jk} is consistent, according to Definition 3, we have:

$$Rcd(a_1, a_p)+D(a_{p+1}, a_{jk}) \leq fd(a_{jk})\text{-}S(a_1) \tag{12}$$

At the same time, according to the build-time consistency of the temporal dependency between fixed-date temporal constraints at a_{jk} and a_{jl}, we have:

$$D(a_{jk+1}, a_{jl}) \leq fd(a_{jl})\text{-}fd(a_{jk}) \tag{13}$$

In fact, if we add (12) and (13), we have: $Rcd(a_1, a_p)+D(a_{p+1}, a_{jk})+D(a_{jk+1}, a_{jl}) \leq fd(a_{jk})-S(a_1)+fd(a_{jl})-fd(a_{jk})=fd(a_{jl})-S(a_1)$, i.e. $Rcd(a_1, a_p)+D(a_{p+1}, a_{jl}) \leq fd(a_{jl})-S(a_1)$. According to Definition 3, the fixed-date constraint at a_{jl} is consistent. So, Theorem 3 holds.

According to Theorems 2 and 3, when we conduct the temporal verification for fixed-date constraints in Figure 1 and Figure 2 at a checkpoint, starting from the first fixed-date constraint after it, we conduct the verification computation one after another until we meet a consistent fixed-date constraint or finish all fixed-date constraint verification. Suppose we now reach the fixed-date constraint at a_{jk} and the checkpoint is at a_p ($p<jk$). We compute $Rcd(a_1, a_p)$ and $D(a_{p+1}, a_{jk})$, and add them together to derive a sum. Then, we compare the sum with the difference between $fd(a_{jk})$ and $S(a_1)$. If the sum is less than or equal to the difference, the fixed-date constraint at a_{jk} is consistent and according to Theorem 2, we need not conduct further verification computation for any fixed-date constraint after a_{jk}. This will save some verification computations and improve the efficiency of the temporal verification. If the sum is more than the difference, the fixed-date constraint at a_{jk} is violated and we still need to verify the next one.

Based on the above discussion, we can further derive Algorithm 2 for run-time verification.

symbol definitions:
  ArrayDE: an array of all fixed-date constraints after checkpoint a_p;
end definitions
Algorithm 2: temporal verification at checkpoint a_p at the execution stage for fixed-date constraints after a_p whose dependency is like the situation in Figure 2
Input: ArrayDE, $E(a_p)$, $S(a_1)$, maximum durations of all activities;
Output: consistent or inconsistent report for fixed-date constraints;
while (not end of ArrayDE) **do**
    Pop up the current fixed-date constraint from ArrayDE, say at activity a_n;
    $Rcd(a_1, a_p) = E(a_p)- S(a_1)$; Compute $D(a_{p+1}, a_n)$;
    if ($(D(a_{p+1}, a_n)+ Rcd(a_1, a_p)) > (fd(a_n) - S(a_1))$) **then**
      Output 'fixed-date constraint at a_n is inconsistent'
    else
      Output 'fixed-date constraint at a_n is consistent and consequently, other fixed-date constraints after a_p are also consistent'; exit;
    end if
end while

Algorithm 2. Temporal verification algorithm at a checkpoint at the execution stage for fixed-date constraints

6 Comparison and Evaluation

Comparing with the previous relevant verification work, in our paper, the clear differences are that we have analysed the dependency between fixed-date constraints and its impact on the temporal verification of them in depth. The discussion in Sections 3 and 4 has shown its impact on the effectiveness of the temporal verification. We can see that, regardless of the temporal dependency, some temporal verifications are not effective as we need to re-verify them later. Section 5 has further illustrated its impact on the efficiency of the temporal verification. In addition, in Sections 4 and 5, based on the temporal dependency, we have derived some new methods and algorithms for more effective and efficient temporal verification. For the temporal verification effectiveness, we can see its improvement clearly from the discussion in Sections 3 and 4.

To better understand the improvement on the temporal verification efficiency, we give the quantitative analyses detailed below. We take the situation in Figure 2 as an example to demonstrate the efficiency improvement because Figure 2 is more representative than Figure 1. In Figure 2, suppose there is a checkpoint, a_p, between a_l and a_{j1}, and there are N fixed-date temporal constraints. When we conduct the temporal verification, the main computation is focused on the sum of the maximum durations between two activities. Therefore, we take each computation for addition as a computation unit. And we compare the number of the computation units based on the temporal dependency, i.e. with the temporal dependency, with that neglecting the temporal dependency, i.e. without the temporal dependency. We denote these two numbers as fd_{with} and $fd_{without}$ respectively. Because in real-world grid workflow environments, normally there are lots of grid workflow instances, we discuss the values of fd_{with} and $fd_{without}$ in a statistical way. Suppose there are M inconsistent fixed-date constraints in Figure 2, according to Definition 3, Theorems 2 and 3, for the verification of the fixed-date constraint FDk at a_{jk}, we can deduce that the number of the computation units is jk-p. Therefore, we can derive the following three computing formulas:

$$fd_{with} = \sum_{k=1}^{M+1} (jk - p) \text{ where } 0 \leqslant M \leqslant N\text{-}1 \tag{14}$$

$$fd_{with} = \sum_{k=1}^{M} (jk - p) \text{ where } M=N \tag{15}$$

$$fd_{without} = \sum_{k=1}^{N} (jk - p) \tag{16}$$

Intuitively, fd_{with} is less than or equal to $fd_{without}$ because $M \leqslant N$. Now, we further analyse to what extent fd_{with} is less than $fd_{without}$ with the inconsistent fixed-date constraint number M changing. For simplicity, we assume the distance between any two adjacent fixed-date constraints in Figure 2 is the same, denoted as Q. Then, based on (14), (15) and (16), we can derive:

$$fd_{with} = \frac{M(M+1)}{2} Q + (M+1)(j1 - p) \text{ where } 0 \leqslant M \leqslant N\text{-}1 \tag{17}$$

$$fd_{with} = \frac{M(M-1)}{2} Q + M(j1 - p) \text{ where } M=N \tag{18}$$

$$fd_{without} = \frac{N(N-1)}{2} Q + N(j1 - p) \tag{19}$$

We take a set of values to see how they perform. Suppose Q=3, *j1-p*=4, *N*=10. The choice of these values does not affect our analyses because what we want is to see the trend of how fd_{with} is less than $fd_{without}$ with the inconsistent fixed-date constraint number *M* changing. Based on these values, with *M* changing, we list the corresponding fd_{with} and $fd_{without}$ in Table 1.

Table 1. Computation unit number change of fixed-date constraint verification by inconsistent fixed-date constraint number *M*

M	0	1	2	3	4	5	6	7	8	9	10
fd_{with}	4	11	21	34	50	69	91	116	144	175	175
$fd_{without}$	175	175	175	175	175	175	175	175	175	175	175

From the above computing formulas and Table 1, we can see the following points:

- If *M*=0, that is to say, all fixed-date constraints are consistent, then fd_{with} is the smallest. In fact, in this case, based on Algorithm 2, we only need to conduct the temporal verification for the first fixed-date constraint. This is the best case and fd_{with} is much less than $fd_{without}$, i.e. 4 vs 175. If *M*=*N*, fd_{with} is equal to $fd_{without}$, i.e. 175 vs 175. If *M*=*N*-1, because the Mth fixed-date constraint is not consistent, we still need to verify the next one, namely the Nth fixed-date constraint. Therefore, fd_{with} is still equal to $fd_{without}$, i.e. 175 vs 175. These two cases are worst ones because all *N* or *N*-1 fixed-date constraints are inconsistent. For all other *M*, fd_{with} is less than $fd_{without}$, as indicated in Table 1 clearly.
- With *M* decreasing, fd_{with} is decreasing. This means that based on the temporal dependency, the more consistent fixed-date constraints, the less the amount of the verification computation. In contrast, no matter how *M* is changing, $fd_{without}$ is always the same. This means that, if we neglect the temporal dependency, no matter how we improve the activity execution for more consistent fixed-date constraints, we always conduct the same amount of the verification computation.

In conclusion, only under the worst cases where all *N* or *N*-1 fixed-date constraints are violated, the amount of the fixed-date constraint verification computation based on the temporal dependency is equal to that neglecting the temporal dependency. In all other cases, based on the temporal dependency, we can conduct more efficient temporal verification. In real-world grid workflow system environments, normally, the above two worst cases seldom happen. Otherwise, the corresponding grid workflow specifications or grid workflow execution environments would be difficult to use and need to be improved. More importantly, if based on the temporal dependency, when we improve the activity execution by grid services and the grid workflow specifications in terms of the execution time and allowed maximum durations, we can improve the temporal verification efficiency significantly. However, if we neglect the temporal dependency, it does not make any difference.

The proposed concepts, principles and new verification methods and algorithms can be regarded as a refinement of the grid workflow temporal verification. Firstly, at the build-time stage, besides the temporal verification for all fixed-date temporal constraints, we still need to verify the dependency between them. Secondly, at the execution stage, we use these new verification methods and algorithms based on the temporal dependency to verify fixed-date constraints as described in this paper.

7 Conclusions and Future Work

In this paper, the temporal dependency between fixed-date constraints in grid workflow systems is explored and its impact on the temporal verification is analysed. Furthermore, based on the temporal dependency, some new verification methods and algorithms are presented. The comparison and evaluation show that based on the temporal dependency, with these new methods and algorithms, we can conduct more effective and efficient temporal verification for fixed-date constraints. All these discussions, relevant concepts, principles and new verification methods and algorithms further reinforce the grid workflow time management.

With these contributions, we can further consider some problems such as temporal adjustment methods when a fixed-date constraint is violated, the predictive mechanisms by which we can predict future possible violations.

Acknowledgements

The work reported in this paper is partly supported by Swinburne Vice Chancellor's Strategic Research Initiative Grant 2002-2004. It is also partly supported by the National Natural Science Foundation of China under grant No.60273026 and grant No.60273043.

References

1. N.Adam, V.Atluri and W.Huang. Modeling and Analysis of Workflows Using Petri Nets. Journal of Intelligent Information Systems, Special Issue on Workflow and Process Management, 10(2), 131-158, 1998.
2. K.Amin, G.von Laszewski, M.Hategan, N.J.Zaluzec, S.Hampton and A.Rossi, GridAnt: A Client-controllable Grid Workflow. In Proc. of the 37th Annual Hawaii International Conference on System Sciences (HICSS'04), 210-219, Hawaii, Jan. 2004.
3. D.Cybok. A Grid Workflow Infrastructure. In Proc. of Workflow in Grid Systems Workshop in GGF10, 2, Berlin, Germany, Mar. 2004
4. J.Chen and Y.Yang. Temporal Dependency for Dynamic Verification of Temporal Constraints in Workflow Systems. In Proc. of the 3rd International Conference on Grid and Cooperative Computing, Springer-Verlag, LNCS 3251, 1005-1008, Oct. 2004.
5. J.Chen, Y.Yang and T.Y.Chen. Dynamic Verification of Temporal Constraints on-the-fly for Workflow Systems. In Proc. of the 11th Asia-Pacific Software Engineering Conference (APSEC'04), IEEE CS Press, 30-37, Busan, Korea, Dec. 2004.
6. S.Chinn and G.Madey. Temporal Representation and Reasoning for Workflow in Engineering Design Change Review. IEEE Transactions on Engineering Management, 47(4), 485-492, 2000.

7. J.Eder, E.Panagos and M.Rabinovich. Time Constraints in Workflow Systems. In Proc. of the 11th International Conference on Advanced Information Systems Engineering (CAiSE'99), Springer Verlag, LNCS 1626, 286-300, Germany, June 1999.
8. J.Eder, H.Pichler, W.Gruber and M.Ninaus. Personal Schedules for Workflow Systems. In Proc. of the Conference on Business Process Management (BPM'03), 216-231, Eindhoven, The Netherlands, June 2003.
9. I.Foster, C.Kesselman and S.Tuecke. The Anatomy of the Grid: Enabling Scalable Virtual Organizations. International Journal of Supercomputing Applications, 15(3), 200-222, 2002.
10. I.Foster, C.Kesselman, J.Nick and S.Tuecke. The Physiology of the Grid: An Open Grid Services Architecture for Distributed Systems Integration. In Proc. of the 5th Global Grid Forum Workshop (GGF5), Edinburgh, Scotland, July 2002.
11. Y.Huang, JISGA. A JINI-BASED Service-Oriented Grid Architecture. The International Journal of High Performance Computing Applications, 17(3), 317-327, 2003.
12. S. Krishnan, P. Wagstrom, and G. von Laszewski. GSFL: A Workflow Framework for Grid Services. In Technical Report Preprint ANL/MCS-P980-0802, Argonne National Laboratory, 9700S. Cass Avenue, Argonne, IL 60439, U.S.A., 2002. Available online: http://www-unix.globus.org/cog/papers/gsfl-paper.pdf
13. H.Li, Y.Yang and T.Y.Chen. Resource Constraints Analysis of Workflow Specifications. The Journal of Systems and Software, 73(2), 271-285, 2004.
14. H. Li and Y. Yang. Dynamic Checking of Temporal Constraints for Concurrent Workflows. Electronic Commerce Research and Applications, Elsevier, in press. Available online at Publisher's Web Site: http://www.sciencedirect.com/science/journal/15674223.
15. O.Marjanovic, and M.E.Orlowska. On Modeling and Verification of Temporal Constraints in Production Workflows. Knowledge and Information Systems, 1(2), 157-192, 1999.
16. O.Marjanovic. Dynamic Verification of Temporal Constraints in Production Workflows. In Proc. of the Australian Database Conference, IEEE Press, 74-81, Canberra, Australia, 2000.
17. E.Panagos and M.Rabinovich. Escalations in Workflow Management Systems. In Proc. of the Workshop on Databases: active and real time, ACM Press, 25-28, Rockville, Maryland, United States, Nov. 1996.
18. E.Panagos and M.Rabinovich. Predictive Workflow Management. In Proc. of the 3rd Workshop on the Next Generation Information Technology and Systems (NGITS-97), 193-197, Neve Ilan, ISRAEL, June 1997.
19. E.Panagos and M.Rabinovich. Reducing Escalation-related Costs in WFMSs. In A.Dogac et al., editor, NATO Advanced Study Institute on Workflow Management Systems and Interoperability. Springer, Istanbul, Turkey, Aug. 1997.
20. H.Pozewaunig, J.Eder, and W.Liebhart. ePERT: Extending PERT for Workflow Management Systems. In Proc. of the 1st EastEuropean Symposium on Advances in Database and Information Systems (ADBIS'97), 217-224, St. Petersburg, Russia, Sept. 1997.
21. Workflow Management Coalition. The Workflow Reference Model, TC00-1003, http://www.wfmc.org/, Jan. 1995.
22. A.Zaidi. On Temporal Logic Programming Using Petri Nets. IEEE Transactions on Systems, Man, and Cybernetics, Part A: Systems and Humans, 29(3), 245-254, 1999.

A New Method for Online Scheduling in Computational Grid Environments

Chuliang Weng, Minglu Li, and Xinda Lu

Department of Computer Science and Engineering, Shanghai Jiao Tong University, Shanghai, 200030, People's Republic of China
{weng-cl, li-ml, lu-xd}@cs.sjtu.edu.cn

Abstract. A crucial issue for the efficient deployment of distributed applications on the grid is that of scheduling. In this paper, a modified cost-based online scheduling algorithm is presented for computational grids with theoretical guarantee. Firstly, a scheduling framework is described, where the grid environment is characterized, and the online job model is defined. Secondly, the modified cost-based online scheduling algorithm is presented where costs of resources are exponential functions of their loads. Finally, we test the algorithm in the grid simulation environment, and compare the performance of the presented algorithm with the greedy algorithm.

1 Introduction

Advances in networking technology and computational infrastructure make it possible to construct large-scale high-performance distributed computing environments, or computational grids [1]. There are a number of projects that deal with a variety of problems in a grid environment such as resource specification, information service, resource allocation and security issue, etc. However, A crucial issue for the efficient deployment of distributed applications on the grid is that of scheduling [2].

In this paper, we focus on the online scheduling issue in the grid context, and present a modified cost-based scheduling algorithm for grid computing with experiments, which predecessor is described in [3] and theoretical guarantee was analyzed there. We borrow ideas from the economics concept for converting the total usage of heterogeneous resources into a homogeneous cost, although there are many methods for determining the price of resources in the grid [4]. For testing scheduling algorithms in grid environments, we build the simulator based on SimGrid Toolkit [5].

2 Assumption and Problem Statement

In Fig.1, a grid system consists of *resource domains* that are individual and autonomous administrative domains, which usually are in the range of Local Area Network (LAN). It is the *metascheduler* that receives requirements of users in the grid environment and assigns users' jobs to geographically distributed resource domains, and

Y. Zhang et al. (Eds.): APWeb 2005, LNCS 3399, pp. 832–837, 2005.

the metascheduler is connected to resource domains by Wide Area Network (WAN). One data repository is available at the metascheduler and input data needed by users' jobs are stored in the data repository in advance.

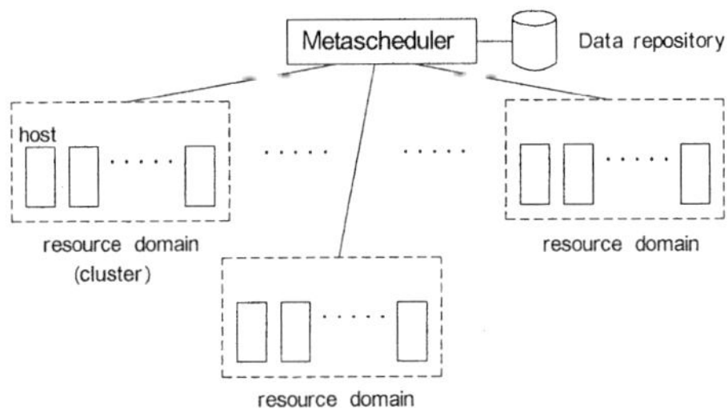

Fig. 1. Topology of the computational grid

It is assumed that the computational grid consists of m resource domains that are geographically distributed. Resource domain rd_i and the metascheduler are connected with bandwidth $r_b(rd_i)$. Compared to communication overhead of transferring job applications and input data from the metascheduler to resource domains in WAN, communication overhead inside a resource domain is ignored. Host rd_{ij} in resource domain rd_i has a CPU resource of speed $r_c(rd_{ij})$, and for simplicity it is assumed that each resource domain has n computational hosts. All other resources associated with the host will be abstracted out, although the framework can be extended to handle additional resources such as memory.

The *unrelated machines* model [6] is chosen for studying the scheduling algorithm, because there are many different factors that will influence the effective load of hosts and the execution time of jobs in the grid context. That is, the load of a given host added by a given job is known, but the load doesn't need to have any relationship to the load the job would add to other hosts.

In this paper, jobs arrive online and each job has to be immediately assigned to one of hosts in the computational grid, i.e. online scheduling. We adopt jobs arrive over time [6] as our online paradigm, i.e., the attribute of a job is known when it arrives, and we define each job jb_k by following parameters:

- The number of CPU cycles required by the job, $n_c(jb_k)$.
- The communication amount it requires, $n_b(jb_k)$. In the following, $n_b(jb_k)$ denotes the size of input data needed by job jb_k for that usually the size of a job application can be ignored compared to the size of input data required by the job.

It is assumed that $n_c(jb_k)$ and $n_b(jb_k)$ are known upon job's arrival with the lack of knowledge of jobs arriving in the future. After assigned to a host in the computational grid immediately when it arrives, a job will not be reassigned to other hosts later. The input data required by a job should be transferred to the corresponding assigned host before the execution of the job.

We adopt a classic performance metric: makespan, which is the length of the schedule, or equivalently the time when the first job starts running subtracted from the time when the last job is completed. The scheduling goal is to minimize the makespan of a given job sequence.

3 Algorithm and Experiments

In this paper, we just borrow ideas from the economics concept for converting the total usage of different kinds of resources, such as CPU and bandwidth, into a homogeneous cost. The cost of a resource is an exponential function of the load assigned on the resource since the first job arrives in the sequence of jobs.

$S(rd_i, jb_k)$ denotes the set of jobs assigned in resource domain rd_i after job jb_k has been assigned on the computational grid, and $S(rd_{ij}, jb_k)$ denotes the set of jobs assigned in host rd_{ij} after job jb_k has been assigned on the computational grid. Then they satisfy the following relation:

$$S(rd_i, jb_k) = \bigcup_{j=1}^{n} S(rd_{ij}, jb_k) \tag{1}$$

The *load* on a given resource equals its usage divided by its capacity. After job jb_k was assigned, the load of the network connecting resource domain rd_i and the metascheduler is defined by:

$$l_b(rd_i, jb_k) = \sum_{jb_p \in S(rd_i, jb_k)} n_b(jb_p) / r_b(rd_i) \tag{2}$$

After job jb_k was assigned in the grid system, the CPU load of host rd_{ij} in resource domain rd_i is defined by:

$$l_c(rd_{ij}, jb_k) = \sum_{jb_p \in S(rd_{ij}, jb_k)} n_c(jb_p) / r_c(rd_{ij}) \tag{3}$$

For simplicity we will abbreviate $l_b(rd_i, jb_k)$ as $l_b(i, k)$, and $l_c(rd_{ij}, jb_k)$ as $l_c(i, j, k)$.

In our early theoretical work [3], we assumed that for a given sequence of jobs the maximum load produced by the optimal offline algorithm is known in advance. In practice, usually for a given sequence of jobs the maximum load produced by the optimal offline algorithm is not known. The doubling approach can be adopted to approximate the maximum load produced by the optimal offline algorithm. Therefore, a positive parameter Δ is introduced, and utilized to normalize $\bar{x} = x/\Delta$ for load x, and the value of Δ is determined in the presented algorithm.

The *marginal cost* of a job jb_k assigned to host rd_{ij} in the grid is denoted by $Cost(i, j, k)$, which consists of the marginal cost of network $Cost_b(i, k)$ and the marginal cost of CPU $Cost_c(i, j, k)$, and they are defined by:

$$Cost_c(i, j, k) = \alpha^{\bar{l}_c(i,j,k-1) + \bar{n}_c(jb_k)/r_c(rd_{ij})} - \alpha^{\bar{l}_c(i,j,k-1)} \tag{4}$$

$$Cost_b(i, k) = \beta^{\bar{l}_b(i,k-1) + \bar{n}_b(jb_k)/r_b(rd_i)} - \beta^{\bar{l}_b(i,k-1)} \tag{5}$$

$$Cost(i,j,k) = Cost_c(i,j,k) + Cost_b(i,k) \tag{6}$$

where, α, β are a constant, and $\alpha>1$, $\beta>1$.

The modified cost-based online scheduling algorithm assigns a job on the host where its resource consumption has the minimum marginal cost according to equation (6). The algorithm is presented as Fig.2.

```
the first job jb_1 arrived;
Δ = min_{i,j}{n_b(jb_1)/r_b(rd_i), n_c(jb_1)/r_c(rd_ij)};
while (job jb_k arrives) {/*include job jb_1 */
   flag = 1;
   while(flag){
      Cost(i, j,k) = Cost_b(i,k) + Cost_c(i, j,k);
      (I, J) = arg min_{i,j}(Cost(i, j,k));
      Δ' = max{l_b(I,k), l_c(I,J,k)};
      if (Δ' > ((log(n+1)m)*Δ))  { Δ = 2*Δ;  flag = 1;}
      esle                        {flag = 0;}
   }
   Assign: jb_k → rd_IJ;
   Update : l_b(i,k), l_c(i, j,k);
}
```

Fig. 2. The modified cost-based online scheduling algorithm

Theorem 1. The modified cost-based online scheduling algorithm is $O(\log(n+1)m)$-*competitive* in the computational grid environment illustrated as Fig.1.

Proof. It can be proved in the similar way as in paper [3].

Table 1. Parameters used in the experiment

Grid Computing Environment		
m (the number of resource domains)	9	fixed
n (the number of hosts in each resource domain)	5	fixed
r_c (the speed of CPU) (Mflop/s)	[200,1800](interval=200)	uniform distribution
Average CPU load	0.2	fixed
Variant coefficient of CPU load	[0.2, 1.8]	uniform distribution
r_b (the bandwidth of network) (Mbit/s)	[0.25, 2.0]	uniform distribution
Job attributes		
Average interval of job arrivals (s)	2/4/6/8/10	poisson arrivals
Total of jobs	600	fixed
n_c (the number of CPU cycles) (Mflop)	1000*[100, 300]	uniform distribution
n_b (the size of input data) (M)	6/12/18/24/30	
Scheduling parameters		
α (coefficient in the cost function)	1.9	
β (coefficient in the cost function)	1.9	
Simulation runs for each scenario	500	

To run the experiments, we developed a simulator based on the SimGrid toolkit [5]. The parameters chosen in the simulation experiment are listed as Table 1. Each experimental result is the average of values produced by 500 runs of simulation.

For testing the performance of the modified cost-based online algorithm, we will compare this presented algorithm with the existing greedy algorithm, and analyze some parameters' influence on its performance with experiments.

Greedy algorithm is an effective online scheduling algorithm. In this paper, greedy algorithm can be correspondingly considered as follows: for each arrival job, the metascheduler immediately assigns the job to the host with the minimum sum of the current load of CPU and the current load of network connecting the metascheduler and the resource domain it located in.

In Fig.3 (a), the size of input data is 6M. As the average interval of job arrivals increases from 2 to 10 seconds, the makespan of two algorithms increases correspondingly.

Fig.3 (a) shows that the modified cost-base algorithm can attain less makespan than the greedy algorithm, and indicates that the modified cost-based algorithm can obtain better performance than the greedy algorithm. This result can be explained from two aspects. Firstly, the greedy algorithm determines the candidate host just according to the current load, and does not consider the CPU speed of the host and the bandwidth of the network link through which the input data will be transferred, so performance estimation of the greedy algorithm will lead to less accurate than the modified cost-based algorithm which has taken these factors into account. Secondly, the marginal cost in the modified cost-based algorithm is an exponential function of resource load, which also benefits to determine the optimal candidate host. The merit of exponential function is that for assigning a job to the system, not only increase in resource load created by the new job but also the current resource load have influence on the marginal cost of the new job.

Fig. 3. Experimental results. (a) Makespan vs. the average interval of job arrivals, (b) Makespan vs. the size of input data

In Fig. 3(b), the average interval of job arrivals is 6 seconds. We compare the two algorithms with the size of input data varying, and makespans of the two algorithms are increasing as the amount of job's input data increases. And it shows that the makespan of the modified cost-based algorithm is less than the makespan of the greedy algorithm. It can also be explained as that the modified cost-based algorithm considers more effective factors for performance estimation and exponential function benefits to determine the optimal candidate host.

4 Conclusions

In this paper, a modified method for determining the cost of resources is presented with theoretical guarantee, which is an exponential function of the load. We implement the algorithm and test the performance of the algorithm in the simulation environment, and experimental results indicate that the presented algorithm could obtain good performance in practice. So we conclude that the modified cost-based online scheduling algorithm is an effective algorithm for online scheduling in the computational grid environment with theoretical guarantee.

Acknowledgements

This research was supported by the National 863 Program of China (No.2004AA104340 and No.2004AA104280), the National Natural Science Foundation of China (No. 60173031 and No. 60473092), ChinaGrid Program of MOE of China, and the grand project (No.03dz15027) of the Science and Technology Commission of Shanghai Municipality.

References

[1] Foster, I., Kesselman, C., Tuecke, S.: The Anatomy of the Grid: Enabling Scalable Virtual Organizations. The International Journal of Supercomputer Applications, 15(3): 200-222, 2001.

[2] Foster, I., Kesselman, C.: The GRID: Blueprint for a New Computing Infrastructure. Morgan Kaufmann, San Francisco, USA, 1998.

[3] Weng, C., Lu, X.: A Cost-Based Online Scheduling Algorithm for Job Assignment on Computational Grids. In: Proceedings of the 5th International Workshop on Advanced Parallel Processing Technologies (APPT'03), Lecture Notes in Computer Science, Vol.2834, Springer-Verlag, 2003, pp.343-351.

[4] Buyya, R., Abramson, D., Giddy, J., Stockinger, H.: Economic Models for Resource Management and Scheduling in Grid Computing. The Journal of Concurrency and Computation: Practice and Experience, 14(13-15): 1507-1542, 2002.

[5] Legrand, A., Marchal, L., Casanova, H.: Scheduling Distributed Applications: the SimGrid Simulation Framework. In: Proceedings of the 3rd IEEE/ACM Symposium on Cluster Computing and the Grid (CCGrid'03), 2003, pp.138-145.

[6] Sgall, J.: On-line Scheduling – A Survey. In: Fiat, A., Woeginger, G. (eds.): Online Algorithms: The State of the Art. Lecture Notes in Computer Science, Vol.1442, Springer-Verlag, 1998, pp.196-231.

Influence of Performance Prediction Inaccuracy on Task Scheduling in Grid Environment

Yuanyuan Zhang[1] and Yasushi Inoguchi[2]

[1] Graduate School of Information Science,
[2] Center for Information Science,
Japan Advanced Institute of Science and Technology,
1-1 Asahidai, Tatsunokuchi, Ishikawa, 923-1292, Japan
{yuanyuan, inoguchi}@jaist.ac.jp*

Abstract. In this paper, we study the influence of performance prediction inaccuracy on task scheduling in grid environment from the context of task selection and processor selection, which are two critical phases in task scheduling. Formulas are established for the degree of misprediction, the probability that the predicted values for the performance of tasks and processors reveal different ordering characteristics from their real values. The impacts of different parameters on the degree of misprediction are also investigated extensively. Evaluation results show that an underestimate of performance can result in greater influence on task scheduling compared with an overestimate, while higher heterogeneity results in smaller influence.

Keywords: grid computing, task scheduling, performance prediction, task selection, processor selection.

1 Introduction

Grid computing[1] is becoming increasingly popular recently. Task scheduling, the problem of scheduling tasks to processors so that all the tasks can finish their execution in the minimal time, is a critical component for achieving high performance in grid environment. Usually the scheduling process of a task scheduling algorithm involves two phases: task selection and processor selection. In task selection phase, the tasks are sorted in a list according to some criterion related with the workloads of the tasks; while in processor selection phase, the first task in the list is allocated to a processor based on another criterion typically related with the speeds of the processors. Therefore, the prediction for the task workloads and processor speeds is critical for achieving satisfying performance in grid task scheduling system. Usually such prediction are executed by some performance prediction tools such as NWS[2].

* This research is conducted as a program for the "21st Century COE Program" by Ministry of Education, Culture, Sports, Science and Technology, Japan.

Y. Zhang et al. (Eds.): APWeb 2005, LNCS 3399, pp. 838–844, 2005.

Existing scheduling algorithms typically assumed that the task scheduler has perfect knowledge about the performance of both tasks and processors. However, although nowadays the performance prediction tools can provide increasingly accurate prediction, it is still impossible to achieve absolutely accurate prediction since grid is a highly dynamic environment[1]. Therefore the performance of task scheduling algorithms will be influenced by such inaccurate prediction, and different task scheduling algorithms reveal different degrees of sensitivity to the inaccurate prediction. In this paper, we would focus on the study of the influence of performance prediction inaccuracy on task scheduling from the perspectives of task selection and processor selection in grid environment.

The remainder of this paper is organized as follows: in next section, we analyze the influence of prediction inaccuracy on task scheduling, introduce the concept of degree of misprediction, and establish related formulas. The impact of the parameters in the formulas for the degree of misprediction is evaluated in section 3. Finally, the paper is concluded in section 4.

2 Analysis of the Influence of Prediction Error on Task Scheduling

2.1 Task Selection

Grid computing is a highly heterogeneous and dynamic environment. Task scheduling problem in such a heterogeneous and dynamic environment is much more difficult than that in homogeneous system. Furthermore, since it is impossible to obtain absolutely accurate prediction for the workloads of tasks because of the dynamicity, the actual workloads of tasks will be different from the predicted values, and this will influence the performance of task scheduling algorithms. For example, if the actual workload of task T_i is less than that of task T_j, while because of prediction error, the predicted value of T_i is more than that of T_j, then we will make wrong scheduling decision if we schedule the tasks based on their workloads.

In this paper we focus on the study of a grid application which is composed of a set of independent tasks. The actual workloads of these tasks are independent identical distribution(i.i.d.) random variables. In grid scheduling system when performance prediction tools are used to predict the performance of the tasks, the predicted errors usually lie in an interval of the actual workloads according to some probability distribution.

Suppose T_1 and T_2 are two tasks in a grid application and their actual workloads are denoted by positive numbers x_1 and x_2 respectively. The prediction errors of T_1 and T_2, y_1 and y_2, are independent random variables and follow some probability distribution in the ranges of $[-ax_1, bx_1]$ and $[-ax_2, bx_2]$, where the possible value fields of a and b are [0,1) and [0,∞) respectively. The probability density function of prediction error is denoted by $g(y)$. For the predicted workloads of T_1 and T_2, denoted by z_1 and z_2, we have the following equations:

$$z_1 = x_1 + y_1; \qquad z_2 = x_2 + y_2. \tag{1}$$

Usually the task scheduling algorithms schedule tasks based on their predicted workloads, for example, schedule the task with the largest workload first or with the smallest workload first, so the prediction inaccuracy has remarkable influence on the performance of scheduling algorithms when the actual workload of T_1 is smaller than that of T_2 while because of the prediction errors, the predicted value of T_1 is greater than that of T_2. We call such situation *misprediction.* Because different performance prediction tools have different degrees of prediction inaccuracy, they can arouse different degrees of misprediction. Therefore, what we are interested in is the probability of the misprediction to happen, i.e., $P(z_1 > z_2|x_1 < x_2)$, which is called *degree of misprediction* for two tasks here.

The above probability can be converted into:

$$P(z_1 > z_2|x_1 < x_2) = P(y_1 > y_2 + x_2 - x_1|x_1 < x_2) \tag{2}$$

where $y_1 \in [-ax_1, bx_1]$, and $y_2 \in [-ax_2, bx_2]$.

In the coordinate system of y_1 and y_2, the inequality $y_1 > y_2 + x_2$ - x_1 is the area above the line L: $y_1 = y_2 + x_2$ - x_1, and the probability of P($y_1 > y_2 + x_2$ - $x_1|x_1 < x_2$) can be expressed by the area of the overlapping region between L and the rectangle surrounded by the lines y_1 = -ax_1, y_1 = bx_1, y_2 = -ax_2 and y_2 = bx_2 in the y_1, y_2 coordinate system.

About the overlapping region, we have the following conclusion:

There are only two cases for the overlapping between L and the rectangle: they either don't overlap or overlap in a triangle region.

Proof. Case(1): This case is shown in figure 1. The line which is parallel to L and passes the point (bx_1,-ax_2) is y_1 = y_2 + ax_2 + bx_1. If L is above this line, then we can see intuitionally that there is no overlapping between L and the rectangle. That is to say, if x_2 - $x_1 \geq$ ax_2 + bx_1, i.e., if (1-a)$x_2 \geq$ (1+b)x_1, the probability P($y_1 > y_2 + x_2$ - $x_1|x_1 < x_2$) equals to 0. It can be expressed mathematically as:

$$P(y_1 > y_2 + x_2 - x_1|x_1 < x_2) = 0 \qquad \text{if } (1-a)x_2 \geq (1+b)x_1, x_2 > x_1.$$

Case(2): If L is under the line y_1 = y_2 + ax_2 + bx_1, then it will overlap with the rectangle. The probability for the misprediction to happen equals to the area

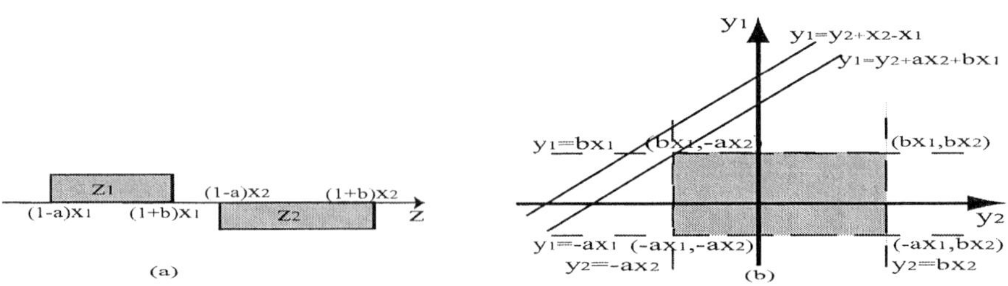

Fig. 1. The case when there is no misperception. (a)the value fields of predicted workloads which don't overlap; (b)the situation of the degree of misperception

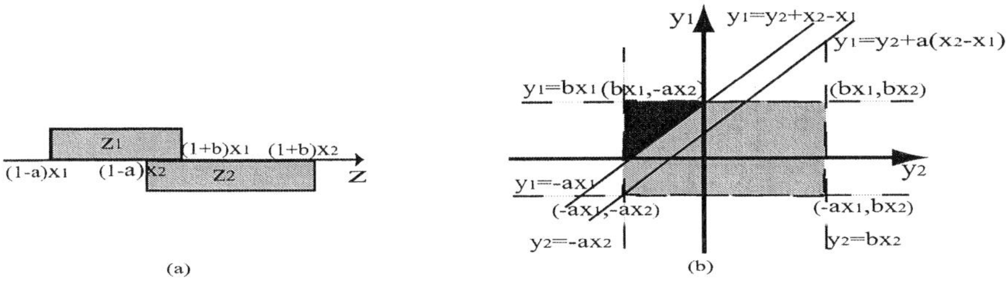

Fig. 2. The case when misperception happens. (a)the value fields of the predicted workloads which overlap; (b)the situation of the degree of misperception

of the overlapping region. The line which is parallel to L and passes the point (-ax_1,-ax_2) is: y_1 = y_2 + a(x_2 - x_1). Since 0 ≤ a < 1, a(x_2 - x_1) < x_2 - x_1. So L must be above the line y_1 = y_2 + a(x_2 - x_1) in any way. From figure 2 we can see that the overlapping region can only be a triangle.

So the proof is completed.

In the case L and the rectangle overlaps in a triangle, the area of the overlapping region, i.e., the probability P(y_1 > y_2 + x_2 - x_1|x_1 < x_2), can be expressed by the double integral of the probability density functions g(y_1) and g(y_2). So we have the following equation:

$$P(y_1 > y_2 + x_2 - x_1 | y_1 < y_2) = \int_{-ax_2}^{(1+b)x_1 - x_2} \int_{y_2+x_2-x_1}^{bx_1} g(y_1)g(y_2)dy_1dy_2$$

$$\text{if}(1-a)x_2 < (1+b)x_1.$$

If the probability density function of the actual workload of a task in the grid application is f(x) and the value field of the actual workload x is [xl,xu], then the *degree of misprediction for the grid application,* which is denoted by *DM*, is defined as the average of the degree of misprediction between any two tasks in the application. In virtue of the equation for the degree of misprediction between two tasks as shown before, *DM* can be expressed as:

$$\text{DM} = \int_{xl}^{xu} \int_{xl}^{\frac{1+b}{1-a}x_1} \int_{-ax_2}^{(1+b)x_1-x_2} \int_{y_2+x_2-x_1}^{bx_1} f(x_1)f(x_2)g(y_1)g(y_2)dy_1dy_2dx_2dx_1$$

This result is independent with the specific function for $f(x)$ and $g(y)$.

2.2 Processor Selection

In processor selection phase, usually a task scheduling algorithm selects a processor according to the predicted computational speed of the processors, for example, select a fastest processor or a slowest processor, while because grid is a highly dynamic environment, the performance prediction tools usually can not provide entirely accurate prediction for the processor speeds, and such prediction inaccuracy will affect the performance of the task scheduling algorithm.

Suppose there are m heterogeneous processors in the grid system. The actual computational speed of processor $P_i(1\leq i \leq m)$ is denoted by s_i. The prediction error of s_i, which is denoted as t_i, typically lies in a range of s_i following some probability distribution. The prediction errors of different processors are independent random variables. Let s_i and s_j be the actual speeds of processor P_i and P_j respectively. The prediction errors for them are t_i and t_j. t_i and t_j are independent random variables. The value fields of t_i and t_j are respectively $[-as_i, bs_i]$ and $[-as_j, bs_j]$ with the probability density function h(t), where $0 \leq a < 1, b \geq 0$(a and b here are different from that in the above subsection). The predicted speeds of P_i and P_j are w_i and w_j. We have the following equations:

$$w_i = s_i + t_i; \qquad w_j = s_j + t_j. \tag{3}$$

The degree of misprediction for two processors is defined as the probability of the event that the actual computational speed s_i is smaller than s_j, while because of prediction errors, the predicted speed w_i is greater than w_j, that is, the probability $P(w_i > w_j|s_i < s_j)$. This can be further transformed to:

$$P(w_i > w_j|s_i < s_j) = P(t_i > t_j + s_j - s_i|s_i < s_j). \tag{4}$$

Following a similar way as that in task selection, we can derive the equation for processor selection:

$$P(t_i > t_j + s_j - s_i|s_i < s_j) = \begin{cases} 0 & if(1-a)s_j \geq (1+b)s_i \\ \int_{-as_j}^{(1+b)s_i - s_j} \int_{t_j+s_j-s_i}^{bs_i} h(t_i)h(t_j)dt_i dt_j & else \end{cases}$$

The degree of misprediction for the scheduling of a task in a grid system with m processors, which is denoted by DM_P, is defined as the average of the degree of misprediction between any two processors. In virtue of the equation for the degree of misprediction between two processors as shown before, DM_P can be expressed as:

$$DM_P = \frac{1}{C_m^2} \sum_{i=1}^{m-1} \sum_{j=i+1}^{m} P(t_i > t_j + s_j - s_i|s_i < s_j). \tag{5}$$

3 Study of Evaluation Results

We present the results from our evaluations which assess the impact of the parameters in formula (5), the influence of prediction inaccuracy on processor selection. The results are shown in figures 3(a)-(f), where the horizontal axis in every figure is the combination of the values of a and b, and the vertical axis is DM_p, the degree of misprediction for processor selection.

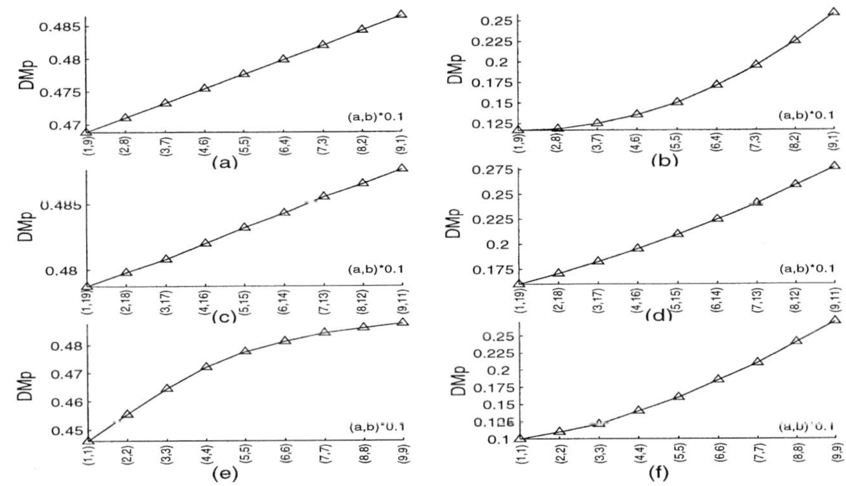

Fig. 3. Influence of parameters a,b and processor heterogeneity on the degree of misprediction. (a),(c),(e): low heterogeneity, (b),(d),(f): high heterogeneity

The parameters in formula (5) are a, b, m, $s_i(1 \leq \mathrm{i} \leq \mathrm{m})$ and h(t). Uniform distribution for the prediction error of processor execution speed is assumed, that is, the probability density function of h(t) is assumed to be

$$h(t) = \frac{1}{(a+b)s},$$

while s is the actual execution speed of a processor. We also assume that there are 6 processors in the grid computing system(m=6) and the actual execution time of the first processor is s_1=500. To evaluate the impact of the grid heterogeneity on the degree of misprediction, two groups of estimations are conducted: in figure 3(a), (c) and (e) the actual execution times of the processors increase successively by the increment of 5(s_{i+1} - s_i = 5, 1 $\leq$ i $\leq$ m-1), while in figure 3(b), (d) and (f) the increment is assumed to be 250(s_{i+1} - s_i = 250, 1 $\leq$ i $\leq$ m-1).

From the comparison of the graphs on the left with that on the right, we can see that, the degree of misprediction decreases as the heterogeneity of grid computing system increases. In figure 3(a) and (b) the range of (a,b) shifts gradually from (0.1,0.9) to (0.9,0.1), that is, the prediction error shifts gradually from overestimate to underestimate. From figure 3(a) and (b) we can see that the degree of misprediction increases as the prediction inaccuracy changes from overestimate to underestimate, moreover, such increase is fleet in highly heterogeneous grid system, while in grid system with low heterogeneityp, the degree of misprediction increases slowly with the shift of (a,b). In figure 3(c) and (d), the predicted error shifts from [-0.1s_i,1.9s_i] to [-0.9s_i,1.1s_i]. Comparing figure 3(c) with (a) and (d) with (b), we can see that the degree of prediction increases as the range of prediction error increases, and higher heterogeneity results in faster increase. In figure 3(e) and (f), (a,b) increases from (0.1,0.1) to (0.9,0.9), while the average prediction error remains constantly to be 0. In figure 3(e) and (f), the degree of misprediction increases as the range of prediction error increases.

Although we only present the results for the case of resource selection here, it is expected that the task selection phase can reveal similar results.

4 Conclusion

The prediction inaccuracy for the performance of tasks and processors usually exists so that influences the performance of task scheduling algorithms in grid computing. This paper studies such influence from the perspective of task selection and processor selection. Evaluation results show that an underestimate of performance can result in greater influence on task scheduling compared with an overestimate, while higher heterogeneity results in smaller influence. We hope our results can provide some references for task scheduling in grid environment.

References

1. I. Foster and C. Kesselman, *The Grid: Blueprint for a New Computing Infrastructure*, Morgan Kaufmann Publishers, San Fransisco, CA, 1999.
2. R. Wolski, N. Spring, and J. Hayes, "The Network Weather Service: A Distributed Resource Performance Forecasting Service for Metacomputing," *Journal of Future Generation Computing Systems*, pp. 757-768, Vol. 15, , Oct., 1999.

Grid Accounting Information Gathering System with Access Control

Boeb Kyun Kim[1], Dong Un An[1], Seung Jong Chung[1], and Haeng Jin Jang[2]

[1] Dept. of Computer Engineering, Chonbuk National University, South Korea
{kyun, duan, sjchung}@chonbuk.ac.kr
[2] Korea Institute of Science and Technology Information
hjjang@kisti.re.kr

Abstract. Grid computing represents the fundamental computing shift from a localized resource computing model to a fully-distributed virtual organization with shared resources. Accounting is one of the main obstacles to widespread adoption of the Grid. Accounting has until recently, been a sparsely-addressed problem, particularly in practice. In this paper, we design and implement the accounting information gathering system. Implemented system is based on OGSA, following GSAX framework of RUS-WG in GGF. To provide end-to-end user identity of accounting information, we use a Grid access control system, called PGAM. And the schema of accounting information is following Usage Record Fields of UR-WG in GGF. Also, the accounting information monitoring tool for system management in the Grid environment is implemented.

1 Introduction

Grid computing represents the fundamental computing shift from a localized resource computing model to a fully-distributed virtual organization with shared resources [1][2][3]. With the Grid, companies achieve a cost efficient and effective mechanism for building and deploying applications across a wide spectrum of devices.

Several commercial obstacles, most notably security and accounting, have impeded the widespread adoption of the Grid. Several projects around security and authentication have begun both within and outside the Grid community, enabling companies to confidently use Grid services. Accounting for these services has until recently, been a sparsely-addressed problem, particularly in practice. The Grid community has yet to produce either framework or, better still, an implementation of Grid accounting [4][5].

We design and implement the accounting information gathering system. Implemented system is based on OGSA (Open Grid Service Architecture) [2], following GSAX (Grid Service Accounting Extension) framework [4] of RUS-WG (Resource Usage Service) in GGF.

To provide end-to-end user identity of accounting information on each resource, we use a Grid access control system, called PGAM [6]. PGAM uses globus toolkit. PGAM tries to support site autonomy, a factor which encourages a site to get into the Grid environment, and provides template account mechanism.

Y. Zhang et al. (Eds.): APWeb 2005, LNCS 3399, pp. 845–850, 2005.

And the schema of accounting information is followed Usage Record Fields of UR-WG (Usage Record) in GGF. The system comprises of several modules which work independently from each other. In addition, the accounting information monitoring tool for the system management in the Grid environment is implemented.

2 Related Works

The area of Grid accounting has also been investigated by others [4][7]. Some of these have provided guidance in outlining the accounting information gathering system architecture.

GSAX [4] is an extensible OGSA accounting and logging framework. It is designed to provide a functionally modular accounting framework which can be expanded by adding or changing components, to allow use of accounting at many levels of application and user understanding, to provide information at different levels of granularity (from real-time information to data on a per-job basis), to integrate QoS and service-level agreements into the accounting framework. This framework is not tied to Grid or OGSA and can easily be adapted to scale with the growth in accountable web services.

DGAS (DataGrid Accounting System) [7] model, developed by DataGrid Project, envisions a whole new economic Grid market, where supply and demand of Grid resources work in unison to strive towards equilibrium where all resources are fully utilized to the lowest possible price. But, DataGrid employs a centralized resource broker intercepting all job within the Grid. Such centralized solutions are not in agreement with the decentralized nature of the Grid. So, the system, designed in this paper, is follows GSAX framework.

3 Design of Accounting Information Gathering System

Designed and implemented system uses the globus toolkit as its middleware which is the most widely adopted grid middleware but is lack of end-to-end user identity.

3.1 Identity in Globus Toolkit

Globus toolkit comprises a set of components that implement basic services for resource management, information service, data management, grid security, etc. GRAM (Grid Resource Allocation Manager) is responsible for access to remote resources, co-allocation of distributed resources, and processing of heterogeneity of resource management. The gatekeeper is an extremely simple component that responds to a request by doing three things: performing mutual authentication of user and resource, determining a local user name for the remote user, and starting a job manager which executes as that local user and actually handles the request.

Normally, when a request for access is received, the gatekeeper attempts to find the corresponding local username in the "grid-mapfile." This file lists pairs of certificate subjects (e.g., "/O=Grid/O=Globus/OU=chonbuk.ac.kr/CN=hdg") and usernames (e.g., gw1). If no line is found for the current subject, access request is denied.

```
"/O=Grid/O=Globus/OU=chonbuk.ac.kr/CN=hdg" gw1
"/O=Grid/O=Globus/OU=chonbuk.ac.kr/CN=dgs" gw2
"/O=Grid/O=Globus/OU=chonbuk.ac.kr/CN=kyun" gw2
"/O=Grid/O=Globus/OU=chonbuk.ac.kr/CN=duan" gw3
```

Fig. 1. An example of "grid-mapfile"

In the original syntax of this file, several certificate subjects can be mapped to one local username. But, this mechanism cannot guarantee end-to-end user identity: who is the owner of local process or job. If the site administrator wants to trace the usage of local resource, he must deploy other special monitoring or tracing tool. Sharing of the same right to local files, directories and mails by multiple grid users can cause security problem, digging into privacy.

To guarantee end-to-end user identity, we adopted PGAM. It uses only 1-to-1 mapping of certificate subject and local username. But 1-to-1 mapping can cause a heavy load on the site administrator and local system. So, PGAM implements template account mechanism [8] to reduce the burden of administrator and local system.

When a grid user requests a right for access to local resource with his credential and personal information and job specification, new thread is created to process it. Each thread processes interaction from client, logs all the record during operation, enforce local resource management policies (e.g., pool of available local usernames, client host policy, stage policy, personal information policy, local resource's status policy).

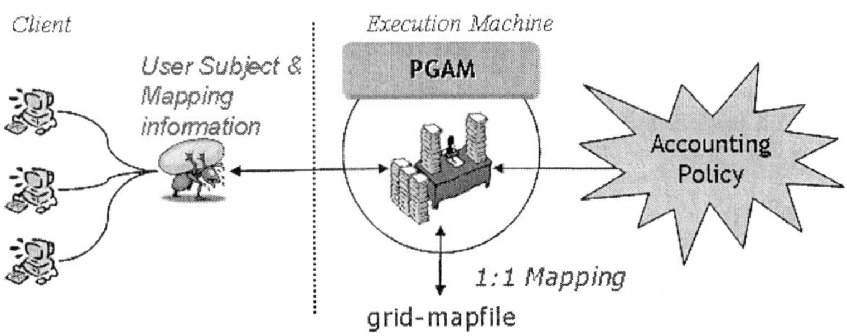

Fig. 2. Function of PGAM

3.2 Schema of Usage Record and Accounting Information Service

Accounting in the grid environment is very different from that in the traditional computing environment, because the concept of the user is different from the local user and the format of accounting data of each system is different from each other.

Accounting information in the grid environment is produced by the grid user. The format of accounting data on linux is different from that on other operating system. We chose Usage Record format, proposed by UR-WG in GGF, as a common usage record format in the grid environment.

Because of characteristics of the grid environment, most of grid programmers try to keep the autonomy of each site with minimum intrusion. Thus, the use of the output of the local accounting system is preferred. Designed accounting information service is independent from any other services or resources and to follow the GSAX. Each resource sends its accounting data to the accounting information service. To obtain his or her accounting information, user uses a service call following OGSA.

3.3 Gathering Process Accounting Information

Most of Unix operating systems provide utilities for monitoring process activities on each system. For the Linux, psacct package contains several utilities for monitoring process activities. The result of the process monitoring is saved into the file "pacct". This file contains information sufficient for Minimum Set of Usage Record.

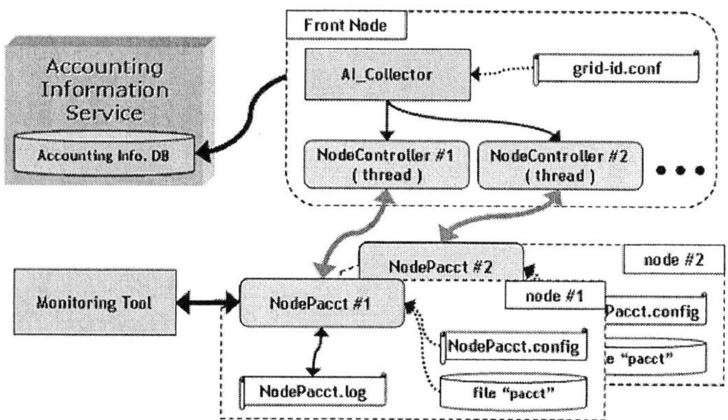

Fig. 3. Architecture for gathering process accounting information

Figure 3 shows the architecture for gathering process accounting information. If a machine is structured as a cluster, AI_Collector is located in the front node only and creates NodeController for each slave node. For each slave node, NodePacct is created by the Monitoring Tool which may locate outside of this machine. NodePacct collects process accounting information from the file "pacct" and interacts with NodeController. Process accounting information in each NodeController is gathered by AI_Collector and sent to accounting information database in the Accounting Information Service. Configuration file "grid-id.conf" contains the list of local usernames that allocated to the grid user. Each NodePacct collects process accounting information which is produced by these users.

We designed this architecture to be scalable. NodeController is created against each NodePacct in the slave node. So, if new slave node is added, NodeController is created automatically. That is, adding and controlling of slave node is very easy.

3.4 Gathering Accounting Information from Job Manager

The system can collect accounting information produced by job manager. We applied to LoadLeveler, the job manager for IBM AIX machine. So, we use this accounting information of the machine to gather grid accounting information. Figure 4 shows the architecture for LoadLeveler. AI_Collector in Figure 4 is the same module in Figure 3. AI_Collector initiates LoadL_Acct to collect accounting information. LoadL_Acct extract accounting information from the history file of LoadLeveler. Application to PBS (Portable Batch System) or other Job Manager is very easy to achieve by developing only the module, which plays the role for LoadLeveler.

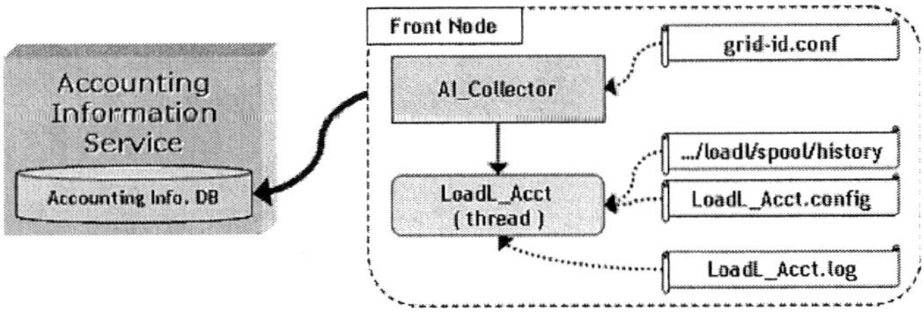

Fig. 4. Architecture for gathering accounting information produced by LoadLeveler

4 Implementation

We implemented this system in the following environments. For the portability of this system, Java is selected. We use MySQL for DBMS.

Figure 5 shows an example of gathered process accounting information. We can see all the required information without the grid user identity. To find the grid user who creates these processes, utility for grid access control is needed. Also, we implement the monitoring tool for process accounting (Figure 6). With this tool, the administrator can manipulate NodePacct. This tool can be applied to job managers.

HostName	CommandNam	UserId	Tty	BeginTime	EndTime	RealTime	SystemTin	UserTim	CharsIO	BlockR\	CpuFacto	HogFactc	MeanMemSiz	KcoreMir	ActFlag	ExitStat
node20.chonbuk.ac.kr	#globus-g	hjhwang	?	20021117200041	20021117200044	3.22	0.02	0.94	43544	0	0.984	0.296	1136	18.05	2	0
node20.chonbuk.ac.kr	date	hjhwang	?	20031117200049	20031117200049	0	0	0	31	0	0	0	0	0	0	0
node20.chonbuk.ac.kr	globus-j	hjhwang	?	20021117200044	20021117200049	5.61	1.06	0.27	192394	0	0.2	0.237	410	9.08	0	0
node20.chonbuk.ac.kr	#globus-g	hjhwang	?	20021117202245	20021117202246	1.58	0	0.62	43544	0	1	0.396	1121	11.68	2	0
node20.chonbuk.ac.kr	date	hjhwang	?	20031117202251	20031117202251	0	0	0	31	0	0	0	0	0	0	0
node20.chonbuk.ac.kr	globus-j	hjhwang	?	20021117202247	20021117202252	5.52	1.03	0.33	192320	0	0.241	0.246	519	11.76	0	0
node20.chonbuk.ac.kr	#globus-g	hjhwang	?	20021117202358	20021117202400	2.69	0.02	0.89	43536	0	0.983	0.337	1140	17.22	2	0
node20.chonbuk.ac.kr	ls	hjhwang	?	20031117202405	20031117202405	0	0	0	5	0	0	0	76	0	0	0
grid.chonbuk.ac.kr	#globus-g	griduser01	?	20031118162118	20031118162120	1.2	0.8	0.35	28040	0	0.53	0.18	2230	16.02	2	0
grid.chonbuk.ac.kr	df	griduser01	?	20031118162120	20031118162120	0	0	0	21	0	0	0	0	0	0	0
grid.chnbuk.ac.kr	globus-j	griduser01	?	20031118162118	20031118162120	5.5	1.02	0.33	4218	0	0.1	0.212	84	7.02	0	0
tea01.chonbuk.ac.kr	#globus-g	user01	?	20031118163847	20031118163852	2.82	0.02	0.92	43532	0	0.887	0.282	1124	16.02	2	0
tea01.chonbuk.ac.kr	cpl	user01	?	20031118163849	20031118163849	0	0	0	20	0	0	0	0	0	0	0
tea01.chonbuk.ac.kr	globus-j	user01	?	20031118163848	20031118163852	4.81	0.8	0.25	185020	0	0.228	0.326	1138	8.06	0	0

Fig. 5. An example of gathered process accounting information

5 Conclusion and Future Works

In this paper, we design and implement the accounting information service. This service can integrate the accounting information of process and from job manager. This service follows the GSAX framework and the accounting information is formatted to follow Minimum Set of Usage Record. It is very easy to add or delete slave node. Because the architecture of the gathering system is layered, extension to other job manager or other kind of platform is very easy. Application to other Job Manager is very easy to achieve by developing only the module, which plays the role for LoadLeveler. But, for the future application, the native XML database would be used as DBMS. And more various kind of Job Manager would be considered.

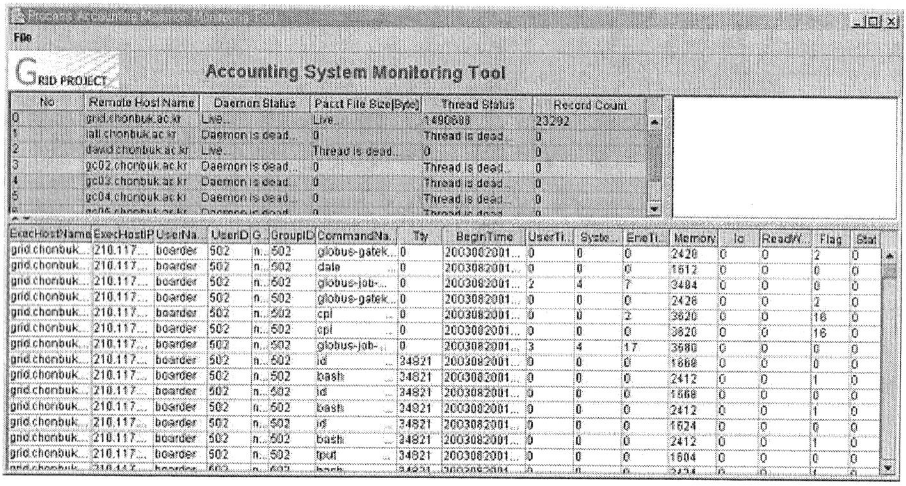

Fig. 6. Monitoring tool for process accounting service

References

1. I. Foster, C. Kesselman(eds), S. Tuecke Q.25, "The Anatomy of the Grid:Enabling Scable Virtual Organizations", Intl. J. Supercomputer.
2. Global Grid Forum, http://www.ggf.org
3. The Globus Alliance, http://www.globus.org
4. A. Beardsmore et al, "GSAX(Grid Service Accounting Extensions)", (draft), GGF6, 2002
5. S. Mullen et al, "Grid Authentication, Authorization and Accounting Requirements Research Document", (draf), GGF8, 2003
6. Beob Kyun Kim et al, "Implementation of Access Control System for Site Autonomy in Grid Environment", Proceedings of The 30th KISS Fall Conference, KISS, 2003
7. The DataGrid Project, http://eu-datagrid.web.cern.ch/eu-datagrid
8. Thomas J. Hacker, Brian D. Athey, "Account Allocations on the Grid", Center for Parallel Computing University of Michigan, 2000

Neural Network Modeling of Transmission Rate Control Factor for Multimedia Transmission Using the Internet

Sung Goo Yoo[1], Kil To Chong[2], and Soo Yeong Yi[2]

[1] Chonbuk National Univ., Control and Instrumentation,
664-14 1ga, Duckjin-Dong
Duckjin-Gu Jeonju Jeonbuk 561-756, South Korea
ding5@chonbuk.ac.kr

[2] Chonbuk National Univ., Electronics and Information,
664-14 1ga, Duckjin Dong
Duckjin-Gu Jeonju Jeonbuk 561-756, South Korea
{kitchong, suylee}@chonbuk.ac.kr

Abstract. This study proposes a prediction model which functions by estimating the bandwidth of the Internet over the time period used for data transmission, that is the RTT (Round Trip Time) and PLR (Packet Loss Rate), which are the most important factors to consider for transmission rate control. The prediction model improves the number of valid transmitted packets by predicting the one-step-ahead transmission rate control factors. A method of prediction modeling was developed using a neural network, which makes it possible to model a nonlinear system and the LMBP algorithm was used to training the neural networks. RTT and PLR data was collected by the TFRC transmission method, which is a kind of adaptive transmission control based on UDP, and used as the training data for the neural network prediction model. Through the training of the neural network, the prediction model can predict the RTT and PLR after one step. It can also be seen that the error in the predicted values is small. This result shows that the congestion situation of the Internet can be predicted by the proposed prediction model. In addition, it shows that it is possible to implement a mechanism, which allows for a substantial amount of data to be transmitted, while actively coping with a congestion situation.

1 Introduction

Most Internet traffic utilizes protocols based on TCP, such as HTTP (Hypertext Transfer Protocol), SMTP (Simple Mail Transfer Protocol), FTP (File Transfer Protocol) and various other protocols [1][2]. However, with the increasing demand for real-time audio/video streaming applications such as IP telephony, audio players using the Internet and VOD, UDP based transmission is becoming an important factor in Internet traffic. Generally, real-time applications don't use TCP [3], which is based on a complex retransmission algorithm, but rather the

Y. Zhang et al. (Eds.): APWeb 2005, LNCS 3399, pp. 851–862, 2005.

simpler UDP [3] algorithm, which doesn't take congestion control into consideration. If congestion occurs on a single link shared by TCP and UDP traffic, TCP will react by reducing the transmission rate, in an attempt to solve the congestion problem. However, under the same circumstances, UDP will aggravate the congestion problem, due to its occupying almost all of the available bandwidth, by maintaining its initial transmission rate. In addition to the congestion problem, this will also lead to unfair use of the Internet.

In order to solve these problems, it is necessary to apply to non-TCP traffic the same mechanism that is used for adjusting the transmission rate of TCP traffic. This revised mechanism for non-TCP traffic should be designed to include the TCP-friendly property for the non-TCP applications. In addition, this system should support the equal distribution of traffic. There are several TCP-friendly algorithms which have been proposed to solve the problem of unequal distribution [4][5][6]. These include the Rate Adaptation Protocol (RAP) [7] and TCP Friendly Rate Control (TFRC) [8], and various other protocols.

One of the important properties of the TCP-friendly algorithm is that it controls the transmission rate adaptively, by measuring the congestion situation in the present Internet. However, this algorithm stresses only the question of fairness with respect to TCP flow, but doesn't consider QoS (Quality of Service) which affects the quality of the transmitted images [9]. In addition, the TCP-friendly algorithm controls the transmission rate using the round trip time (RTT) and packet loss rate (PLR). This study presents a prediction model which operates by estimating the bandwidth of the Internet corresponding to the estimated time period of the future data transmission. The parameters used are the RTT and PLR, which are the most important factors to consider, in order to be able to transmit data with an improved data transmission rate, while actively coping with problems of congestion. To accomplish this, the proposed method controls the transmission rate based on the prediction values obtained using a neural network.

The available methods which can be used for prediction modeling include the decision tree, decision rule, neural network and others. This study uses a neural network that can model and implement an uncertain nonlinear system . A multi-layer perceptron structure [10] that can extract the properties of nonlinear input and output is used as the neural network model. In addition, Levenberg-Marquardt Back-propagation (LMBP) [11] is used to resolve the problem of convergence for the local minimum point that is a drawback of the Back-Propagation algorithm [12][13].

In order to collect the data to be used for the modeling, two computers equipped with the Linux operating system were installed at Seoul National University and Chonbuk National University, respectively, each performing packet transmission by means of the TFRC algorithm. Moreover, IPERF, which is a kind of traffic generator, was used to generate various situations of network congestion. This paper is constructed as follows. Chapter 2 describes the TFRC algorithm used in the transmission test; Chapter 3 presents the structure of the neural network and LMBP training algorithm; Chapter 4 describes the results of the simulation for this study. Finally, in Chapter 5, we present our conclusions and future study directions.

2 TFRC: TCP-Friendly Rate Control

Any method based on TCP Friendly congestion control should calculate the transmission rate based on a TCP model [14][15][16], in which the average transmission rate over time can modeled by considering the operation of TCP in the steady state. This depends on the operation of the TCP protocol, but can basically be expressed as Eq. (1).

$$R = f\left(PLR, RTT\right) \tag{1}$$

where R is the transmission rate, PLR is the packet loss rate, and RTT is the round trip time.

Figure 1 presents the principle of operation of the TCP Reno model [17][18] and shows an operation that reduces the size of the congestion window by half when packet loss occurs.

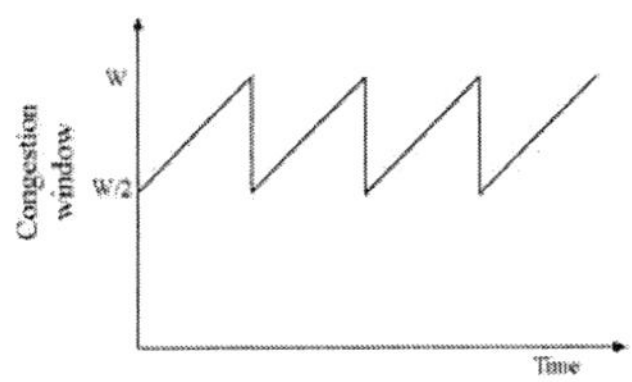

Fig. 1. Operational mechanism of the TCP Reno model in the steady state

If we consider that the size of the congestion window is W and the packet size is s, then the transmission rate before the loss of the packet can be expressed by $R = \frac{W \times s}{RTT}$. Then, the transmission rate after the loss of the packet is $R = 0.5 \times \frac{W \times s}{RTT}$ when the size of the window is reduced to $\frac{W}{2}$. Therefore, the average transmission rate for the whole series of four saw tooth cycles can be expressed as $R = 0.75 \times \frac{W \times s}{RTT}$. The loss rate, p, for a single saw tooth, as shown in Fig. 1, is $\frac{1}{p} = \left(\frac{W}{2}\right)^2 + \frac{1}{2}\left(\frac{W}{2}\right)^2$ and can be expressed as $W \approx \sqrt{\frac{8}{3p}}$. Therefore, finally, the effective transmission rate, $R(t)$, for time t can be represented in the form of the approximate expression shown in Eq. (2) [19][20].

$$R\left(t\right) = \frac{1.22 \times s}{RTT\left(t\right) \times \sqrt{p\left(t\right)}} \tag{2}$$

In this paper, we collect data pertaining to the RTT and PLR through an experiment involving the use of Eq. (2).

3 Neural Network

3.1 Structure of the Neural Network

The structure of the neural network used in this study is the multi-layer perceptron neural network and consists of an input layer, hidden layer and output layer, as shown in Figure 2.

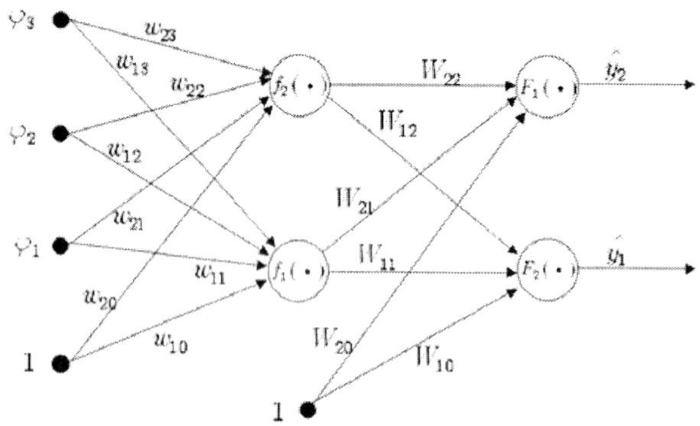

Fig. 2. Structure of the Multi-layer perceptron neural network

The output of the multi-layer perceptron, $\hat{y}$, is presented in Eq. (3) [21].

$$\hat{y}_i(t) = g_i[\varphi, \theta] \; F_i \left[\sum_{j=1}^{n_h} w_{i,j} f_j \left(\sum_{l=1}^{n_\varphi} w_{j,l}\varphi_l + w_{j,0} \right) + W_{i,0} \right] \tag{3}$$

where θ is a parameter vector that includes all of the adjustable parameters in the neural network structure, and $\{w_{j,l}, W_{i,j}\}$ are weights and biases, respectively. Typically, the bias is applied by means of equation 1. A set of training data including the relationship between the output, $\hat{y}_i$, and the input, φ_l, are required to define the weights. The process that defines the weights using this training data is referred to as training.

The error function, E, that represents the error between the output of the training data and the output of the neural network can be defined as in Eq. (4)

$$E = \frac{1}{2}\sum_{n=1}^{k} (y_n - o_n)^2 \tag{4}$$

where y_n is the target value of the training data and o_n is the output of the neural network.

3.2 LM-BP Training Method

Training algorithms used for training neural networks can be classified into three main categories, namely the Steepest Descent, Newton and Gauss-Newton methods [21]. Among these methods, the Steepest Descent method suffers from a problem of convergence. On the other hand, the Newton method, which uses the secondary derivative function, has excellent convergence but is computationally expensive. Therefore, the Gauss-Newton method is normally used for actual neural network training.

The LM algorithms, which are based on the Gauss-Newton method, can solve dynamically the problems presented by the Steepest Descent and Newton methods. These algorithms operate in three stages. Firstly, the weight value is set to a large value, and the Steepest Descent method is applied in the early stages of training. This then provides the weight value for the Newton method, which is applied when convergence has occurred to a certain extent, corresponding to the state in which training is sufficiently advanced to produce a locally minimized convergence. Finally, the algorithm converges rapidly to the optimal solution, by reusing the Steepest Descent method.

That is, the weight value, w, can be obtained by means of training using Eq. (5).

$$w_{i+1} = w_i - (H + \lambda I)^{-1} \nabla F(w_i) \tag{5}$$

where

$$\nabla F(w_i) = \frac{\partial F}{\partial w_i} : \textit{gradient},\ w_i \text{ is the } i\text{th weight value} \tag{6}$$

$$F = \sum_{k=0}^{N} e_k^2 \text{ is SSE(square-sum error)}, k \text{ is the } k \text{ th sample} \tag{7}$$

$$H = \nabla^2 F(w) \text{ is the Hessian matrix} \tag{8}$$

and λ can be controlled dynamically.

However, the LMBP algorithm adopts the Gauss-Newton method that approximates the value of H since the second derivative produces computational problems. That is, the value of H used in the Newton method can be obtained by means of Eq. (9).

$$H = \left[\nabla^2 F(w)\right]_{ij} = \frac{\partial^2 F(x)}{\partial w_i \partial w_j} = 2\sum_{k=0}^{N}\left[\frac{\partial e_k(w)}{\partial w_i}\frac{\partial e_k(w)}{\partial w_j} + e_k(w)\frac{\partial^2 e_k(w)}{\partial w_i \partial w_j}\right] \tag{9}$$

where the second term of Eq. (9) can be neglected, hence

$$\left[\nabla^2 F(w)\right]_{ij} \cong 2\sum_{k=0}^{N}\frac{\partial e_k(w)}{\partial w_i}\frac{\partial e_k(w)}{\partial w_j} = 2J^T(w)\,J(w) \tag{10}$$

where $J_{ki} = \frac{\partial e_k}{\partial w_i}$ is a Jacobian matrix.

By using this approximation, the necessity to use the second derivative can be eliminated. $\nabla F(w_i)$ presented in Eq. (10) is defined by

$$\nabla F(w_i) = J^T(w_i)\, e(w_i) \tag{11}$$

Therefore, the modified LMBP algorithm can be expressed as Eq. (12).

$$w_{m+1} = w_m - \left[J^T(w_m)\, J(w_m) + \lambda_m I\right]^{-1} J^T(w_m)\, e(w_m) \tag{12}$$

Eq. (12) is a weight parameter that is adjusted in the mth repeated process.

4 Modeling of a Prediction Neural Network

4.1 Data Collection

The experimental configuration used to collect the data used in the training and verification processes is shown in Figure 3. The transmission processor (tp), receiving-retransmission processor (rp), and RTT-PLR estimation processor (RTT-PLR ep) were implemented using a socket program written in the ANSI C language. The transmission processor and RTT-PLR estimation processor were installed on the server at Chonbuk National University, while the receiving-retransmission processor was installed on the client at Seoul National University.

Fig. 3. System used for the Experiment

The transmission processor can transmit packets using the TCP-Friendly method, as mentioned in Chapter 2. The packet transmission test was conducted using Eq. (2). The initial transmission speed is 100kb/s, and the whole packet size is 625 bytes, of which 64 bytes are reserved for the probe header. The probe header is attached to the header of the transmission packet, in order to estimate the RTT and PLR. In addition, it has a storage area used to store numbers, so as to keep track of the order in which the packets are transmitted from each processor and their transmission time [19]. When the transmission processor transmits a packet to the receiving-retransmission processor, the receiving-retransmission processor separates the probe header from the received packet, inserts the packet number and current time into the probe header, and then retransmits it to the RTT-PLR estimation processor.

In the case where traffic congestion occurs on the Internet, the values of RTT and PLR are likely to fluctuate rapidly. Even though controlling the transmission rate can help to reduce the amount of traffic problems by rapidly applying these

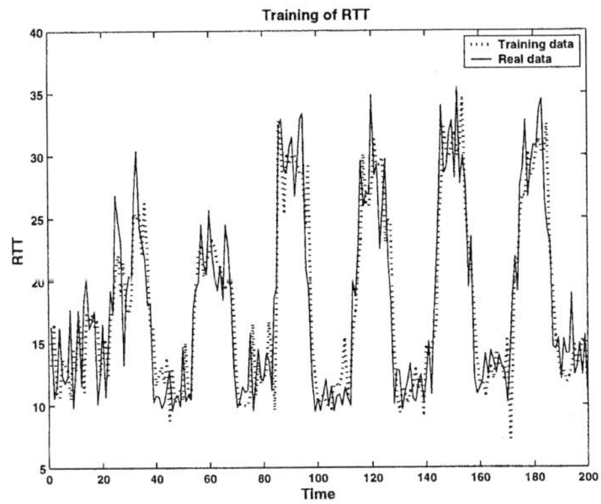

Fig. 4. Results obtained for the training of the round trip time delay from the prediction neural network model

suddenly changed values of RTT and PLR directly to the TFRC mechanism, the quality of service of real-time applications will rapidly deteriorate. In order to prevent this problem, the RTT and PLR of the TFRC algorithm should adhere to the calculation method used by the RTT and PLR of the TCP algorithm. The TCP protocol can change the estimated values of RTT and PLR naturally by using a low-pass filter. The estimated values of RTT and PLR can be obtained by using the moving average as described in Eq. (13).

$$\mathrm{RTT}^* = \alpha \mathrm{RTT}^* + (1-\alpha)\,\mathrm{newRTT}\ ,\ \mathrm{PLR}^* = \alpha \mathrm{PLR}^* + (1-\alpha)\,\mathrm{newPLR} \quad (13)$$

where α is a parameter that has a recommended value of 0.9, and newRTT and newPLR are recently estimated values of RTT and PLR, respectively. The moving average can be used to control the transmission rate, by reducing any sudden changes in the values of the RTT and PLR when traffic problems occur. In the transmission test, the RTT and PLR are estimated at every round (2 seconds), and the moving average RTT and moving average PLR are determined using Eq. (13). In this paper, we train the RTT, PLR, moving average RTT and moving average PLR, and verify the results of the prediction.

The packet transmission experiment was performed every 30 minutes for a period of one week. The RTT and PLR were estimated every round or, in other words, every 2 seconds.

4.2 Modeling

The amount of data collected for RTT and PLR through the experiment described in this paper was about 150,000 for each item. 70% of the experimental data was used in the training phase performed to measure the parameters, while the other 30% was used in the verification phase, for the purpose of measuring the performance of the neural network.

The prediction model was based on the multi-layer perceptron structure shown in Figure 2, in which a multi-layer neural network was constructed con-

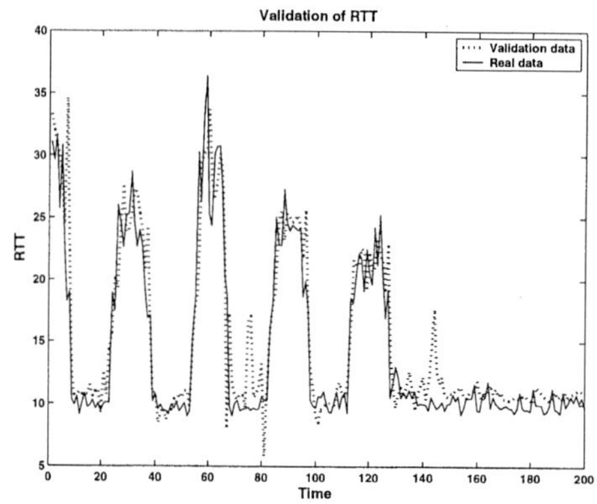

Fig. 5. Verification of the round trip time delay obtained from the prediction neural network model

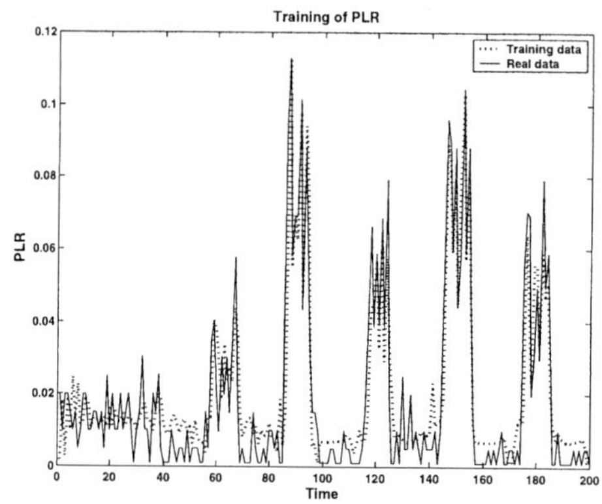

Fig. 6. Results of the training of the packet loss rate by the prediction neural network model

sisting of 20 nodes for the input layer, 8 nodes for the hidden layer, and 1 node for the output layer. In addition, LMBP was used for the training, as described in Chapter 3 [12].

Figure 4 shows part of the results for the training of the round trip time delay. Figure 5 presents the results of the verification phase, involving the application of the remaining data to the neural network. The time period that shows an increase of the values of RTT in the figure corresponds to that where the load was controlled by the traffic generator. From the results of the training, it can be seen that, in the case where a substantial load is applied to the network, i.e. the period in which the value of RTT increases rapidly, the error is small. Although some errors were observed in the results of the verification conducted using data that wasn't used in the training phase, it can be seen that the error in the prediction values is generally quite small when a load is applied to the

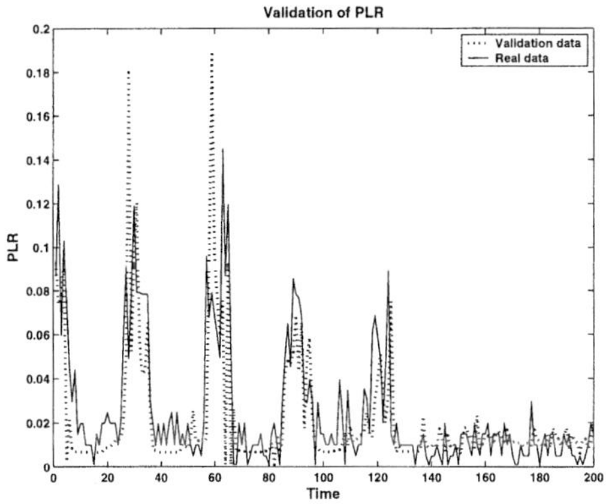

Fig. 7. Verification of the packet loss rate obtained from the prediction neural network model

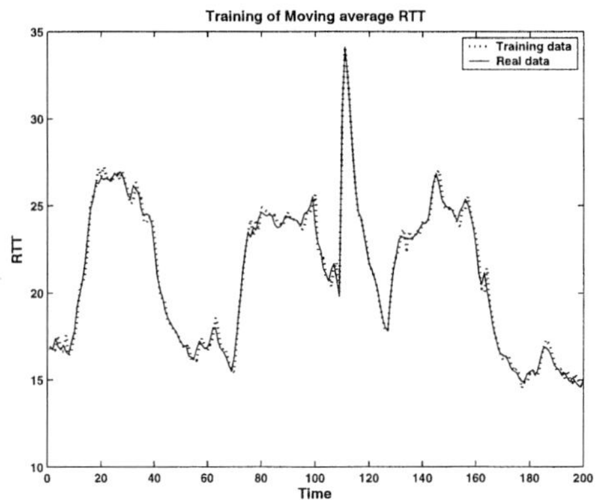

Fig. 8. Results of the training of the moving average RTT by the prediction neural network model

network. The mean square error of the prediction value is 0.34ms for the training data and 1.004ms for the verification data, which represents a very small range of error in proportion to the entire range of RTT.

Figures 6 and 7 show part of the results obtained from the training and verification of the neural network for different packet loss rates. A small change in the value of the packet loss rate has a large impact in the graph, because the measured values are very small. However, it can be seen that the errors in the prediction values are small when the network load is high. The mean square errors of the results of the training and verification phases are 1.52 (%) and 3.82 (%), respectively.

Figures 8 and 9 show the results of the training and verification phases used for the prediction of the moving average RTT using Eq. (13). It can be seen that the improvement obtained from the training and prediction in the case of the

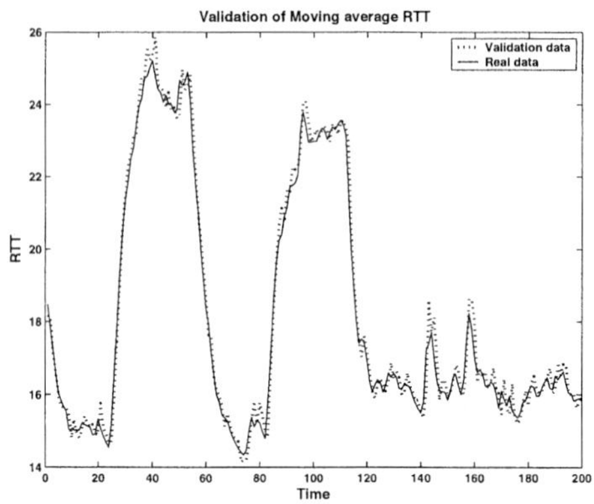

Fig. 9. Verification of moving average RTT obtained from the prediction neural network model

moving average RTT was better than that for the RTT shown in Figures 4 and 5, because the moving average RTT shows a smooth variation, as compared with the RTT which shows a wider fluctuation. The performance of the prediction system is confirmed by the results, which show that the mean square error is 0.680ms, and the verification error is 0.7502ms.

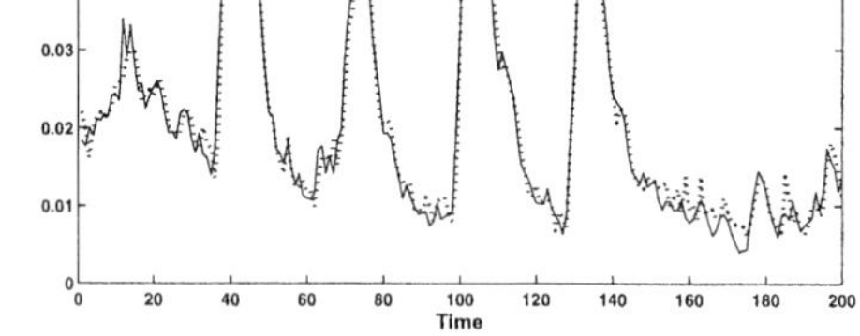

Fig. 10. Results of the training of the moving average PLR by the prediction neural network model

Figures 10 and 11 show the results of the training and verification for the moving average PLR. It can be seen that the improvement in the moving average PLR obtained from the training and prediction is similar to that for the PLR, which shows a rapid change. The mean square errors for the training and prediction performance are 0.87 (%) and 0.9 (%), respectively.

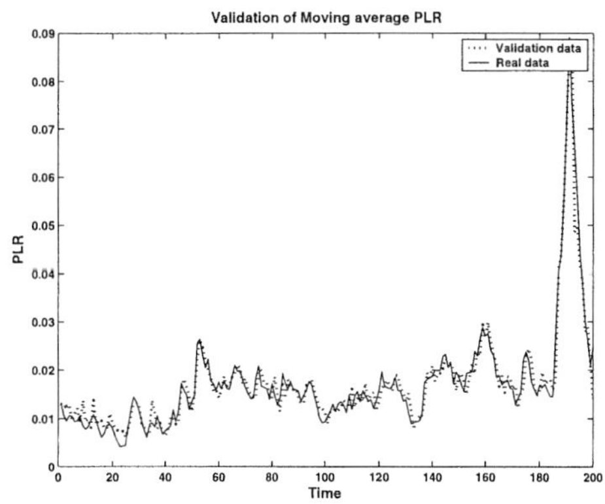

Fig. 11. Verification of moving average PLR obtained from the prediction neural network model

5 Conclusion

In this paper, we designed a prediction model that can be used to predict the most important parameters of the transmission rate control mechanism used for data transmission through the Internet, in order to take into consideration the available bandwidth. A method of prediction modeling was developed using a neural network, which makes it possible to model a nonlinear system and the LMBP algorithm was used to training the neural networks. RTT and PLR data was collected by the TFRC transmission method, which is a kind of adaptive transmission control based on UDP, and used as the training data for the neural network prediction model. Through the training of the neural network, the prediction model can predict the RTT and PLR after one step is completed. It can also be seen that the error in the predicted values is small. This result shows that the congestion situation of the Internet can be predicted using the proposed prediction model. In addition, it shows that it is possible to implement a mechanism, which allows for a substantial amount of data to be transmitted, while actively coping with a congestion situation. The complete verification of the prediction algorithm will be the subject of a future work, which involves configuring the system that controls the transmission rate of an actual multimedia application using the neural network prediction model proposed in this study and comparing its performance with that of the existing methods.

Acknowledgements. The authors thank KEPCO (R-2004-B-120) and RRC (KOSEF) (R-12-1998-026-02003) for their financial support.

References

1. Yin Li, Futai Zou, Zengde Wu, Fanyuan Ma: PWSD: A Scalable Web Service Discovery Architecture Based on Peer-to-Peer Overlay Network. APWeb. LNCS3007 (2004) 291-300

2. Zhiming Pan, Yizhong Wu, Kun Yue, Xiaoling Wang, Aoying Zhou: Efficient Community Management and Optimization Strategies of Web Services in Peer-to-Peer Environments. APWeb. LNCS3007 (2004) 301-310
3. A.S Tanenbaum: Computer Networks(third edition). Prentice Hall International, Inc. (1996)
4. Joerg Widmer, Robert Denda, Martin Mauve: A Survey on TCP-Friendly Congestion Control. IEEE Network, vol 3 (2001) 28-37
5. L. Rizzo: Pgmcc: A TCP-Friendly single-rate multicast Congestion control scheme. Proc. ACM SIGCOMM, Stocholm, Sweden (2000) 17-28
6. S. Sisalem, A. Wolisz: MLDA: A TCP-Friendly Congestion Control Framework for Heterogeneous Multicast Environments. 8th Intl. Wksp. QoS (2000)
7. D. Rajate, M. Handley, D. Estrin: RAP : An end-to-end rate-based congestion control mechanism or realtime streams in the Internet. INFOCOM'99, vol 3 (1999) 1337-1345
8. J. Mahadavi and S. Floyd: TCP-Friendly unicast rate-based flow control. Tech. Rep., Technical note sent to end2end interest mailing list (1997)
9. Zhe Wang, Bin Wang, Chunguang Zhou, Xiujuan Xu: Clustering Data Streams On the Two-Tier Structure. APWeb. LNCS3007 (2004) 416-425
10. K. S. Narendra and K. Parthasarathy: Identification and control of dynamical systems using neural network. IEEE Trans. Neural Networks, vol 1 (1990) 4-27
11. Finschi: An implementation of the Levenberg-Marquardt algorithm. clausiusstrasses 45, CH-8092, Zuerich (1996)
12. Jacek M. Zurada: Introduction to Artificial Neural Systems. West Publshing Company (1992)
13. S. Haykin: Neural Networks. MacMillan (1994)
14. V. Jacobson: Congesion Avoidance and contro. SIGCOMM Symposium on Communications Architectures and Protocols (1988) 214-329
15. Michael J. Donahoo, Kenneth L. Calvert: The Pocket Guide to TCP/IP Socket : C Version. Morgan Kaufmann Publishers, Inc. (2001)
16. Shining Li, Jiping Fang, Fan Yu: On Analysis and Comparison Performance of TCP in Wireless Network. APWeb. LNCS3007 (2004) 341-352
17. V. Paxson: Automated packet trace analysis of TCP implementation. IN Proceedings of SIGCOMMM 97 (1997)
18. Jitendra Padhye, Victor Firoiu, Don Towsley, Jim Kurose: Modeling TCP Throughput : A simple Model and its Empirical Validation. ACM SIGCOMM (1998)
19. Ikjun Yeom: ENDE An End-To-End Network Delay Emulator. PhD Dissertation, Texas A & M University (1998)
20. M. Mathis, J. Semke, J. Mahdavi, T. Ott: The macroscopic behavior of TCP Congesiton Avoidance Algorithm. ACM Computer Communication Review (1997) 67-82
21. M. Norgaard, O. Ravn, N.K. Poulsen, L. K. Hansen: Neural Networks for Modeling and Control of Dynamic System. A Practitioner's Handbook, Springer

A Peer to Peer Proxy Patching Scheme for VOD Servers

Chun Ja Kwon[1], Chi Kyu Choi[1], Geun Jeong Lee[1], and Hwang Kyu Choi[2,*]

[1] Dept. of Computer and Communication Engineering, Kangwon National University, 192-1 Hyoja2dong, Chuncheon, Kangwon, Korea 200-701
{cjkwon, starflower22, phinex}@mail.kangwon.ac.kr

[2] Dept. of Electrical and Computer Engineering, Kangwon National University, 192-1 Hyoja2dong, Chuncheon, Kangwon, Korea 200-701
hkchoi@kangwon.ac.kr

Abstract. The main bottleneck for a VOD system is bandwidth of storage or network I/O due to the high bandwidth requirements and long-lived nature of digital video. Patching is one of the most efficient techniques to overcome the bottleneck of the VOD system through the use of multicast scheme. In this paper, we propose a new patching scheme, called P2P proxy patching, for improving the typical patching technique by jointly using the prefix caching and P2P proxy. In our proposed scheme, each client plays a role in a proxy to multicast a regular stream to other clients that request the same video stream. Due to the use of the P2P proxy and the prefix caching, the server bandwidth is required significantly less than that of the typical patching technique. In the performance study, we show that our patching scheme can reduce the server bandwidth requirements compared with the existing patching techniques.

1 Introduction

Video-on-Demand (VOD) service is one of the most important technologies for many multimedia applications, such as home entertainment, digital video libraries, distance learning, electronic commerce, and so on. A typical VOD service allows that a number of remote clients playback a desired video from a large collection of videos stored in one or more video servers. The main bottleneck for a VOD service is the storage bandwidth of the VOD server and the network bandwidth connecting to the VOD server to the client due to the high bandwidth requirements and long-lived nature of digital video.

Many previous researches have shown that VOD server can be greatly improved through the use of multicast or broadcast scheme. Patching is one of the most efficient techniques to capitalize on the benefits of multicast for VOD services [1], [9]. The patching is a dynamic multicast scheme for extending the capability of standard multicast to support true VOD services by joining new users to an existing multicast

* This paper was supported by BK21 project of Kangwon National University and University Research Program supported by Ministry of Information and Communication in republic of Korea.

Y. Zhang et al. (Eds.): APWeb 2005, LNCS 3399, pp. 863–874, 2005.

stream. This technique allows requests to be served immediately without having to wait for next multicast by using additional channels to transmit a prefix stream to clients. However, the performances of the existing patching schemes, such as Grace Patching and Optimal Patching in [3], are restricted within the limited patching window size and the client buffer size. Recently peer-to-peer (P2P) media streaming schemes have been introduced in the several papers [6], [8]. An important advantage of P2P media streaming is to carry system scalability out with a large number clients' stream sharing. But since the behavior of clients is unpredictable in P2P network, failure recovery mechanism is required for the departure of clients.

In this paper, we propose a new patching scheme, called P2P proxy patching, for improving the typical patching technique by jointly using prefix caching in proxy and regular stream caching in P2P proxy. In our system, clients arriving close in time within patching window size form a group, and then the typical proxy prefix patching is carried out for the clients in the group. Except for the first client in a group who receives the entire stream from the server or other client peer, all other clients will miss the initial part of the stream and will require a patch, where the proxy server serves the prefix to all clients requiring the patch in a group. When the first client in a group starts to play a video stream, the client caches the recent part of video stream in the client buffer. As soon as the buffer is full, the stream is forwarded into other clients in multicast manner. As a result, the output stream from the client is delayed as much as the buffer length in time from the original input stream of the client. Each client system plays an important role as a proxy caching server for regular stream to reduce the server bandwidth usage. This can drastically reduce the server bandwidth requirement. In the performance study, we show that our patching scheme can reduce the server bandwidth requirements compared with the existing patching techniques.

The remainder of this paper is organized as follows. Section 2 describes the related work to the patching scheme and P2P approaches for VOD systems. In section 3, we represent our P2P proxy patching scheme. Section 4 analyzes the performance of the proposed patching scheme. Finally, we conclude this paper in section 5.

2 Related Works

During the past decade, there has been a large amount of research works on the topic of VOD systems. We first investigate the related research works for VOD systems, especially focused on the techniques for reducing server bandwidth requirement. Although a VOD server has high capacity of computation and storage resources, the performance of VOD system can be constrained by increasing more clients. In order to overcome several drawbacks caused by limited server bandwidth, many techniques based on multicast have been proposed, such as patching [1] and batching [7]. Recently, peer-to-peer (P2P) media streaming techniques, in which each client plays a role in a peer that brings computation and storage resources into the system to reduce the workload placed on the server, have been studying [6], [8].

A VOD system adapted standard multicast has a response delay waiting to regular stream start. The patching technique extends the capability of the standard multicast to support true VOD services by joining new clients to an existing multicast stream by use of additional patching channel [1]. This technique allows requests to be served immediately without having to wait for next multicast by using additional channels to transmit a prefix stream to clients. In patching scheme [2], Greedy Patching has at most one regular channel at any time. In contrast, Grace Patching starts a new regular channel whenever a client arrives more than B time units, where B is a client buffer size, and thus the patching window size is limited by the size of client buffer. The patching channel is only used to patch the missing prefix portion of a service, thus the patching scheme is very efficient due to using two channel only for reducing server load. However, according to each new regular channel is generated in every patching window, it can give heavy load to VOD server.

Another efficient technique for enhancing the performance of VOD services is proxy caching. Because the VOD server needs the high server bandwidth and QoS requirements of video data, it is necessary to distribute server side load into local proxy servers. Moreover, since a remote server has a long-term response time and network jitter, proxy caching can be a good solution of these problems. Due to these advantages a proxy prefix caching scheme has been proposed [3], [4], which minimizes the network bandwidth by serving initial part of popular streams stored in proxy and thus provides high-quality video to its clients with low playback delay.

Recently peer-to-peer (P2P) media streaming schemes have been introduced in the several papers [6], [8]. P2P consumes the bandwidth of source peer efficiently by capitalizing the bandwidth of a client to provide services to other clients. An important advantage of P2P media streaming is to carry system scalability out with a large number clients' stream sharing. But the behavior of clients is unpredictable; they are free to join and leave the service at any time, thus abandoning their descendant peers. To prevent this drawback, it is necessary failure recovery by clients' departure. Chaining is the first P2P streaming technique [5], in which the delivery tree is built as rooted at the source and including all and only the clients. This technique re-transmits stream to clients through the delivery tree. A similar approach, called P2CAST, has been proposed in [6]. P2Cast extended the IP multicast patching scheme to the unicast-only network by exploring the idea of P2P network. In P2Cast, the entire video is streamed over the application-level multicast tree, so that it can be shared among clients. For clients who arrive later than the first client in the session, which is formed by clients arriving close in time, and thus miss the initial part of video, the missing part can be retrieved from the server or other clients. But this technique demands additional server load due to constituting regular channel periodically between server and clients in every session.

3 P2P Proxy Patching Scheme

3.1 Overview of P2P Proxy Patching

In this section, we describe our proposed P2P proxy patching scheme which combines prefix caching in proxy and regular stream caching in P2P proxy to improve the typical patching technique. We first illustrate the overall system architecture for the proposed scheme in Fig. 1. The architecture of our VOD system is similar to the typical VOD system with proxy server. The system consists of a central VOD server that serves the entire video files, several proxy servers that store the initial parts of popular videos (called prefix), and multiple clients that are connected to the closest proxy through LAN.

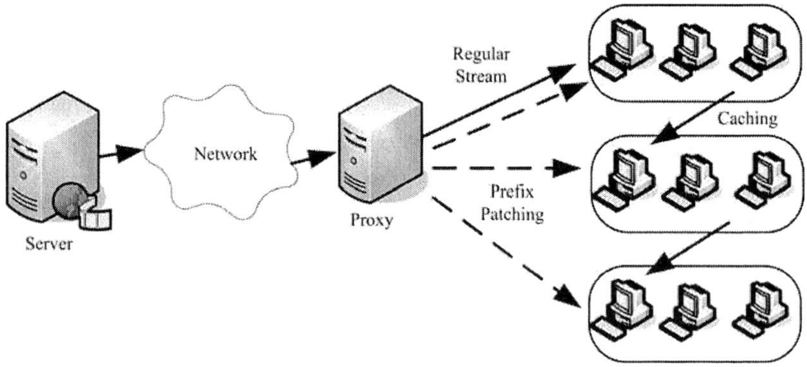

Fig. 1. Overall system architecture for P2P proxy patching

In our system, clients arriving close in time within patching window size form a group, and then the typical proxy prefix patching is carried out for the clients in the group. Except for the first client in a group who receives the entire stream from the server or other client peer, all other clients will miss the initial part of the stream and will require a patch, where the proxy server serves the prefix to all clients requiring the patch in a group. When the first client in a group starts to play a video stream, the client caches the recent part of video stream in the client buffer. The size of buffer is the same as the patching window size. As soon as the buffer is full, the stream is forwarded into other clients in multicast manner. As a result, the output stream from the client is delayed as much as the buffer length in time from the original input stream of the client. Each client system plays an important role as a proxy caching server for regular stream to reduce the server bandwidth usage.

In the typical patching scheme, all clients within the same patching window receive one regular multicast stream from VOD server. A multicast stream is periodically created in each unit time of patching window size, because the patching window size is limited by client buffer size in many cases, i.e. Grace Patching. In our scheme, a proxy server in a LAN can maintain multiple patching groups, which are served by one regular multicast stream from a server. This can drastically reduce the server bandwidth requirement.

In P2P proxy patching scheme, the departure of a client or an underlying network failure, such as link breakdown or available bandwidth fluctuation, can disrupt the delivery of a regular multicast stream from a client to all clients in another group. The proposed scheme provides failure recovery by replacing the failure client to another client in the same group or the central VOD server. In order for the failure recovery we need a stable system to maintain and to manage the information for clients and patching group states. The proxy server is used as an index server to maintain the information. Therefore, a proxy server plays roles of both the prefix caching and information provider in a LAN environment. In the next section, we describe the functions of the proxy server to maintain the information for failure recovery in detail.

3.2 Proxy Server Architecture

In the typical VOD system using proxy server, the proxy has to maintain its session information and update the session state to send a video stream to a client. For example, in the proxy prefix patching scheme [3], the proxy server manages the information for multicast groups and a client list to implement the multicast as well as it serves the prefixes for the popular videos for patching. In this paper, we reorganize the information to index each client and group state for the P2P prefix patching. The proxy server plays role of an index server for P2P clients, and thus it manages a client list and controls failure recovery mechanism.

Fig. 2 describes the information structure in a proxy server. It is a simple index structure representing clients and groups. The index includes information to identify real clients, e.g., IP address or host name. It should be synchronized with the real client state and real group state. Thus the proxy server has to maintain the client's session information between the proxy and clients in a LAN. In Fig. 2, a patching group is represented as the shade circle, and a client participated in a patching group is represented as the white oval. Suppose that each client of C1, C2, ..., and C8 requests the same video stream at time t1, t2, ..., and t8, respectively. Each patching group of G1, G2, G3, and G4 is generated whenever the cached stream size is exceeded to prefix size. Each group has own regular stream from a central VOD server or the previous patching group.

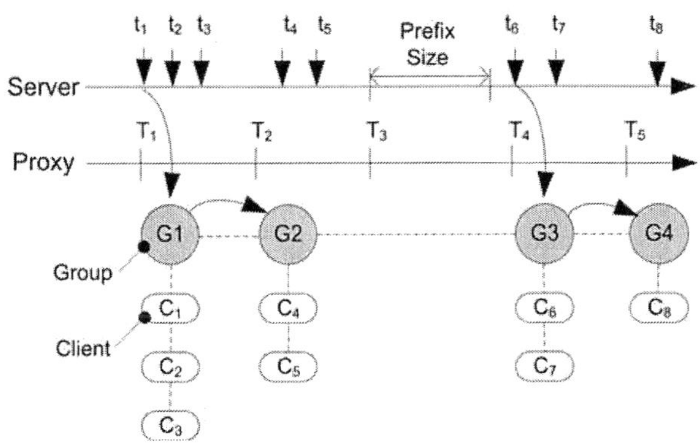

Fig. 2. Index framework for P2P proxy patching scheme

When the first client request C1 arrives at time t1, the VOD server creates a patching group and then a regular channel between the server and the client is established.

As soon as the channel is set up, the client starts to receive the regular stream from the server. The next requests closed in time arrive at time t2 and t3, and the clients join into the first patching group G1. All clients in the same patching group receive a regular stream through the same regular channel and then store into their buffers. For a client C4 the proxy server creates a new patching group G2, because the difference between request time t1 and t4 is larger than prefix size and thus the client cannot patch a prefix from the proxy server. In this case, the proxy server selects one client among clients in the previous patching group G1 as a transmitter of the regular stream for a new group G2. Therefore, a VOD server needs not to create additional channel to transmit a regular stream for patching group G2. In case of a patching group G3, however, clients cannot receive the regular stream from the previous group G2 because the difference between the last stream stored in previous patching group G2 and a request time of clients C6 is larger than the patching window size. Therefore, the patching group G3 should receive their regular stream from a VOD server.

3.3 New Client Admission

When a client requests to play a video through its proxy server, first the proxy server looks for its prefix. If a prefix stream is stored in the proxy, it sends the prefix to the client. Otherwise, it requests the prefix from the central VOD server. Concurrently, the proxy server updates its information structure to manage its multicast group and client session. When a new client session is created by its request, the proxy server registers this session information to its index structure. Moreover, the proxy server should decide whether a regular stream come from a VOD server or the previous patching group consisting of near by clients.

In this process, a proxy server uses its index information to find the last patching group and the most recently regular stream in its client buffer. Then, the system decides whether this client should join into the existing group or it should generate a new patching group for this client. It also decides whether a VOD server dedicates an additional regular channel for this new patching group or it can receive a retransmitted regular stream buffered in a client of the previous group. If the difference between the created time of the last group and the request time of a new client has smaller than the prefix size, this client will join into the existing group. Otherwise, if the difference is larger than the prefix size, a new patching group is generated and this client joins into the new group.

For example, when client C3 requests a video stream at time t3 in Fig. 2, the client C3 joins into the existing group G1 because the difference between the current patching group G1's initial time t1 and the request time t3 is smaller than the prefix size. In other case, when the client C4 requests a video stream at time t4, the client C4 participates in a new patching group G2 because the difference of the init time of the previous patching group G1 and the request time t4 is larger than the prefix size. Similarly, the client requests C6 and C8 generate each patching group G3 and G4, respectably. Finally, when a new patching group is generated, a proxy decides where a regular stream comes from. In Fig. 2, the patching groups G2 and G4 receive regular streams from the previous patching groups G1 and G3. In this case, each difference between the requests time and the most recent stream buffered in the previous group is smaller than the prefix size, thus the clients patch a prefix stream. But the patching group G3 cannot receive its regular stream from the previous patching group. It receives the stream from a VOD server because the difference between its initial time t6 and the most recent stream in the previous group G2 is larger than the prefix stream size.

3.4 Client Caching and Re-transmission

In the typical prefix patching scheme, a client performs caching a regular stream as large as prefix size, which is the same as the difference between a request time and a regular stream's start time. In P2P proxy patching scheme, a client stores the constant size of its video stream as large as its patching window size. Although a part of stream has been played already, a client should maintain the stream waiting to retransmit. This mechanism makes sure that all clients in the same patching group maintain the same video stream in their buffer. It means that a client can be replaced with another client in the same patching group.

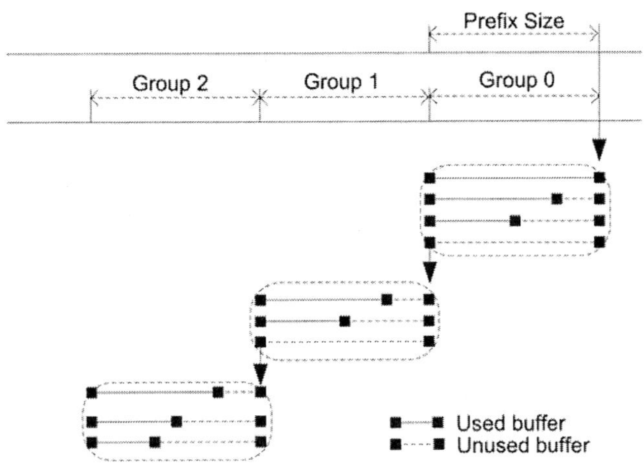

Fig. 3. Regular stream caching by a patching group

Fig. 3 illustrates a process of our cached re-transmission from the previous patching group to the next group. All clients in the same patching group cache their regular streams, and one of them retransmits the stored stream to the next patching group in multicast manner. In Fig. 3, each horizontal line represents a client buffer space. In our scheme, because a client maintains its video stream in the client buffer although it has been played already, the cached stream is divided into 3 categories; wait-to-transmit stream, wait-to-play stream, and current-playing point. In Fig 3, solid line represents a wait-to-transmit stream in the buffer and dashed line represents a wait-to-play stream in the buffer, and current-playing point is placed at the boundary of them.

Therefore, through a process of cached re-transmission, a video stream in the buffer passes 3 steps: wait-to-play, current-playing, wait-to-transmit.

3.5 Failure Recovery

Since we use unstable client system as a cached re-transmitter for regular stream, a re-transmitter may leave its patching group by irregular behavior of the client. In this case, a proxy system should select another client in their group and replace the role. Otherwise, a proxy server should request the remainder of video stream to a central VOD server with an additional channel. In order to recover the failure we use index information managed in a proxy server.

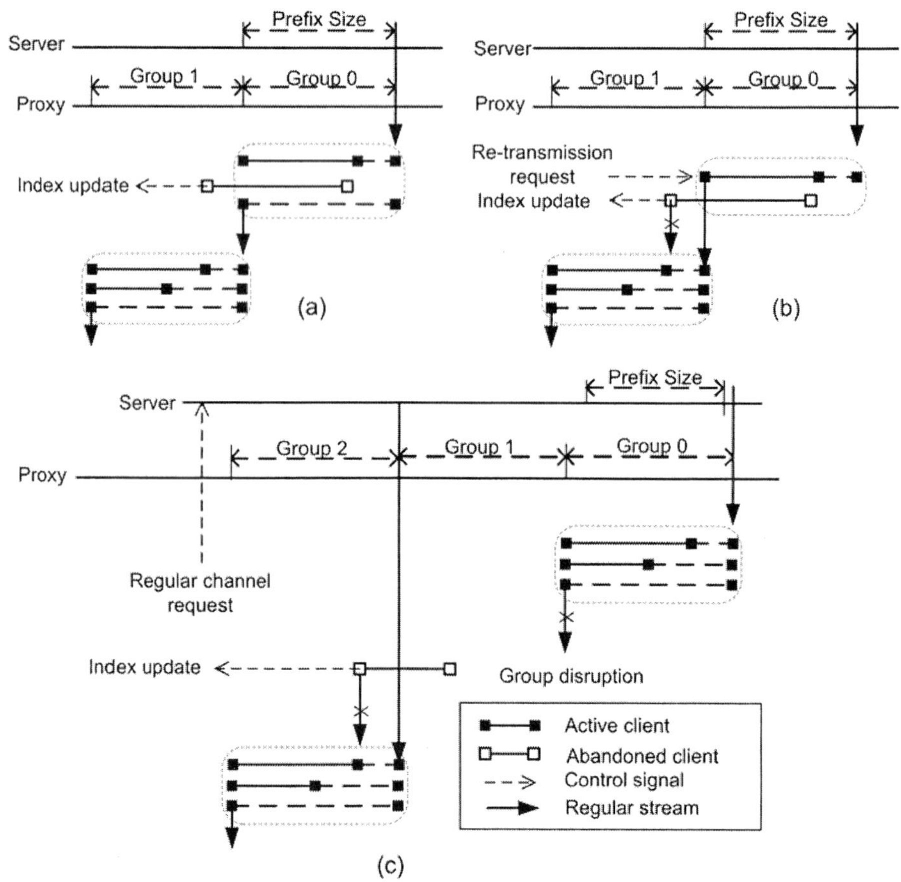

Fig. 4. Failure recovery processes caused by departure of an independent client (a), departure of a re-transmitting client (b), and group disruption (c)

Fig. 4 illustrates regular stream recovery process, which is caused by departure of a client. In this section, we discuss failure recovery process to provide a continuous stream to the receiver. In Fig. 4, (a) represents that an independent client, who does not participate in a re-transmission, has left the patching group. In this case, the client sends a teardown signal to their proxy server. Then, the proxy server updates its index information and the client session is removed. In Fig. 4, (b) represents a case that a re-transmitter leaves. In this case, a proxy server updates its session state to index information, and then searches this index to find a new re-transmitter. As a result, if there is another client in the group it decides and transmits signal. In Fig. 4, (c) represents that there is no client in the group since all clients leave. In this case, a proxy server should send a request for the remainder of the stream to a VOD server.

4 Performance Evaluation

In this section, we evaluate the performance of the P2P proxy patching scheme through simulation experiments. We then compare the performance of our scheme with the existing patching technique. The parameter used in the simulation study is shown in Table 1. In our simulation model, we suppose that a proxy server stores a prefix portion of most popular 10% videos and the default prefix size stored in a proxy is 10 minutes. Also, we assume that client request rate to VOD server follows the Poisson distribution with the default request frequency λ. We suppose that access pattern to videos follows Zipf-like distribution with skew factor θ and the default skew factor for our simulation is 0.271. A uniform distribution corresponds to the value of 1, and a value of 0 represents a highly skewed distribution. The request probability to video i obtains by the following formula, $P_i = \frac{c}{i^{1-\theta}}$.

Table 1. Performance parameters

Parameter	Default	Variation
Number of videos	100	N/A
Video length (minutes)	90	N/A
Mean inter-arrival time (seconds)	10	5~100
Prefix size (minutes)	10	0~20
Normal playback rate b (Mbps)	1.5	N/A
Skew factor	0.271	0.0~1.0
Number of proxy servers	7	N/A
Simulation duration (hours)	10	N/A

Fig. 5 represents the effect of a prefix size in proxy server for the mean server bandwidth requirements. We assume that a proxy server stores only 10% of most popular videos, and the mean request interval time in default is 10 seconds. The prefix size in a proxy is equivalent to the patching window size. Fig. 5 shows that our proposed scheme decreases the mean server bandwidth requirement compared to the typical proxy prefix patching schemes [1], [3]. It shows that the larger prefix size requires the lower server side bandwidth in our proposed scheme. But the effect of prefix size in the typical patching scheme is smaller than that of our proposed scheme.

Fig. 6 represents the effect of mean request interval time for the mean server bandwidth requirements. We assume that the default prefix size in the proxy server for the popular 10% video is 10 minutes. Fig. 6 shows that proposed scheme requires the network bandwidth significantly less than that of the typical patching scheme along with the mean request interval is shorter.

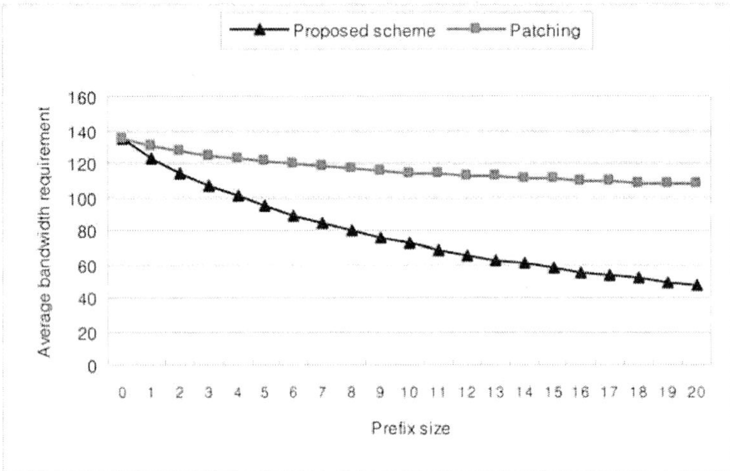

Fig. 5. Server bandwidth requirements for varying prefix size

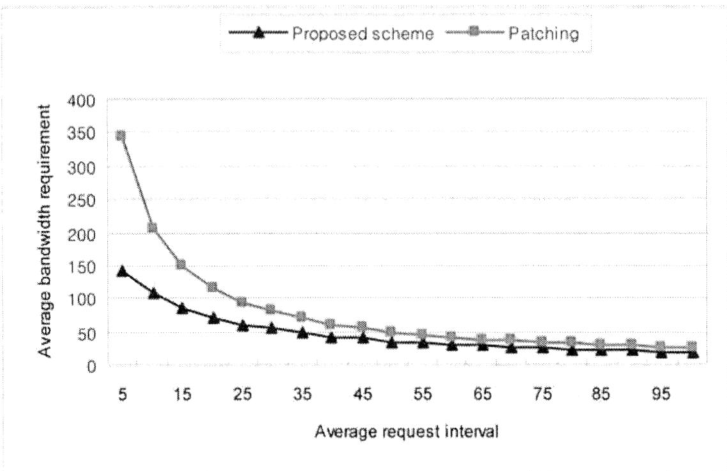

Fig. 6. Server bandwidth requirements for varying mean request interval

Fig. 7 represents the effect of skew factor θ for the mean server bandwidth requirements. We suppose that a video access pattern follows the Zipf-like distribution

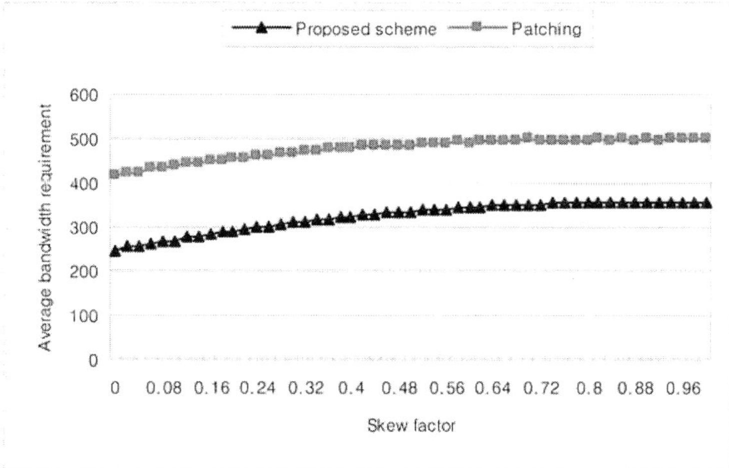

Fig. 7. Server bandwidth requirements for varying skew factor

and then θ is varying from 0.0 to 1.0. The value of 1 represents a uniform distribution, and the value of 0 represents a highly skewed distribution. In Fig. 7, it shows that our proposed patching scheme requires the lower bandwidth than the typical prefix patching scheme significantly. It shows also that the mean server bandwidth requirement is lower when the access pattern is highly skewed.

5 Conclusions

The main bottleneck for a VOD service is the storage bandwidth of the VOD server and the network bandwidth connecting to the VOD server to the client due to the high bandwidth requirements and long-lived nature of digital video. Patching is one of the most efficient techniques to overcome the bottleneck of the VOD system through the use of multicast scheme. In this paper, we proposed the P2P proxy patching scheme which combines the prefix caching in proxy and the regular stream caching in P2P proxy to improve the typical patching technique. In our proposed scheme, each client plays a role in a proxy to multicast a regular stream to other clients that request the same video stream.

In the typical patching scheme, all clients within the same patching window receive one regular multicast stream from VOD server. A multicast stream is periodically created in each unit time of patching window size, because the patching window size is limited by client buffer size. In our scheme, a proxy server in a LAN can maintain multiple patching groups, which are served by one regular multicast stream from server. This can drastically reduce the server bandwidth requirement. In the performance study, we show that our patching scheme can reduce the server bandwidth requirements compared with the existing patching techniques.

References

1. Hua, K.A., Cai,Y., Sheu, S.: Patching: A Multicast Technique for True Video-on-Demand Services. Proc. of ACM Multimedia '98. Bristol, U.K. (1998)
2. Cai, Y., Hua, K.A., Vu, K. : Optimizing Patching Performance. Proc. of SPIE's Conference on Multimedia Computing and Networking '99. San Jose, CA (1999)
3. Sen, S., Rexford, J., Towsley, D. : Proxy Prefix Caching for Multimedia Streams. Proc. of the IEEE Infocom, Vol. 3 (1998)
4. Wang, B., Sen, S., Adler, M., Towsley, D. : Optimal Proxy Cache Allocation for Efficient Streaming Media Distribution. Proc. of the IEEE Infocom, Vol. 3. New York, NY (2002)
5. Sheu, S., Hua, K.A., Tavanapong, W. : Chaining: A Generalized Batching Technique for Video-On-Demand Systems. Proc. of IEEE International Conf. on Multimedia Computing and Systems (ICMCS'97). Ottawa, Canada (1997)
6. Guo, Y., Suh, K., Kurose, J., Towsley, D. : P2Cast: Peer-to-Peer Patching Scheme for VoD Service. Proc. of the 12th World Wide Web Conference (WWW-03). Budapest, Hungary (2003)
7. Dan, A., Sitaram, D., Shahabuddin, P. : Dynamic Batching Policies for An On-Demand Video Server. Multimedia Systems, 4(3). (1996) 112-121
8. Do, T., Hua, K.A., Tantaoui, M. : P2VoD: Providing Fault Tolerant Video- on-Demand Streaming in Peer-to-Peer Environment. Technical Report 2003, SEECS, UCF. http://www.cs.ucf.edu/tdo/
9. Kwon, C.J., Choi, C.K., Choi, H.K. : An Improved Patching Scheme for Video-On-Demand Servers. Proc. of the International Conference on Parallel and Distributed Processing Techniques and Applications. Las Vegas, NV (2004)

An Indexing Method for Two-D Pattern Matching with Applications to Digital Image Searches

Fei Shi and Ahmad AlShibli

Computer Science Department,
Suffolk University,
Beacon Hill, Boston, MA 02114, USA
shi@mcs.suffolk.edu

Abstract. The two-dimensional pattern matching problem is to find all occurrences of a two-dimensional $m \times m$ matrix P (called the pattern) in another (larger) two-dimensional $n \times n$ matrix T (called the text). Most known algorithms for the problem first pre-process the pattern or patterns to make subsequent searches fast. Since each search still takes time proportional to the size of the text, such algorithms are inappropriate in applications in which the text is large and fixed and one will search for many different patterns in the text. We propose an algorithm that first processes the text into an index structure in such a way that subsequent searches with different patterns can be performed very quickly. The construction of the index takes $O(n^2 \log n)$ time and $O(n^2)$ space. The algorithm may produce false matches, in which the algorithm claims a "match" between P and some submatrix of T while they are actually not equal. However, as will be seen, the probability that a false match can occur is negligible. All occurrences of P in T, probably with a few false matches, can be found in $O(m^2)$ time in the worst case, regardless of the distribution of the elements in T and P. Under the assumption that both T and P are random matrices, the algorithm can find all (correct) occurrences of P in T in $O(m + \log n)$ expected time. We applied our algorithm to a digital image search problem and we will present experimental results.

1 Introduction

The two-dimensional pattern matching problem is: given an $n \times n$ matrix $T[0..n-1,\ 0..n-1]$ (called the text) and another $m \times m$ matrix $P[0..m-1,\ 0..m-1]$ (called the pattern) over a finite alphabet Σ, $m \leq n$, find all occurrences of P in T. In recent years, there has been growing interest in two or higher dimensional pattern matching, largely motivated by its applications in low-level image processing and in image database searches.

Baker [Bak78] and Bird [Bir77] independently developed the first algorithms for the problem, which use Aho and Corasick's one-dimensional dictionary matching algorithm [AC75] and run in $O(n^2 \log |\Sigma|)$ time. Amir, Benson and Farach

Y. Zhang et al. (Eds.): APWeb 2005, LNCS 3399, pp. 875–884, 2005.

[ABF92] gave an algorithm that takes $O(n^2)$ time to process the text and $O(m^2 \log |\Sigma|)$ time to process the pattern. Galil and Park [GP92] improved the time bound to $O(n^2 + m^2)$, which is truly independent of the alphabet size.

Algorithms for the two-d matching problem can be generally classified into two classes, based on whether they process the pattern first (*Class 1*) or process the text first (*Class 2*). All the algorithms mentioned above belong to the first class. They are inappropriate when we wish to search for many different and relatively small patterns in a large fixed text, since each search still takes time proportional to the size of the text. The only algorithms known to us that first process the text are due to Zhu and Takaoka [ZT89] and Giancarlo [Gia93, GG97].

Zhu and Takaoka presented two algorithms. Their first algorithm, which is a combination of Knuth, Morris and Pratt's algorithm [KMP77] and Karp and Rabin's algorithm [KR87], uses $O(n^2)$ time and space to process the text. After preprocessing the text, the search can be done in $O(n^2 + m^2)$ time in the worst and average cases. Their second algorithm uses Boyer and Moore's algorithm [BM77] to search the preprocessed text and runs in $O(n^2 \log m/m + m^2)$ time on the average.

The preprocessing part of Giancarlo's algorithm builds a two dimensional suffix tree LT and (since the outdegree of a node in LT can be very large) then transforms it into a trie defined over Σ, which takes $O(n^2(\log n + \log |\Sigma|))$ time and $O(n^2)$ space. The trie can be queried in $O(m^2 \log |\Sigma|)$ time. From this trie, three arrays can be computed in $O(n^2(\log n + \log |\Sigma|))$ time. The arrays allow a search query to be answered in $O(m^2 + \log n)$ time. The Giancarlo algorithm requires that both the text and the pattern should be square matrices.

The algorithm we present in this paper first processes the text into an index structure and therefore belongs to the second class (The same class as Zhu-Takaoka and Giancarlo's algorithms). It applies to rectangular matrices including, of course, square matrices (Giancarlo's algorithm can only deal with square matrices). It is conceptually simple and easy to implement. It preprocesses the text in $O(n^2 \log n)$ time using $O(n^2)$ space. The algorithm is randomized in the sense that during the running time it may produce false matches, i.e., it may claim a "match" between the pattern and some submatrix of the text while they are actually not equal (the "Monte-Carlo" type algorithm). However, as will be seen later, the probability that a false match can occur is negligible. All occurrences of the pattern in the text, probably with a few false matches, can be found in $O(m^2)$ time, regardless the distribution of the letters in the pattern and the text.

Our algorithm can be easily converted into a "Las-Vegas" type algorithm where there is no error and the randomization is on the running time only. Under the assumption that at each position in T and P, each letter of the alphabet occurs equally likely, after preprocessing the text, our "Las-Vegas" version algorithm can find all occurrences of P in T in $O(m + \log n)$ expected time. To the best of our knowledge, this algorithm is the average-case fastest one in its class (Class 2).

Table 1. Comparison of Algorithms in Class 2

Algorithm	Preprocessing	Searching	
		worst case	average case
Zhu-Takaoka-1	n^2	$n^2 + m^2$	$n^2 + m^2$
Zhu-Takaoka-2	n^2		$\frac{n^2}{m} \log m + m^2$
Giancarlo	$n^2(\log n + \log \lvert\Sigma\rvert)$	$m^2 + \log n$	
ours-1	$n^2 \log n$	$m^2 + \log n$	
ours-2	$n^2 \log n$		$m + \log n$

Table 1 shows the time order of the known algorithms in Class 2. All algorithms in Table 1 need $O(n^2)$ extra space for preprocessing the text and Algorithm ours-1 is a probabilistic algorithm.

We implemented our algorithm and used it to search a digital image database for images that contain given patterns. We will report on the experimental results in Section 6.

2 Outline of the Approach

The two main tools applied in our algorithm are Karp and Rabin's hashing technique [KR87] and the *generalized suffix arrays* [Shi96]. To simplify the presentation, we assume that both the text and pattern are square matrices, although our approach applies to rectangular matrices as well. Let the text T and pattern P be

$$T = \begin{pmatrix} t_{0,\,0} & t_{0,\,1} & \cdots & t_{0,\,n-1} \\ t_{1,\,0} & t_{1,\,1} & \cdots & t_{1,\,n-1} \\ \cdots & \cdots & \cdots & \cdots \\ t_{n-1,\,0} & t_{n-1,\,1} & \cdots & t_{n-1,\,n-1} \end{pmatrix} \tag{1}$$

and

$$P = \begin{pmatrix} p_{0,\,0} & p_{0,\,1} & \cdots & p_{0,\,m-1} \\ p_{1,\,0} & p_{1,\,1} & \cdots & p_{1,\,m-1} \\ \cdots & \cdots & \cdots & \cdots \\ p_{m-1,\,0} & p_{m-1,\,1} & \cdots & p_{m-1,\,m-1} \end{pmatrix} \tag{2}$$

Elements of T and P are from some sorted finite alphabet $\Sigma = \{c_1, c_2, \cdots, c_a\}$.

For any string $X = x_0 \cdots x_{m-1}$, define

$$H_p(X) = \sum_{i=0}^{m-1} \bar{x}_i \times a^{m-i-1} \bmod p \tag{3}$$

where $\bar{x}_i = j$ if $x_i = c_j$ (that is, x_i is the $j-$th letter in Σ) and p is some positive integer to be specified later.

We call $H_p(X)$ the *fingerprint* of string X.

Let T_i denote the $m \times n$ submatrix of T whose first row is the i-th row of T. That is,

$$T_i = \begin{pmatrix} t_{i,\,0} & t_{i,\,1} & \cdots & t_{i,\,n-1} \\ \cdots & \cdots & \cdots & \cdots \\ t_{i+m-1,\,0} & t_{i+m-1,\,1} & \cdots & t_{i+m-1,\,n-1} \end{pmatrix} \quad (0 \leq i \leq n-m). \tag{4}$$

Let $T_i(j)$ denote the j-th column of T_i. We represent each column $T_i(j)$, viewed as a string, by its fingerprint $H_p(T_i(j))$. Thus, each $m \times n$ submatrix T_i of T is represented by a string $V_i = H_p(T_i(0)) \cdots H_p(T_i(n-1))$ of length n. Let $v_{i,\,j}$ denote $H_p(T_i(j))$. We then have $V_i = v_{i,\,0}\, v_{i,\,1} \, \cdots \, v_{i,\,n-1}$. We call V_i the *fingerprint string* of the $m \times n$ submatrix T_i.

We process the $m \times m$ matrix P (the pattern) in the same way. Let $P(i)$ denote the i-th column of P, viewed as a string. P is transformed into the string $W = H_p(P(0)) \cdots H_p(P(m-1))$ of length m. Let w_j denote $H_p(P(j))$. We then have $W = w_0\, w_1 \, \cdots \, w_{m-1}$. We call W the *fingerprint string* of the pattern P.

Basic Idea. The basic idea of our approach is as follows. If P matches a part of submatrix T_i of T then the fingerprint string W of P must match a substring of the fingerprint string V_i of T_i. A match between $W = w_0\, w_1 \, \cdots \, w_{m-1}$ and a substring $V_i(j) = v_{i,\,j}\, v_{i,\,j+1} \, \cdots \, v_{i,\,j+m-1}$ of V_i starting at position j implies a possible match between P and the $m \times m$ submatrix of T whose upper left corner lies on position (i, j) of T. We then test whether the corresponding matrix elements are really equal.

A match between W and $V_i(j)$ is called a *false match* if $W = V_i(j)$ but P is not equal to the submatrix of T corresponding to $V_i(j)$. We will show in the next section that the probability that a false match occurs is negligible if the integer p in the fingerprint function $H_p(.)$ is chosen at random from a set $S = \{q \mid q$ is a prime and $q \leq M\}$ and the integer M is sufficiently large.

We will also show that the set of fingerprint strings $V = \{V_0, V_1, \cdots, V_{n-m}\}$ of T can be computed in $O(n^2)$ time and in $O(n^2)$ space. Our two dimensional pattern matching problem is then reduced to a one-dimensional string matching problem. We will use a data structure, called the generalized suffix array, to store the set of fingerprint strings $V = \{V_0, V_1, \cdots, V_{n-m}\}$ of T.

The generalized suffix array for a set of strings [Shi96] is an extension of Manber and Myers' suffix array for a single string [MM93]. Informally, a generalized suffix array of a given set S of strings consists of three arrays, *Pos*, *Llcp* and *Rlcp*. *Pos* is a lexicographically sorted array of all suffixes of strings in S. *Llcp* and *Rlcp* are two arrays of the information about the lengths of the longest common prefixes of the suffixes in *Pos*. Let N denote the sum of the lengths of all strings in S and n the length of the longest string in S. Then the generalized suffix array of S can be constructed in time $O(N \log n)$ in the worst case using $O(N)$ storage. Given the suffix array, on-line string search query of the type "Is X a substring of any strings in S? If so, where does it occur within strings of S?" in $O(m + \log N)$ time in the worst case where m is the length of X. For more detailed information on the generalized suffix array, see [MM93, Shi96].

The construction of the generalized suffix array for V takes $O(n^2 \log n)$ time and $O(n^2)$ space. Using the generalized suffix array for V, we can find all occurrences of W in V in $O(m + \log n)$ time.

The algorithm consists of two phases:

Constructing index

1. We represent every $m \times n$ submatrix T_i of the text T with its fingerprint string V_i ($i = 0, 1, \cdots, n-m$). So we get a set of fingerprint strings $V = \{V_0, V_1, \cdots, V_{n-m}\}$;
2. Build the suffix array for V.

Searching

1. Transform the pattern into a fingerprint string W;
2. Search the suffix array for the occurrences of W. Each occurrence of W in V implies an occurrence of the pattern P in the text T.

In the next section we show how to represent a two-dimensional text by a set of one-dimensional fingerprint strings.

3 Computing Fingerprint Strings

Define $H(X)$ of string $X = x_0 x_1 \ldots x_{m-1}$ as follows:

$$H(X) = \sum_{i=0}^{m-1} \bar{x}_i \cdot a^{m-i-1} \tag{5}$$

where $\bar{x}_i = j$ if $x_i = c_j$ (That is, x_i is the j-th letter in Σ), $i = 0, 1, \cdots, m-1$ and $a = |\Sigma|$. Then, $H(X)$ represents string X uniquely.

Define

$$H_p(X) = H(X) \bmod p \tag{6}$$

for some positive integer p to be specified later. We call $H_p(X)$ the fingerprint of string X. And we call m the *fingerprint height* of $H_p()$. $H_p(X)$ may not represent string X uniquely, as it is possible that $H_p(X_1) = H_p(X_2)$ for two different strings X_1 and X_2.

Denote by T_j the j-th column of T. We may think of T_j as a string; that is, $T_j = t_{0,j}\, t_{1,j} \cdots t_{n-1,j}$. Denote by $T_j(i)$ the substring of length m of string T_j that starts at position i, i.e., $T_j(i) = t_{i,j}\, t_{i+1,j} \cdots t_{i+m-1,j}$. Then

$$H(T_j(i+1)) = (H(T_j(i)) - t_{i,j} \cdot a^{m-1}) \cdot a + t_{i+m,j}. \tag{7}$$

Thus

$$H_p(T_j(i+1)) = (H_p(T_j(i)) \cdot a + \xi \cdot t_{i,j} + t_{i+m,j}) \bmod p \tag{8}$$

where $\xi = -a^m \bmod p$.

Let $v_{i,j}$ denote $H_p(T_j(i))$. Then

$$v_{i+1,j} = (v_{i,j} \cdot a + \xi \cdot t_{i,j} + t_{i+m,j}) \bmod p \tag{9}$$

By setting

$$v_{0,j} = \sum_{i=0}^{m-1} t_{i,j} \cdot a^{m-i-1} \bmod p \tag{10}$$

and then applying Eq(9) for $i = 0, 1, \ldots, n-m-1$, we obtain the fingerprints of all length m substrings of column j of T.

Let $V_i = v_{i,0}\, v_{i,1} \cdots v_{i,n-1}$. That is, V_i is the fingerprint string of the $m \times n$ submatrix T_i of T whose first row is the i-th row of T (see Eq(4)). Assuming that each application of Eq(9) takes constant time (we can keep constants ξ, p and the last computed fingerprint in fast registers), the time needed to compute the fingerprints of all length m substrings of column j of T is $O(n)$. Thus the total time needed to compute $V = \{V_0, V_1, \ldots, V_{n-m}\}$ is $O(n^2)$.

4 False Matches

Let X and Y be any two $m \times m$ matrices. Let $X(i)$ denote the i-th column of X, viewed as a string. Let

$$V = H_p(X(0)), H_p(X(1)), \ldots H_p(X(m-1)), \text{ and}$$
$$W = H_p(Y(0)), H_p(Y(1)), \ldots, H_p(Y(m-1))$$

where $H_p(\cdot)$ is the fingerprint function defined before. We say that $H_p(\cdot)$ leads to a *false match* if $V = W$ but $X \neq Y$.

We now study the probability that a false match can occur employing Karp and Rabin's results [KR87]. Let $\pi(u)$ denote the number of primes $\leq u$.

Lemma 1 (Karp and Rabin [KR87]). *If $u \geq 29$ and $b \leq 2^u$, then b has fewer than $\pi(u)$ different prime divisors.*

Lemma 2 (Rosser and Schoenfeld [RS62]). *For all $u \geq 17$*

$$\frac{u}{\ln u} \leq \pi(u) \leq 1.25506 \frac{u}{\ln u}.$$

Proof. The result is established by Corollary 1 to Theorems 1 and 2 of [RS62].

Lemma 3 (Rosser and Schoenfeld [RS62]). *For all $u \geq 59$*

$$\frac{u}{\ln u}(1 + \frac{1}{2\ln u}) < \pi(u) < \frac{u}{\ln u - 1.5}.$$

Proof. The result is established by formulas (3.1) and (3.4) of [RS62].

Theorem 1. *Let X and Y be any two $m \times m$ matrices over Σ. Let $X(i)$ denote the i-th column of X, viewed as a string. Let*

$$V = H_p(X(0)), H_p(X(1)), \ldots H_p(X(m-1)), \text{ and}$$
$$W = H_p(Y(0)), H_p(Y(1)), \ldots, H_p(Y(m-1))$$

where $H_p(\cdot)$ is the fingerprint function defined before. Suppose $V = W$, then if the prime p in $H_p(\cdot)$ is chosen at random from the set $S = \{q \mid q$ is a prime and $q \leq M\}$, then the probability that a false match occurs (i. e. $X \neq Y$) is less than

$$\frac{\pi(m^2 \log_2 a)}{\pi(M)},$$

provided $m^2 \log_2 a \geq 29$ where $a = |\Sigma|$.

Proof. Let $R = \{0, 1, \cdots, m-1\}$. We use $a|b$ to denote that a divides b. For any prime p, the event that $V = W$ and $X \neq Y$ is equivalent to each of the following statements:

1. For some $r \in R$, $H_p(X(r)) = H_p(Y(r))$ but $X(r) \neq Y(r)$.
2. For some $r \in R$ such that $X(r) \neq Y(r)$, $p \mid H(X(r)) - H(Y(r))$.
3. $p \mid \Pi_{\{r|X(r) \neq Y(r)\}} |H(X(r)) - H(Y(r))|$.

Since for each r, $|H(X(r)) - H(Y(r))| < a^m$, $(a = |\Sigma|)$, thus $\Pi_{\{r|X(r) \neq Y(r)\}} |H(X(r)) - H(Y(r))| < a^{m^2}$. By Lemma 1, the product has fewer than $\pi(m^2 \log_2 a)$ different prime divisors. Thus, p is chosen at random from $\pi(M)$ primes, of which fewer than $\pi(m^2 \log_2 a)$ lead to a false match. Hence, if p is chosen at random from $S = \{q \mid q \leq M$ and q prime $\}$, the probability that a false match occurs is less than

$$\frac{\pi(m^2 \log_2 a)}{\pi(M)}.$$

Theorem 2. *Suppose the prime p in $H_p(\cdot)$ is chosen at random from the set $S = \{q \mid q$ is a prime and $q \leq M\}$. Let $M = \log_2 a \cdot mn^3$. Then the probability that a match is a false one is less than*

$$\frac{1.25506\, m}{n^3} (1 + \frac{3 \ln n}{2 \ln m}).$$

Proof. Apply Lemma 2 to Theorem 1.

For example, suppose our algorithm is applied to a problem instance in which $a = |\Sigma| = 2^8$, $m = 2^9$ and $n = 2^{12}$. We choose $M = 2^{48}$. Then for any prime $p \leq M$, the range of the fingerprint function H_p is $\{0, 1, \cdots, p-1\}$ and each fingerprint can be represented by a 6-byte word. The probability that a match is false is less than

$$\frac{1.25506\, m}{n^3} (1 + \frac{3 \ln n}{2 \ln m}) < 3.02 \times 10^{-8}.$$

5 A Filtering Approach

For an $m_1 \times m_2$ matrix $P[0\,..\,m_1 - 1,\, 0\,..\,m_2 - 1]$, the value m_1 is said to be the height of P. One restriction of our approach presented in the previous sections is that the heights of pattern matrices should be known to the preprocessing portion of the algorithm before the preprocessing begins. We now sketch a way to lift this restriction. We preprocess the $n_1 \times n_2$ matrix $T[0 \mathinner{..} n_1 - 1,\ 0 \mathinner{..} n_2 - 1]$ (the text) in the same manner as was described in the previous sections for a series of values of m: $m = 1,\ 2^1,\ ,2^2,\ \ldots\ 2^{\lfloor \log_2 n_1 \rfloor}$, respectively. Then when presented with an $m_1 \times m_2$ matrix $P[0 \mathinner{..} m_1 - 1,\ 0 \mathinner{..} m_2 - 1]$ (the pattern), we choose $m_1' = 2^i$ such that $2^i \leq m_1 < 2^{i+1}$. We pick any $m_1' \times m_2$ submatrix P' of P. We first look for all occurrences of P' in T in the same way as was described before. Then, for each such occurrence found, we check if it is really an occurrence of P in T using symbol by symbol comparisons.

If we choose $m = m_1' = 2$ we get the simplest version of our approach. Given the preprocessed text, this simple algorithm can find all (correct) occurrences of P in T in $O(m + \log n)$ expected time assuming both the text and pattern are random matrices (A matrix A over some finite alphabet Σ is called a random matrix if at each position of A each element of Σ can occur with the same probability). This is perhaps the average-case fastest algorithm known in its class.

Because of the limit of space allowed for this paper, we cannot give more details about this filtering approach in this paper.

6 Experimental Results

We have implemented our technique and used it to search digital images. Our program, which is written in C, was tested on a (old and slow) PC (Pentium III 450MHZ with 256 MB RAM) that run Redhat Linux.

The text and patterns used in our test were digital images of 256 color values (i.e., $|\Sigma| = 256$). The prime number used in our fingerprint function is $p = 2^{31} - 1$. The size of the text array tested was 480×640 and three different pattern sizes were tested: 15×200, 150×200, and 300×200.

Table 2 shows the time used to construct the index. The total construction time is broken down into the time for converting the text into fingerprint strings and the time for building the suffix array.

Table 2. Index construction

Fingerprint height	Text processing	Building suffix array	Total
15	.06 sec.	0.12 sec.	0.18 sec.
150	.07 sec.	0.07 sec.	0.14 sec.
300	.07 sec.	0.04 sec.	0.11 sec.

Table 3 shows the average time used to search for a pattern in the text.

In our implementation we used a simple and easy-to-implement algorithm for constructing the suffix array which takes $O(N^2)$ time in the worst case- we did not use more efficient algorithms that can construct a suffix array in only $O(N \log N)$ time in the worst case (N denotes the total length of the strings).

Table 3. Searching for patterns

Pattern size	No. of pattern files	Average search time
15×200	1,000	0.006 sec.
150×200	1,000	0.014 sec.
300×200	1,000	0.022 sec.

Our experiments show that the time we have to spend on building the index is acceptable in most cases; once the index is available subsequent searches can be done very quickly.

7 Future Work

We plan to compare empirically our algorithm with other known algorithms such as Zhu-Takaoka algorithm [ZT89] and Giancarlo algorithm [Gia93, GG97].[1]

References

[ABF92] A. Amir, G. Benson and M. Farach, Alphabet Independent Two-dimensional Matching. *Proc. the 24th annual ACM Symposium on Theory of Computing*, 1992, pp. 59-68.

[AC75] A. V. Aho and M. Corasick, Efficient string matching: an aid to bibliographic search. *Communications of the ACM*, June 1975, Vol. 18, No. 6, pp. 333 - 340.

[AL91] A. Amir and G. Landau, Fast parallel and serial multidimensional approximate array matching, *Theoretical Computer Science* 81 (1991), Elsevier, pp. 97-115.

[Bak78] T. J. Baker, A Technique for Extending Rapid Exact-Match String Matching to Arrays of More Than One Dimension. *SIAM J. on Computing,* 7:533-541, 1978.

[Bir77] R.S. Bird, Two Dimensional Pattern Matching. *Information Processing Letters,* 6(5): 168-170, 1977.

[BM77] R.S. Boyer and J.S. Moore, A fast matching algorithm. *Commun. ACM* 20, 10 (Oct. 1977), 762-772.

[Gia93] R. Giancarlo, The Suffix of a Square Matrix, with Applications. *Proc. Fourth Symposium on Discrete Algorithms.* ACM-SIAM, 1993, pp. 402-411.

[GG97] R. Giancarlo and R. Grossi, Suffix Tree Data Structures for Matrices, in Pattern Matching Algorithms, A. Apostolico e Z. Galil Eds.,Oxford University Press, (1997), pp. 293-340.

[GP92] Z. Galil and K. Park, Truly Alphabet-Independent Two-dimensional Pattern Matching. *Proc. 33th Symposium on Foundations of Computer Science*, IEEE, 1992, pp. 247-256.

[1] Giancarlo algorithm is rather complex and hard to implement. We recently contacted Dr. Giancarlo requesting for an implementation of his algorithm and were told that they have not implemented their algorithm yet.

[KMP77] D.E. Knuth, J.H. Morries, and V.B. Pratt, Fast pattern matching in strings. *SIAM J. on Computing*, 6:189-195, 1977.

[KR87] R. Karp and M. Rabin, Efficient Randomized Pattern Matching Algorithms. *IBM J. Res. Develop.*, Vol. 31, No. 2, March 1987, pp. 249-260.

[MM93] U. Manber and G. Myers, Suffix Arrays: A New Method for On-Line String Searches. *SIAM Journal on Computing 22* (1993), pp. 935-948.

[RS62] J. B. Rosser and L. Schoenfeld, Approximate Formulas for Some Functions of Prime Numbers. *Illinois J. Math. 6*, 64-94, 1962.

[Shi96] Fei Shi, Suffix arrays for multiple strings: a method for on-line multiple string searches, in *Concurrency and Parallelism, Programming, Networking and Security: Proceedings Second Asian Computing Science Conference (ASIAN'96)*, Vol. 1179 of LNCS, Springer-Verlag, Berlin, 1996, pp. 11-22.

[ZT89] R.F. Zhu and T. Takaoka, A Technique for Two-Dimensional Pattern Matching. *Communications of the ACM* 32 (9), 1989, 1110-1120.

Indexing Text and Visual Features for WWW Images

Heng Tao Shen[1], Xiaofang Zhou[1], and Bin Cui[2]

[1] School of Info. Tech. and Elec. Eng.,
The University of Queensland, Brisbane, Australia
{shenht, zxf}@itee.uq.edu.au
[2] Singapore-MIT Alliance, National University of Singapore
cuibin@comp.nus.edu.sg

Abstract. In this paper, we present a novel indexing technique called *Multi-scale Similarity Indexing* (MSI) to index image's multi-features into a single one-dimensional structure. Both for text and visual feature spaces, the similarity between a point and a local partition's center in individual space is used as the indexing key, where similarity values in different features are distinguished by different scale. Then a single indexing tree can be built on these keys. Based on the property that relevant images haves similar similarity values from the center of the same local partition in any feature space, certain number of irrelevant images can be fast pruned based on the triangle inequity on indexing keys. To remove the "*dimensionality curse*" existing in high dimensional structure, we propose a new technique called *Local Bit Stream* (LBS). LBS transforms image's text and visual feature representations into simple, uniform and effective bit stream (BS) representations based on local partition's center. Such BS representations are small in size and fast for comparison since only bit operation are involved. By comparing common bits existing in two BSs, most of irrelevant images can be immediately filtered. Our extensive experiment showed that single one-dimensional index on multi-features improves multi-indices on multi-features greatly. Our LBS method outperforms sequential scan on high dimensional space by an order of magnitude.

1 Introduction

WWW provides a super big pool for interesting images. Recently, WWW image retrieval has been a very challenging research area. Such images are typically described by both high-level (text) and low-level (visual) features. To retrieve relevant images from large image database, two issues are essential: effectiveness and efficiency. However, most known research results [1] are on retrieval effectiveness. There is no clearly known research achievement on how to index this particular type of large image database described by multi-features for efficient retrieval, especially on indexing completely different representations: text and visual features. Current method is to build one structure for every single feature. Given an image query, it has to access all individual structures and integrate results from each index to get the final results. Furthermore, these known indexing structures suffer from "*dimensionality*

Y. Zhang et al. (Eds.): APWeb 2005, LNCS 3399, pp. 885–899, 2005.

curse". When the dimensionality of data space reaches 20 or greater, indexing techniques fail to outperform sequential scan [2] for nearest neighbor search.

In this paper, we propose a new method called Multi-scale Similarity Indexing (MSI) that can index WWW images' multi-features in a single structure. MSI exhibits a means of indexing different features in different representations in a single tree, such as image text and visual features, where text feature is in Weighted Lexical Chain model [3] or others, and visual feature is in standard high dimensional data space. MSI first partitions each feature space into clusters. Then the similarity of each image in each feature space to its corresponding cluster's center is computed as the indexing key. By a simple mapping function, we can keep the keys for each cluster in different feature space distinct in different scale level. Thus a standard B+ tree can be easily built on these indexing keys.

However, like other existing indexing technique, MSI also suffers from "*dimensionality curse*". To release MSI from such curse, we propose a novel technique called Local Bit Stream (LBS). LBS exhibits a way to transform the high dimensional feature representation (big size) into a uniform, accurate and compact representation (small size). Given clusters in each feature space, LBS encodes each point in different feature space into a uniformly dimensional bit stream (BS). The BS of a point in a feature space is generated by comparing this point and its cluster's center. Thus such transformation is localized at cluster level. The effectiveness of LBS depends on how to generate the BS for each feature point. Due to the completely different nature of text and visual features, both are encoded in different schemes. We present different encoding strategies for text and visual features. However, both encoding strategies can produce the same uniformly BS representations for text and visual feature points. BS is an approximate representation of original data. It's compact, much smaller in size, and accurate for similarity measures. Furthermore, BS comparisons involve bit operations only. Thus it is much faster in terms of efficiency.

We implement our indexing techniques on top of MYSQL server. An extensive performance study is conducted to evaluate our methods. Our results show that single indexing structure is supreme to multi-indexing structures, and LBS breaks the dimensionality curse by improving the response time faster than sequential scan and iDistance [4] by an order of magnitude without sacrificing the retrieval precision.

The rest of paper is organized as follows. In section 2, we review some related works. In section 3, some preliminary work on image features and similarity measures are introduced. In section 4, we present the single one-dimensional indexing structure – MSI, and in section 5 we propose the LBS and its encoding schemes. An extensive performance study is presented in section 6. Finally, we conclude our paper in section 7.

2 Related Work

Our related works cover several research areas: WWW image retrieval, evidence integration, high dimensional indexing, and multi-feature query processing.

Several WWW image retrieval systems have been proposed in literature. Existing known systems, such as AMORE [5], ImageRover [6], and WebSeek [7], allow the WWW image retrieval on combination of multi-features, like keywords, color, shape and texture. Recently, the high-level features of WWW images were explored by a Weight ChainNet model [3] since low level features cannot represent the high level semantic meanings for WWW images. More recently, the textual and Hyperlink information are extracted from blocks of Web pages to improve the accuracy [24]. And relevance feedback techniques are also applied in WWW image retrieval [8, 25]. However, most of systems focus on retrieval accuracy only.

To integrate multi-features together, most of systems used linear combination by assuming that text and visual features are linearly important. Recently, Dempster Shafer Theory, one technique to handle uncertainty, has been also employed on indexing of face retrieval on the web [9]. In this paper, we examine more techniques, including Certainty Factor and Compound probability.

Recently, Nearest Neighbor (NN) search in high dimensional spaces has been a very active research topic. Several indexing structures [2, 4, 10, 11, 12, 13] have been proposed. However, all these techniques are for indexing an individual feature space purpose, and they all suffer from known "*dimensionality curse*". Their performances degrade rapidly as dimensionality increases. As dimensionality reaches high (>20), they even fail to outperform sequential scan. Most existing systems build one index for every feature space. Given a query, each index has to be accessed. ImageRover [6] tried to combine multi-features by first performing dimensionality reduction on each feature then used existing indexing structure to index *concatenated feature vector* from every reduced feature space. Anne et al [14] applied non-linear neural network techniques with dimensionality reduction method, then used the similar way to index reduced multi-visual features by existing indexing structure. However, both have the following drawbacks. First the dimensionality curse still remains. Their techniques reduce the spaces into a level where the retrieval accuracy is reasonably affected. Image features spaces are typically in dimensionality of a range of tens to hundreds. For images with multi-features, it is usually not practical to reduce the total dimensionality of all reduced feature spaces to be less than 20 while remaining high retrieval accuracy. Second, there was no clear report on their indexing efficiency. Third, neural network is tedious and hard for training, especially for WWW image database with text features. In this paper, we aim to index multi text and visual features in a one-dimensional single index and leave the dimensionality curse to the past.

Another category of our related work is on processing multi-feature queries. Such problem appears obviously on multi-features images database. Given a query image, the typical steps are first to compute the similarity among the same feature space, then combine the score from all feature spaces, and finally rank them based on the final score. Some optimization job can be done to reduce the overall cost [15, 16]. We will not present multi-feature query processing problem in this paper, but on indexing issues.

3 Preliminary

In this section, we briefly present the features we used to describe the WWW images and respective similarity measures.

3.1 WWW Image Features

Without losing the generality, we use text feature and one visual feature as the descriptors of WWW images.

3.1.1 Text Feature

Text descriptions of WWW image carry high-level semantic meanings. We choose a recently proposed representation model called Weighted ChainNet Model [3] as the text feature. Weighted ChainNet constructs a Lexical Chain (or sentence) network given the WWW image's surrounding text in its embedded web page, by assigning different weight for different type of Lexical Chain (LC). And there are six types of lexical chains were introduced: Title Lexical Chain Alt Lexical Chain, Page Lexical Chain, Sentence Lexical Chain, Reconstructed Sentence Lexical Chain, and Caption Lexical Chain. The first three types are constructed by image's title, image's alternate text, and web page's title respectively, and the last three are constructed by image caption. To simplify the problem and illustration, here we summarize the chain network into a single weighted lexical chain by summing all the weight in each type of lexical china for each word in the network. The following formula is used to compute the total weight for each word.

$$Word_{weight} = \sum_{i=1}^{6} Word^{i}_{weight}$$

Where $Word^{i}_{weight}$ is the weight of *Word* in type *i* lexical chain, and *i* ranges from 1 to 6.

Thus all the weighted words form a single *weighted lexical chain*, which is used as our WWW image's text feature. For simplicity, we denote image's text feature as T.

3.1.2 Visual Feature

Wavelet transform is a useful tool in effectively generating compact representation that exploits the structure of visual features of images. By using wavelet sub band decomposition, and remain the most important sub bands (largest coefficients), we can get fixed size dimensional feature vectors independent of resolution and scaling. Wavelets produce the wavelet coefficients for an image as its description. And such coefficients construct a coarse overall approximation of image's visual feature. This approximation captures image's shape, texture and location information in a single signature. We use daubechies' wavelets [17] to generate WWW image's visual features. In this paper, we truncate the 64 most dominating coefficients as our image's visual feature. Thus our WWW image's visual feature is in 64-dimensional feature vector. For simplicity, we denote image's visual feature as V.

3.2 Image Similarity Measurements

For text feature, we employ the cosine formula as follows:

$$Sim^{text}(T_i, T_j) = \frac{T_i \bullet T_j}{\|T_i\| * \|T_j\|}$$

where T_i and T_j is image *i*'s and image *j*'s text feature respectively.

For visual feature, the similarity between two images is computed as follows based on Manhattan Distance:

$$Sim^{visual}(V_i, V_j) = 1 - \frac{(\sum_{d=1}^{D} |V_{i.d} - V_{j.d}|)}{D}$$

where $V_{i.d}$ and $V_{j.d}$ is the dth dimensional value for image *i*'s and image *j*'s visual feature respectively. D is the dimensionality of visual feature space.

4 Index Multi-scale Similarities

4.1 Building Indexing Structure

In this section, we present the one-dimensional single indexing technique for image's multi-features, called Multi-scale Similarity Indexing (MSI). MSI is mainly inspired from the following observations. First, in the same cluster, relevant images have close similarities to the cluster's center. And this property is hold for both text feature space and visual feature space. Second, based on the similarities to the cluster center, images can be ordered within that cluster. Third, similarities are one-dimensional values. If we can map each image into corresponding similarity value and each cluster in each feature space can be scaled into different interval, a single one-dimensional index like B+-tree can be easily built on these similarities. Thus in MSI, high dimensional features spaces are transformed into one-dimensional space. Certain amount of irrelevant images can be fast pruned based on these one-dimensional values' comparisons.

To build MSI, we need first to cluster each feature space into partitions and compute their centers. Let's assume that there are m clusters in text feature space and n clusters in visual feature space. in text space, each cluster is assigned with a cluster ID from 1 to m, and similarly to visual feature space with cluster ID from 1 to n. Given an image with feature T and V, its indexing keys in different feature space are computed as follows:

$$key^{text} = T\_SCALE + i * C + Sim^{text}(T, O_i^T)$$

$$key^{visual} = V\_SCALE + j * C + Sim^{visual}(V, O_j^V)$$

where key^{text} and key^{visual} are the indexing keys, *i* and *j* are cluster Ids for its T and V in text feature space and visual feature space, with cluster center O_i^T and O_j^V respectively. *T_SCALE* and *V_SCALE* are two constant scales with large gap to distinguish text and visual spaces. *C* is a constant to stretch the similarities range so that features in different cluster have different range. Thus features in different clusters can be distinguished easily. For example, an image with feature T and V, T is in cluster *i* in text feature space, and V is in cluster *j* in visual feature space, then its two indexing keys will be transformed into the ranges [*T_SCALE+i*C, T_SCALE+(i+1)*C*] and [*V_SCALE+j*C, V_SCALE+(j+1)*C*] respectively.

A single B+-tree can be used to index the similarity keys for fast retrieval. And an additional auxiliary array is used to store the clusters centers and their minimum and maximum radii/similarity values that define the cluster's data space, where the minimum and maximum radii are used to facilitate searching. When there is only one feature, MSI is similar to iDistance[4], except the keys are computed based on the similarity, rather than distance values.

4.2 Query Processing

Given a query image *Q* to search for the K top relevant images (K nearest neighbors), the searching algorithm works as follows. For each feature space, the query is first divided into two sub queries, Q_T and Q_V respectively, where Q_T and Q_V are image's text and visual features. Then nearest neighbor searching is performed to get K_T and K_V top ranked image Ids from text and visual feature space such that the intersection of both set of Ids has at least K Ids in common. Evidence combination methods are then applied to compute the final list of results.

For each subquery, the searching starts with a query sphere by a *relatively* small radius R around Q_T and Q_V respectively. To find the desired number of most relevant images, the searching radius cannot be predetermined. Hence an iterative method that examines the *increasing larger* query sphere in each iteration has to be used. Searching in MSI begins with scanning the auxiliary array to determine which cluster whose data space overlaps with the searching sphere of Q_T and Q_V. This can be determined by the following triangle inequality property:

$$Sim^{text}(Q_T - O^T) \leq Sim^{text}(Q_T - P) + R \quad \text{or}$$

$$Sim^{visual}(Q_V - O^V) \leq Sim^{visual}(Q_V - P) + R$$

where P is a feature point in either text or visual feature space.

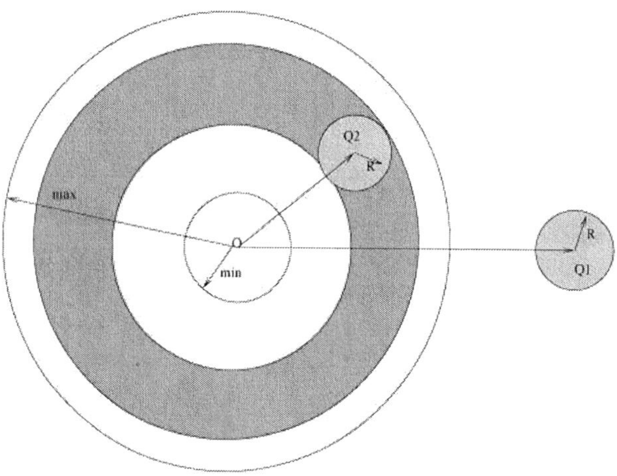

Fig. 1. Searching spaces for two queries

Figure 1 shows the searching spaces for two queries Q_1 and Q_2 corresponding to a cluster O which covers a space defined by its minimum and maximum radii. From the above triangle inequality property, for Q_1, cluster O can be directly pruned since the similarity between Q_1 and O is greater than cluster's maximum radius/similarity plus query searching radius R. The same situation occurs when the similarity between

Q_1 and O is less than the cluster's minimum radius/similarity minus query searching radius R. And this pruning situation is common to both text and visual feature spaces.

On the other hand, if both query sphere and cluster's data space intersect, such as Q_2's searching sphere in figure 1, range searching has to be performed in MSI. Given an image with Q_T and Q_V intersect with cluster O_i^T and O_j^V in text and visual space respectively, their ranges searched in MSI are:

$$\begin{bmatrix} T\_SCALE + i * C + Sim^{text}(Q_T, O_i^T) - R, \\ T\_SCALE + i * C + Sim^{text}(Q_T, O_i^T) + R \end{bmatrix}$$

and

$$\begin{bmatrix} V\_SCALE + j * C + Sim^{visual}(Q_V, O_j^V) - R, \\ V\_SCALE + j * C + Sim^{visual}(Q_V, O_j^V) + R \end{bmatrix}$$

Note that query sphere R is an increasing parameter with number of iterations. Searching for both sub queries is concurrent. It stops when there are at least K common image Ids are discovered in two sets of results searched from two sub queries. Thus MSI can provide approximate K nearest neighbors quickly using one dimensional data comparisons.

So far, we have built a single one-dimensional indexing for WWW image's multi-features. However, similarity-indexing key mapping function is lossy in nature. Searching the data whose similarities to cluster's center are close to query point may introduce certain number of '*false positives*'. For instance, in figure 1, although certain amount of points that are out of searching range can be pruned immediately (white area), the candidates for data access still include a number of points far away from query (green area, named as '*false positive*'). It will be perfect if we can remain only the points inside of query searching sphere (pink area). In next section, we propose Local Digital Coding to effectively filter most of these '*false positives*'.

4.3 Clustering Techniques

As mentioned earlier, the first step for building MSI is to partition each feature space.

For WWW image text feature, every image is in weighted lexical chain model. We observed that WWW images are usually categorized by different topics. Here we propose a method called Topic-driven Clustering, to partition the text space into clusters.

Topic-driven Clustering Algorithm:

1. select the top K hottest keywords, and each keyword is assigned as a center.
2. assign images into these K clusters based on similarities to each center.
3. reconstruct each cluster's center by summarizing its images' weighted lexical chains.
4. reassign images into K clusters based on similarities to each new center.
5. merge K clusters into a desirable number of clusters.

In this algorithm, images are initially clustered into K clusters based on the most frequent keywords appearing in the images (step 1 and 2). Obviously, not all of the images can be assigned into clusters since K keywords cannot cover all images. A reclustering process is performed. In step 2, we expand each cluster's center to be a weighted lexical chain by summarizing all images' lexical chains in the same way as summarizing the image's representation from a lexical chain network. By doing so, the center of cluster can be properly adjusted and represent the cluster's complete information. Then images are partitioned again corresponding to these new centers. Finally we merge closely related clusters into one, until we get a desirable number of cluster we want. After we apply Topic-driven clustering algorithm, the image's text feature are clustered into partitions, each of which has a weighted lexical chain as the center.

To partition the high dimensional data space, such as image's visual feature, several clustering methods [18, 19, 20] have been proposed in literature. In this paper we use the elliptical K-means [21] method to detect the *correlated* clusters in the space. The main purpose of finding correlated cluster is to perform the dimensionality reduction on these clusters locally. Recently research [23] has shown that dimensionality reduction on local correlated/elliptical cluster achieved much better effectiveness compared to reduce the dimensionality on the whole dataset. This is because dimensionality reduction methods such as Principle Component Analysis (PCA) are effectively only when the data space is well correlated. Otherwise, the retrieval accuracy should be affected greatly.

5 Local Bit Stream

In this section, we introduce our new indexing technique applied in MSI to break the dimensionality curse by filtering the irrelevant images greatly.

LBS is inspired by the following observations. First, digital bit (0 or 1) is the smallest data representation. If each dimension of feature space can be represented by digital bit, the memory space can be reduced dramatically. Second, bit operation is always fastest. However, in high dimensional space, the similarity computation on original data is very expensive.

Realize that for WWW images, its text feature and visual feature are in different representation models. Here, we use weighted lexical chain to represent text feature and standard high dimensional point to represent visual feature. Both have the following main differences. First, text feature is discrete in nature since each dimension of lexical chain is a word basically, while visual feature is continuous value along each dimension. Second, the dimensionality of text feature is dynamic, while that of visual feature is fixed. Different images may have different number of words to describe its semantics. To generate the uniform bits representation (we name it as Bit Stream, or BS) for both features, different encoding scheme have to be used.

Except the uniform BS representation, how to produce an effective BS for each image feature is a challenging task. Here we associate the generation of BS with the cluster center where an image belongs. That is, for an image's feature, we first allocate its cluster, and then compare it with its cluster center to generate its BS. Thus we localize the BS generation at cluster level, rather than the whole database level.

Next, we present the two encoding algorithms for text and visual features to produce a D-bit long uniform BS representation, where D is the dimensionality of feature space.

5.1 BS Generation for Text Feature

In text feature space, due to its discrete nature, two preliminary steps are needed before we start encoding by using the property of ordered data. We first order every image's lexical chain and the cluster center's lexical chain based on alphabet order of the words. Second, every word in each image lexical chain is labeled with its position index in the center's lexical chain. Since the center contains all the words appearing in all the images within the cluster, we use the center as the axis to generate the BS representation for images inside of cluster.

The encoding algorithm for an image text feature T in a cluster O^T is shown below.

Text Encoding:

1. BS=0;
2. range = O^T .size()/D + 1;
3. for every word in T
4. pos = word.index / range
5. BS | = 1 << pos;
6. end for

The BS is initialized to be 0. For an ordered center O^T, we divide it into D intervals (line 2). For each word in a text feature T, since we know its corresponding index in O^T, we first compute which interval it lies in (line 4), then update the bit value at that position counted from left to be 1 (line 5). For example, if T contains two words "ACM" and "Multimedia" and their respective position index in the cluster center is 10 and 100. The center contains 1000 words. We want to construct a 64-bit BS. Based on the above encoding method, the interval range is 16. That is, the first interval is [0, 16), second is [16, 32), and so on. Words "ACM" and "Multimedia" are in interval 0 and 6. Thus the BS for T is $2^{\wedge 6} + 2^{\wedge 0}$=65. If more bits are needed than integer, multi-integer or character can be used.

Due to text feature's discrete property, if two are similar, the AND (&) operation on two BSs must be greater than 0. By checking this result, lots of irrelevant images can be pruned immediately. This encoding algorithm can make sure the retrieval precision is exactly the same as sequential scan. Further more, the space occupied by BS is fixed in D bits. However, each original text feature generally takes hundreds of bytes.

5.2 BS Generation for Visual Feature

Different from text feature, visual features are in high dimensional uniform. And along each dimension, the data value is continuous. In text feature space, the fixed number of intervals divided from cluster center is used to produce a uniform D-bit BS representation since the dimensionality of text feature for each image is different.

However, in visual feature space, the dimensionality is fixed. Meanwhile, the similarity measurements between both spaces are also different. Thus we present a different encoding algorithm for continuous and fixed dimensionality feature spaces.

Visual Encoding:

```
1. BS=0;
2. for i =0 to D-1
3.     if (V[i]> O^V [i])
4.         BS | = 1 << i;
5. end for
```

Given a D-dimensional feature space, the above algorithm encodes each feature V into a D-bit BS representation given its cluster center O^V. Initially, the BS is set to be 0 (line 1). For each dimension, if its value is greater than the center value, we set the bit value to be 1 at that dimension for BS (line 3-4), else remain 0. Thus in visual space, the BS is a coarse approximation of original data.

BS for visual feature is derived from comparing its cluster's center. If two images are similar, their BSs should also be similar. To decide whether two BSs are similar, we use a threshold parameter - φ to indicate minimum number of *common bits* that two similar BSs should have. Along a dimension, if both BSs have same bit value, either 0 or 1, we say both BSs have one *common bit*. That is, along a dimension, if two visual features are both greater than the center or both less than the center, then their BSs have one common bit. Clearly, BS representation for a visual feature reflects its approximate trend/signal around its local cluster center. If both BSs have more than φ number of common bits, we say two BSs are similar. Given a 64-dimensional feature space, usually the values are float type – 4 bytes long. Thus for each feature, it occupies 64*4 bytes space. However, a BS occupies 64/8 bytes. There are 32 times differences. Again, by performing bit operations on BSs, we can fast prune irrelevant images before we access the original data. Since φ is a threshold parameter, it has certain side effects. If it is too small, the pruning may not be very effective. On the other hand, if it is too big, some relevant images may be filtered. In the experiments, we will see that while we keep the same accuracy as sequential scan, the retrieval speed can still be faster than sequential scan by times.

So far, we have looked the encoding method to produce BSs for text and visual features. And both encoding algorithm use the *local cluster's center* as a basis. The final outputs from both algorithms have the same representation model – BS.

LBS builds a new simple feature representation called BS for each image in respective feature space. BS is small in size, and fast comparison since it's only involved bit operations. BSs can be embedded into MSI lower than the indexing keys level and upper than the original data level. An example tree structure is shown in figure 2. Thus, after the first level pruning in MSI, a second level pruning by comparing BSs is performed to filter most of 'false positives' included in the first level pruning. The images whose BSs are similar to query BS are then accessed at data level. Experiments showed that while keeping the accuracy high, 90% more 'false positives' could be effectively pruned.

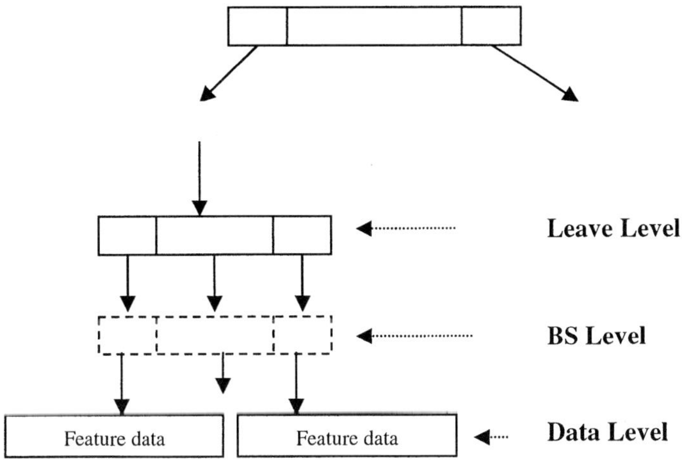

Fig. 2. Overall Structure of MSI with LBS

6 Performance Study

In section, we present our experiments results on our proposals. We compare our indexing technique with sequential scan and multi-indices built by iDistance method [4], where the indexing keys are computed by similarity rather than distance. In the following, we refer our MSI with LBS as LBS only.

6.1 Experiments Set Up

Our database contains 100,000 WWW images downloaded by our web crawler randomly from around 40,000 websites. And we use the weighted lexical chain and wavelet descriptors as image's text and visual features as explained in section 3. We manipulated these databases in MYSQL server. We implement our method in the environment of Ultra-10 SunOS 5.7 processor (333 MHz CPU and 256 MB RAM).

Two parameters are used as measurements: Precision and Efficiency. Since our database is large, it's impossible to compute the retrieval recall. Here we use fixed KNN (K nearest neighbor) to compute the precision. Obviously, within this K results, if the precision is higher, recall is higher also. We set K=20, and test 20 image queries for each experiment. Efficiency is measured by the *Total Response Time* (TRT), which includes the communication time to the MYSQL server.

6.2 Tuning φ

In our LBS method, the important parameter φ which is used to measure the similarity between two BSs has to be tuned. For text feature's BS, due to discrete nature, we have to access every feature point whose BS AND (bit operation &) query's BS is greater than 0. So we need tune φ for visual features only.

In this experiment, we use image's visual features only – the 64- data to see the changing of φ for different dimensional data space. Here we the *relative precision* by comparing LBS with sequential scan. The relative precision is defined as precision by LBS divided by precision by sequential scan. The following figure 3 and 4 show the effect of different φ values on retrieval precision and efficiency for two sets of visual features.

From figure 3, we can see that for 64-dimendional original data, LBS can remain the same precision as sequential scan when φ is less than 36. When φ is greater than 36, there is rapid decreasing on precision. This is reasonable. When φ is larger, more points can be pruned. As φ becomes too large, there may be only less than K candidates remained. When φ becomes 64, only the query image is the candidate to access the original data. Thus a φ value which is a bit larger than the half size of the dimensionality of data space can remain the precision high.

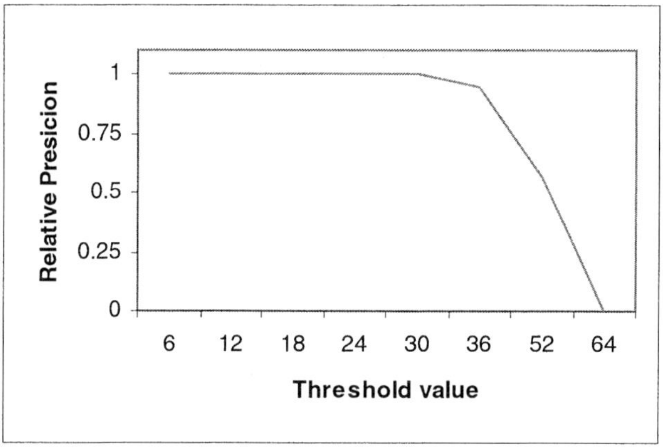

Fig. 3. φ Effects on precision

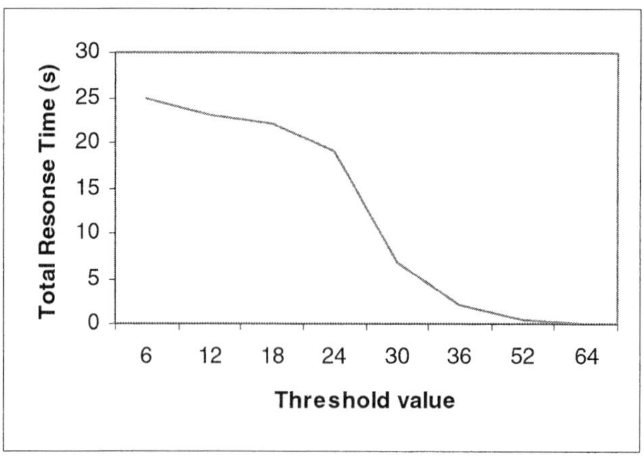

Fig. 4. φ Effects on total response time

Figure 4 shows the φ effects on the total response time. TRT for sequential scan is the result when φ=0. For 64-dimensional space, when φ is less than 24, there is no obvious reduction on TRT. This is clear that in high dimensional space, most of points have few common bits along few dimensions with query point, while they may not be necessary to be the top K nearest neighbors to the query point. However, when φ increases to be larger than the half size of the dimensionality of data space (36 in this case), the TRT is reduced dramatically. This indicates that most of the irrelevant points can be distinguished when φ reaches around the half size of the dimensionality. As φ becomes too large, more points can be filtered, but precision may be affected as shown in figure 3. Thus there is a tradeoff between precision and TRT. From figure 3 and 4, we can see that good values for φ could be a bit larger than the half size of the dimensionality. At these values, TRT can be reduced greatly, while precision is still high. In our later experiments, we chose φ as 36 for our 64-dimensional feature.

6.3 Comparative Study

Now we want to compare our indexing method LBS with sequential scan and multi-indices by iDistance [4], based on the retrieval speed. This experiment tested 3 datasets: text feature only, visual feature only, and text combined with visual features. The following table shows their differences in terms of total response time (s).

Table 1. Comparative study on retrieval speed

	Text Feature	Visual Feature	Combination
LBS	0.8	2.1	3.2
Sequential Scan	3.5	21	33
Multi-indices by iDistance	5.7	32	41

From table 1, we can see that multi-indices method built by iDistance performs even worse than sequential scan. There are two possible reasons. First, accessing and searching multi-indices take more time. Second, dimensionality curse resists in such purely similarity based one-dimensional index because too many 'false positives' are searched. By employing single index structure and LBS, the performance is improved significantly. LBS is more than an order of magnitude better than sequential scan. Clearly, our LBS is an effective method to filter those irrelevant points.

7 Conclusion

In this paper, we presented a novel indexing technique called MSI to index WWW image's multi-features in a single one-dimensional structure. Combined with Local

Bit Stream, our method can outperform sequential scan and multi-indices by iDistance significantly without degrading the retrieval precision.

References

[1] A Review of Content-Based Image Retrieval Systems, http://www.jtap.ac.uk/reports/htm/jtap-054.html

[2] R. Weber and H. Schek and S. Blott, A Quantitative Analysis and Performance Study for Similarity-Search Methods in High-Dimensional Spaces, VLDB, pp 194—205, 1998.

[3] H.T Shen, B. C. Ooi, and K.L. Tan. Giving meanings to WWW images. In Proc. of 8th ACM Multimedia Conference, pp 39-47, 2000.

[4] C. Yu, B.C. Ooi, K.L. Tan and H.V. Jagadish: Indexing the Distance: An Efficient Method to KNN Processing. VLDB, pp421-430, 2001.

[5] Sougata Mukherjea, Kyoji Hirata, and Yoshinori Hara. Amore: A World Wide Web image retrieval engine.The WWW Journal, 2(3): 115-132, 1999.

[6] Stan Sclaro, Leonid Taycher, and Marco La Cascia. Imagerover: A content-based image browser for the World Wide Web. In Proc. IEEE Workshop on Content-Based Access of Image and Video Libraries, 1997.

[7] J. R. Smith and S.-F. Chang, An Image and Video Search Engine for the World-Wide Web, Proceedings, IS&T/SPIE Symposium on Electronic Imaging: Science and Technology (EI'97) - Storage and Retrieval for Image and Video Databases V, 1997.

[8] Zheng Chen, Liu Wenyin, Chunhui Hu, Mingjing Li, and Hongjiang Zhang. iFind: A Web Image Search Engine, SIGIR 2001.

[9] Y. Alp Aslandogan and Clement T. Yu, Evaluating strategies and systems for content based indexing of person images on the Web, ACM Multimedia, pp313-321, 2000.

[10] B. C. Ooi, K. L. Tan, C. Yu and S. Bressan, Indexing the Edges - A Simple and Yet Efficient Approach to High-Dimensional Indexing, PODS, pp 166-174, 2000.

[11] K. Chakrabart and S. Mehrotra, The Hybrid Tree: An Index Structure for High Dimensional Feature Spaces, International Conference on Data Engineering, pp 322-331, 1999.

[12] V. Gaede and O. Gunther, Multidimensional Access Methods, ACM Computing Surveys, 30(2), pp 170-231, 1998

[13] Y. Sakurai, M. Yoshikawa, S. Uemura and H. Kojima, The A-tree: An Index Structure for High-Dimensional Spaces Using Relative Approximation, VLDB, pp 516-526, 2000.

[14] Anne H. H. Ngu, Quan Z. Sheng, Du Q. Huynh, and Ron Lei: Combining multi-visual features for efficient indexing in a large image database. VLDB Journal 9(4): 279-293 (2001).

[15] U. Guntzer, W-T. Balke, and W. Kiessling. Optimizing Multi-Feature Queries for Image Databases, VLDB, pp. 261-281, 2000.

[16] R. Fagin, A. Lotem and M. Naor, Optimal Aggregation Algorithms for Middleware, PODS, 2001.

[17] James Z. Wang, G. Wiederhold, O. Firschein, Sha Xin Wei, Content-based image indexing and searching using Daubechies' wavelets, International Journal of Digital Libraries, 1(4), pp. 311-328, 1998.

[18] R. Aggrawal and J. Gehrke and D. Gunopulos and P. Raghavan, Automatic Subspace Clustering of High Dimensional Data for Data Mining Applications, Proceedings of the ACM SIGMOD Conference, pp 94-105, 1998.

[19] Charu C. Aggrawal and Joel L. Wolf and Philip S. Yu and C. Procopiuc and J. S. Park, Fast Algorithms for Projected Clustering, Proceedings of the ACM SIGMOD Conference, pp 61-72, 1999.

[20] Hinneburg and D. A. Keim, An Optimal Grid-Clustering: Towards Breaking the Curse of Diminsionality in High Dimensional Clustering, VLDB,1999.

[21] K. K. Sung and T. Poggio, Example-Based Learning for View-Based Human Face Detection, PAMI, 20(1):39-51, 1998.

[22] Shortliffe, E. H. Computer-based medical consultation: MYCIN. New York: Elsevier North-Holland.

[23] H. Jin, B.C. Ooi, H. T. Shen, C. Yu, and A. Zhou. An Adaptive and Efficient Dimensionality Reduction Algorithm for High-Dimensional Indexing, ICDE, page 87-98, 2003.

[24] D. Cai, X. He, Z. Li, W.-Y. Ma and J.-R. Wen, Hierarchical Clustering of WWW Image Search Results Using Visual, Textual and Link Analysis. ACM Multimedia 2004.

[25] S. Yu, D. Cai, J.-R. Wen and W.-Y. Ma, Improving Pseudo-Relevance Feedback in Web Information Retrieval Using Web Page Segmentation, World Wide Web, 2003.

Chinese Named Entity Recognition with a Hybrid-Statistical Model

Xiaoyan Zhang, Ting Wang, Jintao Tang, Huiping Zhou, and Huowang Chen

National Laboratory for Parallel and Distributed Processing,
Changsha, Hunan, P.R.China 410073
{zhangxiaoyan98, wonderwang70}@hotmail.com

Abstract. With the rapid growth of the available information on the Internet, it is more difficult for us to find the relevant information quickly on the Web. Named Entity Recognition (NER), one of the key techniques in some web information processing tools such as information retrieval and information extraction, has been paid more and more attention. In this paper we address the problem of Chinese NER using a hybrid-statistical model. This study is concentrated on entity names (personal names, location names and organization names), temporal expressions (dates and times) and number expressions. The method is characterized as follows: firstly, NER and Part-of-Speech tagging have been integrated into a unified framework; secondly, it combines Hidden Markov Model (HMM) with Maximum Entropy Model (MEM) by taking MEM as a sub-model invoked in Viterbi algorithm; thirdly, the Part-of-Speech information of the context has been used in MEM. The experiment shows that the hybrid-statistical model could achieve preferable results of Chinese NER, in which the F1 value ranges from 74% to 92% for all kinds of named entities on an open-test data.

1 Introduction

With the rapid growth of the Internet, huge volume of information available on the Web brings people great challenges. The need for tools that can help users to find, filter and manage the information easily and quickly on the Web is growing accordingly. Named Entity Recognition (NER) is such a technology which is useful in many Web applications, for example, information retrieval, information extraction, digital libraries, question answering, etc.

The NER task was first introduced as Message Understanding Conference (MUC) subtask in 1995 (MUC-6) [1]. Named Entities were defined as entity names (personal names, location names and organization names), temporal expressions (date expressions and time expressions) and number expressions. Compared with the entity names recognition, the recognition of temporal expressions and number expressions is simpler. However the recognition of entity names is harder because of their opening, expansibility and randomness.

There have been a lot of researches on English NER and great successes achieved on it. However, for Chinese, NER is still on the way. Chinese NER has its own

Y. Zhang et al. (Eds.): APWeb 2005, LNCS 3399, pp. 900–912, 2005.

segmentation is Forward Maximum Length Matching. In Viterbi algorithm, when the current word is an indicative word and its context satisfies the entity constructing rules, there will be a potential ambiguity: combing the current words with the context as a candidate entity, or teat them as separate common words. The ambiguity will be kept until Part-of-Speech tagging. When this kind of ambiguity is detected, some new states would be added into the state spaces of corresponding words to mark all the possible positions in the candidate entity. And the observation probability of the candidate entity is calculated by MEM. The above process would be repeated on every word in the sentence to make the complete states space. Viterbi algorithm works to find the most likely Part-of-Speech sequence through traversing the states space.

4 Hybrid-Statistical Model and Named Entity Filtering

This section will introduce two key techniques in this paper: integration of two statistical models and Named Entity Filtering.

4.1 Integration of Two Statistical Models

The flow of our method is: at first, the original input, a Chinese sentence, is segmented; then the NER and Part-of-Speech tagging begin to work, in which the searching space is built before Viterbi algorithm begins to find the best Part-of-Speech sequence; at last we will combine the NE-states into Named Entity tags from the final Part-of-Speech sequence and update the global cache.

Firstly, we define some symbols in Table 4.

Table 4. The Defination of Some Symbols

$\lambda=(\Omega_X, \Omega_O, A, B, \pi)$	HMM
$O=O_1, O_2, \ldots, O_T$	A word sequence
$Q^*=q_1^*, q_2^*, \ldots, q_T^*$	the most likely Part-of-Speech sequence
$\delta_t(i)$ and $\varphi_t(i)$	$\delta_t(i)$ is the maximum probability of generating the sub-sequence $(O_1, O_2, \ldots, O_t)$ under a state sequence $(q_1, q_2, \ldots, q_t)$ which ends with θ_i. $q_t=\theta_i$, $\varphi_t(i)=q_{t-1}$
$T(i)$, N and $T_i(j)$	$T(i)$ is the possible states set of O_i. $N(i)$ is the size of $T(i)$. $T_i(j)$ is the jth element (θ_j) in $T(i)$.
nr, ns, nt, t, and m	personal name, location name, organization name, temporal expression and number expression

Secondly, we define the state transition probabilities between NE-states and Part-of-Speech tags and the observed probabilities under the NE-states. NE-states consist of nine elements (*nrfirst, nrmid, nrlast, nsfirst, nsmid, nslast, ntfirst, ntmid, ntlast*). The first three elements correspond to *nr*, the middle three ones correspond to *ns*, and the last three ones correspond to *nt*. The definitions of are shown in Table 5 and 6.

The following is the description of our algorithm which is framed in Viterbi algorithm, invoking MEM to calculate the observation probabilities of candidate entity names. In the algorithm, the recognized temporal expressions and number expressions are contained in the known lists. And besides, all number strings are recognized as number expressions for the moment. Grouping of these strings will be done in the filtering procedure.

Table 5. The Definition of Observation Probability

$T_t(j)$	$b_j(O_t)$
nr, ns, nt, m, t	1 (ensuring this state will be contained in the best state sequence)
nrfirst, nrmid, nsmid, nslast, ntmid, ntlast	1(the probability is computed when encountered nrlast, nsfirst, ntfirst)
nrlast, nsfirst, ntfirst	The return of ME model
others	The corresponding element in B

Table 6. The Definition of Transition Probability

θ_i/θ_j	a_{ij}
nrfirst/nrmid, nrfirst/nrlast, nrmid/nrlast, nsfirst/nsmid, nsmid/nsmid, nsmid/nslast , ntfirst/ntmid, ntmid/ntmid, ntmid/ntlast	1(ensuring that the unique path between NE-states)
nrlast/nrfirst , nrlast/nsfirst , nrlast/ntfirst , nslast/nrfirst , nslast/nsfirst , nslast/ntfirst , ntlast/nrfirst , ntlast/nsfirst , ntlast/ntfirst	A(the correspond tag of θ_i, the corresponding tag of θ_j)
θ_i is one of *nrlast, nslast or ntlast.* θ_j is one element in the Part-of-Speech set.	A(the corresponding tag of θ_i, θ_j)
θ_i is one element in the Part-of-Speech set. θ_j is one of *nrfirst, nsfirst or ntfirst.*	A(θ_i, the corresponding tag of θ_j)
θ_i is one element in the Part-of-Speech set. θ_j is one element in the Part-of-Speech set.	A(θ_i, θ_j)
others	0

The use of Viterbi algorithm here consists of two parts: making the state spaces and traditional Viterbi algorithm (Initialization, Iteration, Ending and Finding the likely sequence). We take the sentence "7 2 岁 的 五保户 王 俊 大娘 双目 失明" as an example.

1) Viterbi algorithm

1.1) making the state spaces:

For each word O_i:

Firstly, T(i) is initialized by the Part-of-Speech dictionary, global cache and lists of named entity. For example, when processing the third word "的", we will receive its Part-of-Speech information (auxiliary) from the Part-of-Speech dictionary.

If O_i is a number string, then tag *m* is added into the state space of O_i. The first word "７２"is an example.

If O_i is a surname, *nrfirst* and *nrlast* are separately added into the sets of O_i and O_{i+1} provided that "O_iO_{i+1}" satisfies the structure rule of personal name. So does "$O_iO_{i+1}O_{i+2}$". When encountered the fifth word "王", this circumstance will be invoked. Then the state space of "王" will consist of *nrfirst*, and the state space of "俊"will consist of *nrlast*.

If O_i is one of location name suffixes, then *nsfirst* and *nrlast* are separately added into the sets of O_{i-1}, and O_i provided that "$O_{i-1}O_i$" satisfies the structure rule of location name. So do "$O_{i-2}O_{i-1}O_i$" and "$O_{i-3}O_{i-2}O_{i-1}O_i$".

If O_i is one of organization name suffixes, then *ntfirst* and *ntlast* are separately added into the spaces of O_{i-1}, and O_i provided that "$O_{i-1}O_i$" satisfies the structure rule of organization name. So do "$O_{i-2}O_{i-1}O_i$" and "$O_{i-3}O_{i-2}O_{i-1}O_i$".

If the states set of O_i is still null, then *nr*, *ns* and *nt* are added ensuring that Viterbi algorithm can run smoothly.

1.2) traditional Viterbi algorithm:

At last, we will combine the NE-states into Named Entity tags, group temporal expressions and number expressions.

2) The Use of MEM

For many entity names are unknown words, MEM is invoked to calculate the observation probability of this kind of words.

2.1) Feature Matching: matching the features in MEM with information of the context and the current word sequence.

2.2) Calculating the observation probability.

The probability calculated by MEM is in the form of *P(a|b)*, where *a* stands Part-of-Speech, and *b* stands for a word. However the expected probability is in the form of *P(b|a)*. So, use formula (1) to get *P(a|b)*, and then calculate the observation probability *P(b|a) as*:

$$P(b|a)= P(a|b)*P(b)/P(a) \tag{1}$$

The final identification result is as follows:

７２/m 岁/q 的/u 五保户/n 王俊/nr 大娘/n 双目/n 失明/v

4.2 Named Entity Filtering

After analyzing the recognizing result, we found that all knowledge used in our system is on the set level, that is to say, the elements in a same set are not treated respectively. This ignorance caused much misrecognition. So in Named Entity Filtering we will use information about the usage of single words. The experiment results show that it acquires a great increase in the precision.

Filtering is used within and after Viterbi algorithm. The filtering of location names and organization names has been carried on within Viterbi algorithm. For the complexity of location names and organization names, it would cause more extra participial work if doing it after the algorithm. As for personal names, which are relatively simpler, the filtering is put after Viterbi algorithm. In addition, there is another task in the second filtering which is incorporating number string and its suffix. The threshold value of each kind of entity is acquired on empirical observation from corpus.

1) Filtering within Viterbi algorithm

Only the word sequence with the probability larger than the corresponding threshold value is regarded as a candidate location name or organization name, then its NE-states will be added into the state spaces of the word sequence, otherwise NE-states are not added. Table 7 introduces the probability calculating method of a word sequence as a location name. The processing on organization names is similar.

Table 7. The Probability Computing Method of a Word Sequence as a Location Name

The word sequence	Probability (P)
word1 (a) + word2 (b) + word3 (c) + suffix of location name (d) : abcd	P=p(a)*p(b)*p(c)*p(d) p(a)= count(a) in all location names / number of all words in all location names p(b) and p(c) are similar to p(a). p(d) = count(d) in all location name suffixes /number of all words in all location name suffixes
word1 (a) +word2 (b) + suffix of location name (d) : abd	P= p(a)*p(b)*p(d)
word1 (a) + suffix of location name (d): ad	P= p(a)*p(d)

2) Filtering after Viterbi algorithm

This filtering consists of two parts. One is entity names filtering and the other is grouping temporal expressions and number expressions.

Because some words are marked as entities just for ensuring that Viterbi algorithm can run smoothly, they need to be filtered out. This filtering is mainly on personal names filtering. The process is similar to the location names or organization names filtering. Only when the probability of the character sequence as a personal name is larger than the threshold value, it is regarded as a personal name, otherwise the sequence is segmented again. If the sequence consists of two single characters, it is segmented in the form of “one character + one character”. If the sequence consists of three single words, it is segmented in the form of “one character + two characters” or “two characters + one character”. Table 8 is the probability calculating method of a character sequence. For example, some character sequences such as "那黑人", "万余", "齐放" will be filtered. Although they accord with rules of personal name structure, the frequency about the usage of single words is relatively fewer. Therefore they will be segmented again as "那 黑人", "万 余", "齐 放".

In Viterbi algorithm we have recognized some temporal expressions and number expressions which are in known entities lists. All number strings in the algorithm are recognized as part of temporal expressions and number expressions. So in this second filtering we will group them with their suffixes. For example, if the current number string is "12" and the following of it is "月"(mean month), then a temporal expression is recognized as "12月"(means December).

Table 8. The Probability Computing Method of a Character Sequence as a Personal Name

The character string	Probability (P)
character1 (a) + character2 (b) + character3 (c)	P=p(a)*p(b)*p(c) p(a)= count(a) as a surname/number of all surnames in personal names p(b)= count(b) as a name word /number of all name words in personal names p(c) is similar to p(b).
character1 (a) + character2 (b) or character1 (a) + word2 (b)	P=p(a)*p(b)

5 Experiment Result

5.1 Training Corpus and Testing Corpus

The corpus used in our experiment is from People's Daily on January 1998. It is divided into training corpus and testing corpus at the ratio of 1:4. The training data contains 28603 sentences (about 716815 Chinese words), including 11138 personal names, 14229 location names, 6745 organization names, 13287 temporal expressions and 39612 number expressions. The testing data contains 6987 sentences (about 163619 words), including 5874 personal names, 3545 location names, 2056 organization names, 3433 temporal expressions and 9226 number expressions.

5.2 Resource of Knowledge

The knowledge is acquired from various linguistic resources, shown in Table 9.

5.3 Experimental Results

We have carried out two kinds of experiments with filtration or not, the results are shown in Table 10. The numbers before "/" are the results without filtering, and the ones after "/" are the results with filtering.

Table 9. Resource of knowledge in the experiment

Knowledge	Resource
Parameters (A, B, π) in HMM	The training corpus
Features in ME model	The training corpus
Segment dictionary	The training corpus and the testing corpus
Part-of-speech dictionary	The training corpus and the testing corpus
Information of character in personal names	People's Daily in 1998
Information of word in location names and organization names	The training corpus and the testing corpus
Lists of entities and expressions	From web resource.

Table 10. Experiment results (with and without filtration)

(%)	Personal names	Location names	Organization names	Temporal expressions	Number expressions
Precision	70.78/85.66	69.29/81.57	64.81/71.23	85.98/85.97	88.95/88.37
Recall	81.78/79.96	87.09/86.64	78.31/78.42	97.65/97.69	92.31/91.69
F1	75.88/82.71	75.88/84.03	70.92/74.66	91.45/91.45	90.59/90.00

5.4 Analysis of the Experimental Results

The results without filtration show that the recalls are better than the precisions. This is because the knowledge used in NER is on the set level and all elements in one set are regarded indistinguishably, which causes many pseudo entities to be recognized. So we add filtering during and after the recognizing procedure. The great increase in precision can be seen in the result with filtration, especially for personal names, which is fifteen percents. We also find that the results of organization are worse than those of other entities. The reasons maybe lie in two aspects -- one is the complexity of organization, the other is that our method has not looked further enough to recognize some very long nested organization names such as "日本 东京 地方 检察厅 特别 搜查 部". In addition, the improvement on time and number expressions filtering is very little. The reason is that the filtering is mainly on entity names, not on expressions so as to cause little influence on temporal and number expressions.

We can also find from the recognition results that there are quite a few pseudo entities which are general nouns although they contain the indicative words. Some examples of these entities are "贫困地区、各部门、地方政府、服务机构", the indicative words of which are "地区、部门、政府、机构". A method of avoiding this phenomenon is using semantic knowledge as much as possible.

In our method the global cache can ensure the coherence of the same named entities in a text. However some entities will probably be classified as different types, especially in location names, organization names and general nouns. Some samples are as follows: " 五角大楼、白宫、中南海 ". So we should consider the context information and the tradeoff of space-time seriously.

Form the above results and analyses, we will focus on some work as follows in our future research.

1. Introducing more features into MEM.
2. Threshold value selection with more scientific measure.
3. Improving temporal and number expressions recognition in more detail.
4. Finding more trigger points of recognition.

6 Conclusions

Chinese NER is a more difficult task than English NER. Though many approaches have been tried, the results are still not satisfying. In this paper we present a hybrid-statistical model integrating knowledge into two statistical models, in which NER and Part-of-Speech have been combined into a unified framework. The results are preferable. However we should realize that there is still much work to do to improve our method, such as feature selection and finding more trigger points.

Acknowledgement

This research is supported in part by the National Natural Science Foundation of China (60403050) and the National High Technology Research and Development Program.

References

1. 1. Beth M. Sundheim.: Named entity task definition, version 2.1. In Proceedings of the Sixth Message Understanding Conference(1995) 319–332.
2. Jian Sun, Jianfeng Gao, Lei Zhang, Ming Zhou, Changning Huang.:Chinese Named Entity Identification Using Class-based Language Model1. Proceedings of COLING02 (2002)
3. Chen H.H., Ding Y.W., Tsai S.C., Bian G.W.: Description of the NTU System Used for MET2. Proceedings of 7th Message Understanding Conference (1998)
4. Black W.J., Rinaldi F., Mowatt D.: Facile: Description of the NE System Used For MUC-7. Proceedings of 7th Message Understanding Conference (1998)
5. Fukumoto J., Shimohata M., Masui F., Sasaki M.: Oki Electric Industry: Description of the Oki System as Used for MET-2. Proceedings of 7th Message Understanding Conference (1998)
6. GuoDong Zhou., Jian Su.: Named Entity Recognition using an HMM-based Chunk Tagger. In Proceedings of the 40th Annual Meeting of the ACL, Philadelphia, PA (2002) 473–480
7. Adwait Ratnaparkhi.: A simple introduction to maximum entropy models for natural language processing. Technical Report 97-08, Institute for Research in Cognitive Science, University of Pennsylvania (1997)

8. Sekine S., Grishman R., Shinou H.: A decision tree method for finding and classifying names in Japanese texts. Proceedings of the Sixth Workshop on Very Large Corpora, Montreal Canada (1998)
9. Brill E.: Transform-based Error-Driven Learning and Natural Language Processing: A Case Study in Part-of-speech Tagging. Computational Linguistics, 21(4) (1995) 543-565
10. Collins M.: Ranking Algorithms for Named-Entity Extraction: Boosting and the Voted Perceptron. Proceedings of the 40th Annual Meeting of the ACL, Philadelphia July (2002) 489-496,.
11. Jansche M.: Named Entity Extraction with Conditional Markov Models and Classifiers. The 6th Conference on Natural Language Learning (2002)

Towards a Formal Framework for Distributed Identity Management

Jingsha He and Ran Zhang

School of Software Engineering,
Beijing University of Technology,
Beijing 100022, China
Tel/Fax: +86-10-67396061
jhe@bjut.edu.cn

Abstract. In this paper, we propose a framework for identity management in a distributed environment. In addition to achieving convenience, which is the primary objective for identity management in most related work, we believe that user privacy and controlled information disclosure are equally important. Therefore, we look beyond the so-called single-sign-on (SSO) suitable mainly for a federated environment [2] because the requirement that a trust relationship be established between network applications and services so that a central authority can act on behalf of the applications and services in identity management and access authorization is not practical in the Internet where distributed control and management is the mainstream. We show how convenience can be achieved without the requirement for such a central authority in our framework. We also show how multiple identities can be managed for users to access network applications and services and how users can control the disclosure of identity information and hence ensure their privacy. Consequently, the framework can serve as the foundation for the development of the next generation of network identity management systems that are both practical and flexible.

1 Introduction

The emergence of the Internet and e-commerce requires that corporations and governments provide partners, clients and users with easy access to their systems, applications and services. As the result, the management of user identity information in a secure and effective way has become more important and increasingly critical in the successful deployment and provision of web-based applications and services. Identity management not only can help to centralize and simplify the management of user identities and support secure and convenient access to web-based applications and services that require user identification and authentication, it can also help to ensure user privacy by acting on the user's behalf as well as by enforcing applicable laws and policies. Therefore, identity management has received a great deal of attention in the network research community and, as the result, a lot of progress has been made in recent years.

Y. Zhang et al. (Eds.): APWeb 2005, LNCS 3399, pp. 913–924, 2005.

Identity management comes with a broad spectrum of meanings. On one hand, we can find approaches that aim at unifying a diverse set of user identities assigned to and accumulated by an individual user. One example is that an employee in a large organization may have established multiple identities for different computer and network systems following different requirements and guidelines. Another example is that a web user on the Internet may have registered with different web-based applications and services using the same or different identities as requested following different requirements and guidelines. It is obvious that there exists the real need to unify the many different identities to provide convenience to the user and to improve security that may deteriorate as the number of identities increases.

On the other hand, we can find approaches that aim at respecting and protecting user privacy and at reducing the potential risk of exposing user or communication profiles to unauthorized parties [6]. Although current approaches that try to unify user identities may help to ease some of the concerns, they have severe limitations. One such a limitation is that these approaches work only in a so-called federated network environment in which member users, systems, applications and services yield the management of identities to a central authority. In the open Internet environment, however, it is generally very hard to establish a large-scale federated network because different businesses have different needs and different value propositions on their clients and customers, which requires that businesses manage their own users and user identities. This probably explains why popular single-sign-on (SSO) services such as Microsoft .NET Passport could not continue its rapid expansion after reaching certain scale in corporate membership. Liability on user privacy concerns and user ownership has also played some role in slowing down the adoption of SSO services in the open Internet environment. In general, identity management encompasses definitions and lifecycle management of user identities and associated profile information, as well as the environment for exchanging and validating such information [4]. Identity management is essential for building and maintaining trust relationships in different interconnected systems.

The rest of the paper is organized as follows. In the next section, we review some related work. In Section 3, we analyze the network environment and discuss several key requirements for distributed management of identities in such an environment. In Section 4, we present our framework for distributed management of identities and discuss some of the related issues. Finally, we conclude this paper in Section 5.

2 Related Work

Managing multiple versions of user identities in a network environment is crucial for the development of the next generation of distributed applications and services. Most of the work in identity management, therefore, has focused on providing solutions and mechanisms that can help users to create and maintain multiple identities easily. One approach to address this issue is to establish a network-wide standard for the management of multiple identities to ensure the interoperability among different identity management systems. At present, the two popular identity management standards are the Microsoft .NET Passport (www.passport.com) and the Liberty Alliance's open standards for federated network identity [9]. Microsoft .NET Passport consists of a set of web-based service components, provides the single-sign-on (SSO) capability for users, and makes use of encryption technologies such as SSL (i.e., secure socket layer) and triple-DES (i.e., data encryption standard). It helps users to avoid remembering multiple sets of user names and passwords. Users can also use many forms of devices to check and update their profiles associated with their identities, such as PCs and hand-held devices. For a business, Microsoft .NET Passport provides a high-visibility marketing image and trust relationship in the maintenance of user identities. In addition, Microsoft .NET Passport provides a single identity to each user for access to multiple web-based applications and services. Therefore, companies can use this single identity to create a database of user profiles. Similarly, Liberty Alliance has been engaged in developing a set of open standards for federated networks in which identities can be managed collaboratively by member companies [5]. The Alliance currently has over 40 member companies who have been working together to realize the following goals:

- To allow individual consumers and businesses to maintain personal information securely.
- To provide a universal open standard for single-sign-on (SSO) services.
- To provide a universal open standard for identities to span across all network devices.

It should be noted that the standard approach that addresses the issue of managing multiple identities has focused primarily on providing the SSO capability and, therefore, suffers certain limitations [8]. First, SSO is suitable only for a federated network environment in which all member users, systems and applications and services trust a central authority to manage identities and to provide authentication services on their behalf. This is not generally practical in the open Internet in which majority of web sites and applications prefer to remain independent and maintain their own user identities and profiles for flexibility and diversity. Second, there are many other equally important issues besides SSO that an identity management system should address, such as how to help users to ensure privacy and to control the sharing and exposing sensitive user information. Convenience that SSO can provide should by no means sacrifice the capability and flexibility for ensuring user privacy as well as that for businesses to safeguard the most valuable information they possess for their businesses.

Damiani, et al, [4] presented an overview of identity management, identified the major issues and discussed an approach to controlling multiple identities in an electronic world. However, the work lacks many specific details for establishing a framework for the development of an identity management system. Pfitzmann, et al, [11] examined a flaw discovered in the Liberty Alliance protocol and discussed the general nature of third party authentication methods. As pointed out earlier, SSO is the main focus of the Liberty Alliance effort and, therefore, other major issues related to identity management still remain unaddressed in this work. Finally, the trust negotiation framework proposed in [12] relies on a state-based language for trust management that offers a potential solution for trust negotiation in changing environments but, unfortunately, only addressed some of the issues in identity management.

With a general understanding of the major issues in the management of multiple identities as well as the limitations of the current work, we will proposes a framework for distributed management of identities in this paper to meet the requirements and objectives of identity management in an open network environment. Another objective of this framework is to achieve broad interoperability and dynamic scalability among identity management systems.

3 Requirements and Objectives

A network identity is a user identity that can be used to uniquely identify and subsequently authenticate the user in a network environment, especially over the Internet, to provide the user with access to web-based applications and services. In general, any solution for identity management should meet the following three requirements:

- Convenience

Convenience implies support and services that should at least be equivalent to what the current SSO can offer to the user. In a federated environment in which a central authority takes the full responsibility of managing user identities and making authentication decisions, convenience is straightforward. However, a federated architecture is generally suitable only for a single organization or a group of organizations that have very close business relationships. Therefore, it is not generally a practical solution on the Internet. To a large number of unrelated businesses and organizations, forming a federation and becoming members in it presents a great deal of difficulty because the federated architecture would take away from the members the ability of directly managing the most important and valuable information for their businesses, i.e., user identities and associated user profiles. Such architecture also requires that all authentication decisions be made by the central authority, which implies that the central authority has to take a full responsibility in the event of security breaches and that members have to have a full trust on the central authority, both of which are difficult, if not impossible, to achieve. Therefore, achieving convenience without requiring dramatic changes to current business practices is a very important consideration in our framework for distributed identity management.

- Controlled information disclosure

Without a central authority to manage user identities and associated information, the sharing of identities and information among web-based applications and services becomes necessary to meet the requirement for convenience. However, sharing of user identity information without the knowledge and control of the user could lead to unauthorized disclosure of sensitive information, harming the concerned user. For well-behaved businesses, sharing of user identity information should not be allowed without explicit authorization by the concerned user. For less-well-behaved businesses, the lack of explicit user authorization and control provides the possibility to abuse the acquired user identity information to gain unfair business advantages. Consequently, the ability of the user in controlling the disclosure of identity information is essential in our framework for distributed identity management.

- Confidentiality and privacy

Safeguarding user identity information and ensuring user privacy is something that could go beyond what the user can imagine and control. Although the ability of controlling information disclosure provides the user with the necessary means of protecting information and ensuring privacy, there are often times when the user may misjudge the situation or be misled to act in a way that may violate the general policy for protecting user privacy. Furthermore, although authentication decisions based on user identities and associated profiles can provide convenience while preserving user privacy [7], such profiles cannot be generalized for all cases and for all applications and services. Instead, national legislations and policies are being established gradually as the guidelines and laws for businesses to follow in interacting with users over the Internet. Such legislations and policies established by and for businesses should be an integral part of a solution for the management of identities in a network environment.
Our objectives for proposing a framework in this paper are to define the relationships between the various network entities and their identities and to identify necessary means and mechanisms for distributed management of these identities that can meet the three general requirements that we just described.

4 The Framework

We assume, in our framework, that a user has already established one or more identities with different applications and services in a network environment. A user could establish a network identity with an application or service through the registration process required by the application or service. The user could also establish a network identity with an application or service through employment. In a word, a network identity is a name that relates a user to a network application or service and is a unique way of presenting the user to the application or service. A network identity of a user is also an abstraction of all the information about the user that the application or service desires to know and is used to uniquely identify the user within the domain of the application or service. Therefore, a user could use the same name as the network identities with different applications and services as long as the name is unique within each individual application or service.

We now describe the several key elements in our framework for distributed management of network identities.

Users: A user is an active entity that seeks to use a network service offered through a web-based application to accomplish a set of functions advertised by the application.

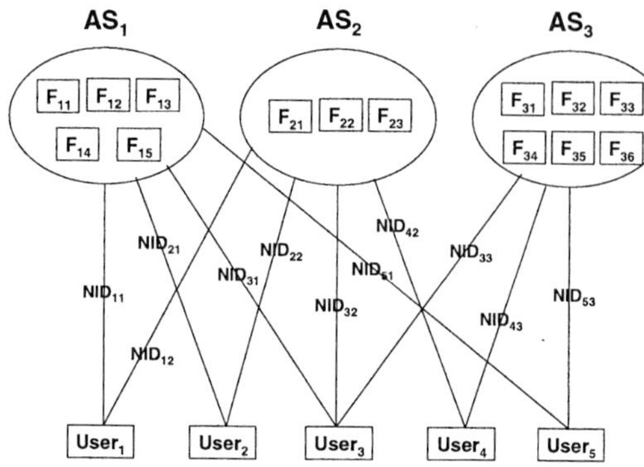

Fig. 1. Relationships between Users and ASs

Application or service (AS): An application or service is the representation of a set of functions that are considered to be valuable to some users and can be activated for the users.

Network identity (NID): A network identity is a name that can uniquely identify a user to an AS, It is also an abstraction of all the information that the AS desires to know about the user. Most important among all the information in a network identity is a secret code or password that is shared by the user and the AS and is used by the AS to authenticate the user in order to relate the user to a subset of the functions that the AS offers. Thus, an NID determines how much of the AS can be used by the user and, therefore, forms a relationship between the user and the AS.

The relationships between a set of users and a set of ASs are depicted in Fig. 1, using NIDs to define the relationships. Note that each AS may choose to offer a different subset of functions to different NIDs, which is an internal service issue for the AS and, therefore, is not a consideration in the framework.

With the NIDs being defined as relationships between users and ASs, the management of NIDs becomes the issue of managing such relationships, which

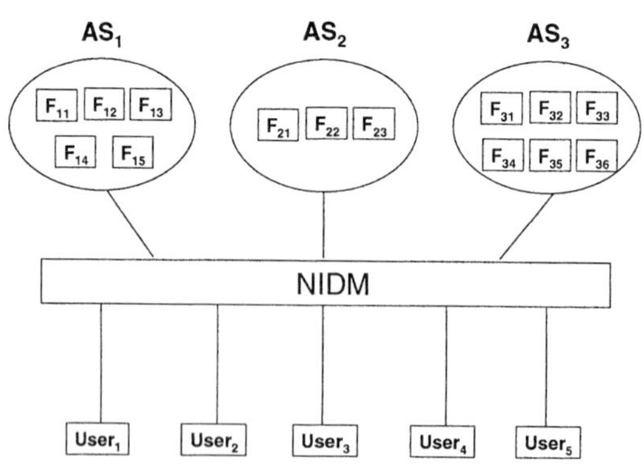

Fig. 2. NIDM as a Set of Management Function

includes establishing and maintaining such relationships, to meet the requirements and objectives we set in this paper. Therefore, mechanisms and management functions are required between the users and the ASs to manage the NID relationships and to realize the management functions on the network identities.

Fig. 2 illustrates the introduction of such management functions, denoted as a component NIDM. Note, however, that the NIDM component is just for the management of NIDs in the framework and doesn't imply that the NIDM can only be implemented as a centralized management module. Rather, the NIDM component should be viewed as a set of middleware management functions, some of which are supported at the user side, some others at the AS side and still other as independent

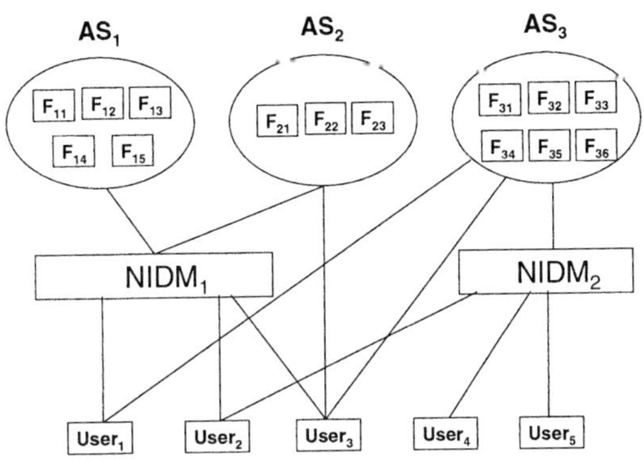

Fig. 3. Distributed Management of Network Identities

middleware network functions or services. Furthermore, a particular function can be supported in more than one form and different forms of support may be used to manage different NIDs according to user requests as well as specific network environments. Therefore, the framework for distributed management of network identities is a very general statement about how network identities can be managed effectively to achieve the requirements and objectives. Fig. 3 illustrates this distributed concept in which different NIDs can be managed in different ways. As an example, Microsoft .NET Passport is an independent network service that can be used for managing the NIDs for a group of applications and services. However, this group is still relatively small and users can choose not to use Microsoft .NET Passport to access some of the applications and services in this group but rather to manage the NIDs in different manners. Furthermore, as pointed out earlier, a management scheme like Microsoft .NET Passport requires a federated architecture in which all the ASs delegate NID management as well as the subsequent user authentication functions to an independent component, which may not be very consistent with business practices and goals. Therefore, it could be very difficult to make such a generic middleware network service appealing to a majority of network applications and services. Therefore, different ways of NID management must be supported to suit the needs and requirements of different network ASs.

We now illustrate how we can meet the requirements in our framework for distributed management of network identities in which we also identify some of the essential functions that are required to achieve our objectives.

- Convenience

Convenience, in the most straightforward way, means that a user, when dealing with multiple ASs, doesn't have to enter the same user information, including critical network identity information, repeatedly unless the user chooses to do so. Therefore, convenience requires that mechanisms be developed for the following two scenarios. In the first scenario, we consider a federated environment in which a central management module is present to aid the user in managing NIDs and to perform user authentication on behalf of the ASs that are members of the federation. Microsoft .NET

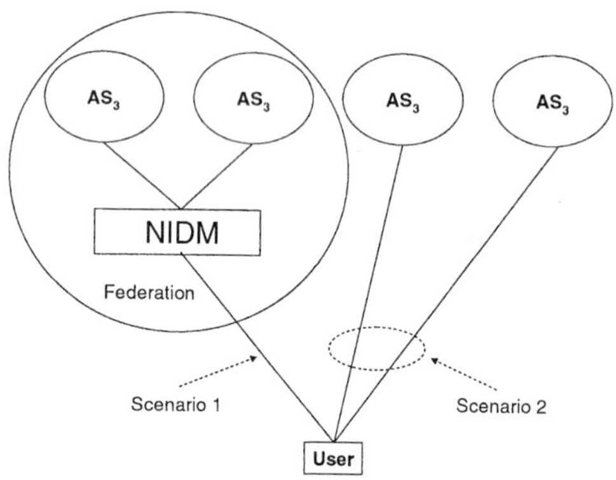

Fig. 4. NID Management Scenarios

Passport is one of the most popular central NID management solutions that serve member ASs in a federated environment. With such a solution, after a user is registered with Microsoft .NET Passport, the user needs only identity and authenticate with Microsoft .NET Passport once before accessing the ASs that belong to the Microsoft .NET Passport federation. However, as pointed out earlier, it would be very hard to imagine that a single federation could ever be formed for all ASs over the Internet. Actually, having a single or a few numbers of federations of ASs for the entire Internet is contradictory to the basic design principles of the Internet in which distributed control and management ought to take the central role. Therefore, in the second scenario, we consider a truly distributed environment in which there is no central NID management module but mechanisms still need to be developed to provide convenience for the users to manage multiple NIDs. Fig. 4 illustrates the two NID management scenarios that we must consider in dealing with the issue of convenience. It is especially true that, due to the lack of a central management module for the distributed management, some different mechanisms must be developed to make it effective and convenient for the users to interact with multiple ASs using NIDs.

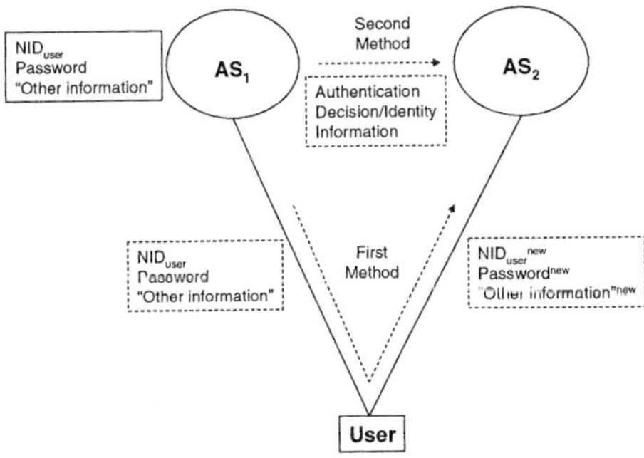

Fig.5. NID Establishment with a NEW AS

In the distributed scenario, we assume that the user has already established an NID with an existing AS. If it is the first time ever that the user has to establish an NID with an AS, the user has no other ways but to go through the process of creating an NID with the AS and to provide user information requested by the AS. Convenience becomes the central issue when this user needs to establish a relationship with another AS in which most, if not all, essential information about the user is primarily the same. Fig. 5 illustrates this situation in which the user has already established an NID with AS_1 and now desires to establish an NID with AS_2. There are at least two

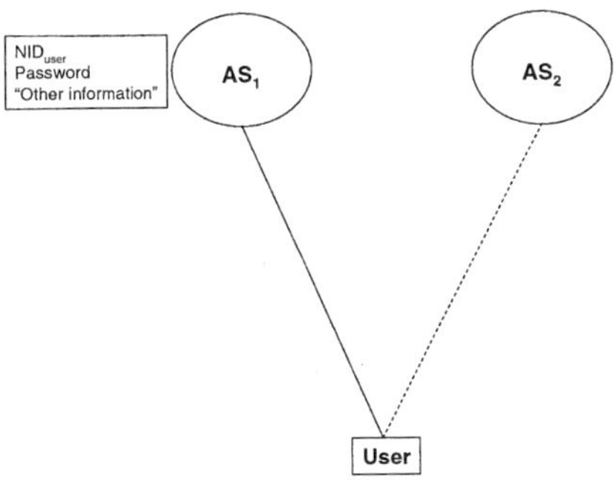

Fig. 6. Methods for Establishing a NEW NID

methods in which convenience can be realized in this case. The first method requires that a protocol be developed in which the user, after successful identification and authentication with AS_1, retrieves information from AS_1 and pass it over to AS_2 to establish an NID with AS_2. The second method requires that a protocol be developed in which the user, after successful identification and authentication with AS_1, requests that the authentication result be sent directly to AS_2 from AS_1. Obviously, with the second method, the user is in effect using AS_1 as a proxy for identification and authentication to AS_2 and, hence, AS_2 will not have an independent NID with the user. Fig. 6 illustrates the two methods, both of which can provide convenience to the user in managing multiple NIDs. Note that the second method may appear to resemble the scheme used for the federated scenario in which AS_1 is the central management module. However, there are some fundamental differences because the second method is a totally distributed solution in which AS_1 is not a centralized default module that performs NID management for the user. Rather, AS_1 is just acting in response to user request in this particular instance. The user may request different ASs with which the user has already established NIDs to perform such identification and authentication functions on its behalf at different instances when interacting with a new AS such as AS_2 in Fig. 6. This is useful because the user may wish to obtain different services at different times from AS_2 by using different NIDs. This also allows the user to maintain desired privacy by using different NIDs when interacting with AS_2 because the different NIDs used gives AS_2 different views about the user.

- Controlled information disclosure

It is obvious that the way in which convenience is achieved in the framework also provides the necessary support for the user to control the disclosure of identity information to a new AS. If the identity information is sent from a present AS to the new AS through the user (i.e., in the first method), for controlled information disclosure, some mechanism must be developed so that the user can examine, edit (i.e., add, modify or delete) and confirm the identity information before the information is sent to the new AS. If the identity information is passed directly from the present AS to the new AS (i.e., in the second method), some mechanism must also be developed so that the user can specify the class of information that can be sent by the present AS to the new AS. Therefore, the methods that help to achieve convenience in our framework also provide the necessary foundation for realizing controlled information disclosure. What we need are the actual mechanisms described above and their implementations to allow the user to exercise the control, which is our current research effort.

- Confidentiality and privacy

With controlled information disclosure, confidentiality and privacy become possible provided that necessary mechanisms be developed to support such functions. For example, to achieve confidentiality, encryption techniques must be employed for data

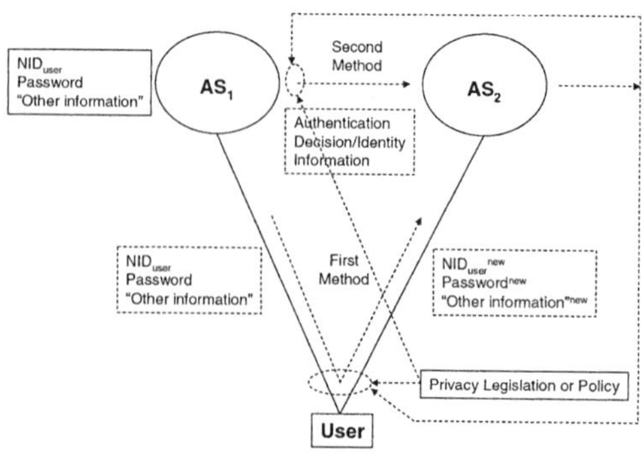

Fig. 7. Mandatory Enforcement of User Privacy

exchanges among the user, the present AS and the new AS using a widely available key distribution scheme such as PKI. The user can also ensure privacy by selectively passing identity information to the new AS with necessary support mechanisms.

However, there is one additional element that must be considered for the purpose of ensuring user privacy, that is, the mandatory and legal aspect of privacy. This is important because an ordinary user often lacks the necessary knowledge about how to effectively protect his/her privacy in the real world. Moreover, business vendors that offer legitimate ASs often tend to request the user to send more personal information than what is necessary for undisclosed business purposes. To gain access to a desired AS, the user usually satisfies the request, which consequently could result in compromises to user privacy. Therefore, we include an element that embodies national legislation or policy for the protection of user privacy over the Internet in our framework and expect with full confidence that such legislation or policy will be fully developed in which businesses will be classified based on the nature and type of ASs they offer and privacy statements will be in place to clearly define what kind of user information can be collected by the businesses. This mandatory privacy policy will offer the badly needed help in eventually achieving the goals of ensuring user privacy. In anticipation of the arrival of such mandatory policy in the future, we incorporate such considerations and the necessary mechanisms in our framework. As the result, we not only have the discretionary control by the user but also have the mandatory control based on legislation or policy over the disclosure of user identity information to a new AS. Fig. 7 illustrates such privacy considerations and the mechanisms that can help to achieve the privacy goals. Note that the privacy enforcement module will take, in addition to the privacy legislation or policy statements, some information about the new AS such as the nature or type of the business or the new AS to apply the policy statements and derive the necessary information to be forwarded to the new AS. Such information can be obtained through a protocol that needs to be developed and must be certified to prevent the new AS from providing inaccurate or even false information that could lead to the violation of the privacy policy. All the mechanisms for obtaining the AS information and for enforcing user privacy accordingly are being developed as a part of the current research effort.

5 Conclusions

We presented a framework for distributed management of network identities to meet the three requirements we identified, namely, convenience, controlled information disclosure and confidentiality and privacy, without the necessary requirement for establishing a federation. We showed that the assumptions that we made for establishing the framework are more realistic in today's Internet environment and the framework can suit any businesses and organizations that have a web presence and provide applications and services that rely on user identity information for authentication and access control and for service differentiation and management. The major contribution of the framework is to define and provide the necessary means for the users to control the disclosure of sensitive identity information to protect information confidentiality and to ensure user privacy. Therefore, the framework addresses both the needs of businesses and organizations and those of the users in today's complex network environment and, thus, can be used as the foundation for the development of the next generation of identity management systems beyond the so-called single-sign-on offered in today's identity management solutions and services.

There are, however, many research and development challenges to face and technical problems to solve before seamless distributed network identity management can become a reality. Chief among them are the methods and mechanisms that we identified and briefly described in this paper that implement and support convenience, controlled information disclosure and confidentiality and privacy which are our current focus in the research on distributed identity management.

References

1. Bonatti, P. and Samarati, P.: A Unified Framework for Regulating Service Access and Information Release on the Web. Journal of Computer Security, Vol. 10, No. 3 (2003) 241-272
2. Buell, D. and Sandhu, R: Identity Management. IEEE Internet Computing, Vol. 7, No. 6 (2003) 26-28
3. Claub, S. and Kohntopp, M.: Identity Management and Its Support of Multilateral Security. Computer Networks, Vol. 37 (2001) 205-219
4. Damiani, E., De Capital di Vimercati, S. and Samarati, P.: Managing Multiple and Dependable Identities. IEEE Internet Computing, Vol. 7, No. 6 (2003) 29-37
5. Hallam-Baker, P. and Malers, E. (ed.): Assertions and Protocol for the Oasis Security Assertion Markup Language (SAML). Oasis Standard (2002) (www.oasis-open.org/committees/security/docs/cs-sstc-core-01.pdf)
6. Kai, R.: Identity Management in Mobile Cellular Networks and Related Applications. Information Security Technical Report, Vol. 9, No. 1 (2004)
7. Millett, L. and Holden, S.: Authentication and Its Privacy Effects. IEEE Internet Computing, Vol. 7, No. 6 (2003) 54-58
8. Kormann, D. and Rubin, A.: Risks of Passport Single Signon Protocol. Computer Networks, Elsevier Science Press, Vol. 33 (2000) 51-58
9. Liberty Alliance Project, "Liberty Architecture Overview," v1.0 (2002) (www.projectliberty.org)
10. Mishra, P. (ed.): Bindings and Profiles for the Oasis Security Assertion Markup Language (SAML). Oasis Standard (2002) (www.oasis-open.org/committees/security/docs/cs-sstc-bindings-01.pdf)
11. Pfitzmann, B. and Waidner, M.: Analysis of Liberty Single-Sign-On with Enabled Clients. IEEE Internet Computing, Vol. 7, No. 6 (2003) 38-44
12. Skogsrud, H., Benatallah, B. and Casati, F.: Model-Driven Trust Negotiation for Web Services. IEEE Internet Computing, Vol. 7, No. 6 (2003) 45-52

Address Extraction: Extraction of Location-Based Information from the Web

Wentao Cai[1], Shengrui Wang[1], and Qingshan Jiang[2]

[1] Department of Computer Science, Universite de Sherbrooke, Sherbrooke, Quebec, Canada
{Wentao.Cai, Shengrui.Wang}@USherbrooke.ca
[2] Software School, Xiamen University, Xiamen, Fujian 361005, P. R. China
qjiang@xmu.edu.cn

Abstract. Updating and retrieving location-based data is an important problem in Location-Based Service (LBS) applications. The Web is a valuable pool of location-based information. Such information can be retrieved and extracted on the basis of corresponding postal addresses. This paper proposes an information extraction method to help collect location-based information from the Web automatically. The proposal applies an ontology-based conceptual information retrieval approach combined with graph matching techniques. Experimental evaluation shows that the method yields high recall and precision results.

1 Introduction

The development of wireless telecommunication has ushered in an era of mobile communicating and computing. As a result, Location-Based Service (LBS) has become a fashionable theme in the industry. It involves the ability to find the geographical location of a mobile device and provide services based on this location information. Updating and retrieving large amounts of location-based data is a significant problem in LBS applications. On the other hand, the ever-growing collection of texts available on the Web constitutes a valuable pool of up-to-date location-based information. Modern Web information retrieval and information extraction approaches can thus be useful in collecting location-based data through the Internet.

Address extraction from the Web can be used to accomplish location-based information extraction, as much location-based information may be identified on the basis of corresponding postal addresses. For example, www.yellowpages.ca provides a large and valuable database containing abundant services with their addresses. However, address extraction is still a difficult problem. As Figure 1 shows, this process involves the ability to scan textual content, identify possible lexical address descriptions, and finally label text segments as understandable address structures.

A postal address is a knowledge structure. It includes suite information, municipal location and regional position, as shown in Figure 2. Based on this observation, address extraction should consider adequate information. Considering the text segment "Kingston Street will be under construction from June 9 to July 15", "Kingston" and "Street" are concepts in the postal address domain, but "Kingston Street" is not a valid address. On the other hand, "Loblaws supermarket, located at 125 Kingston Street, Toronto" contains the address descriptor "125 Kingston Street, Toronto".

Y. Zhang et al. (Eds.): APWeb 2005, LNCS 3399, pp. 925–937, 2005.

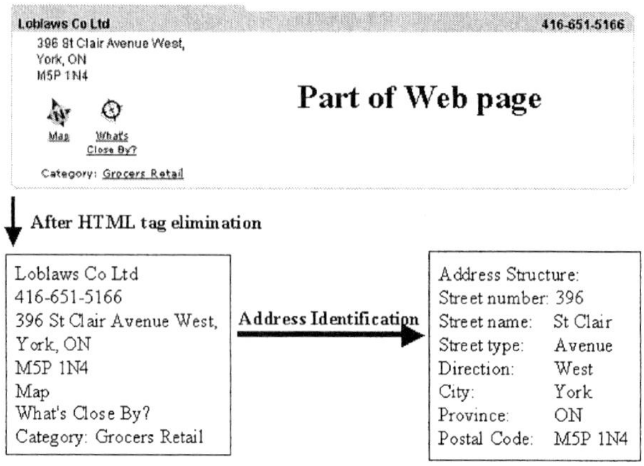

Fig. 1. An illustration of address extraction

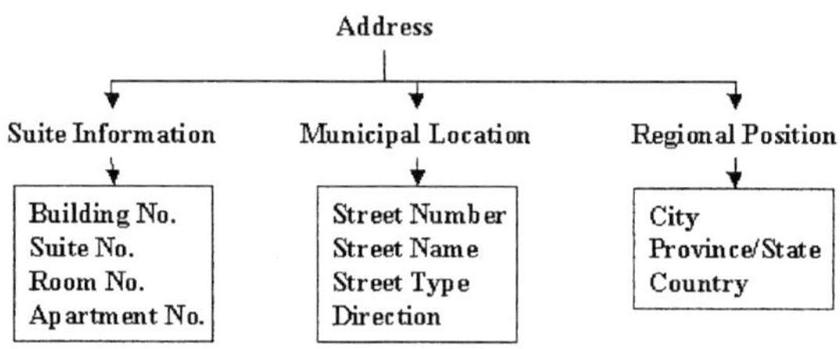

Fig. 2. Postal address structure

Postal address inscriptions are more diverse than general descriptions. A real mailing address can be written as “Suite 113, 100 Kingston Street, Toronto, ON” or “100 Kingston Street, Suite 113, Toronto, ON”. On the other hand, not all address elements have to appear in a real address. For example, the above address does not contain a “direction” description. Some addresses may not have suite information. Another problem is vocabulary [1,2]. Language use may cause semantic misunderstanding due to synonyms (different words for the same meaning) and polysemy (the same word with different meanings). In the synonym case, for example, “Street” is often written as its short form “St”, “St.” or “Str”; “West” is often abbreviated as “W”. To illustrate the polysemy problem, “Quebec” is a province in Canada, but it is also a city name in the province of Quebec; “Ontario” is a province in Canada but it may also be a street name in some city; “Sherbrooke” may also appear as a city name or a street name.

In this paper, we propose a method for retrieving location-based information from the Web. The method employs an ontology-based conceptual information retrieval approach combined with graph matching methods to automatically identify possible address structures in a Web page. Section 2 reviews recent research in the field of content-based information retrieval. Section 3 details our method and Section 4 evaluates our experiments. Finally, Section 5 gives the conclusion.

2 Related Work

The idea of identifying the information in a document with a tabular structure is not new. Many research groups, such as the Message Understanding Conference (MUC) and the Text REtrieval Conference (TREC), have given considerable attention to the information extraction approach over the last decade. Postal address extraction is a new problem, however. The tasks of MUC-7 allowed researchers to extract street address information for a vehicle launch event [4], but most of their proposals are not accurate enough for location-based data identification. Other researchers utilize a standard address database to perform geo-parsing of Web pages [5, 6]. However, this approach is not able to handle diverse address inscription forms.

In the field of content-based information retrieval, recent studies utilize the conceptual analysis of unstructured texts. In such systems, researchers tend to use the domain ontology as a conceptual structure to accomplish concept extraction by combining human knowledge and computing techniques. Mapping the words onto a set of predefined concepts (knowledge) is one way to discover a text's underlying meanings. In this context, an ontology specifies a conceptualization of a particular knowledge domain [7], in which each concept is formalized as a node in the ontology and a relationship between concepts is represented by an edge linking concept nodes.

Some approaches, such as those in [8, 9, 10], suggest applying the concept space model to represent documents. Each document is normalized to a concept-element vector and each element value is determined by concept frequency. An ontology or thesaurus is used to merge synonyms and other related syntax. However, a common vector cannot exhibit the relationship among concepts. Philosophers and linguists have found that graph structures are a better way to represent human knowledge. Conceptual graphs [11] and semantic networks are academic efforts towards machine understanding. Graph-based document representation can easily preserve implicit knowledge in the context of texts. However, transforming plain texts into graphs is not an easy task, since concepts or their relationships have to be identified automatically. Graph matching is also a difficult problem (NP-complete). These two drawbacks obstruct the application of graph structures in information retrieval.

3 Our Proposal

A document is described as a subgraph of a predefined ontology, after concepts in the document are identified and mapped onto this ontology. Comparing concepts corresponds to node similarity. Approximate graph matching is used in this paper.

3.1 Ontology Construction

Ontologies play an increasingly important role in real-world modeling. An ontology is "a specification of a conceptualization" [12]. Such a conceptualization can be defined as a structure $<D, R>$, where D is a domain and R represents relevant relations on D. Based on this view, the ontology itself is actually a set of concepts in a specific domain and defines underlying relations between these concepts.

The concept set in the ontology of the postal address domain is actually a gazetteer, in which each concept can be described as a duple *c=(inscription, meaning)*, where *inscription* corresponds to the lexical inscription form of the concept and *meaning* is the syntactic sense of the concept. For example, the word "Sherbrooke" will be transformed into two concepts: "street_name:Sherbrooke" and "city:Sherbrooke", as "Sherbrooke" can actually be either a street name or a city name. The top-level ontology in the postal address domain (Figure 3) is the abstract understanding of a real mail address. These concepts are the basic entities and general descriptors. On the other hand, factual concepts located in the lower level of the ontology graph are the instances of street name, street type, direction, city and province. Concepts are linked together by means of their semantic relations, classified as vertical and horizontal:

(1) The **PartOf** relation (vertical relationship) organizes concepts according to a decomposition hierarchy. For instance, *municipal location* can be composed of *street-number*, *street-name*, *street-type*, etc. Figure 3 gives a PartOf relation for the top-level ontology in the address domain.

(2) The **InstanceOf** relation (vertical relationship) provides a specific instance of the concept being defined. For example, *Northeast* is an instance of *Direction*, and *Toronto* is an instance of *city*. Figure 4 shows an InstanceOf relation.

(3) The **Similar** relation (horizontal relationship) gives a set of concepts similar to the concept being defined. Fig. 5 gives a Similar relation for the concept *NE.*

(4) The **SyntacticNeighbor** relation (horizontal relationship) defines the neighborhood relation when two concepts are linked together in the document, either in the same sentence or in two adjacent sentences. For example, in "20 Jutland Road, Etobi-

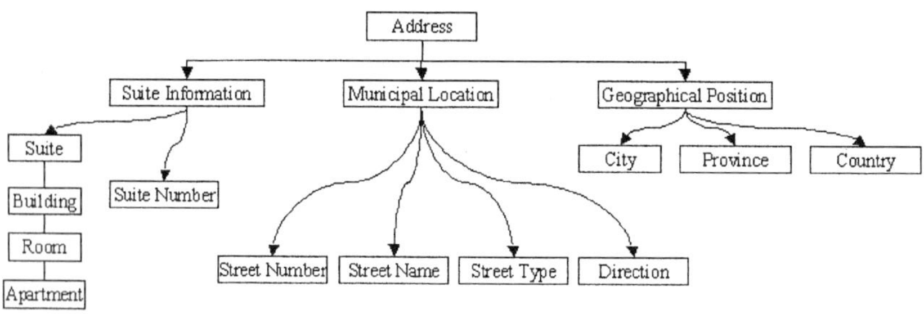

Fig. 3. PartOf relation segment for a top-level ontology in the address domain

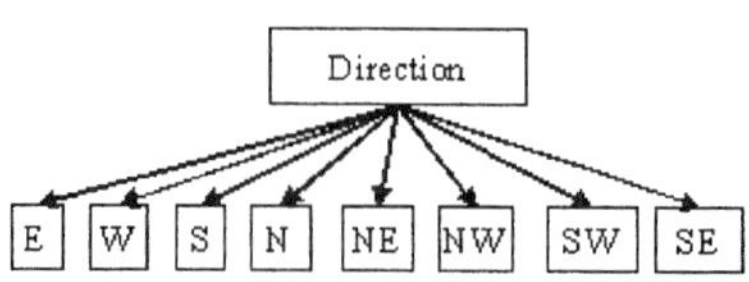

Fig. 4. InstanceOf relation segment for the concept *Direction*

coke, Ontario", "Jutland" is a SyntacticNeighbor of "Road", and "Road" is a SyntacticNeighbor of "Jutland" and "Etobicoke". Figure 6 gives an example of this relation.

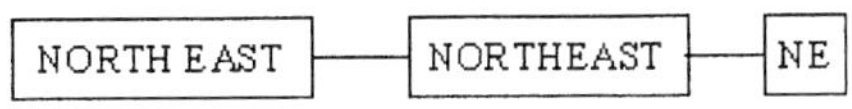

Fig. 5. Similar relation segment for the concept *NE*

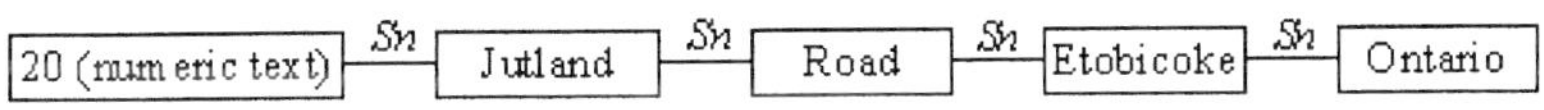

Fig. 6. The SyntacticNeighbor relation in the address domain

When a concept is entered in the ontology, relations are determined. Therefore, the intentional definition of an ontology is represented by $G_o = (N, E)$, where G_o is the ontology graph. N is the set of concept nodes corresponding to $N = (n, d)$, where n is the inscription form of the concept, d is the description of the concept and E is the set of edges linking concept nodes to represent relationships. It is a 4-tuple $E = (Pa, In, Si, Sn)$, where *Pa* is the PartOf relation, *In* is the InstanceOf relation, *Si* is the Similar relation and *Sn* is the SyntacticNeighbor relation.

3.2 Concept Identification

To represent a text segment in a document using a predefined ontology, concepts must first be identified from the unstructured text. However, documents do not contain concepts explicitly, but rather words. Once concepts are expressed in a language (words and grammar), it is possible to identify them by analyzing phrases [10]. We use the following rules with regard to the relationship categories mentioned above.

Rule 1: The SyntacticNeighbor relation can be identified if two concepts are contiguous in the document. For example, the phrase "Maple Street in Canada" indicates that the concept "Maple" is a SyntacticNeighbor of the concept "Street"; the concept "Street" has the SyntacticNeighbor "Maple" but not "Canada".

Rule 2: If a concept is an instance of its parent node, that parent node is also identified. For example, in Figure 2, if the concept "East" is spotted, the "direction" concept should be selected.

Rule 3: If a concept is found, its similar sibling concepts must be identified. For example, in Figure 3, when the concept "NE" is identified, its similar siblings "NORTHEAST" and "NORTH EAST" will also be picked out.

Rule 4: If an identified concept has more than one meaning, all the related concept nodes are highlighted and their parent nodes are also picked out. For example, "Sherbrooke" can be either "street_name" or "city". If "Sherbrooke" is identified in the document, both "street_name:Sherbrooke" and "city:Sherbrooke" are highlighted and their InstanceOf relation parent nodes "street_name" and "city" are also picked out.

Rule 5: The SyntacticNeighbor relation is transferred from the child node to its parent node, following the InstanceOf relation edge. For example, in the phrase "Maple Street in Canada", we know that "Maple" and "Street" are syntactic neighbors, "Maple" is a child node of "street_name" under the InstanceOf relation and "Street" is a child node of "street type" under the InstanceOf relation.

Given "*20 TORONTO ROAD ETOBICOKE ON*", we identify "*20*" as a possible instance of "suite_number" or "street_number", "*TORONTO*" as a possible instance of both "street_name" and "city", "*ROAD*" as an instance of "street_type" (its synonym "*RD*" is also selected), "*ETOBICOKE*" as being in the same situation as "*TORONTO*", and finally "*ON*" as an instance of "Province" (its synonym "*ONTARIO*" is also selected). Following the above five rules, general concepts, "suite_number", "street_number", "street_name", "street_type", "city", "province" are determined, with their relations. Figure 7 illustrates the resulting ontology graph.

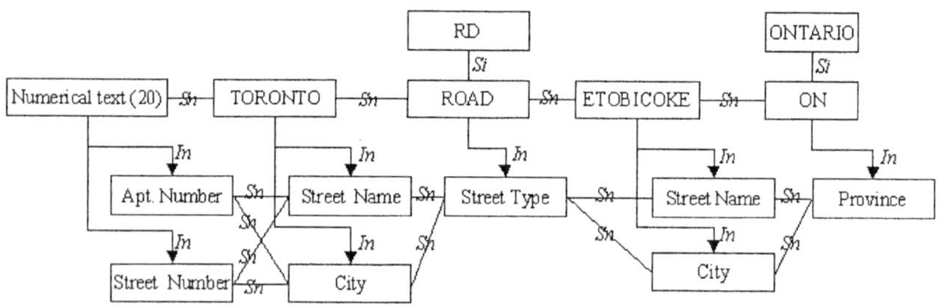

Fig. 7. Ontology graph of "20 TORONTO ROAD ETOBICOKE ON". "*Si*" is the Similar relation edge, "*Sn*" is the SyntacticNeighbor relation edge, "*In*" is the InstanceOf relation edge

3.3 Graph Matching

Graph matching allows us to compute similarity and map common concept nodes between knowledge structures. The similarity between the graph of a text segment and the predefined template graph of the address structure is used to determine whether a phrase is a real address. On the side of node-to-node mapping, ambiguous nodes can be resolved by coherent correspondences and then used to fill out the tabular address structure. Hence, the process involves two steps: graph similarity measurement and node mapping.

Template Graph and Abstract Descriptor Subgraph

To perform graph matching, two definitions have to be given: the template graph, which utilizes a graph to state predefined knowledge of address structure, and the abstract descriptor subgraph, which concentrates the general concepts extracted from a text segment graph to present abstract knowledge of the text.

A **template graph** describes human understanding of address structure. In the postal address domain, a real address is always written according to some official, uniform rules. Although it has diverse orders in different countries or regions, the elements contained in an address are usually the same and their number is limited. In Canada, these elements are "*suite descriptor*", "*suite number*", "*street number*", "*street name*", "*street type*", "*direction*", "*city*", "*province*", and "*country*". A template graph can be predefined to simulate conceivable cases of addresses. Figure 8 presents the SyntacticNeighbor relations between these elements and includes all possible connections in an address expression. This graph is actually a predefined knowledge structure representing a general address conceptualization.

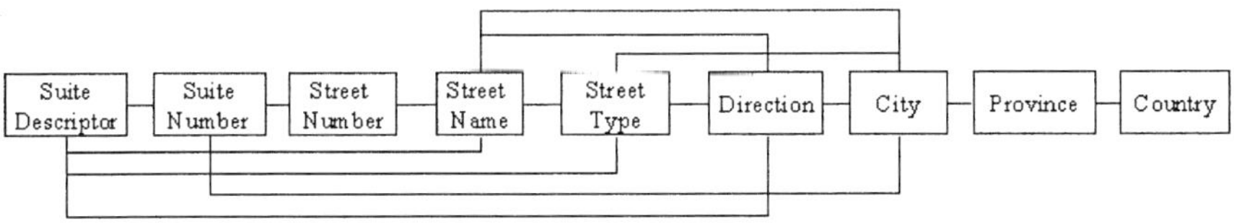

Fig. 8. Template graph in the address domain

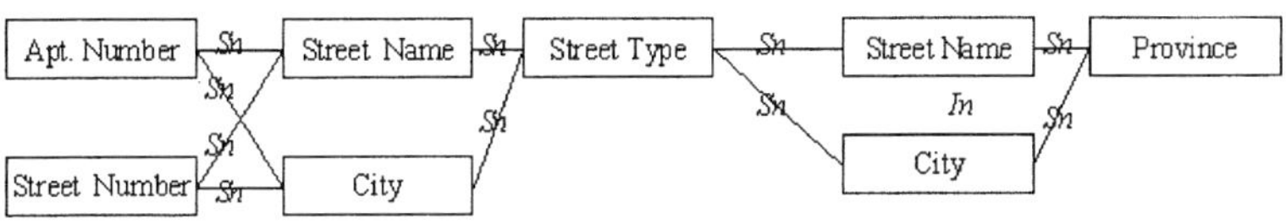

Fig. 9. Abstract descriptor subgraph of "20 TORONTO ROAD ETOBICOKE ON"

An **abstract descriptor subgraph** is the subgraph of concentrated general concepts in the top level of the text segment graph. This notion is based on human analysis of postal address structure. For example, "100 Kingston St, Toronto, ON" has a StreetNumber(100)-StreetName(Kingston)-StreetType(St)-City(Toronto)-Province (ON) structure. Here, we call the general concept "StreetName" as an abstract descriptor of the concept "Kingston", the general concept "StreetType" as an abstract descriptor of the concept "St", etc. After these concepts are identified, their abstract descriptors (InstanceOf or PartOf parent of top-level concept nodes) can be induced by following InstanceOf and PartOf relation edges. These general concepts are then extracted and their SytacticNeighbor relations are determined by transferring from the SyntacticNeighbor relation concepts in the lower level of the ontology. For example, in "*20 TORONTO ROAD ETOBICOKE ON*" and its graph representation in Figure 7, we can acquire the abstract descriptor subgraph in Figure 9, where each concrete concept has been mapped onto its general concept along an InstanceOf edge.

Similarity Measurement

Graph similarity measurement in the information retrieval field has received considerable attention from researchers such as [13, 14]. Most of their proposals define graph similarity based on the similarity between concepts and the similarity between relations, corresponding to separate node and edge comparisons. In the address domain, however, the graph similarity problem is relatively simple. The similarity between two graphs can be defined by the following formula:

$$sim = \frac{N_c(G, G_T) + E_c(G, G_T)}{N(G_T) + E(G_T)}$$

where $N_c(G, G_T)$ is the number of nodes shared by the text segment's abstract descriptor subgraph G and the template graph G_T, $E_c(G, G_T)$ is the number of edges common to G and G_T, $N(G_T)$ is the number of nodes in graph G_T, and $E(G_T)$ is the number of edges in G_T. Taking the example illustrated in Figure 7 for the text segment "20 TORONTO ROAD ETOBICOKE ON", if we compare its abstract descriptor subgraph (Figure 9) with the template graph (Figure 8) and prune off duplicated elements (for instance, by regarding the two "street_name" nodes as a single "street_name", and the two edges connecting "street_name" and "street_type" as one edge), we determine that $N_c(G, G_T) = 6$, $E_c(G, G_T) = 7$, $\mathrm{N}(\mathrm{G_T}) = 9$ and $\mathrm{E}(\mathrm{G_T}) = 15$. We can then derive the similarity between the two graphs as 0.54167.

Structure Mapping

Structure mapping is a node-to-node mapping problem, also called graph isomorphism in mathematical terminology. The goal is to find a one-to-one correspondence of nodes, conserving adjacency, between two graphs or subgraphs. It is well known that isomorphism can be determined by means of a brute-force tree-search enumeration procedure. Although studies such as [15, 16] and the recent work in [17] give more innovative and optimized solutions, this problem still belongs to the class NP-Hard. In the address domain, however, it can be simplified for practical purposes. The trick we have used is to obtain an isomorphism between the template graph and the abstract descriptor subgraph by following InstanceOf relation edges. For a real address structure and its abstract descriptor subgraph, we admit the following two facts:

Fact 1: A node of the template graph may be present only once in the abstract descriptor subgraph. For example, in the address "*20 TORONTO ROAD ETOBICOKE ON*", "street_number(*20*)", "street_name(*TORONTO*)", "street_type(*ROAD*)", "city(*ETOBICOKE*)" and "province(*ON*)" appear once, and other address elements, such as "direction", "suite_descriptor" and "suite_number" do not appear.

Fact 2: An edge in the abstract descriptor subgraph must have its counterpart in the template graph. For example, "suite_number" can never connect with "street_name" directly (in the real world, "suite_descriptor" always precedes "suite_number"); an edge linking "suite_number" and "street_name" in the abstract descriptor subgraph is false and probably caused by word polysemy and ambiguity.

Based on the above facts, a tree-search method can be applied to find node correspondences between the template graph and the abstract descriptor graph in a two-step task:

Step 1: Eliminate edges found in the abstract descriptor subgraph but not in the template graph (Fact 2). For example, in Figure 9, the edges linking "suite_number" and "street_name", "street_number" and "city", "street_name" and "province" do not exist in the template graph. They should be pruned off as in Figure 10.

Step 2: Find a path along SyntacticNeighbor edges in the abstract descriptor subgraph subject to the following conditions: (1) each instance concept node is mapped to a unique abstract descriptor node; (2) no abstract descriptor node is duplicated. For example, a path through Figure 9 can be determined as shown by the heavy line in Figure 11.

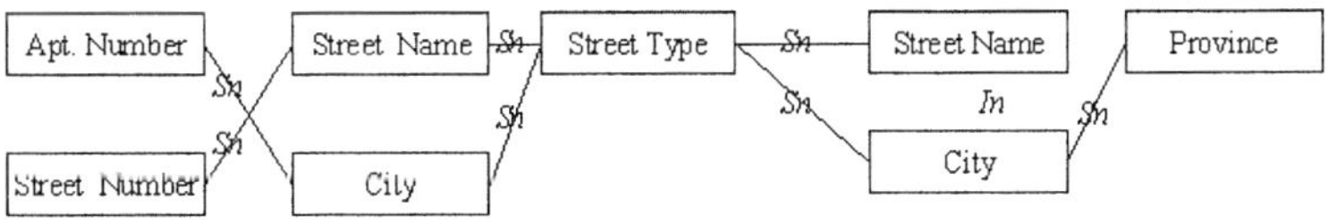

Fig. 10. Eliminating abstract descriptor subgraph edges according to Fact 2

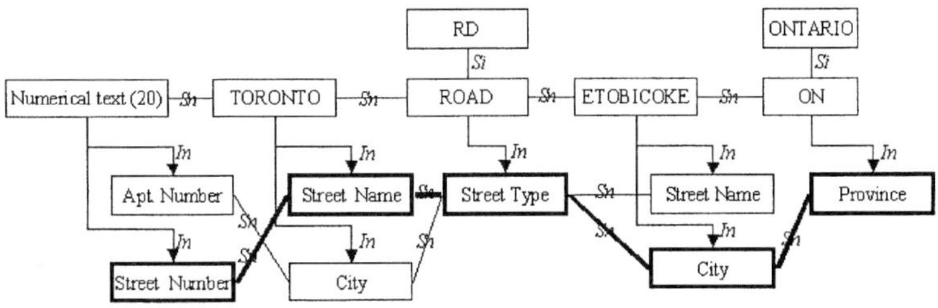

Fig. 11. Determining a path based on Fact 1

After these two steps, a path in the abstract descriptor subgraph can be regarded as an address candidate. The instance concept will now be fit into the tabular structure as its abstract descriptor representative. If no path can be found in the abstract descriptor subgraph, it means that the representable address candidate cannot be parsed to a valid address structure. On the other hand, the existence of two or more paths in the abstract descriptor subgraph means that there are ambiguous meanings for the address candidate. In that case, human intervention is required to validate these possibilities.

4 Experiments and Evaluation

Our ontology construction for the address domain makes use of the DMTI GIS database, which provides instance concepts such as "street_name", "street_type", "direction" and "city" for Ontario, Canada. We used www.yellowpages.ca as a test Web document set to evaluate our proposal.

The concept identification process is carried out after transformation from HTML to plain text. As the SyntacticNeighbor relation is examined in this process, any text segment including two or more nodes can be regarded as an address candidate and transformed into a graph. The graph similarity measurement is then compared. We set the threshold of similarity for extracting the most likely addresses at 0.29. In fact, this threshold value depends on the ontology graph. Since the template graph contains a total of 9 nodes and 15 edges, a possible address structure should contain at least 4 of the nodes in the template graph and the corresponding 3 edges. Thus the minimum of the similarity value, according to Formula 5, should be 0.291667. Filtering by the threshold yields the list of extracted address candidates shown in Table 1.

Table 1. List of address candidates extracted from the Web page http://www.yellowpages.ca/searchBusness.do?what=supermarket&srchtype=business&city=toronto&sType=simpleSearch&action=homeSearch&step=getDirectory&Se=smp&x=28&y=13

Extracted Addresses	Similarity	Real address?
EAST YORK 4 ETOBICOKE 11 NORTH YORK 21 SCARBOROUGH 39 TORONTO 57 YORK 14 ONTARIO	0.2916667	No
25 MALLEY ROAD SCARBOROUGH ON	0.4166667	Yes
73 RAILSIDE ROAD NORTH YORK ON	0.4166667	Yes
73 RAILSIDE ROAD TORONTO ON	0.4166667	Yes
310 MILLWAY AVENUE CONCORD ON	0.2916667	Yes
151 CARLINGVIEW DRIVE ETOBICOKE ON	0.3333333	Yes
151 CARLINGVIEW DRIVE ETOBICOKE ON	0.3333333	Yes
400 SEWELLS ROAD SCARBOROUGH ON	0.4166667	Yes
20 NUGGET AVENUE SCARBOROUGH ON	0.4583333	Yes
2889 DUFFERIN STREET NORTH YORK ON	0.4583333	Yes
790 MILITARY TRAIL SCARBOROUGH ON	0.4583333	Yes
1966 WESTON ROAD YORK ON	0.4166667	Yes
247 SPADINA AVENUE TORONTO ON	0.4583333	Yes
3813 SHEPPARD AVENUE EAST SCARBOROUGH ON	0.5833333	Yes
483 OLD WESTON ROAD YORK ON	0.4166667	Yes
1230 KING STREET WEST TORONTO ON	0.4583333	Yes
0 1 2 3 4 5 6 7 8 9 A B C D E	0.2916667	No

The above table shows all the address candidates from the sample Web page whose computed similarity exceeds the threshold value. Two of these candidates, "EAST YORK 4 ETOBICOKE 11 NORTH YORK 21 SCARBOROUGH 39 TORONTO 57 YORK 14 ONTARIO" and "0 1 2 3 4 5 6 7 8 9 A B C D E", are rejected at the stage of structure mapping, since no valid path can be found in their abstract descriptor subgraphs.

We have performed a preliminary evaluation of the proposed system by using precision and recall measurements, as suggested by MUC. MUC defines scores of precision and recall by comparing the system response to an answer key [3]. Let N_{key} be the total number of real addresses in the answer key, $N_{response}$ the total number of address candidates in the system response and $N_{correct}$ the number of correct addresses in the system response. Then $precision = \frac{N_{correct}}{N_{response}}$ and $recall = \frac{N_{correct}}{N_{key}}$. The "F score", combining recall and precision scores, is also used to measure both factors.

The "F score" is defined as $F = \frac{2 \times precision \times recall}{precision + recall}$. Since there is no benchmark document corpus available for evaluating postal address extraction, we tested our system manually on two Web databases: www.yellowpages.ca and Yahoo! Business-Finder. The results are listed in Table 2.

Table 2. Precision and recall results in 6 experiments using yellowpages and 5 experiments using Yahoo pages. The number of addresses in each page (N_{key}) and the number of correctly extracted addresses (N_{corr}) were determined by a human experimenter

Web Database (Page link)	N_{key}	N_{rese}	N_{corr}
http://www.yellowpages.ca/searchBusiness.do?what=gasoline+station&srchtype=category&city=Etobicoke&sType=simpleSearch&action=homeSearch&step=getDirectory&Se=smp&x=27&y=7	14	15	13
http://www.yellowpages.ca/searchBusiness.do?action=homeSearch&start=16&srchtype=category&Se=smp&directoryId=092462&provinceId=ON&cityId=ETOBICOK&categoryName=Service+Stations+Gasoline%2C+Oil+%26+Natural+Gas&showMsgBox=1&what=gasoline+station&Dir=092462&sType=simpleSearch&categoryId=01186800&step=getDirectory&city=Etobicoke	15	16	14
http://www.yellowpages.ca/searchBusiness.do?action=homeSearch&start=31&srchtype=category&Se=smp&directoryId=092462&provinceId=ON&cityId=ETOBICOK&categoryName=Service+Stations+Gasoline%2C+Oil+%26+Natural+Gas&showMsgBox=1&what=gasoline+station&Dir=092462&sType=simpleSearch&categoryId=01186800&step=getDirectory&city=Etobicoke	15	15	14
http://www.yellowpages.ca/searchBusiness.do?action=homeSearch&srchtype=category&Se=smp&directoryId=092826&provinceId=&cityId=&categoryName=&showMsgBox=1&what=gasoline+station&Dir=&sType=simpleSearch&step=getCategory&city=Kingston	14	12	10
http://www.yellowpages.ca/searchBusiness.do?action=homeSearch&start=16&srchtype=category&Se=smp&directoryId=092826&provinceId=&cityId=&categoryName=Service+Stations+Gasoline%2C+Oil+%26+Natural+Gas&showMsgBox=1&what=gasoline+station&Dir=092826&sType=simpleSearch&categoryId=01186800&step=getCategory&city=Kingston	14	9	7
http://www.yellowpages.ca/searchBusiness.do?action=homeSearch&start=31&srchtype=category&Se=smp&directoryId=092826&provinceId=&cityId=&categoryName=Service+Stations+Gasoline%2C+Oil+%26+Natural+Gas&showMsgBox=1&what=gasoline+station&Dir=092826&sType=simpleSearch&categoryId=01186800&step=getCategory&city=Kingston	15	13	11
http://ca.yp.yahoo.com/ysp?C=gasoline+station&N=&yloc=reup&T=Kingston&S=ON&R=N&SRC=yahoo&STYPE=S&PG=L&Search=Find+It	13	12	8
http://ca.yp.yahoo.com/ysp?C=gasoline+station&N=&yloc=reup&T=Etobicoke&S=ON&R=N&SRC=yahoo&STYPE=S&PG=L&Search=Find+It	15	17	12
http://ca.yp.yahoo.com/ysp?CID=&C=gasoline+station&T=Etobicoke&PG=L&STYPE=S&R=N&SRC=yahoo&S=ON&AL=&PM=001d3abe&MC=&NA=&PP=&paging=1&PI=16&next=1	15	16	9
http://ca.yp.yahoo.com/ysp?CID=001D7200152&C=auto+repair&T=Kingston&PG=L&STYPE=S&R=N&SRC=yahoo&S=ON&MC=1&PI=1	8	8	4
http://ca.yp.yahoo.com/ysp?CID=001D7200152&C=auto+repair&T=Kingston&PG=L&STYPE=S&R=N&SRC=yahoo&S=ON&AL=&PM=0025b52b&MC=1&NA=&PP=&paging=1&PI=16&next=1	7	8	3

Hence, the precision and recall evaluation of our system is as follows: $precision = 0.745$, $recall = 0.724$ and $F = 0.734$.

5 Conclusion and Future Work

The aim of the work described here is to achieve automatic location-based data updating from the Web. Most location-awareness information can be recognized by postal addresses. Node mapping of an address graph fits an identified address segment into slots in a tabular structure. This technique can not only be utilized in mobile applications, but can also be applied in geo-marketing and other applications of location-based services. On the other hand, since the method itself is based on domain ontology, it can also be extended to the automatic extraction of lightweight knowledge.

There are several ways to improve the proposed system. First, the typing-error problem needs to be considered in the process of address identification and extraction. To achieve this goal, string similarity has to be integrated as part of the node similarity measurement. However, such a consideration undoubtedly increases the computation complexity of the address extraction process, since not only does the string edit distance computation itself consume system running time, but word-by-word and phrase-by-phrase comparison within the document must also be executed. Hence, tradeoff solutions between typing-error detection and address identification performance have to be found. Other problems include noise elimination and separation of joined address phrases. For example, "20 Portland Blvd Sherbrooke Quebec 100 King Street Cockville Quebec" (two joined addresses) would be regarded as one address segment by the procedure described here.

References

1. Chen, H.: The Vocabulary Problem in Collaboration of Text from Electronic Meetings, IEEE Computer, Special Issue On CSCW, Vol. 27, No. 5, 1994.
2. Furnas, G. W.: The Vocabulary Problem in Human-System Communication, Communications of the ACM, Vol. 30, No. 11, 1987.
3. Grishman, R.: Information Extraction: Techniques and Challenges, Information Extraction (International Summer School SCIE-97), Spinger-Verlag, 1997.
4. Chinchor, N.: MUC-7 Named Entity Task Definition, in Proceedings of the 7th Message Understanding Conference (MUC-7), 1997.
5. Morimoto, Y., Aono, M., Houle, M.: Extracting Spatial Knowledge from the Web, in Proceedings of the 2003 IEEE Symposium on Applications and the Internet, 2003.
6. Sagara, T., Kitsuregawa, M.: Yellow Page Driven Methods of Collecting and Scoring Spatial Web Documents, in Proceedings of the Workshop on Geographic Information Retrieval, SIGIR, 2004.
7. Guarino, N.: Formal Ontology and Information Systems, in Proceedings of the 1st International Conference on Formal Ontology in Information Systems, 1998.
8. Chen, H., Schatz, B. R.: Semantic Retrieval for the NCSA Mosaic, in Proceedings of the 2nd International World Wide Web Conference, 1994.

9. Chen, H., Martinez, J. ,Ng, T., Schatz, B. R.: A Concept Space Approach to Addressing the Vocabulary Problem in Scientific Information Retrieval: An Experiment on the Worm Community System, Journal of the American Society for Information Science, Vol. 48, 1997
10. Loh, S., Wives, L. K., de Oliveira, J. P. M.: Concept-Based Knowledge Discovery in Texts Extracted from the Web, ACM SIGKDD Explorations, Vol. 1, No. 1, 2000.
11. Sowa, J.: Conceptual Structures: Information Processing in Mind and Machine, Addison-Wesley, 1984.
12. Gruber, T.: Toward Principles for Design of Ontologies Used for Knowledge Sharing, International Journal of Human and Computer Studies, Vol. 43, No. 5, 1993.
13. Zhong, J., Zhu, H., Li, J., Yu, Y.: Conceptual Graph Matching for Semantic Search, in Proceedings of the 10th International Conference on Conceptual Structures, ICCS 2002, Lecture Notes in Artificial Intelligence 2393, Spinger-Verlag, 2002.
14. Montes-y-Gomez, M., Gelbukh, A., Lopez-Lopez, A., Baeza-Yates, R.: Flexible Comparison of Conceptual Graphs, Lecture Notes in Computer Science 2113, Spinger-Verlag, 2001.
15. Ullman, J.: An Algorithm for Subgraph Isomorphism, Journal of the ACM, Vol. 23, 1976.
16. Corneil, D., Gotlieb, C.: An Efficient Algorithm for Graph Isomorphism, Journal of the Association for Computing Machinery, Vol. 17, 1970.
17. Hlaoui A., Wang, S.: A New Algorithm for Inexact Graph Matching, in Proceedings of the 16th International Conference on Pattern Recognition (ICPR 2002), 2002.

PlusDBG: Web Community Extraction Scheme Improving Both Precision and Pseudo-Recall

Naoyuki Saida[1], Akira Umezawa[2], and Hayato Yamana[1]

[1] Waseda University, 3-4-1 Okubo Shinjuku-ku Tokyo, Japan
[2] FUJITSU LIMITED, 1-5-2 Higashi-Shimbashi, Minato-ku, Tokyo, Japan
nao@yama.info.waseda.ac.jp

Abstract. This paper proposes PlusDBG to improve both precision and pseudo-recall by extending the conventional Web community extraction scheme. Precision is defined as the percentage of relevant Web pages extracted as members of Web communities and pseudo-recall is defined as the sum of the number of relevant Web pages extracted as members of Web communities. The proposed scheme adopts the new distance parameter defined by the relevance between a Web page and a Web community, and extracts the Web community with higher precision and pseudo-recall. Moreover, we have implemented and evaluated the proposed scheme. Our results confirm that the proposed scheme is able to extract about 3.2-fold larger numbers of members of Web communities than the conventional scheme, while maintaining equivalent precision.

1 Introduction

A Web community is defined as a set of related Web pages concerning a same topic. Web community extraction is usually used for the clustering of Web pages into semantic sets. Conventionally, e.g. in Web directory services, Web pages are clustered into various well-known topics by hand. However, it is impossible to cluster all the Web pages properly by hand because they are updated frequently and their number is huge. Thus, the Web pages should be clustered automatically into a set of Web communities.

Automatic Web community extraction has two different purposes. Purpose 1, which is represented by HITS [1] proposed by Kleinberg, is to extract the authoritative pages related to a specified seed topic. Purpose 2, which is represented by Trawling [2] proposed by Kumar *et al.*, is to extract the Web communities related to unknown seed topics. However, these conventional schemes are not satisfactory with regard to both precision and pseudo-recall. This results in the inclusion of unrelated pages or the exclusion of related pages from the extracted Web community. Here, precision and pseudo-recall is defined as followings.

Definition 1. *Precision is the percentage of relevant Web pages extracted as members of Web communities.*

Y. Zhang et al. (Eds.): APWeb 2005, LNCS 3399, pp. 938–943, 2005.

Definition 2. *Pseudo-recall is the sum of the number of relevant Web pages extracted as members of the Web communities.*

To extract the usable and comprehensible communities, both precision and pseudo-recall should be high if at all possible. That is, the community with overly low precision or overly low pseudo-recall is not desired.

This paper proposes a new Web community extraction scheme called PlusDBG that improves upon both precision and pseudo-recall. We extend the DBG (Dense Bipartite Graph) extraction scheme [3] proposed by Reddy *et al.* In particular, we adopt a new parameter called "distance" defined by the relevance between a Web page and a Web community.

2 Related Works

The WWW is denoted as a large directed graph [5]: whole nodes are Web pages and whole edges are links. Web community extraction schemes [1, 2, 3, 4] extract Web communities by finding characteristic structures from such a Web graph.

Reddy *et al.* proposed an algorithm for extracting dense bipartite graphs (DBGs) from a large Web graph to extract Web communities without specifying any topics [3]. A DBG is defined as a bipartite graph consisting of both $Fans$ and $Centers$. In DBGs, each Web page of $Fans$ links to at least u $Center$ pages, and each page of $Centers$ is linked from at least v Fan pages. The DBG extraction algorithm consists of two steps. The first step iteratively extracts the candidate Web pages forming a Web community. The second step extracts Web pages constructing a DBG from the extracted candidate Web pages. In this algorithm, every Web page is given as a seed page.

However, conventional schemes have not aimed to satisfy both precision and pseudo-recall. Especially, conventional schemes are infirm at the effect of multiple topic pages. Therefore, the extracted Web community may include unrelated pages and exclude related pages.

3 Proposed Algorithm: PlusDBG

The purpose of this study is to develop a method extracting as many Web communities as possible from a large Web graph without specifying any topics, satisfying both precision and pseudo-recall. Precision and pseudo-recall is defined in Definition 1 and Definition 2. To achieve this purpose, we extend the DBG extraction algorithm [3]. When a Web page includes multiple topics, the DBG extraction scheme tends to extract Web pages including unrelated topics as candidate Web pages forming the Web community. To solve the above problem and to improve precision, we adopt the "distance" defined by the relevance between a Web page and a Web community. Moreover, to improve pseudo-recall, we adapt a termination condition in the first step of DBG described in Section 2. In the conventional DBG extraction algorithm, loop count, which is fixed for all communities, is given as the termination condition. In our proposed scheme, threshold value of the "distance" is given as the termination condition and loop count of each community is determined by itself.

3.1 Definition of the "Similarity" and the "Distance"

The similarity ratio $Sim(p, F)$ between the Web page p and the Web page set F is defined by Equation 1, where $children(p)$ is a set of pages linked from the Web page p and $children(F)$ is a union of Web pages linked from each page in the Web page set F. Then, $Sim(p, F)$ represents the interest ratio of the Web page p to the Web page set F.

$$Sim(p, F) = \frac{|children(p) \cap children(F)|}{|children(p)|} \tag{1}$$

By adopting $Sim(p, F)$ as part of the "distance," we are able to avoid the inclusion of multiple topic pages, because multiple topic pages tend to have lower ratio of outward links to one topic.

The distance between a Web page p_n and Web page set F_{n-1}, denoted by $Dis(p_n, F_{n-1})$, is defined by Equation 2. $Dis(p_n, F_{n-1})$ represents the semantic distance from the topic of the Web page p_n, which is a page added in the n-th iteration, to the topic of Web page set F_{n-1}, which is a page set added in the n-1-th or less iterations. The "distance" is designed so that the Web page added later has a larger distance than the Web pages added previously. This is because, we think that the relevance between a Web page and a seed page becomes highest, when the Web page is directly related to the seed page. That is, the Web pages added in the n-th iteration are directly related to the Web pages added in the n-1-th iteration but indirectly related to the Web pages added in the iteration less than n-1-th.

$$\begin{aligned} Dis(p_n, F_{n-1}) &= (1 - Sim(p_n, F_{n-1})) + Dis(q_{n-1}, F_{n-2}), \text{ for } n \geq 2 \\ Dis(p_1, F_0) &= (1 - Sim(p_1, s)), \text{ for } n = 1 \end{aligned} \tag{2}$$

where, s is a seed page, and $q_{n-1} = \{x | \exists x \in F_{n-1}, \forall y \in F_{n-1}, |children(p_n) \cap children(x)| \geq |children(p_n) \cap children(y)|\}$.

3.2 PlusDBG Algorithm

In PlusDBG, every Web page is given as a seed page in the same way as in the DBG extraction algorithm [3]. PlusDBG consists of two steps, similarly to the DBG extraction algorithm. The first step extracts the candidate Web pages forming a Web community. The second step extracts Web pages constructing a DBG from the extracted candidate Web pages. PlusDBG extends the first step of the DBG extraction algorithm to satisfy both precision and pseudo-recall by using the "distance."

First step is described below. Given a seed page s, PlusDBG extracts the candidate Web pages forming a Web community related to the seed page s from a Web Graph $G(N, E)$, where N is the node set and E is the edge set of the Web graph, iteratively by using the "distance."

1. Assign dis_border as a threshold value of "distance," and set $F = F^+ = \{s\}$.
2. Iterate (a) and (b) while $|F^+| > 0$.
   (a) Find $P = \{p|p \in N, p \notin F, |children(F^+) \cap children(p)| > 0\}$. Then, calculate the "distance" $Dis(p, F)$ for each $p \in P$.
   (b) $F^+ = \{p|p \in P, Dis(p, F) \leq dis\_border\}$. Then, $F = F^+ \cup F$.
3. Output F.

Second step is described below. Given a Web page set F, PlusDBG extracts a set of Web pages forming a DBG as a Web community in the same way as the DBG extraction algorithm from a Web Graph $G(N, E)$.

1. Assign the out-degree threshold of $Fans$ u and the in-degree threshold of $Centers$ v. Then, set $Fans = F$ and $Centers = \{p|p$ is linked from any in $F\}$.
2. Iterate (a) to (c) until both $|Fans|$ and $|Centers|$ are converged.
   (a) Find $P_F = \{p|p \in Fans, |\{q|q \in Centers, q$ is linked from $p\}| < u\}$.
   (b) Find $P_C = \{q|q \in Centers, |\{p|p \in Fans, p$ links to $q\}| < v\}$.
   (c) Remove P_F from $Fans$ and P_C from $Centers$.
3. Output $Fans$ and $Centers$ as a DBG.

4 Evaluation

We use the NTCIR-4 [6] WEB task's test collection for our evaluations.The test collection consists of 11,038,720 Web pages. In the evaluation, only the links between different Web servers are extracted as the data set for evaluation.

In the evaluation, with regard to PlusDBG (hereafter referred to as PDBG), the threshold value of "distance" is set to 1. With regard to the conventional DBG extraction algorithm, the maximum iteration number in the first step is set to 1 (hereafter referred to as DBG1) or 2 (hereafter referred to as DBG2). In PDBG, DBG1 and DBG2, both the out-degree threshold of $Fans$ and in-degree threshold of $Centers$ are also set to 3. Finally, all the Web pages are adopted as the seed pages in the evaluation. Then, each $Center$ is extracted as a Web community. Thus, a Web page may become a member of multiple communities.

4.1 Precision

In this section, the precision of the PDBG, DBG1 and DBG2 are compared. The precision is calculated by random sampling of 25 communities extracted with each algorithm. In each community, 50 Web pages are selected at random to confirm their precision. In the evaluation, Web pages that fulfilled either of the following criteria are counted as pages matching the topic of the community. Criteria 1 is that the page is an entrance page of the Web site covering the topic. Criteria 2 is that the page is a page containing topic-related contents. Here, a Web site is defined as a set of pages written by the same author. In the evaluation, the usefulness of a page is not taken into consideration.

Table 1 shows the precisions of PDBG, DBG1 and DBG2 for the 25 communities selected at random. As shown in Table 1, PDBG achieves almost the same precision as DBG1. In contrast, DBG2 shows the worst precision among

Table 1. Precision for 25 Communities

Community ID	1	2	3	4	5	6	7	8	9	10	11	12	13	14
(1) DBG1	0.93	0.45	0.60	0.72	0.70	1.00	1.00	0.50	0.88	0.62	0.87	0.60	0.60	0.70
(2) PDBG	0.84	0.46	0.59	0.69	0.58	0.99	1.00	0.59	0.88	0.55	0.89	0.59	0.62	0.69
(3) DBG2	0.14	0.00	0.10	0.17	0.04	0.18	0.85	0.39	0.21	0.02	0.02	0.05	0.03	0.07
(2)/(1)	0.90	1.02	0.99	0.96	0.83	0.99	1.00	1.17	1.00	0.89	1.02	0.98	1.03	0.98
(3)/(1)	0.15	0.01	0.17	0.24	0.05	0.18	0.85	0.78	0.24	0.04	0.02	0.09	0.06	0.10

Community ID	15	16	17	18	19	20	21	22	23	24	25	average
(1) DBG1	0.07	0.56	0.86	1.00	0.86	0.30	0.53	0.75	0.50	0.74	0.78	0.68
(2) PDBG	0.24	0.59	0.70	1.00	0.90	0.28	0.69	0.88	0.46	0.74	0.79	0.69
(3) DBG2	0.22	0.10	0.00	0.02	0.00	0.01	0.02	0.02	0.06	0.00	0.08	0.11
(2)/(1)	3.37	1.06	0.80	1.00	1.05	0.93	1.30	1.17	0.92	1.00	1.02	1.10
(3)/(1)	3.08	0.19	0.00	0.02	0.00	0.04	0.04	0.03	0.13	0.01	0.10	0.26

the three algorithms. The precision ratio of PDBG in comparison with DBG1 is about 0.8 to 1.3 in most communities. In contrast, the precision ratio of DBG2 in comparison with DBG1 is under 0.1 in most communities. Hence, PDBG and DBG1 are able to extract communities with comparable precision. However, DBG2 is not able to extract communities with sufficient precision.

4.2 Pseudo-Recall

In this section, the pseudo-recall of PDBG, DBG1 and DBG2 are compared. Pseudo-recall is defined in Definition 2. In Definition 2, pseudo-recall is determined by the number of relevant Web pages in each Web communities and the number of extracted Web communities. However, for all extracted pages, we cannot evaluate whether a page is relevant to a topic. Thus, pseudo-recall is calculated by "*total number of pages*" × "*average precision*" instead. Figure 1 shows the pseudo-recall and the distribution of the extracted communities from the data set. Here, a Web page may become a member of multiple communities. Thus, the total number of pages forming communities may exceed the total number of Web pages in the data set.

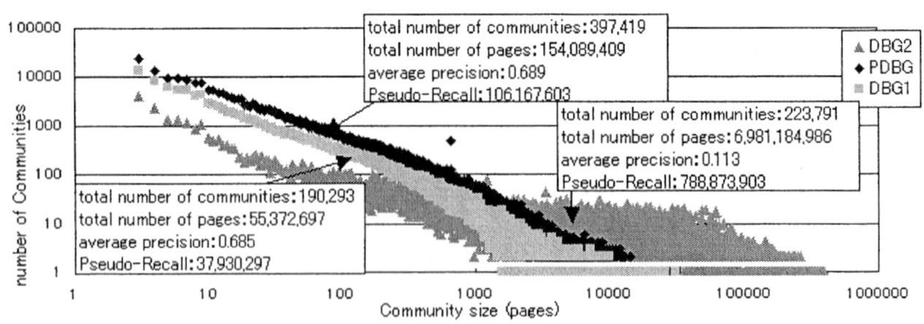

Fig. 1. Distribution of the Extracted Communities

As shown in Figure 1, the pseudo-recall of PDBG is 2.8 times larger than that of DBG1, however, it is smaller than that of DBG2. The reason is discussed below.

As shown in Figure 1, PDBG extracts about 3.2-fold more Web pages than DBG1. Moreover, PDBG extracts about 200,000 communities not extracted in DBG1. For DBG2, the total number of extracted communities is just 223,791, which is about half of the number of extracted communities by PDBG. However, the total number of Web pages forming communities is 6,981,184,986, which is larger than that of PDBG.

This means that PDBG extracts related Web pages more appropriately than DBG2. That is, DBG2 tend to form many large communities such as consisting of more than 10,000 pages including unrelated Web pages.

5 Conclusions

In this paper, we proposed a new Web community extraction scheme, PlusDBG, with improved precision and pseudo-recall. PlusDBG extracts DBGs from the Web page set using the threshold value called "distance." Our experiment results have confirmed that the proposed scheme extracts about 3.2-fold larger numbers of members of Web communities as compared with conventional schemes, while maintaining equivalent precision.

Acknowledgment

This research was founded in part by both "e-Society" and "21-century COE Programs: ICT Productive Academia" in Japan.

References

1. J.Kleinberg, "Authoritative sources in a hyperlinked environment," In Proc. of the 9th Ann. ACM-SIAM Symp. on Discrete Algorithms, pp.668-677, 1998.
2. S.R.Kumar, P.Raphavan, S.Rajagopalan and A.Tomkins, "Trawling the Web for emerging cyber communities," In Proc. of the 8th WWW Conf., 1999.
3. P.K.Reddy and M.Kitsuregawa, "An approach to relate the Web communities through bipartite graphs," The 2nd Int. Conf. on WISE, 2001.
4. G.Flake, S.Lawrence and C.Giles, "Efficient identification of Web communities," In Proc. of the 6th ACM SIGKDD Conf., pp.150-160, 2000.
5. A.Broder, R.Kumar, F.Maghoul, P.Raghavan, S.Rajagopalan, R.Stata, A.Tomkins and J.Wiener, "Graph structure in the Web," In Proc. of the 9th WWW Conf., 2000.
6. NTCIR-4 Workshop, http://research.nii.ac.jp/ntcir/workshop/work-en.html

Fuzzy Inference System with Probability Factor and Its Application in Data Mining

Jiacheng Zheng[1] and Yongchuan Tang[2]

[1] College of Economics, Zhejiang University,
Hangzhou, Zhejiang Province, 310027, P. R. China
zjcheng@zj.com

[2] College of Computer Science, Zhejiang University,
Hangzhou, Zhejiang Province, 310027, P. R. China
yongchuan@263.net

Abstract. In the fuzzy inference system, the construction of the fuzzy rule-base is a key issue. In this paper we provide an identification method for fuzzy model by interpreting the importance factor of each fuzzy rule as the conditional probability of the consequent given the premise. One method of computing the conditional probability is presented. We call this fuzzy model as the fuzzy inference system with probability factor (FISP). One learning process of FISP is also presented in this paper. The application of FISP in time series predication manifests that FISP is very effective.

1 Introduction

During the past several years, fuzzy sets and fuzzy inference systems have reached a popular level within technology, especially fuzzy control based on different kinds of fuzzy inference systems has emerged as one of the most active and fruitful areas for research. Fuzzy if-then rules are an appropriate form to describe the human knowledge under the uncertainty due to fuzziness. On the other hand, the uncertainty due to randomness can be dealt with by the theory of probability (subjective or objective), and the human knowledge under this situation can be represented by the probability distributions. It should be clear that fuzzy sets and probability can live side by side in providing tools for uncertainty analysis in complex, real-world problems[1, 2, 4, 7, 8, 9, 11].

In designing the fuzzy inference system, due to the knowledge imprecision, there is a great need of learning, and tuning the fuzzy if-then rules and associated parameters to achieve a desired level of performance. In order to tune only a particular rule, the fuzzy inference system is extended and each rule is assigned an importance factor or certainty factor, this factor has been explained by many researchers the degree of truth of a rule [10], and some experiments manifest that the importance factor enhances the robustness, flexibility and modelling capability of the system [6].

In this paper, we also discuss the fuzzy inference system in which each fuzzy if-then rule associates a factor, but here the factor is interpreted as the condi-

Y. Zhang et al. (Eds.): APWeb 2005, LNCS 3399, pp. 944–949, 2005.

tional probability of the consequent given the premise, it means how certain the casual relationship between the premise and the consequent is, so in this paper the importance factor or certainty factor is named as the probability factor. The experiments manifest this fuzzy inference system with probability factor is efficient.

In what follows, we review the fuzzy inference system, and proceed to build our fuzzy inference system with probability factor. We introduce the quasi-newton optimization technique and adopt it in the learning process of fuzzy inference system with probability factor. Finally, this new fuzzy model is applied to the data mining — a time series prediction.

2 The Fuzzy Inference System

There are two types fuzzy inference systems: Mamdani-type and Sugeno-type. These two types of inference systems vary somewhat in the way outputs are determined. In this investigation we use Mamdani-type fuzzy inference system.

If $U_1, \ldots, U_n$ are the input variables and V is the output variable we can represent the non-linear function by a collection m "rules" of the form

$$R(r) \text{ If } (U_1 \text{ is } A_{r1}) \text{ and } \ldots \ (U_n \text{ is } A_{rn}) \text{ then } V \text{ is } B_r \text{ with factor } \alpha_r; \quad (1)$$

where if X_j is the universe of discourse of U_j then A_{ij} is a fuzzy subset of X_j and with Y the universe of discourse of V then B_i is a fuzzy subset of Y. And $r = 1, 2, \ldots, m$, m is the total number of rules, α_r $(0 < \alpha_r \leq 1)$ is the importance factor or certainty factor of the rth rule.

Assume the input to the Mamdani-type fuzzy inference system consists of the value $U_j = x_j$ for $j = 1, \ldots, n$. The procedure for reasoning consists of the following steps:

1. Calculate the firing level of each rule τ_i

$$\tau_i = \bigwedge_j [A_{ij}(x_j)] \text{ or } \prod_j [A_{ij}(x_j)] \quad (2)$$

2. Associate the importance or certainty factor α_i with τ_i

$$\pi_i = \tau_i \times \alpha_i \quad (3)$$

3. Calculate the output of each rule as a fuzzy subset F_i of Y where

$$F_i(y) = \bigwedge [\pi_i, B_i(y)] \quad (4)$$

4. Aggregate the individual rule outputs to get a fuzzy subset F of Y where

$$F(y) = \bigvee_i [F_i(y)] \quad (5)$$

5. Defuzzify the aggregate output fuzzy subset

$$\overline{y} = \frac{\sum_i y_i F(y_i)}{\sum_i F(y_i)} \quad (6)$$

3 The Fuzzy Inference with Probability Factor (FISP)

Let P is a probability measure over R^n. Then, the probability of a fuzzy event A is defined by the Lebesgue-Stieltjes integral:

$$P(A) = \int_{R^n} \mu_A(x)\, dP \tag{7}$$

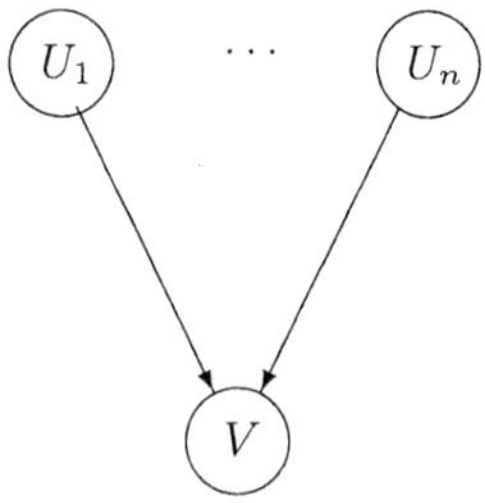

	$A_{11} \cdots A_{1n}$	$\cdots$	$A_{m1} \cdots A_{mn}$
B_1	$P(B_1 \vert A_{11} \cdots A_{1n})$	$\cdots$	$P(B_1 \vert A_{m1} \cdots A_{mn})$
$\vdots$	$\vdots$	$\vdots$	$\vdots$
B_m	$P(B_m \vert A_{11} \cdots A_{1n})$	$\cdots$	$P(B_m \vert A_{m1} \cdots A_{mn})$

CPT assigned to the node V

Fig. 1. The Bayesian belief network of the fuzzy rules

Based on the concept of fuzzy event, we can construct a directed graph. The nodes can be the linguistic variables which have a finite number of possible linguistic values. And this graph has two levels of nodes (see Fig.1). There are n nodes representing the linguistic variables $U_1, \ldots, U_n$ in the first level nodes; and just one node representing the linguistic variable V is in the second level. There is a conditional probability table (CPT) assigned to the node V, this CPT includes the probabilities $P(V|U_1, \cdots, U_n)$ of all possible instantiation of V and $U_1, \ldots, U_n$. In fact this directed graph also represents a fuzzy rule-base which is a multiple input and single output, the first level nodes represent the input variables, and the node in the second level means the output variable. So for any instantiation of input variables $U_1 = A_{r1}, \ldots, U_n = A_{rn}$ and output variable $V = B_r$, there is a corresponding fuzzy if-then rule:

$$R(r) \text{ If } (U_1 \text{ is } A_{r1}) \text{ and } \ldots (U_n \text{ is } A_{rn}) \text{ then } V \text{ is } B_r \text{ with factor } p_r; \tag{8}$$

where for each j, $\{A_{rj} \text{ for all } r\}$ is the fuzzy partition of the universe of discourse X_j of input variable U_j, and $\{B_r \text{ for all } r\}$ is the fuzzy partition of the universe of discourse Y of the output variable V. Here p_r is the conditional probability of the variable V given its parents:

$$p_r = P(V = B_r | U_1 = A_{r1}, \cdots, U_2 = A_{rn}) \tag{9}$$

Given the fuzzy partitions of the input space and output space, we provide an estimate method of p_r. Let there exists a training data set TD in which the ith element is a $n+1$-dim vector $[X_i\ y_i]$, and X_i is n-dim vector $(x_i^1, \ldots, x_i^n)$. So we have

$$p_r = \frac{\sum_i \tau_r(X_i) B_r(y_i)}{\sum_j \sum_i \tau_r(X_i) B_j(y_i)} \tag{10}$$

where $\{B_j\}$ is the collection of all fuzzy subsets in Y. And $[X_i\ y_i]$ is the element in the training data set, $\tau_r(X_i)$ is the firing level of the rth rule defined in eq.(2).

So we have given a new interpretation for the fuzzy if-then rule and its factor using a directed graph. The factor of each rule is the conditional probability of the consequent given the premise.

4 The Application in Time Series Prediction

We construct the fuzzy inference system with probability factor to predict a time series that is generated by the following Mackey-Glass (MG) time-delay differential equation.

$$\dot{x}(t) = \frac{0.2x(t-\tau)}{1+x^{10}(t-\tau)} - 0.1x(t) \tag{11}$$

This is a benchmark problem in the neural network and fuzzy modeling research communities [5]. The training data set and checking data set used in this experiment are shown in [3].

4.1 The Initial Model FISP

This system has four input variables and one output variable. We assume that the "and" operator is production and the domain interval of the ith input variable U_i is divided into K_i fuzzy sets labelled as $A_{1i}, A_{2i}, \ldots, A_{K_i i}$ for $i = 1, 2, 3, 4$, here let $K_i = 3$. Then the 4-dim input space is divided into $3^4 = 81$ fuzzy subspaces:

$$(A_{j_1 1}, A_{j_2 2}, A_{j_3 3}, A_{j_4 4}),\ j_i = 1, 2, 3; i = 1, 2, 3, 4.$$

And the domain interval of the output variable V is divided into 3 fuzzy sets labelled as B_1, B_2, B_3. The gauss-shaped fuzzy sets $A_{j_i i}$ and B_i are adopted:

$$\mu_{A_{j_i i}}(x) = \exp\frac{(x-a_{j_i i})^2}{-2\sigma_{j_i i}^2}, \quad \mu_{A_i}(y) = \exp\frac{(x-a_i)^2}{-2\sigma_i^2}.$$

We assume that all initial fuzzy partitions are even partitions. After using 500 data values to compute the conditional probability of each rule, for each $i = 1, 2, 3$ considering all rules whose consequents involve the fuzzy set B_i, we select 2 rules whose conditional probabilities are the largest to construct the final fuzzy rule-base. So the final fuzzy rule-base has 6 rules whose conditional probabilities are larger. Then we use this fuzzy rule-base to reason, the prediction result is shown in Fig.2. This figure shows that the fuzzy inference system with probability factor can memorize the shape of the data set, and can predict the changing tendency of data values with time.

It is noticeable that the process of selecting the rules whose conditional probabilities are enough large is necessary. Fig. 2 illustrates the prediction output of the FISP which includes all possible rules (the total number is $3^5 = 243$), it's clear that the performance is bad.

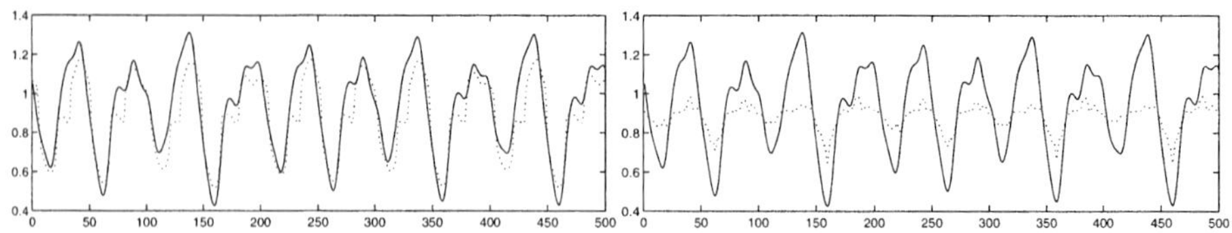

Fig. 2. The left figure shows that the prediction result of FISP which includes 6 rules without learning process. The right figure shows that the prediction result of FISP which includes all possible rules without learning process. The solid line is the expected output, the doted line is the prediction output

4.2 Learning Process of FISP

In order to improve the prediction precision further, we will adjust the parameters (a, σ) which determine the fuzzy partitions of the input and output spaces. Here we take the quasi-newton optimization technique.

Define the least square error function:

$$E = \sum_{i}^{500} \frac{(\overline{y}_i - y_i)^2}{2} \tag{12}$$

where $\overline{y}_i$ is the predicted output of the inference system, and y_i is the expected output in the training data set.

Of the methods that use gradient information, the most favored are the quasi-Newton methods. Because in each iteration the structure of the fuzzy rule-base changes, the gradient information of E can not be supplied analytically, we derive the partial derivatives using a numerical differentiation method via finite differences. This involves perturbing each of the design parameters (a, σ) in turn and calculating the rate of change in the objective function. After 70 iteration,

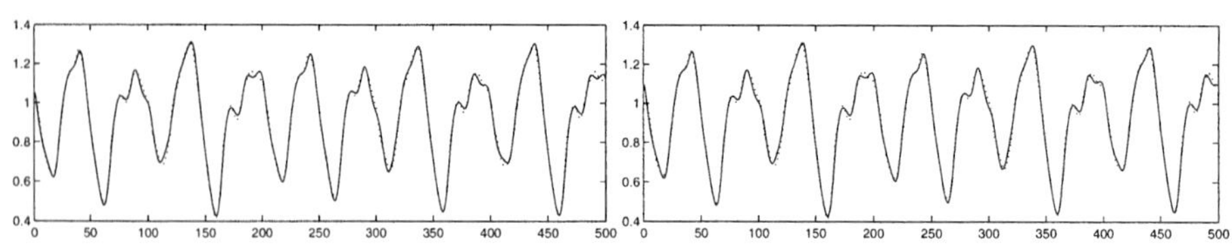

Fig. 3. Comparison of the prediction value of the final model and the expected value using the training (left figure) and testing (right figure) data. The solid line is the expected output, and the doted line is the prediction output of the final model

we get the desired performance, Fig. 3 shows the prediction result, it is hardly to distinguish the difference of the predicted output and the expected output.

5 Conclusions

In this paper we discuss the inner relationship between the body of the fuzzy rule and its associated factor. The factor of a fuzzy rule is interpreted as the conditional probability of the consequent given the premise. In order to compute the probability factor in this kind of fuzzy inference system, a computing method is given in this paper.

Acknowledgements

This work has been supported by Natural Science Foundation of Zhejiang Province, China Postdoctoral Science Foundation (No. 2003034514), Department of Education of Zhejiang Province (No. 20040115), National Natural Science Foundation of China (60475025).

References

1. D. Dubois and H. Prade, "Random sets and fuzzy interval analysis", *Fuzzy Sets and Systems*, Vol. 42, pp. 87–101, 1991.
2. H. T. Nguyen, "Fuzzy sets and probability", *Fuzzy Sets and Systems*, Vol. 90, pp. 129–132, 1997.
3. Jiacheng Zheng, Yongchuan Tang, "Fuzzy Modeling Incorporated with Fuzzy DS Theory and Fuzzy Naive Bayes", *Lectuer Notes in Artificial Intelligence*, Vol. 3339,pp. 816–827, 2004.
4. J.A. Drakopolulos, "Probabilities, possibilities, and fuzzy sets", *Fuzzy Sets and Systems*, Vol.75, pp. 1–15, 1995.
5. M. Russo, "Genetic fuzzy learning", *IEEE transactions on evolutionary computation*, Vol. 4, No. 3, pp. 259-273, September 2000.
6. Kuhu Pal (nee Dutta) and Nikhil R. Pal, "Learning of rule importance for fuzzy controllers to deal with inconsistent rules and for rule elimination", *Control and Cybernetics*, Vol. 27, No. 4, pp. 521–543, 1998.
7. Ronald R. Yager,Dimitar P. Filev, "Including Probabilistic Uncertainty in Fuzzy Logic Controller Modeling Using Dempster-Shafer Theory", *IEEE transactions on systems, man and cybernetics*, Vol. 25, No. 8, pp. 1221–1230, Augest 1995.
8. Sylvia Fruhwirth-Schnattter, "On fuzzy bayesian inference", *Fuzzy Sets and Systems*, Vol. 60, pp. 41–58, 1993.
9. R. Viertl, "Is it necessary to develop a fuzzy Bayesian inference? " in: R. Viertl (Ed.), *Probability and Bayesian Statistics* (Plenum Publishing Company, New York, 1987) pp. 471-475.
10. D. S. Yeung, E.C.C. Tsang, " Weighted fuzzy production rules", *Fuzzy Sets and Systems*, Vol. 88, pp. 299–313, 1997.
11. L.A.Zadeh, "Probability measures of fuzzy events", *J.Math. Analysis and Appl.*, Vol. 10, pp.421–427, 1968.

Interactive Semantic-Based Visualization Environment for Traditional Chinese Medicine Information*

Yuxin Mao[1], Zhaohui Wu[1], Zhao Xu[1], Huajun Chen[1], and Yumeng Ye[2]

[1] Grid Computing Lab, College of Computer Science, Zhejiang University, Hangzhou 310027, China

[2] Zhejiang Mobile Communication CO., LTD. Hangzhou Branch, China

{maoyx, wzh, xuzhao, huajunsir}@zju.edu.cn

Abstract. Vast amount of Traditional Chinese Medicine (TCM) information has been generated across the Web nowadays. Semantic Web opens a promising opportunity for us to share Web TCM information by standardizing the protocols for metadata exchange. To fulfill its long-term goal, we need to build universal and intelligent clients for end-users to retrieve and manage useful information based on semantics and services. In this paper, we propose a set of design principles for such an intelligent information client and describe a novel semantics-based information browser, Semantic Browser, to resolve the problem of sharing and managing large-scale information towards data-intensive fields like TCM.

1 Motivation

Traditional Chinese Medicine (TCM) is a very huge and complex system of medicine knowledge, most of which is human experience from generation to generation. At the same time, thousands of scientific studies that support traditional Chinese medical treatments are published yearly. Due to the rapid development of Web and information technology, innumerable disparate isolated medical databases have been developed in the field of TCM [1] across the Web nowadays. Manifold and decentralization of the Web raise new challenges for Web clients to share and manage information effectively. Semantic Web [2] provides a common framework that allows information resources to be shared and reused across the Web. It has opened a promising opportunity for us to retrieve and share large-scale information in a distributed environment by standardizing the protocols for metadata exchange. To fulfill this long-term goal, we need to build an intelligent environment for end-users to make use of large-scale and heterogeneous information. In this paper, we indicate a series of design principles for such an environment and propose a novel semantic-based Web information client, called Semantic Browser [3][4], oriented data-intensive fields like TCM.

* The work is supported by China 973 fundamental research and development project: The research on application of semantic grid on the knowledge sharing and service of Traditional Chinese Medicine; Intel / University Sponsored Research Program: DartGrid: Building an Information Grid for Traditional Chinese Medicine; and China 211 core project: Network-based Intelligence and Graphics.

Y. Zhang et al. (Eds.): APWeb 2005, LNCS 3399, pp. 950–959, 2005.

A lot of works has been done for sharing and exploiting distributed Web information on the client-side and semantics has been used broadly in organizing and integrating information. Haystack [13] is an RDF based individual information management tool, which aims to enable users to define whichever arrangements of, connections between, and views of Web information they find most effective. However, the way it explores and annotates Web pages makes Haystack not differ from traditional Web browsers very much in essence. Protégé [5] is an ontology development and knowledge acquisition environment with a graphical user interface and various ontology-based plugins. The server mode of Protégé supports multiple users working simultaneously and users can remotely browse and edit ontologies in Protégé, but it's difficult to integrate distributed information resources into the Protégé server dynamically and the form-based interface is not intuitive for exploration of information. OntoRama [11] is a prototype ontology browser, which takes RDF/XML as input format and models ontology as a configurable graph. However, the functionalities of OntoRama are restricted to browsing and querying is not supported yet.

In this paper, we propose a set of principles for designing an intelligent and interactive information client and describe a novel semantic-based information client, called Semantic Browser, to resolve the problem of sharing and managing large-scale Web information towards data-intensive fields like TCM.

2 Traditional Chinese Medicine Information

TCM is a large-scale information system and has its own knowledge structure with a set of special and complex disciplines and concepts, so when constructing Web client for sharing and managing TCM information resources, we should consider the characteristics of the domain well. However, most of the existent researches and applications in this area fail to domain requirements.

2.1 TCM Information Structure

As a medical science that embodies Chinese culture and philosophical principles, TCM has its own particular information structure. With the rapidly growing popularity of computers and the development of the Web, most TCM information has been organized into information bases.

Definition 2.1 (*Information Base*). Information Base is a container of structured or semi-structured information, which can be processed by computers to some extent. Databases, knowledge bases and Web pages all can be categorized as Information Base.

There are so many concepts in the field of TCM and each may be related to innumerable individuals. The relations between these concepts and individuals compose a complex network and even sophisticated TCM doctors cannot understand them well. A TCM concept or relation may refer to several information bases at the same time. However, within different genres or regions, the same concept may be represented by totally different terms in different information bases. For example, many **Chinese medical formulas** are retrieved from ancient literatures or synthesized

medical formulas are retrieved from ancient literatures or synthesized from **single flavor drugs** in laboratories yearly in China. The information about those formulas can be stored in databases of different institutions. In database **A**, the title of **Chinese medical formula** is *formula name* and in database **B**, the title may be *Chinese medical formula name*. When end-users query information about **Chinese medical formulas** that can treat specific diseases in **A**, computer programs cannot link to **B** automatically, as they are two physically independent information resources, though the information in the two databases refers to the same concept.

2.2 Web Semantics

We introduce semantics to resolve the problems above. RDF(S) is the basic framework for the Semantic Web and we can use RDF(S) to integrate distributed and heterogeneous information bases in the Web environment. We propose a blueprint of architecture for semantic-based Web applications in figure 1.

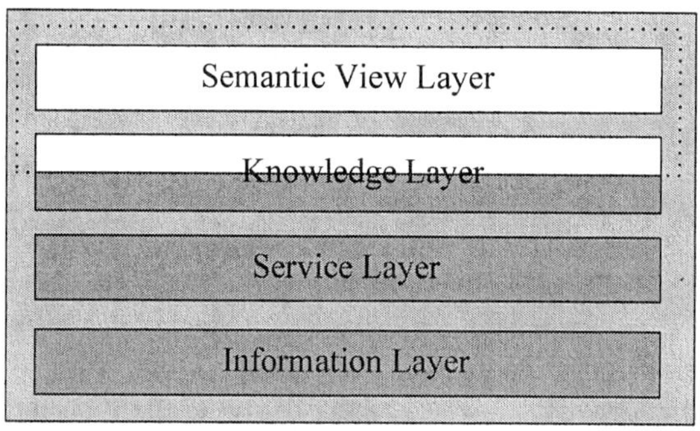

Fig. 1. The architecture for semantic-based Web applications

1) Information bases such as TCM databases compose the **Information Layer**.
2) The **Service Layer** publishes various Web / Grid services.
3) The **Knowledge Layer** embodies well-defined semantics like Web ontologies, which function as a mediator between clients and services.
4) The **Semantic View Layer** is dynamically constructed by Web clients and provides end-users with intelligent interactions.

We have taken an important step in abstracting semantic information about TCM information bases and extract ontologies from vast amount of original TCM information. We classify various TCM concepts into eight top classes and each can be subdivided into several sub-classes. The inherited relations between TCM concepts form a class hierarchy tree about TCM knowledge (see figure 2).

We can use semantic links (URI [2]) to organize complex relations within semantic information as intuitive relational graphs, which are so called **Semantic Graphs**. We herein give the generic definition of semantic graph as follow:

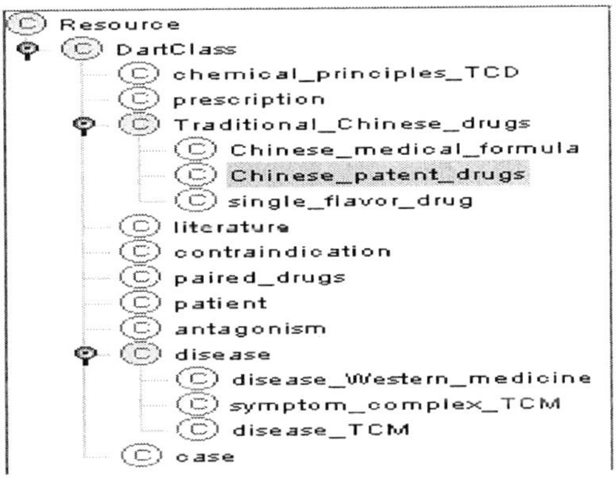

Fig. 2. The class hierarchy tree of TCM knowledge

Definition 2.2 (*Semantic Graph*)**.** A generic semantic graph is defined by the following items: (1) an acyclic relational graph with a central concept or individual of semantic information is a semantic graph; (2) nodes labeled with a semantic link stand for concepts or individuals and arcs stand for properties in a semantic graph. A set of <arc, node> pairs with a set of inter-operations constitute a semantic graph; (3) two joint parallel semantic graphs with no cross also constitute a semantic graph.

Therefore, we can represent the complex relational network of TCM semantic information as a class hierarchy tree and a set of semantic graphs. The TCM ontology is developed by Protégé [5] as RDF(S) and promoted to be Unified Traditional Chinese Medical Language System (UTCML) [1].

2.3 Information Integration

We can dynamically create **Semantic Mappings** between semantics of ontologies and distributed information bases. The RDF model is very directly connected with the schemata of relational databases [6] (see figure 3).

Definition 2.3 (*Semantic Mapping*) The following items define a generic semantic mapping with databases:

(1) $\mathrm{M}_{ci}(Table_1, Table_2 \cdots, Table_n) = Class_i$;

(2) $\mathrm{M}_{pij}(Field_{i1}, Field_{i2} \cdots, Field_{in}) = property_j$;

(3) $\mathrm{M}_i = \langle \mathrm{M}_{ci}, \mathrm{M}_{pi1}, \mathrm{M}_{pi2} \cdots, \mathrm{M}_{pim} \rangle$. M_i is a semantic mapping.

(4) A record in $Table_i$ can be mapped to a direct instance of $Class_i$ by M_i .

By creating semantic mappings through Semantic Registration, database resources can dynamically join a virtual organization [7]. Other kinds of information bases can be mapped to semantic information in similar way. In this way, distributed and heterogeneous information bases are dynamically integrated and we can construct an effective and intuitive semantic view [8](see figure 4) based on various services with large-scale information bases for end-users.

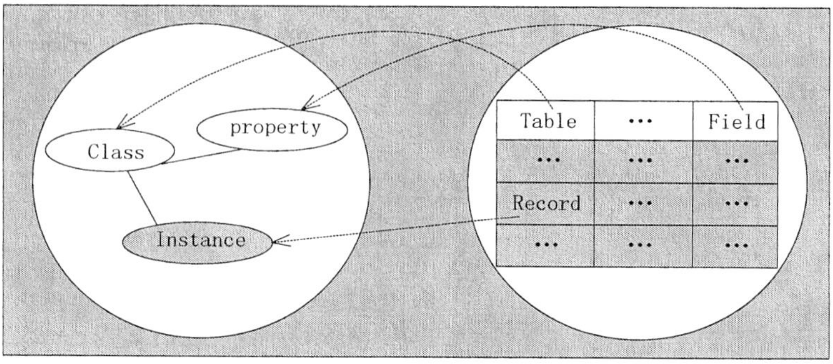

Fig. 3. The semantic mapping between databases and semantics

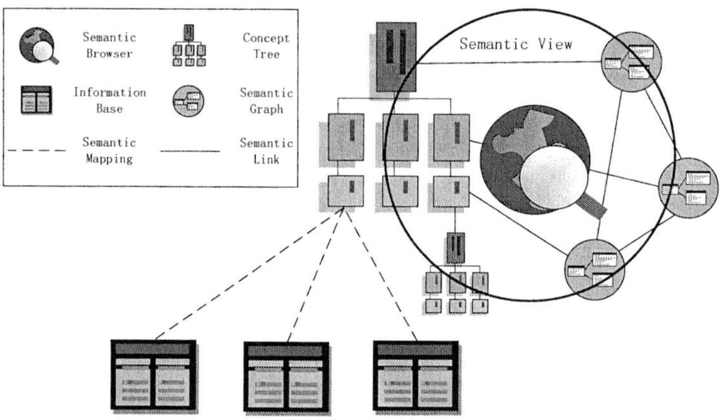

Fig. 4. Integrating distributed information bases with semantics

3 Semantic-Based Visualization Environment

Semantics eliminates the inconsistency of information resources and distributed information bases join together as a virtual organization at Semantic Layer. However we still need a semantic-based universal and visual environment for end-users to retrieve and manage large-scale information and the status of clients is shown as the frame with dotted line border in figure 1. The semantic-based clients will provide end-users with a series of intelligent and effective interactions.

3.1 Design Principles

Here we just propose several basic principles for designing and implementing such a semantic-based Web information client.

Extendable Principle. As a service-based information system, the client accesses various Web services or Grid services to provide high-level operations. Hence it should not be too heavyweight but flexible and alterable on demand. Services of a virtual organization may be delivered and updated at times, but it's unpractical to change the structure of the client frequently according to services. So clients should have the built-in support for extending its functionalities according to the change of services without the main structure being modified.

Visualization Principle. Unlike HTML contents, which are readable for human being, semantic information aims at machine processing. The structure of semantic information is unsuitable for users to read directly. To give end-users an intuitive and universal view on semantic information, the client should provide a mechanism to visualize semantic information as semantic graphs.

Limitation Principle. For large-scale knowledge systems like TCM, the corresponding domain ontologies are huge in most cases. However, the acceptability of end-users is limited and they can't catch anything fed back during once, so the semantic information returned from services should be restricted to some bound.

There are two kinds of semantic links in semantic information. If a resource (a unique concept or individual in semantic information) can be related to another resource with no more than two properties, there is a **Heavy Semantic Link** between these two resources. If a resource cannot be related to another resource within two properties, there is a **Weak Semantic Link** between these two resources.

Clients should represent information with more strong semantic links and discard that with too many weak semantic links. When the scale of semantic information returned from services is terrifically huge, the structure of corresponding semantic graph will get so complex that a lot of nodes and arcs will overlap with each other in the user area of the client, so the design should think much of graph layouts.

Interactive Principle. Besides visualizing semantic information, end-users need more interactions such as querying to gain useful information from distributed information bases, so the semantic graphs visualized by clients should provide end-users with high-level interactions and each element in the graph can interact with users to assist them managing and sharing information.

3.2 Semantic Browser

According to the principles before-mentioned, we implemented a novel semantic-based information browser, Semantic Browser (see figure 5) to resolve the problem of representing and managing large-scale information towards information-intensive field like TCM. Semantic Browser manipulates distributed information bases at Semantic Layer and construct a semantic view for end-users with a series of semantic-based interactions. Semantic Browser is a lightweight client, which accesses the Grid services [9] of DartGrid [10].

According to the Extendable Principle, we develop various semantic plugins, which are independent and optional functional modules in Semantic Browser. A semantic plugin usually contains some Grid Service stubs and remotely accesses a specific category of Grid Services. Semantic Browser reserves slots for extended plugins accessing possible services in the future. This extendable plugin mechanism allows Semantic Browser to extend its functionalities according to the change by adding and updating new plugins, without the basic structure of system being modified.

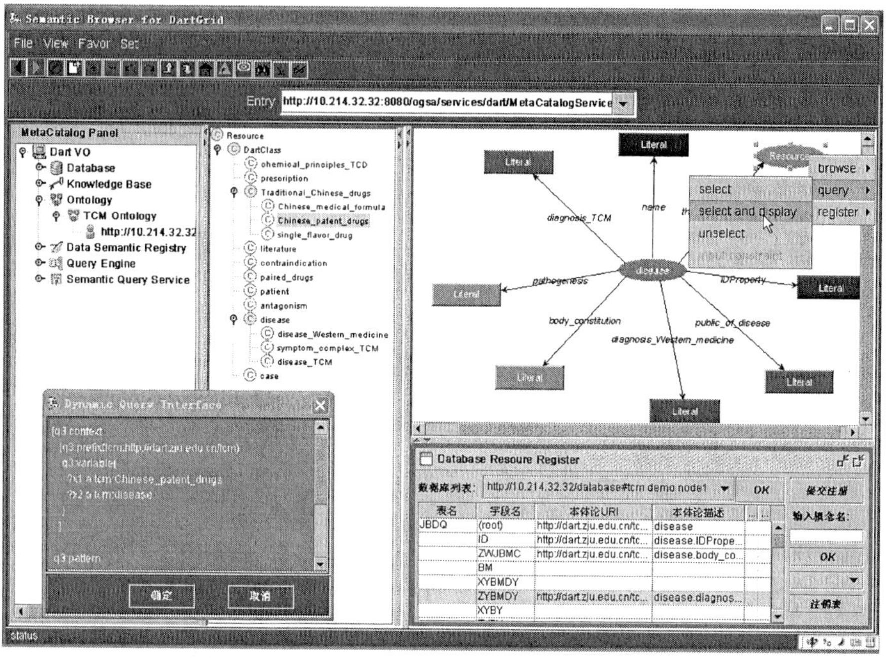

Fig. 5. A screen shot of Semantic Browser

```
SGL ::= '<SGL>' namespacelist,graph* '</SGL>'
graph ::= '<graph' idAttr depthAttr '>' subgraph* '</graph>'
subgraph ::= '<subgraph' idAttr typeAttr weightAttr'>' root,
(arc, node | subgraph)* '</subgraph>'
root ::= '<root' idAttr resourceAttr localnameAttr labelAttr
radiusAttr? SonAttr? AngleAttr? SpaceAttr? DisplayAttr? '>'
'</root>'
arc ::= '<arc' idAttr resourceAttr directionAttr '>' '</arc>'
node ::= '<node' idAttr ((resourceAttr localnameAttr labelAttr)
| (literalAttr operatorAttr inputAttr)) angleAttr? spaceAttr?
DisplayAttr?'>' '</node>'
```

Fig. 6. A part of SGL definition

According to the Visualization Principle, Semantic Browser visualizes semantic information as intuitive Semantic Graphs. A semantic graph in Semantic Browser is represented and comprised by operational vectographic components in Semantic Browser. In order to get a better effect of visualization, we develop an XML-based visual graph language for semantic information, Semantic Graph Language (SGL) [3] and the radial layout algorithm is implemented inside SGL. Unlike common visual graph languages or graph exchange languages, SGL takes semantics into account and treats them as part of graph elements (see figure 6). Semantic Browser has the built-in support for converting various formats of semantic information into SGL.

Browsing operation in Semantic Browser is defined as Semantic Browsing, which is to visualize concepts with their instances that are explicitly described and the relationships among them as semantic graphs and assist users to browse semantic information through semantic links.

According to the Limitation Principle, Semantic Browser slices semantic information according to the granularity of semantics and adopts the radial layout algorithm [11] to arrange the global layout of a semantic graph by each slice of semantic information, to avoid overlapping of nodes and arcs.

According to the Interactive Principle, vectographic components of semantic graphs provide end-users with a series of semantic interactions including Semantic Registration and Semantic Query in a visual environment. In Semantic Browser, end-users can interact with Grid services to retrieve semantic information through the URI rather than querying in local information bases directly.

```
q3:query
  q3:pattern [
      a  tcm: Chinese_medical_formula;
      tcm:name     [];
      tcm: usage_and_dosage [];
      tcm: composition [];
      tcm:treat [ a  tcm: disease ;
              tcm:name "influenza";
              tcm: pathogenesis [];
              tcm: symptom_complex []
            ]
  ].
```

Fig. 7. Querying statements about a Chinese medical formula, which can treat influenza

Table 1. Mapping from Q3 to SGL and relevant operations

Q3 BNF	*Item Example*	*SGL Element*	*Mapping Operation*
operator	q3:query		
pattern	q3:pattern	sgl:graph	initialization
blank_node	[...]	sgl:subgraph	select
verb object	a tcm: Chinese_medical_formula	sgl:root	select and display
prop	tcm:name	sgl:arc	select / select and display
node	[ ]	sgl:node	select / select and display
literal	"influenza"	sgl:node	input constraint

To perform querying at the Semantic Layer, we develop a Semantic Query Language, Query3 (Q3) [12]. Every query in Q3 can be viewed as an OWL class definition; and query processing is reduced as computing instances satisfying the uerying concept definition. The set of statements in figure 7 is a Semantic Query about the **name**, **usage**, **dosage** and **composition** of a **Chinese medical formula**, which can attend **influenza**. The querying statements above can be visually constructed based on semantic graphs and there is a direct mapping from SGL to Q3 (see table 1).

Q3 statements can be generated dynamically in the Dynamic Query Interface (**DQI**, the floating panel in figure 5) of Semantic Browser, by visual mapping during the process of Semantic Browsing. The semantic graph components in Semantic Browser offer four mapping operations, "select", "select and display", "unselect" and "input constraint" (see figure 5). When end-users perform one of the operations at a graph component, a corresponding Q3 item will be automatically produced or updated in the **DQI**. By combining a group of sequential operations, a set of Semantic Query statements will be constructed automatically. The Semantic Query request is sent to the Semantic Query Service of DartGrid and the process of query dispatching and optimizing is packed by the service. Querying results are returned from the virtual organization as semantic information and displayed as semantic graphs.

4 A TCM Use Case

TCM researchers and doctors, who have known basic TCM knowledge, can gain valuable information by performing interactions in the visualization environment of Semantic Browser. Considering the following scenario: a TCM doctor wants to know the compositions of some new Chinese medical formulas for cough.

- First, the doctor can start with browsing the TCM ontology and extracts the top concepts through the Ontology Service as a class hierarchy tree.
- Next, he expands tree nodes to browse sub-classes until he finds the class, *Chinese_medical_formula*, which is related to hundreds of tables from distributed databases. The class and its properties are displayed as a semantic graph.
- During the process of Semantic Browsing, when the doctor performs one of the querying operations at a semantic graph node, a Q3 statement like [*tcm:treat a tcm:disease tcm:name "cough"*] will be automatically generated in the DQI.
- After submission, the Semantic Query Service dispatches the querying request among distributed databases. All information that exactly fits user' requirements will be returned as semantic information and displayed as semantic graphs.
- All properties of the class are displayed in a semantic graph. The compositions of the drug can be visualized as property values intuitively in the graph. If the doctor wants to know more about the composition *liquorices*, he can trace the property value node and a detailed semantic graph about *liquorices* will be displayed.

5 Conclusion

In this paper, we draw out the paradigm of an intelligent visual environment towards manipulating large-scale Web information and indicate a set of design principles. As an implementation to those principles, Semantic Browser dynamically constructs an interactive semantic view based on various Grid services for end-users to perform high-level interactions. In collaboration with the China Academy of Traditional Chinese Medicine, we have built a semantic-based information-sharing platform for TCM databases based on Semantic Browser and DartGrid, which involves tens of large databases from several institutions.

References

1. Xuezhong, Z., Zhaohui, W., Aining, Y. et al.: Ontology Development for Unified Traditional Chinese Medical Language System. Special issue "AIM in China" of the International journal of Artificial Intelligence in Medicine (2004)
2. Tim, B., James, H., Ora, L.: The Semantic Web. Scientific American (2001)
3. Yuxin, M., Zhaohui, W., Huajun, C.: Semantic Browser: an Intelligent Client for Dart-Grid. COMPUTATIONAL SCIENCE - ICCS 2004, PT 1, PROCEEDINGS LECTURE NOTES IN COMPUTER SCIENCE 3036: 470-473 (2004)
4. Yuxin, M., Zhaohui, W., Huajun, C.: SkyEyes: A semantic browser for the KB-Grid. GRID AND COOPERATIVE COMPUTING, PT 2 LECTURE NOTES IN COMPUTER SCIENCE 3033: 752-759 (2004)
5. Natalya, F. N., Michael, S., Stefan, D., Monica, C., Ray, W. F., Mark, A. M.: Creating Semantic Web Contents with Protege-2000. IEEE Intelligent Systems 16(2): 60-71 (2001)
6. Tim, B.: What the Semantic Web can represent. http://www.w3.org/DesignIssues/RDFnot.html
7. Ian, F., Carl, K., Steven, T.: The Anatomy of the Grid: Enabling Scalable Virtual Organizations. Int'l J. High-Performance Computing Applications (2001)
8. Zhaohui, W., Yuxin, M., Huajun, C.: Semantic View for Grid Services. Proceedings of the International Conference on Services Computing (2004) p 329-335
9. Steven, T., Carl, K., Ian, F. et al.: Open Grid Services Infrastructure (OGSI) Version 1.0. Global Grid Forum Draft Recommendation (2003)
10. Zhaohui, W., Huajun, C., Lican, H. et al.: Dart-InfoGrid: Towards an Information Grid Supporting Knowledge-based Information Sharing and Scalable Process Coordination. CNCC (2003)
11. Peter E., Nataliya R., Steve G.: OntoRama.: Browsing RDF Ontologies Using a Hyperbolic-style Browser. The First International Symposium on CyberWorlds, pp.405-411, Theory and Practices, IEEE press (2002)
12. Huajun, C., Zhaohui, W., Yuxin, M.: Q3: a Semantic Query Language for Dart Database Grid. GRID AND COOPERATIVE COMPUTING, LECTURE NOTES IN COMPUTER SCIENCE 3251: 372-380 (2004)
13. David, F. H., Dennis, Q., David, R. K.: User Interaction Experience for Semantic Web Information. The Twelfth International World Wide Web Conference (2003)

Components for Building Desktop-Application-Like Interface in Web Applications*

George Chang[1], Jung-Wei Hsieh[2], and Pedro Calixto[1]

[1] Kean University, Mathematics and Computer Science Department,
1000 Morris Avenue, Union N.J. 07083
gchang@kean.edu

[2] Parsons School of Design, Design and Technology,
10th Floor, 2W 13th Street,
New York, N.Y. 10011

Abstract. Web-based applications have become ubiquitous over the past few years. These applications rely on a simple document markup language called HTML. However, the click-and-link interface provide by HTML-based technology is too limited for building next generation highly interactive Web applications. Hence, we investigate a technique based on a highly interactive rich internet application approach for building desktop-application-like web applications. We discuss the design and architecture of our client and server components, show the efficient use of client, server, and network resources, and conduct server-side component performance evaluations. Usability, universality, reusability and usefulness of our components are our primary objectives. Desktop graphical user interface features such as drag-and-drop, image zoom-in, and folder navigation are now possible for building web-based applications using our components.

1 Introduction

Hypertext-style interface in Internet applications has been around since the inception of the World Wide Web (Web). What makes hypertext a reality is a standard Web language called Hypertext Markup Language (HTML). HTML brought the so-called *non-linear* navigation paradigm from science fiction stories and research laboratories into our daily lives.

The simplicity of HTML has captivated many skillful programmers and creative Web developers, enabling them to create websites of all sorts. Over the years, HTML has withstood many challenges and evolved with new features as the web technology advances at an astonishing pace. Today, HTML is still the predominant technology for website designs. These websites provide mostly

* Supported in part by the RTR 2004-2005 and SpF 2004 Research Grant from ORSP at Kean University.

Y. Zhang et al. (Eds.): APWeb 2005, LNCS 3399, pp. 960–971, 2005.

browseable-only contents with form interaction using Common Gateway Interface (CGI).

Dynamic Web content generation and interaction are achieved by using a database system as the backend data storage and retrieval system in conjunction with a client Web browser, and a Web server. The majority of these types of Internet applications are most used by the e-commerce and entertainment sectors. However, most of these more sophisticated interactive applications still provide only simple interactions such as product navigation, shopping cart storage, and form processing. More complex interaction is achieved by using Javascripts embedded in HTML or plug-ins.

While emerging Web technologies such as Web services and Semantic Web are gaining momentum, the click-and-link interface provided by HTML-based technology is too limited for building highly interactive applications that might someday utilize these emerging technologies. The original intent of HTML was for building hyperlink-style applications with simple interactions and not for highly interactive applications. This paper discusses the techniques used for creating highly-interactive graphical user interface (GUI) components for building desktop-application-like Web applications.

These components complement HTML-based technology. In fact, they integrate well together. Using these components we have built a highly interactive image retrieval Web application as a proof of concept. Our image application is easy to use because it has desktop-application-like GUI features such as folder navigation, icon representation of images, image zoom-in capability, and drag-and-drop functionalities.

The rest of this paper is organized as follows. Section 2 describes some background information and related work. Section 3 describes the component architecture and application design. Section 4 discusses the usability of our components and Section 5 concludes the paper.

2 Background

Displaying and manipulating high-resolution images across the Internet (via a web browser) becomes a daunting challenge due to the massive amounts of data that need to be transferred and the limitation of hypertext-style interface. Hence, providing a desktop-application-like interface for image manipulation and displaying is the primary challenge for web-based application designers.

There are several image file formats, research prototypes, and commercial systems capable of presenting an on-demand imagery delivery (zoom and pan) service over the Internet such as ER Mapper[1], Express Server[2], FlashPix[3], GIS Viewer[4], GridPix[5], TilePic[6], Zoomifyer[7], and ZoomView[8]. All these image formats and systems use variants of tiled-based, multi-resolution-tier method and pre-processed static images. However, all these systems provide view-only functionality and no highly-interactive, desktop-GUI-like environment. On-demand large image delivery with user specified region of interest[9], progressive on-demand with optimal tiling and compression[10], client-caching[10, 11], and server prefetching[11] have also been studied.

This paper discusses the results on the design and implementation of highly-interactive components for building a Web-based image application using Flash component technology. These components can address the shortcomings of previous works. Second, our components can achieve a desktop-application-like interface in the web browser. Third, our components can be extended to provide additional real-time interaction with images stored on the server. Lastly, our component can be used by web developers (non-programmers) easily.

The components that we have developed are client-side GUI components, which require the support of server-side components that we also have developed. Client component objectives are: desktop-application-like GUI, drag-and-drop capabilities, virtual desktop, on-demand image zoom-in, client side image caching, usable by non-programmers and deployable on multiple platforms. Server component objectives are: remote folder/icon management, on-demand image cropping, on-demand image resize and compression, server image caching, and deployable on multiple platforms.

3 Component and Application Design

We introduced four client-side GUI components that are commonly found in windows-based operating systems' GUI environment: Folder, Icon, ImagePane, and ProcessingStatus components.

- Folder component can be used for creating a special file that holds other files and folders (sub-folders) located in a remote server. It reveals its contents when opened and iconized when minimized.
- Icon component can be used for creating a small graphic image or object that points to a file, program, folder (minimized) or object in a remote server, and it responses to drag-and-drop mouse actions.
- ImagePane component can be used for creating an on-demand remote image retrieval and manipulation application. It supports region-of-interest (ROI) zoom-in.
- ProcessingStatus component can be used for status notification for a remote processing call.

Using these components we were able to build a prototype image retrieval web-application with a desktop-like environment called Web Desktop Environment (WDE). The system architecture, user interface, and server-cache management will be discussed in this section.

3.1 System Architecture

Our client components require the support of server-side components as shown in Figure 1. The client requests image, files and directories on demand; the server performs image processing, directory and file lookup requests sent from

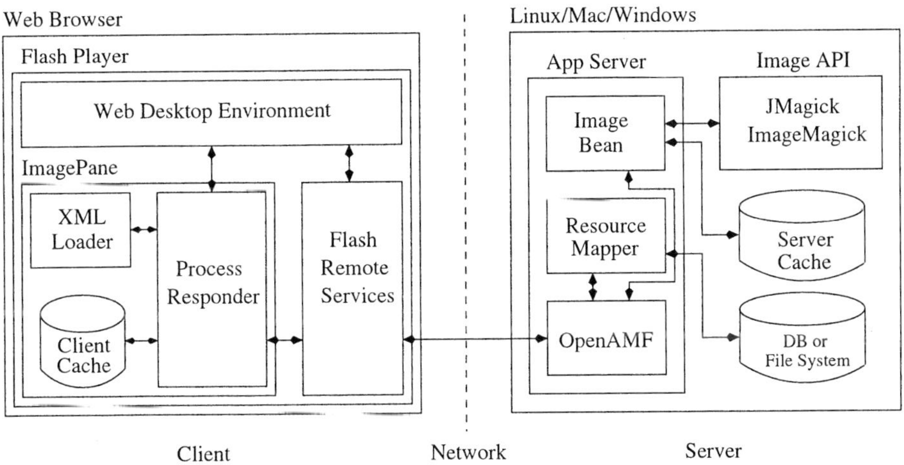

Fig. 1. Client and Server Components

Fig. 2. Four Components in Flash MX 2004

the client; the network is used to transfer the images and date between the server and client.

All four components are developed in Macromedia Flash MX 2004 using Actionscript 2.0. The components are packaged into a Macromedia Extension Package (MXP file) for distribution. Figure 2 illustrates what the web developers will see under their Flash environment after the MXP file is installed.

To use the components the developers just need to drag-and-drop the desired icon, as shown in Figure 2, into a Flash project and change some parameter settings with no programming involved. Once the Flash project is compiled and published, it becomes a Macromedia Flash File (SWF file) that can be linked from an HTML file. See Figure 3 and Figure 9 for screenshots of deployed components in action.

The server components as shown in Figure 1 is developed in Linux using J2SE 1.4.2 SDK, Tomcat 5.0.16, Open AMF 1.0CR5, JMagick and ImageMagick 5.5.6. It is also deployable on OS X and Windows. Open AMF is a free open-source alternative to Macromedias Java Flash Remoting Gateway that implements Flash remoting protocol Actionscript Message Format (AMF). The communication between the Flash Player and the OpenAMF is request-driven which is similar to Simple Object Access Protocol (SOAP). ImageMagick is a robust collection of tools and libraries for image manipulation in various formats. The Image Bean is responsible for making ImageMagick library calls through Java API provided by JMagick.

3.2 The User Interface

Windows-based GUI design was chosen for our prototype image application due to its universality and ease of use. Figure 3 is a screenshot of our Web Desktop Environment (WDE) taken directly from Mozilla Firefox browser. WDE was created using Folder, Icon, ImagePane and ProcessingStatus components that we have developed. WDE behaves like a window manager that is similar to GUI in Windows, Mac, and Linux operating systems. It handles graphical display elements (such as folder and icons), folder open and close actions, drag-and-drop of icon actions, and execution of applications.

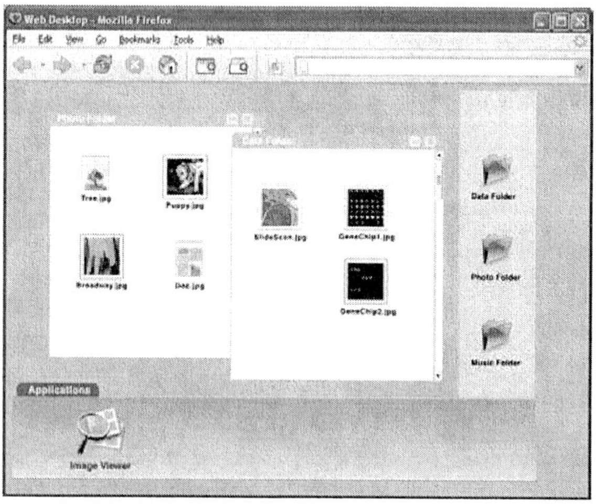

Fig. 3. Web Desktop Environment. Two windows represent two opened folders and Image Viewer Icon on the bottom is the image application icon

Folders and icons are graphical representation of folders and files stored on the remote server. The mapping between client folders to server directories and client icons to server files are handled by the Resource Mapper module. Double click on a folder triggers dynamic retrieval of folder content from the remote server as illustrated in the two opened windows in Figure 3. Drag-and-drop of an icon between folders triggers file organization updates on the server. Drag-and-drop of an icon onto a program icon causes the application represented by the program icon to be executed.

For example, if SlideScan.jpg icon in Figure 3 is drag-and-dropped onto the ImageViewer icon, the action will trigger ImageViewer (based on ImagePane component) to be dynamically downloaded from the server and executed with SlideScan.jpg (a 6.85 MB JPEG file, resolution: 3344x3344 pixels) as its input.

Figure 9 shows six screenshots that illustrate zoom-in interactions between the user client component (ImageViewer), and server component. The ImageViewer frame size in the browser was set to 500x500 (pixels).

Figure 9(a) illustrates the initial screen after the drag-and-drop of SlideScan.jpg icon onto the ImageViewer. First, the ImagePane component is dynamically downloaded from the application server (web server) to the web browser and executed by the Flash Player. The processing status will appear first while the following series of ImagePane component initialization steps are being performed:

1. The XML Loader module retrieves from the server and processes the XML file that contains the metadata about the image. The file contains the following information: image filename, original width, and original height as illustrated in Figure 4.
2. The Flash Remote Services module sends a request to the server for the initial image to be displayed in the ImagePane. Parameters sent to the server include: image name, ImagePane frame size (width and height of the frame within the browser where the image will be displayed).
3. The Process Responder module retrieves the image and display in the ImagePane after the server completes the processing from request sent by the Remote Services in step 2.

```
<?xml version="1.0"?>
<image>
  <imageFilename>
    /dir/images/imagename.jpg
  </imageFilename>
  <width>2048</width>
  <height>1536</height>
</image>
```

Fig. 4. Sample image metadata XML file

Figure 9(b) illustrates the screenshot after the initial image is loaded in the ImagePane. The left hand side of the image is the actual tissue slide scan image (about 50KB). The right hand side is a thumbnail panel for quick navigation.

Figure 9(c) illustrates a zoom-in action in progress. To specify a region of interest (ROI), the user has to left-mouse-click-and-drag to create a white rectangular mask as shown in Figure 9(c). As soon as the left-mouse-button is released, a request is sent to the server with following parameters: image name, ImagePane frame size, coordinates of the ROI. A processing status will appear and thumbnail panel updates as shown in Figure 9(d).

The following steps will be performed by the server component upon receiving of the ROI parameters from the client:

1. Crop the ROI from the original image.
2. Resize the cropped image from step 1 to the ImagePane frame size.
3. Compress resized image from step 2 with 75% JPEG compression level.
4. Save the cropped-resized-compressed image in the web server.
5. Return the URL that links to the saved image from step 4 back to the client and to be used by the Process Responder module.

Figure 9(e) illustrates the screenshot after the ROI from 5(c) has been retrieved from the web server by the Process Responder. Figure 9(f) illustrates the screenshot after another zoom-in action is requested.

3.3 Server-Side Cache Management

Image processing algorithms such as image cropping and resizing are time consuming processes for large images (see Performance Evaluation section). However, it is reasonable to assume that a particular ROI will be requested by the same or different users for more than once. Therefore, we developed an approximate caching algorithm that utilizes cached images to speed-up retrieval time based on the locality of ROI requests.

To better understand the overall idea of this caching algorithm the following pseudocode illustrates its major steps. This caching algorithm uses a hash-based indexing structure to ensure constant search time. It is important to mention that the minimum overlapping threshold was pre-specified at 80%.

```
given (x, y) as the starting point of the requested ROI
foreach (x', y') within 5% of ROI's width and height from (x, y)
    foreach cached image (IMG) under (x', y')
        if overlapping area of IMG and ROI ≥ minimum threshold
            return IMG's URL
save ROI in the cache
```

This approximation algorithm run in O(1/100 x ROI width x ROI height). Using this caching algorithm, time consuming ROI imaging processing steps are eliminated after the initial retrieval. Server side cache is managed by using least recently used (LRU) image queue when the size of overall storage used for caching gets too large.

4 Performance Evaluation

In order to know how well our server components can perform, we conducted responsiveness and stress tests. We evaluated the server performance under four image sizes as listed in Table 1 and shown in Figure 5. The hardware used for the experiments is a Pentium 4 2.4GHz with 512MB RAM running Linux 2.4 Kernel and with 1GB of swap space. Unfortunately, we were unable to compare our system with others due to the fact that previous works only provide viewing

Table 1. JPEG image information

No.	*Dimension(WxH)*	*Size*
1	2270 x 1704	1.40 MB
2	2048 x 3072	3.50 MB
3	3344 x 3344	6.85 MB
4	5000 x 4333	28.00 MB

only functionality on pre-processed static images, while ours is more about real-time interactivity on dynamic processing of images.

The first experiment is designed to investigate the effect of different ROI sizes on the server processing time. The image pane size is set to 500x500 pixels. ROI being used to conduct the experiment is an N x N (pixel) square at a random location (x, y) within the target image. The details of how our server component processes the request are described in the previous section. The experiment is essentially a simulation of client requests on 10 different NxN ROI sizes from 100x100 to 1000x1000 at 100 increments. The average server processing time for 20 requests on each of the 10 ROI sizes is shown in Figure 6.

The second experiment involves random ROI sizes at a random location (x, y) within the target image. The random ROI size (width and height) is constrained within seven different ranges. The seven ranges are classified by the maximum ROIs width and height in respect to the target image's width and height. Ranges are 1/32 (3.13%), 1/16 (6.25%), 1/8 (12.5%), 1/4 (25%), 1/3 (33.33%), 1/2 (50%), and 1/1 (100%) of the target images width and height. One hundred requests for each of the seven ranges are performed. The average processing time for each range on four images is shown in Figure 7.

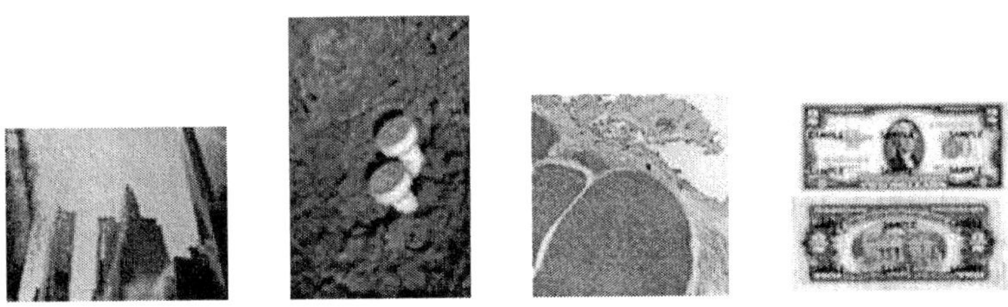

Fig. 5. Four JPEG images of various dimensions and sizes

The last experiment was to investigate the effect of concurrent requests on the server processing time. In this experiment a fixed size ROI (400x400) at a random location (x, y) within the target image was used. Figure 8 shows the effect of up to fourteen concurrent requests on the average processing time for all four images.

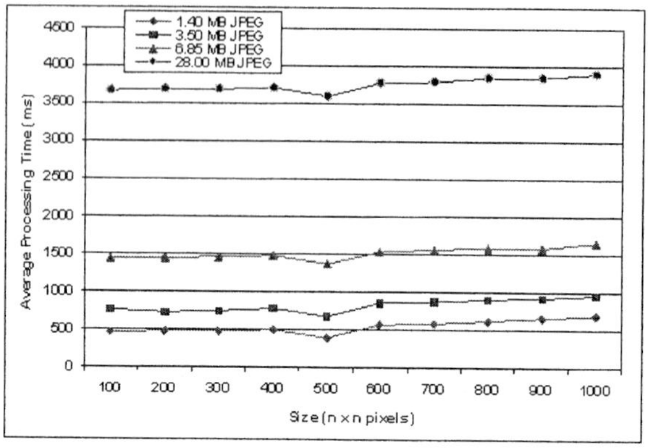

Fig. 6. The effect of ROI sizes on the image processing time

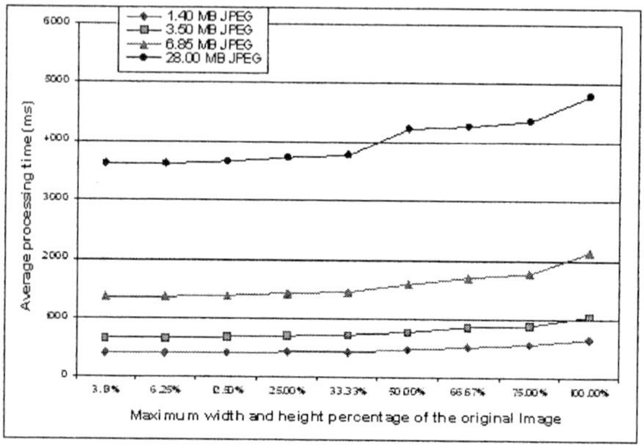

Fig. 7. The effect of range restricted random ROI on the processing time

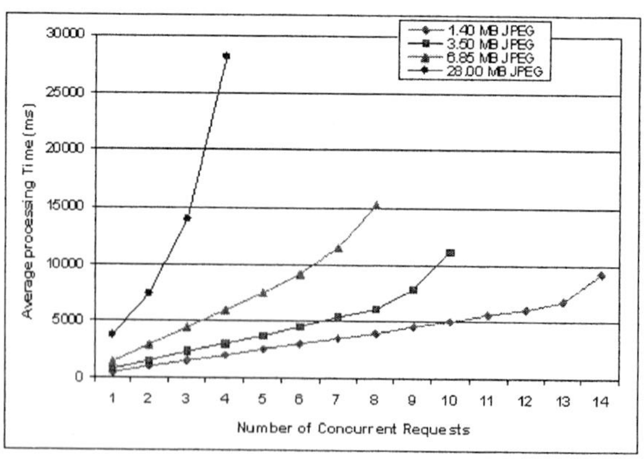

Fig. 8. The effect of concurrent ROI requests on the processing time

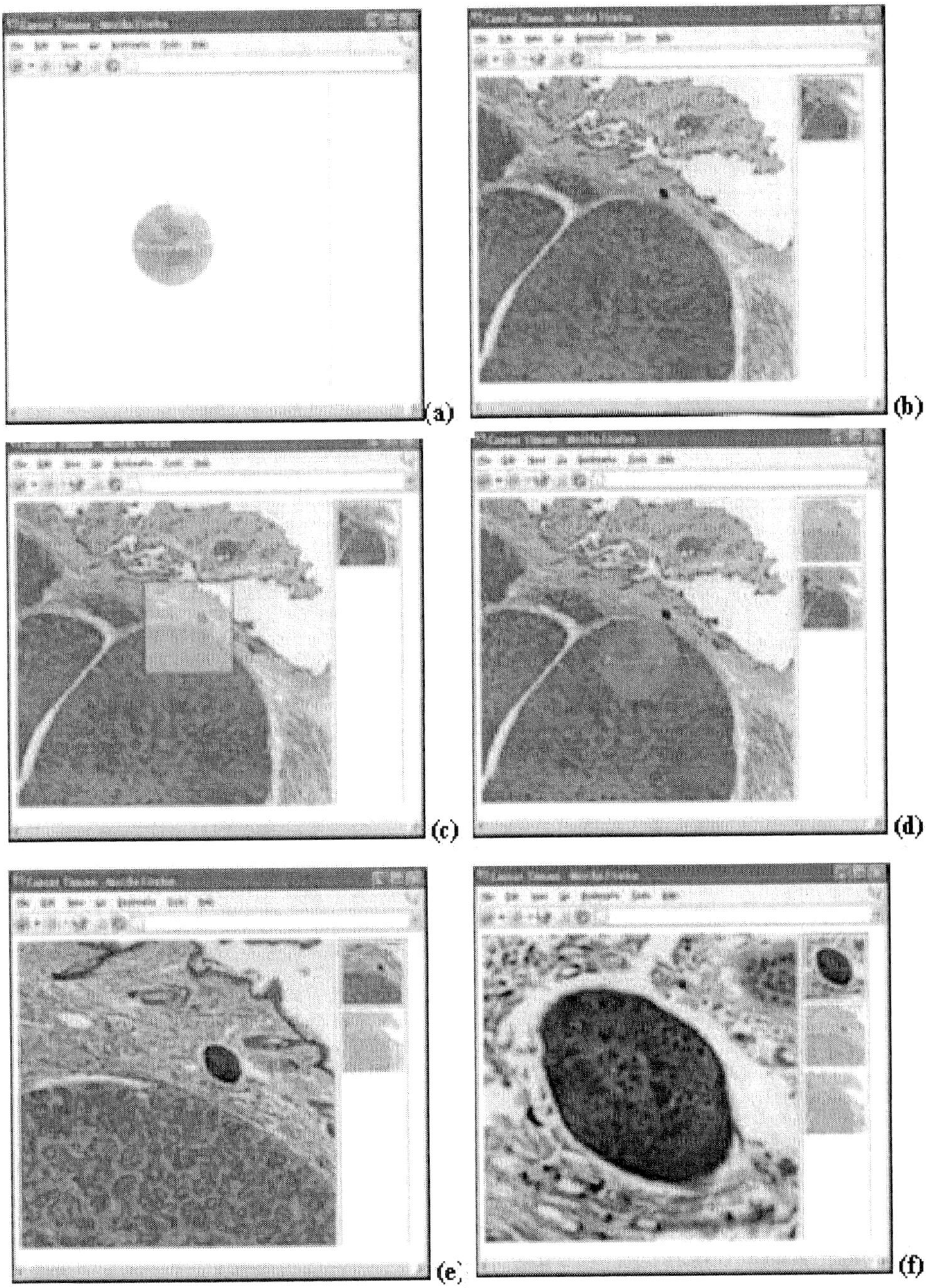

Fig. 9. Image retrieval interaction screenshots. (a) initial loading, (b) after loading, (c) specify ROI, (d) waiting for ROI from the server, (e) ROI returned, and (f) another zoom-in operation performed

5 Discussion

One of our primary objectives is to minimize the resources needed and reduce the response time of our components. Intelligent image data delivery ensures that only the ROI portion of an image that fits within the defined display area is delivered. In this case, ROI is extracted from the original image using ImageMagick crop library routine, followed by a resize routine to ensure that ROI fits within ImagePane frame size (500x500), then a 75% JPEG compression level further reduced the image size. This typically reduces the ROI image to less then 50KB without any detectable image detail loss on the screen and yet it is small in size for delivery over the Internet.

Efficient client side image caching ensures that image data will never be delivered twice. Desired image can be quickly retrieved and displayed in the ImagePane by left-mouse-click on the thumbnail images in the thumbnail panel. Thumbnail panel automatically rearrange the thumbnails as zoom in/out operations are being performed. Server-side image caching ensures that the same or approximate ROI will never be processed twice.

Based on our four test images, the size of ROI does not have much effect on the processing time when the width and height of ROI are both less then 33% of the target image's width and height (see Figure 7). Since ROI tends to be small comparing to the original image, therefore the longer processing time associated with larger ROI sizes will not be an issue.

The results of the concurrent processing benchmark in Figure 8 shows a linear relationship between increases in the number of concurrent requests and increase in the average processing time. This trend holds for as long as the workload fits within the main memory. In the absence of network connectivity issue, a sharp increase in the average processing time indicates the utilization of virtual memory. At which point concurrent processing is then suspended due to the unpredictability of thrashing on the average processing time. The results indicate that 5-10 concurrent users on small/medium size images and only 1-2 concurrent users on large image is possible based on our server hardware setup.

Lastly, Flash platform was chosen due to its highly efficient use of graphic and sound elements produces smaller, more self-contained files than Java applets, thus faster downloading and loading is achieved. As of September 2004, flash player has a market penetration of 98.2% (512.8 million users) [12].

6 Conclusions

Based on the performance statistic of this image delivery system, our goal of providing reusable imaging components for building an on-demand, real-time, highly-interactive, desktop-application-like, and web-based image application has been achieved. Leveraging the enormous install base of Flash Player in web browsers, our client component is developed as a Flash component. Hence, it can be independently deployed and distributed to the web application developers.

Since the supporting server component is written in Java, it can also be deployed in many platforms.

As we have envisioned, our components eliminated hypertext style navigation and in favor of an interface that has the look and feel of a desktop application. In summary, what set our image component apart from those mentioned in previous works are: (1) real-time on-demand interaction and (2) a desktop-application-like interface. Performance is inversely proportional to server-request load, hence issues related to server-side performance improvement are of our future interests.

Future work will include: (1) tile-based client and server-side caching, (2) extend the client platform to include wireless mobile devices, (3) more features such as image filtering and transformation implemented, (4) user session and workflow management, and (5) research other methods to improve the performance of the server components.

References

1. Earth Resource Mapping: http://www.ermapper.com/ (2004)
2. Lizard Tech: http://www.ermapper.com/ (2004)
3. The Digital Imaging Group: http://digitalimaging.com/ (2004)
4. UC Berkeley Digital Library Project: GIS Viewer: http://dlp.cs.berkeley.edu/gis/ (2004)
5. Asami, S., Patterson, D.: GridPix: Presenting large image files over the internet. Technical report, Report No. UCB/CSD-00-1099, May 2000, Computer Science Division, EECS, University of California at Berkeley, CA 94720-1776 (2000)
6. Anderson-Lee, J., Wilensky, R.: Tilepic: A file format for tiled hierarchical data. In: Proceedings of the JCDL, Roanoke, Virginia (2001) 343–344
7. Zoomify: http://www.zoomify.com/ (2004)
8. ZoomView, ViewPoint: http://www.viewpoint.com/ (2004)
9. Rauschenbach, U., Schumann, H.: Demand-driven image transmission with levels of detail and regions of interest. Computers and Graphics **23** (1999) 857–866
10. Owen, M.J., Lui, A.K., Lo, E.H.S., Grigg, M.W.: The design and implementation of a progressive on-demand image dissemination system for very large images. In: Proceedings of the 24th Australasian conference on Computer Science, Gold Coast, Queensland, Australia (2001) 148–155
11. Lin, C., Zheng, Y.: Fast browsing of large-scale images using server prefetching and client caching techniques. In: Proceedings of the SPIE, Applications of Digital Image Processing XXII, Denver, Colorado (1999) 376–387
12. Macromedia: http://www.macromedia.com/ (2004)

Supervised Semi-definite Embedding for Email Data Cleaning and Visualization

Ning Liu[1], Fengshan Bai[1], Jun Yan[2], Benyu Zhang[3], Zheng Chen[3], and Wei-Ying Ma[3]

[1] Department of Mathematical Science, Tsinghua University, Beijing, P.R. China
liun01@mails.tsinghua.edu.cn
fbai@math.tsinghua.edu.cn
[2] LMAM, Department of Information Science, School of Mathematical Science, Peking University, Beijing, P.R. China
yanjun@math.pku.edu.cn
[3] Microsoft Research Asia, 49 Zhichun Road, Beijing, P.R. China
{Byzhang, zhengc, wyma}@microsoft.com

Abstract. The Email systems are playing an important and irreplaceable role in the digital world due to its convenience, efficiency and the rapid growth of World Wide Web (WWW). However, most of the email users nowadays are suffering from the large amounts of irrelevant and noisy emails everyday. Thus algorithms which can clean both the noise features and the irrelevant emails are highly desired. In this paper, we propose a novel Supervised Semi-definite Embedding (SSDE) algorithm to reduce the dimension of email data so as to leave out the noise features of them and visualize these emails in a supervised manner to find the irrelevant ones intuitively. Experiments on a set of received emails of several volunteers during a period of time and some benchmark datasets show the comparable performance of the proposed SSDE algorithm.

1 Introduction

The email services are becoming more and more important in our modern life. Nowadays, a typical user receives about 40-50 email messages every day[5]. For some people, hundreds of messages are usual. Thus, users spend a significant part of their working time on email processing. With the rapid growth of World Wide Web[10], the popularity of email communication is growing; and the time spent on reading and replying emails is increasing. Despite their usefulness, however, email systems nowadays suffer one major problem: information overloading. In other words, people receive a lot of junk or irrelevant emails such as advertisements everyday. The number of these junk emails is so large that a significant amount of efforts have to be put to get rid of them to save space. Generally, the main tool for email management to solve this problem is text classification [10]. However, emails are always short documents with noise information which could decrease the performance of text classification algorithms dramatically. Thus an effective approach to clean the noise of the short text data is highly desired.

Y. Zhang et al. (Eds.): APWeb 2005, LNCS 3399, pp. 972–982, 2005.

Dimension reduction techniques such as Principal Component Analysis (PCA)[6] and Linear Discriminant Analysis (LDA) are traditional linear approaches which could clean the noise features of data [8, 14]. Their goal is to obtain compact representations of the original data that are essential for higher-level analysis while eliminating unimportant or noisy factors. On the other hand, nonlinear dimension reduction algorithms such as Local Linear Embedding (LLE)[9, 11] and Isomap [2] are of great interesting due to the reason that there are many real world tasks in which linear algorithms do not work well [16]. However, little work has focused on the data cleaning problem by nonlinear dimension reduction approaches for text data. This is due to the reason that the nonlinear techniques typically do not scale well for very high dimension text data. In contrast to the traditional text data or web pages, email data are always lower dimensional vectors in Vector Space Model (VSM)[1]. Thus the effective nonlinear dimension reduction algorithms are possible to be applied on the email data.

In this paper, we propose a novel supervised nonlinear dimension reduction algorithm called as Supervised Semi-definite Embedding (SSDE) to clean the noise features of email data. Through this supervised learning procedure, the new arrived email data could be classified into different classes. Then the user could ignore the emails in the irrelevant class. Furthermore, the experimental results on synthetic data showed that we can project the original data into two or three dimensions by our proposed algorithm with data structure preserved. This property could help the user to select the most important emails and ignore the irrelevant emails intuitively.

From the geometrical point view, the data cleaning problem by dimension reduction can be formulated as discovering a low-dimensional embedding of high-dimensional data assumed to lie on a nonlinear manifold. It is highly desirable that this embedding preserved local geometry of the original data, i.e., close points in the high-dimensional space must remain close in the embedded space. Recently, a new nonlinear dimensionality reduction technique based on semi-definite programming, namely Semi-definite Embedding (SDE)[17, 18], is proposed for unsupervised nonlinear dimensionality reduction of image manifold. SDE is based fundamentally on the notion of *isometry*. Like Isomap and LLE, it relies on efficient and tractable optimization that is not plagued by spurious local minima. Isomap estimates geodesic distances between inputs; LLE estimates the coefficients of local linear reconstructions; SDE estimates local angles and distances. Comparing the algorithms, the theoretical and experimental results of SDE showed that it overcomes certain limitation of previous works interestingly. However, the original SDE algorithm is unsupervised and was originally intended for multidimensional image data visualization. The unsupervised algorithms ignore the valuable label information used in classification problems. Our contribution in this paper is a supervised variant of SDE for email data. To learn a mapping from a high-dimensional space into low-dimensional space, a nonlinear regression analysis [7, 12] is used, i.e. mapping new arrival email data points into the embedding space, where the classification of these points is done by the K Nearest Neighbor (KNN) classifier. Our experimental results on various benchmark data sets form the UCI Machine Learning Repository [4] and the real email data of several volunteers show that this algorithm is effective for email classification problems in contrast to PCA, LDA,

LLE, and SDE. Besides this, there is an interesting observation: SSDE could visualize the information of the different classes of data in the reduced space.

The rest of this paper is organized as follows. In Section 2, we introduce some necessary background knowledge of dimension reduction. In Section 3, we present our proposed Supervised SDE algorithm mathematically. In Section 4, we demonstrate the experimental results on some benchmark data sets and the real world email data. Conclusion of this paper is given in Section 5.

2 Background

In this paper, our main contribution is to propose a supervised nonlinear dimension reduction (manifold learning) algorithm to clean the noise features of email data and help to visualize these data for users. Our algorithm originated from an unsupervised manifold learning algorithm called as Semi-definite Programming. For better comprehension, the mathematical definitions of manifold learning problems are given firstly. Following that, some necessary basic ideas of unsupervised SDE are shown in this section.

2.1 Dimension Reduction for Data Cleaning

The world is made of a huge amount of complex data. Discovering the hidden dimension of data, i.e. cleaning the noise features of the data can be seen as a dimension reduction problem. The dimension reduction problem could be mathematically defined as: given N high dimensional inputs $X_i \in R^D$ (where $i = 1, 2, \ldots, N$) with noise features. Here R^D denotes the space of all the D dimensional vectors. The problem is to give a proper algorithm to compute output $Y_i \in R^d$, in one-to-one correspondence with the input X , that provides a faithful embedding in $d < D$ dimensions. Here $X \in R^{N \times D}$ is a matrix with each line a data point.

PCA and LDA are the classical linear techniques for dimensionality reduction. However, many real data sets such as web documents and short emails contain essential nonlinear manifold that are invisible to PCA and LDA [9]. In the last few years, researchers have uncovered a large family of algorithms for computing such nonlinear problem, named as manifold learning.

For manifold learning, it is best described as a problem at the intersection of statistics, geometry, and computation. Given high-dimension data sampled from a low-dimension manifold and a prescription for identifying "neighboring" inputs, the problem is how to efficiently compute a nonlinear embedding such that the outputs preserve local geometry of the original data.

2.2 Semi-definite Embedding

To propose our Supervised SDE algorithm for email data, in this section, we would like to introduce the basic idea of SDE algorithm for manifold learning firstly: *isometry*. Then we present the detail steps of the SDE algorithm in the following subsection.

2.2.1 Isometry

As a novel approach of manifold learning, SDE preserve more local information of the original data than the other nonlinear dimension reduction approaches. SDE utilizes the definition of isometry while mapping a high-dimensional data into a low dimensional space. As the theory of Riemannian manifolds, two manifolds are said to be isometric if they can be bent (or transformed in anyway) one onto the other without changing distances as measured along the surfaces. We can translate the above definition into mathematical form as below.

As a beginning, we give the definition of "neighbor" to describe what local information is. Using the symbols proposed in section 2.1, Consider two data sets $X \in R^{N \times D}$ and $Y \in R^{N \times d}$ that are in one-to-one correspondence $X \to Y$. Let matrix $\Gamma_x = (\tau_{ij}) \in R^{N \times N}$ and $\Gamma_y \in R^{N \times N}$ indicate a neighborhood relation matrix (adjacent matrix) on a data matrix X and Y respectively, in other words, we regard X_j as a neighbor of X_i if and only if $\tau_{ij} = 1$ (the same to Y_j and Y_i). Then we can say that X and Y are locally isometric if and only if X_i and X_j are themselves neighbors (that is, $\Gamma_x = \Gamma_y$), we have:

$$|Y_i - Y_j|^2 = |X_i - X_j|^2 \tag{1}$$

Let $G_{ij} = X_i \cdot X_j$ and $K_{ij} = Y_i \cdot Y_j$ denote the Gram matrices of the inputs and outputs, respectively. Then we can rewrite eq. (1) as by simple linear algebra transformations:

$$K_{ii} + K_{jj} - K_{ij} - K_{ji} = G_{ii} + G_{jj} - G_{ij} - G_{ji} \tag{2}$$

Eq. (2) expresses the conditions for local isometry purely in terms of Gram matrices; it is in fact this formulation that will form the basis of SDE algorithm for manifold learning that we will introduce in the next section.

2.2.2 Semi-definite Embedding

The recently proposed SDE algorithm is proposed to maximize the sum of pairwise squared distances between outputs while the input data and outputs are locally isometric, i.e. it pulls the outputs as far apart as possible, subject to unfolding a manifold without any furling or fold. Mathematically, SDE obtains:

$$\max \text{D(Y)}=\sum_{i,j} |Y_i - Y_j|^2 \tag{3}$$

In addition, SDE also constrain the outputs Y_i to be centered on the origin:

$$\sum_i Y_i = 0$$

Then, Eq. (3) can be translated into the following form by adding the constraint:

$$\text{D(Y)}=\sum_{i,j} |Y_i - Y_j|^2 = \sum_i |Y_i|^2 = Tr(K) \tag{4}$$

So the problem of SDE is to maximize the variance of the outputs $Y_i \in R^d$ subject to the constraints that they are centered on the origin and locally isometric to the inputs $X_i \in R^D$. The optimization problem can be written as an instance of semi-definite programming problem below:

$$\begin{gathered} Max\ Tr(K) \text{ subject to } \mathrm{K} \geq 0, \sum_{\mathrm{ij}} \mathrm{K} = 0, \\ \text{and } \forall ij \text{ such that } \tau_{ij} = 1: \\ K_{ii} + K_{jj} - K_{ij} - K_{ji} = G_{ii} + G_{jj} - G_{ij} - G_{ji} \end{gathered} \quad (5)$$

The problem we discussed above is an illustration of semi-definite programming (SDP) [15]. There are a large amount of papers focusing on efficiently solving the SDP problem, as well as a number of general-purpose toolboxes. The experimental results in this paper were obtained using the SeDuMi and CSDP 4.7 toolbox[3, 13] to solve the semi-definite programming in a supervised manner.

After compute the Gram matrix K by semi-definite programming, we can regain the outputs $Y_i \in R^d$. That $V_{\alpha i}$ denotes the ith element of the αth eigenvector, with eigenvalue λ_α. Then the Gram matrix can be written as:

$$K_{ij} = \sum_{\alpha=1}^{N} \lambda_\alpha V_{\alpha i} V_{\alpha j}$$

A d-dimensional embedding that is locally isometric to the inputs $X_i \in R^D$ is obtained by identifying the αth element of the output Y_i as:

$$Y_{\alpha i} = \sqrt{\lambda_\alpha} V_{\alpha i}$$

The three steps of the SDE algorithm are summarized as following, using the unlabeled data:

Input: data matrix $X \in R^{N \times D}$

***Step 1*:** (Nearest Neighbors) compute the k nearest neighbors of each input.

***Step 2*:** (Semi-definite Programming) compute the Gram matrix of the maximum variance embedding centered on the origin, the preserves the character of locally isometric.

***Step 3*:** (Spectral Embedding) extract a low dimensional embedding from the dominant eigenvector of the Gram matrix learned by semi-definite programming.

Output: new reduced data matrix $Y \in R^{N \times d}$.

3 Mathematical Description of the Supervised SDE Algorithm

SDE is an unsupervised dimensionality reduction algorithm. It aims at taking a set of high dimensional data and mapping them into a low dimensional space while preserving local isometry structure of the data. However, it discards the class information, which is significant for classification tasks such as face recognition and email text categorization. To complement the original SDE with the additional class information, we propose a supervised SDE algorithm (SSDE) which utilizes the classes label information efficiently. Let ω_i to denote the label of sample data X_i, $i = 1,2,\cdots,N$. The name of this proposed algorithm implies that membership information is employed to form the neighborhood of each point, that is, neatest neighbors of a given X_i are chosen only from representatives of the same class as X_i. In other words, the idea of SSDE is to select the neighbors of X_i in SDP (5) from only the class that X_i itself belongs to. This nearest neighbor finding procedure is possible to be conducted since we assume that all the training data are labeled.

The essence of the supervised SDE is consisted of the following steps. Suppose the dataset $\Delta = \{X_i, i = 1,2,\cdots,N\}$ includes all the labeled training sample data. First, the whole data set Δ is divided into subsets $\Delta_{1,}\Delta_{2,}\ldots\Delta_m$ such that $\Delta = \Delta_1 \cup \Delta_1 \ldots \cup \Delta_m$ and $\Delta_i \cap \Delta_j = \phi$, $\forall i \neq j$. Each Δ_i holds the data of one class only and m is the total number of classes known a priori.

Table 1. SSDE algorithm

Training process: using the training data X and the label. ω_i with each X_i

Step 1 select the neighbors of X_i just from the class that X_i itself belongs to. Get the binary matrix Γ, such that X_j is the neighbor of X_i if and only if $\tau_{ij} = 1$.

Step 2 compute the Gram matrix *K* through the following optimize problem with $G_{ij} = X_i \cdot X_j$:

$$Max\ Tr(K) \text{ subject to } \mathrm{K} \geq 0, \sum_{\mathrm{ij}} \mathrm{K} = 0,$$

$$\text{and } \forall ij \text{ such that } \tau_{ij} = 1:$$

$$K_{ii} + K_{jj} - K_{ij} - K_{ji} = G_{ii} + G_{jj} - G_{ij} - G_{ji}$$

Step 3 extract a low-dimension embedding from the dominant eigenvector of the Gram matrix *K*.

Testing process: using unlabeled data

Project all of the unlabeled data u to a low-dimensional representation by nonlinear regression. Then, the classification of these points is done by the K Nearest Neighbor (KNN) classifier.

Each Δ_i is treated separately from others as follows. For each data point $X_i \in \Delta_1$, we look for its K nearest neighbors also belongs to Δ_1, i.e., both X_i and its neighbors have the same class membership. When applied to all data points, this procedure leads to a construction of the neighborhood matrix Γ_x. Thus, whenever X_j is the neighbor of X_i and they belong to the same class, $\tau_{ij} = 1$. After that, Step 2 and 3 in Section 2.2.2 are carried out just as in case of the unsupervised SDE.

Since SSDE is a supervised algorithm, the discussion above is only the training process. For the testing process after embedding, to learn a mapping from a high-dimensional space into low dimensional space, a nonlinear regression analysis approach [13] is used, i.e. mapping unseen points into the embedding space, where the classification of these points is done by the K Nearest Neighbor (KNN) classifier. The detail steps of the SSDE algorithm are summarized in Table 1.

Then we could apply this algorithm on email data to reduce their dimension so as to clear the noise features. Moreover, we could visualize these email data by projecting them into a two or three dimensional space for the users to classify them intuitively.

4 Experiments

To illustrate the property of our proposed Supervised Semi-definite Embedding (SSDE) algorithm, we give an intuitive illustration of this algorithm on a synthetic data set in the first subsection. Since it is not easy to find suitable scale public real email data, we then test the SSDE on a real email data set collected from six volunteers. The data were labeled by the volunteers themselves. To give experimental results on public dataset, we conduct our proposed algorithm on some benchmark datasets of UCI and we take PCA, LDA, LLE and the original unsupervised SDE as the baselines in the third subsection. The results of experiments show that the supervised SDE performs very well on text data which exhibits a manifold structure. Our proposed SSDE achieves average 8% improvement on the precision of classification on the UCI dataset .Due to the nonlinear structure of the email data, our proposed SSDE improved 6%.

4.1 The Synthetic Data

For better comprehension of our proposed SSDE algorithm, we give a group of intuitive pictures on the traditional synthetic data [17] of nonlinear dimension reduction algorithms to illustrate the nonlinear property of it in Figure 1. The picture on the left panel of Figure 1 is the original dataset which is composed of four classes, i.e. dots, tri-angles, circles and stars respectively. They are mixed together in this 2 dimensional picture. The picture on the right panel is these four classes of data after calculated by our algorithm. It can be seen that they are separated into different groups clearly.

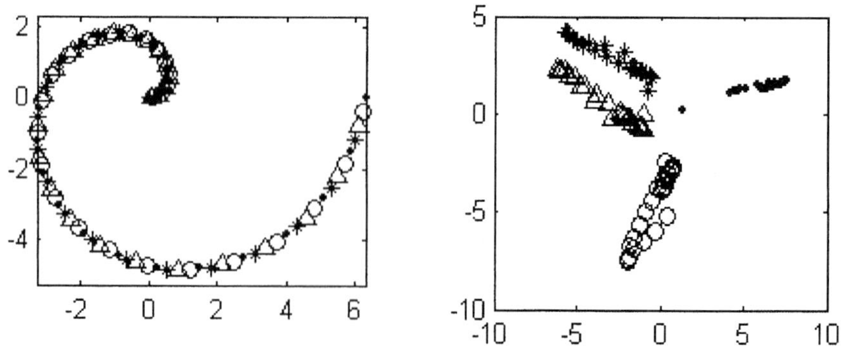

Fig. 1. Nonlinear property of SSDE

4.2 The Real Email Data

To demonstrate the classification performance of the proposed algorithm, the real email data was used here. Since it is hard to find public email data on the Web to the best of our knowledge, we choose the real email data of six volunteers which contains 302 to 485 emails respectively. The experimental results are the average of the six volunteers. Before running the experiments, some preprocessing steps are applied to the dataset. Given an email as input, we ask these volunteers to identify the class label of it by themselves. We predefined the number of classes which is three and they contain: emails about daily work, emails for fun and junk emails (including advertisements) as irrelevant data. Then, we use the Bag of Words algorithm [10] to translate each email text data to a vector. Similarly, the email dataset was randomly split into a training set (80%) and a test set (20%) for 10 times. The experimental results are the average of the ten runs. Moreover, a nonlinear regression analysis algorithm to project the test data and a KNN classifier with k=3 are used. Figure 2 shows the error rate on the test data. The X-axis denotes the algorithms used for comparison.

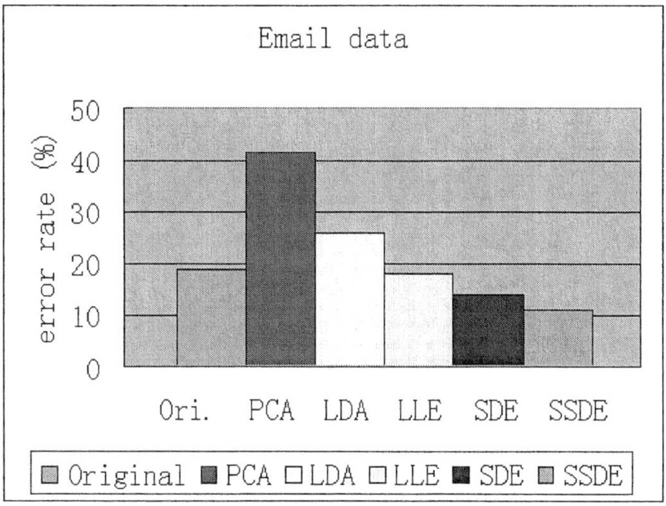

Fig. 2. The error rates of the email data with different algorithms

Figure 2 presents average errors on the email dataset (in %) over the 10 runs. The experimental results show that our proposed SSDE significantly reduced the error rate to 6% while the traditional linear approach even increased the error rate of classification results. This demonstrates that SSDE can extract nonlinear manifold on the email dataset and outperform the unsupervised approaches such as LLE and SDE.

4.3 The UCI Data

The readers may argue that all our experiments are conducted on the synthetic data or the data of our own. What should the performance of the SSDE algorithm be on some public datasets? To answer this question, we conduct it on the UCI machine learning dataset, which is a repository of databases, domain theories and data generators that are used by the machine learning community for the empirical analysis.

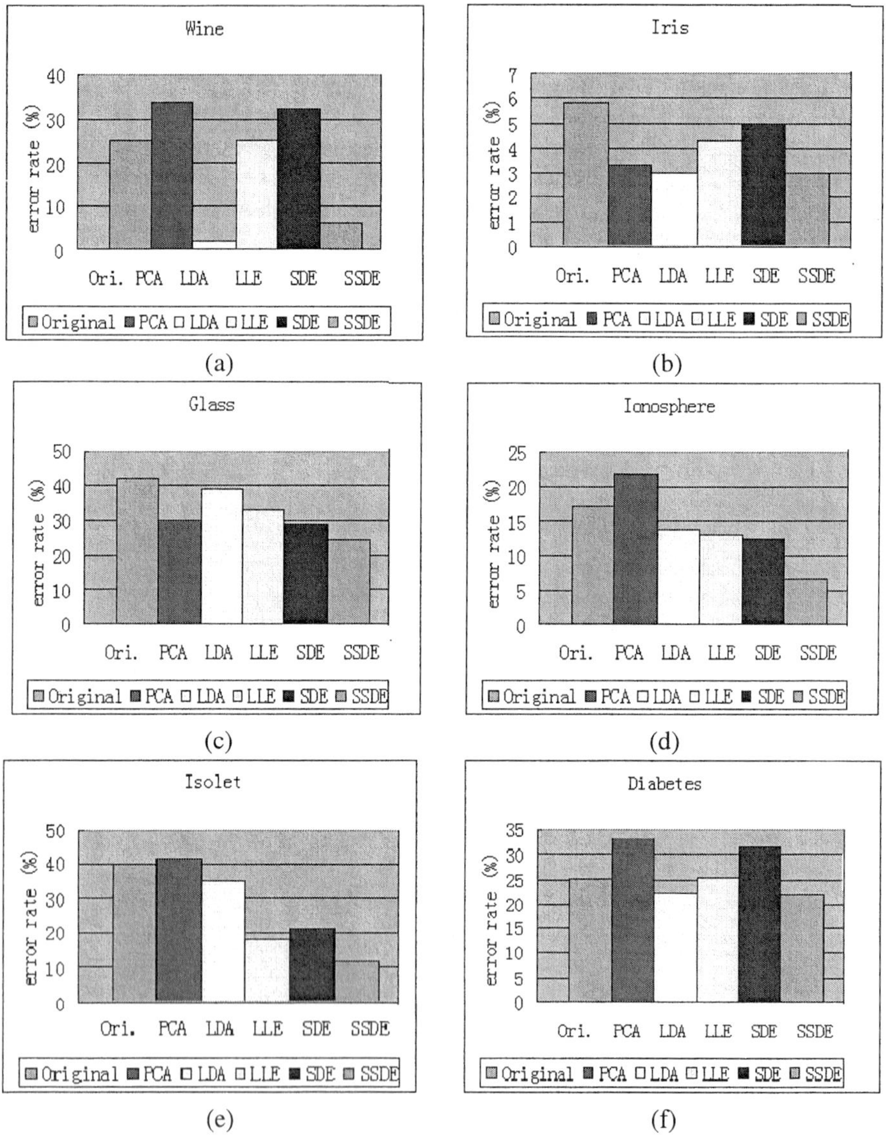

Fig. 3. The error rate pictures on UCI dataset

To verify the classification capabilities of SSDE, it was applied to a number of data sets varying in the number of samples N, dimensions D and classes C. All the data sets were obtained from the UCI repository [4]. Table 2 gives a detailed description of all the datasets used in this paper. For later comparisons, the number of dimensions needed by global PCA to retain 90% of the variance, the global intrinsic dimensionality D_L, is shown in the table as well. To compare the SSDE method with more traditional techniques, we still use PCA (unsupervised linear algorithm), LDA (supervised linear algorithm), LLE (unsupervised nonlinear algorithm) and original SDE as our baseline systems here since they covers almost all the research areas of dimension reduction by feature extraction.

Table 2. Properties of datasets used in this paper

Data	Data Number	Class Number	Dimension	low-dimension
Wine	178	3	13	2
Iris	150	3	4	3
Glass	214	6	9	3
ionosphere	315	2	34	4
Isolet	6,972	26	617	10
diabetes	768	2	8	4

Very similar to Section 4.2, the experiments were set up as follows: a dataset was randomly separated into 10 splits and we take training set (80%) and a test set (20%). To learn a mapping from a high dimensional space into low dimensional space, a nonlinear regression analysis is used, i.e. mapping unseen points into the embedding space. And then the classification of these points is done by the K Nearest Neighbor (KNN) classifier with k=3.

The results of Figure 3 confirm that SSDE generally leads to better classification performance than SDE and other mapping technique used by us. This is to be expected, as SSDE can extract nonlinear manifold in a supervised way.

5 Conclusion and Future Works

In this paper, we propose a novel supervised learning of short text manifold by semi-definite programming. We use this algorithm to clean the email data and visualize them for the email service users. Unlike the original unsupervised SDE algorithm, we studied this algorithm when initial dataset were drawn from several classes. It aims at taking a set of high dimensional data and mapping them into a low dimensional space while preserving not only the local isometry structure of the data but also the class information of the data. In contrast to other dimension reduction algorithms, which could be used to clean the noise features, such as PCA, LDA, LLE and the original SDE, experiments on the real email data and a number of benchmark datasets which clearly exhibit manifold structure demonstrated that SSDE is a powerful embedding. As an interesting observation, SSDE could visualize the different classes of data in the reduced space.

For future work, we will deeply explore the generalisibility of the SSDE method on more different datasets. Further research will address the problem of choosing D_L in a more well-founded way for SSDE.

References

[1] Baeza-Yates, R. and Ribeiro-Neto, B. Modern Information Retrieval. Addison Wesley Longman, 1999.

[2] Balasubramanian, M., Schwartz, E.L., Tenenbaum, J.B., Silva, V.d. and Langford, J.C. The Isomap Algorithm and Topological Stability. Science, 295.

[3] Borchers, B. CSDP, a C Library for Semidefinite Programming. Optimization Methods and Software, 11. 613-623.

[4] C.L., B. and C.J., M. UCI Repository of machine learning databases Irvine. CA: University of California, Department of Information and Computer Science.

[5] Ducheneaut, N. and Bellotti, V. E-mail as Habitat: An Exploration of Embedded Personal Information Management. Interactions, 8. 30-38.

[6] Jolliffe, I.T. Principal Component Analysis. Springer-Verlag, 1986.

[7] Mardia, K.V., Kent, J.T. and Bibby, J.M. Multivariate Analysis. Academic Press, 1979.

[8] Martinez, A.M. and Kak, A.C. PCA versus LDA. IEEE Transactions on Pattern Analysis and Machine Intelligence, 23 (2). 228-233.

[9] Roweis, S.T. and Saul, L.K. Nonlinear Dimensionality Reduction by Locally Linear Embedding. Science, 290. 2323--2326.

[10] Salton, G. and McGill, M.J. Introduction to Modern Retrieval. McGraw-Hill Book Company, 1983.

[11] Saul, L.K. and Roweis, S.T. Think Globally, Fit Locally: Unsupervised Learning of Low Dimensional Manifolds. Machine Learning Research, 4. 119-155.

[12] Seber, G.A.F. and Wild, C.J. Nonlinear regression. Wiley, New York, 1989.

[13] Sturm, J.F. Using SeDuMi 1.02, a MATLAB toolbox for optimization over symmetric cones. Optimization Methods and Software. 625-653.

[14] Torkkola, K., Linear Discriminant Analysis in Document Classification. In Proceedings of the, (2001), 800-806.

[15] Vandenberghe, L. and Boyd, S. Semidefinite Programming. SIAM Review, 38. 49-95.

[16] Vlachos, M., Domeniconi, C., Gunopulos, D. and Koudas, G.K., Non-Linear Dimensionality Reduction Techniques for Classification and Visualization. In Proceedings of the 8th SIGKDD, (Edmonton, Canada, 2002), 645-651.

[17] Weinberger, K.Q. and Saul, L.K., Unsupervised Learning of Image Manifolds by Semidefinite Programming. In Proceedings of the IEEE Computer Society Conference on Computer Vision and Pattern Recognition ,CVPR, (Washington, DC, 2004).

[18] Weinberger, K.Q., Sha, F. and Saul, L.K., Learning a Kernel Matrix for Nonlinear Dimensionality Reduction. In Proceedings of the 21 International Conference on Machine Learning, (Ban, Canada, 2004).

Visual Mining for Customer Targeting

Ji Young Woo[1], Sung Min Bae[2], Chong Un Pyon[1], Minn Seok Choi[3], and Sang Chan Park[1]

[1] Department of Industrial Engineering, Korean Advanced Institute of Science and Technology (Kaist) Guseong-dong, Yusaong-gu, Daejeon, Korea
{jywoo,pcu,sangchanpark}@major.kaist.ac.kr

[2] Department of Industrial & Management Engineering, HANBAT National University DuckMyoung-dong, Yusong-gu, Daejeon, Korea
loveiris@hanbat.ac.kr

[3] Electronic and Telecommunication Research Institute (ETRI) 161Gajeong-dong, Yusong-gu, Daejeon, Korea
cooldenny@etri.re.kr

Abstract. In this paper, we propose the customer map - the information visualization method for customer targeting. To develop the customer map, we classify customer data into customer needs, customer characteristics, and customer value. We suggest an analysis framework to derive key dimensions of the customer map by data mining techniques and a network mapping method to detect meaningful combinations of key dimensions. The customer map is built visually in terms of these key dimensions. The proposed visual targeting model helps a decision maker to build customer-oriented strategies and offers them the ability to monitor and perceive real time state of customer value distribution based on their information without preconception. We apply the visual targeting model to a credit card company, and acquire managerial implications from this study.

1 Introduction

Many data mining techniques have proven to be critical in extracting significant patterns in large data sets. Visualization is one of the best data mining techniques because graphical representation of analysis results often offers superior results compared to other conventional data mining techniques [3]. In the recent customer-centric business environment, the analysis on customer data becomes a major application domain of data mining including visual mining. In today's customer-centered business environment, customer targeting and segmentation to create value through core customers are major concerns [8], [1]. Target market identification, evaluation, and selection are considered to be necessarily undertaken prior to determining specific strategies in corporate. To find target customers, customers have been examined and segmented in terms of their data sources. Many data mining techniques have been introduced to support decisions relevant to customer targeting.

Most of researches on customer targeting and segmentation focus on algorithms and data sources. The criteria for segmentation algorithms emphasizes how much

Y. Zhang et al. (Eds.): APWeb 2005, LNCS 3399, pp. 983 – 990, 2005.

heterogeneous each group is clustered. As to data sources, segmentation and targeting models have been developed from demographics, psychographics, usage/behavioral patterns, value, and needs based segmentation successively reflecting their managerial implications [1]. However, they neglect the opportunity of maximizing the efficiency that they can get when they consider all kinds of customer information together and discover the relationship between information. Also, customer related databases have grown so large that even the marketers or analysts do not always know what information might be represented for customer targeting. In addition, existing targeting models and mining techniques for customer targeting are lack of knowledge presentation ability to visualize and present the mined knowledge to decision-makers. Especially for senior managers, visualization tools are very useful because of their quick and easy knowledge discovery without preconception [3].

In this paper, we will propose a novel customer-targeting model. The model integrates numerous customer data from various data sources. Then, it will derive key information for targeting using data mining techniques and the network mapping method, and visualizes the information using the customer map. We will apply the customer map in a Korean credit card company, and derive strategies from customer maps obtained from its data.

2 Related Works

Customer targeting is finding and keeping right customers, who are profitable and loyal. Customer segmentation is the pre-requisite for customer targeting. It involves the subdivision of the entire market for a product or service into smaller market groups of segments, consisting of customers who are relatively similar within each specific segment [1]. The assumption underlying segmentation is that customers vary widely with respect to their needs and preferences for product and service and their behaviors and information, and with respect to the way they perceive and respond to marketing offerings [1]. To find target customers, customers have been examined and segmented in terms of their data sources. Therefore, segmentation methodologies are deeply dependent on their data sources, such as demographic, lifestyle, preference data, and so on. In this manner, segmentation methods are categorized into three groups, that is, descriptive segmentation, value-based segmentation, and need-based segmentation.

There have been efforts of visualization on customer segmentation. Self Organizing Map (SOM), which is unsupervised neural network technique, has been adopted for customer segmentation. It outperforms in clustering and visualizing data. SOM has advantages for financial, economic and market analyses. It has been used to analyze markets based on customer data, especially to segment customers [5].

Mulhern's research is a cornerstone of the proposed visual targeting model. His research [4] suggested a combined framework of customer profitability and customer portfolio. He emphasized the importance of segment-based target marketing in customer-emphasized environments. With the evaluation of profit distribution across customer, he showed how to assess the distribution of customer profitability by visually inspecting of profit curves. Also, he suggested diagnosing a portfolio of customers and determined what factors either cause or correlate with profitability.

3 Visual Targeting Model

3.1 Customer Information

Customer data can be classified into three categories: customer characteristics, customer needs, and customer value according to the content and interaction types. Customer characteristics information is personal and transaction data about a customer [2]. They include demographics, socioeconomics, life styles and preferences which are stored in customer databases, survey databases, and transaction databases. Customer needs are the non-transactional customer feedback information that includes customer complaints, propositions, claims, and A/S information [2]. One of the major sources of customer needs is customers' evaluation through surveys such as the Customer Satisfaction Index (CSI) survey. Customer needs are diverse on products, services, channels, brand image, and price. Customer value is evaluated from the history of customers' transactions. Customer value is maintained in forms of current value, loyalty, cost, and risk according to business perspectives.

These three categories of customer data will organize the three axes of the customer map. The goal of customer targeting is value creation through focusing the most promising customers. To maintain or mature promising customers, corporate should answer what the customers want. Furthermore, the customer needs can be varied on who the customers are. Therefore, we consider customer value with customer needs to resolve targets' needs and examine their characteristics to catch how customer needs are affected by their characteristics.

3.2 Customer Information Analysis

Customer information analyses are unfolded into customer characteristics and customer needs. Through these analyses, we extract key information from numerous raw data, which are questionnaires from customer surveys and customer information from internal databases. The extracted key information will be a criterion of customer targeting, so it will organize major axes of the customer map.

As the first step, data reduction is performed because raw data of customer characteristics and customer needs consist of numerous variables. As a data reduction technique, we adopt factor analysis. After checking the correlation matrix of variables, we apply principal component analysis which is one of factor analysis methods [6]. Then, key driver analysis is performed for customer needs. In key driver analysis, we use customer satisfaction (CS) as a dependent variable because it is a requisite of customer value and each evaluation on customer needs affects to overall customer satisfaction. Discriminant analysis will derive key customer needs which are significant to overall customer satisfaction. We use decision tree method, especially C5.0 because customer satisfaction index (CSI) is categorical data which is evaluated by 5 or 7-scale measure in the customer survey. Decision tree method will derive key customer needs of each cluster in order to explain how the cluster may vary on relevant dimensions, the derived customer needs.

3.3 Dimension Filtering via Network Map

The customer information analysis outputs several key customer needs and customer characteristics. When the number of key information sets to two, only one customer map will be organized with these two dimensions. In the case that many key drivers are derived, it is necessary to detect meaningful combinations of customer needs and characteristics. For dimension filtering, we apply the network method of link analysis. Building network is the process to expose relationship through interconnected variables.

Key customer needs and characteristics represent nodes in the network. Networking in link analysis expresses the thickness of the link as the number of connections between nodes. However, in our model, the thickness of the link depends on the average of customer value. The network map is divided into customer needs part and customer characteristics part. Each node in different parts is connected with value-based linkage. We select the variables that represent highly connected nodes as criteria of visual targeting. The histogram on the node indicates the number of customers on each attribute of the variable.

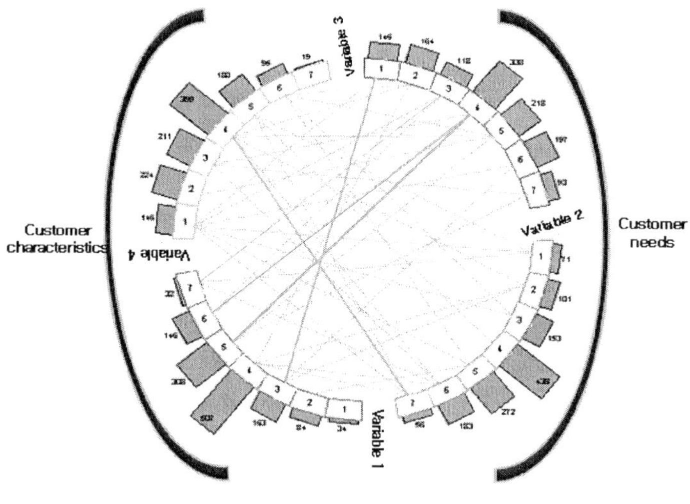

Fig. 1. Network map

3.4 Visual Targeting via Customer Map

After setting a value component and deriving key factors from customer characteristics and customer needs, we visualize the key factors onto the customer map. The customer map evaluates the customer value distribution based on key customer characteristics and customer needs. To implement the customer map, we organize a two-dimensional plane using a key customer characteristic and a key customer need. All customers will have their own positions in the space constituted with (x, y) coordinates. Then, the value component sets up the third dimension, z axis. The average of the value component of the customers in each position represents the value of the third dimension. When we connect all neighbored points, customer map exposes a form of the contour plot. A three-dimensional graph can be projected into a two-dimensional plane by expressing altitude as colors.

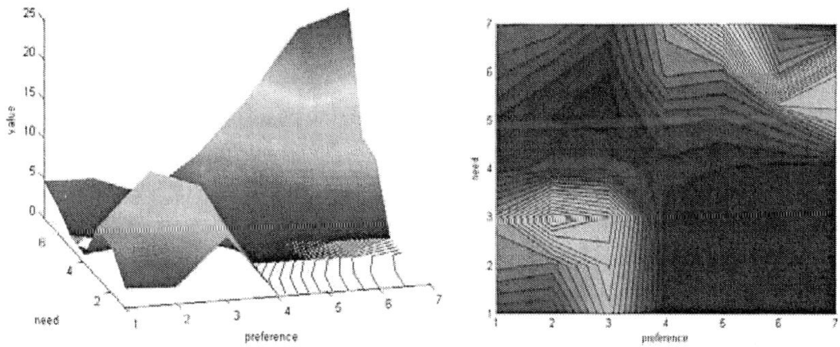

Fig. 2. Three dimensional customer map and two dimensional customer map

3.5 Segmenting and Targeting Through Visualization

Through the value distribution on the customer map, we can diagnose portfolio of target customers and determine what factors relate to customer value. Then, we can derive strategies to increase customer satisfaction of the target by their needs, and to eventually connect their satisfaction to value creation.

From the customer map, customer segmentation can be performed in two ways. One is based on market requirements, which are defined with two dimensions of the map: a customer need and a customer characteristic. This market segmentation is denoted with 'm' starting letters in Fig.3. The other segmentation is based on the customer value which organizes the third dimension of the customer map. This value segmentation is denoted with 'v' starting letters in Fig.3.

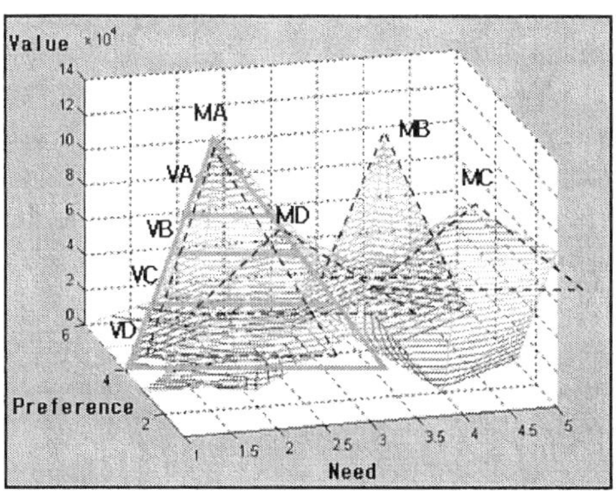

Fig. 3. Customer segments in customer map

With regard to customer targeting, customers are examined in terms of all three dimensions. Target segment is the most profitable or the most cost-consuming customer group. By the Pareto's rule, target customers are defined as the customers whose z dimension values reach to 80% of altitude on the customer map. In Fig.2, the highest area in the 3-dimensional map and the highlighted part in the 2-dimensional map indicate target customers.

There are three check points geometrically in the customer map. The height which represents the average of a value component in each position is a measure to evaluate value of each target. The magnitude of the target measures how big the base of the target is, and the degree of homogeneousness of target customers. The distance between targets on the map with same axes is an index which shows similarities in terms of a customer need and a customer characteristic.

4 Application to Credit Card Industry

We applied our proposed model to a service industry especially to a credit card company. The company performs the CSI surveys twice in a year and maintains various kinds of customer information in the data warehouse. For evaluation of our methodology, we used 3,200 CSI data from two customer surveys. The company updates the customer value as forms of current value, lifetime value and risk value. The current value is enumerated based on the dollar amount of card usage a month. The loyalty value is a long-term value which expresses how long and steady the value remains. The risk value is a cost-sided value component which measures the degree of bad credit.

Data reduction on customer characteristics especially customer lifestyles derived four factors: "stable finance pursuing (q36_2)", "sociability pursuing (q35_3)", "showing off pursing (q36_9)", and "saving pursuing (q36_7)". Data reduction and key driver analysis on customer needs ranked "flexible limits (q4_2)", "special treatment (q6_3)", "financial benefits (q9_5)", and "noble image (q10_2)" as key dimensions of customer targeting. We adopted the current value and the loyalty value as a third dimension and compared their results.

We built the network map with the four customer needs and the four customer preferences. Each need was connected to preference nodes, and each link was represented with the average current value. From the network, we found that "showing off pursing" and "noble image" are good combination to derive a target because the links between them gives a high-valued link. On the other hand, "flexible limit" nodes are connected evenly to all preference nodes; it means it will be difficult to detect a high-end target.

From the customer map built with "showing off" and "noble image", we found that current value is very sensitive to the customer need and the customer preference, but the loyalty value is not sensitive as much as the current value. The customer map shows that target customers are pursuing "nobility image of credit card" and this need appears strongly to the persons who spend money to show off. The customers who have consuming behavior of showing off extremely and are very satisfied to "noble image of credit card" have low loyalty value. Also, this segment is close to the high-end target with respect of current value. This state indicates that those customers are profitable at present, but these profits will not go long.

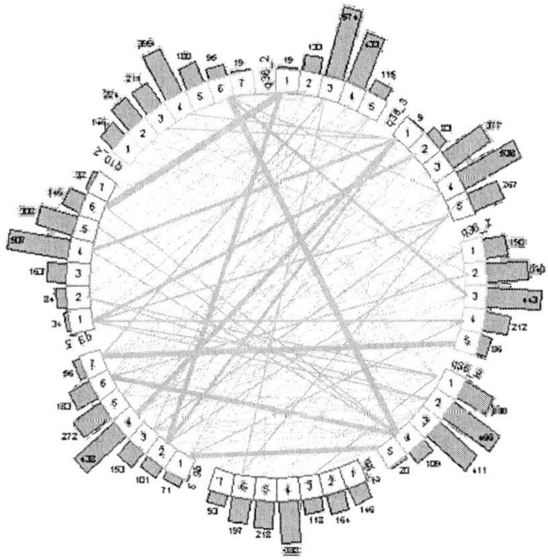

Fig. 4. Network map with key customer needs and preferences

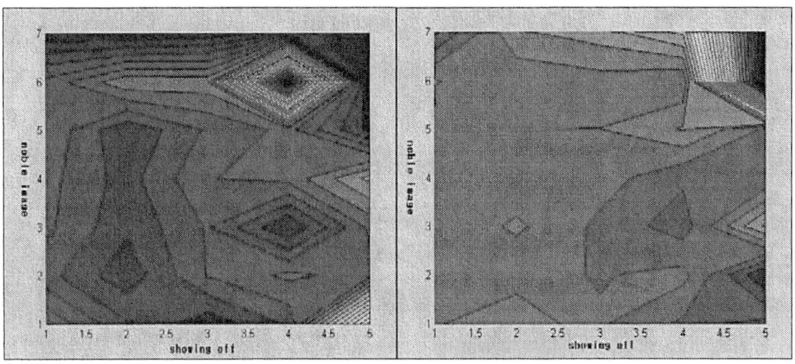

Fig. 5. Customer map with "showing off pursuing" and "noble image"

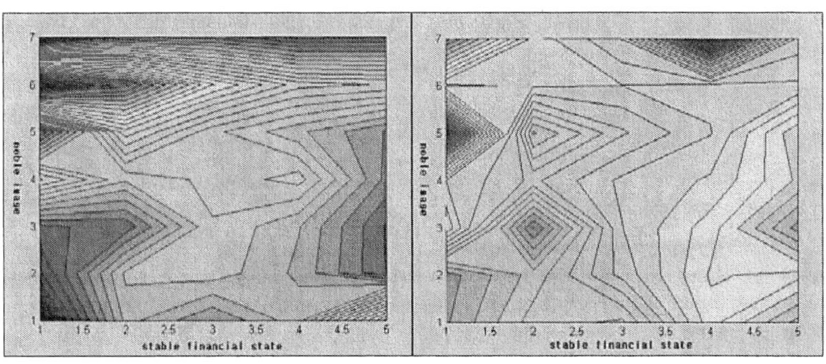

Fig. 6. Customer map with "stable finance" and "noble image"

We also demonstrated the customer map with "stable finance" and "noble image", which is somewhat evenly connected in the network of current value, is but not evenly connected in the network of loyalty value differing from other combinations. We found that current value is sensitive to "noble image," but the customer need on "noble image" is not sensitive to the customer preference of "stable financial state". The loyalty value in this case is a little more sensitive than the first case.

5 Conclusion

We suggested a visualization method, the customer map for customer targeting. Customer map identifies the homogeneous target groups in terms of customer needs, customer characteristics and customer value. To build a customer map, we classified them into three; customer value, customer characteristics and customer needs. Then, we derived key information which will be major axes of the customer map using the multivariate analysis techniques and the link analysis method. We applied the visual targeting model to a credit card company. Using the customer survey data, we derived customer maps and derived marketing strategies toward target customers.

The visual targeting method that we proposed in this paper has contributions to data mining and decision making in business practices. First, it enables decision makers to segment and target right customers. Second, the targeting method does not end up with indicating target customers; it shows what target customers need and how their needs can be varied on customer characteristics. It enables decision-makers to derive long term strategies for maintaining targets. Last, it affords them the ability to make a quick observation of the current state and its change of customer distribution based on customer information without preconception due to the visualization ability of customer map.

References

1. Art Weinstein: Market Segmentation Revised Edition. Probus Publishing Company (1994)
2. Chung-Hoon Park, Young-Gul Kim: A Framework of Dynamic CRM: Linking Marketing with Information Strategy. Business Process Management Journal, Vol. 9, No. 5 (2003) 652-671
3. Christopher Westphal, Teresa Blaxton: Data Mining Solution. John Wiley & Sons, Inc. (1998) 123-147
4. Francis J. Mulhern: Customer Profitability and Diagnosing a Customer Portfolio. Kellogg on Integrated Marketing. John Wiley &Sons, Inc. (2003)
5. Teuvo Kohonen, Guido Deboeck: Visual Exploration in Finance with Self-Organizing Maps. Springer (1998)
6. Vincent-Wayne Mitchell: How to Identify Psychographic Segments: Part1, Part2. Marketing Intelligence & Planning, Vol. 12, No. 7 (1994)

On Designing a Novel PI Controller for AQM Routers Supporting TCP Flows

Nai-xue Xiong[1], Yan-xiang He[1], Yan Yang[2],
Bin Xiao[3], and Xiaohua Jia[4]

[1] The State Key Lab of Software Engineering,
Computer School of Wuhan University, Wuhan Hubei, 430079, PR. China
N.Xiong@mail.ccnu.edu.cn, yxhe@whu.edu.cn
[2] Computer Science Department of Central China Normal University,
Wuhan 430079, PR. China
Y.Yang@mail.ccnu.edu.cn
[3] Department of Computing, Hong Kong Polytechnic University,
Hung Hom, Kowloon, Hong Kong
bxiao@utdallas.edu
[4] SMIEEE, Member of IEEE Communication Society,
Department of Computer Science,
City University of Hong Kong, Kowloon, Hong Kong
csjia@cityu.edu.hk

Abstract. Active Queue Management (AQM) is an effective method to enhance congestion control, and to achieve tradeoff between link utilization and delay. The de facto standard, Random Early Detection (RED), and most of its variants use queue length as congestion indicator to trigger packet dropping. As an extension of RED, a novel AQM algorithm, called NPI-RED, is proposed in this paper. The NPI-RED is based on a novel proportional and integral controller, which not only considers the average queue length at the current time slot, but also takes into consideration the past average queue lengths within a round trip time. We provide a guideline for the selection of the feedback gains for TCP/RED system to stabilize the dynamics, make the queue length converge at a certain target and improve the network performance. We present the condition of asymptotic stability for the model in terms of the average queue length, by using a method, in which we construct a Routh table associated with the characteristic polynomial. Based on the stability condition and control gains selection method, the extensive simulation results by ns2 demonstrate that the NPI-RED algorithm outperforms than the existed AQM schemes in robustness, drop probability and stability.

1 Introduction

Internet congestion occurs when the aggregated demand for a resource (e.g., link bandwidth) exceeds the available capacity of the resource. Resulting effects from such congestion include long delays in data delivery, waster resources due to lost or

Y. Zhang et al. (Eds.): APWeb 2005, LNCS 3399, pp. 991–1002, 2005.

dropped packets, and even possible congestion collapse [1]. Therefore it is very necessary to avoid or control network congestion. Internet congestion control has two parts: 1) the end-to-end protocol TCP and 2) the active queue management (AQM) scheme implemented in routers [2]. AQM can maintain smaller queuing delay and higher throughput by purposefully dropping packets at intermediate nodes.

Several AQM Schemes have been studied in recent literatures to provide early congestion notification to users, e.g., random early detection (RED) [3] and its variant [4], such as Proportional Integral (PI) controller [5], REM [1, 6], BLUE [7], adaptive virtual queue (AVQ) algorithm [8] and PD-RED controller [2]. These schemes can be classified: 1) rate based which controls the flow rate at the congested link and 2) queue based which controls the queue at the congested link. RED [3] is the most prominent and widely studied AQM scheme, which is implemented in routers for congestion control of the Internet. Dynamic-RED (DRED) attempts to stabilize router queue occupancy at a level independent of the active connections by using EWMA as an integral control (I-control) [9]. In [5], the proportional-integral (PI)-controller has been proposed to improve responsiveness of the TCP/AQM dynamics and to stabilize the router queue length around the target. Based on a Proportional-Integral-Derivative (PID) model, an adaptive control mechanism is proposed to improve the system stability and performance under changing network conditions [10]. In these approaches, feedback control theory is used to describe and analyze the TCP/AQM dynamics. However, the current version of RED does not succeed in the goal of stabilizing the queue length. The main reason is probably that the present RED does not use any exact mathematical model to characterize the complex TCP congestion control process; it is thus difficult to provide any systematic and robust law to configure RED's parameters. Unfortunately, its control gain selection is based on empirical investigation and simulation analysis. As can be expected, this method is often ad hoc in nature, and may only be useful for certain class of processes or under certain conditions. A theoretic guideline to choose proper control gain to optimize network performance is still required.

In this paper, a novel proportional integral (NPI) feedback control scheme is proposed for TCP/RED dynamic model developed in [11, 12]. By using control theory and regulating the router queue length to approach the expectative value, the proposed AQM algorithm can decrease the responsive time and improve the stability and robustness of TCP/AQM congestion control. Based on the time-delay control theory, we investigate its asymptotic stability and provide a guideline for the selection of the feedback gains (the proportional and integral parameters) for TCP/RED system, which can make the queue length converge at the expected target, stabilize the RED and improve the network performance.

The remainder of the paper is organized as follows. In Section 2, we present a novel algorithm called NPI-RED and give a theoretic law of choosing the proportional and integral parameters to achieve the system stability. The simulation results demonstrate that the better network performance of NPI-RED can be achieved compared with other AQM schemes in different network conditions by ns2 in Section 3. Finally, we conclude our work and give the further work in section 4.

2 The NPI-RED Algorithm

2.1 Algorithm Description

There are three parameters, i.e., $\{q_{ref}, K_p, K_I\}$ that need to be set in RED. They are specified in the table 1.

We consider the following dropping formula as the feedback controller:

$$\delta p(t) = \frac{K_p(avgq(t) - q_{ref})}{B} - \frac{K_I}{B}\int_{(t-1)-R}^{t-1}(avgq(v) - q_{ref})dv, \quad (1)$$

where $avgq(t)$ denotes the average queue length at time t. We use the average queue length in calculating drop probability instead of the current queue length in order to avoid the sudden change of queue length causing by some short flows or non-TCP flows. From the view of control theory, it is very necessary to ensure the network system stability for an effective system. If the control gains are selected in the stability areas, it can enable the system stability and therefore the network may have better performance, such as less loss ratio, less queue delay and higher network throughput. Then we make the analysis on the system stability and give a theoretic guideline to choose proper control gains to optimize network performance.

Table 1. Parameters of RED

Parameter	Description
q_{ref}	Desired queue size (packets);
K_p	The proportional control gain;
K_I	The integral control gain;
B	The buffer size of the congested router;
p	Probability of packet drop

2.2 Stability Analysis and Control Gain Selection

The stability of the congested buffer occupancy is significantly important because the large oscillation in the buffer can cause a large of data drop, the lower link utilization and the lower system throughput. It influence seriously on the Quality of Service (QoS) of the network. Therefore, in order to meet QoS requirement (e.g., acceptable delay), it is important to consider the stability of the bottleneck link and reduce the steady-state queue length at the routers, and this is the objective of queue management. In this section, we make analysis on the stability based on the dynamic model of TCP and the control theoretic approach, and give the design method in detail. We use the simplified dynamic model of TCP behavior [12] as shown in the following equations:

$$\begin{cases} \delta\dot{W}(t) = -\dfrac{2N}{R_0^2 C}\delta W(t) - \dfrac{R_0 C^2}{2N^2}\delta p(t-R_0) \\ \delta\dot{q}(t) = \dfrac{N}{R_0}\delta W(t) - \dfrac{1}{R_0}\delta q(t) \end{cases} \tag{2}$$

In system (2), we denote $\delta W(t) = W(t) - W_0$, $\delta q(t) = q(t) - q_0$, $\delta p(t) = p(t) - p_0$, where (W_0, q_0, p_0) is the equilibrium point of the system. Here, $\dot{W}(t)$ and $\dot{q}(t)$ denote the time-derivative of $W(t)$ and $q(t)$ respectively, and we denote the parameters of equations (2) in Table 2.

Table 2. Parameters of model (2)

Parameter	Description
W	Expected TCP window size (packets)
q	Current queue length (packets)
R_0	Round-trip time (second)
C	Link capacity (packets/second)
N	Load factor (number of TCP connections)

In [7], Exponentially Weighted Moving Average (EWMA) queue size is used, i.e., the average queue size *avgq(n)* as a measure of congestion of the network. Specifically, with RED, a link maintains the following equation

$$avgq(n) = (1 - w_q)avgq(n-1) + w_q q(n) \tag{3}$$

where *avgq(n)* denotes the average queue length at the nth interval, *q(n)* is the instantaneous queue size at the nth interval and w_q is a weight parameter, $0 \le w_q \le 1$. Let the sampling interval equal to 1, and then we can reach the continuous-time form of equation (3) as follows:

$$q(t) = \frac{1}{w_q}avgq(t) + (1 - \frac{1}{w_q})avgq(t-1) \tag{4}$$

By differentiating both sides of equation (4), we have

$$\dot{q}(t) = \frac{1}{w_q}avg\dot{q}(t) + (1 - \frac{1}{w_q})av\dot{g}q(t-1) \tag{5}$$

In this paper our objective is to develop the active queue management to improve the stability of the bottleneck queue in the network. A linear dynamic TCP model in document [12] is introduced in this paper.

By substituting (4) and (5) into (2), we have

$$\begin{cases} \delta\dot{W}(t) = -\dfrac{2N}{R_0^2 C}\delta W(t) - \dfrac{R_0 C^2}{2N^2}\delta p(t-R_0) \\ \dfrac{1}{w_q}avg\dot{q}(t) + \left(1-\dfrac{1}{w_q}\right)avg\dot{q}(t-1) + \dfrac{1}{R_0}\left(\dfrac{1}{w_q}avgq(t) + \left(1-\dfrac{1}{w_q}\right)avgq(t-1)\right) \\ \qquad = \dfrac{N}{R_0}\delta W(t) + \dfrac{1}{R_0}q_0 \end{cases} \quad (6)$$

The dynamics (2) and (6) are illustrated in the following block diagram:

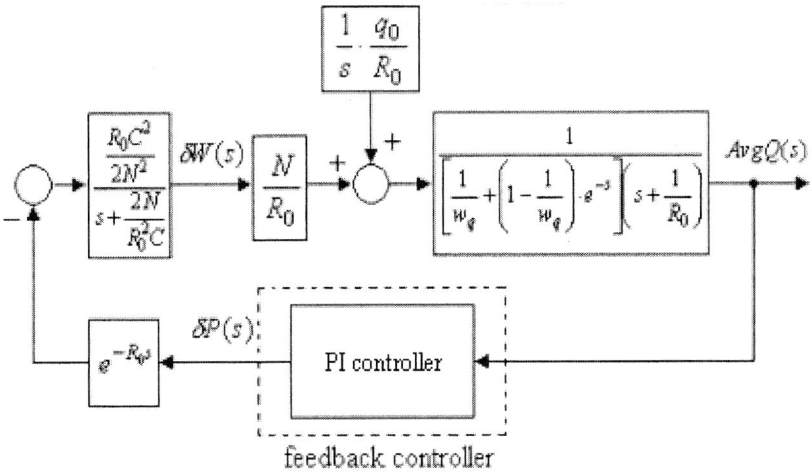

Fig. 1. Block-diagram of the dynamics (2) and (6)

By performing Laplace Transform of (5) and (6), we can derive

$$\begin{cases} \left(s+\dfrac{2N}{R_0^2 C}\right)\delta W(s) = -\dfrac{R_0 C^2}{2N^2}\cdot e^{-R_0 s}\cdot \delta P(s) \\ \left[\dfrac{1}{w_q} + \left(1-\dfrac{1}{w_q}\right)\cdot e^{-s}\right]\left(s+\dfrac{1}{R_0}\right)AvgQ(s) = \dfrac{N}{R_0}\delta W(s) + \dfrac{1}{s}\cdot\dfrac{q_0}{R_0} \\ \delta P(s) = \dfrac{K_P}{B}\left(AvgQ(s) - \dfrac{q_{ref}}{s}\right) - \dfrac{K_I}{Bs}\left(e^{-s} - e^{-(R_0+1)s}\right)AvgQ(s) \end{cases} \quad (7)$$

where $\delta W(s)$, $AvgQ(s)$, $\delta P(s)$ denote the Laplace Transform of $\delta W(t)$, $avgq(t)$, $\delta p(t)$ respectively. For similarity, we assume that $K_P > 0$, $K_I > 0$. Finally, we can get the following polynomial equation

$$\Delta(s)AvgQ(s) = -\frac{R_0C^2e^{-R_0s}}{2}\frac{K_p q_{ref}}{Bs} - (s+\frac{2N}{R_0{}^2C})\frac{Nq(0)}{s},$$

where $\Delta(s)$ is the characteristic equation is

$$\Delta(s) = -(s+\frac{2N}{R_0{}^2C})[\frac{1}{w_q} + (1-\frac{1}{w_q})e^{-s}](NR_0s + R_0s + 1)$$
$$+\frac{R_0C^2}{2N}e^{-R_0s}[\frac{K_P}{B} - \frac{K_I}{Bs}(e^{-s} - e^{-(R_0+1)s})].$$

Then we suppose $e^{-R_0s} = 1 - R_0s + \frac{1}{2}R_0s^2$ and the $\Delta(s)$ is the characteristic equation

$$\Delta(s) = s^4[\frac{1}{2}R_0{}^3(1-\frac{1}{w_q})] + s^3[-R_0{}^2(1-\frac{1}{w_q}) + \frac{1}{2}(1-\frac{1}{w_q})(R_0{}^2 + \frac{2NR_0}{C})$$
$$+\frac{R_0{}^5C^2K_I}{8NB} + \frac{R_0{}^4C^2K_I}{4NB}] + s^2[R_0 - R_0(1-\frac{1}{w_q})(1+\frac{2N}{R_0C}) + \frac{N}{C}(1-\frac{1}{w_q})$$
$$+\frac{R_0{}^3C^2K_P}{4NB} - \frac{R_0{}^4C^2K_I}{2NB} - \frac{R_0{}^3C^2K_I}{2NB}] + s^1[1 + \frac{2N}{R_0Cw_q} - \frac{R_0{}^2C^2K_P}{2NB}$$
$$+\frac{3R_0{}^3C^2K_P}{4NB} + \frac{R_0{}^2C^2K_I}{2NB}] + s^0(\frac{R_0C^2K_P}{2NB} + \frac{2N}{R_0{}^2C} - \frac{R_0{}^2C^2K_I}{2NB}).$$

Suppose the coefficients in the above equation of s^4, s^3, s^2, s^1 and s^0 are respectively a_4, a_3, a_2, a_1 and a_0, i.e.,

$$a_4 = \frac{1}{2}R_0{}^3(1-\frac{1}{w_q}),$$

$$a_3 = -R_0{}^2(1-\frac{1}{w_q}) + \frac{1}{2}(1-\frac{1}{w_q})(R_0{}^2 + \frac{2NR_0}{C}) + \frac{R_0{}^5C^2K_I}{8NB} + \frac{R_0{}^4C^2K_I}{4NB},$$

$$a_2 = R_0 - R_0(1-\frac{1}{w_q})(1+\frac{2N}{R_0C}) + \frac{N}{C}(1-\frac{1}{w_q})$$
$$+\frac{R_0{}^3C^2K_P}{4NB} - \frac{2R_0{}^4C^2K_I}{4NB} - \frac{R_0{}^3C^2K_I}{2NB},$$

$$a_1 = 1 + \frac{2N}{R_0 C w_q} - \frac{R_0^{\;2} C^2 K_P}{2NB} + \frac{3R_0^{\;3} C^2 K_I}{4NB} + \frac{R_0^{\;2} C^2 K_I}{2NB} \text{ and}$$

$$a_0 = \frac{R_0 C^2 K_P}{2NB} + \frac{2N}{R_0^{\;2} C} - \frac{R_0^{\;2} C^2 K_I}{2NB}.$$

Based on the Routh-Hurwitz stability test [13], we get the following Routh Table (in Table 3), where $\gamma_{31} = \dfrac{a_3 a_2 - a_4 a_1}{a_3}$ and $\gamma_{41} = \dfrac{r_{31} a_1 - a_3 a_0}{r_{31}}$.

The whole network system is stable if and only if the valves of the second column are all greater than zero, i.e., $a_4 > 0$, $a_3 > 0$, $\gamma_{31} > 0$, $a_0 > 0$ and $\gamma_{41} > 0$ (i.e., $f(K_P) = a_1 a_2 a_3 - a_1^2 a_4 - a_0 a_3^2 < 0$). We set K_{P1} and K_{P2} are the roots of the function $f(K_P) = 0$ and $K_{P1} < K_{P2}$.Therefore, the range of control gains K_P and K_I in the case of the system stability are as follows:

Table 3. The Routh table

s^4	a_4	a_2	a_0
s^3	a_3	a_1	0
s^2	γ_{31}	a_0	0
s^1	γ_{41}	0	0
s^0	a_0	0	0

$$0 < K_I < \frac{(w_q - 1)(0.5CR_0 - N)}{w_q R_0^{\;3} C^3 (R_0 + 2)}, \quad K_P < R_0 K_I - \frac{4N^2 B}{R_0^{\;3} C^3}, \quad \frac{(K_{P2} + K_{P1})}{2} < K_P < K_{P2},$$

and

$$K_P < \frac{0.5R^3(\frac{1}{w_q} - 1)(1 + \frac{2N}{R_0 C w_q} + \frac{R_0^{\;2} C^2 K_I}{2NB} + \frac{3R_0^{\;3} C^2 K_I}{4NB})}{\frac{R_0^{\;4} C}{4B} + \frac{R_0^{\;5} C^2}{8NB} - \frac{R_0^{\;4} C}{4Bw_q} - \frac{R_0^{\;5} C^2}{8NBw_q} + \frac{R_0^{\;7} C^4 K_I}{16NB^2} + \frac{R_0^{\;8} C^4 K_I}{32NB^2}} + (R_0 + \frac{N(1 - w_q)}{Cw_q}$$

$$+ R_0 (1 + \frac{2N}{R_0 C})(1 - \frac{1}{w_q}) + \frac{R_0^{\;3} C^2 K_I (1 - R_0)}{NB})[R_0^{\;2} (\frac{1}{w_q} - 1) + (\frac{NR_0}{C} + \frac{R_0}{2})(1 - \frac{1}{w_q})$$

$$+ \frac{C^2 R_0^{\;4} K_I (1 + \frac{R_0}{2})}{4NB}] / (\frac{R_0^{\;4} C}{4B} + \frac{R_0^{\;5} C^2}{8NB} - \frac{R_0^{\;4} C}{4Bw_q} - \frac{R_0^{\;5} C^2}{8NBw_q} + \frac{R_0^{\;7} C^4 K_I}{16NB^2} + \frac{R_0^{\;8} C^4 K_I}{32NB^2}).\text{sss}$$

2.3 The Specific Algorithm of NPI-RED

Based on the above stability analysis, we can select the proper control gains that can ensure the system stability and therefore improve the network performance. The computations of $p(n)$ for time n (the nth sampling interval) can be summarized in Fig. 2.

1) Sample the average queue length $avgq(n)$;
2) Compute current error signal by the equation $e(n) = avgq(n) - q_{ref}$;
3) Estimate the number of current active TCP connections N using the technique of flow monitoring and accounting [14], and measure the round trip time R; then compute the range of K_p and K_I based on the above stability condition.
4) Compute current drop probability by (3);
5) Use the equation $p(n) = \frac{K_P \cdot e(n)}{B} + K_I \sum_{i=n-R-1}^{n-1} e(i)$ in RED as the drop probability until time $(n + 1)$ when a new p is to be computed again;
6) Store the $p(n)$ to be used at time $(n + 1)$.

Fig. 2. The NPI-RED algorithm

3 Performance Evaluation

In this section, we evaluate the performance of the proposed NPI-RED algorithm by a number of simulations performed using ns2 [15]. The performance of NPI-RED is compared with RED [3] and other RED variants such as PI-RED [5], PD-RED [2] and adaptive RED [18]. The network topology used in the simulation is the same one used in [16-17]. It is a simple dumbbell topology based on a single common bottleneck link of 45 Mb/s capacity with many identical, long-lived and saturated TCP/Reno flows. In other words, the TCP connections are modeled as greedy FTP connections, that always have data to send as long as their congestion windows permit. The receiver's advertised window size is set sufficiently large so that the TCP connections are not constrained at the destination. The ack-every-packet strategy is used at the TCP receivers. For these AQM schemes tested, we maintain the same test conditions: the same topology (as described above), the same saturated traffic and the same TCP parameters.

The parameters used are as follows: the round-trip propagation delay is 100 ms, the mean packet size is 500 bytes, and the buffer size is set to be 1125 (twice the bandwidth-delay product of the network). The basic parameters of RED (see notation in [6]) are set at min_{th}=15, max_{th}=785, max_p=0.01 and w_q=0.002. For Adaptive RED, the parameters are set as the same in [5]: $\alpha = 0.01$, $\beta = 0.9$, *intervaltime*=0.5s. For PD-RED, the parameters are set as same as [10], i.e., $\delta t = 0.01$, k_p = 0.001 and k_d = 0.05. For NPI-RED, we set $K_P = 12$ and $K_I = 0.01$.

In this simulation, we focus on the following key performance metrics: goodput (excluding packet retransmissions), average queue length, average absolute queue deviation, and packet loss ratio. The average queue length is defined as the arithmetic mean value of instantaneous queue length. The average queue deviation is defined as the absolute deviation between instantaneous queue length and its mean value.

3.1 Simulation 1: Stability Under Extreme Conditions

In this experiment, all TCP flows are persistent, and the stability of the AQM schemes are investigated under two extreme cases: 1) light congestion with a small number of TCP flows N ($N=100$), 2) heavy congestion with a large N ($N=2000$). We set the queue target at 200. Other parameters are the same as those in the second paragraph of the performance evaluation part.

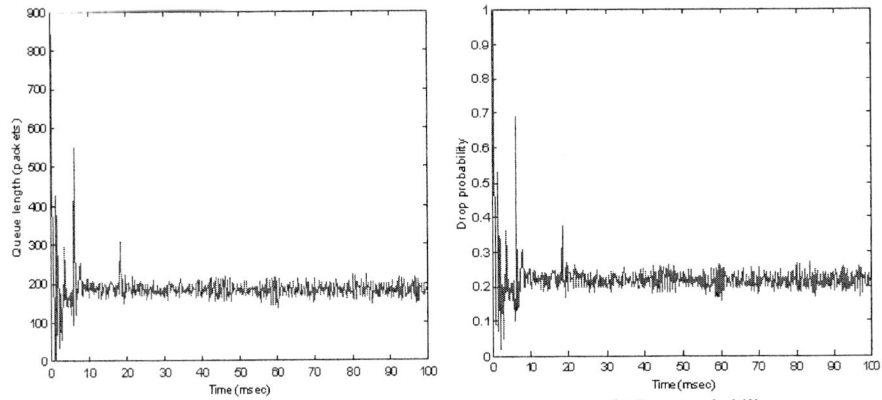

a) Queue length (b) Drop probability

Fig. 3. Light congestion ($N = 100$)

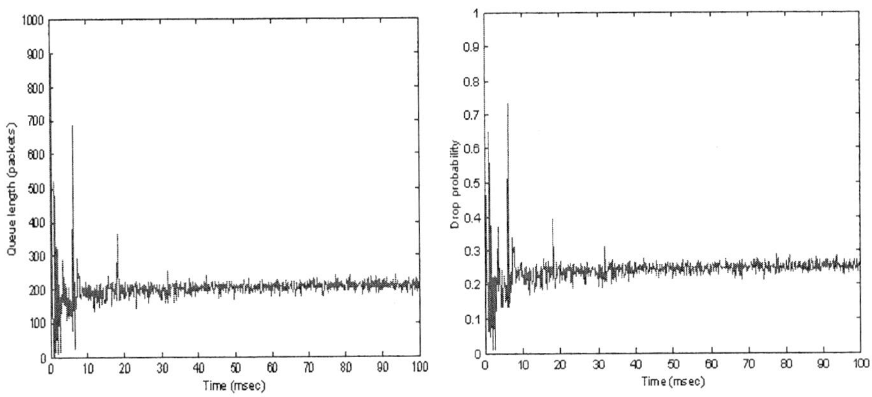

(a) Queue length (b) Drop probability

Fig. 4. Heavy congestion ($N = 2000$)

Fig. 3 and Fig. 4 demonstrate the dynamic change of the average queue length and the drop probability of the NPI-RED algorithm under the light congestion ($N = 100$) and the heavy congestion ($N = 2000$). It can be seen that, although the queue length and the drop probability fluctuate at first, they can be stable quickly, and be near to the queue target 200 and 0.22 respectively. Both the fluctuation amplitude of NPI-RED queue length and the variance of the drop probability are small. In summary, NPI-RED shows better stability and quick response under either light congestion or heavy congestion.

3.2 Simulation 2: Response Under the Variable Number of Connections

In this section, the simulation is performed with the variable number of TCP connections. In the first, the initial umber of connections is set to 2000 and, in addition, 200 TCP connections join in the link at 50.1 ms. Other parameters are the same as those in simulation 1.

Fig. 5 shows the queue length and the drop probability for the variable number of connections. We can find that in the first half queue length can be approximately stabilized at the queue target 200, and the drop probability can also be approximately stable at 0.22. At 50.1 ms, the queue length and the drop probability fluctuate with 200 TCP connections joining in the link, and after that they can be quickly stable. From these figures we can find that NPI-RED achieves a short response time, good stability and good robustness.

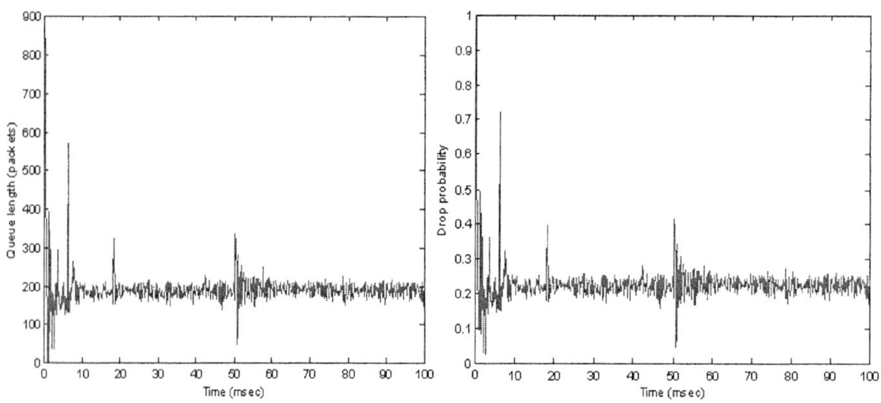

(a) Queue length (b) Drop probability

Fig. 5. Queue length and drop probability for variable number of connections starting at 2000

4 Conclusion and Future Work

In this paper, a novel AQM scheme called NPI-RED is proposed to improve the performance of RED. We have explored the queue length stability of NPI-RED, and have provided guidelines based on theory and simulations for control gain optimization.

Based on the stability condition and control gains selection method, the extensive simulation results by ns2 demonstrate that the NPI-RED scheme outperforms than recently proposed AQM algorithms in robustness, drop probability and stability.

Future work would cover the extension of the proposed approach from the model of a single bottleneck link only with TCP flows to the case of the multiple bottleneck links and to the case where the TCP and non-TCP traffic (e.g., UDP flows) share a single queue. The performance under short flows, and burst traffic loads will also be investigated. In addition, issues such as fairness and protection against non-responsive flows will be addressed, and all other relevant problems that the current RED is facing.

References

1. S. Athuraliya, S. H. Low, V. H. Li, and Q. Yin: REM: active queue management, IEEE Networking, Vol. 15, pp. 48-53, May/June, 2001.
2. Jinsheng Sun, King-Tim Ko, Guanrong Chen, Sammy Chan, and Moshe Zukerman: PD-RED: to improve the performance of RED, IEEE Communications letters, vol. 7, no. 8, August 2003.
3. S. Floyd and V. Jacobson: Random early detection gateways for congestion avoidance, IEEE/ACM Trans. On Networking, Vol. 1, pp. 397-413, Aug. 1993.
4. E. C. Park, H. Lin, K. J. Park, and C. H. Choi: Analysis and design of the virtual rate control algorithm for stabilizing queues in TCP networks, Computer Networks, vol. 44, no. 1, pp. 17-41, 2004.
5. C. V. Hollot, V. Misra, D. Towsley and W. B. Gong: Analysis and design of controllers for AQM routers supporting TCP flows, IEEE Transactions on Automatic Control, Vol. 47, pp. 945-959, Jun. 2002.
6. C. N. Long, J. Wu and X. P. Guan: Local stability of REM algorithm with time-varying delays, IEEE Communications Letters, Vol. 7, pp.142-144, March 2003.
7. W. Fang, Kang G. Shin, Dilip D. Kandlur, and D. Saha: The BLUE active queue management algorithms, IEEE/ACM Trans. On Networking, Vol. 10, No. 4, pp. 513-528, Aug. 2002.
8. S. Kunnivur and R. Srikant: Analysis and design of an adaptive virtual queue (AVQ) algorithm for active queue management, Proc. Of ACM SIGCOMM 2001, San Diego, USA, August 2001, pp. 123-134.
9. J. Aweya, M. Ouellette, and D. Y. Montuno: A Control Theoretic Approach to Active Queue Management, Computer Networks, vol. 36, no. 2-3, pp. 203-235, 2001.
10. X. Deng, S. Yi, G. Kesidis, and C.R. Das: A Control Theoretic Approach for Designing Adaptive Active Queue Management Schemes, Proceedings of IEEE GlOBECOM'03, San Francisco, CA, Dec. 2003.
11. S. Ryu, C. Rump, and C. Qiao: Advances in Internet Congestion Control, IEEE Communications Surveys & Tutorials, Third Quarter 2003, vol. 5, no. 1, 2003.
12. C. V. Hollot, V. Misra, D. Towsley, and W. B. Gong: A Control Theoretic Analysis of RED, Proceedings of IEEE /INFOCOM 2001, Anchorage, AL, April 2001.
13. G. F. Franklin, J.D. Powell, and A. Emami-Naeini, Feedback control of dynamic systems, Addsion-Wesley, 3rd ed., 1995
14. T. J. Ott, T. V. Lakshman, and L. Wong: SRED: Stabilized RED, in Proceedings of IEEE INFOCOM, vol. 3, New York, Mar. 1999, pp. 1346-1355.

15. USC/ISI, Los Angeles, CA. The NS simulator and the documentation. [Online] Available: http://www.isi.edu/nsnam/ns/
16. C. V. Hollot, Vishal Maisra, Don Towsley and Wer-Bo Gong: On designing improved controllers for AQM routers supporting TCP flows, Proc. IEEE INFOCOM, 2001, available at http://www.ieee-infocom.org/2001/paper/792.pdf
17. G. lannaccone, M. May, and C. Diot: Aggregate traffic performance with active queue management and drop from tail, ACM SIGCOMM Computer Communication Rev., vol. 31, no. 3, pp. 4-13, July 2001.
18. S. Floyd, R. Gummadi, S. Shenker, and ICSI: Adaptive RED: An algorithm for increasing the robustness of RED's active queue management, Berkeley, CA. [Online] http://www.icir.org/floyd/red.html.

Call Admission Control with Multiple Priorities Erlang B System

Dali Zhang

Department of Electrical and Computer Engineering,
Queen's University,
Kingston, Ontario, K7L 3N6, Canada
zhangd@ee.queensu.ca

Abstract. Erlang B system has been widely used in modelling and evaluating network performance. For example, guard channels are allocated for handover calls in cellular networks, which is a two-priority Erlang B model. This paper discusses multi-priority fractional guard channel scheme, a generalized Erlang B model, and develops recursive algorithms to reduce computational complexity. Simulation results are presented for the NSFNET topology model when applying the scheme to the Internet. Routing algorithms' influence on system performance is studied.

1 Introduction

Traditional circuit-switched networks such as telephony networks can provide good service to end users in that a physical communication path is established for source and destination. The users have exclusive access for the resource until either end terminates the conversation. In order to find whether a network has enough resources to establish such a connection, call admission control (CAC) is performed during the signaling stage before a connection is made.

The current Internet is a packet-switched network. Compared to circuit-switched networks, it allows larger degree of multiplexing and have lower cost. However, the Internet's poor quality of service has long been criticized. Researchers have been working on different layers to improve it. One branch of such researches aims to mimic circuit-switched network on the Internet by establishing a virtual connection between source and destination with bandwidth reservation, which results in Integrated Services (IntServ), RSVP protocol and their extensions. ATM and MPLS technology are also such examples. Wireless access becomes popular in recent years, and cellular networks begin to carry data services, such as short message service (SMS). As more and more applications found their demands in cellular networks, researchers discuss the third generation (3G) wireless communication networks that aim to provide integrated services for voice, data and multimedia on existent wireless infrastructure.

Since call admission control can limit the number of connections, it is studied extensively in wireless networks and wireline networks as a tool of congestion control. By purposely admitting certain users and limiting others, call admission

Y. Zhang et al. (Eds.): APWeb 2005, LNCS 3399, pp. 1003–1014, 2005.

control can provide differentiated service. For example, researchers have realized that the disconnection for a handoff call will lead to more user dissatisfaction than a normal call in cellular networks, guard channel scheme is proposed to give high priority to handoff calls by reducing blocking probability [7].

Erlang B system is an effective model for telephony networks [2]. It assumes a fixed capacity system with Poisson arrivals. The connections' holding time are independently and identically distributed. Any blocked/rejected call will disappear and never come back again. When certain resources are reserved for high priority traffic, the scheme is named trunk reservation in wireline networks [8]. Erlang B system is also widely used in modelling cellular networks with two priorities [3, 6, 7, 11]. It is frequently called guard channel scheme. Ramjee *et al.* proposed a two-priority generalized Erlang B system, fractional guard channel, for cellular networks [9]. In all studies, call blocking probability, or rejection rate, is considered the most important metric in evaluating the performance.

Fang generalizes Ramjee *et al.*'s work to multi-priority Erlang B system [4], and this paper proposes a recursive algorithm to avoid computational complexity. For guard channel scheme, a special case of fractional guard channel that worth studying itself, we generalize Haring *et al.*'s two-priority recursive algorithm to random priorities. Two general cases, a handoff model and the NSFNET model, which are difficult to analyze with mathematics in this paper, are simulated. Simulation results show that guard channel (or trunk reservation) scheme can effectively provide differentiated services for different priority classes.

The paper is organized as follows: Section 2 discusses the generalized fractional guard channel scheme, with a recursive algorithm and its proof; Section 3 describes multi-priority guard channel scheme and its recursive algorithm, and the general formulas are provided in appendix; Section 4 evaluates the performance of guard channel scheme in handoff model and the NSFNET model; in Section 5, we conclude the paper.

2 Multi-priority Fractional Guard Channel Scheme

Ramjee *et al.* proposed *fractional guard channel* (FGC) policy in cellular networks, which consists of two types of traffic: handoff calls and new calls, where the former is considered as high priority [9]. Fractional guard channel scheme states that high priority calls are admitted whenever system capacity permits, while low priority ones are only allowed with certain probability $\beta(i)$, where i is the number of busy channels. Intuitively, $\beta(i)$ should be a non-increasing function of i so that high priority requests can be protected with lower blocking probability upon heavy traffic.

When more applications are integrated in cellular networks, a multi-priority Erlang B model is needed. Fang generalizes Ramjee *et al.*'s model to a multi-priority system [4], and we present a recursive algorithm to calculate the blocking probability in order to avoid computational problem.

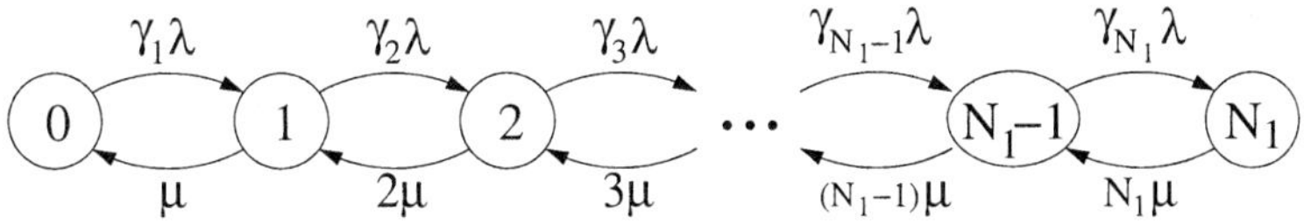

Fig. 1. Multi-priority Fractional Guard Channel Scheme

2.1 Model and Analysis

Upon a multi-priority system, assume all traffic classes from 1 to p are independent. Class i's arrival is Poisson with rate λ_i, and all classes have the same mean service rate μ. The system capacity is N_1, and each incoming request will take one channel. Denote total arrival rate is $\lambda = \sum_{i=1}^{p} \lambda_i$ for all p classes, and α_i the percentage of class i's traffic in total traffic, i.e., $\lambda_i = \alpha_i \cdot \lambda$, and $\sum_{i=1}^{p} \alpha_i = 1$. Further, the traffic intensity, or traffic load, ρ is measured in *erlangs* and $\rho = \lambda/\mu$.

Define a $p \times N_1$ admission probability matrix $\mathcal{B}$, where $\beta_{i,j}$ is the admission probability for class i when the system has $j-1$ channels busy. $0 \le \beta_{i,j} \le 1$ for all $i = 1, 2, \ldots, p$ and $j = 1, 2, \ldots, N_1$. Suppose class 1 has the highest priority and class p the lowest, and we aim to decrease the blocking probability for high priority, then we have the following rules for all elements in the admission probability matrix $\mathcal{B}$:

1. $\beta_{i,j} \ge \beta_{i,j+1}$ for $i = 1, 2, \ldots, p$ and $j = 1, 2, \ldots, N_1 - 1$;
2. $\beta_{i,j} \ge \beta_{i+1,j}$ for $i = 1, 2, \ldots, p-1$ and $j = 1, 2, \ldots, N_1$.

The first rule guarantees a stable system, and the second rule defines the priority order as from 1 to p. Normally, we take $\beta_{1,j} = 1$ for all $j = 1, 2, \ldots, N_1$. Note that the main difference between two priority in [9] and multi-priority fractional guard channel scheme in [4] and this paper is the definition of admission probability matrix $\mathcal{B}$ and γ_i. The following analysis process is much the same as in [9].

We can model the system with a N_1-state Markov chain, illustrated in Figure 1. Denote P_i the probability of system in state i, when there are i channels busy, $0 \le i \le N_1$. Then the state transition function can be put as

$$P_i \cdot \gamma_{i+1} \cdot \lambda = P_{i+1} \cdot (i+1) \cdot \mu$$

for $0 \le i < N_1$, where $\gamma_j = \sum_{i=1}^{p} \alpha_i \cdot \beta_{ij}$ for all channels j, $j = 1, 2, \ldots, N_1$.

Therefore we have

$$P_i = P_0 \cdot \frac{\rho^i}{i!} \cdot \Pi_{k=1}^{i} \gamma_k \tag{1}$$

for $0 \le i \le N_1$, where

$$P_0 = \frac{1}{\sum_{i=0}^{N_1} \left(\frac{\rho^i}{i!} \cdot \Pi_{k=1}^{i} \gamma_k \right)}$$

Define $\beta_{i,N_1+1} = 0$, the blocking probability for class i, $i = 1, 2, \ldots, p$, is

$$B_i = \sum_{k=0}^{N_1} P_k \cdot (1 - \beta_{i,k+1}) \tag{2}$$

2.2 Recursive Algorithm for Computation

Simple as the blocking probability expression is, the computation proves extremely complex with the increment of system capacity, traffic intensity and number of priority classes [10]. Both the numerator and denominator in Equation (1) tend to get overflow for most mathematic softwares upon large capacity. In this subsection, we provide a recursive algorithm for computing blocking probability, which can effectively avoid any overflow or underflow problems.

Given traffic load ρ, this algorithm calculates the blocking probability for each priority class by recursion on the capacity, each time increased by 1. For $t = 0, 1, 2, \ldots, N_1$, the blocking rate for class i, $i = 1, 2, \ldots, p$ is

$$B_i(t) = B_i(t-1) + \frac{1 - B_i(t-1) - \beta_{i,t+1}}{X(t)} \tag{3}$$

where $X(t)$ can be obtained recursively with

$$X(t) = 1 + X(t-1) \cdot \frac{t}{\rho \cdot \gamma_t}. \tag{4}$$

Specifically, we have $B_i(0) = 1 - \beta_{i,1}$, $X(0) = 1$ and $\beta_{i,N_1+1} = 0$.

In what following of this subsection, we are to derive the above recursive algorithm. According to Equations (1) and (2), we can express B_i as

$$\begin{aligned} B_i(N_1) &= P_0 \cdot \sum_{k=0}^{N_1} \left[(1 - \beta_{i,k+1}) \cdot \frac{\rho^k}{k!} \cdot \Pi_{j=1}^{k} \gamma_j\right] \\ &= \frac{\sum_{k=0}^{N_1} \left[(1 - \beta_{i,k+1}) \cdot \frac{\rho^k}{k!} \cdot \Pi_{j=1}^{k} \gamma_j\right]}{\sum_{k=0}^{N_1} \left(\frac{\rho^k}{k!} \cdot \Pi_{j=1}^{k} \gamma_j\right)} \\ &= \frac{\sum_{k=0}^{N_1} \left(\frac{\rho^k}{k!} \cdot \Pi_{j=1}^{k} \gamma_j\right) - \sum_{k=0}^{N_1} \left(\beta_{i,k+1} \cdot \frac{\rho^k}{k!} \cdot \Pi_{j=1}^{k} \gamma_j\right)}{\sum_{k=0}^{N_1} \left(\frac{\rho^k}{k!} \cdot \Pi_{j=1}^{k} \gamma_j\right)} \\ &= 1 - \frac{\sum_{k=0}^{N_1} \left(\beta_{i,k+1} \cdot \frac{\rho^k}{k!} \cdot \Pi_{j=1}^{k} \gamma_j\right)}{\sum_{k=0}^{N_1} \left(\frac{\rho^k}{k!} \cdot \Pi_{j=1}^{k} \gamma_j\right)}. \end{aligned}$$

Denote

$$\begin{cases} \phi(t) = \frac{\rho^t}{t!} \cdot \Pi_{j=1}^{t} \gamma_j \\ Y(t) = \sum_{k=0}^{t} \left(\frac{\rho^k}{k!} \cdot \Pi_{j=1}^{k} \gamma_j\right). \end{cases}$$

Then we will be able to perform the following recursive calculation:

$$\begin{cases} \phi(t) = \phi(t-1) \cdot \frac{\rho}{t} \cdot \gamma_t \\ Y(t) = Y(t-1) + \phi(t) \end{cases}$$

with $\phi(0) = 1$ and $Y(0) = 1$. In order to derive the relationship between $B_i(t)$ and $B_i(t-1)$, we have

$$\begin{cases} B_i(t) = 1 - \frac{\sum_{k=0}^{t} \left(\beta_{i,k+1} \cdot \frac{\rho^k}{k!} \cdot \Pi_{j=1}^{k} \gamma_j\right)}{Y(t-1) + \phi(t)} \\ B_i(t-1) = 1 - \frac{\sum_{k=0}^{t-1} \left(\beta_{i,k+1} \cdot \frac{\rho^k}{k!} \cdot \Pi_{j=1}^{k} \gamma_j\right)}{Y(t-1)}. \end{cases}$$

From the above two equations, $B_i(t)$ can be expressed with $B_i(t-1)$ as

$$B_i(t) = \frac{B_i(t-1) \cdot Y(t-1) + (1-\beta_{i,t+1}) \cdot \phi(t)}{Y(t-1) + \phi(t)}.$$

For brief notation, define $X(t) = \frac{Y(t)}{\phi(t)}$, then we have the recursive Equations (3) and (4) with $X(0) = 1$.

3 Multi-priority Guard Channel Scheme

Guard channel scheme has long been proposed in cellular networks to provide differentiated service for handoff calls and new calls [7]. In wireline networks, especially telephony networks, it is called trunk reservation [8]. Take two-priority system as an example, resource is allocated to high priority requests as long as it is available, i.e., admitted with 100% probability. When the total number of busy channels reaches a threshold, low priority calls will be rejected (admitted with 0% probability). Resources beyond the threshold are specifically reserved for high priority users.

One may notice that guard channel is a special case for fractional guard channel scheme. In a two-priority system with 6 channels and 2 of them are guard channels for handoff calls, for instance, the admission probability matrix becomes

$$\mathcal{B} = \begin{pmatrix} 1 & 1 & 1 & 1 & 1 & 1 \\ 1 & 1 & 1 & 1 & 0 & 0 \end{pmatrix}.$$

Guard channel, or trunk reservation scheme, is worth studying itself in that it is easy to implement with just an array of thresholds instead of an admission probability matrix.

3.1 Guard Channel Model

We follow the aforementioned fractional guard channel model and notations. Specifically, we use thresholds instead of admission probability matrix. A class i request will be blocked when current busy channels are no less than N_i, $i = 1, 2, \ldots, p$. Since class 1 has the highest priority, we have $N_i > N_{i+1}$. Specifically, denote $\lambda_{1:r} = \sum_{i=1}^{r} \lambda_i$ and $\rho_{1:r} = \sum_{i=1}^{r} \rho_i$.

The state transition function is given by

$$P_i \cdot \lambda_{1:r} = P_{i+1} \cdot (i+1) \cdot \mu$$

for $N_{r+1} \le i \le N_r - 1$. $N_{p+1} = 0$. Then it is easy to deduce that the highest priority class blocking probability is

$$B_1 = P_1 = P_0 \cdot \frac{\Pi_{i=1}^{p} \rho_{1:i}^{N_i - N_{i+1}}}{N_1!} \tag{5}$$

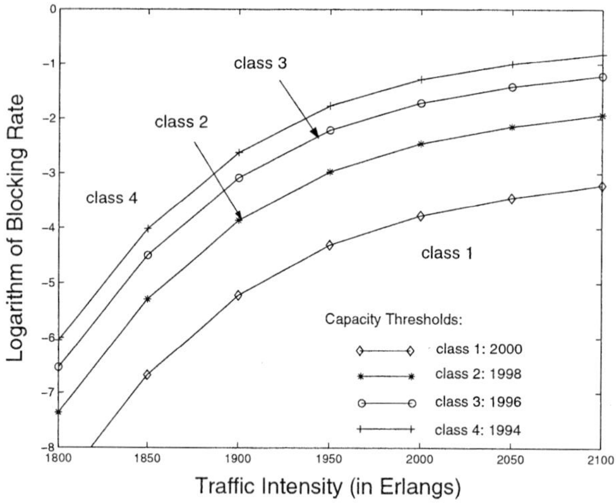

Fig. 2. Analytical Results Computed with Recursive Algorithm $\rho_i = \rho/4$

where we define $N_{p+1} = 0$ and have

$$P_0^{-1} = \sum_{i=0}^{N_p-1} \frac{\rho_{1:p}^i}{i!} + \sum_{i=N_p}^{N_{p-1}-1} \frac{\rho_{1:p}^{N_p} \cdot \rho_{1:p-1}^{i-N_p}}{i!} + \sum_{i=N_{p-1}}^{N_{p-2}-1} \frac{\rho_{1:p}^{N_p} \cdot \rho_{1:p-1}^{N_{p-1}-N_p} \cdot \rho_{1:p-2}^{i-N_{p-1}}}{i!}$$
$$+ \cdots + \sum_{i=N_2}^{N_1} \frac{\rho_{1:p}^{N_p} \cdot \rho_{1:p-1}^{N_{p-1}-N_p} \cdot \rho_{1:p-2}^{N_{p-2}-N_{p-1}} \cdot \cdots \cdot \rho_{1:2}^{N_2-N_3} \cdot \rho_{1:1}^{i-N_2}}{i!}.$$

For priority class r, $2 \leq r \leq p$, the blocking probability is

$$B_r = P_1 + P_0 \cdot \sum_{j=2}^{r} \sum_{i=N_j}^{N_{j-1}-1} \frac{\rho_{1:j-1}^{i-N_j} \cdot \Pi_{k=j}^{p} \rho_{1:k}^{N_k-N_{k+1}}}{i!}. \quad (6)$$

3.2 Recursive Algorithm for Guard Channel Computation

The above blocking probability calculations (Equations (5) and (6)) encounter overflow problem too. Although the recursive algorithm in Subsection 2.2 can be applied to guard channel case with matrix-to-threshold conversion, we would study it specifically. Pioneering works on recursive algorithms have been carried on in single-class Erlang B system [1, 5] as well as two-priority classes Erlang B system [6, 11]. Best result was presented in [6]. In this section, we are going to generalize the methods proposed by Haring *et al.* to multi-priority Erlang B system, with minor correction to their algorithm.

For the highest priority's blocking probability $B_1(t)$, we have

1 . $B_1(0) = 1.0, \quad i = p+1, \quad k = 1 \quad \text{and} \quad N_{p+1} = 0;$

2 . $B_1(N_i + k) = \dfrac{B_1(N_i + k - 1)}{\frac{N_i+k}{\rho_{1:i-1}} + B_1(N_i + k - 1)};$

$$3\,.\ k = k+1, \quad \text{go to step 2 until} \quad k = N_{i-1} - N_i;$$
$$4\,.\ i = i-1, \quad k = 1, \quad \text{go to step 2 until} \quad i = 2.$$

The resultant B_1 would be the blocking probability for priority 1. Now that for priority class r, $B_1(i)$ can all be obtained with above process,

$$1\,.\ B_r(N_r) = B_1(N_r), \quad i = r \quad \text{and} \quad k = 1;$$
$$2\,.\ B_r(N_i + k) = \frac{B_1(N_i + k - 1) + \frac{N_i + k}{\rho_{1:i-1}} \cdot B_r(N_i + k - 1)}{\frac{N_i + k}{\rho_{1:i-1}} + B_1(N_i + k - 1)};$$
$$3\,.\ k = k+1, \quad \text{go to step 2 until} \quad k = N_{i-1} - N_i;$$
$$4\,.\ i = i-1, \quad k = 1, \quad \text{go to step 2 until} \quad i = 2.$$

The above recursive algorithm is very fast, stable, accurate and easy to implement. A four-priority system with capacity $N_1 = 2000$, $N_2 = 1998$, $N_3 = 1996$ and $N_4 = 1994$ has been implemented with around 30 lines C program. With different traffic load, the calculated blocking probabilities are illustrated in Figure 2. For some smaller capacities, we compare the recursive calculation results with those produced by special mathematic software, such as MathCAD, the blocking probabilities are even identical in 10^{-10} order. Capacity as large as one million is tested and the calculation has not encountered any difficulty. General formulas are given in appendix.

4 Simulation Results

As mentioned earlier in this paper, multi-priority Erlang B model can be used to provide differentiated service in both cellular networks and wireline networks. In this section's simulation, we provide a cellular network model and the NSFNET model as representatives.

One should notice that the above analytical models have very strong restrictions: loss network, Poisson arrival, all priority classes having the same mean service time and requesting for unit system resource, etc. In this section, a simulator is developed to remove some of the restrictions. Simulation results are more likely to reflect actual network performance.

In evaluating the system, we consider blocking probability the most important metric. Since rejection rate of about 1% is mostly concerned, figures are illustrated around that. Again, the traffic load, or traffic intensity, $\rho = \lambda/\mu$, is measured in erlangs.

4.1 Cellular Networks Model

In this subsection, we adopt a single cell model with fixed capacity of 20 and Poisson arrivals. No user mobility model is considered. Further, assume handoff calls' mean service time is only half as long as new calls. Note that previous analysis only holds when they have the same mean value. In order to give high

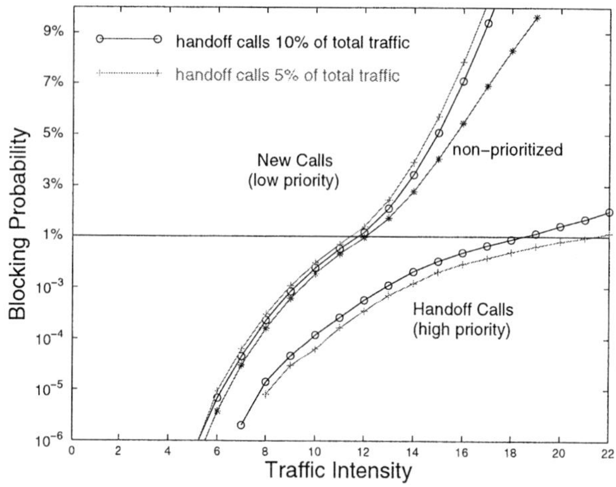

Fig. 3. Guard Channel Simulation Results for Single Cell Model

priority to handoff calls, 1 guard channel is reserved for them. That is, new calls are only blocked when there are 19 channels busy or the system is full.

Figure 3 illustrates $\lambda_1 = 0.1\lambda$ and $\lambda_1 = 0.05\lambda$ cases, and compares their blocking probability with non-prioritized situation. We may observe that, with shorter service time and small percentage traffic, handoff calls achieve much lower rejection rate than new calls in the cell. Meanwhile, new calls blocking probability does not increase much compared to non-prioritized case.

Simple as the model is, it shows that guard channel scheme is effective in providing differentiated service to various priority classes. Our other simulations indicate an increment of blocking probability with bursty traffic (non-stationary Poisson arrivals). When tested with multiple priority classes, the above conclusions still hold.

4.2 The NSFNET Model

The complexity to analyze or simulate cellular networks lies in users' mobility, which ultimately results in fluctuated traffic instead of stationary Poisson process. In wireline networks, things are more complicated in that both network traffic and network topology tend to have significant influence on system performance. This is far beyond aforementioned Erlang B models. Therefore, in this subsection, we use the NSFNET (National Science Foundation NETwork, illustrated in Figure 4) as topology model to study trunk reservation's performance.

The 14-node 21-link NSFNET model is one of the most frequently used models in simulation. For simplicity, assume all links are bidirectional and have the same capacity of 20, and the source-destination pairs are randomly generated with uniformly distributed traffic, i.e., traffic for each node, which confirms to Poisson process, has approximately the same arrival rate. Two priority classes are considered, with the same portion of traffic, $\rho_1 = \rho_2 = 0.5\rho$. Each connection

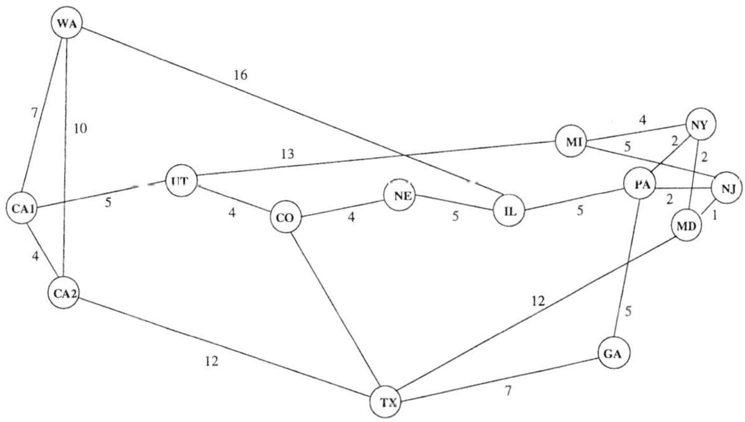

Fig. 4. The NSFNET Backbone Network Topology

request demands the same share of bandwidth, and has exponentially distributed connection holding time with the same mean value.

We adopt Dijkstra's routing algorithm in selecting the least cost path for given source-destination pair. Routes are dynamically calculated. For example, if a link is 100% utilized, it cannot accept more incoming connection requests. Then it is removed from the adjacent matrix which describes the network topology. If there does not exist a path for given source-destination, the request is blocked. For low priority traffic, whenever a link's available resource is equal to or less than the guard channels, the link becomes invalid for the call.

Figure 5 demonstrates the performance for both priority classes with varying number of guard channels. As the number of guard channels increases, class 1 traffic can be better protected at the cost of higher blocking probability for the other priority class. It would be interesting to study the optimal number of guard channels for a given traffic load.

Note that in Figure 5, we perform shortest-distance routing. The distances are shown on Figure 4. Upon simulating a complex topology network, routing algorithm tends to have significant influence on system performance. Two other parameters are considered as adjacent matrix weight: number of hops and traffic load, and thus result in least number of hops routing and load-balanced routing. The former would select a path with smallest number of hops for given source-destination pair, while the latter would choose the one with lightest traffic load.

The three routing algorithms are simulated and the results are illustrated in Figure 6. It shows evidently that load-balanced routing outperforms the other two, especially under light traffic. Indeed, if traffic load is balanced on all links, more connection requests can be admitted rather than blocked. The reason least hops routing also has lower blocking probability than shortest path routing is that the latter would quickly introduce heavy traffic on short links while leave long links under-utilized. Single link's congestion could lead to unexpected high blocking probability.

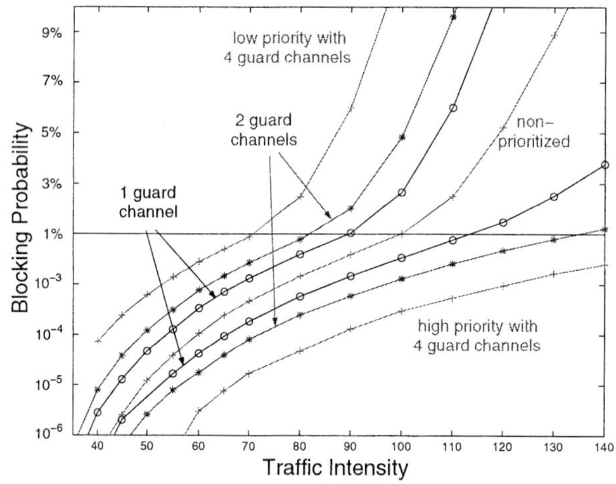

Fig. 5. Guard Channel Simulation Results for the NSFNET Model

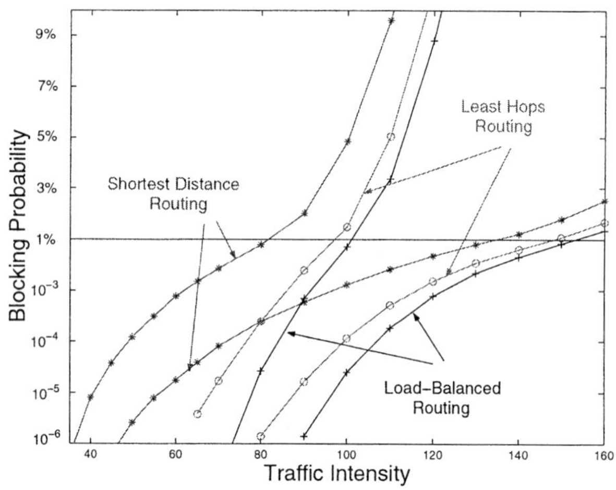

Fig. 6. Routing Algorithms' Influence. 2 Guard Channels

Other of our simulation results prove that hop numbers for all three algorithms do not have much difference, and shortest distance routing does achieve shorter average distance under light traffic than the other two; load-balanced routing has a much smaller average variance for the 21 links' utilization. Load balanced routing is no doubt the best routing algorithm among the three. However, in practical implementation, this does not come for free. In order to find the lightest load links, each node should maintain a real-time updated table of all links' traffic conditions. Even if this is possible, it can cost lots of control messages.

5 Conclusion

This paper studies call admission control problem in multi-priority Erlang B system by mathematical analysis and computer simulations. A recursive algorithm is derived to simplify the computation of multi-priority fractional guard channel scheme. Guard channel, or trunk reservation scheme is a special case of fractional guard channel. We provide a multi-priority recursive algorithm as well. More complex situations are investigated via simulations, which show that trunk reservation scheme can effectively provide differentiated service in wireless networks and wireline networks.

References

1. Akemaru, H., Kawashima, K.: Teletraffic: Theory and applications. Springer-Verlag, Inc., New York, U.S.A. (1993)
2. Bellamy, J.: Digital telephony, 2nd edn. Wiley, New York, U.S.A. (1991)
3. Fang, Y., Zhang, Y.: Call admission control schemes and performance analysis in wireless mobile networks. IEEE Transactions on Vehicular Technology, Vol. 51, No. 2, (2002) 371-382
4. Fang, Y.: Thinning schemes for call admission control in wireless networks. IEEE Transactions on Computers, Vol. 52, No. 5, (2003) 685-687
5. Freeman, R.L.: Reference manual for telecommunications engineering, 2nd edn. Wiley, New York, U.S.A. (1994)
6. Haring, G., Marie, R., Puigjaner, R., Trivedi, K.: Loss forumlas and their application to optimization for cellular networks. IEEE Transactions on Vehicular Technology, Vol. 50, No. 3, (2001) 664-673
7. Hong, D.Y., Rappaport, S.S.: Traffic model and performance analysis for cellular mobile radio telephone systems with prioritized and nonprioritized handoff procedures. IEEE Transactions on Vehicular Technology, Vol. 35, No. 3, (1986) 77-92
8. Le Gall, F., Bernussou, J.: Blocking probabilities for trunk reservation policy. IEEE Transactions on Communidations, Vol. COM-35, No. 3, (1987) 313-318
9. Ramjee, R., Towsley, D., Nagarajan, R.: On optimal call admission control in cellular networks. Wireless Networks, Vol. 3, No. 1, (1997) 29-41
10. Ross, K. W.: Multiservice loss models for broadband telecommunication networks. Springer-Verlag, Inc., London, U.K. (1995)
11. Santucci, R.: Recursive algorithm for calculating performance of cellular networks with cutoff priority. IEE Electronics Letters, Vol. 33, No. 8, (1997) 662-664

Appendix: Guard Channel Recursive Algorithm

Given the blocking probability for class 1 and class r in Equations (5) and (6) respectively, we apply [6]'s method, and generalize Haring *et al.*'s work from two-priority Erlang B system to multi-priority Erlang B system. The capacity is reduced by 1 for given traffic intensity. The general form of class 1's blocking probability $P_1(N_1)$ is given by

$$
\begin{aligned}
P_1(N_2+k) &= \frac{P_1(N_2+k-1)}{\frac{N_2+k}{\rho_{1:1}} + P_1(N_2+k-1)} && k=1,2,\cdots,N_1-N_2;\\
&\vdots \qquad\qquad \vdots\\
P_1(N_r+k) &= \frac{P_1(N_r+k-1)}{\frac{N_r+k}{\rho_{1:r-1}} + P_1(N_r+k-1)} && k=1,2,\cdots,N_{r-1}-N_r;\\
&\vdots \qquad\qquad \vdots\\
P_1(N_p+k) &= \frac{P_1(N_p+k-1)}{\frac{N_p+k}{\rho_{1:p-1}} + P_1(N_p+k-1)} && k=1,2,\cdots,N_{p-1}-N_p;\\
P_1(k) &= \frac{P_1(k-1)}{\frac{k}{\rho} + P_1(k-1)} && k=1,2,\cdots,N_p;\\
P_1(0) &= 1.0.
\end{aligned} \tag{7}
$$

For class-r blocking probability, $2 \le r \le p$

$$
\begin{aligned}
B_r(N_2+k) &= \frac{P_1(N_2+k-1) + \frac{N_2+k}{\rho_{1:1}} \cdot B_r(N_2+k-1)}{P_1(N_2+k-1) + \frac{N_2+k}{\rho_{1:1}}} && k=1,2,\cdots,N_1-N_2;\\
&\vdots \qquad\qquad \vdots\\
B_r(N_{r-1}+k) &= \frac{P_1(N_{r-1}+k-1) + \frac{N_{r-1}+k}{\rho_{1:r-2}} \cdot B_r(N_{r-1}+k-1)}{P_1(N_{r-1}+k-1) + \frac{N_{r-1}+k}{\rho_{1:r-2}}} && k=1,\cdots,N_{r-2}-N_{r-1};\\
B_r(N_r+k) &= \frac{P_1(N_r+k-1) + \frac{N_r+k}{\rho_{1:r-1}} \cdot B_r(N_r+k-1)}{P_1(N_r+k-1) + \frac{N_r+k}{\rho_{1:r-1}}} && k=1,2,\cdots,N_{r-1}-N_r;\\
B_r(N_{r+1}+k) &= P_1(N_{r+1}+k) = \frac{P_1(N_{r+1}+k-1)}{\frac{N_{r+1}+k}{\rho_{1:r}} + P_1(N_{r+1}+k-1)} && k=1,2,\cdots,N_r-N_{r+1};\\
&\vdots \qquad\qquad \vdots\\
P_1(N_p+k) &= \frac{P_1(N_p+k-1)}{\frac{N_p+k}{\rho_{1:p-1}} + P_1(N_p+k-1)} && k=1,2,\cdots,N_{p-1}-N_p;\\
P_1(k) &= \frac{P_1(k-1)}{\frac{k}{\rho} + P_1(k-1)} && k=1,2,\cdots,N_p;\\
P_1(0) &= 1.0.
\end{aligned} \tag{8}
$$

Thus, the general recursive expressions for computing blocking probability are given by Equations (7) for class 1, and Equations (8) for class r ($2 \le r \le p$), which are in consistent with the recursive algorithm in Subsection 3.2.

ACDN: Active Content Distribution Network

Yan Chen, Zeng-zhi Li, and Zhi-gang Liao

Department of Computer Science and Engineering,
Xi'an Jiaotong University, 710049, Xi'an, Shaanxi, China
{chenyan,lzz}@mail.xjtu.edu.cn, zgliao_xjtu@163.com

Abstract. A novel dynamic and active CDN architecture based on active network (ACDN) is proposed. The programmable character of active network makes it easier and quicker to configure new replica servers as well as deploy new policies on demand. A genetic algorithm (GA) based replica server placement optimization algorithm is designed and implemented, as well as active anycast-like user request routing method and policy-based content distribution mechanism. To demonstrate the utility of ACDN model, we implemented a prototype of ACDN, which using extended ANTS active network execution environment. The results show that our approach is reasonable and can satisfied access delay of web application.

1 Introduction

Content Distribution Network (CDN) replicates the content from the place of origin to the replica servers scattered over the Internet and serves a request from a replica server close to where the request originates. Tradition CDN is not flexible and can't be configured in real-time due to the static deployment of replica servers.

A number of previous works have studied how to efficiently and dynamically place web server replicas on CDN. RaDaR architecture [1] proposes a mechanism enable monitoring the load of a large pool of servers and migrating or replicating objects among them to distribute their load and to move replicas closer to the requesting clients. Glen MacLarty et al. propose content delivery architecture [2] that allows individual users to define behavior by specifying content delivery or transcoding proxylets through user-defined policies. Much of traditional work in dynamic replication has concentrated on protocol aspects, without considering the architecture. RaDaR proposes architecture for dynamic web replication, but to deploy replicas dynamically is very different in traditional network. In [2], active network is used to provide dynamic ability, but it's designed for dynamic content delivery not for dynamic replicas deployment.

In this paper, we propose a novel active CDN architecture – ACDN that allows replicas to be deployed dynamically according to server load or user defined policies. ACDN is designed and implemented based on active network to provide dynamic object replication and migration. While the idea of dynamic replication is by no means new, the programmable character of active network makes the deployment and replication process more flexible and easy. To construct a capable CDN, we also

Y. Zhang et al. (Eds.): APWeb 2005, LNCS 3399, pp. 1015–1020, 2005.

focus on the critical algorithms in CDN, such as replica placement optimization algorithm, request routing method and content distribution mechanism.

2 System Model of ACDN

The critical part in ACDN architecture is replica servers. In order to configure replica server dynamically and quickly, we use active node to work as candidate for replica server.

Fig. 1 depicts the system model of ACDN. We assume the Internet environment can be organized into many areas (such as OSPF areas). Active nodes are spread all over the network according to the following rules:

- each area has at least one active node,
- all active nodes in the same area are clustered into a replica group,
- active nodes in the same replica group work together to provide integrated services for all clients in the area.

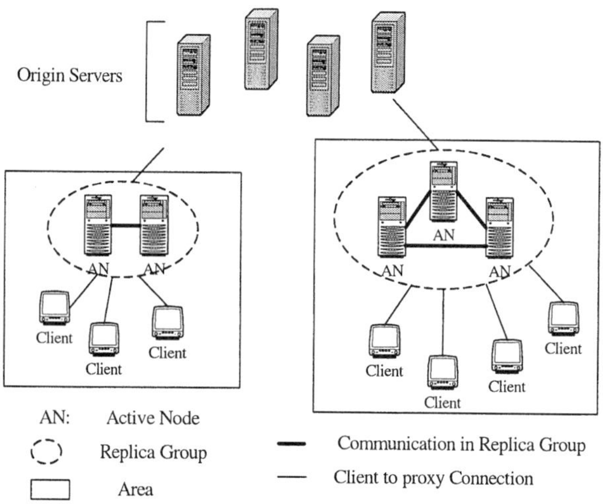

Fig. 1. An example of system model

Active nodes are deployed between web server and client, which can act as:

- Traditional routing node. To servers that don't want their content to be cached, active node do nothing except traditional routing function,
- Web caching node. Active node provides content storage for most web servers to reduce access delay of client,
- Web replica node. Active node replicates all content of a certain web server, and the request of client will be routed to active node.

What active node acts for a certain web server depends on the workload of web server and user defined polices. Normally, an active node works as a shared cache proxy serves clients in the same area. It can upgrade itself to be a replica server of a certain origin server passively or actively:

Passive method: An active node installs and executes active code which causing the active node become a replica server.

Active method: Each replica group keeps the load estimate of origin server. When the gathered message shows that the load of a certain origin server exceeding a threshold, the replica group will elect an active node to negotiate with the origin server and install relevant active code to let itself become a replica server.

3 Algorithms

3.1 GA-Based Replica Placement Algorithm

Assume our concerned web server is *S*, *S* has *k* replicas, which are located in different regions and provide services to the clients of their local regions. The objective of this problem is to optimize the performance of *S* by deploy *k* replicas in right place.

The network is modeled by a connected and directed graph *G(V,E)*, where $V = S \cup C \cup R$ is the set of node, *S* represents web server, C = $\{C_1,C_2......C_m\}$ is the set of clients, R = $\{R_1,R_2......R_n\}$ is the set of candidate replica servers (active nodes). P = $\{P_1,P_2......P_k\}$ is the set of replica servers, which is subset of *R*. For each link $l(u,v) \in E$, $d(u,v)$ indicates the distance of the link.

Definition 1. $\forall u \in C$, $\exists f(u)$ represents the access frequency of node u. P_u is the closer replica server of *u,* the access cost of client *u* to access *S* is defined as:

$$Cost\,(u) = f(u) \times d(u, P_u) \tag{1}$$

Definition 2. The overall (anticipated) cost of all clients to access *S* is:

$$CS = \sum_{u \in C} Cost(u) \tag{2}$$

The objective of replica placement problem is to minimize the overall cost of *S*, that is *min(CS)*. We design a simple but efficient code strategy which use bit strings to represent solution of the problem (chromosome) ψ_t (t=1,2,...,T). ψ_t =$\{R_1, R_2,...,R_n\}$, $R_i \in [0,1]$. Where *n* represents the number of candidate replica server, R_i represents a certain candidate replica server. If R_i has been chosen as replica server then $R_i = 1$, otherwise $R_i = 0$.

Suppose *Csmax* is the maximize value of objective function among the chromosome population, then we define the fitness function as follows:

$$\mathrm{CS}(\Psi_t) = \mathrm{CSmax} - \min(\sum_{u \in C} f(u) \times d(u, P_u)) \tag{3}$$

For replica placement problem, typical two parents crossover and mutation operation may cause invalidated solution. For example, the total number of "1" in chromosome is not equal to *k*. In our approach, we introduce single parent crossover and mutation operators to improve speed and efficiency.

Single parent crossover and mutation operator selects and transforms a chromosome into a new one. Once a chromosome is selected, the crossover operator simply picks crossover length and two crossover points randomly then exchanges the portions of the chromosome around the crossover points. For example, the origin chromosome is: 1 1 0 1 0 1 1 0,the crossover points are 2 and 6, the crossover length is 2. Then the crossover result is: 1 1 1 1 0 1 0 0.

Compare with single parent crossover operator, single parent mutation operator creates offspring quicker by randomly reverses portion of parent chromosome around mutation point. For example, the origin chromosome is: 1 1 0 1 0 1 1 0, the mutation points are 2 and 6, the mutation length is 4. Then the result is: 1 0 1 0 1 1 1 0.

3.2 Content Distribution Policy

The primary difference between active network and tradition network is dynamic programmability. In ACDN, we introduce a policy-based content distribution method, which allows individual users to define behavior by specifying content distribution through user-defined policies. As we have mentioned in section 3.1, all replica servers are active node, all user-defined policy are encapsulated in active code. When being chosen as replica server, an active node should download and execute relevant active code first to maintain content consistency with web server. We have implemented the following typical content distribution active codes in ACDN:

1. Periodic-polling: active node polls the origin server periodically and pull changes to contents it caches. Such mechanism is often used by origin servers whose contents changing frequently.
2. Time-to-refresh (TTR) method [3]: The idea here is to provide user-desired fidelity or consistency guarantees by making replicas track the rate of change of objects they cache.

3.3 Request Routing and Server Selection Algorithm

In ACDN, we propose an active anycast-like mechanism to achieve above operations. Miki Yamamoto et al. proposed a network paradigm for server load balancing using active anycast [4]. In this system, they assume that all routers can support anycast technology (using IPv6 to support anycast address), which is impossible in Internet nowadays. Thus we propose a new active anycast mechanism, which use IPv4 unicast address instead of IPv6 anycast address.In this case, our approach can only be called as active anycast-like.

After deploying replicas throughout Internet, a web server will send IP address of all replicas to active nodes. Active nodes keep the address mapping of web servers and their replicas, as well as measure and record the workload of each replica. When a request to web server comes, the request and response process is depicted in Fig. 2.

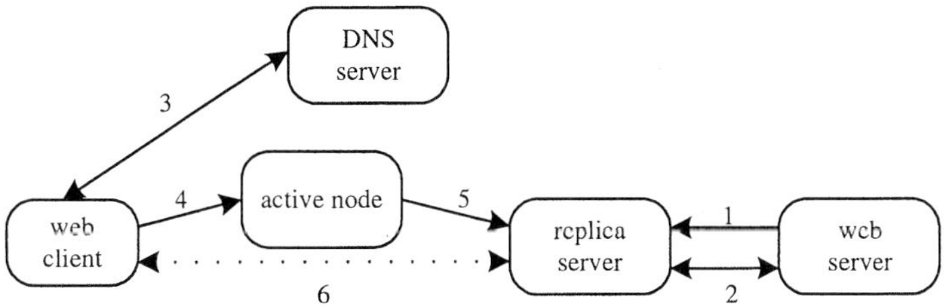

Fig. 2. Active anycast-like request routing

Step 1. Web server distributes active code to its replica servers.
Step 2. Replicas execute active code to maintain consistency with origin server.
Step 3. Client sends a name resolution query to Domain Name Server (DNS) and gets a resolved IP address.
Step 4. Client sends a SYN packet whose destination address field indicates web server address that try to establish a TCP connection.
Step 5. When the SYN packet arrives at an active node, it chooses an adequate server from candidate replicas from the viewpoint of load balancing, and changes the destination address of this SYN packet to the IP address of the select replica server.
Step 6. When the selected replica server receives this SYN packet, it negotiates with the client to establish the TCP connection. After that, the ordinary information exchange phase is started between the replica server and the client.

4 Performance Evaluation

The performance evaluation of proposed ACDN is realized on top of an active networking environment ANTS [5]. In our simulation, we ignore the download time and the processing time of active code, and pay more attention to access latency of client which is affect by network delay and server delay. Furthermore, we make the following assumptions.

- in the network, there are four replica servers (in cluding the web server) which have the same web content,
- the server is modeled as M/M/1 queueing model with capacity of 1.0 contents/sec,
- access to servers are generated as Poisson process.

Fig. 3 shows the result of performance simulation. Fig. 3(a) shows that with the increasing of the number of active nodes in network, the latency can be reduced singnificantly. Since the more active nodes, the more opportunities the client request to be routed to "nearer" replica server by active node. When the number of active nodes reachs 6, the average latency of client is stable, in this instance, the latency mainly depends on processing time of server than network delay. Fig. 3(b) shows the relation between resourse comsumption of web server and number of active nodes. Where resourse comsumption implys the combination of the comsumption of CPU and memory. The result is similar to Fig. 3(a), when the number of active nodes reachs 6, the resourse comsumption is stable, due to the fact that most requests have been routed to replica servers. From these results we can see that ACDN can reduce client latency, consumption of network bandwidth and web server by deploying active node reasonably.

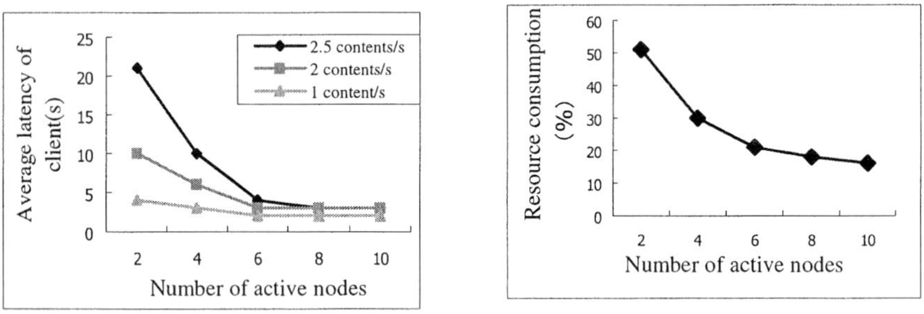

(a) Average latency of client (b) Resource consumption of web server

Fig. 3. Results of ACDN performance

5 Conclusion

The ACDN project is in its early development stages. So far, we have implemented prototypes of ACDN. The programmable character of active node enable configure replica server on demand as well as deploy new algorithm and policy dynamically in ACDN. It expects that ACDN is more flexible and scalable than tradition CDN. And the algorithms designed for ACDN can also be used in traditional CDN.

References

1. M. Rabinovich and A. Aggarwal, RaDaR: A scalable architecture for a global Web hosting service, *Proceeding of the 8th Int. World Wide Web Conf* (1999) 1545 – 1561.
2. G. MacLarty and M. Fry, Policy-based Content Delivery: an Active Network Approach, *Computer Communications,* Vol.24, No. 2 (2001) 241-248.
3. B. Urgaonkar, A. Ninan, M. Raunak, P. Shenoy, et al.: Maintaining mutual consistency for cached Web objects. *Proceeding of The 21st International Conference on Distributed Computing Systems* (2001) 371-380.
4. Miki Yamamoto and Kenji Nishimura, A Network-Supported Server Load Balancing Method: Active Anycast, IEICE Trans. Commun., Vol.E84-B (2001) 1561 - 1568.
5. D. J. Wetherall, J. Gutter and D. Tennenhouse, ANTS A toolkit for building and dynamically deploying network protocol, *Proceeding of Open Architectures and Network Programming* (1998) 117 – 129.

A Real-Time Multimedia Data Transmission Rate Control Using a Neural Network Prediction Algorithm

Yong Seok Kim[1] and Kil To Chong[2]

[1] Samsung Electronics co., Mobile R&D Group2,
416 Maetan-3dong Yeongtong-gu, Suwon Gyeonggi-do 442-600, South Korea
yongseok528.kim@samsung.com

[2] Chonbuk National Univ., Electronics and Information,
664-14 1ga Duckjin-Dong Duckjin-Gu,
Jeonju Jeonbuk 561-756, South Korea
kitchong@chonbuk.ac.kr

Abstract. Both the real-time transmission and the amount of valid transmitted data are important factors in real-time multimedia transmission over the Internet. They are mainly affected by the channel bandwidth, delay time and packet loss. In this paper, we propose a predictive rate control system for data transmission, which is designed to improve the number of valid transmitted packets for the transmission of real-time multimedia through the Internet. A real-time multimedia transmission system was implemented using a TCP-Friendly algorithm, in order to obtain the measurement data needed for the proposed system. Neural network modeling was performed using the collected data, which consisted of the round-trip time delay and packet loss rate. The experiment results show that the algorithm proposed in this study increases the number of valid packets compare to the TCP-Friendly algorithm.

1 Introduction

The use of web servers located on the Internet is constantly increasing, not only for the transmission and reception of text information, but also for all kinds of multimedia applications such as audio and video. Multimedia services using the Internet are rapidly establishing themselves as important applications. In addition, the demand for real-time broadcasting and interactive video services, such as video telephony and video conferencing is also on the increase.

There are a number of studies of the characteristics of networks involving the use of end-to-end pointers to reduce congestion during the transmission of multimedia data [1]. In addition, a useful simulator called ENDE [2], which can simulate end-to-end time delay in a single computer, by analyzing the characteristics of the time delay observed when transmitting real-time data over networks has been developed. Moreover, a network simulator called NS-2 [3][4] has also been developed and used in numerous studies. Based on these simulators, various

Y. Zhang et al. (Eds.): APWeb 2005, LNCS 3399, pp. 1021–1026, 2005.

studies have been performed concerning the transmission rate to use in real-time applications and the protection of the packet loss rate [5][6].

In this paper, through the implementation of a real system, we investigate the changes in the transmission rate according to the variation in the round-trip time (RTT) delay and packet loss rate (PLR), which are two important factors to consider in the transmission of multimedia data. The experiment was performed using the TCP-Friendly algorithm. Moreover, in this paper, we propose a real-time multimedia transmission rate prediction algorithm, using both the TCP-Friendly congestion control algorithm and a neural network prediction algorithm [7][8][9]. The proposed neural network prediction algorithm was trained using the data collected by means of the TCP-Friendly algorithm. The model so obtained was validated using data not used in the training process. In addition, the neural network prediction algorithm was applied to an actual system, using the data transmission rate determined by the one-step-ahead round-trip time delay and the packet loss rate. The round-trip time delay and the packet loss rate was determined with respect to a unit of round-trip. In order to confirm that this algorithm provides effective congestion control, it was applied to a real system for one week at a certain hour of the day. Through this experiment, the effectiveness of the proposed algorithm was verified.

2 TCP-Friendly Rate Control

The existing methods of multimedia transmission can be classified into two different categories. Firstly, the method in which the entire file is downloaded from a web server before being processed and, secondly, the method of streaming, in which only a part of the entire file is downloaded before processing begins and processing continues while the rest of the file is being downloaded. The method of streaming is well suited for the real-time broadcasting of audio and video data.

In the case of multimedia transmission via the Internet, packet loss can occur, mainly because of transmission errors and congestion. In this case, the TCP protocol reduces the transmission rate by applying its own method of congestion control. Therefore, if a number of TCP connections having a similar RTT delay share the same channel, then these TCP connections will have to share the available bandwidth equally. The problem of bandwidth distribution has not previously been studied in detail because, in the past, almost all traffic used a TCP based protocol. However, it has now become the most important issue, due to the increasing use of real-time application services such as IP telephony, video conferencing, at the same time as Non-TCP traffic such as audio/video streaming services. The TCP protocol reduces the transmission rate when congestion occurs, but applications using the Non-TCP protocol will increase the overall amount of traffic by continuing to transmit at the original transmission rate, because there is no mechanism of interaction between the Non-TCP traffic and the TCP traffic. Therefore, it is necessary for Non-TCP traffic to also have a transmission rate control mechanism that is compatible with that of the TCP protocol. In addition, it is necessary to distribute the available bandwidth, by making the Non-TCP traffic conform to the TCP-Friendly protocol, in order to solve the problem known as TCP-Friendly congestion control.

The TCP-Friendly congestion control method calculates the transmission rate based on a TCP model [3][10], in which the average transmission rate over a given period of time can be modeled by considering the operation of the TCP protocol in the steady state. This can be expressed in various ways, depending on the operation of the TCP, but can be basically expressed as Eq. (1).

$$R = f\,(PLR, RTT) \tag{1}$$

If we assume that the size of the congestion window is W and the packet size is s, then the transmission rate before the detection of packet loss can be expressed by $R = \frac{W \times s}{RTT}$, whereas it will become $R = 0.5 \times \frac{W \times s}{RTT}$ when the size of the window becomes $\frac{W}{2}$ following the onset of packet loss. Therefore, the average transmission rate for the entire section of the four saw tooth cycles can be expressed by $R = 0.75 \times \frac{W \times s}{RTT}$. The loss rate, p, for a single saw tooth, can be calculated from the equations $\frac{1}{p} = \left(\frac{W}{2}\right)^2 + \frac{1}{2}\left(\frac{W}{2}\right)^2$ and $W \approx \sqrt{\frac{8}{3p}}$, therefore, the effective transmission rate, $R\,(t)$, for time t can be approximated using the expression shown in Eq. (2) [1].

$$R\,(t) = \frac{1.22 \times s}{RTT\,(t) \times \sqrt{p\,(t)}} \tag{2}$$

In this paper, the RTT and PLR data were collected by means of a test using Eq. (2).

3 Data Transmission Experiment

An experimental configuration was organized to collect the data to be used in the training and validation of the Neural Network. The server and client were built using two computers operating under the Linux operating system and which were installed at Seoul National University and Chonbuk National University in Korea, respectively.

The transmission processor can transmit packets using the TCP-Friendly method. The initial transmission speed is 100kb/s, and the packet size is 625 bytes, of which 64 bytes are reserved for the probe header. The probe header is attached to the header of the transmission packet, in order to estimate the RTT and PLR. In addition, the probe header includes a storage area used to store numbers so as to keep track of the order in which the packets are transmitted from each processor, as well as the transmission time [1]. When the transmission processor transmits a packet to the receiving-retransmission processor, the receiving-retransmission processor separates the probe header from the received packet and then retransmits it to the RTT-PLR estimation processor after inserting the packet number and current time in the storage area of the probe header.

A traffic generator of IPERF [11] is used to implement the various situations involving network control in this experiment. The average RTT is about 10.3ms for the condition in which there is no traffic, and the average PLR is about 0.5%. The RTT and PLR rapidly increased when the traffic load increased. The packet transmission test was performed every 30 minutes over a period of one week.

4 Neural Network Modeling and Transmission Rate Control

A neural network was used to predict the RTT delay and PLR. The training data used for the RTT and PLR were collected by means of a transmission experiment using the TCP-Friendly processing rate produced by the modeling of the TCP Reno congestion control algorithm.

As regards the training method used for the neural network, LMBP was used. The neural network structure was constructed by applying 20 nodes for the input layer, 8 nodes for the hidden layer, and 1 node for the output layer. The actual transmission experiment was performed several times, in each case for 30 minutes. 70% of the experimental data was used for training and the remaining 30% was used for validation.

4.1 Round-Trip Time Delay for the Actual System

Figure 1 shows the predicted actual round-trip time delay produced by the neural network model proposed in this study and the actual round-trip time delay observed in the actual system. As shown in this figure, those data marked by * were collected from the actual system and those marked by ∘ represent the prediction data obtained from the neural network. It can be seen that the round-trip time delay was in the range of 20 to 40ms, in the case where the load was applied to the network, while the round-trip time delay in the steady state was about 10ms in the case of the actual system. Moreover, it was also verified that the neural network model has the capability to predict the round-trip time delay.

4.2 Prediction of the Packet Loss Rate Using the Neural Network Model

Figure 2 shows the results of the test involving the packet loss rate. As presented in this figure, those data marked by * represent the packet loss rate that was observed in the actual system, while those marked by ∘ represent the prediction data resulting from the neural network. It can be seen that the packet loss rate was in the range of 0 to 0.01% in the steady state and was about 5% in the case where the load was applied to the network. Moreover, it was also verified that the neural network prediction algorithm predicts the packet loss rate.

4.3 Accumulated Available Packets in the System Using the Prediction Model

A transmission experiment was performed using the predicted data, followed by the prediction of the one step ahead round-trip time delay and the one step ahead

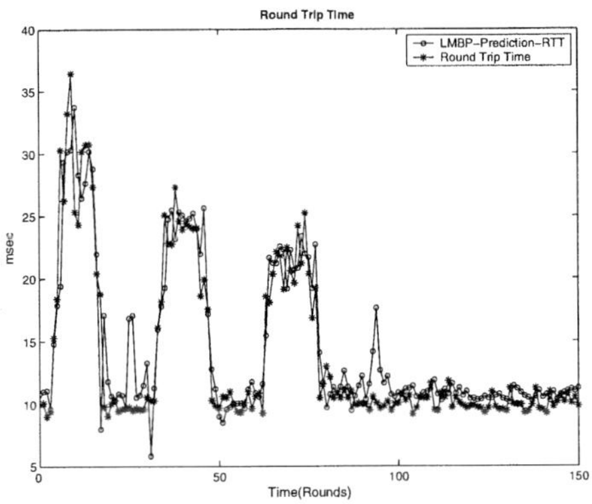

Fig. 1. Predicted and actual values of the packet loss rate in the actual system

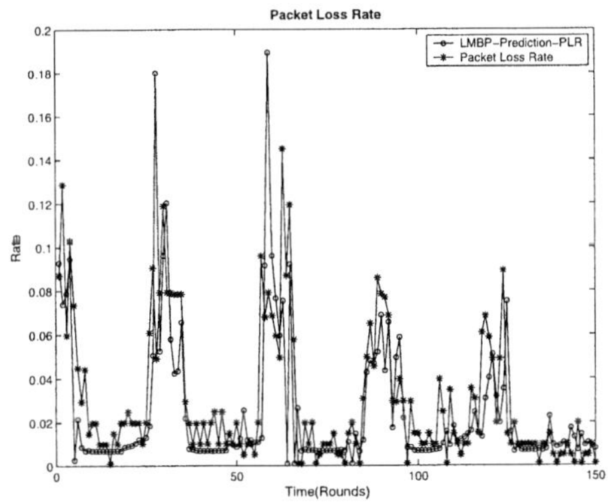

Fig. 2. Accumulated available packets in the client

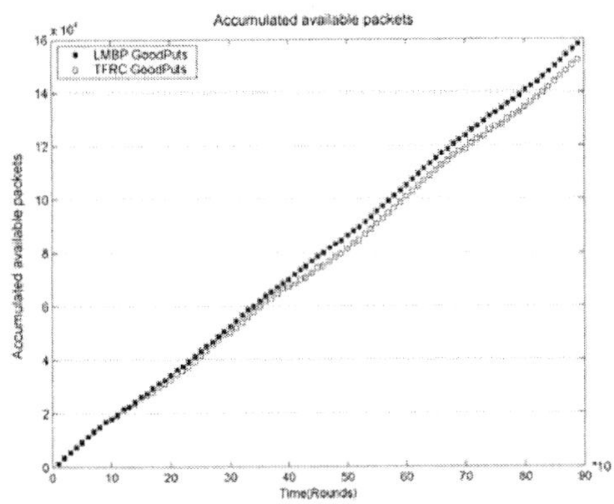

Fig. 3. Accumulated available packets in the client

packet loss rate using the neural network and to obtain the packet transmission rate using the predicted data. Figure 3 shows the results of the experiment involving the TCP-Friendly algorithm and of that using the neural network prediction algorithm proposed in this study. The proposed system can control the transmission rate properly according to the conditions of the network load. In addition, it was confirmed that it sends more valid packets than the TCP-Friendly system does.

5 Conclusion

In this paper, we proposed a system that predicts the parameters using a prediction algorithm and determined the optimum transmission rate by using these predicted parameters, in order to improve the performance of real-time multimedia data transmission over the Internet. A real-time multimedia data transmission system using the TCP-Friendly algorithm was constructed to analyze the performance of the proposed system. A neural network was used as a prediction model and the LMBP method was used to train the neural network. In addition, a neural network model, which was obtained by using the collected data from the actual test, was utilized. The performance of the neural network prediction model was verified through the validation process. By using this neural network model, the one-step ahead round-trip time delay and packet loss rate can be predicted, and the transmission rate of the actual system can also be determined by means of these predicted factors. Furthermore, a multimedia data transmission experiment was performed using these factors. The transmission experiment conducted for the actual system shows that the proposed algorithm increases the number of available packets compared with the TCP-Friendly algorithm.

Acknowledgements. The authors thank KEPCO (R-2004-B-120) and RRC (KOSEF) (R-12-1998-026-02003) for their financial support.

References

1. V. Paxson: End-to-End Internet packet dynamics. In Proceedings of SIGCOMM97 (1997)
2. Ikjun Yeom: ENDE An End-To-End Network Delay Emulator. Texas A & M University (1998)
3. The Network Simulator version2: http://www.isi.edu/nsnam/ns/ns-build.html
4. NS2 : http://www.isi.edu/nsnam/ns/ucb-tutorial.html
5. Q. Zhand, G. Wang, W. Zhu, Y. Zhang: Robust scalable video streaming over Internet with network-adaptive congestion control and unequal loss protection. Technical Paper. Microsoft Research, Beijing, China (2001)
6. W. Zhu, Q. Zhang, Q. Zhang: Network-adaptive rate control with unequal loss protection for scalable video over the internet. Journal of VLSL (2002)
7. R. Yasdi: Prediction of Road Traffic using a Neural Network Approach. Neural Computing and Applications, vol 8 (1999) 135-142
8. Hanh H. Nguyen, Chirstine W. Chan: Multiple Neural Networks for a Long Term Time Series Forecast. Neural Computing and Applications, vol 13 (2004) 90-98
9. R. Baratti, B. Cannas, A. Fanni, F. Pilo: Automated Recurrent Neural Network Design to Model the Dynamics of Complex Systems. Neural Computing and Applications, vol 9 (2000) 190-201
10. V. Jacobson: Congesion Avoidance and contro. SIGCOMM Symposium on Communications Architectures and Protocols (1988) 214-329
11. The IPERF: http://dast.nlanr.net/Projects/Iperf/

Stratus: A Distributed Web Service Discovery Infrastructure Based on Double-Overlay Network*

Jianqiang Hu, Changguo Guo, Yan Jia, and Peng Zou

School of Computer, National University of Defense Technology,
410073 Changsha, China
jqhucn@hotmail.com

Abstract. The Web is moving toward a collection of interoperating Web services. A critical factor to achieving this interoperability is a scalable, flexible and robust discovery mechanism. Yet, a centralized architecture has the limitations of single point failure and performance bottleneck. In order to solve this problem, this paper first proposes a distributed Web Service Discovery Infrastructure called **Stratus**, and then analyzes some key technologies such as Dynamic Tuple Model, topology constructing approach, unified publication and inquiry API etc. Furthermore, the simulation results show that, **Stratus** is scalable, well self-organized, and high efficient for service discovery.

1 Introduction

Web services are self-contained, self-describing modular applications that can be published, located, and invoked across the Web. The Web is moving toward a collection of interoperating Web services. Achieving this interoperability requires dynamic discovery of Web services.

The Web services architecture supports the discovery and binding of services. Web Service registries maintain information describing Web Services produced by service providers, and are queried by service requesters. These registries are important to the ultimate utility of the Web Services and must support scalable, flexible and robust discovery mechanisms. Traditionally, registries have a centralized architecture consisting of multiple repositories that synchronize periodically. However, as the potential number of Web Services grows and becomes more dynamic, such a central approach quickly becomes impractical [1]. Meanwhile, Web Services discovery is further complicated by the natural tendency of the environment to evolve over time with the registries joining and leaving. In order to avoid all these disadvantages, a number of decentralized approaches have been proposed and some systems based on P2P technologies and ontologies have been used to publish and inquire Web Services descriptions [7, 8].

* This work was supported by National Natural Science Foundation of China under the grant No. 90104020 and National 863 High Technology Plan of China under the grant No.2003AA5410, No.2002AA116040.

Y. Zhang et al. (Eds.): APWeb 2005, LNCS 3399, pp. 1027 – 1032, 2005.

In this paper, we present a methodology for establishing some dynamic, scalable, distributed registries with flexible search capabilities, to support Web Service discovery. The proposed infrastructure named **Stratus** can be executed on top of a set of registries to provide the discovery service. **Stratus** is divided into three different layers: the Data layer, the Communications layer and the Operator layer.

The rest of this paper is structured as follows. Section 2 describes the layered architecture of **Stratus** and some key technologies including Dynamic Tuple Model, topology constructing approach and unified publication and inquiry API, etc. Section 3 summarizes related works. Section 4 concludes and outlines the future works.

2 Overview of Stratus

2.1 Layered Architecture

Stratus is divided into three different layers: the Data layer, the Communications layer and the Operator layer. The Data layer is comprised of the Web Service registries that are parts of **Stratus**. The communications layer allows all the distributed components to communicate with each other. The Operator layer enables Registry Peers to support unified interfaces to publish and inquire Web Services. The layered architecture is shown in Fig.1.

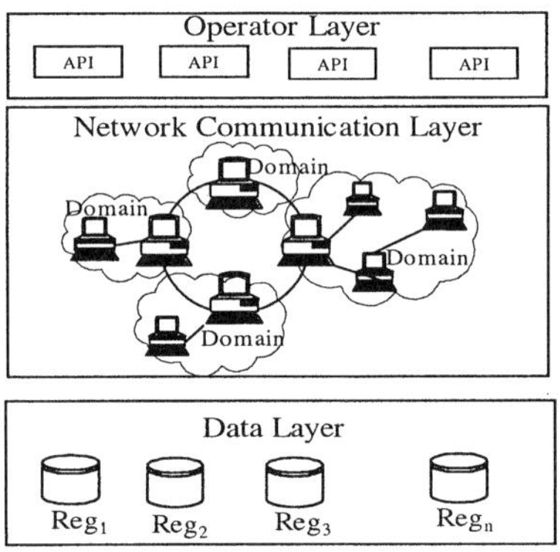

Fig. 1. Layered architecture for **Stratus**

1. Data Layer

As the registries in **Stratus** may have two types of heterogeneity in descriptions: structural heterogeneity and semantic heterogeneity. Therefore, we use tuple model to contain different Web Services descriptions. For broad acceptance, adoption and easy integration of legacy service descriptions, an HTTP hyperlink is chosen as an identifier and retrieval mechanism (*service link*). To address dynamic state maintenance problems, we introduce some time stamps to Dynamic Tuple Model.

2. Communication Layer

Registry Peer runs on top of Web Service registries with each proxy controlling a registry. The Communication Layer is used to establish peer community and manage communication between different registries. Naive registries could be categorized based on business domains (e.g. NAICS, ISO3166, GeoWeb). Each business domain is represented as unique name. A *Service Domain* is usually composed of different registries which have not only similarities but competing business purpose as well, which provides a simplified but exhaustive view of the Web Services registry community, enables logical partitioning of all Web Services.

3. Operator Layer
This layer provides simplified access to registry data and protects users from intricate details in registry. Even if an organization has its own implementation of Web Services registry, it can make the registry available for public access by providing a suitable API as the operator layer. **Stratus** defines unified publication and inquiry API to access Web Services registry.

2.2 Dynamic Tuple Model

Web Services can be described in different ways, such as WSDL, OWL-s, etc. Furthermore, these description documents are often maintained by different data model. As compared to UDDI [2] hierarchical model, Dynamic Tuple Model for maintaining service information is more flexible (by containing different description languages), more efficient (by eliminating data elements complexity), and more simple.

Definition 1 (Dynamic Tuple Model). A dynamic tuple is a soft state data container, where "service Link" is HTTP URL for a description document, "Name" is service name, "Timestamps" is a finite set of time, "Relation" is a finite set of service relations, "Metadata" is a simple structured or semi-structured document(e.g. secure digital XML signature, contact).

$$Tuple=<Link, Name, Timestamps, Relation, Metadata> \quad (1)$$

For reliable, predictable and simple distributed state maintenance, registry tuples are maintained as *soft state* [3]. A tuple may eventually be discarded unless it is refreshed by a stream of timely confirmation notifications from service provider. In according to timestamps, a tuple can be in one of three states (*unknown*, *not cached* or *cached.*) and transition automatically.

2.3 Double-Overlay Topology

Stratus adopts double overlay networks. The upper layer is a backbone consisting of Border Registry Peers (BRP); the lower layer has service domains with each domain consisting of Registry Peers (RP). A dynamical topology construction based on peer trustworthiness and consistent hash in upper overlay network. Therefore, the upper topology is more stable than traditional structured DHT network. Yet, the lower overlay network is unstructured for adapting to registry peer dynamic and autonomic characteristics. Fig.2 depicts a double-overlay network of **Stratus**. (1) Each Border Registry Peer acts as an entry point for registries to join a *Service Domain*. It coordinates admission of each registry in to the *Service Domain*. Based on Chord protocol [4], Border Registry Peers build the structured network. Each peer maintains routing information of about **O**(log*N*) other peers, and resolves all lookups via

O(log*N*) messages to other peers. Meanwhile, Border Registry Peer is aware of inter-domain request. (2) Registry Peers run on top of Web Service registries with each peer controlling a registry. Therefore it is an atomic unit for service publication and inquiry. Based on Gnutella protocol [5], Registry Peers communicate with each other in *Service Domain*. Each Registry Peer is composed of two engines: communication engine and local query engine [6], standing for the two roles that a peer plays. The communication engine is responsible for communication and collaboration with its neighbors in the peer-to-peer network. Meanwhile, it receives and responds service queries from service requesters. The local query engine receives queries from the communication engine and queries the registry for matching services.

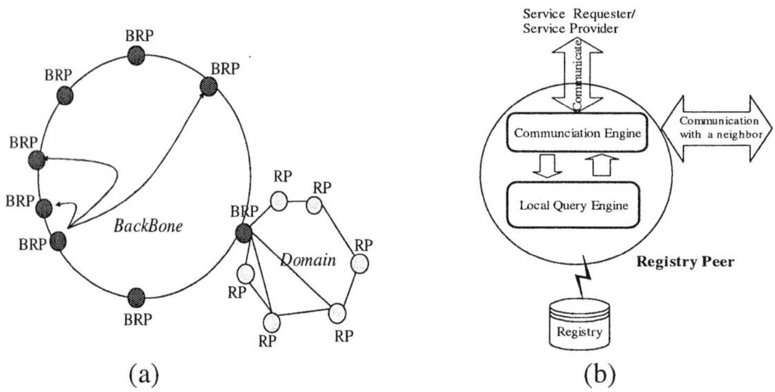

Fig. 2. Double-overlay topology for **Stratus**. (a) **Stratus** consists of structured layer and unstructured layer; (b) A Registry Peer is composed of communication engine and local query engine

2.4 Unified Publication and Inquiry API

Stratus maintains a collection of information about Web Services, including service links, service name and simple description, etc. Each Registry Peer offers unified publication and inquiry API, which allows service providers to publish service information and service requests to inquire service. Furthermore, it shields the implementing complex of different query languages in Web Services registries. It is unreasonable to assume that a single global standard query mechanism can satisfy all present and further needs of a number of registries. Consequently, unified publication and inquiry APIs are deliberately separated and kept as minimal as possible. Besides, finding service with approximate or partial element values might be sufficient.

The three **Stratus** interfaces and their operations are summarized as following: publish(tuple), inquire(tuple) and XML getDescription(URL).Within a tuple, a tuple is uniquely identified by tuple *ID*, which is the pair <*Name*, *Relation*>. If a tuple *ID* doesn't exist, it is inserted into the registry database via publish(tuple) operation. Conversely, inqure(tuple) interface provides powerful XQuery mechanism. XQuery can dynamically integrate external data sources via getDescription(URL) operation, which can be used to process the XML results of remote operations invoked over HTTP.

3 Related Work

The centralized approach includes UDDI, where registries are used to store Web Service descriptions with tree data structure. Although it is simple to discover the maximum number of Web Services with keyword match, the approach does not scale and has performance bottleneck. Conversely, a decentralized approach for the Web Services discovery service is more scalable, more fault tolerant, and more efficient. Neuron [7] system constructs a virtual share space which allows the Web Services to be described in arbitrary forms, and can be executed on top of Tornado. It guarantees that all existing data elements matching a query will be found at bounded cost. Yet, it cannot support range and fuzzy queries. MWSDI [8] system makes use of ontologies and Gnutella protocol to organize Web Service registries and addresses scalability of discovery architecture. It lacks efficient query propagation algorithm and topology optimization policies. These systems cannot keep *soft state* for each query.

We compared latency, space overhead and robustness of **Stratus** with UDDI.

(1) Fig.3 shows the effect of number of peers on latency. Experimental results reveal that the latency of UDDI is roughly 79. This is because of the logical hops of UDDI is 1, and has nothing to do with the number of peers *N*. The latency and the number of **Stratus** are in approximately logarithmic relationship with *N*.

(2) Fig.4 shows that the space overhead of **Stratus** is between 24100 and 25800 bytes, while overhead of UDDI Business Registry between 2.3×10^6 and 5.9×10^7 bytes. Space overhead of **Stratus** is much better than that of UDDI.

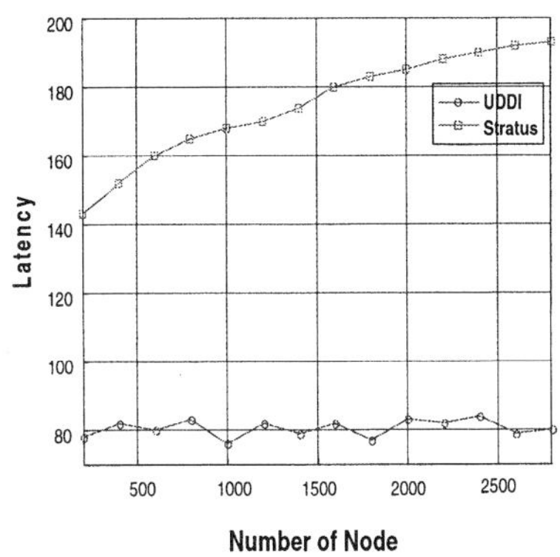

Fig. 3. Number of peers vs. latency

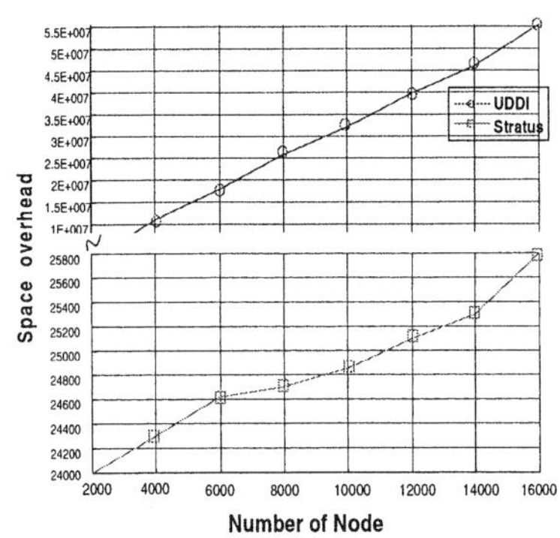

Fig. 4. Number of peers vs. space overhead

(3) UDDI does not scale and single performance bottleneck. We test the ability of **Stratus** to still successful discovery services after a large percentage of peer fail simultaneously. Considering 4000 peers with each peer maintaining 3 pieces of service descriptions, we randomly choose a part of the peers to fail. After the failures occur and **Stratus** is stable, we write down the number of services that could not be queried correctly. Fig.5 depicts the effect of peer failure on service search.

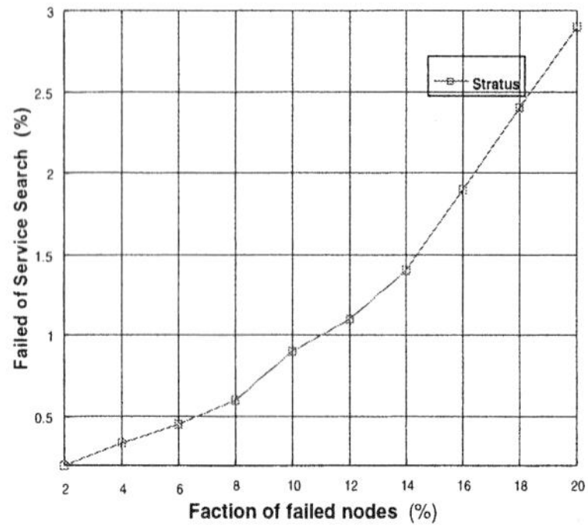

Fig. 5. Peer failure vs. failure of service search

4 Conclusion

This paper presents an infrastructure called **Stratus** for the Web Services discovery. Some key features of **Stratus** are: (1) Using Dynamic Tuple Model to contain different service descriptions and keep *soft state*; (2) Using double overlay network to organize all registries. Besides, we have tested the scalability and discovery efficiency of **Stratus** by using a configurable simulator, and the results prove it to be viable. Issues not covered in this paper that are planned as future enhancements are: (1) query propagation algorithm; (2) load distribution according to registry capabilities.

References

1. Cristina Schmidt, Manish Parashar: A Peer-to-Peer Approach to Web Service Discovery. World Wide Web, Internet and Web Information Systems, Kluwer Academic Publishers, August 2003.
2. UDDI.org: http://www.uddi.org/
3. W Hoschek: A Unified Peer-to-Peer Database Framework for Xqueries over Dynamic Distributed Content and Its Application for Scalable Service Discovery. PhD Thesis, Technical University of Vienna, March 2002.
4. Stoica I, Morris R, Karger D, *et al.*: Chord: A Scalable Peer-To-Peer Lookup Service for Internet Applications In: Proceedings of ACM SIGCOMM 2001
5. M Ripeanu: Peer-to-Peer Architecture Case Study: Gnutella Network. In Int'l. Conf. on Peer-to-Peer Computing (P2P2001), Linkoping, Sweden (2001)
6. Farnoush Banaei-Kashani, Ching-Chien Chen *et al:* WSDPS: Web Services Peer-to-Peer Discovery Service.
7. H.-C. Hsiao, C.-T. King: Neuron-A Wide-Area Service Discovery Infrastructure.
8. K. Verma , K. Sivashanmugam, *et al*: METEOR-S WSDI: A Scalable P2P Infrastructure of Registries for Semantic Publication and Discovery of Web Services. http://lsdis.cs.uga.edu
9. Yin Li, Futai Zou, Zengde Wu, and Fanyuan Ma: PWSD: A Scalable Web Service Discovery Architecture Based on Peer-to-Peer Overlay Network. APWeb 04, LNCS3007, pp.291-300.

ShanghaiGrid: A Grid Prototype for Metropolis Information Services

Minglu Li[1], Min-You Wu[1], Ying Li[1], Linpeng Huang[1], Qianni Deng[1], Jian Cao[1], Guangtao Xue[1], Chuliang Weng[1], Xinhua Lin[1], Xinda Lu[1], Changjun Jiang[2], Weiqin Tong[3], Yadong Gui[4], Aoying Zhou[5], Xinhong Wu[6], and Shui Jiang[7]

[1] Department of Computer Science and Engineering, Shanghai Jiao Tong University, Shanghai 200030, China
[2] Tongji University, Shanghai, China
[3] Shanghai University, Shanghai, China
[4] Shanghai Supercomputer Center, Shanghai, China
[5] Fudan University, Shanghai, China
[6] Shanghai Urban Transportation Information Center, Shanghai, China
[7] East China Institute of Computer Technology, Shanghai, China
{li-ml, wu-my, liying}@cs.sjtu.edu.cn

Abstract. The goal of ShanghaiGrid is providing information services to the people. It aims at constructing a metropolitan-area information service infrastructure and establishing an open standard for widespread upper-layer applications from both communities and the government. A typical application named as Traffic Information Grid is discussed in detail.

1 Introduction

ShanghaiGrid is a long-term project sponsored by Science and Technology Commission of Shanghai Municipality with \$6 million from the government and other participants. It aims at constructing a metropolitan-area Information Services Grid (ISG) and establishing an open standard for widespread upper-layer applications from both communities and the government. Different from other Grid projects in China that are designed mainly for scientific usage, ShanghaiGrid focuses on information collections and services.

Compared to the Computational Grid where provision of computational power, data access, and storage resources is the central task, the Shanghai Information Service Grid focuses on services to the people. ISG will provide information and services including: news, weather reports, traffic status, financial information, community security, ticket service, culture exchange, society education, video conferencing, and many digital government functions such as information sharing, documentation services, regulation and law enforcement, and so on. For example, an instant poll system is able to collect responses from citizens for an important decision; an emergency system can coordinate the rescue activity in a disaster event.

Y. Zhang et al. (Eds.): APWeb 2005, LNCS 3399, pp. 1033 – 1036, 2005.

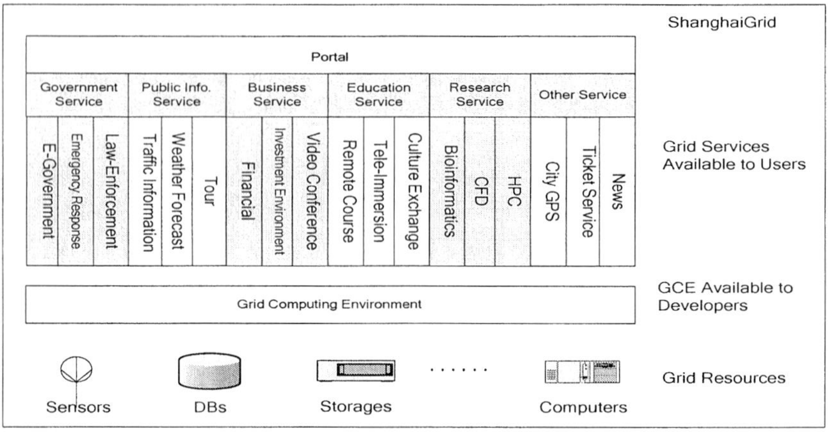

Fig. 1. The potential services provided by ShanghaiGrid

The ongoing ShanghaiGrid project is application-driven. In the perspective of usage, like the traditional web portal, ShanghaiGrid provides various information services such as traffic information service and weather information service which can be accessed by browsers, PDAs, or mobile phones. The potential services that ShanghaiGrid could provide are shown in Fig.1.

2 Background and Overview of ShanghaiGrid

Shanghai is a municipality of eastern China at the mouth of the Yangtze River. Today, it has become the largest economic center and important port city in China, with a land area covering 6,340 square kilometers and a population of 16 million people. It is the entrepreneur city of 2010 Shanghai World Expo. The municipal government is working towards building Shanghai into a modern metropolis and into a world economic, financial, trading and shipping center by 2020. Information technology is a key approach to achieve these goals. Building the City Grid can improve the efficiency of government, build a platform for enterprise, provide citizens with various services, and can keep Shanghai at the top of the world information technology as well. The municipal government has been always paying attention to the development and establishment of information industry and society.

ShanghaiGrid project is one of five top grand Grid projects in China. It is based on the current four major computational aggregations and networks in Shanghai, i.e. the CHINANET (public internet backbone built by China Telecom), the SHERNET (Shanghai Education and Research Network), the STN (Shanghai Science & Technology Network), Shanghai Supercomputing Center (SSC), and various campus networks in Shanghai Jiao Tong University (SJTU), Tongji University (TJU) and Shanghai University (SHU), and is planned to enable the heterogeneous and distributed resources to collaborate into an information fountain and computational environment for Grid services, seamlessly and transparently.

3 Information Service Grid Toolkit

We have developed an Information Service Grid Toolkit (ISGT) for ShanghaiGrid, which provides more middleware services and tools to satisfy the needs of ISG. Moreover, the ISGT hides the complexity of the Grid technique for developers to build Grid applications.

ISGT could be regarded as Information Grid service development kit that may include: Portal design tools, Resource encapsulation tools, Job and workflow design tools, a set of middleware and high level services (Information Service, Workflow Service, Accounting Service and etc.), ISG management tools, Service package tools and etc.

4 Case Study - Traffic Information Grid (TIG)

Traffic jam control is a big problem to large cities. Some ITSs (Intelligent Transportation Systems) have already been put into use in Shanghai, but these systems belong to different government agencies and the traffic information cannot be shared with each other. People cannot get traffic information from these systems directly and there exist many drawbacks such as bottlenecks of data storage, and limitation of computing capacity. TIG is a typical domain Grid in ShanghaiGrid which provides the traffic information and guidance to people. It utilizes grid technology to integrate traffic information, share traffic data and traffic resources, provide better traffic services to traffic participators, help to remove traffic bottlenecks, and resolve traffic problems. Fig.2 shows the detail.

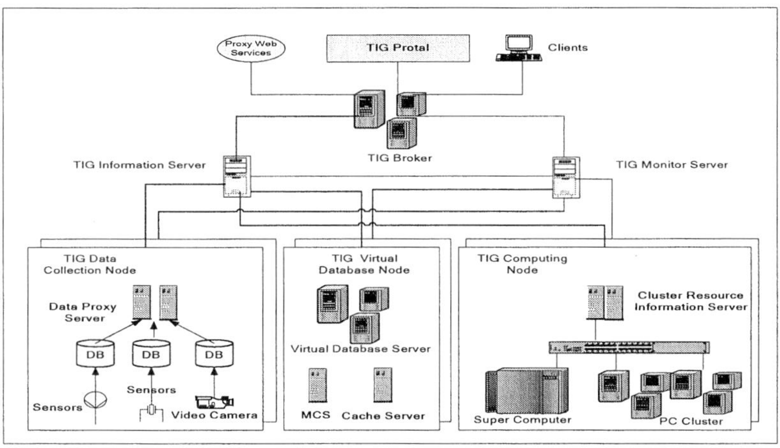

Fig. 2. A typical application of ShanghaiGrid: Traffic Information Grid

The main function of the Data Collection Nodes (DCN) is to provide the dynamic traffic information from various ITSs where traffic data are usually stored in distributed heterogeneous databases. The Data Proxy Servers (DPS) are used to provide Grid data services to other Grid application.

TIG Virtual Database Nodes (VDBN) provides Virtual Database Services (VDBS) which supports uniform access to retrieve data from DPSs. The returned data are cached in cache server and will be automatic destroyed after a certain period of time defined by the Time To Live (TTL) property.

TIG Computing Node (CN) performs the computing task. It is a grid node that provides cluster computing services. Each CN contains a Cluster Resource Information Server (CRIS), a PC cluster (Linux Server), and a Supercomputer. For example, in the SCC Computing Node, the supercomputer is Drawing 3000, the PC cluster contains about 30 Linux PC Servers. The SJTU, FDU, SHU, TJU computing nodes have the similar configuration. The CN exposes itself through the CRIS. The CRIS not only provides the cluster resource information to TIG Information Service, but also manages the backend cluster systems which are used to run MPI application routines such as Computing Optimal Dynamic Path (CODP), demonstrating traffic road states, querying road or crossing information, forecasting traffic flow and so on. CODP consumes most of the CPU time, it is the key problem of lowering the computing time. We use parallel computing technique to solve that problem in CN .

TIG Information Server (IS) provides Information Service. All Grid nodes are registered in IS. It provides the Information about the Grid resources.

In CODP scenarios a user needs input the start and end points. The broker will send the request to the cache server first and check if there is any path in the cache matching the start and end point. If not, the broker will query the Information Service, acquire the suitable CN, start the Grid Service in the CN, and get result after the task is finished. The returned data are cached in cache server. In order to provide users real time guidance there is a TTL property defined by the system. The data in cache server will be automatic deleted according to the value of TTL.

5 Conclusion

ShanghaiGrid is an ongoing project aimed at constructing a metropolitan-area information service infrastructure. The Information Service Grid Toolkit can facilitate the development of the services and applications which include a set of middleware, high level services, design tools, package tools and etc. TIG is a typical domain Grid in ShanghaiGrid providing the traffic information and guidance to public using the computing power of the Grid. The Information Grid will push the information construction of Shanghai and meet the requirement of its citizens.

Acknowledgments

This work is supported by the 973 program of China (No.2002CB312002, 2003CB317000), the 863 program of China (No.2004AA104340, 2004AA104280), National Natural Science Foundation of China (No.60473092, 60433040), ChinaGrid program of MOE of China and ShanghaiGrid project from Science and Technology Commission of Shanghai Municipality (No.03dz15026-03dz15029).

Sentential Association Based Text Classification Systems

Jianlin Feng[1], Huijun Liu[1], and Yucai Feng[2]

[1, 2] Dept. of Computer Science Huazhong Univ. of Sci. & Tech., Wuhan 430074, Hubei, China
[1]{Fengjl, Huijunliu}@mail.hust.edu.cn, fyc@dameng.cn

Abstract. We recently proposed a novel sentential association based approach SAT-MOD for text classification, which views a sentence rather than a document as an association transaction, and uses a novel heuristic called MODFIT to select the most significant itemsets for constructing a category classifier. Based on SAT-MOD, we have developed a prototype system called *SAT-Class*. In this demo, we demonstrate the effectiveness of our text classification system, and also the readability and refinability of acquired classification rules.

1 Introduction

Text classification (TC, also called *text categorization*) is to realize the task of assigning one (*single-labeled*) or more (*multi-labeled*) predefined category labels to unlabeled natural language text documents based on their contents. TC has become more and more important due to the proliferation of digital documents in our daily life. It has extensive applications in online news classification, email filtering, and the like. Many methods have been proposed for TC, including Naïve Bayes, decision trees, *k*-NN, support vector machines (SVM) and *association rule* based (or simply *association* based) methods [2-5].

An association rule for TC is indeed similar to an IF-THEN rule which is manually defined by knowledge engineers in the *knowledge engineering* (KE) method, which is the most popular real-world approach to TC in the 1980s. Naturally association based TC methods have inherent readability and refinability of acquired classification rules. To the best of our knowledge, all the current association based TC methods mainly exploit document-level co-occurring words, which are a group of words co-occurring in the same document [4,5]: words in a document are considered as *items*, and each document is considered as a *transaction* [1], i.e., a set of items. Frequent words (*itemsets*) are then mined from such transactions to capture document semantics and generate IF-THEN rules accordingly. Usually some heuristic such as *database coverage* [3,4,5,9] is used to select the most significant itemsets.

However, the basic semantic unit in a document is actually a sentence. Words co-occurring in the same sentence are usually associated in one way or the other, and are more meaningful than the same group of words spanning several sentences in a document. For example, when word *wheat* occurs in the first sentence of a document

Y. Zhang et al. (Eds.): APWeb 2005, LNCS 3399, pp. 1037–1040, 2005.

consisting of 100 natural sentences, the co-occurrence of word *farm* in the same sentence appears to be more meaningful than its co-occurrence in the 28th sentence.

According to above observations, we view sentences rather than documents as the basic semantic units and have presented a novel association based TC method called *SAT-MOD* ("SAT" means Sentence as Association Transaction and "MOD" means the following *MODFIT* heuristic) [6]. Based on SAT-MOD, we have developed a prototype system called *SAT-Class* for text classification.

The left parts are organized as follows: Section 2 briefly reviews the basic ideas of SAT-MOD. Section 3 describes the system framework and core components of SAT-Class. We give demonstration scenario in Section 4.

2 SAT-MOD: Moderate Itemset Fittest for Text Classification

In our daily life, usually people are liable to emphasize some core ideas by repeating some *representative words* in different sentences, thus frequently repeated words tend to represent a facet of the whole "*document subject*" of a document. Those representative words are captured by Document Frequent Itemsets (abbr. DFIs) in our SAT-MOD method. A DFI is a group of words co-occurring in a minimum number of sentences in a document. With each word as an item, and each natural sentence as a transaction, we can use frequent itemsets mining algorithm such as Apriori [1, 10] to mine DFIs in a document, and represent each training document as a set of DFIs.

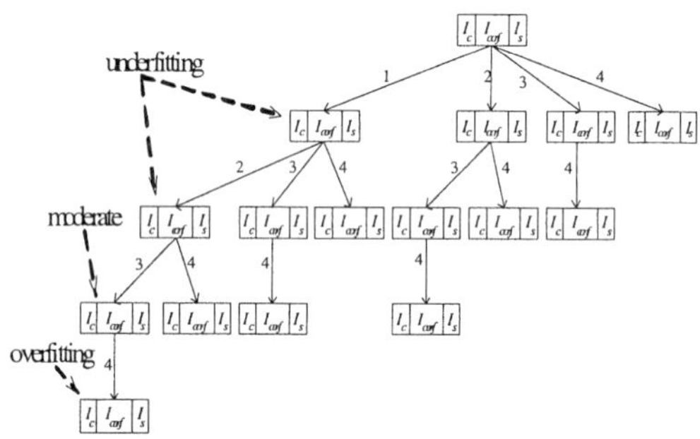

Fig. 1. A category prefix-tree for items 1, 2, 3, and 4

DFIs are then used to generate Category Frequent Itemsets (abbr. CFIs). A *category frequent itemset* with respect to a pre-defined category is an itemset which is simultaneously *document frequent* in a user-specified minimum number of documents in that category. All the CFIs are collected using a *category prefix-tree*, and the tree is then pruned by our novel heuristic called MODFIT. Intuitively, the MODFIT heuristic chooses word groups with moderate number of co-occurring words, which equals to moderately extending a single word with other words along a natural sentence. Using MODFIT pruning, more synonymies are kept to form the classification rules. In addition, we need not apply the step of removing the covered documents, and hence the MODFIT pruning is less expensive. The pruned tree is finally taken as the category classifier. Figure 1 is just an illustration of a category prefix-tree.

3 System Overview

Our text classification system SAT-Class is implemented by three-tiers architecture, which is shown in figure 2. In the database server tier, the RDBMS "DM4" [11] is adopted. In the application server tier, web server "tomcat" is leveraged to provide the http service. The core of application server consists of four primary modules: *Preprocess, GenClassifier, Classify, and Maintain.*

The details of *Preprocess* module are described as figure 3. Firstly, input documents are tokenized. In this tokenization procedure, characters such as numbers and html labels are removed, and the boundary symbols of words and sentences are extracted. If the documents are written in orient language, the tokenizer also does word segmentation by exploiting an orient language dictionary. Then, sentence segmentation, stop word removal, stemming, and encoding are performed sequentially. Only for training documents, association rule mining algorithm implemented by Dr. Borgelt [10] is applied, and every training document is represented as a set of DFIs. Finally, both training documents represented by DFIs and unlabeled documents represented by sentences are stored in text DB.

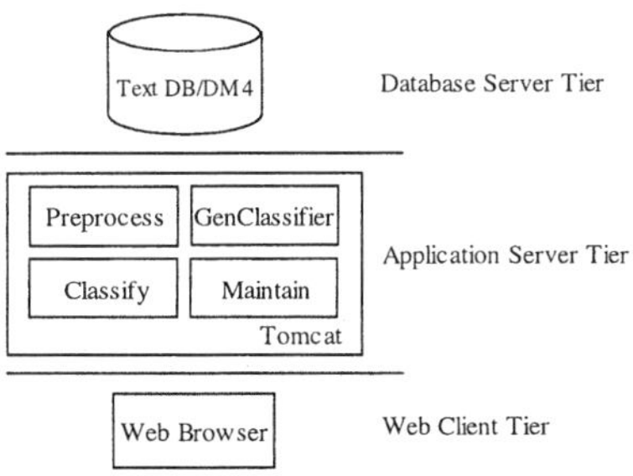

Fig. 2. System Architecture of SAT-Class

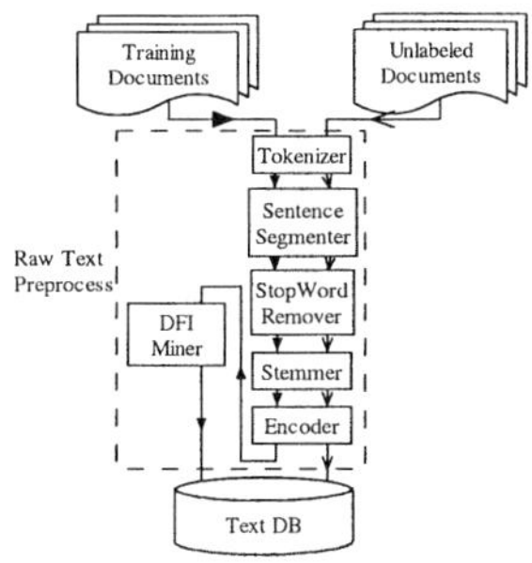

Fig. 3. Raw Text preprocess

After the preprocessing, the *GenClassifier* module constructs classifiers by invoking the MODFIT pruning procedure. During the classifying procedure performed by the *Classify* module, the similarity scores of an unlabeled document with respect to all the predefined categories are first computed, and then that document is assigned to its target categories accordingly. In each category, for the sake of easy browsing, all its subordinate documents are kept in a descendant order of rank scores. Each document is associated with a rank score, which is computed as the ratio of the document's similarity score to the maximum one realized among all the subordinate documents in the category. In the *Maintain* module, three functions are implemented as follows:

- Reading and modifying rules of classifiers

Readable classification rules can help users to understand the classification process. In our system, users can read classification rules in the format of natural language character or words instead of numeric coding. User can also manually refine the rules of classifiers by operations such as "adding", "deleting" or "updating". Those functions can be exploited to integrate domain experience into our system.

- Saving and loading classifiers

The procedure of classifier training is time-consuming, especially when there are too many training documents and/or too many categories. Thus in our SAT-Class system, we provide function of saving and loading classifiers. Saved classifiers are stored in XML files. We can deploy our SAT-Class in another application server by just loading the classifiers previously stored in the XML files, rather than do another training from the very scratch again.

- Adding and deleting class node of taxonomy

Users can utilize these two functions to create new nodes or delete existing nodes. During the adding and deleting operations, only the operated node and corresponding subtree nodes are affected. Thus re-classification is restricted on those nodes. Function of moving class node from one branch to another is not provided yet, for we can accomplish that function by combining functions of saving and loading classifiers.

4 Demonstration Scenario

In our demo, the classification results of two English datasets the Reuters-21578 [7] and the Enron [8], and also one Chinese dataset will be exhibited. The attendees will be invited to experience the system. They can browse the rule sets of taxonomy nodes, and modify the rules by adding, deleting and updating operation. They also has the freedom to perform maintenance operation such as creating, deleting a node.

References

1. R. Agrawal and R. Srikant. Fast Algorithms for Mining Association Rules. In Proc. of the 20th Very Large Data Bases, pages 487-499, 1994.
2. F. Sebastiani. Machine Learning in Automated Text Categorization. ACM Computing Surveys, 34(1): 1-47, 2002.
3. B. Liu, W. Hsu, and Y. Ma. Integrating classification and association rule mining. In SIGKDD, pages 80-86, 1998.
4. M. Antonie and O. R. Zaiane. Text Document Categorization by Term Association. In Proc. of IEEE Intl. Conf. on Data Mining, pages 19-26, 2002.
5. D. Meretakis, D. Fragoudis, H. Lu, and S. Likothanassis. Scalable Association-based Text Classification. In Proc. of ACM CIKM, 2000.
6. J. Feng, H. Liu, and J. Zou. SAT-MOD: Moderate Itemset Fittest for Text Classification. Submitted to www2005.
7. The Reuters-21578 Dataset.
8. http://www.daviddlewis.com/resources/testcollections/reuters21578/.
9. B. Klimt and Y. Yang. The Enron Corpus: A New Dataset for Email Classification Research. In Proc. European Conf. on Machine Learning, Pisa, Italy, 2004.
10. J. R. Quinlan and R. M. Cameron-Jones. FOIL: A Midterm Report. In Proc. European Conf. MachineLearning, pages 3-20, 1993.
11. C. Borgelt. Efficient Implementation of Apriori and Eclat. In Proc. of the first Workshop on Frequent Itemset Mining Implementations, 2003.
12. The RDBMS DM4. http://www.dameng.cn.

Q-GSM: QoS Oriented Grid Service Management*

Hanhua Chen, Hai Jin, Feng Mao, and Hao Wu

Cluster and Grid Computing Lab,
Huazhong University of Science and Technology,
Wuhan, 430074, China
hjin@hust.edu.cn

Abstract. Effective and efficient *Quality of Service* (QoS) management is critical for a service grid to meet the requirements of both grid users and service providers. We introduce Q-GSM, a scalable framework for service management in grid environments, to address this problem. Main characteristics of our framework are 1) grid level resource reservation mechanism; 2) mapping application level service quality to sufficient quantitative reserved resources through negotiating with resources reservation interface; and 3) contract-like service level agreement management of grid services.

1 Introduction

Service oriented grid architecture presents a vision of an integrated approach to supporting both e-science and e-business [1]. In a highly competitive service grid environment, *Quality of Service* (QoS) is one of the substantial aspects for differentiating among similar service providers. QoS problem results from resource sharing among applications. Unless the resource has provisioning as a fundamental capability, predictable quality of service cannot be delivered to a grid consumer.

Research on QoS in grid services is still at its infancy. [2] introduces an efficient wide-area distributed service discovery strategy. It uses caching and propagation of discovery results with client QoS feedbacks in the discovery server hierarchy. QCWS project [3] is a web service architecture that guarantees QoS of multimedia web services by deploying a QoS Broker between web service clients and web service providers. However QCWS does not relate QoS of web services with the supporting resources. G-QoSM [4] provides an application level service management system.

Q-GSM aims at using existing reservation mechanisms to map service level capacity into sufficient quantitative reserved resources. Q-GSM enables service capacity predictability, which is required for proper service scheduling in a service grid. The QoS obligation terms described in a SLA are negotiated before use and monitored during the service lifetime. Q-GSM is also responsible for managing the lifecycle of the service level agreement for a grid service.

* This paper is supported by National Science Foundation under grant 60273076 and 90412010, ChinaGrid project from Ministry of Education, and the National 973 Key Basic Research Program under grant No.2003CB317003.

Y. Zhang et al. (Eds.): APWeb 2005, LNCS 3399, pp. 1041–1044, 2005.

2 Q-GSM Architecture

In our previous work [5], we proposed the model of *Service Virtualization* in grid environment. The main idea of *Service Virtualization* is encapsulating diverse implementations, which may have different QoS capacities, behind a common service interface that standardizes the business function. Based on this model, we design Q-GSM to provide a more available framework to guarantee QoS of grid services.

Fig.1 shows the architecture of the framework of G-QSM, with three components: client components, grid middleware components, and grid server components.

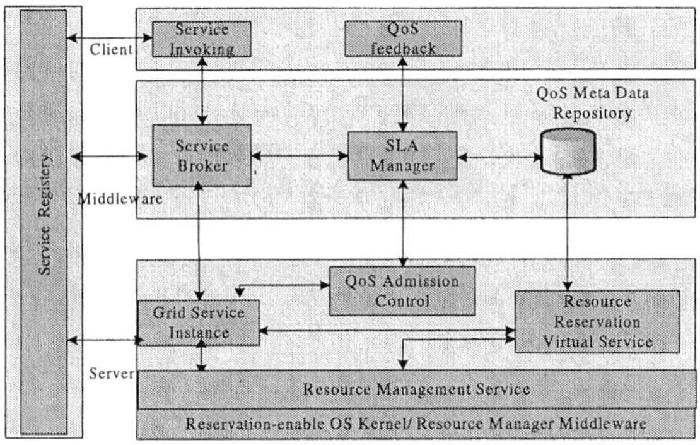

Fig. 1. Architecture of Q-GSM

Grid server is the host environment of grid services. It consists of an admission controller, reservation enabled resource management service, and a virtual resource reservation service. They work together to provide sufficient resources to guarantee the QoS of grid services.

Admission controller is responsible to create grid service instances. During the creation of the grid service instances, the service instance interacts with the resource reservation virtual service to bind sufficient resource to the service instance. The server admits a request only when it can reserve a sufficient amount of resources to achieve the desired service quality.

The resource management service can be any type of the existing reservation enabled resource management system, which has the ability to assign different amount of system resources to different service instances. The virtual resource reservation service serves as an abstract interface to different resource reservation system. It is responsible for function semantics abstraction and protocol transmission.

Different reservation systems are implemented at different levels. *Globus Architecture for Reservation and Allocation* (GARA) provides a flexible architecture that makes it possible for the application to make advance reservation for networks, CPUs, disks, and so on. Q-GSM uses existing reservation mechanisms to map service level capacity into sufficient quantitative reserved resources.

The main responsibility of the service middleware is service virtualization and service QoS management. Service middleware consists of a service broker, *Service Level Agreement* (SLA) manager and the QoS metadata repository.

We deploy a service broker of every common service on the grid as a virtual service and the services located on local resources are called physical services. A broker acts as an intermediary between a client and a set of physical services by providing a single point of submission for request. The requests with QoS requirements from the client to the service broker are scheduled to physical services according to QoS capacity of physical services in the QoS metadata repository.

The QoS metadata repository helps to predictable quality of service delivered to a grid consumer. It is responsible for querying the QoS capacity of the every physical service registered to the virtual service and identifying those services whose QoS capacities match those desired by the service consumer. The selection is driven by high-level application criteria, such as time to completion, reliability, or cost.

The distributed nature of the grid environment makes precise determination of the service state impossible. The QoS metadata repository does not imply any commitment. QoS metadata repository only gives a prediction of the QoS capacity of physical services. To actually allocate the request, the SLA manager will interact with every candidate server to make sure that the service provider will guarantee the QoS of the request and negotiate a contract like SLA. The QoS metadata is assumed to be specified and be updated by the service provider according to the resource status and the feedbacks of the client are also used to adjust the QoS metadata.

The client of the virtual service is for the end user to send their service request with QoS requirements to the service broker. When the client receives the response of the service, it sends the feedback information of the QoS to the SLA manager. Such feedback will help to enhance the precise of the predication. SLA manager determines whether the QoS requirement of the user has been met or not.

Fig 2 shows a sequence diagram among service client, service middleware component and server side component.

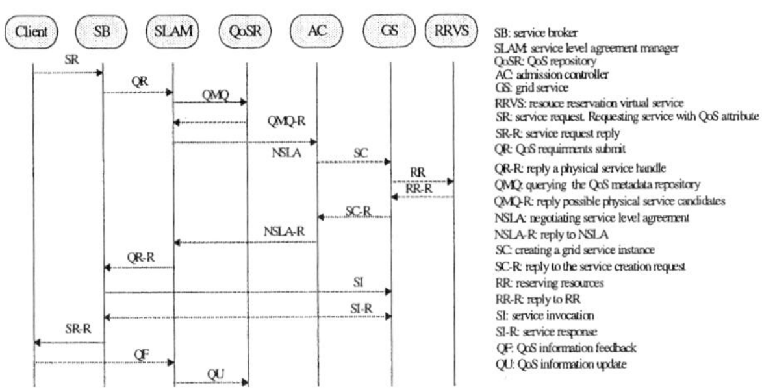

Fig. 2. Sequence Diagram among the Components of the Framework

3 SLA Management of Grid Services

Service management in Q-GSM is SLA-driven. The SLAM dynamically determines whether enough spare capacity is available to accommodate additional SLAs. Fig.3. shows the management framework for the SLA instances during the lifetime. When there is a request from the service broker, the SLAM queries the QoS metadata repository and selects candidate services with the proper QoS metadata.

SLA manager is responsible for negotiating SLA contracts between client and service provider. It is also responsible for SLA management during the service lifetime. QoS objective terms specified in SLAs are monitored during the service lifetime and actions are taken upon violation occurs.

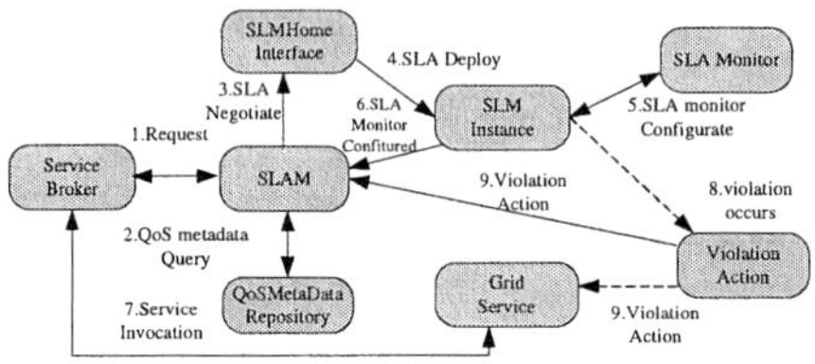

Fig. 3. Service Level Agreement Management Framework

The SLAM is designed in Factory pattern. SLMHomeInterface creates a SLM instance to manage the deployed SLA instance. SLM instance has a lifecycle longer than SLA instance. It configures the SLA monitor service, which has been specified in SLA document. During the access to a grid service, SLA Monitor monitors the SLA Obligations. SLM Instance evaluates the obligations whether they are violated or not. Once violation occurs ViolationAction service will take necessary action. ViolationAction is a grid service specified in SLA. The monitor interfaces can be implemented by service provider or be treated as out-sourcing to third-party.

4 Conclusions

We propose Q-GSM, a QoS oriented grid service management framework. We design an abstract interface to existing resources reservation mechanisms and the management system of the SLA. Our framework makes it easier to build complex application with QoS management.

References

[1] I. Foster, C. Kesselman, J. M. Nick, and S. Tuecke, "Grid Service for Distributed System Integration", *IEEE Computer*, Vol.35, No.6, June 2002, pp.37-46.

[2] D. Y. Xu, K. Nahrstedt, and D. D. Wichadakul, "QoS-Aware Discovery of Wide-Area Distributed Services", *Proceedings of the First IEEE/ACM International Symposium on Cluster Computing and the Grid(CCGrid 2001)*, Brisbane, Australia, May 2001, pp.92-99.

[3] H. G. Chen, T. Yu, and K. J. Lin, "QCWS: an implementation of QoS-capable multimedia Web services", *Proceedings of the Fifth International Symposium on Multimedia Software Engineering*, December 10-12, 2003, pp.38-45.

[4] R. J. AI-Ali, O. F. Rana, D. W. Walker, S. Jha, and S. Sohail, "G-QoSM: Grid Service Discovery Using QoS properties", *Journal of Computing and Informatics*, 2003.

[5] H. Jin, H. Chen, J. Chen, P. Kuang, L. Qi, and D. Zou, "Real-time Strategy and Practice in Service Grid", *Proceedings of The 28th Annual International Computer Software & Applications Conference (CompSac'04)*, September, 2004, Hong Kong, pp.161-166.

Skyhawk Grid System[1]

Nong Xiao, Yingjie Zhao, and Wei Fu

School of Computer, National University of Defense Technology,
410073 Changsha, China
xiao-n@vip.sina.com

1 Introduction

SkyHawk Grid system is a summarizing production of our years of research and developing work, which integrates various heterogeneous distributed computation and data resources into a virtual Super Computer. It provides global uniform access and management mechanism, and supports autonomy characteristics for local systems.

SkyHawk Grid system includes two components:

- Data grid software: GridDaEn
- Grid monitoring software: GridEye

2 What Is GridDaEn

The Grid Data Engine (GridDaEn) is a general data grid system to support uniform and secure access and management of various heterogeneous distributed storage and data resources, such as file systems (e.g., Linux ext2, Windows NTFS), network file systems (e.g. NFS, CIFS), etc. It is the first realized data grid prototype system at home.

- Integrate heterogeneous storage systems (e.g., file systems, datasets, DBs)
- Aggregate various computers (e.g., PCs, clusters, supercomputer)
- Provide uniform seamless access to distributed datasets
- Support virtual dataset composed of distributed data items
- Provide replication and caching mechanism

GridDaen is implemented in Java and can be installed on various platforms.

3 GridDaEn Components

GridDaEn consists of five parts: resource aggregator, data service, metadata service, security service and system management service.

[1] Supported by the National Natural Science Foundation of China (No. 60203016) and 973-2003CB316908.

Y. Zhang et al. (Eds.): APWeb 2005, LNCS 3399, pp. 1045 – 1048, 2005.

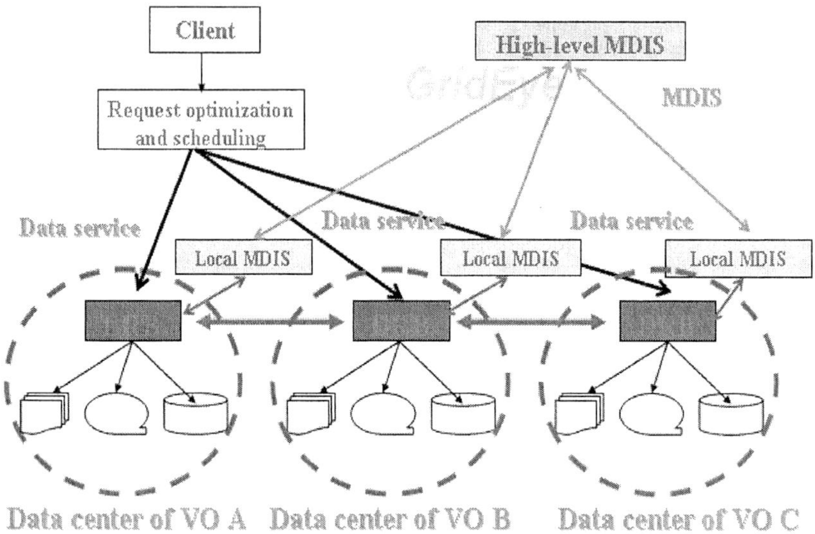

Fig. 1. GridDaen components:DRB stands for Data Request Broker, MDIS for Metadata Information Server. They organize and manage data centers of VO to provide uniform data services

4 GridDaen Features

1. Global Logical View

- Utilize a uniform three-layer naming scheme
- Provide global logical view of data resources in multiple domains
- Shield users from low-level heterogeneous storage resources

2. Uniform Access

- Provide a set of uniform APIs and SDKs based on Web Service to access and manage geographically distributed data resources

3. User-friendly interface

- Provide special GUI, Web Portal and Command Line tools for users

4. Federated services

- Federated services between DRBs and MDISs
- Federated services among DRBs or MDISs
- Distributed data replication and caching
- High performance data transfer
- Flexible, scalable, and highly available

5. Security

- Authentication and authorization by X.509 certificates
- CAS (Community Access Service) based access control

6. Multiple-Domain Management

- Support uniform access and management of resources in different administrative domains
- Provide mapping & management between grid users and local users

5 What Is GridEye

The GridEye is a wide-area grid resource monitoring prototype system, which can real-timely monitor different kinds of information such as computation capability and overload , status of software , hardware resources of heterogeneous platforms.

- Design and realize a flexible and effective information model
- Integrates cluster's (e.g. , PBS, LSF, Ganglia, Dawning Cluster) and single PC's (e.g. , Windows, Linux) native resource monitoring system
- Provide a global uniform status view, including static & dynamic information view and historic statistical view
- Provide a set of service interfaces which is independent of the underlying system details

6 GridEye Functionality

1. Scalable Architecture

- Conformed to Grid Monitoring Architecture (GMA) using producer/consumer model
- Service-oriented design consists of four relatively parts: Monitoring information provider, Register center, Monitoring proxy and Domain monitoring service
- Multi-level structured Web Service based grid monitoring service: local monitoring domain and global monitoring domain

2. Open and Flexible Information Model

- Multi-level structured Web Service based grid monitoring service: local
- Main resource entities form basic hierarchy structure, including: Organization, Services, Cluster, Host and File
- Assistant entities form extended branches, including: Person, Processor, Memory, Network, Application and so on

3. Uniform Access Interface

- Web service is introduced to provide uniform interfaces
- Different systems comprehend access mode by self-described WSDL document from Register Center

4. Robust Storing Mechanism and Intelligent update Policy

- Monitoring information is distributed stored and replicated in different sites, avoiding single-point failure
- Flexible and intelligent monitoring and update policy

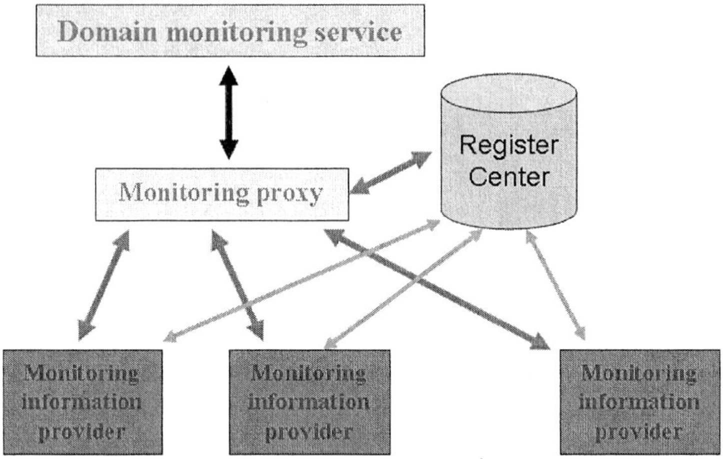

Fig. 2. GridEye's architecture: a provider/consumer model

Cooperative Ontology Development Environment CODE and a Demo Semantic Web on Economics*

He Hu[1], Yiyu Zhao[1], Yan Wang[1], Man Li[1], Dazhi Wang[2], Wenjuan Wu[1], Jun He[1], Xiaoyong Du[1], and Shan Wang[1]

[1] School of Information, Renmin University of China, Beijing 100872, P.R. China
[2] Chengdu Institute of Computer Application, Chinese Academy of Sciences, Chengdu 610041, China
{hehu, duyong}@ruc.edu.cn

Abstract. Ontology is the backbone of Semantic Web. Ontology has drawn more and more concerns with the research works developing in the Semantic Web. The construction of large-scale ontologies will involve collaborative efforts of multiple developers. In this paper, we give a demonstration of our Cooperative Ontology Development Environment CODE and discuss a demo Semantic Web on Economics.

1 Background

Internet and WWW have become important sources for information acquisition. More and more individuals and enterprisers set up homepages on the Web, publishing various related information. In theory, we can get almost all kinds of information we need by Web searching; but in practice, the problems of the unstructured Web pages, the chaos of Web links, the explosion of Web sizes and the diversity and dynamics of Web contents all make it not an easy job to find the accurate information.

Current search requests must be specified as key words separated by boolean operators. Search engines can only retrieve data on a purely syntactic basis. It is not possible to embed domain specific knowledge into the search engines' queries. Ontology approach can solve this problem by providing a semantic foundation in these systems. Tom Gruber [2] has defined ontology as "a specification of a conceptualization". Ontologies provide a deeper level of meaning by providing equivalence relations between concepts; they can standardize meaning, description, representation of involved concepts, terms and attributes; capture the semantics involved via domain characteristics, resulting in semantic metadata and "ontological commitment" which forms basis for knowledge sharing and reuse. Ontologies can provide a domain theory using an expressive language

* This research was supported by NSFC of China (project number: 604963205).

Y. Zhang et al. (Eds.): APWeb 2005, LNCS 3399, pp. 1049–1052, 2005.

for capturing the domain. One of the properties of ontologies is that all relevant knowledge has been made explicit; this constitutes in the necessity of specifying many relationships that are otherwise left implicit and are only made explicit in the applications developed for working with the ontology.

The Semantic Web has been regarded as the next version of current Web, which aims to add semantics and better structure to the information available on the Web. Underlying this is the goal of making the Web more effective not only for humans but also for automatic software agents. The basic idea is to create an environment for intelligent programs to carry out tasks independently on behalf of the user. Ontologies in fact turn out to be the backbone technology for the Semantic Web, Tim Berners-Lee [3] has portrayed Semantic Web as a layered architecture where ontology layer lies in the middle of the other layers.

2 Cooperative Ontology Development Environment CODE

Our cooperative ontology developing environment is based on role-based collaborative development method (RCDM)[1]. The tool has been applied in constructing law and economics ontology in the project for subject-oriented semantic web in Renmin University of China. As the base of building the subject-oriented

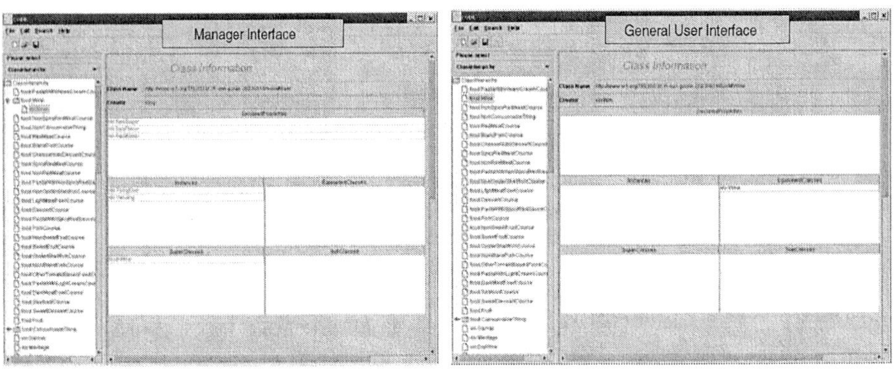

Fig. 1. Cooperative Ontology Developing Environment

semantic web about law and economics, large-scale ontologies on law and on economics are needed. The development environment based on RCDM is the first step towards the final goal, and it has been proven to be proper and effective. The project is a medium but comprehensive system, and we will continue to test and improve our system in practice.

3 A Demo Semantic Web on Economics

3.1 Economic Ontology

Economic ontology is constructed from the resources in digital library of humanities and social science in Renmin University of China (RUC). RUC is one of the most important researching centers in humanities and social science. The economic ontology includes the basic concepts and relations used in economic field. The ontology covers information about experts and scholars, science institutions, science conferences, science and research projects, statistic information, case information, information sources and glossary entry etc.

3.2 A Combination with Digital Library

During the process of building the Economic Semantic Web, we work closely with the Digital Library team of RUC. The quick development of Web information retrieval has posed new challenges and opportunities to traditional library researchers. The Digital Library team of RUC is creating tools and services needed by the RUC Libraries to create, manage and employ digital resources, as well as those needed by the RUC University community and the world beyond to access and use the libraries' digital collections. As cited above, the Economic ontology is constructed from the resources of the Digital Library in RUC. The demo Semantic Web we are currently building is planned to be deployed to the Portal of the Digital Library, making it a good Semantic Web demonstration.

3.3 Economic Semantic Web

The Economic Semantic Web is a subject-oriented Semantic Web, with its focus on economic field. The Economic Semantic Web uses multi-layered representation framework. XML is used to describe the structure of documents in an unifying way. RDF brings the ability of describing the semantics of document structures. With the development of Semantic Web research, we are more and more concerned with the problem of representing and retrieving information content on the Web. The ontology language layer building on top of RDF schema is used to formally describe the meaning of terms in the Web documents vocabularies, which plays a key role in building Semantic Web. Web ontology language (OWL [5]) is the standard Web ontology language proposed by W3C, it is used in Economic Semantic Web to define economic ontology. OWL has three sublanguages: OWL Full, OWL DL and OWL Lite.

OWL is the basic file format in our Economic Semantic Web system. An OWL document can include an optional ontology header and any number of class, property, and individual descriptions or axioms. A named class in an OWL ontology can be described by a class identifier. An anonymous class can be described by exhaustively enumerating all the individuals that form the instances of this class (owl:oneOf), by a property restriction (owl:Restriction), or by logical operation on two or more classes (owl:intersectionOf, owl:unionOf, owl:complementOf). Property restrictions include value (owl:allValuesFrom) and cardinality restrictions (owl:cardinality, owl:maxCardinality, owl:minCardinality). The semantics of OWL is defined based on model theory, in the way analogous to the semantics of Description Logic[6]. OWL DL sub-language can be mapped to SHIQ description logic.

The reasoning capabilities of the system is provided by Description Logic. Description Logic is a subset of Predicate Logic. It allows specifying a terminological hierarchy using a restricted set of first order logic formulas; therefore it is well suited for modelling. Latest research proposes that it is possible and even more efficient to transfer Description Logic into Horn Logic Programs. Description Logic provides a reasonably sophisticated facility for defining categories in terms of existing relations.

3.4 IIR on the Economic Semantic Web

Intelligent Information Retrieval is supported on the Economic Semantic Web. Keyword (Syntactic)-based retrieval has been popularized by current Web search services. However, due to the problems associated with polysemy and synonym [4], web users are often unable to get the accurate information they are looking for. Concept retrieval is one of solutions to this problem. Using the concepts and relations defined in economic ontology, the Economic Semantic Web supports concept retrieval on economic field, gains a better recall and precision performance than the traditional search services.

4 Conclusion

We give a brief demonstration of our Cooperative Ontology Development Environment CODE in the paper, and discuss the design and functionalities of the Economic Semantic Web being built at RUC.

References

1. Man Li, Dazhi Wang, Xiaoyong Du and Shan Wang, Ontology Construction for Semantic Web: A Role-based Collaborative Development Method , to be appeared in APWeb05, 2005
2. Gruber T. R., Toward Principles for the Design of Ontologies Used for Knowledge Sharing, International Journal of Human and Computer Studies, 43(5/6): 907-928, 1995
3. Tim Berners-Lee, James Hendler and Ora Lasilla, The Semantic Web, The Scientific American, May 2001
4. Jiawei Han, Kevin Chen-Chuan Chang, Data Mining for Web Intelligence. IEEE Computer 35(11): 64-70 , 2002
5. W3C,"OWL Web Ontology Language Overview ", http://www.w3.org/TR/owl-features/, 2004
6. The Description Logic Handbook - Theory, Implementation and Applications, F. Baader, D. Calvanese, D. McGuiness, D. Nardi, and P. Patel-Schneider, editors, Cambridge University Press, 2003

Dart Database Grid: A Dynamic, Adaptive, RDF-Mediated, Transparent Approach to Database Integration for Semantic Web*

Zhaohui Wu, Huajun Chen, Yuxing Mao, and Guozhou Zheng

College of Computer Science, Zhejiang University,
Hangzhou, 310027, China
{wzh, huajunsir, dengsg, maoyx}@zju.edu.cn

Abstract. This paper demonstrated the Dart Database Grid system developed by Grid Research Center of Zhejiang University. Dart Database Grid is built upon several Semantic Web standards and the Globus grid toolkits. It is mainly intended to provide a Dynamic, Adaptive , RDF-mediated and Transparent (DART) approach to database integration for semantic web. This work has been applied to integrate data resources from the application domain of Traditional Chinese Medicine.

Keywords: Semantic Web, Grid Computing, Database Integration, Ontology.

1 Overview

The rapid growth of web along with the increasing decentralization of organizational structures has led to the creation of a vast interconnected network of distributed electronic information. In present of such a new setting, one maybe needs to perform dynamic database integration over perhaps hundreds of or even thousands upon thousands of geographically distributed, semantically heterogeneous data sources that are subject to different organizations or individuals. Building upon techniques from both Semantic Web and Grid development, we have developed an operational prototype called Dart Database Grid [†] [1] to address above problems. DartGrid exhibits a Dynamic, Adaptive , RDF-mediated and Transparent (DART) approach to database integration for semantic web. With DartGrid, the user can:

- Integrate heterogeneous, cross-enterprise databases using RDF/OWL semantic.
- Query a relational database using RDF-based semantic query language.
- Publish a relational database onto the Semantic Web by web/grid service.

* This work is supported by China 973 fundamental research and development project: The research on application of semantic grid on the knowledge sharing and service of Traditional Chinese Medicine; China 211 core project: Network-based Intelligence and Graphics; Data Grid for Traditional Chinese Medicine, subprogram of the Fundamental Technology and Research Program, China Ministry of Science and Technology.

† DartGrid Homepage: http://grid.zju.edu.cn. An easy-install demo is available at the website.

Y. Zhang et al. (Eds.): APWeb 2005, LNCS 3399, pp. 1053 – 1057, 2005.

- Dynamically aggregate a set of database resources for integration at runtime.
- Visually specify the mapping from relational schema to mediated RDF schema.
- Visually construct a RDF-based semantic query .
- Graphically browse the query result as RDF graph.

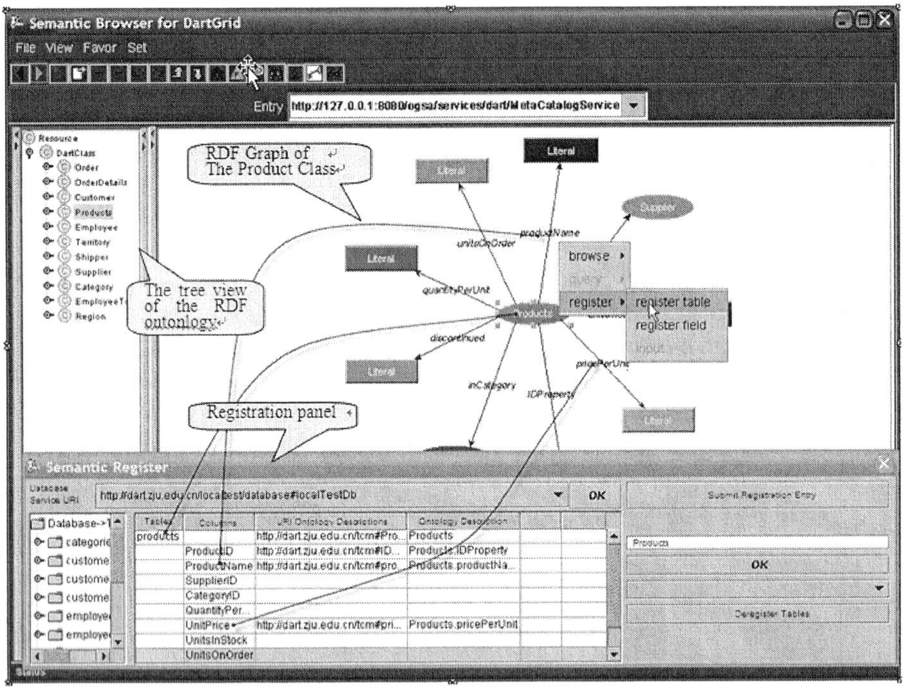

Fig. 2. Visual tool for Relational-to-RDF schema mapping

DartGrid is built upon the Globus toolkit, the widely accepted grid development platform. As Figure 1 displays, a set of grid services are developed within DartGrid. For examples:

- The Ontology Service (OntoS) is used to expose mediated RDF/OWL ontologies;
- The Semantic Query Service (SemQS) is used to accept RDF queries and transform them to corresponding SQL queries;
- The Semantic Registration Service (SemRS) is used to expose the mapping information from source relational schema to mediated RDF schema;
- The Database Grid Service is used to expose the data and schema of RDBMS.

These set of services provide the developer with the necessary facilities to develop web/grid-service-oriented client applications. The DartBrowser [2] of DartGrid is such kind of client application. With DartBrowser, the user can graphically browser RDF ontologies retrieved from the ontology service, visually construct a RDF-based semantic query and submit it to the semantic query service; visually specify the mapping between a relational schema to mediated RDF schema and submit the registration entry to the semantic registration service. At last, we note that DartGrid effort was motivated by the application of web-based data sharing and database integration for Traditional Chinese Medicine (TCM)[3] . Currently, in our deployed testbed, an ontology service, with about 10,000 records of TCM ontology instances contained, has been set up, and ten nodes with 50+ TCM-related databases have been deployed.

2 RDF-Based Relational Schema Mediation

The task of schema mapping from relational model to RDF model has proven to be burdensome and erroneous. DartGrid provides offers a visual tool to facilitate the task of schema mapping. This releases the user from costly and erroneous task of manually editing a mapping file. As Figure 2 displays, The user can specify which table should be mapped onto which classes and which column should be mapped onto which properties. When finishing the mapping definition, the tool will automatically generate a registration entry in RDF/XML format, and this entry will be submitted to the semantic registration service .

3 Semantic Query Processing

DartGrid offers a semantic browser [2] enabling user to interactively specify a semantic query. The typical working scenario is :1)User visits a Ontolog Service and browses ontologies graphically; 2)User selects classes and properties of interest, specifies the constraints, and a semantic query string will be generated simultaneously; 3)User submits this semantic query string to the Semantic Query Service; 4)When the result (also in RDF/XML format) is returned, the user can browse the result graphically again. Figure 3 and 4 illustrate an example from our TCM application. It showcases how user can step-by-step specify a semantic query to find out Chinese *CompoundFormulas* constituted by some Chinese *UnitMedicine* that can help *influenza.* In the first step (the upper-left part of the figure), the user selects the *tcm:CompoundFormulas* class (labeled with "1" in the figure) and its three

properties: *tcm:name* (labeled with "2"), *tcm:madeBy* (labeled with "3"), and *tcm:usage* (labeled with "4"). The user also specifies a relationship between *tcm:CompoundFormulas* class and *tcm:UnitMedicine* class (labeled with "6" in the figure) in this query. The relationship is called *tcm:constituedBy* (labeled with "5") . In the second step (the upper-right part), the user selects the *tcm:UniteMedicine* class and one of its properties (*tcm: name*) and one relationship (*tcm:cure*) as well as do in the first step. The *tcm:cure* (labeled with "7") relate the *tcm:UniteMedicine* and *tcm:Disease* class(labeled with "8"). In the third step, the user selects the *tcm:Disease* class and one of its properties (*tcm: name*) as well as dose in the last two steps, and input a constraint which specify that the *tcm:name* of the *tcm:Disease* should be "influenza".

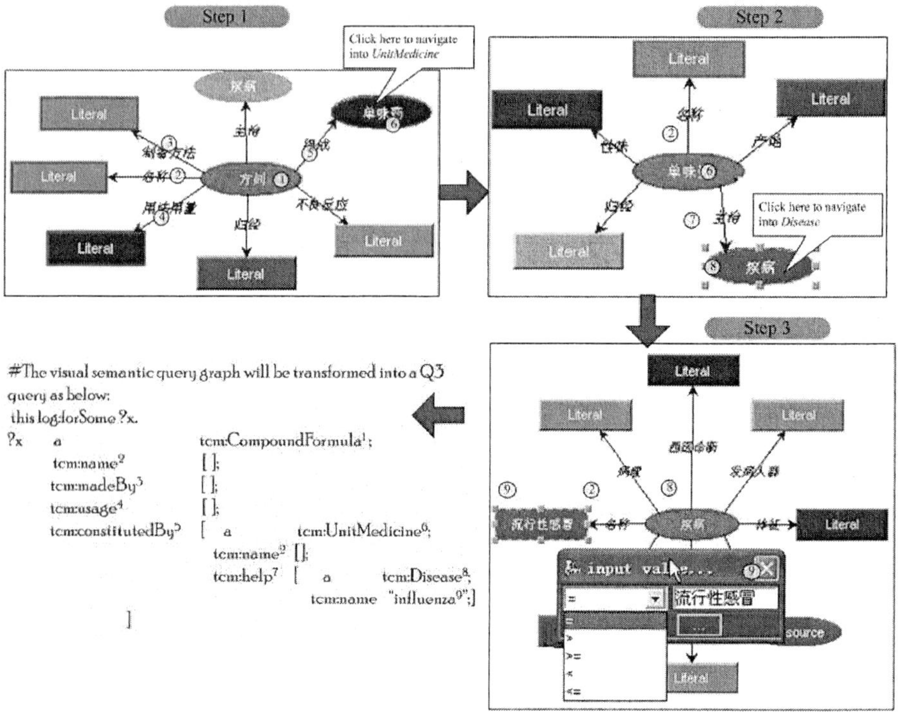

Fig. 3. An example of visual semantic query

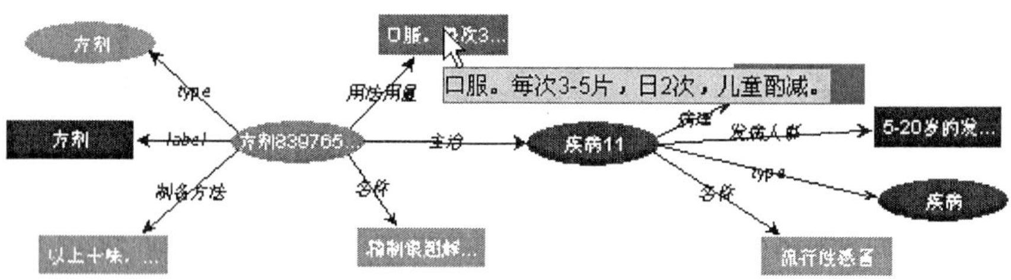

Fig. 4. The query result. The result retrieved from databases will be wrapped by RDF semantic and converted to RDF/XML format before returned to the semantic browser

4 Summary

We finally give a summary of the characteristics of DartGrid . Firstly, DartGrid exposes database resources as web/grid services. The semantic query interface for processing RDF queries is also implemented as a web/grid service, so that the user can develop service-oriented RDF applications. This web-service-oriented architecture is quite important for web-oriented database integration. Secondly,

synthesized speech, digitized audio, recognition of spoken and DTMF (Dual Tone Multi-Frequency) key input, recording of spoken input, telephony, and mixed initiative conversations. VoiceXML uses natural dialog. Its major goal is to bring the advantages of Web-based development and content delivery to interactive voice response applications [1]. Since the technology uses XML syntax, it can be easily used with other XML based technologies, such as Web Services, to send and receive data/information via the Internet.

Designing a VUI is very different from designing other user interfaces. Most user interfaces usually offer some visual information for users to interact with. With VUI, users have to listen, memorize, and speak to interact with the system. The VUI cannot provide rich content information because users are not able to memorize pages of verbal information. The design has to be simple, with short and clear dialogs so that users can navigate through the service without any problem. Speech recognition technology is still imperfect, and users encounter failure for various reasons. It is important to accommodate errors when designing a VUI. Also users possess a wide variety of voice, speech skills and vocabularies, and all these factors must be considered.

3 VUI Design for a Telephone Application

A VUI for a 'Cinema Service' telephone application is designed using Jakob Nielsen Ten Usability Heuristics [2] and hosted by a voice hosting service provider. The application provides the following functions:

- Search for movie by name, genre, classification, release date and actor
- Listen to movie reviews, ratings and trailer
- Find session times

The following is a sample VoiceXML code as part of VUI design for the telephone application:

```
<?xml version="1.0" ?>
<vxml version="2.0">
<form id="greeting"><block>Welcome to the Cinema service.
<goto next="#main"/></block>
</form>
<menu accept="approximate" dtmf = "false" id = "main">
<prompt>You can book movie tickets, find session times, ...
What would you like to do?</prompt>
</menu>
<form id="book">
<block> Booking movie tickets. <goto next = "book.vxml" />
</block>
</form>
...
</vxml>
```

4 Experiments

Designing a VUI is a relatively new experience for most developers. There are very few good VUI guidelines available today mainly because VUI design is so new and requires ample usability testing [3]. In order to improve the initial VUI design, a series of experiments are conduced on the 'Cinema Service' telephone application.

4.1 Experiment 1 – Navigation

The aim of this experiment is to find out the experience of users in navigating through the application. Users are not given any instructions.

During the experiment, users perform the following sequence of tasks:

Task 1: Find out the running time of the movie "Superman 5".
Task 2: Find the five-star rating of the movie "Matrix 4".
Task 3: Find all session times for "Aliens vs. Predator" on Friday night.
Task 4: Book two movie tickets for "Predator 3" at noon on Tuesday.
Task 5: Find all movies staring "Tom Jones".

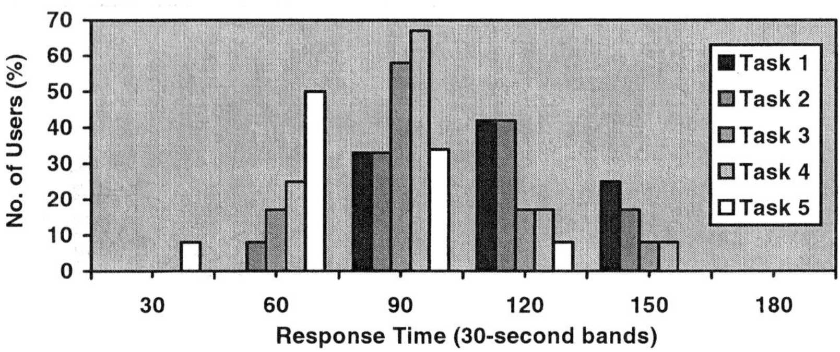

Fig. 1. Results of Experiment 1

The experimental results in Fig.1 show that all the users are slow at the beginning and become more comfortable with the application and improve their skills progressively. In the end users start to predict and 'barge in'. It indicates that an advanced user interface should be created for experienced users.

4.2 Experiment 2 – Memory and Age Group

The second experiment aims to find out how long and how many voice prompts can be spoken to a user before the user forgets previous prompts or gets confused.

Four separate menus are created for this experiment.

Menu 1: Four links, each link has a brief description
Menu 2: Four links, each link has a long description
Menu 3: Eight links, each link has a short description
Menu 4: Eight links, each link has a long detailed description

Users find all the menus easy to remember, except for the last menu which is long and detailed. However, the experimental results show that there is no correlation between age groups (18 to 39 and 40 plus) and the number of links that can be memorized.

4.3 Experiment 3 – TTS Settings and Pre-recorded Prompts

This experiment intends to investigate user-preferred application settings. Users are asked to answer the following questions:

- Do you prefer a male or female voice?
- How do you understand the TTS (Text-to-Speech) voice?
- Do you prefer TTS or pre-recorded human voice prompts?

Table 1. Results of Experiment 3

Gender	
Female	75%
Male	25%

Understanding TTS	
All	75%
Most	25%

Voice Preference	
TTS (Computer)	33%
Pre-recorded (Human)	67%

As indicated in Table 1, majority of users prefer female TTS voice. Nearly all users can understand TTS voices. And pre-recorded human voice is preferred over the computer generated TTS voice. Due to the fact that all the dynamic contents have to be played to users via the TTS, female TTS voice is the choice.

5 Conclusions

A VUI for a VoiceXML telephone application has been designed and a number of experiments carried out. From the experimental results, it can be concluded that two separate user interfaces should be created so that users with different levels of experience can choose a different interface. Multiple, long and descriptive prompts make navigation difficult and female TTS voice is preferred for dynamic VUI.

References

1. McGlashan, S. et al.: Voice Extensible Markup Language (VoiceXML) Version 2.0, http://www.w3.org/TR/voicexml20/, W3C Recommendation 16 March 2004.
2. Nielsen, J.: Heuristic Evaluation of User Interfaces, Proc. of ACM CHI'90 Conference. Seattle, WA, 1-5 April (1990) 249-256.
3. Yankelovich, N.: Designing Effective Speech Interfaces, John Wiley & Sons, Inc. (2000)

Content Browsing by Walking in Real and Cyber Spaces

Satoshi Nakamura, Sooyeon Oh,
Mitsuru Minakuchi, and Rieko Kadobayashi

National Institute of Information and Communications, Japan
3-5, Hikaridai, Seika-cho Soraku-gun, Kyoto, 619-0289, Japan
{gon, sooyeon, mmina, rieko}@nict.go.jp
http://www2.nict.go.jp/jt/a133/indexe.html

Abstract. "Walking" style operations for browsing content are described. This style is intuitive and enjoyable and enables the daily use of digital content. We illustrate the concept with two examples. One is EnergyBrowser, a physical walking interface for browsing Web pages. The other is a comparative 3D archive browser, which is for 3D archives. It automatically controls the viewpoint in comparing content based on the user's view control in focused content.

1 Introduction

Though a vast amount of digital media content has become available, browsing and manipulating methods are mainly restricted to interfaces of a computer, e.g. a graphical user interface with a mouse and a keyboard. This limitation makes browsing content unintuitive: for example, complicated links among Web pages cause the user to feel lost easily, and browsing 3D content with a mouse and menus is quite difficult.

"Walking" style operations serve to make browsing content much more intuitive and as casual as physical movement and looking around. In this paper, we introduce two elemental techniques to achieve this concept: a physical walking interface for browsing Web pages and automatic viewpoint control for comparing 3D content.

2 EnergyBrowser: Walk in the World Wide Web

EnergyBrowser is a web browser that renders web pages incrementally in proportion to the amount of walking/jogging the user has done.

Figure 1 is the appearance and the schematic of the EnergyBrowser system. An accelerometer (energy-acquisition equipment in Fig. 1), an instrument that is worn around the user's waist, detects the user's motion. EnergyBrowser estimates the tempo, the intensity, and the number of steps from the sensor data. Then, EnergyBrowser calculates the amount of energy consumed by walking and converts it into Web pages imaginarily. Thus, the user sees more web pages the more he or she walks.

An example of actual usage is as follows: First, EnergyBrowser selects a target web page and pre-fetches it. Next, *EnergyBrowser* analyzes the page and displays its

Y. Zhang et al. (Eds.): APWeb 2005, LNCS 3399, pp. 1062–1065, 2005.

background image. At the same time, EnergyBrowser converts the page into the format that is preferable for incremental rendering, for example, eliminating unnecessary frames and enlarging font sizes, if needed. After that, EnergyBrowser renders a fragment of the body of the page. The size of the fragment is proportional to the amount of walking. EnergyBrowser scrolls down the display area automatically when a displaying fragment exceeds the size of the display area. Figure 2 shows an example of incremental displaying of a web page. When a whole page is displayed, EnergyBrowser selects the next target page.

There are many web browsers for looking at web pages on the World Wide Web, but they only render pages as they are. In contrast, EnergyBrowser proceeds rendering based on the user's physical input. The feeling that the user controls the process of the browser is very enjoyable and is a novel experience.

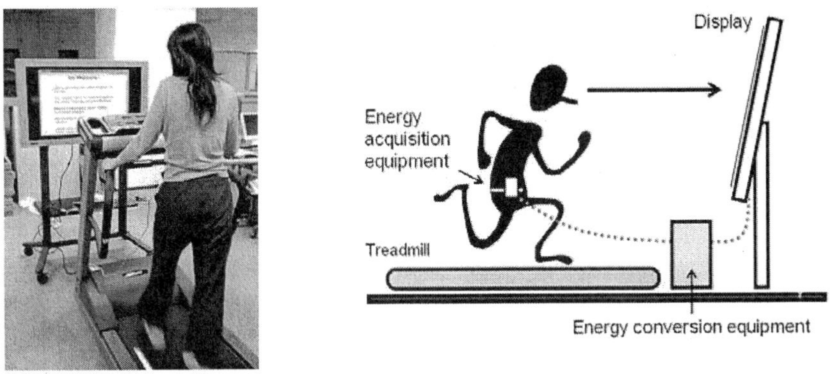

Fig. 1. Appearance and schematic of EnergyBrowser

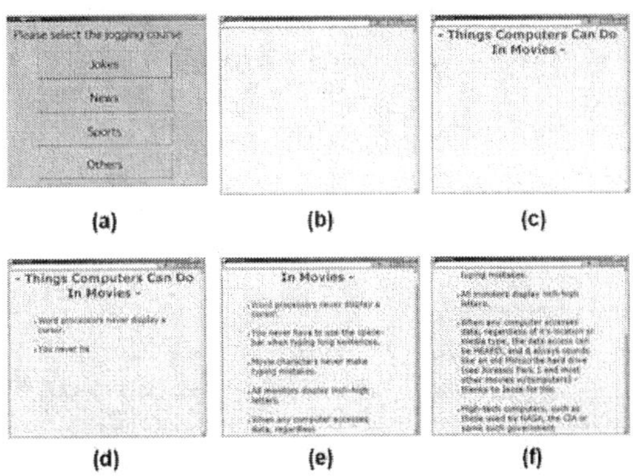

Fig. 2. Example of gradual rendering of a web page. (a) shows an initial menu. (b - d) show an incremental rendering sequence

3 Comparative 3D Archive Browser

As for 3D content, many digital archives of ruins and restoration by 3D CG have been created. However, only looking at the content is not enough. The user needs to understand. Systems that support the user's understanding of content are therefore required.

An effective method of helping understanding is comparison. However, comparing the present situation (ruin) to the past (restoration) with existing systems is difficult because the user has to operate their viewpoints separately.

Fig. 3. Function of Walkthrough

Fig. 4. Function of comparison

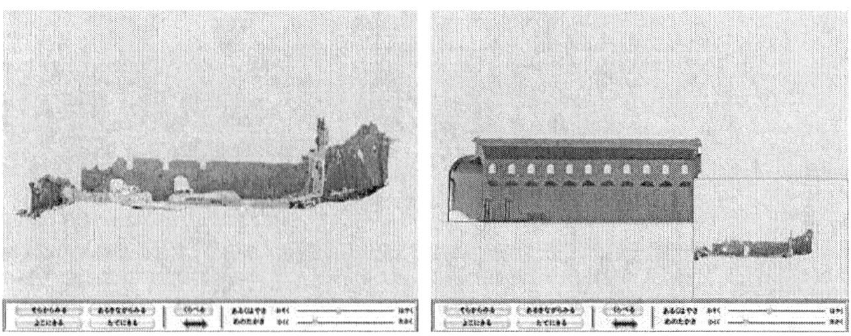

Fig. 5. Function of section

We therefore created a browser that displays other content simultaneously while controlling the viewpoint automatically to compare it to the content that the user is viewing. A comparative Web browser [1] enables comparison between Web pages by displaying related parts of other Web pages automatically. Our comparative 3D archive browser is semantically a 3D extension of this. The user can walk through only one space in real space. However, in virtual space, the user can walk through plural spaces at the same time. It is the key concept of the system, and it is intuitive and effective.

We are constructing a prototype system using the 3D digital archives of the ruins of the Turkish Republic Gemiler Island. We have implemented the following functions.

- A walkthrough function, which enables the user to move freely in 3D digital archives (Fig. 3).
- A concurrent navigation function, which enables comparison between the present condition and a proposed restoration on the same screen (Fig. 4).
- A cross-section function, which displays a cross-section view of the ruins or the whole historical building (Fig. 5). The user can control the cutting plane. This is useful for understanding the inner structure in detail.

Thus, the user can walkthrough 3D archives freely, and the system provides comparative views of other related content, such as restorations.

4 Conclusion

We illustrated physical and virtual walking interfaces for browsing content. Our public demonstration showed they are intuitive and popular, especially with children.

The current interface of a comparative 3D archive browser is a keyboard or game controller, but a real walking interface can be imported, such as the one used in EnergyBrowser. Though this combination is similar to the system proposed by Kadobayashi et al. where the user can walk around in virtual ancient villages [2], it can provide more effective browsing by comparison and gradual reading of annotations attached into 3D space.

References

1. Nadamoto, A. and Tanaka, K. A Comparative Web Browser (CWB) for Browsing and Comparing Web Pages. In Proceedings of the 12th International World Wide Web Conference (WWW2003), pp. 727-735, 2003
2. Kadobayashi, R., Nishimoto, K., and Mase, K.: Immersive Walk-through Experience of Japanese Ancient Villages with the VisTA-walk System, Barcelo, J.A., Forte, M., and Sanders, D. (Eds.), Virtual Reality in Archaeology, Archaeopress, pp.135-142, 2000.

A Personal Web Bulletin Board with Autonomic Behaviors and Virtual Portal Function

Yutaka Kidawara[1], Tomoyuki Uchiyama[2], Yukiko Kawai[1], Yuhei Akahoshi[2], and Daishuke Kanjo[1]

[1] Interactive Communication Media and Contents Group,
National Institute of Information and Communications Technology,
3-5 Hikaridai,Seika-cho,Soraku-gun,Kyoto,619-0289 Japan
TEL: +81-774-98-6886, FAX: +81-774-98-6959
{kidawara, yukiko, kanjo}@nict.go.jp

[2] Department of Social Informatics, Graduate School of Informatics,
Kyoto University, Yoshida-Honmachi,
Sakyo-ku, Kyoto, 606-8501 Japan
TEL: +81-75-753-5385, FAX: +81-75-753-4957
{tomoyuki, akahoshi}@dl.kuis.kyoto-u.ac.jp

Abstract. We propose a new concept for displaying, browsing, and retrieving web content that works by adding autonomic behaviors to *Field* on browser. The mechanism provides autonomic operation for web content when users search their interested information. We also discuss the Personal Web Bulletin Board (PWBB), which is an implementation of our concept. PWBB provides interactive user operation and personalized view for web content to us.

1 Introduction

In the not too distant future, network-accessible devices will be ubiquitously installed ubiquitously in urban areas. Moreover communication device technologies are evolving towards a communications tool, called the "ubiquitous Internet" by which we can use multiple device for web content operations. Fusion of real and cyber world will be accelerated by the ubiquitous Internet. Users operate equipments in real world through a digital content [6] . User's activity is stored in user's digital devices and replayed on particular digital devices [4, 5]. and a digital content can be operated by real materials[7]. A way of using web content will also change by the new communication technology. Future web content will be used as a sign-board on the ubiquitous Internet. Users will use a web content like a poster on the bulletin board. Users may expect that the information can be copied from a digital bulletin board to other devices such as PDA, memory device and so on [1], operated on the display screen directly[2], and changed browser's appearance by user's preference [3].

In this paper, we describe a new web browsing system, which is a content operation mechanism that can be used as a bulletin board.The system has a *Field*

Y. Zhang et al. (Eds.): APWeb 2005, LNCS 3399, pp. 1066–1069, 2005.

with autonomous behaviors, and each *Field* enables us to retrieve, browse and integrate web content intuitively .We also describes a practical implementation of the system called the Personal Web Bulletin Board (PWBB).

2 Field with Autonomic Behaviors

Today's paradigm of web browsing is on a PC or PDA display screen will no doubt have to be modified to take full advantage of ubiquitous computing technology. In particular, through ubiquitous computing, we may be able to have easy access to multiple screens on which we can to retrieve, browse and edit web contents. Let us assume that individual screens can be assigned a number of operations,such that regions on the screens will be devoted to these operations. We call such a region is *Field*. The user can assign an autonomic behaviors to *Field* . Users will likely expects that each *Field* acts the role autonomically when a web content is put on it. Each *Field* will also conform to an individual user's content view. By selecting the kind of function,a user can develop a personal virtual portal interface for viewing web contents on the Internet. We have already developed a prototype, "Personal Web Bulletin Board" , that can operate autonomically and be viewed like a portal web site on a *Field*.The following section describes the prototype's applications.

3 A Personal Web Bulletin Board

The "Personal Web Bulletin Board" has two kinds of functions. First, the board can implement several web retrieval functions and editing functions. Second, users can develop their own style of viewing web content aggregations. The function enables us to acquire our necessary information easier.

3.1 Autonomic Web Content Operation on Field

The application is for acquiring information from the Internet. Users find some web contents by using conventional web search engines, and they put the web content onto the *Field* on the screen. Our prototype has five different functions, and each *Field* has an autonomic behavior depending on its function. For example, a *Retrieval Field* is assigned a tf/idf web content retrieval mechanism. The prototype functions are illustrated in Fig.1. They are:

1. Retrieval of web content by using a conventional web search engine.
2. Selection of web content by dragging it onto a *Similar Content Retrieval Field*. The field executes the tf/idf retrieval function autonomically and displays retrieved web content around the dragged content.
3. Dragging the selected content onto the *Linked Content Retrieval Field*. The field can display linked web pages.
4. Dragging the content onto the *Clipping Field*. The field can clip a part of the content when the user selects region on the screen.

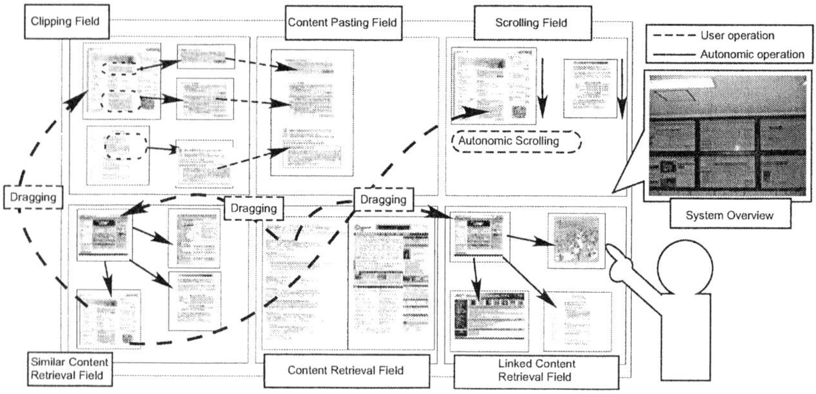

Fig. 1. Example of web content operation on prototype system

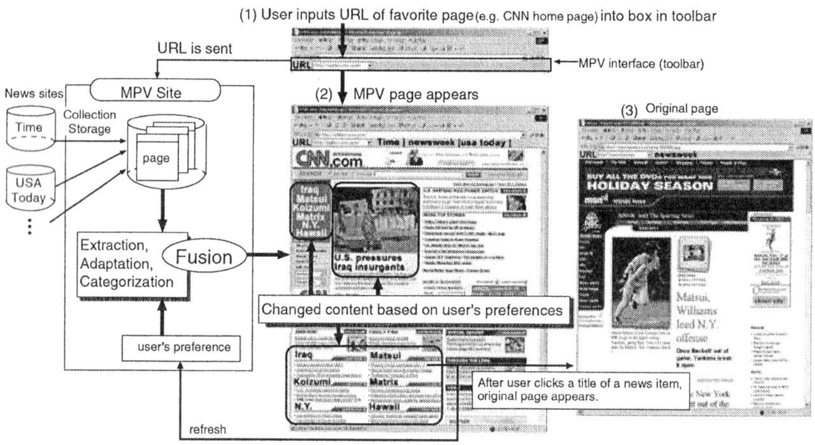

Fig. 2. An example of web content operation on prototype system

5. A *Scrolling Field* that scrolls autonomically. The function is especially useful for long web pages without a keyboard or mouse.
6. Creating new web pages by using clipped web content on the *Content Pasting Field.*

Users can browse various information related to their interested web content at a glance because a number of functions are executed on the *Field.*

3.2 Personal Virtual Portal Function

Fig.2 shows the personal virtual portal can provide the integrated web content according to the user's own style[3]. The function of the personal virtual portal automatically categorizes and integrates articles from numerous pages based on the user's preference after gathering these pages from various web sites. This function has two unique features: (1)application of the "look" and "feel" of the dragged top page from another Field, with part of the original content being replaced by the integrated content, and (2)automatic categorization and integration of collected information based on the user's preferences. Whenever a user accesses an integrated page after browsing pages in another Field, he/she can obtain the desired content efficiently because the integrated page presents pages refreshed on the basis of the user's behavior, which reflects his/her interests and knowledge. In addition to the integrated page framework, methods based on the user's preferences for replacing and categorizing content have been developed using an HTML table model and a vector matching model.

4 Conclusion

We have described a new concept of displaying, browsing, and retrieval for web contents, which is executed by adding autonomic behaviors to *Field* on browser. The behaviors are executed when web content puts on the *Field* or user preferences are provided to the *Field*. We also described the Personal Web Bulletin Board (PWBB). PWBB provides autonomic web retrieval, scrolling, clipping functions assigned to *Field*, which enables us to browse the integrated web content according to the user's own style. These functions can work effectively as an new web content operation. Users can acquire their necessary information browsing the integrated web content through their own style and operating various web content on the screen interactively.

References

1. Y. Kidawara, K. Zettsu, WebBoard: A New Display and Browsing Concept for Web Content in Public Areas, ICME2004, PD6, June 2004.
2. Y. Kidawara, K. Zettsu, T. Uchiyama, K. Tanaka, Device Cooperative Web Browsing and Retrieving Mechanism on Ubiquitous Networks, Database and Expert systems Applications(DEXA2004), Springer LNCS3180, pp. 874-883, Sep. 2004.
3. Y. Kawai, D. Kanjo, K. Tanaka, My Portal Viewer for Content Fusion based on User's Preferences, ICME2004, June 2004.
4. B. Ullmer, H. Ishii, and D. Glas: MediaBlocks: Physical Containers, Transports, and Controls for Online Media, In Computer Graphics Proceedings of SIGGRAPH'98, pp. 379-386, Jul. 1998.
5. B. Ullmer and H. Ishii: MediaBlocks: Tangible Interfaces for Online Media. In Extended Abstracts of CHI'99, pp. 31-32, May 1999.
6. K. Gronbak, J. F. Kristensen, P. Orbak, and M. A. Eriksen: Physical Hypermedia: Organizing Collections of Mixed Physical and Digital Material, In Proceedings of ACM HyperText '03, pp. 10-19, Aug. 2003.
7. L. Romero and N. Correia: HyperReal: A Hypermedia Model for Mixed Reality, In Proceedings of ACM HyperText '03, pp. 2-9, Aug. 2003.

ImageAspect Finder/Difference-Amplifier: Focusing on Peripheral Information for Image Search and Browsing

Shinsuke Nakajima[1] and Koji Zettsu[1,2]

[1] National Institute of Information and Communications(NICT), 3-5 Hikaridai Seika-cho Soraku-gun Kyoto 619-0289, Japan
{snakajima, zettsu}@nict.go.jp

[2] Graduate School of Informatics, Kyoto University, Yoshida Honmachi, Sakyo, Kyoto, 606-8501, Japan
zettsu@dl.kuis.kyoto-u.ac.jp

Abstract. Conventional image search/browse systems are not useful enough. Because there is a limit to representing characteristics of images though image data has a diversity of characteristics. We develop Difference-Amplifier and ImageAspect finder that are image search and browsing system focusing on peripheral information of query/answer images. The Difference-Amplifier for relevance feedback can extract user's requirements for image retrieval by amplifying difference between a user-selected image and unselected peripheral images. The ImageAspect Finder for image browsing can extract context of the image and other images that are used in the same context by analyzing surrounding text of link anchor that refers to the query image.

1 Introduction

Recently, image search/browse systems on the Web, such as Google Image search, become very popular. However, they seem to be not useful enough. Traditional image retrieval systems focus on identifying answer images based on specific properties of image content, such as annotated keyword, colors, textures, or objects. Because there is a limit to representing characteristics of images though image data has a diversity of characteristics.

Namely, in the case of querying for content based image retrieval, users cannot represent which characteristics they pay attention to by one query image, since a query image has a diversity of characteristics. Moreover, in the case of browsing images retrieved by image search engine, users cannot understand why answer images are retrieved, since it cannot show relations between users' query and answer images.

Consequently, we propose Difference-Amplifier (abbreviated by DA) for relevance feedback and ImageAspect finder that are image search and browsing system focusing on peripheral information of query/answer images.

Y. Zhang et al. (Eds.): APWeb 2005, LNCS 3399, pp. 1070–1074, 2005.

The image retrieval based on relevance feedback with DA is one of content-based image retrieval methods. A conventional content-based image retrieval system retrieves answer images that are the most similar to query image selected among several images browsed by a user. However, the user must be not satisfied with selected answer image because he/she continues image retrieval. Thus, the retrieval system should extract real user's requirements from a diversity of characteristics of query image. The DA for relevance feedback regards unselected browsed images with selected query image as peripheral information, so that it can extract user's requirements for image retrieval by amplifying difference between a query image and its peripheral image.

The ImageAspect Finder for image browsing analyzes surrounding text of link anchor that refers to a target image. Then, it can extract context of the image and other images that are used in the same context. By considering not only metadata of the image but also usage context of the image as its peripheral information, the ImageAspect Finder can retrieve context for the given images and image for the given context. Therefore, the ImageAspect Finder can help users to understand a diversity of characteristics of the images. Namely, in addition to the content properties, image content is also characterized by the context in which it is exposed. For example, if we browse a flower image in sightseeing brochure, we may understand the image as a symbol of beautiful nature.

2 Difference-Amplifier for Relevance Feedback

Relevance-feedback with DA is different from conventional relevance-feedback in that it also uses unselected images browsed with the selected image to generate the next query. "Relative Query"[1] is also an image retrieval method using both user-selected image and unselected peripheral images to generate query. However, it does not amplify difference between selected one and unselected ones to emphasize user's retrieval intention.

Prototype image retrieval system of relevance-feedback with DA presents clustered images as similar images are placed at neighbor each other, and it retrieves the answer image based on user-selected image as positive sample and unselected peripheral images that are placed around selected one and similar to it. By using the selected image and its peripheral ones, system can extract user's rough requirement and some elements of feature vector that the user is interested in.

Relevance-feedback with DA is defined as follows:

$$\mathbf{Q_{k+1}} = \alpha \cdot \mathbf{Q_k} + \beta \cdot \left\{ \mathbf{S_p} + \gamma \cdot \frac{\sum_{S \in peripheral(S_p)} (\mathbf{S_p} - \mathbf{S})}{N_{S_p}} \right\}$$

$\mathbf{S_p}$ and $peripheral(S_p)$ corresponds to a feature vector of a user-selected positive image and a set of feature vectors of unselected peripheral images. $\mathbf{N_{S_p}}$ corresponds to a number of elements of $peripheral(\mathbf{S_p})$. $(\mathbf{S_p} - \mathbf{S})$ means difference of feature vector between a positive image and one of peripheral images.

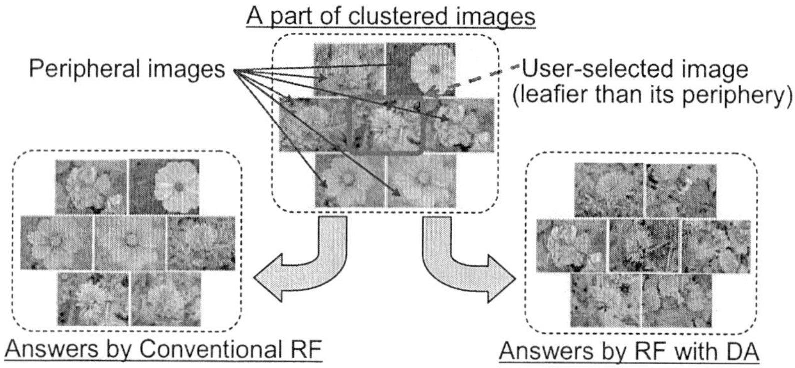

Fig. 1. Example of Relevance-Feedback with Difference-Amplifier

$\mathbf{Q_k}$ and $\mathbf{Q_{k+1}}$ correspond to the present query and the next query. The α, β and γ correspond to weights. Particularly, dependence on present query can be changed by α.

Fig. 1 shows example of relevance-feedback with DA. Let us suppose that a user selects an image as positive sample for image retrieval, which is leafier than its peripheral images. As the figure indicates, in the case of conventional relevance-feedback, user's requirement is not reflected enough in answer images because conventional relevance-feedback uses only a user-selected image that he/she is not satisfied sufficiently. On the other hand, in the case of relevance-feedback with DA, user's requirement, which is that he/she wants to a leafier image than its periphery, is reflected in answer images. Consequently, our system enable users to retrieve an answer image more effectively than conventional method.

3 ImageAspect Finder

Images on the Web are particularly incorporated into Web pages, and recognized as a part of the page contents. For example, when we view the image showing car traffic in the Web page entitled by "air pollution gives you heart disease", we understand that the image is used in the context of environment pollution. As a result, we may recognize the image as a picture implying air pollution caused by traffic fumes. In this way, surrounding contents of an image indicate the context in which the image is exposed, and provides an viewpoint on the image. Analyzing contexts of images facilitates understanding their roles, reputations or intended usages.

Traditional image retrieval systems applied to Web contents allow users to search and browse images solely by image content. In contrast, we propose an approach for discovering typical contexts of images from the Web, which we call *aspects* of the images[2]. Fig. 2 illustrates basic concepts of our approach. ImageAspect Finder consists of two processes: context extraction and context clustering. For a given image, the context extraction process extracts a coherent semantic range of Web contents surrounding the image. We extend the notion of "surroundings" to incorporate the Web contents associated by Web document structure and link structure. By expanding the surrounding contents from a link anchor to its upper paragraphs, the context extraction mechanism detects a significant change of surrounding contents. The context clustering process clusters similar contexts. Each cluster represents an aspect. The clustering process extracts common keywords from the contexts in each cluster as a description of the corresponding aspect. Finally, ImageAspect Finder displays the keywords and/or images typically appear in the aspect in order to "visually" acquire the surrounding contents for the given images.

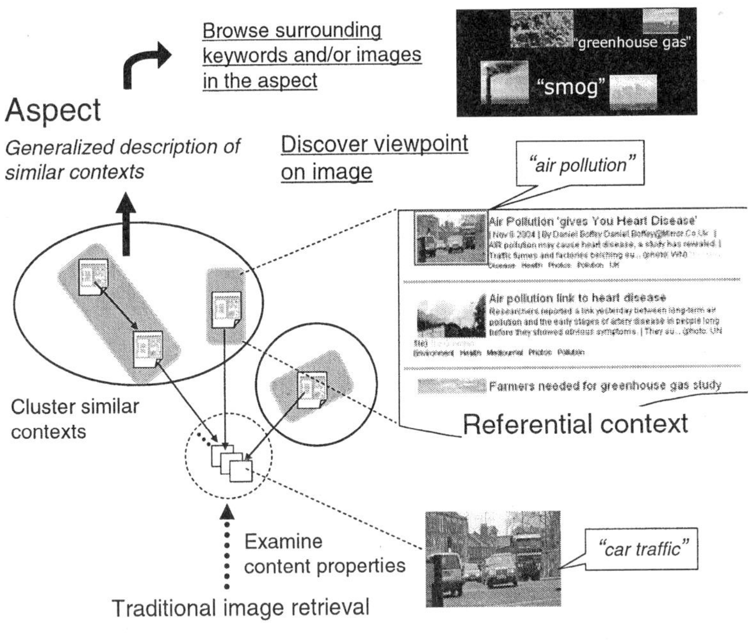

Fig. 2. Basic concept of ImageAspect Finder

4 Conclusion

We propose and develop Difference-Amplifier and ImageAspect finder that are image search and browsing system focusing on peripheral information of query/ answer images.

References

1. Shinsuke Nakajima, and Katsumi Tanaka, : Relative Queries and the Relative Cluster-Mapping Method, Proc. of 9th International Conference on Database Systems for Advanced Applications (DASFAA 2004), pp.843-856, (Mar. 2004)D
2. Zettsu, K., Kidawara, Y. and Tanaka, K.: Discovering Aspect-based Correlation of Web Contents for Cross-media Information Retrieval, Proceedings of the 2004 IEEE International Conference on Multimedia and Expo (ICME2004), Taipei, Taiwan (June, 2004).

Tools for Media Conversion and Fusion of TV and Web Contents

Hisashi Miyamori, Akiyo Nadamoto, Kaoru Sumi, and Qiang Ma

Interactive Communications Media and Contents Group,
National Institute of Information and Communications (NICT),
3–5, Hikari-dai, Seika-cho, Souraku-gun, Kyoto, 619–0289 Japan
{miya, nadamoto, kaoru, qiang}@nict.go.jp

Abstract. This paper describes tools for media conversion and fusion of TV and web content. Conventionally, web pages are browsed on a personal computer (active browsing) and TV programs are watched on TV (passive watching). However, if TV and web content is converted and integrated, it can be viewed in different ways, depending on one's mood, age, or situation. Two kinds of tools are presented in this paper: tools for converting web content to TV content and tools for converting and integrating TV content to web content. As examples of the former, we explain tools for converting web content, after stage-managing, in the form of comic talkshows or animated picture books for easier understanding by children. As examples of the latter, we describe tools for converting TV content in the form of a storyboard, followed by searching related web pages that complement the original TV content, and integrating the results into a single storyboard-style web page.

1 Introduction

We are developing technologies for converting and integrating TV and web content. Conventionally, web pages are browsed on a personal computer (PC) (active browsing) while TV programs are watched on TV (passive watching). However, if TV program and web content is converted and integrated, it can be viewed in different ways depending on one's mood, age, or situation. For instance, when web content is converted into a TV program, you can obtain information in the same way as you do from TV. With our systems, you do not have to operate a PC to get web content, and you can get web content while you are working on other tasks such as cooking. Conversely, when TV programs are converted into web pages, you can quickly browse the content of each program just like you look through web pages. You can also find specific scenes in program easily without fast-forwarding or rewinding a video. This leads to a new viewing style where the content from TV programs and web pages is blended together. In this way, we are aiming to establish technologies for converting and integrating TV and web content, enabling users to "watch" web pages as TV programs and "browse" TV programs in the form of web pages. Tools for such conversion and integration are described in the following two sections.

Y. Zhang et al. (Eds.): APWeb 2005, LNCS 3399, pp. 1075–1078, 2005.

2 Tools for Converting Web Content into TV-Program-Like Content

We developed two types of tools for converting web content into TV-program-like content. One system is based on the talkshow metaphor and the other on the picture-book metaphor. The characteristics of our systems are:

- Passive manner interface
  Our systems enable users to get web content in a way similar to watching a TV program. Even young children, who cannot operate computers well, can obtain web content from our systems.
- Transforming into easy content
  Our systems transform difficult web content into easy content by using dialogs or paraphrasing. Thus, young children can understand desired web content easily.

The key technologies of our systems are: dialogue generation, Q&A generation, paraphrase, choreography composition.

Web2Talkshow
Web2Talkshow transforms declarative-based web content into humorous dialog-based TV-program-like content that is presented through cartoon animation and synthesized speech[1]. A typical Web2Talkshow display is shown in Fig. 1. Web2Talkshow lets users get desired web content easily, pleasantly, and in a user-friendly way while they continue work on other tasks, so it will be much like watching TV.

Interactive e-Hon: Translating Web contents into a storybook world
Interactive e-Hon (Fig.2)[2] is a word translation medium using animation and dialog explanation to help children understand contents on the Web, e.g., news, episodes, and novels. In the natural language processing, each subject or object is transformed into a character, and each predicate is transformed into the behavior

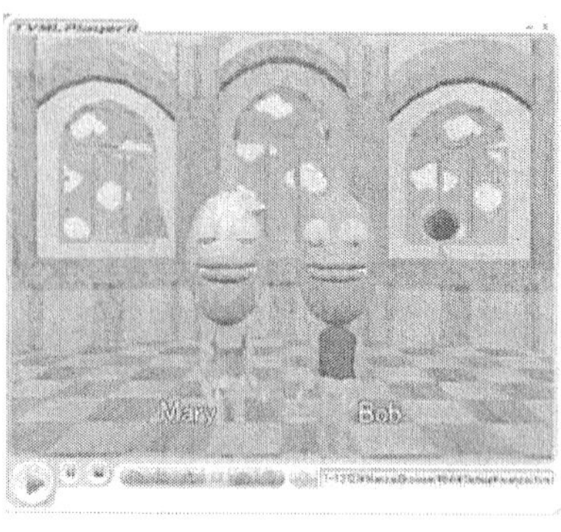

Fig. 1. Image displayed by Web2-Talkshow

Fig. 2. Example view of Interactive e-Hon

of a character. An animation plays in synchronization with dialog output from a voice synthesizer.

3 Tool for Converting and Integrating TV Content to Web Content

We developed "**WA-TV**"(**W**ebification[3] for **A**ugmenting **TV**) as a tool for converting and integrating TV content to web content. It is a prototype system of a next-generation storage TV with video augmented by "webification". The characteristics of our systems are:

- Active manner interface, improvement of scene search efficiency
  Simple zooming operation smoothly transforms the appearance of TV content between the list screen and the normal playback screen. Users can easily grasp the overview of the program and search specific scenes.
- Augmentation of TV content
  Complementary information retrieval enables automatic search for the information which was not provided by a TV program. The system integrates the search results into the list screen of TV content, resulting in augmenting the original information.

The key technologies of our systems are: segmentation[3][4], metadata extraction[3], complementary information retrieval[4], zooming crossmedia[3].

Fig. 3 shows an example screen of WA-TV. Groups of caption texts and videos segmented at different levels of details, such as in topics, subtopics, and sentences, are displayed vertically in the form of a storyboard. Hyperlinks to the search results for complementary information are integrated below the caption texts. If necessary, users can access to more detailed or expanded inforamation than provided by the original program.

Fig. 4 illustrates the transformation of the screen appearance of WA-TV. Zooming operation smoothly changes the size of thumbnails as well as switches to another storyboard of different level of detail. As a result, users can seamlessly move back and forth among the storyboard screens of different levels of details and the normal playback screen, and thus, can search specific scenes efficiently.

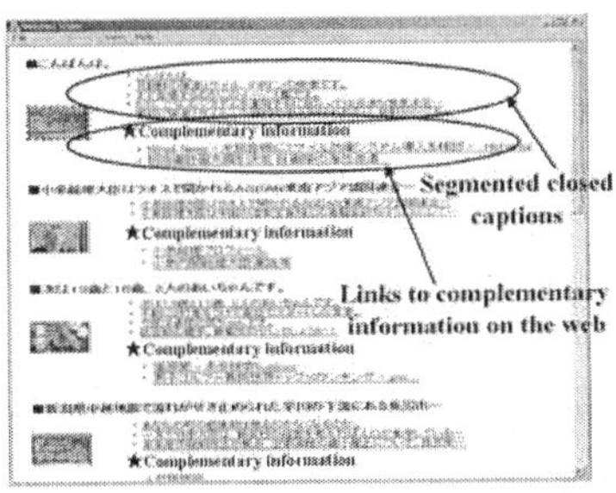

Fig. 3. Example screen of WA-TV

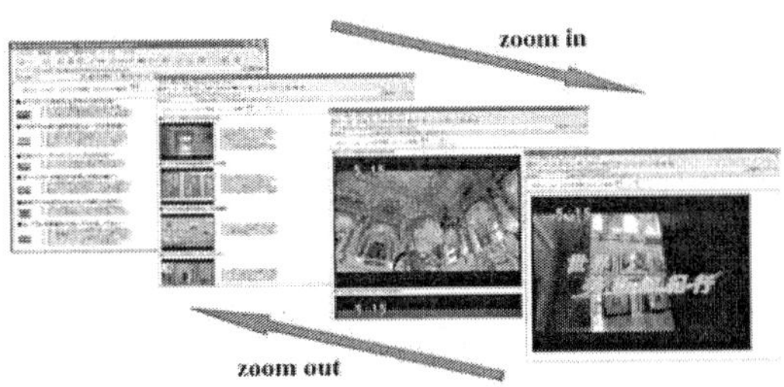

Fig. 4. Transformation of screen appearance by WA-TV

4 Summary

This paper described several tools for media conversion and fusion of TV and web content. These tools enable new viewing styles, such as "watching" web pages as TV programs and "browsing" TV programs in the form of web pages. These tools are expected to be applied for push services and streaming services for web content and for interactive services and data broadcasting for TV programs (Fig. 5). They are also expected to become fundamental technologies to establish the Content Convergence Environment (CCE), where in the future users will be able to view web and TV content as if they were blended together (Fig. 5).

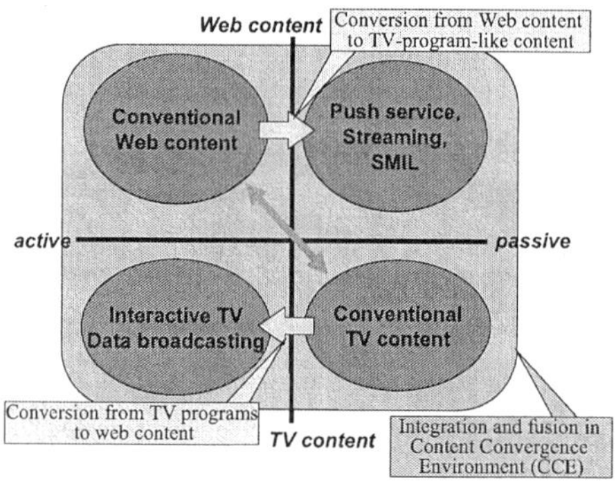

Fig. 5. Media conversion and fusion of TV and Web contents

References

1. Akiyo Nadamoto, and Katsumi Tanaka: Passive viewing of Web page based on automatic dialog generation, IPSJ SIG, 2004-DBS-134, pp. 183-190, 2004.
2. Kaoru Sumi and Katsumi Tanaka: Interactive e-Hon: Translating Web contents into a storybook world, AISB 2005 Symposium on Conversational Informatics, to appear in 2005.
3. Hisashi Miyamori, and Katsumi Tanaka: Webified Video: webification of video and its metadata, IPSJ2004-DBS-132, pp.49-56, 2004.
4. Qiang Ma, Akiyo Nadamoto, and Katsumi Tanaka: Complementary Information Retrieval for Cross-Media News Contents, Proc. of ACM MMDB, 2004.

Author Index

Lecture Notes in Computer Science

For information about Vols. 1–3339

please contact your bookseller or Springer

Vol. 3452: F. Baader, A. Voronkov (Eds.), Logic for Programming, Artificial Intelligence, and Reasoning. XI, 562 pages. 2005. (Subseries LNAI).

Vol. 3448: G.R. Raidl, J. Gottlieb (Eds.), Evolutionary Computation in Combinatorial Optimization. XI, 271 pages. 2005.

Vol. 3442: M. Cerioli (Ed.), Fundamental Approaches to Software Engineering. XIII, 373 pages. 2005.

Vol. 3441: V. Sassone (Ed.), Foundations of Software Science and Computational Structures. XVIII, 521 pages. 2005.

Vol. 3440: N. Halbwachs, L.D. Zuck (Eds.), Tools and Algorithms for the Construction and Analysis of Systems. XVII, 588 pages. 2005.

Vol. 3436: B. Bouyssounouse, J. Sifakis (Eds.), Embedded Systems Design. XV, 492 pages. 2005.

Vol. 3433: S. Bhalla (Ed.), Databases in Networked Information Systems. VII, 319 pages. 2005.

Vol. 3432: M. Beigl, P. Lukowicz (Eds.), Systems Aspects in Organic and Pervasive Computing - ARCS 2005. X, 265 pages. 2005.

Vol. 3427: G. Kotsis, O. Spaniol, Wireless Systems and Mobility in Next Generation Internet. VIII, 249 pages. 2005.

Vol. 3423: J.L. Fiadeiro, P.D. Mosses, F. Orejas (Eds.), Recent Trends in Algebraic Development Techniques. VIII, 271 pages. 2005.

Vol. 3422: R.T. Mittermeir (Ed.), From Computer Literacy to Informatics Fundamentals. X, 203 pages. 2005.

Vol. 3421: P. Lorenz, P. Dini (Eds.), Networking - ICN 2005, Part II. XXXV, 1153 pages. 2005.

Vol. 3420: P. Lorenz, P. Dini (Eds.), Networking - ICN 2005, Part I. XXXV, 933 pages. 2005.

Vol. 3419: B. Faltings, A. Petcu, F. Fages, F. Rossi (Eds.), Constraint Satisfaction and Constraint Logic Programming. X, 217 pages. 2005. (Subseries LNAI).

Vol. 3418: U. Brandes, T. Erlebach (Eds.), Network Analysis. XII, 471 pages. 2005.

Vol. 3416: M. Böhlen, J. Gamper, W. Polasek, M.A. Wimmer (Eds.), E-Government: Towards Electronic Democracy. XIII, 311 pages. 2005. (Subseries LNAI).

Vol. 3415: P. Davidsson, B. Logan, K. Takadama (Eds.), Multi-Agent and Multi-Agent-Based Simulation. X, 265 pages. 2005. (Subseries LNAI).

Vol. 3414: M. Morari, L. Thiele (Eds.), Hybrid Systems: Computation and Control. XII, 684 pages. 2005.

Vol. 3412: X. Franch, D. Port (Eds.), COTS-Based Software Systems. XVI, 312 pages. 2005.

Vol. 3411: S.H. Myaeng, M. Zhou, K.-F. Wong, H.-J. Zhang (Eds.), Information Retrieval Technology. XIII, 337 pages. 2005.

Vol. 3410: C.A. Coello Coello, A. Hernández Aguirre, E. Zitzler (Eds.), Evolutionary Multi-Criterion Optimization. XVI, 912 pages. 2005.

Vol. 3409: N. Guelfi, G. Reggio, A. Romanovsky (Eds.), Scientific Engineering of Distributed Java Applications. X, 127 pages. 2005.

Vol. 3408: D.E. Losada, J.M. Fernández-Luna (Eds.), Advances in Information Retrieval. XVII, 572 pages. 2005.

Vol. 3407: Z. Liu, K. Araki (Eds.), Theoretical Aspects of Computing - ICTAC 2004. XIV, 562 pages. 2005.

Vol. 3406: A. Gelbukh (Ed.), Computational Linguistics and Intelligent Text Processing. XVII, 829 pages. 2005.

Vol. 3404: V. Diekert, B. Durand (Eds.), STACS 2005. XVI, 706 pages. 2005.

Vol. 3403: B. Ganter, R. Godin (Eds.), Formal Concept Analysis. XI, 419 pages. 2005. (Subseries LNAI).

Vol. 3401: Z. Li, L.G. Vulkov, J. Waśniewski (Eds.), Numerical Analysis and Its Applications. XIII, 630 pages. 2005.

Vol. 3399: Y. Zhang, K. Tanaka, J.X. Yu, S. Wang, M. Li (Eds.), Web Technologies Research and Development - APWeb 2005. XXII, 1082 pages. 2005.

Vol. 3398: D.-K. Baik (Ed.), Systems Modeling and Simulation: Theory and Applications. XIV, 733 pages. 2005. (Subseries LNAI).

Vol. 3397: T.G. Kim (Ed.), Artificial Intelligence and Simulation. XV, 711 pages. 2005. (Subseries LNAI).

Vol. 3396: R.M. van Eijk, M.-P. Huget, F. Dignum (Eds.), Agent Communication. X, 261 pages. 2005. (Subseries LNAI).

Vol. 3395: J. Grabowski, B. Nielsen (Eds.), Formal Approaches to Software Testing. X, 225 pages. 2005.

Vol. 3394: D. Kudenko, D. Kazakov, E. Alonso (Eds.), Adaptive Agents and Multi-Agent Systems III. VIII, 313 pages. 2005. (Subseries LNAI).

Vol. 3393: H.-J. Kreowski, U. Montanari, F. Orejas, G. Rozenberg, G. Taentzer (Eds.), Formal Methods in Software and Systems Modeling. XXVII, 413 pages. 2005.

Vol. 3391: C. Kim (Ed.), Information Networking. XVII, 936 pages. 2005.

Vol. 3390: R. Choren, A. Garcia, C. Lucena, A. Romanovsky (Eds.), Software Engineering for Multi-Agent Systems III. XII, 291 pages. 2005.

Vol. 3389: P. Van Roy (Ed.), Multiparadigm Programming in Mozart/OZ. XV, 329 pages. 2005.

Vol. 3388: J. Lagergren (Ed.), Comparative Genomics. VII, 133 pages. 2005. (Subseries LNBI).

Vol. 3387: J. Cardoso, A. Sheth (Eds.), Semantic Web Services and Web Process Composition. VIII, 147 pages. 2005.

Vol. 3386: S. Vaudenay (Ed.), Public Key Cryptography - PKC 2005. IX, 436 pages. 2005.

Vol. 3385: R. Cousot (Ed.), Verification, Model Checking, and Abstract Interpretation. XII, 483 pages. 2005.

Vol. 3383: J. Pach (Ed.), Graph Drawing. XII, 536 pages. 2005.

Vol. 3382: J. Odell, P. Giorgini, J.P. Müller (Eds.), Agent-Oriented Software Engineering V. X, 239 pages. 2005.

Vol. 3381: P. Vojtáš, M. Bieliková, B. Charron-Bost, O. Sýkora (Eds.), SOFSEM 2005: Theory and Practice of Computer Science. XV, 448 pages. 2005.

Vol. 3380: C. Priami, Transactions on Computational Systems Biology I. IX, 111 pages. 2005. (Subseries LNBI).

Vol. 3379: M. Hemmje, C. Niederee, T. Risse (Eds.), From Integrated Publication and Information Systems to Information and Knowledge Environments. XXIV, 321 pages. 2005.

Vol. 3378: J. Kilian (Ed.), Theory of Cryptography. XII, 621 pages. 2005.

Vol. 3377: B. Goethals, A. Siebes (Eds.), Knowledge Discovery in Inductive Databases. VII, 190 pages. 2005.

Vol. 3376: A. Menezes (Ed.), Topics in Cryptology – CT-RSA 2005. X, 385 pages. 2005.

Vol. 3375: M.A. Marsan, G. Bianchi, M. Listanti, M. Meo (Eds.), Quality of Service in Multiservice IP Networks. XIII, 656 pages. 2005.

Vol. 3374: D. Weyns, H.V.D. Parunak, F. Michel (Eds.), Environments for Multi-Agent Systems. X, 279 pages. 2005. (Subseries LNAI).

Vol. 3372: C. Bussler, V. Tannen, I. Fundulaki (Eds.), Semantic Web and Databases. X, 227 pages. 2005.

Vol. 3371: M.W. Barley, N. Kasabov (Eds.), Intelligent Agents and Multi-Agent Systems. X, 329 pages. 2005. (Subseries LNAI).

Vol. 3370: A. Konagaya, K. Satou (Eds.), Grid Computing in Life Science. X, 188 pages. 2005. (Subseries LNBI).

Vol. 3369: V.R. Benjamins, P. Casanovas, J. Breuker, A. Gangemi (Eds.), Law and the Semantic Web. XII, 249 pages. 2005. (Subseries LNAI).

Vol. 3368: L. Paletta, J.K. Tsotsos, E. Rome, G.W. Humphreys (Eds.), Attention and Performance in Computational Vision. VIII, 231 pages. 2005.

Vol. 3367: W.S. Ng, B.C. Ooi, A. Ouksel, C. Sartori (Eds.), Databases, Information Systems, and Peer-to-Peer Computing. X, 231 pages. 2005.

Vol. 3366: I. Rahwan, P. Moraitis, C. Reed (Eds.), Argumentation in Multi-Agent Systems. XII, 263 pages. 2005. (Subseries LNAI).

Vol. 3365: G. Mauri, G. Păun, M.J. Pérez-Jiménez, G. Rozenberg, A. Salomaa (Eds.), Membrane Computing. IX, 415 pages. 2005.

Vol. 3363: T. Eiter, L. Libkin (Eds.), Database Theory - ICDT 2005. XI, 413 pages. 2004.

Vol. 3362: G. Barthe, L. Burdy, M. Huisman, J.-L. Lanet, T. Muntean (Eds.), Construction and Analysis of Safe, Secure, and Interoperable Smart Devices. IX, 257 pages. 2005.

Vol. 3361: S. Bengio, H. Bourlard (Eds.), Machine Learning for Multimodal Interaction. XII, 362 pages. 2005.

Vol. 3360: S. Spaccapietra, E. Bertino, S. Jajodia, R. King, D. McLeod, M.E. Orlowska, L. Strous (Eds.), Journal on Data Semantics II. XI, 223 pages. 2005.

Vol. 3359: G. Grieser, Y. Tanaka (Eds.), Intuitive Human Interfaces for Organizing and Accessing Intellectual Assets. XIV, 257 pages. 2005. (Subseries LNAI).

Vol. 3358: J. Cao, L.T. Yang, M. Guo, F. Lau (Eds.), Parallel and Distributed Processing and Applications. XXIV, 1058 pages. 2004.

Vol. 3357: H. Handschuh, M.A. Hasan (Eds.), Selected Areas in Cryptography. XI, 354 pages. 2004.

Vol. 3356: G. Das, V.P. Gulati (Eds.), Intelligent Information Technology. XII, 428 pages. 2004.

Vol. 3355: R. Murray-Smith, R. Shorten (Eds.), Switching and Learning in Feedback Systems. X, 343 pages. 2005.

Vol. 3354: M. Margenstern (Ed.), Machines, Computations, and Universality. VIII, 329 pages. 2005.

Vol. 3353: J. Hromkovič, M. Nagl, B. Westfechtel (Eds.), Graph-Theoretic Concepts in Computer Science. XI, 404 pages. 2004.

Vol. 3352: C. Blundo, S. Cimato (Eds.), Security in Communication Networks. XI, 381 pages. 2005.

Vol. 3351: G. Persiano, R. Solis-Oba (Eds.), Approximation and Online Algorithms. VIII, 295 pages. 2005.

Vol. 3350: M. Hermenegildo, D. Cabeza (Eds.), Practical Aspects of Declarative Languages. VIII, 269 pages. 2005.

Vol. 3349: B.M. Chapman (Ed.), Shared Memory Parallel Programming with Open MP. X, 149 pages. 2005.

Vol. 3348: A. Canteaut, K. Viswanathan (Eds.), Progress in Cryptology - INDOCRYPT 2004. XIV, 431 pages. 2004.

Vol. 3347: R.K. Ghosh, H. Mohanty (Eds.), Distributed Computing and Internet Technology. XX, 472 pages. 2004.

Vol. 3346: R.H. Bordini, M. Dastani, J. Dix, A.E.F. Seghrouchni (Eds.), Programming Multi-Agent Systems. XIV, 249 pages. 2005. (Subseries LNAI).

Vol. 3345: Y. Cai (Ed.), Ambient Intelligence for Scientific Discovery. XII, 311 pages. 2005. (Subseries LNAI).

Vol. 3344: J. Malenfant, B.M. Østvold (Eds.), Object-Oriented Technology. ECOOP 2004 Workshop Reader. VIII, 215 pages. 2005.

Vol. 3343: C. Freksa, M. Knauff, B. Krieg-Brückner, B. Nebel, T. Barkowsky (Eds.), Spatial Cognition IV. Reasoning, Action, and Interaction. XIII, 519 pages. 2005. (Subseries LNAI).

Vol. 3342: E. Şahin, W.M. Spears (Eds.), Swarm Robotics. IX, 175 pages. 2005.

Vol. 3341: R. Fleischer, G. Trippen (Eds.), Algorithms and Computation. XVII, 935 pages. 2004.

Vol. 3340: C.S. Calude, E. Calude, M.J. Dinneen (Eds.), Developments in Language Theory. XI, 431 pages. 2004.